WITCHCRAFT
IN OLD AND NEW ENGLAND

WITCHCRAFT
in Old and New England

BY

GEORGE LYMAN KITTREDGE

Quicquid mortale creamur

New York

RUSSELL & RUSSELL

TO

MY WIFE

PREFACE

MY SALEM friends will expect me to remind the reader that the great outbreak of 1692 occurred in Salem *Village*, now Danvers, though the trials were held at Salem.

In view of some recent works on witchcraft, it seems only prudent to avow that I have no belief in the black art or in the interference of demons in the daily life of mortals.

Three of my eighteen chapters have already been published: the first, in the American Historical Review for October, 1917 (now reprinted by permission of the editor, Professor Jameson, and the publishers, the Macmillan Company); the seventeenth, in Studies in the History of Religions Presented to Crawford Howell Toy, 1912 (reprinted by permission of the Harvard University Press); the eighteenth, in the Proceedings of the American Antiquarian Society, 1907 (reprinted by permission of the Society). Each of these chapters has undergone some slight revision.

G. L. K.

CAMBRIDGE, MASSACHUSETTS
    December 28, 1928

CONTENTS

I. A Typical Case 3

II. English Witchcraft Before 1558 23

III. Image Magic and the Like 73

IV. Love and Hate 104

V. Madness, Curses, and the Elfshot . . . 124

VI. Venefica 136

VII. Charms Ghoulish and Profane 141

VIII. Wind and Weather 152

IX. The Witch in the Dairy 163

X. Metamorphosis 174

XI. Mirrors and Thieves 185

XII. Treasure Trove 204

XIII. Haunted Houses and Haunted Men . . . 214

XIV. The Seer 226

XV. Cold Water 232

XVI. The Compact and the Witches' Sabbath . . 239

XVII. King James the First 276

XVIII. Witchcraft and the Puritans 329

Notes 375

Index 599

WITCHCRAFT
IN OLD AND NEW ENGLAND

CHAPTER I

A TYPICAL CASE

THE accessible materials for a history of Elizabethan witchcraft are scattered and fragmentary. Much is lost, and much remains inedited. Yet we cannot hope to understand the prosecutions of the last sixty years of the seventeenth century, whether in Old England or in New, until we arrive at a substantially accurate comprehension of what was thought and done at the close of the great queen's reign. It is not only the dogmas of the theologians, the tenets of the physicians, and the rules of the law that we need to know, but, above everything else, the beliefs and feelings of the populace — of the folk itself. For it is in this matter of witchcraft, if anywhere, that public opinion is supreme. The populace may, perhaps, be restrained by the more enlightened part of the community, but the so-called governing classes cannot prosecute with success if the populace does not approve. Witch-hunting never flourishes unless the common people are eager for it. It is to them that the officers of the law must look for testimony, and it is the jury of the vicinage that renders the verdict. Experience has taught, over and over again, how hard it is for the most skeptical judge to bring about an acquittal in a particular case when the neighborhood from which the jury comes is convinced of the reality of the crime in general.

There was a famous witch-trial at Exeter, England, in 1682. Roger North was present, and here is his account of the state of public opinion:

The women were very old, decrepit, and impotent, and were brought to the assizes with as much noise and fury of the rabble against them as could be shewed on any occasion. The stories of their arts were in everyone's mouth, and they were not content to belie them in the country, but even in the city where they were to be tried miracles were fathered upon them, as that the judge's coach was fixed upon the castle bridge, and the like. All which the country believed, and accordingly persecuted the wretched old creatures. A less zeal in a city or kingdom hath been the overture of defection or revolution, and if these women had been acquitted, it was thought that the country people would have committed some disorder.[1]

This was a case in which it seems clear that the judges would have preferred a verdict of "not guilty" if they had been left to themselves.

Another striking example is that of Jane Wenham, who was condemned to death for witchcraft in 1712. Her trial is notable for its recent date. By that time there was much incredulity on the subject in the minds of educated men. Chief Justice Powell, who presided, made open fun of the evidence and summed up strongly in the defendant's favor, but in vain. He was obliged to sentence the woman to death and to content himself with procuring her pardon from the crown.[2] Nor was it until 1736 that the English and Scottish statutes against witchcraft were repealed. In considering the tenacity of the popular belief on this subject, we should never forget that the essence of witchcraft is *maleficium*. The hatred and terror which a witch evokes is due to her will and her power to inflict bodily injury. Compacts with the devil, the suckling of imps, the violation of graves, the abominations of the Witches' Sabbath — these are mere incidentals, the paraphernalia of the art. They aggravate the offence, to be sure, and proof that a woman is implicated in such horrors may send her to the scaffold or the stake. But, in the last analysis, every witch is prosecuted, not because she amuses herself with riding a broomstick or because she has taken a fiend for a lover: she is hunted down like a wolf because she is an enemy to mankind. Her heart is full of malignity. For a harsh word, or the refusal of a bit of bread, she becomes your mortal foe. And her revenge is out of all proportion to the affront, for she is in league with spirits of evil who are almost infinite in strength. She sends blight upon your crops, the rot upon your sheep, the murrain on your cattle; your house takes fire; your ship is cast away. She visits you and your family with strange wasting diseases — with palsy, with consumption, with raging fever, with madness, with death. Witch-trials are not prompted by theological hair-splitting, by systems of devil-lore, by the text, "Thou shalt not suffer a witch to live." *These all come after the fact*. It is self-protection that incites the accuser. His cause is fear — and fear of bodily harm. The witch is a murderer, or may become a murderer on the slightest provocation. She cannot be spared, for there is no safety for life, body, or estate until she is sent out of the world.

Now the mere creed — the belief that witches exist and that they can work supernaturally to the injury and even to the destruction of their enemies — is the heritage of the human race. The Englishman of the sixteenth or seventeenth century did not excogitate or dream it for himself, or borrow it from the Continent, or learn it from his spiritual advisers whether before the Reformation or after. He inherited it in an unbroken line from his primeval ancestors. And along with it came another dogma, likewise of abysmal antiquity — the theory that all diseases are of supernatural origin. This dogma had, to be sure, been somewhat limited in scope as the shaman developed into the physician, but it was still extant and still vigorous. Every malady that baffled the doctors was ascribed to witchcraft, often by the doctors themselves; and all sudden or virulent or wasting maladies lay under suspicion. These things are truisms, but they are continually lost sight of by the investigators of English witchcraft. There is a constant assumption that such beliefs are abnormal, a persistent tendency to ignore the fact that it was rather a mark of exceptional enlightenment in popular diagnosis to look to natural causes than a mark of positive credulity or superstition to look to supernatural causes. In brief, the ordinary Elizabethan, in this essential particular — the doctrine of *maleficium* and its application to disease — had not yet emerged from barbarism. And it was the doctrine of *maleficium*, and nothing else, that made the witch-creed terrible.

After a witch had been arrested, it is true, she often fell into the hands of the learned who asked her questions based on an elaborate system of demonology, and, when so interrogated, she often confessed strange things, which the industry of scholars may trace to foreign creeds or imported philosophies. Some of this erudite material, through the pulpit or otherwise, did certainly attach itself to the native and popular beliefs. And thus we may easily be led to fancy that judges, philosophers, divines — and even King James I — were to blame for the prevalence of English witchcraft in the seventeenth century. But such elaborations were merely incidental. They came into a particular case, if at all, only when the witch had once been cried out upon. Somebody falls sick, and the doctors cannot cure him; a child has hysterical fits and is grievously tormented. There are aged women in the village at whom we have long looked askance. They are foul-mouthed, perhaps, and prone to curse when we offend them; or they have laid claim to occult power, and have traded on the terror they inspire. They may even imagine themselves to hold intercourse with Satan, for they share the current superstitions and are not very strong in their wits. One of these beldames is mentioned as the bewitcher, perhaps because the patient's distempered fancy has seen a face and called a name. Then old rumors are revived: Smith's cattle died year before last, or Jones's little son. For there is ever at hand a huge mass of such latent evidence, all connected with the primitive doctrine of *maleficium*, and only waiting for a prosecution to bring it before the courts. When the trial begins, we may hear of compacts with Satan, of flights through the air, of sordid and hideous revels at the Witches' Sabbath. But such things are mere confirmatory details. The essential point, the really efficient impulse, is always *maleficium* — injury to goods or body or life through supernatural means.

For England, the worst period of witch-prosecution is, by common consent, the seventeenth century — the century of the Lancashire witches, of Matthew Hopkins and John Stearne, of Glanvil's *Saducismus Triumphatus*. The reign of James, we remember, covers exactly twenty-two years, from March, 1603, to March, 1625. In 1604 Parliament enacted a famous statute against witchcraft, usually called the statute of James I. The idea has been prevalent that the delusion was dying out at the close of Elizabeth's reign, and that the advent of the British Solomon gave it fresh vigor.

My purpose is to report an extremely interesting case of alleged witchcraft which occurred in Devonshire in 1601 and 1602, just before James came to the throne. This alone would make it significant enough. But it is still further noteworthy because it exhibits the phenomena in what we may call a pure form. We have only the testimony of voluntary, and for the most part aggrieved, witnesses. There are no arguments, no confessions, no comments from the bench. There is nothing but the beliefs and experiences of the witnesses themselves, honestly detailed according to their lights. Hence the documents afford us a perfect picture of the witchcraft creed as held by the common people. And we find, as we should expect, that the sum and substance of it all was *maleficium* — injury to the property and the health of the victims, amounting even to ruin and death.

The documents consist of eleven "examinations," * taken before a Devon justice of the peace, Sir Thomas Ridgeway, in 1601 and 1602. The manuscript was acquired by the Harvard College Library, in loose sheets, in 1905.[3] The papers are the original records, each examination being written out by a clerk and signed by the magistrate. Most of them are in duplicate, both copies bearing Ridgeway's signature, and one is in triplicate. Such examinations were regularly taken to perpetuate testimony, and were offered as evidence at the assizes. The method may be conveniently seen in Thomas Potts's account of the Lancashire witch-trials of 1612, at which he acted as clerk of the court.[4] Thus our Devon record contains a considerable body of material of unquestionable authenticity.

Sir Thomas Ridgeway was a man of first-rate intelligence, and is remembered as one of the Planters of Ulster. He was born about 1565. In 1600, shortly before the date of our examinations, he was appointed high sheriff of Devon and received the honor of knighthood. In 1616 he was raised to the Irish peerage by the title of Lord Ridgeway, and in 1623 he became Earl of Londonderry.

The scene of the trouble was Hardness, a village close to Dartmouth. Here lived Michael Trevisard, a fisherman, with his wife Alice and his son Peter. All were defamed for witchcraft, and suspicion against Michael and Alice was of long standing. The witnesses against them were persons of their own humble condition, belonging in Hardness or the vicinity.

* One of these includes the testimony of a man and his wife, so that we really have twelve witnesses.

There is no trace of influence from the clergy or the gentry. It was the villagers themselves who appealed to the magistrate for protection. One witness speaks of a number of them as going to Tunstall, to the house of Sir Thomas Ridgeway, to make a complaint, and as meeting Alice Trevisard on the way back. Whether the accused persons were ever brought to trial we do not know, but it is clear that Ridgeway had these documents prepared for eventual use at the assizes.

The whole essential body of the witchcraft doctrine occurs, in a highly condensed form, in the examination of Alice Butler, of Hardness. This is in two parts, and may be quoted in full. The duplicate shows a number of variant readings, some of which I have inserted in brackets. I have modernized the spelling and regulated punctuation and capitals, and so elsewhere.

Devon Th' examination of Alice Butler of Hardness, in the County aforesaid, widow, taken before Sir Thomas Ridgeway, Knight, the second of October, 1601.

1. This examinate saith that she, sitting at a door or bench in Hardness aforesaid about Christide last was twelvemonth with one Michael Trevysard of Hardness aforesaid, used these words: "I would my child were able to run as well as any of these children that run here in the street!" Then said Trevysard, "It shall never run!" "No? That's hard!" says this examinate again. "No, it shall never run," answered Trevysard, "till thou hast another," repeating the same words a dozen several times at the least with great vehemency. Whereupon this examinate, being much troubled in mind, especially upon a fear conceived by her before through the general bad report that went of him, departed from him. And the very same week the same child sickened, and consumed away, being well one day and ill another, for the space of seventeen weeks or thereabout, and then died.

2. This examinate further saith, that Peter Trevysard, son of the said Michael Trevisard, came to this examinate's house to borrow a hatchet, which Alice Beere, servant to this examinate, denied, to whom the said Michael answered [var. and he answered], "Shall I not have it? I will do thee a good turn ere twelvemonth be at an end." And shortly the said Alice Beere sickened, continuing one day well and another day ill, for the space of eleven weeks, and then died. In which case both the husband of this examinate and a [var. another] child of theirs fell sick, and so continued seventeen or eighteen weeks, and then died.

TH: RIDGWAY.

The regular fashion of commenting on such utterances as these is to cry out against the malicious folly of the accuser and to lament the hard lot of the accused. May I be permitted, for once, to abandon custom, and to express my sympathy with poor Alice Butler, who had lost her husband and two of her children by some strange wasting sickness, for which she had no name, and who could only revert to the primeval tenets of savage man in her attempt to explain so dreadful a visitation? Few utterances in any records are more artlessly pathetic.

To the student of English witchcraft the document is very valuable on account of the purity and simplicity of type which it exemplifies. *Maleficium* is the gist of the whole matter, and the process described is perfectly accordant to rule. We have the *damnum minatum* and the *malum secutum*. That is all. There are no complications whatever. There is not a trace of those foreign and learned elements that are often thought to constitute the bulk of the English witchcraft doctrine after the Reformation. There is no Black Man, no book to sign, no compact with Satan. There are no infernal revels, no fiendish lovers. In short, there is nothing that is non-essential. Alice Butler's evidence is precisely the kind of testimony that might have been offered against a witch in any land and in any stage of civilization, from the Stone Age to day-before-yesterday. It would be quite pertinent at the trial of a witch of Ashantee or Congo or the Australian bush. It exhibits the primitive and universal creed of the whole human race, preserved without the contamination of culture or education, and surviving every religious vicissitude, to the beginning of the seventeenth century, in one of the most enlightened countries in the world. Incidentally, it was quite enough to send Michael Trevisard to the scaffold if he came to trial and the jury believed Alice's story. Finally, nobody was to blame. The responsibility lay not upon the jurists or the theologians or the neighborhood: it was the burden of the human race as a whole.

An equally distressing case was that of Joan Baddaford. Alice Trevisard, it appears, had fallen out with John Baddaford, Joan's husband, and had "said unto him that he should go to Pursever Wood and gather up his wits." The precise meaning of this railing speech escapes me, but I fancy it was equivalent to calling John a scatter-brained fool. The phrase reminds one, though perhaps whimsically, of Pandar's con-

temptuous "Yea, hazelwood!" in Chaucer's Troilus.⁵ We
may also adduce, tentatively, the common saying, "Your wits
are gone wool-gathering." It was manifestly possible, if the
sequel should warrant, to interpret Alice's jeering words as a
threat that John should lose his mind. The sequel did so
warrant.

Within three weeks after [Joan alleged], the said John Baddaford made a
voyage to Rochelle, in the Hope of Dittsham, and returned home again out
of his wits, and so continued by the space of two years, tearing and renting
his clothes, in such sort as four or five men were hardly able to bind him
and keep him in order.

In like manner, as we learn from Potts's Wonderfull Discoverie of Witches in the Countie of Lancaster, John Bulcock
and his mother Joan were indicted, in 1612,

for that they feloniously had practiced, exercised, and used their divelish
and wicked arts, called witchcraft, enchantments, charms, and sorceries,
in and upon the body of Jennet Deane, so as the body of the said Jennet
Deane, by force of the said witchcrafts, wasted and consumed, and after
she, the said Jennet, became mad.

But we must return to the testimony of Joan Baddaford.

On the occasion of the same quarrel, Joan averred, Alice
Trevisard had "further threatened this examinate that
within seven years after she should not be worth a groat, nor
have a house to dwell in, nor a coat to her back." And these
threats came true, for "whereas she had at that time the fee
simple of an house worth one hundreth pounds, now is she
worth nothing."

Let us bear in mind that the things to which poor Joan
Baddaford bore witness must have been facts. Her insane
husband and her fallen fortunes were neither delusions nor
superstitions. We cannot ridicule or denounce; we can only
pity. If Joan was a bad logician — if she reasoned post hoc
ergo propter hoc — so do we, every day of our lives. And as
to threats, they are still admissible as evidence against an
accused murderer.

The next section of Joan's examination may seem trivial,
but it was significant of inveterate malice on the part of the
alleged witch, and thus was clearly pertinent. Some three
years before the date of this document, Joan had asked

a penny of Alice Trevisard "for washing of clothes." Alice paid the debt, but added that the penny should do Joan "little good." Joan spent the coin for drink, "and when the drink came, she had no power to drink thereof, but the same night fell sick, and continued so by the space of seven weeks following." This is an excellent instance of primeval magic. It is notoriously dangerous to receive anything from a witch, whether by way of gift or of payment. Joan's inability to drink is a typical symptom. We meet with it again in the Lancashire trials of 1612, as reported by Thomas Potts. One Peter Chaddock, in testifying against Isabel Robey, deposed that at one time he

> was very sore pained, and so thirsty withal, and hot within his body, that he would have given anything he had to have slaked his thirst, having drink enough in the house, and yet could not drink until the time that . . . James the Glover came to him; and this examinate then said before the said Glover, "I would to God that I could drink!" whereupon the said Glover said to this examinate, "Take that drink, and in the name of the Father, the Son, and the Holy Ghost, drink it," — whereupon this examinate then took the glass of drink, and did drink it all, and afterwards mended very well.

Joan Baddaford's experiences, or some of them, convinced her that Alice Trevisard was a witch. This, indeed, was the general opinion in those parts. At all events, Joan, with several of her neighbors, went to Sir Thomas Ridgeway's house at Tunstall to lay a complaint against her. On the way back, Alice met them. A dispute ensued, as was natural, and Alice said to Joan, "Thou or thine may be burned before long be!" The taunt, we may conjecture, was in answer to some such remark as that Alice deserved to be burnt for a witch. It is easy to imagine the scene. The sharp-tongued Alice, a common railer and brawler, baited by a group of villagers, all of whom believed that they had suffered at her hands, was determined to give as good as she got, regardless of the risk that anything she said might be used against her. The encounter was on a Monday. From that day until the next Thursday Joan Baddaford made no fire in her house, whether from fear or from poverty we cannot tell. On Thursday, however, Joan began to build a fire. She laid a few coals in her chimney — brought from a neighbor's cottage, no doubt — and turned aside to break up some wood. Her child was sitting upon the hearth. Suddenly she heard the child scream, and saw that the band about his neck was burning. Looking into his neck, she found that the flesh was "burned to the bone." Yet the child had not fallen into the fire, but was "sitting on the hearth as before." Indeed, the fire was not kindled at all, but the coals lay there just as she had put them in. These facts Joan "presently shewed to divers of the chief of Dartmouth, and sought the best remedy she could, but found neither salve nor anything else that did it any good, but within three weeks after the child consumed and died." Here again is a grim fact — superstition or no superstition — the child perished miserably, and no one could understand his disease.

The examination of William Tompson, of Dartmouth, is uncommonly lively and picturesque. William was a sailor. Some six years before, he and a comrade (one William Furseman, also of Dartmouth) had chanced to meet Alice Trevisard upon the Force in that town. It was about midnight. She was dressed in a "long grayish cape down to her foot," and wore a hood which covered almost all her face, "so that they took her for some Seminary priest." They asked her what she was doing in the street at that time of night. Probably the sailors were not quite sober. At any rate, they were uncivil, and if, as William alleged, they mistook Alice for a priest, we may be sure they were rough-handed. An altercation followed — but we will let Tompson tell his own story:

> She fell out with them, and they were no sooner gone from her than this examinate fell, and was in great danger of breaking his neck. Whereat the said Alice laughing, this examinate said to her, "Dost thou laugh at a shrewd turn [i.e. a bad accident]?" And then he struck her with a musket rod; whereupon she threatened this examinate, saying, "Thou shalt be better thou hadst never met with me!"

Vengeance was swift. Within three weeks after the *damnum minatum*, William Tompson went to sea. His ship caught fire — none knew how — and foundered. Out of twenty-five on board, only six were saved. As for William, he was picked up by a Portuguese vessel ("by a Portingalle") and carried to Spain, where he was imprisoned for a whole year. On his return Alice Trevisard said to Elizabeth Tompson, his wife, "Is he come home on life? He hath better luck than a good man! But it is no matter. He shall be there again within this twelve months." And the prophecy was fulfilled. In less than half a year William was captured once more, this time by the Spaniards, and he was kept in confinement for twenty-five months. "Elizabeth Tompson," adds the record, "being examined upon these last speeches of her husband's oath, affirmeth them to be true."

William Tompson's sufferings inevitably bring us thoughts of a famous passage in Macbeth. The temptation to linger a moment over the comparison is not to be resisted. The witch in Shakspere had been flouted by the wife of the master of the Tiger. The ship has reached Aleppo in safety.

> But in a sieve I'll thither sail,
> And, like a rat without a tail,
> I'll do, I'll do, and I'll do!

The horrid vagueness of these menacing words has misled many. "She threatens," runs the usual note, "in the shape of a rat, to gnaw through the hull of the Tiger and make her spring a leak." So one might imagine, were it not that the Weird Sister proceeds to interpret her own oracle in the plainest terms.

> I will drain him dry as hay!
> Sleep shall neither night nor day
> Hang upon his pent-house lid.
> He shall live a man forbid.
> Weary se'nnights nine times nine
> Shall he dwindle, peak, and pine.
> Though his bark cannot be lost,
> Yet it shall be tempest-tost!

Nothing can be clearer than the witch's intentions. Arrived at Aleppo, she will take the shape of a rat in order to slip on board the Tiger unnoticed. This, and not to use her teeth, is the object of the transformation. Then she will bewitch the craft and lay a spell upon the captain. There is no question of scuttling the ship. The witch, as she tells us herself, controls the winds. She will make them contrary, so that the Tiger, though destined to reach port at last, shall be tossed about in storm and distress for nine times nine weeks, until the water is all gone and the provisions are exhausted. The master shall pine away with hunger and thirst and lack of sleep, until the full measure of vengeance is exacted. Then, and not till then, shall he come home to the fat ronyon, his wife, who denied the hag a chestnut and bade her begone for a foul witch. Alice Trevisard's revenge was equally swift and terrible — a fire at sea, an open boat, and a Spanish prison. Our document is of 1601, and Macbeth was written not far from 1605. The one falls just before the accession of James I, the other shortly after his accession. Surely, in view of such stories as William Tompson's, we should hesitate to affirm that the interest in witchcraft which manifested itself in England soon after James ascended the throne was due to the king's influence. Let us rather infer that his accession found the agitation already under way and of long standing. Such an inference, by the way, is amply supported by the records of the time. But let us return to the sea.

A tale of all but incomparable wildness concerning a bewitched ship is reported by one Captain Silas Taylor, writing from Harwich, in England, to Joseph Williamson, keeper of state papers. The letter is dated November 2, 1667.

They tell a strange story at Ipswich [says the captain] of one of their ships that was lost in the late storms; that another of the same town passing by them, and being well acquainted, they sent their remembrances to friends; the master, Jonathan Banticke, to his parents, one Hornegild, a passenger who had lost his ship at Scarborough Road, his love to his wife and children, and all the other seamen to their relations. When asked the reason, and whether their ship was leaky, or what they wanted, the first ship replied that they had long labored to free their maintop, where sat a couple of witches, but by all that they could do, could not remove nor get them down, and so they were lost people. The master named the two witches to the second ship's master and his company, insomuch that they are now in jail at Ipswich. The story is credibly reported by the second ship, and generally believed.[6]

Thomas Heywood repeats a story which he got from an old acquaintance ("a woman of good credit and reputation"). This lady, while at Amsterdam, awaiting passage for England, lent an old woman some money, taking a brass kettle as security, "which she did, knowing it to be serviceable for her to keep a charcoal fire in at sea, to comfort her and her child." The debtor could not pay, and yet objected vigorously to having the kettle go out of the country. They parted on ill terms: "Carry it away if thou canst!" cried the hag defiantly. "Marry, and I will trie what I can doe!" replied the lady, with some spirit.

The Maister called aboord, the wind stood faire, the Sea was calme, and the weather pleasant: but they had not beene many houres at Sea, when there arose a suddene, sad, and terrible tempest, as if the winds and waters had beene at dissention, and the distempered ayre at warre with both. A mightie storme then arose, insomuch that the Maister protested, that in his life he had not seene the like, and, being in despaire of shipwracke, desired both Saylers and passengers to betake themselves to their prayers. This word came from them that laboured above the Hatches to those that were stowed under: their present feare made them truly apprehend the danger, and betake themselves to their devotions; when suddenly one casting up his eyes, espyed an old woman sitting on the top of the maine Mast: The Maister saw her, and all those that were above, being at the sight much amased. The rumor of this went downe, which the gentlewoman hearing (who was then sitting with her child in her Cabbin and warming it over a Charcoale fire made in the Kettle). "O God!" sayth she (remembring her former words) "then the old woman is come after me for her Kettle;" the Maister, apprehending the businesse, "Marrie and then let her have it!" saith he, and takes the Kettle, coales and all, and casts them overboord into the Sea. This was no sooner done, but the Witch dismounts her selfe from the Mast, goes aboord the Brasse Kettle, and in a moment sailes out of sight: the Ayre cleared, the Windes grew calme, the tempest ceased, and she had a faire and speedie passage into England.

This tough yarn Heywood certifies he had heard confirmed by other passengers on the same voyage.[7]

The next deposition in the manuscript is that of Christian Webbar. We will pass it over for a moment, to take up the examination of Christopher Honywell, since that, like William Tompson's, has to do with the sea. Christopher's deposition is unique. He was a lad of thirteen, and seems to have been playing about the harbor with another boy, Peter Trevisard, Michael and Alice's son, when the strange thing happened which tended to show that no member of the family was free from the taint of sorcery. The document is short and I shall append it entire. It would be quite charming in its naïve wonder if it were found in less sinister company.

Th' examination of Christopher Honywell aged thirteen years or thereabout, taken as aforesaid the 2 of October, 1601.

This examinate saith that about Whitsuntide last he was with Peter Trevisard, son of the said Michael Trevisard, at a place at Hardness where the fishermen use to hang their nets; where the said young Trevisard did put off his father's boat, saying, "Go thy ways to New Quay, and go between the two lighters, and I will meet thee there." And farther this examinate saith that he ran with the young Trevisard to the New Quay presently after, and found the boat there between the two lighters, the said quay being distant near two flight-shoots from the place where the boat was so thrust off, as aforesaid, and not right against [i. e. opposite] the same place, but on one side, the said two lighters also being so near together that there was but room enough for the boat to go in.

TH: RIDGWAY.

Enchanted boats that obey their master's will, or guide themselves without the helmsman's touch, are well known in the realm of faery. Here belong the Argo with its talking figurehead, and the ships of the Phæacians, which knew men's minds and the way to every port; here, too, the self-moving ship in Marie's Lai de Guigemar. Frithiof had a ship which understood his words and obeyed them. Svend Ranild, in the Danish ballad, stood upon the shore in great need of his ship, which was anchored in the offing. He blew such a blast that his horn burst into three pieces: "'Come ye not in?' quoth Ranild."

> That was Ranild's golden ship
>   That heard the horn so good;
> She broke asunder cables nine,
>   And came to where he stood.
> "Be thou welcome," quoth Ranild.[8]

The bearing of young Christopher's testimony should not be misconceived. It was merely confirmatory of the general proposition that the Trevisards possessed uncanny powers. To insist on its frivolity and hold up our hands in horror at the criminal folly of our forefathers in sending men and women to the gallows on such grounds is *parum ad rem*. No English witch was ever convicted on evidence like this, nor were such harmless feats of seamanship punishable at all under the law. There was plenty of serious evidence against the Trevisards, as we have seen. And with this caveat we may revert to the deposition of Christian Webbar, which is quite different from anything we have had before, and of very particular interest.

Christian was a widow in Hardness. She had let a tenement in the village to Michael Trevisard at a yearly rent

of twenty-six shillings and eightpence. He had paid only
six and eightpence, and Christian demanded the pound that
was in arrears. "It shall be the worse for you!" was Alice
Trevisard's response. Then followed a very curious piece of
malignant sorcery. Alice cast water upon Christian's stairs.
One Isabel Tozar saw it done, and warned Christian to

beware how she went up her stairs, which this examinate refrained accordingly for a space, in which mean space the said Alice Trevisard herself happened to pass through some part of the said stairs. And within one hour
after, the said Alice, and this examinate also, fell grievously sick, and part
of the hands, fingers, and toes of the said Alice rotted and consumed away,
as yet appears by her.

The singularity of this piece of sorcery consists in the fact
that the maleficent magic took effect on the witch herself
when she heedlessly came under its influence. Alice fell into
the pit which she had dug for another. Christian suffered
too, on the principle of sympathy, but the virulence of the
infection was felt chiefly by its contriver.

Joan Davye testified that her husband George had a quarrel with Michael Trevisard. Within a se'nnight thereafter
Joan was sitting by the fire with a young child in her arms
when the child leapt into the fire and was "very much
scalded." When Trevisard heard of it, he said that he could
help the child in twenty-four hours, if he wished, but that he
would never do good to George Davye or any of his family.
Davye seems to have been at sea at the time. At all events,
the very week after, on "the same voyage" (so runs the testimony) "the said George Davye was hurt very grievously in
shooting off a piece for pleasure." Joan also declared that
one Henry Oldreeve had some differences with Trevisard,
and that soon after Oldreeve lost twenty fat wethers in one
week and "he himself languished and died."

William Cozen was another person who had fallen out with
Trevisard. In this case the vengeance, though deferred, was
none the less certain. Within a quarter of a year, William's
daughter-in-law was sadly afflicted. Without a blow or
any visible cause "her neck shrunk down between her two
shoulders, and her chin touched her breast, and so remaineth
still in a very strange manner." This accusation, like some
others that we have already looked at, finds its parallel in

the Lancashire case of 1612. Alison Device was the grand-daughter of old Elizabeth Demdike, who had been a devotee of sorcery for fifty years and is described as "a general agent for the devil in those parts." Alison bore witness against both her mother and her grandmother; but she herself was im-plicated, confessed, and was hanged. Her offence was the laming of Abraham Law, a peddler. Abraham excited the compassion of the court by his miserable plight. Before his encounter with Alison Device, he

was a verie able sufficient stout man of Bodie, and a goodly man of Stature. But by this Devilish art of Witch-craft his head is drawne awrie, his Eyes and face deformed, his speech not well to bee understood; his Thighes and Legges starcke lame; his Armes lame especially the left side, his handes lame and turned out of their course, his Bodie able to indure no travell: and thus remaineth at this present time.[9]

Alison was asked if she could cure the poor creature, and, though repentant, insisted that this was beyond her power. As in the case of Christian Webbar's infected stairs, the spells acted dynamically, when once they were set in motion, and passed quite beyond the witch's control. "The gods them-selves cannot recall their gifts."

William Cozen's deposition closes with a bit of graphic horror which defies commentary in its simple impressiveness: "Further this examinate saith that Joan Cozen, wife of this examinate, being in her deathbed, requested this examinate that if Alice Trevisard, wife of the foresaid Michael Trevi-sard, did come to her grave, he should beat her away."

The evidence of Susan Tooker (or Turke) is very definite. It involves all three Trevisards, Michael and Alice and Peter their son. About four years ago, she declared, Alice Trevisard threatened her in plain terms: "I will not leave thee worth a gray groat!" Walter Tooker, Susan's husband, was just starting on a voyage. He lost both ship and goods, though the weather was fair. Further, it appears that young Peter Trevisard had been refused drink by Susan, whereupon he said "that it had been better to have delivered him drink." Next day Susan sickened, and she suffered for seven weeks. Finally, averred Susan, Mr. Martin, in the year of his mayor-alty, set up a fold, or pound, at Hardness, to keep timber in. Michael Trevisard said: "Martin, hast thou made a fold?

Wind and weather shall tear up all!" And so it happened, nor could Mr. Martin keep his fold in place. "Since that time it hath been set up in the millpool, where no stormy weather can annoy it. Yet sithence it hath been plucked up very strangely, for it riseth up altogether, being timber of an exceeding great weight and bigness."

The trivial nature of some of the charges brought against alleged witches and wizards often excites the contemptuous mirth of the modern. But there is no sense or reason in such an attitude of mind. The importance of a piece of evidence should not be measured by the actual importance of the occurrence testified to, but by its significance with regard to the point at issue, that is, with regard to the question whether the defendant was or was not a practiser of "arts inhibited and out of warrant." Nobody scoffs at a prosecuting attorney now-a-days for spending his energies over scraps of paper or thumb-prints or scratched hands when a murder trial is in progress. It is just as absurd to jeer at our ancestors for troubling themselves about exploding ale-barrels or butter that would not "come." The malice of a witch, according to the general hypothesis, may show itself in small things as well as in great. Jeering is poor business anywhere, but, if we must be contemptuous, let us concentrate our energies on the doctrine itself. No true philosopher will see anything ridiculous in the testimony of Joan Laishe, except the essential absurdity of the whole underlying thesis.

Joan, it seems, had once refused Alice Trevisard a half-pennyworth of ale, and Alice had retorted in the customary fashion. "That shall be a hard halfpennyworth!" and "I will not leave you worth a groat!" Two days after, one of Joan's ale-casks "on the sudden leapt up of itself," and fell on the ground. The cask burst, and all the ale was lost.

Among the secondary causes of witch prosecution, the "healer," or white witch, regularly plays a conspicuous rôle. When consulted in sickness, she is quick to ascribe the ailment to evil arts, and is often ready enough to name the culprit. There need be no malice in this rôle of the white witch. She is simply in the same primitive stage of medical science which ascribes every malady to the personal enmity of a sorcerer. As to designating the guilty party, that is of course requisite. We must know who our enemy is if we are to resist or forestall his assault.

I have said that our Devon documents include all or most of the typical features of an English witchcraft case. Accordingly, the wise woman is not lacking. Her name was Blachford, Mother Blachford of Bridgetown. Alice Trevisard, it appears, called at John Denman's house in Kingswear, alleging that she had a letter for his wife. Mistress Denman was not at home. Alice showed a piece of paper to Denman's daughter, but the girl would not touch it, because she had heard that Alice was a witch. Soon after, one of Denman's children fell sick. Mother Blachford, to whom he resorted for medicine, told him that Alice Trevisard had bewitched the child. "When you go home," said Mother Blachford, "you shall find that Alice was at your house this morning with what she said was a letter." Denman inquired accordingly, and learned what had happened in his absence. There is some vagueness at this point, which cross-questioning might have dissipated. It is obvious, however, that the paper was suspected to be a charm. At all events, Denman declared that he never heard of the letter again. What became of the child is not stated. Probably it recovered, in spite of Alice's spell and Mother Blachford's remedy.

Oddly enough, I find among my notes a fragment of New England tradition attaching to a Massachusetts witch named Blatchford. I obtained it, about forty years ago, from a lady of eighty-four, who had heard the story from "old Mr. David Loring's wife," the victim of the spell. It is a small matter, but has not only the coincidence of name to excuse one for telling it, but also a certain relation of locality. Barnstable, where the thing happened, is named after the Devonshire Barnstaple. It was settled in 1639, and the spelling with *b* instead of *p* was a common method of writing the name of the Devonian town in the seventeenth century and is still a common local pronunciation. Some of the pioneers of the Old Colony town were Devon men. The Indian trail from Barnstable Harbor straight across Cape Cod is now a public highway, known as Mary Dunn's Road, from an Indian woman who once lived in a hut near a pond which the trail passes. The pond, too, is called after Mary Dunn. It is a pretty little sheet of water, lying quite solitary in the midst of the woods. One day, as Mrs. Loring reported, she was returning on horseback to Barnstable from the village of Hyannis, at the southern end of the trail, and, when she was nearing the pond, one Lizzie Blatchford, a witch, who lived on the margin, bewitched her horse, so that he insisted on going round and round the pond for a long time. To all intents and purposes, as we see, old Mrs. Loring was "pixey-led," and we have in her little anecdote a good instance of the connection between the fairies and witchcraft. Her remedy, if she had only known it, was to turn her cloak inside out and so reverse the spell. Bishop Corbet, best known to literature as the author of The Fairies' Farewell, had a similar adventure not far from 1620, and has left us a humorous account of it in his Iter Boreale. Corbet, not yet a bishop, was lost with his companions in Charley Forest, on the way from Newark to Bosworth.

> Whilst in this mill wee labour and turne round
> As in a conjurers circle, William found
> A menes for our deliverance: "Turne your cloakes,"
> Quoth hee, "for Puck is busy in these oakes:
> If ever yee at Bosworth will be found,
> Then turne your cloakes, for this is Fayry-ground!"
> But, ere this witchcraft was perform'd, wee mett
> A very man, who had no cloven feete;
> Though William, still of little faith, doth doubt
> 'Tis Robin, or some sprite that walkes about.
> "Strike him!" quoth hee, "and it will turne to ayre;
> Crosse your selves thrice and strike it!" "Strike that dare,"
> Thought I, "for sure this massy forrester
> In stroakes will prove the better conjurer."

There is one more deposition in our manuscript — that of John Galsworthie of Hardness. It affords no novelties, but may be given in full to complete the record.

The examination of John Galsworthie of Hardness in the County aforesaid, husbandman, taken before Sir Thomas Ridgway, Knight, the eighth of April, 1602.

This examinate sayeth that about four years sithence, his wife demanded certain money of Alice Trevisard, the wife of Michael Trevisard of Hardness, which she owed her; whereunto the said Alice Trevisard answered, "I pray God that thou never prosper in body nor goods!" And never sithence did he, this examinate, or his wife, prosper in body or goods; for in very short time after that the said Alice Trevisard had spoken those words, he was taken lame in all his body and went by two crutches twelve-month after. And further this examinate saith that his wife was never well in her body, sithence, but consumed away, and died at Christmas last past. And also this examinate sayeth that he had a sow great with pigs, which pigs rotted in the sow's belly within six weeks after his wife had demanded the money of the foresaid Trevisard, as aforesaid.

TH: RIDGWAY.

These documents are interesting enough as pictures of life and manners. But, as already suggested, their chief claim to our notice rests upon their date and upon the pure and un-mixed form in which they exhibit the essential element in all witchcraft. The latter point needs no emphasis. The outcry against Michael Trevisard and his family was raised by the people itself — by the unadulterated, unsophisticated "folk," instigated only by its own primeval philosophy of *maleficium*. There were no social or political or theological complications. We have simply an upheaval from below, from the abysmal pit of savagery out of which the human race has had to strug-gle up. And such uncontaminated testimony, coming at this particular moment (in 1601 and 1602), is of very special con-sequence. If we are to comprehend the history of witchcraft in England, we must keep in mind, for this exact time, a clear idea of the intellectual condition of just that class to which Alice Butler and Joan Baddaford and William Tompson and all the other complainants belonged. Queen Elizabeth died in 1603, and King James's witchcraft act was passed in 1604. There is a more or less general impression that this act was momentous, and that the accession of James gave an extra-ordinary impulse to prosecution. If, as all will agree, our documents are typical of the state of popular feeling in 1601 and 1602, they offer an instant challenge to this idea. Any-how, they make short work of the notion that English witch-craft was a theological importation from the Continent.

CHAPTER II

ENGLISH WITCHCRAFT BEFORE 1558

IN THE present chapter we shall trace the history of English witchcraft from Anglo-Saxon times to the accession of Elizabeth in 1558. In this process we shall convince ourselves, by the mere logic of plain facts, that the Elizabethans did not import their ideas or practices in this regard from the Continent, as some scholars have maintained, through the agency of the returning Marian exiles, whether Bishop Jewel or others: on the contrary, they inherited these ideas and practices from their forefathers in an unbroken line of tradition. Incidentally we shall observe that the various articles of the witch-creed — as held both by the deluded witches themselves and by their prosecutors — are identical with the articles of the witch-creed of uneducated folk to-day, and likewise with that of contemporary savages throughout the earth. Thus it will appear beyond question that the tradition is continuous, not merely from the Anglo-Saxons to the present time, but — what is even more significant — from remote ages and from conditions of all-but-primitive barbarism.

Witches may be white or black — beneficent or malefic — and it is, of course, only the latter that are hated and feared by the people at large, for white witches, who heal diseases and undo the spells of malignant sorcery — are regarded as friends of mankind. But the distinction is, in practice, often ignored or forgotten, since the same person may use the arts of sorcery for good or for ill. And there is ever a tendency among theologians to include both sorts of witches under the same condemnation, as dealing with evil spirits, and among the folk to suspect the white witch of mischief on occasion. Still, the driving force in all prosecution is the fear that the black witch inspires.

At the outset we must guard against a possible misapprehension. "Magic itself," says a distinguished scholar, "is actual and universal. But witchcraft never was. It was but a shadow, a nightmare: the nightmare of a religion, the shadow of a dogma. Less than five centuries saw its birth, its vigor, its decay." [1] This statement is accurate if by witchcraft is meant the fully developed and highly complicated system set forth in the Malleus Maleficarum and Del Rio's Disquisitiones Magicae, — what Hansen calls "der verhängnisvolle Sammelbegriff des Hexenwesens," [2] — which was not possible until scholasticism had codified the motley notions about magic and demonology and sorcery and devil-worship which Christian superstition and Christian theology had derived from the most various sources — from Judaism, classical antiquity, Neoplatonism, and the thousand-and-one notions of pagan converts. But, momentous as this fully developed system was, — and true though it may be that without the schematizing influence of scholastic philosophy the witch-prosecution which was epidemic on the Continent from 1400 to 1700 could hardly have taken place, — yet we should never forget that the essential element in black witchcraft is *maleficium* — the working of harm to the bodies and goods of one's neighbors by means of evil spirits or of strange powers derived from intercourse with such spirits. This belief in *maleficium* was once universal; it was rooted and grounded in the minds of all European peoples before they became Christian; it is still the creed of most savages and of millions of so-called civilized men. Throughout the history of witchcraft (in whatever sense we understand that word) it remained the ineradicable thing — the solid foundation, unshakably established in popular belief, for whatever superstructure might be reared by the ingenuity of jurisconsults, philosophers, theologians, and inquisitors. Without this popular belief in *maleficium*, the initial suspicions and complaints which were the starting-point of all prosecutions would have been impossible and inconceivable. *With* this popular belief, the rest was easy.

Besides, we must make a sharp distinction between English witchcraft and Continental witchcraft. The trials of the Elizabethan age, as we have noted in A Typical Case, did not involve acceptance, either by the people or by the judges, of the complicated and systematized doctrine which formed the basis for the inquisitorial proceedings on the Continent. For England, then, we have to do, in the main, with isolated phenomena, with concrete facts (or what were taken for facts) which prompted the folk to defend themselves; not with theories which prompted the spiritual guardians of the people to eradicate heresy. There was no Holy Inquisition. Scholars might theorize, but action was taken because John Doe's cow had fallen strangely sick or Richard Roe's child had languished and died of some mysterious ailment. In a word, Elizabethan witchcraft (as brought to trial) was simple and primitive. It shows no trace whatever of the elaborate abominations of the Witches' Sabbath.[3] The impulse to prosecution, in most instances, came not from the learned or ruling classes but from humble folk, who clung tenaciously to their primeval belief in *maleficium*, lived in constant fear of it, and always had definite persons in view who passed for witches and in many cases professed the black art and actually supposed themselves able (as they certainly were willing) to practise it. Scot, though he directs his arguments largely against the bookish witchmongers like Bodin and Danæus and Institoris, refers clearly to the ignorant populace as the source of such opinions and insists that educated men should free themselves from the superstition of the masses. "See also," he exclaims, "what persons complaine upon them, whether they be not of the basest, the unwisest, and most faithles kind of people"; and he goes on to construct a typical instance of such a complaint, involving not only the *damnum minatum* and the *malum secutum* but also consultation with a "wise woman." [4] John Gaule, in 1646, distinctly refers to the "common people" the impulse to the prosecution of witches: "Every poore and peevish olde Creature (such is their Ignorance and Uncharitablenesse) cannot but fall under their suspicion, nay their infamous exprobation; every Accident, (more then ordinary) every disease whereof they neither understand the Cause, nor are acquainted with the Symptomes must bee suspected for witch-craft. His Cow or his Hog, cannot be strangely taken, but straight it must bee reckoned and rumored for bewitcht." [5] As late as 1704 John Toland, in a striking passage, accounts for the errors of the higher ranks in society on the ground of their contact with nurses and servants in childhood. "We are presently after our Birth deliver'd to Nurses, ignorant Women of the meanest Vulgar, who infuse into us their Errors with their Milk, frightning us into quiet with the menaces of Rawhead and Bloody-bones, Bugglebows and Bullbeggars. And lest we shou'd be lost by wandring abroad, or drop into Wells or Rivers, they terrify us with storys of Spirits and Hobgoblins, making us believe that all lonesome places are haunted, and that the invisible Powers are principally active and mischievous in the night-time. . . . From our Nurses we are brought home, where we are still put into worse hands among idle and ignorant Servants, whose chiefest Entertainments are Discourses of Fairys, Elves, Witchcrafts, walking Ghosts, Fortune-telling, consulting Astrologers, or such other chimerical Doings; delighting to fright and delude one another, not seldom to carry on their private Intrigues: which things, however intended, never fail to make fatal impressions on the Children: and for the most part our Parents are not wiser." [6]

The general and specific identity of the English witch-creed in both Elizabethan and pre-Elizabethan times with that of uncivilized races at the present day might be illustrated by a multitude of testimonies from travellers and anthropologists. Three or four quotations will suffice. Among the Bueni of Madagascar, we are told, "in almost every village there is some old and very ugly woman who is accused of being a witch. It is she who causes all the misfortunes and all the maladies. She is feared and hated. Children run away when she approaches and adults do not accost her without terror." [7] Among the East African Barundi, in like manner, witches and sorcerers, old women for the most part, "bear the blame if a person falls sick or dies, if a storm lays waste the fields, if cattle are injured or plague-stricken, if women are barren, if children do not thrive, if thefts occur, and so on." [8] In Morocco the sorcerer "operates both for good and for ill. He cures, he relieves pain, he inspires hope, he consoles; he grants love and alienates affection; he causes impotence and sterility; he infuses, modifies, or develops friendship; he makes his enemies pine away with debility or disease; some persons he corrupts, others he makes his accomplices; his influence brings into his service not only human beings but animals, things, and the elements. He causes the moon to descend in foam upon plants; [9] he fills the air and the earth with mirages and the night with phantoms." [10] Compare the testimony of the eminent theologian William Perkins, whose life was almost exactly coincident with Queen Elizabeth's reign: "The wonders done by Inchanters are: 1. The raising of stormes and tempests; windes and weather, by sea and land: 2. The poysoning of the ayre: 3. Blasting of corne: 4. Killing of cattell, and annoying of men, women, and children: 5. The procuring of strange passions and torments in mens bodies and other creatures, with the curing of the same: 6. Casting out of deuills." [11] There is scarcely a single item of malefic witchcraft in Elizabethan annals that cannot be matched in the beliefs of the ancient Assyrians. Their witches and wizards had the evil eye, controlled demons for their own vile purposes, brought on storms, took away one's wealth, caused accidents, spoiled food and drink, sent bad dreams, thwarted the marital relation by impotence and barrenness, had charms for both love and hatred, afflicted their enemies with disease and madness even unto death. They moved rapidly from place to place, waylaid travellers, slipped into houses in strange manner. Their use of image magic is dwelt on, and so is the employment of images in abolishing their spells. [12]

The prevalence of every form of witchcraft and sorcery in England before the Norman Conquest might be inferred from the richness of the native vocabulary, even if we had no other proofs: for *witch, wizard, enchanter, seer, diviner*, and so on, there are more than thirty Anglo-Saxon terms. [13] But there are other proofs in abundance. In 747 the Council of Clovesho directed bishops to traverse their dioceses yearly and, calling the people together, to teach the word of God, which forbids, among other sins, pagan observances, defined as "soothsayers, sorcerers, auguries, auspices, amulets, spells, or all the filth of the impious and errors of the heathen." [14] King Alfred's edict merely repeats the Law of Moses (Exodus, xxii, 18) in an oddly distorted form: "Those women who are wont to receive enchanters and magicians and wizards or witches — thou shalt not suffer them to live." [15] In the Laws of Edward and Guthrum (before A.D. 940), wizards and witches, soothsayers, perjurers, secret murderers, and harlots are classed together; [16] and there is an identical clause in the Laws of Æthelred (1008) [17] — which adds magicians (*scin-cræftcan*) [18] to the list — and of Cnut (ca. 1030) : [19] all such offenders are to be banished or destroyed unless they reform and make amends. This clause was a favorite bit with the preachers of the time.[20] We may compare also the Ecclesiastical Law of King Edmund (ca. 942), which excommunicates perjurers and those who practise magic, but with a similar proviso.[21] Hell, according to the tenth-century Blickling Homilies, is the destination of those wizards that practise incantations and conjuring and thus beguile the unwary and seduce them from God by their witcheries and illusions.[22] When Antichrist comes, another homilist prophesies, "he shall have with him wizards and sorcerers and diviners and those who know how to chant spells; . . . and cursed spirits shall be his teachers and his companions." [23] Witchcraft or evil magic is also mentioned in various forms of the Ritual for the Ordeal of Swimming (ninth century and later),[24] and in a Formula of Excommunication of the first half of the eleventh century.[25] Attempts to frustrate the ordeal of hot iron or hot water by witchcraft are also contemplated in rituals.[26]

The Secular Laws of Cnut (ca. 1030) forbid paganism,[27] which they define as follows: "to worship the heathen gods, or sun or moon, fire or flood, wells or stones or trees of any kind, or to love witchcraft or to work secret murder in any wise, or to practise anything in the way of sacrifice or soothsaying or such delusions." [28] This enactment comes mostly from one of the so-called Canons of King Edgar, which it substantially reproduces.[29] By secret murder (not mentioned in the canon), Cnut means particularly homicide by witchcraft, as the context indicates.[30] His ordinance was in part repeated in the Laws of the Northumbrian Priests of York in the same century.[31] Cnut, by the way, was of course familiar with the superstitions of his native Denmark, and Scandinavian wizards and witches, according to Saxo Grammaticus, could brew poisons, slay by their curse, take animal form and in that shape kill; they could procure love by spell or philtre, bring mist and glamour and rain and bad weather, strike panic fear, blunt steel weapons, summon a person against his will, and devise protective charms.[32] English witchcraft was equally varied and comprehensive.

Homicide by witchcraft, then, came under the general head of secret murder (morð, murdrum),[33] but it is particularly designated in the Laws of Æthelstan (ca. 930)[34] and in the Modus of King Edgar's time (ca. 965),[35] as well as in the vernacular Confessional[36] and Penitential[37] falsely ascribed to Archbishop Ecgbert of York and in the Latin penitentials (Irish, English, and Frankish) to which the names[38] of Finnian, Columban,[39] Theodore, Bede, and Ecgbert[40] are attached. The legal treatise of ca. 1114 known as the Leges Henrici pronounces the crime of homicide by poison or witchcraft punishable with death; if, however, the victim survives but has suffered sickness or bodily injury, the offender is let off with the requirement of compensation. This clause in the Leges specifies as one means of such homicide, a form of witchcraft known from very ancient times, and still prevalent — namely, invultuacio (envoûtement), that is, the maltreatment of an image or effigy representing the person to be afflicted or destroyed.[41] This occult method of murder is also mentioned in the Anglo-Saxon Modus Imponendi Poenitentiam of King Edgar's period and, in identical terms, in the Anglo-Saxon Penitential of Pseudo-Ecgbert.[42] An actual case of the kind, from the ninth or tenth century, is recorded (along with the witch's punishment by drowning) in an account of the title to a piece of land in Northamptonshire. We shall return to this matter presently.[43]

That the Anglo-Saxons believed in murderous witches who could fly through the air, would be probable anyhow, since their Germanic kin on the Continent lived in fear of such creatures in the sixth, seventh, and eighth centuries and even charged them with cannibalism,[44] as their laws demonstrate.[45] Such superstition is condemned by an Irish synod of about A.D. 800,[46] and is mentioned as existent in full force by the tenth-century German penitential known as the Corrector — a document embodied in his Decretum by Burchard of Worms about 1020.[47] But when to this general probability is added the use of the word walcyries for "witches" in King Cnut's Proclamation of 1020, and in other texts of the same century, the case must be taken as proved.[48] This word, which properly designated the "killers" or winged battle-goddesses of Germanic mythology (originally, no doubt, acting as independent agencies, but later reduced to subjection to Woden),[49] was used to gloss *Bellona* and *Erynnis* and *Allecto* and *Tisiphone*.[50] Its application, therefore, to a human witch is highly significant.

That madness may be caused by witchcraft is one of the most persistent of superstitions. It is not mentioned in the secular laws of the Anglo-Saxons, but the Penitential of Pseudo-Theodore prescribes five years' penance for a *mathematicus*, which it explains as one who perverts a man's mind by invocation of demons; and the same provision is found in Pseudo-Cummean and many other penitentials (with some variety in the punishment).[51]

For amatory magic we have ample evidence. The Anglo-Saxon Modus of about A.D. 965 prescribes appropriate penances for clerics or laymen who, to win love, work witchcraft in food or drink or by spells,[52] and a similar clause occurs in the Anglo-Saxon Penitential of Pseudo-Ecgbert and elsewhere.[53] Love potions are also denounced by Ælfric.[54]

Thrilling stories of the adventures of holy men with heathen wizards formed the subject matter of Anglo-Saxon sermons. Thus in Ælfric we may still read, in our ancient vernacular, of St. James's encounter with Hermogenes and his pupil;[55] of St. Matthew's triumph over Zaroes and Arphaxat, who, driven by him out of their native Ethiopia,[56] appeared later in Persia in a violent attempt to thwart the mission of Sts. Simon and Jude;[57] and, of course, of the vain struggles, historical and legendary, of Simon Magus against St. Peter and St. Paul.[58] Ælfric preaches also of the devils Ashtaroth and Berith, who contended with St. Bartholomew.[59]

The church, naturally, has always forbidden soothsaying in every variety, augury (by birds or otherwise), *sortes*, and the employment of seers or diviners.[60] Such prohibitions are conspicuous in the laws and penitentials of the Anglo-Saxon period [61] as well as in the homilies of Wulfstan, Ælfric, and others.[62] "In time of need it is better to call upon Christ in prayer than to have recourse to a wizard and a diviner for help."[63]

White witchcraft for the cure of disease [64] and other purposes innocent in themselves, was of course rife among the Anglo-Saxons and, equally of course, it was condemned as heathenish and diabolical. We hear, accordingly, of mothers who put their children on the roof or in the oven to drive away fever,[65] or who pass them through the earth at the cross-roads (a rite styled "devil's craft" in one text and coupled, in another, with healing "by any witchcraft");[66] of wives who taste their husband's blood as a medicine;[67] of misguided Christians who burn grain (*pro sanitate viventium et domus*) on the spot where a man has died or is buried,[68] or who "fast in honor of the moon" to regain their health.[69] Here too belongs the general prohibition of women's incantations and divinings (which are styled "diabolical" but are not thereby restricted to black magic),[70] for this ban covers every kind of soothsaying and all manner of spells, whether to heal the sick, to ensure or increase the potency of herbs,[71] to consecrate amulets,[72] or to accomplish any other desirable object. The doctrine was that to recite the Pater Noster and the Creed — which every Christian should learn [73] — is proper, but that all other forms of words are dangerous, or at best suspicious.[74] St. Cuthbert, in the seventh century (so Bede informs us), used to leave his monastery of Mailros in times of pestilence and preach to the people of the villages round about, who, abandoning the sacraments, sought help from idolatrous remedies, as if "by incantations or amulets or any other secrets of demonic art they could check the plague that God had sent." [75] The English healers and wise women so often brought to book in the middle ages were true-bred descendants of their forefathers.[76] So intertwisted were Christianity and paganism that even the Pater Noster itself was treated by learned and pious men in a manner that approaches witchcraft. This comes out grotesquely in the Anglo-Saxon "Salomon and Saturn," where to each letter of the prayer as written in runic symbols, is ascribed a peculiar virtue in grappling with the fiend — a manifest transference from the runic sorcery of heathen days.[77] The same poem, indeed, mentions in plain terms such sorcery when it tells how the fiends "sometimes fetter the hands of a fighting man and make them heavy when he has to defend his life against a hostile host"; how they "scratch deadly signs, baleful letters, upon his weapon, and by written symbols bewitch his sword and take away the glory of his blade." [78]

Charms and spells in abundance are preserved to us from
Anglo-Saxon England (as from other Germanic territory) [79]
— charms to heal wounds [80] and staunch blood,[81] to expel or
ward off poison [82] and the venom of spiders and serpents,[83] to
protect one against wild animals and savage dogs,[84] to cure
ailments (natural or demonic) in man and beast[85] or to shift
them to other objects,[86] to shield one from witches and elves
and goblins and terrors by night or day,[87] to help in childbirth [88] and prevent barrenness or miscarriage,[89] to enhance
the virtue of medicinal herbs,[90] to increase fertility of the soil
and guard the fields from blasting witchcraft,[91] to call down a
swarm of bees,[92] to keep one safe and sound on a journey and
counteract fatigue,[93] to calm a storm and drive away hail and
control the winds,[94] to gain favor,[95] to detect or thwart
thieves and recover stolen goods and strayed or stolen horses
and cattle,[96] to ensure victory in fight.[97] Witchcraft against
men and cattle is mentioned in the famous Nine Worts
Charm [98] and in several other spells.[99] In an extremely elaborate description of a remedy for "elf-disease" we find the possibility of meeting a demon in the dark contemplated with
calm resolution. "Go on Thursday evening at sunset to the
place where you know [the herb] helenium grows. Then sing
Benedicite and Pater Noster and a litany; and stick your
knife into the plant; let it stick therein. Go away. Return
when day and night are just dividing; in the same morning
hour go first to church and cross yourself and commit yourself to God. Then go in silence, and *though anything horrible
should come to meet you*, or a man, speak no word to it or him
until you come to the plant that you marked the evening
before." [100] Charms and recipes for the bite of a snake or
other venomous creature are common enough in the Anglo-
Saxon collections.[101] One theory was that a devil might enter
the body of a serpent, or assume its shape, and in this guise
might sting the cattle in the field.[102] Such spells, mostly
remedial (*inania carmina* as John of Salisbury called them in
the twelfth century — "idle charms, which the whole medical profession condems"),[103] occur in manuscript in every
period from the Norman Conquest to the present day, and
there is plenty of evidence for their constant use.[104] One of
these venerable rigmaroles has run a career of triumphant

popularity for a thousand years and is still chanted with as
much efficacy as ever — the famous charm for toothache
which begins "St. Peter sat upon a marble stone." [105]

To the general department of white witchcraft belong also
the trivial offerings mentioned in the penitentials: "They
who sacrifice to devils *in minimis* shall fast for one year, but
they who sacrifice *in magnis* shall fast for ten." In one manuscript the trifling sacrifices are explained as those offered at
well-springs or at trees. [106] Such worship of wells, trees, and
stones might be either white magic or black, but in any case
it was strictly forbidden as pagan and devilish. [107] Satan,
Wulfstan teaches us, often sends disease or injury upon a
man to induce him to offer alms at a well or a stone "or some
other lifeless thing," and then relieves him. [108]

Of black magic at wells there is a vivid instance in the saga
of Hereward. When William the Conqueror despaired of
taking the Isle of Ely, one of his knights made a suggestion:
"I have long been acquainted with an old woman who, if she
were with us, would by her art alone deprive the defenders of
their valor and drive tham all out of the island in panic."
The hag was summoned and every precaution was taken to
keep her presence a secret from the garrison; but Hereward,
suspecting that something was in the wind, went out to investigate, disguised as a potter. [109] Chancing to spend the
night at the house of the widow where the witch lodged, he
overheard the two women conversing in French, which they
wrongly assumed he could not understand, about their sorcery. At midnight the pair went down to springs of water on
the border of the garden. Hereward dogged their steps and
heard them ask "responses" of the "guardian of the springs"
(obviously a water-demon). When the enemy made their
next attack, the witch was stationed on a high place in the
midst of them, in order to be protected while she plied "her
art." But her spells were bootless, and in the Norman rout
that followed she fell and broke her neck. [110] How she meant
to bewitch the defenders of Ely is not disclosed, but manifestly she was proceeding on information derived from the
spirit or elemental demon that inhabited the springs.

Thus witchcraft is combined with well-worship. [111] Such
worship in varying forms has maintained itself to the present

day. Most of the holy wells [112] which are found all over Britain were originally honored with pagan ceremonies, relics of which persist in many instances. "Cursing wells" are well-known,[113] and "wishing wells," which abound, are available as well for banning as for blessing.[114] In 1410 Bishop Robert Mascall of Hereford learned to his sorrow that, although the adoration of wells and stones is canonically stigmatized as idolatry, yet his subjects resorted in great numbers to a certain spring and stone in the parish of Turnaston.[115] Warkworth's Chronicle (*ad ann.* 13 Ed. IV, 1473–74) tells of springs that give omens of dearth, pestilence, and battle.[116] Such were the "hunger borns" near Rockley which, as Dr. Pocock heard in 1754, "break out" to "denote an approaching scarcity, and I was told," he adds, "that the hoarders of corn rejoyce whenever they rise." [117] One remembers Shakspere's farmer "that hanged himself on th'expectation of plenty." In 1528 we find among the York Visitations a record of the thrilling half-heathen ceremonial used by Isabel Mure of Bishopwilton: "Shee took fier and ij yong women with hir and went to a rynnyng water, and light a wyspe of straw and sett it on the water, and saide thus, 'Benedicite. Se ye what I see? I se the fier burne and water rynne and the gryse grew and see flew [i. e. and the grass grow and the sea flow], and nyght fevers and all unkowth evils that evil flee, and all other, God will,' and after theis wordes sais xv Pater noster, xv Ave Maria and thre credes." [118]

We may linger awhile in the fifteenth century and examine a highly significant document of 1538 — John Bale's "Comedy concerning Three Laws, of Nature, Moses, and Christ." Bale was born in 1495 and died in 1563.

The character Idolatry is "decked lyke an olde wytche." Let us see what Bale's idea of such a personage was. Fortunately he is explicit as well as abundant in the information he supplies. The old witch Idolatry can tell fortunes; by saying Ave Mary and "by other charmes of sorcerye" she can ease men of the toothache, can cure the ague and the pox, can recover lost property, can fetch the devil from hell, can milk cows and draw drink out of a post. She is a good midwife and can charm children so that spirits cannot hurt them. She can work wiles in war, can keep corn and cattle from thriving, can make the ale in the vat lose its head and strength. No man can brew or bake successfully if she opposes. She can dry up wells and cause trees and plants to wither. She can kill poultry by her arts. If she is favorably disposed, her charms speed the plough and make the cows give plenty of milk; the mill, the cradle, and the mustard-quern shall "go apace" if she is pleased. She can play tricks akin to table-tipping — can cause phenomena like those which we read of in many narratives of *poltergeister* and haunted houses: merely by throwing her glove she makes stools dance and earthen pots prance. She knows spells to protect chickens from foxes and other vermin as well as to cure sick ducks and geese; so likewise to cure colts of "lampes" and of the bots. She has drinks for coughs and for "hyckock" and the "chycock," and charms for the pip. Headache she can prevent, and insomnia vanishes if you will follow her directions.[119]

> Besydes these charmes afore,
> I haue feates many more
> That I kepe styll in store.

Some of her curative and prophylactic charms involve the use of formulas of the old religion or recourse to certain saints. Such means, however, become sorcery under her manipulation, precisely as we find to be the case in divers bits of folklore which have survived to the present day and of which examples enough occur in the records of the ecclesiastical courts in pre-Elizabethan times. Bale's description of the occult powers of his Old Witch covers both beneficial and malefic witchcraft: she is both a white witch and a black witch, according as one enjoys her favor or incurs her enmity, and this accords with experience and with the everyday creed of the folk.

Nobody who has even a superficial acquaintance with popular superstitions, ancient and modern, will imagine for a moment that Bale imported these things from the Continent or derived his knowledge of them from the learned tomes of theologians and demonologists. And the date of his scurrilous but for us invaluable comedy is exactly twenty years before the accession of Queen Elizabeth.

In the comic interlude of Thersytes, written in 1537,

young Telemachus gives Thersites a letter from Ulysses,
which the recipient reads aloud. It begs pardon for past
enmity and prays Thersites to help the boy to find a physician

> That hym may wyselye charme
> From the wormes that do hym harme.

Ulysses has heard men say

> That better charmer is no other
> Then is youre owne deare mother.
> I praye you of her obtayne
> To charme away his paine.

Thersites assents and conducts Telemachus to the charmer,
assuring him that he shall be the better for seven years. She
refuses: "Charme that charme wyll, he shal not be charmed
of me." The undutiful Thersites threatens her with his club:

> Charme olde witche in the deuils name
> Or I wyll sende the to him to be his dame.

After some acrimonious discussion, she gives way:

> Come hyther pretye childe
> I will the charme from the wormes wylde.

First he must tell her his name; then he must lie down "upright" (on his back) on the ground and stir not once for a
thousand pound. Telemachus obeys and the witch pronounces a charm of tremendous length and amazing bur-
lesquery.[120] One remembers that in old popular medicine a
large variety of ailments were ascribed to worms.[121]

No better commentary on Bale and Thersytes can be desired than the actual cases of witchcraft and sorcery recorded
in Archdeacon Hale's extracts from the Act-Books of the
Commissary of London.[122] In 1477 John Bere was before the
Commissary on the charge of defaming his neighbors and believing in sorcery, but he cleared himself: probably this was a
case of stolen goods.[123] In 1480 John Stokys was accused of
"using incantations of sorcery for fevers." [124] In 1527 William Browne, charged with using "art magic and incantation
of horses," confessed that he cured horses of "the fasshyns"
with herbs, reciting the Lord's Prayer and the Angelic Salutation each five times and the Apostles' Creed thrice.[125] In

1528 Margaret Hunt made a similar confession. The details are highly significant. For a lame or sore arm Margaret prescribed the juice of certain herbs. The patient was also to repeat the Lord's Prayer and the Angelic Salutation five times and the Apostles' Creed once and then to apply a blue clout. So ran the testimony of one of her patients. Margaret herself confessed to further ceremonies. First she prays the Blessed Trinity to save and heal her patients from all their wicked enemies. "Then she techeth them ix nights for to sey v pater nosters, v aves and a crede, and iii pater nosters, iii aves and credes, in the worshyp of Seynt Spyrite; and when the[y] take ther chamber and go to bedde at night, to sey one pater, one ave and one crede in the worshypp of Seynt Ive, to save them from al envy." For the ague "she techeth them to gether herbe-grace [i. e. rue], peneriall, redde sage, redde fenell, and the barre rote, before the son downe, so that it be the last dryncke that the syke drincketh at night." For sores "she techeth them to gether herbe-grace, dyll, verveye [i. e. vervain, verbena], marygoldes, put a lyttill holy water to them, and sey sume prayers; and when she stampethe [i. e. brays the herbs in a mortar], to sey iii pater nosters, iii aves, and a crede, in the worshyp of our Lady, yf it be a woman that stampeth; and if it be a man, he must se[y] iii pater nosters, iii aves, and a crede, in the worshypp of Jesus." [126] It is interesting to note dill (anise) and vervain among Margaret's simples. These plants were *fuga daemonum*: they kept off devils and "hindered witches of their will." [127] The prescription of such herbs, as well as what Margaret says about "envy" (i. e. malice), indicates that she believed the ailments were (or might have been) caused by witchcraft. She learned her practice, she declares, in Wales from one Mother Emet. In the same year (1528) Elizabeth Fotman confessed that she took a rod "and put it to the horse bely that was syke of the botts, and made crosses on a caryers horse bely . . . and the horse rose up by and by and was hole." She was charged also with curing toothache and worms.[128] Other pre-Elizabethan cases from similar sources are not lacking. About 1426 the accounts of Bishop Langley of Durham disclose an entry of ninepence paid to Thomas Egliston for "signing" sixteen head of cattle with St. Wilfred's signet to ward off the

murrain; but the entry is crossed out, as if disapproved —
whether for conscience' sake, or because the treatment failed,
or because the fee was exorbitant![129] The case of Agnes Hancok, the healer, in 1438, will be cited later (p. 145, below). In
1448 Mariot Jacson was before the Durham ecclesiastical
court as an *incantatrix*; in 1450 Agnes Bowmer was arraigned
at the same tribunal for sortilege, and so in 1452 was Alice
Davison for using sorcery "in the medical art."[130] At about
this time "sorcery or witchcraft" is mentioned among the
"more greuous defautes" in certain additions to the Rule of
St. Saviour and St. Bridget.[131] In 1457 Thomas Hull of Hertford made his confession and abjured in the parish church in
the presence of the Bishop of Lincoln: "That I haue yeven
ayde, counsell, help, and fauour vnto oon Thomas Curteys,
to thentent that he exercised and vsed nigromancy and
heresy."[132] In 1472 William Hull, Vicar of Cawnton, being
convicted of sortilege on abundant testimony, was forced to
swear, on pain of deprivation, that he would resign his cure
before Michaelmas, or at least exchange it.[133] In 1481 John
Parkyn was presented before the York ecclesiastical court for
"using incantations" for some purpose, and Agnes Marshall
was presented for the same offence in her practice as a midwife.[134]

The prevalence of wandering practitioners of magic at the
end of the fifteenth century is suggested by an entry in Bishop
Redman's visitation of Sulby monastery, Northamptonshire,
in 1500. One of the brethren named Thomas Wryght was
presented for using "books of experiments," and besides
for rewarding a certain "vagabond" liberally for teaching
him this science. His books were seized, but he was treated
leniently because he protested that he had used them "for
speculation merely and never for operation."[135]

The medical act of Henry VIII was passed in 1511. The
preamble recites that medicine and surgery are practised by
"a grete multitude of ignoraunt persones," so that "common
Artificers, as Smythes, Wevers, and Women, boldely and
custumably take upon theim grete curis and thyngys of great
difficultie, In the which they partely use socery and which-
crafte, partely applie such medicyne vnto the disease as be
verey noyous and nothyng metely."[136]

In 1538 (the very year of Bale's Comedy) Agnes Robson confessed that she cured little pigs and other animals by a charm, and the charm itself is recited at full length in the Visitation Book of the Bishop of Lincoln: After a prayer ("God almyghty, god and saincte charyte, I beseche you of your blessyd goodnes to helpe this same thing"), Agnes uttered the following magic formula:

> John is thy christen name, John,
> And thre bytter bytter hathe the bytten,
> Thre bytter bytter hathe the nyppen,
> And thre bytter bytter hathe the stryken,

Besechyng almyghty god, whedder itt were eye or tong or hert, the better shall be your heale and boote, the father the son and the holy gooste.

On the same occasion Johanna Connyngton confessed to reciting a similar spell for sick children: "Three byttes haue ye bytten with hert and tong and eye." [137] Almost a hundred years later Anne Whittle alias Chattox, one of the Lancashire witches who were hanged in 1612, confessed that when she was sent for "to helpe drinke that was forspoken or bewitched" she successfully "vsed this Prayer for the amending of it, viz.

> ### "A CHARME.
>
> Three Biters hast thou bitten,
>   The Hart, ill Eye, ill Tonge:
> Three bitter shall be thy Boote,
> Father, Sonne, and Holy Ghost
>   a Gods name.
> Fiue Pater-nosters, fiue Auies,
>   and a Creede,
> In worship of fiue woundes
>   of our Lord." [138]

Anne's use of this old charm is a very curious circumstance, for she had ignorantly perverted its function from mankind to malt. In 1616 Isobel Harvie at Kirkcaldy admitted using a version of the charm which she had learned from "ane wayfaring man"; [139] other versions were employed in Scotland for sick horses in 1641 and 1656, [140] and still another is reported from the Orkneys in recent days. [141]

One of Elynour Rummyng's guests in Skelton's poem was a white witch, but she dabbled also in magic of a more questionable sort:

> She semed halfe a leche,
> And began to preche
> Of the tewsday in the weke
> Whan the mare doth keke;
> Of the vertue of an vnset leke;
> Of her husbandes breke;
> Wyth the feders of a quale
> She could to Burdeou sayle;
> And wyth good ale barme
> She could make a charme
> To helpe wythall a stytch.
> She semed to be a wytch.[142]

Skelton died in 1529.

In 1549 Bishop Hooper registered the fact that a few years before "a poor man that erred by ignorance," had assured him that "this medicine could heal all diseases, ' + *Jesus* + *Job* + *habuit* + *vermes* + *Job* + *patitur* + *vermes* + *in* + *nomine* + *Patris* + *et* + *Filii* + *et* + *Spiritus Sancti* + *Amen* + *lama* + *zabachthani* + .'"[143] Obviously this formula, which the Bishop's informant regarded as a panacea, was a charm for worms.[144] In rationale it is identical with the famous charm against toothache, *Petrus sedebat*: some holy personage, like Job or St. Peter, has suffered from the ailment in question and has been cured; to recite these facts in proper form will heal the patient. The toothache formula, as we have seen, has had a continuous popularity in Britain for something like a thousand years, and this is undoubtedly true of many another charm. The same principle underlies one of the most precious relics of Germanic paganism — the Second Merseburg Spell, which has survived to recent times in Scandinavia, Finland, Scotland, England, and Germany.[145] The form is widespread and very ancient, beginning with an epic portion — a narrative — and applying what happened once upon a time to the remedial purpose in the present. We have a striking example in the Great Demotic Papyrus, where a charm for wounds tells at the outset how the son of the goddess Isis was wounded and how his mother prepared the oil of healing.[146]

But we must revert to chronology and pick up the thread of our discourse at the beginning of the Norman period.

When Duke William's *lorica* was put on hindside before at

Hastings, he said: "If I believed in sorcery, I should not go to battle to-day; but I have never put my trust in sorceries nor loved sorcerers. For in every business — whatever I had to do — I have always committed myself to my Maker." [147]

In 1075 the Council of London forbade the hanging up of dead beasts' bones to ward off the cattle plague; likewise *sortes*, soothsaying, divination, and all such works of the devil.[148] About 1114 the law-book called Quadripartitus translated Cnut's decree against paganism, which includes lots and soothsaying,[149] and in 1126 a London synod threatened with excommunication and everlasting infamy all sorcerers, soothsayers, and practisers of any kind of augury, as well as all persons who assent to such acts.[150] This canon was appropriate to the times, for not long before had flourished Gerard (Hugo Gerold), Archbishop of York, who died in 1108. He was, we are told, an acute and learned man (*homo quidem acutus et literatus*), but was thought to be rather too skilful in "cleaning out the purses" of his subjects, and, as many did not scruple to assert, he practised the black art. He died suddenly, and was so hated by the people that the boys threw stones at his bier.[151] An English homily of about this time describes the Emperor Julian (the Apostate) as believing in witchcraft and serving the devil, and tells how he once sent a demon on an errand to a foreign shore.[152]

In the twelfth and thirteenth centuries, indeed, we have ample evidence for the currency in Britain of almost every superstitious belief or practice that enters into the witch-creed, be the witchcraft white or black. We hear of charms and sortilege and soothsaying and divination and prophecy and necromancy, of detective sorcery for stolen goods, of mirror magic or crystal gazing, of abuse of the consecrated wafer and of baptismal water for good purposes and bad; of holy texts repeated backward or intermingled with profane formulas or misapplied to occult ends; of the winning of love and favor by spells or secret arts; of witchcraft for murder or bodily harm; of familiar spirits and house-haunting *poltergeister* and serviceable domestic cobolds; of demons of the storm; of demoniacal possession; of devils in the guise of pygmies or of animals; of witches in beast-form who, if wounded, show the wound when they return to humanity; of milk-stealing witchcraft; of spectral evidence, when devils appear in the likeness of innocent women; of incubus and succubus and demon offspring; of invocation and conjuration of evil spirits; of the diabolical compact and homage to Satan — of everything, in short, except the Witches' Sabbath, and that is an institution that does not appear at all in the trials of the Elizabethan age. For Germany in the thirteenth century we have a vivid picture of rustic witchcraft in a sermon of Berthold of Regensburg. "O ye village folk, many of you would go to heaven but for that same little axe [half-heresy], which murders all that believe in witchcraft (*zouberie*) and in divination and seeresses and in cunning women and in night-ladies and such goblins and in Robin Goodfellow." Some put their trust in holy wells and holy trees. Foolish women try to win a husband by witchcraft. While they are about it, why don't they cast their spells on a king instead of contenting themselves with a farmer's son or a laborer? One woman baptizes an image of wax, another an image of wood, another a dead man's bone. One works witchery with herbs, another with the holy chrism, another with the sacred wafer — the body of God. They practise magic when they get their husbands, and after they get them; before childbirth; before the christening and after the christening. They even believe that they can take a man's heart out of his body and replace it with a bunch of straw! [153] It is a wonder that your husband does not become leprous. Fie! do you really believe that you can take a man's heart out of his body and put in a bunch of straw? — This, in substance, is Berthold's account of contemporary superstition among the folk. [154] Who that knows the middle ages can doubt that his homily might have been delivered with equal force in Essex or Somerset or Yorkshire? Examples will be furnished under appropriate heads, but a few miscellaneous bits of testimony may here be cited.

Zoroaster passed with our ancestors as the inventor of magic, on the authority of St. Augustine. [155] He was regularly identified with Noah's wicked son Ham; [156] so by Capgrave, for example, in his fifteenth-century Chronicle. [157] Herbert de Losinga, first Bishop of Norwich, who died in 1119, writes, "The ark was of small compass; but yet even there Ham preserved the arts of magic and idolatry." [158]

William Laudun, a brave English knight, came to Gilbert Foliot, then Bishop of Hereford (as he was from 1149 to 1162), and asked counsel: "A Welsh wizard (*maleficus*) recently died in my town. Four nights later he came back, and he keeps coming every night, calling by name certain of his former neighbors, who instantly fall sick and die within three days, so that but few of them are left." The bishop suggested that the evil angel of this dead villain had perhaps reanimated his body, and advised the knight to have it dug up and beheaded, and then buried again after the grave had been sprinkled copiously with holy water. All this proved of no avail, and at length the name of Sir William himself was called. Seizing his sword, he pursued the demonic corpse to the churchyard, and, just as it was sinking into the grave, cleft its head to the neck. There was no further trouble.[159] We have here, to all intents and purposes, a case of vampirism, and it is noteworthy that the vampire was a wizard in this life. Other instances of vampirism in the twelfth century are recorded by William of Newburgh.[160]

The thrilling tale of the Witch of Berkeley, retold in Southey's deservedly famous ballad,[161] had a triumphant career in the middle ages. We discover it first in William of Malmesbury,[162] who appeals for confirmatory evidence to the Dialogues of the great Pope Gregory, in whom, says William, you may read of a wicked man who was buried in a church but was cast out of the building by demons.[163] William's Berkeley legend was repeated by one English historian after another, and the marvel found due recognition in Vincent's Speculum Historiale, in the Northern History of Olaus Magnus, in Hartmann Schedel's Book of Chronicles, and in the Prodigies of Conrad Lycosthenes. Schedel illustrates the event with a terrific woodcut of the Witch carried off on horseback by Satan, and Olaus and Conrad offer us a truly comic delineation of the same prodigious ride.[164] A similar horror, perhaps derived from the Berkeley legend (but without mention of sorcery), is the Priest's Wife Carried off by the Devil, told in French by the Englishman William (of Waddington?) in the thirteenth century and translated by Robert of Brunne in the early fourteenth. She had four sons, who all became priests in their turn, but they could not withhold her body from the clutch of the fiends. The youngest son, we are informed, used the story in his sermons "in many places in England" as an awful warning to "prestresses." [165] No wonder it made its way to Germany and Sweden and even to Iceland. [166] Such stories as that of the Witch of Berkeley did not remain buried in chronicles, nor was their circulation confined to the class or classes of society that could read. They circulated in two ways — first by way of common talk, until the thrill of the original occurrence died out with the generations (a kind of currency that we cannot trace but for which we should always make large allowance); and, secondly, they were embodied in collections of *exempla* (illustrative anecdotes for preachers), were told and retold in sermon after sermon, and thus became household words. [167] The Witch of Berkeley finds a place in more than one of these collections: in the Speculum Laicorum, for instance, probably compiled about 1275 by an English cleric; and in the Alphabetum Narrationum, whence it was translated into our vernacular in the fifteenth century. [168] Who can estimate the influence of so impressive a legend in its demonstrable course of seven centuries?

Peter of Blois, Archdeacon of Bath for twenty-six years, who enjoyed the favor of Henry II and Queen Eleanor, has left us an important letter on the superstitions of his age. One Master William, when about to start on his day's journey, had chanced to meet a monk. This was reputed to be bad luck, [169] and the monk himself had urged him to return, warning him that, if he ventured out, he would run a great risk. But Master William despised such vanities and rode forth unconcernedly with the train of the Archbishop of Canterbury, to whose household he belonged. He had not gone far, however, when horse and rider fell into a deep pit full of water, whence he was rescued with great difficulty. One of the cavalcade was so impressed that he consulted Archdeacon Peter on the whole question of unlucky meetings, dreams, spooks, birds, and sneezes. [170] In replying, the wise Archdeacon reminds his friend that Satan is always trying to undermine our faith by his wiles. To that end he puts fantastic notions into our heads, promising us that we may know the future by the flight of birds, by our meeting with men or beasts, by dreams, and in other ways. His object is to disquiet our hearts with idle curiosity. Some men consult figurecasters; others, astrologers; still others, wizards (*pythonicos*); and because their divination now and then comes out right, heedless persons put confidence in them. But a good Christian ought not to enquire about the future: he should leave it humbly to God. "Then pay no attention to dreams,[171] my dear friend. Do not entangle yourself in the false opinion of those who fear to meet a hare, or a woman with flowing tresses, or a blind man, or a lame man, or a monk, but who look forward joyously to good hospitality on their journey if a wolf meets them, or a doe, or if a martin flies from left to right, or if on setting forth they hear distant thunder or meet a hunchback or a leper. My own opinion is that Master William would have been equally in danger of drowning if no monk had met him!"[172] Mandeville's Voyage and Travel comments on the strange fact that some Christian men "seyn that summe bestes han gode meetynge, that is to seye for to meete with hem first at morwe, and summe bestes wykkyd meetynge": the hare and the swine are ominous; it is favorable to armed men when birds of prey are seen to catch their quarry, unfavorable when the quarry escapes; ravens are unlucky. Is it any wonder, then, that the Indians worship idols?[173]

Eustace the Monk, a famous French pirate,[174] was killed in a sea-fight with the English off Sandwich in 1217. The versified narrative of his career drawn up by a lively French romancer in the same century,[175] credits Eustace with an extensive and peculiar knowledge of the black art. He had spent half a year in an underground chamber at Toledo conversing with the devil, who taught him all kinds of nigromancy and predicted, on bidding him farewell at the close of the curriculum, that he should be killed at sea after waging war with kings and counts. Eustace, the poet assures us, could practise mirror magic by sword and basin, and could divine by turning the psalter or by inspecting a sheep's shoulder-bone: he knew a thousand conjurations, a thousand charms, a thousand "experiments." A prose account of his death in an early fourteenth-century manuscript is marvellous enough. A French fleet under his command entered Sandwich harbor, but he had by magic rendered his own ship invisible. One Stephen Crabbe, however, who had been a friend of his and had learned his arts, boarded the vessel, attacked the freebooter, and cut off his head. In this encounter Crabbe seemed to the beholders to be contending with an invisible antagonist on the surface of the water; but when the pirate fell dead, the glamour came to an end and ship and men were in full view.[176] Eustace's spells in this instance were like those by which Chaucer's Clerk of Orleans in The Franklin's Tale made the rocks vanish on the Breton coast.

In the Synod of Durham under Bishop Richard de Marisco (between 1217 and 1226), sorceries and witchcrafts in cases of marriage are prohibited under pain of excommunication.[177] In 1222 at Oxford a young man and two women were brought before the Archbishop of Canterbury, Stephen Langton, on complaint of the Archdeacon of Oxford. The man, it was said, had let himself be crucified, was in the habit of exhibiting the five wounds (still visible), and was called Jesus[178] by his two feminine companions. One of these women, who was elderly, had long been addicted to witchcraft (*maleficis incantationibus*) and had deluded the young man by her magic arts. Both she and her dupe were convicted and were "shut up between two walls until they died," but the younger woman, the man's sister, was set free because she had revealed the impious conduct of her brother and the witch.[179] If this was an instance of the *stigmata*, it precedes by two years the case of St. Francis and has escaped the researches of Imbert-Gourbeyre, whose "Liste des Stigmatisés" from 1224 to 1891 mounts to the stupendous total of three hundred and twenty-one.[180] In the same year (1222), a chronicle declares, a Jewish necromancer [181] purchased a boy and wrapped him in the skin of a dead man, in order that by means of incantations he might learn the future from the lad's answers to his questions. The idea was that future events would be seen by the medium as if they were taking place at the moment.[182] This performance combines stark necromancy (in which the dead are called back to give responses) with the kind of incubation described by Ovid when he tells how King Numa sacrificed a sheep to Faunus and another to Somnus and slept on their skins spread upon the hard ground, and how Faunus appeared to him in a dream and uttered a dark oracle, which Egeria interpreted.[183] This was an ancient Latin rite, observed (so Virgil testifies) with momentous results by King Latinus himself, who was the son of the god Faunus.[184] Geoffrey of Monmouth, imitating Virgil, makes Brutus seek Britain in obedience to an oracle which Diana had pronounced in a vision as he slept in the open air on the hide of a doe.[185] One of the heathenish New Year's Day rites denounced as idolatry in the penitential known as the Corrector et Medicus (included in the first quarter of the eleventh century by Bishop Burchard of Worms in his Decretum as Book xix) was to sit on a bull's hide at the crossroads in order to learn the future.[186]

Often, in recent days, has a witch been violently assaulted by her victim or by one who feared to become her victim. Thus in 1857 at Wenlock in Shropshire a young man murdered a supposed witch.[187] In 1879 in Norfolk a man accused of assaulting a girl defended his action on the ground that her mother had bewitched him by means of "a walking toad."[188] Cases of scratching or wounding are common. At Poughkeepsie in 1802 Nicholas Toncroy was tried for assaulting an old woman: he thought her a witch and cut her three times across the forehead;[189] for it is an old idea that to draw the witch's blood will annul her spells.[190] Examples of all sorts may be accumulated *ad libitum* from the nineteenth and twentieth centuries;[191] and such panic ferocity was of course no less common in early times, though only now and then did it get into court and thus achieve the dignity and permanence of a record. Of this we have a fine instance as far back as 1279 in the Assize Roll for Northumberland. "A certain unknown witch (*quaedam mulier ignota sortilega*) entered the house of John de Kerneslawe one evening and reviled him because he made the sign of the cross over the lamps. And the said John, defending himself as if from the devil, struck this same witch with a staff so that she died. And afterwards, by the judgment of the whole clergy, she was burned. And the same John after that deed went mad. And afterwards, when he came to his senses, remembering the foresaid deed, for fear he might run into danger, he fled into the bishopric of Durham. And he is not defamed of any felony; therefore let him return if he wishes, but, on account of his flight, let his chattels (£4, 5s.) be confiscated." [192]

One feels sympathy for the Abbot of Sulby, Thomas of Whalley (bad as he was), who, after he had been at the head of that house for ten years, was found, on visitation of the archbishop in 1280, to have squandered a great sum of money upon Elias Favelle, *incantator* and *sortilegus*, whom he employed to discover the body of his brother, drowned in the Ouse.[193] We can but wonder whether Elias resorted to the old method (still practised) of floating a loaf of bread (with or without a candle, or ballast of quicksilver) on the theory that it will come to rest directly over the corpse.[194] At all events, Abbot Thomas was excommunicated for this and other offences.

In 1286 an apostate Cistercian monk of Rievaulx named Godfrey Darel was reported to the Archbishop of York as a vagrant practiser of witchcrafts (*maleficia*) and wicked incantations.[195]

In the Confessional of Bishop Quivil (Synod of Exeter, 1287) various kinds of sorcery and witchcraft are denounced as dishonorable to God — conjurations for detecting theft (by means of sword or basin [mirror magic] or of "names written and enclosed in balls of clay and placed in holy water"), and divinations and sortilege such as "some wretches use for the sake of women with whom they are madly in love." [196]

Adam de Stratton, Chancellor of the Exchequer, the most infamous of extortioners and false stewards in English annals, was arrested and tried in 1289 and 1290. Infinite treasure was found in his possession. There was also seized among his chattels, we are told, a coffer or silk bag containing parings of nails, human hair, the feet of toads and moles, and other "diabolical things." It was sealed up by the king's justiciary, but Adam broke the seal and threw the magic objects into a vault. Therefore he was accounted a sorcerer.[197]

Adam's magic bag has excellent parallels in a French magician's bag described by Gregory of Tours in the late sixth century and in the negro obeah-man's bag described by Monk Lewis in his West Indian journal in the early nineteenth. The French sorcerer, a pretended holy man arrested at Paris about 580, had a great sack full of divers herbs along with moles' teeth, the bones of mice, and bears' claws and fat: all these things were at once recognized as *maleficia*.[198] Similar magical objects have been discovered in Scandinavian grave-mounds of the bronze age.[199] The obeah-man's bag contained "thunder stones [i. e. celts or belemnites, famous charms wherever found],[200] cats' ears, the feet of various animals, human hair, fish bones, the teeth of alligators, &c." [201] A hoodoo bag, according to Central Kentucky negroes, must be made of red flannel: it should contain a pinch of salt, a red pepper, a rabbit's foot, a chicken's spur, and some ashes.[202] A charm left by hostile natives at the door or window of Mr. Ellis in Madagascar "consisted of a small basket, . . . in which were two pieces of granite stone, called 'death stones.' A hole was burned in the basket, which indicated calamity by fire. Amongst the contents were hedgehog's bristles, parts of scorpions or centipedes, hair, earth said to be from a grave, and other strange ingredients." [203] Sorcerers' bags in New Guinea contain, among other miscellaneous rubbish, lizards' jaws, cassowaries' claws, and alligators' teeth.[204] About 1863 in Corisco Island on the West Coast of Africa, a missionary heard a slave girl confess that she had killed the chief's mother by witchcraft. She told him how she had gathered crumbs of the old woman's food, "strands of her hair, and shreds of her clothing; how she had mixed these with other substances, and had sung enchantments with drum and dance, aided by others; had tied all these things together on a stick which she had secretly buried at the threshold of the old woman's door, desiring and expecting that she should thereby die. . . . The old woman had died a month or two later; and the slave believed that what she had done had been efficient to accomplish the taking of life." [205] In modern England bottles are now and then dug up which have been buried by some witch for malefic purposes or by her victim as a counter-charm. These contain hair, clippings of nails, pins, etc.[206] Their occurrence shows the continuity of tradition and throws light on the purposes of Adam de Stratton. He wished to kill somebody who had crossed his path or to torment an enemy (he had plenty of enemies) whom he suspected of be-witching him.

Perhaps Adam meant to use his bag of tricks in the manner described in the extraordinary confession of Bernard de Vignolles in 1496. Bernard accused John Kendal (Grand Prior of the Order of St. John of Rhodes), Sir John Thonge or Thweng (knight of the same order, and Kendal's nephew), and William Horsey (Archdeacon of London) of a plot framed at Rome to destroy King Henry VII, his children, his mother, and certain of his favorites or councillors. Bernard was the agent of the conspirators. After these had returned to England, the prior and the archdeacon sent him to Rome to complete their negotiations with a Spanish astrologer, Master John Disant, who had already afforded them a specimen of his powers by causing the death of "vng Turc, qui estoit seruiter du frere du Grant Turc, a Rome, au pallays du pappe." Master John gave Bernard a little box of ointment which was to be smeared "along and across" some door or gate, so that the king might walk over it: then those who now loved him best would murder him. Bernard opened the box, found the contents nasty and malodorous, and threw the whole thing into a vault. At Orleans, on his way home, he bought of an apothecary a similar box and some quicksilver, mixed the quicksilver with earth and soot and water, and thus prepared a substance of the same color as the ointment; for he feared the magician might have sent a letter of instructions by another messenger. On arriving in England, he delivered the counterfeit; but the prior had lost heart: he dared not touch the accursed stuff and bade Bernard throw it away where it could never be found.[207] King Henry, the "Salomon of England," must have read this strange farrago, for the document is endorsed "La confession de Bernart de Vignolles" in his own royal handwriting; but he seems to have made light of it. "He was indeed full of apprehensions and suspicions," so Bacon tells us; "but, as he did easily take them, so he did easily check them and master them." [208] At all events, Prior John Kendal received a general pardon on June 18, 1496.[209]

The fourteenth century is rich in evidence. Much of this will be considered under appropriate heads. A few specimens of a miscellaneous character will suffice at this point.

The records of the City Court of Exeter in 1302 contain the

complaint of Reginald Kene that John Mody had called Kene's wife a wicked witch and thief. The same roll gives the presentation of the grand jury to the effect that "Dionysia Baldewyne is accustomed to receive John de Wermhille and Agnes his wife, and Joan La Cornwalyse [i. e. Cornish woman] of Teignmouth, who are witches and enchanters." [210] "If ever you have practised nygromauncye," writes Robert of Brunne in 1303, "and have offered sacrifice to the devil through witchcraft, or given reward to anybody to raise the devil in order to discover lost goods, you have sinned. If you have looked into sword or basin or thumb or crystal (or caused a child to do so) — all that sort of thing is called witchcraft. Trust not the pie's chattering — many men are deceived thereby; nor omens from meeting in the morning, nor hansel, nor dreams. Put not your trust in witchcraft. Whenever it is true, that is merely through the devil's craft to make men believe what is hateful to God." So far Robert follows his author, William (conveniently styled "of Waddington"), an Englishman who wrote in French in the previous century. [211] Then, instead of translating William's story of a false dream, Robert illustrates witchcraft by quite a different example — the tale of the Witch and her Milk-sucking Bag, which we shall consider in its place (p. 165). Dan Michel of Kent (1340) has a similar passage censuring those who "for pence" cause Satan to be invoked and practise enchantments; those who "make to look in the sword or the nail of the thumb" to detect thieves or for other purposes; and those who by charms or by witchcraft cause man and wife to hate each other or bring about unlawful love between the unmarried. He mentions also the abuse of host, chalice, and chrism by witches and evil-minded priests. In another place he writes of "the deuines [diviners] and the wichen and the charmeresses that werketh be the dyueles crefte." [212]

In the first decade of this century came the prosecution of the Templars in France and England, involving charges of Satanism and the blackest magic which are too familiar to need specification. [213] The prevalence of occult practices at about this time is emphasized by Bishop Baldock in a mandate "against sorcerers and enchanters" addressed to the official of the Archdeacon of London in 1311. He has learned

that in the city and diocese the horrid crime of sorceries, incantations, and art magic has so increased that the souls
of the people are in peril. Certain persons are resorting to
magic and spells for the recovery of lost property or for knowledge of future events and secrets in the past; some are practising conjurations and divinations, are holding conventicles
and making circles and invoking demons "by loaves and
knives" [214] or otherwise; some pretend to invoke spirits in
nails and mirrors, in stones and rings, and pretend that these
spirits give signs and responses, and so on. The official is to
investigate and send the bishop the names of offenders.[215]
The Lollard Apology is equally emphatic.[216] It denounces the
use of amulets of gospel texts hung about one's neck to drive
away fiends or sickness or to protect the wearer. "Charmis
on no maner are leful [lawful]." Charmers, enchanters, au-
gurs, necromancers, etc. are defined and reprobated. "God
for his endless mercy keep us from the malice of charmers and
conjurers, witches, sorcerers, and others that are put in the
general sentence and cursing of the kirk." [217]

Dame Alice Kyteler's case in 1324 comprises almost every
superstitious curiosity discoverable in the witch-trials of the
sixteenth and seventeenth centuries: [218] denial of Christ and
apostacy from his Church; consultation with demons by sorcery for responses and counsel; the sacrifice of cocks at the
crossroads; the compounding of their entrails, along with
herbs, spiders, black worms like scorpions, serpents, the
brain and clouts of an unbaptized infant, and the hair and
nails of corpses (all boiled together in the skull of a beheaded
robber), in the preparation of drugs, unguents, and powders
to cause love and hate, disease and bodily harm; the employment of these compounds to kill or infatuate her former husbands and to reduce her present husband (her fourth) to a
miserable state of decrepitude; the performance of a mock
rite of excommunication against her husbands; carnal copulation with her familiar spirit (called Robin or Robert Artis
filius), who had appeared in the form of a black dwarf with
two similar companions, but who sometimes took shape as a
cat or a shaggy black dog.[219] These horrors come from the
contemporary narrative, and their truth was admitted by one
of Dame Alice's friends or servants, Petronilla de Midia, who

confessed to sharing in them by her instructions. Thus we have an admirable account of the witch-creed as it existed in the mind of a fourteenth-century English ecclesiastic, the Bishop of Ossory, — for Richard Ledrede, the prosecutor, was an Englishman — and in the minds of the Anglo-Irish of Kilkenny. Later accounts credit Dame Alice with further acts of witchcraft, which need not here occupy us.[220]

One of the last crimes of the tyranny of Roger Mortimer was the condemnation of Edmund, Earl of Kent (brother of the murdered Edward II) in the Winchester Parliament of 1330. Kent had heard, somehow, that Edward was still alive, and his consequent activity in Edward's interest was the pretext for his conviction and execution on March 19.[221] The whole affair was engineered by Mortimer, for the young Edward III had not yet got a free hand. On the 24th Mortimer addressed a letter to the Pope, in the name of Edward III, explaining and justifying this crime. To aggravate Edmund's alleged offences, he declares that Edmund confessed that he had heard from a certain friar, on the authority of a demon whom the friar had conjured, that the elder Edward was not dead.[222] When Mortimer was condemned in the Westminster Parliament in the following November, the accusers obviously had this matter of the demon in mind. Among the charges is included the statement that Mortimer had managed through his corrupt agents to convey to Kent a report that Edward was still living, whereupon (the bill adds) the Earl investigated the question "by all the *good* means that he knew of" (*ce fist espier par totes les bones voies q'il savoit*).[223]

In 1336 Pope Benedict XII wrote to the Bishop of Paris to send to the papal court one William Altafex, described as "nigromanticus de Anglia," and with him certain metal plates or tablets (*laminas*) that he was said to use in his magical operations.[224]

In 1355 a wager of battle between the hired champions [225] of the Bishop of Salisbury and the Earl of Salisbury was postponed, because, when the bishop's champion was searched by the judges, several rolls of prayers and charms were discovered in his coat.[226] This was a pretty good joke on the bishop, or so it seems to us when we reflect that trial by combat was an ordeal (or judgment of God) and that the appellant had to swear that he was not fortified by magic: "that ye shull have . . . nor stone of vertue, nor hearb of virtue; nor charme, nor experement, nor none other enchauntment by you, nor for you, whereby ye trust the better to overcome the said C. de D. your Adversarie." [227] Tricks of this nature, however, must have been common. The Arundel Penitential prescribes three years' penance for one who attempts by any witchcraft (*maleficio*) to subvert trial by combat, or the ordeal by hot iron or by hot or cold water, or any kind of lawful judgment; [228] and Bishop Burchard's Decretum prescribes the penance of a wizard for him who eats, drinks, or carries anything by which he thinks he can turn aside the judgment of God. [229] Such attempts are also contemplated in some of the forms of ritual for the ordeal of hot iron or of hot or cold water in England in the ninth to the twelfth century. [230] The Anglo-Saxon Leech-Book of the tenth century directs a man who is to fight with his foe to boil young swallows in wine or spring water and eat them, [231] and another Anglo-Saxon treatise declares that the right forefoot of a badger (if sanctified by the words "In the name of the living God I take thee for a medicine") is an amulet that will ensure victory in every conflict. [232] One is reminded of the "Ephesian letters" of the ancient Greeks, a charm which a wrestler from that city was detected in wearing in a match with a Milesian. Until the amulet was removed, the Milesian could not wrestle at all; after its removal, the Ephesian was thrown thirty times! [233] In an Old Norse anecdote of a swimming match, one of the champions tears a bag of charms from the other's neck, protesting in extempore verse that *he* has never resorted to such knavery, "and yet he is still alive!" [234]

When Sir Robert Tresilian, condemned in 1388 by the Merciless Parliament, was mounting the scaffold, he boasted that he "could not die so long as he had some things about him." This cryptic utterance was plain enough to the officers. They stripped him accordingly, and found amulets in which were depicted astrological signs, a demon's head, and several diabolical names. After that, he was hanged without difficulty; but, says the contemporary writer to whom we owe this strange story, his throat was cut also, as a measure of additional security. [235] John Heydon, famous in his day as a prac-

titioner of occult arts, testifies in 1664: "Some I have seen
Shot-free in the *Canaries* by wearing Rings, pieces of gold,
&c. Telesmatically prepared." [236] Such a "hardman" was
the notorious Croatian adventurer, Captain Carlo Fantom:
once, when his colonel, Sir Robert Pye, shot at him for stealing a horse, the bullets went through his buff-coat and set his
shirt on fire, but did him no damage. Fantom "tooke the
bullets, and sayd to Sir Robert, 'Here, take your bullets
again.'" Thus Aubrey, most delightful of gossips, on the authority of an eyewitness. [237]

Charms, spells, and amulets to render one invulnerable or
otherwise protect one in battle are in common use everywhere. [238] Such things were carried by many soldiers in the
latest of great wars. [239] Charms to win one's case in court or to
silence or nonplus one's adversary there, are also common
among savage men and civilized. [240] Trite but inevitable is a
quotation from Cicero's *Brutus*. In an important lawsuit in
which he and Curio were counsel on opposite sides, Curio,
while addressing the court, "suddenly forgot the whole case"
— a portentous lapse of memory which he ascribed to
the "spells and witcheries" of Titinia, Cicero's client." [241]
Charms of this nature — to make an opponent forget his
case — are still practised by the natives in Rhodesia. [242] In
the Old Norse Havamál, Odin, in the character of a Scandinavian wizard, claims to know spells for lawsuits, as well as
for almost every other purpose that the heart of man can
devise. [243] Litigation was dogged by uncanny perils in fifteenth-century Cornwall if we may lend credence to the petition which Henry Hoigges of Bodmin, Gentleman, addressed
to the Lord Chancellor about 1440. The prior of Bodmin had
been sued by Richard Flamank, and Hoigges was the plaintiff's attorney. One John Harry, a priest in the prior's
service, by "sotill craftys of enchauntement wycchecraft
& socerye," plotted to destroy Hoigges, and caused him to
break his leg and to suffer such injuries that "he was in
despayr of his lyff." This Harry, moreover, continually from
day to day was practising "the said sotill craft of enchauntement wycchecraft and socerye" and boldly avowed it, as was
notorious in the county, and he openly threatened thereby to
break Hoigges's neck. Therefore, since the common law gave

him no remedy, he besought the Chancellor to help him by forcing Harry to abjure his wicked arts.[244]

> De par le Roi défense *au Diable*
> De faire miracle!

To return to the fourteenth century, — in 1385 two Londoners (John Brugges, chaplain, and John Wyghton, tailor), convicted of practising "the prohibited art of magic," were by the king's command left to the Bishop of London "to do what he deems fit for their imprisonment" until they should submit to judgment and satisfy Holy Church.[245]

In 1396 an Englishman, in preparing a manual of French conversation, included in his dialogue the rumor that at Orleans the devil teaches his disciples "nigromancie" in a head, and refers to a great magician there, an Englishman called "Colin T.," who "knew how to do many marvels by means of his *nigromancie*." Professor Royster has recently identified this wonder-worker with the Colle Tregetour whom Chaucer, in the House of Fame, saw carrying a windmill under the shell of a walnut — "an uncouth thing to telle." [246]

> Ther saugh I pleyen iogelours,
> Magiciens and tregetours
> And phitonesses,[247] chermeresses,
> Olde wiches, sorceresses,
> That use exorsisaciouns
> And eek thise fumigaciouns;
> And clerkes eek, which conne wel
> Al this magyke naturel,
> That craftely don hir ententes
> To make, in certeyn ascendentes,[248]
> Images lo! through which magyk
> To make a man ben hool or syk.[249]

So the Brazen Horse in The Squire's Tale is explained by some of the bystanders as an "apparence ymaad by som magyke, as iogelours pleyen at thise festes grete." [250] The "olde wiches, sorceresses," were not mere creatures of the poet's imagination. The archdeacon whom the Friar celebrates in his Tale was an officer

> That boldely did execucioun
> In punisshinge of fornicacioun,
> *Of wicchecraft* and eek of bauderye.[251]

The Parson mentions

thilke horrible swering of adiuracioun and coniuracioun, as doon thise false enchauntours or nigromanciens in bacins ful of water, or in a bright swerd, in a cercle, or in a fyr, or in a shulder-boon of a sheep. I can nat seye but that they doon cursedly and damnably, agayns Crist and al the feith of Holy Chirche.

What seye we of hem that bileven in divynailes, as by flight or by noyse of briddes, or of bestes, or by sort, by geomancie, by dremes, by chirkinge of dores, or crakkinge of houses, by gnawynge of rattes, and swich manere wrecchednesse? Certes, al this thing is deffended [i. e. forbidden] by God and by al Holy Chirche. For which they been acursed, til they come to amendement, that on swich filthe setten hir bileve. Charmes for woundes or maladye of men, or of bestes, if they taken any effect, it may be pera-venture that God suffreth it, for folk sholden yeve the more feith and reverence to his name.²⁵²

The art of the Clerk of Orleans in The Franklin's Tale is natural magic in the main, perhaps, but he cannot be fully acquitted of demonic invocation.²⁵³

The poet Gower may be taken as a representative of edu-cated opinion among devout and sober-minded Englishmen of the second half of the fourteenth century. Lovers, he tells us, to win their desire, do many strange things "that were better to be left":

> Among the whiche is wicchecraft,
> That som men clepen sorcerie.

And he proceeds to enumerate divers kinds of this black art, with a profusion of curious lore, some of which has not yet been traced by the commentators. Geomancy, hydromancy, pyromancy, and aëromancy he decides are not illicit, if prac-tised by way of nature and with good intent; but lovers also use "nigromance" with incantation and "hot subfumiga-tion." To illustrate sorcery he tells of Circe's transformations and of the wiles of the Egyptian Nectanebus, apparently with full faith in the possibility of both, and concludes his exam-ples with a brief account of Zoroaster, whom he regards as the inventor of magic, and finally of the Witch of Endor.²⁵⁴ In another place Gower couples Nectanebus with Proteus,

> That couthen bothe of nigromaunce
> In what liknesse, in what semblaunce,
> Riht as hem liste, himself transforme.²⁵⁵

And he relates the enchantments of Medea as if they were plain matters of fact.[256] Other cases in this century involving sorcery or witchcraft (for love or favor; for the detection of theft; for death, by images), false prophecy, *poltergeister*, demoniacal possession, demonic appearances and storms, the incubus and his offspring, homage to Satan, and the Satanic compact, as well as one possible instance of the swimming ordeal, will be considered under their several heads.

A Frenchman who had lived in England and who (about 1400) wrote a graphic account of the fall of Richard II, after specifying certain prophecies ascribed to Merlin and Bede which the English nobility accepted as forecasting the king's captivity and death, described the English as "of such a nature that they put perfect trust in prophecies and illusions (*fantosmes*) and sorceries and willingly make use of them." "In my opinion," he adds, "this is not well done, but is a great defect in their [Christian] faith." [257]

In the fifteenth century the evidence is practically uninterrupted throughout: we have, in fact, some pertinent item from more than fifty several years of the hundred, beginning with John Kyme, "soothesegger," in 1401,[258] and ending with Thomas Wryght in 1500, a monk of Sulby in the diocese of Lincoln, who, in Bishop Redman's visitation, was found to have used "books of experiments" and also to have rewarded lavishly a vagabond professor of occult science for instructing him. Brother Thomas protested that he had "speculated" only and had not proceeded to "operation," and his case was continued.[259] A number of these cases have already been registered in our study of Bishop Bale's witch (pp. 36–38, above), and others will be taken up when we come to special subjects. This leaves, however, a good many for our present consideration.

In the summer of 1402, so John Capgrave informs us, there were strange doings near Bedford and Biggleswade. "Fast by the townes of Bedforth and Bikilhswade, appered certeyn men of dyvers colouris, renning out of wodes, and fytyng horribly. This was seyne on morownyngis and at midday: and whan men folowid to loke what it was, thei coude se rite nawt." [260]

On January 2, 1406, after due deliberation in the Privy Council, the king's writ went to the Bishop of Lincoln:

"Since we are given to understand that there are in your diocese very many sorcerers, magicians, enchanters, nigromancers, diviners, soothsayers, and wizards,* who perpetrate from day to day divers horrid and detestable acts, whereby they . . . cause very many of our people in the foresaid diocese to be led astray by their malefic arts and defamed . . ., to the disturbance of our people, the scandal of holy mother church, and the manifest overthrow of the Catholic faith, we appoint you to summon such persons, examine them, and imprison them until they abandon their arts or you receive further instructions." [261] In the April following we have a remarkable mandate addressed by the spiritual administrators of Durham (the see being then without a bishop) to the Chaplain of the Collegiate Church of Chester-le-Street. This document recites that by civil and canon and divine law the practice of sorcery and magic, as well as consultation with sorcerers and magicians, is forbidden under the severest penalties. Therefore the Chaplain is to warn all sorcerers and magicians, and all who resort to them or trust them, that within six days they must make good the injuries they have done to any person, and must abandon their evil ways. [262] At about this time a versified manual for parish priests instructs the parson to forbid witchcraft, divination, and charms. When he examines his penitents' consciences he must ask them if they have "made any conjuring or any witchcraft" to recover stolen goods or for other purpose or have practised sorcery to win women. [263]

In 1410 Bishop Mascall of Hereford was grieved to learn that very many persons in the diocese were resorting with idolatrous practices to a spring and a stone in Turnastone parish. He refers the matter to his official and to the dean. [264]

In 1444 a man was pilloried in London "the whyche wrought by a wycckyd spyryte, the whyche was callyd Oberycom, and the maner of hys proces and werkyng was wretyn and hanggyd abowte hys necke whenne he was in the pellery." [265]

Cases of slander are particularly interesting since they show how common and easy an accusation this of sorcery or

---

* "Sortilegi, magici, incantatores, nigromantici, divinitores, arioli, et phitones" — a trim reckoning!

witchcraft was. Thus in 1452 Johanna Smythson appeared in the ecclesiastical court of Durham and brought two witnesses to prove that Agnes Thomson had publicly defamed her for sortilege, and had also reported that a certain chaplain was her lover and had spent so much for gifts as to be imprisoned for debt.[266] Agnes was held to sufficient compurgation. In 1567, on January 26, Margaret Lambert had a case against Elizabeth Lawson in the Durham ecclesiastical court, and John Lawson, Elizabeth's husband, declared that Margaret was an exorcist in that "for certaine things lackinge she turned a seve upon a pair of sheres." Thereupon, nine days later, Margaret accused John of slander in alleging that she was a "chermer." John appeared and said that he had no witnesses against Margaret, — he had spoken from hearsay. Another notable instance of village gossip! [267] Other cases of slander might be cited,[268] but these will suffice to define the category. Meantime let us take one instance from ancient days and one from the age of prose and reason. A leaden plate from Cnidos contains a Greek curse in which Antigone devotes to the infernal gods and goddesses the person who has falsely accused her of giving poison to Asclepiades (probably her husband) and of employing a witch to destroy him. She invokes the same curse upon herself if she is guilty.[269] In the Norwich Gazette of February 11, 1725, Hester Brown Percy prints an advertisement to the following effect: She has charged Mary Parker with being a witch and with being in great part the cause of her present sufferings. This charge she wishes now to retract publicly.[270] *Alter et idem!*

On June 13, 1483, was enacted that strange scene in the Council when Richard of Gloucester accused Queen Margaret ("yonder sorceres, my brothers wife") and Jane Shore of bewitching him. The *locus classicus* is a racy passage in the History of Richard III which passes as Sir Thomas More's: "Then said the protectour: ye shal al se in what wise that sorceres and that other witch of her counsel, Shoris wife, with their affynite, haue by their sorcery and witchcraft wasted my body. And therwith he plucked vp hys doublet sleue to his elbow vpon his left arme, where he shewed a werish withered arme and small, as it was neuer other. And thereupon euery mannes mind sore misgaue them, well perceiuing that this matter was but a quarel. For wel thei wist, that the quene was to wise to go aboute any such folye. . . . And also no man was there present, but wel knew that his harme was euer such since his birth." [271] In this same year one of the accomplices in the treason of Buckingham when he "ymagined and compassed" the death of King Richard, was Thomas Nandik, late of Cambridge, "nigromansier." [272]

In 1486 or 1487 a young son of John Adowne was afflicted with terrible pains and could neither walk nor stand upright. The most skilful physicians and surgeons were consulted, — for the boy's father was of Archbishop Morton's household, — but they were helpless and some of them declared that in their opinion it was "nothing natural," and that little John was suffering from the "venomous touch of a malign spirit." His mother commended him to the prayers of the dead King Henry VI, as to the intercession of a saint, and he soon recovered. [273]

A typical case of fraud dates from 1492, when, on the basis of common rumor (*fama publica referente*), the Commissary of the Bishop of London was informed that Richard Laukiston, some dozen years before, had said to Margaret Geffrey, "Thow arte a poore widow, and it wer almes to helpe the to a mariage, and if thow wilt do any cost in spendyng any money, thow shalt have a man worth a thousand pounds." "How may that be?" asked the widow. "My wif," replied Laukiston, "knoweth a connyng man, that by his connyng can cause a woman to have any man that she hath favour to," but, he added, "This shall cost money." Then said Margaret, "I have no good [i. e. goods] save ii masers for to fynde me, my moder, and my children, and if thei wer sold and I faile of my purpose, I, my moder, and my children wer undoen." Richard reassured his dupe, however, and she handed over the two bowls, valued at five marks and ten shillings. Apparently nothing came of the investment. Both parties were summoned before the Commissary and confessed. Richard was required to restore the bowls or their value in money within eight days on pain of the major excommunication; his punishment was deferred and is not recorded. Margaret was to do public penance on three Sundays by walking before the procession of the cross barefoot, having her head covered with a knotted kirtle of flame color and carrying in her right hand a candle worth a penny.[274] The offences of the two were regarded as pertaining to heresy and sorcery; but the case was plainly one of barefaced fraud.[275] We should note that the accusation arose — as so often happened — from the common talk of the neighborhood.

About 1500 Sir William Tyndale, knight, petitioned the Lord Chancellor for relief against Sir William Carrowe, who had sued him at common law on a bond for ten pounds. Tyndale declares that this bond was extorted from him by Carrowe, who had maliciously arrested Tyndale's wife for "wytchecraft and socery" and had refused to release her until Tyndale had given him the bond in question. While she was in Carorwe's custody, "he dyde raunsake hyr, surmysyng [i. e. alleging] that sche hadde on hyr wrytyng of socery and wytchecraft," and threatened her so that she was in great fear. Yet no "defawte" had been found in her.[276]

In 1502 Eleanor Dulyne was brought before the Commissary of London for "devising certain magic arts" to destroy her husband and for plotting his death by poison. She cleared herself and was discharged, but Anna Miller, one of her neighbors, was brought to book as a "common defamer" — and in particular for having slandered Mistress Dulyne in this matter.[277]

In 1523 the Earl of Surrey informed Wolsey of a disastrous stampede of the horses belonging to Lord Dacre's troop in the Scottish campaign: "I dare not write the wonders that my Lord Dacre and all his company doo saye they sawe that nyght, vj. tymys, of sprits and fereful sights. And unyversally all their company saye playnely, the Devill was that nyght amongs theym vi. tymys." [278] Whether Satan was acting on his own initiative or in deference to witches' incantations, we are not informed.

In 1532 Thomas Sall, precentor of Norwich Priory, was charged with absenting himself often from service. "Also," the record reads, "he has places and houses which he frequents for the practice of his arts, on which account great infamy and scandal arise because of those who resort to such places" — manifestly to consult the clerical wizard.[279]

The troubles of Sir William Neville, Lord Latimer's

brother, in 1532 introduce us to a couple of wizards, Nashe of
Cirencester and Richard Jones of Oxford. Nashe was a regular practitioner, whom Sir William consulted as to the whereabouts of some missing silver spoons; but this trivial matter
was soon forgotten in the revelations that ensued. For Nashe
assured Sir William that great things were in store for him:
his wife should die and he should marry an heiress and suc-
ceed to his brother's title. At Nashe's suggestion he had recourse to Jones, an operator of a higher type, and incidentally
an alchemist. In Jones's chamber he saw "styllatoryes,
alembykes, and odre instruments of glasse," also a sceptre
and other things that pertained "to the conjuration of the
iiij kyngs." Jones raised four "king devils," and these
brought the magician "into a tower, and showed him there
the picture of the said William Nevyll standing in a robe of
velvet and a cronall on his head, and said it was he that
should be Earl of Warwick." A friend warned Neville that
demons are liars, but he replied that Jones could "so bind
them that they shall not lie." Neville lost his head completely and indulged in much wild talk of his brilliant pros-
pects, mentioning by the way certain prophecies about the
king; and so he was arrested, and the Council undertook to
investigate the whole affair. Jones was called to account and
drew up a confession in which, of course, he did his best to
exculpate himself. Neville had asked him (so runs the conjuror's story) if it were not possible "to have a ring made
that should bring a man in favour with his prince; seeing my
Lord Cardinal had such a ring, that whatsomever he asked of
the King's Grace, that he had." And, added Neville, Master
Cromwell (when he and I were servants in Wolsey's house)
"did haunt to the company of one that was seen in your
faculty [i. e. skilled in your art]; and shortly after no man so
great with my Lord Cardinal as Master Cromwell was!" "I
shewed him," Jones continues, "that I had read many books,
and specially the works of Solomon, and how his ring should
be made, and of what metal; and what virtues they had after
the canon of Solomon." But he protests that he never made
such a thing himself. A fortnight later, he goes on, Neville
visited him at Oxford and informed him that he had at his
house a person named Wayd, who "did shew him that he

should be a great lord in a place where there was a fair castle," which Neville thought must be the Castle of Warwick. Thereupon Jones recounted an alleged dream: "that an angel took him [Neville] and me by the hands, and led us to a high tower, and there delivered him a shield, with sundry arms which I cannot rehearse." Jones admits that he "wrote a foolish letter or two according to his [Neville's] foolish desire, to make pastime to laugh at." In at least one of these, as it appears from other evidence, Jones addressed his dupe as Earl of Warwick. Jones also admits that he once made certain "molds" for "Sir Gr. Done, Knight, to the intent he should have had Mistress Elizabeth's gear," i. e. "property." We have no details about this piece of knavery. He further confesses that now and then he had, at the request of friends, "cauled to stone" (that is, conjured spirits into a crystal) for the recovery of stolen goods. He had often been asked "by foolish fellows of the country" to assist them in the search for treasure trove, but had "never meddled with it at all." One thing, however, Jones takes seriously, and that is his alchemical researches. "To make the philosopher's stone I will jeopard my life, so to do it," if the king wishes. He requires but twelve months "upon silver" and twelve and a half "upon gold," and is willing to be kept in prison until he succeeds. He makes a similar offer in a letter to Cromwell.[280]

In 1533 and the following year, there was intense excitement about the Holy Maid of Kent, Elizabeth Barton, whose visions and prophecies so alarmed the government that she was put to death as a traitor in 1534. Some regarded her as inspired, others as a demoniac, still others as a mere impostor.[281] By the violently Protestant author of The Image of Ypocresye, a contemporary satire, à la Skelton, she is styled "this witche" and is said to have been sent from the devil —

> A virgyne ffayre and gent,
> That hath our yees blent.[282]

Certain passages in her case, be they true or false, excuse this rating if they do not justify it. She feigned, it was alleged, that Satan sought to make her his wife;[283] and she certainly told Sir Thomas More "that of late the Devil, in likeness of a Bird, was flying and fluttering about her in a Chamber, and suffered himself to be taken; and being in hands, suddenly changed, in their sight that were present, into such a strange ugly-fashioned Bird, that they were all afraid, and threw him out at a Window." [284] Reginald Scot ranks her among the *ventriloqui*.[285]

In 1535 Friar John Colsell was to be arrested for practising "the decitful arte of magike and astronomye," [286] and a priest (not named) was found by officers of Abbot Thomas of Abingdon to have in his possession a conjuring book. He was likewise apprehended.[287]

In 1537 John Butler wrote to Cranmer from Calais of a priest, William Richardson (called Good Sir William) who was so ill-advised as to instruct his parishioners to keep the day of St. Thomas the Martyr a holiday, as of old. Butler wishes to know what to do with him, for he is a great enemy to the truth. Once he was about to be punished for sorcery, but "such suit was made for him that nothing was done." [288] There are many papers on file about Richardson, who was taken to London and imprisoned in the Fleet.[289] In 1540 he was executed, along with William Peterson (another Calais priest), for doubting the king's supremacy in the English Church.[290]

In 1538, or earlier, Sir Richard Holonde, of Yatton, Somerset, was of ill repute for "nigromansy." [291] In 1539 John Misselden, merchant, along with his son Robert, had a writ of privy seal to exercise his "science or cunning" to transmute base metals to gold or silver, provided they used no necromancy, but only "plain science of philosophy." [292]

On July 29, 1540, the notorious Walter Lord Hungerford was executed for treason along with Thomas Cromwell. Hungerford was somehow involved in a horrible scandal, into which we need not enquire. For our purpose it suffices to know that, according to the bill of attainder, he had "procured Sir Hugh Woodes, chaplain, Dr. Mawdelyn, and one Mother Roche to conjure and show how long the king should live." [293] The French ambassador wrote home that, among other things, he was attainted "d'avoir usé d'art magique et invocation de Dyables." [294] One must not fail to note the association of a professional witch, for such Mother Roche undoubtedly was, with the more exalted practisers of wicked arts. A certain Mother Huntley was also involved.²⁹⁵ In the same year John Heron's house in Kent was searched and "a sceptre and certain charactes in a plate touching conjuracions" were found. He confessed to the Privy Council "his foly in using of fantastical practises in astronymye," and was released under bonds not to "practise use or exercise any maner of necromancye astronymye calculacions or other experimentes" and to inform against any who did.²⁹⁶ I suspect that this was the same Heron, a "professor" of physic and surgery, who Scot says was a friend of Mother Bungie, the great witch of Rochester, "reputed among all men for the cheefe ring-leader of all other witches." She admitted on her deathbed "that hir cunning consisted onlie in deluding and deceiving the people: saving that she had . . . some sight [i. e. skill] in physicke and surgerie, and the assistance of a freend of hirs, called *Heron*, a professor thereof." ²⁹⁷ Scot was born about 1538. He seems to have known Mother Bungie's husband, and speaks of her having practised her arts "manie yeares." I think there is no doubt that a considerable part of her career fell before the Elizabethan age. Mother Bungie was not merely a white witch, for her curse was dangerous, at least to pigs. Her prophecies remained in credit among the ignorant after her death.²⁹⁸

In 1541 Thomas Walpole confessed conspiracy with one Forde, a physician of East Dereham in Norfolk, "touching certain conjuracions," and the Council issued orders to arrest Forde, search his house, and send him up with his instruments of conjuration.²⁹⁹ On October 21, 1542, John Morris, yeoman, of Brampton, Leicestershire, had a pardon under the privy seal for all felonies, "being crimes of the magic arts, etc., committed since Mayday." ³⁰⁰ This was the year of the Witchcraft Act of Henry VIII. In 1545, Dr. Nicholas Wotton, Dean of Canterbury and York, ambassador to the Emperor, writes from Mechlin to Sir William Paget: "Here is a strange report that a certain hermit confessed to have by sorcery procured the death of the duke of Lorraine's father and mother and the Duke's own disease, and, being in prison, promised to heal the Duke if he might have his pardon; but the Duke would believe nothing of it, and now the hermit is dead in prison, so that there seems no help for the Duke." ³⁰¹

The extraordinary case of Harry Lord Nevell, son and heir of Ralph, Earl of Westmoreland, in 1546 merits close attention for two reasons: first, because there can be no possible doubt as to the main facts, since we have them in Nevell's own words; second, because the affair illustrates the prevalence of various kinds of sorcery in the reign of Henry VIII, and the proneness of persons of high social position, and not merely the humble, to dabble in these arts, malefic and other. Nevell, a young profligate of twenty-one, tired of his wife (to whom he was married when he was eleven years old) and addicted to gaming and fleshly lusts, was looking forward impatiently to the death of his father. In 1546, before October 1, he was arrested and confined in the Fleet, whence he wrote several letters of confession or petition to the Chief Secretary, Sir William Paget, and one to the king. To Paget he professes to reveal "the whole circumstance of his grievous offences." The tempter and chief agent was, it seems, Ninian Melville (or Menville). About two years before (a month before Christmas, 1544) Melville suggested the preparation of a ring to help Lord Harry at play,[302] for he was an inveterate loser, he tells us, and was already in debt. One Stafford, who was approached, at first objected, "because of the Act" (the Witchcraft Statute, then but two years old), but gave way, and next morning introduced a man named Wisdom, henceforth the Mephistopheles of the drama. Lord Harry was impressed by Wisdom's good clothes: he was "not in a threadbare coat as commonly these imperfect multipliers [alchemists] be." Wisdom declared that he "could work the ring by two ways, by good or evil spirits," but this time "he would work it by the holy angels." [303] He "only did such things for friends, most of his practice being in physic." He asked an annuity of twenty pounds, but Lord Harry was a bargainer and beat him down to ten, payable after the Earl's decease. Thereupon Wisdom became an inmate of Lord Harry's household for a month — till Christmas. We may infer that the magic ring was provided, though we hear no more of it. Wisdom promised to enable his client to "play as well on the lute and virginals as any man in England." This was to be effected on St. Stephen's Day by raising "the god Orpheus," who would appear in the form of a little boy;

but the invocation was interrupted and came to naught. Wisdom also told Sir Harry that he had learned from Melville (who had in his turn learned it from "a blind man which was a Jew born and a practiser of the same art") that near a town of the Earl's in the North there was a huge mass of treasure buried under a cross; what the sum was, Wisdom added, he would that night enquire of "a spirit that he had in a crystal stone." On the morrow he reported that it was two thousand pounds "in Portegewes." Melville and Wisdom visited the spot and overturned the cross, but found nothing. Somewhat later, they offered to kill Sir Harry's wife for him, obviously by magic and probably by the usual trick of a waxen image. But this was too much, even for him (so he avers) and he refused. Not long after, Wisdom told him that "he had practised the death both of his [Sir Harry's] father and of his wife." Sir Harry was astonished. He protests, in another letter to Paget, that "he never consented to his father's destruction, or knew of it till the deed was done." The Earl did not die, however, until some years after (in 1549). In his petition to the king Lord Harry praises his wife: she is kind and good and will assuredly forgive him. We are left to infer that he is lying when he protests that he did not consent to the attempt upon her life and his father's.[304] What became of Melville and Wisdom we do not know. If they were hanged, as the statute directs, the world was well rid of a pair of knaves. But Sir Harry was spared and succeeded to the earldom of Westmoreland on his father's death.[305]

From 1550 we have the testimony of Roger Hutchinson in a work intended to instruct the laity: "I think our Sadducees will be edified more by a conjurer, than by the words of godliness. Wherefore I send them to conjurers, sorcerers, enchanters, charmers, witches; which will learn and persuade them that there be devils, and that they be not lusts of the flesh, but spiritual substances and spirits created for vengeance; which now, in the end of the world, shall pour out their strength, to pluck the Lamb of God out of the minds of all men." [306] Hutchinson was educated at St. John's College, Cambridge, where he was Senior Fellow in 1547; he died in 1555. His contemporary, Dr. John Caius, affords us similar evidence in 1552 from the point of view of a physician. He warns his readers to avoid quacks as they would the plague. Such are "simple women, carpenters, pewterers, brasiers, sopeballesellers, pulters, hostellers, painters, apotecaries (otherwise then for their drogges), auaunters themselues to come from Pole, Constantinople, Italie, Almaine, Spaine, Fraunce, Grece and Turkie, Inde, Egipt or Jury: from ye seruice of Emperoures, kinges & quienes, promising helpe of al diseases, yea vncurable, with one or twoo drinckes, by waters sixe monethes in continualle distillinge, by *Aurum potabile*, or *quintessence*, by drynckes of great and hygh prices, as though thei were made of the sunne, moone, or sterres, by blessynges and Blowinges, Hipocriticalle prayenges, and foolysh smok- ynges of shirtes Smockes and kerchieffes, wyth suche others theire phantasies, and mockeryes, meaninge nothinge els but to abuse your light belieue, and scorne you behind your backes with their medicines (so filthie, that I am ashamed to name theim) for your single wit and simple belief, in trusting them most, whiche you know not at al." [307]

The Wall Spirit was famous in London in 1554. Nashe alludes to the affair: "What a piteous noyse, like a spirit in a wal, doth he here make!" [308] The medium, a "poore maide" of sixteen or seventeen named Elizabeth Croft, stood at Paul's Cross as a penitent, confessing her imposition. [309]

In 1555 Dr. John Dee was examined by the Privy Council. He had been accused by George Ferrys of striking one of Ferrys's children blind by magic and killing another. He was also charged with directing his arts against Queen Mary's life. After a brief confinement in the Fleet, he was released under bonds. Besides Dee there were involved Sir Thomas Benger, John Field, and Christopher Cary, all of whom made some kind of confession as to "lewde and vayne practises of calculing and conjuring." [310]

One of Reginald Scot's helpers in the search for material for The Discoverie of Witchcraft was "T. E.," Master of Arts, a physician and "practiser of certeine vaine sciences," whose penitent letter, written in 1583 under sentence of death, is printed in full. T. E. declares that he has associated with conjurors for twenty-six years, and this puts his initiation back into Queen Mary's reign. Some phrases in the docu- ment suggest that he had been employed by the Earl of

Leicester, who is known to have dabbled in the occult. Who
T. E. was and what became of him I do not know. When he
wrote to Scot, he had been reprieved, apparently at Leicester's request. He once had a book, he avers, composed "in
the old Saxon toong, by one Sir John Malborne a divine of
Oxenford, three hundred yeares past; wherein he openeth all
the illusions & inventions of those arts and sciences," but
this he had deposited with the parson of Slangham in Sussex.
Scot bestirred himself to borrow the manuscript, but the parson refused to let it go out of his hands.[311]

Bishop Hooper was burned for heresy in 1555, so that he
cannot well be held to have brought in foreign notions from
the Continent at Elizabeth's accession three years later. Let
us see what he thought about witches and wizards. In 1548
or 1549, in full accord with Bishop Quivil's canon of 1287
and with Anglo-Saxon doctrine,[312] Hooper reckoned among
idolaters "such as give faith unto the conjuration or sorcery
of superstitious persons" — as, for example, "to witches
or soothsayers, where they abuse the name of God to singe
out the fire of him that hath burned his hand, and to stanch
blood, to heal man or beast." [313] Among offences he specifies
"seeking the help of damned spirits, or of such souls as be
departed out of this world, as Saul did"; and necromancy
pure and simple — the attempt "to resuscitate dead bodies,
or call spirits departed into the body again." "These men,"
he tells us, "in English be called conjurers, who useth arts
forbidden by God's laws, and also by the laws of ethnicks, before Christ was born." He denounces those "that by the
abuse of God's name use superstitious conjurations and enchantments, when they seek the truth of the devil and dead
bodies." [314] He condemns astrology; "over-much faith unto
medicines, or the nature of stones and herbs"; divination as
to future events, crops, health or sickness; healing by the
abuse of God's name "through the help of the devil"; palmistry and physiognomy.[315] In one of his later writings he denounces as "the greatest and most abominable evil (one of
them) that can be done against God" — "witchcraft, and
calculation by astronomy and such other like." [316] For all
these crimes he seems to approve the punishment of death.[317]
In his visitation as Bishop of Gloucester in 1551, Hooper in-

cludes among the enquiries to be made of the parishioners concerning the ministers: "Whether any of them teach, talk, reason, or defend any prophecies and lies of men besides God's holy word, or use themselves, or suffer any other to use, witchcraft, palmistry, and such other forbidden arts: or whether any of them put their trust in such forbidden and damnable crafts." [318]   In this same year Elizabeth Hicks, Joan Clerk, and William Baker were enjoined in his diocesan court "not to use certain specified sorceries." The two latter were obliged openly on Sunday to express sorrow for their offences. In the same year and court William Newport, vicar of St. Owen's, was presented for using the sorcery of key and book for discovery of theft. On one occasion he had practised this form of divination in the church chancel! In his case a book of magic appears — it belonged to one Sibill, appropriately named.[319] When William Wycherley, tailor and sorcerer, was examined in 1549, he deponed that "there be within England above v hundred conjurers as he thinketh . . .; and specially in Norfolk, Hartfordshire, and Wourcestershire and Gloucestershire a great number." [320] Gloucester was Hooper's diocese from 1550 to 1552, when he was created Bishop of Worcester.

The common resort to sorcerers and white witches is certified by Latimer in 1552. When we pray "Hallowed be thy name," he tells his congregation, "we require [i. e. ask] that all witchcrafts be removed; that art magic and sorcery be pulled out, necromancy taken away; and so nothing be left but his holy word, wherewith we may daily praise the name of God. For I fear me there be a great many in England which use such sorceries, to the dishonour of God and their own damnation." And again, "Some of us, when we be in trouble, do run hither and thither to sorcerers and witches, to get remedy." And yet again, Jairus in the Bible "did not as a great many of us do, when we be in trouble, or sickness, or lose any thing, we run hither and thither to witches or sorcerers, whom we call wise men; when there is no man so foolish and blind as they be: for the devil leadeth them according unto his will and pleasure, and yet we run after them, seeking aid and cure at their hands." [321]

Let us see what we have found in 900–1557. We have

read of magic books and amulets and scrolls and fumigations and potent herbs; of fortune-telling and soothsaying and prophecy; of divination in great variety (by geomancy and hydromancy, by birds and beasts and meetings, by *sortes*, by balls of clay, by bible and key, by sieve and shears, by loaf and knives, by the shoulder bone of a sheep, by sleeping in or on a hide, by the promptings of a familiar spirit or of a voice from the wall) and for divers purposes (to learn the secrets of the past or future, to detect thieves and get back what is lost or stolen, to forecast luck in travel, to recover a drowned man's body); of crystal gazing and the magic mirror (including the use of swords and knives and basins and thumbnails); of spells and charms and incantations — for the healing of man and beast, for protection against disease or injury or the assaults of demons and elves or the depredations of animals, for abundance of milk and corn and mustard, for skill in music and luck with the dice, for safety at the ordeal or in the wager of battle, for love or hate, for finding buried treasure; of *poltergeister* and their antics and of similar tricks that witches play; of demon apparitions and demoniacal possession; of evil spells to hinder corn and cattle from thriving, to spoil the ale, to dry up wells, to blast plants and trees, to destroy poultry; of milk-stealing witchcraft; of witchcraft to bind a man or break his leg or wither his arm or strike him blind or drive him mad or cause his death; of image witchcraft for love and murder; of magic powders and unguents and the conjure-bag; of mist and storm brought about by demons with or without a witch's agency; of witch-wiles in war; of vagrant practitioners of magic or witchcraft both lay and cleric; of jugglers and tregetours who work illusion whether by spells or by sleight of hand; of the vampire-wizard who summons men to the next world; of profanation not only of prayers and holy texts but of the mass, the font-water, the chrism, the consecrated wafer, and the wine of the chalice; of homage to Satan and compact with him and fleshly union with fiends; of familiar spirits in the shape of dwarf and cat and dog; of the swimming test for witchcraft; of the devil's carrying off the witch's body when she dies. Once more there is nothing of importance that does not come in except the Sabbath, and that is unknown to the Elizabethan cases.

CHAPTER III

IMAGE MAGIC AND THE LIKE

NO DEPARTMENT of witchcraft affords more convincing evidence of continuity than Image Magic, technically termed *invultuacio* or *envoûtement*. From remote periods of history in Egypt, Assyria, Babylonia,[1] and India,[2] from classic times and lands,[3] from the middle ages, and so on down to the present day, the practice of image magic has been prevalent, and it is still common the world over, among savage men and civilized.[4] It depends, of course, on the doctrine of sympathy. An effigy of wax, clay, wood, metal, or almost any substance, is pierced with nails, pins, or thorns, and burned or slowly roasted. The victim suffers corresponding torments, pines away as the puppet melts or crumbles, and dies when it is stabbed to the heart. Sometimes the image is buried or drowned instead of being consumed by fire, and there are other varieties which the sequel will illustrate. As for the end in view, that may be either enmity pure and simple, or self-defence against a witch. Often, also, the object is to torture a person with the pangs of love or to recall a truant sweetheart. The same method in general may be applied to remedial purposes — the image being treated in such a manner as to benefit the patient. This branch of therapeutics is celebrated by Chaucer in describing his Doctor of Physic:

> Wel coude he fortunen the ascendent
> Of his images for his pacient.[5]

And the poet knew also of evil art in this kind. Along with the magicians and charmeresses and olde wicches in the House of Fame he mentions

> Clerkes eek which conne wel
> Al this magyke naturel,
> That craftely don her ententes
> To make, in certeyn ascendentes,
> Images, lo! through which magyk
> To make a man ben hool or syk.[6]

Agrippa sums up malefic image magic very well. The figure, he tells us, is buried in the earth or sunk in a river; or it is hung up in the chimney or on a tree, head down in some cases; or it may be plunged into hot water or thrown into the fire.[7] Dr. Primrose (who died in 1659), in his chapter "Of the Weapon-salve," duly ascribes the efficacy of wax figures to the principle of sympathy: "As the Image laid to the fire, or exposed to the frost, doth burn, or congeale him that is absent; so doth the unguent laid upon the weapon." In neither case does he doubt the possibility of the operation, which he thinks comes from the devil.[8]

In ancient *defixiones* [9] it was sufficient to scratch a name on a leaden plate, which was then buried, preferably in a tomb or grave, with appropriate ceremonies; but often the word of defixion (καταδῶ, i. e. καταδέω, "I bind fast") was added, and also, frequently, invocations of the chthonic gods or of demons were engraved, with other spells to curse the victim. A nail might be driven through the rolled tablet. At times, too, a picture of the victim was inscribed, or images were buried along with the roll.[10] Such a leaden doll is portrayed by Wünsch: the head has been cut off, the arms and legs are bent backward and tied with strips of lead, the trunk is crossed by a fetter, there is an iron nail in the breast and another in the belly.[11] A good example is the celebrated find at Pozzuoli — eight puppets of clay lying on the burnt bones in a tomb, each of them inscribed with a name, masculine or feminine, in Greek letters.[12] A miracle of Saints Cyrus and John, as told by Sophronius, deals with a similar puppet. Theophilus, an Alexandrian, disabled in hands and feet, prayed to these saints, who forthwith appeared in a dream and directed him to have himself carried to the shore, and there, when he saw a fisherman casting nets, to give him money to make a cast for him: "Whatever the net brings up will cure you." The first cast brought up a small basket, which contained a bronze figure, like Theophilus in all respects; both feet and both hands were pierced, each with a nail. When these were pulled out, Theophilus recovered.[13] In 1903 there was washed ashore at Calicut a lifesize female effigy with long iron nails in head, body, and limbs.[14]

The Anglo-Saxon Penitential falsely ascribed to Ecgbert,[15]

Archbishop of York, provides for three years' fasting (one year on bread and water, and two on the same for three days in the week) for this kind of sorcery; if the victim dies, the fast is for seven years (three on bread and water, and four on the same for three days in the week), precisely as for murder by *veneficium* ("mid wicce-cræfte": iv, 16). So also in the Penitential enacted under King Edgar.[16] The twelfth-century Latin compilation known as the Laws of Henry I rates *invultuacio* as murder (along with poisoning, sorcery, and any other malefic magic), if the man dies.[17] An actual case of such murder is mentioned in an Anglo-Saxon charter of ca. 963–975. A certain widow and her son had forfeited an estate at Ailsworth, Northamptonshire, "because they drove iron nails (*stacan*) into Ælsi, Wulfstan's father." The image was apparently discovered in the woman's chamber. She was drowned at London Bridge, and her son fled and was outlawed.[18]

John of Salisbury (1120–1180) was of course acquainted with image magic. He speaks of the use of figures of wax or clay as love-charms, and he quotes Virgil's Eclogue, as well as Hypsipyle's charge against Medea from Ovid's Heroides, which includes the making and piercing of waxen images:

> Deuouet absentes simulacraque cerea fingit,
> Et miserum tenues in iecur urget acus.[19]

And Peter of Blois, Archdeacon of Bath in the latter part of the same century, gives similar evidence.[20] Giraldus Cambrensis (ca. 1146– ca. 1220) reproves the abominable conduct of contemporary priests who pervert the sacrament of the altar to black magic "by celebrating masses over images of wax in order to curse some person." There are others, he adds, "who sing the mass Fidelium [21] against a man ten times or more, that he may die before the tenth day or soon after, and be buried with the dead." [22]

If such practices had not been known to the Anglo-Saxons, full information would have come in with the Norman Conquest, for they were familiar to the French. In the very year of the Battle of Hastings, Evrard, Bishop of Trèves, met his death by this means. He had issued an edict that all Jews not baptized by Easter should be banished from the city.

Certain of this "evil race" thereupon made a waxen image in his likeness, and bribed a priest — "Christian in name, not in deed" — to baptize it. On Easter Sunday, when the bishop was about to perform the rites of baptism, they melted the image. The bishop collapsed at the fontstone, was helped into the sacristy by attendant priests, and died there in his sacred vestments kneeling before the cross.[23]

In 1308 Guichard, Bishop of Troyes, was accused of murdering Jeanne, queen of Philip IV, by sorcery three years before. The details are thrilling. He consulted a witch and caused a demon to be invoked by a friar who was skilful in this art; he did homage to the demon and received full instructions how to proceed. With the friar and the witch he visited a hermitage in disguise, and had a waxen image made and baptized by the name of Jeanne. This was pierced with a needle or stylus in the head and other parts of the body. Jeanne fell sick then or soon after, and no physician could either diagnose the case or find a remedy. The bishop caused the figure to be pierced again and again by the witch, but still the queen refused to die. Then crying out in anger, "How, devil? Will this woman live forever?" he broke the limbs of the image, tore it into bits, trampled on it, and threw it into the fire, where it was consumed. At or near that time the queen died. The intimate association of one or two notorious local witches with these and other diabolical performances is noteworthy.[24] The affair must have been matter for conversation in English court circles, for the victim had been at one time betrothed to a son of Edward I, and her mother (Blanche d'Artois) had in 1275 married Edmund of Lancaster, brother of the same king Edward. The prosecution lasted from 1308 to 1313. Even more closely connected with England was the case of Enguerrand de Marigny, hanged at Paris on April 30, 1315; for he had been in favor with Edward II, to whom he had lent much money, and who had assigned him an interest in the customs of the port of London.[25] Enguerrand, who had been chamberlain, chief councillor, and so special a favorite of Philip IV that many thought he had bewitched him, was accused of embezzlement and treason, but was to have been let off with banishment to Cyprus during the pleasure of Louis X, when his accuser (Charles de

Valois, the king's uncle) learned that one Jacobus de Lor and his wife and manservant had (at the instance of Enguerrand's wife and sister and perhaps of himself) moulded wax images to effect the culprit's deliverance and also to injure the king and Charles and others, though the ladies alleged that the end in view was to win Louis's favor or forbearance. The sorcerer Jacobus hanged himself in prison, and his wife was burned. These revelations changed Enguerrand's sentence to one of death, though he denied every accusation. In 1317 he was taken down from the gallows and honorably buried — he had a full rehabilitation from Philippe le Long.[26] In this same year Hugues Géraud, Bishop of Cahors, was flayed alive and burned for plotting the death of Pope John XXII by poison and image magic.[27]

We may now return to England. On the last day of November, 1323, so runs the testimony of Robert le Mareschal of Leicester, more than a score of the inhabitants of Coventry, most of them burghers, visited the house of Master John de Notingham in that town, a professed magician (*nigromauncer*), with whom Robert was lodging. "Will you keep a secret — to your own profit?" they asked. The magician and his lodger replied that they would. Then the visitors declared that they could no longer endure the oppression of the Prior of Coventry, backed as he was by the king and the two Despensers, father and son; and they asked Master John if he would kill the king, the Despensers, and the prior, together with his cellarer and his seneschal, "par sa nigromancie et ses artz." The bargain was struck: Master John was to receive twenty pounds "et sa gareison" in any house of religion in England that he should elect, and Robert le Mareschal fifteen. Shortly after, the burghers made a payment on account and delivered seven pounds of wax and two ells of canvas. The miscreants Robert and John went to work at once in an old house half a league from Coventry and continued their operations until almost the end of the following May (1324). They made six images of wax, each to represent one of the persons to be destroyed, and a seventh image in the shape of one Richard de Sowe, which was to be used in testing the efficacy of their diabolical attempts ("prover les autres images s'il furent certeyns ou ne mye"). On the 27th of

April, about midnight, as they were "about their work"
Master John gave Robert a sharp spit of lead and bade him
stick it into the forehead of Richard's image. Next day he
sent Robert to Richard's house to see how he was, and he
found him out of his mind, shrieking and crying "Harrow!"
And so Richard continued to suffer until Sunday, the 20th of
May (1324), when Master John pulled out the spit and stuck
it into the heart of the image. There it remained until the
following Wednesday, when Richard died. Thus it appeared
that the experiment was a complete success. Such is the substance of Robert le Mareschal's statement before the Coroner
on November 30, 1324. Probably the death of Richard de
Sowe was being investigated by this official, and Robert,
finding himself under suspicion, had decided to "appeal"
(i. e. accuse) the master magician and the burghers "of felony" — thus (to use the nearest modern equivalent in such a
case) turning king's evidence. At all events, he was the ap-
pellor both in the coroner's court and also in the Court of the
King's Bench, to which the case was called up by a writ of
certiorari (dated Nov. 6, 18 Ed. II [1324]). It was tried in
June, 1325. By this time John de Notingham had died in
prison. The Coventry burghers were acquitted. Robert le
Mareschal was held in custody, and what became of him we
cannot tell.[28] An echo of this case is a letter sent in 1324 by
Pope John XXII to the younger Despenser (one of the intended victims). In reply to Despenser's complaint "that he
is threatened by magical and secret dealings, the pope recom-
mends him to turn to God with his whole heart, and make a
good confession and such satisfaction as shall be enjoined.
No other remedies are necessary beyond the general indult
which the pope grants him." [29]

Later in this century (1376) a learned friar in the service of
Alice Perrers is said to have moulded figures of wax to infatuate King Edward (see p. 105).

The ordinary mental pabulum of Englishmen in the fourteenth century may be illustrated by an often-quoted story
from one of the most popular of all collections of exempla, the
Gesta Romanorum. While a certain knight was in Rome on
his way to the Holy Land, his wife at home had an intrigue
with a clerk skilled in *nigromancia*. At her request the clerk

undertook to kill the husband in order to marry her himself. He prepared an image of wax like the knight and gave it the knight's name; then he fastened it to the wall. Meanwhile, as the knight was walking in a public square in Rome, a cunning man (*magister quidam peritus*) accosted him: "This day you are a son of death unless you have my help, for your wife has made arrangements to kill you!" The knight accepted the friendly offer, whereupon the magister had him get into a bath and gave him a polished mirror and bade him look therein. He saw a room in his own house, and there stood the clerk, ready to shoot an arrow at the image. By the master's orders, the knight ducked under at the moment when he saw the arrow leave the bow. The clerk missed. So, too, at the second shot. Then the clerk was much distressed: "If I do not hit the image the third time, I shall lose my life." And so he shot, and the arrow turned back and slew him. All this was seen and heard by the knight as he looked in the mirror. [30] The tale was deservedly popular. It was turned to good account by Holkot [31] and Barham adapted it as "The Leech of Folkestone" in his Ingoldsby Legends. [32]

A famous case of the early fifteenth century probably involved image magic, but the details are lacking. In October, 1419, Henry V prosecuted his stepmother, Joan of Navarre, for attempting to kill him by witchcraft. It was set forth in Parliament, "on information given the king as well by relation and confession of a friar, John Randolf, of the Order of Friars Minors, as by other credible evidences," that she "had compassed and imagined the death and destruction of our lord the king in the most horrible manner that one could devise," as had been openly published throughout the realm; and that the Council had ordered her goods and chattels to be confiscated,[33] as well as the rents of her estates, dower and other. She was committed to Leeds Castle in the custody of Sir John Pelham. The means used to destroy King Henry, vaguely expressed in the parliamentary record, is made clear by contemporary historians. It was "sorcery and nigromancy," and Friar Randolf, who had been her confessor, admitted his guilt in this regard.[34] Singularly enough he was not put to death, but merely imprisoned for life, or during the king's pleasure. In 1429, however, he was murdered. A priest — the "parson of the Tower" according to one of the chroniclers — smashed his head with a stone, finished him off with a hatchet, and hid the corpse under sand and dung. The priest was mad, we are told, but no doubt he had long regarded Brother Randolf as a servant of the devil.[35] King Henry died on the first of September, 1422. On the 13th of July he wrote a letter directing that Queen Joan's dower should be restored. She petitioned parliament accordingly, in 1423, and her prayer was granted.[36]

Henry V was undoubtedly worried about witchcraft, and so were his prelates. In the month preceding the parliament of 1419 the Archbishop of Canterbury ordered prayers and processions for the king and his army in France, especially to protect him against the operations of necromancers. In his mandate to the Bishop of London he says that the king desires such services, in order that God may protect him from all the wicked, malicious, and unjust plots of his enemies, and from the "superstitious operations of necromancers, especially such as (according to report) have lately been devised by some persons for the destruction of his person." [37] And in the month following the parliament we have the case of Richard Walker, a chaplain, arrested by the Prior of Winchester for sorcery and brought before Convocation by the Archbishop of Canterbury on November 8, 1419. Among his paraphernalia were a beryl stone, two little images of yellow wax, and two books containing conjurations and figures. Richard confessed that he had practised art magic in divers ways according to the precepts of one of the books, but he declared that he did not believe in these things, but felt sure that all such operations were false, because he had never succeeded in any of his occult experiments. This form of confession of course cleared him of heresy.[38]

In 1426 commissions were issued to men of standing in the counties of Somerset, Dorset, and Cornwall, to investigate the complaint of William Lord Botreaux that Sir Ralph Botreaux and William Langkelly had employed three persons (said to practise "soothsaying, necromancy, and art magic") to "weaken and annihilate, subtly to consume and altogether to destroy by the said arts the body of the said William." [39]

Shortly before the middle of the fifteenth century we note a capital instance of witchcraft. The accident that it involved a lady of rank is the reason why we have so many details. Such things must have been common enough among the lowly, but they either passed without notice from the authorities or the records are lost or unpublished. In 1441 Eleanor Cobham, Duchess of Gloucester, was accused of conspiring with Master Roger Bolingbroke, clerk, Canon Thomas Southwell, and Margery Jourdemayne, to procure the king's death by sorcery.[40] Roger, who made some kind of confession implicating the duchess, was convicted of high treason and was hanged, drawn, and quartered; Margery was burned at Smithfield, either as a female traitor or perhaps as a relapsed heretic,[41] for she had been arrested for sorcery before and may have abjured; Southwell died in prison. The duchess did elaborate public penance and was sentenced to imprisonment for life.

That Bolingbroke was a practitioner of sorcery and that he was employed by the duchess to exercise his art in some way, there can be no manner of doubt. On Sunday, July 23, 1441, his paraphernalia were exhibited. A sermon was preached at Paul's Cross and meanwhile Master Roger stood upon a high stage in the churchyard "aboue alle mennes heddis." He was clad in his conjurer's robe: — "holdyng a suerd in his right hand and a septre in his lift hand, araid in a marvaillous aray whereynne he was wont to sitte whanne he wroghte his nygromancie." Upon the scaffold was also "a chaier ypeynt-ed, wherynne he was wont to sitte whanne he wroughte his craft, and on the iiij corners of the chaier stood iiij swerdis, and vpon euery swerd hanggyng an ymage of copir." Besides this there were on view "meny other instrumentis ac-cordyng to his said craft."[42] The copper images were probably effigies of demons rather than of the king; but one chronicler mentions among the exhibits, "ymages of siluer, *of wexe*, and other metalles,"[43] and here we have undoubtedly the figure of the king which was to cause his death. The same authority adds that later, when "all his [Roger's] Instrumentes that were shewed at Seint Paules Crosse afore-tyme" were shown to Dame Eleanor, she "seyd it was not so; bot that she did it forto haue borne a child by hir lord, the

Duke of Gloucestre." [44] This means obviously that the duchess alleged that the waxen image (as well as other things) was not designed to compass the king's destruction but to procure her a child. Frazer has accumulated from all over the world examples of imitative magic with a puppet either for offspring or for easy delivery.[45] Yet that the waxen image was to be consumed with the usual result on the victim's health and life is expressly stated by Fabyan and Hall.[46]

It may be that, at the duchess's request, Roger "wroughte the said nygromancie" merely, as he declared, "to knowe what sholde falle of hir and to what astat she sholde come." [47] Perhaps his denial of "eny treson ayens the kyngis persone" was true, coupled as it was with a confession that "he presumed to fer in his konnyng." [48] His attempt to forecast Eleanor's future rank doubtless involved a treasonable calculation as to the time of the king's death (as often in similar cases), and this is probably the excessive presumption that he confessed. But the chroniclers are practically a unit in asserting that the conspirators aimed to kill the king. Anyhow, I cannot believe that Roger limited his experiments to astrological mathematics. The function of Canon Southwell was to "say massis . . . in the logghe of Harnesey Park beside London vpon certayn instrumentis" which Roger was to use in his "craft of nygromancie" [49] — and this kind of profane rite was characteristic of the blackest of black magic.[50] If a waxen image was actually fashioned, perhaps Southwell was to baptize it by the king's name — a regular ceremony in such cases.[51] It is interesting to read in William Wyrcester (a competent witness) that Bolingbroke was the "most famous scholar in the whole world in astrology and magic," and that many "lamented him extremely." [52]

We are particularly concerned, however, with Margery Jourdemayne, for she was a witch pure and simple — humble in station, but eminent enough in her profession to be engaged by a lady of high rank. Such persons were more than once involved in high-life scandals of this sort. What part she played in Roger's conjurations we shall never know. She may have acted quite independently — but, with his confession to convict the duchess of nigromancy, there would seem to be no sense in pursuing Margery merely because she had furnished

Dame Eleanor with philtres from time to time. If there was a wax figure at all, we must infer that Margery Jourdemayne had a hand in its manufacture or manipulation; for male sorcerers in other cases more than once found the coöperation of a witch desirable in such matters. So in the historic prosecution of Guichard, Bishop of Troyes (1308–1313), the hermit confessed that, to procure the death of Queen Jeanne, the bishop employed a witch to torment the image.⁵³ And Enguerrand de Marigny, we are told, in adopting similar means to destroy Louis X, employed not only a magician but an old lame witch as well.⁵⁴ Finally, it makes no difference whether any of the charges were true or whether the whole affair was hideous political chicanery. Anyhow, it reveals the beliefs and the practices of the age.

Margery Jourdemayne had long been notorious as "the Witch of Eye" — that is, of the manor of Eye-next-Westminster.⁵⁵ Eleven years before, in 1430, she had been under arrest for "sorcerye" along with Friar John Asshewell of London and John Virley, *clericus*, and was confined for a time in Windsor Castle.⁵⁶ In 1432 the trio were discharged by the Privy Council: the two Johns found security for their good behavior, and Margery was released on her husband's bond.⁵⁷ Both these years are rather notable in the history of witchcraft. In 1430, a chronicler informs us, seven witches (*maleficae*) from different parts of the realm were apprehended in London and committed to the Fleet: they had plotted King Henry's death.⁵⁸ It was also in 1430 that Joan of Arc was captured and delivered into the hands of the English. As a London chronicler has it, " ther was a woman takyn y-armed [armed] in the ffeld, . . . the whiche was called Pucell de Dieux, a false witche." ⁵⁹ Compare the report of the Duke of Bedford in 1428 after the death of the Earl of Salisbury at the Siege of Orleans: " a Disciple and Lyme of the Feende, called the Pucelle, that used fals Enchauntementes and Sorcerie." ⁶⁰ The Maid, we remember, was believed by her enemies to have been trained in witchcraft by hags of her neighborhood, which — so the articles of accusation aver — was infamous of old for such practices.⁶¹ In 1432, on May 7, the king commanded two officers to arrest Thomas Northfelde of Worcester, a Dominican friar, to seize his books of sorcery, and other suspected materials, and to bring him before the Council to answer charges.[62]

We have no trace of Margery Jourdemayne between 1432 and 1441 except the statement of one chronicler that Dame Eleanor had for a long time (before 1441) used her "sorcerie and wicchecraft," and that by "suche medicines and drynkis as the said wicche made" the lady had "enforced" the Duke "to loue her and to wedde her." [63] Duke Humphrey's marriage to Eleanor Cobham took place at least as early as 1431. In the interim Margery had doubtless plied her trade industriously among her neighbors, and would have died in her bed instead of being burned at the stake if she had refrained from mingling in high society. It is noteworthy that both in 1432 and 1441 she was somehow associated with ecclesiastics — men of education — in her nefarious practices.

It is interesting to note that Foxe registers Roger (whose surname he gives as Onley) as a red-letter martyr in his Kalender, and Dame Eleanor as a confessor. As Gairdner remarks, "the fact that she was condemned for something by the Church of Rome seems to have been sufficient in Foxe's eyes to give her a place in the 'Kalender.'" [64] Bishop Bale also regards both Roger and the Duchess as sufferers for religion's sake.[65] Anyhow the lady's unquiet spirit haunted her prison, Peel Castle, in the Isle of Man, as recently as the eighteenth century.[66]

On January 22, 1470, Jacquette de Luxembourg, Duchess of Bedford, was cleared of a slanderous accusation of witchcraft brought against her by Thomas Wake. He had exhibited an image of lead, "made lyke a Man of Armes, conteynyng the lengthe of a mans fynger, and broken in the myddes, and made fast with a Wyre," which he asserted she had fashioned; and he had also urged John Daunger, a parish clerk of Northamptonshire, to testify that the duchess had manufactured two other images, one representing Edward IV and another Elizabeth Grey, whom the king married. On the day mentioned, both Wake and Daunger were examined before the Bishop of Carlisle, and the accusation broke down, for Daunger refused to give any such evidence.[67] The old scandal was revived by Richard III in 1483 in his attempt to show that there had never been a valid marriage between

King Edward and Queen Elizabeth. It was then asserted that "the pretensed Mariage" was brought about "by Sorcerie and Wichecraft" committed by Elizabeth and her mother, according to "the common opinion of the people and the publique voice and fame thorough all this Land." [68] Obviously the notion was that two of the figures were used in love magic.

In 1490 Johanna Benet was called before the Commissary of London for sorcery with a candle of wax: "as the candle consumes, the man must waste away." [69] A similar story was told at Norwich as late as 1843 in the course of a prosecution for assault, and candle witchcraft is still practised in England, it seems, to torment and recall a truant lover. [70] About 1500 Alice, wife of John Huntley of Southwark, was charged with image magic. She had, it was said, long "used and exercised the feetes of Wychecraft and Sorsery ayenst the lawe of the Chirche and of the kyng." There were found in her house, according to the petition in Chancery filed by John Knyght, chaplain, one of the searchers, "dyverses mamettes [images] for wychecraftes and enchauntementez, with other stuffe beryed and depely hydd under the erthe." What the outcome was we cannot tell. Our sole information is derived from Knyght's petition, from which it appears that he had been arrested, probably at Mistress Alice's suit, and was then in the Marshalsea. [71] It was likewise about the year 1500 that the Bishop of St. David's undertook to discipline Thomas Wyriott, Gentleman, and a woman named Tanglost for adultery. This was the beginning of troubles. Wyriott's wife died soon after, and it was common fame that she was killed by witchcraft worked or procured by Tanglost. The bishop banished Tanglost from the diocese. Thereupon she hired a witch at Bristol, one Margaret Hackett, and brought her to Wyriott's house, where, in a room inappropriately styled Paradise Chamber, the two women made a pair of waxen images in order to destroy the prelate. Margaret was arrested, and she confessed; but another witch was hired and a third figure of wax was fashioned. Tanglost was then examined for heresy by four doctors of divinity, who referred her to the bishop for "correction." Wyriott, however, kept her out of his hands by legal chicanery. At present — so the bishop declares in his bill in chancery — she is conveyed from place to place by Wyriott and his friends to the intent that she may continue her sorcery against him. In order, therefore, to safeguard his life, he petitions the Lord Chancellor to order the case of Tanglost before the Court of Chancery. In her answer Tanglost denies the charge of witchcraft and contends that the prosecution is purely malicious. What the outcome was we do not know.[72]

The legend of the Scottish king Duff turns up in Hector Boece, whose History appeared in 1527.[73] The age of the tradition is indeterminable. Later chroniclers repeat the tale, which was known to Shakspere. He did not utilize this particular feature, though he adopted and adapted some of the details for Macbeth.

In 1527 (the year of John Dee's birth), Dr. Thomas Benet of Salisbury, afterwards Precentor and Chancellor of the cathedral, writes to Wolsey. He is sending him a Frenchman named Maturyn Bensart, a practitioner of physic at Sherborne, who is suspected of necromancy, especially because his servant had caused four metal images of men and women to be cast. These were found on searching, as well as some suspicious-looking knives and "divers instruments." Bensart admitted that he had made *aurum potabile* in his native country.[74]

In 1538 there was great excitement about a wax baby with two pins stuck in it, discovered when about to be buried in a London churchyard. A scrivener named Poole, skilled in sorcery, was consulted. He declared that the maker of the puppet, whoever he was, "was not his craft's master, for he should have put it either in horse dung or in a dunghill." The authorities looked into the affair. The talk at Oxford was that the image represented Prince Edward, that there was a knife through the head or heart, and that as the image "did consume, so likewise should the Prince." [75] The preamble to the Witchcraft Statute of Henry VIII (1542) expressly notes the prevalent manufacture of "dyvers Images and pictures of men women childrene Angelles or develles beastes or fowles."[76]

Reginald Scot tells a good story about "Brandon the juggler," whom I cannot date. He "painted on a wall the picture of a dove, and seeing a pigeon sitting on the top of a

house, said to the king; Lo now your Grace shall see what a
juggler can doo, if he be his craftes maister; and then pricked
the picture with a knife so hard and so often, and with so
effectuall words, as the pigeon fell downe from the top of the
house starke dead." He was forbidden "to use that feat anie
further, least he should emploie it in anie other kind of murther." "This storie is," Scot adds, "untill the daie of the writing hereof, in fresh remembrance, & of the most part beleeved
as canonicall, as are all the fables of witches." [77]   Scot also
gives directions for hurting or killing a person by means of a
waxen image — also for images of brass and of "the earth of
a dead man," and for waxen images to procure love.[78] He
contends that all this is folly. "But," he adds, "concerning
these images, it is certaine that they are much feared among
the people, and much used among cousening witches."
In proof he furnishes details of an occurrence "not long
sithence" at New Romney in Kent. A young woman fell sick
and "a famous witch called mother Baker" was consulted.
Mother Baker, learning that the family suspected a woman of
the neighborhood, declared that this woman was guilty, for
she had made a heart of wax and pricked it with pins and
needles. Mother Baker, to support her fiction, concealed
such an image in the victim's house. Her fraud was detected.[79]

That image witchcraft went on through the reigns of
Elizabeth and James I, was a matter of course. Indeed, it has
continued to the present time in uninterrupted succession
from remote antiquity.

In the examinations of witches arrested at Windsor in 1579
it appeared that "they have made away and brought to their
deathes by certen pictures of waxe certen persons." So we
learn from the Acts of the Privy Council (January 16, 1578–
79), which go on to assert that "there hath bene latelie discovered a practise of that device very likelie to be intended to
the distruction of her Majesties person." [80] This lately discovered plot is doubtless that implied in the letter of the
Privy Council of August 22, 1578, to the Lord Mayor and the
Bishop of London and other officials, "advertising them of
the receipt of their letters of the xv[th] of this present, with a
boxe fast sealed wherein weare conteyned three pictures of

waxe and certen examinacions taken by them towching the maner of finding the said pictures." [81] This affair is treated by Scot with due scorn: "Were there not three images of late yeeres found in a doonghill, to the terror & astonishment of manie thousands? In so much as great matters were thought to have beene pretended [i. e. intended] to be doone by witchcraft." [82] Bodin reports that these three images of wax were found in the possession of a "Prestre Sorcier" who was curé d'Istincton (Islington), and were intended "pour faire mourir la Royne d'Angleterre, & deux autres proches de sa personne." They were discovered, he adds, "dedans un fumier" and the names of the queen and others were written on them.[83] Mendoza, the Spanish ambassador, gives further details in a despatch to his home government. A country-man found the three figures buried in a stable. They were two spans high and broad in proportion. "The centre figure had the word Elizabeth written on the forehead and the side figures were dressed like her councillors, and were covered over with a great variety of different signs, the left side of the images being transfixed with a large quantity of pig's bristles as if it were some kind of witchcraft." [84] The fact is, if we may trust Scot, that "an olde cousener, wanting monie," had made the three puppets for a young gentleman, promising him that thereby the love of three women might be gained. Ben Jonson, long afterward, mentioned the business as something of which he remembered the current rumor, "being then very young." [85] Soon after the Islington scandal, there was information before the Council (February 3, 1578–9) of certain persons in the bishopric of London who were "privie to the secrett keping of certaine images which are reserved to some ill purpose of sorcerie or idolitrie." The Council wrote at the same time to the Bishop of Norwich of a report that at Thetford and other places in his diocese "there hath bene sene, not long since, in some mens houses certen images" of a similarly dubious character. [86] Again, in 1580 Nicholas Johnson was accused of sorcery by "making of her Majesties picture in wax," [87] and five years later Lord Burghley received a letter alleging that William Awder (schoolmaster, minister, and physician) claimed the power to kill or cure by means of such an image.[88]

In 1590 a Mistress Dewse was informed against for dealing with a conjurer to kill her enemies: she wished their pictures of wax to be made and pricked to the heart. It appears that, when the conjurer said he was "lame" (in his hands, I suppose) and therefore could not make the wax "pictures" for Mrs. Dewse, she made them herself under his supervision — three figures, to wit, one for Mr. Younge ("& put a pynne into his harte"), another for Sir Rowland Heyward ("& putt a pynne to his harte & another under his ribbes"), and one for Sye ("& putt two pynnes in his eyes"). Two of these images were found by the sheriff in her cupboard and were at the date of the record (January, 1589 [-90]) in the custody of the town clerk of London. A point of particular interest in Mrs. Dewse's case is her suggestion to the conjurer that, if the waxen images failed to work, he should destroy her enemies "in a dampe," as she had heard some were destroyed at the Oxford assizes.[89] Doubtless she had in mind the Black Assize of 1577, when typhus (jail fever) killed off judges, jury, lawyers, and townspeople. In this mortality Catholic writers discerned "a wonderful judgment of God" upon heretical persecutors; but the science of the day explained it as due to a poisonous "damp" (i. e. steam or vapor) that exhaled from the prisoners or perhaps from the soil. The most popular theory, however, ascribed the fatal damp to the sorcery of Roland Jenks, a bookseller tried on this occasion for vending Catholic literature. From strange and frightful materials, it was said, Jenks had moulded a candle, which he lighted "as soon as ever he was condemned." [90] This was the story which Mrs. Dewse had heard.

In 1591 a surgeon of Burton-on-Trent named Richard Batte (or Bate) was under vehement suspicion. He had threatened to make a picture of wax and thereby to consume his mother-in-law and her children. This, at all events, was the allegation of his wife's brother. Indeed, Batte himself admitted that he had hired a painter to prepare such an image, averring, however, that he needed it to cure a patient who suffered from a sharp attack of dysentery. The painter, too, deposed to the same effect. We do not know the outcome.[91] In 1611, to be sure, one *William* Bate had King James's pardon, and the record states that he was "indicted twenty years since for practising of invocation of spirits for finding treasure." The ground for this long-deferred grace was that the evidence was "found weak." [92] The date fits, but the name and the offence do not.

In 1594 an image of wax was found in the bedroom of Ferdinando, fifth Earl of Derby, who had died suddenly. An old woman was suspected. One of her hairs was "prict directly in the heart" of the image, or, according to another account, hair like the earl's was "twisted through the belly thereof." [93] In 1596 Thomas Lodge teaches the orthodox view that it is a sin to seek cures by witches or enchanters, but he concedes the propriety of thwarting them by pulling a needle out of an image of wax if you find such a thing. [94] About 1600, to round out the century, Lady Blake's son was suspected of "being a practiser" with one Elkes for treasure, and for making images to procure love. [95]

Clay figurines played their part in the Lancashire witch tragedy of 1612; [96] image magic of a peculiar sort emerged in 1615 in the trial of Mrs. Ann Turner for poisoning Sir Thomas Overbury; [97] and the English witch literature of that century abounds in material on the subject. [98] Examples from Massachusetts are not wanting. The Rev. George Burroughs, it was testified, "had been at Witch-Meetings," and "brought Poppets to them, and thorns to stick into those Poppets, for the afflicting of other People." And there were discovered in the wall of Bridget Bishop's cellar "several Poppets, made up of Rags, and Hogs Brassels, with Headless Pins in them, the points being outward." [99] In Goody Glover's house were found and "brought into Court, several small Images, or Puppets, or Babies, made of Raggs, and stufft with Goatshair, and other such Ingredients. When these were produced, the vile Woman acknowledged, that her way to torment the Object of her malice, was by wetting her Finger with her Spittle, and stroaking of those little Images." [100]

Caroline of Brunswick, when Princess of Wales, was comically addicted to image magic. Under date of 1814 Lady Charlotte Campbell (afterwards Bury) furnishes details in her diary: "After dinner, her Royal Highness made a wax figure as usual, and gave it an amiable addition of large horns; then took three pins out of her garment, and stuck them through and through, and put the figure to roast and melt at the fire.... Lady——says the Princess indulges in this amusement whenever there are no strangers at table; and thinks her Royal Highness really has a superstitious belief that destroying this *effigy* of her husband will bring to pass the destruction of his royal person." [101]

If we had newspapers or folklorists from the middle ages, such cases would be countless, for they turn up constantly in recent times and even at the present day, despite the progress of science and what is called rationalism. One remembers the experiments of de Rochas as detailed in his treatise on L'Extériorisation de la Sensibilité, which are accepted by Jules Bois as demonstrating the possibility of *envoûtement*, whether for love or malignity. [102] I need not multiply examples of image witchcraft from modern Britain, where it is still going on; but two or three may be cited. About 1861 a Devonshire girl, dying of consumption, believed that the rival who had stolen her sweetheart was so inveterate in malice as to make an image of her in wax and drive pins into it every night. More recently a London woman made a wax figure of her husband's mistress and set it inside the fender, with the formula, "Burn, you white witch! burn!" [103] In 1909, in a Somerset parish, an old servant warned the rector: "Mrs. —— is a witch, and I fear she will do you some harm; she will make an image of you in wax, or clay, stick it all over with pins and burn it; you will have great trouble, perhaps be very ill and die." [104] A West Sussex vicar reports that a sick woman among his parishioners, who suffered from delusions, showed him in 1916 "a rude figure cut out of a turnip. She pointed out two pins stuck into that part which represented the chest. She told me that her husband had made it with the object of her suffering in the same places. She complained much of pains in the chest and finally died of diabetes." [105] A cake stuck with pins and burned in a pan may replace the witch's image and make her appear. [106] Image magic to bewitch one to death is known to our Southern negroes. An image is made of snake oil mixed with flour or sand; a name is given to the puppet; when it is baked at the fire or pins are stuck in, the victim suffers; a pin in the heart means death. [107] In the Scottish Highlands, [108] the magic figure is known as a

corp criadhach ("body of clay").[109] Not long ago, we are
told, a young woman in the Western Islands almost died from
envoûtement, but fortunately the image, stuck with pins, was
discovered in time: it lay in a running stream, which was
gradually washing it away. A similar case has recently been
reported from Uist.[110] At Inverness in 1883 a woman charged
with assault alleged, in her defence, that the grandmother of
the girl she had attacked was a witch, and she exhibited in the
police court the clay puppet used to bewitch her: [111] "The
legs had been broken off the image, and since then the prisoner believed that her own legs were losing their strength."
A *corp criadhach* from Islay, with dozens of pins in the breast,
is exhibited in the Museum of Archæology at Cambridge in
England.[112]

A recent lawsuit in the Upper Congo grew out of image
magic. Two men quarrelled. *A* had heard that *B* paid a
witch-doctor to call up *A*'s image, which was then repeatedly
stabbed by *B*. But *B* insisted that it was another person's
image, not *A*'s, that the sorcerer had evoked.[113] Among the
Northern Bantu and elsewhere you may kill your enemy by
spearing his shadow.[114] So, in an ancient Irish saga, Find
"saw before him Cuirrech's shadow, and throughout the
shadow he hurled a spear, chanting a spell over its head, and
it strikes into Cuirrech, who fell thereby." [115] A wizard of
Lincoln once revealed a thief by making his shadow appear
on a wall.[116] In Africa you may stab your enemy's outline
drawn in sand; [117] in North Carolina, if you mark out his
figure on a board and shoot it, he feels pain in the corresponding part of his body.[118] In 1903 a mountaineer in that state,
finding that butter would not come when his wife churned,
declared that a woman of the neighborhood had bewitched
the milk, pinned up a portrait of her on the wall, and shot a
silver bullet through it.[119] In Nova Scotia, "if bewitched,
draw a figure of the witch on a board and fire a charge of shot
into it. This, done before sunrise, will break the spell." [120]
Henslowe, the Elizabethan theatrical manager, jotted down
the following spell in his famous Diary: "To make a fowle
fialle downe picture yt in paper & when yt is makinge leat one
say m.a.n. to the eand with battes blude behold her wth
thine eies & pricke the picture in the head wth a pyne & she

will falle downe Jmedyately." [121] The reluctance of savages
to have their portraits drawn is shared by some civilized persons. A Belgian girl, to torment her faithless lover, sent him
back his portrait with the eyes pricked out with pins.[122] It
was an old superstition in New Hampshire that you would
soon die if you allowed yourself to be photographed.[123] To
break a mirror, as everybody knows, is a sign of death in the
family, or at best of seven years' bad luck.[124] Faded almost
beyond recognizing was the image magic which came out in
a case before a Taunton (Somerset) magistrate in 1881. A
"witch-doctor" of that town had tapped a sick woman's palm
with his finger, assuring her that every stroke was a stab in
the witch's heart.[125]

To use an animal instead of a figurine as representative of
the person to be injured was common enough in ancient *defixiones*.[126] Thus along with the cursing tablet there might be
buried a cat or a cock that had been tortured or mutilated.
The object was, of course, to cause one's enemy to be afflicted
or disabled in like manner.[127] So in the county of Durham in
1861, when a woman was thought to be suffering from witchcraft, pins were run into a live pigeon by each member of her
family, and the bird was roasted. The witch, it was hoped,
would feel these torments and thus would be forced to come
and remove the curse.[128] About 1920 in Devon a cockerel was
tortured to death with pins; then the feathers were singed off
and the carcass was thrown away. A spell was recited, beginning:

> With this pin I thee prick,
> My enemy's heart I hope to stick.[129]

Here we have a performance and a spell precisely like those of
the ancients. Compare a Latin tablet from the proconsular
Province of Carthage: "This cock's tongue I have torn out
while he was alive. . . . So may the tongues of my enemies be
made dumb against me!" [130] and a Greek tablet from the
same region: "As this cock is fast bound in feet and hands
and head, so bind the legs and the hands and the head and
the heart of Victoricus the charioteer." [131]

Sometimes the animal thus maltreated was regarded as an
offering to the infernal gods; and this idea has descended to

our own times, for the sacrifice of a cock is a recognized feature of ancient, mediæval, and modern sorcery. In the proceedings against Dame Alice Kyteler in 1324 it was alleged
that she had offered cocks at the crossroads to a demon, tearing them limb from limb, and had used the entrails in the preparation of magical powders and unguents.[132] In 1879 in Ireland a black cock was cut into quarters and offered at the four
corners of a field to bring ill fortune upon the owners of the
land.[133] To baptize a dog or a cat was a powerful rite to command demons, and sometimes, in such cases, the creature was
slaughtered as if it were a human sacrifice.[134] This comes out
unmistakably in the trial of two treasure-digging sorcerers in
1465: they had promised their demon "the body of a Christian man," but they cheated him by offering up a cock which
they had baptized by a Christian name.[135] "A redd cock
beinge dead" was seized among the miscellaneous paraphernalia of two men caught in the act of "witchcrafte or conjuringe" in a field near London in 1590; presumably it had
been sacrificed to a demon, for they also left behind in their
flight "a fayre cristall stone" with *Sathan* written on it.[136]

With the sacrificial purpose [137] is sometimes confused the
idea of transferring an ailment. In former days persons
afflicted with fits used to throw money into St. Tecla's well in
Denbighshire, and then to sleep all night under the altar-
table in the church, holding a live cock in their arms. "In the
morning they would let the cock go, when the bird took off all
the fits with him and died soon after." An aged parishioner,
about the middle of the last century, told the clerk that he
remembered seeing the cocks stagger about from the effects
of the fits.[138] Transference is more or less the idea, apparently, in the common practice of curing warts by rubbing
them with a snail and impaling the creature on a thornbush.[139]
Similar customs are — the enclosing of a live spider in a box
or a hollowed nut for ague or whooping cough; [140] the cure of
ague by putting a live snail in a bag, wearing the bag round
the neck for nine days, and then throwing the snail into the
fire; [141] the burying of a shrewmouse alive in a hole in an ash
tree.[142] For whooping cough you may wear a live spider or
caterpillar as an amulet: it wastes away, and the cough
slackens; or you may draw a black ribbon three times

through the body of a live frog and let the patient wear the ribbon round his neck.[143] Such transference to animals, sticks, and running water occurs in the Anglo-Saxon Leech Book.[144] In 1580 Mother Gawe undertook to cure a sow by shifting the disease to a cat, but the sow died after all — thus testifies the old Chronicle of Shrewsbury.[145]

Here belongs, though also conceived as a sacrifice, the ancient Germanic rite of burying an animal alive to check the cattle plague.[146] In Queen Elizabeth's time a man was brought before the Commissioners for Ecclesiastical Causes for burying "a quick dogg and a quick cowe."[147] A dead creature, feet up, may also be buried under the threshold of the stable or cowshed, to save the herd.[148] In Scotland, in 1597, a cock was buried alive to cure insanity.[149] In the Hebrides and the Highlands a remedy for epilepsy (a demonic affliction) is to bury a black cock under the bed or the floor, with clippings of the patient's hair and nails;[150] or the cock may be buried on the spot where the epileptic falls.[151] Here the rationale may be to transfer the epilepsy to the cock, or to propitiate the demon by an oblation, or to torment the witch until she reverses the spell. Transference is frankly the motive in the Highlands when one buries in a neighbor's ground a beast that has perished from the blight of the evil eye.[152] An English spell for black magic is or was to hang up nine living toads on a string and then bury them: as they pine away, your enemy will languish until death comes.[153] In Devonshire it was once customary to bury three live puppies, arranged in a triangle, in the corner of a field to clear it of weeds.[154] In these two instances the rationale is plain enough, but often the various motives get confused in people's minds with time, and in the upshot the process is merely a means of injury or of remedy, with no clear notion of the whys and wherefores.

Similarly the folk do not always distinguish between sacrifice and torturing the witch when they burn a live creature to stop a pestilence among domestic animals.[155] We have a fine example reported by Sir Roger Wilbraham in 1605: "Mʳ Harley my host at Huntingdon told me this night, supping with me, that he being before a farmer & 24 horses for plows 12 horses & xxx cattall were bewitched & died in ii daies, sod-

dainlie sick, crying & grynnyng & staringe: in th'end was advised to burne a sick horse alive & so did, and after had no
more died: another did so by his shepe by Harley's advise:
non after died: & Harley said a knowen witch advised him to
burne the hart by rosting on a spitt, & the witch wold come to
the dore before the hart was rosted."[156] To burn an animal
alive in order to check a cattle plague or the like must have
been a settled practice in England long before Elizabeth came
to the throne. Ravens burnt alive are specified as a cure for
gout and the falling sickness in an English medical manuscript of the middle ages.[157] The Essex parson, George Giffard, mentions the custom in 1587: "They take a Hogge or
some other beast and burne it aliue";[158] and he returns to the
subject in his Dialogue (1593): witches can be baulked, so his
parishioners imagined, by burning "some liue thing, as hogge
or henne," for this drives away the devils they send; a pig was
burnt alive and the witch said that her demon cat would
never go thither any more; a woman's "hennes began to die
vp, vntil she burnt one henne aliue";[159] one of the interlocutors remarks that, to stop a pestilence, some of his neighbors
wished him "to burne some thing aliue, as a henne or a
hogge."[160] In 1624 John Crushe was presented in the archdeacon's court of Giffard's county because he had burnt on
Hawkwell common a lamb which he declared was bewitched,
and so had set fire to the common, which was full of rubbish.[161] In Essex also, in the last century, when a man's goslings died, their death was ascribed to the evil eye of a notorious witch of Thorpe, and two live goslings were baked in
the oven; this killed the witch, whose body showed burns.[162]
The same Thorpe witch, a Mrs. Gardner, once "overlooked"
a boy, who kept "a-pindling away." His grandmother
burned some of his hair and bits of his nails, and the witch
soon came, with piteous entreaties: the spell was broken.[163]
Early in the nineteenth century, at Wherstead in Suffolk, a
duck was baked alive when the ducks ceased to lay; near
Ipswich, in the same county, a sheep was burned in the eighteenth century, and thereby the witch was burned to death in
her house.[164] In 1833 a pig was roasted to death in Huntingdonshire to save the sickly litter.[165] Similar cases are known
in the United States.[166] Less drastic was the action of the

Lincolnshire farmer whose pigs were dying: he scored a live pig's back with a redhot poker, and the witch died of a sore back soon after.[167] In Norfolk it may suffice to cut off and burn a bit of a pig's tail and ear.[168] So in 1657 a Connecticut colonist whose pigs had died "in a strange way," cut off the tail and one ear of the last sickly survivor and threw them into the fire, "and after put the pigg vpon the fire till it was dead." This sorcery with ear and tail was, he averred, "a meanes vsed in England by some honest people to finde out witches." [169] Instead of a living animal one may burn, with equal efficacy, the carcass of a creature that has died of the witch-sent disease,[170] or the straw on which a diseased beast has been bled to death.[171] Timothy Crowther (1694–1760), Yorkshire parish clerk and wizard, had a "Remedy for a Horse or Cow that hath harme dun by a Witch," which must needs be quoted entire: "Take hair of each Quarter, som of each Hoof and horn; sew it up in a Cloth, & in yᵉ form of a ball; prick it full of pins and put in 3 Needls. Boil it in yᵉ afflicted Water til yᵉ pan be like to burn, then Throw it in to yᵉ fire and say (3 times), 'Witch, Witch, Witch, thus shalt Thou Burn in Hell.'" [172]

It is even now a common practice to torment an enemy by sticking pins, needles, or thorns in an animal's heart [173] and (often) roasting it [174] or parching it in the chimney. Here the beast's heart serves your malefic sorcery as well as an image of wax or the whole animal would do. The custom is manifestly of immemorial antiquity and differs in no essential from the burial of a mutilated cat or cock in the ancient *defixiones*: indeed, the heart may be cut out of a living animal.[175] About 1842, by a white wizard's directions, six bullocks' hearts — two stuck with pins, the others with new nails — were slowly melted, and thus the witch's heart was to be melted too; then nails were driven into a butt and it was rolled downhill, to torture the witch further; she was killed by this treatment and showed the marks.[176] In Yorkshire, in the eighteenth century, a cow's heart was boiled and stuck with pins to check the cattle plague.[177] In the South Downs, rather recently, when pigs had been "overlooked" (made sick by the evil eye), a heart was pierced with nails and pins and then roasted.[178] A similar case occurred in Somerset in 1875.[179] In

Devonshire, some years ago, when a pony went lame, an animal's heart was burned; the witch came and tried to buy apples, which were refused; the pony got well.[180] The classic cock reappears in the county of Durham: about 1855, to cure a sick horse, a black fowl's heart stuck with pins was roasted.[181] In Somerset, in 1882, as a counter-charm when a woman had gone mad, an animal's heart with pins in it was to be roasted and then put in the chimney to waste away and thus rot the witch's heart.[182] In South Devon, also as a counter-charm to avenge the black witchcraft that had killed cows or sheep, a sheep's heart was pierced with pins and nails.[183] Against bad luck in fishing, caused by witchcraft, a pigeon's heart was filled with pins and roasted in Yorkshire.[184] To keep out Dorset witches a piece of bacon stuck with pins used to be hung up in the chimney.[185] An elaborate piece of sorcery to stop death of cattle is reported by the Rev. J. C. Atkinson from Cleveland: an ox-heart was pierced with nine new pins, nine new needles, and nine new nails and burned at midnight to the accompaniment of two verses of a [cursing] psalm.[186] About 1897 a Devonshire woman, tormented by witchcraft, laid a sheep's heart stuck with pins on the bar that holds up the pothooks in the fireplace and repeated the following spell:

> May each pin
> Thus stuck in
>   This poor heart
> In hers go
> Who hurts me so
>   Till she departs.

The patient recovered and the witch died, so they say.[187] Sometimes the heart, instead of being burned, is buried in the ground or concealed in the fabric of a house or under the foundation.[188] The process may be purely malefic [189] or may be resorted to as a counter-spell.[190] The heart may be extracted from a living animal: in Yorkshire, for example, to ward off witchcraft, take a black hen's heart out of the living bird, stick it full of pins, and bury the hen.[191]

We must remember that these performances are not fictitious. A calf's heart, thus pierced, was exhumed in 1827 opposite the threshold of an old Dalkeith tenement (apparently under the flagstones of the floor) and was sent to Sir Walter Scott as a curiosity. Scott sent it to the Society of Antiquaries, in whose museum it may still be seen.[192] The Taunton Museum shows two dried pigs' hearts, thick set with pins, both found in an old chimney in Somerset.[193] In 1884 a bullock's heart pierced with whitethorn prickles, nails, and pins, was found in a Dorset chimney.[194] In 1902 a bullock's heart, with pins and black thorns, was discovered tied up under the roof of an outhouse in Devon.[195] In 1917 there was exhibited in London a sheep's heart, prepared in similar fashion by a Devonshire woman who had practised witchcraft in the metropolis as recently as 1908.[196] About 1862 a woman was brought before the Durham magistrates for larceny: she had committed the theft to cure her bewitched child; the process was to steal a fowl, take out the heart, stick this full of pins, and roast it at midnight over a slow fire.[197] In 1905 there were witches in Devon who professed to be able and willing to torture anybody by means of a sheep's heart or a toad full of pins hung up in the chimney.[198]

In 1610 Joan Bayly of Rye, an octogenarian, deposed that, thinking Thomas Hart's child bewitched, she told Mistress Hart to get a piece of red cloth, sixty needles, and a halfpennyworth of pins. Then, to force the witch to come, Joan stuck the pins and needles in the cloth, put it in the fire, and pierced it with a dagger. After a long time the cloth was consumed, and, says Joan, "at length it did seem to be like unto a toad, but no party came in," and she declares that she does not know who bewitched the child.[199] Probably the cloth was cut to the shape of a heart. A corked greybeard jug containing clippings of hair and of fingernails along with such a cloth heart stuck full of bent pins, was dug up at Westminster in 1904.[200] In Yorkshire "when a child was born, and it proved either unhealthy or deformed, it was generally supposed some evil-disposed person must have pricked its name with pins on a pin-cushion. When such a discovery was made by an expectant wife, nothing was said to the person working the evil, but the cushion was stolen, the pins withdrawn one by one, and stuck into the heart of a calf. This had to be buried in the churchyard." [201]

The same kind of sorcery (with images, animals, or hearts)

may be applied to love matters, whether for revenge or to summon one's sweetheart.[202] In 1867 a doll "stuck about the heart with tin tacks" was found in a Lincolnshire stable, where a young fellow had hidden it as a charm to make a girl meet him.[203] In Cambridgeshire a pigeon's heart dried at the fire and pierced with redhot pins was an instrument of vengeance on a faithless lover or a seducer.[204] In Lincolnshire, in 1890, a pigeon's insides were taken out while it was alive and were put over the house door: the girl's lover came.[205] A pigeon's heart, taken out while it is alive, and stuck with pins, if placed under one's pillow will recall a faithless sweetheart. A frog stuck with pins and buried alive serves a similar purpose. Sometimes this latter process is accompanied by a spell beginning: "I do not want to hurt this frog."[206] In Buckinghamshire one thrusts two pins through a lighted candle so as to pierce the wick and form a cross, repeating the formula:

> It's not this candle alone I stick,
> But A. B.'s heart I mean to prick;
> Whether he be asleep or awake,
> I'd have him come to me and speak.[207]

A Staffordshire charm reported in 1902 consists of a heart-shaped bit of red flannel stuck with three pins pointing toward the centre and sprinkled with the red liquid known as dragon's blood. Burn this on a Friday at midnight, and say —

> 'Tis not this blood I wish to burn,
> But —— 's heart I wish to turn.
> May he neither rest nor sleep
> Till he returns to me to speak.[208]

There are varieties of the spell: sometimes the shoulder-bone of a lamb (famous in divination)[209] is used, and is pricked with a penknife.[210] The bladebone of a rabbit stuck with nine pins and put under your pillow will make you dream of your sweetheart.[211] The so-called dragon's blood is, of course, a substitute for the blood of the bespelled person.[212] A queer story, incident to a trial for assault, was told to the Norwich magistrates in 1843. Mr. and Mrs. Curtis declared that Mrs. Bell had bewitched them. Mrs. Curtis saw her light a candle and fill it with pins.[213] She then put some dragon's blood and

water into an oyster shell and repeated a form of words over
it. Instantly Mr. Curtis's arms and legs were "set fast."
Mr. Curtis corroborated his wife's testimony, adding that to
the mixture in the shell the witch added parings of her own
nails and put the dish on the fire.[214] For the rhyming spell we
may compare the incantation that, in 1894, a "wise man" of
Wells taught a patient as a means of breaking a witch's
charms: about the hour of midnight she and her husband
were to sit by the fire and burn salt, repeating —

> This is not the thing I wish to burn
> But Mrs. ——'s heart of Somerset to turn,
> Wishing thee neither to eat, drink, sleep, nor rest
> Until thou dost come to me and do my request,
> Or else the wrath of God may fall on thee and cause thee to be con-
> 　　sumed in a moment. Amen.[215]

The Malays have a similar formula: earth from an enemy's
footprint is beaten while the operator chants —

> It is not earth that I switch,
> But the heart of So-and-so.[216]

In Somerset an onion may replace the puppet or the heart:
write your enemy's name on a scrap of paper and fasten it to
the onion with as many pins as possible; put it up the chimney; as it withers, so will your victim waste away. Such an
onion was found in a chimney about 1880.[217] A lemon stuck
with pins was found some years ago in a churchyard in Brad-
ford, Yorkshire.[218] This kind of substitution occurs in many
countries, civilized and savage.[219] Neapolitan malefic witchcraft is worked by sticking an orange, a lemon, or a potato
with pins and nails.[220] In Sicily an egg, an orange, or a lemon
is often used.[221] In Bombay to pierce a nut with needles is one
way to keep off a witch.[222] In Fiji a plantain sucker, set out
at midnight with spells and curses, is clubbed, speared, and
buffeted until it wilts and dies; and one's enemy suffers and
dies along with the plantain.[223] Some Fijians bury a cocoanut
(which bears a grotesque resemblance to a human head),
"with the eye upward, beneath the temple-hearth, on which
a fire is kept constantly burning; and as the life of the nut is
destroyed, so the health of the person it represents will fail
till death ensues."[224] In the Dekkan and the Konkan there is

strange black magic with an image and a lime pierced with pins: the lime goes to the victim and kills him.[225] The Malays pierce a lime to cause love-pangs in the heart of the beloved.[226] In Pomerania to bind an egg with green silk, and then bury it in hot ashes in the name of a thief, will so torment him that he must bring back the booty.[227] Elsewhere on the Continent similar witchcraft is wrought with a sod bearing the thief's footprint: hang it up, for instance, in the chimney smoke, and, as it dries, so he pines away, or suffers from a withered foot.[228] To drive a nail (preferably redhot), or pins or a knife, into a person's footmark makes him lame, and this means of detection or vengeance is often utilized against a witch.[229] In the Scottish Highlands a square of turf is pierced with pins and put in the fire to punish the hag who has afflicted a child.[230] Burning a handful of thatch from a witch's cottage forces her to reveal herself, according to a theory long accepted by country people in England; [231] so, in Joan Cason's case (1586), a tile from the witch's house, put in the fire, compelled her to come in person.[232]

A bottle buried, or put by the fire, with pins or spikes from a thornbush in it — or pins, needles or nails (sometimes also hair, bits of fingernails, etc.) — will work malefically, and is a good remedy, therefore, against witchcraft. In Lincolnshire, jugs called greybeards and other vessels are found now and then beneath the foundation or threshold or hearthstone of old buildings; they may contain horseshoe nails, scraps of iron, needles, pins, etc.[233] In West Sussex about fifty years ago, if you filled a quart bottle with pins and heated them redhot, they would prick the heart of the witch that had given you epilepsy and make her take off the spell.[234] Boiling pins in urine will force a Sussex wizard to come to your house (1919).[235] To bury a bottle containing the urine of a bewitched person or animal will afflict the witch with strangury: this (as well as to draw the witch's blood or hang up a horseshoe) Increase Mather regards as an illicit measure of protection. His son Cotton also disapproves "the Urinary experiment" by which "the Urine must be bottled with Nails and Pins, and such Instruments in it as carry a shew of Torture with them, if it attain its end." [236] To ascertain who was afflicting Mr. Parris's children at Salem Village, it was said that his "Indian Man, and Woman, made a Cake of Rye Meal, and the Childrens water, baked it in the Ashes, and gave it to a Dog, since when" (adds Mr. Lawson) "they have discovered, and seen particular persons hurting of them." A similar performance is reported from England in 1626.[237] According to Drage (1665), "stopping up Bottles of that Drink that hath been bewitched, hath made the Witch able neither to urine or deject, until they were opened."[238] For bewitched cattle, according to a "cunning man" cited by Gifford, the Essex parson, in 1593, one may "set on a posnet or some pan with nayles, and seeth them, and the witch shal come in while they be in seething, and within a fewe dayes after, her face will be all bescratched with the nailes."[239] So in Nova Scotia, by recent report, if your cows are bewitched, you may boil the milk with pins: the witch will suffer and will come to your house and ask about the cows.[240]

Charm bottles have often come to light.[241] One found in a Wharfedale garden in 1845 was filled with pins, needles, human hair, fragments of fingernails, brimstone, etc.[242] Another, buried upside down,[243] filled with dark water and containing nine bent pins, was under the clay floor of a cottage in Staffordshire.[244] A jar containing spikes from a thornbush as well as pins was exhumed in a Devon churchyard in 1895, and a bottle with pins in the cork was turned up in 1900 in digging a grave in the same county.[245] A similar discovery was made some sixty or seventy years ago in a grave at Bodmin.[246] Tombs, we remember, were the favorite places of deposit for cursing tablets in antiquity. Two large coils of human hair, recently deposited, were uncovered about 1900 in a kistvaen near Postbridge.[247] The following elaborate recipe comes from the same county (Devon): "To destroy the power of a witch. Take three small-necked stone jars: place in each the liver of a frog stuck full of new pins, and the heart of a toad stuck full of thorns from the holy thorn bush. Cork and seal each jar. Bury in three different churchyard paths seven inches from the surface and seven feet from the porch. While in the act of burying each repeat the Lord's prayer backwards. As the hearts and livers decay, so will the witch's power vanish. After performing this ceremony no witch can have any power over the operator."[248]

CHAPTER IV

LOVE AND HATE

WHEN Parliament in 1542 made it felony to "use devise practise or exercise, or cause to be used devysed practised or exercised, any invocacions or conjuracions of Sprites wichecraftes enchauntementes or sorceries, to thentent . . . to provoke any persone to unlawfull love," [1] the legislators were merely faithful to the witch-creed of the world, ancient and modern, civilized and savage. [2] To work witchcraft for love by spells, or by philtres in food or drink, is forbidden in an Anglo-Saxon penitential of the tenth century as well as in other kindred documents, insular and Continental, of the ninth century or earlier. [3] Unseemly English nursery jingles about fishes and cocklebread [4] go back somehow to strange rites of love-magic described by Burchard of Worms about 1020 and in a manuscript written in England in the thirteen-hundreds. [5]

At the Synod of Exeter in 1287 sorcery for love was treated by Bishop Peter Quivil as a sacrifice to demons in violation of the First Commandment. [6] In an English fabliau, contemporary with the bishop, a lecherous cleric calls upon Dame Sirith to help him to his obdurate lady, who is married. The old procuress is loud in her disclaimers: "I am a holy woman; no skill have I in witchcraft. May his life and soul be shent that sent thee to me on this errand!" Yet, after binding him to secrecy, for she fears to be "brought before the Chapter for such works," the dame wins the wife's consent by a wile, persuading her that a certain dog was once a woman, but had been transformed by a clerk's witchery because she would not listen to his suit. The tale comes from the Orient, but is adapted to English conditions: the husband has gone to the fair at Botolphston (the Lincolnshire Boston), the wife is named Margery, and the suitor is called Wilekin. [7] Dame Sirith herself is precisely the kind of person whom moral Gower contemplated when he described the bawd-witch a century later. Such a witch, he tells us, is one "who, in her old age, when she cannot otherwise afflict men's hearts with love, becomes *d'amour la sorceresse*. She is a worse *diablesse* than the devil himself. He who by her means procures love, devotes himself to Satan and renounces his God." [8] Here we have the implicit covenant with Satan which, as well as the definite compact, is so marked a feature of the witch-creed of later times.

England narrowly escaped a visit from one powerful sorcerer in the thirteenth century, — a Toledo Master of Arts who seems to have had a truant disposition. At Maestricht, after describing the customary circle, he skinned a cat and gave it to three anonymous demons, who straightway devoured it; then he sacrificed two doves to the great fiend Epanamon, whom he conjured into a vessel of glass (the Bottle Imp!). Thereupon his clients expressed their wishes: one desired the favor of a woman, another the friendship of the Duke of Brabant, another a boon so foul that the demon declared he could not grant it. The magician embarked for England and was lost at sea. [9]

The infatuation of Edward III for Alice Perrers, which was of course ascribed to occult arts, is learnedly discussed by the Monk of St. Albans, who refers to Nectanebus, the famous Egyptian magician (the real father of Alexander the Great), and mentions the Rings of Moses. Alice, it seems, had in her service a friar who professed to be a physician but was in fact a sorcerer. He made figures of wax, representing King Edward and Alice, and, operating with these and using powerful herbs and charms, he had brought the king completely under her control. He had also prepared rings of oblivion and of memory, as Moses did in ancient times, and so long as the king used these (i. e., apparently, so long as he wore a ring of memory which his mistress had given him), he could never forget her. [10] When this friar was arrested in 1376, one of Alice's maids jeered at him: "Could not you, who were wont to prophesy to others, foresee what was to happen to yourself?" "I foresaw the event," he replied, "but could not tell when it was to come." [11] The same scornful jest—to all intents and purposes — was uttered by Alexander when he pushed Nectanebus into the pit, [12] and by the Thracian girl (so Plato tells us) when Thales tumbled into the well, and it became popular in an Æsopic fable.[13] However, there is nothing very brilliant about the quip, which may well have been invented more than once. A similar taunt from a modern Yorkshire farmer has been noted.[14] A wizard in Radnorshire was asked by a child, "Why do you not charm that lump off your head, as you are such a great conjurer?" [15] A native Tongan magistrate, about 1870, after exposing the shams of a witch-finder, had the man tied up and laid in the sun, bidding him keep off the flies by his powerful magic! [16] "Physician, heal thyself!" As for the Rings of Moses, the legend runs that, when the Ethiopians invaded Egypt, Tarbis, the daughter of their king, fell in love with Moses and surrendered to him the city of Saba (afterwards called Meroe) on condition that he should marry her. When he wished to return to Egypt, she refused to let him go. So Moses, who was skilled in astrology, engraved on a gem a figure that conferred memory; on another a figure that caused forgetfulness. Setting the stones in rings that were alike, and pretending that these were symbols of mutual affection, he kept the ring of remembrance for himself but gave that of oblivion to the princess. Thus Tarbis forgot her love for Moses, and he abandoned her. This is the version of Peter Comestor, from whom the legend was borrowed by Gervase of Tilbury, Vincent of Beauvais, and others.[17] Especially important for England was its inclusion in the book of exempla known as Convertimini (ascribed to Robert Holkot) and in the Gesta Romanorum. The Gesta transfers the tale to Vespasian or, in some texts, to "Fridericus." [18] Chaucer was aware that Moses, as well as Solomon, had the name of skill in the art of rings.[19]

In the fifteenth century, Dame Eleanor Cobham was said to have "enforced" Duke Humphrey "to loue her and to wedde her" by "medicines and drynkis" prepared by Margery Jordemayne, the Witch of Eye, burned as a relapsed heretic (or perhaps as a traitor) in 1441.[20] In 1484 the Act of Settlement of the crown on Richard III contains the allegation that the marriage of the late King Edward with Elizabeth Grey was brought about "by Sorcerie and Wichecraft, committed by the said Elizabeth, and her mother Jaquett Duchesse of Bedford, as [is] the common opinion of the people, and the publique voice and fame thorough all this Land." [21]   In 1536 Chapuys reported to his home government a rumor that King Henry declared that his marriage to Anne Boleyn was null and void because he had been seduced by witchcraft. The report came to Chapuys from two authorities unnamed (a lady and her husband), who told him that they were informed by an important person that the king had said this *to somebody*! [22]

So much for high life! A sheaf of humbler testimonies follows herewith.

In 1446 Mariot de Belton was brought before the Durham ecclesiastical court as a witch (*sortilega*); she was said to be in the habit of telling unmarried women that by her arts she could procure whomsoever they desired for their husbands. Another woman, Isabella Brome, was similarly accused at the same time. Both were admitted to compurgation.[23]   In 1481 Johanna Beverley was brought to bar in the Commissary's Court of the diocese of London as a sorceress (*sortilega*). She had induced two witches to win her the love of Robert Stanton and also of a second gentleman. These rivals, it was said, had fought for her, and one had almost killed the other. Her husband, for his part, stood in such fear of them that he durst not live with her. She was likewise a common harlot and bawd, and was willing to use poison when her art failed her.[24]   In 1492, Richard Laukiston confessed that he had received two mazers (or bowls), worth five marks and more, of Widow Margaret Geffrey on his promise to get her a husband by means of "a connyng man." [25]

In 1519 Richard Hall, a chaplain of Alne in Yorkshire, dealt in love potions (*pocula amatoria*).[26]   In 1526 Margaret Williamson was brought before the London Commissary for using a love drink (*potu amatorio*) and possessing suspected books. She gave information that a certain parchment volume was in the hands of Henry Devell, and was discharged.[27]   In 1552 Joan Hall of Norwich, a servant, deposed before the mayor and aldermen that she had been defrauded by an old acquaintance, Mrs. Hudson, a shoemaker's wife, who had extracted from her more than twenty shillings on pretence of consulting a cunning man in order to procure for Joan "a rich marriage." For a good while she was afraid to make any

complaint, for she had been told that, if the quest were abandoned, "the spirit which the cunning man had raised would
have a leg or an arm or an eye from her." [28]

In 1582 the Archdeacon of Canterbury in his visitation
took up the case of Goodwife Swane, "vehemently suspected
to be a witch." "She herself hath reported that she can make
a drink, which she saith if she give it to any young man that
she liketh well of, he shall be in love with her." [29] In 1585
John Meere of Dorset, student of the Temple, was accused
of using sorceries and threats to win the love of Mistress
Edetha Best. In particular he had threatened to trouble her,
it was alleged, with the sight of the devil unless she consented.[30] In 1591 John Prestall of London, it was charged,
"practised sorcery, witchcraft, or magic, to draw the affections of men and women." One of his customers was Edmund
Carlton, Gent., to whom he had promised a drink.[31]

Black magic to ingratiate one's self with royalty was an ancient practice in France. In the year 583 the infant son of
King Chilperic died of dysentery. Mummolus, a high official,
was suspected of procuring his death at the hands of certain
witches of Paris. These confessed, under torture, that they
were in fact witches and were guilty of many such murders:
the little boy, they said, they had "given for the life of Mummolus" (that is, to preserve the life of the official they had
sacrificed the child).[32] Mummolus denied this, admitting,
however, that he had often received from these women *inunc-
tiones et potiones* which were to procure him the favor of the
king and queen.[33] A charge of sorcery was, indeed, a natural
thing enough for any courtier's enemies to bring against him
when he stood high in his sovereign's regard. Thus in 1232
the Chief Justice Hubert de Burgh, Earl of Kent (Shakspere's Hubert in King John), was accused, among other
crimes, of winning the royal favor by incantations and sorceries.[34] Hubert was also accused of stealing from the royal
treasury a gem which made the wearer invincible and with
giving it to the king's enemy Llewellyn.[35] In the time of
Edward II (1307–1327) that king's fondness for his insolent
minion Piers Gaveston was explained by many as due to
wizardry.[36] Sorcery to win a prince's favor was a feature of
French high life at the time. Thus, in 1308, Guichard, Bishop

of Troyes, was accused of consulting a demon to learn how he could either win the favor (not love) of Jeanne de Navarre, wife of Philip IV, or cause her death; he was told by a witch that she had no power to win over the queen but could destroy her.[37]　Magic was also suspected to account for the high standing of Enguerrand de Marigny, Philip's chief counsellor, hanged for malefic sorcery in the next reign (1315). Both these cases were of course familiar matters to Englishmen.

The famous legend of Charlemagne's ring (familiar to English readers in Southey's ballad of "King Charlemain") was known to the satirist Skelton from Petrarch [38] and was utilized in his savage attack on Wolsey in "Why Come Ye Nat to Courte?" Tyndale also tells the story.[39] It is wonderful, writes Skelton, that the king is so fond of the Cardinal and so blinded that he cannot see how the wily prelate deceives him:

> I dought [i. e. fear] lest by sorcery
> Or suche other loselry,
> As wychecraft or charmyng,
> For he is the kynges derlyng,
> And his swete hart rote.

I well know, the poet continues, that, according to Francis Petrarch, Charlemagne was out of his mind with like dotage:

> It was by nycromansy,
> By carectes * and coniuracyon
> Vnder a certeyne constellacion,
> And a certeyne fumygacion,
> Vnder a stoon on a golde ryng,
> Wrought to Charlemayn the king,
> Whiche constrayned him forcebly
> For to loue a certayne body
> Aboue all other inordinatly.
> This is no fable nor no lye.

But let my mathematical masters tell you the rest —

> For I abhore to smatter
> Of one so deuyllysshe a matter.[40]

The innuendo is obvious. Hardly anybody doubted that Wolsey had somehow enchanted his royal master. He "calked [calculated] the king's nativity and birth," writes

---

* That is, by astrological or magical figures.

Tyndale, and "as I heard it spoken of divers, he made by craft of necromancy graven imagery to bear upon him, wherewith he bewitched the king's mind, and made the king to dote upon him more than ever he did on any lady or gentleman, so that now his Grace followed him, as he before followed the king." [41] Tyndale seems to think that this kind of thing was a weakness incident to prelates: in the time of Henry VII, he tells us, "Cardinal Morton had a licence of the pope for fourteen to study necromancy, of which he himself was one." [42]

Many supposed that Wolsey had a familiar demon in his service. William Stapleton, an ex-Benedictine, who himself possessed at one time a little ring that he thought might be useful in searching for buried treasure, had heard from a friend (ca. 1527) that the parson of Lesingham and another called up three spirits, — Andrew Malchus, Oberion, and Inchubus, — but that Oberion refused to speak, because, as Andrew Malchus explained, he "was bound unto my Lord Cardinal." [43] Richard Jones, another dabbler in the black art, confessed in 1532 that Sir William Neville asked him if it were not possible "to have a ring made that should bring a man in favour with his Prince; seeing my Lord Cardinal had such a ring, that whatsomever he asked of the King's Grace, that he had." [44] Neville also told him that Cromwell once associated with a sorcerer, and "shortly after no man so great with my Lord Cardinal as Master Cromwell was!" Stapleton replied that he "had read many books, and specially the works of Solomon, and how his ring should be made, and of what metal; and what virtues they had after the canon of Solomon," but that he never made one himself and knew of their virtues "only by hearsay." [45] A priest named Dr. Clene, in 1538 boasted that he had lived some years with Cardinal Wolsey and had made for him "a ring with a stone that he wrought many things with." This Doctor Clene was also known as Sir John Skarme, "because he can cumber the devil, as is said." [46] *Skarme* should be *Shorn*. Master John Shorn (or Schorn), rector of North Marston in Buckinghamshire about 1290, won lasting fame by conjuring the devil into a boot. Old figures of Master John, boot in hand, with a little devil peeping out at the top, still exist. [47] John Hey-

wood's Palmer (in the interlude of The Foure PP) mentions
his shrine among many others that he has visited in his long
career as a vowed pilgrim.[48]

Magical rings are so abundant in ballads and romances
that a "valued file," a mere catalogue with the briefest note
of their powers, whether due to art magic or to the natural
virtue of the stone, would fill page after page.[49] They
may confer invisibility like Gyges' ring in Plato,[50] or ensure
the wearer against discomfiture and his horse's stumbling,[51]
or make him invulnerable and fireproof,[52] or double his
strength,[53] or keep him in good health and spirits,[54] or tell him
how another fares (as whether his wife is alive or dead, true
or false).[55] When the Queen of Spain is about to restore the
Good Werewolf to his human figure, she binds about his neck
a rich and noble ring containing a stone "of so stiff virtue"
that he who wears it shall "nevermore be witched with witchcraft [56] nor perish with poison, nor wrongly shall he never
wive." [57] The hero of Jean de Condé's Dit dou Levrier has a
ring with an Indian stone which changes color when it feels
poison or sorcery or treachery, and which wins favor as well.[58]

The admirable *novella* of the young man who put his ring
on a finger of a statue of Venus and who found himself betrothed to the goddess until he was set free by the arts of
Palumbus, sorcerer and Christian priest, was introduced to
English readers by William of Malmesbury and was copied
by chroniclers and others until it became an item of what
we call general information.[59] It is best known to modern
readers from The Earthly Paradise.[60]

There are many love-charms — either for divination or to
enforce the passion — still known to the English folk, and
some of them involve the darkest and profoundest magic.[61]
I do not think that these were imported by Bishop Jewel or
by any of the Marian exiles! At all events, it is apposite to
cite two or three ancient examples of similar superstition. A
Jewish-Greek love-charm, engraved on a leaden tablet dug
up in the great necropolis at Hadrumetum in the Roman
province of Africa, had for its object to inspire Urbanos with
mad love for Domitiana and to force him to marry her.[62]
Another tablet of lead to procure love, dating from the third
or fourth century and showing a characteristic mixture of

Greek, Egyptian, and Hebrew elements, not only invocates gods and spirits (both celestial and infernal) to fire the damsel's heart, but calls particularly upon the spirit of the dead man in whose grave the spell was buried.[63] A leaden tablet from Cnidos in Caria devotes to the infernal gods the woman, whoever she may be, that estranged Nacon from his wife Prosodion and his children.[64] In another from the same place an abandoned wife curses her rival, Dorothea.[65] An Attic tablet lays a spell upon Theodora that Callias may forget her.[66] A Latin tablet found amongst tombs in a vineyard near Rome deserves translation: "As the dead man who is buried here can neither speak nor converse, so may Rhodine be dead with regard to Marcus Licinius Faustus and unable to speak or converse. And as this dead man is not pleasing to gods or men, in the same way may Rhodine be pleasing to Marcus Licinius Faustus and may she have as much strength as the dead man who is buried here. Father Dis, to thee I entrust Rhodine, that she may always be hateful to Marcus Licinius Faustus."[67] In a Latin tablet from Carthage five demons, whose names are written in Greek characters and two of whom are styled Egyptian, are called upon to win the love of a woman. "Take away sleep from her until she comes to me and satisfies my desire." "Compel her to come to me in love." "Drive her away from her parents and her chamber and force her to love me."[68] One, in Greek and Latin, from Hadrumetum, containing magic signs and words (including *Sabaoth*), calls for the love of Victoria. It figures two hearts intertwined and transfixed with a sword or a spike.[69] In another, in Latin, from the same place, Felix bespells Vettia, the daughter of Optata, that "for his love she may neither sleep nor eat, and that she may forget her father and her mother and her kindred and all her friends and all other men."[70]

That love-potions are more likely to cause madness or death than love is noted by Wier and after him by Scot.[71] In his index Wier notes that "love is to be won by love, not by philtres." Thus he forecasts the reply of the old Aztec woman, reputed to be wise in magic, to Señor Casanova when he asked her what he should do to make a woman love him: "Love her!" said the beldame. "If you wish her to love you, love her!" — and she refused him any other charm.[72] This is even better psychology than Ovid's *amabilis esto*.

Impotence could be induced by witchcraft or sorcery: such was the universal belief, which had often come before the ecclesiastical courts since the scandalous divorce proceedings of Lothaire I in the ninth century.[73] It was of course shared by our Anglo-Saxon forefathers,[74] is still an article of faith among savages, the world over, and holds its place in civilized and half-civilized folk-lore. By the middle of the twelfth century such a condition, thus caused, was an accepted ground for divorce, and for the next three hundred years these cases were so numerous that this species of sorcery became an everyday matter. It is beautifully illustrated by a suit for defamation before the Prior's court at Durham in 1435. Margaret Lyndyssay accused three men of saying that she was an *incantatrix* who, with another woman, had used very black magic of the sympathetic order to this end. She cleared herself with five compugators (all women), and the men were warned, on pain of excommunication, not to repeat the slander.[75] The witchery in this Durham case was identical with that employed for a somewhat similar purpose in the seventeenth century, as recorded by John Webster.[76] Both find a striking parallel in the means by which the Homeric Iphiclus was kept childless, as told by Pherecydes in the fifth century B.C.[77] And so I may dismiss the subject, together with that of barrenness, by referring to the note, where is cited a small selection from the superabundant literature.[78]

The continuity of popular tradition independently of the Reformation and of prosecution on the Continent in the sixteenth century is well illustrated in the ballad of "Willie's Lady." Willie's wife is not acceptable to his mother, who is a "vile rank witch of vilest kind." She arrests her daughter-in-law's delivery by evil spells: — nine witch knots in that lady's locks, combs of care in her hair, a bush of woodbine between the two bowers, etc.; and she denies her all relief. Then the Belly Blind, a serviceable household goblin, shows Willie how to balk the witch: he is to make a wax baby and invite her to the christening. The mother, in anger, calls out

> Oh, wha has loosed the nine witch knots
> That was amo' that ladie's locks?

and so on, revealing the whole plot. Willie undoes the spells, and "now he's gotten a bonny young son." [79]

"Willie's Lady" is Scottish, but the same plot is preserved in numerous versions from Scandinavia, and in tales from Scotland, Germany, Italy, and elsewhere,[80] as well as in the classical legend of the birth of Apollo. Latona's sufferings, according to the Homeric Hymn, were prolonged for nine days and nights by the malice of Hera until Ilithyia was induced to relieve them.[81] More elaborate is Ovid's account of the birth of Hercules. Here Lucina, bribed by Juno, sits before Alcmena's door, with her right knee crossed over her left and her fingers interlocked. At last Galanthis (*media de plebe*) suspects the trick, and calls upon the stranger to wish Alcmena joy; whereupon Lucina springs up, unclasping her hands, and Hercules is born. Ovid's tale occurs substantially in the Metamorphoses of Nicander, as early as the second century B.C. There is further pertinent material in Pausanias, Pliny, and Apuleius.[82] We observe that the Greek Ilithyia in this myth is nothing more or less than a witch-midwife who can help or hinder [83] childbirth by occult means, precisely like a modern woman in the same profession.[84]

Spells and charms have always been a resource on the part of midwives to assist delivery, and the Church has felt bound to repress such practices.[85] Midwives had to receive episcopal license and were held strictly accountable. In 1481 Agnes Marshall was presented in a York visitation for practising obstetrics without competent knowledge and for using incantations.[86] In 1538 Nicholas Shaxton, Bishop of Salisbury, cautioned every curate to charge midwives "to beware that they cause not the Woman, being in Travaile, to make any folishe Vowe, to go in Pilgrimage to this Ymage, or that Ymage, after her Deliveraunce, but only to call on God for Helpe. Nor to use any Girdels,[87] Purses, Mesures of our Lady,[88] or such other Superstitious Things, to be occupied about the Woman while She laboureth, to make her beleve to have the better Spede by it." [89] In 1554 Bonner, Bishop of London, enquired in his visitation "whether any midwife or other woman, coming to the travail of any woman with child, do use or exercise any witchcraft, charms, sorcery, invocations or prayers, other than such as be allowable, and may stand with the laws and ordinances of the Catholic Church," [90] and he expressly forbade such practices in his Acts for the next year.[91] Queen Elizabeth's Royal Acts of 1559 are quite in accord with Bonner: "Whether you knowe anye that doe vse charmes, sorcerye, enchauntmentes, inuocations, circles, witchecraftes, southsayinge, or any lyke craftes or ymaginations inuented by the Deuyll, and specyallye in the tyme of womens trauayle." [92] Much the same thing may be read in Grindal's Acts in 1571 [93] and 1576,[94] in Parker's in 1575,[95] and in Barnes's in 1577.[96] Particularly significant is the enquiry in the Visitation of the Commissary of St. Mary's, Salop, in 1584, because it actually mentions the unlocking charm: "Whether any mydwife within your parishe in tyme of weomens travill be knowne or suspected to use sorcerie, witchcrafte, charmes, *unlockynge of chests and dores*, . . . or to saye unlaweful praiers or superstitious invocations." [97] It is a widespread belief that, when a woman is in labor, all knots must be untied and all locks unlocked.[98] This piece of sympathetic magic is well-known to savage men. In New Guinea, "should labour be unduly prolonged, the child's father is sent for. He, after having opened any boxes there may be in the house, . . . sits down near his wife and proceeds to untie the cord which confines her hair, and to remove the *gana* from his arms." [99]

The kind of charm that midwives employed is exemplified in a fifteenth-century specimen. This recites that "St. Mary bore Christ; St. Anne bore Mary; St. Elizabeth bore John; St. Cecilia bore Remigius," and it summons the unborn child in impressive language: "O infans, siue viuus, siue mortuus, exi foras, quia Christus te uocat ad lucem!" [100] A similar adjuration was in Anglo-Saxon times written on virgin wax and bound under the mother's right foot.[101]

Margery Jourdemayne, the Witch of Eye, doubtless was an adept in such practices. There is some evidence that Dame Eleanor Cobham employed her, not to cause the death of King Henry VI by spells with an image of wax, but to make it possible for her to bear a child.[102]

Whatever we may think of other elements in witch-lore, there is at least one dogma about which there can be no disputing — the dogma of Incubus. That mortals may have husbands, wives, or lovers from the Other World is an article of the popular creed that has come down from the remotest times to which we can trace history whether by record or by inference. The psychological and physiological basis [103] for this notion has been amply set forth by scholars and men of science and need not here detain us. Theologians, from St. Augustine down, accepted it (from the folk) as a fact of human experience.[104] No other view was possible in the case of ancient kings and notables reputed to be the sons of gods or goddesses, for the pagan deities were regarded as devils who had deceived and misled mankind in days of yore and who were still active to beguile the world. Such was the parentage of Alexander, Seleucus, Plato, the elder Scipio, and Augustus,[105] to say nothing of Hercules, the story of whose begetting is paralleled or reproduced in the legend of King Arthur.[106] By the year 1100 — to take a safe date — the Incubus Dogma was solidly established as an article of learned faith throughout Western Europe.[107] The whole race of Huns was of demonic ancestry according to a tradition which, whatever its origin, became widespread in the literature of *exempla*.[108] Demons might be male or female, and could shift their sex at will. For Britain we may instance the case of Merlin, recorded by Geoffrey of Monmouth [109] and repeated with unction by Cæsarius of Heisterbach in the thirteenth century. After mentioning the "fortissima gens Hunnorum," descended from outcast Gothic women and *incubi daemones*, Cæsarius continues: "We read that Merlin, the prophet of the Britons, was the son of such a demon and a nun. So too the kings who down to the present day hold sway in that same Britain, now styled England, are reported to be the descendants of a *mater phantastica*. But Merlin was a rational man and a Christian. He foretold many things that should come to pass, and his prophecies are fulfilled daily." [110] Reginald Scot, in one of his best arguments *ad absurdum*, touches up the Merlin legend which William of Newburgh had attacked long before.[111] "If *Incubus* could beget *Merlins* among us, we should have a jollie manie of cold [i. e. false] prophets." [112] In mentioning the English kings Cæsarius has reference to the family legend of the Plantagenets — a tale which in the English metrical romance of Richard Coer de

Lion has resulted in giving Richard a demon mother who flies off through the roof of the church when King Henry tries to detain her at the moment of the elevation of the host. Giraldus Cambrensis, rehearsing the same legend of an unnamed Countess of Anjou, avers that King Richard used to mention it in jest.[113] Such tales as Robert le Diable and Sir Gowghter, as well as the Lai de Yonec,[114] belong here as confirmatory evidence to the prevalent belief. Merlin's fame as the son of a demon, as Cæsarius indicates, was kept alive by his prophecies, which persisted as a potent influence in politics until recent times.[115]

Cæsarius registers several other examples of *incubi* or *succubae*, and his book was justly popular, for he was a born *raconteur*.[116] Of course the same sort of thing turns up in various collections of *exempla*, so that the matter was kept steadily before the popular mind by the mediæval preachers, and thus the folk-idea received the constant endorsement of the keepers of the people's conscience. So, in a manuscript written in England in the thirteenth century, we have an anecdote of a woman who resisted the importunities of a demon wooer so valorously that he murdered her husband and one of her sons and smote her with blindness.[117] The same collection informs us that demons, once plentiful in Scotland, had been driven out by the Dominicans, but this was an oversanguine remark, for Hector Boece chronicles a particularly horrible instance from the latter part of the fifteenth century, as well as a fairy-mistress story from the same era. The hideous tale is, to all intents and purposes, the myth of Cupid and Psyche fallen upon evil days.[118]

Walter Map was well acquainted with the notion of incubi and succubi and tells several stories concerning them, and Gervase of Tilbury (ca. 1211) speaks of unions between women and demons as not uncommon in his day.[119] In the Anglo-Saxon Leech-Book one may find the recipe for a salve "against elf-kin and night-walking demons and those persons with whom a devil has sexual intercourse."[120]

In 1249 in Herefordshire was born a demon's child who within six months had a full set of teeth (like Richard III) and was as tall as a boy of seventeen; his mother went into a decline and died soon after.[121] The trial of Guichard, Bishop of Troyes, which lasted from 1308 to 1313, must have been common talk in English court circles; for he had stood high in favor with Blanche d'Artois, who had married Edmund of Lancaster, brother of Edward I, in 1275, and with her daughter Jeanne, who was at one time betrothed to King Edward's son. Guichard was accused of divers sorceries. It was matter of general knowledge that he was the son of a demon (there were twenty-seven witnesses on that point), and his nickname at school had been *fils de neton*.[122] In An Alphabet of Tales, a fifteenth-century English translation of the Alphabetum Narrationum (a Latin handbook of exempla compiled, it seems likely, by Arnold of Liége in 1308), we read of a demon who visits a woman by night and gives her rings and jewels of gold and many other presents. The case should be interesting to modern students of materialization and ectoplasm, for the uncanny wooer appeared "with grete lightis aboute hym, so that all the chawmer myght be seen with the light, and the droppis of the seargis [candles] might be sene." [123] The Alphabet also borrows three tales of this class from Cæsarius.[124] In one of them a young man has a love-tryst with a woman and her place is taken by a fiend.[125] A variation on this theme occurs in a frightful story about a woman named Joan, living in 1337 at Kingsley in the diocese of Winchester, who was deceived by an evil spirit in the shape of her lover, William. Returning from a tryst in the forest of Wolmer, she learned from William that the assignation was none of *his* doing, and so the truth came to light. Poor Joan soon died, and her corpse was so heavy that eight men could hardly bear her body to the grave. There are other details full of horror. The affair was duly entered in the chronicles, and Rinaldi thought it notable enough to deserve a place in his Annals of the Church.[126] This tale makes a good note on Chaucer, since the tragedy occurred at about the time when he was born, and it well illustrates the popular creed of England in those days — the creed so tellingly utilized by the Wife of Bath (who was pretty well emancipated) for a dig at the Friar who ventured to laugh at the length and volubility of her preamble:

> For ther as wont to walken was an elf,
> Ther walketh now the limitour him-self

In undermeles and in morweninges,
And seyth his matins and his holy thinges
As he goth in his limitacioun.
Wommen may go saufly up and doun
In every bush or under every tree;
Ther is noon other incubus but he.[127]

The author of The Pilgrim's Tale (ca. 1540) adapts Chaucer [128] and names him. Reginald Scot quotes Chaucer,[129] and Harsnet follows Scot's example.[130] The Wife's words are mythologically significant, for they mark the passage of the old Teutonic belief in elves or trolls or hillmen that woo or abduct mortal women [131] into the theological conception that explains all such creatures as devils. Sometimes the folk clung to the older idea, sometimes they accepted the newer. Native tradition is well represented in a number of our most famous ballads — Hind Etin (Child, No. 41), for example, which has many relatives in Scandinavia and Germany, and Lady Isabel and the Elf-Knight (No. 4), in which the wooer is rather murderous than lustful. Here too belongs The Dæmon Lover (No. 243), at least in some of its varieties. In one of the oldest of these pieces, extant in a manuscript of about 1450, the foul fiend promises to teach a maiden "all the wisdom of the world" if she will accept him as her lover.[132]

A Perthshire woman was wooed by the devil in recent years, but she was rescued in time.[133] A homely variant of the fairy-mistress *motif* turns up in modern England. A tailor, returning from his daily tasks, met a beautiful lady in a solitary place, and they made an appointment for the next evening. But the canny tailor had his doubts and consulted the vicar. He advised him to keep the tryst, for the devil (if devil it were) might resent his absence and work him harm, but he was "to do everything contrary or *crosswise*" to the lady's suggestions, whatever they might be. The spell worked, and the tailor was saved.[134] Meilerius of Caerleon in the twelfth century was not so well-advised, and he went mad when his mistress revealed herself in the shape of a hideous fiend.[135]

The persistency of tradition is well illustrated by St. John's wort and vervain. "I remember," wrote Walter Scott in 1812, "to have heard a ballad, in which a fiend is introduced paying his addresses to a beautiful maiden; but disconcerted by the holy herbs which she wore in her bosom, makes the following lines the burden of his courtship:

> Gin ye wish to be layman mine,
> Lay aside the St Johns wort and the vervain." [136]

We have the same tale recorded in 1625 by a Durham worthy, the Rev. Dr. Thomas Jackson (1579–1640), afterwards President of Corpus Christi College, Oxford: "I well remember a tradition, that was old, when I was young, better believed by such as told it, then if it had been Canonical Scripture. It was of a maid that liked well of the devil making love to her in the habit of a gallant young man, but could not enjoy his company, nor he hers, so long as she had *Vervine* and *S. Johns* grass about her: for to this effect he brake his mind unto her at last in rime:

> If thou hope to be Lemman mine;
> Lay aside the St. Johns grass, and the Vervine." [137]

Our next step is back to the twelfth century — to the Great Life of St. Hugh, Bishop of Lincoln (born ca. 1135, died 1200). A certain woman had long had an intrigue with a demon who took the shape of a handsome young man. She had often confessed, fasted, and done penance, but could not be rid of him. The bishop prayed for her, and this is what happened. One day another spirit in the form of a fair youth came and promised to free her if she would follow his directions. He showed her an herb growing near her house and bade her hide some of it in her bosom and scatter some about her dwelling. By-and-by the demon lover came in his accustomed figure, looked in at the window by which he was wont to enter, and said: "What pray is that foul and horrid thing which you have scattered about in the house? Throw it away quickly!" She refused, and he departed with furious threats. Soon after came the other youth and congratulated her; but he added, "Put away the herb now, for it is hateful to all our kind; and, after I go, take it again." She would not, and he too went away with threats. Thereafter she always kept the herb in her bosom, and she had no further trouble. The writer afterwards learned what the herb was, for the woman had shown it to a Canterbury monk, who told him. This monk said that he knew of a youth and an Essex girl who had been similarly relieved. The Greeks call it *hypericon*, the English call it St. John's grass (*herba Sancti Johannis*).[138] A similar story occurs in two collections of *exempla* made in England in the thirteenth century.[139] In the next century Robert Holkot is our authority for the prevalence of the opinion that "herba Johannis que dicitur perforata fugat demones per naturam."[140] Drayton, in The Muses Elizium (1630), makes the hermit Clarinax include, in his list of "powerfull simples,"

> Heere holy Veruayne, and heere Dill,
> Against witchcraft much auailing.[141]

The ditty

> Vervain and Dill
> Hinders Witches from their Will

is a rhyme known to Aubrey in 1696, and he vouches for a similar efficacy in St. John's wort, on the authority of Henry Lawes, Milton's friend.[142] The rhyme is still current in this form,[143] as well as in the following more elaborate shape:

> Trefoil, vervain, John's wort, dill
> Hinder witches of their will — [144]

which was known to Meg Merrilies.[145] According to some Devon wiseacres, the spirits of the air will become visible if you anoint your eyes for three days with the mixed juices of dill, vervain, and St. John's wort.[146] Vervain, then, like St. John's wort, is *fuga daemonum*. If you carry it about you by day or night, it keeps off "the deuel of helle" according to a mediæval English poem on medicinal herbs.[147] But this same poem informs us that vervain gathered in May at dawn, when pulverized and thrown between a man and a woman, causes dissension: "Though they love each other never so well, they shall quarrel and strive" —

> Thow thei lowyn hem neuer so wel,
> Thei schul flytyn and strywyn that sel: [148]

queer doctrine, since vervain also makes a good charm to win the favor of great lords: "Qhwo-so beryth it vp-on hym, he shal hawe lowe [have love] of grete maystrys, and thai shal nowth refuse his askyngis but graunt him with good wyll that that he wele." [149]   But probably the month of May has something to do with it. "Malae nubunt Maio." It is significant that both vervain and dill were ingredients in one of the favorite remedies of Margaret Hunt, who was called to account for illicit medical practice in the Commissary's Court of London in 1528. "For them that hath ony sorys on ther bodys, she techeth them to gether herbe-grace [i. e. rue], dyll, vervey[n]e, marygoldes, put a lyttill holy water to them, & sey sume prayers." She learned her art in Wales from a woman called Mother Emet. From some phrases in Margaret's confession we may infer that she believed that the ailments treated were or might have been induced by witchcraft.[150]

For the time of Henry VIII we can call an expert witness in the person of Andrew Boorde, the distinguished physician, who died in 1549. Boorde is judicial. Though his own opinion, like Reginald Scot's, is that the nightmare or incubus is caused by "some euyll humour" in the patient's bodily constitution, yet he admits the alternative that it may be a demon, and cites a contemporary example — an anchoress of St. Albans who (so she told him) "was infested of such a spirite." And, "yf it be a spirite," Boorde knows the remedy: St. John's wort, which, as he has read, is *fuga daemonum* and is "of that vertue that it doth repell suche malyfycyousnes of spirites." [151]   But Harsnet, in 1603, inveighing against the Catholic exorcists of his day, scouts the demonophobic virtue of St. John's wort: "Whereas your prescript is compounded of these delicate simples, Brimstone, *Assa fœtida*, *Galbanum*, *S. Iohns Wort, and Rue*; *Porphyrie*, and *Iamblichus*, men acquainted with the nature, and disposition of deuils, afore your whip had ere a string to it, doe affirme, that those forcible violent sauours and stinking odours, are the very delicacies for deuils, and allectiues to their noses." [152]

The Incubus Dogma was brought into close relation with witchcraft in the trial of Dame Alice Kyteler of Kilkenny in 1324. This lady, four times married, was charged with killing some of her husbands by sorcery and with so bewitching others that they gave all their property to her and to William Outlawe, her son by her first marriage. Her present husband,

John le Poer, she had afflicted with a wasting disease. She had a familiar demon named Filius Artis, also called Robin (or Robert) Filius Artis, who showed himself now as a cat, now as a shaggy dog, now as a black man. All these details (with a mere change of names and social station) might be extracted from the narrative of the Chelmsford witch-trials of 1566. Now this Robin, according to the confession of one of Dame Alice's confederates, was an incubus, and as such was the lady's lover.[153] The Kyteler case, though staged in Ireland, is rather English than Irish in its connections. The town of Kilkenny was founded by Strongbow, and the persons concerned were obviously not Celts. The prosecutor, William Ledrede, Bishop of Ossory, was a Franciscan friar of London, who addressed the people in English and French,[154] and whose English birth was more than once cast in his teeth: — "an English foreigner," "that good-for-nothing rustic runaway from England."[155]

CHAPTER V

MADNESS, CURSES, AND THE ELFSHOT

THAT a witch or wizard can drive a man mad, either by spells or by sending a demon to buffet him, is an old article of faith which descended as a matter of course from Anglo-Saxon times [1] to the Elizabethan age. In and for itself demoniacal possession is due to the immediate action of an evil spirit which enters into the victim and controls his thoughts, his speech, and his deeds, either constantly or by intermittent attacks.[2] Whether a witch sent the demon,[3] or he operated without human initiative, the result was the same.

In any given instance of violent madness or weird seizure, two views were possible, apart from a strictly medical diagnosis. The theologians, though not excluding witchcraft as a potential factor, were likely to have recourse to the doctrine of possession or obsession. The difference between these two forms of demonic assault, though plain enough in words, was seldom grasped, and is, indeed, rather a matter of psychical hair-splitting than anything that could concern the layman.[4] People in general, on the other hand, were prone to think some witch to blame, and there were two or three professed or suspected hags available in every village. The whole subject of demoniacs, then, is inseparable from witchcraft. Instances of possession might be cited without limit, for a multitude of saints inherited the ancient and divine function of healing, in this as in other departments of the medical art.[5] For our present purpose a few such cures worked by holy men in England will suffice.[6]

Benedict, a cleric of Winchester, and John, a layman from Ireland, both possessed, were cured by the merits of Edward the Confessor in 1267, when his body was translated for the second time.[7] The shrine of St. Cuthbert, Bishop of Lindisfarne, was the scene of several cases of this nature. There, about 1140, one Walter, possessed of a devil in the shape of a black dog (which he alone could see, though others heard it

speak), was freed by the saint's merits: the narrative is derived in part from Walter's brother.[8] Another patient was a
boy whom the demons tossed about at times (spasms!) and at
times carried through the air to distant spots.[9] Still another
was a woman whom a devil buffeted exceedingly.[10]

St. Hugh of Avalon, Bishop of Lincoln in the same century,
cast out a devil in the cathedral. When the bishop saw the
madman led towards him, he sprinkled him with holy water
and adjured the evil spirit to come out of him and torment
him no more. The patient fell to the ground and lay as one
dead. St. Hugh poured over him a great quantity of holy
water, and he was permanently cured.[11] St. Godric, the hermit of Finchale (who died in 1170), cured several demoniacs,
according to his contemporary, Reginald, monk of Durham.[12]
One example will serve: it is good for its classical touch and
also for the coöperation of St. Cuthbert and St. Godric. A
woman was so tormented by demons for sixteen years that
she had almost lost her understanding. She prayed to St.
Cuthbert at Durham. As she rose from her knees, she had a
vision of the saint walking before her to Finchale. Thither
she followed him and there was freed, as she merited, from all
diabolical assaults and illusions.[13] A girl was so maddened by
a demon that she scratched and bit whomsoever she could
reach. Her parents brought her to the tomb of St. Oswin the
Martyr, remained there all night with her in prayer, and took
her home cured.[14] One is strongly reminded of the ancient
practice of incubation.[15] Another cure that suggests incubation is that of Edwin, a young monk of Ely, as described in
the twelfth-century Liber Eliensis. A holy man from Winchester, who happened to be present when Edwin suddenly
went mad at compline, saw what was invisible to all others
— a creature like a black boy that kept a tight grip on the
sufferer's cowl. Edwin was very violent, kicking and trying
to bite those who restrained him; but his faithful brethren
watched with him all night at St. Ætheldreda's shrine. Towards morning he fell asleep, and when he awoke he was
sane.[16]

In 1355, according to a brief entry in the Annals of Worcester, "many men were driven mad at the sight of demons."
Knighton's chronicle is more expansive: In this summer

there raged a strange sickness, as it were from the assault of evil spirits. For people went mad in town and country, everywhere in the realm. They ran into woods and thickets to hide like wild beasts — fleeing from human society. Some ran from the fields to the villages and from the villages to the fields, now here and now there, and could with difficulty be caught. Many, when taken, were led to the church, and there they lay bound until they received their enlightenment from God. In some churches you might see ten or twelve of them at once, and it was great pity to behold their possession.[17] Here we have plain demoniacal possession, the devil working directly upon his victims; but eleven years later (in 1366) madness as the result of witchcraft was in the minds of the mayor and alderman of London when they furnished a kindly Fleming with a Latin letter to keep him clear of possible accusations in this regard. They certify "that Ortillus Frank van Nerynbergh . . . having accidentally fallen down on Saturday, the Feast of the Assumption of the Blessed Virgin, A.D. 1366, in an infirmity of frenzy and lost his senses, he had been removed in that state out of the city by one Hankyn Fleming, who out of charity undertook to convey him to his own country, in the hope that he might recover his health, please God; so that no evil suspicion might fall on the said Hankyn in respect of the infirmity aforesaid." [18]

A sudden attack of possession during sermon time is recorded in Gregory's London Chronicle under the year 1469. It was on a Sunday afternoon in Lent. A young man who attended one of the officers of the royal household "was soore vexyd and bound with the devylle." After he was loosed, he lay for a long time speechless; "and as sone as he myght speke men of worschippe com to hym, and sum grete statys [i. e. persons of high position] alle-so com to hym and desyryd hym to telle hem of hys syghtys that he had sene in hys ferfulle vexacyon." He made known his vision in confession to the Prior of Charterhouse and to "many dyvers docters" of theology.[19] When the miracles of King Henry VI were collected with a view to his canonization, there was turned in an account of a boy named William Sawndie. It is not expressly asserted that he was a demoniac, but his case fits one of the older instances. He often lost his mind, and twisted his head completely round toward his back. A mere vow to visit the holy king's tomb cured him. The dead king's merits, however, healed a real demoniac on another occasion.[20]

The affliction of Sir Roger Wentworth's children, and especially of his daughter Anne, as described by Sir Thomas More, might be transported bodily into the Elizabethan age or even into the reign of James I, without any anachronism. Anne was "a very fayre yonge gentylwoman of .xii. yeres of age" when Satan attacked her. She was "in merueyllous maner vexed & tourmented by our gostly enemy ye deuyll, her mynd alyenated & rauyng with dyspysing & blasphemy of god, and hatred of all halowed thynges, with knowledge and perceyuynge of the halowed from the vnhalowed, all [i. e. although] were she no thynge warned thereof." In the presence of the image of our Lady at Ipswich she was "so greuously tourmented, and in face, eyen, loke and countenaunce so grysely chaunged, with her mouthe drawen asyde, and her eyen layde out vpon her chekes, that it was a terrible syght to beholde." All the demoniacs, however, were "in the presence of all the company restored to theyr good state perfytely cured and sodeynly." Sir Thomas insists that there was no chance for trickery or imposture; the family was too respectable and too intelligent. Besides, "the mayde her selfe [was] to yonge to fayne, and the fassyon it selfe to straunge for any man to fayne." Mistress Anne forsook the world, despite her father's remonstrances, and when More wrote (in 1528) she was living "well and gracyously."[21] Some one, writing under Cranmer's name in Queen Mary's time, reported the case in a hostile spirit: She "told many men the secrets of their hearts, which they thought no man could have told, but God only. She cut stomachers in pieces, and made them whole again; and caused divers men that spake against her delusion to go stark mad. All which things were proved, and openly by her confessed, to be done by necromancy and the deceit of the devil."[22]

Sometimes wizardry and sanctity vied with each other in treating demoniacs. Gregory the Great tells a terrifying anecdote of a possessed lady whose relatives entrusted her to *malifici*. These ducked her in the river and tried to expel the demon by incantations, with the result that, "by the wonderful judgment of God," when one devil was driven out, a legion took his place. Bishop Fortunatus, however, relieved her permanently by assiduous prayer.[23]

The ancient Germanic (and, indeed, universal) idea that madness may be caused by spells[24] coalesces with the belief in demoniacal possession in the popular as well as the learned witch-creed. So experience proved that philtres were quite as likely to cause insanity or death as to procure love.[25]

Abnormal fasting[26] may be a token of sanctity, and as such it often achieves a place in legend and chronicle. One of these fasts, about A.D. 824, lasted for three years.[27] Though the Fasting Nun of Leicester, who died in 1225, had taken no food for seven years except the communion on Sunday, yet her face was always like a white lily suffused with rosy red.[28] A similar case, that of Jewet Metles (i. e. Meatless), is reported from the neighborhood of Walsingham in 1336.[29] Foreign tidings of the kind made their way into England, as in or about 1434, when the Brut celebrates "an holy maid in Holand, called Lydwith, which lyued onely bi miracle, not etynge any mete."[30] Less marvellous, but more humanly interesting, is the history of Cecilia de Rygeway, to whom King Edward III accorded a free pardon in 1357. Accused of murdering her husband, she had refused to plead, and had therefore been committed to prison to be starved into docility — a milder discipline than the *peine forte et dure*. For twoscore days she had "sustained life in close confinement without food or drink, marvellously and as it were against human nature." "In honor of the Virgin, from whom this miracle is believed to proceed," so runs the entry in the Patent Rolls, "the king has granted her his grace.[31] But Satan, as *simia Dei*, is ever at hand to deceive the world by false miracles, and so, in 1289, we learn of a boy who went without food for twenty-four months "by the illusion of demons of the incubus sort."[32] It is a pity we have no details, for these demons may possibly have been the fairies, who enabled a Scottish woman (whom the Rev. Mr. Kirk examined toward the end of the seventeenth century) to keep life afoot though she had taken "verie little or no Food for several years past." She was "prettie melanchollyous and silent, hardly ever seen to laugh. Her natural Heat and radi-

cal Moisture seem to be equally balanced, lyke ane unextin-
guished Lamp, and going in a Circle, not unlike to the faint
Lyfe of Bees, and some Sort of Birds, that sleep all the Winter
over, and revive in the Spring." [33]

All these curiosities, as well as many others that might be
adduced,[34] may seem remote from witchcraft, but we should
remember Mercy Short of Boston (1692). One of the "mis-
eries" with which she was afflicted by demonic spectres (sent,
it was inferred, by a witch of Salem) was "an Extreme Fasting for many Days together." [35] In 1701, too, the London
Post-Angel for August printed an account of a man in Old
Street Square, "who now lives without *Eating* and *Drinking*"
and "is thought to be *Bewitch'd.*" His fast had lasted above
three weeks, and he had "voided several crooked Pins." [36]
At York in 1538 was executed for treason one Mabel Brigge,
who had performed the terrible rite of "fasting upon" a person to bring about his death. For this service she had been
hired by another woman, and it was alleged in extenuation
that the end in view was merely to recover stolen money; but
Mabel herself had declared, according to one witness, that
"she had never so fasted but once for a man, and he brake his
neck or [i. e. before] it were well fasted, and so she trusted
that they should do that had made all this business, and that
was the King and this false Duke" — the Duke of Norfolk.
So profound was the belief in the hideous spell that rumor was
soon rife in the neighborhood that King Henry was dead.[37]
The ceremony (known as the Black Fast or St. Trinian's
[Ninian's] Fast, and manifestly related to the venerable Irish
custom of fasting upon a person as a means of distress — to
force him, that is, to accede to one's legal claims[38]) was legiti-
mately practised in England as an extreme act of religious
mortification, involving abstinence not only from flesh but
from milk and all food prepared with milk. To apply the
Black Fast profanely, as for the detection of robbers, was
manifestly outrageous, but Mabel's crime was even worse
than that, for she had turned the ancient rite to purposes of
murder and treason. Of course the Black Fast was altogether prohibited later by the reforming clergy. Thus, in
1577, Bishop Barnes of Durham enjoined "that no popishe
abrogated hollydaies be kept hollydaies, . . . nor any super-

fluous faste be used as those called the Lady fast, or Saint Trinyons fast, the Blacke fast, Saint Margaret fast, or suche other, invented by the devill, to the dishonouringe of God and damnacion of the sowles of idolatrous and supersticious persons." [39]

The efficacy of a witch's imprecation [40] and her own belief therein are well illustrated by the trial of Elena Dalok in 1493. Elena was clearly a bad woman. She was accused not only of being a common slanderer (*skandilizatrix*) of her neighbors, but also of professing to own a book which told her all things that were to come, of claiming the power to bring rain at her command, and of declaring that whomever she cursed was sure to die: — "She says that she has cursed very many who never lived in this world thereafter." * If she could have heaven *here*, she cared nothing for heaven in the world to come. She wished that she might be in hell for as long a time as God shall be in heaven, that with the hooks of hell (*uncis infernalibus*) she might revenge herself on a certain John Gybbys, who was dead. [41] In 1596 the wife of Maurice Jones of Barking was presented before the Archdeacon's Court of Essex. One Robgente's wife had sent to ask some medicine for the colic. Instead of acquiescing, Goody Jones "fell downe upon her knees, and after many curses and evill speches, praied, that the said Robgentes wife might never be cured; but that she might abide the extremest tormentes that ever was abiden: since which time, the said Robgentes wife hath lien, and yet dothe lye in great misery, and can find no ease." [42]

These lurid records may be illustrated by the ferocious picture of a village termagant in a view of frank-pledge held at Godmanchester, Huntingdonshire, in 1634. The bailiffs, to guard against fire, had thrown out of several houses a quantity of "gleanes" and peas that were drying "at the backs of their chimneys" and in other dangerous places. Widow Dorothy Walpoole "did take a fire stick in her hand and swore by God's blood she would set the gleans and peaze the Bailiffs had cast out of her house on fire, and bid a red plague of God light upon the Bailiffes and all that came with them

---

* "Ipsa dicit quod anatimazavit quamplurimos qui nunquam postea in hoc seculo vitam duxerunt."

and that they might rotte like dewe against the sunne." She
was set in the stocks and afterwards sent to the house of correction, "and ther punished according to her deserts and to
the terror of all other lewde queanes not conformable to good
government." [43] Luckily for her, the Widow Walpoole was
not (it seems) suspected of witchcraft, but she is a good witness for the continuity of tradition. Her curse was not learned
from Caliban, though it makes a fine note on his outburst: —

> The red plague rid you
> For learning me your language!

In this same year Isabel Oxley was mildly disciplined by
the Court of High Commission for blasphemous words. At
divers times, Ralph Fenwick testified, he had heard her
curse George Fenwick "as followeth: — 'Godes curse, Godes
plague, light of the and all thine.'" And "aboute August or
September last Isabell, in the townegaite of Heddonn and
neere unto the doore of Reede, did revile, and curse, and said
unto him, 'Godes plague and Godes curse light of the and
thine beastes, and God lett never they nor anie thing thou
hast prosper nor doe well.' Beinge neighbour unto Isabell,
hath verie oftenn heard and observed her cursinges." She
submitted and was required to make confession in Heddon
church. [44]

Still in 1634 Thomas Aspinwal of Winwick, a swearer, was
brought before the church authorities for asserting that he
had a prayer that would shorten a man's life. [45] Such ideas
are still cherished, as they have been among all races and nations from the remote past. In the fine old ballad of Robin
Hood's Death, Robin and Little John come to a black water,
over which is laid a plank, and upon the plank there kneels
an old woman who is "banning Robin Hode" — why, we do
not know, for the manuscript is defective, but his death ensues on that same night. [46] In The Wife of Usher's Well, the
mother, learning that her three stalwart sons will never come
back from overseas, for they are dead, curses the waters for
their sake:

> I wish the wind may never cease,
>   Nor fashes in the flood,
> Till my three sons come hame to me
>   In earthly flesh and blood.

And the lads come home from the grave, only to return thither at cockcrow.[47] In 1816 Sir Cuthbert Sharp recorded that a belief in "bad prayers" was still prevalent.[48] About 1865 a wise woman in Somerset, who professed to cure pigs, was summoned as a cheat and confessed fraud; but a death followed her curse.[49] Curses have actually been sold within man's memory in Denbighshire.[50] In 1889 a written curse was sent anonymously to a farmer in Devon:[51] such things differ little from the ordinary anonymous letter, threatening, abusive, or merely slanderous.

Under this rubric, as another illustration of traditional tenacity, I may note that the story of The Beggar's Curse has survived to modern times among the people. Sigebert of Gembloux tells it under date of 606. A poor man asked alms of some sailors. The master of the vessel replied, "We have nothing on board but stones." "Let everything turn to stones then!" retorted the beggar. And this happened forthwith to all the articles of food in the vessel, though they retained their original forms and colors. From Sigebert the tale was copied into English chronicles, as well as into the Alphabetum Narrationum, and we find it still current in Lincolnshire, with some variation — a farmer for the shipmaster, and wheat for bread.[52]

Certain great stones, — associated, no doubt, with pagan worship, — are known in Wales and Ireland as "cursing stones." [53] There are "cursing wells," too, in Great Britain,[54] and "wishing wells," which abound, are available for banning as well as for blessing.[55] Teutonic myth and tradition and mediæval romance are crowded with tales of heroes, and *Weisse Frauen*, and treasures, — all under a ban, — of accursed castles and cities and waste lands.[56]

The burial of metal tablets engraved with spells against an enemy is a learned species of magic to which educated Englishmen resorted now and then in the sixteenth and seventeenth centuries. In 1899 a small leaden plate was dug up at Lincoln's Inn which invokes the spirits of the moon "That Nothinge maye prosper Nor goe forwarde that Raufe Scrope takethe in hande." Scrope was admitted to Lincoln's Inn in 1543; he was treasurer for a year in 1564–65, and one of the Governors from 1570 until his death in 1572.[57] Similar tab-

lets have been discovered at Dymock in Gloucestershire,[58] on
Gatherley Moor in Richmondshire,[59] and near a disused
burial ground at Kettleby near Brigg.[60] In 1540 John Heron
was sent to the Privy Council by Sir Richard Long with a letter about "a sceptre and certain caractes in a plate touching
conjuracions" found in Heron's lodging.[61] But these were
probably not curses.

Men or domestic animals may be elfshot, and the little flint
arrowheads thus projected are often found in field or byre.[62]
This method of injury was and is particularly at home in
Ireland and Scotland; and Scottish examples were of great
interest to Pepys and Dr. George Hickes, as their correspondence shows.[63] But a magnificent verse-charm in Anglo-
Saxon proves the strength of this superstition among our
English ancestors. "Out, little spear, if herein it be! . . . The
mighty witch-wives sent shrieking darts: I will send another
flying arrow back against them. . . . Out, little spear, if
herein it be! Six smiths sat; deadly spears they wrought.
Out, spear — not in, spear! If there be a bit of iron herein,
the work of a witch, it shall melt. If thou wert in skin shot, or
wert in flesh shot, or wert in blood shot, or wert in limb shot,
never be thy life threatened! If it were a shot of the Æsir,[64]
or were a shot of elves, or were a shot of a witch, now will I
help thee. This is cure for thee of shot of Æsir, this is cure
for thee of shot of elves, this is cure for thee of shot of a witch.
I will help thee." [65] "Shotten" (i. e. elf-shotten) horses and
cattle are several times treated in the Old English Leechdoms: the cures involve ointment, prayer, masses, holy
water, and magic rites with knife and rod.[66] A pseudo-Para-
celsan tract declares that witches by their arts insert things
into a man's body which must be extracted if the patient is
to recover, and Richard Baxter gives an instance of such procedure. Samuel Rowlands the satirist in 1602 knew of persons who pretended to have the art of shooting needles into
the flesh.[67] Among the fraudulent pretensions of Elizabethan
sharpers, so Robert Greene tells us, — and he knew if anybody did, for he was a cony-catcher himself, — was the power
"to fill a Letter full of Needles, which shall bee laide after
such a Mathematicall order, that when hee opens it to whome
it is sent, they shall all spring vp and flye into his body as

forceably, as if they had beene blowne vp with gunpowder, or
sent from a Calleeuers mouth like small shotte."[68] An evil
spirit of the poltergeist sort in 1762 stuck pins galore into
various parts of the bodies of Molly and Dobby Giles of Bristol — so Mr. Henry Durbin, Chymist, declares in his circumstantial narrative.[69] Wier finds it necessary to ridicule the
belief of his time that witches, by the devil's aid, send into the
bodies of their victims straws, pigs' bristles, fish-bones, thorns,
etc.[70] So Malay and Nigerian wizards and Melanesian ghosts
shoot darts that kill unless extracted by a medicine man.[71]
Here belongs also the Australian wizardry with "pointing
bones."[72] Very similar were the powers claimed by the
Martha's Vineyard powwaws and credited to them by the
English: "Their Practice was," writes Matthew Mayhew,
"either by desiring the Spirit to them appearing to perform,
what mischief they intended; or to form a piece of Leather
like an *Arrow-head*, tying an Hair thereto; or using some
Bone, as of Fish (that it might be known Witchcraft, to the
bewitch'd) over which they perform'd certain *Ceremonies*;
and dismiss'd 'em to effect their desire." And such things, he
adds, have actually entered the flesh and been extracted.[73]
A Melanesian healer used to cure toothache by removing a
little maggot,[74] which she would show to the sufferer. Others,
in stripping off the poultices which they apply to the sick,
profess to take away at the same time the snake or lizard that
has caused the pain.[75] Medicine men among the Nagas of
India extract from their patients pebbles, fragments of leaf,
scraps of bone, bits of wood (for rheumatism), a lump of hair
from the throat in a case of coughing.[76] Examples of such
trickery may be accumulated *ad libitum*.[77]

Witch narratives from Britain and the Continent abound
in examples of sufferers who vomited or voided bones, pins,
nails, needles, bits of lead, farthings, whetstones, nutshells,
rushes, balls of wool or hair, and so on, which the witch had
somehow conveyed into the system.[78] When Edward Bonavant of Reading (1634) was in his fits, thought to be caused
by the witchcraft of William Walles and his wife, he felt as it
were a mouse inside his body.[79] One of the Essex witches executed in 1645 under the Hopkins régime, told John Stearne
that if a certain imp of hers which tried to get into his mouth

had gone down his throat "there would have been a feast of toads in his belly." Such, at least, was Stearne's evidence.[80] To cure possession, Drage informs us in his "treatise on sicknesses and diseases from witchcraft and supernatural causes" (1665), "herbs are boiled in a Pot, over which the bewitched do hold their heads, when the fit approaches; Maister *Gibbons* of *Harborough* cured one so; and like a Mouse leaped forth of her mouth, and she was absolutely freed; a Gentleman living nigh *Huntingdon*, who told me, was Spectatour. Others were [cured] with some stinking Suffumige cast on Coals; so was a Maid I knew cured, a Mouse in similitude, leaped from her Mouth, held open when the fit approached."[81]

We may conclude with a lively anecdote that points with unmoving finger at the close correspondence between European witchcraft and the beliefs and practices of savage life. Dean Granville of Durham tells the tale as 't was told him by a French physician of Provence. A patient suffering from melancholia was convinced beyond persuasion that he was possessed of the devil. The shrewd doctor, falling in with the man's humor, visited him one day with a priest and a surgeon, and took along a bat in a bag. He explained that he could relieve him if he would consent to a slight operation. Prayer was offered, and the surgeon made a small incision in the man's side. Then the physician, "having the bat in readynesse, just as the cut was given, let flye the bat about the chamber; crying out, 'Behold, there the divel is gon.' The man beleived it and was cured."[82]

CHAPTER VI

VENEFICA

WHEN the plague desolated Athens in the year 430 B.C., the rumor ran that the Lacedæmonians had poisoned the cisterns.[1] In our Civil War many of us in the North believed that the Southerners were trying to spread yellow fever among us by consignments of infected clothes or bedding. In the latest of our wars the Germans were popularly accused not only of well-poisoning and the like but even of attempting to ruin the wheat crop of our Western states by shipments of poisonous pollen.[2] In 1920 Sir Hamar Greenwood, Chief Secretary for Ireland, read in the House of Commons a letter which he said had been captured in a raid. It purported to be from the commander-in-chief of the Republican army and contemplated the spreading of glanders among the British cavalry horses and of typhoid by means of infected milk among the troops.[3] Even in time of peace such rumors are rife. In 1884, during an outbreak of cholera, there was rioting in the country near Turin, because the peasantry suspected the upper classes of endeavoring to poison them.[4] There was more or less excitement in 1911 over the report that unscrupulous speculators, to raise the price of cotton, were spreading the boll weevil in Georgia and the Carolinas.[5] Recent newspapers report the poisoning of a well used by Colorado miners and the local suspicion that it was the work of a "strike sympathizer."[6]

Throughout the years that intervene between the Plague at Athens and our own enlightened age of science, this kind of belief has been prevalent,[7] as, for example, at Rome in the first and second centuries after Christ, when the pestilence was ascribed to the activity of wretches who killed their victims by pricking them with sharp instruments smeared with mortal drugs;[8] and in the first half of the sixteenth century (ca. 1536), when some forty Italian conspirators (one of them a hangman) undertook, it was said, to start the plague

afresh by means of a deadly ointment.[9] A like outbreak at
Milan in 1630 has been immortalized by Manzoni.[10] In 1258
many died of poison in England and a general plot was
feared.[11] Any unpopular class may be suspected: in 1427 a
hundred and fifty casks of sweet wine were condemned; the
fumes had a horrible stench; the Lombards of London were
accused of poisoning the wine.[12] With such plots, of course,
the black art has often been associated, for poisoners have always been suspected of sorcery and sorcerers of poisoning.[13]
Instructed by the devil himself or enabled thereto by their
own diabolical skill (however originating), witches and wizards could compound actual poisons (as no doubt they often
did), or could imbrue harmless things with noxious qualities,[14] so as to destroy not only individual victims, but whole
communities as well.[15] Sometimes they threw their accursed
potions into the wells,[16] sometimes they scattered them in the
air,[17] sometimes they daubed them on walls or on the handles
of doors.[18] Thus came various diseases, even the plague.
Now this accusation was brought against the Jews, now
against the lepers,[19] now against some imagined confederacy
of sorcerers. There is great variety in details, but none in the
main idea.[20] *Venefica* as a stock word for "witch" tells its
own story. Medicine men and white witches are the primitive physicians, and thus they may on fit occasion prove to
be such practitioners as Dr. Palmer and Dr. Pritchard of infamous memory.

　Even Reginald Scot was convinced that many so-called
witches were in fact poisoners. "It appeareth," he tells us,
that women "have been the first inventers, and the greatest
practisers of poisoning, and more naturallie addicted and
given thereunto than men." He quotes many authorities, ancient and modern. In particular he recites, with full credence, the Italian case in 1536, when forty "*Veneficæ* or
witches" renewed the plague by smearing the doors and door-
posts with an ointment and powder to the destruction of
whole families, and he adds two recent Italian instances of
similar crime. "This art consisteth," he tells us, "as well in
poisoning of cattell as of men: and that which is doone by
poisons unto cattell, towards their destruction, is as common-
lie attributed to witches charms as the other. And I doubt

not, but some that would be thought cunning in incantations, and to doo miracles, have experience in this behalf." We observe, too, that Scot is convinced that many pretending witches administer philtres, which potions, he contends, cannot procure love, but "are meere poisons, bereaving some of the benefit of the braine, and so of the sense and understanding of the mind. And from some it taketh awaie life, and that is more common than the other." [21] And he declares expressly that in case persons accused of witchcraft "confesse that, which hath beene indeed committed by them, as poisoning, or anie other kind of murther, which falleth into the power of such persons to accomplish; I stand not to defend their cause." He adds, however, that the judges should take care to ascertain that the means used were adequate to the deed confessed.[22]

Poisoning and sorcery are both involved in the *cause célèbre* of George of Clarence.[23] On the Sunday before Christmas, 1476, his wife Isabella died, and his second son, Richard, followed her on New Year's Day. At the next spring sessions for Warwickshire (1477), the widow Ankerett Twinnewe (or Twynmowe or Twynyho), late servant of the Duke and Duchess, was indicted for poisoning her mistress, and Sir Roger Tocotes, Knight, also of the Duke's household, for abetting. At the same time John Thuresby, yeoman, was indicted for poisoning Clarence's son. The Duke himself was prosecutor. He acted with illegal violence in the arrest of Ankerett and extorted a verdict of guilty by overawing the court. Some of the jurors were so remorseful that they begged her to forgive them. The cases were transferred to the King's Bench by writ of *certiorari*, but Ankerett and Thuresby had already been hanged. Tocotes, who had avoided arrest, surrendered on hearing of the writ, had a fair trial in the higher court, and was acquitted. In 1478, on petition of Ankerett's grandson, the judgment and record in her case were annulled.[24] On May 19, 1477, soon after the execution of the widow Ankerett, three persons, one of them closely associated with Clarence, were convicted of constructive treason: — Thomas Burdett, Gentleman, Clarence's friend; John Stacy, Gentleman; and Thomas Blake, clerk. The indictments make Burdett the instigator. He employed

Stacy and Blake, on November 12, 1474, "to calculate the nativities of the King, and of Edward Prince of Wales," and "to know when the King and the Prince should die," and, on the sixth of February following, this pair "worked and calculated by art magic, necromancy, and astronomy, the death and final destruction of the King and Prince"; and again on May 20, 1475, they "did falsely and treacherously work in the said arts, although according to the determinations of Holy Church, and the opinions of divers Doctors, it is forbidden to any liegeman thus to meddle concerning Kings and Princes in manner aforesaid, without their permission." All were found guilty, but Blake was pardoned.[25]

So far nothing emerges that can definitely be called sorcery. Clarence thought his wife had been poisoned — he may or may not have regarded the widow Twynyho as a witch; Burdett and his accomplices were guilty of using astrology (and possibly incantations in connection therewith) to find out when the king and the prince were to die — and that was treason, even if they used no spells to destroy them. But we have further information. Stacy, it appears, was famous not only as an astrologer (*astronomus*) but as a great magician (*magnus necromanticus*). He had been accused (and perhaps this was the primary charge) of yielding to the solicitation of the adulterous wife of Richard Lord Beauchamp so far as to make leaden images to procure the death of this nobleman, and, when examined under torture concerning his magical practices, he had confessed "many things" against himself and Burdett, presumably including the treasonable calculations just described. At the foot of the gallows both he and Stacy had declared their innocence — Stacy feebly, Burdett with many words and great spirit. This was the same Stacy who had misled the Duke of Suffolk years before by an ambiguous warning to beware of the Tower.[26] On the day after their execution Clarence had the temerity to bring Dr. William Goddard into the King's Council and to have him read the dying declaration of Stacy and Burdett. The king was highly incensed and ordered Clarence's arrest. He never regained his liberty.[27] In the following February (1478) he was convicted by bill of attainder, and among the charges in the bill there are three that particularly concern us: he had spread the report that Burdett "was wrongefully putte to Deth"; "he saide and laboured also to be noysed by suche his Servauntez, apte for that werk, that the Kyng oure Sovereigne Lorde, wroght by Nygromancye, and used Crafte to poyson his Subyettes, suche as hym pleased"; [28] he declared "that the Kyng entended to consume hym [Clarence] in like wyse as a Candell consumeth in brennyng." Perhaps he had suggested that the poisoning of his duchess (which nobody now credits) was done by the king's order or with the king's complicity. The reference to the candle suggests that he had charged the king with the particular kind of murderous magic (*envoûtement*) which we have already discussed. Anyhow, he was condemned, and, according to the usual story, he was drowned in a butt of wine.[29]

CHAPTER VII

CHARMS GHOULISH AND PROFANE

FRAGMENTS of dead mortality have been used in spells and as remedies from ancient times. Pliny enumerates such superstitions in a curious passage.[1] For the blackest of black magic we have the testimony of Tacitus, who tells us that after the death of Germanicus there were found remnants of human bodies, spells and curses and the name of Germanicus engraved on leaden tablets, half-burned ashes smeared with corruption, and other *maleficia* by which souls are believed to be devoted to the gods below.[2] For the middle ages in general the evidence of the distinguished Florentine jurist Paolo Grillando may serve. The cool prose of his catalogue of horrors makes the thing as vivid as it is gruesome: "Some take a small piece of a buried corpse, — especially the corpse of one who has been hanged or has otherwise suffered a shameful death, — and use, in compounding their *sortilegia*, the nails or teeth, the hair, ears, eyes, beard, hand, foot, finger, . . . heart, liver, lungs, . . . sinews, bones, or flesh." [3] "At this day," says Bacon, "the mortalest poisons practised by the West Indians have some mixture of the blood or fat or flesh of men; and divers witches and sorcerers, as well amongst the heathen as amongst the Christians, have fed upon man's flesh, to aid (as it seemeth) their imagination with high and foul vapours." [4] Oldham in his Fourth Satire (1679) mentions

> Felons Bones from rifled Gibbets torn;
> Like those, which some old Hag at midnight steals,
> For Witchcrafts, Amulets, and Charms, and Spells.[5]

Savage wizards are commonly believed to exhume corpses and eat them.[6] In 1904 three men were executed in the West Indian island of Saint Lucia for the murder of a boy. Their motive was to procure his hands and heart (and perhaps also his head) for obeah practice.[7]

Remnants of the dead are still popular in spells or as cures.[8] A dead man's hand (especially if he has been hanged or has met with any violent or untimely death) will cure eczema, wens, tumors, goitre, and the king's evil, and will erase unsightly birthmarks. The efficacy of the dead hand was known to Pliny and is derided by Fernel, the modern Galen.[9] The Cumberland receipt for birthmarks is to stroke the spot with the hands of three heads of families who died on the same day: this is what Sir Thomas Browne calls "committing any maculated part unto the touch of the dead." [10] You can cure toothache or ward it off by biting out a tooth from a corpse or skull, particularly if you carry the tooth in your pocket; [11] or you may rub the gum with a dead finger,[12] or "scarifie the gums in the greefe with the tooth of one that hath beene slaine." [13] Powdered skull is good for fits.[14] Moss scraped from a skull, pulverized and taken as cephalic snuff, cures headache.[15] Drinking from a suicide's skull (or from any human skull if freshly exhumed) cures epilepsy.[16] Chronic headache vanishes if you drive a nail into a dead man's skull.[17] You can cure a corn by cutting it with a razor that has shaved a corpse.[18] For scrofula one should wear the napkin from a dead man's face round the neck and then drop it on his coffin in the grave.[19] For headache "tie a halter about your head wherewith one hath beene hanged" [20] — a suicide's noose, according to Pliny.[21] A hangman's rope is good for scrofula,[22] and a bit of it ensures luck in gambling.[23] A piece of suicide's rope worn as a girdle protects you against all accidents.[24] Chips from a gallows on which several have been hanged, when worn in a bag round the neck, cure the ague.[25] A fragment of a gibbet is good for toothache.[26] Warts disappear when sprinkled with earth from a new-made grave.[27] To lay a child in such a grave is helpful in eye trouble.[28] Churchyard grass will cure the bite of a mad dog.[29] Bits of lead cut from church spouts that empty in the churchyard are good for fits.[30] Churchyard earth is good for stitch in the side and consumption.[31] A two hours' burial in the churchyard may help one's rheumatism.[32] A ring made of a coffin hinge or handle will relieve cramp.[33] In some of these remedies one recognizes the principle of transferring the pain or ailment to the dead man and thus putting an end to it along with the other earthly troubles of the departed.[34] Similar, perhaps, was the rationale of the advice on which Joan Sargeant acted in 1532: "Whereas she had a child syk a certen walkynge man or beggar shewed her that she shold cutt her saide childes gyrdill in fyve peces and then to go to the churche and say v Paternosters and fyve aveyes and then to take the same peces of the gurdill and hide hit in v sondry growndes and so she dyd." [35]

A grisly act of black magic was prescribed in Anglo-Saxon times for a woman who, having lost one child, feared miscarriage or stillbirth: she was to take earth from the grave of her dead baby, wrap it in black wool, and sell it to some merchant, repeating this spell: "I sell it — and may ye sell it — this black wool and the grains of this sorrow!"[36] To burn grain on the spot where a man has died — the object being to cure disease or ward it off — is a custom forbidden along with other pagan superstitions in many penitentials, English and Continental, of the Anglo-Saxon age.[37] From the Visitation Books of York Cathedral for 1510 it appears that a woman in Newbald Parish had recently conducted herself in a strange way ("demey[n]d hir marvelously"). She had taken the covering of the bier, and a ploughstave that had killed a man, and a cloth from under a corpse, and had laid them upon her cow, doubtless as a curative spell, though that is not stated.[38]

The eleventh-century Latin paraphrase of Æthelstan's Laws mentions necromancy,[39] and so do the Canons of Edgar, which, if somewhat later than that king's time, still belong in the tenth century.[40] Nigromantia, writes John of Salisbury, in the twelfth century, is so called because it concerns itself altogether *in mortuorum inquisitione*; its efficacy seems to consist in its power to wake the dead; but it is really the deceit of tricky demons and the perfidy of impostors.[41] Odin in the Old Norse Havamál, speaking in the character of a wizard, declares that he knows many spells, and among them one that will call down a corpse from the gallows and force it to speak.[42] The fourteenth-century Apology for Lollard Doctrines defines "nigramauncers" as those who "by figures or markings upon the dead body of beast or of man, operate to get knowledge or to work [magic] or to influence God." [43] To this department, then, might be referred the divination by the lines in a sheep's shoulder-bone condemned by Chaucer's Parson.[44] The violation of graves so often mentioned in old penitentials, was probably for the sake of rifling the dead in most cases, though the idea of obtaining materials for black magic is not excluded.[45]

In 1371 a Southwark wizard was arrested "with the head and face of a dead man" in his possession, as well as a book of sorcery. He was brought before Justice Knivet in the King's Bench, but, since there was no indictment, he was discharged after taking an oath "that he would never be a sorcerer." The head and the book were burned at the expense of the prisoner![46]

In 1324 Dame Alice Kyteler, it was alleged, used, among other ingredients, the brain and clouts of an unbaptized infant and the hair and nails of corpses (boiled in the skull of a beheaded robber) in the manufacture of the drugs, unguents, and powders with which she worked malefic witchcraft. And this same skull was the pot wherein she prepared the tallow for her infernal candles.[47] The Witch of Endor, in the once-admired Biblical epic of Du Bartas (1544–1590), uses in her necromancy a "puant Flambeau" made of the fat of her own son.[48] In an old East Indian tale a Brahmin carries a candle of human fat while searching for hidden treasure; when it fell from his hand, he knew that he had discovered the right spot.[49] Such a candle, according to a current belief reported by Cardano, reveals the whereabouts of secret hoards by a hissing sound when near the place and by going out when very close.[50] According to Deacon and Walker, distinguished authorities of the early seventeenth century, "A notable experiment of . . . deceiuing of *senses*, may fitly be found in a *candle* of *Adders grease*: which (all the while it be burning alone in the night) will cause all the *russhes* strawed in the *parlour*, to seeme as if they were *crawling snakes*." [51] This quotation dates from 1601. Four years later one Whitehead, brought before the Star Chamber for forgery, confessed or boasted "that he coude turne all the rushes in a Roome into spirites and serpentes." [52] From Southern India we learn that a lighted lamp filled with oil prepared from a kind of tree-snake makes its bearer appear to be covered with running serpents of a green color.[53] This kind of witchery is credited to thieves in Ceylon: they can make a house seem to swarm with serpents by applying a little whip-snake oil to the flame of a lamp.⁵⁴ Burglars' use of the Hand of Glory — a dead man's hand burning as a candle to cause sleep, or to reveal who is asleep in the house and who is awake — is a persistent superstition familiar to every reader of The Ingoldsby Legends.⁵⁵

Throughout the middle ages, and in modern times as well, the Christian Church has had to struggle against the abuse of its sacraments, ordinances, ceremonies, and holy things for profane purposes,⁵⁶ particularly by would-be sorcerers, but also at the hands of well-meaning but ignorant persons who cannot distinguish between a prayer and a spell and who insist on misapplying religious rites and on employing holy objects in unauthorized ways — for "white magic," for instance, as a means of cure.⁵⁷ The superstitious in Sussex in the sixties of the last century were wont to take the communion whenever they felt ill.⁵⁸ This reminds one of the decree of the Council of Arles (ca. 450) to the effect that baptized demoniacs should be admitted to full communion in order to be freed from the devil who was tormenting them.⁵⁹ To be confirmed over and over again is likewise a common remedy for ailments: one old woman is on record who was bishopped, as she called it, seven times; she said it helped her rheumatism.⁶⁰ Reiterated baptism is forbidden in Anglo-Saxon penitentials and denounced by Ælfric.⁶¹ When the famous Celtic scholar Edward Lhwyd was collecting antiquarian material from different Welsh parishes he learned that in one of them "the ordinary women are hardly brought to look upon Churching otherwise than as a charm to prevent witchcraft and think that grass will hardly ever grow where they tread before they are churched." ⁶²

It has never been easy — even for theologians — to discriminate between a prayer and a spell. The orthodox view, however, is plain enough: normal prayers are proper and commendable, but spells are not removed from the category of illicit magic or witchcraft by the mere intermingling of sacred names and biblical texts (see p. 31). Take, for instance, the case of Agnes Hancok in 1438. She was a healer who professed, among other things, to cure children afflicted by the spirits which the common people call "feyry"; but her practice involved communication with these unclean spirits, whose advice she was said to seek whenever she pleased.[63] Agnes protested that she used only medicines and prayers. However, when she repeated her prayers by the bishop's command, he heard therein "certain strange and unknown words" which she could not interpret; and so she was obliged to abjure.[64]

Even a prayer or a passage of scripture might become a spell if used unlawfully or by unauthorized persons. It was wrong, for instance, to have recourse to the bible for divination, or to wear sacred texts as amulets.[65] Such malfeasance was strictly prohibited by the Anglo-Saxon church (p. 30), but it was hard to control and has persisted in spite of ecclesiastical denunciation.[66] I have heard an old man on Cape Cod — half in jest, perhaps, but assuredly half in earnest — attempt to bespell a snake by reciting over and over again, as fast as he could speak, "The seed of the woman shall bruise the serpent's head! The seed of the woman shall bruise the serpent's head!"[67] This same text was efficacious in the hands of a boy at Nottingham in 1672. After reading the folk-book of Dr. Faustus, he engraved with his knife on a pale "the words of the contract there expressed," sprinkled his blood upon them, and subscribed his name. The devil met him and made brilliant promises; but the boy was frightened, "reformed exceedingly," and "prayed much." One night, while he was at prayer, the devil appeared and bade him give over; but "he prayed still, leaning on his bed-side." Then "the bed lifted up leisurely till it was beyond his reach." Opening his bible at the text in question, he laid it upon the bed, which "came gradually down again." The hero of the incident became a preacher; but he was worried about the contract, for it remained uncancelled in the devil's hands.[68] In a gross form we detect the same idea in the mind of the bewitched Shropshire woman who laid a leaf of the bible over her heart;[69] and of the Welsh farmer who read a chapter to his sick cow;[70] and of the Devonshire yeoman who, after losing pig after pig by witchcraft, bought another and protected it by putting a bible over the door of the sty.[71] In Yorkshire a certain leaf of the bible under the flagstone in front of the

doorstep makes a thief stumble when he enters.[72] Giraldus
Cambrensis records a case in which a sick person was cured
by the application of a copy of the Gospel of Matthew.[73]
Among Cranmer's Articles for visitation in 1548 occurs the
following enquiry: "Whether any persone hath abused the
Ceremonies, as in castyng holy Water vpon his Bed, or bear-
yng aboute hym, holy Bread, saincte Jhons Gospell, ryngyng
of holy Belles, or kepyng of priuate holy daies, as Taylors,
Bakers, Brewers, Smithes, Shoomakers, and suche other." [74]
According to an Anglo-Saxon Leech Book, to make a "holy
drink" for a man afflicted with elf-disease (or nightmare) the
first five verses of St. John's Gospel and other texts were to
be written upon the housel-dish (the sacramental paten);
then five herbs were to be soaked in water that had been
dipped up (against the stream) by a pure person, and the
writing on the paten was to be washed off into the mixture;
then hallowed wine was to be poured in, and three masses
were to be sung over the whole![75] There is a similar use of the
paten in a medicine for fever.[76] William of Malmesbury mentions the biblical *sortes* and also specifies black magic by inversion: a psalm sung backward acts as an evil spell, and the
woman who sings it he styles a witch (*venefica*).[77] The Anglo-
Saxon Leechdoms, which testify abundantly to the belief
that many ailments come from demons, elves, or witches,[78]
make free use of holy water as an ingredient in herb-drinks
for men and animals,[79] as well as in ointment for sick or elf-
shotten cattle and horses.[80] Baptismal water,[81] holy salt,[82]
holy oil,[83] holy bread,[84] hallowed garlic,[85] and lichen from the
rood,[86] are likewise utilized. The recipes are complicated by
divers rites, prayers, and spells, both in the preparation and
in the administration, and masses (one, three, four, seven,
nine, or twelve) are sometimes to be sung over the herbs or
the unguent.[87] Thus the mixture of paganism and Christianity is strikingly manifest.

Giraldus also tells of wicked priests who pervert the sacrament of the altar to black magic, celebrating masses over
waxen images for the sake of cursing some victim, or singing
the *missa Fidelium* ten times or more, with an imprecation, in
order that the person may die before the tenth day or soon
after and be buried with the dead.[88] Here belongs also the

baptism of a waxen image by the name of the man or woman who is to be destroyed by melting or stabbing it (p. 76). To christen a cock or a cat seems to have been rather common in magical rites.[89] On April 30, 1649, Isabella Billington was executed at York for crucifying her mother and offering a calf and a cock as a burnt sacrifice; her husband, too, was hanged as an accomplice: what their object was, does not appear.[90]

A grotesque and rather horrifying mixture of ancient magic with Christian superstition is the Devonshire custom of creeping thrice under the communion table at midnight on Midsummer Eve to be cured of fits.[91] Here the table, replacing the altar, is a substitute for the cleft ashtree or holed stone or loop of turf through which, in accordance with primeval ideas, sufferers creep or children are passed for relief from rickets, hernia, and other troubles [92] — a practice forbidden as devilish in Anglo-Saxon times (p. 31). In recent years in the Hebrides, to guard against whooping cough, a boy was passed three times over the back and under the belly of an ass in the name of the Blessed Trinity; then a bit of bread was broken in two, and one half was eaten by the boy and the other by the donkey.[93] I fear the bread in this instance was originally the consecrated host. In several counties of England a like ceremony (without the bread) is observed for various diseases, and sometimes a piebald or skewbald horse or a bear replaces the ass.[94] The ass is traditionally a sacred animal (as in the mediæval Feast of Asses) because of our Lord's triumphal entry into Jerusalem upon an ass's back,[95] — also, perhaps, because of the Flight into Egypt, — and accordingly it has a cross upon its neck. Hairs from this cross are sometimes administered to a child between two slices of bread as a cure for whooping cough.[96]

The wine of the eucharist is still regarded as efficacious in disease or physical weakness.[97] This idea is mentioned by Reginald Scot, who of course repudiates it: — "*A charme for the choine cough* [i. e. whooping cough]. Take three sips of a chalice, when the preest hath said masse, and swallow it downe with good devotion." [98] The wine is particularly valued for this purpose in modern England if it can be obtained from a Roman Catholic priest.[99] In 1538 there was trouble at Rye because "the curate, as a witch, gave Hamper's child drink three times of the chalice for the chyne cough." [100] Water from a running stream and "hallowed wine" are used in an Anglo-Saxon recipe for a "holy drink" to cure a man who suffers from nightmare or other goblin infestation. [101]

In 1612 James Device, one of the Lancashire group, testified that old Demdike, his grandmother, bade him take the communion on Shere Thursday. He was not to swallow the bread but "to bring it and deliuer it to such a thing as should meet him in his way homewards." However, James did swallow the bread, and the thing that met him, a demon hare, was very angry. [102] Traces of these ideas persist in England. [103] Lincolnshire folk-lore teaches that, if a woman keeps the communion bread in her mouth and feeds it to a toad which is waiting in the churchyard, her man will consent to marry her. Similar action will enable you to be a witch according to Berkshire superstition: the toad is Satan. [104] A young girl in Lincolnshire was informed a little while ago that when she went to her first communion she would become a witch if she kept half of the bread in her mouth. [105] A bit of the host has even been used as a charm to ensure victory in cock-fighting. [106] The host as a love-charm was well-known in the middle ages and later. Grillando prosecuted a clerk of religion who swallowed a part of the host himself and sent the rest, ground to powder, to a woman with whom he was in love, that she might take it in her food or drink. [107] Cæsarius of Heisterbach, whose stories were extremely popular in the middle ages, tells of a lascivious priest who, after saying mass, kept the wafer in his mouth, hoping that, if he thus kissed a woman whom he was vainly wooing, she would yield. He found, however, that he was miraculously prevented from leaving the church. [108] A woman who was a great sufferer confessed that when she was a young girl her garden was infested with caterpillars. One night she told her troubles to a vagabond wench to whom she had given lodging. The woman advised her to pulverize a host and sprinkle the powder over the growing vegetables. This saved the garden, but she paid the penalty by ill health thereafter. [109] There is a twelfth-century story of a peasant who hid the host in a hole in his pigpen to protect the swine from disease. [110] In the same century a poor rustic had heard from some wicked impostor that he would soon grow rich if he carried the *corpus Domini* about with him always: so he kept the bread in his mouth at communion and sewed it up in his cape.[111] A favorite mediæval tale, as old as the twelfth century and told and retold with slight variations, is that of the man or woman who put a bit of the consecrated wafer in a beehive to check disease or to increase the supply of honey; the pious bees built a little church of wax about the wafer, with towers, windows, altar, and all. This legend turns up in Giraldus Cambrensis and in several collections of *exempla*, some of them made in England.[112] Dan Michel of Kent, in 1340, writes of the abuse of the host by witches and evil-minded priests.[113] In a fourteenth-century collection of pious tales, made in England, we learn of a sorceress who broke it into four parts, meaning to use it for incantations.[114] In 1532 (and this is historical fact) three hosts were stolen from a church at Aldgate on Good Friday, perhaps for magical purposes.[115] In 1582 the wife of Edward Jones was required to prove to the satisfaction of the Archdeacon of Lewes "that she did eat the Communion bread and put yt not in hir glove." [116]

The water of baptism is still regarded as efficacious in various complaints — toothache, for instance, and somnambulism — and for a charm to ensure good luck.[117] This points back to an old malpractice, for water "hallowed with font-hallowing" was an ingredient in certain salves of the Anglo-Saxons, the herbs used in one of their fumigations were dipped in font-water, and this was an ingredient in their medicinal draughts.[118] Early in the thirteenth century, in a Council held at Durham by Bishop Richard de Marisco, it was ordered that "fonts should be kept locked on account of sorcery (*propter sortilegia*)," and that chrism and holy oil should be likewise guarded.[119] In 1287, at the Synod of Exeter under Bishop Peter Quivil, it was ordered that each church should have a stone baptistery well locked (*bene seratum*).[120] From this time down, well into the sixteenth century, there is abundant evidence about font-covers, and many complaints turn up in visitations that the font in this or that church is not duly provided with a lock.[121] The highest English authority on canon law, Bishop Lyndewoode (who died in

446), in commenting on these precautions, remarks of the *ortilegia* that it is "more respectable to pass them over in silence than to specify them."[122] One regrets his scruples, but we do not actually need his testimony. Holy water from font or piscina, — as also the holy oil of baptism, of chrism, and of extreme unction, — was regarded as a powerful ingredient in love-potions.[123] Holy water was used to baptize images of wax that were employed in the blackest of black magic — amatory or malefic.[124] Two women at Rome, whom Grillando saw, confessed that they had anointed their lips with baptismal oil to make their kisses seductive.[125]

A silver coin from the offertory is good for sore eyes and other complaints: if carried in the pocket, it keeps off rheumatism. A ring made out of such a coin cures epilepsy, scrofula, paralysis, and fits.[126] Doubtless gold would be still better for the eyes — for everybody knows that gold coins or gold rings (especially wedding rings) are good to rub on styes or weak eyes [127] — but the village offertory is not rich in gold. "Do not all old people," wrote the Rev. George Plaxton to Thoresby in 1709, "wipe their eyes with Jacobuses when they meet with them, as an opthalmique charm to mend the sight?" [128] A pious Quaker in 1699 bequeathed a gold ring for poor Friends to have "to wash sore eyes with." [129] Lead stolen from a church window during service is a curative amulet.[130] Water from the leads or roof of a church is a valuable remedy.[131] Grease from the church bells may be used as an ointment for ringworm, warts, and piles.[132] Here again we touch elbows with our remote ancestors: the Anglo-Saxon Leech Book prescribes for a "fiend-sick man" a medicine compounded of ale, garlic, holy water, church lichen from a cross, and ten different herbs, and directs that the patient shall drink it out of a church bell.[133] It was rather hard measure to put English rustics to their penance for relying on the charms operated by local healers, and at the same time to bid them trust the Royal Touch for the King's Evil and to teach them that consecrated finger-rings were good for cramp.[134]

CHAPTER VIII

WIND AND WEATHER

"VENTOS abigoque vocoque" says Ovid's Medea.[1] Archbishop Agobard of Lyons (who died A.D. 840), in a special tract "Against the Foolish Notions of the People about Hail and Thunder," inveighs against the *tempestarii* or weather-wizards of his time: "wretched creatures who declare that they can not only bring on storms but also can protect the inhabitants from them," and who levy a tariff on their clients, far more punctually paid than the tithes.[2] We find, accordingly, that belief in such witchcraft came to be regarded as superstitious and was treated as a sin that deserved a heavy penance.[3] But folk-lore was too strong for the rational theologians; they had to swing into line, and throughout the middle ages the old doctrine of witches (or devils) and weather, remained in full force — a doctrine inherited from primeval times and still shared by civilized man and savage the world over.[4] The Penitential ascribed to Ecgbert (Archbishop of York from 732 to 766) assigns seven years' penance for any sender-forth of storms (*emissor tempestatum*), and so do the penitentials of Pseudo-Cummean and Pseudo-Theodore.[5] Such *tempestarii* are similarly treated in other manuals of the kind on the Continent as early as the eighth century,[6] and are likewise condemned in the Laws of the Visigoths and in Charlemagne's Capitularies.[7]

Bede tells us that when St. Germanus and Bishop Lupus were sailing from France to Britain to rescue the land from the Pelagian heresy, "the hostile violence of demons" raised a furious tempest.[8] An elaborate Anglo-Saxon charm or prayer (it may well be taken either way) for safety in general, and in particular for protection and favorable winds on a voyage, refers with sufficient clearness to demons: — "the grim terror"; "the great fear that is hateful to every one"; "Let no nightmare harm me"; "that I may be guarded

against the hateful ones that pursue my life." ⁹ According to
the Anglo-Saxon Herbarium, the castor-oil plant or its seed
protects from hail and, on a ship, quells storms; it should be
gathered with a prayer or spell (given in Latin and English)
addressed directly to the herb.¹⁰

Saint Godric, the twelfth-century hermit of Finchale, once
saw a terrible demon who vomited black storm clouds from
his mouth and caused flood and famine in all the region.¹¹
Two famous historical events may be cited in comparison,
both illustrating the ascription of such phenomena to the arts
of sorcery. In a desperate battle with the Quadi (A.D. 174)
the army of Marcus Aurelius was refreshed by a rain when
perishing with heat and thirst, and at the same time the bar-
barians were overwhelmed by a storm of fire and hail; and the
rain which refreshed the Romans, burned like oil when it fell
upon the Quadi. This marvellous storm was said to have
been caused by the magic arts of one Arnuphis, an Egyptian
in the service of the emperor. Christian writers, however,
preferred to ascribe it to a legion of Christians, afterwards
known as the Thundering Legion.¹² Our second example
comes closer to the vision of Saint Godric. At the Battle of
Liegnitz, in 1241, between the Poles and the Mongol invaders,
the standard of the Tartars was inscribed with the Greek letter X, and on the tip was the image of an ugly black bar-
barian's head. When this standard was shaken, the head
breathed forth a smoky mist, dense and fetid, which not only
concealed the Tartars from their enemies, but overcame the
Poles by its stench, so that they were defeated with frightful
slaughter.¹³ So at the Battle of Barnet, in 1471, the Yorkist
lords were confused by a mist, which was said to have been
caused by the spells of Friar Bungay.¹⁴ Such mists are familiar in Druidical and Scandinavian wizard-lore.¹⁵ Mist produced by a miracle due to St. Acca scattered King Malcolm's
army when he invaded England and threatened Durham.¹⁶

Ralph Niger's chronicle tells of a huge dragon sweeping
through the air at St. Osyth in 1171, from whose motion such
a fire was kindled that it burnt to ashes a house with all the
outbuildings. And he illustrates the incident by what once
happened at the monastery of Fossez at the confluence of the
Marne and the Seine: in a terrible thunderstorm a monstrous

serpent came flying across the Marne, spouting fire from mouth and nostrils; one of the monks, with the sacred wafer in his hand, advanced against the dragon and forced it to plunge into the river with a crash which was heard for almost two miles.[17] Some three hundred years earlier (A.D. 857) there was a frightful storm at Cologne. The people took refuge in St. Peter's Church, the bells were set ringing, and all began to pray for God's mercy, when a thunderbolt in the shape of a fiery dragon split the building asunder, and killed a priest at the altar of St. Peter, a deacon at the altar of St. Denis, and a layman at the altar of St. Mary; six others were severely injured by the same stroke.[18]

In England on St. Luke's Day (October 18), 1221, a great northeast wind (the quarter of evil influences — *ab Aquilone omne malum*) blew down trees, houses, and church steeples, and many fiery dragons and wicked spirits were seen flying in the air.[19] In 1323 there was a terrible wind-storm with hideous darkness and a great waterspout: the chronicler attributes the outbreak to "the evil spirit, the head of all iniquity."[20] In 1361 (the year of the Second Great Pestilence), men, beasts, trees, and houses were struck by lightning, "and the devell in mannes lyknes spak to men goynge be the weye."[21] In December, 1365, a west wind (*ventus ille zephyrus*) did much damage to the monastery at Reading, and the devil appeared in hideous guise — and no wonder, the chronicler remarks, when we consider the unseemly costume then in fashion.[22] On July 15, 1441, when Henry VI passed through London with due solemnity, a mighty tempest burst upon the city; "and so it was spoken emonges the peple, that ther were som wikked fendes and spirites arered out of helle by coniuracion, forto noy the peple in the Reame, and to put theym to trouble, discencion and vnrest."[23] Nearly two centuries later the Londoners held the same doctrine: in 1626 the "vulgar" of the city ascribed a great storm to the conjuring of Dr. John Lambe, who happened to be on the river at the time,[24] and in 1628 "Dr. Lambe, the witch, was beaten to death in London streets by the boys and apprentices."[25]

After giving an account of the storm of February 1st, 1445, which set Paul's steeple afire, the chronicler adds a curious detail. A great "standard" that had been set up in the pave-

nent at the Leadenhall in Cornhill and was decked with
ıolm and ivy for the citizens' Christmas sports, was "torne
ʳp and cast downe with [i. e. by] the malign spirite, and the
tones of the pavement all about cast in the strete to dyuers
ıouses, so that the peple were sore agast of the grete fervent
empestes that shewed that tyme." [26] A true-bred weather-
witch appears in 1493 in the person of Elena Dalok, arraigned
ıefore the Commissary of London. "She herself said," so
ʳuns the record, "that if she bids the rain to rain, it rains at
ıer command." [27]

In 1615 Margaret Byx alias Elwin, under sentence of
ıeath as an incendiary, confessed her guilty knowledge of a
ılot to burn the town of Wimondham in Norfolk. It was
Ellen Pendleton alias Flodder who broached the matter to
ıer. "She sayth that ther was a pece of match placed in a
ıtable in length about thre fathomes, wherunto the said
Ellen Pendleton did put fier and kindled the same upon the
Satterdaye at night as she veryly beleeveth," and that Ellen
told her that the town should be set on fire the next day.
"And sayth further that she told her that against that tyme
that the winde should by conjuration so be raysed that the
fier should not be staied nor quenched in hast," and the wind
did rise accordingly. Incidentally "the aforesaid Ellen tould
her that she would send out that which should breake the
neck of Mʳ Fraunces Tilluth and his horse neck eyther by
night or by daye." Ellen too was condemned and executed. [28]
We may note, by way of comparison, that the destruction
of St. Paul's steeple by lightning in 1561 was held by some
persons to have been "mischievously done by art magic." [29]
Others, on the contrary, saw in the catastrophe the just hand
of an avenging God. "It is no maruaile," writes an anonymous pamphleteer, "yf God haue sende downe fire to brinne
parte of the Churche." [30]

It is only natural that the Prince of the Powers of the Air
should manifest his hatred of God by attacking churches. [31]
In 1402 at Danbury in Essex "the Devill appeared in likenesse of a Gray Fryer; who entring the Church, put the
people in great fear, and the same hour, with a Tempest of
Whirlewinde and Thunder, the top of the steeple was broken
down, and half of the Chancell scattered abroad." [32] The

demon mounted the altar and sprang from side to side thereon. The church was filled with an intolerable stench. In departing he passed between the legs of one of the congregation, who soon fell sick of a mortal disease, his feet and part of his legs becoming black.[33] With these antics of the devil on the altar we may compare the precisely similar freaks of the lightning, accompanied by a dreadful stench,[34] in a church at Liége in 1118.[35] The shape assumed by the demon for his exploit at Danbury might well have been ascribed to the plots of certain Friars Minors, for, a few days later, eight brothers of this order were arrested, convicted, and executed for treason.[36] It was in August and September of this same year (1402) that rain, wind, and hail all but destroyed the army of Henry IV in his campaign against "that great magician, damn'd Glendower." On the eve of the Nativity of the Virgin (i. e. on September 8) the king's tent was beaten down and his lance was torn up from the ground and fixed itself in his armor: it would have been his last night on earth if he had not gone to bed in his panoply. Many explained these things as the diabolic arts of the Friars Minors.[37] Three times, John Hardyng tells us, King Henry invaded Wales, and every time he had dreadful weather, which everybody ascribed to witches.

> The king had neuer, but tempest foule & raine
> As longe as he was ay in Wales grounde
> Rockes & mystes, windes & stormes euer certaine
> All men trowed, y̆ witches it made that stounde.[38]

On Twelfth Day, 1534, the devil appeared "with greate tempest and darknes" in St. Alkmond's Church at Shrewsbury, and he went out through the steeple, carrying a pinnacle with him and leaving the print of his claws upon one of the bells.[39] Compare what happened in the parish church at Bungay near Norwich on Sunday, the fourth of August, 1577. "An horrible shaped thing" like a black dog appeared "in a great tempest of violent raine, lightning, and thunder." "This black dog," writes Abraham Fleming in a contemporary pamphlet, "or the divel in such a Likenesse (God hee knoweth al who worketh all)," wrung the necks of two of the worshippers. As he passed another man in the congregation, he "gave him such a gripe on the back, that therwithall he was presently drawen togither and shrunk up, as it were a peece of lether scorched in a hot fire; or as the mouth of a purse or bag, drawen togither with a string." He left "yᵉ marks as it were of his clawes or talans" [40] on the wall and door. Similar wonders the dog wrought in the parish church of Blibery (Bliborough) on the selfsame day, killing three persons, burning the hand of one, and "blasting" several others.[41] The Black Dog of Bungay is familiarly mentioned in John Louthe's Reminiscences, 1579: John Cooke, Registrar of Winchester diocese, when he had to "preche hys owne shame" at Paul's Cross, did so without blushing, "for hys syde panche and Croydon complexyone [42] wolde not suffer hym to blushe, more then the black dogge of Bungay." [43] The Black Dog of Bungay had his prototype in the year 857 at Treves. The Bishop was holding service when the bell-tower was shattered by lightning; the darkness was so dense that the worshippers could scarcely recognize each other; the earth yawned asunder; an enormous dog ran about the altar in a circle.[44] The persistence of such tales is illustrated by legends current on Dartmoor in the first half of the last century with reference to the dreadful storm of Sunday, October 21, 1638, in which Widdicombe church was struck by lightning, several persons being killed and many injured.[45] One tradition is that the devil appeared on a black horse and enquired the way to the church just before the storm; another that he entered the church to fetch away a wicked disciple of his own and flew off with him through the roof.[46] The Rev. John Prince, in his Worthies of Devon (1701), shows himself tempted to believe that evil spirits were active in this storm: "There are some circumstances . . . that seem to confirm this hypothesis, as in particular the throwing down stones from the steeple, so fast as if it had been done by an hundred men." [47] In 1537, Charles Wriothesley, Windsor Herald, found an item of French news (just brought to London from Calais) of sufficient interest to jot it down in his book of annals. On the Tuesday after Passion Sunday, it seems, the steeple of Our Lady's Church at Calais was struck by lightning and set on fire. The day before, in the same vicinity, a spirit in the likeness of a man suddenly appeared in the midst of a merry-making company, and as suddenly "vanyshed awaye, cariinge a parte of the house awaye with him." [48]

Reginald Scot, following Wier [49] as usual, rejects the notion that devils or their disciples control the weather, but his testimony is valuable as to the prevalence of this doctrine among the common sort. Many believe, he assures us, "that neither haile nor snowe, thunder nor lightening, raine nor tempestuous winds come from the heavens at the commandement of God: but are raised by the cunning and power of witches and conjurers; insomuch as a clap of thunder, or a gale of wind is no sooner heard, but either they run to ring bels, or crie out to burne witches." [50] It was a common thing in England, as elsewhere, to ring the church bells in a storm, particularly when it thundered. Cases may be noted in 1450, 1457–8, 1464, and 1519.[51] A York pontifical of the eighth century provides a formula for blessing a church bell: "Wherever this bell sounds, let the power of enemies retire, so also the shadow of phantoms, the assault of whirlwinds, the stroke of lightnings, the harm of thunders, the injuries of tempests, and every spirit of the storm-winds." [52] But the devil was sometimes defiant, as when, in 1534 at St. Alkmond's church in Shrewsbury, he "put the prynt of hys clawes uppon the iiij[th] bell" and "for the tyme stayed all the bells in the churches within the sayd towne that they could neyther toll nor rynge." [53]

Storms often attended the conjurations of men who sought for buried treasure. Thus the vile weather that prevailed in Halifax and vicinity in 1510 was ascribed by common fame to the devil-raising efforts of such adventurers; [54] and when, about 1539, William Wycherley and others (including one Thomas *Goslyng*!) undertook to call up the "orientalle or septentrialle" spirit Baro at a place in Sussex, their spells raised "a terrible wynde and tempest," though Baro failed to appear in person.[55] Meredith Lloyd told Aubrey of the conjuring of Dr. John Dee and associates at a pool in Brecknockshire: "They found a wedge of gold," but "a mighty storme and tempest was raysed in harvest time, the countrey people had not knowen the like." [56] The persistency of these ideas is notable. Not far from 1800 the scholars of Clitheroe grammar school called up Satan: a fearful storm ensued,[57] and that storms are due to conjuring is a belief still or recently current in Wilts.[58] So a tempest may mark the death of a witch or wizard,[59] of a suicide,[60] or of any enormous sinner, — when Satan comes to claim his own. At about the hour of the death of King John there was a fierce storm and many horrid visions were seen.[61] A high wind presaged the death of Henry I, and there were shocking circumstances about his burial that suggest diabolic agency.[62] There was a storm, too, in 1265, when Simon de Montfort was slain at the Battle of Evesham.[63] Modern instances are common enough.[64]

Higden in his fourteenth-century Polychronicon tells us that in the Isle of Man witches sell sailors wind tied up under three knots of thread: as these are untied, the wind freshens.[65] Similar traffic is on record for Lapland, Finland, Pembrokeshire, the Orkneys, Shetland, the Highlands in general, and other places in the North.[66] Odin in a poem in the Elder Edda, speaking in the character of a wizard, claims to know spells to quench fire, to heal feuds, and to calm the waves.[67] Oddo, a famous pirate among the Danes, was so skilled in magic that he could traverse the sea without a ship and could wreck the vessels of his enemies by storms.[68] Alexander Roberts in 1616 cites "the experience of our owne Nauigators, who trade in *Finland, Denmarke, Lapland, Ward-house, Norway*, and other Countries of that Climate, and haue obtained of the inhabitants thereof, a certaine winde for twenty dayes together." [69] Ady in 1656 avers that "it is certain that there are some people in *Germany*, and *Polonia*, that do commonly sell Winds by the Devils help to Sea-men." [70] The Lapland and Northern witches and their traffic in weather became proverbial.[71] The Female Tatler for December 28–30, 1709 (No. 76), prints a humorous advertisement: "*This is to give Notice to all News-Writers, that there is lately come over a* Laplander *that profers to sell all manner of* Winds *at reasonable Rates, to bring the Packet Boats in due time*," etc. Walter Scott and his shipmates bought a wind of Bessie Millie at Stromness in the Orkneys in 1814: they were joking, of course, but she was in earnest.[72] So was Henry More the Platonist when, in 1653, he set down his belief in the sale of winds as well as in the raising of tempests by witches. As means to the latter end he specifies "casting of Flint-Stones behind their backs towards the West, or flinging a little Sand in the Aire, or striking a River with a Broom, and so sprink-ling the Wet of it toward Heaven,[73] the stirring of Vrine or Water with their Finger in a Hole in the ground, or boyling of Hogs Bristles in a Pot."[74] Versified spells for raising and laying the wind may be read in the Second Confession of the famous Scottish witch Isobel Gowdie (1662).[75]

Here we may note the exploit of a Swedish fisherman, Per Mattsson, with a wind-pipe about 1659. One day, when the boat was on the way back from fishing, there was a stark calm. "We shall have wind," said Per, and he blew in a little green tobacco pipe that he had: immediately a light breeze sprang up. Per blew again: the wind freshened, but still was not strong enough to make rowing unnecessary. Then he blew the third time, and they had wind enough. Three wit-nesses who were on board agreed in this testimony when the matter came before the Swedish Witchcraft Commission in 1671.[76]

"To whistle for a wind" is a faded bit of sorcery, and a whistling *woman* is especially dangerous to the ship.[77] In 1459 a woman of the Leventina in Switzerland confessed that she had attended a witches' assembly where "Lucifel" was present in the form of a black cat. The hags wished to cause bad weather, and the fiend bade them whistle three times; a few days later came snow and frost and cold with great dam-age to the crops of the valley. [78]

The parish register of Wells in 1583 contains a tragic entry: "Decemb. Perished upon the West coast, coming from Spain, Richd Waller [and thirteen others, named], whose deaths were brought to pass by the detestable working of an execrable witche of Kings Lynn, whose name was Mother Gabley, by the boiling or rather labouring of certayn Eggs in a payle full of colde water, afterward approved sufficiently at the ar-raignement of ye said Witche."[79] Similar is a tale of New Hampshire witchcraft told by Mr. Stephen Dolloff (born in 1795) to a friend of mine some years ago. He had heard it from his grandmother, whom Old Aunt Patty, reputed a witch, was visiting when the spell was worked.[80] Three "big boys," who had been teasing Aunt Patty, were rash enough to attempt to cross the Squamscot River in a small boat. "'Long about three o'clock in the a'ternoon Patty fetched a pail of water and dipped up the water and tipped it over a little three times, and then over it went, and she said 'There you go, you dogs!' Waal, jest that time them boys was a-crossin' the river, an' a squall struck 'em all of a suddent, an' the boat upsot, an' they was all drownded. 'Tain't safe to hector a witch, noway!'"

Pathetic enough is the confession of Elizabeth Harris at Faversham in 1645: "She further saith that her sonne being drowned in Goodman *Woodcots* High [i. e. hoy, a small vessel] she wished that God might be her revenger, which was her watchword to the Divell, and the High was cast away, and she conceives that her wish was the cause of its being cast away." Joan Williford, executed in this same year, testified "that her Divell told her that *Elizabeth Harris* about six or seven yeeres since curst the Boat of one *Iohn Woodcott*, and so it came to passe." [81]

Cases that illustrate the loss of ships or boats by witchcraft may be accumulated in any desired quantity. [82] Preeminent among such grisly experiences is that which so earnestly occupied the Swedish magistrates in 1669. Tomas Andersson's fishing boat had foundered in a storm with all on board; and the testimony (confession in part) was that the storm was raised by witchcraft, that a wizard and some witches flew out to the boat in divers shapes (as magpie, jackdaw, crow, and raven), resumed their human form when they reached her, broke off the mast, and threw the men overboard though they cried to God for help! [83]

In the early nineteenth century it was a saying among New England mariners, when a contrary wind detained them in port, that "the old woman has got the cat under the half-bushel"; [84] and there is a story of a woman on Block Island "who actually did put a cat under a barrel . . . to prevent the sailing of a certain schooner." [85] The same bit of folk-lore turns up in Ireland. [86] To drown a cat is to raise the wind, as Fielding discovered in his voyage to Lisbon. [87]

When the theory that storms were of Satan's raising was combated, the argument was likely to be that the Almighty sends them to rebuke and punish the sins of the community.

Thus, in 1704, Joseph Hussey, Pastor of the Congregational
Church at our Cambridge, published a tract at London
which tells its own story in the title-page: "A Warning from
the Winds. A Sermon preach'd upon Wednesday, January
xix. 170$\frac{3}{4}$. Being the day of Publick Humiliation, for the
late terrible, and awakening storm of wind, sent in great rebuke upon this kingdom. November xxvi, xxvii. 1703. And
now set forth in some ground of it, to have been inflicted as a
punishment of that General Contempt, in England under
Gospel-Light, cast upon the work of the Holy Ghost, the
Third Person in the Blessed Trinity, as to his divine breath-
ings upon the souls of men. To which is subnected a Laborious Exercitation upon Eph. 2. 2. About the Airy Oracles,
Sibyl-Prophetesses, Idolatry, and Sacrifices of the elder
pagan times, under the influence of the God of this world,
according to the course of it, and as now indifferently working in the Children of Disobedience to defend this text
against the common mistake, that the winds are raised by
Satan, under the divine permission." "Ascribe unto the
Lord," cries the preacher, "the glory due unto his name. Let
God have the honor of these blasts: Entertain not a thought
that the winds were raised by Satan, Witches, Cunning-Men,
or Conjuration. This is dishonor to God, and unworthy of
the Christian name." [88] But, though theories vary and star-
eyed Science advances, folk-lore is stubborn in conservation
and we still say proverbially "as busy as the Old Harry in a
gale of wind."

CHAPTER IX

THE WITCH IN THE DAIRY [1]

WHEN cows "go dry" unaccountably or give bloody milk, witchcraft has always been an easy and natural diagnosis. In 1909 a woman was fined and imprisoned in Pennsylvania for "disorderly conduct": she had invaded a neighbor's barn and had tried to cast a spell over the cow; the milk stopped.[2] The witch's motive may be mere ill-will, but often she is herself stealing the milk in some occult fashion. Such milk-filching is nearly related to the transference of crops forbidden in the Twelve Tables of the Romans.[3] An early witness is a passage in the Corrector, a penitential of the tenth century which was taken over in the first quarter of the eleventh by Bishop Burchard of Worms as the Nineteenth Book of his famous Decretum: "Some women firmly believe that by their charms and incantations they can attract their neighbor's milk or honey to their own cows or bees, or to those of whomsoever they will." [4] This entry is highly significant, for the belief in question is not an article of the learned bishop's creed: he mentions it as a false opinion, a piece of censurable folk-lore. The methods followed by such milk-stealers are, of course, not specified in the Corrector, but later documents describe one of them that was familiar in Germany and France. A woman of the Black Forest confessed in 1486, among other enormities, that a devil had taught her how to rob people of their milk: she was to strike an axe into a post and milk the handle; the confession of her associate witch mentions four wooden spigots of similar efficacy.[5] A Tübingen preacher, Martin Plantsch, in a sermon delivered there apropos of the burning of a witch in 1505, testifies to the current belief that witches can drain their neighbors' cows by milking an image (*statua*) or an axe-handle: his own idea is that the devil milks the cow and then invisibly brings the milk to the object from which it appears to come.[6] Geiler von Kaiserberg (1445–1510) offers the same explanation,[7] and a fine woodcut of an old hag milking an axe-handle adorns his page.[8]   Young Robinson, in 1634, showed his familiarity with such notions when he testified that he had seen some of his Lancashire neighbors pulling ropes in a barn, "presently after which pulling, there came ... flesh smoaking, butter in lumps, and milk as it were flying from the said ropes" (p. 270, below).   Robert Kirk, in or about 1691, speaking of contemporary Scottish witches, remarks: "What Food they extract from us is conveyed to their Homes by secret Paths, as sume skilfull Women do the Pith and Milk from their Neighbours Cows into their own Chiese-hold thorow a Hair-tedder, at a great Distance, by Airt Magic, or by drawing a spickot fastened in a Post, which will bring Milk as farr as a Bull will be heard to roar." [9]   This notion is not obsolete either on the Continent [10] or in Great Britain and Ireland, and it survives in our own country.   About 1780 Ann Allan, a Yorkshire witch, milked one of the legs of a three-legged stool.   In Scotland and the North of England witches draw milk from the cow-tether; in the Highlands and the Isle of Skye they milk the crook or pothook; in Ireland they milk a spit; in Kentucky they get butter by squeezing a fork-handle.[11]

By good fortune we learn — what would be inferential anyhow — that milk-stealing witchcraft was common in England long before Queen Elizabeth came to the throne. Bale's witch (1538), who had charms to make cows give plenty of milk,[12] must also have been able to steal it by sorcery, though she does not expressly claim this power — for she does assert that one of her accomplishments is to "draw drynke out of a rotten post." [13]   "Drink," to be sure, did not mean milk or water in those days, but the principle is the same.   And we may go much farther back than Bale.   We can appeal to Robert of Brunne's Handlyng Synne, freely adapted from Le Manuel des Pechiez, a poem by one William (conventionally styled "of Waddington"), who, though he wrote in French, was an Englishman born, bred, and ordained.   Robert began his "English rhyme" — so he tells us himself — in 1303, and he composed it for the uneducated, who are fond of rhymes and tales.[14]   His treatment of sorcery and witchcraft is therefore much to the point.   If ever you have practised nygromauncye (he writes) and offered

sacrifice to the devil through witchcraft, or given reward to
anybody to raise the devil in order to discover lost goods, you
have sinned. If you have looked into sword or basin or
thumb or crystal, — or caused a child to do so, — all that
sort of thing is called witchcraft. Trust not the pie's chattering — many men are deceived thereby — nor omens from
meeting in the morning, nor hansel, nor dreams. Put not
your trust in witchcraft. Whenever it is true, that is merely
through the devil's craft to make men believe in what is hateful to God. So far Robert follows his author.[15] Then, instead
of repeating William's story of a deceitful dream, he illustrates witchcraft by quite a different example — the tale of
the Witch and her Milk-sucking Bag (vv. 499-562):

> Lo here a tale of a wycche
> That leuede no better than a bycche!

The text is that when one believes in a false thing worked by
witchcraft, the devil shows that thing because of one's belief;
or, in other words, it is not the spell that does the work, but
the devil, because of the witch's faith.

There once was a witch who made a big leather bag, which
she enchanted so that it went and sucked men's cows in the
pasture. This continued for a long time, but was discovered
at length. All the goodmen of the town summoned her before
the bishop and produced the bag. The bishop, incredulous,
bade the witch work the marvel if she could, and she began to
recite her charm; the bag rose up and started on its way; but,
at his command, she made it lie still again. Then the bishop
recited the charm, saying and doing exactly what the witch
had said and done; but the bag did not stir. "Why is this?"
asked he. "Because you do not believe," the witch replied.
"If you would have faith in the words [of the charm] as I
have, then the bag would go and suck cows. You may say
what you like, but your words are wasted unless you have
faith. I have faith in the words I uttered: it is my faith that
did the deed." The tale ends rather lamely: "The bishop
commanded that she should not believe or work as she had
wrought." [16] This experiment in the occult was more successful than that tried by "the illustrious Prince N." in the
fifteenth century with a witch who said she could fly if she

smeared herself with a magic unguent. Her faith, apparently, was perfect; yet, though anointed again and again, she stood motionless, and "nothing unusual happened." [17]   As for milk-stealing in England, we can go much farther back than Robert of Brunne; for the Arundel Penitential, a manuscript written by an English scribe in the thirteenth century,[18] contains the following rule: "Whoever shall work to take away or to acquire for himself the supply of any person's milk or honey or other things by any spell or witchcraft — let him do heavy penance for three years." And an identical clause occurs in the Penitential of Bartholomew Iscanus, Bishop of Exeter from 1161 to 1184.[19]

A witch, as we all know, often takes the shape of a hare,[20] and in this guise she may suck your cow dry or drink up the milk. This method of theft, still credited in Great Britain and Ireland (as well as the Continent),[21] was known to Giraldus Cambrensis in the twelfth century: "That certain old women," he writes, "as well in Wales as in Ireland and Scotland, change themselves into the form of hares in order the more secretly to steal other people's milk by sucking [cows'] udders under a false shape, is an old complaint and still common." [22]

Cows may be dried up by the English goblins called Hobthursts; they may be milked by Scottish and Irish fairies, by hedgehogs (a shape often assumed by imps), or by snakes, especially black snakes.[23] The goatsucker (*caprimulgus*) carries its own condemnation in its name: its supposed sin is duly registered by Pliny.[24] A Yorkshire witch used to send hedgehogs to suck cows and even assumed urchin-form herself with the same design. Witches in Iceland have imps of very frightful origin whom they dispatch on the like errand; in Sweden they employ "milk-hares." [25] An English witch about 1649 was said to have taken the form of a polecat and in that guise to have sucked a brood-sow; when the polecat was injured, the witch suffered the hurt.[26] The German vampire who so impressed the imagination of Henry More, varied his more ghoulish pranks by draining the cows dry.[27] Witches may take away the milk of a nursing mother; they may even suck her breasts till the blood comes — just as they can make a cow give bloody milk.[28] Sometimes, too, they suck the blood of infants. Such were the *striges* of antiquity, who were hags or demons in bird form.[29]

As a witch may dry up your cows, so she may bewitch your cream; then the butter "will not come." [30] Everybody past middle life remembers this piece of folk-lore and is prepared with the remedy: plunge a redhot iron — a poker, a spit, or best of all a horseshoe [31] — into the cream. That will reverse the spell and may burn the witch, who is actually or mystically present in the churn [32] — in the form of a hare, it may be. That such counter-magic was meant to harm the guilty hag was the opinion of Goodwife R. in Giffard's Dialogue (1593): "When they thrust in the spitte they say, If thou beest here haue at thine eie." [33] The churn may be whipped, with good results. Salt (a sacred substance) is sometimes efficacious, especially if you throw it into the fire as well as into the churn. So also is rowan (mountain ash): stir the cream with a rowan twig, or throw rowan twigs in, or bind a rowan chaplet round the churn, or put rowan on top of it. Again, you may put a shilling or a crooked sixpence in the churn or may touch each corner of the house with a redhot poker.[34] Black indeed is the magic involved in a counter-charm from Scotland: to bring butter, boil a pint of milk with seven needles and nine pins and pour it into the churn. In Nithsdale, when milk went wrong, a divot from the witch's roof was stuck with one pin for each cow and plunged into boiling milk; another divot was laid on top of the chimney: the witch came.[35]

Such bewitchment may be pure malice, as in the case of Alse Martyn, arrested in 1565. Some years before, it was alleged, she had entered a house and cried "Gyve no melche"; and "from that day they could make no butter, nor chysse, nor have no melche of kyne." [36] Revenge was the motive alleged in the case of Goodwife Malter, investigated by Sir Thomas Smith in 1570. One witness deposed

That she being Servant to a Farmer's Wife in the said Parish of *Theydon Mount*, this Goodwife *Malter* came to her Mistress, who was going to *London* Market, and desired her to bring her home some Sprats; but she saying she came always loaden from *London*, denied her. Upon this, the Deponent, then her hired Maid, came from Milking; and as she set her Milk in the Pan upon a Loft, there was a Speckled Bird, as she thought, which fluttered among the Milk-Pans, and with her Feet and Wings slubbered therein: Her Mistress in the mean time called her away. But she endeavoured by a Broom to sweep or drive away this Bird. But it would not away, but went fluttering from Pan to Pan; and could not fly, but skip and hop. At the last, it went from the Loft where the Milk and Wheat was, into the Cheese Loft. And then being often called by her Mistress she came down, and being blamed for her long tarrying, she related how she was troubled with such a Bird. And then her Mistress came her self into the Milk Loft, and found it come down Stairs a very Toad. Which after it was once come into the Buttery, she could never see it more. And for the space of six Weeks after by no Means, no Diligence, nor change of Churn, nor Cloths, could they have any Butter; until that her Mistress did bid her carry her Milk, and churn at a Neighbours House; and there the Milk made Butter as it was wont to do before, and in the same Milk Pans.[37]

Sir Thomas Smith was born in 1518. Whatever his opinion may have been on the trustworthiness of this deposition, he can hardly have acquired his views on the general subject from the Marian exiles who returned at Elizabeth's accession. And it is even less likely that the village gossip here recorded was derived from his instructions to his humble Essex neighbors. Often, the witch's intent was to transfer the butter to her own possession.[38] As in the case of dried-up cows, so the prevention of butter's coming is sometimes ascribed to imps or house cobolds, with no mention of a witch.[39] One of Reginald Scot's best touches concerns butter sorcery. After quoting from the Malleus Maleficarum the general rule for guarding against such magic — neither to give nor lend butter, milk, or cheese to a begging witch — he offers a sound scientific explanation of disasters in the dairy, adds an occult receipt to thwart the butter witch, and concludes thus: "There be twentie severall waies to make your butter come, which for brevitie I omit; as to bind your cherne with a rope, to thrust thereinto a red hot spit, &c: but your best remedie and surest waie is, to looke well to your dairie maid or wife, that she neither eat up the creame, nor sell awaie your butter." Scot himself had suffered from thievish maids.[40]

Modern Irish witches perform diabolical rites for stealing butter. They sweep dew from the grass into their hands on a May morning and thrice chant "Come all to me!" They dip a dead man's hand into their churn and bid it "Gather far and near! Gather far and near!" A witch of Fife on the last night of the year, swinging over her head a cow-tether of hair, chanted:

> Hares' milk and mares' milk
> An' a' the beas' that bears milk,
> Come to me! [41]

Similar charms occur on the Continent. From Switzerland we have the formula, "Us jedem Hus en Löffel"; from Silesia, "Hier ein Löffel, dort ein wenig." A witch of Oldenburg repeated "Ut jedem Hus 'n Läpel vull, ut Pastoren Hus 'n Pott vull." [42] Here we come close to a kind of sorcery used by Dame Alice Kyteler (if we may believe Holinshed) in the fourteenth century: "She swept the streets of Kilkennie betweene compleine and twilight, raking all the filth towards the doores of hir sonne William Outlaw, murmuring and muttering secretlie with hir selfe these words:

> To the house of William my sonne,
> Hie all the wealth of Kilkennie towne."

The underlying principle holds good to-day. In Yorkshire "it is advisable that a new broom should sweep something into the house before it is used in the contrary direction, otherwise you sweep good luck away from your threshold." [43]

Dairy magic got into a Welsh court in 1879, when Mrs. Braithwaite's butter would not come. She declared that Mrs. Williams's witchcraft was to blame, and Mrs. Williams appealed to the magistrates for protection: "She assured the Bench she was in danger, as every one believed she was a witch." [44] In recent years a Welsh farmer was brought to trial for an assault: he had drawn blood upon a supposed witch and had forced her to come to his house and bless the churn. [45] Old formulæ of blessing are still in use. The commonest of them all is —

> Come, butter, come;
> Come, butter, come.
> Peter stands at the gate,
> Waiting for a buttered cake.
> Come, butter come. [46]

That this spell is pre-Reformation its very terms demonstrate; but we need not take refuge in mere inference, for there is direct testimony that it was known in England in the days of Queen Mary.[47] And thus the whole matter of butter witchcraft is carried back to the age in which we wish to find it.

In old times, when brewing was as vital a domestic business as butter-making, one of a witch's malicious tricks was to thwart fermentation or to spoil the ale otherwise.[48] "You have some plot now," says the Master Devil to Pug in Ben Jonson's comedy —

> You have some plot now
> Upon a tunning of ale, to stale the yeast,
> Or keep the churn so that the butter come not,
> Spite o' the housewives cord, or her hot spit? [49]

Mother Waterhouse, one of the Chelmsford witches hanged in 1566, "caused Satan [her imp] to destroye the brewing." [50] In this, too, Bale's witch was proficient long before Queen Elizabeth's accession, and she could likewise thwart the baking, as mediæval and modern hags could and can, by hindering the bread from rising, and making it hard.[51]

> Whan ale is in the fatt,
> If the bruar please me natt,*
> The cast shall fall downe flat.[52]
>   And neuer haue any strength.
> No man shall tonne nor bake,
> Nor meate in season make,
> If I agaynst hym take,
>   But lose hys labour at length.[53]

But so long as she was kept in good humor, all would go well:

> I haue charmes for the plowgh,
> And also for the cowgh,
> She shall geue mylke ynowgh,
>   So longe as I am plesed.
> Apace the mylle shall go,
> So shall the credle do,
> And the musterde querne also,
>   No man therwith dysesed.[54]

A blessing for spoiled ale (in Latin with Anglo-Saxon glosses) — that it may be rendered sound and sparkling — with due citation of the wedding at Cana in Galilee, may be read in the

---

* I. e. "unless the brewer gratify me," "give me a gratuity."

Durham Ritual.[55] Herrick knew how to prevent a witch from playing tricks with bread-makers:

> This Ile tell ye by the way,
> Maidens, when ye leavens lay:
> Crosse your dow, and your dispatch
> Will be better for your batch.[56]

This method of prophylaxis still holds good both with dough before baking and with malt before brewing.[57]

Jennet Device, involved in the Lancashire prosecution in 1612, used as a "prayer" to get drink (that is, to transfer other people's beer to her own vessels) the words "Crucifixus hoc signum vitam Eternam. Amen." This her mother taught her. Her brother also knew the spell and told her that within an hour after its repetition "drinke hath come into the house after a very strange manner." [58] Here we have a witch and wizard in the style of Bale's hag who could draw drink out of a rotten post.

That crops may be ruined or soil made barren by witchcraft is still a current belief.[59] It was equally current in Anglo-Saxon times, as an elaborate charm of that age proves: "Here is the remedy for your fields if they will not grow well, or if any unfit thing is applied to them in sorcery or in witchcraft." This charm is a mixture of Christianity and paganism, involving the removal of four sods from different parts of the farm and their replacement after four masses have been said over them. A hole is also to be bored in the ploughbeam, into which certain herbs with holy salt, etc., are to be put. Seed from another man's land must be acquired from a farmer who is in need of charity, and two for one must be paid for it. This seed is to be laid upon the plough with an appropriate formula. A prayer must be offered to God and his saints that the farm may be protected against all enemies and against all bales that sorceries may sow. "Now I pray the Lord who made the world that no woman may be so skilful in speech or no man so cunning as to turn aside the words thus spoken." Then drive the first furrow, reciting another formula: "Hale be thou, Earth, mother of men! Be thou fertile in God's protection, plenteous in food for men's use!" [60] Finally you must make a loaf of different kinds of meal kneaded with milk and holy water, and lay it under this first furrow, calling for God's blessing on the field and closing the whole ceremony with three pater-nosters.[61] Several pious spells for the defence of crops from birds, insects, mice, and "venomous animals" occur in the Durham Ritual, and in some of these we find the devil or demons associated on a par with more tangible enemies of the farmer. Two of them pertinently cite the driving away of Asmodeus by the "fishy fume," as told in the Book of Tobit.[62]

We are now in a position to understand how Bale's witch (1538), when she claims to wield both white magic and black, is the legitimate descendant of her English ancestors. By merely spitting she can "make corn and cattle never thrive." She can dry up wells and "cause trees [63] and herbs to die." But, on the other hand, she has good "charms for the plough" which ensure abundant crops.[64] In the direct line also is the modern spell which concludes thus: "By virtue of this holy charm I bind this ground that no thievery or work of darkness may be committed hereupon." [65]

Witchcraft that destroys or steals a man's crops is forbidden in the Twelve Tables of the ancient Romans and is too well known to need comment.[66] Pliny repeats a truly Roman anecdote about C. Furius Cresimus and his exemplary defence when accused of enriching himself after this fashion.[67] Abt provides abundant references for Mesopotamia, Greece, Italy, and Carthage.[68] Nider, about 1437, knew of two wizards who had the power to transport invisibly from their neighbor's field to their own one third of dung, hay, grain, or anything else. Scottish witches were equally skilful.[69] As to magic transference of grain from one field to another one further example will suffice. In the Deccan, when there is a known witch in the village, the people are always anxious about their crops. They take care to harvest a different kind of grain from that which the witch raises. Then, if they discover a mixture of grain in her field, they resort to counter-magic.[70]

A ready way to destroy crops is, of course, to bring on a storm, especially a hailstorm, and witches have vast power over the weather.[71] Another way is the production of vermin.[72] In Guernsey a few years ago a witch ruined the melons

by means of a small black fly which men of science found it
impossible to recognize.[73] This scurvy trick of sorcery is applied to divers ends. About 1637 Goody Rose of Bedford was
ducked "for bewitching a Maid's pease (that had denied her
some) to be all, and each, worm-eaten; and another fellow to
be alwayes lowsie." [74] In 1843 in the Norwich police court
a woman complained that another woman had bewitched
her "by sending her and her children a vast number of
vermin." [75]

Where fisheries replace agriculture for a livelihood, boats or
nets may be bewitched.[76] Less than a century ago, in Norfolk, a seaworthy fishing craft, because it was bewitched, was
burnt "stick and stem." [77] A witch can bring in schools of
fish,[78] or can "take away" fish as she can milk.[79]

CHAPTER X

METAMORPHOSIS

FROM Elizabeth's accession to the present moment the witch-creed has cherished the notion that demons may have the form of animals, and that in this guise they may serve the witch as familiar spirits to carry out her wicked designs. Or the witch may transform herself into beast-shape: then, if the animal is wounded, she suffers in like manner. "When I goe but into my closes," says the Essex farmer in Giffard's racy Dialogue (1593), "I am afraide, for I see nowe and then a Hare; which my conscience giueth me is a witch, or some witches spirite, shee stareth so vppon me. And sometimes I see an vgly weasell runne through my yard, and there is a foule great catte sometimes in my Barne, which I haue no liking vnto." [1] Of course these doctrines were nothing new in 1558, nor were they imported from the Continent by the Marian exiles. Every child in Britain was familiar with them, for they are primitive and universal, if anything in demonology is entitled to those much-abused adjectives. Said an Australian Blackfellow to Mr. Howitt, "If I saw an old man kangaroo come up hopping close and sit and stare at me, I should keep my eyes fixed upon him, and try to get out of his way, lest he might be a *bŭgin* [wizard], who, getting behind me, would take me at a disadvantage." [2] In South Africa in the fifteenth century, when witches were much feared as causing murrain, blighted crops, sickness, and death, they kept lizards and moles in their service — uncanny creatures still used (in fragments) for evil magic among barbarous races. A famous witch of Tripoli had for her familiars a snake, scorpions, and a hare. Melanesian wizards send snakes or crocodiles to kill their victims. In Nigeria the witch's heart flies abroad in vulture form while her body lies unconscious at home; when the vulture is killed, she dies too. Among the Bakongo, insects trapped by the doctor are witches who have caused disease: if the insect is hurt, the witch suffers.[3] Closely connected is the idea that witch-sent diseases may be extracted from the body in some bestial form (see p. 135). Thus in Nigeria bats or frogs are taken from the mouths of possessed persons.[4] As for England, if transformation to animal form is required as an element in the witch-creed, one may cite the old Germanic belief in werewolves,[5] which is amply certified for Anglo-Saxon England. *Werewolf*, indeed, is on record as a proper name, even (oddly enough) as the name of a learned Mercian priest who assisted King Alfred in his literary work. The devil himself is called "the ravening werewolf" in the Laws of Cnut. As to the middle ages Gervase of Tilbury is a sufficient witness: such transformations, he tells us, have been common in England. For Ireland and Wales the evidence is abundant, and was well known to mediæval Englishmen.[6] Romantic fiction, too, helped to keep the werewolf tradition alive among our English ancestors.[7]

At the moment when William the Second was slain by the arrow of Wat Tyrrel or another in New Forest, the Earl of Cornwall — far away on the Bodmin moors, hunting and alone — met a huge black goat, carrying on his back a man, black, naked, and wounded in the breast. Adjured by the Triune God to tell what he was, the apparition replied: "I am bearing to judgment your king, William Rufus — your tyrant rather. For I am an evil spirit, the avenger of his malice, which raged against the Church of Christ." Direful portents had forewarned the tyrant of his end, and the devil had appeared visibly to men, speaking to wayfarers in woodland glades and solitary paths.[8] The goat is a favorite form with Satan — why, Remigius takes great pains to elucidate.[9] Goat-riding devils — hideous dwarfs with cowls and long beards — haunted a little island near Farne when the pious Bartholomew chose Farne for his hermitage in the twelfth century.[10] To St. Dunstan the devil showed himself often — not only in his own hideous shape, as in the anecdote of the tongs [11] — but as a bear, a dog, and a fox.[12] St. Hugh of Cluny brought a frightful serpent out of a woman's body by means of holy water which he forced thrice into her mouth.[13] In the third decade of the twelfth century a certain Walter, possessed of the devil in the form of a black dog (visible to him alone but heard by others), was cured by the merits of St. Cuthbert, and he lived until 1165.[14] St. Godric, the twelfth-century Hermit of Finchale, was continually haunted by demons. At times they crowded his cell in the guise of black dwarfs or pygmies; but they appeared in all manner of shapes — like a bear, an eagle, a crow; they bellowed like oxen.[15] So poor Mr. Richard Allington, in the latter part of Elizabeth's reign, dying of the smallpox and tormented in conscience for his practices of usury, saw one night in his chamber little creatures "like puppets," which jumped upon his bed and, as he says, "pulled, tossed, stirred, teared, and so vexed mee, as I was neuer in all my lif so sore vexed and troubled." [16]

Owen Glendower possessed a stone which rendered him invisible. It had belonged to the Earl of Arundel who was beheaded by Richard II. This earl had a pet raven, and once, when he was playing chess in his garden, the bird (*vel spiritus in specie corvina*) ejected the magic stone.[17] Grotesque was the apparition that startled the Isle of Portland near Weymouth in 1456. A cock of the hue of a pheasant came out of the sea. He had legs half a yard long and a red beard, and upon his head was a great crest. He stood in the water and crowed three times: "and euery tyme that he crew he turned hym rounde aboute, and bekened wyth his hede towarde the north, the southe, and the weste; . . . and when he had crowe iij. tymes he vanysshed away." [18]

Rural Britain still swarms with demon-dogs (barguests, boggarts, Old Shuck, Hairy Jack, and the rest),[19] to say nothing of such aërial phenomena as Gabriel's Hounds, known from the fifteenth century and celebrated by Wordsworth in not the best (or the worst) of his multitudinous sonnets.[20] Old Shuck comes etymologically of an ancient line, for his name is the Anglo-Saxon *scucca*, "demon." [21] A witch may masquerade as a dog:[22] Stearne, Matthew Hopkins's lieutenant, tells of a hag, wounded in dog shape, who showed the injury when restored to human form.[23] Dog-familiars are likewise common.[24] Small wonder, then, that in the seventeenth century, when Prince Rupert was sojourning at Winwick, Mr. Charles Herle, the rector, recorded that a parishioner "maintained that he saw in Prince Rupert's dog an en-

chanted Camp Lady of intelligence, that is to say, a spy." [25]
This was the Prince's pet dog Boy, killed on Marston Moor,
about whom there are exceedingly curious tracts.[26] The idea
that Boy was a familiar spirit was rather prevalent.[27] But
we can go centuries farther back than Prince Rupert. Jack
Cade, in the proclamation for his arrest in 1450, is accused
not only of using books of magic but of having "rered upp
the Divell in the semblaunce of a black dogge" in his lodging
at Dertford.[28] Among the miracles of the dead King Henry
VI we hear of the rescue of a midnight wayfarer, attacked
by an evil spirit in the guise of a black dog which was about
to eat him up. He called upon the glorious martyr for help
and the creature vanished.[29] A demon in animal form — cat,
shaggy black dog — and three demons like black dwarfs occur in the Kyteler case (1324).[30] Goblin horses (like Tatterfoal and Shagfoal), sometimes demons and sometimes ghosts,
are equally common.[31]

Of the cat-witch, injured in that shape and suffering the
same wounds *in propria persona*, there are countless modern
instances.[32] By this test, indeed, you may often prove that
Goody So-and-So is indeed a witch, as you have long suspected. For the English middle ages, Gervase of Tilbury may
suffice. It is a known fact, he avers, that "women have been
seen and wounded in the shape of cats by persons who were
secretly on the watch, and that the next day the women have
shown wounds and loss of limbs." [33] A pertinent instance
from our own Cambridge about 1660 is recited by Mr. John
Hale in his Modest Enquiry. He is pleased to be able to
testify that the supposed wound turned out to be a boil.[34]
In 1561 there was a wild adventure at Vernon in France.
Witches and wizards used to assemble by night in an "old
and ancient" castle in the shape of an infinite number of cats.
Four or five bold investigators of psychic phenomena spent
the night there. One of the watchers was killed and all of
them were soundly clawed, but they wounded several cats,
and the same hurts were afterwards discovered on men and
women of the neighborhood.[35]

The cat appears as a familiar in the first of the really notable Elizabethan witch-trials, at Chelmsford in 1566. It was
a white-spotted creature named Sathan, which sucked blood;

it took the form of a toad and caused the death of a man who touched it; and it helped its mistress to an unsatisfactory husband. But, in view of all the evidence, I do not think the cat swam the Channel in 1558 or came over on Bishop Jewel's shoulder in 1559. In fact, I know it did not. Elizabeth Frauncis received the cat from her grandmother, kept it for fifteen or sixteen years, and then presented it to Mother Waterhouse, who had cherished it more than nine years when brought to trial. This carries the demon back well into King Henry's days, even if we ignore the period when he was in the service of the Frauncis woman's grandam.[36]

Alanus de Insulis, a favorite author among mediæval English readers, derives the name of the heretic Cathari from *catus*, because they are said to worship Lucifer with obscene rites when he appears to them in that form.[37] King Arthur's fight with the Demon Cat is an ancient feature of his adventurous career.[38]

The tame villatic cat keeps some of her devilish traits in current superstition.[39] Cats may suck a sleeping child's breath: this notion is still common in both Old and New England.[40] There is also a widespread idea that cats must be kept away from a corpse or they may mutilate it. This turns up in our own country in an enlightening form: "Never take a cat near a dead person, lest the cat take the soul of the dead." The soul, we remember, often issues from the mouth of a sleeping man in the shape of a mouse![41] What all these notions have to do with the affliction known as "cat-fear," I shall leave to the psychologists to determine. "There are some," writes Increase Mather, "who if a Cat accidentally come into the Room, though they neither see it, nor are told of it, will presently be in a Sweat, and ready to die away."[42] On this head, indeed, there is literature for every mood. The serious-minded may follow the reasoning of Archbishop Bramhall, in his Vindication of True Liberty against Hobbes: "Those actions which are altogether undeliberated and do proceed from sudden and violent passions, . . . which surprise a man, and give him no time to advise or reason, are not properly and actually in themselves free, but rather necessary actions; as when a man runs away from a cat or a custard, out of a secret antipathy."[43] The amateur of robust humor may recall how Mr. Henry Watson put to flight a redoubtable duellist — "one that," as he happened to know, "would face any thing upon Earth, except a Cat" — by brandishing a pair of kittens. "No sooner," so Mr. Henry writes to Bully Dawson, "did he set eyes upon his little squawling Adversaries, but away he scower'd, as if a Legion of Devils had been in pursuit of him. . . . Since which Retreat I have not yet seen him; but for Self-preservation, which you know is Nature's Law, I have ever since walk'd Arm'd with a brace of Kittens in my Pocket, for fear of farther danger." [44]

For some reason or other the hare passes for an uncanny creature.[45] To meet or be crossed by a hare is very bad luck.[46] Hares may be employed as familiar spirits, and as such may steal milk for their mistress hags by sucking a neighbor's cows.[47] For witches in hare-form we have the authority of Giraldus Cambrensis [48] and of modern folk-lore in profusion.[49] If you wound a witch-hare, the witch herself suffers the injury, of course.[50]

In the Chelmsford trial in 1566,[51] when a white-spotted cat played a leading rôle as familiar spirit, the Queen's Attorney asked Mother Waterhouse, "When dyd thye Cat suck of thy blood?" "Never!" was her reply; but marks were discovered on her face and nose where she had pricked herself to feed the demon. This idea — that witches feed their familiars with their blood — is persistent in the later history of English witchcraft. It is important to observe, therefore, that it was not a doctrine brought in from the Continent by the Marian exiles. Nothing could be better for this purpose than the case of John Steward, ex-schoolmaster of Knaresborough (Yorkshire), in 1510. He was brought to book in the Archbishop's Court for sorcery. The substance of the charges will concern us elsewhere.[52] Here be it noted that one of the witnesses had been told by a certain Sir Thomas Spurret "that he sawe Stewerd have iij. humble bees, or like humble bees, and kepte theyme undir a stone in the erth, and called theyme oute by oone and oone, and gave iche oone of theyme a drop of blode of his fyngor."[53] That an insect should serve as a witch's familiar is natural and proper. Such creatures, therefore, occur in considerable variety

among men, savage and civilized;[54] but the fly and the bee
are especially noteworthy in English tradition.[55] Scot mentions as a ridiculous feature of the witch-creed the notion
that devils may be "made tame, and kept in a box," to do
service to their mistresses.[56] Compare what Thomas Nashe
wrote of the Münster Anabaptists in 1594: "Verie deuout
Asses they were, for all they were so dunstically set forth,
and such as thought they knew as much of Gods minde as
richer men: why, inspiration was their ordinarie familiar,
and buzd in their eares like a Bee in a boxe euerie hower what
newes from heauen, helle, and the land of whipperginnie."[57]
The distinguished Oxford mathematician Thomas Allen
(1542–1632) of Gloucester Hall (now Worcester College),
who passed for a second Friar Bacon,[58] and who, as well as
Dr. Dee, was reputed to be employed by Leicester as a conjurer and figure-caster,[59] "had a great many mathematicall
instruments and glasses in his chamber," so Aubrey informs
us, "which did also confirme the ignorant in their opinion"
of his magical activities, "and his servitor (to impose on fresh-
men and simple people) would tell that sometimes he should
meet the spirits comeing up his staires like [i.e. in the shape
of] bees." He also had a watch which was taken for a devil.[60]
When Archbishop Sharp of St. Andrews was assassinated in
1679, "upon the opening of his tobacco box a living hum-
ming bee flew out," which was regarded as his familiar
demon.[61] Witches in bee-form and a bee as a witch's emis-
sary occur in Scottish trials of that same century.[62] Here is
another tale from pre-Elizabethan days: At Malling, in
Kent, "one of Q. *Maries* justices, upon the complaint of
many wise men, and a few foolish boies, laid an archer by
the heeles; bicause he shot so neere the white at buts. For
he was informed and persuaded, that the poore man plaied
with a flie, otherwise called a divell or familiar. . . . The
archer was severelie punished, to the great encouragement of
archers, and to the wise example of justice; but speciallie to
the overthrowe of witchcraft."[63] Flies of this demonic nature
are good old figures in Germanic lore. They were well-
known in Lappish, Finnish, and Norse sorcery.[64] The Lombard King Kuninkpert, while plotting to murder two of his
nobles, Aldo and Granso, chanced to see a big fly in the

window. He struck at it with his knife and cut off one foot. On their way to the palace Aldo and Granso met a limping man who had lost a foot and had a wooden leg. He warned them to beware of the king and they took sanctuary. The king realized that the fly was an evil spirit.[65] Such stories came down to the English Reformers on their native soil without the need of foreign influences. When Thomas Badby was examined for heresy in 1409 and "was multiplying words without knowledge" in his own defence, a horrible spider was seen to creep over his lips. One of those present wished to remove it, but the Archbishop of Canterbury said: "Let it alone! Now shall we see who teaches him to speak." [66]

Everybody, except here and there a sophisticated and supercilious man of science, agrees with Rosalind's father that the toad is ugly and venomous, though most of us have ceased to look for the precious jewel in its head. Toad poison, from ancient times to the present, has been much in evidence.[67] But, like vipers and other nauseous and deadly creatures, toads are also valuable in medicine. Plague-stricken patients in the seventeenth century wore round the neck a toad (alive or dried), whose stronger venom drew out the poison of the disease.[68] The ashes of a burnt toad are good for dropsy according to the precepts of folk-medicine in Devonshire.[69] This fact makes the following anecdote, which comes from about the middle of the sixteenth century, as exhilarating to the student of the tenacity of tradition as it is comforting to the moralist. A Roman lady, whose husband was in a desperate state of health from dropsy, grew weary of the trouble and expense and attempted to poison him with a pulverized toad: to her chagrin, the dose cured him! [70] King John was poisoned by the venom of a toad administered by a tyrannicide monk in a wassail cup, if we may believe one of the best-told stories in English chronicles.[71]

The devil, who squat like a toad at the ear of Mother Eve in Eden, is always at hand in the churchyard after service, waiting in that guise for some evil-minded communicant to feed him with a bit of the consecrated wafer: whoever thus sacrifices to Satan will straightway become a witch or wizard.[72] The relation of witches to toads (or frogs) [73] is notorious; and, like everything else in this department of superstition, it is founded on fact. Toads are not uncommon in earth-floored huts,[74] and doubtless they were sometimes petted [75] by solitary old women who, esteemed as witches, regarded themselves as such and thought the creatures were really imps or demons. Anyhow, toad-familiars are as commonplace as cats.[76] The Chelmsford witch of 1566, Mother Waterhouse, actually changed her white-spotted cat into a toad without impairing its competency.[77] Oliffe Barthram, executed at Bury St. Edmunds in 1599 for "diuellish and wicked witcheries practized vpon Ioane Iorden," had sent three toads to her victim "to trouble her in her bed." [78] As late as 1879 a man charged with assault excused himself in a Norfolk court by declaring that the woman assaulted was a witch who had bespelled him by means of a "walking toad." [79] Malefic witchcraft by such agency was not obsolete in Devon in 1905.[80] When Saubadine de Soubiete, one of the Labourd witches of the early seventeenth century, was thrown into the fire by the executioner, "a whole swarm of toads came out of the top of her head." [81] The familiar of the witch who tormented Rachel Pindar in 1574 was "sometyme like a doge, and sometyme like a tode." [82] In modern Devonshire an old woman "kept toads in her back kitchen for the purpose of injuring persons against whom she had a grudge; another, who was bedridden, kept toads in her bed, and people used to come to have their fortunes told by them." [83] Nanny Morgan, a Shropshire hag who was murdered in 1857, had a box full of live toads in her cottage.[84] A modern wizard of Somerset kept toads on hand in pots: to make a person pine away and die, he would stick a toad's heart full of pins and hang it up in the chimney.[85] Bodin, with a moderation not always discernible in his treatment of witchcraft, lays down the principle that to keep toads in pots, though a suspicious circumstance, is not sufficient ground for condemnation to death.[86] The frequent confusion between the witch and her familiar occurs in a Maldon case in 1579 and in the case of Mary Smith, executed in 1616: a toad was burned, and she suffered appropriate pains.[87]

From a wild account of the murder of Fair Rosamond penned by an irresponsible chronicler of the fourteenth century (who refers the whole affair to the reign of Henry III

instead of Henry II) we learn that Queen Eleanor put Rosamond into a bath and hired a wicked old woman to lance
her arms; and another old witch (*sorceresse*) brought two
horrible toads, which seized the damsel's breasts and sucked
her blood while two more hags held her arms. The queen had
the reptiles buried with the body in a foul ditch. One of the
witches confessed under torture.[88] Nothing could be absurder
from an historical point of view, but as evidence for what was
believed of witches in mediæval England the item is priceless.

Why it should be good luck to meet a toad (though bad
luck to meet a hare) I cannot divine except on the principle
of *similia similibus curantur*, but such was the notion in
fourteenth-century England.[89]

A dim shadow of the toad-witch haunts the minds of New
England boys if they retain the superstition (current among
them on Cape Cod in my youth) that to kill a toad brings on
a shower of rain; for in this article of faith one recognizes the
old notion that storms attend the death of witches.[90]

Of course a witch may transform a man into an animal (as
in the case, sometimes, of the nightmare hag).[91] The possibility was much debated by men of learning, and the theologians were inclined to hold that such shifts are in appearance only; but the people in general had (and have) no
doubts, having inherited their creed from the beginning of
time. And even among the learned elect there was a trace —
and more than a trace — of the old leaven. Besides, there
were special influences at work. The famous romance of
Apuleius, in outline, got into circulation as historical fact
and was thus made current in twelfth-century England
by William of Malmesbury in his story of the Two Witches
of Rome, which subsequent chroniclers delighted to copy.
These hags, William tells us, who kept a wayside inn,
added to their gains by transforming their guests into domestic animals and selling them. One young man, a professional entertainer, sold in the form of an ass, did not forfeit
his human intelligence and amused his master's friends by
clever tricks. At last he got into a pond, and water restored
him to his proper shape.[92] The occurrence is assigned to the
eleventh century.[93] The starting point for this anecdote
might well have been a chapter of St. Augustine, who, after

citing Circe and the classic werewolves of Arcadia,[94] repeat
a *canard* that he himself heard in Italy — how certain ol‹
women, by means of cheese which they gave to travellers
turned them into beasts of burden, with the retention, how
ever, of their human reason, "just as Apuleius in his Golde‹
Ass has revealed or pretended that by a poison he wa‹
changed into an ass with a human mind." St. Augustine i‹
skeptical but cautious, and does not utterly reject the evi
dence.[95] In Reginald Scot we may read of a young Englis‹
sailor who met with similar treatment at the hands of ‹
witch of Cyprus. Scot regards the tale as a tough yarn.[9‹]
We have now approached the widespread märchen "Sell th‹
Steed but Keep the Bridle," in which a magician drives ‹
good trade in horses by this occult means,[97] and we are no‹
far from the Greek myth of Erysichthon, who sold his daughte‹
over and over again, now as a mare, now as a cow, now as ‹
bird, now as a stag.[98] Once upon a time St. Macarius wa‹
besought to help a girl who appeared to have been trans
formed into a mare "per phantasias magicas." He per
ceived in a moment that the metamorphosis was not actual
but simply due to demonic illusion, for *he* saw the girl wher‹
others saw the mare. By prayer and by anointing he brough‹
it about that she once more looked to others and to hersel‹
like what she really was. This anecdote appears in English i‹
the fifteenth century.[99] Giraldus Cambrensis narrates, as a‹
observed fact of his own time, that some magicians in Irelan‹
make what seem to be pigs out of any material that come‹
handy and sell them on market days. Such pigs, for whatever reason, are always red.[100] As soon as they cross any
body of water, they vanish, reverting to the substance ou‹
of which they were manufactured, and in no event can they
retain their pig-shape for more than three days.[101] Now and
then a holy man may imitate the witch. Etymologizing plays
queer tricks, some of which are due to the primeval idea that
the name is essentially connected with the nature, so that
it is effectual in spells.[102] An amusing instance is the Durham
monk Reginald's account how the surname Todd (which
means "Fox") originated: a thievish monk was transformed
into a fox by his brethren's prayer to St. Cuthbert — but
was restored to humanity when he repented.[103]

CHAPTER XI

MIRRORS AND THIEVES

MIRROR-MAGIC or crystal-gazing in its several species (employing variously a mirror, a beryl or other stone, a basin of water, a swordblade, or a polished fingernail) [1] has a long history in England before we come to Dr. John Dee, Queen Elizabeth's mathematician, who was beyond question the most persevering of all known experimenters in this still-popular department of the occult. The object was ordinarily to detect a thief or to discover the whereabouts of his booty, but then as now it could be applied to any kind of secret. John Wesley in 1761 records in his diary the thrilling story told him by a lad who, when he gazed in the crystal belonging to Timothy Crowther (Yorkshire parish clerk, astrologer, and magician, 1694–1761), beheld a murder in the very act and saw the corpse in the pit where it was afterwards found: the boy declared that he could identify the murderers if he should ever meet them anywhere. [2] Crowther's manuscript charm-book, still in existence, gives the full formula for calling spirits into the stone or beryl. [3] The scryer was regularly a young boy, for the doctrine was that certain demons or angels — their character was equivocal — could not or would not manifest themselves except to the pure alone. [4]

Specularii was the technical name for users of the crystal or the magic mirror. Such persons, according to John of Salisbury (ca. 1115–1180), defend their art on the ground that "they make no offerings [to demons], harm nobody, often do good service by revealing thefts, cleanse the world of evil witchcraft (*maleficiis purgant orbem*), and seek only truth that is useful or necessary." [5] These pretexts, however, are bootless, — so he contends, — and we know well enough that the invocations preceding the scryer's vision were by no means always orthodox. Chaucer's Parson had no doubt on this point: "Lat us go now to thilke horrible swering of

adiuracioun and coniuracioun, as doon thise false enchauntours or nigromanciens in bacins ful of water, or in a bright
swerd, in a cercle, or in a fyr, or in a shulder-boon of a sheep.
I can nat seye but that they doon cursedly and damnably,
agayns Crist and al the feith of holy chirche." [6]   Robert of
Brunne in the same century offers important testimony, ex-
panding his source — the French-writing English author of
Le Manuel des Pechiez — in notable fashion. The French
text censures divination by "turning the psalter" and by
"looking in sword or basin" —

> Si le sauter feites unques turner,
> En espee ou bacin garder.

Robert writes:

> 3yf you yn swerde, other yn bacyn,
> Any chylde madyst loke theryn,
> Or yn thumbe, or yn cristal —
> Wycchecraft men clepyn hyt alle.[7]

When John of Salisbury was a boy he was entrusted to a
priest to learn the psalter. This priest was a practiser of
magic, and he attempted to use John and another boy as
scryers. After invoking certain demons, he had them look
at their fingernails, which were smeared with holy oil, and
at a polished metal bowl. The other boy saw some indistinct
and cloudy images, but William could discern nothing of the
sort, and he was therefore shut out whenever his tutor undertook these experiments in the black art. The whole thing
was horrible to him, he tells us, and his horror was increased,
when he grew up, by what he observed of the fate of such
speculary magicians; for he knew many, and all except two
of them lost their sight either from natural causes or by the
hand of an enemy. These two were the priest, his former
tutor, and a certain deacon, both of whom took warning and
entered religious orders. Yet even so, they suffered many
misfortunes.[8] John's gratitude to God for lack of psychic
power is significant. A boy scryer was likely to dabble in
magic when he grew up. Thus John Wilkynson, canon of
Drax, implicated in a notorious attempt at treasure-digging
sorcery in 1510,[9] confessed that, when a child of twelve, "he
was at an invocacion made at Wakefield by a scholar of

Orlyaunce for a [stolen] pair of bedes [a rosary], when he saw in a glasse a woman that had the beides in her hand, and a sprite like a kyng in a chare of gold." [10] The University of Orléans, by the way, was famous for the study of the occult. Chaucer's magician in The Franklin's Tale was a clerk of that school.

In 1311 Ralph Baldock, Bishop of London, sent a letter to the Official of the Archdeacon, directing him to investigate the matter of sorcery and magic in the city and diocese. He has learned that these arts have many practitioners there. Among other abuses it appears that, for the recovery of lost articles or for revelation of the future, certain persons "profess that they invoke spirits in fingernails, mirrors, stones, and rings, or similar materials, who, as they pretend, give vain responses and make signs." [11]

Among the paraphernalia of Richard Walker, a chaplain of the diocese of Winchester, brought to book for sorcery in 1419, was a beryl stone hung on a black leather strap. [12] In 1440 Will am Sadyngstone, Abbot of the house of Augustinian Canons at Leicester, was accused by his own brethren of this kind of magic as well as of multiplication (i. e. alchemy). Some of his money had been stolen. He called the brethren together and declared that some one of them must be the thief, but nobody would confess, and so he had recourse to sorcery. On the 20th or 21st of September, 1439, after certain incantations, he anointed the thumbnail of a boy named Maurice and bade him tell what he saw. As a result of the boy's vision, the abbot accused Brother Thomas Asty of the theft. Bishop Alnwick allowed the abbot to purge himself of the charge of sorcery *sola manu*. In the course of the same enquiry a witch appears: William Banastre, the abbot's servingman, took counsel of an *incantatrix* for a lost piece of money. [13]

In 1467 William Byg, alias Lech, was accused of heresy and sorcery in the court of the Archbishop of York. He confessed that for the past two or three years he had practised crystal gazing for the recovery of stolen goods, but he never could see anything in the crystal himself. His scryer was a boy of less than twelve years. He put in the boy's hand a crystal stone (*unum lapidem cristallum*) and made him repeat a Pater

Noster, an Ave, and a Credo, as well as the prayer that follows: — "Lord Jesus Christ send us three angels from the right-hand direction who shall tell or show us the truth about these things which we shall ask." Sometimes the boy saw the stolen goods in the crystal, sometimes the thieves, sometimes one or two angels. When the boy saw an angel or angels, Byg adjured them in Latin to reveal the truth, and then the boy saw the thieves and the booty. A score of times the boy had seen nothing. Byg gave examples of goods and money recovered, with names. He had learned the art from Arthur Mitton of Leicester about 1464.[14]

In 1475 or 1476 Nazareth Jarbrey confessed to the Commissary of London that he visited Thomas Barley in Totell Street, Westminster, and (after certain prayers offered by Thomas) looked in a beryl stone and saw a man who stole a casket with pearls and stones and other things from his mother's house. Again, at the request of a cleric of St. George's church, he visited the said Thomas and saw in like manner a man and a woman in the beryl. On describing them, he was told by the cleric that he knew the woman and that her name was Longbele. In this case the client himself was the scryer, and it appears that he was so successful that his fame spread in the neighborhood; hence the cleric of St. George's asked his aid.[15]

Not far from 1485 John Haddon of Coventry, having been robbed of forty pounds, consulted certain persons "usyng the craftes of Sorcery, Wychcraftes, and Nygromancy." These advised him to arrest William Lee, because they perceived that he wore such garments as "they determyned by ther unlawfull wychcraftes that the takers of the seid money had and used at the tyme of the takyng of the seid money." Lee was arrested, but was soon released for lack of evidence; but now Haddon is prosecuting him again in the Mayor's court at Coventry, and Lee despairs of justice there, since he is poor and Haddon is "of gret myght and power and gret alyaunce" in that city. And so Lee petitions in chancery for a writ of *certiorari*. Though the kind of sorcery used is not specified, it seems clear that crystal gazing was the method.[16]

In 1509 we have a case of defamation. Alice Ancetyr slanderously accused Christopher Sandon of stealing a rosary.

t seems that she visited a magician who dwelt in Charterhouse Ward, and he told her that he beheld in a mirror the
picture and image of Christopher. He added that Chris-
opher, standing at a glass window, had seen her hiding the
beads in her bed, and so had entered the chamber and stolen
hem.[17] In 1535 Thomas, Abbot of Abingdon, notified Cromwell of the arrest by the abbot's officers of a priest, in whose
possession were books of conjurations for finding hidden
treasure, and for consecrating not only rings with stones,[18]
but also a crystal "wheryn a chylde shall lokke and se many
hyngs." [19] Crystallomancy for the discovery of treasure or
he recovery of lost or stolen goods is plainly enough men-
ioned in the preamble to Henry VIII's statute of 1542.[20]

In 1549 William Wycherley, of St. Sepulchre's parish,
ailor and conjurer, confesses that he has "used the cristalle
o invocate the spirit called Scariot, which he called dyvers
ymes into the cristall, to have knowledge of thynges stolne,
which spirit hath geven hym knowledge an C. tymes, and
hereby men have been restored to their goodes." "This
practise by the cristalle," he adds, "he hath *at the com-
maundement of my lord protector* executed in the presence of
mr. Thynne" and others, "and by this meane my lord protector's plate was founde, where this deponent told his grace
that it was hidd." The Lord Protector Somerset may or may
not have been aware that so humble a wizard was utilized by
his household. Wycherley was acquainted with one Robert
Bayly, a "scryer of the cristalle stone." He knew also that
"one Lowth, in Flete-streete, a broderer," used the crystal,
and that "Thomas Malfrey of Goldstone besides Yarmouth,
and] a woman besides Stoke Clare" were "skryers of the
glass." [21]

This brings us within sight of the Elizabethan age, and we
need not pursue the subject. There is much material in Reginald Scot,[22] and Dr. Dee's elaborate and long-continued experiments in crystallomancy, published at great length by Meric
Casaubon in 1659, are matters of common knowledge.[23] One
or more of Dee's show-stones seem to be preserved.[24] The
Oriental use of a mirror of Indian ink is familiar to all novel-
readers from The Moonstone,[25] but it may be worth a note
that in 1831 Sir Walter Scott was deeply interested in a story

from Cairo about mirror magic by means of a black square traced in the palm of a Nubian boy.[26] Aubrey heard a similar tale long ago from a London merchant who had been a factor in Barbary: "It was desired to know, whether a Ship was in safety, or no? There appeared in the Woman's Hand the perfect Lineaments of a Ship under Sail." Aubrey adds that "a Parallel Method to this is used in *England*, by putting the White of a New laid Egg in a Beer Glass, and expose it to the Sun in Hot Weather, as *August*, when the Sun is in *Leo*, and they will perceive their Husband's Profession." [27]

Among the practical advantages of witchcraft, the detection of thieves and the recovery of lost or stolen goods have always held a distinguished position.[28] Spells of this kind are universal in their geography and include many varieties of occult lore, from mere clairvoyance or divination (as by crystal, bible and key, sieve and shears) [29] to the direst curses upon the offender. Plenty of records are preserved in Greek and Roman tablets devoting to the infernal gods those persons who have stolen one's property or who dishonestly retain property lent or deposited.[30] Modern magic is equally ferocious at times: the thief shall go blind or lose an eye,[31] or he shall die within a year.[32] One of the uses to which Mabel Brigge, executed in 1539, put her "black fast," we remember, was to recover stolen goods: she "fasted against" the suspect, who was thus forced to confess or to make restitution.[33] Timothy Crowther, Yorkshire parish clerk and cunning man (1694–1761), had a formula "for recovering things stolen by making a plate of wax." [34] Reginald Scot derisively registers several charms to detect or injure a thief, including St. Adelbert's tremendous imprecation and the jocose verses of Sir John the priest who had raided the miller's fishpond:

> All you that have stolne the millers eeles,
> *Laudate Dominum de coelis,*
> And all they that have consented thereto,
> *Benedicamus Domino.*

One of Scot's spells involves crystallomancy with a virgin child as scryer.[35] Henslowe's Diary contains an innocuous charm: "To know wher a thinge is y[t] Js stolen Take vergine waxe & write vpon yt Jasper + melchiser + Balthasar + & put yt vnder his head to whome the good partayneth & he shall knowe in his sleape wher the thinges is become." [36]

Several Anglo-Saxon charms (Latin and vernacular mixed) to detect thieves and recover stolen property, are preserved. [37] Three of these (for cattle, horses, or household goods) are distinctly Christian, though two of the three involve the magical ceremony of thrice dripping wax from three candles into the hoofprints, and one of these two curses the thief by wishing that Abraham may shut up all roads and paths against him, that Job may do the same for rivers, and that he may be brought in bonds to judgment. A fourth, all in Latin, affords a fuller form of the same imprecation. [38] A fifth, in Latin glossed in Anglo-Saxon, calls upon Abraham to protect the livestock against robbers. [39] A sixth charm (for cattle), all in Anglo-Saxon, combines Christian and pagan elements, concluding with a curse upon the robber, who is to "waste away as fire consumes wood." [40] A seventh (against theft in general) is mere gibberish: "Luben luben niga, efith niga efith," etc. [41] We have also a magic diagram to be drawn in silence and put in one's left shoe: then one will soon discover the whereabouts of the missing article. Finally, we learn that madder placed upon a beehive will ensure the bees against being stolen. [42] On the whole, these Anglo-Saxon spells differ in no essential from the illicit formulas which white witches were and are accustomed to mutter, and for which they were often brought before the church courts. [43]

One twelfth-century culprit is fortunately known to us because she happened to come into contact with St. Hugh, who was Bishop of Lincoln from 1186 to 1200. A dean in the diocese informed the bishop that this woman seemed to have a spirit of divination (*spiritum pythonicum*), and that the people resorted to her in crowds. A specialty of hers was to reveal thefts, by whomsoever committed. [44] When the dean or any other man of learning interrogated her, she put him to silence by "impudent verbosity." St. Hugh had an interview with the seeress. Extending his closed right hand, with the edge of his stole folded in it, and addressing not so much her as the demon that possessed her, he said: "Divine what this hand holds!" The evil spirit abandoned her, and she fell as it were lifeless at his feet and could not answer. "I cannot divine," she cried at last, "but I beg the mercy of this holy bishop." St. Hugh found her rustic dialect unintelligible, but the dean acted as interpreter. She was committed to the Prior of Huntingdon for discipline, and she soon reformed.[45]

In the same century we have seen that crystal-gazers defended their art because it enabled them to do good service as detectives.[46] Such thief-catching magic is condemned, however, by Robert of Brunne in 1303: "If you ever had to do with nigromancy, or made sacrifice to the devil through witchcraft, or paid any man to raise the devil in order to disclose anything stolen ('done away'), you have sinned. If you have made any child look in sword or basin, in thumb-[nail] or in crystal — all *that* men call witchcraft." [47] Robert's contemporary, Ralph Baldock, Bishop of London, found various kinds of sorcery prevalent in the city and the diocese in 1311 and issued a mandate accordingly.[48] One of the varieties mentioned is "for the recovery of lost articles." In this same century we may observe a familiar type of religious anecdote as localized at Exeter: it illustrates the efficacy of confession. A ditcher had stolen some food. The master of the house questioned the servants, and, since they all denied, he threatened to consult "a certain nigromantic wizard." The ditcher, alarmed, hurried off to confession and was absolved. The wizard anointed a little boy's nail, and, after appropriate incantations, asked him what he could see. The boy saw the theft, but could not identify the thief.[49] Of such mirror magic for stolen goods we have already noted half a dozen English examples from 1440 to 1549.[50]

In 1382 the Mayor's Court in London sentenced Henry Pot, "a Duchysman," to stand one hour in the pillory for "deceit and falsehood." Simon Gardiner, it appears, had missed a mazer cup. Henry paid him a call and promised to discover the thief; "and hereupon the same Henry made thirty-two balls of white clay, and over them did sorcery or his magic art" and then declared that Cristina, the wife of Nicholas Freeman, had stolen the cup, "falsely and maliciously lying therein." Pot confessed. He admitted also that "he had many times before practised divers like sorceries, both within the city and without, through which various persons had undeservedly suffered injury in their character and good name." [51]   The business of the clay balls is partly explained by a passage in Foxe's Acts and Monuments. He is censuring Bishop Longland of Lincoln for leaving witchcraft unpunished in 1521. John Sparke's wife of Chesham "had certaine money stolne. For the whiche the sayd Sparke her husband sent for the counsaile of two Friers; who gaue him counsaile to make two balles of clay, and to put them in the water, and in the same balles to inclose the names of them whom he suspected: and so doyng the sayd Sparke came to his money agayne." [52]   Bishop Peter Quivil of Exeter, in 1287, refers to this style of divination as a customary thing: "Let the penitent confess if he has broken the First Commandment by rendering unto demons or other creatures the worship due to God alone: to wit, by performing sleights, that is, by having recourse to conjurations, as is wont to be done for theft, in a sword or a basin, or in names written and enclosed in clay and put in holy water." [53]   And more than five hundred years later we find the same method followed by country girls to learn the names of their future husbands. Our source of information this time is a vastly entertaining number of The Connoisseur (February 20, 1755), which is crammed with folk-lore. [54]

Still in 1382 Richard Berewold was prosecuted in the mayor's court for the same offence — "deceit and falsehood." Matilda de Eye had lost a mazer by theft. He undertook to name the thief. The process is curious: "He took a loaf, and fixed in the top of it a round peg of wood, and four knives at the four sides of the same, in form like a cross; and then did soothsaying and the art magic over them." Then he falsely designated Johanna Wolsy as the guilty person. Berewold was pilloried for an hour, "the said loaf, with the peg and knives stuck in it, being hung from his neck." [55] This kind of divination (*per panes et cultellos*) is mentioned as prevalent in the diocese of London by Bishop Baldock in a mandate of 1311. [56]

Again in 1382 the Mayor and Aldermen sentenced William Norhamptone, cobbler, to an hour in the pillory. Alice Trig's "Paris kerchief" had been purloined, and she suspected Alice Byntham, who straightway visited the pretended seer and asked him to vindicate her. She gave him certain private tips about Mistress Trig, which he used to convince the latter that he could reveal the truth about anything whatsoever. Then he assured her that, as truly as these private matters were thus and so, Mistress Byntham was innocent, and, he added, "You will be drowned within a month!" Mistress Trig fell into deep melancholy and almost died. The knavish William confessed, as usual, and "because that the said William pretended to be a wise man, and skilled in such magic arts, whereas he expressly acknowledged that he knew nothing about them, and so deceitfully trifled with Alice," the city fathers sentenced him to one hour in the pillory.[57]

This 1382 was a dismal date for London sharpers. To complete the tale — though at the expense of a digression — we may note what happened to Roger Clerk at the hands of the same court. Roger was arrested for pretending to medical skill, although he was "in no way a literate man" and "altogether ignorant of the art of physic or of surgery." His particular offence was selling to Roger atte Hache a leaf torn out of a book on which was written, as he averred, a good charm for fevers. This was wrapped in cloth of gold. On examination, no charm whatever was found upon the leaf. The Court told Clerk that "a straw beneath his foot would be of just as much avail for fevers as this said charm of his was; whereupon, he fully granted that it would be so." The punishment was exemplary. On a horse without a saddle Clerk was led through the midst of the city to the music of trumpets and pipes, with the charm-packet hung about his neck, and also a whetstone (the sign of a liar); one urinal was suspended at his breast and another at his back.[58]

This penalty is almost identical with that inflicted in the same month on another pretender to medical knowledge, who also professed astrology. He caused it to be proclaimed that a pestilential mist was to come upon the city on May 14th (the vigil of the Ascension), and that all who violated his directions should die suddenly. These directions were simple: Do not leave your chamber until you have repeated the Lord's Prayer five times and broken your fast. Many believed him, broke their fast, and did not go to mass. Next day, when his lying became evident, he was ridden through the city "in the sight of all the physicians and surgeons," with his back toward the horse's head and the horse's tail in his hand for a bridle. A whetstone was hung about his neck, and also "duae ollae, quas *jordanes* vulgo vocamus." [59]

In 1390 John Berkyng, a converted London Jew, got into serious trouble by his fraudulent arts. His case, which also came before the Mayor and Aldermen, is notable for the rank of his clients. One of the complainants was William Shede-water, a servant of Edmund Duke of York. Two silver dishes had been stolen from the Duke's house in Fleet Street. The Duke's Council consulted Berkyng, who was said to be skilled in magic, and he accused William falsely. Two other complainants had been similarly accused with regard to a scarlet mantle of Lady Le Despenser's. Berkyng confessed and begged for mercy. He was pilloried for an hour on Cornhill, imprisoned for a bit, and finally compelled to abjure the city.[60] In 1418 Thomas Forde of Canterbury, sawyer and soothsayer, was convicted by the London court "of hidous trespasses and disseites." He had convinced Widow Jonet Cook of Eastcheap that he could inform her where a little coffer containing more than two hundred pounds had been buried by her husband. She was to pay for his meat and drink as well as for "the sotell instrumentes that longen to his craft," and was to reward him also with her hand in marriage. The widow actually paid him more than forty shillings. He likewise cajoled another woman out of almost a pound by promising to recover half a gown of cloth of gold which was stolen. He was sentenced to stand on the pillory for an hour on three market days with a whetstone about his neck.[61]

A bill in chancery filed by William Paule, parish priest of St. Andrew's, Holborn, shows the prevalence of sorcery in the fifteenth century. In 1484 or 1486 Thomas Fereby, a London goldsmith, had been robbed, and the thieves had thrown a bag containing part of the booty into the grounds of Paule's parsonage. Paule had returned this to the owner, but Fereby, missing "many other goodes," consulted "diverse nigromansiers," who decided that these were in the priest's possession. So Fereby brought an action of trespass in the Common Pleas against Paule with reference to *all* the stolen property, alleging that the priest had robbed him with force and arms and fixing the *ad damnum* at a hundred marks.

Paule petitions for a writ of subpœna summoning Fereby before the Court of Chancery, and also for an injunction to prevent his proceeding further in the Common Pleas until the Lord Chancellor has examined the case.[62] At about the same time Roger Page accused John Holond, husbandman, of breaking into his house and robbing him. Page had consulted "negremaunsers," who named Holond as the guilty man. On this charge Holond was arrested and kept in prison, although he offered sufficient surety. He petitioned the Chancellor to order the bailiffs to bring him and his case before the Court of Chancery.[63] In 1497 Sir Robert, Rector of St. Mary at Nax, was reported as a common defamer of many persons by means of his arts of sorcery. In particular he had slandered Alice Hall, declaring that she had stolen two rings belonging to Robert Draper.[64] In this same year we have in the London Commissary's Court a good case of sorcery by psalter and key [65] — a practice condemned in the thirteenth century by the Englishman William (usually styled of Waddington) in his Manuel des Pechiez.[66] John White of Oldfish Street was the culprit, and he confessed.[67] The modus operandi is briefly described in the record and more fully by Reginald Scot, and is familiar in modern divination.[68] The name of each suspected person is written on a slip of paper. One of these slips the diviner inserts in the pipe (or hollow end) of a big key. Then he lays the key upon the eighteenth verse of the Fiftieth Psalm: "When thou sawest a thief, then thou consentedst with him, and hast been partaker with adulterers." The closed book, with the key inside, is loosely held by the diviner and his client, while the diviner speaks the fateful verse. If the name in the key is that of the thief, the book and key will turn round and may even fall to the floor. White was accused of "practising the magic art" in this manner to discover who had stolen John Ryan's silver spoon, and of putting the guilt upon Elizabeth Doland, whose husband beat her in consequence and drove her out of his house.[69] John Steward, an ex-schoolmaster of Knaresborough, concerned in a sensational case of invocation for hidden treasure in 1510, denied that he ever called up demons or spirits, but admitted that once upon a time he had used the art of inquiry for lost and stolen articles "by the turning of the key in the book," and that on this occasion he recited the biblical verse just quoted.[70] In general, Steward confessed himself a trickster, though he seems to have trusted the oracle of the key. His case will occupy us later (pp. 207–208).

In 1529 John Welford was sentenced by the Lincoln ecclesiastical court to offer a pound of wax before the Blessed Virgin in Liddington church. His offence was — consulting (without success) a man "that reported hym self to be a doctor" in hope to learn who had stolen seven pounds. Welford said that he had heard at Northampton from several persons that this doctor was able to "tell of stollen guddes." He had also attempted to consult another wise man on the same business, but nothing came of it.[71]

In 1549 William Wycherley of St. Sepulchre's parish, tailor, when examined by Sir Thomas Smith[72] for conjuring, gave a full account of the experiment with psalter and key. "And he saith that he hath used this practise so often that he cannot expresse how many the tymes; for people ar so importune upon hym dayly for this purpose, that he is not able to avoyde them."[73] Wycherley declares that the kingdom abounds in sorcerers, and a case of ca. 1545 tends to substantiate his assertion. The parish church of Holbeach, Lincolnshire, had been robbed of property in money and jewels to the value of above three hundred marks (£200), and the people had recourse to John Lamkyn, master of the Holbeach grammar school, and Edmund Nasche of Cirencester, a wheeler by trade, both of whom called themselves soothsayers and claimed skill in "nigramansi." The result was the public defamation of John Patriche as the robber. Patriche, sorely aggrieved, complained to the Star Chamber, which took the matter up, with what result we cannot tell.[74] Nor do we know what species of "nigramansi" Nasche and Lamkyn fancied. In 1551, however, it was for sorcery with key and book in discovery of theft that William Newport, Vicar of St. Owen's, Gloucester, had to do humiliating public penance.[75] To consult a sorcerer to recover church property seems like fighting the devil with fire, but our ancestors did not shrink from such methods. Thus in 1583–84 the churchwardens' accounts of Thatcham, Berkshire, show a payment of one and fourpence "for the ingoing to Burfield to the cunnyng woman for to make enquire for the comunione clothe and the ij outhar clothes that were lost out of the church." [76] And Giffard in his Dialogue (1593) tells of the recovery of a stolen communion cup by the aid of a "wise man." [77]

We have now entered the great queen's reign, and I need not continue, for everybody knows that divination by bible and key is still going on; [78] but I cannot deny myself the pleasure of remarking that complaints for slander or abusive language or assault, involving this method of detecting a thief, came before English judges in Norfolk in 1866, at Ludlow in 1878, and in London (Thames Police Court) in 1884.[79] Now-a-days, however, the trick is usually worked to test love, or to learn the name or initial of one's future husband; and accordingly the Scripture passage is generally taken from the book of Ruth ("Whither thou goest, I will go," etc., i, 16) or from the Canticles ("I am my beloved's, and my beloved is mine," vi, 3; or "Many waters cannot quench love, neither can the floods drown it," viii, 7; or "Set me as a seal upon thine heart, as a seal upon thine arm; for love is strong as death, jealousy is cruel as the grave: the coals thereof are coals of fire, which hath a most vehement flame," viii, 6).[80] Small blame to the superstitious! The most hardened investigator cannot write down words like these without half-believing in their magic power. But there is an anticlimax, after all. With the ridiculous versatility of the occult, the verse from Ruth is sometimes used to detect a thief! [81] And (for in the lowest deep there is a lower deep) it is reported from the Wye Valley that the charm of bible and key will cure nosebleed, if followed by slipping the cold key down the back of your neck.[82]

A companion piece to divination by Bible and Key is coscinomancy or the oracle of Sieve and Shears, of which Wier gives a good description. The sieve is put upon the opened shears, and these are grasped with two fingers and raised so that it balances. An unintelligible charm is recited (*dies, nues, ieschet, benedoefet, donuina, enitemaus*). Finally the names of suspected persons are called: if the sieve trembles, totters, or turns at a name, that person is guilty.[83] In 1554, William Hasylwoode, a cleric, was brought before the Commissary's Court of the Diocese of London on the charge that he is and was accustomed to use "arte magica, seu sortilegio, Anglice wytchecraft, or sorcery, with a seve and a payre of sheeres." He confessed that "in July was twelve monythe last past, he . . . , having then lost his purse, wth xiiii grootes in the same, and thereupon remembryng, that he being a chylde, dyd hear his mother declare, that when any man hadd lost anny thing, then they wold use a syve, and a payre of sheeres, to bring to knowledge who hadd the thing lost; and so this examinante upon occasion thereof, dyd take a seve, and a payre of sheeres, and hanged the seve by the poynte of the sheeres, and sayed these wordes — by Peter and Paule, he hath yt, namyng the partye whom he in that behalf suspected; which thing he never used but ones, and also declared yt to one of his acqueyntaunce." [84] This is highly significant, for Hasylwoode learned his lore not from books, but at his mother's knee. In 1549 William Wycherley deposed that the sieve-and-shears oracle was used by Thomas Shakilton, laborer, of Aldersgate Street; by Christopher Morgan, plasterer, and his wife, of Beche Lane beside the Barbican; and by one Croxton's wife, of St. Giles parish ("and she only speaketh with the fayrayes"); also that Sir Robert Brian, formerly a hermit but then a Highgate priest, not only used psalter and key but was in the habit of conjuring with a sieve and a pair of shears, "invocating saint Paule and Saint Peter." [85] The full incantation runs as follows:

> By St. Peter and by St. Paul,
> If —— —— hath stolen ——'s ——,
> Turn about riddle and shears and all.[86]

A form of the spell was known to Scot and Aubrey,[87] and from a case in the Worcestershire records (1633) we learn that these two apostles were supposed to be the inventors of the process.[88] Almost the same formula has been utilized for the Bible and Key,[89] where, indeed, the saints' names seem more appropriate than in coscinomancy.

Elizabethan (and later) examples of Sieve and Shears are common enough. One of them is rather diverting. In 1573 it was testified that Thomas Somer, a shoemaker of Morpeth, who had lost his shirt, was told by John Bell "that yf he wold geve him 6 names of everye syd of his neighbours, and geve him 4 *d*. that he wold geve a wyf of Newcastell that wold turne the redell, and geat him the shirt within a weack; and the sheart dyd come within 3 dayes after." [90] An amusing scene in Barten Holyday's comedy The Marriage of the Seven Arts brought the sieve-and-shears oracle into play *coram populo*. Geometres is in love with the fair maid Astronomia and consults Magus to learn who shall win her. Magus proposes to work by coscinomancy. The implements are brought in, and the spell is reeled off: *Dies mies, Ieschet, bene doefet, Dowina, Enitemaus*. "Who shall have Astronomia? Shall Poeta?" The sieve remains quiet. "Shall Logicus?" No motion. "Shall Geographus?" The sieve barely stirs. "Shall Geometres?" The sieve turns round! [91] "'T is to be feared," writes Cotton Mather, "The Children of *New-England* have *Secretly* done many things that have been pleasing to the Devil. They say, That in some Towns, it ha's been an usual Thing for People to Cure Hurts with *Spells*, or to use Detestable Conjurations, with *Sieves*, & *Keyes*, and *Pease*, and *Nails*, and *Horse-Shooes*, and I know not what other Implements, to Learn the Things, for which they have a Forbidden, and an Impious *Curiositie*. 'T is in the Devils Name, that such Things are done." And again, "There is the Witchcraft of them, that with a Sieve or a Key, will go to discover how their lost Goods are disposed of," and "It is likewise a sort of Sorcery, for persons to let their Bibles fall open, on purpose to determine what the State of their Souls is, from the first word they light upon." [92] Divination of the sieve-and-shears variety or analogous thereto is in use in India, in Africa, among the Melanesians, among the Malays, and elsewhere. [93] Some form of coscinomancy was practised by the ancients. [94]

Spells and rites to "bind" thieves so that they cannot stir or make off with their plunder are a recognized specialty of both savage and civilized witchcraft. An Elizabethan charm, for example, cramps the guilty man and dims his eyes for the time being. [95] The unlearned might well be pardoned for confusing miracle with magic when the relics of holy men had the same effect as sorcery. Gregory the Great tells of a thief who stole a wether from a monastery garden, but when he was escaping, as he passed the grave of a pious monk, he found himself rooted to the spot and unable to throw down his prize, for he could not unclasp the hand that held it.[96] In like manner a passer-by who tried to steal a staff which a worshipper in St. Cuthbert's church at Durham had left stuck in the ground outside, found that his hand adhered to the staff and that the staff was too firmly planted to be removed. Very similar was the experience of a burglar who attempted to carry off an ivory coffer from the same church.[97] A rascal who was rifling the purse of a pious man at his prayers by St. Ecgwin's bier could not withdraw his hand.[98] One of the miracles of St. Germanus was so to confuse a thief that he wandered round and round (as if pixey-led) and was unable to make off with his booty.[99] Giraldus Cambrensis knew of a young man who, when about to enter St. Mary's church, discovered that he could not pass the portal, though the doors were open; he confessed theft, and the inhibition ceased.[100] Another of Gerald's examples tells of a boy who tried to rob a pigeon's nest in Llanfaes church: his hand stuck to the stone on which the nest was built, and the marks are still visible.[101]

In a diverting but indecorous English *fabliau* of the fifteenth century, the parson, who is an injured husband's brother, works an "experiment" — that is, a trick of magic — with a basin, so that it sticks to a priest's hands: he thought it was "sum wychecrafte" — as indeed it was. And the wife's hands stick there too, and so do the servant-maid's and the clerk's, and the carter's shovel sticks to the maid. Thus the priest's intrigue is revealed and he has to pay a hundred pounds before the parson "charms the basin" loose.[102] The same anecdote occurs as a *märchen*.[103] Danish folk-lore is rich in anecdotes of this nature: one of them — an especial favorite — keeps the pilferer standing with a finger stuck fast in the tap of an ale-cask.[104] Sigrun's nightmare curse in the Elder Edda takes us out of ecclesiastical surroundings: "Let the ship not stir on which thou sailest, though a fair wind rise astern![105] Let the horse not run on which thou ridest, though thou hast need to escape thy foes! Let not that sword cut that thou dost wield, unless it sing round thine own head!"[106] A magic chair which holds fast whoever sits in it, as in Milton's Comus, occurs in Greek mythology and is common enough in Celtic and Germanic saga.[107] Witches now-a-days are just as skilful as of old [108] in bespelling men or horses so that they cannot stir,[109] and popular tales the world over testify to the universality of what we may call paralyzing or adhesive magic.[110] But a witch's charm may loose as well as bind. So in Bede's famous legend of Imma and Tunna. Imma, a captive taken after a battle, is bound; but as soon as he is left alone, his bonds are loosed. The reason is that his brother, finding a body that he thought was Imma's, has had it honorably buried and has taken care that many masses should be sung for the salvation of his soul. The earl who holds Imma prisoner, thinks he must have charms or amulets about him, "such as are said to loosen bonds." Ælfric, who repeats the story, makes the earl ask Imma if he broke his bonds by magic or by means of runes. Robert of Brunne, who also repeats it, makes him ask if he is skilled in sorcery:

> Sum wycchecrafte about thou doust bere
> That thy bondes mow the nat dere [harm].

There is a similar tale in the Dialogues of Gregory the Great.[111]

The most amazing of all spells for the recovery of stolen goods comes from France in 1323. The abbot of the Cistercian monastery at Cercanceau (Seine-et-Marne) had lost much treasure. He consulted a sorcerer (*sortilegus*), who engaged that by his arts it should be restored and the names of the robbers and their fautors should be disclosed. The wizard buried a black cat in a chest with food for three days at a crossroads, with an arrangement of hollow reeds to give the creature air. The food was bread soaked in chrism, holy oil, and holy water. After three days the cat was to be skinned and its skin was to be cut into strips to form a magic circle. Then the magician, entering the circle, was to call up the demon Berith,[112] who would give the information desired. However, some shepherds happened to come along. Their dogs scratched frantically at the place where the cat was buried, and the shepherds heard the animal mewing underground. Horror-stricken, they carried information to the local judge, who dug up the box and saw that sorcery had been at work, though he had no notion who was guilty or what was the intent. The carpenter who had made the chest told the name of his customer, and so the truth came out. The sorcerer (Jean de Persant) and his helper (Johannes Praepositi) were arrested, and the helper made a full confession and died in prison. The abbot was condemned to life imprisonment, and so were an apostate Cistercian and several regular canons who were implicated. The master wizard was burned.[113]

CHAPTER XII

TREASURE TROVE

THE discovery of Octavian's treasures was registered by William of Malmesbury in the twelfth century, and the tale gained currency through repetition by later chroniclers.[1] Every prehistoric barrow or ancient camp — British, Roman, or aboriginal — was and is a strong temptation. "There is apon the tope of one of Mendipe Hills," wrote Leland in his Itinerary (ca. 1535–1543), "a place encampyd caulyd Dolbyn, famous to the people, thus saynge:

> If Dolbyri dyggyd ware,
> Of golde shuld be the share."

This is Dolebury Camp in Somerset.[2] In the same county lies Ruborough Camp, known locally as the Money Field, where, beneath the surface, is an iron castle full of gold and silver, guarded by gnomes and spirits and containing more treasure than the palaces of all the kings in the world. Once a digger got so far as to strike the door with his spade; but horrible groans and shrieks burst forth, and he narrowly escaped being carried off by the demons. So ran the tradition in the last century.[3]

Hill-digging had its peculiar perils. There was always a fair chance that some devil might be on hand where money was stored, for "Radix malorum est cupiditas." Thus when Edward the Confessor visited the royal treasury, his righteous eyes discerned a fiend that was sitting on the chest;[4] and in the thirteenth century a famous Kentish divine told of a miserly peasant who was horrified to see a devil, in the shape of a gigantic toad, squatting upon the hoard that he had so painfully accumulated.[5] In the reign of William the Conqueror a demon clothed with the body of the dead Gogmagog still guarded a vast hoard that the giant had deposited in a specially constructed vault at the town of Chastiel Bran; and the town was in ruins, for the goblin had prevented its rebuilding.[6] In 1344 a Saracen physician applied to the Earl

of Warenne for leave to capture a serpent in his Welsh domain at a place called Brunfeld. Having snared the monster
per incantationem, the doctor declared that there was a cavern
near by, in which it had lived, containing a great treasure;
and this proved to be the fact.[7] Here we have, to all intents
and purposes, the hoard-guarding dragon of Beowulf and
Saxo Grammaticus and many a local legend.[8] The connection of demons with treasure trove is illustrated by certain
forms of blessing in the Durham Ritual and elsewhere, to be
pronounced over vessels found "in ancient places" and presumably used by pagans in days of yore. One such formula
calls for the "departure of the Enemy of mankind" and
prays that the cups and jars may be "free from all phan-
tasmic assault." [9]

Spells and incantations,[10] then, are needful in the quest for
buried riches. Indeed, they are doubly necessary: first, to
call up a spirit who shall disclose the right spot; and second,
to control the demon who keeps the hoard. Such a demon replaces the ancient dragon, but he gets much of his credibility
also from the gnomes and dwarfs of Germanic myth —
"swart fairies of the mine," whose lineal descendants, unaf-
fected by science or theology, are the "knockers" and their
fellows, who are still heard (if seldom seen) by miners and
often warn them of danger. These elementals, as we may call
them, were a subject of reasonable curiosity to Robert Boyle
in the first half of the eighteenth century; he wished to ascertain "whether the diggers do ever really meet with any sub-
terraneous demons; and, if they do, in what shape and manner they appear; what they portend, and what they do." [11]

The Witchcraft Statute of Henry VIII (1542) recites in the
preamble that divers and sundry persons have devised and
practised invocations and conjurations to "get Knowlege for
their own lucre in what place treasure of golde and Silver
shulde or mought be founde and had in the earthe or other
secrete places" and, apparently in the course of these quests,[12]
"have dygged up and pulled downe an infinite nombre of
Crosses within this Realme," and declares that such invocations and conjurations, as well as the removal of any cross,
shall henceforth be punishable as felony.[13] The statute was
repealed in 1547; but the penalty for invocation and conjura-

tion was revived, though with no mention of crosses, by the Elizabethan law of 1563.[14]

Crystallomancy was more or less the regular procedure in searching for treasure. Thus, also in 1465, according to the finding of a jury impanelled by the king's escheator for Norfolk, John Cans and Robert Hikkes called up a spirit of the air (*spiritum aerialem*) at Bunwell, and promised to sacrifice to him "the body of a Christian man" if he would disclose the whereabouts of a hoard. Then the spirit "by the help of a certain crystal" showed them a "vast treasure" buried in Nonmete Hill. They dug up more than a hundred shillings, which they appropriated without regard to the royal rights in treasure trove. The demon was certainly justified in expecting a human sacrifice, which would, indeed, have been quite according to rule: in 1841 some Italian treasure-seekers actually murdered a boy for this purpose,[15] and similar crimes are recorded in Serbia in 1892 and in Russia in 1901.[16] But it is exhilarating to read how Cans and Hikkes jockeyed the fiend: they baptized a cock, gave it a Christian name, and sacrificed it as a burnt offering.[17] Incidentally we may recall that in 1595 Judith Phillips was in trouble for cozening a widow in a search for money supposed to be concealed in a house: "She told the widow she must have a turkey and a capon to give to the queen of the fairi, which the widow provided."[18] Those cunning rascals, Cans and Hikkes, were well instructed in folk-lore, for, in contriving to outwit the fiend, they followed a long and merry line of precedents that has continued in tradition, if not in practice, to the present day. The devil builds a bridge on condition that he is to have the first creature that crosses: he expects to make his prey of a human being, but a dog is driven over first.[19] The Devil's Barn was built by a fiend who was scared away, before he could claim his fee, by the trick of making a cock crow when the work was not quite finished.[20] Still celebrated in New Hampshire is the exploit of General Jonathan Moulton of Hampton, who sold himself to Satan for a bootfull of gold. Satan poured the coins down the chimney; but the general had cut off the sole of the boot, and the fiend gave up in despair, leaving his expected victim safe and very rich.[21] Such stories conform to well-known types.[22]

In 1466 Robert Barker of Babraham was brought before his Bishop in the Lady Chapel at Ely. There had been found in his possession a portentous quantity of apparatus — "a book, and a roll of black art containing characters, circles, exorcisms and conjurations; a hexagonal sheet with strange figures; six metal plates with divers characters engraved; a chart with hexagonal and pentagonal figures and characters, and a gilded wand." Barker alleged that one John Hope "had promised him wealth if he would give him two pounds six shillings and eightpence for the books and instruments, and said he had great hopes of certain spirits appearing to him, who would answer his questions, direct him to gold and silver in abundance, and impart to him all secrets. To this end he found a secret place in a close next William Clerk's house at Saffron Walden. As these things seemed to savour of idolatry and heresy, the Bishop commanded Robert Barker to abjure them, and enjoined as a public penance that Robert should, on the next two Sundays, walk round the market places of Ely and Cambridge, with bare feet and uncovered head, carrying the said plates and charts round his neck, the wand in his right hand and the books in his left hand. Afterwards all the books and instruments were to be burned in Cambridge Market Place. By way of private penance the Bishop ordered that Robert should fast on bread and water the whole of every Friday for a year, and say the seven penitential Psalms, with the Litany, every Sunday throughout the year." [23]

In 1510 there lived at Knaresborough an ex-schoolmaster named John Steward, who practised conjuring and was frequently consulted in cases of theft. Two clerics, Richard Greenwood (parson of Bingley) and John Wilkinson (canon of Drax) suggested that he should join them in a treasure-hunt at Mixindale Head (near Halifax), where (according to local tradition) a certain Leventhorp, then dead, had once upon a time uncovered "the foote of the kist [chest]" and had seen the devil sitting on it. Leventhorp had tried to remove the chest with a sword, but the fiend "nypped it a soundre in the myddist, as it had been a rish [a bulrush]." Steward agreed to help, and soon after mentioned the plan to one of his customers, a priest named James Richardson, who was consulting him professionally, on behalf of Thomas Jameson, as to what had become of some portable property and (coincidently) of a runaway servant. Thus Jameson, a leading citizen of Halifax and formerly Lord Mayor, became likewise interested in the project. Canon Wilkinson had been a scryer or crystal-gazer in his youth and possessed a book of magic (sent to him, he said, by Steward), which he gave or lent to Richardson. Following its rules, Richardson prepared a leaden tablet and inscribed upon it the image of a certain demon, Oberion, and the names of four others, "whereof Storax was one." The adventurers — Steward, Greenwood, Wilkinson, Richardson, and Jameson — agreed to meet at Mixindale by night on the twenty-eighth of January. Three circles of virgin parchment, each thirty feet in circumference, had been made ready in order to protect the operators from the fiends. The final invocation on the spot was to be uttered by Canon Wilkinson, who hoped to raise the spirit Belphares. Unfortunately a dense fog came up, the adventurers lost their way, and the whole scheme came to nothing. However, their proceedings had made so much talk in the neighborhood that Richardson was arrested as a person "publicly defamed of heresy or sorcery." He was turned over to the archiepiscopal court of York and prosecuted by the Vicar General. All the persons implicated took care to deny the actual raising of any devils, but enough was proved or confessed to justify the imposition of a very elaborate penance. As for Steward, the professional, he cheerfully confessed himself a trickster. When people applied to him for information — he averred — his custom was to show them a book of astrology and make believe that he was a cunning man, though in fact "he coude no thing do, but some tyme it hapened as he said, and that was as the blynde man cast his staff." Significant as to the regular ceremonies is his denial that he ever baptized a cock or a cat or any animal, or ever offered sacrifice to devils. Significant, too, is the prevalent rumor that explained the foul weather at about this time as due to the conjurations of Parson Greenwood and the Canon.[24] Finally we must not fail to note that Steward was reputed to have three familiar spirits in the shape of humblebees and to feed them with his blood. This brings him into intimate contact with the witch-creed of the Elizabethan age.[25]

In 1521 the Mayor and Aldermen of Norwich investigated the doings of William Smith, who, with his two associates — picturesquely styled Amylyon and Judy — had extorted money from several persons for hill-digging alleged to be in violation of exclusive rights for Norfolk and Suffolk granted by Henry VIII to Lord Corson or Curson in that year. They had also seized two or more crystal stones and some books. The testimony brought out a number of interesting facts. George Dowsing, a schoolmaster, had "reised a spirett or ij in a glass" or stone while a priest "held the glasse in his hande." On that occasion, however, another priest "began and reised a spiret first." Amylyon was present at the ceremony: "He saieth that George Dowsing dede areyse in a glasse a litill thing of the length of an ynche or ther about, but whether it was a spiret or a shadowe he can not tell, but the seid George said it was a spirett." [26]

In the hill-digging case which came before the Bishop of Lincoln in 1527, conjuration is barely hinted at, but spells are as obvious to one who knows the business as they were to the sixteenth-century judge. John Curson of Kettering had learned that there was three thousand pounds (sterling, I suppose) of gold and silver buried in a bank beside the cross "nygh hand to Kettering" in two pots. This knowledge had cost him twenty nobles: he "dyd speke with a lerned man for the knawledge of the trueth," but "the said John Curson did not name with what clarke he had ben withall." The deponent as to the facts, John Trawlove of Humberstone (a village near Leicester), swore that he himself "neuer dyd counsell with bern man to knaw of enny mony ther, nor in non other place," and that "he neuer dyd shoe to Cursont hat he wold goo to enny cunyng man for that matter, but Curson shoed hym that he hadd been at a Cunnyng man for that matter, and that it had cost him xx^{ti} nobles." Curson's story included some picturesque details. He had attempted to dig before, but had been frightened away by a "lumbring within the ground," and he said "that a man sprite and a woman sprite dyd kepe the said ij pottes." William Godely, who took part with Trawlove in the enterprise, protested "that he was neuer dygging of cross, nor off counsaill of diggyng for noo money but onely this oon tyme." [27]

Between 1527 and 1530 occurred the treasure-hunting efforts of William Stapleton, a secular priest who had once been a Benedictine monk but had found the discipline too rigorous. They involve magic books, a ring, a plate, a circle, a sword, a "shower" or crystallomancer with his boy scryer, and demons named Oberion, Inchubus, and Andrew Malchus. He searched or planned to search in at least five or six different spots, but every attempt was a fiasco. On one occasion he was ordered off by the owner of the land; on another, the spirit of the treasure failed to appear, probably (he thinks) because "there was none there." Lord Leonard tested Stapleton's powers by having a servant bury some money in the garden: "I shewed [i. e. used the show-stone or crystal] for the same, and one Jackson scryed unto me; but we could not accomplish our purpose." These details come from Stapleton's own narrative in a letter to Wolsey.[28] He admits using the crystal "for things stolen," and spins a queer yarn about the Duke of Norfolk, who, it seems, was sorely troubled by a demon sent by Wolsey. Stapleton, being urged to rid him of this infliction, pretended that he had moulded a waxen image in the duke's likeness and had sanctified it: this was mere fraud, however, "to have promotion and favour of the said duke." [29] When Stapleton wrote, he had been deprived of his magic book and all his instruments. The book had been seized by the Duke of Norfolk and the instruments were in the hands of Sir Thomas More. Stapleton's demon Andrew Malchus tempts one to linguistic conjecture. Malchus, to be sure, is an old acquaintance, being the High Priest's servant whose ear was cut off by St. Peter (John, xviii, 10); but I suspect that either Stapleton or the reporter, yielding to the spell of *Volksetymologie*, transmogrified into Andrew Malchus the name of Adram(m)elech, one of the gods to whom the Sepharvites "burnt their children in fire" (2 Kings, xvii, 31).[30] The devil that tormented Molly and Dobby Giles at Bristol in 1762, and played poltergeist tricks in the house, was said by a cunning woman who was consulted to be Malchi, "the chief of the familiar spirits." [31] Indeed, the spirit answered to that name, for a reverend gentleman, among many other questions in Greek and Latin, asked the imp "if it would answer to its true name, if he named it? it scratched it would. He then said, *Si nomen tuum Malchi est, ter scalpe?* which it did." [32]

Sir William Neville's Oxford consultant, the sorcerer Richard Jones, confessed in 1532 that "foolish fellows in the country" had often applied to him for assistance in their search for treasure.[33] In 1538 a London scrivener named Pole was reported to profess skill in "getting money hidden under ground." He and another Londoner had planned to visit Yarmouth on such a quest. Pole had friends in the country who possessed "books enough for all purposes." [34]

The most farcical of all treasure-seekers was William Wycherley, of St. Sepulchre's parish, tailor and professional sorcerer, examined at some length by Sir Thomas Smith in 1549. His main activity was in the detection of thieves and the recovery of stolen property by the time-honored oracle of the Sieve and Shears,[35] but for some ten years he had also applied the crystal to this purpose, invoking "the spirit called Scariot." To the crystal he had also resorted in his quests for treasure, but always in vain. About 1539, with four companions, he had used the *Circulus Salamonis* to call up Baro, "whom he taketh [to be] an orientalle or septentrionalle spirit." One of the four was a "scryer of the cristalle stone." They had sword, ring, and holy water. "A terrible wynde and tempest" arose, but no spirit appeared. On another occasion Wycherley used an unconsecrated sword in his treasure-digging sorcery, but was scared away by a black apparition which turned out to be a blind horse. He had also supplied certain persons with a sword, or sceptre, and a ring for a similar attempt. About nine years before, he had practised conjurations in a great circle with sword and ring, in the presence of a priest, apparently for buried treasure: his intention was to raise a spirit called Ambrose Waterduck ("Waterduke"), but the spirit did not come when he did call for him. The comical Wycherley appends to his personal confession a list of about a dozen conjurers, clerics and laymen, and winds up as follows: "This deponent saith that there be within England above v hundred conjurers as he thinketh, but he knoweth not their names; and specially in Norfolk, Hartfordshire, and Wourcestershire and Gloucestershire a great nomber." [36] We may take it for granted that Sir Thomas Smith, however devoutly he believed in magic, had sufficient sense of humor to appraise the revelations of the half-witted Southwark tailor at their true value.   By his own admission Wycherley was guilty of an offence that was punishable by death under the Statute of 1542 — conjuration and invocation of evil spirits; for Scariot, at least, must fall within that category, whatever the status of Ambrose Waterduck!   Yet all we know of his fate is a brief entry in the Grey Friars Chronicle under date of September 29, 1549. On that day the sermon usually delivered at Paul's Cross was preached in the Shrouds (the Chapel of St. Faith in the cathedral) because of the bad weather; and in front of the preacher stood "one that dwellyd in Charterus lane," with a paper on his breast describing him as a conjurer.[37] This must have been Wycherley. Let us hope that he died in his bed.

Satan is the father of lies. He assured Ann Darker that she should find money hidden "in the hall garden, but she found none."   Katherine Jooly was told by her imp Jackly that "there was a bushell of rusty mony in Sir Robert Brooks closet and he wold fetch her some," but he disappointed her. The fiend, in the shape of a black boy, met Elizabeth Southerne by a whitethorn and there he promised her two and sixpence. He had it not with him, he added "but she shold haue it at the next time she came that way, but he fayled of his promise, he met her indeed but complayned of the hardnes of the times." All these instances of diabolical charlatanry are from confessions made in 1645.[38]

Whoever is still desirous of getting buried treasure away from the devils that watch over it, may find the process fully described in Pseudo-Paracelsus.[39]   Thus he may avoid the contempt of Asmodeus, Prince of Demons, who once laughed to scorn an unsophisticated wizard who was sitting upon the spot where a king's hoard lay hidden and never suspected it.[40]   But candor prompts me to cite the comment of the learned Florentine jurist Paolo Grillando, who regards the whole business as "one of the fouler illusions which the devil works upon men, because," he adds, "in truth I have never read, seen, or heard that any necromancer, magician, or sor-

cerer of this kind ever found any treasures, or gold or silver;
yet I have seen a very great number of such searchers who,
after many labors and diabolical rites, have at last neither
seen nor found anything except the earth." [41]   Besides, if one
invokes angels or good spirits, there is always the risk that
devils may appear instead. [42]

If the recent excavators at Glastonbury, — who resorted to
what is called automatic writing and thus received (as they
supposed) messages from long-dead monks couched in improbable Latin and impossible English, [43] — had practised
this art in the fifteenth century, their bishop would undoubtedly have put them to their purgation.

CHAPTER XIII

HAUNTED HOUSES AND HAUNTED MEN

TO MOLEST a family by impish tricks (such as knocking, stone-throwing, rattling the doors, moving furniture, tossing pots and pans about, twitching off the bedclothes, and so on) is a favorite pastime of goblins, and, like many other elfish businesses, this specialty of haunting houses has often been brought by the folk under the general head of witchcraft: that is to say, the procurer of the turmoil (whoever the immediate agent) is held to be some witch or wizard who has a grudge against the householder. Historical examples are: the disturbances at Woodstock in 1649;[1] the Drummer of Tedworth in Wiltshire, who tormented the Mompessons in 1662 and 1663 and inspired Addison's comedy;[2] the haunting of Volentine Austin's house at the English Cambridge near the end of the same century;[3] the stone-throwing demon of New Hampshire;[4] the troubles of the Wesley family at Epworth parsonage in 1716 and 1717.[5] About 1662 there was a poltergeist at Brightling in Sussex, and somehow the house was burned down; a woman was arrested as a witch.[6]

There is an admirable instance of a poltergeist in the Annals of Fulda, under the year 858, which shows how persistent the type is. It was near Bingen on the Rhine. The demon threw stones,[7] beat against the walls of houses as with a hammer, spoke and revealed thefts, and brought the whole community into an uproar.[8] Such fiends were active in mediæval Britain. Two or three contemporary instances are reported by Giraldus Cambrensis.[9] From an English manuscript of the fourteenth century we learn that mugwort prevents elves and "evyll thynges" from entering a house, and so does "herbe Jon."[10] Similar virtue was attributed to "rud molin, a plant that grows near running water,"[11] by the Anglo-Saxons, who lived in constant dread of house-haunting fiends. Note, for instance, the Latin Benediction of Milk and Honey in the

Durham Ritual, which prays that, in the dwellings of the faithful, all demons may be put to rout, and that all impure and plague-bringing spirits, foes, and diseases may be banished, and all vain terrors [12] whether of midday [13] or of the night.[14] This might well include Puck, whose name, at all events, was familiar in those days,[15] though we have no account of his performances until later. The German Bilwiz, a domestic demon, though not avouched for England in Saxon times, is active in several old ballads under the alias of Billie Blin or Bellie Blind.[16]

We have to do (really) with several classes of imps: house cobolds, stable goblins, lutins, poltergeister, fairies, brownies, dobbies, hobhursts, spirits of wood and field — who are sometimes helpful, but always capricious and of uncertain temper, and who shift or exchange functions in baffling fashion.[17] When a witch is to blame for the hubbub, we have merely that blending of fairy-creed and witch-creed that is incident to the conversion of all elemental spirits into demons in the Christian sense: the goblins that once acted independently have become the witch's familiars or servants.[18] To be pixeyled is an ordinary experience, especially when one is going home from the tavern; [19] and in like manner a witch may lead you astray and keep you wandering about or travelling in a circle.[20] You can undo the spell by turning your coat inside out, whether sprites or witches are to blame.[21] The Will-o'-the-Wisp is a misleading sprite of this nature; but there are cases on record in which a sturdy rustic has beaten Will with his staff and then has boasted that he has "killed the devil." [22] It is hardly necessary to show that the Elizabethans inherited this lore of house cobolds and poltergeister and did not import it, but a few bits of testimony may be entertaining.

There was a house cobold in the time of Richard I in the mansion of Sir Osbern de Bradewelle at Daghewurthe in Suffolk. His name was Malekin and he had the voice and shape of a little child. Sometimes he spoke English in the Suffolk dialect, but now and then he conversed in Latin with the chaplain on Scriptural subjects. He was actually seen but once — and that was by a chambermaid. He often asked for food and drink. This the family left for him on a chest, and it always disappeared.[23] Giraldus Cambrensis in the twelfth century knew of a demon in the form of a red-haired youth who served as seneschal in the house of a Pembroke gentleman: he was the offspring of an incubus who had beguiled a woman by assuming her husband's shape.[24] Gerald appends a similar example from Denmark, where a fiend acted as clerk to an archbishop.[25] Foreign examples were made familiar to Englishmen by report. About 1138 a black dwarf haunted the cellar in the Abbey of Prüm and wasted the wine. He was sent to school, but did not speak; neither would he eat or drink, and it was decided that he was a devil. When stripped of his monastic attire, he vanished like smoke.[26] This goblin reminds one of the Continental Friar Rush, whose diabolically entertaining exploits became the subject of an English chapbook not later than 1569.[27] Captain Cox owned a copy in 1575,[28] and Reginald Scot, in 1584, referred to Rush's printed "storie," styled him "Rush of England," and compared him with the impish Hutgin (Hudgin) of Hildesheim,[29] whose performances are assigned to the year 1132.[30] Friar Rush was known to unlearned Englishmen early enough to be mentioned by the rustic Hodge in Gammer Gurton's Needle, and that seems to put his arrival back into the pre-Elizabethan time:

> Saw ye neuer Fryer Rushe
> Painted on a cloth, with a side long cowes tayle,
> And crooked clouen feete, and many a hoked nayle? [31]

Another Continental spook that the English knew about was Ginnechochet or Guignehochet. Johannes de Garlandia, alias John the Englishman, a rhetorician of the thirteenth century, tells us that he was an evil spirit in France who took up his abode in a cistern and used to give responses to passersby. As a specimen of comic dialogue, John furnishes a Conversation between Ginnechochet and a Countryman.[32] Here might belong also the enchanted knight Chapalu, who also lived in a cistern,[33] were it not that he seems to be really a demonic Cat of high mythological dignity.[34] The spirit named Horton or Orthon, of whom Froissart gives so lively an account, was sent as a poltergeist in the first instance, but proved a highly serviceable creature in the upshot: he made himself visible in the form of a sow.[35] Gaston Phébus, Comte de Foix, was credited with a servitor of the same type, who,

like Horton, used to bring news from a distance with tele-
graphic speed.[36]

To disturb a night's rest by twitching off the bedclothes or
throwing one out of bed is a specialty of sportive demons: so
we learn from Guilielmus Alvernus (Bishop of Paris 1228–
1249), who treats authoritatively of this subject as of countless others in his De Universo.[37] Both pranks are among those
of which Robin Goodfellow boasts in his ballad.[38] We remember, by the way, that the Emperor Otho was tumbled
out of bed by the ghost of his murdered predecessor Galba.[39]
This is what happened in 1389 to Thomas of Ely and his son
William at the hands of a spirit.[40] The Italian Monaciello, a
fantastic little creature, plays the bedclothes trick;[41] so do
English fairies and Highland cobolds.[42] Sometimes a witch is
responsible, as in the case of Oliffe Barthram, executed at
Bury St. Edmunds in 1599.[43] In Essex not very long ago the
bedclothes were pulled off the husband of a late-dead witch,
whether by her damned ghost or by one of her erstwhile
familiars does not appear.[44]

Gervase of Tilbury knew all about poltergeister. They are
called *folleti*, he says (i. e. the French *follets*), they inhabit
peasants' cottages, and, because they are invisible (though
sometimes heard to speak), they pelt those who enter, with
sticks of wood, stones, and household utensils.[45]

Saints, monks, and anchorites have often been distressed
by tricks of the same kind among other molestations from
Satan.[46] For England we may take the experience of St.
Godric of Finchale, who died in 1170. He had every reason
to cast out devils, for they tormented him assiduously. One
of them played all manner of pranks to disturb him at his
prayers, and even entered his oratory, threw the pyx at him,
and drenched him with a horn of wine.[47] One day when he
was gathering apples in his orchard, a very tall man appeared
and begged some. "No!" answered the justly suspicious hermit, "unless you will ask for them for love of God (*pro caritate*)." "I beg them and ask them *pro caritate*," replied the
stranger; but he spoke indistinctly, saying rather *caritat* than
caritate. The holy man gave him some apples, with the
formula: "Here, take them *pro caritate*, and return thanks to
God." This was too much for the demon, who vanished, first

taking on his own hideous form.[48] Of course a devil once tried
to seduce St. Godric by tempting him in the form of a fair
lady.[49] Now and then a devil threw Godric out of bed, once
hitting him on the head with a stool besides.[50] When the
saint grew old and fell sick, the fiend redoubled his efforts.
He showed himself as a bear, as an eagle, as a crow, or in his
own diabolical image; he bellowed like an ox. Sometimes a
multitude of demons crowded the cell: they were very black,
and short of stature like the little dwarfs who are called
half-foot men or pygmies (*Semipedales vel Pigmaei*). They
laughed at him, hissed at him, assailed him with firebrands,
with hammer, with pincers; they scattered dust upon him:
but all was of no avail.[51] So real were they in appearance that
a youthful attendant attacked them with an axe, knowing
no better.[52] In the same century a troublesome poltergeist
ceased his antics when rebuked by Bartholomew, the holy
man of Farne.[53]

Eminent among haunting creatures is the nightmare witch
or god or demon, fear of whom is conterminous with the bad
dreams of the human race.[54] The old Greek physicians, as
faithful disciples of Hippocrates, combated this belief of the
folk,[55] but in vain. So important an element is it in the history of man's thought that Laistner has almost succeeded in
using it as a Key to All the Mythologies.[56] There are plenty
of charms and recipes against nightmares and nocturnal goblins among the Anglo-Saxon Leechdoms, but some of them
designate the creature vaguely as a "walker-by-night" (*nihtgenga*).[57] In two, however, we have plain language: (1) "If a
nightmare (*mare*) ride a person" — and directions for an
amulet follow; [58] (2) certain little stones, found in the bellies
of young swallows, are good "for headache and eye-trouble
and the assault of a fiend and a night-walker and tertian
ague and nightmare . . . and spells." [59] In a third, an obscure
spell "against a dwarf," we are told that the goblin "came
walking in, a spider-wight, had his halter in his hand, said
that thou wert his horse," and "layeth his rope upon thy
neck" — and then "they began to sail away from the land,"
through the air, we must infer, in a wild witch-ride.[60] Some of
the elf-charms may also refer to the nightmare.[61] This, we
should remember, was a very terrible hag or demon to our

ancestors. The Norse hero Vanlandi was ridden to death by "the mare" while his men stood by and could see nothing, though they did their best to help him.[62] The Anglo-Saxons sometimes identified the nightmare with the feminine incubus (the incuba) or with the satyr.[63] John the Carpenter in Chaucer's Miller's Tale, after making the sign of the cross over Nicholas to shield him "from elves and fro wightes," repeats the "night-spell" on the four corners of the house and on the threshold:

> Iesu Crist and Seynt Benedight
> Blesse this hous from every wikked wight,
> For nightes verye, the white Pater Noster!
> Where wentestow, Seynt Petres soster? [64]

That demons or pixies or cobolds (though sometimes serviceable in stables) disturb horses in their stalls, tire them out by night-riding, and plait or tangle their manes, is a widespread modern belief, and there is abundant evidence for similar notions in mediæval and ancient times. Continuous tradition is soundly demonstrable.[65] Among the multitude of cantrips shifted from cobolds to witches this horse-riding, like man-riding, occurs frequently.[66] Ælfric believed and repeated the tale of a cow driven mad by a devil that rode on her back; [67] and the Durham Ritual contains a curious spell in which Abraham is invoked to bless our horses, goats, and swine from thieves, and the guardian angel of "our animals" is called upon to protect them so that "the devil shall not be able to ride upon them." [68] As lately as 1890 some young Cornishmen were arrested for threatening a witch who made their horses kick and jib.[69] Now and then a witch transforms a man into a horse by means of a magic bridle or otherwise, and rides him by night.[70] About 1780 a young Cape Cod man was thus served by an old woman whose doughnuts he had stolen.[71]

For pre-Elizabethan England one must not forget the fine old epic charm preserved in King Lear (iii, 4):

> St. Withold footed thrice the old;
> He met the nightmare and her nine-fold;
> Bid her alight
> And her troth plight,
> And aroint thee, witch, aroint thee! [72]

Close to this is the spell for horses that have the nightmare, repeated with scorn by Blundevill in 1571 as "a fonde foolishe charme" from "an olde Englyshe wryter": — "Take a Flynt Stone that hath a hole of hys owne kynde [i. e. naturally, not artificially made], and hang it over hym [the hag-ridden horse] and wryte in a bill. *In nomine patris*, &c.

> Saint George our Ladyes Knight,
> He walked day so did he night,
> Untill he hir found,
> He hir beate and he hir bounde
> Till truely hir trouth she him plyght
> That she woulde not come within the nignt,
> There as Saint George our Ladys Knight,
> Named was three tymes, Saint George.

And hang this Scripture ouer him, and let him alone." [73] The same charm occurs in Scot and in Fletcher's Monsieur Thomas, and a variant is known in Shetland.[74] The holed stone as a stable-charm was familiar to Scot in the sixteenth century and to both Aubrey and Sir Thomas Browne in the seventeenth, and is still in common use. It is customary, Aubrey tells us, to hang a holed flint "over horses that are hagge-ridden," and Sir Thomas wonders "what natural effects can reasonably be expected when, to prevent the *ephialtes* or nightmare, we hang up an hollow stone in our stables." [75] The custom must be somehow related to the ancient and extensive practice of creeping through prehistoric monuments like the Cornish Men-an-Tol or Crickstone in order to get rid of some disease.[76] Herrick's stable-charm is different, but was doubtless a sovereign prophylactic.

> Hang up hooks and sheers to scare
> Hence the hag that rides the mare
> Till they be all over wet
> With the mire and the sweat:
> This observ'd, the manes shall be
> Of your horses all knot-free.[77]

To the nightmare-witch belongs the goblin that jumps upon your back — the Aufhock or Huckauf, as the Germans call him. He is no stranger to modern Englishmen. Sussex tradition tells of a headless man who leaps up behind you as you ride by. The Yorkshire dobbies, sometimes acting as ser-

viceable house-cobolds, may also play the Aufhock's prank as
you pass a solitary spot where they have their haunt; and the
barghest sits on a gate or a fence, all ready to mount upon
your shoulder.[78] We cannot expect to find much about this
grotesque yet venerable figure in the records of mediæval historians and legend-writers, but one precious example emerges
from the desert of silence. In the Life of King Oswin — a
work dating from the first part of the twelfth century — we
have an account of Brother Arkillus, monk of Tynemouth,
still living at the time. He was tormented in his sleep by
a devil in the form of a black dwarf (*parvulum simulans
Aethiopem*) who "clung heavily to his back." After this infliction had gone on for a long time, Arkillus dreamed one
night that he had pulled the demon off, torn him in pieces,
and hurled him into the fire. He awoke, sore damaged by the
demonic attack, but rejoicing in his victory.[79]

It is a feature of many witch-trials that the afflicted persons
see their tormentor, though she is invisible to everybody else,
and fall in convulsions or incur bodily harm at her hands in
such a vision.[80] If the spectre is injured, the witch may suffer
accordingly,[81] just as when she is wounded in beast-shape.[82]
Here again we come into contact with ancient doctrines and
mediæval experience as well as with the witch-creed of modern savages.

If a sick man slept in a temple of Asclepias (Æsculapius),
the god might reveal to him in a dream the means of healing. Sometimes, indeed, the cure actually took place during
sleep: Asclepias appeared to the patient and healed him, so
that he was well and sound when he awoke. Thus a blind
man dreamt that the god had opened his eyes; in the morning
he could see: a man with crippled fingers dreamt that his
hand was restored, and so he found it next morning.[83] Similar
miracles are related of Saints Cosmas and Damian, Saints
Cyrus and John, and other holy men.[84] In Germany in 944
a man whose hand had been cut off, had it suddenly restored
fourteen years later while he was asleep in the night, "as
those who know him assert," adds the chronicler cautiously.[85]
Cæsarius of Heisterbach informs us that once upon a time the
wounded leg of a nun was anointed by the Blessed Virgin in a
dream, and when the nun awoke it was healed.[86] In Glaston-

bury church a boy with a horribly twisted mouth dreamt that he was cured, and awoke cured in fact through the merits of St. Peter and St. Indract.[87] Through the merits of Simon de Montfort a dropsical man was tapped (*scarificatus*) in a dream; in the morning he was well, for all the corrupt matter had been drawn off.[88]

Cædmon and Coleridge, as everybody knows, learned or composed poetry in dreamland which they remembered on awaking. In this regard the experiences of Hesiod, of the author of the Old Saxon Heliand, and of the Icelander Hallbjörn at the grave-mound of Thorleifr Jarlaskjáld are often cited. Not so well-known, apparently, is the new anthem learned by St. Dunstan in a dream, or the good fortune of the monk that Cæsarius tells of, who received in a dream the power of preaching extempore with such eloquence as to astound all hearers.[89] *In nocte consilium!*

You may suffer bodily injury in a dream as well as get back your health or receive the gift of poesy. So in one of the most famous miracles registered by the Venerable Bede. When Laurentius, St. Augustine's successor as Archbishop of Canterbury, was about to leave England, St. Peter appeared to him in a dream, rebuked him sharply for abandoning his post, and scourged him *flagellis artioribus*. Next morning Laurentius showed King Æodbald the welts and wounds left by St. Peter's whip: "retecto vestimento, quantis esset verberibus laceratus ostendit." The king was converted on the spot.[90] A somewhat similar tale figures as one of Lucian's comic marvels.[91] Capgrave tells how Bishop Grosseteste appealed from the Pope to God; "and in his deth he appered to the Pope, and smet him on the side with a pike of his crosse staf, and said thus: 'Rise, wrech, and come to the dom.' This wordis herd the cubiculeris, and the strok was seyn in his side, for he deyed anon aftir that." [92] Here belongs, psychologically, the miraculous manner in which Æquitius, in a dream, was permanently relieved of his besetting temptation, as recounted by Gregory the Great.[93] Such incidents occur also in romances. There is a fine example in the Prose Perceval. One of King Arthur's squires dreamed that a man stabbed him with a knife: he awoke, and there was the knife sticking in his side up to the haft.[94] Close allied to Bede's legend is an inci-

dent in the ancient heroic literature of Ireland: Cuchulinn in
a dream is flogged by two mysterious women; when he wakes
he is so used up that he takes to his bed and lies speechless for
a whole year.[95]

How closely legends of this kind may approximate the
witch-creed is admirably shown in the Monk Reginald's Memorials of St. Cuthbert. Among the saint's cures was that of
a man afflicted with a constant shaking of the head. The patient recalled that once in his sleep "a matron blacker than
soot" appeared and twisted his head violently, telling him
that he should never be relieved of his affliction. On awaking
he found his head constantly moving.[96] Here we have something that might well have passed for witchcraft if a village
crone had been under suspicion. The date of the cure is 1172.

Such ideas, then, which are the basis of spectral evidence,
were not imported from Strassburg or Zürich when the
Marian exiles came back to England. They were a part of all
Englishmen's inheritance from the backward and abysm of
time. The sufferer from witchcraft when the spectral hag
buffeted him, was in the same stage of belief that Mr.
im Thurn discovered among the Indians of British Guiana:
"Morning after morning, the Indians declared that some absent man, *whom they named*, had visited their hammocks during the night, and had beaten or otherwise maltreated them;
and they always insisted on much rubbing of the supposed
bruised parts of their bodies." [97]

Walter Map, toward the end of the twelfth century, tells a
story which illustrates the danger of trusting spectral evidence. A certain knight found his first three children with
their throats cut on the morning after birth, and no watching
availed. When a fourth was expected, he and his wife fasted,
prayed, distributed alms, and shed many tears. A boy was
born, and, with lamps burning, they and their neighbors
watched. A stranger (*peregrinus*) who asked hospitality for
God's sake and was devoutly received, stood guard too, and
after midnight, when all the rest were asleep, *he* remained
awake. Suddenly he saw a reverend matron approaching the
cradle to kill the child. He seized her. All the rest recognized her as the most noble lady of the town, eminent in character as in position. When questioned, she stood mute. He

declared that she was a demon, held her firmly, and branded her in the face. Next he bade them summon the lady. She came and was seen to be burnt in like manner. Then the stranger explained that the good woman had angered the demons and that they had resorted to this masquerade to bring her to shame.[98] Thereupon he released the fiend, who flew out of the window with wails and shrieks.[99] A similar impersonation (without tragedy) occurs in Symphorien Champier, who draws from the Life of St. Germanus of Auxerre. There are demons who visit houses and for whom food is left out.[100] They are called "good ladies" (*bonae mulieres*) and are obviously house cobolds or serviceable fairies in origin, like the drudging goblin in Milton for whom the cream-bowl is duly set. Yet it appears in Champier's anecdote that they were identified as women of the neighborhood. However, when this was investigated, the suspected persons were found at home in bed: the demons had simply taken their form. The same story may be read in the Legenda Aurea and in the fifteenth-century Alphabet of Tales.[101]

Map's story brings us to the subject of *striges* — demons or witches that steal or devour young children or (as, in 1653, Elizabeth Lambe was accused of doing) [102] suck their blood. These go back to the remotest ages and are practically coextensive with mankind. Sometimes they take bird-form, and rationalists have always contended that they are merely birds of prey, but the people were convinced that they are really cannibalistic hags who may assume bird shape for convenience.[103] The *lamiae* belong to the same general category as the *striges*, and the terms are often used synonymously. In a mosaic of about A.D. 500 two *lamiae* (so labelled) are pictured as birds with women's faces, like the Sirens.[104] The original Lamia was a mortal beloved by Zeus, but her children were destroyed by jealous Hera. She died of grief and now she slaughters the children of others in revenge.[105] There was a somewhat similar myth about Gello, as to whom we have a proverb involving a rather savage pun: "Fonder of children than Gello!" [106] The memory of both survives in Greece, where Gilo or Gylou is a hag who sucks children's blood [107] and Lamia is a demon who strangles them.[108] It was one of the signs that Mauricius was destined to become

Emperor of the East that, when he was a baby, Gilo often took him out of bed as if to eat him, but could do him no harm.[109]

For early Germanic times from A.D. 500 to 650 this grisly piece of folk-lore is proved by the Frankish, Alamannic, and Lombard laws, and by the Saxon laws of Charlemagne for the eighth century, and thereafter evidence abounds.[110] Gervase of Tilbury knew of lamiae who were said to visit houses in the night, drag infants from the cradle, and sometimes torment sleepers (like the nightmare, presumably). John of Salisbury also bears testimony to this article of the demonological creed but discredits it.[111] Witches or female demons of this general sort often deprive nursing mothers of their milk.[112] They may also extract and feed upon a person's heart or entrails.[113]

Lamiae, as we know from Philostratus and Keats, may seek the love of mortals, but they devour their lovers.[114] Here we come close to the subject of incubi and succubae.

The witch records of England abound in stories of infanticide, but such murders are usually perpetrated out of enmity for the parents or in stark malice.[115] On the Continent, however, the motive is usually that of sacrifice to demons [116] or of cannibalism [117] or (frequently) the object is to use the blood or fat or flesh of the victims in charms or unguents.[118]

CHAPTER XIV

THE SEER

PROPHECY[1] is not a department of witchcraft, but it is closely allied; for one of the prime objects of magic is to read the future, and a witch or a wizard may at any moment assume a prophetic rôle. For centuries the English government was about equally concerned with sorcerers and with prophets — with sorcerers because they might attempt to kill the king, with prophets (including astrologers) because they might forecast the hour of his death. Prophecy was always a strong influence with the populace and was regularly invoked in support of every treasonable plot or attempted revolution. We all remember Owen Glendower's allegorical foretellings — "the moldwarp and the ant" — and Hotspur's ridicule. The best comment is still Sir Francis Palgrave's, made some eighty years ago in the Norfolk Archæology, where Glendower's imaginings are visibly pictured. "Tradition in some cases," writes Sir Francis, "poetry in others, mere fancy and fiction in more, attributed these prophecies to celebrated names — Marvellous Merlin, Venerable Bede, the Hermit of Bridlington, and Thomas the Rhymer, as well as the Martyrs of English nationality: Waltheof and Becket, and others, including even the Sybil."[2] The statute of Henry VIII against seditious prophecies was repealed in the first year of his successor's reign, but a new law was soon needed. In the first and fifth years of Elizabeth, acts against conjuration and prophecy proceeded side by side, sometimes, indeed, in combination in a single bill. The connection is almost primeval, descending to the Elizabethan age by every line along which we can trace influences — English,[3] Scandinavian, classical, Christian.

In 1213 King John hanged a popular seer — Peter the Wise, a hermit of Wakefield (or of Pontefract) who had foretold the end of his reign.[4] In 1283, when Llewellyn's head was crowned in mockery and carried through Westcheap to

be set up on the Tower, the people recognized the fulfilment
of the prediction made by a certain witch (*sortilega*) who,
when the Welsh chieftain took up arms, promised that "he
should ride crowned through the midst of Cheap." [5] Such
equivocations of the fiend ("Aio te, Aeacida, Romanos vincere
posse") emerge in all periods:

> For goddes speken in amphilologyes,
> And for a soth they tellen twenty lyes.[6]

"Consuetudo enim daemonis est semper talibus qui eum co-
lunt amphibologice loqui." [7] "Your head shall be the highest
of the field," said the demon to Provenzano Salvani of Siena
before his battle with the Florentines in 1269; and so it was,
for they cut it off and raised it on the point of a lance.[8]

In 1311 the instructions of Bishop Ralph Baldock to the
Official of the Archdeacon of London, include enquiry, along
with various other kinds of sorcery, into that which seeks to
learn the future.[9] This became the regular thing. So, for instance, in the Royal Articles of 1547; [10] in the Articles of
Cranmer in 1548,[11] of Bonner in 1554,[12] and of White as Cardinal Pole's commissioner in 1556; [13] in Queen Elizabeth's
Articles and Injunctions in 1559; [14] in the anonymous Interrogatories in 1560 [15] and Parkhurst's in 1561; [16] in Jewel's
Articles in 1568,[17] Sandys's in 1569,[18] and Whitgift's in
1588.[19]

A professed astrologer, who scared the Londoners in 1382
by a false prophecy about a pestilential fog, was condignly
punished.[20] Late in the reign of Richard II, John Kyme,
"sothesegger," was committed to the Tower. In 1401 two
citizens of London were his mainpernors to the Constable to
bring him before the Council with a view to his release. The
Council required him to swear on the Gospels that "for the
future he would never trust false prophecies or occupy himself with them or speak (either privately or in public) of anything that may run counter to the government of our lord the
King." Then he was discharged.[21]

When, in 1450, William de la Pole, Duke of Suffolk, attempted to escape to France, his ship was captured by a
barque called the Nicholas of the Tower, and his head was
struck off by a sailor on the gunwale of a cockboat. "This

duke of Suffolk hadde axed befor this tyme of on that was an astronomer, what sholde falle of him, and how he sholde ende his lif; and whanne the said astronomer hadde labourid therfore in his said craft, he ansuerde to the duke and said that he sholde die a shameful deth, and counselid him alwey *to be war of the Tour*." [22] The "astronomer" from whom Suffolk derived this ambiguous oracle was John Stacy, Gentleman,[23] whose art, in the long run, proved fatal to the artist. He was executed for treason seventeen years later (1477) because he — with Thomas Blake, Clerk — had "worked and calculated by art magic, necromancy, and astronomy the death and final destruction" of King Edward IV and the Prince of Wales.[24] In 1462 at Cambridge a boy of eleven years met in the street a spirit in the form of an old man with a long beard and in poor attire, who foretold pestilence and famine.[25] In 1466 Robert Barker, a figure-caster, was brought before the Bishop of Ely for discipline.[26] In the thirteenth year of Edward IV (1473–74) "ther was a voyce cryenge in the heyre, betwyx Laicetere and Bambury, uppon Dunmothe, and in dyverse othere places, herde a long tyme cryinge, 'Bowes! Bowes!' whiche was herde of xl. menne; and some menne saw that he that cryed soo was a hedles manne." [27] In 1493 Elena Dalok, a professed witch, claimed to have a book which revealed to her everything that was to come.[28]

A wild case is that of George Cartar, a thresher attached to the Abbey of Saltrey, Huntingdonshire. George was brought before the Bishop of Lincoln in 1525 because he had strange ideas about the sacrament. Clearly he was of unsound mind. When once he began to confess, he told a weird story. Fifteen years before he had seen the heavens open "the breadth of ij brode berne doores," and, at about the same time, he was in the Court of Righteousness "and ther he hard oon call for S[ir] John Wed priest of blakeburne & dean ther, and then he [i. e. Sir John] apered and went vp a gree [a flight of steps] & his gown was full of ashes, as he had been rolled in the ashes, and ther was a black fello met hym & put hym bihynde a walle & ther was many great skrykes and from them cam down ashes . . . whithe & blak, and he told the same preste was deade when he was ten myle fro hym." [29] In the trial of the Duke of Buckingham for treason in 1521 it appeared that he had built his hopes upon a prophecy that he should be king, made by Nicholas Hopkins, a Carthusian monk who claimed to have "revelations." Yet the duke had been warned by a faithful friend "that the monk might be deceived by the devil, and that it was bad to meddle in such things." [30]

Demoniacs often prophesied — as, for instance, Anne, daughter of Sir Roger Wentworth, whose experiences interested her contemporary Sir Thomas More and also Cranmer.[31] They also revealed secrets of past and present. It was a devil who spoke through the possessed person's agency.

In 1535 Dr. Maydland of the Black Friars in London was reported to have said that "he knew by his science of necromancy that the New Learning should be suppressed, and the Old restored by the King's enemies from beyond sea." [32]

Sir John Dobson, Vicar of Muston, executed at York in 1538, was charged with promulgating allegorical prophecies of an elaborate sort concerning the king, the pope, the emperor ("he that beareth the eagle"), the scallop shells, the crumb, and the Cock of the North. He confessed that he had borrowed of Prior Borrowby of Scarborough a prophetic roll "which Merlin and Thomas of Erceldoune made." [33] At the same time was put to death Mabel Brigge, "that fasted a black fast to an abominable intent" against Henry VIII and the Duke of Norfolk. It was rumored that her spell had killed the king.[34] Robert Allen, a professional astrologer and conjurer of London, was in trouble about the middle of this century. He dealt in love spells, recovered lost or stolen goods, and taught his customers how to win at the diceplay; and some of his charms are preserved. His chief offence, however, was his being the "false prophecyer" who, in 1551, "bruted thatt kynge Edward [VI] was deade, too yeres before it came to pas." [35] In 1551 William Tassell was by the King's Council committed to the custody of the Master of the Horses "for casting of figures and prophesieng." [36] In the next year a certain Clerke, formerly the Duke of Norfolk's secretary, was "accused to be a reporter abrode of certaine lewde prophecies and other slaunderous matters touching the Kinges Majestie and dyvers noble men of his Councell." He lodged, it seems, with one Richard Hartlepoole, and there were found in his chamber divers "carractes" (magical or astrological figures and calculations) as well as "bookes of nigromancie and conjuration." Hartlepoole's wife was alleged to be Clerke's helper or confederate — "a doer with [him]," and the Countess of Sussex was somehow implicated. All three were sent to the Tower. What became of Clerke, I cannot say, but Mistress Hartlepoole and the countess were kept in prison for about six months and then set at liberty with an admonition "to beware of sorseries." [37] In 1554 the justices of Norfolk were instructed by Queen Mary to search for the broachers of "vain Prophesies" and "seditious, false, or untrue Rumours," which are "the very Foundation of al Rebellion." [38] In 1556 John Davys, a pretended soothsayer, though he had given bonds not to "use the like practises," was in prison for the same in London. His previous exploits had been in Wales.[39] In that same year a queer case of combined magic and prophecy came to light in Cardinal Pole's metropolitan visitation of the diocese of Lincoln. I translate the Latin record: "Thomas Waller of Alwincle in the diocese of Peterborough, being informed against for applying himself to magic arts and for having consulted a certain William Atkinson of Yardwell, Lincolnshire, and John Tassell of Baltisham, Cambridgeshire, soothsayers (*homines preficos et fatiloquos*), confessed. And being further examined as to what these persons had told him, he replied that one of them had predicted that he, the said Thomas Waller, should be hanged at the next Northampton assizes; and the other had prophesied that he should escape hanging, but narrowly and with great difficulty. While this case was pending before us, the said Thomas Waller was convicted of sacrilege at the assizes, and he would have been hanged at Northampton, as it is said, if he had not absconded." [40]

This brings us to the threshold of Queen Elizabeth's reign. No wonder a bill to punish prophecies was debated in her first parliament (1559) and passed in her second (1563).[41]

Prophets occasionally combined their business of vaticination with other profitable trades, as was the method of one Grig, a poulterer in Surrey,[42] who had not only "bene a very great deceiver of the people in sellinge of his ware" (coneyskins and the like), but also pretended to cure the sick by merely "speaking prayers on them, sayinge he tooke noe mony." He was amazingly popular: the Londoners "would followe him as yf he had bene a God." In 1550, by order of the Council, Gryg was set on a scaffold, in Surrey and elsewhere, "with a paper on his brest" that proclaimed his faults, and was forced to beg public pardon.[43]

CHAPTER XV

COLD WATER

THE ordeal by swimming (*judicium aquae frigidae*),[1] which is so conspicuous in the modern history of witchcraft, was an old Germanic rite.[2] The doctrine is, that the pure element of water will reject a criminal, not suffering him to sink — a notion originally pagan, but reinforced in Christian times by the use of water for baptism. In this regard the distinguished Cambridge theologian William Perkins explodes it, arguing cogently that mere water as water has no sacred quality or character.[3] There is manifest connection with the ancient and all-but-universal belief that water (particularly running water) dissolves a spell or interposes an obstacle to the passage of uncanny beings.[4] The general principle is stated by William of Malmesbury on the authority of an old monk of his acquaintance: "Nihil enim quod per nigromantiam fit potest in aqua aspectum intuentium fallere."[5]

Pliny reports on the authority of the historian Phylarchus (of the third century B.C.) that certain persons in Pontus, who have two pupils in one eye and the figure of a horse in the other, cannot sink in the water, even when weighed down by their clothes. Though nothing is said of their being wizards, their double pupils look suspicious, and they were manifestly a little out of the common run of humanity.[6] Walter Map had read of Scythian women thus provided, who killed by an angry look.[7]

The Gauls are said to have tested the legitimacy of their new-born children by floating them on the Rhine.[8]

The reverse of the regular swimming ordeal is reported from ancient Sicily, where, in the sacred precinct of the Palici, there was a spring which tested oaths. You wrote your affidavit upon a tablet (of wood, apparently) and threw this into the water; if you had sworn truly, it floated; if falsely, it became heavy and sank, and you were burnt (by the holy fire of the spring, it would seem).[9]

In the third century there was a pool at Aphaca in Phœnicia, sacred to Aphrodite, into which offerings were thrown:
if rejected, they floated (even if made of gold or silver); if
accepted, they sank, however light.[10]

Adam of Bremen (about 1070) tells us that there was a
spring in the temple precinct at Uppsala in which men were
drowned as a sacrifice: if the body never came up, that was a
sign that the gods accepted the victim.[11] So the Laconians
at the festival of Ino threw flour cakes into Ino's Pool near
Epidaurus Limera: if they sank and did not emerge, that was
a good omen; if the water sent them back to the surface, it
was bad luck.[12]

The famous Russian preacher Serapion (who died in 1275)
notes that the swimming ordeal was practised by the people,
but he repudiates it as stark folly.[13] As for Western Europe,
the swimming ordeal was certainly an old custom in 829.
In that year it was prohibited by Louis the Pious;[14] but there
is evidence enough that the rite maintained itself in various
places on the Continent.[15] Hence its employment at Lemgo
in 1583, which struck Scribonius as so peculiar, and which
led to a long and complicated discussion among the learned,
was a survival, not an invention.[16]

For England the ordeal by swimming is mentioned in the
Laws of Æthelstan (ca. A.D. 930) and of Æthelred (ca. 1000)
as well as in the so-called Laws of William the Conqueror (ca.
1100), in the Assize of Clarendon (1166) and the Assize of
Northampton (1176),[17] and in borough charters of 1194 and
1207.[18] Of the ritual used in this *judicium aquae frigidae*
several varieties are preserved, dating from the tenth to
the twelfth century.[19] Some of these provide by a formula
against the evil magic to which the culprit might have recourse to enable him to deny his crime or frustrate the ordeal.[20] The swimming test was used, according to these
texts, for theft, adultery, homicide, and witchcraft.[21] The
oldest of them decrees expressly that the accused persons shall
be thrown into the water one by one: "if they sink, let them
be regarded as innocent; if they float, let them be judged
guilty."[22] Another, somewhat later, calls for a pool twelve
feet deep and full of water, describes how the man is to be
tied up (with his hands under his bent knees), and directs that

a cord shall be bound about his loins. In this cord a knot is to be made, a long hair's length from the man's body: if he sinks to the knot, he is innocent.[23]

The Great Roll of the Pipe affords plentiful evidence for the regular application of the cold-water test in felonies throughout England in the second half of the twelfth century. The usual entry is a statement that "the sheriff makes return of the chattels of fugitives and of those who were condemned (*perierunt*) by (or in) the *judicium aquae*"; then follows a list of names and amounts. There are more than a score of these lists in 1166 (the year of the Assize of Clarendon) and about as many in 1176 (the year of the Assize of Northampton).[24] In 1166 two priests received ten shillings for "blessing the pits" at Bury St. Edmunds.[25] In 1168 three shillings was paid for making an ordeal pit (*fossa juisii*) at Windsor, and at Colchester five shillings and fourpence was a priest's fee "for the judgment of two men" and thirteenpence was laid out "for making the pits for the same judgments"; [26] in 1169 the cost of "preparing a judgment pit" in Warwickshire was two and six.[27] Instances of illegal ducking are of particular interest. Thus in 1185 the town of Preston (whose ancient Custumale mentions this kind of ordeal, as well as that of iron and the wager of battle) [28] was fined five marks because some of the inhabitants had subjected a man to the swimming test "without warrant"; [29] one Silvester Fitz-Simon had to pay forty-five shillings and fourpence for putting Warren, son of Baldwin, to the water test unjustly; [30] Robert le Heiward was similarly fined for a like offence, [31] and Roger de Chaurea was mulcted in half a mark for engaging in this ceremony without the supervision of the king's sergeant.[32] In the same year the Sheriff of Yorkshire paid five marks as a penalty for forcing an alleged thief, who had stood this ordeal successfully, to abjure the realm without the consent of the justices.[33] In 1174 a wealthy Londoner, Johannes Senex, convicted of robbery by the *judicium aquae*, was executed, though he offered the king a great sum for a pardon.[34] For the reigns of Richard I and John (1189–1216) there are also many records of the swimming ordeal.[35] In 1219, however, at the latest, it was abolished in England,[36] as well as the ordeal by fire, in deference to the Fourth Lateran Council (1215), which forbade all clerics to perform any rite of blessing or consecration at the ordeal of hot or cold water or of the hot iron; [37] but Roger Bacon, later in the same century, still treats it with respect.[38] In 1300 or 1301 the town of Ipswich gave "the Ordeale pitt in the suburbs" to one Fabate, having no further use for it.[39]

In the seventeenth century the water ordeal, though more or less practised in England, was distinctly under suspicion. King James approved it in his Daemonologie,[40] but I know no evidence that he enforced the principle in practice after he succeeded Elizabeth. The Cambridge theologian William Perkins exploded the theory in his sermons. Dr. Cotta rejected the test in an elaborate argument and was followed by Bernard in his Guide to Grand-Iury Men, who emphasizes its illegality. Matthew Hopkins and his lieutenant John Stearne swam witches until they were forced to discontinue,[41] but Stearne declares that he never swam any "but upon their owne request." "It was then," he adds, "the desire of such persons themselves, thinking thereby to cleare themselves." [42] In 1694 at the Wilts Quarter Sessions certain persons were tried for riotously swimming Margaret Waddam, a suspected witch; [43] in 1699 the widow Coman was swum by the mob three times in July, and died in December.[44] In New England there was some swimming, but Increase Mather and the ministers in general pronounced emphatically against it.[45]

It cannot be proved that the English use of the test by swimming in the seventeenth century was not the result of Continental influence, for we have no satisfactory evidence for the interval, but, in view of the other features of witchcraft and especially of the extraordinary hold which this performance has kept upon the people down to the present, it is reasonable to infer continuity of belief and practice from the pre-Elizabethan age. Anyhow, there is no reason whatever to guess that the Reformers brought this ordeal back from the Continent in or about 1558, for, on that theory, one must explain why we have no records of its practice during the great queen's reign. Manifestly it was never legal after its abolition by Henry III in 1219. Scot mentions the swimming ordeal but once and in such terms as demonstrate that he did not know of its employment in contemporary England.[46]

I should like to think that a Worcestershire case of 1302

belongs here, but the court roll is indecisive. It informs us that Roger Ordrych threw Margery la Leche into a running stream; "and she raised the hue and cry upon him justly; therefore he remains *in misericordia.*" [47] Perhaps this was mere assault, though Margery's surname "la Leche" suggests that she professed to be a healer, or white witch, and we know that even the whitest of witches might be tempted into dark ways or might, at all events, be suspected of such straying. Anyhow, Ordrych took the law into his own hands.

For the eighteenth century we have cases in plenty, both before and after the repeal of the Witchcraft Law in 1736. [48] In 1701 Sarah Morduck was maltreated and threatened with ducking as a witch, though she had been acquitted at the Guildford assizes. [49] Cases of swimming are known in 1704 (London), [50] 1709 (a man and two women; Leicestershire), [51] 1717 (three persons; Leicestershire), [52] 1730 (Somerset), [53] 1735 (Kent), [54] 1736 (Leicestershire), [55] 1737 (Bedfordshire), [56] 1748 (Norfolk), [57] 1751 (Hertfordshire), [58] 1752 (Suffolk), [59] 1760 (Leicestershire), [60] 1760 (attempt; Wiltshire), [61] 1762 (threat; Kent), [62] 1769 (Cambridgeshire), [63] 1776 (Leicestershire), [64] 1785 (Northamptonshire), [65] 1795 (Suffolk). [66] The Tring affair (Hertfordshire) in 1751 was particularly atrocious. The witch died, and Thomas Colley, the ringleader of the mob, was hanged for murder: yet spectators at his execution were heard to complain "that it was a hard case to hang a man for destroying an old wicked woman that had done so much mischief by her witchcraft." [67] In Virginia, Grace Sherwood was swum in 1706. [68] A New Jersey case in 1730 is reported. [69]

In 1808 Ann Izzard, of Great Paxton in the county of Huntingdon, was scratched and wounded and threatened with ducking as a witch. [70] In 1825 a man was swum in Suffolk. [71] At the Monmouth assizes in 1827 four persons were found guilty of assault upon Mary Nicolas, a reputed witch about ninety years old. They had scratched her with a thorny rosebush to draw blood, [72] had searched her for a witchteat and on her head had found a wart, and had proposed to force her into a pool for the ordeal of swimming. They had also taken her to the place where cattle had died, accusing her of causing their death. [73] In 1864 two persons were convicted of assault at the Chelmsford assizes for swimming a supposed

wizard in the previous year.[74] At Dunmow, in 1880, two
more were convicted of attempting to throw a witch into a
pond.[75] In 1897 a rheumatic old woman at Lyme, Connecticut, was ducked by a mob "to drive the devil out of her." [76]

As Neuwald wrote, years and years ago, in his refutation of
Scribonius: "The rabble, when once it takes a notion (even a
very bad one), holds it as tenaciously as a cask keeps long
afterward the odor of that with which it was first imbued.
And nobody sticks to an opinion, however foolish, more
closely than the ignorant mob, which delights in absurdities
of this kind. . . . The populace grows riotous when such
spectacles are abolished, and feels aggrieved at being deprived of sights to which even witches eagerly resort and to
which they offer themselves voluntarily." [77]

The regular swimming ordeal for witchcraft and other offences is known in India and Burma.[78] A Delhi case from the
first part of the fourteenth century is on record: a witch was
convicted by this test and was burned alive; she was a *caftan*
("hyena") and, after the manner of *caftans*, had eaten the
heart of a child.[79] Other varieties of the ducking or diving
ordeal occur in the Orient. Among the Kachins of Burma the
guilty person, standing in the water, finds that he cannot put
his head under.[80] Among the Shans that one of two contes-
tants who remains under water for the longer time is held to
have proved his case.[81] Elsewhere in India the defendant is
cleared if he can remain at the bottom by grasping a fixed
stake until an arrow has been shot and has been brought back
to the bank by a runner, or (in the Malay Peninsula) if there
is a law contest between two persons, the party whose champion holds himself under the longer is the winner.[82] By the
Laws of Hammurabi, King of Babylon in the third millennium B.C., a person accused of witchcraft is to plunge into the
divine river: if drowned, he is guilty; if the river spares him,
his innocence is established. The same ordeal is prescribed
for a wife charged with adultery.[83] A similar reversal of the
usual swimming test was reported from Africa in 1701.[84]

When examined in 1619 on the charge of murdering the son
and heir of the Earl of Rutland by witchcraft, Joan Flower
fell down unconscious, "mumbling in her mouth" a piece of

bread and butter which she was vainly trying to swallow
after wishing "that it might never go through her if she were
guilty," and she died while being carried to Lincoln jail.[85] In
1625 Mrs. Journeman of Axminster, accused of stealing an
apron, "wished that if it were not her own apron, . . . she
might never be able to open her mouth or speak more"; and,
so runs the contemporary record, "since that time, being
three days since, she was never heard to utter any word, or to
open her mouth." [86] This woman may have remembered the
Psalmist's asseveration, "Let my tongue cleave to the roof of
my mouth" (cxxxvii, 6); [87] but Joan Flower's voluntary test
is a good example of "folk-memory," for it goes back to the
venerable ordeal by bread and cheese, used in Anglo-Saxon
times in cases of theft, homicide, adultery, and witchcraft.
The idea was that no guilty defendant could swallow the morsel without choking.[88] Forms of ritual for this procedure are
extant, and it is mentioned in the Laws of Æthelred (1014)
and of Cnut (ca. 1030).[89] In 1053 Earl Godwine was choked
to death, we are told, on subjecting himself (more or less in-
formally) to the ordeal of bread.[90] In Nigeria, as an oath, a
man "takes a head of corn" and wishes, in set terms, that the
next grain he eats may choke him if he swears falsely. There
is a similar ordeal with small stones in the Solomon Islands,
with rice in Chittagong, and with rice or bread in East
Africa.[91]

CHAPTER XVI

THE COMPACT AND THE WITCHES' SABBATH

THE idea of a formal compact with Satan, which plays so important a part in the history of witchcraft, was supported by great fathers of the church. St. Augustine treats it rather fully.[1] St. Jerome appears to have accepted it to explain a dark passage in Isaiah: "Because ye have said, We have made a covenant with death, and with hell are we at agreement" (*Percussimus foedus cum morte et cum inferno fecimus pactum:* xxviii, 15). Widespread was the legend of St. Basil, Bishop of Cæsarea (370–379), who recovered from the fiend a written contract given by a miserable young man in return for the love of a woman; it occurs in fifteenth-century English in An Alphabet of Tales.[2] Greater still was the influence exerted by the legend of Theophilus — precursor of the Faust saga — which was translated from Greek into Latin[3] in the ninth century and has had a triumphant career throughout the Occident for a millennium.[4] Theophilus made his appearance in English about the year 1000, when Ælfric, in a Homily on the Assumption of the Blessed Mary, summarized the legend briefly but competently, with plain mention of the written contract.[5] The whole story in English verse is included both in the South English Legendary (thirteenth century) and in the North English Homilies (fourteenth century), and there is a third version extant in Middle English.[6] Thus there were many manuscript copies of the legend in circulation, to say nothing of its use in the pulpit. Vincent of Beauvais inserted it in his Speculum Historiale, and it is a stock item in mediæval collections of miracles and exempla, appearing for instance in the English Alphabet of Tales.[7] In 1572 William Forrest rhymed it afresh,[8] and a prose version occurs in Thomas Heywood's Hierarchie of the Blessed Angells, 1635.[9] Scenes from the legend have been recognized in sculptures in Beverley Minster and in the Lady

Chapel at Ely.[10] An English poem of the fourteenth century attaches a similar fiction to Pope Cælestinus, who died A.D. 432.[11]

The story of Gerbert and the pact with the devil by means of which he became pope as Silvester II in 999, has been familiar to Englishmen ever since the twelfth century, when William of Malmesbury embodied it in his *Gesta Regum*; and William declares expressly that he is merely writing things down which "per omnium ora volitabant." Several English chroniclers borrowed it from him, and so did Robert Holkot and Vincent of Beauvais. It turns up in the vernacular in the fifteenth-century Alphabet of Tales,[12] and is echoed by Bishop Pilkington (1520–1575): "Silvester the Second and Benet the Ninth gave themselves to the devil, and offered sacrifice to him, that he would make them popes, and promised after their death wholly to be his." [13] To Gerbert, as well as to the two distinguished Englishmen Roger Bacon and Bishop Grosseteste, was ascribed the making of a magical speaking head of brass.[14] In 1181 Walter Map recounted Gerbert's life in a richly romantic fashion which reminds one strongly of the Lai de Lanval by the author's contemporary, Marie de France. In Map, Gerbert's supernatural protector is Meridiana, a *fée*, in whom we recognize a feminine form of the Midday Demon.[15]

Among the good deeds of St. Wulfric, the hermit of Haselbury in Dorset (who died in 1154), we read of a Northern man who, under stress of poverty, became the devil's vassal and did him homage. By-and-by he repented and had recourse to the pious hermit, who compelled the fiend to relinquish his prey.[16]

Walter Map, writing in the same century, tells of Eudo, a rich young baron, reduced to beggary by foolish spending, like the hero of Marie's Lai de Lanval. He was lamenting under a tree when a huge man of ugly countenance appeared and promised to restore his prosperous state if he would subject himself to his orders (*dummodo se suo subiciat dominio*) and follow his counsels. Eudo knew well enough that it was a devil, nor did the fiend attempt to disclaim that character. On the contrary, he delivered a long and instructive lecture on demonology. He was one of the angels, he avowed, who fell with Lucifer: not one who had previous knowledge of Lucifer's plans, but one who had cast in his lot with the rebellious archangel. "God, in his mercy, permits us," he said, "to have our punishment in waste places as well as in those that are inhabited. Of old the peoples, deluded, called us *semideos* or *semideas*. To us belong Monticolae, Silvani, Driades, Oreades, Fauni, Satiri, Nayades." [17] Eudo made his pact with the fiend (*adquiescit in pactis*), and grew rich by robbery and murder; but at last, repentant, he had recourse to the Bishop of Beauvais. Him he found outside the walls by a great pyre that the judges of the city had kindled to burn a witch. The bishop, in scorn and wrath, imposed upon him the penance of leaping upon this pyre. Eudo straightway obeyed and was burned to ashes. [18]

A singular case of alleged homage to Satan dates from the reign of Edward I. Sir John Lovetot the elder was one of the scandalously corrupt justices whose misdeeds confronted Edward I on his return from France in 1289. In 1290 he was fined £3000, but the next year he was pardoned in consideration of this fine, and he continued to sit at the King's Bench until his death in 1294. [19] Soon after 1286 old Sir John had married Joan, the widow of Bartholomew de Briançon (Brianzun), [20] a lady who must have been many years his junior. His son by a former marriage, Sir John the younger, was a man grown [21] and probably felt aggrieved. At all events, he hated his stepmother cordially, and in 1301, after her death, he showed his feelings by bringing terrible accusations against Walter de Langton, Bishop of Coventry and Lichfield and Treasurer of the Realm. Not content with charging him with simony and unlicensed plurality, he alleged that the bishop had committed adultery with the elder Sir John's wife Joan, and had kept her publicly as his mistress after her husband's death. In order to carry on the intrigue more conveniently — so ran the charges — Bishop Walter had caused old Sir John to be strangled in his sleep. Finally, the bishop was a sorcerer: he had often conversed with the devil, had done him homage, and had kissed him *in tergo* — a regular ceremony, it was believed, of such infernal vassalage. [22] Pope Boniface VIII suspended Bishop Walter from all spiritual and temporal functions, and referred the case to a commission headed by the Archbishop of Canterbury; but the trial was soon transferred to the Roman curia itself. King Edward was furious. He wrote at least four letters to the Pope, protesting that the bishop was a model of all the virtues and that Lovetot, a false traitor, was persecuting him out of mere malice, and he sent a missive of similar purport to three cardinals. He even arrested Lovetot, though he released him at the pontiff's request. When the final hearing came on (in June, 1303), the bishop was acquitted, but he was required to clear himself with thirty-seven compurgators and he had to borrow seven thousand florins to pay his expenses at Rome.[23]

John Tannere (alias John Canne), who claimed to be the son of Edward I, was drawn and hanged as a traitor in the eighth year of Edward II (1314–1315). He made public confession that he had "served the devell" for more than three years, and said the fiend had promised him the English crown.[24]

In 1366 there died a certain carpenter (*artifex lignarius*) who had served the devil for fifteen years in order to excel others of his trade. He foreknew his end, and had his fellow-workmen shut him up in a chamber alone. They heard frightful cries, rushed in, and found him tearing out his own entrails. The carpenter confessed his sins, both in private and publicly, received the viaticum, and died in the faith.[25] A similar tale of a fiddler was current in Devon about ninety years ago.[26] Satan, in his quest for souls, is no respecter of persons.

Many stories circulated in the middle ages about wretches who did homage to the devil or sold themselves to him. Such were the tale of "The Three Warnings" versified by Mrs. Thrale;[27] that of the man in the diocese of Rochester who did homage to Satan and gave him a silver spoon as pledge;[28] that of the man whose hand was marked with a black stain from the devil's thumb;[29] that of the Franciscan in Milan who discovered to his horror that his father worshipped the devil in the form of a golden-robed king.[30] All of these were current in England. With the general run of English witches, who belonged to the illiterate class, the agreement with Satan was implicit only, or at most oral;[31] but sometimes a document was drawn up, as in the case of the Nottingham boy in 1672, and in that of Thomas Browne of Middlesex, acquitted in 1643 on an indictment for selling himself to the devil by a written compact.[32]

The Witches' Sabbath in its developed form is a combined religious service and business meeting followed by a debauch of feasting, dancing, and wild lust. Satan is visibly present — as man, or monster, or huge demonic goat, — to receive homage as a feudal lord and worship as a deity. The rites are in elaborate profanation of Christian ceremonies, which they reverse or parody or burlesque. Proselytes are brought in, to make or confirm their formal compact with the devil: they renounce their baptism and all "seals and symbols of redeemèd sin," abandon their faith in God and in his Church, and abjure their redemption through Christ. Satan, for his part, promises them riches and pleasure so long as they live and happiness in the world to come. To each is assigned a familiar demon, who shall come at call to serve as operating agent in every malefic design. To and from the Sabbath the worshippers are swiftly transported through the air, often for long distances, riding on staffs or broomsticks, or on fiends in bestial form; or they may fly thither and home again by virtue of a magic ointment with which they smear themselves. This ointment, which has other occult properties, is sometimes prepared at the meetings from the fat and marrow of stolen infants who are sacrificed to Satan or of buried infants whom the hags have clawed up from their graves.[33] Such were the orgies of the Witches' Sabbath as systematized in the fourteenth and fifteenth centuries by the scholastic ingenuity of devout theologians and described in confessions innumerable wrung by torture from ignorant and superstitious defendants in response to leading questions framed by inquisitors who had the whole system in mind before the trial began.

Two elements in the system are clearly distinguishable — the religious service with its attendant debauch, and the demonic transportation.

For the demonic transportation, which accords in essence with the ancient and practically universal belief in the power of witches and demons to take various shapes and to fly through the air, we have a text of paramount significance, the so-called Canon Episcopi. This document, first recorded in the collection of ecclesiastical decrees made by the Abbot Regino of Prüm about the year 906, is of unknown authorship, but it is doubtless the genuine enactment of some council, and must be considerably older than Regino's time, though it certainly did not emanate, as succeeding legists and theologians supposed, from the Synod of Ancyra (A.D. 314). It denounces the errors of certain women who are "seduced by the illusions and phantasms of demons." These "believe and declare that they ride upon beasts with Diana, goddess of the pagans, and a countless multitude of women, passing through many regions in the dead of night, and that on appointed nights they are called out to her service. A vast number, misled by this false opinion, accept these things as true, and thus deviate from the faith, since they think that something of divine nature and power exists apart from the one true God." Priests should preach that such notions are mere demonic fancies put into the mind by the evil spirit. "For Satan (who transforms himself into an angel of light), when he has once taken possession of a woman's mind and subjected her to his power by infidelity and wrong belief, straightway changes himself into the likeness of divers persons and deludes the minds of his subjects in sleep, so that the victim believes that these things, which only her spirit experiences, she really experiences in the body." [34] This enlightened canon was included in the authoritative collections of Ivo of Chartres and Gratian, and became the accepted law of the church. [35] If it had been consistently applied throughout the witch prosecutions on the Continent, the whole apparatus of the Witches' Sabbath would have been relegated to the domain of disordered intellects and bad dreams, where, in large part, it certainly belongs.

The Canon Episcopi, we observe, has in and for itself nothing to do with witchcraft. The women whom it contemplates are merely deluded creatures whose sin consists in their faith in a heathen goddess, their willingness to attend her in aërial frolics, and their acceptance of dream phenomena, in this regard, as genuine experiences. In short, they have relapsed to paganism. But they are not witches, even in intent. Their imagined flight involves no purpose of evil magic: they have neither the power nor the wish to kill their neighbors or blight their crops or send the murrain upon their cattle. In the mind of the folk, however, the coursers with Diana became crossed or confused with another breed of uncanny creatures — the *striges*, vampire-hags who ranged the air by night and slaughtered new-born infants or sucked their blood (p. 224). Such beings were immemorial figures of the popular creed, and they have continued to haunt men's minds to the present day. Even in Regino's book, the deluded women of Diana are brought into close connection with witchcraft; for in his rules for a bishop's visitation we find a brief extract from the Canon Episcopi combined with a passage which deals specifically with the black art: "The bishop must inquire whether there is any woman [in the parish] who by certain witcheries and incantations says that she can change men's minds from hate to love or from love to hate, or damages or steals their goods; and whether there is any who says that, with a horde of demons in the likeness of women, on appointed nights she rides upon certain beasts and joins their company." Other prescribed enquiries concern divination, superstitious ceremonies at trees or springs or stones, and charms and rites to transfer the pestilence from one's own animals to the flocks and herds of a neighbor.[36]

With all this, however, we are still far removed from the Witches' Sabbath. For *that* we have to look in quite another direction.

The religious meetings of any body of Non-conformists are a natural object of suspicion to the orthodox, particularly if the sectaries hold them in secret, as they must in times of persecution, and very particularly if the service involves ceremonies of a mysterious character. In that case the assemblies, however decorous, are likely to be regarded by the uninitiated majority as orgies of demonolatry and licentiousness. Such were the conventicles of the early Christians in the estimation of pagan Rome; and such, in the estimation of orthodox Christianity, were the conventicles of the heretical sects that arose successively as time went on — of the Manichæans from the third to the sixth century, of the Paulicians from the seventh to the ninth, of the Cathari and the Waldenses in the middle ages. Nor does history lack instances in which the ill repute has been justified, as in the case of the Anabaptist disciples of Jan Matthys and John of Leyden.

In the course of the fourteenth century the papal inquisitors discovered (so they thought) a new heretical sect — the sect of devil-worshipping witches. These, it logically followed, must hold meetings, and such meetings must resemble those of the other heretics. The belief in witchcraft was ancient, primeval, and of the folk; but the folk had always feared and hated witches as individuals, not as members of an organized body or as adherents to a system. The idea of a Sabbath of Witches was neither ancient nor of popular origin. It was a mere transference. What was already established in the inquisitorial mind with regard to the Satanic Synagogue of the Cathari was shifted, as a matter of logical course, to the alleged assemblies of the new heretical sect, the devotees of witchcraft. The process was complete by the early fifteenth century.

Thus originated the momentous doctrine of the Witches' Sabbath, which included, from this time on, the ancient folk-belief in the aërial flight, already emergent now and then in cases of heresy. To be sure, the Canon Episcopi had to be explained away; but this was no difficult feat for scholastic reasoners. The Canon, they argued, teaches merely that certain deluded women imagine themselves to fly abroad in troops with other worshippers of Diana. It applies, therefore, to a specific form of false belief, which it condemns. Such delusions are no doubt possible. However, the Canon does *not* apply to the witches of our own time, members of this strange sect of demonolaters. These are undoubtedly often transported through the air to their Sabbath, where they do homage to Satan, render an account of their evil deeds, and dance and revel with their demon lovers.[37]

Now the papal inquisition, as everybody knows, never gained a foothold in England. In the English middle ages, therefore, no extensive prosecution for heresy took place; there was nothing, that is to say, at all comparable to the pursuit of the Cathari and Waldenses on the Continent. The result, with reference to witchcraft, is a striking contrast between England and the Continent not only in the number of cases but in the nature of the several accusations. In England, when a witch was brought to trial, she was charged with specific crimes, with killing men and cattle, with afflicting her neighbors with disease, and so on. She might have accomplices, to be sure, but she was not supposed (as on the Continent) to belong to an heretical sect: she was an individual offender and was prosecuted as such. There was no great central authority charged with the sacred duty of extirpating a new and dangerous league of demonolaters which threatened the very existence of the Church.

Then came the break with Rome, and when, by 1542, the king and his advisers felt that sorcery and witchcraft required their more earnest attention, it was the civil authorities that took charge of the matter. And the act of parliament, passed in that year, is true to English tradition. It penalizes incantation and conjuring, witchcraft that kills or wastes or maims a person or destroys or impairs his goods and chattels, and other offences of kindred nature. It does not in the remotest way recognize the existence of Satanic assemblies or of demon-worship *en masse*. Elizabeth's law of 1563 is little more than a preciser enactment with a modification of penalties, and the law of James I is a mere revision of Elizabeth's.

Here, then, we discern a fundamental distinction between Elizabethan witchcraft in England and Continental witchcraft during the same period. The English trials conform to the law. In no single recorded witch-trial during the reign of Elizabeth is there the slightest trace of the Witches' Sabbath.[38] The charges, the testimony, the confessions never hint at such assemblies. The common people, who brought the complaints, knew that some witch by her uncanny arts had killed or injured their cattle or their children or themselves, or had somehow damaged their property. The culprits confessed that they had familiar spirits in the shape of dogs and cats and toads. They admitted the practice of evil magic. But neither the complainants nor the defendants showed any knowledge of the Witches' Sabbath. And the judges, however familiar some of them may have been with Continental matters, never thought of examining suspects on that subject, and consequently never suggested such notions to the witches themselves or to the people at large. Through out the Elizabethan age the trials proceeded precisely as if n Witches' Sabbath had ever existed.[39] If we had only thes trials to go by, we should not know that anybody had eve believed in such a thing at any period of the world's history

Sir Thomas Smith, for example, took testimony agains two witches in his own parish in 1570, but the evidence has n touch of the Sabbath.[40] The same is true of the Chelmsfor cases of 1566 and 1579 and 1589, of the St. Osyth cases o 1582 (which were the chief cause of Scot's book), and of th Warboys cases of 1593. In all of these we have the evidenc in sufficient detail to assure us that, if the Sabbath ha emerged, we should find it in the record. Take, for instance the confession of Ursley Kempe of St. Osyth. She informe against Mother Bennet and Alice Hunt, but made no sug gestion of being associated with them in meetings. On th contrary, her first knowledge that each of them had a familia spirit came from her looking in at their windows when the were from home and seeing an imp like a ferret peep out from under a cloth. Further information about her neighbor Ursley derived from her own familiar, Tyffyn, who "did tel her alwaies (when she asked) what the other wytches ha done." [41] Individual and private action is the theme in thi whole case — not concerted villany or associated devil worship.[42]

A witness of the highest character is the Rev. George Gif fard, whose tract came out in 1593 and was reissued in 1603 It gives us a remarkably full account of the witch belief of th country people in Essex, but without any suggestion of thei holding feasts or conventicles. "The deuils," he writes "make the witches in some places beleeue, that they ar turned into the likenesse of wolues, that they rend and tear sheepe, that they meet together at a banquet, that some times they flie or ride in the ayre, which thinges indeed ar nothing so, but they strongly delude the fantasies of th witches." [43] But this is information given by the learne man in Giffard's dialogue (Daniel — "come to judgment" to his less intelligent neighbors, and it is clear that Daniel i not speaking of English conditions, for he prefaces this iten by the phrase "in Germany and other countries."

Reginald Scot's attitude is especially significant. He tells much of witches' assemblies, to be sure, and derides the superstition that believes in their existence; but his object in dealing with them is to discredit the absurdities of Continental writers, to whom (in this matter) he carefully refers, especially the authors of the Malleus Maleficarum, and Bodin, and Danaeus. He nowhere mentions the Sabbath as known to English witches or as alleged against them by English authorities, or even hints at it. And he scouts the idea that witches are organized and that they are bound by oath to augment their fellowship.[44] He is manifestly anxious to prevent this Continental doctrine from getting a hold upon educated English belief, and his treatment of the subject confirms (if confirmation were needed) the evidence derived from the records of trials, which, as I have said, demonstrates that the creed of the English common people in his time (with whom the prosecutions originate) did not include the Sabbath at all.

The Malleus, we should remember, was familiar to educated Englishmen. Sir Thomas Smith had a copy in his library in 1566, and Dr. Dee lent his copy to Mr. Edward Hopwood in 1597. Bodin's Demonomanie was also familiar. Gabriel Harvey, who commends Scot in the main, remarks that he wishes he had treated Bodin more courteously or confuted him more effectually.[45] Danaeus appeared in an English translation in 1575.[46] Scottish witchcraft included the Sabbath and it forms a part of the confessions in Newes from Scotland published in 1591.[47] These facts only make the absence of this feature from the Elizabethan trials the more striking and significant.

William Perkins, the famous Cambridge theologian, although a firm believer in witchcraft and in the actuality of compacts with Satan, gives no credence to the Witches' Sabbath. Those who deny the existence of witches, he informs us, argue that "they which confesse of themselues things false, and impossible, must needs be parties deluded, but our Witches* doe this, when they be examined or consulted with, as that they can raise tempests, that they are carried through

---

* By "our Witches" Perkins means "witches of our times" (a phrase that he uses on p. 191), not "English Witches."

the aire in a moment, from place to place, that they passe through keyholes, and clifts of doores, that they be sometimes turned into catts, hares, and other creatures; lastly, that they are brought into farre countries, to meete with Herodias, Diana, and the Deuill, and such like; all which are mere fables, and things impossible." But these very delusions, Perkins contends, arise from the witches' league with Satan. "Becoming his vassalls, they are deluded, and so intoxicated by him, that they will run into thousands of fantasticall imaginations, holding themselues to be transformed into the shapes of other creatures, to be transported in the ayre into other countries, yea to do many strange things, which in truth they doe not." [48] Nowhere, however, does he refer to the Sabbath as an English institution. It is manifest that, in this regard, he is thinking of Continental matters, and this inference is clinched by his marginal citation of Pico della Mirandola and Remigius. Perkins is a good witness for Elizabethan times, for he was born in 1558 and died in 1602, so that his life was almost exactly coincident with Elizabeth's reign.

Two facts, then, are of immense significance: (1) The Witches' Sabbath, though well-known on the Continent, is never mentioned or even suggested in the records of English trials in the Elizabethan period; and (2) It is never mentioned by the Elizabethan writers on witchcraft unless they are referring to Continental beliefs and practices. Add to these two facts a third, of equal moment, which has been fully established in preceding chapters: There is no single detail of witchcraft that emerges in any Elizabethan trial which was not an article of English belief before 1558. The conclusion is plain and unescapable: There is no ground whatever for imagining that the Anglican exiles — Jewel and Bentham and Grindal and Cox and Parkhurst and the rest — who returned from Germany and Switzerland on the death of Queen Mary, introduced foreign ideas on witchcraft into their native country. For the witch-creed of the English people throughout the reign of Elizabeth remained identical with their witch-creed before her accession. There was but one new element which the returning exiles could have contributed — the Witches' Sabbath; and this doctrine emerges in no English witch-case until after the accession of James I. Indeed, as we shall see presently, it is not until 1612 that the Sabbath is mentioned in any English trial.

I have not forgotten Jewel's famous sermon before Queen Elizabeth. On the strength of a brief passage in this discourse, an eminent authority has ventured the assertion that "we have every right to believe that Jewel introduced foreign opinion on witchcraft," and that "Jewel's words put the matter formally before the queen and her government." [49] The first of these propositions is confuted by the character of Jewel's remark; the second by the evidence of chronology.

On July 19, 1559, Jewel had been appointed on a commission for the settlement of church affairs in the West and South of England. He left town soon after the first of August and made a circuit of about seven hundred miles, which included Reading, Abingdon, Gloucester, Bristol, Bath, Wells, Exeter, Cornwall, Dorchester, and Salisbury. In the course of the visitations incident to this pious pilgrimage he was horrified by the prevalence of Romanist practices and of witchcraft. In a letter to Peter Martyr of Zürich, written on November 2, the day after his return to London, he remarks: "It is incredible how great a crop and forest of superstitions has sprung up in the darkness of the Marian time. Everywhere we found relics of the saints, nails by which foolish persons imagined that Christ had been crucified, and I know not what fragments of the holy cross. *The number of sorceresses and witches had increased immensely everywhere.* The cathedrals were mere dens of thieves." [50]

The sentence that I have italicized is repeated, with expansions, in a striking passage in Jewel's (undated) sermon at court, which must have been delivered, therefore, after November 1, 1559. [51] The text is Luke, xi, 15, "But some of them said, He casteth out devils through Beelzebub, the chief of the devils." The subject, however, is neither witchcraft nor demonology. The sermon is an orderly defence of the Reformers against the Romanists, involving, of course, a counter-attack. We are the true Christians, Jewel argues, yet they call us heretics. Such has always been the lot of the godly. Moses, for the "many and strange wonders" that he wrought, was called a sorcerer. Our Lord himself did not escape. The scribes and Pharisees "made light of Christ's miracles, and said to the people: 'He casteth out devils through Beelzebub.'" His answer was that "every kingdom that is divided in itself shall be brought to desolation," but "all the angels of Satan agree and conspire together to the upholding of their kingdom": "Therefore must you needs confess that I have removed this devil by some other greater power, and not by the power of Beelzebub." "Here," Jewel continues, "perhaps some man will reply, that witches and conjurers oftentimes chase away one devil by the mean of another. Possible it is so; but that is wrought not by power, but by collusion of the devils: for one devil, the better to attain his purpose, will give place, and make as though he stood in awe of another devil. And by the way, to touch but a word or two of this matter, for that the horrible using of your poor subjects enforceth thereunto; it may please your grace to understand that this kind of people (I mean witches and sorcerers) within these few last years are marvellously increased within this your grace's realm. These eyes have seen most evident and manifest marks of their wickedness. Your grace's subjects pine away even unto death, their colour fadeth, their flesh rotteth, their speech is benumbed, their senses are bereft. Wherefore, your poor subjects' most humble petition unto your highness is, that the laws touching such malefactors may be put in due execution. For the shoal of them is great, their doings horrible, their malice intolerable, the examples most miserable. And I pray God they never practise further than upon the subject. But this only by the way: these be the scholars of Beelzebub." And so the preacher, after this brief digression, returns to his argument — for two-thirds of the sermon is yet to come — and demonstrates to his own satisfaction that the Reformers' doctrines are the doctrines of "the ancient fathers, the doctors, and the apostles." Judge us by our fruits: "Superstition is removed, idolatry is taken away, the sacraments are rightly and duly used, . . . the prayers are in such sort as the people may take profit and comfort by them. . . . If this be heresy, then, alas! what is true religion? Can these be done by the power of Beelzebub?" [52]

I should perhaps crave pardon for spending so much time

over the plan and scope of Jewel's sermon. Not otherwise, however, could I present the witchcraft paragraph in its due relation to the whole. It occupies about one quarter of a page in a ten-page sermon. It is a mere *aside*, brought in, as Jewel himself says, "by the way." Doubtless it impressed the queen and the congregation, but it was not the burden of the prophet's message; it was not what they were to "carry away with them."

And what of the paragraph itself? Why, its bearing is as clear as day. It contemplates witchcraft merely in its primitive and fundamental and world-wide aspect — as *maleficium* pure and simple, as the black art by which the people are daily injured in life, body, and estate. It shows no trace of Continental influence; it conveys no suggestion of the Witches' Sabbath and its enormities. If we are to hold that Jewel's imagination had been inflamed by anything that he had heard or seen during his exile, then neither this passage nor the parallel sentence in his letter to Peter Martyr can be cited in support of such a view; [53] and these are the only utterances of the kind that have been discovered in all Jewel's published works, which extend to thousands of pages. [54]

In his three months' visitation of the Southwest of England [55] (from early August to the end of October, 1559) [56] it was Jewel's duty as commissioner not only to establish the reformed practices in the church but to investigate the morals of the laity. And we are fortunate in having, in contemporary print, the identical Articles of Inquiry which he was bound by royal command to use. The order of proceedings was to summon the parishioners and churchwardens and to call upon them to furnish, under oath, "their detections and answers." [57] One of the Articles runs as follows: "Whether you knowe anye that doe vse charmes, sorcerye, enchauntmentes, inuocations, circles, witchecraftes, southsayinge, or any lyke craftes or ymaginations inuented by the Deuyll, and specyallye in the tyme of womens trauayle." [58] This is almost word for word a copy of the corresponding item in the Royal Articles of Edward VI, drawn up for a similar visitation in 1547. [59] Lest we should infer, however, that its tenor was inspired by Protestant ideas, we must observe that Bishop Bonner's articles for the diocese of London in 1554 contain an identical enquiry: "Whether there be any that do use charms, witchcraft, sorcery, enchantments, false sooth-sayings, or any such-like thing, invented by the craft of the devil." [60] And a similar clause appears in Bishop White's articles (as Cardinal Pole's commissary) for Lincoln diocese in 1556, and in Pole's own articles for the diocese of Canterbury in 1556 and 1557.[61] Other episcopal interrogatories both before and after Elizabeth, agree in substance.[62] In this regard, then, the Reformation made no difference. In asking his questions about witchcraft Jewel was no innovator: he was following the regular practice of the church; he might perfectly well have taken them from the tenth-century manual of Regino (p. 245, above). Nor was he looking for novelties in the replies of the laymen. At no period of English history from King Alfred to day-before-yesterday would such questions have failed to bring out a mass of complaints against the wizards and witches of the neighborhood.

Conjuration and witchcraft were not absent from the minds of the English administration when Jewel landed. How could they be? Only four years before, in 1555, Sir Thomas Benger, with the famous Dr. John Dee and two others, had been arrested and examined by order of the Privy Council concerning "matters of conjuring or witch-crafte." Dee was accused by George Ferrys of striking one of Ferrys's children blind and killing the other and of directing his arts against Queen Mary's life. His reputation was against him, for the mass of the people were convinced that he practised black magic, and later, we remember, his library at Mortlake was burned by the mob (p. 318). After a short imprisonment, however, he was discharged under bonds.[63] In the same year a picturesque case, involving a bewitched woman and bewitched cattle and a white witch who associated with the fairies,[64] occurred at Taunton. The witch, Joan Tyrrye, told a story which often turns up elsewhere in folk-lore. "At one time she met with one of the 'fayre vayres,' being a man, in the market of Taunton, having a white rod in his hand, and she came to him, thinking to make an acquaintance of him, and then her sight was clean taken away for a time, and yet hath lost the sight of one of her eyes." [65] This was an experience not unusual. "Mortals," to quote Child, "whose eyes have been touched with fairies' salve can see them when they are to others invisible, and such persons, upon distinguishing and saluting fairies, have often had not simply this power but their ordinary eyesight taken away." [66]

Queen Mary died on November 17, 1558. Just one week later we read in the records of the Council that John Thirkle, tailor, "detected [i. e. accused] of conjuringe," is to be examined and kept in custody, and that one Richard Parlaben is to be similarly treated.[67] In the same month Sir Anthony Fortescue and two associates, Kele and Prestall, were also arrested, but soon released.[68] Fortescue and Prestall were later implicated in the Pole conspiracy of 1562 (p. 260), in the course of which, according to the indictment, there were incantations and conjurations — Prestall being one of the conjurers. Probably something of the kind was suspected on the present occasion. On December 18 the Council sent "certein examynacions taken of some that practysed conjuring in the Cytie of London" to the Bishop of London, with orders "to procede by such severe punishement against them that shalbe proved culpaple herein, according to thorder of thecclesyasticall lawes." [69] This bishop was Bonner, one of the most zealous of the Catholic prelates. The ecclesiastical laws were invoked by the Council because there was at this time no statute against conjuring and witchcraft, for the law of 1542 had been repealed in 1547. Here, then, we find the administration showing an active interest in these arts for reasons of state. And all this took place two or three months before Jewel reached London — some weeks, indeed, before his departure from Zürich on the homeward journey.[70]

When Jewel reached England, shortly before March 20, 1559, Elizabeth's First Parliament had been in session since the 25th of January. On March 15 "an act wherby the use and practice of enchantmentes, witchcrafte, and sorcery is made felonye" had received its first reading in the House of Commons; on April 4 it was read for the second time and ordered to be engrossed; on the 25th it was read for the third time and passed. It went up to the Lords on the 27th, where it was read for the first and the second time on the 28th and the 29th; but it got no farther. Doubtless it would have passed in due course; but the main purpose of the session was now achieved: the great business of the Supremacy Act and the Act of Uniformity was completed, and on May 8th parliament was dissolved, not to reassemble until 1563.[71]

What had the returning exiles to do with this Witchcraft Bill? Nothing, so far as one can ascertain or reasonably conjecture. The dates tell the story. The rapid progress of the bill when it reached the upper house indicates practical unanimity, and we must infer that the measure was acceptable to the bishops. And who were the bishops? They were survivors from the Marian period — Heath and Tunstall and Bayne and Bonner and the rest, the same prelates who were soon to be deprived for refusing the oath of supremacy. Jewel and Parker and Bentham and Grindal and their associates were not yet in office and had no seats in parliament. There is no indication, and no likelihood, that they drafted the bill or felt any particular interest in it. In Jewel's case, we have a strong argument *ex silentio*. If he returned from Zürich equipped with new ideas on witchcraft derived from Peter Martyr and full of zeal for the prosecution of witches, why did he not mention the subject in his long letter to that same Peter written at London on March 20, 1559, five days after the bill was brought up in the Commons? This letter, by the way, is significant not only for what it does not contain, but for what it *does*. "The bishops," Jewel writes, "are a great hindrance to us. Since they are, as you know, among the nobility and leaders in the upper house, and since not one of our men has a seat there who can refute their artifices and falsehoods by speaking face to face with them, they reign as sole monarchs, among men unskilled in affairs, and easily hold our weak senators in check, either by their numbers or by reputation for learning." [72] Three more letters Jewel despatched to Peter Martyr before the dissolution of parliament, and still there is no mention of witchcraft.[73] I need not continue. There is not a particle of evidence to connect Jewel and the Marian exiles with the Witchcraft Bill of 1559. Who drafted it we cannot tell. Probably it was brought into the Commons at the instance of the Council, which, as we have seen, had been for some time active in the investigation of conjuring cases and had felt the lack of a statute.[74] Clearly it was not a party measure. Doubtless it was as acceptable to the Reformers as it certainly was to the Romanist bishops, for there cannot have been any difference of opinion about the heinousness of witchcraft. Anyhow, the bill was a mere revival of the Statute of 1542.[75]

Between the dissolution of parliament on May 8, 1559, and the session that began on January 12, 1563, cases enough of witchcraft and conjuration came up to convince the queen and her council that some such law was needed as that which had been on the point of passing when the First Parliament rose. The evidence, though scattered and fragmentary, is ample. In August, 1559, Lady Chandos was writing to Secretary Cecil and others in favor of her daughter Lady Frances Throgmorton, who had been arrested for bewitching and poisoning her husband, George Throgmorton.[76] On November 26, less than a month after Jewel's return from his Western circuit, and before the earliest date that has ever been suggested for his sermon, Sir Richard Sakevyle and others by them of certain persons accused of sorcery, witchcraft, reported to the queen the "particulars of examinations taken poisoning, enchantment, etc.; particularly in the case of George Throgmorton and Lady Frances Throgmorton, his wife, who was accused of poisoning her husband." [77] In 1560 the parishioners of St. Lawrence in Thanet, Kent, reported at the visitation of the archdeacon that one Mother Bushe was "suspected to be a witch." [78] In the same year the Court Rolls of Gillingham Manor, Dorset, record the presentation of Cecilia Lambert as a woman of ill fame under grave suspicion of practising incantations.[79] In 1561 the Act Book of the City of Exeter tells of Frances Dyrim, who for her unquiet life among her neighbors and "for her suspected wytchecraft" had already been punished and "also exyled out of the Citie," but had returned.[80] In the same year, when lightning struck the steeple of St. Paul's, some persons declared "it was maliciously done by art magic." [81] Still in 1561, the Londoner Henry Machyn enters in his diary three several instances of men pilloried for sorcery. The first, on February 13, was a Southwark scrivener, "and ther was a paper sett ouer ys hed wrytten for sondrys and practyses of grette falsode and much on-trowthe, and sett forthe vnder coller of sowth-sayng." Then, on June 23, "was sett on the pelere for kungeryng on prest, ys name ys master Belissun [at] Westmynster." On the 25th "was sett in Chepesyde ij peleres for vij men that was sett on the pelere at Westmynster on Mydsomer evyn for kungeryng, and odur matters." [82]   One of the seven was Francis Cox, whose "unfained retractation" is extant in a broadside, from which it appears that his punishment was ordered by the Council for "the use of certayne sinistral and divelysh artes." Cox avows "that from a child he began to practise the most divelish and superstitious knowledge of Necromancie and Invocations of Spirites, and curious Astrology." [83] Soon after, he published "A Short Treatise, declaringe the Detestable Wickednesse of Magical Sciences." [84] From the records of the Queen's Bench we learn that Francis Cox (Cocks) and Leonard Bilson (Machyn's "Belissun"), with seven other men, were brought to the bar of that court on June 23, 1561, by the warden of the Fleet in obedience to a royal mandate. All nine had been arrested in London "for certain trespasses, contempts, conjurations, sorceries, and incantations practised there and elsewhere" and had been imprisoned by the Council's orders. They made confession in open court. Since there was no record in the case and no prosecutor appeared, the justices, using their "discretion," required them to abjure. Immediately after the oath they were set in the Westminster pillory by order of Council. Two of the nine were Winchester clerics, one of them (Bilson) a prebendary; two, a "clerk" and a miller, were from Worcestershire; two, an ironmonger and a yeoman (Francis Cox), were Londoners; one was a salter of Middlesex, one a goldsmith of Westminster, one a merchant of Bristol. The Bristol "merchant," Hugh Draper by name, was a prosperous innkeeper. He had been arrested "by the accusation of one John Man, an astronomer" (i. e. astrologer), who charged him with being a "conjurer or sorcerer" and with directing his arts "againste Sr William St Lowe and my ladie." Francis Cox owed his arrest to the same informer, who alleged that he was also implicated in the "practise" (i. e. plot) of Draper "and others" against the St. Loes. This was the Sir William St. Loe who was Captain of the Guard to the Queen, and my lady was his wife Elizabeth, known to fame as Bess of Hardwick, who after his death married George Earl of Shrewsbury

in 1568.[85] The plot involved an attempt to poison Lady
Elizabeth, in which one of her husband's nieces was implicated. Draper and Cox seem to have cleared themselves of
this particular crime, but both were undoubtedly guilty of
sorcery and conjuration. The exact terms of the oath of abjuration taken by the nine wizards are fortunately preserved:

Yee shall sweare, that from henceforth ye shall not vse, practize, deuise,
or put in vre or exercise, or cause, procure, counsell, agree, assist, or consent
to be vsed, deuised, practized, put in vre, or exercised any Inuocations or
Coniurations of spirits, witchcrafts, inchantments, or sorceries, or any
thing whatsoeuer, touching or in any wise concerning the same, or any of
them, to the intent to get or find any money or treasure, or to wast, consume, or destroy any person in his members, bodie, or goods, or to prouoke
any person to vnlawfull loue, or to know, tell, or declare, where goods lost
or stollen be come, or for any other purpose, end, or intent whatsoeuer, so
helpe you God, and the holy contents of this booke.[86]

*Here we have almost the very words of that Witchcraft Statute of
Henry VIII which was to have been revived in the parliament of
1559.* Note further that the proceedings in this case originated not with the ecclesiastics but with the Privy Council.
True, Grindal, the Bishop of London, examined one of the
culprits, a priest named John Cox (perhaps a relative of
Francis), but he did so at the request of Secretary Cecil, to
whom he forwarded Cox's confession. Grindal's covering
letter indicates that he was in favor of legislation against sorcery,[87] but so, as we have seen, were the Romanist bishops in
the First Parliament.

Not only the civil authorities but the physicians at about
this time were troubled by the prevalence of sorcery and
witchcraft. In 1562 Thomas Gale, Master in Chirurgery,
saw in the two London hospitals more than three hundred
poor people in such a desperate condition that sixscore of
them could never recover without the loss of a leg or an
arm or some other permanent disability. Quacks, male and
female, were to blame. "I think there be not so few in London as three score women that occupieth the arte of Physicke
and Chirurgerie. These women, some of them be called wise
women, or holie or good women, some of them be called
Witches and useth to call on certaine spirits." [88] Dr. William
Bullein, writing early in 1563, pays his respects to the same

sort of charlatans who deceive the people "with their Knacks, Pricks, Domifying and Figuring . . . Faining, that they have Familiers and Glasses; whereby they may find things that be lost. And beside them are infinite of old dotish Witches with Blessings for the Fair, and conjuring of Cattel." Bullein also mentions some witches of Suffolk whom he had known.[89]

John Halle, Chyrurgyen, is another witness. One of his examples of the "beastlye Abusers, bothe of Chyrurgerie, and Physyke, in oure tyme," is a certain Valentyne, who set up practice in 1560 at Staplehurst in Kent. "Thys abhominable deceaver made the people beleve that he could tel al thinges present, past, and to come; and the very thoughtes of men, and theyr diseases, by onlye lokinge in theyr faces." Sometimes, when consulted, he pretended "that he wente to aske councel of the devel, by going a litle asyde and mumblynge to him selfe." He was imprisoned and whipped, but resumed his business, whereupon the parson of Staplehurst brought him before the ecclesiastical court "as an adulterer, and a woorker by divlishe and magicall artes," and he was excommunicated. In 1562 he absconded to avoid arrest by the civil authorities.[90]

In October, 1562, Arthur and Edmund Pole (the Cardinal's nephews) with Anthony Fortescue (their brother-in-law) were arrested, and on February 19, 1563, with five associates, they were indicted for treason, in that on September 1, 1562, at Lambeth, they did "conspire not only to depose the Queen, but to effect her death and total destruction, and to erect and place Mary Queen of Scots in the Royal authority." Two of the conspirators, John Prestall and Edward Cosyn, according to the indictment, had, at Southwark on September 10, "practised various incantations and conjurations of evil spirits in working their said affairs: and inquired of an evil spirit how to carry their treasons into effect." Six of the group were arraigned on February 26, before a special commission. Fortescue confessed, and the others were convicted.[91] "Their onely defence," we are told, "was that they ment to attempte nothing in the Quenes life tyme, who by conjuration they had fownde should not lyve passinge the nexte spring." [92] Their lives were spared, but all of them were imprisoned in the Tower. Prestall and Cosyn had gone abroad before the arrest of their companions, and were not tried with the others.

This John Prestall was a gentleman of Surrey and was somehow of kindred to the Poles.[93] He was deeply involved in Scottish and Spanish plots against Elizabeth, in which he was closely associated with Dr. John Story, executed for high treason in 1571. Though sentenced to death in that same year, Prestall was spared by the queen. His contacts with the occult are highly curious. He was one of the two conjurers in this Pole affair of 1562. In 1567 he was released from the Tower on his offer to convert silver into gold.[94] In 1569 it was reported that he was in Scotland, "daily accompanying the Lord Maxwell, and sometimes . . . with the Laird of Coghill, where, having got two other persons, he coins both gold and silver," whether as an alchemist or as a counterfeiter does not appear.[95] In 1578 he informed against a priest named Emerson, an accomplice apparently, who practised conjuration.[96] In 1590 and 1591, when at large in London after some ten years in the Tower, he was engaged in "sorcery, witchcraft, or magic, to draw the affections of men and women," and it is on record that he had promised one Edmund Calton "a drink," manifestly a love potion.[97] After this he is lost to view.[98]

Just before the Poles and their accomplices were tried, the Second Parliament of Elizabeth convened, on January 12, 1563. On the 18th, a bill to revive the witchcraft law of Henry VIII was introduced in the House of Commons. On the 21st it was read for the second time and was referred to Sir Henry Sydney for report. As a result, a new bill was brought in on the 8th of February. This passed the House on the 11th, and went up to the Lords on the 15th, when it had its first reading, but it did not pass. On the 9th of March a new witchcraft bill was read in the Lords. This was read a second time next day and referred for report and advice to the Lord Chief Justice of the Common Pleas. It was passed on the 13th, and brought down from the Lords "by Mr. Solicitor" on the same day. It passed the Commons on the 19th.[99] This act, which was the law of the land until 1604, is more exact and detailed than the statute of 1542 which the Commons had intended to revive; but it is also somewhat milder; it discriminates grades of offence and fixes the penalties accordingly (see p. 282). Jewel and several of his fellow-exiles were bishops by this time and sat in the House of Lords, but there is nothing to indicate that they were any more in favor of the law than the Romanist bishops had been in favor of the more drastic bill that had come before them in 1559. Again we have letters — three in number — from Jewel to his Zürich friends, written during this three months' session, and there is no word of witchcraft in any of them.[100] From 1559 to 1602, indeed, we have in print about two hundred letters written by the English reformers to their friends on the Continent and some fifty letters from Continental correspondents to Englishmen. Every conceivable topic is discussed or touched upon, some of them again and again: — the mass, the Royal Visitation, the coinage, the Westminster Conference, the plague, the wars, vestments, the queen's marriage, the Ubiquitarians, Parkhurst's epigrams, the state of the universities, the silver cross in Elizabeth's chapel, the lightning that struck the Salisbury steeple, candles, the Anabaptists, organs in the churches, the Rising in the North, the ring in betrothal, the opposition in parliament, the murder of Darnley, the churching of women, a sheep in Essex that revealed a murder,[101] monstrous births,[102] etc., etc. But demonology and witchcraft are barely mentioned. I have searched these letters more than once, and — except for Jewel's solitary sentence, already quoted (p. 251) — I have found but three instances:

(1) 1566. Rizzio was "skilled in the necromantic art." [103]

(2) 1571. The Papists endeavor to cause the death of Elizabeth "by poison and violence and witchcraft and treason." [104]

(3) 1574. A Dutch girl at Norwich and the son of an M. P. were possessed of a devil, but were set free by God's help. [105]

In two letters of 1563 from Bishop Parkhurst to Henry Bullinger is this silence particularly eloquent. In the first, written shortly after the prorogation of the parliament that enacted the Witchcraft Law, he tells of the Poles' conspiracy but ignores the sorcery it involved. In the second, which dates from August, he reports the news from Scotland just brought by a young preacher of that nation. "They have decreed in parliament," so runs one of the items, "that adultery shall be punished with death." [106] But Parkhurst neglects to add that the same penalty has been fixed by the Scottish legislators for practising any kind of witchcraft, sorcery, or necromancy, or for pretending to any knowledge of such arts, or for consulting any person who thus pretends. Yet this Draconic statute had been enacted, like that against adultery, in the Scottish parliament of the preceding June, and precedes it immediately in the record.[107] Surely, if the returning exiles had been so eager in this matter as some scholars would have us believe, — and particularly if such eagerness had been due to their Continental lessons and experiences in Mary's reign, — Bishop Parkhurst, one of the most eminent of those exiles, writing to a Zürich friend in August, 1563, might be expected to advert both to the English witchcraft law (passed in March of that year) and to the Scottish witchcraft law (passed in June) as matters of interest not only to himself but to his correspondent. *Praefulget per absentiam!*

I have no thought of denying that Jewel and the other bishops probably favored the Witchcraft Act of 1563. Indeed, there is one piece of evidence, heretofore overlooked, which proves their interest in that measure. The Convocation of 1563 met on the same day as Parliament (January 12), and for Convocation William Alley (or Allein), Bishop of Exeter, prepared a "Judgment for Doctrine and Discipline." This contains, among many other proposals, a recommendation "That there be some penal, sharp, yea, Capital Pains for Witches, Charmers, Sorcerers, Inchanters and such like." [108] My point is — and I think I have proved it amply — that the opinions of Jewel and his confrères on sorcery and witchcraft did not differ from those of the Romanists, and, further, that the legislation (abortive in 1559, effectual in 1563) was not due to their initiative, but rather to the general government as represented by the Privy Council. Anyhow, it is perfectly clear that they introduced no Continental ideas on the subject. The varieties of witchcraft and sorcery specified in the Statute of 1563 are identical with those in the Statute of 1542. In view of the activity of the civil authorities before the return of the exiles, of what was done by the parliament of 1559, when the Marian bishops were still in the House of Lords, and of the general excitement on the subject of conjuring and witchcraft between the parliament of 1559 and that of 1563, it is hard to understand why to the exiles and to Jewel in particular should be ascribed the bringing forward in 1563 of the same proposition to revive the Statute of Henry VIII that had all but passed on the previous occasion. And it is still more difficult to comprehend the point of view of those scholars who maintain that a few sentences in Jewel's sermon of 1560 made such an impression as to cause the drafting and passage of the Witchcraft Statute of 1563.[109]

One curiosity of learned opinion remains to be noted before we come back to the Witches' Sabbath. In 1582 one W. W. (not hitherto identified) published Brian Darcey's circumstantial account of the St. Osyth witchcraft cases of that year. From this a distinguished investigator makes the following quotation: "There is a man of great cunning and knoweledge come ouer lately vnto our Queenes Maiestie, which hath aduertised her what a companie and number of Witches be within Englande: whereupon I and other of her Iustices haue receiued Commission for the apprehending of as many as are within these limites." Who was this newcomer? "Probably Jewel" is the reply of the investigator, and he ventures to suggest that "the impression produced" by the appeal in Jewel's sermon "was responsible probably not only for the passage of the law [of 1563] but also for the issue of commissions to the justices of the peace to apprehend all the witches they were able to find in their jurisdictions."[110] Now "lately," one must confess, is an elastic word, but there must be some ultimate in its capabilities in the way of stretching. Darcey was writing in 1582: Jewel had come over *twenty-three years* before, and, at the moment of composition, he had lain for *eleven years* in his grave, for he died in 1571. And that is not all. Let us look at the context. Ursley Kempe had informed against Elizabeth Bennet, and Elizabeth was being examined by Squire Darcey. She made a general denial. "Then," writes Darcey, "I calling her vnto mee, saide, Elizabeth as thou wilt haue favour confesse the truth. For so it is, there is a man of great cunning and knoweledge come ouer lately vnto our Queenes Maiestie, which hath aduertised her what a companie and number of Witches be within Englande: whereupon I and other of her Iustices haue receiued Commission for the apprehending of as many as are within these limites, and they which doe confesse the truth of their doeings, they shall haue much fauour: but the other they shall bee burnt and hanged. At which speeches shee the saide Elizabeth falling vpon her knees distilling teares confessed as hereafter followeth." [111] When read thus in its context, Darcey's dictum takes on a quite peculiar complexion. *Falsus in uno, falsus in omnibus.* Darcey was lying when he promised "favour" in return for a full confession, for Elizabeth Bennet was executed in due course.[112] He was lying when he threatened her with burning, for he knew (though she did not) that the halter was the worst punishment she had to fear. He was almost certainly lying when he talked of a special witch-hunting commission; for his ordinary powers as a justice of the peace needed no such reinforcement to enable him to arrest and prosecute witches. The inference is compulsive. It is idle to guess at the identity of the "man of great cunning and knowledge." There was no such person. He was a bugbear of Brian Darcey's own manufacture.

But we must return to the Witches' Sabbath. No suggestion of this is perceptible, as we have seen, in any English trial during the Elizabethan period, although the Continental notions about it are mentioned by Reginald Scot and other English writers from 1584 on. In Scotland, however, the famous case of Dr. Fian and his associates in 1590 and 1591 involves the Sabbath system in an elaborate form [113] — a fact which emphasizes once more the distinction between England and the Continent in this regard.

Ben Jonson's Masque of Queens (1609) exhibits the Sabbath in full career, but he got his material — so he says himself — "out of the fulness and memory of [his] former readings," and in his erudite notes (written at Prince Henry's request) he has exerted himself "to retrieve the particular authorities." [114]

The first trace of the Witches' Sabbath in any English case appears in the trials of the Lancashire Witches in 1612. On May 19 in that year Anne Whittle (alias Chattox) confessed to the Mayor of Lancaster that, some fourteen years before, Elizabeth Southerns (alias Demdike) had induced her to become a witch. Soon after, she said, the devil came to Demdike's house about midnight, and the two women went out to meet him. A meal was served, *al fresco* apparently, and their she-familiars, Fancie and Tibbe, carried off what was left. "There was victuals, *viz.* Flesh, Butter, Cheese, Bread, and Drinke . . . although they did eate, they were neuer the fuller, nor better for the same." [115] Assuredly this is a faint reflection of the Sabbath, but there is more to come. Among the accused was old Demdike's daughter, Elizabeth Device, a widow, who lived with her mother in a house called Malkin Tower.[116] Here, on Good Friday about noon, so Elizabeth's nine-year-old daughter Jennet testified, was held a meeting of some twenty persons, only two of whom were men. Her mother told her, Jennet continued, that these were all witches and that they came "to giue a name" to the familiar spirit of Jennet's elder sister, Alizon. They "had to their dinners Beefe, Bacon, and roasted Mutton." The mutton, so Jennet's brother James informed her, "was of a Wether of Christopher Swyers of Barley: which Wether was brought in the night before . . . by the said Iames Deuice . . .: and in this Examinates sight killed and eaten." [117] Brother James in his examinations, supplied further details. The meeting had three objects: *first*, to christen Alizon's familiar ("but [they] did not name him, because shee was not there"); *second*, to release the witches confined in Lancaster Castle (namely, his sister Alizon, his grandmother Demdike, Anne Whittle, and Anne's daughter Redferne), to murder the jailer, and to blow up the castle; *third*, to plot the death of a certain Master Thomas Lister.[118] Neither James nor Jennet says anything of any demon's actual presence at the feast. Thus the affair is reduced to the prosaic level of a noonday dinner of neighbors who were concerned for their incarcerated friends and relatives. Very likely some such gathering occurred, and there may have been wild talk among the guests. The stolen sheep, at all events, sounds authentic. James admitted the theft,[119] which, by the way, was enough to hang him in those days even if he had not confessed (as he did) to murder by witchcraft.[120] Though Satan did not attend this rural banquet, there were devils waiting outside, for, James tells us, all the witches left the house "in their owne shapes and likenesses," and, as soon as they were "forth of the dores," they were on horseback — on creatures, that is to say, that had the form of "Foales, some of one colour, some of another; and *Prestons* wife was the last: and when shee got on Horsebacke, they all presently vanished out of this Examinates sight. And before their said parting away, they all appointed to meete at the said *Prestons* wiues house that day twelue-moneths; at which time the said *Prestons* wife promised to make them a great Feast. And if they had occasion to meete in the meane time, then should warning be giuen, that they all should meete vpon *Romleyes* Moore." [121] Both James Device and his little sister gave the names of several persons present at the meeting, and their testimony was repeated, in almost identical terms, at several trials. On one of these occasions Jennet added the circumstance that John Bulcocke turned the spit when the wether was roasted.[122] Elizabeth Device, their mother, would confess nothing until she learned of her daughter's evidence, but by-and-by she admitted the dinner at Malkin Tower. "And shee also confesseth, in all things touching the Christening of the Spirit, and the killing of Master *Lister* . . ., as the said *Iames Deuice* hath before confessed; but denieth of any talke was amongst them, . . . to her now remembrance, at the said meeting together, touching the killing of the Gaoler, or the blowing vp of Lancaster Castle." [123] Old Demdike died in prison before trial. Anne Whittle and Anne Redferne were executed. So were Elizabeth Device (old Demdike's daughter) and Elizabeth's children, Alizon and James, as well as five of the persons whom James and Jennet recognized at the meeting. Their crime, of course, was not attendance at this feast, but murder or injury by witchcraft, which some of them confessed.

In the same year (1612), on August 19, the Three Witches of Salmesbury were arraigned at Lancaster for afflicting Grace Sowerbutts. Grace, who was an hysterical patient of fourteen, swore that she witnessed a meeting of the three (one of whom was her grandmother and another her aunt) at Red Bank on the River Ribble. Such meetings were held after dark every Thursday and Sunday "by the space of a fortnight." "Foure black things, going vpright, and yet not like men in the face," carried the three witches, and Grace too, across the river. "And when they came to the said Red

Banck, they found some thing there which they did eate.
But this Examinate saith, shee neuer saw such meate; and
therefore shee durst not eate thereof. . . . And after they had
eaten, the said three Women and this Examinate danced,
euery one of them with one of the black things aforesaid,'
and so on. "*Being further examined touching her being at Red-
bancke*, she saith, . . . that at their said meeting . . . , there
did come also diuers other women, . . . some old, some
yong," but these were mere spectators and did not join the
dance. The phrase that I have italicized is significant. The
examining magistrate, it is clear, wished to hear about a real
Witches' Sabbath, not a mere assignation between three
individuals and their familiars — and he questioned Grace
accordingly; but his suggestion elicited nothing that approxi-
mates the published accounts of Satan's Synagogues on the
Continent. Still, there were horrors enough in Grace's story.
On another occasion (not a Sabbath, however), her grandmother had thrust a nail into a child and sucked its blood.
The child languished and died. Grace's grandmother and
aunt dug up the body and cooked it, and ate of it, but Grace
refused. Afterwards they "did seethe the bones of the said
child in a pot, and with the Fat that came out of the said
bones, they said they would annoint themselues, that thereby
they might sometimes change themselues into other shapes."
Altogether we seem to have enough in Grace's evidence to
show that by 1612 the main features of the Continental Sabbath had become articles in the creed of the English country
people. But alas for such a theory! The judge, though a firm
believer in witchcraft, was suspicious. He committed Grace
to a preacher and two justices for further examination, and
she finally confessed that she had lied from start to finish, and
that all she had testified had been taught her by a Catholic
priest.[124] We need not share the judge's indignation. To him
the priest was, of course, a deviser of malicious falsehoods.
To us, on the contrary, he may appear honest but deluded. In
either case, he was manifestly familiar with learned material,
and no good witness, therefore, for native folk-lore. Yet one
must cheerfully admit that by 1612 — nine years after Queen
Elizabeth's death — the Continental Sabbath had won a
place — if a shadowy and unstable one — in the prosecution

of English witches. The account of the Lancashire witches published by Thomas Potts in 1613 familiarized the public with all the details of the feast on stolen mutton at Malkin Tower.

Dr. Cotta almost ignores the Sabbath in his elaborate treatise, The Triall of Witch-craft (1616). He mentions the Italian Porta's narrative of the woman who declared that she had ridden through the air over the mountains and "met in conventicles" with other hags, though in fact she was sound asleep in her chamber all the time; [125] adds that some writers "of worthy credit" report "that the bodies of Sorcerers and Witches haue beene really carried, and locally remoued from one place into another by the Diuell," and concludes that such transportation is possible. [126] But he says nothing of English witch-conventions and even ignores the alleged feast of conspirators at Malkin Tower, though he was acquainted with the Lancaster prosecution and cites it as proof of image magic. [127]

Thomas Cooper in 1617 describes witch-meetings in church, with the fiend in the pulpit preaching and divers profane rites. [128] His sources are mainly King James and perhaps the Continental authorities, but he may intend to ascribe such services to the English disciples of Satan. "Hath not *Couenrie*," he asks, "beene vsually haunted by these hellish Sorcerers, where it was confessed by one of them, that no lesse then three-score were of that confedracie?" [129]

From 1612 to 1634 the English witch-trials are barren of evidence about the Sabbath. The witches accused of tormenting the Fairfax children from 1621 to 1623 were thought to belong to a band of seven, and there is mention of their meeting to confer with their Master "in what sort to proceed." On another occasion Helen Fairfax was found on a high moor a good way from home. She had been carried thither, she said, by one of the hags and a demonic cat, and there she saw many women together at a great fire. Again, in a trance, the children "were told that all the witches had a feast at Timble Gill: their meat was roasted about midnight. At the upper end of the table sat their master, viz., the devil, at the lower end Dibb's wife, who provided for the feast, and was the cook." [130] Some of these details may have come before the York assizes in April and August, 1622; but on the former occasion the defendants were acquitted and on the latter the judge "withdrew the offenders from trial by the jury of life and death, and dismissed them at liberty." [131] Fairfax's narrative remained in manuscript until the nineteenth century. Nothing further transpires on the subject of the Witches' Sabbath in any English trial until we reach 1634.

In that year, however, Edmund Robinson, a lad of ten or eleven who lived in the same vicinity as the Lancashire witches of 1612, told a weird tale. Goody Dickinson, he testified, had carried him off on a white horse (which was a boy transformed by a magic bridle) to a house in the neighborhood. There he saw divers persons about the door, and others came riding up "on Horses of several colours." About threescore entered, "where they had a fire, and meat roasting." A young woman "gave him Flesh and Bread upon a Trencher and Drink in a Glass, which after the first tast he refused and would have no more, but said, it was naught." Presently he followed some of the company into the barn. There he saw six of them pulling six several ropes, from which came milk, and butter in lumps, and smoking meat, and fell into basins. "And after that these six had done, there came other six which did so likewise." He also saw "three Woman take six Pictures from off the beam, in which Pictures were many Thorns or such like things sticked in them." Scared by the "ugly faces" made by the rope-pullers, he ran for home; but he had identified nineteen of the witches and wizards and gave their names.[132]

Widow Margaret Johnson, examined soon after young Robinson, declared that she was not "at the greate meetinge" on All Saints Day, but admitted her presence at a second meeting of between thirty and forty witches on the following Sunday. The object of such gatherings was, she averred, "to consult for the killinge and hurtinge of men and beastes." Besides the witches and their familiars there was present "one greate grand Divell or spirit, more eminent then the rest." The regular time for "a yearlie generall meetinge" was Good Friday. As to the aërial flight, Margaret had things to tell which tempt one to suspect that there were leading questions asked by the justices. If the witches "desire to bee in anie place vpon a suddaine, theire Divell or spiritt will vpon a redd dogg, or any thinge also presentlie convey them thither yea into any roome of a mans howse, but shee saith, it is not the substance of theire bodies, but theire spirit assumeth such forme of shape as goes into such roomes." [133] Trials followed, and several were found guilty. Three or four died in prison, but none were executed, for young Robinson soon after confessed that his story was a mere fabrication; "that he had heard the neighbours talk of a witch feast . . . at Mocking Tower in Pendle Forest about twenty years since, . . . and thereupon he framed these tales concerning the persons aforesaid, because he heard the neighbours repute them for witches." [134]

Young Robinson's lies, however, are good evidence of the folk-belief of the time. What he told accorded with his own notions and found ready credence with his neighbors and the jury. All the more striking is the enormous and persistent contrast between the Continental Sabbath and its seventeenth-century English representative. Robinson's romance came upon the stage of the Globe in 1634 in the form of The Late Lancashire Witches, a comedy by Thomas Heywood and Richard Brome. It was "well received" and was published in the same year. [135]

With the advent of Matthew Hopkins the Witches' Sabbath in its attenuated English form reappears in the reports of trials and achieves a more or less permanent status. Hopkins, who was a man of some learning, believed in it devoutly. He tells us that "in *March* 1644. he had some seven or eight of that horrible sect of Witches living in the Towne where he lived, a Towne in Essex called *Maningtree*, with divers other adjacent Witches of other towns, who every six weeks in the night (being alwayes on the Friday night) had their meeting close by his house, and had their severall solemne sacrifices there offered to the Devill." [136] It was this experience that embarked him on his witch-finding career. The details are ludicrously meagre in comparison with the flamboyant debauches of the hags and demons of France and Germany. John Wynick, executed at Huntingdon in 1646, knew of an assembly of more than twenty witches at Tilbrooke Bushes in Bedfordshire, and at Burton-Old "there met above fourescore at a time." John Stearne, Hopkins's lieutenant, who furnishes these statistics,[137] informs us that Satan binds his witches "to imitate Christ in many things, as his Assemblies and Sabbaths, Baptism and Covenants." All these Satan has, "after his manner, as *Rebecca West* and *Elizabeth Clarke* confessed, as well in these as in other particulars, as you may finde as well by theirs and others Confessions, as also by the Writings of learned men who have writ concerning the same." [138] Stearne's appeal to scholarly authors sounds rather helpless: he realized, I fear, the jejune character of the native evidence about the Sabbath. Rebecca West was acquitted in 1646, despite her confession that she and four other witches met with Elizabeth Clark at Elizabeth's house in Manningtree (Essex), "where they together spent some time in praying unto their Familiars, and every one in order went to prayers; afterwards some of them read in a book, the book being *Elizabeth Clarks*; . . . forthwith their Familiars appeared" and the several witches assigned them tasks. Hopkins adds details from Rebecca's confession to him: "The Devill appeared to them in the shape of a dogge; afterwards in the shape of two Kidyns" and two dogs; the familiars kissed all the witches except Rebecca, and her the devil kissed after she had taken an oath to serve him; later, when she was alone, he visited her and she submitted to his embraces.[139] Joan Cariden, one of three Kentish witches executed at Faversham in 1645, confessed that Jane Hott, another of the three, told her "that there was a great meeting at Goodwife Panterys house, . . . and the Divell sat at the upper end of the Table." [140]

Between the Hopkins cases and the efflorescence — for England — of the Sabbath in 1665 we have one puny specimen in 1650, when Widow Dorothy Swinow of Chatton in Northumberland was indicted for witchcraft. The burden of the complaint was her alleged afflicting of three children. Margaret White confessed upon oath that "Mrs. Swinow, and her sister Jane, and her selfe were in the Divels company in her sister Janes house, where they did eate and drinke together (as by her conceived) and made merry." [141]

As to the Sabbath, the connecting link between the Hopkins cases and the Lancashire trials of 1612 is Richard Bernard's manual entitled A Guide to Grand-Iury Men, which was published in 1627 and again in 1629. Bernard sets forth in parallel columns twenty-nine points comparing "what the Lord doth" with "what Satan doth," with intent to exhibit "how Satan obserueth the Lords doeings and sayings, and therein striues to bee like him." Four of these points concern the devil's "set meetings for his Magicians and Witches to come together"; but the only rite he specifies as there performed is the christening of the familiar spirit, which he derives from the Lancaster cases.[142] No other English instance of a Sabbath is cited by Bernard, but he was we'l versed in Continental lore. When persons are under suspicion, he instructs us, it is an indication of guilt "if they haue beene heard to speake of their transportation from home to certaine places of their meetings with others there, of which transportations stories make mention: and also the relations of the Lancashire Witches meeting at Malkin Tower, some 20. together, and were carried by spirits in likenesse of Foales, as those witches confessed."[143] For the "stories" there is a marginal reference to Bodin and Del Rio.[144] And Bernard instructs the grand jury to examine witnesses specifically on such matters: "Whether they haue heard the suspected to foretell of mishaps to befal any, or heard them speake of their power to hurt this or that, or of their transportation, to this or that place, or of their meetings in the night there?"[145] Now John Stearne's book is an outstanding instance of extensive and peculiar plagiarism. He copies page after page from Bernard, changing the order at times but following the phraseology almost or quite word for word. Practically every item of his labored argument (including proof texts from Scripture) is borrowed without credit;[146] but Stearne enriches the discussion with a vast number of concrete details drawn from the great witch-hunt of his own period. So in the matter of the Sabbath. It is an indication of the witches' guilt, writes Stearne, "if they have been heard to speak of their transportation from home to certain places of their meetings with others there, as was at Manningtree, Burton-Old, Tilbrook-bushes, and other places."[147] Thus we are enabled to trace the antecedents of the Sabbath as it

emerges in the activities of Witch-finder Hopkins and Lieutenant Stearne. Bernard was their handbook of inquisition
and Bernard's native material was, in this particular, the report of the Lancaster cases of 1612 that was published by
Thomas Potts in 1613.

In 1665 we have good accounts of witch-meetings in the
famous examinations of Elizabeth Style and others conducted
by the Somerset justice, Robert Hunt.[148] At some of these
conventicles there were but four persons besides the devil;
at one there were twelve; at another, fourteen. The witches
were borne through the air by the virtue of a magic ointment.
The devil was there in the form of a man in black, and received their homage. "They had Wine, Cakes and Roast-
meat (all brought by the Man in black) which they did eat
and drink. They danced and were merry." Sometimes the
devil played upon a pipe or cittern. The main business, apart
from festivity, was the baptizing of waxen images. The
witches were carried "sometimes in their Bodies and their
Clothes, sometimes without"; and now and then (so Elizabeth believed) their Bodies were "left behind" at home and
"only their Spirits" were present. Elizabeth's confession was
"drawn from her" on at least three different occasions "by a
gentle Examination, meeting with the Convictions of a guilty
Conscience." Several "grave and Orthodox Divines" were
present. It requires no great acumen to perceive the real
source of some of these details. The remark about bodily or
spiritual presence indicates a distinction which Elizabeth
herself could never have thought of. It must have been
elicited, of course, by a definite question from one of the educated examiners who was acquainted with the age-old debate
on this point among theologians, philosophers, and physicians.

Mr. Hunt's investigations might have rivalled those of
Matthew Hopkins if he had not been checked by the higher
powers. "Had not his discoveries and endeavours," writes
Glanvil, "met with great opposition and discouragements
from some then in Authority, the whole Clan of those hellish
Confederates in these parts [i. e. Somerset] had been justly
exposed and punished." [149] However, Hunt left enough on
record to prove that by Restoration times the Witches' Sab-

bath had at length achieved a place in the witch-creed of England.[150] Yet, even then, the English Sabbath was a feeble reflection of its foreign original. The more one studies its history, the more clearly the fact emerges: the Witches' Sabbath was not at home on English soil. Every other point in the beliefs and practices, actual and imagined, of the English witches of the sixteenth and seventeenth centuries can be traced back for hundreds of years in the island itself. The doctrine of a Sabbath, on the contrary, was a learned importation and made its way slowly and with difficulty among the folk. Opinions will always differ as to any basis of fact that may underlie the Continental stories; but the theory that English witches were keeping alive a pagan ritual, and were meeting in orgiastic mysteries that had descended from pre-Christian times, will not stand the test of the most elementary historical criticism. There is not the slightest evidence that they were ever organized at all. Some of the accused were innocent, some were guilty in intent. Now and then, like other criminals, a few of them may have met to eat a stolen wether or to plot a murder. But "covens" and devil-priests and Satanic orgies are, for England, out of the question.[151]

CHAPTER XVII

KING JAMES THE FIRST

COMMON fame makes James I a sinister figure in the history of English witchcraft. The delusion, we are told, was dying out in the later years of Elizabeth, but James fanned the embers into a devouring fire. His coming was the signal for a violent and long-continued outburst of witch-hunting, for which he was personally responsible. He procured the repeal of the comparatively mild Elizabethan law and the enactment of a very cruel statute. He encouraged and patronized witchfinders, and was always eager for fresh victims. His reign is a dark and bloody period in the annals of this frightful superstition.

Many authorities might be adduced in support of these views, but I must rest content with quoting three writers who have had some influence in propagating them, — Mrs Lynn Linton, Mr. Robert Steele, and Mr. G. M. Trevelyan.

In 1861 Mrs. E. Lynn Linton published a volume of Witch Stories, which was reissued in 1883 and has met with deserved favor. Mrs. Linton has no mercy on James I. His "name stands accursed for vice and cruel cowardice and the utmost selfishness of fear." [2] "Treacherous, cruel, narrow-minded, and cowardly," she calls him, "beyond anything that has ever disgraced the English throne before or since." He had a "mania against witches," [4] a "lust for witch blood." [5] "There was no holding in of this furious madness after James I had got his foot in the stirrup, and was riding a race neck and neck with the Devil." [6] These are hard words; yet Mrs. Linton knows that the beliefs which she has in mind were "rampant in England when good Queen Bess ruled the land," [7] and her own book contains facts enough to give us pause.

Let us take a leap of thirty-odd years and read what Mr. Robert Steele has to tell us in his article on witchcraft in the fourth volume of a well-reputed work of collaboration, Social England, edited by Mr. H. D. Traill:

> With the accession of James a change came over the feelings of those in power. During the later years of Elizabeth tract after tract appeared, calling for severe punishment upon witches, but with no result: the English trials, up to now, had been characterised rather by folly than ferocity, the new rule was marked by ferocious folly. For forty years Scotland had been engaged in witch-hunting, with the result that 8000 human beings are believed to have been burnt between 1560 and 1600; and for the last ten years of the century the king had been at the head of the hunt. . . . In the first Parliament of James the more merciful Act of Elizabeth was repealed; a new and exhaustive one was enacted. . . . Under this Act 70,000 persons were executed up to 1680.[8]

I stand aghast at these figures. There is no sense or reason in them. No records have been published or examined which would justify the assertion that *a seventieth part* of this monstrous number met their death in the period named. As for the time from the passage of the act of 1604 till the death of James in 1625, Mr. Steele would find it hard to make out an average of more than two or three executions a year. I half suspect that he had got hold of some statistics of mortality from the plague.

Mr. Trevelyan is vaguer, but no less emphatic:

> The skeptical Elizabeth, perhaps with some pity for her sex, had refused to yield when the pamphlet press called on the Government to enact fiercer laws "not suffering a witch to live." The outburst came with the accession of a Scottish King, who, though he rejected the best part of the spirit of Knox, was crazed beyond his English subjects with the witch-mania of Scotland and the continent. His first Parliament enacted new death-laws; at once the Judges and magistrates, the constables and the mob, began to hunt up the oldest and ugliest spinster who lived with her geese in the hut on the common, or tottered about the village street mumbling the inaudible soliloquies of second childhood. [9]

In this witch-hunt, Mr. Trevelyan tells us, "learning, headed by the pedant King, was master of the hounds." [10]

So much for the current opinion.[11] Let us try to discover to what extent it is justified by the facts. And first we must consider two things that have created an enormous prejudice against King James, — his Scottish record and his authorship of the Dæmonologie.

The history of witchcraft in Scotland is a difficult subject, and it is particularly hard to determine just what degree of responsibility attaches to King James. To sift the matter thoroughly would require much time and space. Still, a few facts are patent. (1) James did not make the Scottish law of witchcraft. The statute was enacted in 1563, before he was born. (2) He did not teach the Scottish nation the witch-creed. That creed was the heritage of the human race, and was nowhere less questioned by all classes and all professions than in Scotland, where, indeed, it survived in full vigor for more than a century after James was dead. (3) The worst period of Scottish prosecution does not fall in his reign. The three great prosecutions were in 1590-1597, in 1640-1650, and in 1660-1663. The second was worse than the first, and the third (which began with the Restoration) was the worst of all. (4) James did not initiate the prosecutions of 1590.[12]

Upon this last point we must dwell for a moment. In 1583, when James was a boy of seventeen, the Scottish clergy called for a sharper enforcement of the law. In 1590 began the trials of John Fian and his associates, with which the name of the king is indissolubly connected. It seems quite clear that these trials were not James's own idea. His intellectual curiosity — well known to be one of his most salient characteristics — led him to attend the examinations. But he was not naturally credulous in such matters (as we shall see later), he found the confessions beyond belief, and he pronounced the witches "extreame lyars." When, however, Agnes Sampson, to convince him, repeated in his private ear a conversation that he had held with the queen on the marriage-night, he "acknowledged her words to bee most true, and therefore gaue the more credit" to their stories.[13] It makes little difference what we think of this feat of Agnes Sampson's: the value of the anecdote lies in the light it throws on the king's skepticism. Agnes also implicated the Earl of Bothwell in a charge of witchcraft against the king's life. James's dislike and fear of Bothwell are notorious; they appear in a striking passage of the Basilikon Doron.[14] He looked on Bothwell as his evil genius and was ever ready to listen to anything to his discredit. Chancellor Maitland, who was Bothwell's enemy, had the king's confidence.[15] Numer-

ous executions followed, and the great prosecution of 1590–
1597 was now under way. It had started, however, not with
James, but, as usual, among obscure persons. The king had
simply become involved in the affair. No doubt he counte-
nanced the general witch-hunt that followed; but he cannot
be said to have encouraged it, for no encouragement was
needed. The clergy were eager, and the people lived in constant terror of witches. If ever there was a spontaneous popular panic, this was such an outbreak. James and his Council
had only to let the forces work. And, indeed, it seems pretty
certain that they had no power to stem the current. Mr. Andrew Lang, who censures the king, says in plain terms that he
'could not have controlled the preachers.' [16] Add to this the
testimony of Pitcairn, a hostile witness, that the period from
1591 to 1596 was distinguished by "open defiance of the King
and Parliament, and by the frequent and daring conspiracies
enterprised against the Royal person." [17] Altogether, it does
not appear that James is to blame for the events of 1590–
1597, or that the prosecution proves him either exceptionally
credulous or exceptionally devoted to witch-hunting. If a
whole nation believes in witchcraft, outbreaks of prosecution
(like other outbreaks) are likely to happen whenever there
are troublous times. This has been seen over and over again,
— in the tumult of the English Civil War, for instance, and
just after the Revolution, and in our own Salem at a critical
moment in New England history. [18] James was not riding the
storm like Odin. He was only a mortal man, swept off his feet
by the tide.

Whether these considerations are just or not, one thing is
certain — by 1597 James was convinced that matters had
gone too far. Indictments were piling upon indictments,
there was no telling the innocent from the guilty, and no end
was in sight. Commissions of justiciary for witchcraft were
being held throughout Scotland, and the king, by a stroke of
the pen, revoked them all. [19] It is noteworthy that the proxi-
mate cause of his action was the discovery that many de-
nunciations were fraudulent. Compare James's incredulity
at the outset, and the skill which he showed later in life (as we
shall see presently) in detecting similar impostures. From
1597 to James's accession to the English throne in 1603, there

were abundant witch-trials in Scotland, but the annual number of executions was much smaller, and there is no reason to
suppose that the king pressed for more. When he succeeded
to the English crown, the intensity of the Scottish witch-
quest had ceased, by his own act, and that period was associated in his mind with a time of anarchy. England looked to
him like a haven of rest. He was certainly thinking of other
matters than witches when he came into the promised land.

So much for the first of the two things that have led men to
approach James's English witch record with a prejudiced
opinion. Let us pass to the second, — his authorship of the
Dæmonologie.

The importance of King James's Dæmonologie has been
greatly exaggerated, both as to its bearing on his supposed
career as a prosecutor and as to its effect on English sentiment in his time. The book is a confession of faith, not an
autobiography. It is proof of what James *thought*, not of
what he *did*. The publication of the Dæmonologie did not
cause the death of any Scottish witches, either directly or
indirectly. Nor did it convert a single Scottish skeptic, for
there were none to convert. The book did not appear until
1597, — the very year in which James, by a stroke of the pen,
checked the great prosecution that had been going since 1590.
As to England, the case against the Dæmonologie is pitifully
weak. The treatise, though well-constructed and compendious, is not original. It adduces neither new facts nor new
arguments. Gardiner is perfectly right when he says that
James "had only echoed opinions which were accepted freely
by the multitude, and were tacitly admitted without inquiry
by the first intellects of the day." [20] Certainly there is no
reason to think that the Dæmonologie had any appreciable
effect on English sentiment.

I am well aware that King James's Dæmonologie was reissued in London in 1603. But this was a mere bookselling
speculation,[21] like the Latin translation by Germberg that
appeared at Hanover in 1604.[22] There is no parade about the
volume, no hint that it was published at the king's instance.
Contrast the circumstances attending the publication of the
Basilikon Doron in the same year. This had been privately
printed in 1599. When it came before the public in 1603

there was a long, defensive preface, entirely new, in which the king exerted himself to stand well with his English subjects.[23] James, as we have already remarked, had other things than witchcraft to occupy his thoughts when he mounted the English throne. If it can be shown that he immediately engaged in a campaign for new witch-laws or for more vigorous prosecution, then we may regard the Dæmonologie of 1603 as a campaign document. But first one must show that he did engage in any such campaign; otherwise the question is begged. And, as we shall soon discover, he did nothing of the kind.

Clearly, then, we must study the witch-law and the witch-trials of James's English reign on the basis, not of prejudice, but of evidence. And first we may consider the Statute of 1604.

The current ideas about the English laws against witchcraft are very inaccurate. For these misapprehensions Thomas Wright is in large part responsible. His learned and interesting Narratives of Sorcery and Magic, which has enjoyed a deserved popularity for more than seventy-five years, is surprisingly loose in its statements about legal history.

"The first act in the statute-book against witchcraft," says Wright, "was passed in the thirty-third year of Henry VIII, A.D. 1541, whereby this supposed crime was made felony without benefit of clergy." [24] So far he is quite correct, except for the year of our Lord, which should be 1542. "In 1547," he adds, "when the power was entirely in the hands of the religious reformers under Edward VI, his father's law against witchcraft was repealed." This assertion, though technically indisputable, is rather misleading. The act to which Wright refers (1 Edward VI, c. 12) does not once mention sorcery, magic, or witchcraft. The third section wipes out of the statute-book "all offences made felony by any act or acts of Parliament, statute or statutes, made sithence the xxiiith day of April in the first year of the reign of the said late King Henry theight, not being felony before." Among these offences was witchcraft.

Wright's next statement is highly objectionable. It amounts to a serious, though inadvertent, *suppressio veri*. "Under Elizabeth," he avers, "in 1562 [this should be 1563], a new act was passed against witchcraft, punishing the first conviction only with exposure in the pillory." [25]   Now the truth is that Elizabeth's law was much severer than one would infer from these words. It fixes the death penalty (1) for all who "use, practise, or exercise invocations or conjurations of evil and wicked spirits to or for any intent or purpose," quite irrespective of the result of such invocations or conjurations, and (2) for all who practise witchcraft that causes a person's death. Under the former provision — to take a good example — Edmund Hartlay lost his life in Lancashire in 1597. He was a professed conjurer, and had been employed to relieve the children of Mr. Nicholas Starkie, who were thought to be possessed with devils. Hartlay caught the hysterical affection himself and was tormented in like manner. "The next day, beinge recouered, he went into a little wood, not farr from the house, where he maide a circle about a yarde and halfe wyde, deuiding it into 4. partes, making a crosse at every Diuision: and when he had finished his worke, he came to *M. Starchie* and desiered him to go and tread out the circle, saying, I may not treade it out my selfe, and further, I will meete with them that went about my death," [26] — that is, in effect, I wish to raise the devils that tried to kill me yesterday. There were other charges against Hartlay, but none of a capital nature. "The making of his circle was chefly his ouerthrowe." [27] He denied the fact, but, the rope breaking, confessed it before he died.[28]

Furthermore, the Elizabethan statute provided that "witchcraft, enchantment, charm, or sorcery" which caused bodily injury to human beings or damage to goods or chattels should be punished with a year's imprisonment (with quarterly exposure in the pillory) for the first offence, and *with death for the second offence*. And finally, the statute provided imprisonment and the pillory, with *life imprisonment* for the second offence, for all who should "take upon" themselves to reveal the whereabouts of hidden treasure or of lost or stolen goods, or should practise witchcraft with intent to provoke unlawful love or to "hurt or destroy any person in his or her body, member, or goods." It must now be manifest how unduly Wright extenuates the grimness of Elizabeth's law.

Thus we reach the reign of James I. In his first year was passed the statute of 1604, which remained in force until

1736. The relation of this act to the statute of Elizabeth, which it repealed, becomes a matter of great importance to determine. Here Wright leaves us in the lurch. James, he tells us, "passed a new and severe law against witchcraft,[29] in which it now became almost a crime to disbelieve." [30] We are led to infer that, whereas Elizabeth's law was mild and hardly objectionable, James's statute was both novel and severe. The facts are quite different. James's statute follows Elizabeth's in the main, even in phraseology. (1) The new statute (like the old) provides death as the penalty for *invocation or conjuration of evil spirits* for any purpose and without regard to the issue. But it inserts two clauses making it also felony to "consult, convenant with, entertain, employ, feed, or reward" any such spirit for any purpose, or to dig up any dead body, or part thereof, for use in sorcery. (2) For *witchcraft that kills*, death is the penalty (as in the Elizabethan enactment). (3) For *witchcraft that causes bodily harm*, but does not kill, the new law imposes death for the *first* (instead of the *second*) offence. (4) For the *minor varieties* of sorcery and witchcraft, *death* is substituted for *life imprisonment* as the penalty for the second offence.[31] Clearly the statute of 1604 is not so great a novelty as we have been led to think. It is, to be sure, more severe than the Elizabethan enactment, but only in some respects. Let us study the two a little further.

The substitution of *death* for *life imprisonment* as the penalty for the second offence in certain minor grades of sorcery can hardly be called an increase in severity. The appalling state of the prisons is notorious. There was a dreadful outbreak of jail fever at the Oxford assizes in 1577,[32] and another at the Exeter assizes in 1586.[33] Prisoners often died while awaiting trial or execution. In 1608 the Earl of Northampton, as Warden of the Cinque Ports, induced the mayor of Rye to admit to bail a woman condemned to death for aiding and abetting a witch. Her execution had been stayed, and it was feared that she would succumb to the "lothsomness of the prison." [34] Under such conditions, the change from a life sentence to hanging was rather mercy than rigor.

The penalty for digging up the dead (unknown to the Elizabethan law) was not excessive, in view of the general severity of the penal code. The thing was certainly done now and then. It was a real — not an imaginary — crime, and deserved punishment. However, no case has ever been cited in which a man or woman was put to death for this offence alone, and we may therefore disregard that clause as of no practical effect.

As for the new provision about consulting or covenanting with evil spirits, or feeding them, it was capable of operating with great severity. In fact, however, I do not believe that a single case can be found during James's reign in which anybody suffered death under this clause who was not otherwise liable to the extreme penalty.[35]

There remains, then, one change in the law, and only one, — death for the *first* (instead of the *second*) offence in witchcraft that injures the body without killing, — to justify the common opinion that James's statute of 1604 was so stern an enactment as to make an era in English witch-prosecution.

At the outset, candor impels us to inquire whether James's statute was really severe at all. Our judgment must be based, not on our present penal code, but on that of the sixteenth and seventeenth centuries. When death was the penalty for stealing a sheep, or breaking into a house, or taking a purse on the highway, or stealing thirteenpence, was it harsh to hang a witch for driving her neighbor mad or smiting him with epilepsy or paralysis?[36] To object that witches could not do such things is no answer. This objection might hold against the passing of *any law whatever*, but has nothing to do with the question of *severity*. It is quite as silly to fine or imprison a man for an impossible crime as to hang him for it. However, we may waive this point, for we are more directly concerned with the question whether James's law was so much severer than Elizabeth's as to make its passage a momentous event. This is to be tested, of course, by observing how the two laws worked, not by weighing their words.

To get the perspective, let us look at one of the most notorious of Elizabethan cases, that of St. Osyth in Essex. One Ursula (or Ursley) Kempe, alias Grey, was a woman of ill repute, who lived, with Thomas Rabbet, her bastard son, in the little village of St. Osith's (now St. Osyth), near Colchester. She had long lain under suspicion of witchcraft.

There was sickness in the family of a neighbor, Grace Thurowe, and Grace fancied that Ursula was to blame. The local magistrate, Brian Darcey, lent a ready ear to her complaint. Witnesses came forward in abundance, and one revelation led to another, as usual. Thomas Rabbet gave evidence against his mother. Ursula confessed her crimes, with many tears. A whole nest of offenders was uncovered, and, in conclusion, no less than thirteen witches were convicted. This was in 1582.[37] The affair made a great noise, and appears to have been the chief immediate impulse to Reginald Scot's famous book, The Discoverie of Witchcraft.

Of the thirteen persons convicted on this occasion, all but three were found guilty of "bewitching to death," and consequently suffered the extreme penalty under the statute of Elizabeth. James's statute would have hanged the other three as well. To this extent, and to this extent alone, would it have operated more severely than its predecessor.

The St. Osyth tragedy took place about twenty years before James I succeeded to the English crown. Will it be believed, in the face of the vehement denunciation to which this king is traditionally subjected as a besotted persecutor, that nothing comparable to it occurred in his reign until 1612, when he had been on the throne for nine years? Yet such is the indisputable fact.

An analysis of these Lancashire trials of 1612, on the basis of Thomas Potts's official narrative, yields the following results. Nineteen persons were tried, of whom eight were acquitted. Of the eleven convicted, one (whose offence was the killing of a mare) was sentenced to the pillory. This leaves ten who were hanged.[38] Six of these were indicted for murder by witchcraft, and therefore would have suffered death under Elizabeth's law as surely as under James's. Four, then, were executed who might have got off with imprisonment if the older statute had remained in force. But it is by no means certain that all of the four would actually have escaped the gallows. For there was evidence of murder by witchcraft against two of them, and they might have been tried on that charge if the lesser accusation of driving a woman insane had not sufficed to send them out of the world. There remain but two, therefore, of the eleven convicted, who, so far as we can see, would have been in no danger of death under Elizabethan conditions. And one of these exemptions may be balanced by the case of the woman sent to the pillory for killing a mare, inasmuch as there was testimony that she too had confessed to a couple of murders, so that the prosecutors might have found an excuse for hanging her, even under Elizabeth's statute, if they had so desired. In the same year, Jennet Preston was hanged at York. She was convicted of murder by witchcraft, and would have suffered death by Elizabeth's law. Likewise in 1612, there was an outbreak of prosecution in Northamptonshire, which ended in the execution of five persons. Every one of these, however, had been found guilty of murder by witchcraft.[39] Hence their fate under the statute of James was precisely what it would have been if Elizabeth's statute of 1563 had never been supplanted.

Two facts of immense significance are now clear: first, that James's accession was not the signal for an outbreak of witch-prosecution, for he had been on the throne for nine years before any such outbreak occurred; second, that the statute of 1604 was not appreciably more severe, in its practical working in 1612, than the Elizabethan statute would have been at the same time if it had continued in force.

Before leaving the events of 1612, however, we must inquire whether James had any hand in the prosecutions. The answer is unequivocal. There is not a particle of evidence that he either suggested or encouraged the trials, or, indeed, that he ever heard of the cases until the defendants had been hanged. A contrary view is sometimes expressed with regard to the Lancaster trials,[40] but there is no foundation for it. The source of the error is nothing more or less than William Harrison Ainsworth's romance entitled The Lancashire Witches. This was published in 1849, and appears to have proved more entertaining to some historians than the study of authentic documents.

One of Ainsworth's most amusing characters is Master Thomas Potts, a London lawyer. Potts happens to be in Lancashire on legal business, and, on coming into contact with the rumors and petty intrigues of the neighborhood, grasps the chance to ingratiate himself with King James by gathering evidence and fomenting prosecution. "So there ιre suspected witches in Pendle Forest, I find," says Master ᵖotts; "I shall make it my business to institute inquiries con-᷐erning them, when I visit the place to-morrow. Even if ᷉nerely ill-reputed, they must be examined, and if found inno-᷐ent cleared; if not, punished according to the statute. Our ᷊overeign lord the king holdeth witches in especial abhor-᷐ence, and would gladly see all such noxious vermin extir-᷊ated from the land, and it will rejoice me to promote his ᷊audable designs. . . . He is never so pleased as when the ᷐ruth of his tenets are proved by such secret offenders being ᷊rought to light, and duly punished." ⁴¹ And again: — "If ᷄ can unearth a pack of witches, I shall gain much credit from ᷉ny honourable good lords the judges of assize . . . , besides ᷊leasing the King himself, who is sure to hear of it, and re-᷆ard my praiseworthy zeal." ⁴²

Ainsworth is quite within his rights as a novelist, but we ᷊hould not read him as if he were an historian. Potts had ᷉othing to do with getting up the evidence or fomenting the ᷊rosecution. He was a London lawyer, or law-writer, who ᷄cted as clerk at the Lancaster assizes. Probably he was ac-᷐ompanying the justices on their circuit. At the instance of ᷐hese justices, as we know, he prepared an official narrative, ᷆hich was published in 1613 after revision by one of them ᷄Sir Edward Bromley). The king is mentioned only once in ᷐his tract (except, of course, in legal formulas), and that in ᷊assing: "What hath the Kings Maiestie written and pub-᷊ished in his *Dæmonologie*, by way of premonition and pre-᷉ıention, which hath not here by the first or last beene exe-᷐uted, put in practise or discouered." ⁴³ If James had known ᷄nything about the case, Potts would surely have brought ᷉him in.

But we are not done with Ainsworth's contributions to his-᷐tory. In the third volume of the romance he introduces King James in person, talking broad Scots, profoundly impressed by the evidence, causing the witches to be brought into his presence, and urging on the prosecution. These scenes occur while he is the guest of Sir Richard Hoghton at Hoghton Tower.⁴⁴ All this is very good fiction indeed. But it should not pass as history. The Pendle witches were hanged in August, 1612. James made a progress that summer, but not in Lancashire. His visit to Hoghton Tower was five years later, in August, 1617.[45]

Ainsworth wrote The Lancashire Witches at the suggestion of Mr. James Crossley, to whom he dedicated it. Mr. Crossley was an admirable antiquary, and the world is in his debt for a first-rate edition of Potts's Discoverie and for many other things. But, though very learned in the literature of witchcraft, he was far astray in his estimate of James's attitude and in other pertinent matters. He ignores the Elizabethan statute and lays stress on that of James, "enacted," he avers, "as the adulatory tribute of all parties, against which no honest voice was raised, to the known opinions of the monarch."[46] Mr. Crossley could not fail to observe that the passage of the "execrable statute" of 1604 was not followed by an instant fury of prosecution. He knew well that eight years elapsed before anything took place that was at all notable. And this is how he expresses himself: the statute, he suggests, "might have been sharpening its appetite by a temporary fast for the full meal of blood by which it was eventually glutted."[47] This is not merely personification, — it is pure mythology.

The plain and simple truth is this: During the twenty-two years of James's reign (1603–1625), there was no more excitement on the subject of witchcraft, and there were no more executions, than during the last twenty-two years of Elizabeth (1581–1603).[48] James's accession was not in any sense the signal for an outburst of prosecution. As we have just noted, the first bad year was 1612, when he had been on the throne for almost a decade. It is certain that the statute of 1604 was not more severe, in its practical workings, than the statute of Elizabeth.[49] Nor can a single fact be brought forward to prove that James was eager, during his English reign, to multiply the number of victims.

We must now examine the prevalent opinion that the statute of 1604 was passed to please King James or at his instance, or, indeed, that he wrote the bill himself. Most readers will be surprised to learn that not a particle of direct evidence has ever been adduced in favor of any of these propositions. They rest entirely upon assumption or inference. The earliest testimony that I can discover[50] is Hutchinson's n 1718, — more than a century late; and Hutchinson, *more suo*, is commendably cautious. He does not profess to have any authority for his views. "I cannot forbear thinking" — such are his words — "that it was the King's Book and Judgment, more than any Encrease of Witches, that influenc'd the Parliament to the changing the Old Law." [51]   And again, "I cannot but think, that if King *James* himself was not the first Mover and Director in this change of the Statute, yet there might probably be a Design of making Court to the King by it." [52]   He frankly labels his theory "the best Guess I can make." [53]   The "juryman" (his interlocutor in the dialogue) accepts the theory: "I am the apter to believe this Account; because I have often heard, that our Law did come from thence," that is, from Scotland along with the new king. [54] Dr. William Harris, in his account of James I (1753), follows Hutchinson, whom he cites, remarking that the statute was "formed out of compliment (as has been well conjectured)." [55]   Scott, in 1810, follows Hutchinson, remarking that the statute "probably had rise in the complaisance of James's first Parliament." [56]   By 1829 the tradition had hardened considerably, so that a writer in the Gentleman's Magazine asserted that James "is said to have penned [the statute] himself." [57]   So much for the external evidence, — now for the probabilities.

In the first place, the text of the statute is sufficient proof that James did not draft it himself. For it is *not a new law*. It follows, in the main, the Elizabethan statute word for word. At the utmost, James can be suspected of penning only a few phrases. This part of the charge we may therefore dismiss without ceremony. But what of the view that James fathered or fostered the bill, that it was introduced at his instance, or passed with an eye to his favor? Was there, or was there not, such a state of public opinion in England as will account for the statute without our having recourse to the conjecture that it was passed under James's influence or out of complaisance to him?

If this were merely a question of the rank and file of the people, there would be no room for argument. The last few years of Elizabeth's reign abounded in witch-prosecutions and were marked by intense popular excitement on the subject. A typical outbreak was that in Devon in 1601 and 1602, when the Trevisard family was complained of before Sir Thomas Ridgeway.[58] But we are now occupied with the law-makers, who, though constantly exposed to pressure from the populace, may conceivably have preferred the *status quo.* Was there, or was there not, before James's accession, a movement among the better-educated classes for a revision of the law and a sharpening of the penalties? To test this question, we may consult four well-known treatises which are seldom scrutinized from this point of view. We will begin with Perkins's Discourse.

William Perkins, the eminent theologian, born in 1558, was Fellow of Christ's College, Cambridge, from 1584 to 1594. He died in 1602, leaving behind him A Discourse of the Damned Art of Witchcraft, which was published in 1608 by Thomas Pickering, B.D. of Cambridge, and Minister of Finchingfield, Essex. Pickering dedicated the volume to Coke. Though not issued in the author's lifetime, this treatise is good evidence as to what the views of learned Englishmen were at the turn of the century. Nor was it without influence before Perkins died, for, as the title-page sets forth, the discourse was "framed and delivered" by him "in his ordinarie course of Preaching." It came from the press of the Cambridge University Printer.

Perkins's book is a masterpiece. It is cogently reasoned, and marked by that concise and simple style for which this author was distinguished above his contemporaries. We may shudder at his opinions, but are forced to admire his candor and ability. Perkins warns his readers against convicting on slender evidence. His virile and methodical intellect draws the line sharply between presumptions that justify suspicion, and proofs that warrant a verdict of guilty.[59] Certain superstitious popular tests he rejects utterly, — such as scratching the witch, and firing the thatch of her cottage, and the ordeal by swimming.[60] Some of these, he declares, "if not all, are after a sort practises of Witchcraft, hauing in them no power or vertue to detect a Sorcerer, either by Gods ordinance in the creation, or by any speciall appointment since." In scouting the water ordeal, Perkins may have had his eye upon King James's defence of it in the Dæmonologie. "It appeares," the king had written, "that God hath appointed (for a super-naturall signe of the monstrous impietie of Witches) that the water shall refuse to receiue them in her bosome, that haue shaken off them the sacred Water of Baptisme, and wilfully refused the benefite thereof." [61] Note the brevity and force of Perkins's refutation: — "To iustifie the casting of a Witch into the water, it is alledged, that hauing made a couenant with the deuill, shee hath renounced her Baptisme, and here-upon there growes an Antipathie betweene her, and water. *Ans.* This allegation serues to no purpose: for all water is not the water of Baptisme, but that onely which is vsed in the very act of Baptisme, and not before nor after. The element out of the vse of the Sacrament, is no Sacrament, but returnes again to his common vse." [62] Let us remark, in passing, that Thomas Pickering, a beneficed clergyman, did not hesitate to publish this unceremonious denial of the king's argument in 1608, when James had been five years on the throne, and to dedicate the work which contains it to Chief Justice Coke. This may serve to correct, *pro tanto*, the too prevalent opin-ion that James I expected his English subjects to receive his Dæmonologie as but little, if at all, inferior in authority to the Holy Scriptures.

Our immediate concern, however, is with the general ten-dency of Perkins's treatise, and in particular with his precepts as to punishment. He admits the witch-dogma in its entirety. The ground of all sorcery is a league or covenant with the devil, which may be either express or implicit. There are two kinds of witchcraft, — namely, divining and working.[63] The second class includes the raising of storms, the poisoning of the air (which brings pestilence), the blasting of corn, "the procuring of strange passions and torments in mens bodies and other creatures, with the curing of the same." [64] It is an error to hold that melancholia so deludes women that they imagine themselves witches when indeed they are none. Per-haps, after the witch has made her contract with the fiend, she may credit herself with imaginary powers, but the won-ders already enumerated she can certainly perform, with Satan's aid.[65] Thus Perkins opposes himself squarely to Wierus and Scot. His refutation of their theories is solid and convincing, if we admit what nobody dreamt of denying, —

the existence of evil spirits. His book, indeed, may be taken as a measure of the slight effect which these dissentients had produced on the minds of sixteenth-century Englishmen.

As to the law against witchcraft, Perkins is an invaluable witness. He wrote when the Elizabethan statute was in force, and he was of course not under the sway of King James of Scotland, with whose theories, indeed, we have seen him at outspoken variance. Perkins believes that the law of Moses should continue in force, and that "all Witches beeing thoroughly conuicted by the Magistrate," should be put to death.[66] He expressly declares that this punishment ought to be inflicted not only upon those who kill by means of witchcraft, but upon all witches without any exception whatever, — upon "all Diuiners, Charmers, Iuglers, all Wizzards, commonly called wise men and wise women." He includes in plain terms all so-called "good Witches, which doe no hurt but good, which doe not spoile and destroy, but saue and deliuer." Here he uses a really unanswerable argument, which shows in the most striking fashion how ill-equipped we are, with our mild penal laws, to sit in judgment on the severity — whether actual or comparative — of the Jacobean statute. "By the lawes of England," writes Perkins, "the thiefe is executed for stealing, and we think it iust and profitable: but it were a thousand times better for the land, if all Witches, but specially the blessing Witch might suffer death. For the thiefe by his stealing, and the hurtfull Inchanter by charming, bring hinderance and hurt to the bodies and goods of men; but these are the right hand of the deuill, by which he taketh and destroieth the soules of men. Men doe commonly hate and spit at the damnifying Sorcerer, as vnworthie to liue among them; whereas the other is so deare vnto them, that they hold themselues and their countery blessed that haue him among them, they flie vnto him in necessitie, they depend vpon him as their god, and by this meanes, thousands are carried away to their finall confusion. Death therefore is the iust and deserued portion of the good Witch." These are the closing words of Perkins's weighty treatise.[67]

Perkins was a vital force in forming English opinion while he was alive, especially during the last decade of the sixteenth century and at the beginning of the seventeenth. Few Cambridge lecturers were more authoritative, and Cambridge was in close contact with public men. He "was buried with great solemnity at the sole charges of *Christs Colledge*, the University and Town striving which should expresse more sorrow at his Funeral; Doctor *Montague* Preached his Funeral Sermon upon that Text, *Moses my Servant is dead.*" [68] This was James Montagu, first Master of Sidney Sussex College, afterwards Bishop of Bath and Wells (1608) and of Winchester (1616). Bishop Hall, who was at Cambridge while Perkins was active, commends Perkins warmly. "A worthy divine," he calls him, "whose labors are of much note and use in the Church of God." [69] Fuller is also among his admirers.[70] How the Discourse worked when its substance was orally delivered "in his ordinarie course of preaching" may be inferred from the respect with which the printed book is continually cited, — by Cotta, for example, in his Triall of Witch-craft (1616).[71] Cotta's treatise is likewise dedicated to Coke.

John Cotta was of Trinity College, Cambridge, in 1590, and later of Corpus Christi. He received the degree of M.A. in 1596, and that of M.D. in 1603. His first book appeared in 1612. It contains a good deal about witchcraft. In 1616 he published a systematic treatise, A Triall of Witch-craft, of which a second edition came out in 1624. The main object of this work is to prove that any given case of alleged sorcery ought to be examined by methods of the senses and reason, like other objects of investigation. Cotta, then, is on the right side. He follows Wierus in maintaining that many so-called bewitched persons are suffering from natural disease. When he wrote, he was practising at Northampton, where he had resided ever since he took his medical degree in 1603. His rationalizing attitude was largely the result of his own experience as a physician during this interval.

The whole ground of Cotta's argument is an acceptance of the traditional witch-dogma. He believes that there are witches in plenty; that they make contracts with the devil; that supernatural deeds are performed by the fiend, in which the witch "hath a property and interest" by virtue of her covenant with him; that, in this way, witches may be implicated in afflicting their fellow-creatures with diseases or in causing their death. As concrete examples, we may take the witches of Warboys (1589–1593) and the Lancashire witches (1612), for both of those notorious cases are accepted by Cotta without demur.[72] And, just as he is confident that the guilt of a witch may be discovered with certainty by methods of reason and perception which he develops elaborately, so he is content to leave her to the courts, to be "arraigned and condemned of manifest high treason against Almighty God, and of combination with his open and professed enemy the Diuell."[73] The statute of 1604 was none too rigorous for Dr. Cotta. If these were his sentiments in 1616, when he was writing a cautionary and corrective treatise, we may be certain that his views were quite as orthodox at the turn of the century, when he was still at the University of Cambridge and subject to the influence of Perkins, whom he cites with so much respect.

From Cambridge we turn to Oxford. Thomas Cooper, of Christ Church, was A.B. in 1590, A.M. in 1593, B.D. in 1600. In 1601 he was presented by his college to a living in Cheshire, which he resigned in 1604. From 1604 to 1610 he was vicar of Holy Trinity, Coventry.[74] His volume entitled The Mystery of Witch-craft was not published until 1617, but it embodies information enough about the author's experiences and opinions in the time preceding the accession of James to make it available for our present purposes. Cooper's acquaintance with magic began while he was a student at Oxford. There was a time, he tells us, when he "admired some in the Vniuersitie famozed in that skill." "Did not," he exclaims, — "did not the Lord so dispose of mee, that my *Chamber-fellow* was exceedingly bewitched with these faire shewes, and hauing gotten diuers bookes to that end, was earnest in the pursuit of that glorie which might redound thereby? Did not wee communicate our Studies together? was not this skill proposed and canuased in common? And did not the Lord so arme his vnworthy seruant, that not onely the snare was gratiously espied; but, by the great mercie of my God, the Lord vsed mee as a meanes to diuert my *Chamber-fellow* from these dangerous studies?"[75] Thus we learn that when Cooper received his Cheshire living, in 1601, he was deeply impressed with the horror of dealing with devils. Between this date and 1610 he had several encounters with witchcraft, — at Northwich (near Chester), in Lancashire, and at Coventry.[76] Some of these are perhaps too late for us to use, but the Northwich incident falls in 1601 and 1602.[77] At all events, we are safe in believing that the sentiments which Cooper expresses in his volume do not differ appreciably from those which he entertained before James's accession. Now Cooper agrees in all essentials and in most particulars with Perkins, from whom he borrows largely without due acknowledgment.[78] Writing after the passage of the statute of 1604, he rejoices that the law has been made severer.[79] Yet he is not satisfied. Like Perkins, he holds that "the *Blesser or good Witch* . . . is farre more dangerous then the *Badde or hurting Witch*," [80] and that both kinds ought to be extirpated. Thus it appears that Cooper, though he wrote after the passage of the statute of 1604, may serve as a witness to the opinions that prevailed among many of the clergy at about the turn of the century.

Our fourth witness is a very strong one, and his testimony is not complicated by inferences about dates. He is George Giffard, another Oxford man. Giffard's Dialogue concerning Witches and Witchcrafts was first published in 1593, — a year otherwise notable in the annals of English sorcery, as we shall see in a moment. It was reissued in 1603, three years after his death.[81] Giffard was an eminent preacher of Maldon, in Essex. He passes for one of the earliest opponents of the witchcraft delusion, and with some reason, for he held that sickness and death ascribed to witchcraft were due to natural causes, he repudiated spectral and hearsay evidence, and he argued against convicting anybody except on conclusive testimony. Yet it never entered his head to deny the existence of witches or to doubt that they have dealings with the fiend. He tells us that the times were devil-haunted. "It falleth out in many places euen of a sudden, as it seemeth to me, and no doubt by the heauie iudgement of God, that the Diuels as it were let loose, do more preuaile, then euer I haue heard of. . . . Satan is now heard speake, and beleeued. He speaketh by coniurers, by sorcerers, and by witches, and his word is taken. He deuiseth a number of things to be done, & they are put in practise and followed." [82] Giffard is here speaking in his own person. Elsewhere in the dialogue he gives us a first-rate account of the popular terror. One of the interlocutors is "Samuel," an honest and well-to-do goodman. "They say," declares Samuel, "there is scarse any towne or village in all this shire, but there is one or two witches at the least in it." [83] And the annals of Essex bear out Samuel's views. Thirteen witches, as we have seen, were convicted and ten of them hanged in that county in 1582, and there were other executions there in 1566, 1579, and 1589. It was an outbreak in that same county in 1645 that started Matthew Hopkins on his career; and the evidence and confessions went back, in some instances, for twenty and even thirty years.[84] Giffard was a man of unusual humanity and strong common sense, as his book shows. Yet he was heartily in favor of a severer law than the statute of Elizabeth. The following passage from his Dialogue is a precious document for our present purposes. "Daniel" is the speaker who presents Giffard's own views; "M. B." is a schoolmaster.

Dan. A witch by the word of God ought to die the death, not because she killeth men, for that she cannot (vnles it be those witches which kill by poyson, which either they receiue from the diuell, or hee teacheth them to make) but because she dealeth with diuels. And so if a Iurie doe finde proofe that she hath dealt with diuels, they may and ought to finde them guiltie of witchcraft.

M. B. If they finde them guiltie to haue dealt with diuels, and cannot say they haue murdered men, the law doth not put them to death.

Dan. It were to be wished, that the law were more [p]erfect in that respect, euen to cut off all such abhominations. These cunning men and women which deale with spirites and charmes seeming to doe good, and draw the people into manifold impieties, with all other which haue familiarity with deuils, or vse coniurations, ought to bee rooted out, that others might see and feare. (Sig. K3.)

Here we have a highly intelligent preacher, a man of real influence, pressing for precisely that change in the law — the extension of the death penalty to witchcraft that produces bodily injury without death — which was actually embodied in the statute of 1604. And Giffard, like Perkins, condemns the "white witch" utterly. The evidence speaks for itself.

Perkins's Discourse and Giffard's Dialogue are strongly contrasted works. Giffard addresses his teaching to the unlearned: he throws his book into the form of a conversation (so he tells us) "to make it fitter for the capacity of the simpler sort." Perkins, on the other hand, writes for educated persons, — for those who can follow a close-knit scholastic argument. Giffard's aim is to free the minds of the common people from needless terrors and to prevent the shedding of innocent blood. Perkins, though he warns his readers (as Giffard does) against condemning on slender evidence, is chiefly bent on defending the witchcraft dogma against the assaults of Wierus and Reginald Scot. Yet both Giffard and Perkins hold tenaciously to the inherited belief. There *are* such things as witches; they *do* ally themselves with the devil; they *should* be punished. And in this matter of the penalty — which is our chief concern at the moment — Giffard and Perkins are in perfect accord. Both maintain that *all witches ought to be put to death, irrespective of the question whether they have killed men by their arts or not.* In other words, the Elizabethan statute seemed to them insufficient, and they urged the enacting of a law of greater severity. Could there be more illuminating evidence? Nothing can be clearer than that, about the turn of the century, before Elizabeth was dead and James had taken her place, there was strong pressure for a revision of the witchcraft law, and for revision in the direction taken by the statute of 1604. This was the kind of pressure to which the legislators yielded — nothing loth, to be sure. They were not browbeaten by King James, nor did they vote with an eye to the royal favor. They followed their own consciences, incited by the feelings of the populace and stimulated by the exhortations of the gravest counsellors they knew.

The four books that we have just examined would suffice to prove, even if there were no other evidence, that the accession of James found the English public — both in its educated and its uneducated classes — deeply impressed with the actuality of witchcraft as an ever-present menace to soul and body, intensely excited on the subject, and pressing hard for the extermination of witches.[85] But there is other evidence in plenty. The records from 1582 to 1603 abound in specific cases. Two items call for particular notice: the Darrel affair (1586–1601), and the affair of the Witches of Warboys (1589–1593). There is a close psychological connection between them.

John Darrel, a Cambridge graduate, was a Puritan preacher in Derbyshire when (in 1586) he began his career as a caster-out of devils. In 1598 he was summoned before an ecclesiastical commission over which Archbishop Whitgift presided. Bishop Bancroft and Chief Justice Anderson were members of the commission. More than forty witnesses were called. Some of the demoniacs confessed fraud, and Darrel, with his associate George More, was convicted of imposture and imprisoned.[86] There had been an uproar over the possessions and the exorcisms, and popular opinion sided with Darrel. Samuel Harsnet, the cleverest of Bishop Bancroft's chaplains, was delegated to write up the case. His famous Discovery came out in 1599, and was expected to overwhelm Darrel with ridicule and odium. In the long run it has had this result, for Darrel is usually treated now-a-days as an impostor. But it had no such effect at the time. Both Darrel and More wrote long replies, and printed them surreptitiously in defiance of the authorities.

Bancroft soon discovered that Harsnet's skirmishing was not sufficient, and he brought his heavy troops into action. Two treatises, of unimaginable ponderosity in style and matter, each elaborated in concert by two preachers, John Deacon and John Walker, came out in 1601.[87] Harsnet had railed and ridiculed and "exposed," but he had steered clear of dialectics. Deacon and Walker toiled to supply the desideratum. Using all the scholastic machinery, they tried to prove, by logic and Scripture, that there is no such thing as demoniacal possession now-a-days, and that Darrel's demoniacs were either counterfeiting or else afflicted with natural diseases. Darrel promptly replied to both books, printing his answers surreptitiously, as before.

Strange as it may seem, Darrel has the best of the argument. For his opponents admit both too little and too much. They admit too little, since they wish the fits to appear fraudulent, whereas these were, beyond a shadow of doubt, genuine hysteria, of which lying and imposture are well-recognized symptoms. Darrel was sharp enough to see that, as managed by his opponents, the hypothesis of fraud and the hypothesis of disease thwarted each other, and left some kind of demonic assault in possession of the field. They admit too much, because they themselves grant the existence of evil spirits of vast power (nay, take pains to demonstrate their existence), and because they accept demoniacal possession as a fact in ancient times, though they reject it for the present age. This rejection was, of course, quite arbitrary, and their attempts to justify it from Scripture were pitifully weak. Darrel could appeal to facts and experience. His patients had manifested the same symptoms as the demoniacs of old, and it was obviously absurd to force a distinction. If the afflicted persons in Bible times were possessed with devils, then his patients were possessed with devils; and if he had relieved them (as he surely had), then there was no reason which Deacon and Walker could make valid to reject the corollary of dispossession.

But what connection has this strange affair with witchcraft? Here we must walk circumspectly, for misapprehensions are rife. It is often inferred that Bancroft and Harsnet, because they denounced Darrel and his patients as tricksters, had no belief in witchcraft. This is a false conclusion. A demoniac is not necessarily bewitched. He may owe his dire condition to some witch's malice, or, on the other hand, the devil may have assailed him immediately, without a witch's agency. Further, there are many evil things done by witches which have no reference to demoniacal possession. In all of Darrel's cases, to be sure, witches were accused. To some extent, then, Bancroft and his assistants were, in effect, attempting to discredit the witch-dogma, since they were attacking the genuineness, or the diabolical origin, of certain phenomena ascribed, in these particular instances, to witchcraft. But (and we cannot be too careful in making the distinction) *they did not deny either the existence or the criminality of witches in general*, any more than they denied the existence of wicked spirits. They strove to explode the theory of demoniacal possession; but they did not attack the witchcraft dogma. Indeed, they took care to avoid committing themselves on that head. For, even if they had no faith in the dogma, they knew that to assail it would throw them out of court, inasmuch as the belief in witchcraft was, in some form or other, universal among all classes and all persuasions.

Further, Bancroft and his aids, in their opposition to Darrel, were not espousing the cause of alleged witches, — or, if so, they were doing it in a purely incidental way. Their object was quite definite and unconcealed. They were warring against the Puritans [88] and the Roman Catholics, whom they regarded as foes to Church and State. Puritan preachers and Roman Catholic priests both professed to cast out devils. In Bancroft's eyes these were absurd pretensions. Yet the people and many of the clergy were much impressed. There was danger ahead, so the Bishop thought. A vigorous campaign was necessary. But the campaign was political and ecclesiastical, not humanitarian. Its aim was not to save witches, but to crush exorcists.[89]

Here is a significant bit of evidence on this point. In 1602 Mary Glover, the daughter of a merchant in Thames Street, had weird seizures, which she attributed to the malign spells of Elizabeth Jackson. The neighbors were eager to prosecute, but a physician informed Chief Justice Anderson that "the maid did counterfeit." Anderson directed Sir John Croke (Recorder of London) to summon the girl to his chamber in the Temple and test the matter. Croke did so in 1603, having both the maid and the witch present, with divers neighbors and certain ministers. He was convinced, by various drastic tests, that there was no imposture, and committed Mother Jackson to Newgate. At the Recorder's instance, several ministers undertook to relieve the girl by fasting and prayer. They were completely successful. One of them, Lewis Hughes, was despatched to Bishop Bancroft with the tidings. He was not well received. "I . . . could have no audience," he writes, "and for my paines I was called Rascall and varlot, and sent to the Gatehouse, where hee kept me foure moneths." [90] But Mother Jackson was arraigned and convicted in due course. Bancroft, we observe, was certain that this was not demoniacal possession, and he imprisoned the exorciser. But he made no effort, so far as we can learn, to rescue the witch. He left her to the courts with a good conscience.

This episode fell just after the so-called exposure of Darrel. The date makes it instructive. The Recorder, we note, was still a believer in possession, despite the arguments of Bancroft's literary bureau, and so were many (perhaps most) of

the clergy. Indeed, we must not too hastily assume that all
the bishops even were ready to subscribe to Bancroft's extreme tenets. Take the case of Thomas Harrison, the Boy of
Northwich, in Cheshire. His fits began in 1600 or 1601 and
lasted a year or two. He was kept for ten days in the Bishop
of Chester's palace and carefully watched, but no fraud was
detected. The bishop (Richard Vaughan) and three other
commissioners issued an order that, "for [his] ease and deliverance" from "his grievous afflictions," public prayers
should be offered for him in the parish church "before the
congregation so oft as the same assembleth." They delegated seven clergymen to visit him by turns, and "to use
their discretions by private prayer and fasting, for the ease
and comfort of the afflicted." Some held, this document informs us, "that the child [was] really possessed of an uncleane
spirit." This Bishop Vaughan and the other commissioners
doubted. But they did not think he was shamming. They
had "seene the bodily affliction of the said child," and observed in sundry fits very strange effects and operations, they
tell us, "either proceeding of naturall vnknowne causes, or of
some diabolical practise." [91] And Harvey, one of the clergymen appointed by the bishop to fast and pray, wrote to a
friend that nothing like the "passions [i. e. sufferings], be-
hauiour, and speeches" of the boy had "ever come under his
observation or occurred in his reading." "Few that haue
seene the variety of his fits, but they thinke the diuell hath
the disposing of his body. Myselfe haue diuers times seene
him, and such things in him as are impossible to proceed from
any humane creature. The matter hath affected our whole
countrey. The Diuines with us generally hold, that the child
is really possessed." [92] A contemporary memorandum assures us that once, when the bishop was praying with him,
"the Boy was so outragious, that he flew out of his bed, and
so frighted the Bishops men, that one of them fell into a
sown, and the Bishop was glad to lay hold on the boy, who
ramped at the Window to have gotten out." [93]

Joseph Hall, afterwards Bishop of Exeter (1627) and of
Norwich (1641), in disputing with a Belgian priest in 1605,
asserted roundly that "in our church, we had manifest proofs
of the ejection of devils by fasting and prayer." [94] Hall was a

firm believer in witchcraft and approved of the statute of 1604.[95]

And now we will go back a few years in order to see what the bishops and the judges thought, and how they acted, when a case combining demoniacal possession with witchcraft was not complicated by Puritan or Roman Catholic exorcism. Let us examine, as briefly as may be, the celebrated case of the Witches of Warboys. The story has been told again and again, but its actual bearing on the history of English witch-prosecution has never been pointed out. The Warboys case lasted from 1589, when the fits of the afflicted persons began, until 1593, when the witches were hanged.

Robert Throckmorton, Esquire, was a Huntingdonshire gentleman of excellent family and connections. He was of Ellington, but had removed to Warboys shortly before our story begins. Both these places are near the county town, and therefore not far from Cambridge. The disturbance began in November, 1589, when Jane, Mr. Throckmorton's daughter, a girl of about ten years, was attacked with violent hysteria. In her fits, she called out against Mother Samuel, an aged neighbor. Two first-rate physicians of Cambridge were consulted, Dr. Barrow (a friend of Mr. Throckmorton's) and Master Butler. The latter was William Butler (1535–1618) of Clare Hall, of whom Aubrey tells several amusing anecdotes. Aubrey informs us that he "never tooke the degree of Doctor, though he was the greatest physitian of his time." [96] Both Barrow and Butler were baffled, and Barrow ascribed the fits to witchcraft, remarking that he himself "had some experience of the mallice of some witches." [97] This speech is worth noting, for it throws light on the state of mind of university men. Within two months, Mistress Jane's four sisters — ranging in age from nine to fifteen years — were similarly attacked, and they all cried out against Mother Samuel. This affliction lasted until April, 1593, or about three years and a half. In the interval six or seven women-servants (for the Throckmorton ménage was of course somewhat unstable) suffered from just such fits, — and also the wife of one of the girls' maternal uncles, Mr. John Pickering of Ellington. Mother Samuel was believed to be the cause of it all. Yet the children's parents acted with exem-

plary caution. They had no wish to prosecute Mother
Samuel, but treated her kindly and gave their attention to
caring for the girls and urging her to confess. Her confession
and repentance, it was hoped, would put an end to the fits.

About Christmas, 1592, Mother Samuel admitted her
guilt. Even then there was no immediate thought of bringing her to justice. She was in great distress of mind, and
both Mr. Throckmorton and Dr. Dorington, the parson of
Warboys, exerted themselves to give her Christian consolation as a repentant sinner. However, she almost immediately
retracted, whereupon Mr. Throckmorton, losing patience at
last, took her before the Bishop of Lincoln (William Chaderton) and certain justices. She again made admission of guilt.
Soon after the girls fell into their fits afresh, and they now
accused the old woman of the death of Lady Cromwell, the
second wife of Sir Henry Cromwell of Hinchinbrook, the
great landowner of those parts, known for his splendor as the
Golden Knight.

The Cromwells and the Throckmortons were friends, and,
in September, 1590, Lady Cromwell, being then at Ramsey,
only two miles from Warboys, had made a call of sympathy
on the family. Mother Samuel, who lived next door, had
been summoned. The Samuels were Sir Henry's tenants, and
the lady spoke roughly to the old woman, accusing her of
witchcraft, and snatched off her cap and clipped off a lock
of her hair. This she told Mistress Throckmorton to burn.
Mother Samuel uttered some words which, when later remembered, passed for the *damnum minatum*. That night
Lady Cromwell was strangely attacked, and she died after an
illness of a year and a quarter, — that is, about the beginning
of 1592. Nobody appears to have connected Mother Samuel
with her death until, in 1593, the afflicted girls charged her
with it in their ravings. They extended the accusation to John
Samuel, her husband, and Agnes, her daughter. All three were
tried at Huntingdon before Justice Fenner on April 5th,
1593. Mother Samuel confessed, and, with her husband and
daughter, was hanged, according to the Elizabethan statute.
There was no doubt of their guilt in anybody's mind. Mother
Samuel herself thought the girls bewitched, and old Samuel
was finally convinced that his wife was guilty.

Several causes combined to make this the most momentous witch-trial that had ever occurred in England. The long continuance of the phenomena and the station of the victims were alone sufficient to give the affair wide currency. The family was connected with many persons of importance. Mr. Robert Throckmorton was related to the Warwickshire and the Gloucestershire Throckmortons. One of his first cousins, also named Robert, lived at Brampton, Northants, close by, and often witnessed the girls' fits. The girls' maternal uncle, Mr. (afterwards Sir) Gilbert Pickering of Tichmarsh, and his brothers, John and Henry, were deeply interested, and gave evidence at the assizes. So did Dr. Francis Dorington, the Warboys rector, who was the husband of Mr. Throckmorton's sister. Robert Poulter, vicar of Brampton, another witness, was also connected with the family.[98] Francis Cromwell, Sir Henry's brother, was one of the justices to whom Mother Samuel confessed. The Cromwells were among the best-known commoners in the kingdom. Dr. Dorington's brother John, a Londoner, visited the children in their attacks, and of course he talked of the affair in the capital.

The connections with Cambridge were also very intimate. The physicians consulted by Mr. Throckmorton, as we have noticed, lived there, and they were both university men. Dr. Francis Dorington, the parson of Warboys, who had married Mr. Throckmorton's sister, and Thomas Nutt, the vicar of Ellington, were also Cambridge graduates.[99] Both were deeply interested in the case, and gave evidence at the trial. Henry Pickering, one of the children's maternal uncles, was at Christ's College when the fits began.[100] He not only visited the Throckmortons in 1590, "being then a Scholler of Cambridge," and stayed there three or four days, but he took two other scholars of his acquaintance to see the witch, and we have a pretty full account of the interview. Mr. Pickering was fully persuaded that Goody Samuel was a witch. Being somewhat moved, he told her that "there was no way to preuent the iudgements of God, but by her confession and repentance: which if she did not in time, he hoped one day to see her burned at a stake, and he himselfe would bring fire and wood, and the children should blowe the coales." [101] This Mr. Henry Pickering became, in 1597, rector of Aldwincle All Saints, in Northamptonshire. His daughter Mary married Erasmus Dryden (son of Sir Erasmus), and became the mother of the illustrious poet, who was born at the parsonage house of Aldwincle All Saints in 1631.[102] Thus it appears that the five tormented Throckmorton girls were first cousins of the poet's mother, and that Mrs. Throckmorton was his great-aunt. We note that William Perkins, whose treatise on witchcraft we have examined, was a fellow of Christ's College during most of the time when these fits were going on. It is curious, too, that the publisher of Perkins's posthumous treatise (another Cambridge man) was Thomas Pickering,[103] doubtless a relative, though we cannot be certain of that. Both Sir Henry Cromwell and his son Oliver had been at the university.

The Warboys case, then, demonstrably produced a deep and lasting impression on the class that made laws. The gentlemen concerned were not ignorant country squires in the remote districts; they were intelligent, well-educated men, in close contact with one of the universities and with the capital.

Nor was the impression allowed to die out. It was perpetuated in two ways — by a remarkable book and by a permanent foundation. The presiding judge, Edward Fenner, was so much struck by what he had seen and heard (for the children had their fits in his presence) that he joined with others to further the publication of a narrative, — The Most Strange and Admirable Discoverie of the Three Witches of Warboys, — which was printed in London in 1593. Full notes had been kept from the outset (as befitted the intelligence and education of the families concerned) and these were used by the author. This is no mere catchpenny tract. It is a careful and temperate report of the girls' malady from first to last. Nothing comparable to it, considered as a report on a long-continued case of epidemic hysteria, had ever appeared in England. The details, at which modern writers on witchcraft are wont to jeer, are no more ridiculous than the details in recent and esteemed treatises on *la grande hystérie*, or on multiple personality. That it kept the Warboys case alive long after the accession of James I is certain, for Dr. John Cotta, in 1616 and again in 1624, refers to the "Treatise

of the Witches of Warbozys" as authoritative.[104] He had
no doubt whatever that the Throckmorton girls were bewitched.[105]

Finally, Sir Henry Cromwell took effectual measures for
perpetuating the impression made by the long-continued
phenomena, the trial, and the book. Certain goods and chattels of the executed felons were forfeited to him as lord of the
manor. He disdained to keep the money and wished to de-
vote it to public uses. Hence he established an annual sermon
at Huntingdon, to be delivered by a fellow of his own college,
Queen's of Cambridge. The appointee was to "preache and
invaye against the destestable practice, synne, and offence of
witchcraft, inchantment, charm, and sorcereye." The sermon was maintained until 1812, but toward the end its burden was turned to the explosion of the old belief.[106]

And now, when we come to apply what we have observed
of the state of educated public opinion and to estimate its
presumable effect on the legislators of 1604, who passed the
revised statute, we are struck with a fact which all investigators have overlooked or ignored. *Two gentlemen were sitting
in the House of Commons who had the strongest personal interest
in the Warboys case.* The Samuels had been hanged, not for
tormenting the Throckmorton girls,[107] but for bewitching
Lady Cromwell to death. As we run our eye down the list of
Members of Parliament, it is arrested by two names, — Sir
Oliver Cromwell and Henry Cromwell, — one the member
for the County of Huntingdon, the other for the borough.
These were sons of that Sir Henry whose wife had died (as all
believed) from Mother Samuel's arts, and who had founded a
sermon in perpetual memory of the murder.

Both Sir Oliver and Henry Cromwell might therefore be
presumed to have an effective knowledge of the case. But
we are not left to conjecture. Their uncle, Francis Cromwell,
was one of the justices to whom Goody Samuel confessed.[108]
Mr. Henry Cromwell himself had visited the Throckmorton
house with one of Sir Henry's men and had observed two of
the girls in their fits.[109] This was in 1593, shortly before the
actual trial, and after the girls had begun to accuse the
Samuels of Lady Cromwell's murder. As for Sir Oliver, his
wife had accompanied her mother-in-law on the fatal visit to

the Throckmortons, and had been present at her interview with Goody Samuel. That night, Lady Cromwell was "strangly tormented in her sleep, by a cat (as she imagined) which mother Samuel had sent vnto her." Mistress Oliver Cromwell was sleeping in the same bed (her husband being from home), and was awakened by the "strugling and striuing of the Lady . . . and mournfull noise, which shee made speaking to the cat, and to mother Samuel." Mistress Oliver roused her mother-in-law, who told her all about her dream. Lady Cromwell had no more sleep that night, and soon after sickened, as already told.[110] We may be sure that when Mr. Oliver Cromwell returned, he was put in full possession of both ladies' experiences. Surely neither Sir Oliver Cromwell nor his brother stood in need of instruction in the witch-dogma from James I, or required any royal influence to persuade them to vote for the statute of 1604.

It is worth while to follow the clue a little farther, and to glance at the parliamentary history of the statute. Most writers have been quite innocent of any knowledge that it even had such a history. Yet there it stands in the Lords' and Commons' Journals, and an instructive history it is.

The bill originated in the House of Lords. The first reading took place on March 27, 1604. On the 29th it was read a second time and referred to a committee consisting of six earls, sixteen other peers, and twelve bishops. The committee was to have the most expert advice conceivable, and to that end an imposing array of legal talent, learning, and experience was requested "to attend the Lords" in their deliberations. Here is the list: the Chief Justice of the Common Pleas (Anderson), the Chief Baron of the Exchequer (Sir William Peryam), two justices of the King's Bench (Sir Christopher Yelverton and Sir David Williams), Serjeant Croke, the Attorney-General (Coke), and Sir John Tindall, a distinguished ecclesiastical lawyer. Nor was all this a mere flourish. The committee and its eminent counsel took their duties seriously. They rejected the draft that had been referred to them, and, on the 2d of April, the committee reported a new bill, "framed" by the committee. This was brought into the Lords by the Earl of Northumberland. It received certain amendments, and, on May 8th, after the third reading, was passed and sent to the House of Commons. Here, too, there was careful deliberation. On May 11th the bill had its first reading; and on the 26th it was read a second time and referred to a committee of seventeen, including the Recorder of London and two serjeants-at-law (Hobart and Shirley), which was directed to meet on the first of June in the Middle Temple Hall. On the 5th, Sir Thomas Ridgeway, for the committee, reported the bill "with alterations and amendments." On June 7th it came up for the third reading, was passed as amended, and on the 9th was sent up to the Lords.[111]

This bare statement of recorded facts disposes of the myth that King James was the author or the father of the statute which has so long been associated with his name and fame. Whether the measure was good or bad, — whether its results were great or small, — the Lords and Commons of England, and not the king, must shoulder the responsibility.[112] And it is in complete accord with what we should expect from the caution with which both houses proceeded and the care which their committees took, that the statute, when finally it left the hands of Parliament, was not really a new law at all, but simply a modification and extension of the statute of Elizabeth.

Two names on the Lords' Committee catch the eye immediately, — the Earl of Derby and the Bishop of Lincoln. Ten years before, in 1594, a short time after the witches of Warboys were hanged, Ferdinando, fifth Earl of Derby, had died at Latham after a ten days' illness. The physicians (he had four) ascribed his disease to a surfeit combined with over-exertion. But there were grave suspicions of sorcery. The Earl had dreamed strange dreams; he had been "crossed" by an apparition "with a gastly and threatning countenance." An image of wax was discovered in his bedroom. "A homely Woman, about the age of fifty yeeres, was found mumbling in a corner of his honours Chamber, but what God knoweth." Three other suspected witches appear in the case at divers times and in sundry manners. The Earl himself "cryed out that the Doctors laboured in vaine, because hee was certainely bewitched." In the end, the opinion seems to have prevailed that he died from natural causes.[113] But it

would be extraordinary if all the circumstances had not made
a profound impression on his younger brother, who succeeded
him, and this is the Earl of Derby whom we have noted in the
Lords' Committee on the bill. Another person who must also
have been deeply affected by these strange happenings was
the Bishop of Chester, who attended the dying man. This
was Dr. William Chaderton, who was translated to Lincoln
in 1594, and he, too, sat in the Lords' Committee.

Henry Percy, Earl of Northumberland, who reported the
second draft from the committee, was a famous student of
the occult sciences and was popularly known as "the Wizard
Earl." Like Dr. Dee, he believed that his own investigations
were free from the taint of diabolism, but, like Dee, he must
also have felt convinced that there were others who *did* traffic
with the infernal powers, and that such persons deserved
punishment.

Henry Howard, Earl of Northampton, another member of
the Lords' Committee, had the reputation of being the most
learned of the peers. He was a firm believer in the actuality
of communication between mortals and wicked spirits. In
his erudite Defensative against the Poyson of Supposed Prophecies, written in 1582 and 1583, he declared that one of the
means "whereby the contagion of vnlawfull Prophesies is
conueyed into the mindes of mortall men, is conference with
damned Spirits or Familiars, as commonly we call them." [114]
And he unhesitatingly ascribed the clairvoyance of cunning
men and women to such revelations, — taking as an example
their disclosure of the thief in a case of cutting a purse. [115]

Let us turn to the Commons' Committee. Here we find
several interesting names. Sir Roger Aston had been English
resident in Scotland. This may be held to be a two-edged
argument, but we do not need it, for there are plenty more.
Two of the most notoriously witch-haunted counties in England were Lancaster and Essex. Now, Lancashire was represented on the committee by Sir Richard Molyneux of Sefton.
As for Essex, not only was the county member, Sir Francis
Barrington, on the committee, but also Sir Robert Wroth,
who lived principally at Loughton Hall, in Essex. He was a
man of forty-odd when Brian Darcey's great St. Osyth cases
were tried and ten witches (perhaps more) were hanged in that

county. Other executions took place at Chelmsford in 1579 [116] and 1589.[117] Giffard, we remember, was an Essex preacher, and his Dialogue, published in 1593 and reissued in 1603, had urged the sharpening of the statute in the precise direction which this parliament took. Wroth had large possessions in Middlesex and sat for that county.[118] Now of the twenty-nine years from 1573 to 1601 there were witch-records for thirteen. Serjeant Hobart (later Sir Henry) was likewise a committeeman. What he thought of witchcraft we may infer from his conduct when Lord Chief Baron of the Exchequer at the trial of Margaret and Philip (i. e. Philippa) Flower, who were executed in 1619 for bewitching to death the son of the Earl of Rutland.[119] Nobody will suggest that he learned his creed from James I. If any should be so absurd, we may balance him by Sir Humphrey Winch, also an M.P., though not on the committee, who, in 1619, incurred the wrath of the king by condemning nine witches to death in a case which James himself shortly after exposed as an imposture. We shall return to this in a moment.[120] There was a Mr. Throckmorton on the committee. This was John Throckmorton, M.P. for Gloucestershire. The Throckmortons of that county were related to those of Huntingdonshire. It is likely that Mr. John had felt some share of the universal interest roused by the experiences of his distant kinswomen of Warboys. The Recorder of London also sat on the Commons' Committee. This was Henry Montagu,[121] afterwards Chief Justice of the King's Bench (1616) and Earl of Manchester (1626). He was of Christ's College, Cambridge, where he had been a younger contemporary of William Perkins, whose strong advocacy of more stringent laws against witchcraft we have already noted. Later, he was a patron of Thomas Cooper, whose book about witchcraft we have examined.[122] James Montagu, who preached Perkins's funeral sermon, was his younger brother.[123] Their father, Sir Edward Montagu, was likewise on the Commons' Committee. Can there be any doubt of the opinions of this family on the subject of witchcraft? Must we look to James I as the source of their views? Finally, we note with peculiar interest that the bill was reported, with amendments, from the committee to the House by Sir Thomas Ridgeway, of Devon, before whom, in 1601 and 1602, were taken an extraordinary series of examinations accusing the Trevisard family of witchcraft.[124]

It is time to study the advisory board of legal experts who were attached to the Lords' Committee on this most earnestly debated bill. Three of these attract our particular attention, Chief Justice Anderson, Serjeant Croke, and Coke, then Attorney-General.

Sir Edmund Anderson had been chief justice for twenty-two years. He knew all about the workings of the Elizabethan statute. At first sight one might think him opposed to witch-prosecution, for he had taken a leading part in "exposing" Darrel, and he had a lively sense of the danger of popular excitement to the innocent in such matters. But a moment's thought will set us right. Perkins and Giffard and Dr. Cotta — nay, James himself, as we shall see presently [125] — thought that judges ought to be very careful to sift the evidence and protect the innocent, but none of them doubted that a witch whose guilt was proved ought to be condemned. So the majority of civilized men to-day believe in the wisdom and righteousness of the death penalty for a certain grade of crime, but all are agreed that care should be taken to clear the innocent. An instructive example of the distinction that we must make may be seen in the person of Sir Edward Bromley. At the same assizes, in 1612, Bromley presided over two sets of witch-trials, those of the Pendle witches and those of the witches of Salmesbury. In the Pendle cases, he could not doubt the evidence, and he condemned ten to death with complete assurance that he was doing right. Cotta, himself, in 1616, speaks of the evidence in these cases with regard to sorcery by means of "pictures" (i. e. images) as "proued" by "testimonies beyond exception." [126] In the Salmesbury cases, on the contrary, Bromley saw reason to suspect the veracity of the chief witness for the prosecution, and followed up the clue so well that the defendants were acquitted.[127] Students of demonology will not forget that modern writers have seen fit to gird at Bromley, not only for his supposed cruelty and superstition in condemning the witches of Pendle, but also — strange to say — for the ground on which he first entertained the suspicion that led to the acquittal of the other group. But it is hard to satisfy modern writers on witchcraft, who insist on censuring the sixteenth and seventeenth century on a basis of modern rationalism. It is quite certain that if some of those who now sit in judgment on the witch-prosecutors had been witch-judges, no defendant would ever have escaped.

But we must return to Chief Justice Anderson, who, as well as Sir John Croke, sat on the committee of advisers to the Lords. Anderson and Croke had been associated, in 1603, in the affair of Mary Glover, which we have already considered. This happened before the accession of James. Croke appears therein as a devout believer in both demoniacal possession and witchcraft, and there is no reason to suppose that Anderson was in any way dissatisfied with his proceedings.[128]

Now for Coke, the Attorney General. There is a new provision in the statute of 1604 (not found in the Elizabethan law) imposing the death penalty on any one who shall "take up any dead man, woman, or child out of his, her, or theire grave, or any other place where the dead bodie resteth, or the skin, bone, or any other parte of any dead person, to be imployed or used in any manner of Witchcrafte, Sorcerie, Charme, or Inchantment." Hutchinson [129] conjectured that this provision was due to King James, noting that such ghoulish outrages were a part of the confession of Agnes Sampson, one of the first Scottish witches examined in the king's presence in 1590.[130] I am willing to add to this guess whatever support may be derived from the fact that the king, in his Dæmonologie, more than once adverts to the witches' habit of "joynting," or dismembering, corpses.[131] But, when all is said and done, this is a poor refuge, in view of what now appears to be the history of the statute, especially when one remembers that the use of the dead for purposes of sorcery dates, not from the confession of Agnes Sampson, but from the "backward and abysm of time." The lawmakers, cleric or lay, did not learn of this habit from King James, unless they were so ignorant as never to have heard of Lucan's Erichtho,[132] whom Marston actually brought upon the stage at about this very time in a tragedy which contains a speech, in description of the sorceress, that out-Lucans Lucan.[133] But we need not appeal to the classics. Sir Edward Kelley,

far-famed as Dr. Dee's scryer in crystallomancy, had already
emulated Erichtho. Years before, "vpon a certaine night, in
the Parke of Walton in le dale, in the county of Lancaster,
with one Paul Waring," he had "inuocated some one of the
infernall regiment, to know certaine passages in the life, as
also what might bee knowne by the deuils foresight, of the
manner and time of the death of a noble young Gentleman,
as then in his wardship." The black rites finished, Kelley
learned of the gentleman's servant about a poor man's corpse
that had been buried in a neighboring churchyard that very
day. "Hee and the said *Waring* intreated this foresaid seruant, to go with them to the graue." The servant complied,
"and withall did helpe them to digge up the carcase of the
poor caitiffe, whom by their incantations, they made him (or
rather some euill spirit through his Organs) to speake, who
deliuered strange predictions concerning the said Gentleman." All that we know of the prodigious Kelley inclines us
to credit him with an attempt at necromancy on this occasion. Weever, who told the tale in 1631, had it from the servant who was present, as well as from the young gentleman to
whom the servant had revealed the affair.[134] It is safe to say
that the crime of violating graves was as common in England
as in Scotland. It surely was an offence quite as worthy of the
gallows as sheep-stealing, or theft above the value of twelve-
pence. And it was natural enough to insert a clause to cover
it in the revised law. Now Coke was just the man to do this,
for he knew of a fourteenth-century case which showed that
the law was imperfect in this very point, and he reports the
occurrence in his Institutes:

A man was taken in Southwark with a head and a face of a dead man,
and with a book of sorcery in his male, and was brought into the king's
bench before Sir John Knevett [135] then chief justice: but seeing no indictment was against him, the clerks did swear him, that from thenceforth he
should not be a sorcerer, and was delivered out of prison, and the head of
the dead man and the book of sorcery were burnt at Tuthill at the costs of
the prisoner. So as the head and his book of sorcery had the same punishment, that the sorcerer should have had by the ancient law, if he had by his
sorcery praied in aid of the devil.[136]

Who was so likely as Coke to instruct the Lords' Committee as to the defect in the former statute in this regard? At

all events, his exposition of the statute of 1604 shows how thoroughly he believed in witchcraft, and leaves no doubt as to the general bearing of whatever advice he gave the committee. Nor need we quote his celebrated charge to the jury in Mrs. Turner's trial for the murder of Overbury, as we might otherwise be tempted to do.[137] Among the magical exhibits at this trial was a parchment on which "were written all the names of the *holy Trinity*; as also a figure, in which was written this word *Corpus*, and upon the *parchment* was fastned a little piece of the *skin* of a *man*." [138] This was, it appears, a charm of Forman's. He certainly did not import it from Scotland! [139]

I think we may now regard the following propositions as proved: (1) The last twenty years of Elizabeth's reign were a time of intense and continuous excitement in the matter of witchcraft, with repeated trials and a good many executions. (2) The doctrine was not dying out when James came to the throne. It was held with great tenacity, not only by the masses, but by a vast majority of the educated and influential, — nobility, country gentry, divines, judges, and citizens. (3) The Elizabethan law was generally thought to be imperfect, and there was strong pressure for new legislation. (4) The statute of 1604 was carefully considered and fully discussed. It was not a king's bill, nor was it rushed through under royal whip and spur, or passed out of complaisance to the new sovereign. There is no evidence that the king took any particular interest in the act. It reflected the conscientious opinions of both Houses of Parliament.[140] (5) It followed the language of the Elizabethan statute at almost every point, though somewhat more severe. (6) In its practical working, however, in James's time, the statute of 1604 was not appreciably severer than the Elizabethan law.

But the case against James I as a witch-hunter during his English reign is not merely destitute of every kind of evidence in its favor, — it has to meet an overwhelming array of direct proof on the other side. And to this evidence we must now pass. It is quite conclusive.

First, we will consider certain pardons that are matters of record. The list is short — for there were few convictions — but it is significant.[141] On April 16, 1604, when the new statute was still under deliberation, Christian, the wife of Thomas Weech, of County Norfolk, received the royal pardon for witchcraft.[142] In 1608, Simon Reade was pardoned for conjuration and invocation of unclean spirits.[143] This case is mentioned by Ben Jonson in The Alchemist (1610).[144] Reade was a medical practitioner and cunning man of Southwark.[145] One Toby Mathew of London had lost £37, 10 shillings, by theft, and Reade invoked three devils — Heawelon, Faternon, and Cleveton — to learn the name of the thief and recover the money. There were several séances, — the first on November 8, 1606, the others before the 10th of the following January.[146] Apparently Mathew blabbed, perhaps because the devils did not find his money for him. No doubt Reade, when he saw that his trickery was to cost him his life, confessed that the conjuration was pure humbug, and so was pardoned. In 1610, Christian Weech received a second pardon, this time for the murder of Mary Freeston by witchcraft.[147] In 1611, William Bate, "indicted twenty years since for practising invocation of spirits for finding treasure," was pardoned.[148] In Bate's case the ground is expressly stated,— the evidence was "found weak." Of course this was also the reason for royal clemency in the other three cases. We have precisely the same situation that confronts us in Jane Wenham's case, in 1712, when the judge was dissatisfied with the verdict of a credulous jury and saved the condemned prisoner in the only way open to him, then as now, by procuring the royal pardon.

The bearing of these records is unmistakable. They prove both that James was no bigoted and undiscriminating witchfinder and witch-prosecutor, and that the judges tried to get at the truth in this crime as in others. Here, then, is the place to quote a passage from Francis Osborne, with whom King James was no favorite: "What his Judgement was of Witchcraft, you may, in part, find by His Treatise on that Subject, and Charge he gave the Judges, to be Circumspect in Condemning those, Committed by Ignorant Justices, for Diabolical Compacts. Nor had he Concluded his Advice in a Narrower Circle, (as I have heard) Then the Denyal of any such operations, but out of Reason of State: and to gratifie the Church, which hath in no Age, thought fit to explode out of the Common-peoples minds, An Apprehension of Witch-craft." [149] The latter part of this dictum may pass for what it is worth. The whole passage is valuable for the light it throws upon the king's reputation with his contemporaries. They thought him skeptical rather than credulous.

There is a close relation between the general purport of Os-borne's testimony and the attitude of James with regard to the curative power of the royal touch.[150] His incredulity on this point was manifested at the very beginning of his reign. "The King," wrote Scaramelli to the Doge of Venice, in 1603, shortly before the coronation, "says that neither he nor any other King can have power to heal scrofula, for the age of miracles is past, and God alone can work them. However," adds the Venetian, "he will have the full ceremony [*sc.* of coronation, anointing included], so as not to lose this preroga-tive [*sc.* of touching for the king's evil], which belongs to the Kings of England as Kings of France." [151] And we know that he actually touched for the evil on various occasions, for rea-sons of state,[152] knowing well that the ceremony could not harm the sufferers and might work beneficially upon them through the imagination. "He was a King in understand-ing," says Arthur Wilson, "and was content to have his Sub-jects ignorant in many things. As in curing the *Kings-Evil*, which he knew a *Device*, to aggrandize the *Virtue* of Kings, when *Miracles* were in fashion; but he let the World believe it, though he smiled at it, in his own *Reason*, finding the strength of the *Imagination* a more powerful *Agent* in the *Cure*, than the *Plasters* his *Chirurgions* prescribed for the *Sore*." [153]

Along with the pardons which we have noted may be classed the toleration which James extended to Forman and Lambe and Dee. This is a curious circumstance which has never received the attention it deserves.

Simon Forman was undoubtedly a rascal.[154] He seems, however, to have been a likeable fellow. Lilly's anecdote of his predicting his own death is charming and proves that Forman had a good measure of *bonhomie*.[155] It also goes far to show that he put some trust in his own occult powers, though in the main he must have been a charlatan. Cer-tainly he passed for a sorcerer. For years he made a public profession of necromancy and magic at Lambeth, and was much consulted by the ladies. On the 26th of June, 1603, Forman was licensed by the University of Cambridge to practise medicine, and on the next day the university conferred upon him the degree of M.D. How he contrived to obtain these certificates of professional respectability is a puzzle.[156] King James never molested Forman, and the Doctor died peacefully in 1611. The full extent of his rascality did not come out until the trial of Mrs. Turner, in 1615, for the murder of Overbury,[157] but that makes no difference. He was a notorious conjurer, and it would have been easy to find evidence during his life that would have hanged him a hundred times.[158]

Dr. John Lambe was in the same kind of business as Forman but was even less reputable. He was convicted at the Worcester assizes on two separate indictments, each of them for a capital crime. The first was for "wasting and consuming" Thomas Lord Windsor by witchcraft; the second for "invoking and entertaining" evil spirits.[159] Sentence was suspended, and Lambe was imprisoned in Worcester Castle. Shortly after, he was removed to the King's Bench in London,[160] where he remained a long time. But his confinement was not rigorous. He lived in prison quite at his ease, receiving his patients and clients and doing a thriving business as physician and sorcerer.[161] He was convicted of a rape committed while in confinement,[162] but the chief justice reported that the evidence was dubious, and in 1624 he was pardoned.[163] Soon after, he was released from custody and took up his residence near the Parliament House.[164] In 1628 he met his death at the hands of the London mob while returning from a play at the Fortune.[165] Lambe was protected by Buckingham, and was known as the "Duke's devil." [166] But Buckingham was not always friendly. Thus, in 1625, the duke was clamorous against him on account of his connection with Lady Purbeck's case. "If Lambe" — so Buckingham wrote to Attorney General Coventry and Solicitor General Heath — "be allowed to get off by saying he was only juggling [i. e. not really practising sorcery], . . . the truth can never be known; Lambe has hitherto, by such shifts, mocked the world and preserved himself." [167] I am far from maintain-

ing that King James's indulgence to such scoundrels as Forman and Lambe was altogether creditable to him, but it certainly tends to prove that he was not a rabid prosecutor of
witches and sorcerers.[168]

Dr. Dee is in a different category, for he was a profound
scholar and a man of a sincere and simple character, whom it
would be profanation to class with Lambe and Forman. Yet
there is no manner of doubt that his occult experiments (of
which voluminous documentary evidence is still extant)
might have convicted him of sorcery on literally a thousand
counts. His sole defence would have been that he was invoking and consulting good angels, not demons, but the theologians could have made short work of that allegation. True,
Dee had been examined on a charge of witchcraft in the Star
Chamber in 1555 and acquitted.[169] But his subsequent proceedings were enough to condemn him, and he constantly had
to protest against the aspersion of being "a companion of
Hell-hounds and conjuror of wicked and damned spirits," [170]
and "the arche coniurer of this whole kingdom." [171] In 1583
the mob had destroyed his library at Mortlake.[172] Anecdotes
that descended to Aubrey give ample testimony to his fame
as a conjurer.[173] Dee seems to have been agitated by the passage of the statute of 1604, for, on June 5 of that year, while
the act was still in debate, he petitioned King James to have
him "tryed and cleared of that horrible and damnable, and to
him most grievous and dammageable sclaunder, generally,
and for these many yeares last past, in this kingdom raysed
and continued, by report and print against him, namely, that
he is or hath bin a conjurer or caller or invocator of divels." [174]
No attention was paid to his entreaty, but the king did not
molest him, and he died in his bed in 1608. James doubtless
respected Dee's learning, and he may have been assured of his
innocence by the aged scholar's friends, who were numerous
and influential, — Sir Julius Cæsar, for instance. Indeed,
Dee was styled "the King his Mathematitian," [175] — a title
which appears to imply some degree of royal favor.

James's pardons and his toleration of Dee and Lambe and
Forman would go far to show that he was not a bigoted
witch-prosecutor. But there is evidence of an unequivocal
nature. It concerns the king's personal activity in the detec-

tion of imposture. On this point the records are decisive, and, when we consider the prevalent impression as to James's character as a witch-finder, they are nothing less than astounding.[176]

First of all we have a charming letter from James to the young Prince Henry. It bears no date, but unbiassed judges put it at the very beginning of the reign, and Sir Henry Ellis believes that it was written before the Prince had left Scotland.

> My Sonne I ame glaid that by youre Letre I maye persave that ye make some progresse in learning. . . . I ame also glaide of the discoverie of yone litle counterfitte Wenche. I praye God ye maye be my aire [i. e. heir] in such discoveries. Ye have ofte hearde me saye that most miracles nou a dayes proves but illusions, and ye maye see by this hou waire judgis should be in trusting accusations withoute an exacte tryall; and lykewayes hou easielie people are inducid to trust wonders. Lett her be kepte fast till my cumming; and thus God blesse you my sonne.[177]

In 1604 we find James, in his Counterblast to Tobacco, deriding exorcism in a style worthy of Bancroft and Harsnet. "O omnipotent power of Tobacco!" he ejaculates. "And if it could by the smoke thereof chace out deuils, as the smoke of *Tobias* fish did (which I am sure could smel no stronger) it would serue for a precious Relicke, both for the superstitious Priests, and the insolent Puritanes, to cast out deuils withal."[178]

Another letter of the king's should be given in full, if space allowed. It begins by reminding the recipient "how that in late time we discovered and put to flight one of those counterfeits, the like whereof ye now advertise us." "By this bearer," adds King James, "we send unto you instructions suited for such an occasion, willing you leave nothing untried to discover the imposture." It appears that the patient was a woman who lay in a trance and had supported life for a long time on one small cup of wine. The king gives wise directions and remarks that "miracles like those of which you give us notice should be all ways and diligently tested." And he concludes with the words, "It . . . becomes us to lose no opportunity of seeking after the real truth of pretended wonders, that if true we may bless the Creator who hath shown such marvels to men, and if false we may punish the impudent inventors of them."[179]

In 1605 Sir Roger Wilbraham notes in his Journal, immediately after telling a witch-story:— "The King's maiestie, sithence his happie comyng, by his owne skill hath discovered 2 notorious impostures: one of a phisicion that made latyne & lerned sermons in the slepe: which he did by secret premeditacion: thother of a woman pretended to be bewitched, that cast up at her mouth pynnes, & pynnes were taken by divers in her fitts out of her brest." [180]

The first of these two impostors was Richard Haydock of New College, Oxford, the celebrated Sleeping Preacher. He made a great noise in the world. In 1605 James summoned him to court, where he preached three times. The king felt sure he was shamming. He soon fathomed Haydock's mystery, brought him to repentance, and treated him kindly afterwards.[181] The doctor's confession, addressed to King James, is extant among the State Papers.[182] Though witchcraft was not involved, the incident throws light on the king's frame of mind.

King James's detection of Haydock took place in April, 1605. In November of the same year the Gunpowder Plot was discovered. James, it will be remembered, boasted rather pedantically in an address to Parliament that he had unriddled a dark sentence in the Mounteagle letter and so was in effect the discoverer of the conspiracy.[183] He made similar pretensions in a conversation with Giustinian, the Venetian ambassador.[184] There is a plain connection between his pride in this exploit and the shrewdness he had just exhibited in the affair of the Sleeping Preacher and in that of the bewitched woman, for Salisbury gave out that he and other Councillors had submitted the Mounteagle letter to the king because of "the expectation and experience they had of His Majesties fortunate Judgement in cleering and solving of obscure Riddles and doubtful Mysteries." [185] It makes no difference whether this consultation was *pro forma*, mere courtly complaisance, or whether the Councillors really got some help from the king. On either hypothesis, the penchant of James for playing the detective is equally clear.

The second case mentioned by Wilbraham was pure witchcraft. The symptom of vomiting pins was regarded by most scholars as decisive against fraud. Thus Cotta, in 1616, in enumerating various tests by which (in contradistinction to swimming, scratching, and other things that he repudiates) witchcraft may be recognized, accepts this as one that is "palpable and not obscure to any eye without difficulty, offering [itself] to plaine and open viewe." [186] It now appears that James, more than ten years before Cotta wrote, had confuted this infallible test. Yet we are told that Cotta "was in advance of his age," that "he published his book in 1616, when King James's doctrines prevailed in full force, and it attracted little attention." [187] I agree that Cotta was in advance of his age. Be it so — but what shall we then say of James I?

Another undated example is preserved by Aubrey.[188] A gentlewoman named Katharine Waldron, who "waited on Sir Francis Seymor's lady of Marlborough," pretended to be "bewitched by a certain woman." The phenomena were similar to those in the case of Mary Glover, which misled the Recorder of London in 1603.[189] The king "detected the cheat" by a clever, though somewhat indecorous, device.

More than once, when James was unable to investigate these matters in person, he intrusted the business to somebody else. Thus, in 1605, a warrant was issued for "such sums as the Earl of Salisbury shall require, for the charges of two maids suspected to be bewitched, and kept at Cambridge for trial." [190] *Trial* in this record of course does not mean *trial in court* (for it was not a crime to be bewitched), but *test*, *investigation*. Obviously it was thought that the girls might be shamming. Again, in 1611, instructions were sent to the Bishop of Bangor and the Judges of Assize for County Carnarvon "to search out the truth of a supposed witchcraft committed on six young maids." [191] This was another cautionary measure to prevent false accusation and the arraignment of innocent persons. It reminds one of the action of Charles I in 1634, when he delegated Bishop Bridgman to investigate the second Pendle case.[192] We shall have occasion to consider the attitude of King Charles presently.

A case in which we have a precise record of King James's action is that of Anne Gunter, a Windsor girl who was "troubled with such strange and unusual symptoms, that she was generally thought and reported by all that saw her to be bewitched." The king summoned Anne and, "pretending great pitty to her, told her, he would take care for her relief." He entrusted the investigation to Dr. Edward Jorden, a well-reputed London practitioner who had distinguished himself by proving in 1602 that young Mary Glover was not bewitched but suffered from hysteria. Jorden soon reported that Anne was, in his opinion, an impostor. The king, "confirmed in what he had suspected before," urged the girl to confess; and she, "upon [his] importunity and promise to her of making up what damage should accrue for the discovery," acknowledged the fraud: she had acted, she said, under the instructions of her father, who wished to throw suspicion upon a woman of the neighborhood with whom he had taken offence. King James gave Anne a portion and she was happily married.[193]

And now we come to the most distinguished of all King James's exploits in the detection of fraudulent bewitchment. It is a case which, even if it stood absolutely alone, might suffice, in the absence of adverse testimony, to clear his reputation.

In 1616, on the 18th day of July, nine persons were hanged at Leicester. Their crime was the bewitching of a boy of twelve or thirteen, named Smythe,[194] who suffered from fits [195] like those of the Throckmorton girls of Warboys.[196] Indeed, the influence of that famous case is unmistakable. Justice Fenner, in 1593, made old Samuel recite a formula devised by one of the hysterical girls: "As I am a Witch, and did consent to the death of the Lady Cromwell, so I charge the deuil to suffer Mistres Iane to come out of her fitt at this present." [197] Thereupon the girl was instantly relieved. So at Leicester in 1616 the accused were obliged to say, "I such a one chardge the hors [one of the devils], if I be a wiche, that thou come forthe of the chilld," whereupon young Smythe ceased to be tormented.[198] The judges were Sir Humphrey Winch, Justice of the Common Pleas, and Sir Randolph Crew (Serjeant),[199] — the former a member of the Parliament that passed the Statute of 1604.[200]

About a month after the execution of these nine witches, King James chanced to be at Leicester on a royal progress. He stayed there not more than twenty-four hours.[201] The

Smythe boy was still having his fits, and six more accused persons were in jail awaiting trial at the autumn assizes. Nobody can doubt what the issue would have been. But now James intervened. I will let Francis Osborne (1593–1659) tell the story. "The King being gratified by nothing more, then an Opportunity to shew his Dexterity in Discovering an Imposture, (at which, I must confess Him, The Promptest Man Living) upon his Arrival convented the Boy. Where, before Him, (possibly daunted at his Presence, or Terrified by his Words) he began to faulter, so as the King discover'd a Fallacy. And did for a further Confirmation, send him to Lambeth; where the Servants of *George Abbot*,[202] did in a few Weeks discover the whole Deceit. And He was sent back to his Majesty, before the end of the Progress. Where upon a small Entreaty, He would repeat all his Tricks oftentimes in a Day.'[203]

The result we learn from a contemporary letter written by a Leicester alderman.[204] Five of the six alleged witches were released without a trial; the sixth had died in prison. Nor did the king neglect to let the judges see that he was not pleased with their lack of acumen. "Justice Winch," writes Mr. John Chamberlain to Sir Dudley Carleton on October 12, "and Serjeant Crew are somewhat discountenanced for hanging certain Witches in their circuit at Leicester; whereas the King, coming that way, found out the juggling and imposture of the boy, that counterfeited to be bewitched."[205]

King James's action in the Leicester case of 1616 took instant effect. The clamor of the populace against witches was not silenced, but the judges henceforth used extraordinary circumspection. They had no mind to incur the royal displeasure. The result should be carefully noted. From July, 1616, until James's death on March 27, 1625, almost exactly nine years, only five persons are known to have been executed for witchcraft in England.[206] Two of these were hanged at Bristol in 1624, and I have no details.[207] One — Elizabeth Sawyer of Edmonton — confessed after conviction.[208] The other two were Margaret and Philippa Flower, who were executed at Lincoln on March 11, 1619. Their case is very remarkable. A bare statement of facts will prove how impossible it was for any jury to acquit them or any king to show them favor. Incidentally, we should observe that they would have been hanged under the Elizabethan statute.

Joan Flower was a foul-mouthed old woman, much given to cursing, and suspected by her neighbors of being a witch. She was incensed at the Countess of Rutland for discharging her daughter, Margaret Flower, from service at Belvoir Castle, though there were good grounds for it, and though the countess had treated the girl with much kindness. Soon after, the earl's eldest son died, and some years later his other son fell sick and his daughter as well. The earl, it seems, had no suspicion against the Flowers. Ultimately, however, Joan and her two daughters were arrested, doubtless as a result of local gossip. Joan Flower was never tried for the crime. At the time, as it appears, of her examination, she defiantly subjected herself to a strange test. She "called for bread and butter, and wished it might neuer goe through her if she were guilty of that wherevpon she was examined; so mumbling it in her mouth, neuer spake more words after, but fell downe and dyed as she was carried to Lincolne Jaile." Both her daughters confessed and were hanged.[209] There can be no vestige of doubt in any unprejudiced mind that these three women were guilty in intent. They had practised what they supposed to be witchcraft in order to destroy the children, and they believed they had succeeded. We may pity them for their malicious infatuation, but we cannot deny that their fate was deserved. Nor was it conceivable that they should escape it when God himself seemed to have pronounced their guilt.

Five executions, then, make the whole account for the last nine years of King James's reign, and with regard to two of these, there could be no suspicion of counterfeiting. The earl's son and heir had really died, and the accused had certainly tried to kill him by sorcery. Here there was no ground on which the king's acumen in detecting imposture could work, nor could any amount of caution on the part of the judges avoid the plain conclusion.[210]

But the effect of King James's rebuke of the Leicester justices is visible not only (by inference) in the lack of executions. It may also be traced in more positive ways. In 1620 occurred the notorious fraud of William Perry, the Boy of

Bilson. The supposed witch was acquitted at the Stafford assizes, August 10, 1620, and the judges intrusted Perry to Bishop Morton, who was present. Morton detected the trick, and at the next summer assizes, June 26, 1621, the boy made public amends, asking forgiveness of the alleged witch, who was there to receive this rehabilitation.[211] James was not personally active — so far as we know — in this exposure, but that it was pleasing to him we can infer, not only from our general knowledge, but from the fact that Arthur Wilson, in his History of Great Britain, published in 1653, appends to the story the following observation: "The King took delight by the *line* of his *Reason* to sound the depth of such *brutish Impostors*, and he discovered many." Then, after reporting the case of Haydock, the Sleeping Preacher, Wilson continues: "Some others, both men and women, inspired with such *Enthusiasms*, and *fanatick fancies*, he reduced to their right *senses*, applying his *Remedies* suitable to the *Distemper*, wherein he made himself often very merry . . . but some of their Stories being a little *coarse*, are not so fit to be here related." [212]

In 1624 John Gee, in a sermon at Paul's Cross tells of a young woman in London "who pretendeth to be vexed and *possessed by a Deuill*." He concludes his account with the significant remark: "I leaue the examination of this to him that sits on our *Throne*, his *Maiestie*, who hath a happy gift in discouery of such *Impostures*." [213]

Tributes to King James's interest in detecting fraudulent cases are offered not only by Osborne (who speaks of "the Charge he gave the Judges, to be Circumspect in Condemning those, Committed by Ignorant Justices, for Diabolical Compacts"),[214] but by Bishop Goodman (1583–1656), by Bernard, and by Fuller. Goodman's testimony is brief, but to the purpose. James, he says, "was ever apt to search into secrets, to try conclusions [i. e. experiments], as I did know some who saw him run to see one in a fit whom they said was bewitched." [215] "Did not our late King *Iames*," writes Bernard, "by his wisedome, learning and experience, discouer diuers counterfeits?" [216] Fuller provides an elaborate *testimonium*.[217] After telling of the Boy of Bilson, he continues as follows:

Indeed, all this KING's Reign was scattered over with Cheaters in this kinde. Some Papists, some Sectaries, some neither, as who dissembled such *possession*, either out of malice to be revenged on those whom they accused of *Witchcraft*, or covetousnesse to enrich themselves.

Then, after giving several examples, which he calls "a few out of many," [218] he concludes thus: —

K. *James* . . . was no lesse dexterous than desirous to make discovery of these Deceits. Various were His waies in detecting them, awing some into confession with His presence, perswading others by promise of pardon and fair usage. He ordered it so, that a Proper Courtier made love to one of these bewitched Maids, and quickly *Cupid* his Arrows drave out the pretended Darts of the Devil. Another there was, the Tides of whose Possession did so Ebbe and Flow, that punctually they observed one hour till the KING came to visit her. The Maid loath to be so unmannerly as to make His MAJESTY attend her time, antedated her Fits many houres, and instantly ran through the whole Zodiac of tricks which she used to play. A third, strangely-affected when the first verse of S. *John's* Gospel was read unto her in our Translation, was tame and quiet whilst the same was pronounced in Greek, her English Devil belike understanding no other language. The frequency of such forged Possessions wrought such an alteration upon the judgement of King JAMES, that he receding from what he had written in his *Demonologie*, grew first diffident of, and then flatly to deny the workings of *Witches* and *Devils*, as but Falshoods and Delusions.[219]

It seems probable that Fuller goes too far in this last statement, though Osborne says something to the same effect.[220] It is not likely that King James ever gave up his theoretical belief in witchcraft.[221] It is clear, however, that, in his later years, he came close to the opinion pronounced, in 1711, by Addison in a famous passage (echoed by Blackstone): "I believe in general that there is, and has been such a thing as witch-craft; but at the same time can give no credit to any particular instance of it." [222] But we must return to King James's good influence on the judges.

This influence comes out very clearly in the Fairfax case, six years after James's rebuke to Justice Winch and Serjeant Crew.[223] In 1622, Edward Fairfax, the translator of Tasso, brought six women before the York assizes on the charge of bewitching his two daughters. The fits had lasted for several months and were similar to those of the Throckmorton girls: the Warboys narrative was still doing its work. At the same assizes, one of Fairfax's neighbors, a gentleman named John Jeffray, accused the same defendants of bewitching his daughter Maud. The grand jury was exceptionally intelligent, including six justices of the peace. It had already "received a good *caveat* by a message from the judge to be very careful in the matter of witches." [224] Yet it found a true bill, and the trial began.

The six women were arraigned on August 9, 1622.[225] Mark the course of proceedings. All three of the afflicted girls fell into a trance in the presence of the court and were carried out insensible. Sir George Ellis and some other justices, leaving the bench, followed, and exerted themselves to discover the imposture that they suspected. They soon returned, declaring that the Jeffray girl had confessed that she had acted throughout by the direction of her parents. Maud Jeffray denied that she had made the alleged admissions; but her father was sent to jail forthwith, and his charge was dismissed.[226] The Fairfax girls, however, had not been found to be counterfeiting, and the trial of that case went on. But the court was determined to avoid the mistake made at Leicester in 1616. The presiding justice, after some witnesses had been heard, instructed the jury that the evidence "reached not to the point of the statute," stopped the trial, and discharged the defendants.[227] Thereafter it was "given out," as Fairfax tells us, that "Jeffray and his family devised the practice, to which they drew my eldest daughter, and she the younger." Fairfax himself was exonerated.[228]

Here we see the influence of the king's precept and example at every turn. The grand jury was warned to be careful, the judges were eager to discover an imposture, and, thinking they had done so, yet not daring to trust the jury to acquit, they found that the facts alleged did not bring the case under the statute and took it away from the jury. And finally — as if to leave to posterity no doubt whatever of the first source of all this caution and circumspection — Fairfax mentions King James in the most unequivocal way. His narrative is, in effect, an appeal from the judges to public opinion. *His* daughters, he maintains, are certainly no tricksters; they are in an altogether different category from "*those whose impostures our wise king so lately laid open.*" [229]

Nor did the good effects of King James's skeptical temper and of the lesson he taught the judges cease with his death. I can find but one execution for witchcraft in the first seven years of Charles I. Then occurred the famous case of the Lancashire Witches of 1633. On this occasion seventeen persons were convicted, but the judge did not believe in their guilt, and brought the matter to the king's attention. A careful investigation ensued, and none of the alleged witches suffered death. Hitherto this case has been regarded as marking a contrast between Charles's creed and practice and the acts and belief of his father. Mr. Crossley, who is so severe on King James, praises King Charles warmly for thus "distinguishing himself . . . in days when philosophy stumbled and murder arrayed itself in the robes of justice — by an enlightened exercise of the kingly prerogative of mercy." [230] Wright remarks that "Charles I had not the same weak prejudices in these matters as his father." [231] It is well to approve King Charles, whose personal record in this matter of witchcraft is laudable, but it must now be quite clear that he was merely following his father's praiseworthy example.

Our scrutiny of King James's record is finished. No summing up is necessary. The defendant is acquitted by the facts. One final remark, however, may be made, in lieu of a peroration. Diligent search has so far brought to light less than forty executions for witchcraft throughout England in the reign of James I, or an average of about *two a year*.[232] Contrast with this statement the fact that in ten years of the same reign (6–15 James I), at least thirty-two persons were pressed to death in the single County of Middlesex for refusing to plead in cases of felony (not witchcraft), or an average of over *three a year*, and that, in the same county for the same period, at least seven hundred persons were hanged for felonies other than witchcraft, or an average of *seventy a year*.[233] These figures call for no commentary. We may double or treble the number of witch-hangings, if we will, in order to allow for incompleteness in the published records, and it still remains true that the reign of James I was not, in this regard, a dark and bloody period.

CHAPTER XVIII

WITCHCRAFT AND THE PURITANS

WE ARE all specialists now-a-days, I suppose. The good old times of the polymath and the Doctor Universalis are gone forever. Yet signs are not wanting that some of us are alive to the danger of building our party-walls too high. In one respect, at all events, there can be no doubt that the investigators of New England antiquities are aware of their peril, though they occasionally shut their eyes to it, — I mean, the tendency to consider the Colonists as a peculiar people, separated from the Mother Country not only geographically, but also with regard to those currents of thought and feeling which are the most significant facts of history. True, there is more or less justification for that kind of study which looks at the annals of America as ends-in-themselves; but such study is ticklish business, and it now and then distorts the perspective in a rather fantastic way. This is a rank truism. Still, commonplaces are occasionally steadying to the intellect, and Dr. Johnson — whose own truths have been characterized by a brilliant critic as "too true" — knew what he was about when he said that men usually need not so much to be informed as to be reminded.[1]

The darkest page of New England history is, by common consent, that which is inscribed with the words Salem Witchcraft. The hand of the apologist trembles as it turns the leaf. The reactionary writer who prefers iconoclasm to hero-worship sharpens his pen and pours fresh gall into his inkpot when he comes to this sinister subject. Let us try to consider the matter, for a few minutes, unemotionally, and to that end let us pass in review a number of facts which may help us to look at the Witchcraft Delusion of 1692 in its due proportions, — not as an abnormal outbreak of fanaticism, not as an isolated tragedy, but as a mere incident, a brief and transitory episode in the biography of a terrible, but perfectly natural, superstition.

In the first place, we know that the New Englanders did not invent the belief in witchcraft.[2] It is a universally human belief. No race or nation is exempt from it. Formerly, it was an article in the creed of everybody in the world, and it is still held, in some form or other, and to a greater or less extent, by a large majority of mankind.[3]

Further, our own attitude of mind toward witchcraft is a very modern attitude indeed. To us, one who asserts the existence, or even the possibility, of the crime of witchcraft staggers under a burden of proof which he cannot conceivably support. His thesis seems to us unreasonable, abnormal, monstrous; it can scarcely be stated in intelligible terms; it savors of madness. Now, before we can do any kind of justice to our forefathers, — a matter, be it remembered, of no moment to them, for they have gone to their reward, but, I take it, of considerable importance to us, — we must empty our heads of all such rationalistic ideas. To the contemporaries of William Stoughton and Samuel Sewall the existence of this crime was not merely an historical phenomenon, it was a fact of contemporary experience. Whoever denied the occurrence of witchcraft in the past, was an atheist; whoever refused to admit its actual possibility in the present, was either stubbornly incredulous, or destitute of the ability to draw an inference. Throughout the seventeenth century, very few persons could be found — not merely in New England, but in the whole world — who would have ventured to take so radical a position. That there had been witches and sorcerers in antiquity was beyond cavil. That there were, or might be, witches and sorcerers in the present was almost equally certain. The crime was recognized by the Bible, by all branches of the Church, by philosophy, by natural science, by the medical faculty, by the law of England. I do not offer these postulates as novelties. They are commonplaces. They will not be attacked by anybody who has even a slight acquaintance with the mass of testimony that might be adduced to establish them.

It is a common practice to ascribe the tenets of the New Englanders in the matter of witchcraft to something peculiar about their religious opinions, — to what is loosely called their Puritan theology. This is a very serious error. The doc-

trines of our forefathers differed, in this regard, from the doctrines of the Roman and the Anglican Church in no essential,
— one may safely add, in no particular. Lord Bacon was not
a Puritan, — yet he has left his belief in sorcery recorded in a
dozen places.[4] James I was not a Puritan, but his Dæmonologie (1597) is a classic treatise, his zeal in prosecuting
Scottish sorcerers is notorious, and the statute of 1604 [5] was
the act under which Matthew Hopkins, in the time of the
Commonwealth, sent two hundred witches to the gallows in
two years, — nearly ten times as many as perished in Massachusetts from the first settlement to the beginning of the
eighteenth century.

Matthew Hopkins, the Witch-Finder General, apparently
was a Puritan. Indeed, it is his career, more than anything
that ever happened in New England, which has led to the
reiterated statement that Puritanism was especially favorable, by its temper and its tenets, to prosecution for witchcraft. For his activity falls in the time of Puritan power, and
the Parliament granted a Special Commission of Oyer and
Terminer, in 1645, to try some of the witches that he had detected, and Edmund Calamy was associated with the Commission. But, on the other hand, it must be noted that John
Gaule, who opposed Hopkins and is usually credited with
most influence in putting an end to his performances, was
also a Puritan, — and a minister likewise, and a believer in
witches as well. The Hopkins outbreak, as we shall see, must
be laid to the disturbed condition of the country rather than
to the prevalence of any particular system of theology.
Under Cromwell's government, witch-trials languished, not
because the belief in witchcraft changed, but because there
was order once more. So in Scotland, the conquest by Cromwell checked one of the fiercest prosecutions ever known.
The Restoration was followed, both in England and in Scotland, by a marked recrudescence of prosecution.[6]

But we must return to Matthew Hopkins. Let us see how
his discoveries affected James Howell. In 1647 Howell writes
to Endymion Porter: "We have likewise multitudes of
Witches among us, for in *Essex* and *Suffolk* there were above
two hundred indicted within these two years, and above the
one half of them executed: More, I may well say than ever

this Island bred since the Creation, I speak it with horror. God guard us from the Devil, for I think he was never so busy upon any part of the Earth that was enlightned with the beams of *Christianity;* nor do I wonder at it, for there's never a Cross left to fright him away." [7]   In the following year, Howell writes to Sir Edward Spencer an elaborate defence of the current tenets in witchcraft and demonology. [8]   One striking passage demands quotation: — "Since the beginning of these unnatural Wars, there may be a cloud of Witnesses produc'd for the proof of this black Tenet: For within the compass of two years, near upon three hundred Witches were arraign'd, and the major part executed in *Essex* and *Suffolk* only. *Scotland* swarms with them now more than ever, and Persons of good Quality executed daily."

It is confidently submitted that nobody will accuse Howell of Puritanism. The letters from which our extracts are taken were written while he was a prisoner in the Fleet under suspicion of being a Royalist spy. [9]   His mention of the disappearance of crosses throughout England will not be overlooked by the discriminating reader. It will be noted also that he seems to have perceived a connection — a real one, as we shall see later — [10] between the increase in witchcraft and the turmoil of the Civil War.

Jeremy Taylor was surely no Puritan; but he believed in witchcraft. It is a sin, he tells us, that is "infallibly desperate," [11] and in his Holy Living (1650) he has even given the weight of his authority to the reality of sexual relations between witches and the devil. [12]

It was not in Puritan times, but in 1664, four years after the Restoration, that Sir Matthew Hale, then Chief Baron of the Exchequer, pronounced from the bench the following opinion in the Bury St. Edmunds case: — "That there were such Creatures as *Witches* he made no doubt at all; For *First,* the Scriptures had affirmed so much. *Secondly,* The wisdom of all Nations had provided Laws against such Persons, which is an Argument of their confidence of such a Crime. And such hath been the judgment of this Kingdom, as appears by that Act of Parliament [13] which hath provided Punishments proportionable to the quality of the Offence. And desired them [the jury], strictly to observe their Evidence; and desired the great God of Heaven to direct their Hearts in this weighty thing they had in hand: *For to Condemn the Innocent, and to let the Guilty go free, were both an Abomination to the Lord.*" [14] Hale's words were fraught with momentous consequences, for he was "allowed on all hands to be the most profound lawyer of his time," [15] and the Bury case became a precedent of great weight. "It was," writes Cotton Mather, "a Tryal much considered by the Judges of New England." [16]

Hale's conduct on this occasion has of course subjected him to severe criticism. Lord Campbell, for example, goes so far as to declare that he "murdered" the old women, — a dictum which shows but slight comprehension of the temper of the seventeenth century. More creditable to Campbell's historical sense is the following passage: — "Although, at the present day, we regard this trial as a most lamentable exhibition of credulity and inhumanity, I do not know that it at all lowered Hale in public estimation in his own life." [17] Bishop Burnet, as is well known, makes no mention of the case in his Life of Hale. [18] One might surmise that he omitted it out of respect for his hero's memory, since his little book is rather an obituary tribute than a biography. More probably, however, Burnet did not regard the case as any more significant than many other decisions of Hale's which he likewise passed over in silence. Unequivocal evidence that the Bury trial did not injure Hale's reputation may be found in the silence of Roger North. North's elaborate character of Hale, in his Life of the Lord Keeper Guilford, [19] is notoriously prejudiced in the extreme. Though admitting Hale's legal learning and many good qualities, North loses no opportunity to attack his record. Besides, North praises the Lord Keeper for his conduct in procuring the acquittal of an alleged witch. If, then, the Bury case had seemed to him especially discreditable, or if he had thought that it afforded an opening for hostile criticism, we cannot doubt that he would have spoken out in condemnation. His complete silence on the subject is therefore the most emphatic testimony to the general approval of Hale's proceedings. Highly significant, too, is the fact that even Lord Campbell does not blame Hale for believing in witchcraft, but only for allowing weight to the evidence in this particular case. "I would very readily have pardoned him," he writes, " for an undoubting belief in witch-craft, and I should have considered that this belief detracted little from his character for discernment and humanity. The Holy Scriptures teach us that, in some ages of the world, wicked persons, by the agency of evil spirits, were permitted, through means which exceed the ordinary powers of nature, to work mischief to their fellow-creatures. . . . In the reign of Charles II, a judge who from the bench should have ex-pressed a disbelief in [magic and the black art] would have been thought to show little respect for human laws, and to be nothing better than an atheist." We may profitably compare what Guilford himself (then Francis North, Chief Justice of the Common Pleas) wrote of the Devonshire witches in 1682, — nearly twenty years after the Bury case: — "We cannot reprieve them, without appearing to deny the very being of witches, which, as it is contrary to law, so I think it would be ill for his Majesty's service, for it may give the faction oc-casion to set afoot the old trade of witch-finding, that may cost many innocent persons their lives which the justice will prevent." [20]

Sir Thomas Browne, the author of the Religio Medici, was no Puritan, and he was one of the leading scientific men of his day. Yet he gave his opinion, as an expert, at the request of the Court in this same Bury St. Edmunds case, to the follow-ing effect: — "That the Devil in such cases did work upon the Bodies of Men and Women, upon a Natural Foundation, (that is) to stir up, and excite such humours super-abound-ing in their Bodies to a great excess," [21] and further, that "he conceived, that these swouning Fits were Natural, and noth-ing else but what they call the Mother [i. e. hysteria], but only heightned to a great excess by the subtilty of the Devil, co-operating with the Malice of these which we term Witches, at whose Instance he doth these Villanies." [22]

Browne has been much blamed for this dictum, but there is nothing unreasonable or unscientific in it, if one merely grants the actuality of demoniacal obsession and possession, which was then to all intents and purposes an article of faith.[23] If the devil can work upon our bodies at all, of course he can intensify any natural fits or spasms from which we happen to be suffering. Thus Browne's diagnosis of the disease in this case as hysteria, by no means excluded the hypothesis of *maleficium*. But most modern writers refuse to discuss such subjects except *de haut en bas*, — from the vantage-ground of modern science.

Sit Thomas Browne's view was, it seems, substantially identical with that of his predecessor, the famous Robert Burton, — no Puritan either! — who has a whole subsection "Of Witches and Magitians, how they cause Melancholy," asserting that what "they can doe, is as much almost as the Diuell himselfe, who is still ready to satisfie their desires, to oblige them the more vnto him." [24]

Joseph Glanvil, the author of The Vanity of Dogmatizing, was no Puritan,[25] but a skeptical philosopher, a Fellow of the Royal Society, and Chaplain in Ordinary to King Charles II; neither was his friend, Dr. Henry More, the most celebrated of the Cambridge Platonists. Yet these two scholars and latitudinarians joined forces to produce that extraordinary treatise, Saducismus Triumphatus: or, A Full and Plain Evidence concerning Witches and Apparitions. This book, an enlarged form of Glanvil's Philosophical Considerations concerning Witchcraft (1666), was published in 1681, and went through no less than five editions, the last appearing as late as 1726.[26] It was thought to have put the belief in apparitions and witchcraft on an unshakable basis of science and philosophy.[27] No English work on the subject had a more powerful influence. When the Rev. John Hale, of Beverley, wrote his Modest Enquiry,[28] which deplored the Salem excesses and protested against spectral evidence, — a notable treatise, published, with a prefatory epistle from the venerable Higginson,[29] in 1702, — he was able to condense the affirmative part of his argument, because, as he himself says, Glanvil "hath strongly proved the being of Witches." [30]

Dr. Meric Casaubon, Prebend of Canterbury, was not a Puritan; yet the second part of his Credulity and Incredulity (1668) contains a vigorous assertion of demonology and witch-lore, and was republished in 1672 under the alluring title, A Treatise Proving Spirits, Witches and Supernatural Operations by Pregnant Instances and Evidences.[31]

Ralph Cudworth, the antagonist of Hobbes, was not a Puritan. Yet in his great Intellectual System he declares for the existence of sorcery, and even admits a distinction between its higher operations — as in the θεουργία of Apollonius of Tyana [32] — and the vulgar performances of everyday wizards.[33] There is some reason, too, for supposing that Cudworth took part with Henry More in examining certain witches at Cambridge, and heard one of them try to recite the Creed and the Lord's Prayer, as she had offered to do "as an argument she was no witch." [34]

Robert Boyle, the improver of the air-pump and the discoverer of Boyle's Law, had "particular and considerable advantages to persuade [him], upon good grounds," that some witch stories are true, and he thought that Glanvil's investigations would do "a good service to religion." [35] This was in 1677. In the following year Boyle declared his belief [36] in the performances of the devil of Mascon.[37] Boyle's religious views did not hinder him from being a leader in that fervor of scientific experimentation which is one of the glories of the latter half of the seventeenth century. And he too was not a Puritan.

Isaac Barrow, the master of Newton, was not a Puritan. Yet he left on record, in one of his sermons, one of the most powerful and eloquent of all protests against disbelief in the kind of phenomena which our ancestors are so often attacked for crediting. The passage is long, but must be quoted in full, for every word is of weight: —

I may adjoin to the former sorts of extraordinary actions, some other sorts, the consideration of which (although not so directly and immediately) may serve our main design; those (which the general opinion of mankind hath approved, and manifold testimony hath declared frequently to happen) which concern apparitions from another world, as it were, of beings unusual; concerning spirits haunting persons and places, (these discerned by all senses, and by divers kinds of effects;) of which the old world (the ancient poets and historians) did speak so much, and of which all ages have afforded several attestations very direct and plain, and having all advantages imaginable to beget credence; concerning visions made unto persons of especial eminency and influence, (to priests and prophets;) concerning presignifications of future events by dreams; concerning the power of enchantments, implying the coöperation of invisible powers; concerning all sorts of intercourse and confederacy (formal or virtual) with bad spirits: all which things he that shall affirm to be mere fiction and delusion, must thereby with exceeding immodesty and rudeness charge the world with extreme both vanity and malignity; many, if not all, worthy historians, of much inconsiderateness or fraud; most lawgivers, of great silliness and rashness; most judicatories, of high stupidity or cruelty; a vast number of witnesses, of the greatest malice or madness; all which have concurred to assert these matters of fact.

It is true, no question, but there have been many vain pretences, many false reports, many unjust accusations, and some undue decisions concerning these matters; that the vulgar sort is apt enough to be abused about them; that even intelligent and considerate men may at a distance in regard to some of them be imposed upon; but, as there would be no false gems obtruded, if there were no true ones found in nature; as no counterfeit coin would appear, were there no true one current; so neither can we well suppose that a confidence in some to feign, or a readiness in most to believe, stories of this kind could arise, or should subsist, without some real ground, or without such things having in gross somewhat of truth and reality. However, that the wiser and more refined sort of men, highest in parts and improvements both from study and experience, (indeed the flower of every commonwealth; statesmen, lawgivers, judges, and priests,) upon so many occasions of great importance, after most deliberate scanning such pretences and reports, should so often suffer themselves to be deluded, to the extreme injury of particular persons concerned, to the common abusing of mankind, to the hazard of their own reputation in point of wisdom and honesty, seems nowise reasonable to conceive. In likelihood rather the whole kind of all these things, were it altogether vain and groundless, would upon so frequent and so mature discussions have appeared to be so, and would consequently long since have been disowned, exploded, and thrust out of the world; for, as upon this occasion it is said in Tully, "Time wipeth out groundless conceits, but confirms that which is founded in nature, and real."

Now if the truth and reality of these things, (all or any of them,) inferring the existence of powers invisible, at least inferior ones, though much superior to us in all sort of ability, be admitted, it will at least (as removing the chief obstacles of incredulity) confer much to the belief of that supreme Divinity, which our Discourse strives to maintain.[38]

Dr. George Hickes, of Thesaurus fame, was one of the most eminent scholars of his time. He was also a Non-juror, and titular Bishop of Thetford. In other words, he was not a Puritan. Yet in 1678 Hickes published an account of the infamous Major Weir, the most celebrated of all Scottish wizards, which betrays no skepticism on the cardinal points of sorcery.[39] There is also an extremely interesting letter from the Doctor to Mr. Pepys, dated June 19, 1700, which indicates a belief in witchcraft and second sight. The most curious part of this letter, however, deals with Elf Arrows. "I have another strange story," writes Dr. Hickes, "but very well attested, of an Elf arrow, that was shot at a venerable

Irish Bishop by an Evil Spirit in a terrible noise, louder than thunder, which shaked the house where the Bishop was; but this I reserve for his son to tell you, who is one of the deprived Irish Clergymen, and very well known, as by other excellent pieces, so by his late book, entitled, 'The Snake in the Grass.'" [40] What would the critics say if this passage were found in a work of Cotton Mather's?

Finally, it is not amiss to remember that the tolerant, moderate, and scholarly John Evelyn, whom nobody will accuse of being a Puritan, made the following entry in his Diary under February 3, 1692–1693: "Unheard-of stories of the universal increase of Witches in New England; men, women and children devoting themselves to the devil, so as to threaten the subversion of the government. At the same time there was a conspiracy amongst the negroes in Barbadoes to murder all their masters, discovered by overhearing a discourse of two of the slaves, and so preventing the execution of the designe." There is no indication that Evelyn regarded either of these conspiracies as less possible of occurrence than the other.[41]

Most of these passages are sufficiently well known, and their significance in the abstract is cheerfully granted, I suppose, by everybody. But the cumulative effect of so much testimony from non-Puritans is, I fear, now and then disregarded or overlooked by writers who concern themselves principally with the annals of New England. Yet the bearing of the evidence is plain enough. The Salem outbreak was not due to Puritanism; it is not assignable to any peculiar temper on the part of our New England ancestors; it is no sign of exceptional bigotry or abnormal superstition. Our forefathers believed in witchcraft, not because they were Puritans, not because they were Colonials, not because they were New Englanders, — but because they were men of their time. They shared the feelings and beliefs of the best hearts and wisest heads of the seventeenth century. What more can be asked of them? [42]

I am well aware that there are a few distinguished names that are always entered on the other side of the account, and some of them we must now consider. It would be unpardonable to detract in any manner from the dear-bought fame of such forerunners of a better dispensation. But we must not forget that they *were* forerunners. They occupy a much more conspicuous place in modern books than they occupied in the minds of their contemporaries.[43] Further, if we listen closely to the words of these voices in the wilderness, we shall find that they do not sound in unison, and that their testimony is not in all cases precisely what we should infer from the loose statements often made about them.

Johann Wier (1515–1588) deserves all the honor he has ever received. He devoted years to the study of demonology, and brought his great learning, and his vast experience as a physician, to bear on the elucidation of the whole matter.[44] He held that many of the performances generally ascribed to devils and witches were impossible, and that the witches themselves were deluded. But there is another side to the picture. Wier's book is crammed full of what we should now-a-days regard as the grossest superstition. He credited Satan and his attendant demons with extensive powers. He believed that the fits of the so-called bewitched persons were due in large part to demoniacal possession or obsession, and that the witches themselves, though innocent of what was alleged against them, were in many cases under the influence of the devil, who made them think that they had entered into infernal compacts, and ridden through the air on broomsticks, and killed their neighbors' pigs, and caused disease or death by occult means. And further, he was convinced that such persons as Faust, whom he called *magi*, were acquainted with strange and damnable arts, and that they were worthy of death and their books of the fire. One example may serve to show the world-wide difference between Wier's mental attitude and our own.

One of the best-known symptoms of bewitchment was the vomiting of bones, nails, needles, balls of wool, bunches of hair, and other things, some of which were so large that they could not have passed through the throat by any natural means.[45] Such phenomena, Wier tells us, he had himself seen. How were they to be explained? Easily, according to Wier's general theory. Such articles, he says, are put into the patient's mouth by the devil, one after another, as fast as they come out. We cannot see him do this, — either because he acts so rapidly that his motions are invisible, or because he fascinates our sight, or because he darkens our eyes, perhaps by interposing between them and the patient some aërial body.[46]

The instability of Wier's position should not be brought against him as a reproach, since he was far in advance of his contemporaries, and since his arguments against the witch-dogma are the foundation of all subsequent skepticism on the subject.[47] Besides, it is certain that such a thoroughgoing denial of the devil's power as Bekker made a century later would have utterly discredited Wier's book and might even have prevented it from being published at all.[48] Yet, when all is said and done, it must be admitted that Wier's doctrines have a half-hearted appearance, and that they seemed to most seventeenth-century scholars to labor under a gross inconsistency. This inconsistency was emphasized by Meric Casaubon. "As for them," writes Dr. Casaubon, "who allow and acknowledge *supernatural operations* by Devils and Spirits, as *Wierius;* who tells as many strange stories of them, and as *incredible*, as are to be found in any book; but stick at the business of *Witches* only, whom they would not have thought the Authors of those mischiefs, that are usually laid to their charge, but the Devil only; though this opinion may seem to some, to have more of *charity*, than *Incredulity*; yet the contrary will easily appear to them, that shall look into it more carefully." And Casaubon dwells upon the fact that Wier grants "no small part of what we drive at, when he doth acknowledge *supernatural operations*, by Devils and Spirits." [49] Indeed, the apparent contradiction in Wier's theories may also excuse Casaubon for the suggestion he makes that Wier's intention "was not so much to favour *women*, as the *Devil* himself, with whom, it is to be feared, that he was too well acquainted." [50] This reminds us of what King James had already written of "Wierus, a German Physition," who "sets out a publike Apologie for all these craftes-folkes, whereby, procuring for their impunitie, he plainely bewrayes himselfe to have bene one of that profession." [51]

Reginald Scot's Discoverie of Witchcraft appeared in 1584. Scot, who was largely indebted to Wier, goes much farther than his Continental predecessor. Of course he does not deny the existence of evil spirits; [52] but he does not believe, like Wier, that evil spirits are continually occupied in deluding mankind by all manner of false (or præstigious) appearances. Such deceits he ascribes to juggling, and he accordingly gives elaborate directions for the performance of various tricks of legerdemain. [53]

There seems to be a more or less prevalent impression that Scot's book explodes witchcraft so thoroughly that the whole delusion might soon have come to an end in England if James I had not mounted the throne a short time after it was published. True, King James's Dæmonologie is expressly directed "against the damnable opinions" of Wier and Scot. [54] But, to tell the truth, Scot's treatise did not require a royal refutation. To us moderns, who are converted already and need no repentance, its general air of reasonableness, together with its humor and the raciness of the style, makes the Discoverie seem convincing enough. But this is to look at the matter from a mistaken point of view. The question is, not how Scot's arguments affect us, but how they were likely to affect his contemporaries. Now, if the truth must be told, the Discoverie is deficient in one very important respect. It makes no satisfactory answer to the insistent questions: "What are these evil spirits of which the Bible and the philosophers tell us, and which everybody believes in, and always has believed in, from the beginning of time? And what are they about? If they are powerful and malignant, why is it not likely that the effects which everybody ascribes to them are really their work? And if they are eager not only to torment but to seduce mankind, why is it not reasonable to suppose that they accomplish both ends at the same time — kill two birds with one stone — by procuring such evil effects by means of witches, or by allowing themselves to be utilized by witches as instruments of malice?" It was quite proper to ask these questions of Scot. He admitted the existence of evil spirits, but declared that we know little or nothing about them, denied that they can produce the phenomena then generally ascribed to their agency, and alleged fraud and delusion to account for such phenomena. Even to us, with our extraordinary and very modern incredulity toward supernatural occurrences, the lacuna in Scot's reasoning is clear enough if we only look at his argument as a whole. This we are not inclined to do; at least, few writers on witchcraft have ever done it. It is easier and more natural for us to accept such portions of Scot's argument as agree with our own view, to compliment him for his perspicacity, and to pass on, disregarding the inadequacy of what he says about evil spirits. Or, if we notice that his utterances on this topic are halting and uncertain, we are tempted to regard such hesitancy as further evidence of his rational temper. He could not quite deny the existence of devils, we feel, — that would have been too much to expect of him; but he waves them aside like a sensible man.[55] A moment's consideration, however, will show us that this defect in Scot's case, trifling as it appears to us now-a-days, was in fact a very serious thing. To us, who never think of admitting the intervention of evil spirits in the affairs of this world, the question whether there are any such spirits at all has a purely theoretical interest. Indeed, we practically deny their existence when we ignore them as we do: *de non apparentibus et non existentibus eadem est lex.* — But to Scot's contemporaries, the question of the existence of evil spirits involved the whole matter in debate, — and Scot granted their existence.

A curious particular in the history of Scot's Discoverie should also be considered in estimating its effect on the seventeenth century. The appearance of a new edition in 1665, shortly after the famous Bury St. Edmunds case,[56] may at first sight seem to indicate powerful and continuing influence on the part of the Discoverie. When we observe from the title-page, however, that the publisher has inserted nine chapters at the beginning of Book xv, and has added a second book to the Treatise on Divels and Spirits, our curiosity is excited. Investigation soon shows that these additions were calculated to destroy or minimize the total effect of Scot's book. The prefixed chapters contain directions for making magical circles, for calling up "the ghost of one that hath hanged himself," and for raising various orders of spirits. These chapters are thrust in without any attempt to indicate that they are not consistent with Scot's general plan and his theories. They appear to be, and are, practical directions for

magic and necromancy. The additional book is even more
dangerous to Scot's design. It is prefaced by the remark: —
"Because the Author in his foregoing Treatise, upon the
Nature of Spirits and Devils, hath only touched the subject
thereof superficially, omitting the more material part; and
with a brief and cursory Tractat, hath concluded to speak the
least of this subject which indeed requires most amply to be
illustrated; therefore I thought fit to adjoyn this subsequent
discourse; as succedaneous to the fore-going, and conducing
to the compleating of the whole work." [57]

How far "this subsequent discourse" is really fitted to
complete Scot's work may be judged by a statement which it
makes on the very first page, to the effect that bad spirits
"are the grand Instigators, stirring up mans heart to attempt
the inquiry after the darkest, and most mysterious part of
Magick, or Witchcraft." And again a little later: — "Great
is the villany of Necromancers, and wicked Magicians, in
dealing with the spirits of men departed; whom they invocate, with certain forms, and conjurations, digging up their
Carkasses again, or by the help of Sacrifices, and Oblations
to the infernal Gods; compelling the Ghost to present it self
before them." [58] All this is quite opposed to Scot's view and
the whole intention of his book. The insertion of such worth-
less matter was, of course, a mere trick of the bookseller to
make a new edition go off well. But the fact of its insertion
shows that Scot was thought to have left his treatise incom-
plete or unsatisfactory in a most important point. And the
inserted matter itself must have gone far to neutralize the
effect of republication in a witch-haunted period. And so we
may leave Reginald Scot, with our respect for his courage
and common sense undiminished, but with a clear idea of the
slight effect which his treatise must have had on the tone and
temper of the age that we are studying.

John Webster's Displaying of Supposed Witchcraft, which
appeared in 1677 — the Preface is dated "February 23.
1673" — was particularly directed against Glanvil and
Meric Casaubon. It holds a distinguished place in the history of witchcraft, and demands our careful scrutiny. What
is usually thought of it has been eloquently expressed by the
late Mr. James Crossley. "In this memorable book," writes

Mr. Crossley, "he exhausts the subject, as far as it is possible to do so, by powerful ridicule, cogent arguments, and the most varied and well applied learning, leaving to [Francis] Hutchinson, and others who have since followed in his track, little further necessary than to reproduce his facts and reasonings in a more popular, it can scarcely be said, in a more effective form." [59]

A few of Webster's opinions must be specified, that the reader may judge how far The Displaying of Supposed Witchcraft deserves to rank as a work of sober and scientific reason, and to what extent the author merits the position that seems to be traditionally assigned to him as an uncompromising assailant of superstition.

Angels, good and bad, are "really and truly corporeal" and not spirits, except "in a relative and respective" sense.[60] Since devils are corporeal, Webster admits that "they may move and agitate other bodies." Their strength, however, is limited, "for though one Devil may be supposed to move or lift up that which would load an Horse, yet it will not follow that he can move or lift up as much as would load a Ship of a thousand Tun." [61] Webster grants that "God doth make use of evil Angels to punish the wicked, and to chastise and afflict the godly, and in the effecting of these things that they have a power given them to hurt the earth and the Sea and things therein, as to bring tempests, thunder, lightning, plague, death, drought and the like." [62]

Webster has a profound belief in apparitions and tells some capital ghost stories [63] — "unquestionable testimonies," he calls them, "either from our own Annals, or matters of fact that we know to be true of our own certain knowledge, that thereby it may undoubtedly appear, that there are effects that exceed the ordinary power of natural causes, and may for ever convince all Atheisticall minds." [64] One of these tales concerns the murder of one Fletcher by Ralph Raynard, an innkeeper, and Mark Dunn, a hired assassin. One day "the spirit of *Fletcher* in his usual shape and habit did appear unto [Raynard], and said, Oh *Raph*, repent, repent, for my revenge is at hand." The result was a full confession. "I have recited this story punctually," writes Webster, "as a thing that hath been very much fixed in my memory, being then but young, and as a certain truth, I being (with many more) an ear-witness of their confessions and an eye-witness of their Executions, and likewise saw *Fletcher* when he was taken up, where they had buried him in his cloaths, which were a green fustian doublet pinkt upon white, gray breeches, and his walking boots and brass spurrs without rowells." The spectre, Webster is convinced, was an "extrinsick apparition to *Raynard*," and not the mere effect of a guilty conscience "which represented the shape of *Fletcher* in his fancy." The thing could not, he thinks "be brought to pass either by the Devil, or *Fletchers* Soul," and therefore he "concludes that either it was wrought by the Divine Power, . . . or that it was the Astral or Sydereal Spirit of *Fletcher*, seeking revenge for the murther." [65]

Webster also believes fully in the "bleeding or cruentation of the bodies of those that have been murthered," particularly at the touch of the murderer or in his presence, and he gives a very curious collection of examples, in some of which "the murtherers had not been certainly known but by the bleeding of the body murthered." [66] The most probable explanation of such phenomena he finds in the existence of the astral spirit, "that, being a middle substance, betwixt the Soul and the Body doth, when separated from the Body, wander or hover near about it bearing with it the irascible and concupiscible faculties, wherewith being stirred up to hatred and revenge, it causeth that ebullition and motion in the blood, that exudation of blood upon the weapon, and those other wonderful motions of the Body, Hands, Nostrils and Lips, thereby to discover the murtherer, and bring him to condign punishment." [67] In some cases, however, Webster holds that the soul has not actually departed, "and God may in his just judgment suffer the Soul to stay longer in the murthered Body, that the cry of blood may make known the murtherer, or may not so soon, for the same reason, call it totally away." [68]

These specimens of Webster's temper of mind might perhaps suffice to show with what slight justification he has been regarded as a scientific rationalist. We must not dismiss him, however, until we have scrutinized his views on the subject of witchcraft itself. He passes for a strong denier of the whole business of sorcery. We shall find that this is a great mistake. So far from denying the existence of witches, Webster is indignant at the imputation that his theories and those of other like-minded scholars should be interpreted in any such sense. "If I deny that a Witch cannot flye in the air, nor be transformed or transsubstantiated into a Cat, a Dog, or an Hare, or that the Witch maketh any visible Covenant with the Devil, or that he sucketh on their bodies, or that the Devil hath carnal Copulation with them; I do not thereby deny either the Being of Witches, nor other properties that they may have, for which they may be so called: no more than if I deny that a dog hath rugibility (which is only proper to a Lion) doth it follow that I deny the being of a Dog, or that he hath latrability?" [69] This sentence contains, in effect, the sum and substance of Webster's negative propositions on the subject.[70] Let us see what he holds as affirmatives.

Though rejecting the theory of an external covenant between the devil and a witch, Webster acknowledges "an internal, mental, and spiritual League or Covenant betwixt the Devil and all wicked persons." Further, "this spiritual League in some respects and in some persons may be, and is an explicit League, that is, the persons that enter into it, are or may be conscious of it, and know it to be so." [71] Now there are certain persons, commonly called witches, who are full of "hatred, malice, revenge and envy," of which the devil is the "author and causer," [72] and these, by Satan's instigation, "do secretly and by tradition learn strange poysons, philters and receipts whereby they do much hurt and mischief. Which most strange wayes of poysoning, tormenting, and breeding of unwonted things in the stomach and bellies of people, have not been unknown unto many learned men and Philosophers." [73] Among these effects of "an art more than Diabolical," which has "been often practised by most horrible, malevolent, and wicked persons," is the production of the plague. There is no doubt of the fact. There are "undeniable examples." An unguent may be prepared which is of such power that, when it is smeared upon the handles of doors, "those that do but lightly touch them are forthwith infected." In 1536 there was a conspiracy of some forty persons in Italy, who caused the death of many in this way.[74]

To such arts Webster ascribes the dreadful outbreak of jail-fever at the Oxford assizes in 1579. This was not, and could not be, the ordinary "prison infection." It was brought about by the contrivances of one Roland Jenks, "a Popish recusant," who was condemned for seditious words against the queen. Jenks, it seems, had procured strange poisons of a local apothecary, and had made a kind of candle out of them. As soon as he was condemned, he lighted his candle, from which there arose such a "damp," or vapor, that the pestilence broke out as we have seen.[75] It is manifest, Webster holds, "that these kind of people that are commonly called Witches, are indeed (as both the Greek and Latin names doe signifie) Poysoners, and in respect of their Hellish intentions are Diabolical, but the effects they procure flow from natural Causes." [76] This last proposition is, indeed, perhaps the chief point of Webster's book. Witches exist, and they do horrible things, but they accomplish their ends, not by the actual intervention of the devil and his imps, but by virtue of an acquaintance with little-known laws of nature. Another example, which cannot be quoted in detail, will make Webster's position perfectly clear. A man was afflicted with a dreadful disease. The cause was discovered to be the presence of an oaken pin in the corner of a courtyard. The pin was destroyed and the man drank birchen ale. He made a complete recovery. It is plain, according to Webster, that the pulling up and burning of the oaken pin "was with the help of the Birchen Ale the cure; but it can no wayes be judged necessary that the Devil should fix the Oak pin there, but that the Witch might do it himself. Neither can it be thought to be any power given by the Devil to the Oaken pin, that it had not by nature, for in probability it will constantly by a natural power produce the same effect; only thus far the Devil had a hand in the action, to draw some wicked person to fix the pin there . . . , thereby to hurt and torture him." [77]

One is tempted to still further quotations from Webster's utterances on this topic, especially because his book has been much oftener mentioned than read. But we must rest content with one passage which sums up the whole matter: — "The opinions that we reject as foolish and impious are those we have often named before, to wit, that those that are vulgarly accounted Witches, make a visible and corporeal contract with the Devil, that he sucks upon their bodies, that he hath carnal copulation with them, that they are transubstantiated into Cats, Dogs, Squirrels, and the like, or that they raise tempests, and fly in the air. Other powers we grant unto them, to operate and effect whatsoever the force of natural imagination joyned with envy, malice and vehement desire of revenge, can perform or perpetrate, or whatsoever hurt may be done by secret poysons and such like wayes that work by meer natural means." [78]

It is true that Webster opposed some of the current witch-dogmas of his time. There are passages enough in his elaborate treatise which insist on the prevalence of fraud and melancholia. In his Epistle Dedicatory, which is addressed to five Yorkshire justices of the peace, he lays particular stress on the necessity of distinguishing between impostors and those unfortunate persons who are "under a mere passive delusion" that they are witches, and warns the magistrates not to believe impossible confessions. For all this he deserves honor.[79] Nor do I intend for a moment to suggest that the queer things (as we regard them now-a-days) which I have cited are in any manner discreditable to Webster. He was not exceptionally credulous, and he belonged to that advanced school of English physicians who, in the second half of the seventeenth century, upheld the general theories of Paracelsus and van Helmont in opposition to the outworn follies of the Galenists or regulars. He was a man of great erudition, of vast and varied experience, of uncommon mental gifts, and of passionate devotion to the truth. I admire him, but I must be pardoned if I am unable to see how he can be regarded as a tower of skeptical strength in the great witchcraft controversy. Even his admissions on the subject of the fallen angels are enough to destroy the efficiency of his denial of current notions about witchcraft. Once grant, as Webster does, that our atmosphere is peopled by legions upon legions of evil angels, delighting in sin, eager to work mischief, inimical to God and man, furnished with stores of acquired knowledge, and able to devise wicked thoughts and put them into our minds,[80] and it was idle to deny — in the face of the best philosophic and theological opinion of the ages — that these demonic beings can make actual covenants with witches or furnish them with the means of doing injury to their fellow-creatures.

"*A Witch*," according to Glanvil's definition, "*is one, who can do or seems to do strange things, beyond the known Power of Art and ordinary Nature, by vertue of a Confederacy with Evil Spirits. . . .* The *strange things* are *really* performed, and are not all *Impostures* and *Delusions.* The Witch *occasions*, but is not the *Principal* Efficient, she seems to do it, but the *Spirit* performs the wonder, sometimes immediately, as in *Transportations* and *Possessions*, sometimes by applying other Natural Causes, as in raising *Storms*, and inflicting *Diseases*, sometimes using the *Witch* as an *Instrument*, and either by the Eyes or Touch, conveying Malign Influences: And these things are done by vertue of a *Covenant*, or *Compact* betwixt the *Witch* and an *Evil Spirit.* A *Spirit*, viz. an *Intelligent Creature* of the Invisible World, whether one of the Evil Angels called *Devils*, or an Inferiour *Dæmon* or *Spirit*, or a wicked *Soul* departed; but one that is able and ready for mischief, and whether altogether Incorporeal or not, appertains not to this Question." [81] Glanvil's book was well known to the Mathers. So was Webster's Displaying of Supposed Witchcraft.[82] Could there be a moment's doubt which of the two would appeal the more powerfully to their logical sense? Why, even we ourselves, if we look at the matter fairly, — taking into consideration Webster's whole case, and not merely such parts of it as accord with our preconceived opinions, — are forced to admit that Glanvil's position is much the stronger.

In a well-known passage, in which the intellectual temper of Massachusetts before 1660 is contrasted with that of the next generation,[83] our classic New England essayist remarks that after 1660 the Colonists "sank rapidly into provincials, narrow in thought, in culture, in creed." "Such a pedantic portent as Cotton Mather," Lowell continues, "would have been impossible in the first generation; he was the natural growth of the third." To discuss these epigrammatic theses would take us far beyond the limits of our present subject. One thing, however, must be said. Pedantry in the latter half of the seventeenth century was not confined to New England, nor to the ranks of those who were controversially styled the witchmongers. Meric Casaubon and Joseph Glanvil were not pedantic, but John Webster's Displaying of Supposed Witchcraft — which in some respects comes very near to being a great book — is a monument of pedantry, and John Webster was not a product of New England.

In Thomas Hobbes, whom we may next consider, we find a philosopher who was altogether incredulous on the subject of witchcraft. "As for witches," he writes, "I think not that their witchcraft is any real power; but yet that they are justly punished, for the false belief that they have that they can do such mischief, joined with their purpose to do it if they can; their trade being nearer to a new religion than to a craft or science." [84] This dictum may accord with reason, but one must admit that it was cold comfort for persons accused of diabolical arts. And so was the more famous remark of Selden: "The Law against Witches does not prove there be any; but it punishes the Malice of those people, that use such means, to take away mens lives. If one should profess that by turning his Hat thrice, and crying Buz; he could take away a man's life (though in truth he could do no such thing) yet this were a just Law made by the State, that whosoever should turn his Hat thrice, and cry Buz; with an intention to take away a man's life, shall be put to death." [85] Bayle, shortly after the beginning of the eighteenth century, agreed with Selden as to the justice of putting "sorciers imaginaires" to death.[86] Thomas Ady, believing (like Scot, to whom he often refers) that the witches and sorcerers of the Bible were mere cheats, and that the same is true of all who pretend to similar arts in modern times, is ready to admit the justice of the death penalty in cases of fraud. In describing the case of a certain Master of Arts who was "condemned only for using himself to the study and practice of the Jugling craft," he concludes: — "if he had been a Jugler, or practiser of that Craft to this end, to withstand the Prophets when they wrought true miracles, as *Pharaohs* Juglers withstood *Moses*, or if he were one that practised it to seduce the people after lying delusions, to magnifie himself as a false Prophet, like *Simon Magus* in the *Acts*, or to cause people to ascribe miraculous power to him, or to seek to the Devil as our common Deceivers, called good Witches, do, he was deservedly condemned." [87]

Four dissenters from the current witchcraft dogma we must pass over in silence — John Wagstaffe, Sir Robert Filmer, Robert Calef, and Dr. Francis Hutchinson. Calef came too late to be really significant in our discussion; Filmer's tract is a kind of *jeu d'esprit*, not likely to have had any influence except upon lawyers; [88] and Wagstaffe's book is a quite inconsiderable affair. Yet, in parting, we must not neglect an odd remark concerning two out of the four — as well as one other, John Webster, whose lucubrations we have already criticised — a remark which, occurring as it does in a work of much learning and unusual distinction, illustrates in striking fashion the inaccuracy which we have already had occasion to notice, now and again, in recent writers who have busied themselves with the abstruse and complicated subject of witchcraft. President White, in his Warfare of Science with Theology, expresses his admiration for Webster, Wagstaffe, and Hutchinson in the following terms: — "But especially should honour be paid to the younger men in the Church, who wrote at length against the whole system: such men as Wagstaffe and Webster and Hutchinson, who in the humbler ranks of the clergy stood manfully for truth, with the certainty that by so doing they were making their own promotion impossible." [89] Of the three men whom Dr. White thus commends for renouncing all hope of ecclesiastical preferment, the first, John Webster, was sixty-seven years old when he published his book; he had long been a Non-conformist, and he describes himself on his title-page as "Practitioner in Physick." The second, John Wagstaffe, was a gentleman of independent means who damaged his health by "continual bibbing of strong and high tasted liquors" [90] and who was not in orders at all; the third, Dr. Francis Hutchinson, was Chaplain in Ordinary to King George I when he published his Essay and was advanced to a bishopric two years after the first edition of the book appeared. [91]

When, in 1691 and 1693, we come to The Enchanted World (De Betoverde Weereld) [92] of the Dutch preacher and theologian Balthasar Bekker, we arrive at a method of opposing the witch-dogma different from anything we have so far examined. Bekker was fully aware of the difficulties of his theme, and he had an uncommonly logical head. His method is perfect. He first sets forth the spiritual beliefs of the Greeks and Romans and their practices in the way of sorcery. Then he shows — with an anticipation of the process so often used by the modern anthropological school — that the same doctrines and practices are found among "the pagans of the present day," — in Northern Europe, in Asia, in Africa, and in America, as well as among the ancient Jews. The Manichæan heresy, he contends, was a mélange of pagan and Jewish doctrines. These doctrines — heathen, Jewish, and Manichæan — early became current among Christians. Hence, Christians in general now hold that all sorts of extraordinary happenings are due to the activity of the devil. Thus Bekker succeeds in explaining the primary conceptions of modern demonology and witchcraft as derived from heathen sources.[93]

Bekker's next task is to define body and spirit, according to reason and the Bible. Both body and spirit are creatures. God, being perfect and increate, is neither body nor spirit, but superior to both. He is called a spirit in the Bible, simply because there is no better word to express the divine nature, but that nature is different from what is ordinarily meant by the term. God being the governor of the world, we have no ground for believing that there are demigods (dæmons in the Greek sense) or vice-gods. Apart from the Scriptures, reason affords us no proof that there are any spirits except men's souls. The Scriptures, however, teach that there are good angels, of whom Michael is the chief, and bad angels, whose prince is the devil. Beyond this, we learn practically nothing from the Bible with regard to a hierarchy of angels or of devils. Demoniacal possession was a natural disease: it had nothing to do with evil spirits. Such devils as are mentioned in Scripture are not said to be vassals of Satan; in many cases we are to understand the word "devil" merely as a figure of speech for a wicked man. There is no warrant in Holy Writ for the belief that Satan can appear to mortals under different forms, nor for the powers vulgarly ascribed to him and his supposed demonic household. In particular, there is no scriptural warrant for the opinion that Satan or his imps can injure men bodily or even suggest evil thoughts to them. The devil and the evil angels are damned in hell; they have not the power to move about in this world. The only way in which Satan is responsible for the sins which we commit is through his having brought about the fall of Adam, so that men are now depraved creatures, prone to sin. There is no place in the divine government for particular suggestions to wickedness, made from time to time, since the Fall, either by Satan himself or by any of his train. Diabolical influence upon mankind was confined to the initial temptation in Eden. Since Adam, neither Satan nor any evil spirit has been active in this world in any manner whatever, spiritual or corporeal. God rules, and the devil is not a power to be reckoned with at all. These revolutionary propositions Bekker proves, to his own satisfaction, not only from reason, but from the Word of God.[94]

Here at last we have a rational method. Bekker is not content with half-measures; he lays the axe to the root. There is a devil, to be sure, and there are fallen angels; but neither the one nor the other can have anything to do with the life and actions of mortal men. Practically, then, the devil is non-existent. We may disregard him entirely. If Bekker's propositions are admitted, the stately fabric of demonology and witchcraft crumbles in an instant. And nothing less drastic than such propositions will suffice to make witchcraft illogical or incredible. Bekker's argument, we see at once, is utterly different from anything that his predecessors had attempted.

It now becomes necessary for Bekker to proceed to discuss those passages in the Bible which appear to justify the common beliefs in sorcery and witchcraft. These beliefs are contrary to reason, but, if they rest upon revelation, they must still be accepted, for Bekker regards himself as an orthodox Christian of the Dutch Reformed Church. Accordingly Bekker takes up every scriptural passage which mentions witches, enchanters, diviners, and the like, and interprets them all in such a way that they lend no support to current beliefs in the reality of compacts with the devil, of magic, or of witchcraft. Whatever magicians and witches, so-called, may think of their own performances, there is nothing in Scripture, as interpreted by this bold and expert theologian and unsurpassed dialectician, to warrant us in believing in intercourse with Satan, or in his intervention, with or without the mediation of sorcerers and witches, in human life as it is to-day.[95]

But, Bekker hastens to admit, there remains a huge mass of recent testimony which is regarded by almost everybody as sufficient to establish the existence of sorcery and witchcraft, whether such things are recognized in the Bible or not. To this testimony Bekker devotes the Fourth (and last) Book of his treatise.

He first points out that all such testimony is prejudiced, since it comes from persons who have a fixed and, so to speak, an inherited belief in the truth of the marvels whose very existence is in question. He then examines a great body of material, with splendid sobriety and common sense. This is perhaps the most interesting part of his work to us, — though in fact it is less original than much of what precedes, since all opponents of the witch-dogma, beginning with Wier, had attacked the evidence in many particulars, and since even those scholars and theologians who supported the dogma most effectively — like Glanvil — had granted without hesitation that fraud and delusion played a large part in the accumulation of testimony. Bekker's treatment of the subject, however, is better than anything of the kind that had been written before. Fraud, terror, hysteria, insanity, illusion of the senses, — due to disease or to what we should now call hypnotic or semi-hypnotic conditions, — unknown laws of nature — these are the sources from which he derives his interpretation of the evidence. This part of his work, then, has a singularly modern tone, and gives the author a valid claim to rank as an enlightened psychologist.

It has seemed advisable to give particular attention to Bekker's Enchanted World because of its singular merits, as well as on account of the distinguished position which it deservedly holds among the books which oppose the belief in witchcraft. In strictness, however, we are not bound to include this work in our survey of seventeenth-century opinion, since it did not appear in season to exert any influence on New England at the time of the Salem prosecution. The first two Books of Bekker's work were published in 1691; the second two, which deal specifically with witchcraft, in 1693. The trouble in Salem began in February, 1692, and the prosecution collapsed in January, 1693. It is certain that New England scholars knew nothing about the first two Books when they were engaged in witch-trials, and the last two were not published until the trials had come to an end. But this matter of dates need not be insisted on. Even if our ancestors had received advance sheets of The Enchanted World, their opinions would not, in all probability, have been in the slightest degree affected. Indeed, the reception which Bekker's treatise met with in his own country is a plain indication of the temper of the times in this business of witchcraft. The publication of the first two Books in 1691 was the signal for a storm of denunciation. The Dutch press teemed with replies and attacks. Bekker was instantly called to account by the authorities of the Reformed Church. Complicated ecclesiastical litigation ensued, with the result that the Synod of North Holland issued a decree declaring Bekker "intolerable as teacher in the Reformed Church" and expelling him from his ministerial office (August 7, 1692).[96] Soon after, the Church Council of Amsterdam voted to exclude him from the Lord's Supper (August 17),[97] and he was never admitted to communion again. He died on June 11, 1698.[98]

Another reason for going so fully into Bekker's arguments is that they give us an excellent chance to take up a question which is of cardinal importance in weighing the whole matter of witchcraft. I refer, of course, to the question of Biblical Exegesis.

If we wish to treat our forefathers fairly, we are required to criticise the few opponents of the witch-dogma in a really impartial way. We ought not to commend such portions of their argument as chance to square with our own ideas, and ignore the rest. We must review their case as a whole, so as to discover how far it was right or reasonable on the basis of their own postulates. We must test the correctness of their premises, as well as the accuracy of their logic.

This process we have gone through with already in several instances. We have seen that all the opponents of witchcraft so far examined struggle to maintain a position that is strategically indefensible, either because they admit too much, or because they ignore certain difficulties, or because they are frankly eccentric. It does not help their case to contend that what they admit or what they ignore does not signify from our present scientific point of view. It *did* signify *then*. The only man whose argument covers the ground completely and affords a thorough and consistent theory on which a seventeenth-century Christian was logically justified in rejecting witchcraft and demoniacal possession as facts of everyday experience is Balthasar Bekker.

Now the truth or falsity of Bekker's very radical conclusions hinged — for Bekker himself and for his contemporaries — on the soundness of his Biblical exegesis. If his way of disposing of those passages which mention devils and witches and diviners and familiar spirits is not justifiable — if the Biblical writers did not mean what he thinks they meant — then his whole case goes to pieces. In discussing the witchcraft dogma of the seventeenth century, we must accept the Bible, for the nonce, as the men of the seventeenth century (Bekker included) accepted it — as absolutely true in every detail, as dynamically inspired by the Holy Ghost, as a complete rule of faith and practice. Modern views on this subject have no *locus standi*.

Now, if we only keep these fundamental principles firmly in mind, we shall have no doubt as to the outcome. Beyond question, the Bible affords ample authority for belief in demoniacal possession, in necromancy, in the ability of Satan and his cohorts to cause physical phenomena, and in the power of sorcerers to work miracles.[99] True, not all the details of the witchcraft dogma rest upon Biblical authority, but enough of them do so rest to make the case of those who uphold the traditional opinion substantially unassailable, except upon the purely arbitrary assumption that all these wonders, though formerly actual, have ceased in recent times.[100] Bekker's exegesis is erroneous in countless particulars and presents an altogether mistaken view of Biblical doctrines. As interpreters of the language of Scripture, the orthodox theologians of his time, who pinned their faith to witchcraft, were nearer right than he was. And what is true of Bekker's exegesis, is equally true of that followed by all previous opponents of the witchcraft dogma. My reason for not referring to this point in criticising their books is obvious. Bekker has gone farther, and succeeded better, in explaining away the testimony of Scripture than any of the others. It is more than fair to them to rest this part of the case upon his success or failure. If Bekker falls, all of them certainly fall, — and Bekker falls.[101]

From our cursory examination of the works put forth by some of the chief opponents of the witch-dogma, it must be evident that none of these works can have had a very profound influence on the beliefs of the seventeenth century, — their function was rather, by keeping discussion alive, to prepare for the change of sentiment which took place soon after 1700, in what we are accustomed to call "the age of prose and reason." Such an examination as we have given to these books was necessary to establish the proposition with which we set out, — that our ancestors in 1692 were in accord with the practically universal belief of their day. It has shown more than this, however, — it has demonstrated that their position was logically and scripturally stronger than that of their antagonists, provided we judge the matter (as we are in honor bound to do) on the basis of those doctrines as to supernaturalism and the inspiration of the Bible that were alike admitted by both sides. We may repeat, then, with renewed confidence, the statement already made: Our forefathers believed in witchcraft, not because they were Puritans, not because they were Colonials, not because they were New Englanders, but because they were men of their own time and not of ours.

Another point requires consideration if we would arrive at a just judgment on the Salem upheaval. It is frequently stated, and still oftener assumed, that the outbreak at Salem was peculiar in its virulence, or, at all events, in its intensity. This is a serious error, due, like other misapprehensions, to a neglect of the history of witchcraft as a whole. The fact is, the Salem excitement was the opposite of peculiar, — it was perfectly typical. The European belief in witchcraft, which our forefathers shared without exaggerating it, was a constant quantity. It was always present, and continuously fraught with direful possibilities. But it did not find expression in a steady and regular succession of witch-trials. On the contrary, it manifested itself at irregular intervals in spasmodic outbursts of prosecution. Notable examples occurred at Geneva from 1542 to 1546;[102] at Wiesensteig, Bavaria, in 1562 and 1563;[103] in the Electorate of Trier from 1587 to 1593;[104] among the Basques of Labourd in 1609;[105] at Mohra in Sweden in 1669 and 1670.[106] In the district of Ortenau, in Baden, witchcraft prosecution suddenly broke out, after a considerable interval, in 1627, and there were seventy-three executions in three years.[107] From the annals of witchcraft in Great Britain one may cite the following cases: — 1581, at St. Osyth, in Essex;[108] 1590–1597, in Scotland;[109] 1612, at Lancaster,[110] and again in 1633;[111] 1616, in Leicestershire;[112] 1645–1647, the Hopkins prosecution;[113] 1649–1650, at Newcastle-on-Tyne;[114] 1652, at Maidstone, in Kent;[115] 1682, at Exeter.[116] The sudden outbreak of witch-trials in the Bermudas in 1651 is also worthy of attention.[117]

It is unnecessary for us to consider how much of the evidence offered at witch-trials in England was actually true. Some of the defendants were pretty bad characters, and it would be folly to maintain that none of them tried to cause the sickness or death of their enemies by maltreating clay images or by other arts which they supposed would avail. Besides, now and then an injury is testified to which may well have been inflicted without diabolical aid. Thus Ann Foster, who was hanged for witchcraft at Northampton in 1674, confessed that she had set a certain grazier's barns on fire, and there is much reason to believe her, for she was under considerable provocation.[118] As to occult or super-normal powers and practices, we may leave their discussion to the psychologists. With regard to this aspect of the Salem troubles, we must accept, as substantially in accordance with the facts, the words of Dr. Poole: "No man of any reputation who lived in that generation, and saw what transpired at Salem Village and its vicinity, doubted that there was some influence then exerted which could not be explained by the known laws of matter or of mind."[119] Even Thomas Brattle, in speaking of the confessing witches, many of whom he says he has "again and again seen and heard," cannot avoid the hypothesis of demoniacal action. They are, he feels certain, "deluded, imposed upon, and under the influence of some evil spirit; and therefore unfit to be evidences either against themselves, or any one else." [120]

One common misapprehension to which the historians of witchcraft are liable comes from their failure to perceive that the immediate responsibility for actual prosecution rests frequently, if not in the majority of instances, on the rank and file of the community or neighborhood. This remark is not made in exculpation of prosecutors and judges, — for my purpose in this discussion is not to extenuate anybody's offences or to shift the blame from one man's shoulders to another's. What is intended is simply to remind the reader of a patent and well-attested fact which is too often overlooked in the natural tendency of historians to find some notable personage to whom their propositions, commendatory or damaging, may be attached. A prosecution for witchcraft presupposes a general belief among the common people in the reality of the crime. But this is not all. It presupposes likewise the existence of a body of testimony, consisting of the talk of the neighborhood, usually extending back over a considerable stretch of years, with regard to certain persons who have the reputation of being witches, cunning men, and so on. It also presupposes the belief of the neighborhood that various strange occurrences, — such as storms, bad crops, plagues of grasshoppers and caterpillars, loss of pigs or cattle, cases of lunacy or hysteria or chorea or wasting sickness, — are due to the malice of those particular suspects and their unknown confederates. These strange occurrences, be it remembered, are not the fictions of a superstitious or distempered imagination: they are — most of them — things that have really taken place; they are the *res gestae* of the prosecution, without which it could never have come about, or, having begun, could never have continued. And further, in very many instances of prosecution for witchcraft, there have been, among the accused, persons who believed themselves to be witches, — or who had, at any rate, pretended to extraordinary powers and — in many instances — had either used their uncanny reputation to scare their enemies or to get money by treating diseases of men and cattle. And finally, the habit of railing and brawling, of uttering idle but malignant threats, and, on the other hand, the habit of applying vile epithets — including that of "witch" — to one's neighbors in the heat of anger — customs far more prevalent in former times than now — also resulted in the accumulation of a mass of latent or potential testimony which lay stored up in people's memories ready to become kinetic whenever the machinery of the law should once begin to move.[121]

Nobody will ask for evidence that railing and brawling went on in colonial New England, that our forefathers sometimes called each other bad names, or that slander was a common offence.[122] That suspicion of witchcraft was rife in various neighborhoods years before the Salem outbreak, is proved, not only by the records of sporadic cases that came before the courts,[123] but by some of the evidence in the Salem prosecution itself.

That the initial responsibility for prosecution usually rested with the neighborhood or community might further be shown by many specific pieces of testimony. The terrible prosecution in Trier toward the close of the sixteenth century is a case in point. "Since it was commonly believed," writes Linden, an eyewitness, "that the continued failure of the crops for many years was caused by witches and wizards through diabolical malice, the whole country rose up for the annihilation of the witches." [124] To like purpose are the words of the admirable Jesuit, Friedrich Spee, in the closing chapter of the most powerful and convincing protest against witch-trials ever written — that chapter which the author begged every magistrate in Germany to mark and weigh, whether he read the rest of the book or not: — "Incredible are the superstition, the envy, the slanders and backbitings, the whisperings and gossip of the common people in Germany, which are neither punished by magistrates nor reproved by preachers. These are the causes that first rouse suspicion of witchcraft. All the punishments of divine justice with which God has threatened men in the Holy Scriptures are held to come from witches. God and nature no longer do anything, — witches, everything. Hence it is that all demand, with violent outcry, that the magistracy shall proceed against the witches, whom only their own tongues have made so numerous." [125]

As for England, the annals of witchcraft are full of instances which show where the initial responsibility rests in particular prosecutions. Two examples will serve as well as many.

Roger North, the distinguished lawyer, who was at Exeter in 1682, when a famous witch-trial occurred, [126] gives a vivid account of the popular excitement: — [127] "The women were very old, decrepit, and impotent, and were brought to the assizes with as much noise and fury of the rabble against them as could be shewed on any occasion. The stories of their acts were in everyone's mouth, and they were not content to belie them in the country, but even in the city where they were to be tried miracles were fathered upon them, as that the judges' coach was fixed upon the castle bridge, and the like. All which the country believed, and accordingly persecuted the wretched old creatures. A less zeal in a city or kingdom hath been the overture of defection and revolution, and if these women had been acquitted, it was thought that the country people would have committed some disorder." [128]

Our second example is a very notable case, which occurred in 1712, — that of Jane Wenham, the last witch condemned to death in England. Jane Wenham had a dispute with a neighboring farmer, who called her a witch. She complained to the local magistrate, Sir Henry Chauncy. He referred the dispute to the parson of the parish, who, after hearing both sides, admonished the wranglers to live at peace and sentenced the farmer to pay Jane a shilling. The old crone was not pleased. Shortly after, one of the clergyman's servants, a young woman, was strangely afflicted. Jane was brought to trial. Every effort seems to have been made by the court to put a stop to the affair, but the local feeling was so strong, and the witnesses and complainants were so many (including the clergymen of two parishes) that nothing could be done. The official who drew up the indictment endeavored to make the whole affair ridiculous by refusing to use any other phraseology in describing the alleged crime than "conversing with the devil in the form of a cat." But the well-meant device only intensified the feeling against the witch. Mr. Justice Powell, who presided, did what he could to induce the jury to acquit, but in vain. They brought in a verdict of guilty, and he was obliged to pass sentence of death. He suspended the execution of the sentence, however, and secured the royal pardon, — to the intense indignation of the neighborhood. Here we have a jury of the vicinage, accurately reflecting the local sentiment, and insisting on carrying out its belief in withcraft to the bitter end, despite all that the judge could do.[129] It is well to note that the clergymen involved in the prosecution were not New England Puritans, and that the whole affair took place just twenty years after the last execution of a witch in Massachusetts. Of itself, this incident might suffice to silence those who ascribe the Salem outbreak to the influence of certain distinguished men, as well as those who maintain that the New Englanders were more superstitious than their fellow-citizens at home, that their Puritanism was somehow to blame for it, and that witchcraft was practically dead in the Mother Country when the Salem outbreak took place.[130]

Yet Thomas Wright — never to be mentioned without honor — speaks of the New England troubles as "exemplifying the horrors and the absurdities of the witchcraft persecutions more than anything that had occurred in the old world," [131] and Dr. G. H. Moore, — in an important article on The Bibliography of Witchcraft in Massachusetts — declares that the Salem outbreak "was the *epitome* of witchcraft! whose ghastly records may be challenged to produce any parallel for it in the world's history!" [132] In further refutation of such reckless statements I need add but a single instance. In 1596 there was an outbreak of some pestilence or other in Aberdeen. The populace ascribed the disease to the machinations of a family long suspected of witchcraft. A special commission was appointed by the Privy Council, "and before April, 1597, twenty-three women and one man had been burnt, one woman had died under the torture, one had hanged herself in prison, and four others who were acquitted on the capital charge, were yet branded on the cheek and banished from the sheriffdom." [133]

There was a very special reason why troubles with the powers of darkness were to be expected in New England, — a reason which does not hold good for Great Britain or, indeed, for any part of Western Europe. I refer, of course, to the presence of a considerable heathen population — the

Indians. These were universally supposed to be devil-worshippers, — not only by the Colonists but by all the rest of the
world, — for paganism was held to be nothing but Satanism.[134]
Cotton Mather and the Jesuit fathers of Canada were at one
on this point.[135] The religious ceremonies of the Indians were,
as we know, in large part an invocation of spirits, and their
powwaws, or medicine men, supposed themselves to be wizards, — *were* wizards, indeed, so far as sorcery is possible.[136]
The Colonial government showed itself singularly moderate,
however, in its attitude toward Indian practices of a magical
character. Powwawing was, of course, forbidden wherever
the jurisdiction of the white men held sway, but it was punishable by fine only, nor was there any idea of inflicting the
extreme penalty [137] — although the offence undoubtedly
came under the Mosaic law, so often quoted on the title-
pages of books on witchcraft, "Thou shalt not suffer a witch
to live."

The existence of all these devil-worshipping neighbors was
a constant reminder of the possibility of danger from witchcraft. One is surprised, therefore, to find that there was no
real outbreak until so late in the century. It argues an uncommon degree of steadiness and common sense among our
forefathers that they held off the explosion so long. Yet even
this delay has been made to count against them, as if, by
1692, they ought to have known better, even if they might
have been excusable some years before. In point of fact, the
New Englanders, as we have seen, made an end of trying
witches nearly twenty years earlier than their English fellow-
citizens. But we shall come back to this question of dates
presently.

Much has been written of the stupendous and criminal
foolishness of our ancestors in admitting "spectral evidence"
at the Salem trials. Nothing, of course, can be said in defence
of such evidence in itself; but a great deal might be said in
defence of our ancestors on this score. The fact is, — and it
should never be lost sight of, — there was nothing strange in
their admitting such evidence. It was a matter of course that
they should admit it. To do so, indeed, was one of the best
established of all legal principles. Spectral evidence was admitted, for example, in England, either in examinations or in

actual trials, in 1593,[138] 1612,[139] 1616,[140] 1621,[141] 1633,[142] 1645,[143] 1650,[144] 1653,[145] 1654,[146] 1658,[147] 1660,[148] 1661,[149] 1663,[150] 1664,[151] 1665,[152] 1667,[153] 1670,[154] 1672,[155] 1673,[156] 1680,[157] 1682,[158] 1683.[159] Even Chief Justice Holt, whose honorable record in procuring the acquittal of every witch he tried is well-known, did not exclude spectral evidence: it was offered and admitted in at least two of his cases, — in 1695 and 1696,[160] — both later than the last witch-trial in Massachusetts. In the 1697 edition of that very popular manual, Michael Dalton's Country Justice, spectral evidence ("Their Apparition to the Sick Party in his Fits") is expressly mentioned as one of the proofs of witchcraft.[161] What may fairly be called spectral evidence was admitted by Mr. Justice Powell, anxious as he was to have the defendant acquitted, in the trial of Jane Wenham in 1712.[162] The question, then, was not whether such evidence might be heard, but what weight was to be attached to it. Thus, in Sir Matthew Hale's case, Mr. Serjeant Keeling was "much unsatisfied" with such testimony, affirming that, if it were allowed to pass for proof, "no person whatsoever can be in safety." [163] He did not aver that it should not have been admitted, but only protested against regarding it as decisive, and in the end he seems to have become convinced of the guilt of the defendants.[164] It is, therefore, nothing against our ancestors that they heard such evidence, for they were simply following the invariable practice of the English courts. On the other hand, it is much to their credit that they soon began to suspect it, and that, having taken advice, they decided, in 1693, to allow it no further weight. We may emphasize the folly of spectral evidence as much as we like.[165] Only let us remember that in so doing we are attacking, not New England in 1692, but Old England from 1593 to 1712. When, on the other hand, we distribute compliments to those who refused to allow such evidence to constitute full proof, let us not forget that with the name of Chief Justice Holt we must associate those of certain Massachusetts worthies whom I need not specify. It is not permissible to blame our ancestors for an error of judgment that they shared with everybody, and then to refuse them commendation for a virtue which they shared with a very few wise heads in England. That would be to proceed on the principle of "heads I win, tails you lose," — a method much followed by Matthew Hopkins and his kind, but of doubtful propriety in a candid investigation of the past. We shall never keep our minds clear on the question of witchcraft in general, and of the Salem witchcraft in particular, until we stop attacking and defending individual persons.

Sir John Holt, Chief Justice of the King's Bench from 1682 to 1710, has a highly honorable name in the annals of English witchcraft. A dozen or twenty cases came before him, and in every instance the result was an acquittal.[166] Chief Justice Holt deserves all the credit he has received; but it must be carefully noted that his example cannot be cited to the shame and confusion of our ancestors in Massachusetts, for most of his cases, — all but one, so far as I can ascertain, — occurred after the release of the New England prisoners and the abandonment of the prosecution here. As to that single case of acquittal, we must not forget that there were also acquittals in Massachusetts, — in 1673, 1675, 1676, 1680, and 1683.[167] As to acquittals in England *after* 1693, let it be remembered that there were *no trials at all for witchcraft* in New England subsequent to that year. If Chief Justice Holt is to be commended for procuring the acquittal of a dozen witches between 1693 and 1702, what is to be ascribed to our forefathers for bringing no cases to trial during that period?

The most remarkable things about the New England prosecution were the rapid return of the community to its habitually sensible frame of mind and the frank public confession of error made by many of those who had been implicated. These two features, and especially the latter, are without a parallel in the history of witchcraft. It seems to be assumed by most writers that recantation and an appeal to heaven for pardon were the least that could have been expected of judge and jury. In fact, as I have just ventured to suggest, no action like Samuel Sewall's on the part of a judge and no document like that issued by the repentant Massachusetts jurymen have yet been discovered in the witch records of the world.[168]

But it is not for the sake of lauding their penitential exercises that I lay stress upon the unexampled character of our forefathers' action. There is another aspect from which the outcome of the Salem trials ought to be regarded. They fell at a critical moment, when witchcraft was, for whatever reason, soon to become a crime unknown to the English courts. They attracted attention instantly in the Mother Country.[169] Can there be any question that the sensational recovery of the Province from its attack of prosecuting zeal, accompanied as that recovery was by retraction and by utterances of deep contrition, had a profound effect in England? The mere dropping of the prosecution would not have had this effect. In 1597, James I, alarmed at the extent to which witch-trials were going in Scotland, revoked all the existing special commissions that were engaged in holding trials for this offence.[170] But the evil was soon worse than ever. What was efficacious in the New England instance was the unheared-of action of judge and jury in recanting. This made the Salem troubles the best argument conceivable in the hands of those reformers who, soon after 1700, began to make actual headway in their opposition to the witch-dogma.

I am not reasoning *a priori*. By common consent one of the most effective arraignments of the superstition that we are discussing is the Historical Essay on Witchcraft of Dr. Francis Hutchinson, which appeared in 1718 and again in 1720. Now Hutchinson, who gives much space to the New England trials, refers to Sewall's action, and prints the recantation of the jurors in full. Nor does he leave us in doubt as to the purpose for which he adduces these testimonies. "And those Towns," he writes, "having regained their Quiet; and this Case being of that Nature, that Facts and Experience are of more Weight than meer rational Arguments, it will be worth our while to observe some Passages that happened after this Storm, when they had Time to look back on what had passed." [171]

Whatever may be thought of these considerations, one fact cannot be assailed. In prosecuting witches, our forefathers acted like other men in the seventeenth century. In repenting and making public confession, they acted like themselves. Their fault was the fault of their time; their merit is their own.

We must not leave this subject without looking into the question of numbers and dates. The history of the Salem

Witchcraft is, to all intents and purposes, the sum total of witchcraft history in the whole of Massachusetts for a century. From the settlement of the country, of course, our fathers believed in witchcraft, and cases came before the courts from time to time, but, outside of the outbreak in 1692, not more than half-a-dozen executions can be shown to have occurred.[172] It is not strange that there should have been witch-trials. It is inconceivable that the Colony should have passed through its first century without some special outbreak of prosecution — inconceivable, that is to say, to one who knows what went on in England and the rest of Europe during that time. The wonderful thing is, not that an outbreak of prosecution occurred, but that it did not come sooner and last longer.

From the first pranks of the afflicted children in Mr. Parris's house (in February, 1692) to the collapse of the prosecution in January, 1693, was less than a year. During the interval twenty persons had suffered death, and two are known to have died in jail.[173] If to these we add the six sporadic cases that occurred in Massachusetts before 1692, there is a total of twenty-eight; but this is the whole reckoning, not merely for a year or two but for a complete century. The concentration of the trouble in Massachusetts within the limits of a single year has given a wrong turn to the thoughts of many writers. This concentration makes the case more conspicuous, but it does not make it worse. On the contrary, it makes it better. It is astonishing that there should have been only half-a-dozen executions for witchcraft in Massachusetts before 1692, and equally astonishing that the delusion, when it became acute, should have raged for but a year, and that but twenty-two persons should have lost their lives. The facts are distinctly creditable to our ancestors, — to their moderation and to the rapidity with which their good sense could reassert itself after a brief eclipse.[174]

Let us compare figures a little. For Massachusetts the account is simple — twenty-eight victims in a century. No one has ever made an accurate count of the executions in England during the seventeenth century, but they must have mounted into the hundreds.[175] Matthew Hopkins, the Witch-finder General, brought at least two hundred to the gallows from 1645 to 1647.[176] In Scotland the number of victims was much larger. The most conscientiously moderate estimate makes out a total of at least 3,400 between the years 1580 and 1680, and the computer declares that future discoveries in the way of records may force us to increase this figure very much.[177] On the Continent many thousands suffered death in the sixteenth and seventeenth centuries. Mannhardt reckons the victims from the fourteenth to the seventeenth century at millions,[178] and half a million is thought to be a moderate estimate. In Alsace, a hundred and thirty-four witches and wizards were burned in 1582 on one occasion, the execution taking place on the 15th, 19th, 24th, and 28th of October.[179] Nicholas Remy (Remigius) of Lorraine gathered the materials for his work on the Worship of Demons,[180] published in 1595, from the trials of some 900 persons whom he had sentenced to death in the fifteen years preceding. In 1609, de l'Ancre and his associate are said to have condemned 600 in the Basque country in four months.[181] The efforts of the Bishop of Bamberg from 1622 to 1633 resulted in six hundred executions; the Bishop of Würzburg, in about the same period, put nine hundred persons to death.[182] These figures, which might be multiplied almost indefinitely,[183] help us to look at the Salem Witchcraft in its true proportions, — as a very small incident in the history of a terrible superstition.

These figures may perhaps be attacked as involving a fallacious comparison, inasmuch as we have not attempted to make the relative population of New England and the several districts referred to a factor in the equation. Such an objection, if anybody should see fit to make it, is easily answered by other figures. The total number of victims in Massachusetts from the first settlement to the end of the seventeenth century was, as we have seen, twenty-eight, — or thirty-four for the whole of New England. Compare the following figures, taken from the annals of Great Britain and Scotland alone. In 1612, ten witches were executed belonging to a single district of Lancashire.[184] In 1645 twenty-nine witches were condemned at once in a single Hundred in Essex,[185] eighteen were hanged at once at Bury in Suffolk [186] "and a hundred and twenty more were to have been tried, but a sudden movement of the king's troops in that direction obliged the judges to adjourn the session."[187] Under date of July 26, 1645, Whitelocke records that "20 Witches in Norfolk were executed," and again, under April 15, 1650, that "at a little Village within two Miles [of Berwick], two Men and three Women were burnt for Witches, and nine more were to be burnt, the Village consisting of but fourteen Families, and there were as many Witches," and further that "twenty more were to be burnt within six Miles of that place."[188] If we pass over to the Continent, the numbers are appalling. Whether, then, we take the computation in gross or in detail, New England emerges from the test with credit.

The last execution for witchcraft in Massachusetts took place in 1692,[189] as we have seen; indeed, twenty of the total of twenty-six cases fell within the limits of that one year. There were no witch-trials in New England after 1693. The annals of Europe are not so clear. Six witches were burned in Renfrewshire in 1697.[190] In England, there were trials, one or more, in almost every year from 1694 to 1707, though always with acquittal.[191] Then, in 1712 Jane Wenham was condemned to death for witchcraft, but she was pardoned. Two clergymen of the Church of England, as well as a Bachelor of Arts of Cambridge,[192] gave evidence against her. Just before the arrest of Jane Wenham, Addison in the Spectator for July 11, 1711, had expressed the creed of a well-bred and sensible man of the world: "I believe in general that there is, and has been such a thing as Witch-craft; but at the same time can give no Credit to any particular Instance of it." Blackstone, it will be remembered, subscribed to the same doctrine, making particular reference to Addison.[193] The last witch-trial in England was apparently Jane Wenham's. In 1717 three cases came before the grand jury at Leicester, but no bill was found.[194] Prompted, one may conjecture, by the stir which the Wenham trial made, the Rev. J. Boys, of Coggeshall Magna, in Essex, transcribed, in this same year, from his memoranda, A Brief Account of the Indisposition of the Widow Coman. This case had occurred in his own parish in 1699, and he had given it careful investigation. Both in 1699, when he jotted down the facts, and in 1712, Mr. Boys was clearly of the opinion that his unfortunate parishioner was a witch. His narrative, which remained in manuscript until 1901,[195] may be profitably compared with Cotton Mather's account of his visit to Margaret Rule in 1693.[196] Such a comparison will not work to the disadvantage of the New England divine. Incidentally it may be mentioned that the mob "swam" the widow Coman several times, and that "soon after, whether by the cold she got in the water or by some other means, she fell very ill, and dyed." Let it not be forgotten that this was six years after the end of the witchcraft prosecutions in Massachusetts. In 1705, a supposed witch was murdered by a mob at Pittenween in Scotland.[197] In 1730, another alleged witch succumbed to the water ordeal in Somersetshire.[198] The English and Scottish statutes against witchcraft were repealed in 1736,[199] but in that same year Joseph Juxon, vicar, preached at Twyford, in Leicestershire, a Sermon upon Witchcraft, occasioned by a late Illegal Attempt to discover Witches by Swimming,[200] and in 1751 Ruth Osborne, a reputed witch, was murdered by a mob in Hertfordshire.[201] The last execution for witchcraft in Germany took place in 1775. In Spain the last witch was burned in 1781. In Switzerland Anna Göldi was beheaded in 1782 for bewitching the child of her master, a physician. In Poland two women were burned as late as 1793.[202]

That the belief in witchcraft is still pervasive among the peasantry of Europe, and to a considerable extent among the foreign-born population in this country, is a matter of common knowledge.[203] Besides, spiritualism and kindred delusions have taken over, under changed names, many of the phenomena, real and pretended, which would have been explained as due to witchcraft in days gone by.[204]

Why did the Salem outbreak occur? Of course there were many causes — some of which have already suggested themselves in the course of our discussion. But one fact should be borne in mind as of particular importance. The belief in witchcraft, as we have already had occasion to remark, was a constant quantity; but outbreaks of prosecution came, in England — and, generally speaking, elsewhere — spasmodically, at irregular intervals. If we look at Great Britain for a moment, we shall see that such outbreaks are likely to coincide with times of political excitement or anxiety. Thus early in Elizabeth's reign, when everything was more or less unsettled, Bishop Jewel, whom all historians delight to honor, made a deliberate and avowed digression, in a sermon before the queen, in order to warn her that witchcraft was rampant in the realm, to inform her (on the evidence of his own eyes) that her subjects were being injured in their goods and their health, and to exhort her to enforce the law.[205] The initial zeal of James I in the prosecution of witches stood in close connection with the trouble he was having with his turbulent cousin Francis Bothwell.[206] The operations of Matthew Hopkins (in 1645-1647) were a mere accompaniment to the tumult of the Civil War; the year in which they began was the year of Laud's execution and of the Battle of Naseby. The Restoration was followed by a fresh outbreak of witchprosecution, — mild in England, though far-reaching in its consequences, but very sharp in Scotland.

With facts like these in view, we can hardly regard it as an accident that the Salem witchcraft marks a time when the Colony was just emerging from a political struggle that had threatened its very existence. For several years men's minds had been on the rack. The nervous condition of public feeling is wonderfully well depicted in a letter written in 1688 by the Rev. Joshua Moodey in Boston to Increase Mather, then in London as agent of the Colony. The Colonists are much pleased by the favor with which Mather has been received, but they distrust court promises. They are alarmed by a report that Mather and his associates have suffered "a great slurr" on account of certain over-zealous actions. Moodey rejoices in the death of Robert Mason, "one of the worst enemies that you & I & Mr. Morton had in these parts." Then there are the Indians: — "The cloud looks very dark & black upon us, & wee are under very awfull circumstances, which render an Indian Warr terrible to us." The Colonists shudder at a rumor that John Palmer, one of Andros's Council, is to come over as Supreme Judge, and know not how to reconcile it with the news of the progress their affairs have been making with the King. And finally, the writer gives an account of the case of Goodwin's afflicted children, which, as we know, was a kind of prologue to the Salem outbreak: — "Wee have a very strange th[ing] among us, which we know not what to make of, except it bee Witchcraft, as we think it must needs bee.'' [207] Clearly, there would have been small fear, in 1692, of a plot on Satan's part to destroy the Province, if our forefathers had not recently encountered other dangers of a more tangible kind.

In conclusion, I may venture to sum up, in the form of a number of brief theses, the main results at which we appear to have arrived in our discussion of witchcraft: [208]

1. The belief in witchcraft is the common heritage of humanity. It is not chargeable to any particular time, or race, or form of religion.

2. Witchcraft in some shape or other is still credited by a majority of the human race.

3. The belief in witchcraft was practically universal in the seventeenth century, even among the educated; with the mass of the people it was absolutely universal.

4. To believe in witchcraft in the seventeenth century was no more discreditable to a man's head or heart than it was to believe in spontaneous generation or to be ignorant of the germ theory of disease.

5. The position of the seventeenth-century believers in witchcraft was logically and theologically stronger than that of the few persons who rejected the current belief.

6. The impulse to put a witch to death comes from the instinct of self-preservation. It is no more cruel or otherwise blameworthy, in itself, than the impulse to put a murderer to death.

7. The belief in witchcraft manifests itself, not in steady and continuous prosecution, but in sudden outbreaks occurring at irregular intervals.

8. Such outbreaks are not symptoms of extraordinary superstition or of a peculiarly acute state of unreason. They are due, like other panics, to a perturbed condition of the public mind. Hence they are likely to accompany, or to follow, crises in politics or religion.

9. The responsibility for any witch-prosecution rests primarily on the community or neighborhood as a whole, not on the judge or the jury.

10. No jury, whether in a witch-trial or in any other case, can be more enlightened than the general run of the vicinage.

11. Many persons who have been executed for witchcraft have supposed themselves to be guilty and have actually been guilty in intent.

12. Practically every person executed for witchcraft believed in the reality of such a crime, whether he supposed himself to be guilty of it or not.

13. The witch beliefs of New England were brought over from the Mother Country by the first settlers.

14. Spectral evidence had been admitted in the examinations and trials of witches in England for a hundred years before the Salem prosecutions took place.

15. Trials for witchcraft, and one conviction and death sentence, occurred in England after they had come to an end in Massachusetts, and executions occurred on the Continent a hundred years later than that time.

16. Spectral evidence was admitted in English witch-trials after such trials had ceased in Massachusetts.

17. The total number of persons executed for witchcraft in New England from the first settlement to the end of the century is inconsiderable, especially in view of what was going on in Europe.

18. The public repentance and recantation of judge and jury in Massachusetts have no parallel in the history of witchcraft.

19. The repentance and recantation came at a time which made them singularly effective arguments in the hands of the opponents of the witch-dogma in England.

20. The record of New England in the matter of witchcraft is highly creditable, when considered as a whole and from the comparative point of view.

21. It is easy to be wise after the fact, — especially when the fact is two hundred years old.

NOTES

CHAPTER I

A TYPICAL CASE

1. Roger North, Autobiography, ed. Jessopp, 1887, pp. 131–132.

2. See p. 334, above.

3. The manuscript is now numbered 24241.5. The examinations are divided into sections, numbered by a clerk, and the sheets are now bound in the order thus indicated. The contents of the manuscript are as follows (no folio numbers in the original): Leaf 1a: Alyce Butler, October 2, 1601 (§§ 1, 2). Leaf 1b: blank. Leaf 2a: Johan Baddaford, October 2, 1601 (§§ 3, 4, 5 begins). Leaf 2b: Johan Baddaford concluded (§ 5 ends); William Tompson (§ 6) and Elizabeth, his wife (§ 7), October 2, 1601. Leaf 3a: Christian Webbar, October 2, 1601 (§§ 8, 9); Christofer Honywell, October 2, 1601 (§ 10). Leaf 3b: blank. Leaf 4a: Johan Davye, January 20, 1601 (i. e. 1602) (§ 10 [*bis*]). Leaf 4b: blank. Leaf 5a: William Cozen, October 2, 1601 (§§ 11, 12); Suzan Tooker, October, 1601 (§§ 13, 14, 15 begins). Leaf 5b: Suzan Tooker concluded (§ 15 ends, § 16). Leaf 6a: Johan Laishe, October 2, 1601 (§ 17). Leaf 6b: blank. (The lower half of leaf 6 has been torn off and is lost. It must have contained another examination [§ 18]. Johan Laishe's examination is complete.) Leaf 7a: John Denman, before Ridgeway, March 13, 1601 (i. e. 1602) (§ 19). Leaf 7b: blank. Leaf 8a: John Denman, before Ridgeway, March 13, 43 Elizabeth (i. e. 1602) (§ 20), duplicate of § 19. Leaf 8b: blank. Leaf 9a: John Galsworthie, April 8, 1602 (§ 33). Leaf 9b: blank. Leaf 10a: Alice Buttler, October 2, 1601 (§ 36), duplicate of §§ 1, 2. Leaf 10b: blank. Leaf 11a: Johan Baddaford, October 2, 1601 (§ 37), duplicate of §§ 3–5. Leaf 11b: blank. Leaf 12a: William Tompson and Elizabeth, his wife, October 2, 1601 (§§ 38, 39), duplicate of §§ 6, 7. Leaf 12b: blank. Leaf 13a: Christian Webbar, October 2, 1601 (§ 41), duplicate of §§ 8, 9. Leaf 13b: blank. Leaf 14a: Johan Davye, October 2, 1601 (§ 45), duplicate of § 10 [*bis*]. Leaf 14b: blank. Leaf 15a: John Denman, before Henry Hayward, October 2, 1601 (see below) (§ 46), duplicate of § 19 and § 20; Suzan Turke, October 2, 1601 (§ 47), duplicate of §§ 13–16 (there called Suzan Tooker). Leaf 15b: blank. Leaf 16a: Christofer Honywell, October 2, 1601 (§ 48), duplicate of § 10.

Thus it appears that there are duplicates of all the examinations but three (William Cozen, Johan Laishe, and John Galsworthie), and that John Denman's testimony appears thrice. Denman appears to have been first examined before Henry Hayward, mayor of Dartmouth. This examination is found on leaf 15a (§ 46). It is headed "Thexaminacon of John Denman of Kingsweare taken before *Sr. Thomas Ridgwaie Knight the second* daye of October, 1601. et Ao R Rne Eliz etc. xliijmo." But the words here italicized are crossed out, and another hand has interlined

"Henry Heyward Mayor of Dartmth." Since "the second" is included in the cancellation, the date is left doubtful. Ridgeway does not sign § 46, though his signature is appended to § 47 (Suzan Turke's examination), which follows on the same page. Denman was reëxamined, this time before Ridgeway, on March 13, 1601 (i. e. 1602), and of this examination we have two copies, both signed by Ridgeway, one on leaf 7a (§ 19), the other on leaf 8a (§ 20). There are slight variations among the three copies, and this is true of the duplicates in the case of the other witnesses.

The examinations are in two clerkly hands. One clerk wrote § 20 (Denman's examination, March 13, 1602) and § 33 (Galsworthie's examination, April 8, 1602). Another clerk wrote all the other examinations. All are dated October 2, 1601, except § 10 [*bis*] (Johan Davye, January 20, 1601 [*i. e.* 1602]), and the two just noted (§§ 20, 33, Denman and Galsworthie). Johan Davye's duplicate (§ 45) is dated October 2, 1601, though the other copy (§ 10 [*bis*]) bears date January 20, 1601 [1602].

That several examinations are lost is shown by the torn leaf (6), on the lower half of which must have stood § 18 (missing in the numbering), and also by the fact that there are no §§ 21–32, 34–35, 40, 42–44. Some of these missing sections, however, undoubtedly contained duplicates.

4. Potts, The Wonderfull Discoverie of Witches in the Countie of Lancaster, 1613.

5. Chaucer, Troilus, v, 505. Cf. iii, 890; v, 1174.

6. Calendar of State Papers, Domestic, 1667–1668, p. 4.

7. Thomas Heywood, Γυναικειον or Nine Bookes of Various History concerning Women, 1624, pp. 414–415. Cf. pp. 152ff., above.

8. Grundtvig, Danmarks Gamle Folkeviser, No. 28, I, 374. Since my version is a trifle free, I subjoin the original stanza (28):

> Ded ware denn for-gyldene snecke,
> der hand den liud feck:
> hun seigled i sønder di acker-strenge nie,
> och hun thill Ranelld geck.
> Wer du well-kommen! sagde Ranild.

9. Potts, The Wonderfull Discoverie of Witches, 1613, sig. S.

CHAPTER II

English Witchcraft Before 1558

1. G. L. Burr, The Literature of Witchcraft, reprinted from the Papers of the American Historical Association, New York, 1890, p. 238 (38). Cf. the same scholar's Preface to his Narratives of the Witchcraft Cases 1648–1706, 1914, pp. xv–xvi, xvii, note. For a discussion of Jewel and his assumed influence see Chapter XVI.

2. Joseph Hansen, Zauberwahn, Inquisition und Hexenprozess im Mittelalter und die Entstehung der Grossen Hexenverfolgung, 1900, p. 35. On *maleficium* see especially Hansen, pp. 9–14. Nothing could be truer than his words: "Wie viel auch immer im Laufe der Zeit in den Begriff der Zauberei und Hexerei hineingetragen worden ist, so ist doch sein Kern stets das

Maleficium geblieben. Aus dieser Vorstellung erwächst die angstvolle Furcht der Menschen und das Verlangen nach gesetzlichem Schutze und blutig strenger Strafe; von ihr hat die strafrechtliche Behandlung dieses Wahns ihren Ausgang genommen" (p. 9). "Das Maleficium, mit Ausnahme des Wettermachens, ist ohne alle Unterbrechung von der kirchlichen und bis in das 17. Jahrhundert auch von der staatlichen Autorität als Realität angenommen, seine Kraft ist nie ernstlich in Abrede gestellt worden; es bildet den roten Faden auch durch die Geschichte der strafrechtlichen Verfolgung" (pp. 13–14). Everybody knows that the most convincing evidence of witchcraft — short of confession or of denunciation by a confederate — was held to be threats followed by injury, the *damnum minatum* and the *malum secutum*. The difference between England and the Continent in the development of the witchcraft idea and in the history of prosecution is recognized by Hansen (p. 34), whose treatment of the whole subject is limited to Continental matters. President White in his Warfare of Science with Theology, 1896, I, 350 ff., also has his eye primarily on the Continent, like Professor Burr in The Literature of Witchcraft (note 1, above).

3. See Chapter XVI.

4. Scot, Dedication, ed. Nicholson, pp. xiii–xiv. Cf. xi, 15, pp. 203–205 (147–149), ed. Nicholson, pp. 164–165; xvi, 2, pp. 471–472 (340), ed. Nicholson, p. 397; xvi, 6, p. 483 (348), ed. Nicholson, p. 406. He thinks that he has so thoroughly refuted the writers on witchcraft that "they must coine new stuffe, or go to their grandams maids to learne more old wives tales, whereof this art of witchcraft is contrived" (xvi, 1, p. 470 [339], ed. Nicholson, p. 396). He looks backward to Catholic times for the English witch-creed, for it never occurs to him that it came in with the Marian exiles! See i, 8; ii, 10; vii, 15; xv, 39; pp. 16 (11), 35 (24), 152–153 (112–113), 462 (333), ed. Nicholson, pp. 13, 27, 123, 389. He testifies that professing witches abound, some of whom believe in their own powers. See i, 3, and iii, 9, pp. 7–9 (5–6), 52–53 (43), ed. Nicholson, pp. 5–7, 41. Cf. i, 2, and xv, 1, pp. 4 (3), 376–377 (265–266), ed. Nicholson, pp. 3, 313. See also Ady, A Candle in the Dark, 1656, p. 169: "Old Wives Fables, who sit talking and chatting of many false old Stories of Witches, and Fairies, and *Robin Good-fellow*, and walking Spirits, and the Dead walking again; all which lying fancies people are more naturally inclined to listen after than to the Scriptures." Cf. Bernard, A Guide to Grand-Iury Men, 2d ed., 1629, pp. 11, 23–25, 75. A typical example may be seen in Bacon's letter of May 15, 1619, in which he asks Sir Thomas Leigh and Sir Thomas Puckering to investigate a case: "Being informed by the petition of Mr. Thomas Porten, a poor Yorkshireman, of a heavy accident by fire, whereby his house, his wife, and a child, together with all his goods, were utterly burnt and consumed, which misfortune the petitioner suggests (with much eagerness) was occasioned by the wicked practices and conjurations of one John Clarkson . . . and his daughter (persons of a wandering condition); affirming, for instance, that one Mr. Hailes of Warwick did take from the said Clarkson certain books of conjuration and witchcraft," etc. (Life and Letters, ed. Spedding, VII, 30–31). For an admirable study of the attitude of

the folk toward all varieties of witchcraft see U. Jahn, Baltische Studien, XXXVI (1886), 171–207.

5. Gaule, Select Cases of Conscience touching Witches and Witchcrafts, 1646, pp. 85–86.

6. Toland, Letters to Serena, 1704, Letter I, The Origin and Force of Prejudices, pp. 4–5.

7. "Il est rare que, dans chaque village, on n'accuse pas quelque vieille femme bien laide d'être *mpamo vavy;* c'est elle qui cause tous les malheurs et toutes les maladies; elle est crainte et détestée, les enfants fuient à son approche et les grandes personnes ne l'abordent qu'avec terreur. Elle est l'objet de toutes les haines, mais personne n'ose le lui faire sentir, par crainte des ses représailles" (Bénévent, Étude sur le Bouéni, Colonie de Madagascar, Notes, Reconnaissances et Explorations, Revue Mensuelle, 1st Year, 1897, II, 56).

8. "Diesen *abarosi* . . . genannten Hexen und Schwartzkünstlern wird zunächst die Schuld zugeschoben, wenn ein Mensch erkrankt oder stirbt, wenn Unwetter die Felder verwüstet, wenn Vieh verunglückt oder von Seuchen befallen wird, wenn Weiber unfruchtbar bleiben, Kinder missraten, Diebstähle vorkommen usw." (Hans Meyer, Die Barundi, 1916, p. 133).

9. For the *virus lunare* see Lucan, Pharsalia, vi, 669, which Steevens quotes to illustrate the "vaporous drop profound" in Macbeth, iii, 5.

10. "Suivant les circonstances, indifféremment, il [le sorcier] opère pour le bien ou pour le mal, il guérit, il soulage, il sème l'espérance, dispense le dictame de la consolation, il donne l'amour, et le rompt, lie les forces de la génération, infuse l'amitié, la modifie ou la développe, dessèche les adversaires en leur inculquant des langueurs ou des maux; il déprave les uns, rend complices les autres, influe sur les gens, les bêtes, les choses et les éléments en les mettant à son service. Il fait descendre la lune écumante dans les herbes, remplit de mirages l'air et la terre, de fantômes la nuit; il suggère, illusionne, il crée les factices merveilles" (Mauchamp, La Sorcellerie au Maroc, pp. 201–202). Cf. van der Burgt, Un Grand Peuplade de l'Afrique Équatoriale, 1904, p. 55; Claridge, Wild Bush Tribes of Tropical Africa, 1922, pp. 170–185; Crooke, Religion and Folklore of Northern India, 1926, pp. 421–422; Sir J. M. Campbell, The Indian Antiquary, XXIX (1900), 46–56.

11. Perkins, A Discourse of the Damned Art of Witchcraft, 1608, p. 128. Cf. Orchard, The Doctrine of Devils, 1676, pp. 53, 63; Nider, Formicarius, v, 3, ed. 1517 (1516), fol. lxxiii v°; Ulrich Molitoris, De Lamiis et Phithonicis Mulieribus, 1489.

12. Tallqvist, Die Assyrische Beschwörungsserie Maqlû, I, 15–19, and *passim.* Cf. Pike, History of Crime in England, I, 33–34; Reitzenstein, Hellenistische Wundererzählungen, 1906, p. 83.

13. See Brie, Englischen Studien, XLI (1910), 20–27.

14. Council of Clovesho (A.D. 747), canon 3 (Haddan and Stubbs, Councils, III [1871], 363–364): "prohibens et inter caetera peccamina paganas observationes, id est, divinos, sortilegos, auguria, auspicia, fylacteria, incantationes, sive omnes spurcitias impiorum gentiliumque errata." On the

whole matter of Anglo-Saxon witchcraft and magic see the extensive collections of Jente, Die Mythologischen Ausdrücke im Altenglischen Wortschatz (Anglistische Forschungen, ed. Hoops, LVI), 1921, pp. 235–271 ("Los und Weissagung"), 272–338 ("Zauber").

15. Laws of Alfred, Introduction, § 30: "gealdorcræftigan and scinlæcan and wiccan" (Liebermann, Die Gesetze der Angelsachsen, I, 38–39; Thorpe, Ancient Laws, folio, 1840, p. 23). The word *wiccan* undoubtedly includes both genders, as is often true of "witch" in later English.

16. Edward and Guthrum, § 11 (Liebermann, I, 134; Thorpe, p. 74): "wiccan oððe wigleras, mansworan oððe morðwyrhtan oððe . . . horcwenan." The Quadripartitus (ca. 1114) translates by "sortilege uel incantatrices, periuri et uenefici uel mortem facientes, . . . meretrices" (Liebermann, I, 135).

17. Æthelred, vi, 7: "wiccan oððe wigeleras, scincræftcan oððe horcwenan, morðwyrhtan oððe mansworan" (Liebermann, I, 248; Thorpe, p. 135). The eleventh-century paraphrase reads, "incantatores autem, magos, phithonicos et ueneficos necne idolorum cultores" (Liebermann, I, 249). In its version of Æthelred, vi, 28 (a clause which does not mention witchcraft, unless this is included under the general terms *morðweorcum* and *swiccræftan*), the same paraphrase specifies *necromantię, sortilegia, idolatrię, maleficia,* and *ueneficia* (Liebermann, I, 254–255).

18. For *scin, scincræft, scinlæca,* etc., see Jente, pp. 155–161.

19. Cnut, ii, 4a: "wiccean oððe wigleras, morðwyrhtan oððe horcwenan" (Liebermann, I, 310; Thorpe, p. 162). The Latin versions (Liebermann, I, 311) have: "sage uel incantatrices, ueneficę aut murdri operarii uel meretrices" (Quadripartitus, ca. 1114); "incantatores et incantatrices et malefici aut . . . meretrices" (Instituta Cnuti, ca. 1100); "uenefici aut magi uel latrones homicide siue meretrices" (Consiliatio Cnuti, ca. 1125). Cnut, i, 5 (Liebermann, I, 284; Thorpe, p. 155), speaks of a priest's being accused of "evil arts" (*uncræftum*), which suggests black magic. Here the Instituta has "de latrocinio aut de incantatione uel de huiusmodi re"; the Consiliatio, simply "calumpnia et uicio."

20. For this clause utilized by preachers see anonymous homilies in Napier's Wulfstan, 1883, pp. 114–115, 309; cf. pp. 26–27 (genuine Wulfstan), 203–204, 298 (cf. Brotanek, Texte und Untersuchungen, 1913, pp. 51–52). See Liebermann, III, 175, 202.

21. Edmund, i, 6 (Synod of London): "ða ðe . . . liblac wyrcað" (Liebermann, I, 186; cf. III, 124, § 9a; Thorpe, p. 105). A homilist exhorts us to beware of *liblacas* and *attorcræftas* (Napier, Wulfstan, p. 290; cf. pp. 135, 253).

22. Blickling Homilies, ed. Morris, 1880, p. 61: "þa scinlæcan þa þe galdorcræftas and gedwolan begangaþ, and mid þæm unwære men beswicaþ and adwellaþ, and hi aweniaþ from Godes gemynde mid heora scinlacum and gedwolcræftum." Cf. p. 63: "þæm mannum þe gedwolcræftas begangaþ." See a similar passage in Ælfric's Homilies, ed. Thorpe, II (1846), 330; in the same (II, 592), drycræft and wiccecræft are included in a list of chief sins (cf. Napier's Wulfstan, pp. 135, 253, 290).

23. De Antichristo (Napier's Wulfstan, p. 194). This Anglo-Saxon homily is in the main translated from the Libellus de Antichristo written before 954 by Adso, afterwards Abbot of Montier-en-Der. For the present passage (cf. 2 Thessalonians, ii, 9-10; Matthew, xxiv, 24) see the Libellus in Migne, XL, 1132; CI, 1293; Haupt's Zeitschrift, X, 267. Cf. Pseudo-Bede, Sibyllinorum Verborum Interpretatio, Migne, XC, 1185; Hincmar, De Praedestinatione II, cap. 27, Opera, 1645, I, 215 (Migne, CXXV, 280). See also St. Augustine on Psalm IX, cap. 24 (Opera, IV [1835], 78), and De Civitate Dei, xx, 20 (VI [1838], 960); Bede, Explanatio Apocalypsis, ii, 13 (Migne, XCIII, 169). On Adso's tract (which has been wrongly ascribed to Alcuin and Rabanus Maurus) see von Zezschwitz, Vom Römischen Kaisertum, 1877, pp. 36-43, 155; W. Meyer, Der Ludus de Antichristo, 1882, pp. 3-4; Preuss, Die Vorstellungen vom Antichrist, 1906, pp. 17, 277. On Antichrist's magical education, etc., see Malvenda, De Antichristo, 1604, ii, 22, pp. 105-106; v, 5, p. 249; vi, 4, pp. 319-320; vii, 20, pp. 392-393. Adso's Libellus is also the source of the account of Antichrist in The Prick of Conscience, vv. 4047-4622, ed. Morris, 1863, pp. 110-126 (for his education by witches and magicians see vv. 4211-4216); also of that in the Cursor Mundi, vv. 21971-22426, ed. Morris, pp. 1256-1283 (see vv. 22111-22116).

24. See Chapter XV, note 21.

25. Excommunicatio V, § 2 (Liebermann, I, 435): *maleficium*.

26. Ritual II, § 4 (ninth or tenth century), Liebermann, I, 407 ("aut per herbas uel quaecunque temptamenta siue molimina maleficiosa"); Ritual IV, § 4 (ninth century), I, 410-411 ("per aliquid maleficium aut per herbas maleficas et diabolicas"; "ðerh hvoelc yfelwoerc oððe ðerh wyrto yfelwyrcendo and diovblica"); Ritual XII, §§ 17, 19 (eleventh or twelfth century), I, 421 ("per aliqua maleficia aut per herbas diabolica arte infectas"; "per aliquod maleficium aut per herbas terre").

27. Good King Josiah, Ælfric tells us (Lives of Saints, xviii, 461-465, ed. Skeat, I, 412-413), forsook heathenism "and destroyed the *wiccan* and drove out the *wigleras* and cast down *drycræft*" (see 2 Kings, xxiii, 24).

28. Cnut, ii, 5 (Liebermann, I, 312; Thorpe, p. 162). For well-worship and witchcraft at springs see pp. 33-34, above.

29. Canons of Edgar, § 16 (Thorpe, p. 396). See Liebermann, I, 313; II, 742, s. v. *Zauber*, § 1a. The canon mentions well-worship, stone-worship, necromancy (*licwiglunga*), sortilege (*hwata*), spells (*galdra*), etc. One manuscript (Thorpe, p. 396, note 5) mentions also the passing of a child through the earth (see p. 31, above).

30. Liebermann, II, 503, s. v. *Heidentum*, § 11; II, 587, s. v. *Mord*, § 4a.

31. Laws of the Northumbrian Priests, § 48 (Liebermann, I, 383; Thorpe, p. 419); cf. § 54 for wells, trees, and stones.

32. See references in York Powell's Introduction to Elton's Saxo, 1894, pp. lxxvii-lxxx. For evidence from the sagas see The Antiquary, XLII (1906), 106-110; Folk-Lore, XVII (1906), 421-426.

33. See Liebermann, II, 587, s. v. *Mord*, §§ 3b-4b. Cf. Cnut, ii, 56 (Liebermann, I, 348; Thorpe, p. 175, § 57), with Leges Henrici, lxxi, 1-1a

(Liebermann, I, 590; Thorpe, p. 251). Modern cases of death ascribed to witchcraft may be noted from Lincolnshire ca. 1850 (Lincolnshire Notes and Queries, II [1891], 233), Devonshire in 1875 (Transactions Devonshire Association, VII [1875], 261; The Reliquary, XVIII [1877–78], 146), Somerset in 1883 and 1887 (Elworthy, The West Somerset Word-Book, p. 548), Suffolk in 1890 (Folk-Lore, VI [1895], 119), and Yorkshire in 1904 (Folk-Lore, XV [1904], 463–464).

34. Æthelstan, ii, 6: "be þam wiccecræftum ond be liblacum ond be morðdædum, gif mon þær acweald wære," etc. (Liebermann, I, 152–155; Thorpe, p. 86, i, 6).

35. Modus Imponendi Poenitentiam, § 37 (Thorpe, p. 409): "Gif hwa oðerne mid wiccecræfte fordo, fæste .vii. gear." Cf. Pseudo-Theodore, xxvii, 9 (Thorpe, p. 292); Pseudo-Cummean, vii (ix), 1 (Schmitz, II, 626). On Cummean see Zettinger, Archiv für Katholisches Kirchenrecht, LXXXII (1902), 501–540.

36. The Anglo-Saxon Confessional of Pseudo-Ecgbert, § 29 (Thorpe, p. 355), after prescribing (a) the graduated penance to be undergone by a woman who practises "drycræft and galdor and unlibban," goes on to impose (b) seven years' penance if she kills anybody "mid hire unlybban." The first part of this (a) agrees with Theodore as represented by Discipulus Umbrensium, i, 15, 4 (Haddan and Stubbs, Councils, III, 190; Schmitz, II, 556), with Pseudo-Bede-Ecgbert, ii, 30, 2 (Schmitz, II, 694), and with Pseudo-Cummean, vii (ix), 12 (Schmitz, II, 627); cf. Schmitz, II, 237, 496. Both parts (a and b) are found in Excarpsus Ecgberti, vii, 6–7 (Haddan and Stubbs, III, 424; Schmitz, II, 667), in Pseudo-Bede-Ecgbert, ii, 15, 3 (Schmitz, II, 690–691), and (separated) in Pseudo-Theodore (xxvii, 13, and xxi, 6, Thorpe, pp. 292, 288), which explain *arte sua malefica* (the cause of death) by "id est per poculum aut per artem aliquam."

37. Pseudo-Ecgbert, Anglo-Saxon Penitential, iv, 16 (Thorpe, p. 379), agreeing almost word for word with Modus Imponendi Poenitentiam, § 37 (Thorpe, p. 409). See note 35, above.

38. The origin and history of these penitentials need not here detain us. Whether they developed from Celtic and Anglo-Saxon usage or otherwise, they were certainly well-known in England long before the Norman Conquest. See also penitentials in Schmitz, I, 307, 378, 413, 429–430, 683; II, 181, 236, 296, 320, 324, 334, 351, 360, 377.

39. Vinnianus, § 18 (Schmitz, I, 504); Columbanus, § 6 (Schmitz, I, 597).

40. See notes 35 and 36, above.

41. Leges Henrici, lxxi (Liebermann, I, 590; Thorpe, p. 251): "Si quis ueneno uel sortilegio uel inuultuacione seu maleficio aliquo faciat homicidium, siue illi paratum sit siue alii, nichil refert, quin factum mortiferum et nullo modo redimendum sit . . . Si autem insortiatus non fuerit mortuus, set cutis uariationem uel probabilem corporis contrahat egritudinem, emendetur sapientum antiquis diffinicionibus, sicut acciderit." This is, in effect, as Liebermann notes, from Lex Ribuaria, cap. 83 (Monumenta, Leges, V, 265).

42. Modus Imponendi Poenitentiam, § 38 (Thorpe, p. 409); Pseudo-Ecgbert, Anglo-Saxon Poenitentiale, iv, 17 (Thorpe, p. 379). See pp. 74–75, above.

43. See Chapter III.

44. On these *strigae* or *lamiae* see Hansen, Zauberwahn, pp. 58–61, 84–85, 132–140. On witchcraft and sorcery in old Germanic laws see Vordemfelde, Die Germanische Religion in den Deutschen Volksrechten (Religionsgeschichtliche Versuche und Vorarbeiten, XVIII, i), 1923, pp. 125–149.

45. See references to Frankish, Alamannic, and Lombard laws in Hansen, Zauberwahn, pp. 58–59.

46. Haddan and Stubbs, Councils, II, ii (1878), 329.

47. Corrector, § 170 (Schmitz, II, 446).

48. Cnut's Proclamation of ca. 1020, § 15, Liebermann, I, 274 ("morð-slagan and mansworan and wiccan and wælcyrian"; cf. III, 189); interpolation (?) in Wulfstan's famous Sermo ad Anglos (Napier, p. 165: "wiccan and wælcerian"); anonymous homily (Napier, p. 298: "wyccan and wæl-cyrian and unlybwyrhtan").

49. Cf. Golther, Munich Academy, Abhandlungen, Philosophisch-Philologische Classe, XVIII, ii (1889), 401–438; the Same, Handbuch der Germanischen Mythologie, 1895, pp. 109–116.

50. Wright and Wülcker, Anglo-Saxon and Old English Vocabularies, 1884, I, 360, 3; 527, 17; 417, 12; 347, 32; 533, 26; 189, 11. *Gorgoneus* is explained by *wælkyrginc* in the Anglo-Saxon De Rebus in Oriente Mirabilibus, x, ed. Knappe, 1906, p. 49. The name of the goddess Venus in Aldhelm's "Veneris stuprorum amatricis" (De Laudibus Virginitatis, cap. 47, ed. Giles, p. 62; ed. Ehwald, p. 301) is glossed by *gydene, wælcyrie* (Napier, Old English Glosses, 1900, p. 115, line 4449). *Hægtes(se)*, the same word as the German *Hexe*, is used to gloss *striga* and *Pythonissa* and *Erinnys* and *Furia* and *Eumenides* and *Parcae* (Wright and Wülcker, I, 48, 18; 188, 33; 392, 18 [cf. 19, 33]; 404, 33; 404, 34; 533, 21; 392, 19; 189, 12). *Parcarum* is glossed by *wyccena* and *wiccyna* (Napier, p. 159, line 137; p. 166, line 113).

51. Pseudo-Theodore, xxvii, 20 (Thorpe, p. 293); Pseudo-Cummean, vii (ix), 7 (Schmitz, II, 626). Cf. Burchard, x, 28. See also Schmitz, I, 303, 414, 683; II, 238, 296, 322, 325, 329, 336, 343, 346, 353, 362, 496; cf. II, 425.

52. Modus Imponendi Poenitentiam, § 39 (Thorpe, p. 409): "Gif hwa wiccige ymbe oðres lufe and hym sylle on æte oþþe on drince oþþe on galdorcræftum." Cf. Cockayne, Leechdoms, I, xliv–xlv.

53. Pseudo-Ecgbert, Anglo-Saxon Penitential, iv, 18 (Thorpe, pp. 379–380); Pseudo-Theodore, xxvii, 10 (Thorpe, p. 292: cf. Summa de Judiciis, i, 58, Schmitz, II, 484); Pseudo-Cummean, vii (ix), 2 (Schmitz, II, 626). See also Schmitz, I, 306, 429–430, 462, 504 (Finnian), 597 (Columban), 683; II, 236, 296, 320, 324, 334, 342, 351, 360, 425. For the use of semen see Theodore as represented by Discipulus Umbrensium, i, 14, § 15 (Schmitz, II, 555), by the Canones Gregorii, § 191 (Schmitz, II, 541), by the Poenitentiale Sangallense Tripartitum, ii, 26 (Schmitz, II, 184), and by Capitula Judiciorum, xxiii, 2 (Schmitz, II, 241); Pseudo-Theodore, xvi, 30 (Thorpe,

p. 282); Pseudo-Ecgbert, Anglo-Saxon Confessional, § 29 (Thorpe, p. 355); Pseudo-Cummean, i (iii), 36 (adds blood, Schmitz, II, 608). Cf. other penitentials in Wasserschleben, Die Bussordnungen der Abenländischen Kirche, 1851, pp. 560 (adds "urinam vel stercus"), 692 (adds "alia sortilegia vel causas illicitas"); Schmitz, I, 314, 382, 413, 453, 683 (adds blood), 749 (adds blood); II, 356, 366, 445. For menstrual blood see Schmitz, I, 459; II, 448 (cf. I, 683); Schönbach, Vienna Sitzungsberichte, Philosophisch-Historische Classe, CXLII (1900), No. 7, p. 133; cf. De Groot, The Religious System of China, IV (1901), 397–398. Compare the tasting of a husband's blood as a remedy: Theodore as represented by Discipulus Umbrensium, i, 14, § 16 (Schmitz, II, 555), by the so-called Canones Gregorii, § 190 (Schmitz, II, 541), by the Capitula Judiciorum, xxiii, 2 (Schmitz, II, 241), by the Poenitentiale Sangallense Tripartitum, ii, 37 (Schmitz, II, 184); Pseudo-Ecgbert, Anglo-Saxon Confessionale, § 31 (Thorpe, p. 356); Pseudo-Theodore, Poenitentiale, xvi, 31 (Thorpe, p. 282); Pseudo-Cummean, i (iii), 35 (Schmitz, II, 608). See also Schmitz, I, 413, 453, 691.

54. Ælfric, Lives of Saints, xvii, 157–161, ed. Skeat, I, 374.

55. Ælfric's Homilies, ed. Thorpe, II (1846), 412–419. See Pseudo-Abdias, De Historia Certaminis Apostolici, iv, 2–4, ed. 1566, foll. 41–47r⁰ (Fabricius, Codex Apocryphus Novi Testamenti, 1719, I, 517–521).

56. Ælfric's Homilies, II, 472–477. See Acta Sanctorum, September 21, VI, 221–223.

57. Ælfric, II, 482–491. See Pseudo-Abdias, vi, 7–20, ed. 1566, foll. 75–81 (Fabricius, I, 608–629).

58. Ælfric, I, 370–383. See Pseudo-Abdias, i, 6–18, ed. 1566, foll. 5v⁰–13 (Fabricius, I, 411–437). Cf. Ælfric's Lives of Saints, ed. Skeat, I, 372.

59. Ælfric's Homilies, I, 454–469. See Pseudo-Abdias, ed. 1566, foll. 97–101 r⁰ (Acta Sanctorum, August 25, V, 34–37).

60. On the whole matter see the large collections of Jente, pp. 235–271.

61. Soothsayers (wigleras): Laws of Edward and Guthrum, ca. A.D. 921–940, § 11 (Liebermann, I, 134; Thorpe, p. 74); Æthelred, ca. A.D. 1008, vi, 7 (Liebermann, I, 248; Thorpe, p. 135); Cnut, ca. A.D. 1030, ii, 4a (Liebermann, I, 310; Thorpe, p. 162). — So-called Canons of Edgar, § 16 (Thorpe, p. 396: lic-wiglunga, hwata, on mislicum gewiglungum); Cnut, ii, 5 (Liebermann, I, 312; Thorpe, p. 162: on blote [var. hlote] oððon fyrhte), based on Canons of Edgar, § 16; Law of Northumbrian Priests, ca. A.D. 1028–1060, § 48 (Liebermann, I, 383; Thorpe, p. 419: on blot oððe on firhte), based on Cnut, ii, 5 (cf. Old Norse ganga til fréttar, Gering, Ueber Weissagung und Zauber im Nordischen Altertum, 1902, pp. 7–8); Pseudo-Ecgbert, Anglo-Saxon Poenitentiale, ii, 23 (Thorpe, p. 371: idele hwatunga, tida hwatinga), from Halitgar, iv, 26, Schmitz, II, 285 (both mention astrological observations and the use of spells in herb-gathering); the Same, iv, 19 (Thorpe, p. 380: hlytas, hwatunga); Dialogus Ecgberti, § 15 (Thorpe, p. 323; Haddan and Stubbs, III, 410). See the canon of the Council of Clovesho, A.D. 747 (note 14, above). Cf. Ælfric's Homilies, ed. Thorpe, I (1844), 100, 102; Old English Homilies, ed. Morris, 1873, II, 11. Augury, divination, soothsay-

ing, and consultation of those who practise these arts are forbidden in the
Penitential of Pseudo-Theodore, xxvii, 6, 11 (agreeing with Pseudo-Cummean, vii [ix], 3 and 5, Schmitz, II, 626) and 23 (Thorpe, pp. 292, 293), and
in a multitude of other penitentials in terms that agree substantially with
Pseudo-Theodore, xxvii, 6 and 11 (see Schmitz, I, 310, 414, 462; II, 181,
236, 296, 321, 324, 328, 335, 342–343, 352–353, 361, 377, 378). See also
Excarpsus Ecgberti, viii, 4 (Haddan and Stubbs, III, 424; Schmitz, II,
668), agreeing with Pseudo-Bede-Ecgbert, ii, 30, § 3³ (Schmitz, II, 695);
Pseudo-Bede-Ecgbert, i, 18 (Schmitz, II, 682). Cf. Capitularia Regum
Francorum, ed. Boretius, I (1883), 25, 45; Epistolae Merowingici et Karolini Aevi, ed. Dümmler, I (1892), 351. The *sortes sanctorum* and *sortes* in
general are forbidden in Pseudo-Theodore, xxvii, 12 (Thorpe, p. 292), in
Pseudo-Cummean, vii (ix), 4 (Schmitz, II, 626), and in many other manuals (see Schmitz, I, 327–328, 379, 414, 462, 684; II, 181, 236, 296, 321, 324,
328, 336, 343, 347, 353, 361, 378; cf. Concilia Aevi Merovingici, ed. Maassen, 1893, pp. 9, 180, Monumenta, Leges, Sect. III, Vol. I; Homilia de
Sacrilegiis, ed. Caspari, 1886, pp. 7, 21–23). The Arundel Penitential, § 91
(Schmitz, I, 462), styles them also "so-called *sortes patriarcharum vel apostolorum*" (cf. Grillando, De Sortilegiis, i, 2, ed. 1592, p. 2); the Poenitentiale Parisiense, § 20, mentions their use in hunting and fishing (Schmitz, I,
684). As from "Theodorus" the Summa de Judiciis, vii, 16 (Schmitz, II,
496), specifies forty days' penance for those who seek to learn the future
"in tabulis" or "in codicibus," who presume to use *sortes* in the psalter or
the gospel or otherwise, or to observe divinations, adding, however, the remark "Brocardus x dies." The passage comes in the main from Burchard's
Decretum, x, 26: see also x, 27, and Corrector, § 67 (Schmitz, II, 425: cf.
Wasserschleben, p. 707; Schmitz, I, 463). For *sortes Homericae* and *Virgilianae* see Sir Thomas Browne, Pseudodoxia Epidemica, v, 24, 7, Works, ed.
Wilkin, 1852, II, 97–98. For Ὁμηρομαντεία see British Museum Papyrus
CXXI (Kenyon, I, 83–89); cf. Philologus, LXXII (1913), 552–556. Theodore, as represented by Discipulus Umbrensium, i, 15, § 4 (Haddan and
Stubbs, III, 190; Schmitz, II, 556: accepted as genuine by Liebermann, II,
728, s. v. *Wahrsagung*), penalizes women's "incantationes vel divinationes
diabolicas" and goes on to quote (inexactly) the 24th canon of the Council
of Ancyra (A.D. 314), which imposes heavy penance on "οἱ καταμαντευόμενοι καὶ ταῖς συνηθείαις τῶν ἐθνῶν ἐξακολουθοῦντες ἢ εἰσάγοντές τινας εἰς
τοὺς ἑαυτῶν οἴκους ἐπὶ ἀνευρέσει φαρμακειῶν ἢ καὶ καθάρσει," or, according to the paraphrase of Isidorus Mercator, those who "auguria, vel
auspicia, sive somnia vel divinationes quaslibet secundum morem Gentilium observant" or bring into their houses men of this kind "in exquirendis
aliquibus arte malefica, aut ut domos suas lustrent" (Mansi, Concilia, II
[1759], 521, 534, cf. 522, 275–528; Hefele, Conciliengeschichte, 2d ed., I
[1873], 241–242). This canon is quoted also by Pseudo-Theodore (xxvii,
17, Thorpe, p. 293), by Halitgar (iv, 25, cf. 27, Schmitz, II, 284, 285), by
Pseudo-Cummean (Excarpsus, vii [ix], 16, Schmitz, II, 627), and elsewhere (see Schmitz, I, 379, 431, 683; II, 236, 422; Wasserschleben, p. 291).
The Excarpsus Ecgberti, viii, 1 (Haddan and Stubbs, III, 424; Schmitz, II,
667), like Pseudo-Bede-Ecgbert, ii, 30, § 3 (Schmitz, II, 694), couples the

employment of *sortes sanctorum* with "quarumcumque scripturarum inspectione." On lots and soothsaying see Jente, pp. 235–271.

62. Wizards and soothsayers (*wiccan* and *wigleras*) are threatened with hell-pains by Wulfstan (ed. Napier, 1883, pp. 26–27). Another homily copies him with some variation (Napier, pp. 203–204). Still another (Napier, p. 309) copies either Æthelred, vi, 7, or Cnut, ii, 4a, which are practically identical (see Liebermann, III, 175, 202). Ælfric associates idolatry with witchcraft and soothsaying: "to bysmorfullum deofolgylde ne to wiccecræfte ne to wiglungum" (Assmann, Angelsächsische Homilien und Heiligenleben, 1889, p. 28); cf. an anonymous homily in Assmann, p. 143; Sermo de Baptismate, Napier's Wulfstan, p. 40 ("Ne gyman ge galdra ne idelra hwata ne wigelunga ne wiccecræfta; ne weorðian ge wyllas," etc.). A homily ascribed to Ælfric condemns those who divine in any way, whether by animals or by birds: "þa þe on ænegum þingum wigliað, oððe be nytenum oððe be fugelum" (Brotanek, Texte und Untersuchungen, 1913, p. 20). The Latin source reads "omnes qui caragios et divinos vel praecantores aut propter se aut propter suos inquirunt" (Brotanek, p. 107): it is a Latin sermon extant in a tenth-century manuscript written in England (Brotanek, pp. 103–104). See also Ælfric, Lives of Saints, xvii, 88–123, ed. Skeat, I, 370–373 (auguries from birds, sneezes, horses, dogs; in wiving, travelling, brewing, etc.; Jamnes and Mambres, Simon Magus: partly from Pseudo-Augustine, Sermon 278, § 1, Migne, XXXIX, 2269; cf. Pseudo-Augustine, De Rectitudine Catholicae Conversationis, cap. 5, Migne, XL, 1172). Cf. Excarpsus Ecgberti, viii, 4 (Haddan and Stubbs, III, 424; Schmitz, II, 668), and Pseudo-Bede-Ecgbert, ii, 30, § 3 (Schmitz, II, 695), which condemn "caraios et divinos praecantatores": see also Schmitz (I, 234, 568, 581), who cites canon 4 of the Synod of Auxerre, ca. A.D. 573–603 (Concilia Aevi Merovingici, ed. Maassen, 1893, p. 180). Pseudo-Theodore's Penitential, xxvii, 24 (Thorpe, p. 293), mentions "divinos vel praecantatores" but not "caraios."

63. Napier's Wulfstan, p. 171. Cf. Pseudo-Augustine, Sermon 265, Migne, XXXIX, 2238–2239.

64. Ælfric, Lives of Saints, xvii, 75–81, ed. Skeat, I (1881), 368–370 (from Pseudo-Augustine, Sermon 278, De Auguriis, § 1, Migne, XXXIX, 2269); xvii, 124–128, I, 372 (Sermon 278, § 3, XXXIX, 2270). Cf. Sermon 279, § 4, XXXIX, 2272.

65. Theodore as represented by Discipulus Umbrensium, i, 15, § 2 (Haddan and Stubbs, III, 190; Schmitz, II, 556), by the Poenitentiale Sangallense Tripartitum, ii, 34 (Schmitz, II, 184), by the Canones Gregorii, § 116 (Schmitz, II, 535), by the Capitula Judiciorum, xvi, 4 (Schmitz, II, 237); Pseudo-Theodore, Poenitentiale, xxvii, 14 (Thorpe, p. 292); Pseudo-Ecgbert, Anglo-Saxon Confessionale, § 33 (Thorpe, p. 356); Excarpsus Ecgberti, viii, 2 (Haddan and Stubbs, III, 424; Schmitz, II, 667); Pseudo-Bede-Ecgbert, i, 34 (Schmitz, II, 682); Summa de Judiciis, vii, 10 (Schmitz, II, 496: "Beda"); Pseudo-Cummean, vii (ix), 14 (Schmitz, II, 627). See also Schmitz, I, 316, 464, 684, 749; II, 365, 430; Wasserschleben, Bussordnungen, 1851, p. 543; Burchard, x, 14 (Migne, CXL, 835: "Beda"). Cf. Dieterich, Mutter Erde, 3d ed., 1925, pp. 8–12; Samter, Geburt, Hochzeit

und Tod, 1911, p. 55; Zeitschrift des Vereins für Volkskunde, XXV (1915), 228–241 (the roof in folk-lore); Korrespondenzblatt des Vereins für Siebenbürgische Landeskunde, XXIII (1900), 145 (oven).

66. Canons of Edgar, § 16 (Thorpe, p. 396, note 5); Pseudo-Ecgbert, Anglo-Saxon Poenitentiale, iv, 20 (Thorpe, p. 380). See also an anonymous sermon in Assmann, Angelsächsische Homilien und Heiligenleben, 1889, p. 143; Ælfric's Lives of Saints, ed. Skeat, I (1881), 374. Cf. Hauksbók, ed. 1892–96, p. 167; Corrector, § 179 (Schmitz, II, 448); Schmitz, I, 464; Jente, pp. 57–58, 306–307. Compare the use of a bramble of which both ends grow in the ground (Leechdoms, II, 290, 292). See Chapter VII, note 92.

67. See note 53, above.

68. See p. 143, above.

69. Pseudo-Theodore, xxvii, 26 (Thorpe, p. 293).

70. Theodore as represented by Discipulus Umbrensium, i, 15, § 4 (Haddan and Stubbs, III, 190; Schmitz, II, 556); Pseudo-Theodore, xxvii, 13 (Thorpe, p. 292); Excarpsus Ecgberti, vii, 6 (Haddan and Stubbs, III, 424; Schmitz, II, 667); Pseudo-Ecgbert, Anglo-Saxon Confessionale, § 29 (Thorpe, p. 355: *drycræft, galdor, unlibban*); Pseudo-Bede-Ecgbert, ii, 15, § 3, and 30, § 2 (Schmitz, II, 691, 694); Pseudo-Cummean, vii (ix), 12 (Schmitz, II, 627). See also Burchard, x, 24; Schmitz, II, 237, 496; Wasserschleben, p. 282.

71. Pseudo-Ecgbert, Anglo-Saxon Poenitentiale, ii, 23 (Thorpe, p. 371), forbids the gathering of herbs with any spell (*galdre*) except Pater Noster and Creed. This is from Halitgar, iv, 26 (Schmitz, II, 285); cf. Summa de Judiciis, vii, 13 (Schmitz, II, 496). Cf. Ælfric, Homilies, ed. Thorpe, I, 476. See also Pseudo-Augustine, De Rectitudine Catholicae Conversationis, cap. 5, Migne, XL, 1172; Corrector, § 65 (Schmitz, II, 424); Burchard, x, 20, Migne, CXL, 836; Schmitz, II, 338, 344, 497. For such spells see Leechdoms, I, 120, 314; II, 154; III, 30–37 (cf. I, 318; II, 116, 138); Marcellus Burdigalensis, ed. Niedermann (Corpus Medicorum Latinorum, V), xxv, 13, p. 189; cf. A. Franz, Die Kirchlichen Benediktionen, 1909, I, 395–396, 421. On Anglo-Saxon superstitions about plants see Hoops, Ueber die Altenglischen Pflanzennamen, 1889, pp. 41–67.

72. *Ligaturae:* Pseudo-Bede-Ecgbert, ii, 39, § 1 (Schmitz, II, 696); Pseudo-Theodore, Poenitentiale, xxvii, 22 (Thorpe, p. 293); practically the same (though sometimes corrupted) in Schmitz, II, 296, 322, 325, 329, 343; fuller ("Si quis ligaturas per herbas vel quolibet ingenio malo incantaverit et super Christianum ligaverit"), Schmitz, I, 312; II, 353, 362. Cf. Corrector, § 63 (Schmitz, II, 423–424; cf. I, 463); Wasserschleben, pp. 545, 707. On the custom see Schmitz, I, 312–314; II, 306–307. — *Fylacteria:* Council of Clovesho (A.D. 747), § 3 (Haddan and Stubbs, III, 364); Excarpsus Ecgberti, viii, 4 (Haddan and Stubbs, III, 424; Schmitz, II, 668); Pseudo-Bede-Ecgbert (Wasserschleben's Pseudo-Bede, p. 272), ii, 30, § 3 (Schmitz, II, 695); Pseudo-Theodore, Poenitentiale, xxvii, 8, 24 (Thorpe, p. 293). Cf. Corrector, § 92 (Schmitz, II, 429). See, for amulets, Leechdoms, I, 326, 328; II, 138, 140. Cf. A. Franz, II, 435–438; Homilia de Sacrilegiis, ed. Caspari, 1886, pp. 9–10, 11, 29–30, 39–40; Ælfric, Homilies, ed.

Thorpe, I, 476; Pseudo-Augustine, Sermon 265, Migne, XXXIX, 2239; Pseudo-Augustine, De Rectitudine Catholicae Conversationis, cap. 5, Migne, XL, 1172; Eitrem, Ein Christliches Amulett auf Papyrus (Forhandlinger i Videnskapsselskapet i Kristiania, 1921).

73. Bede, Letter to Ecgbert (Haddan and Stubbs, III, 316); Legatine Synod, A.D. 787 (the same, III, 448); Canons of Edgar, §§ 17, 22 (Thorpe, pp. 396, 397); Ecclesiastical Institutes (Thorpe, p. 477); Napier's Wulfstan, p. 307; Brotanek, Texte und Untersuchungen, 1913, pp. 25, 127; Cnut, i, 22 (Liebermann, I, 302; Thorpe, pp. 159–160); Ælfric, Lives of Saints, ed. Skeat, I, 280.

74. See Homilia de Sacrilegiis, ed. Caspari, 1886, pp. 9, 27–29; Martin of Bracara, De Correctione Rusticorum, ed. Caspari, 1883, p. 35; Burchard, x, 49; Schmitz, II, 338, 344, 497. Cf. Klapper, Das Gebet im Zauberglauben des Mittelalters, Mittheilungen der Schlesischen Gesellschaft für Volkskunde, IX, ii, Heft 18 (1907), pp. 5–41; Lyndewoode, Constitutiones Provinciales, 1st ed., ca. 1480, sig. giiij, lf. 3v°.

75. Bede, Historia Ecclesiastica, iv, 25 (27), ed. Plummer, I, 269; cf. II, 266.

76. On spells see Hälsig, Der Zauberspruch bei den Germanen, 1910. Prayers for the benediction of herbs were, of course, permissible, and we have several specimens from Anglo-Saxon times. See, for example, Cockayne, Leechdoms, III, 79–80; Leonhardi, Kleinere Angelsächsische Denkmäler, I (1905), 154–155. Cf. Ælfric, Homilies, ed. Thorpe, I, 476: "Ne sceal nan man mid galdre wyrte besingan, ac mid Godes wordum hi geblestian, and swa ðicgan."

77. Salomon and Saturn, ed. Kemble, 1848, pp. 140–143; ed. Wülker, Bibliothek, III, ii (1898), 63–65 (309–311). Cf. Schipper, Germania, XXII (1877), 56; von Vincenti, Die Altenglischen Dialoge von Salomon und Saturn (Münchener Beiträge, XXXI), I (1904), 56–58. On the profane use of ave, pater, etc., in curative spells and the addition or intermixture of other words or characters see Grillando, De Sortilegiis, i, 2, ed. 1592, p. 2; vi, 21–22, pp. 81–82.

78. Ed. Kemble, p. 144; ed. Wülker, III, ii, 66 (312).

79. See especially Grendon, Journal of American Folk-Lore, XXII (1909), 105–237; Brie, Mitteilungen der Schlesischen Gesellschaft für Volkskunde, VIII, xvi (1906), 1–36; J. F. Payne, English Medicine in the Anglo-Saxon Times, 1904; Singer, Proceedings British Academy, 1919–1920, pp. 341–374. Cf. A. Franz, Die Kirchlichen Benediktionen, 1909; Kögel, Geschichte der Deutschen Literatur, I, i (1894), 77–95.

80. Leechdoms, II, 112–115; III, 10.

81. Leechdoms, I, 330–333, 394; II, 54. Cf. The Book of Cerne, ed. Kuypers, 1902, Appendix, pp. 207, 223; Jörimann, Frühmittelalterliche Rezeptarien (Beiträge zur Geschichte der Medizin, ed. Sigerist, I), 1925, p. 13.

82. Leechdoms, I, 312–315. Cf. I, 170; II, 154, 336; Franz, I, 294–334.

83. Leechdoms, I, 202, 312–315; II, 112–115; III, 10, 30–37. Cf. II, 142–145, 328. For herbs and other things that drive or keep snakes away or make one snake-proof, see I, 92, 166, 198, 208, 242–245, 252, 276, 280,

338, 366. See also p. 146. Cf. Franz, I, 294–334; II, 171–175; Bang, Norske Hexeformularer, 1901, pp. 164–165, 168, 169, 174–175, 527; W. de Gray Birch, An Ancient Manuscript, 1889, p. 90; Jörimann, p. 74.

84. Leechdoms, I, 312, 360, 372. Cf. I, 92, 170; Franz, II, 139–170.

85. Leechdoms, I, 98, 112, 120, 214, 312–315, 332, 386–389, 393–394; II, 112, 136–141, 290–293, 322, 344–353; III, 8–15, 24, 30–43, 52–57, 62, 64–71, 74, 288–291, 294–295; Haupt's Zeitschrift, XXXI (1887), 45–52. Cf. Franz, II, 124–140, 399–615.

86. Leechdoms, II, 76, 104, 142, 144, 306, 318; III, 52, cf. 68. See Chapter III, note 144.

87. See pp. 133, 147, 215, 218. For herbs that thwart evil charms, protect one against witches and wizards, and are *fuga daemonum*, see Leechdoms, I, 102 (evil eye), 176, 190, 224, 248, 312; cf. I, 318, 360, 364. For clear mention of witches and wizards or their malefic charms see I, 102, 190, 398, 402; II, 138, 298, 306, 342 (cf. Grendon, pp. 212–213, 236); III, 36, 52, 54, 295. Cf. Jörimann, pp. 28, 29, 30, 31, 53; Revue des Langues Romanes, V, 103–105.

88. Leechdoms, I, 392; III, 64. Cf. I, 218–221, 266. See Franz, II, 186–208.

89. Leechdoms, II, 328; III, 66–69. Cf. I, 330; II, 10, 114, 306.

90. Leechdoms, I, 314; II, 154; III, 30–37. Cf. I, 318; II, 116, 138. Cf. Franz, I, 393–421; Corpus Medicorum Latinorum, IV (1927), 11, 166–167, 231, 295–298; Schönbach, Vienna Sitzungsberichte, Philosophisch-Historische Classe, CXLII (1900), No. 7, pp. 140–148.

91. Leechdoms, I, 395 (cf. Singer, Proceedings British Academy, 1919–1920, pp. 360–363), 398–405. Cf. Franz, I, 361–393. See pp. 171–172.

92. Leechdoms, I, 384; cf. I, 96–99, 397. Cf. von Steinmeyer, Die Kleineren Althochdeutschen Sprachdenkmäler, 1916, pp. 396–397; Franz, II, 135–137; Ebermann, Bienensegen, Festschrift Eduard Hahn, 1917, pp. 332–344.

93. Leechdoms, I, 388–391; II, 154. Cf. I, 102, 176; Franz, II, 261–289; Hyde, The Religious Songs of Connacht, II, 50–55; Ivens, Melanesians of the South-East Solomon Islands, 1927, pp. 331–333.

94. Leechdoms, I, 302, 308, 326, 390. Cf. Franz, II, 1–123.

95. Leechdoms, I, 312–315; III, 290.

96. Leechdoms, I, 384, 390–393, 396; III, 58, 60, 286–289. Cf. Franz, II, 139–140. See Chapter XI.

97. Leechdoms, I, 328; III, 154. Cf. Franz, II, 299–300.

98. Cockayne, III, 36 (*malscrung*); Wülker, Bibliothek, I, 320–323; Grendon, pp. 192–193 (cf. pp. 226–229); Skemp, Modern Language Review, VI (1911), 300–301; Singer, Proceedings British Academy, 1919–1920, pp. 353–357.

99. Cockayne, I, 402 (witchcraft against crops); Wülker, I, 315; Grendon, pp. 176–177. — Cockayne, II, 138–141 (*leodrune*, "sorceress," "witch"); Leonhardi, p. 42; Grendon, pp. 202–203, 233. — Cockayne, I, 190, from Herbarium Apuleii ("if any evil-working person bespells [*begalep*] another through any malice"). — Cockayne, II, 298 (drycræft); Leonhardi, p. 90; Grendon, pp. 200–201, 232. — Cockayne, II, 306 (*wip*

.. *malscra and yflum gealdorcræftum*); Leonhardi, p. 94; Grendon, pp. 200–201, 232. — Cockayne, II, 342 (*wiþ wifgemædlan*); Leonhardi, p. 104; Grendon, pp. 212–213, 236. — Cockayne, III, 52, 54 (ða mihtigan wif; hægtesse); Wülker, I, 317–318; Grendon, pp. 164–165, 214–215.

100. Cockayne, II, 346; Leonhardi, p. 105.

101. Leechdoms, ed. Cockayne, I, 78, 82, 92–96, 108, and *passim*; II, 110–115 (Leonhardi, pp. 33–35), 142–145 (Leonhardi, p. 43; Grendon, pp. 199, 231), 328 (Leonhardi, p. 100); III, 30–37 (Wülker, I, 320–323; Grendon, pp. 190–195).

102. Salomon and Saturn, i, 152–154, ed. Kemble, 1848, pp. 143–144; Wülker, III, ii (1898), 66 (312).

103. Johannes Sarisburiensis, Policraticus, i, 13, Leyden ed., 1595, p. 42. Cf. St. Augustine, De Doctrina Christiana, ii, 20, 30: "Ad hoc genus pertinent omnes etiam ligaturae atque remedia, quae medicorum quoque disciplina condemnat," etc.

104. Charms and spells. Eleventh century: Napier, Herrig's Archiv, LXXXIV (1890), 323. — Twelfth century: Zupitza, Haupt's Zeitschrift, XXXI (1887), 45–52; Priebsch, Modern Language Review, XVII (1922), 81 (thief); Das Herbarium Apuleii, ed. Berberich (Anglistische Forschungen, ed. Hoops, V), 1902, pp. 95, 118, 120–121; M. R. James, Catalogue of MSS., Gonville and Caius College, II (1908), 431. — Thirteenth century: Yorkshire Archæological Journal, XVII (1903), 402–404, 407–408; M. R. James, Catalogue, as above, II, 444 (rats and mice). — Fourteenth century: Henslow, Medical Works of the Fourteenth Century, 1899, pp. 32–33, 71–72, 144–145; Holthausen, Anglia, XIX (1897), 78–85; Harland and Wilkinson, Lancashire Folk-Lore, 1867, p. 77; Arderne, Practica de Fistula, ed. Power, 1910, pp. 102–104; the Same, De Arte Phisicali et de Cirurgia, ed. Power, 1922, pp. 6, 32; Archæologia, XXX (1844), 420. — Fifteenth century: Reliquiae Antiquae, 1845, I, 126–127, 315; Priebsch, Haupt's Zeitschrift, XXXVIII (1894), 14; Förster, Anglia, XLII (1918), 217–219; Ein Mittelenglisches Medizinbuch, ed. Heinrich, 1896; Sloane MSS., Scott's Index, s. v. *Magic*. — Sixteenth century: Holthausen, Anglia, XIX (1897), 87–88; J. G. Nichols, Narratives of the Days of the Reformation, pp. 326–329; Halliwell, Popular Rhymes and Nursery Tales, 1849, p. 207. — Seventeenth century: Rye, Norfolk Archæology, XIV (1901), 131–132; McBryde, Modern Language Notes, XXI (1906), 181–182 (thief); Folk-Lore, XXI (1910), 376–378; Archæological Journal, XXIX (1872), 75–76 (mad dog); Transactions Cumberland and Westmorland Antiquarian and Archæological Society, New Series, XII (1912), 82–85; Sloane MSS., Scott's Index, s. v. *Magic*. — Eighteenth century: Transactions Cumberland and Westmorland Antiquarian and Archæological Society, 1st Series, XIV (1897), 371–372; The Reliquary, XXIII (1882–83), 198–201; Dawson, History of Skipton, 1882, pp. 392–395; Cowper, Hawkshead, 1899, pp. 314–315. — Nineteenth century: Transactions Lancashire and Cheshire Antiquarian Society, XXVII (1910), 105–107 (cattle, house, nightmare, fairies, wealth and health, etc.).

105. I. For the regular St. Peter charm for toothache (with slight variations in some instances, as "at the gates of Jerusalem" instead of "on a

marble stone") see Leechdoms, ed. Cockayne, I, 394; III, 64; Anzeiger für Deutsches Alterthum, XV (1889), 145; J. F. Payne, English Medicine in the Anglo-Saxon Times, 1904, p. 129; Ebermann, Blut- und Wundsegen (Palaestra, XXIV), 1903, pp. 19–22; Heinrich, Ein Mittelenglisches Medizinbuch, 1896, pp. 102–103; Brie, Mitteilungen der Schlesischen Gesellschaft für Volkskunde, VIII, ii (1906), 25–26; Hälsig, Der Zauberspruch bei den Germanen, 1910, pp. 46–47, 79–80; Haupt's Zeitschrift, XXVII (1883), 308; William Carr, The Dialect of Craven, 1828, II, 264; Digby MS. 86, fol. 30, Notes and Queries, 11th Series, XI (1915), 294; W. G. Black, Folk-Medicine, 1883, p. 77; Halliwell, Popular Rhymes and Nursery Tales, 1849, p. 212; Köhler, Germania, XIII (1868), 178–184 (Kleinere Schriften, III [1900], 544–552); Northall, English Folk-Rhymes, 1892, p. 135; Henderson, The Folk-Lore of the Northern Counties, 1879, p. 172; Harland and Wilkinson, Lancashire Folk-Lore, 1867, pp. 75–76; Burne and Jackson, Shropshire Folk-Lore, p. 183; Hewett, Nummits and Crummits, 1900, p. 67; Baring-Gould, Devonshire Characters, 1908, p. 77; Leather, The Folk-Lore of Herefordshire, 1912, pp. 74–76; E. M. Wright, Rustic Speech and Folk-Lore, 1913, p. 249; Denham Tracts, II (1895), 9–10; Hammond, A Cornish Parish, 1897, p. 353; E. Owen, Welsh Folk-Lore, pp. 264–265; Trevelyan, Folk-Lore and Folk-Stories of Wales, 1909, p. 227; Couch, The History of Polperro, 1871, p. 148; A. W. Moore, The Folk-Lore of the Isle of Man, 1891, p. 98; Gregor, The Folk-Lore of the North-East of Scotland, 1881, p. 48; J. G. Campbell, Witchcraft and Second Sight in the Highlands and Islands of Scotland, 1902, pp. 69–70; Celtic Magazine, XIII (1888), 40; Alexander Macdonald, Story and Song from Loch Ness-side, 1914, p. 181; Polson, Our Highland Folklore Heritage, 1926, p. 33; Douglas Hyde, The Religious Songs of Connacht, II, 58–61 (Patrick for Peter in one version); Journal of American Folk-Lore, VIII (1895), 287 (Bergen, Current Superstitions, 1896, p. 96; Knortz, Der Menschliche Körper in Sage, Brauch und Sprichwort, 1909, p. 136); Notes and Queries, 1st Series, I (1850), 293, 349, 397, 429; III (1851), 20, 259; X (1854), 221; 2d Series, XII (1861), 501 (cf. 7th Series, V [1888], 262); Bye-Gones for 1876–77, pp. 300, 305, 314, 339; for 1888, p. 79; for 1895–96, p. 438; Journal of the British Archæological Association, XXXIV (1878), 329–330; Proceedings Dorset Natural History and Antiquarian Field Club, XIII (1892), 50; XXXV (1914), 82; Transactions Devonshire Association, XXXII (1900), 92; Folk-Lore Record, I (1878), 40; Folk-Lore Journal, II (1884), 33, 94–95; V (1887), 201; Folk-Lore, VI (1895), 203; XV (1904), 196–197, 350; XVI (1905), 167; Müllenhoff and Scherer, Denkmäler Deutscher Poesie und Prosa, 2d ed., 1873, pp. 466–467 (3d ed., 1892, II, 281); Zeitschrift des Vereins für Volkskunde, I (1891), 175; VI (1896), 91–92, 195–196; Gaster, Ilchester Lectures, 1887, pp. 85–86; Leland, Gypsy Sorcery, pp. 38–39; Bang, Norske Hexeformularer og Magiske Opskrifter (Videnskabssellskabet i Christiania), 1901, No. 133, p. 68 ("a man" instead of Peter). Cf. the charm in Sloane MS. 1580, fol. 44 v°.

The Virgin Mary may replace St. Peter in this or a similar charm. See Leather, The Folk-Lore of Herefordshire, 1912, pp. 75–76; Archæologia Cambrensis, 7th Series, III (1923), 172–173; Mitteilungen der Schlesischen

Gesellschaft für Volkskunde, IX, xviii (1907), 10; Haupt's Zeitschrift, XXXVIII (1894), 16; The Physicians of Myddvai (Meddygon Myddfai), ed. Pughe and Williams, 1861, § 804, pp. 276-277, 453-454 (Bye-Gones for 1876-77, p. 319). So may our Lord's brother, St. James. See Hunt, Popular Romances of the West of England, 1865, II, 215 (3d ed., 1881, p. 414); Black, Folk-Medicine, p. 77; cf. Courtney, Cornish Feasts and Folk-Lore, 1890, p. 149 (Peter is our Lord's brother: so in Folk-Lore Journal, V [1887], 201). Job occurs instead of Peter in a Swedish version: Hyltén-Cavallius, Wärend och Wirdarne, I (1863), 416-417; cf. Skrifter utgivna av Svenska Litteratursällskapet i Finland, XCI (1910), 209; Klemming, Läke- och Örte-Böcker, 1883-84, pp. 227, 228. The person afflicted at the moment supersedes St. Peter in an English variant: Bye-Gones for 1897-98, pp. 233-234. St. Apollonia is invoked in like manner in a related charm that occurs frequently in Romance countries. See Wolf, Beiträge zur Deutschen Mythologie, I (1852), 260; Köhler, Germania, XIII (1886), 180-181; Archivio per lo Studio delle Tradizioni Popolari, IV (1885), 261 (cf. Zanetti, La Medicina delle Nostre Donne, 1892, p. 180); Mélusine, III (1886), 114; Revue des Traditions Populaires, I (1886), 36; Bulletin de Folklore, II (1893-95), 5-6; Sauvé, Le Folk-Lore des Hautes-Vosges, 1889, pp. 35-36; Meyrac, Traditions des Ardennes, 1890, p. 179; Cabanès and Barraud, Remèdes de Bonne Femme, 1907, p. 281; Marin, Cantos Populares Españoles, I (1882), 445. For her connection with toothache see: Legenda Aurea, cap. 66, ed. Grässe, 1850, p. 294; Bale, Select Works (Parker Society), p. 498; Munday, The English Romayne Lyfe, 1582, p. 38 (Bodley Head Quartos, XII); Reginald Scot, Discourse upon Divels, chap. 24, p. 528 (378), ed. Nicholson, p. 443; Archæologia, XXX (1844), 397-398; Anglia, XIX (1897), 84; British Museum Add. MS. 37787, fol. 131 (Catalogue 1906-1910, p. 147); Heinrich, as above, pp. 148-149; Bang, Norske Hexeformularer, 1901, No. 1087, p. 482; Revue Celtique, VI (1883-85), 73-74; Laisnel de la Salle, Le Berry, I (1900), 391; Zanetti, La Medicina delle Nostre Donne, 1892, p. 180; Bartsch, Sagen, Märchen und Gebräuche aus Meklenburg, II (1880), 427; Fossel, Volksmedicin und Medicinischer Aberglaube in Steiermark, 2d ed., 1886, pp. 109-110; Baumgarten, Aus der Volksmässigen Ueberlieferung der Heimat, Linz, 1864, I, 127; Ons Volksleven, III (1891), 62; van Andel, Volksgeneeskunst in Nederland, 1909, pp. 232, 239; A. De Cock, Volksgeneeskunde in Vlaanderen, 1891, pp. 168-169; Archivio per lo Studio delle Tradizioni Popolari, V (1886), 271; Biblioteca de las Tradiciones Populares Españolas, I (1883), 269-270.

II. A related toothache spell, in which St. Peter stands (usually) under an oak and our Lord bids him take water in his mouth, is common in German. See Wolf, Beiträge zur Deutschen Mythologie, I (1852), 255, § 11 (cf. § 13, I, 255-256); Peter, Volksthümliches aus Oesterreichisch-Schlesien, II (1867), 238; Lammert, Volksmedizin und Medizinischer Aberglaube in Bayern, 1869, p. 237; Dunger, Rundâs und Reimsprüche aus dem Vogtlande, 1876, p. 277; Neunzig Geheimnisse, Cologne chapbook, undated, p. 6; Baltische Studien, XXXVI (1886), 307-308; Alemannia, XV (1887), 123; XXV (1898), 130; Zeitschrift für Volkskunde, I (1889), 36-37 (*Loth* for *Peter* in one version); II (1890), 201; Zeitschrift für Oester-

reichische Volkskunde, II (1896), 156; Niederlausitzer Mittheilungen, IV
(1896), 296; Blätter für Pommersche Volkskunde, V (1897), 26; Zeitschrift des Vereins für Volkskunde, VIII (1898), 201; Wuttke, Der Deutsche Volksaberglaube der Gegenwart, ed. Meyer, 1900, p. 172 (cf. p. 352:
Job instead of *Peter*); E. H. Meyer, Badisches Volksleben, 1900, p. 571;
Kleeberger, Volkskundliches aus Fischbach i. d. Pfalz, 1902, p. 53; Zeitschrift des Vereins für Rheinische und Westfälische Volkskunde, II (1905),
285; IX (1912), 150 (cf. VIII [1911], 68); Drechsler, Sitte, Brauch und
Volksglaube in Schlesien, II (1906), 301–302; E. John, Aberglaube, Sitte
und Brauch im Sächsischen Erzgebirge, 1909, p. 107; Seyfarth, Aberglaube
und Zauberei in der Volksmedizin Sachsens, 1913, p. 110 (cf. p. 111: Jakob
cures Joseph); Manz, Volksbrauch und Volksglaube des Sarganserlandes,
Schriften der Schweizerischen Gesellschaft für Volkskunde, XII (1916), 57.
The Virgin replaces St. Peter in a variant in Blätter für Pommersche
Volkskunde, V (1897), 25; so also in a Norwegian variant in Bang, Norske
Hexeformularer, 1901, No. 227, p. 130 (other varieties, Nos. 214 [Job], 235
[a sick man], 237 [Rube], pp. 120, 134, 135). Job and Josaphat are the in-
terlocutors in a version in Mitteilungen des Vereins für Anhaltische
Geschichte und Altertumskunde, VI (1893), 599. For a similar spell in which
St. Jost is the sufferer and in which worms are mentioned see: Kuhn's
Zeitschrift, XIII (1864), 146–147; Germania, XIII (1868), 182; Bartsch,
Sagen, Märchen und Gebräuche aus Meklenburg, II (1880), 427; Der Ur-
Quell, Neue Folge, I (1897), 281.

III. Almost identical with (2), but representing Job as complaining of
scurvy or the like, is another German charm. See Rank, Aus dem Böhmer-
walde, 1843, pp. 275–276 (1851, I, 161–162); Wolf, Beiträge zur Deutschen
Mythologie, I (1852), 256; E. Meier, Deutsche Sagen, Sitten und Gebräuche aus Schwaben, 1852, pp. 523–524; Grohmann, Aberglaube und
Gebräuche aus Böhmen und Mähren, 1864, pp. 174–175; A. Peter, Volksthümliches aus Oesterreichisch-Schlesien, II (1867), 229; Fossel, Volksmedicin und Medicinischer Aberglaube in Steiermark, 2d ed., 1886, pp.
108–109; Am Ur-Quell, I (1890), 170; Alemannia, XXV (1898), 129;
Wuttke, Der Deutsche Volksaberglaube der Gegenwart, ed. Meyer, 1900,
p. 173; Zeitschrift des Vereins für Rheinische und Westfälische Volkskunde, VIII (1911), 67–68; Seyfarth, Aberglaube und Zauberei in der
Volksmedizin Sachsens, 1913, p. 111 (Job's child for Job). St. James
(Jakob) sometimes replaces Job in this charm. See Mittheilungen der
Geschichts- und Alterthumsforschenden Gesellschaft des Osterlandes, VII
(1874), 450; Baltische Studien, XXXVI (1886), 272–273; Zeitschrift für
Volkskunde, II (1890), 162–163; Zeitschrift des Vereins für Rheinische und
Westfälische Volkskunde, II (1906), 285; Seyfarth, Aberglaube und Zau-
berei in der Volksmedizin Sachsens, 1913, p. 111. Cf. Germania, XVII
(1872), 75–76.

IV. St. Peter is the patron in a fever charm which resembles the regular toothache formula. See Archæologia, XXX (1844), 400–401; Anglia,
XIX (1897), 79–80; Haupt's Zeitschrift, XXXVIII (1894), 16–17; Heinrich, Ein Mittelenglisches Medizinbuch, 1896, pp. 166–167, 220–221;
Klemming, Läke- och Örte-Böcker, 1883–86, pp. 39–40; Brie, Mitteilungen

der Schlesischen Gesellschaft für Volkskunde, VIII, ii (1906), 26. For a similar charm for *la teigne* (St. Paul or St. Peter) see Revue des Traditions Populaires, I (1886), 37; Cabanès and Barraud, Remèdes de Bonne Femme, 1907, p. 277.

V. For a very curious thief-charm which has some relation to this group see Dunger, Rundâs und Reimsprüche aus dem Vogtlande, 1876, pp. 283–284; Knoop, Volkssagen aus dem Oestlichen Hinterpommern, 1885, p. 170. Cf. also the Sicilian wolf charm in Zeitschrift für Romanische Philologie, XXXII (1908), 580–583.

Among the miracles of St. Cuthbert is registered the relief of a dreadful toothache that had defied both charms and medicines: Reginald, Libellus de Admirandis S. Cuthberti Virtutibus, cap. 130, ed. Raine (Surtees Society, I), pp. 278–279.

106. Theodore as represented by Discipulus Umbrensium, i, 15, § 1 (Haddan and Stubbs, III, 189; Schmitz, II, 556; cf. Burchard, x, 12), by Canones Gregorii, § 115 (Schmitz, II, 535), by Capitula Judiciorum, xvi, 4 (Schmitz, II, 237: Vatican MS. 1349 reads "in minimis causis idest ad fontes vel ad arbores"); Pseudo-Theodore, xxvii, i (Thorpe, p. 292); Ecgbert, Anglo-Saxon Confessionale, § 32, Thorpe, p. 356 ("Gif man medmycles hwæt-hwega deoflum onsægð, fæste he .i. gear; gif he mycles hwæt onsecge, fæste .x. winter"); Excarpsus Ecgberti, iv, 12 (Haddan and Stubbs, III, 420; Schmitz, II, 664); Pseudo-Bede-Ecgbert, ii, 29 (Schmitz, II, 694); Pseudo-Cummean, vii (ix), 13 (Schmitz, II, 627). Sacrifice to devils, without distinction as to the grade of the offence, is punished in the laws of King Wihtræd of Kent (A.D. ca. 695) by a fine (*healsfang*) or by forfeiture of all one's cattle; in the case of a slave, the culprit must make amends to his lord with six shillings or with "his hide," i. e. with a flogging (§§ 12, 13; Liebermann, I, 13; cf. II, 503, s. v. Heidentum, § 5; II, 621, s. v. Prügel; Thorpe, p. 18).

107. Canons of Edgar, § 16 (Thorpe, p. 396); Cnut, ii, 5 (Liebermann, I, 312; Thorpe, p. 162); Laws of Northumbrian Priests, § 54 (Liebermann, I, 383; Thorpe, pp. 419–420); Pseudo-Ecgbert, Anglo-Saxon Poenitentiale, ii, 22 (Thorpe, p. 371), and iv, 19 (Thorpe, p. 380); Pseudo-Bede-Ecgbert, i, 18 (Schmitz, II, 682); Pseudo-Theodore, xxvii, 18 (Thorpe, p. 293); Pseudo-Cummean, vii (ix), 6 (Schmitz, II, 626); Ælfric, Lives of Saints, xvii, 129–142, ed. Skeat, I, 372–375 (Pseudo-Augustine, Sermon 278, Migne, XXXIX, 2271: cf. Sermon 265, XXXIX, 2239, and the pseudo-Augustinian De Rectitudine Catholicae Conversationis, cap. 5, Migne, XL, 1172–1173); Ælfric's Homilies, ed. Thorpe, I, 474; homily in Brotanek, Texte und Untersuchungen, 1913, p. 20, cf. pp. 107, 125–126; Napier's Wulfstan, p. 40; anonymous homily, Assmann, Angelsächsische Homilien und Heiligenleben, 1889, p. 143. Cf. Burchard, x, 2, 10, 21, 32; Schmitz, I, 330, 379, 412, 462, 683, 748; II, 181, 237, 296, 321, 324, 328, 335, 336, 343, 353, 361, 378, 424, 430; Grimm, Deutsche Mythologie, 4th ed., I (1875), 484–492; Weinhold, Die Verehrung der Quellen in Deutschland (Berlin Academy, Abhandlungen, 1898), pp. 29–69; Jente, Die Mythologischen Ausdrücke im Altenglischen Wortschatz, 1921, pp. 56–57; R. M. Garrett, Precious Stones in Old English Literature (Münchener Beiträge, XLVII),

1909, pp. 79–82. For councils see Schmitz, I, 330–331; Fournier, Revue d'Histoire et de la Littérature Religieuses, VI (1901), 307; Concilia Aevi Merovingici, ed. Maassen, 1893, pp. 133, 179. Cf. Leechdoms, III, 74. Compare eating and drinking *juxta fanum*: Pseudo-Theodore, xxvii, 2, Thorpe, p. 292 (it is sacrilege and *mensa demoniorum*); Pseudo-Cummean, vii (ix), 10 (Schmitz, II, 627; cf. II, 296, 354, 363); cf. Vordemfelde, Die Germanische Religion in den Deutschen Volksrechten (Religionsgeschichtliche Versuche und Vorarbeiten, XVIII, i), 1923, pp. 64–67. For festivals "in locis abhominandis gentilium" (forbidden by the Council of Ancyra, A.D. 314) see Pseudo-Theodore, xxvii, 5 (Thorpe, p. 292; cf. xlii, 2, p. 300), and cf. Schmitz, I, 303; II, 296, 354, 362.

108. Wulfstan, ed. Napier, pp. 11–12; cf. anonymous homily, p. 303.

109. Cf. Robin Hood and the Potter, and parallel stories (Child, The English and Scottish Popular Ballads, III, 108–115).

110. Gesta Herewardi, in the Rolls ed. of Gaimar, Lestorie des Engles, pp. 384–385, 388–390.

111. Cf. Journal British Archæological Society, XXXII (1876), 60–64; Papers and Proceedings, Hampshire Field Club and Archæological Society, II (1894), 56.

112. Hope, The Legendary Lore of Holy Wells in England, 1893. Cf. The Reliquary, II (1861–62), 126–136; Proceedings Society of Antiquaries of Scotland, XXVI (1892), 63–65; Archæologia Cambrensis, 1st Series, I (1846), 50–54, 184, 466; 4th Series, III (1872), 262; 5th Series, VIII (1891), 8–16.

113. Archæologia Cambrensis, 3d Series, III (1857), 214; IV (1858), 205–206; Bye-Gones for 1888, pp. 47–48, 68; for 1899–1900, pp. 425–426, 431; for 1903–04, p. 197.

114. Hope, pp. 71, 76, 83, 92–93, 107–108, 142, 143, 145, 185, 199.

115. Registrum Roberti Mascall, ed. Parry (Canterbury and York Series, XXI), pp. 74–75.

116. Warkworth's Chronicle, ed. Halliwell (Camden Society), 1839, pp. 24–25.

117. The Travels of Dr. Richard Pocock through England, ed. Cartwright (Camden Society, New Series, XLIV), II, 54. Cf. Archæologia Cambrensis, 6th Series, IX (1909), 71.

118. Visitations, Raine, The Fabric Rolls of York Minster (Surtees Society, XXXV), p. 273. I have corrected the punctuation.

119. Bale, A Comedy concernynge Three Lawes, of Nature, Moses, and Christ, vv. 406–543, ed. Schröer, Anglia, V (1882), 172–174. Since the character Idolatry represents in Bale's mind, in some respects, the Roman Catholic Church, he mixes up a number of the rites or practices of the old faith with the current notions about witchcraft, but this need not confuse us.

120. Child, Four Old Plays, 1848, pp. 74–82. The source of Thersytes is a Latin dialogue by Ravisius Textor, but this episode is not in the source: see Holthausen, Englische Studien, XXXI (1902), 89.

121. Leechdoms, II, 38, 114, 120–127, etc.; Kuhn's Zeitschrift, XIII (1864), 135–151; Müllenhoff and Scherer, Denkmäler, 3d ed., 1892, II,

281; Höfler, Archiv für Religionswissenschaft, II (1899), 98–100, 155–158; A. Franz, Die Kirchlichen Benediktionen, 1909, II, 402–403, 415.

122. A Series of Precedents and Proceedings . . . from Act-Books of Ecclesiastical Courts in the Diocese of London, by Wm. Hale Hale, Archdeacon of London, 1847.

123. Hale, pp. 15–16.

124. Hale, p. 3: "utitur incantacionibus sortilegiae pro febribus."

125. Hale, p. 102.

126. Hale, pp. 107–108.

127. See Chapter IV, notes 140–149.

128. Hale, p. 108. Compare the Anglo-Saxon method of curing an elf-shotten horse, which involves striking him on the back with a rod (Leechdoms, ed. Cockayne, II, 290; ed. Leonhardi, I, 88).

129. Raine, Historiae Dunelmensis Scriptores Tres (Surtees Society, IX), Appendix, p. ccccxl.

130. Durham Depositions, ed. Raine, pp. 29, 33.

131. Arundel MS. 146, Aungier, The History and Antiquities of Sion Monastery, 1840, p. 259.

132. Lincoln Diocese Documents, ed. A. Clark (Early English Text Society, XXXV), pp. 259, 260. For midwives' charms see pp. 114–115, above.

133. Visitations and Memorials of Southwell Minster, ed. Leach (Camden Society, New Series, XLVIII), p. 15.

134. Visitations, in Raine, The Fabric Rolls of York Minster (Surtees Society, XXXV), pp. 259, 260. For midwives' charms see pp. 114–115, above.

135. Collectanea Anglo-Premonstratensia, ed. Gasquet (Royal Historical Society, Camden Third Series, XII), III, 117–118. On the distinction made cf. Pererius, Adversus Fallaces et Superstitiosas Artes, i, 14, ed. 1603, p. 101.

136. 3 Henry VIII, chap. xi (Statutes of the Realm, III [1817], 31–32).

137. Lincoln Episcopal Visitations, Peacock, Archæologia, XLVIII (1885), 262. Cf. the charm "Drei falsche Zungen haben dich geschossen," etc., well-known on the Continent: Wolf, Beiträge zur Deutschen Mythologie, I (1852), 256–257; Zeitschrift für Volkskunde, II (1890), 160–161; Zeitschrift für Oesterreichische Volkskunde, II (1896), 149–150.

138. Potts, The Wonderful Discoverie of Witches, 1613, sigg. E2 v°–E3 r°. See pp. 170–171, above.

139. Macbean, Kirkcaldy Burgh Records, 1908, p. 343; County Folk-Lore, VII (1914), 109.

140. Dalyell, The Darker Superstitions of Scotland, 1834, pp. 23, 27.

141. Notes and Queries, 1st Series, X (1854), 221.

142. Skelton, The Tunnyng of Elynour Rummyng, vv. 447–458. Cf. the celebrated Anglo-Saxon charm "for a sudden stitch" in Leechdoms, III, 52–55.

143. Hooper, A Declaration of the Ten Holy Commaundmentes, Early Writings, ed. Carr (Parker Society), 1843, pp. 328–329.

144. Cf. Lammert, Volksmedizin, 1869, pp. 128–134; Seyfarth, Aberglaube und Zauberei in der Volksmedizin Sachsens, 1913, pp. 17–21; Ger-

mania, XXXII (1887), 460; Zeitschrift für Deutsche Philologie, XL (1908), 433; Alemannia, XXVI (1898), 71–72; Hälsig, Der Zauberspruch bei den Germanen, 1910, pp. 92–96; von Steinmeyer, Die Kleineren Althochdeutschen Sprachdenkmäler, 1916, pp. 370–375; Anzeiger für Deutsches Altertum, XL (1921), 97; Klemming, Läke- och Örte-Böcker, 1883–86, pp. 227, 228, 308–309; Archivio per lo Studio delle Tradizioni Popolari, VII (1888), 569.

145. Grimm, Deutsche Mythologie, 4th ed., II, 1030–1031; Golther, Handbuch der Germanischen Mythologie, 1895, pp. 382–385. See for many variants (most of them Christianized) O. Ebermann, Blut- und Wundsegen (Palaestra, XXIV), 1903, pp. 1–24. Cf. Christiansen, Die Finnischen und Nordischen Varianten des Zweiten Merseburgerspruches (FF Communications, Vol. II, No. 18), 1915 (cf. Ohrt, Danske Studier, XIII [1916], 189–193); Hästesko, Motivverzeichnis Westfinnischer Zaubersprüche (FF, No. 19), p. 5; Transactions Devonshire Association, XXII (1900), 92. I find it impossible to accept the theory that the Second Merseburg Spell is a Christian charm decked out with names of pagan gods. See further, Hälsig, Der Zauberspruch bei den Germanen, 1910, pp. 75–79; R. M. Meyer, Haupt's Zeitschrift, LII (1910), 390–396; K. Krohn, Göttingische Gelehrte Anzeigen, CLXXIV (1912), 212–217; von Steinmeyer, Die Kleineren Althochdeutschen Sprachdenkmäler, 1916, pp. 365–370; Grienberger, Beiträge zur Geschichte der Deutschen Sprache und Literatur, XLV (1921), 232–234; Mackel, Jahrbuch des Vereins für Niederdeutsche Sprachforschung, XLVII (1921), 54–56; Ohrt, Trylleord (Danmarks Folkeminder, No. 25), 1922, pp. 77–80; Preusler, Beiträge zur Deutschkunde (Siebs Festschrift), 1922, pp. 39–45; Wrede, Berlin Academy, Sitzungsberichte, 1923, pp. 85–90; Mogk, Anzeiger für Deutsches Altertum, XLIII (1924), 37–38; Hoffmann-Krayer, the same, p. 178.

146. Griffith, The Demotic Magical Papyrus, 1904, p. 129; new translation by Spiegelberg, in Reitzenstein, Hellenistische Wundererzählungen, 1906, pp. 103–105. For other examples, ancient and modern, see Heim, Incantamenta Magica (Jahrbücher für Classische Philologie, Supplementband, 1893, XIX), Nos. 104–135, pp. 495–507; The [Syriac] Book of Protection, ed. H. Gollancz, 1912, pp. xxxi, xxxviii–xxxix, liv–lv, lxvii–lxxi, lxxxi, lxxxiii; Mansikka, Über Russische Zauberformeln, 1909, pp. 24, 34–74, 168–276. On charms and amulets see the learned paper of Wordsworth, Yorkshire Archæological Journal, XVII (1903), 377–412. Cf. T. J. Pettigrew, On Superstitions connected with the History and Practice of Medicine, 1844, pp. 47–88; O. Ebermann, Blut- und Wundsegen (Palaestra, XXIV), 1903; Tavenner, Studies in Magic from Latin Literature, 1916, pp. 70–123. Sir William Temple sums up the subject capitally in his essay Of Poetry (Works, 1757, III, 417). For a rich collection of Highland charms see Carmichael, Carmina Gadelica, 1900, I, 231–339; II, 1–159. For Irish charms see Douglas Hyde, The Religious Songs of Connacht, II, 46–73.

147. Brevis Relatio (Giles, Scriptores Rerum Gestarum Willelmi Conquestoris, 1845, p. 7): "Si ego in sortem crederem, hodie amplius in bellum non introirem. Sed ego nunquam sortibus credidi, nec sortilegos amavi. In

omni enim negotio quicquid agere debui, creatori meo me semper com-
mendavi."

148. Wilkins, Concilia, I, 363-365: "quasi pro vitanda animalium
peste." Cf. William of Malmesbury, Gesta Pontificum, i, 42, ed. Hamilton,
p. 68.

149. Liebermann, I, 313. See p. 28, above.

150. Wilkins, I, 408; Symeon of Durham, ed. Arnold, I, 280; John of
Worcester, ed. Weaver (Anecdota Oxoniensia, XIII), 1908, p. 21.

151. William of Newburgh, Historia Rerum Anglicarum, Chronicles of
the Reigns of Stephen, Henry II., and Richard I., ed. Hewlett, I, 28. Cf.
Walter Map, De Nugis Curialium, v, 6, ed. Wright, p. 224 (ed. James,
p. 234); Walsingham, Historia Anglicana, ed. Riley, I, 146; William of
Malmesbury, Gesta Pontificum, ed. Hamilton, p. 259, note 6, and p. 260,
note 1.

152. Twelfth-Century Homilies, ed. Belfour, I (1909), 16: "ilyfde on
deofelgylde . . . and lyfede þa drycræft and þæs deofles ðeowdom."

153. See p. 225, above.

154. Berthold von Regensburg (ca. 1220-1272), Sermon 43, ed. Pfeiffer
and Strobl, II (1880), 70-71. Cf. II, 44, 147. See further Kotelmann, Gesundheitspflege im Mittelalter, 1890, pp. 236-242.

155. St. Augustine, De Civitate Dei, xxi, 14. Cf. Aldhelm, De Laudibus
Virginitatis, cap. 43, Opera, ed. Giles, 1844, p. 57.

156. See Bochart, Geographia Sacra, 1681, iv, 1, pp. 231-233 (who rejects the identification); Gaspar Schott, Magia Universalis, 1677, Part I,
lib. i, cap. 3, Vol. I, pp. 14-17 (who accepts it).

157. Capgrave, ed. Hingeston, pp. 25-26. Capgrave calls him "fynder
of witchcraft."

158. Letter 57, Goulbourn and Symonds, The Life, Letters, and Sermons of Herbert de Losinga, 1878, I, 204.

159. Walter Map, De Nugis Curialium, ii, 27, ed. Wright, pp. 103-104
(ed. James, pp. 99-100).

160. William of Newburgh, v, 22-23 (24), ed. 1610, pp. 637-650. Cf.
Havecost, Die Vampirsage in England, 1914, pp. 15-18.

161. Imitated from Southey by Jean Moréas in "La Vieille Femme de
Berkeley" (Les Cantilènes, 1886, pp. 127-136; 1897, pp. 97-106).

162. William of Malmesbury, Gesta Regum Anglorum, ii, 204, ed.
Stubbs, I, 253-256.

163. Gregory, Dialogi, iv, 55, ed. Moricca, 1924, pp. 313-314.

164. Matthew Paris, Chronica Majora, ed. Luard, I, 381-383; Roger of
Wendover, Flores Historiarum, ed. Coxe, I, 286-288; Flores Historiarum,
ed. Luard, I, 420-422; Knighton, ed. Lumby, I, 42-43; Radulfus Niger, ed.
Anstruther, p. 158; Eulogium Historiarum, ed. Haydon, I, 400-403;
Chronicle in De Antiquis Legibus Liber, ed. Stapleton (Camden Society,
XXXIV), p. 179; Higden, Polychronicon (and Trevisa's English translation), vi, 25, ed. Lumby, VII, 194-197; Bromton, Twysden, Scriptores X,
cols. 940-941; Speculum Historiale, xxv, 26, Venice, 1494, fol. 325 r° (also
in Jean de Vignay's French translation); Olaus Magnus, Historia de Genti-
bus Septentrionalibus, iii, 21, Rome, 1555, pp. 126-127; Schedel, Chroni-

carum Liber, Nuremberg, 1493, fol. 189 vº; Lycosthenes, Prodigiorum et Ostentorum Chronicon, 1557, p. 378. See Faligan, Revue des Traditions Populaires, III (1888), 487–491; Tausserat, the same, III, 643–647. William Rufus was carried off to hell on the back of a demon goat (see p. 175, above).

165. William, Le Manuel des Pechiez, vv. 6222–6304 (Handlyng Synne, vv. 7982–8087), ed. Furnivall (Roxburghe Club), 1862, pp. 248–251. William declares that he heard the story told, and that the thing happened in England. Robert of Brunne refers it to the reign of Edward I.

166. Selen Troist, Cologne, 1484, fol. lix vº; Själens Tröst, ed. Klemming, pp. 267–268; Gering, Islendzk Æventyri, No. 36, I, 124–126; II, 100–101 (cf. Köhler's note, II, 101–102).

167. Cf. Owst, Preaching in Medieval England, 1926, pp. 60–64.

168. Herbert, Catalogue of Romances, III (1910), 403, 437; An Alphabet of Tales, ed. Banks, No. 728, pp. 487–488 (thence in Coulton, Social Life in Britain, 1918, pp. 528–529). See also Additional MS. 6716, Herbert, III, 690. For the tale of The Priest's Wife see Herbert, III, 501, 502 (§§ 285, 301); cf. III, 380 (§ 119), 501 (§ 294), 661 (§ 202).

169. See Homilia de Sacrilegiis, ed. Caspari, 1886, pp. 8, 26.

170. For censure of those who trust auguries from birds and sneezes see Pseudo-Augustine, Sermon 278, § 1 (Caesarius of Arles, Migne, XXXIX, 2269), paraphrased by Ælfric, Lives of Saints, ed. Skeat, I (1881), 370; Pseudo-Augustine, De Rectitudine Catholicae Conversationis, cap. 5, Migne, XL, 1172; Homilia de Sacrilegiis, ed. Caspari, 1886, pp. 7, 24–25. For omens from sneezing see, e. g., Cicero, De Divinatione, ii, 40, 84; Pliny, ii, 7, 5, 24; cf. Sir Thomas Browne, Pseudodoxia Epidemica, iv, 9, Works, ed. Wilkin, 1852, I, 410–413; Massam, The Cliff Dwellers of Kenya, 1927, pp. 200–201; P. Saintyves (i. e. É. Nourry), L'Éternuement et le Bâillement dans la Magie, 1921.

171. "Somnia ne cures" — the same precept from Cato's Distichs, ii, 31, quoted by Dame Pertelote in The Nonne Prestes Tale: "Ne do no fors of dremes."

172. Petrus Blesensis, Epistola 65, Opera, ed. Giles, I, 187–192. Cf. Corrector, § 149 (Schmitz, II, 441–442); Le Manuel de Pechiez, vv. 1106–1120, and Robert of Brunne's Handlyng Synne, vv. 363–378, ed. Furnivall (Roxburghe Club), 1862, p. 13; Giffard, A Dialogue concerning Witches and Witchcraftes (1593), ed. 1603, sig. F3, lf. 2vº; Gaule, Πûς-μαντία, 1652, pp. 180–181; Bieber, Kaffa, II (1923), 347 (meeting as omen). In the same letter Archdeacon Peter mentions the fact that by the prompting of the devil certain women mould images of wax or clay to torture their enemies or to fire their sweethearts with love. To be sure, he quotes Virgil, but he is none the less stating the belief of his own time, and its practice too.

173. Mandeville's Travels, chap. 19, ed. Hamelius, 1919, I, 110; cf. the French in The Buke of John Maundeuill, ed. Warner (Roxburghe Club), 1889, p. 83. See for such omens Sébillot, Le Folk-Lore des Pêcheurs, 1901, pp. 176–192; Hopf, Thierorakel und Orakelthiere, 1888; Schell, Zeitschrift des Vereins für Rheinische und Westfälische Volkskunde, XI (1914), 257–265; The Indian Antiquary, V (1876), 21; X (1881), 313; XIII (1884), 57;

XXXII (1903), 432; E. Thurston, Omens and Superstitions of Southern India, 1912, pp. 15–19, 24–25; Crooke, Religion and Folklore of Northern India, 1926, pp. 311–313; North Indian Notes and Queries, IV (1894–95), 182–183; G. W. Briggs, The Chamārs, 1920, pp. 159–161; Hose and Mc-Dougall, The Pagan Tribes of Borneo, 1912, II, 55, 58–59; I. H. N. Evans, Studies in Religion, Folk-Lore, and Custom in British North Borneo and the Malay Peninsula, 1923, pp. 37–38.

174. On Eustace the Monk see Cannon, English Historical Review, XXVII (1912), 649–670.

175. Roman d'Eustache le Moine, ed. Michel, 1834; ed. Foerster and Trost (Wistasse le Moine), 1891.

176. Harleian MS. 636, fol. 201 (Michel, pp. xxxvi–xxxix; Trost, pp. xviii–xix).

177. Wilkins, Concilia, I, 582.

178. Cf. Gregory of Tours, x, 25.

179. Radulphus de Coggeshall, ed. Stevenson, p. 191; Holinshed, II (1807), 353 (from Radulphus); Matthew Paris, Chronica Majora, ed. Luard, III, 71; Flores Historiarum, ed. Luard, II, 175; Ricardus Argentinus, De Praestigiis et Incantationibus Daemonum et Necromanticorum, 1568, p. 148.

180. Imbert-Gourbeyre, La Stigmatisation, 1894, I, xix–xli. Cf. Bianchi, Archivio di Antropologia Criminale, XLVI (1926), 152–175.

181. In 1286 the Bishop of Hereford's Register contains the bull of Honorius IV in which that pope expresses some concern about the Jews and their study of "Thalmamud": Registrum Ricardi de Swinfeld (Canterbury and York Series, VI), pp. 139–140, cf. pp. 120–122.

182. Radulphus de Coggeshall, ed. Stevenson, p. 191.

183. Ovid, Fasti, iv, 652–672. Cf. Nashe, Have with You to Saffron-Walden, 1596, Works, ed. McKerrow, III, 60–61.

184. Æneid, vii, 81–106. Cf. Roscher, Ephialtes, p. 85.

185. Geoffrey of Monmouth, Historia Regum Britanniae, i, 11, ed. San-Marte, 1854, pp. 12–13.

186. Corrector, § 62 (Schmitz, II, 423).

187. Burne and Jackson, Shropshire Folk Lore, p. 161; Bye-Gones for 1882–83, pp. 253–254, 257. See the Slavic and other cases collected by Löwenstimm, Aberglaube und Strafrecht, 1897, pp. 44–52, 57–58, 62–66. An excellent German case of assault is discussed by Hellwig, Archiv für Strafrecht, LIV (1907), 132–146.

188. Folk-Lore Record, II (1879), 207–209; Gomme, Folklore as an Historical Science, pp. 203–204.

189. Boston Weekly Magazine, December 18, 1802, I, 31. I owe this curious reference to Mr. Albert Matthews.

190. George Giffard, A Discourse of the Subtil Practises of Deuilles by Witches and Sorcerers, 1587, sig. H3, lf. 1 v°; the Same, A Dialogue of Witches and Witchcraftes, 1593, sigg. B v°, C3 r°, E3 v°, E4 r°; 1 Henry VI, i, 5, 6 (Talbot to Joan of Arc); Historical MSS. Commission, 13th Report, Appendix, Part IV, p. 108 (1594); Perkins, A Discourse of the Damned Art of Witchcraft, 1608, pp. 206–207; Alexander Roberts, A Treatise of Witch-

craft, 1616, p. 58; Cotta, The Infallible True and Assured Witch, 1624, p. 136; Fairfax, Daemonologia, ed. Grainge, 1882, pp. 88–89; Bernard, A Guide to Grand-Iury Men, 2d ed., 1629, pp. 187–189; A True and Exact Relation, 1645, p. 18; Gaule, Select Cases of Conscience touching Witches and Witchcrafts, 1646, p. 144; Stearne, A Confirmation and Discovery of Witch-craft, 1648, p. 37; Wonderfull News from the North, 1650, p. 10; York Depositions, ed. Raine, pp. 38, 58, 82, 247 (1651, 1653, 1660, 1680); Drage, Daimonomageia, 1665, pp. 10, 21; Ramesey, Ελμινθολογια, 1668, p. 74. Cf. pp. 169, 236, above.

191. See, for example, Mackie, Norfolk Annals, 1901, II, 61–62; Blashill, Sutton-in-Holderness, 1896, pp. 283–284; F. Hancock, The Parish of Selworthy, Somerset, 1897, p. 233; Hewett, Nummits and Crummits, 1900, p. 64; The Reliquary, VII (1866), 128; Folk-Lore Record, III, ii (1881), 292; Transactions Devonshire Association, XV (1883), 102–104; XXXI (1899), 117–118; The Antiquary, IX (1884), 42; Journal of the British Archæological Association, XL (1884), 301–302 (Proceedings Dorset Natural History and Antiquarian Field Club, XIII [1892], 42–44); The Western Antiquary, III (1884), 28–29; IV (1885), 143; VI (1887), 13; Folk-Lore, XI (1900), 111–112; Wickwar, Witchcraft and the Black Art, p. 296 (a case in 1924); Folk-Lore Journal, II (1884), 349–350; Lincolnshire Notes and Queries, II (1891), 144; Norfolk Archæology, II (1849), 306; Page, An Exploration of Exmoor, 4th ed., 1895, pp. 33, 307; Polson, Our Highland Folklore Heritage, 1926, pp. 63–64; Wallonia, VI (1898), 62–64; XVI (1908), 96–97; Revue des Traditions Populaires, XXV (1910), 105–106; Hellwig, Verbrechen und Aberglaube, 1908, pp. 14–18.

192. Three Early Assize Rolls, ed. Page (Surtees Society, LXXXVIII), pp. 343–344.

193. Register of William Wickwane, Lord Archbishop of York (Surtees Society, CXIV), p. 24.

194. Child, The English and Scottish Popular Ballads, II, 143, 512; III, 509; IV, 468; Oliver Heywood, Autobiography (ca. 1664), ed. Turner, III (1883), 89; Gentleman's Magazine, April, 1767, XXXVII, 189; Addy, Household Tales, 1895, pp. 76–77; J. Ll. W. Page, An Exploration of Exmoor, 4th ed., 1895, pp. 33–34; Notes and Queries, 1st Series, IV (1851), 251, 297–298; VI (1852), 311; 4th Series, VIII (1871), 395; 5th Series, IX (1878), 8, 111, 478; 6th Series, VIII (1883), 367, 435–436 (cf. CXLVII [1924], 61–62); Journal British Archæological Association, New Series, V (1899), 339; James Napier, Notes and Reminiscences relating to Partick, 1875, p. 226. Cf. Le Braz, La Légende de la Mort chez les Bretons Armoricains, 1902, II, 5 (with Dottin's note); the same, 1922, I, 395; Mélusine, II (1884–85), 252–253; III (1886–87), 141, 215; Revue des Traditions Populaires, I (1886), 56; XXIII (1908), 391; XXX (1915), 100; La Tradition, IV (1890), 236, 373–374; Wuttke-Meyer, pp. 255–256; Volkskunde, XII (1899–1900), 173; North Indian Notes and Queries, V (1895–96), 191.

195. "Maleficiis et incantationibus nefariis inserviens": The Register of John le Romeyn (Surtees Society, CXXIII), ed. Brown, I, 158, cf. pp. xi–xii.

196. Modus Exigendi Confessiones, Wilkins, Concilia, II, 162.

197. Bartholomew de Cotton, Historia Anglicana, ed. Luard, p. 172 (cf. pp. 171, 180); Annales de Wigornia, Annales Monastici, ed. Luard, IV, 499. Cf. Annales de Dunstaplia, the same, III, 357; Annales Londonienses (Otho Biii), ed. Stubbs, Chronicles of the Reigns of Edward I. and Edward II., I, 97–98. Cf. (though without mention of sorcery) Annales Monastici, III, 467; IV, 321; Knighton, ed. Lumby, I, 279; Johannes de Oxenedes, ed. Ellis, pp. 275–276; Rishanger, ed. Riley, p. 420; Melsa Chronicle, ed. Bond, II, 251; Calendar of Patent Rolls 1281–1292, pp. 338, 346, 396, 473; Calendar of Close Rolls 1288–1296, pp. 64, 340–341, 351–352; the same, 1296–1302, pp. 49, 346; State Trials of the Reign of Edward the First, ed. Tout and Johnstone, 1906, pp. xiii, 85–91, 96–98; Parliamentary Writs, ed. Palgrave, I, 14, note 1. See also Hubert Hall, Introduction to the Rolls ed. of The Red Book of the Exchequer, III, cccxxii–cccxxxi; Christobel M. Hoare, The History of an East Anglian Soke, 1918, pp. 441–446.

198. Gregory of Tours, ix, 6.

199. Annaler for Nordisk Oldkyndighed, 1848, pp. 341–342, 347–350, 352, and Plate V; Aarbøger for Nordisk Oldkyndighed, 1889, pp. 321–322, 334–338. Cf. Helm, Altgermanische Religionsgeschichte, I (1913), 165–167.

200. Blinkenberg, The Thunderweapon in Religion and Folklore, 1911; L'Anthropologie, XX (1909), 31–34; Bellucci, Il Feticismo Primitivo in Italia, 1907, pp. 17–22, 72–76; Revista de Minho, XIII (1898), 118–119; Revue des Traditions Populaires, V (1890), 245–246; XVI (1901), 601–602; XVII (1902), 416; XIX (1904), 41; XX (1905), 138–140; Sir William Brereton's Travels, ed. Hawkins (Chetham Society), I (1844), 41; Lovett, Magic in Modern London, 1925, pp. 49–51.

201. M. G. Lewis, Journal of a West India Proprietor, 1834, p. 95.

202. Thomas, Kentucky Superstitions, 1920, pp. 244–246. In 1912 a Louisiana negro got into trouble by selling "conjure bags" which ensured immunity from arrest (Cedar Rapids, Iowa, Republican, April 4, 1912; Boston Transcript, April 5, 1912).

203. W. Ellis, Madagascar Revisited, 1867, p. 271; cf. Sibree, Madagascar and its People, p. 385.

204. Seligmann, The Melanesians of British New Guinea, 1910, pp. 283–288, and figs. 29–31 (cf. J. H. Holmes, In Primitive New Guinea, 1924, pp. 203–204). See also Pitcairn, Criminal Trials in Scotland, 1833, III, 615; Cross, Studies in Philology (University of North Carolina), XVI (1919), 263–267; Puckett, Folk Beliefs of the Southern Negro, 1926, pp. 231–238; H. J. Bell, Obeah, 2d ed., 1893, pp. 15–16; Kristensen, Danske Sagn, VI, i (1900), 339; Bentley, Pioneering on the Congo, 1900, I, 257–259; K. L. Parker, The Euahlayi Tribe, 1905, pp. 36–37; Journal Anthropological Institute, XXI (1892), 118; XXXIII (1903), 74–81. Cf. Seneca, Medea, 731–739.

205. Nassau, Fetichism in West Africa, 1904, p. 131. Cf. Cavazzi, Istorica Descrizione de' Tre' Regni Congo, Matamba, et Angola, 1687, vii, 123, p. 857; Kemp, Nine Years at the Gold Coast, 1898, pp. 124–125; van der Burgt, Un Grand Peuple de l'Afrique Équatoriale, 1903, p. 55; Talbot, In the Shadow of the Bush, 1912, p. 199 (Nigeria); Tauxier, Le Noir de

Bondoukou, 1921, pp. 180–181; Melland, In Witch-Bound Africa, 1923, pp. 213–214; Statham, Through Angola, 1922, p. 203; Journal of the Straits Branch of the Royal Asiatic Society, LXV (1913), 29; Enthoven, The Folklore of Bombay, 1924, p. 239; Horne and Aiston, Savage Life in Central Australia, 1924, pp. 135–136; Dornan, Pygmies and Bushmen of the Kalahari, 1925, p. 295; D. R. MacKenzie, The Spirit-Ridden Konde, 1925, pp. 258–259, 275; Roscoe, The Baganda, 1911, pp. 344–345; the Same, The Bakitara, 1923, p. 50; Williams and Calvert, Fiji and the Fijians, New York, 1859, p. 195; Deane, Fijian Society, 1921, pp. 161–165; Brewster, The Hill Tribes of Fiji, 1922, p. 233; Stack, The Mikirs, 1908, p. 36; Gimlette, Malay Poisons and Charm Cures, 1923, pp. 68–69, 95; Barnett, Sinhalese Folklore, The Indian Antiquary, XLV (1916), Supplement, p. 79; St. Johnston, The Lau Islands (Fiji), 1918, pp. 48–52, 57–60; Crooke, Religion and Folklore of Northern India, 1926, pp. 431–432; Bergen, Animal and Plant Lore, 1899, pp. 14–15; Nider, Formicarius, v, 3, ed. 1516 (1517), fol. lxxiiii rᵒ (T. Heywood, The Hierarchie of the Blessed Angells, 1635, p. 475); Anania, De Natura Daemonum, 1581, p. 173; Grillando, De Sortilegiis, ed. 1592, iii, 9, 15, 26, 30, pp. 22, 26–27, 37–38, 41–42; v, 7, pp. 52–53; Frazer, The Golden Bough, 3d ed., III, 267–287; Hillebrandt in Bühler's Grundriss der Indo-Arischen Philologie, III, ii (1897), 176; Frischbier, Hexenspruch und Zauberbann, 1870, pp. 17–18; Journal (Royal) Anthropological Institute, XXVI (1897), 151; LV (1925), 229–230, 249; Zeitschrift der Gesellschaft für Schleswig-Holsteinische Geschichte, XLV (1915), 149–150, 199, 200, 212, 231; Seyfarth, Aberglaube und Zauberei in der Volksmedizin Sachsens, 1913, pp. 57–60; Zeitschrift des Historischen Vereins für Niedersachsen, 1878, pp. 101–102.

206. Bogg, Lower Wharfeland, 1904, p. 346 (pins, needles, hair, bits of fingernails, brimstone, etc.); Proceedings Dorset Natural History and Antiquarian Field Club, XXXVII (1916), 59–60 (two vipers and a centipede); cf. Wilde, Ingatestone, 1913, p. 401. As to hair, nails, teeth, saliva, etc., in malefic witchcraft see Grillando, De Sortilegiis, ed. 1545, v, 11, fol. xxvj vᵒ (ed. 1592, v, 7, p. 53); Hartland, The Legend of Perseus, II (1895), 63–78; Roscoe, The Bakitara, 1923, p. 50 (Central Africa); Hans Meyer, Die Barundi, 1916, p. 133 (German East Africa); Routledge, With a Prehistoric People, 1910, p. 276 (British East Africa); Westermann, Die Kpelle ein Negerstamm in Liberia, 1921, p. 206. See also pp. 99–103, above.

207. Bernard's deposition, dated at Rouen, March 14, 1495[-6], is in Cotton MS. Caligula Dvi. It is printed by Madden, Archæologia, XXVII (1838), 205–209 (cf. pp. 171–178); by Gairdner, Letters and Papers Illustrative of the Reigns of Richard III and Henry VII, II, 318–323; and by A. F. Pollard, The Reign of Henry VII, I, 116–123.

208. Bacon's Works, ed. Ellis and Spedding, VI, 237, 243.

209. Calendar of Patent Rolls 1494–1509, p. 49.

210. Journal British Archæological Association, XVIII (1862), 307.

211. Robert of Brunne, Handlyng Synne, vv. 339–498, ed. Furnivall (Roxburghe Club), 1862, pp. 12–17; Le Manuel des Pechiez, vv. 1078–1273, ed. Furnivall, pp. 12–17.

212. Dan Michel, Ayenbite of Inwit, ed. Morris, 1866, pp. 40–41, 43, 19

(a translation of the Somme des Vices et des Vertus of Frère Lorens, 1279: see MS. Harvard College Library, 37591.60, fol. 30 r°, cf. fol. 12 v°). Cf. pp. 148–151, above.

213. For England see the Acta contra Templarios in Wilkins, Concilia, II, 329–393 ("adorabant quendam catum sibi in ipsa congregatione apparentem," art. 14, p. 331; the obscene kiss, art. 30, p. 331; heads as idols, art. 46–61, p. 332); Records of the Northern Convocation (Surtees Society, CXIII), pp. 19–48; Register of John de Halton, Bishop of Carlisle (Canterbury and York Series, XIII), II, 2–9, 15–16, 21–22, 35–36; Knighton, ed. Lumby, I, 333, 407; Adam Murimuth, ed. Thompson, pp. 13–16; Flores Historiarum, ed. Luard, III, 143–145, 332–334; Perkins, English Historical Review, XXIV (1909), 432–447; XXV (1910), 209–230; Ramsay, Genesis of Lancaster, 1913, I, 16–20, 34–39; Lea, A History of the Inquisition, 1888, III, 298–301; Schottmüller, Der Untergang des Templer-Ordens, 1887, pp. 368–407; Gmelin, Schuld oder Unschuld des Templerordens, 1893, pp. 453–466. For English accounts of the French prosecution see Flores Historiarum, ed. Luard, III, 143, 147, 331; Anonymous Annales Regis Edwardi Primi, in Riley's ed. of Rishanger, pp. 492–499.

214. This method of divination was practised in London by Richard Berewold about 1382. See p. 193, above.

215. Registrum Radulphi Baldock (Canterbury and York Series, VII), ed. Fowler, I, 144–145.

216. The mandate of Boniface IX directing the Archbishop of Canterbury to prosecute Lollards (1395) declares that they assert that "exorcisms and blessings in church of wine, bread, water, oil, salt, wax, incense, the altar stone, church walls, vestments, mitres, pastoral or pilgrims staves, are practices of necromancy" (Papal Letters, IV, 515).

217. An Apology for Lollard Doctrines, ed. Todd (Camden Society, XX), pp. 90–98. For such lists and definitions see also Pollux, Onomasticon, vii, 188; Isidore, Origines, viii, 9; John of Salisbury, Policraticus, i, 12, ed. Webb, I, 50–54. The palm must be awarded to John Gaule, who, in his Πῦς-μαντία the Mag-astro-mancer (1652), catalogues more than fifty kinds of -mancy (pp. 165–166).

218. Cf. Hansen, Zauberwahn, pp. 343–344.

219. Contemporary Narrative, ed. Wright (Camden Society, XXIV), pp. 1–3, 32. This was in Ireland, but within the English Pale, and the prosecuting bishop was not an Irishman.

220. See p. 169, above.

221. Knighton, ed. Lumby, I, 452; Adam Murimuth, ed. Thompson, pp. 59–60; Robert of Avesbury, ed. Thompson, pp. 284–285; Walsingham, Historia Anglicana, ed. Riley, I, 192–193 (cf. II, 351); Hemingsburgh (Hemingsford), ed. Hamilton, II, 301–302 (ed. Hearne, 1731, II, 271); Annales Paulini (Chronicles of the Reigns of Edward I and Edward II, ed. Stubbs, I, 349); Gesta Edwardi Tertii (the same, II, 100); Vita Edwardi Secundi (the same, II, 291). Cf. Rymer's Foedera, ed. Holmes, IV, 430; Pike, History of Crime, I, 228–229, 471.

222. Rymer's Foedera, ed. Holmes, IV, 424. The confession is extant in French, English, and Latin, and purports to have been made before Robert

Houell, Coroner of the King's Household, and repeated in Parliament on March 16, 1330: French, Cotton MS. Claudius Eviii (Thompson's edition of Adam Murimuth, pp. 253–255); English, Cotton MS. Julius Cii (Journal of the British Archæological Association, VII [1851], 140–142; Latin, see Riley's edition of Walsingham's Historia Anglicana, II, 351–352. Sorcery or conjuration seems to be hinted by the phrase "quidam pessimi exploratores" in the Annales Paulini (ed. Stubbs, as above, I, 349).

223. Rotuli Parliamentorum, II, 52, 53b; cf. II, 33–34.

224. Hansen, Quellen, p. 8.

225. Cf. Wm. Brown, Yorkshire Archæological Journal, XXIII (1915), 300–307.

226. Year Book 29 Edward III, ed. 1679, p. 12 ("Les Iustices avoient trove in le cote Shawel qui fuit le champion l'Evesque, plusors rolles des orisons et sortileges"); George Neilson, Trial by Combat, 1890, p. 152; Horwood, Year Books of 32–33 Edward I (Rolls Series), p. xvi, note.

227. Dugdale, Origines Juridiciales, 1671, p. 82; cf. Neilson, pp. 91, 159, 163.

228. Arundel Penitential, § 78 (Schmitz, Die Bussbücher, I [1883], 457). Cf. Fournier, Revue d'Histoire et de Littérature Religieuses, IX (1904), 97–98. The MS. was written in England in the thirteenth century; the work itself dates probably from the eleventh or twelfth.

229. Burchard, Decretum, x, 25, Migne, CXL, 836; Summa de Judiciis, vii, 15 (Schmitz, II, 496). See A. Franz, Die Kirchlichen Benediktionen, 1909, II, 329–330.

230. Liebermann, Die Gesetze der Angelsachsen, I, 407, 410–411, 415, 418, 421, 423, 424; cf. the Frankish rituals edited by Zeumer, Formulae Aevi Merowingici et Karolini, 1886 (Monumenta, Leges, Section V), pp. 604–627. Speaking of the duel between the Dukes of Hereford and Norfolk in 1398, Adam of Usk remarks that "quia rex a sortilegio habuerat quod dux Northfolchie tunc prevaleret, ducis Herfordie destruccionem affectando multum gaudebat" (Thompson's 2d ed., 1904, p. 24).

231. Leechdoms, ed. Cockayne, II, 154 (ed. Leonhardi, I, 46).

232. Leechdoms, ed. Cockayne, I, 328, from De Taxone Liber (ed. Howald and Sigerist, Corpus Medicorum Latinorum, IV [1927], 230). One class of the Latin MSS. has an unintelligible charm: "Butabar torthon hydran," etc. See also Medicina de Quadrupedibus, an Early M[iddle] E[nglish] Version, ed. Delcourt (Anglistische Forschungen, ed. Hoops, XL), 1914, pp. 2–5. A badger's foot was one of the magic articles in the collection of de Rojas's Celestina (ed. Cejador y Frauca, 1913, I, 82). Cf. Pliny, xxviii, 29, 116, on the chameleon. Note also the favorite negro talisman, a rabbit's foot.

233. Eustathius on Odyssey, xix, 247, p. 1864; Suidas, s. v. Ἐφέσια γράμματα, ed. Bernhardy, I, 673; Lobeck, Aglaophamus, 1829, pp. 1163–1164, 1330; references in Bernhardy, and in Alberti's Hesychius, I (1746), 1544–1545. Hesychius gives some of the gibberish (ed. M. Schmidt, II [1860], 240). See Kuhnert, Pauly-Wissowa, V, x (1905), 2771–2773.

234. Kormaks Saga, chap. 12, ed. 1832, pp. 116–119; Vigfusson and Powell, Corpus Poeticum Boreale, 1883, I, 362.

235. Thomas Favent, Historia siue Narracio de Modo et Forma Mira-
bilis Parliamenti, ed. McKisack (Camden Miscellany, XIV), 1926, p. 18;
Howell, State Trials, I (1816), 117. Favent's details may or may not be
correct, but they are equally good for our purpose in either case, since they
reflect the superstitious beliefs of the fourteenth century. Compare the use
of charms and amulets to enable one to withstand torture (Bouvet, Les
Manieres Admirables pour Découvrir toutes Sortes de Crimes et Sortileges,
1659, pp. 194-199).

236. Heydon, Psonthonphancia, 1664, p. 86. Cf. Fletcher, The Little
French Lawyer, iv, 4; Ady, A Candle in the Dark, 1656, p. 56.

237. Thoms, Anecdotes and Traditions (Camden Society), 1839, pp.
111-113.

238. For charms, amulets, and girdles that keep one safe from weapons
see, for example, Gaule, Select Cases of Conscience touching Witches and
Witchcrafts, 1646, p. 113; [N. Orchard,] The Doctrine of Devils, 1676,
p. 196; Habington, The Queen of Arragon, i, 1, Collier's Dodsley, IX, 342;
Train, An Historical and Statistical Account of the Isle of Man, 1845, II,
177; Carmichael, Carmina Gadelica, 1900, II, 251 (girdle); O. Berthold,
Die Unverwundbarkeit in Sage und Aberglauben der Griechen (Religionsgeschichtliche Versuche und Vorarbeiten, XI, i), 1911, pp. 56-59;
Dieterich, Kleine Schriften, 1911, pp. 234-251; Martin Plantsch, Opusculum de Sagis Maleficis, 1507, sig. b v, lf. 1 v°; Heinrich von dem Türlîn,
Diu Crône, 4870-4888, 14942-14955, ed. Scholl, 1852, pp. 60, 183-184
(girdle); Scheible, Das Kloster, VI (1847), 214-216; Wuttke-Meyer, pp.
319-320; Haupt's Zeitschrift, III (1843), 42; Germania, XXV (1880), 70;
XXVI (1881), 241; Alemannia, XVII (1889), 240, 242; XIX (1892), 136-
138; XXXVII (1909), 21-22; Am Urdhs-Brunnen, II (1883-85), 176;
VI (1888-89), 93; Baltische Studien, XXXVI (1886), 208-219, 230-232;
Kleeberger, Volkskundliches aus Fischbach i. d. Pfalz, 1902, pp. 58-62;
Hessische Blätter für Volkskunde, I (1902), 17-18; Zeitschrift des Vereins
für Rheinische und Westfälische Volkskunde, VIII (1911), 78-79; Olbrich,
Mitteilungen der Schlesischen Gesellschaft für Volkskunde, X, i, Heft 19
(1908), 45-71; Archiv für Kriminal-Anthropologie, III (1900), 93-94; XXV
(1906), 77, 159-160; XLVII (1912), 345-352; Gering, Ueber Weissagung und
Zauber im Nordischen Altertum, 1902, pp. 16-18; Kristensen, Jyske Folkeminder, VI (1883), 211-212; the Same, Danske Sagn, II (1893), 325-331; VI,
i (1900), 253-254; Wigström, Folktro ock Sägner, Nyare Bidrag till Kännedom om de Svenska Landsmål, VIII, iii (1902), 299; Capello and Ivens, De
Benguella ás Terras de Iácca, 1881, I, 224; D. Kemp, Nine Years at the
Gold Coast, 1898, p. 124; Mary H. Kingsley, Travels in West Africa, 1897,
p. 467; Decle, Three Years in Savage Africa, 1898, p. 155; Tauxier, Le Noir
de Bondoukou, 1921, p. 180; Hewat, Bantu Folk Lore, p. 51; Callaway,
The Religious System of the Amazulu, 1870, p. 441; E. P. Herrick, The
Southern Workman, XXXVI (1907), 401; The Antananarivo Annual, No.
2, Vol. I (1876, reprinted 1885), 318-319; No. 20 (1896), V, 421-425; Skeat,
Malay Magic, 1900, p. 524; Annales du Musée Guimet, XXVI, iv (1900),
79, 85, 105-106; Journal Royal Anthropological Institute, XX (1891), 127;
XLVI (1916), 325; Gillen, Report of the Horn Expedition, ed. Spencer,

1896, Part IV, p. 182 (Australian girdle). Cf. Speed, The History of Great Britain, 1611, chap. 22, § 27, p. 807. See also the seventeenth-century spell in Sloane MS. 631, fol. 224 r°; cf. Sloane MS. 2628, fol. 11 r°. In 1645 Margery Sparam confessed that she had sent her two black imps "after her husband beinge a solier to protect him"; and Ann Smith confessed that "her sone haue one imp wth him in the army" (Add. MS. 27402, foll. 120 v°, 121 r°).

239. Vogt, Die Schutzbriefe unserer Soldaten, Festschrift zur Jahrhundertfeier der Universität zu Breslau, ed. Siebs, 1911, pp. 586–620; Zeitschrift des Vereins für Volkskunde, XXV (1915), 243–245; Lovett, Magic in Modern London, 1925, pp. 10–11, 13–15. Cf. Korrespondenzblatt des Vereins für Siebenbürgische Landeskunde, XXXVIII (1915), 35–37; Niederlausitzer Mittheilungen, VIII (1904), 298–299; X (1909), 331–332.

240. In 1620 the luckless schoolmaster Peacock was imprisoned (and tortured) for attempting "to infatuate the king's judgment by sorcery" in the business of Sir Thomas Lake (Chamberlain to Carleton, February 28, 1620, [Birch,] The Court and Times of James the First, 1848, II, 202; State Papers, Domestic, 1619–1623, p. 125; Spedding, Bacon's Letters and Life, VII, 76–80).

241. Cicero, Brutus, 60, 217: "Idque veneficiis et cantionibus Titiniae factum esse dicebat." Of ancient *defixiones* the four commonest uses were in litigation, in theft, in chariot races, and in love (Audollent, Defixionum Tabellae, 1904, p. lxxxix). In 1663, John Heydon, a devotee of astrology, geomancy, and all the Rosicrucian arts of divination, who practised as an attorney at the King's Bench, Westminster, advertised his superiority to other lawyers in the following terms: "By these Arts we gain credit: for we will undertake no cause that shall go against us; let the Plaintiff or Defendant pretend what they will, we know beforehand what good or evil will end the business; and so we (contrary to others) endeavour peace, save money and trouble" (Theomagia: or, The Temple of Wisdome, 1663, Book iii, chap. 19, p. 125).

242. E. W. Smith and Dale, The Ila-speaking Peoples of Northern Rhodesia, 1920, I, 264. For similar witchcraft see Puckett, Folk Beliefs of the Southern Negro, 1926, pp. 277–278; Hellwig, Verbrechen und Aberglaube, 1908, pp. 113–118; the Same, Archiv für Religionswissenschaft, XVIII (1915), 296–300; Löwenstimm, Aberglaube und Strafrecht, 1897, pp. 128–129; Wolf, Beiträge zur Deutschen Mythologie, I (1852), 258; Bang, Norske Hexeformularer, 1901, pp. 524–525; Bidrag till Södermanlands Äldre Kulturhistoria, I, iv (1883), 76–77; Archiv für Kriminal-Anthropologie, III (1900), 90–91.

243. Havamál, sts. 146–163 (Bugge, Norrœn Fornkvæði, 1867, pp. 62–64; Corpus Poeticum Boreale, ed. Vigfusson and Powell, 1883, I, 26–28).

244. Calendars of the Proceedings in Chancery, I (1827), xxiv.

245. Calendar of Patent Rolls 1385–1389, p. 63.

246. La Maniere de Langage, ed. Stengel, Zeitschrift für Neufranzösische Sprache und Literatur, I (1879), 7; Chaucer, The House of Fame, vv. 1277–1281; Royster, Studies in Philology, University of North Carolina, XXIII (1926), 380–384. On tregetours see Guilielmus Alvernus, De

Universo, ii, 3, 23, Opera, 1674, I, 1062; cf. W. Hertz, Gesammelte Abhandlungen, 1905, p. 427, note 2.

247. The Witch of Endor was a "phitonissa" (Friar's Tale, D 1510).

248. Cf. Canterbury Tales, Prologue, 411–418. See also Symphorien Champier, Dyalogus in Magicarum Artium Destructionem, ii, 2 (Lyons, ca. 1500, sig. b, lf. 2 v°), on golden images "ad fortunandum vel sanandum a certis morbis vel contraria faciendum."

249. House of Fame, 1259–1270.

250. The Squire's Tale, F 216–219.

251. The Friar's Tale, D 1299–1303.

252. The Parson's Tale, §§ 37–38, ed. Skeat, IV, 607.

253. Tatlock, Astrology and Magic in The Franklin's Tale, Kittredge Anniversary Papers, 1913, pp. 339–350.

254. Gower, Confessio Amantis, vi, 1261–2400.

255. The same, v, 6670–6675.

256. The same, 3559–3622, 3690–3718, 3945–4174. See also what Gower says of Achelous, "a soubtil man," who was able to deceive "thurgh magique and sorcerie" (iv, 2075–2078).

257. Jean Creton, ed. Buchon, Collection des Chroniques, XXIV (1826), 413; Archæologia, XX (1824), 374.

258. Palgrave, An Essay upon the Original Authority of the King's Council, 1834, pp. 87–88.

259. Collectanea Anglo-Premonstratensia, ed. Gasquet (Camden 3d Series, XII), III, 117–118.

260. Capgrave, Chronicle of England, ed. Hingeston, p. 281.

261. Rymer, Foedera, 2d ed., VIII, 427; Calendar of Patent Rolls 1405–1406, p. 112; Proceedings and Ordinances of the Privy Council, ed. Nicolas, I, 288.

262. Historiae Dunelmensis Scriptores Tres, ed. Raine (Surtees Society, IX), Appendix, pp. cxciv–cxcv.

263. John Mirk (Myrc), Instructions for Parish Priests, vv. 360–371, 969–974, ed. Peacock (Early English Text Society), 1868, 1902, pp. 12, 30.

264. Registrum Roberti Mascall, ed. Parry (Canterbury and York Series, XXI), pp. 74–75. See pp. 33–34, above.

265. Gregory's Chronicle, ed. Gairdner, The Historical Collections of a Citizen of London (Camden Society, New Series, XVII), p. 185.

266. Durham Depositions, ed. Raine (Surtees Society, XXI), p. 33.

267. Durham Depositions, p. 84.

268. See, for example, Journal of the British Archæological Society, XVIII (1862), 307 (1302); Durham Depositions, ed. Raine, pp. 27, 84, 91, 247, 313, 318 (1435, 1567, 1570, 1572, 1574, 1586); Rotuli Parliamentorum, VI, 232 (1470); Calendar to the Records of Doncaster, III, 151 (1595); Worcester County Records, Historical MSS. Commission, Various Collections, I, 293 (1617); W. H. Hale, A Series of Precedents and Proceedings, 1847, pp. 244–245 (1619); Municipal Records of Dorchester, Dorset, ed. Mayo, 1908, p. 664 (1634); North Riding Record Society, IV (1886), 182 (1640); Wilts Quarter Sessions, Historical MSS. Commission, Various Collections, I, 122, 127 (1650, 1653); Somerset Record Society, XXVIII (1912),

362 (1658); W. J. Hardy, Hertford County Records, Notes and Extracts from the Sessions Rolls, 1905, I, 217 (1669); W. Rye, Extracts from the Court Books of Norwich 1666–1688, 1905, p. 162 (1681); Yorkshire Notes and Queries, I (1888), 239 (1690); North Riding Record Society, IX (1892), 6 (1691); Moule, Descriptive Catalogue of the Charters of Weymouth, 1883, p. 87 (1716). Slander in cases of alleged theft on the basis of a sorcerer's pretended revelations was also common (see pp. 187–197, above).

269. Audollent, Defixionum Tabellae, No. 1, pp. 6–8. Cf. No. 4, pp. 10–11; No. 8, pp. 15–16.

270. The Eastern Counties Collectanea, ed. by J. L'Estrange, 1872–73, p. 207.

271. More's History of King Richard III, ed. Lumby, pp. 46–47; Workes, 1557, p. 54. Cf. Grafton's Chronicle, ed. 1569, p. 779 (II [1809], 98); Hall's Chronicle, ed. 1809, p. 360. See Gairdner, History of the Life and Reign of Richard the Third, 2d ed., 1879, pp. 80–84.

272. Bill of attainder, Rotuli Parliamentorum, VI, 245.

273. The Miracles of King Henry VI, ed. Knox and Leslie, 1923, pp. 172–176. A recipe for a swollen and aching face (ca. 1440) is labelled "Pur le blastyng de mal esprit" (Heinrich, Ein Mittelenglisches Medizinbuch, 1896, p. 171).

274. Hale, pp. 32–33.

275. See John Taylor the Water Poet, The Water-Cormorant his Complaint, 1622, sig. E, lff. 2 v°–F2 r°, for the character of "A Figure flinger, or a couzning cunning man."

276. Tyndale's petition, published by Martin, Archæologia, LX (1907), 376.

277. Hale, p. 77: "Notatur quod ymaginavit quasdam artes divinitarias, ad interficiendum maritum suum."

278. Ellis, Original Letters, 2d ed., I (1825), 217.

279. Visitations of the Diocese of Norwich 1492–1532, ed. Jessopp (Camden Society, New Series, XLIII), pp. 269, 270.

280. Letters and Papers, Henry VIII, V, Nos. 1679–1680, pp. 694–696; VI, Nos. 257, 258, pp. 115–116; VII, No. 923 (xxi), p. 346; Palgrave, Norfolk Archæology, I (1847), 219–223; Froude, History of England, II (1856), 178–182. Jones's unsigned confession is ascribed to Sir Edward Neville by Palgrave, and, in Letters and Papers, to Thomas Wood; but if one compares it with Jones's letter to Cromwell (Letters and Papers, V, No. 1680) and with Wood's accusations (V, No. 1679), the authorship is clear.

281. Statutes of the Realm, III (1817), 446–451; Letters and Papers, VI and VII, index, s. v. Barton; letter to Cromwell, Three Chapters of Letters relating to the Suppression of Monasteries, ed. Wright (Camden Society, XXVI), 14–22; Archæologia Cantiana, I (1853), 40; Chronicle of the Grey Friars, ed. Nichols (Camden Society, LIII), p. 37; Wriothesley's Chronicle, ed. Hamilton (Camden Society, New Series, XI), I, 23, 24, 85; Chronicle in Camden Miscellany, XII, 8, 9; Chronicle in Richard Hill's MS., ed. Dyboski, pp. 163, 164; Stow, Annales, ed. 1631, pp. 569–570; Cranmer, Miscellaneous Writings and Letters, ed. Cox (Parker Society), pp. 65–66, 252, 271–274; Harpsfield, A Treatise on the Pretended Divorce,

ed. Pocock (Camden Society, New Series, XXI), p. 178; Burnet, The History of the Reformation, I (1679), Collection, pp. 123–127; Amos, Observations on the Statutes of the Reformation Parliament, 1859, pp. 39–45; Gairdner, Lollardy and the Reformation, I (1908), 453–462; Gasquet, Henry VIII and the English Monasteries, 5th ed., 1893, I, 110–150; Cheney, Transactions Royal Historical Society, 2d Series, XVIII (1904), 107–129; Mundy, The Home Counties Magazine, VII (1905), 34–40; The Antiquary, XLVI (1910), 213–219; Merriman, Life and Letters of Thomas Cromwell, 1902, I, 118–120, 361, 371, 373–379; II, 291.

282. The Image of Ypocresye, vv. 1685–1706, Furnivall, Ballads from Manuscripts, I, 233–234.

283. Letters and Papers, VII, No. 72, p. 29.

284. More's letter, Burnet, The History of the Reformation, 2d ed., II (1683), Collection, p. 289; cf. Letters and Papers, VII, No. 287, p. 120.

285. Scot, vii, 1, p. 126 (94), ed. Nicholson, p. 101; cf. vii, 3, p. 133 (99), ed. Nicholson, p. 107.

286. Cromwell to the Earl of Rutland, August 9, 1535, Merriman, Life and Letters of Thomas Cromwell, 1902, I, 415.

287. See p. 189.

288. Letters and Papers, XII, ii, No. 231, pp. 97–98.

289. The same, XII, ii, No. 267, pp. 112–113 (Merriman, Life and Letters of Thomas Cromwell, 1902, II, 64–65); No. 272, p. 114; No. 328, p. 134; No. 337, p. 138; No. 424, p. 172; No. 467, p. 184; No. 569, p. 214; Nos. 625–626, pp. 230–232; No. 661, p. 241; No. 697, p. 251.

290. State Papers, Henry VIII, VIII, 218, 219, 300; Letters and Papers, XIV, ii, No. 726, pp. 266–267 (Merriman, II, 243–244); XV, No. 37, p. 14; No. 217, p. 76; XVI, No. 678 (23), p. 327.

291. Letters and Papers, XIII, ii, No. 815, p. 323.

292. The same, XIV, i, No. 278, p. 108.

293. Parliament Roll, 32 Henry VIII, Letters and Papers, XV, No. 498, § 59, p. 216. Cf. the letter from Richard Hilles to Bullinger, Original Letters (Parker Society), I (1846), 202. See also Chronicle of the Grey Friars, ed. Nichols (Camden Society, LIII), p. 44; Wriothesley's Chronicle, ed. Hamilton (Camden Society, New Series, XI), I, 120; London Chronicle, Camden Miscellany, XII, 16; Stow, Annales, ed. 1631, p. 580; Burnet, The History of the Reformation, 2d ed., I (1681), 361.

294. Correspondance Politique de MM. de Castillon et de Marillac, ed. Kaulek, 1885, p. 207.

295. Letters and Papers, XV, No. 784, p. 369.

296. Proceedings of the Privy Council, ed. Nicolas, VII, 12–14, 25, 27, 30, 38; Letters and Papers, XV, Nos. 1006, 1008, 1011, pp. 499, 500; XVI, Nos. 8, 14, 55, pp. 3, 5, 16.

297. Scot, xvi, 3, pp. 473–474 (341–342), ed. Nicholson, pp. 398–399.

298. Scot, viii, 1, pp. 157–158 (116), ed. Nicholson, p. 126.

299. Proceedings of the Privy Council, ed. Nicolas, VII, 106–107; Letters and Papers, XVI, No. 424, p. 214.

300. Letters and Papers, XVII, No. 1012, § 48, p. 567.

301. The same, XX, i, No. 542, p. 256.

302. Cf. Kristensen, Danske Sagn, VI, i (1900), 157–158.

303. To evoke or conjure "the holy angels" is risky business, for it is always possible that a demon may come instead. See Iamblichus, De Mysteriis, ii, 10, ed. Parthey, 1857, p. 91; iii, 31, p. 177; Arnobius, Adversus Gentes, iv, 12, Migne, V, 1024, 1026; Lobeck, Aglaophamus, 1829, p. 58.

304. Letters and Papers, XXI, ii, Nos. 203, 212, 417–421, pp. 101, 103–104, 198–201; Martin, The Archæological Review, II (1889), 280–283.

305. Doyle, Official Baronage, 1886, III, 634–635.

306. Roger Hutchinson, The Image of God or Laie Mans Booke, 1550, chap. 24, Works, ed. Bruce (Parker Society), 1842, p. 142.

307. John Caius, A Boke or Counseill against the Disease commonly called the Sweate or Sweatyng Siknesse, 1552 (in Works, ed. Roberts, 1912, p. 26). Compare the complaint of Antonius Niger, City Physician at Brunswick, in a letter of ca. 1537: "Ita populus hic deditus est mulierculis medicinam incredibili et periculosa stulticia porrigentibus, Empyricis, Iudaeis, Aromatarijs et imperitissimis quibusque" (Zeitschrift des Historischen Vereins für Niedersachsen, 1903, p. 537). See also Cotta, A Short Discoverie of the Vnobserved Dangers of Severall Sorts of Ignorant and Vnconsiderate Practisers of Physicke in England, 1612.

308. Nashe, Have with You to Saffron-Walden, 1596, Works, ed. McKerrow, III, 48.

309. London Chronicle in Camden Miscellany, XII, 36–37; Wriothesley's Chronicle, ed. Hamilton (Camden Society, New Series, XX), II, 117–118; Chronicle of Queen Jane, etc., ed. J. G. Nichols (Camden Society, XLVIII), p. 78; Chronicle of the Grey Friars, ed. J. G. Nichols (Camden Society, LIII), p. 90; Diary of Henry Machyn, ed. J. G. Nichols (Camden Society, XLII), p. 66; Holinshed, IV (1808), 56; Stow, Annales, ed. 1631, p. 624.

310. See Dee's own account in his Compendious Rehearsall, 1592 (Chetham Miscellanies, Vol. I [1851], Chetham Society, XXIV, Autobiographical Tracts of Dr. John Dee, ed. Crossley, pp. 20–21). Cf. Dee's Aduertisement, prefixed to his General and Rare Memorials pertaining to the Perfect Arte of Navigation, 1577 (Crossley, p. 57). See also Acts of the Privy Council, New Series, V, 137, 139, 143, 176; Strype, Ecclesiastical Memorials, Oxford ed., III, i (1822), 348–349.

311. Scot, xv, 42, pp. 466–489 (337–338), ed. Nicholson, pp. 393–395. The letter is dated "From the bench this 8. of March, 1582," i. e. 1583.

312. See pp. 27–31.

313. Hooper, A Declaration of the Ten Holy Commaundementes, 1548 (Early Writings, ed. Carr, Parker Society), chap. 4, p. 308. The Preface is dated November 5, 1549.

314. The same, chap. 6, pp. 326–327, 329.

315. Chap. 4, p. 308, and chap. 6, pp. 328–329 (cf. pp. 330–333).

316. Hooper, Exposition upon Psalm LXXIII (Later Writings, ed. Nevinson, Parker Society, p. 294).

317. Ten Holy Commaundements, chap. 6, pp. 329–330.

318. Later Writings, p. 145.

319. Records of the Diocese of Gloucester, Historical MSS. Commission, Various Collections, VII, 56, 53.

320. Narratives of the Days of the Reformation, ed. J. G. Nichols, p. 335.

321. Latimer, Second Sermon on the Lord's Prayer, 1552 (Works, ed. Corrie, Parker Society, I, 349, 345); Lincolnshire Sermon, 1553 (1552) (Works, I, 534). *Wizards* may be the correct reading instead of *witches*.

CHAPTER III

Image Magic and the Like

1. Budge, Egyptian Magic, 1901, pp. 65–103; the Same, The Life and Exploits of Alexander the Great, 1896, pp. x–xvii; the Same, Facsimiles of Egyptian Hieratic Papyri, I (1910), 10; Moret, La Magie dans l'Égypte Ancienne, Conférences faites au Musée Guimet, 1906, pp. 264–268 (Bibliothèque de Vulgarisation, XX); Fossey, La Magie Assyrienne, 1902, pp. 78–81, 95, 103, 130; Jastrow, Die Religion Babyloniens und Assyriens, I (1905), 285, 296–297, 304–313; R. C. Thompson, The Devils and Evil Spirits of Babylonia, II (1904), xxxv–xxxvii, 98–111; Tallqvist, Die Assyrische Beschwörungsserie Maqlû, I, 18–19, 23, 32–39, 42–53, 64–67, 70–73, 78–79, 100–109.

2. V. Henry, La Magie dans l'Inde Antique, 1909, pp. 169–173, 227–230; Hillebrandt in Bühler's Grundriss der Indo-Arischen Philologie, III, ii (1897), 177; Caland, Altindischer Zauberritual, 1900, pp. 119, 134, 166, 184. For mediæval and modern India see Manucci, Storia do Mogor, transl. by Irvine, III (1907), 207–208, 215–216; Lyall, Asiatic Studies, 1882, p. 88; Oman, Cults, Customs and Superstitions of India, 1908, pp. 317–321; The Indian Antiquary, V (1876), 21–22; XXVIII (1899), 82–83; XXXIII (1904), 57; XXXVI (1907), 20, 310; G. W. Briggs, The Chamārs, 1920, p. 170; Crooke, Religion and Folklore of Northern India, 1926, pp. 109, 432–433; Ivanow, Journal and Proceedings Asiatic Society of Bengal, New Series, XIX (1924), 43–50; Panjab Notes and Queries, I (1883–84), 125; II (1884–85), 94; North Indian Notes and Queries, IV (1894–95), 72; J. H. Hutton, The Angami Nagas, 1921, pp. 241–242; J. P. Mills, The Lhota Nagas, 1922, pp. 168–169; the Same, The Ao Nagas, 1926, pp. 241–242; Hodson, The Nāga Tribes of Manipur, 1911, p. 142; Shakespear, The Lushei Kuki Clans, 1912, p. 109; Mrs. Leslie Milne, The Home of an Eastern Clan, 1924, p. 263; R. V. Russell, The Tribes and Castes of the Central Provinces of India, 1916, III, 562, 563; IV, 140; Enthoven, The Folklore of Bombay, 1924, pp. 241, 258–259; Bombay Gazetteer, IX, ii (1894), 142 (Gujarat); Journal of the Bombay Branch, Royal Asiatic Society, XIV (1879–80), 202–203; E. Thurston, Ethnographic Notes in Southern India, 1906, pp. 328–329, and Plate XIX; the Same, Omens and Superstitions of Southern India, 1912, pp. 120, 246–254; Journal of the Ceylon Branch of the Royal Asiatic Society, IV (1865–66), 68–78; VII, ii (1882), 116–119 (with figure); Hildburgh, Journal Royal Anthropological Institute, XXXVIII (1908), 157–161, 180–181; Geiger,

Aufsätze zur Kultur- und Sprachgeschichte (Kuhn Festschrift), 1916, pp. 185–192 (Ceylon).

3. Plato, Laws, xi, p. 933 B; Theocritus, ii, 28–29; Fahz, De Poetarum Romanorum Doctrina Magica (Religionsgeschichtliche Versuche und Vorarbeiten, II, iii), 1904, pp. 19–23 (125–129); Kuhnert, Rheinisches Museum, XLIX (1894), 43–58; Dedo, De Antiquorum Superstitione Amatoria, 1904, pp. 22–27. See also note 19.

4. For image witchcraft see Du Cange, s. vv. *invultare, vultivoli*; Hansen, Quellen, 1901, index, s. vv. *Zauberei, Bilder*; von Negelein, Bild, Spiegel und Schatten, Archiv für Religionswissenschaft, V (1902), 1–37; Frazer, The Golden Bough, 3d ed., I (1911), 55–78; Feilberg, Sjæletro (Danmarks Folkeminder, No. 10), 1914, pp. 165–204 (also Aarbog for Dansk Kulturhistorie, 1896, pp. 1–55); Lea, A History of the Inquisition, 1888, III, 389–391, 430, 434–435, 453, 455–456, 458–459, 464, 467–468; Nyrop, Dania, VII (1900), 37–42; Cuming, Journal of the British Archæological Association, LV (1899), 161–170; Cabanès and Nass, Poisons et Sortilèges, 1903, I, 197–253, 304–306; von Dobeneck, Des Deutschen Mittelalters Volksglauben, 1815, II, 20–28; Carl Meyer, Der Aberglaube des Mittelalters, 1884, pp. 261–263; Andree, Ethnographische Parallelen und Vergleiche, II (1889), 8–11; Gomme, Ethnology in Folklore, 1892, pp. 51–52; Lewin, Die Gifte in der Weltgeschichte, 1920, pp. 411–415; Haddon, Magic and Fetishism, 1906, pp. 20–22; D. McKenzie, The Infancy of Medicine, 1927, pp. 52–56; Longman and Loch, Pins and Pincushions, 1911, pp. 30–34; Thoms, Anecdotes and Traditions (Camden Society), 1839, pp. 101–102; Hartland, The Legend of Perseus, II (1895), 97–100; Zeitschrift des Vereins für Volkskunde, IX (1899), 333–335; X (1900), 417–420; Alfonso el Sabio, Las Siete Partidas, vii, 23, 2 (ed. 1807, III, 668); Pseudo-Paracelsus, De Summis Naturae Mysteriis, transl. by Dorn, 1584, pp. 82, 84 (Of the Supreme Mysteries of Nature, transl. by R. Turner, 1655, pp. 85, 87–88); Paracelsus, De Ente Spirituali, chaps. 7–8 (Œuvres Complètes, transl. by Gillot de Givrey, 1913, I, 111–114); Nider, Formicarius, v, 3, ed. 1517 (1516), fol. lxxiiii v°; Malleus Maleficarum, Pt. II, qu. 1, cap. 5, 11, 12 (ed. 1620, pp. 192, 223, 228); Martin Plantsch, Opusculum de Sagis Maleficis, 1507, sig. b v, lf. 2 r°; Paolo Grillando, De Sortilegiis, ed. 1545, iii, 11, fol. xx v° (ed. 1592, iii, 15, p. 27); v, 3, xxv v° (v, 2–3, pp. 48–49); v, 11–12, fol. xxvij (v, 9–10, pp. 54–55); vi, 14, fol. xxxij r° (vi, 18, pp. 76–77); x, 6, fol. lj r° (x, 9, p. 158); x, 14, foll. lj v°–lij r° (x, 13, pp. 160–161); Wier, De Praestigiis Daemonum, v, 9, 10, 12, ed. 1568, pp. 477, 480–481, 487–488; Paulus Frisius Nagoldanus, Dess Teuffels Nebelkappen, 1583, sig. B4 v°; Fernel, De Abditis Rerum Causis, ii, 16 (De Morbis Universalibus et Particularibus, 1656, p. 517); Boguet, Discours des Sorciers, 1608, chap. 31, pp. 197–201; van Helmont, Of the Magnetick Cure of Wounds, cap. 87, transl. Charleton, A Ternary of Paradoxes, 1650, p. 55; Charles Sorel, De l'Vnguent des Armes, appended to Des Talismans, 1636, pp. 387–388; Thiers, Traité des Superstitions, 1741, I, 154; IV, 461–463; Calmet, Traité sur les Apparitions des Esprits, 1751, pp. 161–168; Marguerite of Navarre, Heptaméron, i, 1, ed. Frank, I, 39–42; Lehugeur, Histoire de Philippe le Long, I (1897),

416, 436; De Cauzons, La Magie et la Sorcellerie en France, II, 310, 312, 334-335, 346-347; Hecker, Die Grossen Volkskrankheiten des Mittelalters, ed. Hirsch, 1865, pp. 157-158; Doutté, Magie et Religion dans l'Afrique du Nord, 1909, pp. 61-62, 298-300; Mauchamp, La Sorcellerie au Maroc, pp. 293-297; Sudan Notes and Records, II (1919), 133; Farrow, Faith, Fancies and Fetich, or Yoruba Paganism, 1926, pp. 119-121; D. R. MacKenzie, The Spirit-Ridden Konde, 1925, p. 258; P. A. Talbot, The Peoples of Southern Nigeria, 1926, II, 182; Pechuël-Loesche, Volkskunde von Loango, 1907, p. 339; Weeks, Among the Primitive Bakongo, 1914, pp. 225-226; Decle, Three Years in Savage Africa, 1894, p. 153 (Matabele); Puckett, Folk Beliefs of the Southern Negro, 1926, pp. 242-245, 271-272 (U. S. A.); Skeat, Malay Magic, 1900, pp. 45, 430-432, 569-574 (with figures); Gimlette, Malay Poisons and Charm Cures, 1923, pp. 96, 105-106; The Philippine Islands, ed. Blair and Robertson, XLIII (1906), 313, 317-318; Hose and McDougall, The Pagan Tribes of Borneo, 1912, II, 117-119; Hose, Natural Man, 1926, pp. 250-251 (Borneo); Forgues, Revue des Deux Mondes, 2d Series, XLIII (1863), 154 (Borneo); The Native Tribes of South Australia, ed. Woods, 1879, pp. 23-24, 135; Howitt, Journal Anthropological Institute, XVI (1887), 27-29; the Same, The Native Tribes of South-East Australia, 1904, p. 363; Eylmann, Die Eingeborenen der Kolonie Südaustralien, 1908, p. 218; Le Clercq, Nouvelle Relation de la Gaspesie, 1691, pp. 334-335; Charlevoix, Journal, xxv (1721), Histoire et Description Generale de la Nouvelle France, 1744, VI, 88; Alexander Henry, Travels and Adventures in Canada and the Indian Territories between 1760 and 1776, 1809, p. 121; A Narrative of the Captivity and Adventures of John Tanner, 1830, pp. 174, 341; J. G. Kohl, Kitchi-Gami, 1860, pp. 281-282, 395-397; Speck, Memoirs American Anthropological Association, VI (1919), 265-266; Freeland, University of California Publications, American Archæology and Ethnology, XX (1923), 70; Bureau of American Ethnology, 26th Report (for 1904-05), 1908, p. 446 (Tlingit Indians); Archiv für Religionswissenschaft, XV (1912), 313-318 (with figures; Mexico); Journal Ethnological Society of London, New Series, II (1870), 236 (Bolivia and Peru); De Groot, The Religious System of China, V (1907), 920-926; Dennys, The Folk-Lore of China, 1876, pp. 82-83; Wieger, Folk-Lore Chinois Moderne, 1909, pp. 11, 96-99, 237-239, 277-283; Revue Scientifique, 4th Series, XIX (1903), 562 (China); Batchelor, Ainu Life and Lore, pp. 268-269; Fritzner, Historisk Tidsskrift, Kristiania, IV (1877), 203; Maal og Minne, 1921, pp. 43-44; Zeitschrift der Gesellschaft für Schleswig-Holsteinische Geschichte, XXVIII (1898), 293-297 (fifteenth century); Am Ur-Quell, VI (1896), 12; Archiv für Kriminal-Anthropologie, III (1900), 97; Volkskunde, XII (1899-1900), 245; Ebel, Hessische Blätter für Volkskunde, III (1904), 130-146; Seyfarth, Aberglaube und Zauberei in der Volksmedizin Sachsens, 1913, pp. 50-54; Zeitschrift der Gesellschaft für Schleswig-Holsteinische Geschichte, XLV (1915), 199, 211; Chapiseau, Le Folk-Lore de la Beauce et du Perche, 1902, I, 209; Wallonia, XII (1904), 6-8; Pitrè, Usi e Costumi, IV (1889), 134; Archivio per lo Studio delle Tradizioni Popolari, XVIII (1899), 17-18; Mansikka, Ueber Rus-

sische Zauberformeln, 1909, p. 93; Holmberg, Finno-Ugric, in The Mythology of All Races, ed. J. A. MacCulloch, IV (1927), 12–13; von Wlislocki, Volksglaube und Religiöser Brauch der Zigeuner, 1891, pp. 103–108.
Cf. Zeitschrift für Oesterreichische Volkskunde, III (1897), 272; Bonwick, Daily Life and Origin of the Tasmanians, 1870, p. 178; Ribbe, Zwei
Jahre unter den Kannibalen der Salamo-Inseln, 1903, p. 149.

5. Chaucer, Canterbury Tales, Prologue, A 417–418. For elaborate
directions for making images to cause love or hate, fever or torment, to
win favor, to bind the tongue, etc., see Sloane MS. 3556, foll. 11 v°–15 r°.
Iron spikes and thorns are used. Astrology is taken into account. Angels
and demons are invoked.

6. The House of Fame, vv. 1266–1270.

7. Agrippa, De Occulta Philosophia, ii, 49, ed. 1533, p. cxci.

8. Primrose, Popular Errours, translated by Robert Wittie, 1651, Book
iv, chap. 48, p. 428. The original book, De Vulgi in Medicina Erroribus,
appeared in 1638.

9. "Defigi quidem diris deprecationibus nemo non metuit" (Pliny,
xxviii, 2, 4, 19).

10. See Audollent, Defixionum Tabellae, 1904, pp. xlix–liii, lv–lvi; for
figures on tablets, see pp. lxxvi–lxxvii (see also the figures on the Sethian-
ische Verfluchungstafeln, ed. Wünsch, 1898); for external images, see
pp. lxxvii–lxxxi. Cf. Wünsch, Defixionum Tabellae Atticae, 1897 (Inscrip-
tiones Graecae, III, iii); Kuhnert, Pauly-Wissowa, Real-Encyclopädie,
VIII (1901), 2373–2377. Such pictures may also be seen in magical papyri:
for example, in one found at Oxyrhynchus are depicted three human heads
(like busts), and between two of them stands the name of Paulus Julianus
(Papiri Greci e Latini, No. 29, I [1912], 69–71, and facsimile). In modern
magic you may kill your enemy by nailing to a tree a piece of paper inscribed with his name (Manz, Volksbrauch und Volksglaube des Sarganserlandes, Schriften der Schweizerischen Gesellschaft für Volkskunde, XII
[1916], 109–110).

11. Wünsch, Eine antike Rachepuppe, Philologus, LXI (1902), 26–31
(with figures). Cf. his references, and Audollent, Defixionum Tabellae,
pp. lxxv–lxxx (see especially No. 17, p. 32); also Nogara, Ausonia, IV
(1910), 31–39; Mariani, the same, IV, 39–47; Dugas, Bulletin de Correspondance Hellénique, XXXIX (1915), 413–423; Cumont, Comptes Rendus,
Académie des Inscriptions, 1913, pp. 412–421.

12. Notizie degli Scavi, 1897, pp. 529–534 (with figures).

13. Sophronius, SS. Cyri et Joannis Miracula, cap. 35, Migne, Patrologia Graeca, LXXXVII, 3541–3548.

14. Thurston, Ethnographic Notes in Southern India, 1906, Plate XIX.

15. Poenitentiale Ecgberti, iv, 17, Thorpe, Ancient Laws, folio ed.,
1840, p. 379.

16. Modus Imponendi Poenitentiam (canons enacted under Edgar),
§ 38, Thorpe, p. 409 (Wilkins, Concilia, I, 274, § 40). Cf. Liebermann, Die
Gesetze der Angelsachsen, II, 588, 743.

17. Leges Regis Henrici Primi, cap. 71, § 1, p. 251 Thorpe. See Chapter II, note 41.

18. Kemble, Codex Diplomaticus, No. 591, III, 125 (I, lix–lx); Thorpe, Diplomatarium Anglicum, pp. 229–230; Birch, Cartularium Saxionicum, No. 1131, III, 372–373. The text is not perfectly clear. Cf. Kemble, The Saxons in England, 1849, I, 432, 526; Jente, Die Mythologischen Ausdrücke im Altenglischen Wortschatz, 1921, pp. 311–313. On drowning as a punishment for witchcraft see Hansen, Zauberwahn, pp. 115, 222, 381, 383, 431. Cf. Æthelstan's Laws, iv, § 6, 4, Liebermann, I, 172 (iii, 6, in Thorpe, p. 93), and see Liebermann, II, 393.

19. Virgil, Eclogue viii, 80–81; Ovid, Heroides, vi, 91–92; John of Salisbury, Policraticus, i, 12, ed. Webb, 1909, I, 51–52. Such magicians are called *vultiuoli*, John tells us. Another kind of figures are made by *imaginarii*: "Imaginarii sunt, qui imagines quas faciunt, quasi in possessionem praesidentium spirituum mittunt, ut ab eis de rebus dubiis doceantur" (i, 12, I, 52).

20. Petrus Blesensis, Epistola 65, Opera, ed. Giles, I, 192.

21. That is, the mass *In Commemoratione omnium Fidelium Defunctorum*, which begins "Requiem aeternam dona eis, Domine" (Missale Romanum, Lugduni, 1690, pp. lxxxix–xci).

22. Giraldus Cambrensis, Gemma Ecclesiastica, i, 49, Opera, ed. Brewer, II, 137.

23. Gesta Trevirensium Archiepiscoporum, cap. 28 (Martene, Veterum Scriptorum Amplissima Collectio, IV, 172–173; Recueil des Historiens, XI, 194).

24. See Rigault, Le Procès de Guichard, Évêque de Troyes, 1896, especially pp. 67–68, 70, 72–80, 194, 270–273. Cf. Johannes a Sancto Victore, Memoriale Historiarum, Recueil, XXI, 644, cf. 652.

25. Calendar of Close Rolls 1313–1318, p. 163 (cf. pp. 26, 64, 88); Calendar of Patent Rolls 1313–1317, pp. 4, 13, 42, 44, 45, 101, 204, 255.

26. Continuatio Chronici Girardi de Fracheto, Recueil, XXI, 42–43; Continuatio Chronici Guillelmi de Nangiaco, the same, XX, 612–613, 618; Johannes a Sancto Victore, Memoriale Historiarum, the same, XXI, 659–661; Chroniques de Saint-Denis, the same, XX, 693–696, 700; Chronique Rimée, vv. 7055–7096, 7195–7288, cf. vv. 7326–7327, the same, XXII, 159–160; J. Petit, Charles de Valois, 1900, pp. 145–154, 337–338; Lehugeur, Histoire de Philippe le Long, I (1897), 109. The execution is recorded by Adam Murimuth, ed. Thompson, p. 22.

27. Langlois, Le Fin d'Hugues Géraud, La Revue de Paris, 13th year, I (1906), 531–552.

28. Coram Rege Roll, ed. Palgrave, Parliamentary Writs, II, ii (1830), Appendix, pp. 269–271; Wright, Proceedings against Dame Alice Kyteler (Camden Society, XXIV), pp. xxiii–xxix; Calendar of Patent Rolls 1324–1327, p. 44.

29. Avignon, Kal. Sept., 1324, Papal Letters, II, 461.

30. Gesta Romanorum, cap. 102 (94), ed. Œsterley, pp. 428–430, cf. 727; ed. Dick (Innsbruck MS.), cap. 167, pp. 139–141.

31. Robert Holkot, Super Libros Sapientie, Lectio 190, Speyer, 1483, sig. Pj r° (Reutlingen, 1489, sig. Miiij, lf. 4 v°).

32. Barham, The Ingoldsby Legends, ed. 1875, I, 125–166.

33. Rotuli Parliamentorum, IV, 118. See the inventory of Friar Randolf's goods, the same, IV, 225–226. Cf. Devon, Issues of the Exchequer, pp. 368–370, 373; Calendar of Patent Rolls 1416–1422, pp. 276, 294, 304, 362, 396, 402.

34. Devon, Issues of the Exchequer, p. 362; Chronicle of London, 1827, pp. 107–108; Kingsford, Chronicles of London, pp. 73, 80, cf. 298; Brut, ed. Brie, pp. 422–423; Walsingham, Historia Anglicana, ed. Riley, II, 331.

35. Chronicle in MS. Harley 3775, in Riley's edition of John Amundesham, Annales Monasterii S. Albani, I, 38; Kingsford, Chronicles of London, pp. 80, 273; Gregory's Chronicle, ed. Gairdner, p. 164; Brut, ed. Brie, p. 423; Devon, Issues of the Exchequer, pp. 360, 365. For Friar Randolf see Baildon, Archæologia, LXI (1908), 166–174.

36. Rotuli Parliamentorum, IV, 247–249; Calendar of Patent Rolls 1422–1429, pp. 84, 166.

37. Mandate of September 25, 1419, Wilkins, Concilia, III, 392–393.

38. Wilkins, Concilia, III, 393–394.

39. Calendar of Patent Rolls 1422–1429, p. 363.

40. King's order of August 9, 1441 (Rymer's Foedera, 2d ed., X, 851; Calendar of Patent Rolls 1436–1441, p. 559); order of October 26, 1443 (Rymer, XI, 45; Calendar of Patent Rolls 1441–1446, p. 206); Records of the Privy Council, ed. Nicolas, VI, 51; Rotuli Parliamentorum, V, 135; Devon, Issues of the Exchequer, pp. 440–442, 447–448, 459–460; William Wyrcester, Annales (Stevenson, Letters and Papers illustrative of the Wars of the English in France, II, ii, 762–763); Brut, ed. Brie (Early English Text Society), pp. 477–484, 508–509; Three Fifteenth-Century Chronicles, ed. Gairdner (Camden Society, New Series, XXVIII), pp. 63, 149, 150; English Chronicle, ed. Davies (Camden Society, LXIV), pp. 57–60; Gregory's Chronicle (Gairdner, The Historical Collections of a Citizen of London, Camden Society, New Series, XVII), pp. 183–184; Chronicle of London, 1827, pp. 128–130; Chronicles of London, ed. Kingsford, 1905, pp. 148–149, 154–155; Six Town Chronicles, ed. Flenley, 1911, pp. 102, 115–116; Brief Notes (Kingsford, English Historical Literature in the Fifteenth Century, 1913, pp. 340–341, cf. p. 156); Chronicle of the Grey Friars (ed. Nichols, Camden Society, LIII, pp. 17–18; ed. Howlett, Monumenta Franciscana, II, 171); Brief Annals (Songs, Carols, etc., from Richard Hill's Commonplace-Book, ed. Dyboski, Early English Text Society, pp. 144–145); Fabyan, fol. clxxxxvii, ed. Ellis, 1811, p. 614; Hall's Chronicle, ed. 1809, p. 202; Stow, Annales, ed. 1631, pp. 381–382; poem On the Mutability of Worldly Changes (Kingsford, English Historical Literature, p. 396); Drayton, Englands Heroicall Epistles (Poems, Part II, Spenser Society, pp. 267–284, especially pp. 271–272); Mirror for Magistrates, ed. 1587, foll. 140 v°–145 r° (ed. Haslewood, 1815, II, 112–125); Christopher Middleton, The Legend of Humphrey, Duke of Glocester, 1600 (Harleian Miscellany, ed. Park, X [1813], 176–179, 181–184); Vickers, Humphrey Duke of Gloucester, 1907, pp. 269–279, 335; J. W. Flower, Surrey Archæological Collections, II (1864), 157–168. For the poetical Lament of the Duchess of Gloucester ("Thorowout a pales as I can passe") see Wright, Political Poems, II, 205–208; Flügel, Anglia,

XXVI (1903), 177–180; Songs, Carols, etc., from Richard Hill's Common-place-Book, ed. Dyboski, pp. 95–96; Hardwick, Cambridge Antiquarian Society Communications, I (1859), 177–190. See also the ballad of "The Lamentable Fall of the Dutchess of Gloster," T. Evans, Old Ballads, 1784, I, 317–323 (R. H. Evans, Old Ballads, III, 1–8). The First Part of King Henry VI ignores the Witch of Eye and Canon Southwell, but associates Sir John Humm with Roger Bolingbroke and the Duchess. Sir John is mentioned, apparently in connection with this case, by Chronicle, ed. 1827, pp. 129–130: "Roger the clerk afornseyd on the Satirday, that is to sey the xviij day of Novembre, was brought to the Yeldehalle, with Sir John Hom prest, and William Wodham squyer, the which Sr John and William hadden there chartres [i.e. pardons] at that tyme." Robert Bale's Chronicle (Six Town Chronicles, ed. Flenley, p. 116) and the chronicle in Cotton MS. Vitellius Axvi (Kingsford, Chronicles of London, p. 155), which also (though not so clearly) indicate this association, likewise mention John Humme (Hum).

41. This point of relapse is expressly mentioned in An English Chronicle, ed. Davies, p. 59. See also Coke, Institutes, Part III, chap. 6.

42. An English Chronicle, ed. Davies, p. 57. Cf. Stow, Annales, ed. 1631, p. 381; Gregory's Chronicle, p. 183; A Chronicle of London, 1827, p. 128; Kingsford, Chronicles of London, p. 148; Robert Bale's Chronicle, Flenley, Six Town Chronicles, p. 115; William Wyrcester, Annales, as above, II, ii, 763; Brut, ed. Brie, p. 478.

43. Brut (Trin. Coll. Camb. MS. O. 9. 1), p. 478.

44. Brut, p. 480. Cf. Kingsford, English Historical Literature in the Fifteenth Century, p. 93. As to Eleanor's declaring that all she wanted was to have a child by the Duke, see the extraordinary report made to him by his physician, Gilbert Kymer (Dietarium, in Hearne's edition of Liber Niger Scaccarii, 1728, pp. 550–559, especially pp. 553–554, 557–558). Cf. Étienne de Bourbon, Septem Dona Spiritus Sancti, ed. Lecoy de la Marche, 1877, pp. 318–319.

45. The Golden Bough, 3d ed., I (1911), 70–74.

46. Fabyan, fol. clxxxvii, ed. Ellis, 1811, p. 614; Hall, ed. 1809, p. 202.

47. Chronicle, ed. Davies, p. 58.

48. The same, p. 60.

49. The same, p. 57.

50. See pp. 76, 147–148, 151, above.

51. See Lehugeur, Histoire de Philippe le Long, I (1897), 416; Hansen, Quellen, pp. 18, 48, 231.

52. Stevenson, as above, II, ii, 763. Wyrcester mentions no other accomplices of Eleanor except the "Wyche of Eye." His words are: "Quidam clericus famosissimus unus illorum in toto mundo in astronomia et arte nigromantica" and "notabilissimus clericus unus in toto mundo."

53. Rigault, Le Procès de Guichard, Évêque de Troyes, 1896, pp. 79–80.

54. Chroniques de Saint-Denis, Recueil, XX, 696.

55. "Mulier magica, vocata vulgariter Wyche of Eye juxta villam Westmonasterii" (Wyrcester, II, ii, 763); "the wicche of Eye beside Westminster" (Brut, p. 480); "the wycche be syde Westemyster" (Gregory's

Chronicle, p. 184); "surnamed the wytche of Eye besyde Westmynster" (Fabyan, fol. clxxxxvii, ed. 1811, p. 614); "a witch of Eye besides West-minster" (Stow, ed. 1631, p. 381). On "The Manor of Eia, or Eye next Westminster" see W. L. Rutton, Archæologia, LXII (1910), 31–58.

56. Devon, Issues of the Exchequer, p. 410 (Asshewell), p. 409 ("a certain woman," clearly Margery). I have no record of Virley's arrest, but assume it took place about the same time.

57. Rymer, Foedera, 2d ed., X, 505; Records of the Privy Council, ed. Nicolas (May 9, 1432), IV, 114; Wright, Proceedings against Dame Alice Kyteler, p. xii, note. Cf. Tighe and Davis, Annals of Windsor, 1858, I, 301–302. In a document of May 6, 1432 (printed by Palgrave, An Essay upon the Original Authority of the King's Council, 1834, p. 89), Asshe-well is described as "Ordinis Sanctae Crucis Londoniae." An entry in a chronicle under date of June 17, 1433, may throw some light on his repu-tation. That afternoon "was the Clipse [eclipse] that Asshewell the white frere, and other clerkes, spake of longe tyme before; which all peple dowted [i.e. dreaded] and were sore aferd of, thurgh the speche of the said frere" (Brut, ed. Brie, p. 466).

58. Harleian MS. 3775, printed in Amundesham, Annales Monasterii S. Albani, ed. Riley, I, 56–57.

59. MS. Julius Bii, Kingsford, Chronicles of London, p. 96. Cf. Chron-icle in Harleian MS. 3775, ed. as above, I, 42: "foemina malitiosa Fran-ciae, la Puselle dicta."

60. Rymer, Foedera, 2d ed., X, 408.

61. "Quae Johanna in juventute non fuit edocta nec instructa in credu-litate nec primitivis fidei; sed per aliquas vetulas mulieres assuefacta et imbuta ad utendum sortilegiis, divinationibus et aliis superstitiosis operibus sive magicis artibus; quarum villarum plures habitantes notati fuerunt ab antiquo uti praedictis maleficiis": Procès de Condamnation et de Réhabilitation de Jeanne d'Arc, ed. Quicherat, I (1841), 209. Cotta, in 1616, referred to Joan as "that infamous woman" (The Triall of Witch-craft, p. 48).

62. Rymer, 2d ed., X, 504–505; Calendar of Patent Rolls 1429–1436, p. 220; Wright, Kyteler, p. xi, note.

63. English Chronicle, ed. Davies, pp. 58–59.

64. Gairdner, Lollardy and the Reformation, I (1908), 337–338.

65. Bale, Scriptorum Illustrium Maioris Brytanniae Catalogus, viii, 4, I (1557), 584–585. Bale credits two books to Roger's pen: "Contra uulgi superstitiones, Lib. 1" and "De sua innocentia, Lib. 1," but I do not find his name in Bale's notebook (Index Britanniae Scriptorum, ed. Lane Poole and Bateson, 1902).

66. Waldron, A Description of the Isle of Man, ed. Harrison (Manx Society), 1865, p. 14; Flower, Surrey Archæological Collections, II (1864), 166.

67. The Duchess's petition, February 10, 1470, approved by the king on February 16, Rotuli Parliamentorum, VI, 232; also Calendar of Patent Rolls 1467–1477, p. 190, and Earl of Leicester's MSS., Historical Manu-scripts Commission, 9th Report, Appendix, p. 367.

68. Petition in the Act of Settlement, 1484, Rotuli Parliamentorum, VI, 241. Cf. Tyndale, The Practice of Prelates, Expositions and Notes, ed. Walker, Parker Society, pp. 304-305.

69. Hale, p. 20. Cf. H. J. Bell, Obeah, 2d ed., 1893, pp. 60-61.

70. See p. 100, above.

71. Knyght's petition, Archæologia, LX (1907), 373-374.

72. Petition and answer, Archæologia, LX (1907), 374-376.

73. Hector Boëthius, Scotorum Historia, Book xi, Paris, 1574, fol. 221; William Stewart, The Buik of the Croniclis of Scotland, or a Metrical Version of the History of Hector Boece, vv. 35749-35924, ed. Turnbull, II, 512-517. Cf. Wier, iii, 14, ed. 1568, pp. 250-255; Holinshed, V (1808), 233-234. On the whole matter of such magic see Dalyell, The Darker Superstitions of Scotland, 1834, pp. 328-351.

74. Letters and Papers, IV, ii, No. 3743, pp. 1670-1671. Cf. Notes and Queries for Somerset and Dorset, XVII (1923), 291.

75. Letters and Papers, XIII, i, No. 41, p. 13; XIII, ii, No. 1200, p. 505.

76. Statute of 33 Henry VIII, chap. 8, Statutes of the Realm, III (1817), 837.

77. Scot, xiii, 13, p. 308 (217), ed. Nicholson, p. 251.

78. From Wier, v, 10, ed. 1568, pp. 480-481.

79. Scot, xii, 16, pp. 257-259 (185-187), ed. Nicholson, pp. 208-210.

80. Acts of the Privy Council, New Series, XI, 22. These were the four witches (Elizabeth Stile and her three associates) executed at Abingdon in February, 1578-9: see Stationers' Register, ed. Arber, II, 349, 352; Scot, Discoverie, i, 4, p. 10 (7), 8; i, 8, p. 17 (12), 13; iii, 7-8, p. 51 (42), 39-40; ix, 7, p. 176 (129), 142; Discourse of Divels (appended to same), chap. 33, p. 543 (389), 455-456; Notestein, pp. 27-28, 346-347, 387.

81. Acts, X, 309; see also X, 322, 326.

82. Scot, xvi, 3, pp. 474-475 (342-343), 399-400. Cf. Notestein, p. 387. Scot cites Bodin.

83. Bodin, De la Demonomanie des Sorciers, 1580, Preface, sig. éiij, lf. 2 v° (1587, sig. íij r°); ii, 8, 1580, foll. 116 v°-117 r° (1587, foll. 129 v°-130 r°).

84. Mendoza to Zayas, September 8, 1578, State Papers, Spanish, 1568-1579, No. 524, p. 611.

85. Jonson, The Masque of Queens, 1609. He cites Bodin, ii, 8.

86. Acts, XI, 36-37.

87. The same, XII, 251-252.

88. Historical MSS. Commission, Marquis of Salisbury's MSS., III, 106.

89. Gentleman's Magazine, October, 1860, CCIX, 380-385; Hart, Archæologia, XL (1866), 395-396; Calendar of State Papers, Domestic, 1581-1590, p. 644.

90. An Epistle of the Persecvtion of Catholickes in Englande, transl. by G. T., Douay, [1582,] pp. 149-150; Rishton's Addition to Nicholas Sanders, De Origine ac Progressv Schismatis Anglicani, 1586, pp. 430-432; Ribadeneira, Appendix to Sanders's De Origine, in Vera et Sincera Historia, 1628, p. 50; Diego de Yepes, Historia Particvlar de le Persecu-

cion de Inglaterra, 1599, ii, 9, § 11, p. 75; Pollen, Unpublished Documents relating to the Catholic Martyrs (Catholic Record Society, V), 1908, pp. 97–99, 139; Diarium Secundum, Douai, ed. T. F. Knox, 1878, p. 127, cf. p. 217; Register of Merton College, Philosophical Transactions for 1758, L, ii (1759), 699–702; Acts of the Privy Council, New Series, IX, 347, 368–369; Cogan, The Haven of Health, 1589, pp. 272–276; Stow, Annales, ed. Howes, 1615, p. 681; Fuller, Church-History, 1655, Cent. XVI, ix, 3, §§ 23–25, pp. 109–110; Plot, The Natural History of Oxford-shire, 1677, chap. 2, § 10, p. 24; Camden's Annales, ed. 1625, pp. 285–286; Baker's Chronicle, ed. 1660, p. 376; Bacon, Sylva Sylvarum, x, § 914; Wood, The History and Antiquities of the University of Oxford, ed. Gutch, II (1796), 188–192 (cf. the Latin translation, Historia et Antiquitates, 1674, of which Wood complained as both abbreviated and interpolated, I, 294–296); A. Clark, note in his ed. of Wood, Survey of the Antiquities of the City of Oxford (Oxford Historical Society), I (1889), 269; Challoner, Memoirs of Missionary Priests, I (1741), Introd., pp. 6–10; F. Pollard, The Antiquary, XIII (1886), 49–54; A. Clark, Register of the University of Oxford, II, i (1887), 154; John Webster, The Displaying of Supposed Witchcraft, 1677, pp. 245–246. Cf. Nashe, Pierce Penilesse, 1592: "One bad pamphlet is enough to raise a damp that may poison a whole Tearme" (Works, ed. McKerrow, I, 239).

91. Historical MSS. Commission, 12th Report, Part IV, Duke of Rutland's MSS., I, 294–297, 147. There is discrepancy in dates. Was the year 1591 or 1583, or were there two prosecutions?

92. Calendar of State Papers, Domestic, 1611–1618, p. 29.

93. On the case of the Earl of Derby see Lodge, Illustrations of British History, 2d ed., 1838, II, 459–462; Gentleman's Magazine, 1751, XXI, 269–270, 398–399; Stow, Annales, ed. 1631, pp. 767–768; Historical MSS. Commission, 4th Report, Appendix, p. 366; Calendar of the Marquis of Salisbury's MSS., V, 253.

94. Lodge, The Divel Coniured, 1596, pp. 39–40 (Hunterian Club, No. 26, 1875, Complete Works, III). The word *wax* is misprinted *war*.

95. Calendar of State Papers, Domestic, 1598–1601, p. 523.

96. Potts, The Wonderfull Discoverie of Witches, 1613, sig. B3 lf. 1 v°, E, E3 lf. 1 v°–F r°, F3 lf. 2, G2, N3 lf. 2 v°–O2 v°. Cf. Cotta, The Infallible True and Assured Witch, 1624, p. 113. A lump of clay stuck full of pins figured in the trial of a witch acquitted in 1682 (An Account of the Tryal and Examination of Joan Butts, 1682).

97. Truth Brought to Light and Discouered by Time, 1651, pp. 19–20, 43, 137; Howell, State Trials, II (1816), 932–933; The Egerton Papers, ed. Collier (Camden Society), 1840, p. 472. See also, as to a waxen image thought to represent Prince Henry, Spedding, Bacon's Letters and Life, V (1869), 289.

98. James I, Dæmonologie, ii, 5, ed. 1597 (and 1603), pp. 44–46; William Perkins, A Discourse of the Damned Art of Witchcraft, 1608, pp. 148–149; Cotta, A Short Discoverie, etc., 1612, p. 58; the Same, The Triall of Witch-craft, 1616, p. 90; the Same, The Infallible True and Assured Witch, 1624, p. 113; Cooper, The Mystery of Witch-craft, 1617,

p. 259; Fairfax, Dæmonologia, ed. Grainge, 1882, pp. 72–75, 95–96; Bernard, A Guide to Grand-Iury Men, 2d ed., 1629, pp. 175–176; The Lawes against Witches, 1645, p. 4; Stearne, A Confirmation and Discovery of Witch-craft, 1648, pp. 53–54; Beveridge, Cullross and Tulliallan, 1885, I, 238 (1650); Gaule, Πῦσ-μαντία the Mag-astro-mancer, 1652, pp. 174–176, 230–231; Pitcairn, Criminal Trials in Scotland, 1833, III, 605, 612–613, 615–616, 618 (1662); Drage, Daimonomageia, 1665, pp. 12–14; Meric Casaubon, A Treatise proving Spirits, Witches and Supernatural Operations, 1672 (a reissue of his Of Credulity and Incredulity in Things Natural and Civil, 1668), pp. 86–87, 92–94; Glanvil, Sadducismus Triumphatus, 4th ed., 1726, pp. 296–299, 302–303, 307, 309–311; Wilts Quarter Sessions, 1670, Historical MSS. Commission, Various Collections, I, 150–151; Blagrave, Astrological Practice of Physick, 1671, pp. 121–127, 135, 153; A True and Impartial Relation of the Informations against Three Witches, 1682, pp. 7–10, 18–19; Bovet, Pandaemonium, 1684, pp. 227–229; George Sinclair, Satans Invisible World Discovered, 1685, reprint (1871), pp. 1–8, 24; Aubrey, Remaines of Gentilisme and Judaisme (1686–87), ed. Britten, 1881, p. 61; A Collection of Modern Relations of Matters of Fact concerning Witches and Witchcraft, 1693, pp. 47–48 (case in 1644); Sadducismus Debellatus, 1698, p. 39; Boys, The Case of Witchcraft at Coggeshall, Essex, in the Year 1699 (London, 1901), pp. 8–9, 11–13, 15–17; Hickes to Pepys, June 19, 1700, Private Correspondence of Pepys, ed. Tanner, 1926, I, 370–371 (Scotland); A True and Full Relation of the Witches of Pittenweem, 1704, pp. 5, 7, 10. Cf. Primerose, Popular Errours, transl. Wittie, 1651, pp. 426–428; Alexander Ross, The Philosophicall Touch-Stone, 1645, p. 31. Joan Flower, arrested in 1619 for murdering the son and heir of the Earl of Rutland by witchcraft, had (her daughters testified) put a glove of little Lord Henry's into boiling water, pricked it often, and then buried it (The Wonderfull Discoverie of the Witchcrafts of Margaret and Philip Flower, 1619, sigg. C3, lf. 2 v°–D r°). See p. 324, above. Shadwell, who utilizes the pricking of images of wax and wool in his comedy of The Lancashire Witches (published in 1682), remarks in a note: "One in my memory had this kind of witchcraft sworn against her at the Old-Bayley, before Steel, Recorder of London" (The Poetry of Witchcraft, ed. Halliwell, 1853, pp. 28, 35).

99. Cotton Mather, The Wonders of the Invisible World, Boston, 1693, pp. 99, 113. In her Witch-Cult in Western Europe, 1921, pp. 49, 151, Miss Murray accepts Mr. Burroughs as the actual head of a "coven" or witch-conventicle, and so do Mr. Herbert Gorman in his entertaining novel "The Place Called Dagon" (1927) and Mr. Summers in his Geography of Witchcraft (1927, p. 346). All three (pardonably, so far as the novelist is concerned) overlook or ignore the fact that the General Court in 1711 reversed Mr. Burroughs's attainder and awarded damages to his heirs (Goodell, Proceedings Massachusetts Historical Society, 1st Series, XX [1884], 285–294, cf. 313, 315–316, 318–319).

100. Cotton Mather, Late Memorable Providences, 2d impression, London, 1691, p. 8. Cf. the Same, A Brand Pluck'd out of the Burning, 1692 (Burr, Narratives of the Witchcraft Cases 1648–1706, 1914, p. 273);

the Same, Another Brand, in Calef, More Wonders of the Invisible World, 1700, p. 9. See also Burr, p. 440, for the case of Grace Sherwood of Virginia (1706).

101. Lady Charlotte Bury, Diary, 1839, I, 306.

102. A. de Rochas, L'Extériorisation de la Sensibilité, 6th ed., 1909, pp. 85–129; Jules Bois, Le Satanisme et la Magie, 1895, pp. 291–337 (malefic), 338–362 (love).

103. Folk-Lore, XV (1904), 102–103.

104. Notes and Queries for Somerset and Dorset, XI (1909), 328. In 1900 it was reported that an Italian burned a pin-studded wax figure of President McKinley on the steps of the American embassy in London (Boston Herald, March 22, 1923). In Norfolk, not long ago, many pin-studded wax figures were found in the cottage of a reputed (and professional) witch who had just died (Harper's New Monthly Magazine, LXXXVII [1893], 795).

105. Sussex Archæological Collections, LIX (1918), 130. See also Wickham, Records by Spade and Terrier, p. 299 (Somerset); The Reliquary, XV (1874–75), 111–113 (image of dough); Folk-Lore, XV (1904), 103 (Cambridgeshire).

106. Folk-Lore, XII (1901), 176 (Lincolnshire). Cf. Harland and Wilkinson, Lancashire Folk-Lore, 1867, pp. 208–209; Blakeborough, Wit, Character, Folklore and Customs of the North Riding of Yorkshire, 2d ed., 1911, p. 191 (cake baked on shovel; witch's name chalked on shovel; witch made ill; bewitched woman recovered). A charm on paper pierced with pins may torture the witch and fetch her (E. Owen, Welsh Folk-Lore, p. 249).

107. Journal of American Folk-Lore, XXV (1912), 133 (Georgia); cf. IX (1896), 227. See also Puckett, Folk Beliefs of the Southern Negro, 1926, pp. 242–244.

108. See Maclagan, Folk-Lore, VI (1895), 144–148 (with figure); J. G. Campbell, Witchcraft and Second Sight in the Highlands and Islands, 1902, pp. 46–48; The Celtic Magazine, XII (1887), 41; W. Mackay, Urquhart and Glenmoriston, 1893, p. 431; Polson, Our Highland Folklore Heritage, 1926, pp. 35, 72–73. Cf. Pitcairn, Criminal Trials in Scotland, 1833, I, 197, 199, 240; III, 605, 612–613, 615–616, 618 (clay, wax, butter); James Napier, Notes and Reminiscences relating to Partick, 1875, pp. 182–183; Trotter, Galloway Gossip, 1901, p. 247; Train, An Historical and Statistical Account of the Isle of Man, 1845, II, 168; Bottrell, Traditions and Hearthside Stories of West Cornwall, I (1870), 77; Bardan, The Dead-Watchers and Other Folk-Lore Tales of Westmeath, 1891, pp. 60–61; Folk-Lore, VI (1895), 302 (Ireland).

109. Gaelic Dictionary (Herne Bay, 1902), p. 254.

110. Folk-Lore, VI (1895), 144; XIV (1903), 373–374.

111. Antiquarian Magazine, V (1884), 104; Folk-Lore Journal, II (1884), 121. See also Nicholson, Golspie, 1897, pp. 82 (clay figure in running stream), 82–83 (rag image with pins in it burned).

112. Longman and Loch, Pins and Pincushions, 1911, Plate XII, at p. 33; cf. Folk-Lore, VI (1895), 147.

113. Folk-Lore, XIX (1908), 93–94.

114. Roscoe, The Northern Bantu, 1915, p. 285. Cf. Caland, Altindischer Zauberritual, 1900, p. 166; Crooke, Religion and Folklore of Northern India, 1926, pp. 188–189; W. C. Smith, The Ao Naga Tribe of Assam, 1925, p. 96; G. W. Briggs, The Chamārs, 1920, p. 169; Sudan Notes and Records, VII (1924), 79; P. A. Talbot, The Peoples of Southern Nigeria, 1926, II, 183.

115. The Rennes Dindsenchas, § 49, ed. Stokes, Revue Celtique, XV (1894), 443–444. Cf. Pradel, Mitteilungen der Schlesischen Gesellschaft für Volkskunde, VI, ii (1904), 1–36; E. W. Smith and A. M. Dale, The Ila-Speaking Peoples of Northern Rhodesia, 1920, I, 234.

116. Addy, Household Tales, 1895, pp. 36–37.

117. Tremearne, The Ban of the Bori, p. 183. Cf. Archivio per lo Studio delle Tradizioni Popolari, XVIII (1899), 37 (portrait); Speck, Penobscot Shamanism, Memoirs American Anthropological Association, VI, No. 4 (1919), 265–266 (picture outlined in sand or drawn with charred stick on bark — shot, stabbed, clubbed, or burned); Menghi, Flagellum Daemonum, Exorcism 6, in Mallei Maleficarum, 1582, II, 242 (demon's painted image burned as part of exorcism).

118. Bergen, Animal and Plant Lore, 1899, p. 15. Cf. Doddridge, Notes on the Settlement and Indian Wars of the Western Parts of Virginia and Pennsylvania, 1824, p. 162.

119. Boston Herald, March 22, 1923. Cf. Bergen, p. 15 (Alabama).

120. Folk-Lore, XXXII (1921), 125. Cf. Whitney and Bullock, Folk-Lore from Maryland, 1925, p. 79.

121. Henslowe's Diary, ed. Greg, 1904, p. 33. Cf. Sloane MS. 3846, fol. 95 v°.

122. Revue des Traditions Populaires, IX (1894), 12.

123. Bergen, Current Superstitions, 1896, p. 144; cf. Whitney and Bullock, Folk-Lore from Maryland, 1925, p. 79. On "the perils of portraiture" see Abbott, Macedonian Folklore, 1903, pp. 300–301; Andree, Ethnographische Parallelen und Vergleiche, II (1889), 18–20; Holmberg, Finno-Ugric, in The Mythology of All Races, ed. J. A. MacCulloch, IV (1927), 12; Sébillot, Revue des Traditions Populaires, I (1886), 349–354; Seyfarth, Aberglaube und Zauberei in der Volksmedizin Sachsens, 1913, p. 54. Cf. Crooke, Religion and Folklore of Northern India, 1926, pp. 189–190; J. H. Hutton, The Sema Nagas, 1921, pp. 199–200; W. C. Smith and Hutton, The Ao Naga Tribe of Assam, 1925, p. 96; Tremearne, The Tailed Head-Hunters of Nigeria, 1912, p. 195.

124. Bergen, p. 128. Cf. Crooke, p. 189; Zeitschrift für Oesterreichische Volkskunde, XIII (1907), 133; Biblioteca de las Tradiciones Populares Españolas, I (1883), 237; Zeitschrift für Völkerpsychologie, XIII (1882), 343; Puckett, Folk Beliefs of the Southern Negro, 1926, pp. 441–442; Germania, XXIX (1884), 92. See Róheim, Spiegelzauber, 1919, Chap. VI.

125. Somerset County Gazette, January 22, 1881, as quoted by Gomme, Folklore as an Historical Science, pp. 204–205.

126. Compare the black magic with a buried lizard in the Kauçika Sūtra, Caland, Altindischer Zauberritual, 1900, pp. 164–166. See also Sudan Notes and Records, II (1919), 125; Beaver, Unexplored New Guinea, 1920, p. 134.

127. Audollent, Defixionum Tabellae, Nos. 111–112, pp. 167–171; No. 222, pp. 295–296; No. 241, pp. 323–324. Cf. No. 36, p. 66; No. 232, pp. 305–306. See also p. lxxxi.

128. Henderson, Notes on the Folk-Lore of the Northern Counties, 1879, pp. 223–224.

129. Transactions Devonshire Association, LVI (1925), 308. Cf. Wilkinson, Transactions Historic Society of Lancashire and Cheshire, New Series, I (1861), 2–4; Harland and Wilkinson, Lancashire Folk-Lore, 1867, pp. 208–209; W. G. Black, Folk-Medicine, 1883, p. 73. According to Drage, Daimonomageia, 1665, p. 12, "some take a Beast Skin or Hide, and stick it full of Thornes, or Pins and call it such an ones Skin"; and he describes (p. 13) a somewhat similar ceremony in which a certain horse is called by name. Cf. the impaling of a cat in order that a thief may suffer (J. H. Hutton, The Angami Nagas, 1921, p. 242).

130. Audollent, No. 222, p. 295.

131. The Same, No. 241, p. 323.

132. Proceedings against Dame Alice Kyteler, ed. Wright (Camden Society, XXIV), pp. 2–3, 32. Cf. Frischbier, Hexenspruch und Zauberbann, 1870, pp. 20–21; Scheftelowitz, Das Stellvertretende Huhnopfer (Religionsgeschichtliche Versuche und Vorarbeiten, XIV, iii), 1914, pp. 49–50; Eitrem, Les Papyres Magiques de Paris, Skrifter utgit av Videnskapsselskapet i Kristiania, 1923, pp. 6–7.

133. Folk-Lore, XXII (1911), 51. Cf. Pliny, x, 56, 77, 156; Höfler, Die Volksmedizinische Organotherapie, p. 31; De Cock, Volksgeneeskunde in Vlaanderen, 1891, pp. 95, 107–109. For the baptism of a cock see Mr. William Lilly's History of his Life and Times, 2d ed., 1715, p. 41, and p. 148, above.

134. See cases in 1603 and 1604 (cat: Sussex Archæological Collections, XLIX [1906], 53–54); 1605 (John Hawarde, Les Reportes del Cases in Camera Stellata, ed. Baildon, 1894, pp. 250–251); 1632 (Reports of Cases in the Courts of Star Chamber and High Commission, ed. Gardiner, Camden Society, New Series, XXXIX, 275–276). Cf. Pitcairn, Criminal Trials in Scotland, 1833, II, 543; J. B. Baker, The History of Scarborough, 1882, p. 487; Germania, X (1865), 100–101.

135. See p. 206.

136. Document printed by Hart, Archæologia, XL (1867), 397. The blood of a black cock is of much consequence in a seventeenth-century spell and ceremony invoking Sathan, Barentur, and Barbason for money (Sloane MS. 3846, foll. 27 v°–29 r°).

137. Cf. De Cock, Volksgeneeskunde in Vlaanderen, 1891, pp. 104–109.

138. Archæologia Cambrensis, 3d Series, II (1856), 185.

139. Gloucestershire Notes and Queries, I (1881), 43; Henderson, Notes on the Folk Lore of the Northern Counties, 1866, p. 108; Nicholson, Folk Lore of East Yorkshire, 1890, p. 141; Old Yorkshire, ed. by William

Smith, II (1881), 170; The Essex Review, V (1896), 160; Bye-Gones for 1874–75, p. 125; for 1886–87, pp. 465, 478; for 1893–94, p. 25; Folk-Lore Record, I (1878), 218; Folk-Lore, VI (1895), 121; Leather, The Folk-Lore of Herefordshire, 1912, p. 84; Charles Kent, The Land of the "Babes in the Wood," [1910,] p. 86; Frazer, The Golden Bough, 3d ed., IX (1913), 53; Wuttke-Meyer, p. 327; Mélusine, II (1884–85), 550; III (1886–87), 44; Zeitschrift des Vereins für Rheinische und Westfälische Volkskunde, II (1905), 282. Cf. Trotter, Galloway Gossip, 1901, p. 125; Kristensen, Jyske Folkeminder, IX (1888), 64; P. Saintyves (i.e. É. Nourry), La Guérison des Verrues, 1913, pp. 34–37.

140. Bye-Gones for 1871–73, p. 47; Henderson, 1879, p. 150; C. H. Poole, The Customs, etc., of the County of Somerset, 1877, p. 52. Cf. Wuttke-Meyer, p. 326; Marcellus Burdigalensis, De Medicamentis, ed. Niedermann (Corpus Medicorum Latinorum, V), 1916, viii, 52, p. 59; xiv, 25, p. 107; xiv, 68, p. 111; Glyde, The Norfolk Garland, p. 31; E. P. Herrick, The Southern Workman (magazine), XXXVI (1907), 403 (Cuba).

141. Gloucestershire Notes and Queries, I (1881), 43.

142. Brockett, A Glossary of North Country Words, 1825, p. 190; Folk-Lore Record, I (1878), 42. Cf. Dalyell, pp. 191–192.

143. Folk-Lore, XXXV (1924), 356 ("Spider, as you waste away, Whooping cough no longer stay"; Suffolk); Burne and Jackson, Shropshire Folk-Lore, p. 194; Salopian Shreds and Patches, V (1883), 79; Polson, Our Highland Folklore Heritage, 1926, p. 32. Cf. Notes and Queries for Somerset and Dorset, III (1893), 3; Henderson, 1879, p. 141; R. V. Russell, The Tribes and Castes of the Central Provinces of India, 1916, IV, 224.

144. Leechdoms, ed. Cockayne, II, 76, 104, 142, 144, 306, 318; III, 52; ed. Leonhardi, pp. 24, 32, 43, 94, 97, 144. Cf. Marcellus Burdigalensis, De Medicamentis, ed. Niedermann (Corpus Medicorum Latinorum, V), 1916, viii, 50, pp. 58–59; viii, 64, p. 60; xii, 24, p. 99; xxii, 41, p. 177; xxix, 35, p. 233. For ancient spells of transference see Heim, Incantamenta Magica, Nos. 69–74, pp. 483–484. Cf. also W. G. Black, Folk-Medicine, 1883, pp. 34–48; Enthoven, The Folklore of Bombay, 1924, p. 277; Frazer, The Golden Bough, 3d ed., IX, 1–71; Seyfarth, Aberglaube und Zauberei in der Volksmedizin Sachsens, 1918, pp. 180–205; Blau, Das Altjüdische Zauberwesen, 1898, p. 73; Bodin, De la Demonomanie des Sorciers, iii, 2, ed. 1587, foll. 143 v°–146 r°; Cabanès and Barraud, Remèdes de Bonne Femme, 1907, pp. 229–250; Sébillot, Traditions et Superstitions de la Haute-Bretagne, 1882, I, 285–286; Strackerjan, Aberglaube und Sagen aus dem Herzogtume Oldenburg, 2d ed., 1909, I, 81–88.

145. Transactions Shropshire Archæological and Natural History Society, 1st Series, III (1880), 283; cf. VIII (1885), 99–100.

146. Burdick, Magic and Husbandry, 1905, p. 161; Grimm, Deutsche Mythologie, 4th ed., III (1878), 175; U. Jahn, Die Deutschen Opfergebräuche bei Ackerbau und Viehzucht, 1884, pp. 14–18; Wuttke-Meyer, pp. 299–300, 435; John, Sitte, Brauch und Volksglaube im Deutschen Westböhmen, Beiträge zur Deutsch-Böhmischen Volkskunde, VI (1905),

290; Skattegraveren, IX (1888), 73–74; Reutlinger Geschichtsblätter, VI (1895), 47; Kristensen, Danske Sagn, VI, i (1900), 269; VI, ii (1901), 479–482; Henderson, Notes on the Folk-Lore of the Northern Counties, 1866, p. 117 (1879, p. 148); Dalyell, pp. 101, 185 (1629, 1643); Wm. Hunter, Biggar and the House of Fleming, 1867, p. 390. Cf. Thurston, Omens and Superstitions of Southern India, 1912, p. 211 (pig buried alive), cf. p. 210; Roscoe, The Northern Bantu, 1915, pp. 136–137 (cattle plague transferred to one cow, which is then killed). For the burial of living men or animals in Russia to check the cholera see Löwenstimm, Aberglaube und Strafrecht, 1897, pp. 11–15; the Same, Zeitschrift für Socialwissenschaft, VI (1903), 210.

147. Notes and Queries, 1st Series, I (1850), 294.

148. Saga-Book of the Viking Club, III (1902–04), 50; Thiers, Traité des Superstitions, 1741, I, 271, 378. Cf. Mackay, Urquhart and Glenmoriston, 1893, p. 435; The Indian Antiquary, XLI (1912), Supplement, p. 70. See p. 103, above.

149. Dalyell, pp. 190–191, 420.

150. Folk-Lore, VI (1895), 167; XI (1900), 446; XIII (1902), 56; XIV (1903), 370–371. Cf. Gregor, The Folk-Lore of the North-East of Scotland, 1881, p. 140; W. Mackay, Urquhart and Glenmoriston, 1893, p. 435; Roscoe, The Banyankole, 1923, p. 138 (fowl buried alive with disease attached).

151. Proceedings Society of Antiquaries of Scotland, IV (1863), 216, note; Henderson, 1879, pp. 147–148. Cf. Am Ur-Quell, Neue Folge, I (1897), 25; Polson, Our Highland Folklore Heritage, 1926, p. 30.

152. Maclagan, Evil Eye in the Western Highlands, 1902, pp. 217–218.

153. Notes and Queries, 1st Series, I (1850), 429.

154. Transactions Devonshire Association, IX (1877), 90. Cf. Craigie, Scandinavian Folk-Lore, 1896, p. 388; Haupt's Zeitschrift, XXII (1878), 8–9.

155. Rhŷs, Celtic Folklore, 1901, pp. 304–308, has excellent material on burning live animals to stop a pest and on the confusion between the idea of bringing the witch and that of sacrifice. Thus (p. 305), "A . . . woman . . . related to me how she watched while the carcase of a bewitched colt was burning, and how she saw the witch coming," etc. As to plain sacrifice see Transactions Devonshire Association, XXXVIII (1906), 87–88; Archæologia Cambrensis, 4th Series, II (1871), 98.

156. Journal of Sir Roger Wilbraham, January 18, 1604[–5], ed. Scott (Camden Miscellany, X), p. 69.

157. Archæologia, XXX (1844), 397.

158. Giffard, A Discourse of the Subtil Practises of Deuilles by Witches and Sorcerers, 1587, sig. H3 r°.

159. Cf. Pitcairn, Criminal Trials in Scotland, 1833, III, 557.

160. Giffard, A Dialogue concerning Witches and Witchcraftes, 1593, sig. G v°, E r°, L4 v°, B r°; cf. C3 r°, H r°, T4 v°. Cf. Perkins, A Discourse of the Damned Art of Witchcraft, 1608, p. 208; Cotta, A Short Discoverie of the Vnobserued Dangers of Seuerall Sorts of Ignorant and Vnconsiderate Practisers of Physicke in England, 1612, p. 54; the Same,

The Triall of Witch-craft, 1616, pp. 113–114; the Same, The Infallible True and Assured Witch, 1624, p. 136; Fairfax, Daemonologia, ed. Grainge, 1882, p. 35; Bernard, A Guide to Grand-Iury Men, 2d ed., 1629, p. 209; Gaule, Select Cases of Conscience touching Witches and Witchcrafts, 1646, p. 76; Drage, Daimonomageia, 1665, p. 21; Glyde, The Norfolk Garland, p. 54.

161. The Essex Review, XXV (1916), 96.

162. The Essex Review, XII (1903), 104–105. Cf. Wuttke-Meyer, p. 284.

163. The Essex Review, XII (1903), 103–104.

164. Zincke, Wherstead, 2d ed., 1893, pp. 223–225. See also The Examiner, January 1, 1809, II, 6. Cf. Vonbun, Die Sagen Vorarlbergs, 2d ed., 1889, p. 153 (eggs disappear; a hen is thrown into the oven; the witch is burned).

165. Folk-Lore Journal, II (1884), 122. See also Grimm, Deutsche Mythologie, 4th ed., I (1875), 506–507 (1767, Mull; Northamptonshire); III (1878), 175; Forby, The Vocabulary of East Anglia, 1830, II, 395–396; Hunt, Popular Romances of the West of England, 1865, I, 237–239; W. G. Black, Folk-Medicine, 1883, pp. 72–74; Dalyell, The Darker Superstitions of Scotland, 1834, pp. 184–185; Gregor, The Folk-Lore of the North-East of Scotland, 1881, p. 186; Maclagan, Evil Eye in the Western Highlands, 1902, p. 140; Proceedings Society of Antiquaries of Scotland, IV (1863), 216; Henderson, Notes on the Folk-Lore of the Northern Counties, 1879, pp. 148–149; Robert Young, Annals of the Parish and Burgh of Elgin, 1876, p. 81; A. W. Moore, The Folk-Lore of the Isle of Man, 1891, pp. 92–93; Zeitschrift des Vereins für Volkskunde, V (1895), 410; Hartland, The Legend of Perseus, II (1895), 109–110. Erasmus Francisci (Der Höllische Proteus, 2d ed., 1695, p. 109) tells of putting a hare on the fire to make the witch come.

166. Cross, Studies in Philology (University of North Carolina), XVI (1919), 259; Doddridge, Notes on the Settlement and Indian Wars of the Western Parts of Virginia and Pennsylvania, 1824, p. 163 (live puppies burned in glass-blowers' furnaces; cf. The Indian Antiquary, XXVIII [1899], 252).

167. Lincolnshire Notes and Queries, I (1889), 170. Cf. Doddridge, Notes on the Settlement and Indian Wars of the Western Parts of Virginia and Pennsylvania, 1824, p. 163.

168. Harper's New Monthly Magazine, October, 1893, LXXXVII, 797; Charles Kent, The Land of the "Babes in the Wood," [1910,] p. 87. Cf. Henderson, 1879, p. 149; Cowan, The Ancient Capital of Scotland, 1904, II, 132.

169. Records of the Colony or Jurisdiction of New Haven, ed. Hoadly, 1858, pp. 224–225; J. M. Taylor, The Witchcraft Delusion in Colonial Connecticut, pp. 149–150. Cf. Bernard, A Guide to Grand-Iury Men, 2d ed., 1629, p. 209; Pool's narrative (1663) in Glanvil, Sadducismus Triumphatus, 4th ed., 1726, p. 327. Andrew West had an ailing pig. Some said "burne it, other said, cut of the eares and burn them, and so they did, and

then the pig amended by and by" (A True and Iust Recorde, 1582, sig. F). Cf. Sloane MS. 3846, fol. 96 v° (hair and ear-tips).

170. The Most Strange and Admirable Discouerie of the Three Witches of Warboys, 1593, sig. P3, lf. 1 r°; Relation of the Most Remarkable Proceedings at the Late Assizes at Northampton, 1674, pp. 4–5 [many sheep have legs broken by witchcraft; one burnt, "for that (according to their tradition) would make the Witch come to the place"]; Hale, A Modest Enquiry into the Nature of Witchcraft (1697), Boston, 1702, pp. 78–79 (ca. 1659); The Reliquary, XVIII (1877–78), 146; Notes and Queries for Somerset and Dorset, IV (1895), 77; Bye-Gones for 1882–83, p. 335; Gregor, Notes on the Folk-Lore of the North-East of Scotland, 1881, pp. 185–186; Train, An Historical and Statistical Account of the Isle of Man, 1845, II, 159; Journal of American Folk-Lore, XIV (1901), 44; Egerton MS. 2884, article 11, fol. 14, Catalogue of Additions to the Manuscripts in the British Museum 1906–1910, p. 268; Doddridge, as above, p. 163; Whitney and Bullock, Folk-Lore from Maryland, 1925, p. 79. Cf. Bladé, Contes Populaires de la Gascogne, 1886, II, 233–234; Kristensen, Danske Sagn, VI, i (1900), 296–297; Wuttke-Meyer, pp. 259, 436.

171. Hunt, Popular Romances of the West of England, 1865, II, 82–83. Cf. Notes and Queries, 1st Series, VII (1853), 613; Henderson, 1879, p. 186 (blood of elfshot cow boiled with pins brings the witch). See also C. J. Palmer, The Perambulation of Great Yarmouth, II (1874), 148, note; Bye-Gones for 1901–02, p. 95 (burn hay); Ditchfield, The Parson's Pleasance, pp. 192–193; Whitney and Bullock, Folk-Lore from Maryland, 1925, p. 80; Roscoe, The Baganda, 1911, p. 344.

172. Dawson, The Reliquary, XXIII (1883), 200. Giffard (A Dialogue of Witches and Witchcraftes, 1593, sig. E4 r°) tells of burning hair of a sick boy; the witch came and said "John, scratch me." Drage (Daimonomageia, 1665, pp. 9–10) notes that "a great Sign is, If any thing that comes from the Sick be burnt or harmed, and the suspected Woman suffers in such manner, or comes to the House" (cf. p. 21: "burning the Excrements [i.e. hair or nails] of one bewitched"). At the trial of Anne Kerke, hanged at Tyburn in 1599, it was testified that Mother Gillams of the Bankside had pronounced the afflicted child bewitched, and had advised the parents to cut off and burn a piece of the witch's coat "togeather with the childs vnder cloth": this was done and the child was healed (Report, in The Triall of Maist. Dorrell, 1599, p. 100). Cf. Festschrift Louis Gauchat, 1926, p. 425; Hartland, The Legend of Perseus, II (1895), 112–115; Deutsche Volkskunde aus dem Oestlichen Böhmen, V (1905), 28–32; VI (1906), 202–203. See also Giffard, sig. E3 v° (clothes of sick girl burned); G2 v° (nails boiled; witch's face "all bescratched"); The Wonderfull Discouerie of the Witch-crafts of Margaret and Philip Flower, 1619, sig. C2; Bernard, A Guide to Grand-Iury Men, 2d ed., 1629, pp. 132, 209. For New England, Hale (1697) remarks, "I observed that the people laid great weight upon this; when things supposed to be bewitched were burnt, and the suspected person came to the fire in the time of it" (A Modest Enquiry into the Nature of Witchcraft, Boston, 1702, p. 21; cf. pp. 77–81). Cf. Cotton Mather, Late Memorable Providences, 2d impression, London, 1691, p. 115.

173. Mathews, Tales of the Blackdown Borderland (Somerset Folk Series, No. 13), 1923, p. 106; Sébillot, Le Folk-Lore de France, III (1906), 124 (cf. III, 241).

174. Clague, Manx Reminiscences, [1911,] p. 175; [Trotter,] Galloway Gossip, 1877, pp. 45, 98–99 (cock's heart as a counter-charm). For a wax heart see Trotter, pp. 98–99.

175. Logan, The Scottish Gaël, 1831, II, 63. Cf. p. 93, above.

176. Transactions Devonshire Association, XIV (1882), 387–390; cf. XXVIII (1896), 94–95. For the spiked barrel see Child, The English and Scottish Popular Ballads, II, 343; IV, 30, note ‡, 32; V, 48; Train, An Historical and Statistical Account of the Isle of Man, 1845, II, 167–168.

177. Dawson, History of Skipton, 1882, p. 389. Cf. Transactions Devonshire Association, XIV (1882), 390–392.

178. Folk-Lore, XX (1909), 65.

179. Notes and Queries for Somerset and Dorset, IV (1895), 77. Cf. III (1893), 1–2; Elworthy, The Evil Eye, 1895, p. 56.

180. Notes and Queries for Somerset and Dorset, III (1893), 2–3. See also Transactions Devonshire Association, X (1878), 103 (pig). Cf. the case from Radnorshire in Bye-Gones for 1886–1887, p. 310 (calves). See also the Rev. Thomas Jackson, Recollections, 1873, pp. 13–14 (woman in a decline, ox-heart stuck with pins, roasted, to bring witch).

181. Archæologia Æliana, New Series, XXII (1900), 113; Folk-Lore Journal, I (1883), 91. Cf. Longman and Loch, Pins and Pincushions, 1911, pp. 36–37.

182. Wickham, Records by Spade and Terrier, p. 292; Folk-Lore Record, V (1882), 172.

183. Folk-Lore, XXVIII (1917), 100.

184. Folk-Lore Journal, III (1885), 378. Cf. County Folk-Lore, II (1901), 165; Sébillot, Le Folk-Lore des Pêcheurs, 1901, p. 218.

185. George Roberts, The History and Antiquities of the Borough of Lyme Regis and Charmouth, 1834, p. 262.

186. J. C. Atkinson, Forty Years in a Moorland Parish, 2d ed., 1891, pp. 104–106.

187. Transactions Devonshire Association, XLIX (1917), 69–71.

188. Folk-Lore, XII (1901), 176. Cf. Volkskunde, XII (1899–1900), 160.

189. County Folk-Lore, II (1901), 158 (cow's heart buried).

190. Peacock, A Glossary of Words used in the Wapentakes of Manley and Corringham, 1877, p. 193 (heart of bewitched beast stuck full of pins and buried).

191. Nicholson, The Folk Lore of East Yorkshire, 1890, p. 92. Cf. Logan, The Scottish Gaël, 1831, II, 63.

192. Scott's Journal, January 31, 1827, 1890, I, 350; Archæologia Scotica, III (1831), 300–301; figure in Longman and Loch, Pins and Pincushions, 1911, Plate XII, at p. 33 (see p. 37). For a very curious piece of imposture, involving the suspension of a beast's heart stuck with pins in a chimney (for increase of money), see Folk-Lore Journal, I (1883), 332.

193. Elworthy, The Evil Eye, 1895, pp. 53–54, figs. 4 and 5 (cf. p. 55);
the Same, West Somersetshire Word-Book, English Dialect Society, 1886,
pp. 572–573. Cf. Hancock, The Parish of Selworthy, Somerset, 1897,
p. 239; A. L. Humphreys, The Materials for the History of the Town of
Wellington, Co. Somerset, 1889, p. 239; Mathews, Tales of the Blackdown
Borderland (The Somerset Folk Series, No. 13), 1923, pp. 105–106; Transactions Devonshire Association, XLIX (1917), 69.

194. Proceedings Dorset Natural History and Antiquarian Field Club,
XIII (1892), 45–46 (cf. p. 56).

195. Transactions Devonshire Association, XXXV (1903), 136–137.

196. The Times, March 5, 1917, p. 5.

197. Henderson, Notes on the Folk-Lore of the Northern Counties,
1866, pp. 186–187.

198. The Antiquarian, XLI (1905), 363 (as the hearts dry and the pins
drop out, misfortunes come). In Somerset a toad's heart stuck with pins
serves a like purpose (Mathews, Tales of the Blackdown Borderland, 1923,
p. 107). In Wales we hear of a live toad, thus pierced, as an evil charm
(Longman and Loch, Pins and Pincushions, p. 33). A cow's heart, pierced
with pins, has been used to bewitch a cow (T. and K. Macquoid, About
Yorkshire, 1883, p. 294). Cf. Drechsler, Sitte, Brauch und Volksglaube in
Schlesien, II (1906), 107.

For examples of (1) burning or roasting or boiling an animal's heart
or hanging it up to shrivel in the chimney, or (2) piercing it (with thorns,
pins, nails, or the like), or of a combination of such rites, the object being
to torment the witch and make her come and reverse the spell, or to thwart
or kill her, or somehow to stop disease, see Malleus Maleficarum, Pt. II,
qu. 2, ed. 1620, pp. 268–269; van Helmont, De Magnetica Vulnerum
Curatione, capp. 110, 171, Opera, 1682, pp. 723, 731 (transl. Charlemont,
A Ternary of Paradoxes, 1650, pp. 63–64, 89); Thiers, Traité des Superstitions, 4th ed., 1741, I, 155; Burr, Narratives of the Witchcraft Cases
1648–1706, 1914, p. 87 (Pennsylvania, 1684); Notes and Queries, 2d Series,
I (1856), 415; Mathews, Tales of the Blackdown Borderland, 1923, p. 110;
J. Sullivan, Cumberland and Westmorland, 1857, p. 152; Peacock, A Glossary of Words used in the Wapentakes of Manley and Corringham, 1877,
p. 193; F. K. Robinson, A Glossary of Words used in the Neighbourhood of
Whitby, 1876, p. xxii; Blakeborough, Wit, Character, Folklore and Customs of the North Riding of Yorkshire, 2d ed., 1911, pp. 158–159; Lovett,
Magic in Modern London, 1925, pp. 67–69; E. Owen, Welsh Folk-Lore,
p. 241; J. C. Davies, Folk-Lore of West and Mid-Wales, 1911, p. 239;
County Folk-Lore, II (1901), 156, 160; VII (1914), 114–115 (Fifeshire,
1743); Gregor, The Folk-Lore of the North-East of Scotland, 1881,
p. 187; McCulloch, Guernsey Folk Lore, 1903, pp. 293, 390–394, 403–404;
Laisnel de la Salle, Le Berry, I (1900), 364; Sauvé, Le Folk-Lore des
Hautes Vosges, 1889, pp. 200–201; Witzschel, Sagen, Sitten und Gebräuche aus Thüringen (Kleine Beiträge, II), 1878, p. 270; Wuttke-Meyer,
p. 284 (cf. p. 185); E. Meier, Deutsche Sagen, Sitten und Gebräuche aus
Schwaben, 1852, p. 176; Frischbier, Hexenspruch und Zauberbann, 1870,
pp. 19–20; Wallonia, I (1893), 149–150; XV (1907), 104, 303; Knoop,

Volkssagen aus dem Oestlichen Hinterpommern, 1885, p. 167; Baltische Studien, XXXVI (1886), 339–340; Dania, III (1892–94), p. 222. Cf. Folk-Lore Journal, VI (1888), 116; Cabanès and Nass, Poisons et Sortilèges, 1903, I, 225 (malefic); Zeitschrift des Vereins für Volkskunde, V (1895), 93–94; Alemannia, II (1875), 135; Volkskunde, XII (1899–1900), 160; Meyrac, Traditions des Ardennes, 1890, p. 177. Cf. Bodin, Demonomanie, 1580, iii, 5, fol. 146 v° (horse's entrails burned).

199. Rye MSS., Historical MSS. Commission, 13th Report, Appendix, Part IV, p. 145. Cf. County Folk-Lore, I, No. 2 (1893), p. 188; Puckett, Folk Beliefs of the Southern Negro, 1926, p. 296.

200. Proceedings Society of Antiquaries, 2d Series, XX (1904), 155–156 (with figure).

201. Blakeborough, Wit, Character, Folklore and Customs of the North Riding of Yorkshire, 2d ed., 1911, pp. 145–146.

202. In Slavic tales of the type made famous by Bürger's "Lenore" the dead lover is brought back by boiling a dead man's head, bones, or carcass in a pot or by burning a cat in a redhot oven (Child, The English and Scottish Popular Ballads, V, 61).

203. Heanley, Saga-Book of the Viking Club, III, i (1902), 44.

204. Folk-Lore, XV (1904), 103. Cf. Monseur, Le Folklore Wallon, p. 94; Wallonia, V (1897), 37–38; Sébillot, Le Folk-Lore de France, III (1906), 241 (cf. III, 125); Hilton-Simpson, Among the Hill-Folk of Algeria, 1921, p. 150. Samuel Rowlands, satirizing the wizards of his time, describes one of their love-potions (The Letting of Humours Blood in the Head-vaine, 1600, Hunterian Club reprint, p. 60):

> More, he will teach any to gaine their loue,
> As thus (saies he) take me a Turtle Doue,
> And in an Ouen let her lie and bake
> So dry, that you may pouder of her make;
> Which being put into a cuppe of wine,
> The wenche that drinkes it will to loue incline:
> And shall not sleepe in quiet in her bed,
> Till she be eased of her mayden-head.
> This is *probatum*, and it hath bin tride,
> Or els the cunning man cunningly lide.

The Sunday Observer (London), January 29, 1928, reports a recent case in Genoa: a girl pierced a lamb's heart with pins, and was about to bury it in a churchyard along with her false lover's photograph, in order to ensure his return. Wax hearts pierced with needles were among the paraphernalia of the procuress in de Rojas's Celestina (ed. Cejador y Frauca, 1913, I, 86).

205. Lincolnshire Notes and Queries, II (1891), 41.

206. Addy, Household Tales, 1895, p. 79. The skeleton or one of the bones of a toad or frog that has been buried alive in an anthill is a potent love-charm: Bergen, Animal and Plant Lore, 1899, p. 14; Zeitschrift des Vereins für Rheinische und Westfälische Volkskunde, III (1906), 61–62. Cf. Skattegraveren, XI (1889), 205; Wallonia, II (1894), 62–63; V (1897), 38; Am Ur-Quell, I (1890), 19; II (1891), 55; Blätter für Pommersche

Volkskunde, VI (1898), 27; Puckett, Folk Beliefs of the Southern Negro, 1926, p. 265; Scipione Mercurio, De gli Errori Popolari d'Italia, 1603, iv, 14, fol. 207 v°; Scot, vi, 7, p. 124 (92), ed. Nicholson, p. 98.

207. Henderson, Notes on the Folk-Lore of the Northern Counties, 1866, p. 139 (similarly in Durham, p. 138). See also Journal of the British Archæological Association, LV (1899), 165. Cf. Glyde, The Norfolk Garland, p. 12; J. C. Davies, Folk-Lore of West and Mid-Wales, 1911, p. 10; Monseur, Le Folklore Wallon, p. 94; Wallonia, V (1897), 38; Revue des Traditions Populaires, IX (1894), 12; Schönwerth, Aus der Oberpfalz, I (1857), 127–128; Hessische Blätter für Volkskunde, VI (1907), 13–14; Schweizer Volkskunde, IX (1919), 2.

208. Folk-Lore, XX (1909), 221. Cf. Addy, Household Tales, 1895, p. 80; Puckett, Folk Beliefs of the Southern Negro, 1926, p. 273; Notes and Queries, 1st Series, II (1850), 259.

209. See Chapter VII, note 44.

210. Northall, English Folk-Rhymes, 1892, pp. 156–158, has varieties of the charm and mentions (p. 156) the bladebone. See also Hewett, Nummits and Crummits, 1900, p. 69; Addy, pp. 73–74; Henderson, 1866, pp. 140–141; J. C. Davies, p. 9; Glyde, The Norfolk Garland, pp. 11–12.

211. Notes and Queries, 1st Series, VI (1852), 312. In Oxfordshire a girl may make a doughcake, lay it on the hearthstone, and prick her initials on it; her future husband will come and prick *his* initials: Folk-Lore, XXIV (1913), 79. This is a variety of the "dumb cake": see Archæologia, XVII (1814), 166–167; Brockett, A Glossary of English North Country Words, 1825, p. 229; Forby, The Vocabulary of East Anglia, 1830, II, 408; Halliwell, Popular Rhymes and Nursery Tales, 1849, p. 216; Glyde, The Norfolk Garland, pp. 9–10; Lincolnshire Notes and Queries, II (1891), 44; Hewett, Nummits and Crummits, 1900, pp. 11–12; The English Dialect Dictionary, s. v. *dumb*. Cf. the witch-cake, p. 103, above.

212. Cf. Lovett, Magic in Modern London, 1925, p. 21.

213. At Bovey Tracy once a Devonshire witch gave a man a candle to kill a man (Henderson, Notes on the Folk-Lore of the Northern Counties, 1866, p. 145).

214. Norfolk Annals, ed. Mackie, I (1901), 429–430.

215. Notes and Queries for Somerset and Dorset, IV (1895), 157. Cf. The Spectator, February 17, 1894, LXXII, 232.

216. Skeat, Malay Magic, 1900, pp. 568–569.

217. Elworthy, West Somersetshire Word-Book, p. 572; the Same, The Evil Eye, 1895, pp. 54–55. Cf. Mathews, Tales of the Blackdown Borderland (The Somerset Folk Series, No. 13), 1923, p. 106; Monseur, Le Folklore Wallon, p. 94.

218. Notes and Queries, 2d Series, I (1856), 331.

219. For an African example see MacKenzie, The Spirit-Ridden Konde, 1925, p. 258. Cf. Crooke, Religion and Folklore of Northern India, 1926, p. 430; Oman, Cults, Customs and Superstitions of India, 1908, p. 288; G. W. Briggs, The Chamārs, 1920, p. 169; Hobley, Bantu Beliefs and Magic, 1922, p. 181 (eggs); Fossey, La Magie Assyrienne, 1902, pp. 75–77; Haddon, Magic and Fetishism, 1906, p. 48.

220. Folk-Lore, VIII (1897), 6; Elworthy, The Evil Eye, 1895, p. 57 and fig. 6.

221. Pitrè, Usi e Costumi, IV (1889), 129–131, 134–135. Cf. Giambattista Basile, I (1883), 68; La Calabria, II, No. 3 (1889), p. 8.

222. Enthoven, The Folklore of Bombay, 1924, p. 238.

223. A. B. Brewster, The Hill Tribes of Fiji, 1922, p. 234. Cf. W. Deane, Fijian Society, 1921, p. 162.

224. Williams and Calvert, Fiji and the Fijians, New York, 1859, p. 195.

225. Enthoven, p. 241. Cf. Tremearne, The Ban of the Bori, p. 183.

226. Wins edt, Shaman, Saiva, and Sufi, 1925, p. 53.

227. Baltische Studien, XXXVI (1886), 326. Cf. Journal Royal Anthropological Institute, XLIII (1913), 43–44.

228. Bartsch, Sagen, Märchen und Gebräuche aus Meklenburg, II (1880), 334; Germania, XXXI (1886), 346; Am Ur-Quell, II (1891), 126; V (1894), 289–290; VI (1896), 129; Zeitschrift des Vereins für Rheinische und Westfälische Volkskunde, IV (1907), 222; VII (1910), 231. Cf. Bang, Norske Hexeformularer, 1901, pp. 337–338; Mansikka, Ueber Russische Zauberformeln, 1909, p. 93 (love-charm); Archiv für Kriminal-Anthropologie, XXV (1906), 156–157 (malefic); Folk-Lore, XXXV (1924), 47 (earth from footprint heated with nails, needles, and broken glass, until the pot bursts; Czecho-Slovak); Shakespear, The Lushei Kuki Clans, 1912, p. 109.

229. Hollingsworth, The History of Stowmarket, 1844, p. 247 (nail or knife); A. L. Humphreys, The Materials for the History of the Town of Wellington, 1889, p. 238 (redhot nail); Transactions Devonshire Association, XII (1880), 104 (nail in footprint or threshold); XV (1883), 102; Folk-Lore, XI (1900), 216; XV (1904), 80 (Monmouthshire; knife in heelmark); XXV (1914), 367 (pins); The Spectator, February 17, 1894, LXXII, 231; J. Ll. W. Page, An Exploration of Exmoor, 4th ed., 1895, p. 307 (place a nail or other sharp piece of metal in the witch's path or near her house); Saga-Book of the Viking Club, V (1907–08), 149; Whitney and Bullock, Folk-Lore from Maryland, 1925, p. 82; Seyfarth, Aberglaube und Zauberei in der Volksmedizin Sachsens, 1913, pp. 54–57 (footprint nailed or stabbed); American Anthropologist, XXIII (1920), 442 (stabbed); Radin, Bureau of American Ethnology, 37th Report, pp. 268–269 (stabbed); Howitt, The Native Tribes of South-East Australia, 1904, pp. 366–367 (sharp fragment of quartz, glass, bone, or charcoal); Burdick, Magic and Husbandry, 1905, p. 141 (nail in horse's hoofprint; so Wuttke-Meyer, p. 267). For varieties of footprint magic see Lucian, Dialogi Meretricum, iv, 5; Corrector, § 175 (Schmitz, Die Bussbücher, II, 447); Saxo Grammaticus, iv, p. 177 Müller and Velschow (p. 118 Holder); Cardano, De Subtilitate, xviii, Opera, 1663, III, 645; Sir Kenelm Digby, Of Bodies, 1644, chap. 18, ed. 1645, p. 205; Frazer, The Golden Bough, 3d ed., I (1911), 207–214; Hartland, The Legend of Perseus, II (1895), 78–83; Train, An Historical and Statistical Account of the Isle of Man, 1845, II, 156–157; A. W. Moore, The Folk-Lore of the Isle of Man, 1891, p. 95; Rhŷs, Celtic Folklore, 1901, pp. 303–304; St. J. D. Seymour, Irish Witchcraft and Demonology, 1913, pp. 240–241; Wuttke-Meyer, pp. 269,

271; Rantasalo, Der Ackerbau, IV (1924), 159–161 (FF Communications, XVII, No. 55); Tettau and Temme, Die Volkssagen Ostpreussens,
Litthauens und Westpreussens, 1837, p. 267; Zeitschrift des Vereins für
Volkskunde, XV (1905), 180–181; Niederlausitzer Mittheilungen, II
(1892), 47–48; Deutsche Volkskunde aus dem Oestlichen Böhmen, V
(1905), 41; Revue des Traditions Populaires, XXIII (1908), 11; Zeit-
schrift für Socialwissenschaft, VI (1903), 219–220; Archiv für Kriminal-
Anthropologie, XXV (1906), 156–157, 185, 191–192; Krauss, Slavische
Volkforschungen, 1908, p. 167; Andree, Ethnographische Parallelen und
Vergleiche, II (1889), 8, 11, 12; Journal (Royal) Anthropological Institute, XVI (1887), 26–27; XXXI (1901), 140; XXXVIII (1908), 160;
XLIV (1914), 338–339; XLIX (1919), 293; Caland, Altindischer Zauberritual, 1900, p. 165; The Indian Antiquary, XXXVI (1907), 310;
Crooke, Religion and Folklore of Northern India, 1926, pp. 422, 435;
Milne, The Home of an Eastern Clan, 1924, p. 263; Sibree, Madagascar
before the Conquest, 1926, p. 180; Tremearne, The Ban of the Bori, pp.
181–182; Gouldsbury and Sheane, The Great Plateau of Northern Rhodesia, 1911, p. 90; E. W. Smith and A. M. Dale, The Ila-Speaking Peoples
of Northern Rhodesia, 1920, II, 93; P. A. Talbot, The Peoples of Southern
Nigeria, 1926, II, 182; A. C. Hollis, The Nandi, 1909, p. 51; Pechuël-
Loesche, Volkskunde von Loango, 1907, p. 339 (cf. p. 341); Kitching, On
the Backwaters of the Nile, 1912, p. 238; Westermarck, Ritual and Belief
in Morocco, 1926, II, 332; E. C. Parsons, Folk-Lore of the Sea Islands,
South Carolina, 1923, pp. 211–212; Puckett, Folk Beliefs of the Southern
Negro, 1926, pp. 267, 269–274; Skeat, Malay Magic, 1900, pp. 155, 568–
569; Beaver, Unexplored New Guinea, 1920, p. 133; W. J. V. Saville, In
Unknown New Guinea, 1926, p. 268; Thurnwald, Forschungen auf den
Salomo-Inseln und dem Bismarck-Archipel, I (1912), 443; W. E. Armstrong, Rossel Island, 1928, p. 175; Spencer, The Native Tribes of the
Northern Territory of Australia, 1914, pp. 260–261; M. Bartels, Die
Medicin der Naturvölker, 1923, pp. 32–34; Bureau of American Ethnology, 26th Report (for 1904–05), 1908, p. 446; Leland, Gypsy Sorcery,
1891, p. 112; Journal of American Folk-Lore, XL (1927), 169 (Louisiana
negroes).

230. Maclagan, Evil Eye in the Western Highlands, 1902, p. 9.

231. Perkins, A Discourse of the Damned Art of Witchcraft, 1608,
p. 206, disapproves "the burning of the thatch of the suspected parties
house, which is thought to be able to cure the partie bewitched, and to
make the Witch to bewray her selfe." Cf. Gaule, Select Cases of Conscience touching Witchcrafts, 1646, p. 76; Stearne, A Confirmation and
Discovery of Witch-craft, 1648, p. 34; Blagrave, Astrological Practice of
Physick, 1671, p. 154 (thatch or tile heated in urine); Hartland, The
Legend of Perseus, II (1895), 93; Rowley, Dekker, and Ford, The Witch
of Edmonton, 1623, iv, 1, Dyce's Ford, 1869, III, 236–237; Brand-Hazlitt,
III, 76–77.

232. John Waller in Holinshed, IV (1808), 892. Cf. Glanvil's Sadducismus Triumphatus, 4th ed., 1726, pp. 321, 334.

233. Folk-Lore, XII (1901), 176. Cf. Babcock, The American Journal

of Insanity, April, 1895, p. 520 (bottle buried to thwart witch); Whitney and Bullock, Folk-Lore from Maryland, 1925, p. 82.

234. Folk-Lore Record, I (1878), 25–26. A bottle of bent pins under the hearthstone would keep witches out (I, 26). Cf. Peacock, A Glossary of Words used in the Wapentakes of Manley and Corringham, 1877, p. 193; Cross, Studies in Philology (University of North Carolina), XVI (1919), 263, note; H. J. Bell, Obeah, 2d ed., 1893, pp. 4–5 (against thieves).

235. Sussex Archæological Collections, LX (1919), 147. Cf. Durbin, A Narrative of Some Extraordinary Things, 1800, pp. 39–40, 54–55; A Brief Account, prefixed to the Rev. Isaac Nicholson's Sermon against Witchcraft, 1808, p. iii; W. H. B. Saunders, Legends and Traditions of Huntingdonshire, 1888, pp. 156–157; Forby, The Vocabulary of East Anglia, 1830, II, 394–395; J. G. Campbell, Witchcraft and Second Sight in the Highlands and Islands, 1902, p. 14; Alemannia, II (1875), 135; Bang, Norske Hexeformularer, 1901, p. 347; Tremearne, The Ban of the Bori, p. 184; Mitteilungen der Schlesischen Gesellschaft für Volkskunde, VII, i (1905), 91 (cooking needles makes the witch come); Deutsche Volkskunde aus dem Oestlichen Böhmen, IX (1909), 57 (cooking pins brings the tortured witch). In 1683, when Abraham Swift, a child of twelve, suffered strange fits, the physician refused to prescribe for him "until his water had been tryed by fire": the idea was that, if this were done, "the witch that had hurt him would come and discover all" (The Rev. Oliver Heywood his Autobiography, etc., IV [1885], 53–54).

236. Aubrey, Miscellanies, 4th ed., 1857, p. 140; Hunt, Popular Romances of the West of England, 1865, II, 210, note (cf. Bottrell, Traditions and Hearthside Stories of West Cornwall, I [1870], 81–82); Increase Mather, An Essay for the Recording of Illustrious Providences, 1684, pp. 265–280; Cotton Mather, Late Memorable Providences, 2d impression, London, 1691, pp. 59–61. See also Blagrave, Astrological Practice of Physick, 1671, p. 154; Glanvil's Sadducismus Triumphatus, 4th ed., 1726, pp. 334–335; Brand-Hazlitt, III, 77–78. Cf. An Account of the Tryal and Examination of Joan Butts, . . . at the Assizes holden for Southwark, . . . May 27, 1682 (Dr. Bourn advised the afflicted child's parents "to save the Childs water, and put it into a Bottle, stopping it close, and bury it in the Earth, and to burn the Childs Clothes, assuring them, that the Witch . . . would come in." Joan was acquitted, though she did in fact come in). The experiment of heating urine was tried in the Leicestershire cases of 1717 (Add. MS. 35838, fol. 104). For full directions, as well as an elaborate charm or prayer, see Add. MS. 36674, fol. 145 r°, or Sloane MS. 3706, fol. 23 r°. Cf. Sloane MS. 3846, foll. 95 r°–96 r°.

237. Deodat Lawson, A True Narrative, in Increase Mather's Further Account of the Tryals of the New-England Witches, London, 1693, p. 8; Hale, A Modest Inquiry, Boston, 1702, p. 23; Alexander Roberts, A Treatise of Witchcraft, 1616, p. 53. Cf. Rheinische Geschichtsblätter, I (1895), 348–349. See also Bernard, A Guide to Grand-Iury Men, 2d ed., 1629, p. 132. A versified recipe for such a witch-cake ("to bring in the witch") from Henry Bold's Wit a Sporting in a Pleasant Grove of New Fancies, 1657, pp. 76–77, is quoted in Brand-Hazlitt, III, 78; but this,

like several poems in Bold's little volume, is simply conveyed (as "the wise it call") from Herrick's Hesperides (Riverside edition, II, 116). See also Sloane MS. 3846, fol. 98 v°.

238. Drage, Daimonomageia, 1665, p. 21.

239. Giffard, A Dialogue concerning Witches and Witchcraftes, 1593, sig. G2 v° (also ed. 1603).

240. Folk-Lore, XXXII (1921), 125. Cf. Rochholz, Schweizersagen aus dem Aargau, 1856, II, 167–168.

241. See, for example, Notes and Queries, 2d Series, I (1856), 415; Archæologia, XLVI (1880), 132–134; Devon and Cornwall Notes and Queries, XI (1921), 288; Proceedings Dorset Natural History and Antiquarian Field Club, XXXVII (1916), 59–60 (two vipers and a centipede); Halifax Antiquarian Society Papers, 1904–05, pp. 6–7 (cow's hair, parings of hoof, nails, extracts from the Bible). Cf. Bergen, Animal and Plant Lore, 1899, pp. 14–15.

242. Bogg, Lower Wharfeland, 1904, p. 346. Cf. Longman and Loch, Pins and Pincushions, 1911, pp. 37–38.

243. Cf. The Indian Antiquary, XXVII (1898), 239; Enthoven, The Folklore of Bombay, 1924, p. 239.

244. The Reliquary, VII (1866–67), 101.

245. Transactions Devonshire Association, XXVIII (1896), 98–99; XXXII (1900), 89–90.

246. Hunt, Popular Romances of the West of England, 1865, II, 210.

247. Transactions Devonshire Association, XXXV (1903), 139.

248. Hewett, Nummits and Crummits, 1900, p. 74. For magic by inversion see p. 147, above; cf. pp. 21, 119.

CHAPTER IV

Love and Hate

1. 33 Henry VIII, chap. 8, Statutes of the Realm, III (1817), 837.

2. For love-magic see, for example, Fahz, De Poetarum Romanorum Doctrina Magica, 1904, pp. 16–37 (122–143); Kuhnert, Rheinisches Museum, XLIX (1894), 37–56; Grillando, De Sortilegiis, ed. 1545, iii, 10–19, foll. xx r°–xxij v°; v, 3–8, foll. xxv r°–xxvj v° (ed. 1592, iii, 14–24, pp. 26–35; v, 2–6, pp. 47–51); Wier, De Praestigiis Daemonum, iii, 38–39, ed. 1568, pp. 339–347; v, 10, pp. 480–481 (wax image); Carl Meyer, Der Aberglaube des Mittelalters, 1884, pp. 263–265; Hälsig, Der Zauberspruch bei den Germanen, 1910, pp. 53–54; Wuttke-Meyer, pp. 365–368; Schönwerth, Aus der Oberpfalz, I (1857), 125–134; Ebel, Hessische Blätter für Volkskunde, III (1904), 130–154; G. F. Abbott, Macedonian Folklore, 1903, pp. 226–227; Seligmann, The Melanesians of British New Guinea, 1910, pp. 179–180, 289, 302, 645; Ivens, Melanesians of the South-East Solomon Islands, 1927, pp. 87, 280–282, 289–290, 336; Skeat, Malay Magic, 1900, pp. 568, 574–579; J. H. Weeks, Among Congo Cannibals, 1913, pp. 286–287; Tremearne, The Ban of the Bori, pp. 159–165. The superb Scandinavian ballad of "Ridder Stig" illustrates the potency of

runes in love-magic and bears in some ways a striking resemblance to Browning's "Mesmerism": Grundtvig, Danmarks Gamle Folkeviser, No. 76, II, 301–318; Grundtvig and Sigurðsson, Islenzk Fornkvæði, I, 52–59 (cf. I, 66–70).

3. See p. 30, above.

4. Thoms, Anecdotes and Traditions (Camden Society), 1839, pp. 93–96; Halliwell, The Nursery Rhymes of England, 1842, pp. 137, 183; the Same, Popular Rhymes and Nursery Tales, 1849, p. 256; Northall, English Folk-Rhymes, 1892, pp. 153–157; English Dialect Dictionary, s.v. cockelty-bread; Aubrey, Remaines of Gentilisme and Judaisme, ed. Britten, 1881, pp. 43–44, 96, 225; Shadwell, The Lancashire Witches, 1682, ed. Halliwell, The Poetry of Witchcraft, 1853, pp. 41, 56.

5. Corrector (included in his Decretum by Burchard as Book xix), §§ 172, 173 (Schmitz, II, 447); Arundel Penitential, § 81 (Schmitz, I, 459; cf. Fournier, Revue d'Histoire et de Littérature Religieuses, IX [1904], 97).

6. Bishop Peter Quivil's Modus Exigendi Confessiones, Wilkins, Concilia, II, 162.

7. T. Wright, Anecdota Literaria, 1844, pp. 1–13; McKnight, Middle English Humorous Tales in Verse, [1913,] pp. 1–24.

8. Gower, Mirour de l'Omme, 9493–9504, Works, ed. Macaulay, I (1899), 110. Charms and witchcraft to procure unlawful love are condemned by Dan Michel of Kent, Ayenbite of Inwit, ed. Morris, 1886, p. 43 (ca. 1340).

9. Albericus Trium Fontium (Recueil, XXI, 609). For other demons in the same chronicle see XXI, 615–616 (1235; demons as red dwarfs), 628 (1240, 1241; prophetic and tricksy demons), 629 (1241; demons as vultures and ravens seen and heard). Under 1233 Alberic tells of the German Luciferians, who worshipped an image of the infernal prince (XX, 608–609).

10. Samuel Rowlands satirizes a trickster who pretends that he can "frame a ring" that will win love (Greenes Ghost Haunting Conie-Catchers, 1602, Hunterian Club, p. 12, Works, I).

11. Monk of St. Albans, Chronicon Angliae, ed. Thompson, pp. 97–100, 104–105. Cf. the English chronicle, Archæologia, XXII, 233–238, 241–243.

12. Pseudo-Callisthenes, 14.

13. Plato, Theaetetus, 174A; Aesop, ed. Halm, No. 72. See Weinreich, Der Trug des Nektanebos, 1911, pp. 16–17.

14. Old Yorkshire, ed. Wm. Smith, IV (1883), 268–269.

15. Burne and Jackson, Shropshire Folk-Lore, pp. 187–188.

16. St. Johnston, The Lau Islands, 1918, p. 59.

17. Peter Comestor, Historia Scholastica, on Exodus vi (Migne, CXCVIII, 1144); Gervase of Tilbury, Otia Imperialia, iii, 111 (Leibnitz, I, 1001; Liebrecht, p. 49); Vincent of Beauvais, Speculum Historiale, ii, 2, Venice, 1494, fol. 16 r°; Holkot, Super Libros Sapientie, Lectio 113, Reutlingen, 1489, sig. yiij, lf. 2 v°; Bromyard, Summa Predicantium, s.v. Caro, C, ii, § 14; Berchorius (Berçuire), Reductorium Morale, xiv, 71, 3,

Paris, 1521, fol. cccxlix r°. Cf. Josephus, De Antiquitate Iudaeorum, ii, 10, 252, ed. Nader, I, 119.

18. Convertimini, Herbert, Catalogue of Romances, III, 130, 149; Gesta Romanorum, cap. 10, ed. Œsterley, pp. 287–288 (cf. cap. 26, p. 323, and note, p. 714); English Gesta Romanorum (girdle), ed. Madden, 1838, pp. 179–180, cf. p. 517 (ed. Herrtage, 1879, pp. 227–230; cf. Herbert, III, 254); Innsbruck MS. of Gesta, cap. 11, ed. Dick, 1890, pp. 10–11 (Fridericus; cf. Gesta in MS. Harley 5369, Herbert, III, 207).

19. The Squire's Tale, F 247–251.

20. English Chronicle, ed. Davies (Camden Society, LXIV), pp. 58–59. See p. 81, above.

21. Petition, Rotuli Parliamentorum, VI, 241.

22. Letters and Papers, Henry VIII, X, No. 199, pp. 69–70.

23. Durham Depositions, ed. Raine, p. 29.

24. Hale, p. 7. Mary Blandy, hanged at Oxford in 1752 for poisoning her father, alleged that the arsenic which she gave him was furnished by her lover, Captain Cranstoun, as an innocuous potion to conciliate her father. See The Trial of Mary Blandy, ed. Roughead, 1914.

25. Hale, pp. 32–33.

26. Raine, The Fabric Rolls of York Minster (Surtees Society, XXXV), p. 272.

27. Hale, p. 102.

28. Depositions Taken before the Mayor and Aldermen of Norwich, ed. Rye, 1905, p. 34.

29. Archæologia Cantiana, XXVI (1904), 19. Goody Swane had also threatened one of her neighbors, "and it is come to pass this same woman her neighbour hath never been well since."

30. Calendar of State Papers, Domestic, 1581–1590, pp. 241, 246–248.

31. The same, 1591–1594, pp. 17–18, cf. 19. See pp. 260–261, above.

32. Compare the story of King Aun in the Ynglinga Saga, cap. 29 (25) (Konunga Sögur [Heimskringla], I [1816], 33–35; ed. Jónsson, I, i [1893], 45–48).

33. Gregory of Tours, vi, 34–35. The Norse Grógaldr mentions, among other spells, one that changes the hate of enemies to good will (st. 9, Bugge, Norrœn Fornkvæði, 1867, p. 340).

34. Matthew Paris, Chronica Majora, ed. Luard, III, 223 ("per incantationes et sortilegia").

35. Roger of Wendover, ed. Hewlett, III, 33; Matthew Paris, Chronica Majora, III, 222.

36. Anonymous Vita Edwardi II, in Hearne's ed. of Johannes de Trokelowe, Annales, p. 110. Among Gaveston's treasures were a silver-gilt box "pur porter eynz un anel entour le col de un homme," and a (magic?) girdle of lion's skin adorned with gold and gems (Rymer, Foedera, 2d ed., III, 389, 390; cf. Joan Evans, Magical Jewels, 1922, pp. 112, 119).

37. Rigault, Le Procès de Guichard, Évêque de Troyes, 1896, pp. 72, 74, 271. See p. 76, above.

38. Petrarch, Epistolae de Rebus Familiaribus, i, 3, ed. Fracassetti, I, 41–42. Cf. Kornmann, De Miraculis Mortuorum, ii, 14, Opera Curiosa,

1694, pp. 37–40; Garmann, De Miraculis Mortuorum, 1709, i, 9, 2, p. 261; Bullen, Old Plays, III, 166–261 (The Distracted Emperor); Pauls, Der Ring der Fastrada, Zeitschrift des Aachener Geschichtsvereins, XVII (1895), 1–73; G. Paris, L'Anneau de la Morte, 1897; Romania, XXV (1896), 612–617. A similar legend has attached itself to Harold Fairhair and to King Waldemar of Denmark: Haralds Saga hins Hárfagra, cap. 25 (Heimskringla, ed. Unger, 1868, p. 67; Flateyjarbók, I, 567, 582; Agrip, Fornmanna Sögur, X, 379–380); Thiele, Danske Folkesagn, I (1820), 89–90, 188–191; Uhland, Schriften zur Geschichte der Dichtung und Sage, VI, 399. Cf. Moth, Danske Studier, 1915, pp. 97–107.

39. Tyndale, The Practice of Prelates, Works, ed. Russell, 1831, I, 411; Expositions and Notes, ed. Walter (Parker Society), p. 265.

40. Skelton, Why Come Ye Nat to Courte? vv. 654–712.

41. Tyndale, as above, ed. Russell, I, 452–453; ed. Walter, p. 308.

42. The same, I, 450; p. 305. Of course Tyndale approved the Mosaic law in such cases (Prologue to Exodus, Doctrinal Treatises, ed. Walter, p. 413).

43. Stapleton's letter, Norfolk Archæology, I (1847), 59. See p. 210, above.

44. Magic rings were popular in the reign of the eighth Henry. A book of conjuring found in the possession of an Abingdon priest in 1535 contained formulæ for consecrating rings with stones in them (Ellis, Original Letters, 3d Series, III [1846], 41–42; Letters and Papers, IX, No. 551, p. 182). In 1544 a sorcerer named Wisdom made a ring for the profligate Lord Harry Nevell to ensure luck in gambling (Letters and Papers, XXI, ii, No. 417, p. 198; see p. 67, above). Cf. Robert Greene, The Blacke Bookes Messenger, 1592, Bodley Head Quartos, X (1924), 24.

45. See p. 63, above. As to Solomon's rings see Wm. Jones, Finger-Ring Lore, 1877, 1898, pp. 91–92.

46. Letters and Papers, XIII, i, No. 1383, p. 512.

47. Norfolk Archæology, II (1849), 280–290; Notes and Queries, 3d Series, VII (1865), 413–414; Journal British Archæological Association, XXIII (1867), 256–268, 331–332, 370–378; XXV (1869), 334–344; XLI (1885), 262–266; Records of Buckinghamshire, II (1863), 60–74; III (1870), 76, 354–369; Archæologia Cantiana, XI (1877), xxxviii, lxi–lxii; The Reliquary and Illustrated Archæologist, VII (1901), 37–44; Proceedings Society of Antiquaries of Scotland, XI (1876), 65; Hope, The Legendary Lore of the Holy Wells of England, 1893, pp. 3–5.

48. Heywood, The Foure PP, v. 45, Manly, Specimens of the Pre-Shaksperean Drama, I (1897), 485. Cf. Bale's Select Works, ed. Christmas (Parker Society), p. 498 ("Master John Shorne's boot"); S. R. Maitland, Remarks on the Rev. S. R. Cattley's Defence of his Edition of Fox's Martyrology, 1842, pp. 39–40.

49. See Joan Evans, Magical Jewels of the Middle Ages and the Renaissance, 1922; Du Méril, Floire et Blanceflor, 1856, pp. clix–clxiv; Child, The English and Scottish Popular Ballads, I, 200–201; Wm. Jones, Finger-Ring Lore, 1877, 1898, pp. 121–126. Cf. R. M. Garrett, Precious Stones in Old English Literature (Münchener Beiträge, XLVII), 1909; Dickman,

Le Rôle du Surnaturel dans les Chansons de Geste, 1926, pp. 99, 180; J. Kirchmann, De Annulis, 1672, cap. 21, pp. 198–218.

50. Plato, De Re Publica, ii, pp. 359–360.

51. Auberi, Tobler, Mittheilungen aus Altfranzösischen Handschriften, I (1870), 12.

52. Floire et Blanceflor, ed. Du Méril, p. 42. Cf. Yvain, ed. Holland, 1880, vv. 2595–2613, pp. 111–112; Horn, vv. 2051–2057, ed. Stengel, 1883, pp. 108–109; Horn, ed. Hall, 1901, pp. 32–33.

53. Wolfdietrich D, viii, st. 42, ed. Jänicke, Deutsches Heldenbuch, II (1873), 145.

54. Reinfried von Braunschweig, 15066–15091, ed. Bartsch, 1871, pp. 440–441.

55. See Child, Ballads, I, 200–201.

56. Cf. Roman de la Charrette, vv. 2344–2367, ed. Förster, 1899, p. 88.

57. William of Palerne, 4424–4431, ed. Skeat, pp. 141–142; cf. Guillaume de Palerne, 7731–7745, ed. Michelant, 1876, pp. 224–225. The English version dates from ca. 1350.

58. Jean de Condé, Dit dou Levrier, vv. 1326–1333, ed. Scheler, II, 344; ed. Tobler, pp. 137–138.

59. William of Malmesbury, Gesta Regum Anglorum, ii, 205, ed. Stubbs, I, 256–258; Roger of Wendover, Flores Historiarum, ed. Coxe, I, 498–500; Flores Historiarum, ed. Luard, I, 577–578; Eulogium Historiarum, ed. Haydon, I, 393–395; Matthew Paris, Chronica Majora, ed. Luard, I, 527–528; Bromton, Twysden, Scriptores X, cols. 950–951; De Antiquis Legibus Liber, ed. Stapleton (Camden Society, XXXIV), p. 179; Vincent of Beauvais, Speculum Historiale, xxv, 29, Venice, 1494, fol. 325 vº (thence in Guazzo [Guaccius], Compendium Maleficarum, 1608, ii, 4, pp. 110–111); Alphabetum Narrationum (Herbert, Catalogue, III, 437; Toldo, Herrig's Archiv, CXVIII [1907], 76–81); An Alphabet of Tales, No. 730, ed. Banks, II (1905), 488–489. For further references see Baum, Publications Modern Language Association, XXXIV (1919), 523–579; XXXV (1920), 60–62.

60. Riegel, Die Quellen von William Morris' Dichtung The Earthly Paradise (Erlanger Beiträge, II, ix), 1890, pp. 63–65.

61. See Northall, English Folk-Rhymes, 1892, pp. 108–123, 153–158; Brand's Popular Antiquities, ed. Hazlitt, 1870, III, 260–263. Cf. p. 104.

62. Blau, Das Altjüdische Zauberwesen, 1898, pp. 96–112, cf. pp. 24, 52. Cf. Zeitschrift des Vereins für Volkskunde, XXVI (1916), 194–198.

63. Papiri Greci e Latine (Società Italiana per la Ricerca dei Papiri), No. 28, I (1912), 63–69.

64. Audollent, Defixionum Tabellae, 1904, No. 5, pp. 12–13.

65. No. 10, pp. 17–18.

66. No. 68, pp. 95–97.

67. No. 139, pp. 196–198.

68. No. 230, pp. 301–302.

69. No. 264, pp. 362–363.

70. No. 266, pp. 364–365. Cf. Journal Anthropological Institute, XXXIV (1904), 207–210.

71. Wier, iii, 39, ed. 1568, pp. 342–347; Scot, vi, 6–7, pp. 121–124 (90–92), ed. Nicholson, pp. 96–99.

72. Casanova, La Magia del Amor entre los Aztecas, Mexican Folkways, 1925, I, 19.

73. Hansen, Zauberwahn, pp. 71–72, 88–99, 153–166, 287–289; Parisot, Le Royaume de Lorraine sous les Carolingiens, 1898, chaps. 4–8.

74. Leechdoms, ed. Cockayne, I, 330 (De Taxone Liber, ed. Howald and Sigerist, Corpus Medicorum Latinorum, IV [1927], 231); II, 10, 114, 306 (cf. I, xli–xliv); ed. Leonhardi, pp. 4, 35, 94. Cf. Grendon, Journal of American Folk-Lore, XXII (1909), pp. 138, 200–201, 212–213, 232, 236; Jente, Die Mythologischen Ausdrücke im Altenglischen Wortschatz, 1921, p. 310. See also Corrector, § 186, Schmitz, Die Bussbücher, II (1898), 450; Arundel Penitential, § 85, Schmitz, I (1883), 460.

75. Depositions and other Ecclesiastical Proceedings from the Courts of Durham, ed. Raine (Surtees Society, XXI), p. 27.

76. Webster, The Displaying of Supposed Witchcraft, 1677, p. 260. Cf. Sloane MS. 1983, fol. 70 v°.

77. Pherecydes, frag. 26, ed. Sturz², pp. 118–119 (frag. 75, ed. Müller, Fragmenta Historicorum Graecorum, I, 89–90), from Scholium on Odyssey, xi, 287 (ed. Dindorf, II, 499–500); Eustathius on Odyssey, xi, 292, p. 1685; Scholium on Theocritus, iii, 43, ed. Dübner, p. 31; Apollodorus, Bibliotheca, i, 4, 12, 1–8, ed. Heyne² (1803), pp. 73–76. Cf. Mannhardt, Wald- und Feldkulte, II, 30–31; Frazer's excursus in his Apollodorus, 1921, II, 350–355; Frazer, The Golden Bough, 3d ed., I (1911), 158–159.

78. Tuchmann, Mélusine, V (1890–91), 232–236; Hansen, Quellen, index, s. v. Impotenz; Malleus Maleficarum, Pt. i, qu. 8–9, qu. 18, ed. 1620, pp. 87–96, 139; Pt. ii, qu. 1, capp. 6–7, pp. 192–200; qu. 2, capp. 2, 4, pp. 276–280, 284; Jörimann, Frühmittelalterliche Rezeptarien (Beiträge zur Geschichte der Medizin, ed. Sigerist, I), 1925, p. 77; Danaeus (Daneau), De Veneficis, cap. 3, 1575, pp. 51–53 (cf. translation, A Dialogue of Witches, 1575, sigg. Ev, lf. 4 r°–Fj r°); Corpus Medicorum Latinorum, IV (1927), 293 (fragmentary spell "ut mulier non concipiat"); Fernel, De Abditis Rerum Causis, ii, 16 (1656 ed. of De Morbis Universalibus et Particularibus, p. 517); De l'Ancre, L'Incredulité et Mescreance du Sortilege, 1622, pp. 309–359, 766–767, 773; Cardano, De Subtilitate, cap. 18, Opera, 1663, III, 643, 646; Wier, iii, 34, ed. 1568, p. 329; iv, 20, pp. 409–412 (cf. v, 9, p. 478; v, 19, p. 511); Bodin, De la Demonomanie des Sorciers, 1587, ii, 1, foll. 61 v°–64 r°; Scot, iv, 4, pp. 77–78 (60–61), ed. Nicholson, pp. 61–62; iv, 8, pp. 82–83 (63–64), ed. Nicholson, p. 65; Grillando, De Sortilegiis, ed. 1545, iii, 22, fol. xxiij r°; vi, 10–13, fol. xxxj (ed. 1592, iii, 26, pp. 37–38; vi, 13–16, pp. 71–75); Guazzo (Guaccius), Compendium Maleficarum, 1608, ii, 4, pp. 109–113; Del Rio, Disquisitiones Magicae, lib. iii, qu. iv, sect. 8, ed. Venice, 1616, pp. 422–426; Garmann, De Miraculis Mortuorum, 1709, i, 11, 40, pp. 305–307; Heywood, The Hierarchie of the Blessed Angells, 1635, p. 474; T. Lupton, A Thousand Notable Things, 1650, p. 20; Webster, The Displaying of Supposed Witchcraft, 1677, pp. 246–247; Pitcairn, Criminal Trials in Scotland, 1833, I, 206; Folk-Lore, XI (1900), 120–125; XXXIII (1922), 391–392; Linder-

holm, De Stora Häxprocesserna i Sverige, I (1918), 86, 114, 123; Gaupp, Archiv für Kriminal-Anthropologie, XXVIII (1907), 22–48; Seyfarth, Aberglaube und Zauberei in der Volksmedizin Sachsens, 1913, pp. 63–64; Manz, Volksbrauch und Volksglaube des Sarganserlandes, Schriften der Schweizerischen Gesellschaft für Volkskunde, XII (1916), 144; Alemannia, II (1875), 136–137; VIII (1880), 280–284; Am Ur-Quell, III (1892), 269, 276–279; Hessische Blätter für Volkskunde, III (1904), 149–153; Baltische Studien, XXXVI (1886), 317; Salgues, Des Erreurs et des Préjugés, 2d ed., I (1811), 155–169; Revue des Traditions Populaires, XV (1901), 132; Pitrè, Usi e Costumi, Credenze e Pregiudizi del Popolo Siciliano, IV (1889), 127–128; Thiers, Traité des Superstitions, 1741, IV, 567–600; Cabanès, Remèdes d'Autrefois, 1905, pp. 448–474; Scheible, Das Kloster, VI (1847), 203–214; Frazer, The Golden Bough, 3d ed., Taboo, 1911, pp. 299–301; Löwenstimm, Aberglaube und Strafrecht, 1897, pp. 112–113; Samter, Geburt, Hochzeit und Tod, 1911, pp. 123–124; Thorndike, A History of Magic and Experimental Science, 1923, I, 655; von Dobeneck, Des Deutschen Mittelalters Volksglauben, 1815, II, 13–20; Georgeakis and Pineau, Le Folk-Lore de Lesbos, 1894, pp. 344–345; G. F. Abbott, Macedonian Folklore, 1903, pp. 171, note, 226, 232; Gaster, The Exempla of the Rabbis, 1924, p. 149; Atharva-Veda, iv, 4, Whitney and Lanman, VII, 149–151; vi, 138, VII, 384; vii, 90, VII, 454–455 (cf. i, 16, VII, 17–18; vi, 72, VII, 335; vi, 101, VII, 354–355); The Indian Antiquary, LII (1923), 113–115 (ritual murder to procure offspring; cases in 1893, 1896, and 1897); Enthoven, The Folklore of Bombay, 1924, pp. 285–294; De Indische Gids, VII, i (1885), 54; Skeat and Blagden, Pagan Races of the Malay Peninsula, 1906, II, 67; Doutté, Magie et Religion dans l'Afrique du Nord, 1909, pp. 88, 288–296; Mauchamp, La Sorcellerie au Maroc, pp. 201–202, 258–266; Westermarck, Ritual and Belief in Morocco, 1926, I, 571–573; II, 575–576; Hobley, Bantu Beliefs and Magic, 1922, pp. 196–198; Hans Meyer, Die Barundi, 1916, p. 133; Tremearne, The Ban of the Bori, pp. 164, 167; D. R. MacKenzie, The Spirit-Ridden Konde, 1925, pp. 103, 282; Cardinall, The Natives of the Northern Territories of the Gold Coast, p. 48; D. Amaury Talbot, Woman's Mysteries of a Primitive People, 1915, pp. 145–148; P. A. Talbot, The Peoples of Southern Nigeria, 1926, II, 181; Seligmann, The Melanesians of British New Guinea, 1910, p. 288. For a very remarkable case see Pauls, Der Exorcismus an Herzog Johann Wilhelm von Jülich 1604 und 1605, Annalen des Historischen Vereins für den Niederrhein, LXIII (1896), 27–53. For details as to means and cure see Sloane MS. 1983, foll. 70 v°–71 v°. Cf. Sloane MS. 3529, fol. 12.

79. Child, The English and Scottish Popular Ballads, No. 6, I, 81–88.

80. Child, I, 469; V, 285; Gonzenbach, Sicilianische Märchen, 1870, I, 72–73; Journal of American Folk-Lore, XXX (1917), 180 (North Carolina); Didakais and Folk-Lore Gazette, I (1912), 17. Cf. Frazer, The Golden Bough, 3d ed., Taboo, 1911, pp. 298–299.

81. Hymn to the Delian Apollo, 91–119.

82. Ovid, Metamorphoses, ix, 281–315 (cf. Iliad, xix, 114–119); Pliny, xxviii, 6, 17, 59 (cf. Sir Thomas Browne, Pseudodoxia Epidemica, v, 23, 9,

Works, ed. Wilkin, 1852, II, 84). See Child, I, 84–85, with special reference to Böttiger, Kleine Schriften, 2d ed., 1850, I, 61–92. Cf. von Sybel in Roscher's Ausführliches Lexicon der Griechischen und Römischen Mythologie, s. v. *Eileithyia*, I, 1219; Welcker, Kleine Schriften, III (1850), 190–193.

83. See the truly infernal spell εἰς κλείδημα γυναικός printed by Delatte, Le Musée Belge, XVIII (1914), 85; cf. Jacoby, Hessische Blätter für Volkskunde, XXV (1927), 208.

84. Cf. D. Amaury Talbot, Woman's Mysteries of a Primitive People, 1915, p. 22; P. Amaury Talbot, The Peoples of Southern Nigeria, 1926, II, 169.

85. A. Franz, Die Kirchlichen Benediktionen, 1909, II, 207–208.

86. Raine, The Fabric Rolls of York Minster (Surtees Society, XXXV), p. 260.

87. For girdles see Binsfeld, De Confessionibus Maleficorum et Sagarum, 1591, p. 146; Folk-Lore, IX (1898), 79. Agnes Hancok in 1438 was convicted of fortune-telling and incantation. "She used to assert . . . that by the inspection of the shirt or girdle or shoe of a sick person, she could tell when the malady first took the patient, and in what way and for what cause, though she never saw the sick person. That by taking the measurement of the girdle or shoe she could tell whether the sick person would live or die. . . . She used to send the remedy of health by blessing the girdle or shoe or head-band (*tene*)" (Notes and Queries for Somerset and Dorset, XII [1911], 33–34); cf. p. 143, above.

88. Cf. Bourke, 9th Report Bureau of Ethnology (for 1887–88), 1892, pp. 573–575; Simpson, Journal British Archæological Association, XXX (1874), 357–374 (measure of the wounds in Christ's side); Bale, Select Works, ed. Christmas (Parker Society), p. 525 ("St. John's gospels with the five wounds and the length of our Lord for drowning"); Proceedings Society of Antiquaries, 2d Series, XXIII (1909–11), 340–344; Bye-Gones for 1901–02, pp. 95, 111, 145; Pradel, Griechische und Süditalienische Gebete (Religionsgeschichtliche Versuche und Vorarbeiten, III, iii), 1907, p. 383; Beiträge zur Geschichte des Niederrheins, XIII (1898), 234; Durham Depositions, ed. Raine, pp. 99–100; Notes and Queries for Somerset and Dorset, XII (1911), 33; Zeitschrift des Vereins für Volkskunde, XXI (1911), 151–159 (with references); Georgeakis and Pineau, Le Folk-Lore de Lesbos, 1894, p. 347.

89. Burnet, The History of the Reformation, III (1715), Collection, p. 146; Frere and Kennedy, Visitation Articles and Injunctions (Alcuin Club), 1910, II, 58–59.

90. Cardwell, Documentary Annals, 1844, I, 164; Frere and Kennedy, II, 356, cf. 357.

91. Frere and Kennedy, II, 372.

92. Articles to be enquyred in the visitation, in the fyrste yeare of the raygne of our moost drad soueraygne Lady, Elizabeth (London, Richard Iugge and Iohn Cawood, 1559), § 37, sig. Bj r°. Cf. Cardwell, I, 246; Frere and Kennedy, III, 5.

93. Frere and Kennedy, III, 270.

94. Cardwell, I, 413–414. Cf. Transactions Cumberland and West-morland Antiquarian Society, New Series, III (1903), 68 (midwife's oath).

95. Frere and Kennedy, III, 383.

96. The Injunctions etc. of Richard Barnes, ed. Raine (Surtees Society, XXII), p. 18. Cf. Frere and Kennedy, II, 292 (Hooper, 1551–52); III, 221 (Horne, 1569). Note the language of a midwife's license (1675): "You shall in no wise exercise any manner of witchcraft, charms, sorcery, invocation, or other prayers, than such as may stand with Gods laws, and the kings" (Sussex Archæological Collections, IV [1851], 249).

97. Owen and Blakeway, A History of Shrewsbury, 1825, II, 364.

98. Wuttke-Meyer, 1900, p. 378; Fritzner, Historisk Tidsskrift, Christiania, IV (1877), 203–205; Folk-Lore, VII (1896), 180; Child, I, 85; V, 285. On the magic symbolism of the key see Delatte, Le Musée Belge, XVIII (1914), 75–88. On knots to hinder birth see Blau, Das Altjüdische Zauberwesen, 1898, p. 53, cf. p. 25. On magic knots in general see Heim, Incantamenta Magica, Nos. 38, 75, 79, Jahrbücher für Classische Philologie, XIX (1893), 475–476, 484, 486.

99. Seligmann, The Melanesians of British New Guinea, 1910, pp. 84–85. See also A. C. Hollis, The Nandi, their Language and Folk-Lore, 1909, p. 90. Cf. Pliny, xxviii, 4, 9, 42: "Partus accelerat hic mas ex quo quaeque conceperit, si cinctu suo soluto feminam cinxerit, dein solverit adiecta precatione se vinxisse, eundem et soluturum, atque abierit." See Frazer, The Golden Bough, 3d ed., Taboo, 1911, pp. 293–298; Samter, Geburt, Hochzeit und Tod, 1911, pp. 121–130. Cf. R. V. Russell, The Tribes and Castes of the Central Provinces of India, 1916, III, 563.

100. Ein Mittelenglisches Medizinbuch, ed. Heinrich, 1896, pp. 143–144. See also Vassiliev, Anecdota Graeco-Byzantina, I (1893), 339–340; Henslow, Medical Works of the Fourteenth Century, 1899, pp. 32–33; A. Franz, Die Kirchlichen Benediktionen, 1909, II, 197–204; Hälsig, Der Zauberspruch bei den Germanen, 1910, pp. 42–44, 96–98; Klemming, Läke- och Örte-Böcker, 1883–86, p. 213; Anglia, XIX (1897), 85; Germania, XXIV (1879), 311; XXXII (1887), 458; Ploss, Das Weib in der Natur- und Völkerkunde, ed. Bartels, 1897, II, 240–267.

101. Cockayne, Leechdoms, I, 392. For Anglo-Saxon charms and ceremonies for facilitating delivery or preventing miscarriage see Leechdoms, I, 218; III, 64, 66–69; Grendon, Journal of American Folk-Lore, XXII (1909), 206–209, 234. Cf. Bang, Norske Hexeformularer, 1901, pp. 148–149. Abortion by maleficium is penalized in Pseudo-Theodore, xxvii, 10 (Thorpe, p. 292), in Pseudo-Cummean, vii (ix), 2 (Schmitz, II, 626), and in many other penitentials (Schmitz, I, 306; II, 236, 296, 320, 324, 334, 342, 360, 484). Cf. Homilia de Sacrilegiis, ed. Caspari, 1886, pp. 11, 39; St. Bonaventura, Opera, IV (1889), 728. See also the curious charms for childbirth in Sloane MS. 2457, foll. 30 r°–31 r°.

102. See pp. 81–82, above.

103. For a typical case (1516), see Zeitschrift des Bergischen Geschichts-vereins, IX (1873), 103–110.

104. St. Augustine, De Civitate Dei, xv, 23; Isidore, viii, 11, 103; Guilielmus Alvernus, De Universo, ii, 3, 25, Opera, 1674, I, 1070–1073;

Kornmann, De Miraculis Vivorum, Opera Curiosa, 1694, pp. 169–179; Guazzo, Compendium Maleficarum, 1608, i, 11, pp. 34–38; Increase Mather, An Essay for the Recording of Illustrious Providences, 1684, p. 138; P. de l'Ancre, Tableau de l'Inconstance des Mauvais Anges et Demons, 1613, pp. 214–234. Erasmus Francisci has a very curious chapter (79) on "Die gespenstische Buhlschafft" in Der Höllische Proteus, 2d ed., 1695, pp. 839–867; he also tells the story of the water-spirit who wooed a girl at a village dance (pp. 922–923).

105. Malvenda, De Antichristo, 1604, ii, 9, pp. 77–79; Roscher, Ephialtes, p. 35. For Alexander see especially Weinreich, Der Trug des Nektanebos, 1911; cf. Reitzenstein, Poimandres, 1900, pp. 309–310. See also Reitzenstein, Hellenistische Wundererzählungen, 1906, pp. 139–141.

106. Geoffrey of Monmouth, Historia Regum Britanniae, viii, 19, ed. San-Marte, 1854, p. 117. Cf. the Latin metrical Gesta Regum Britanniae, vv. 2918–2927, ed. Michel (Cambrian Archæological Association), 1862, p. 105; Fletcher, The Arthurian Material in the Chronicles (Harvard Studies and Notes, X), 1906, p. 167; Herbert, Catalogue of Romances, III, 175, § 100.

107. Hansen, Zauberwahn, p. 142; cf. pp. 83, 141–144, 179–189. For the popular origin of the idea, see pp. 181–183, 187–188, 207.

108. Herbert, Catalogue of Romances, III, 352.

109. Geoffrey of Monmouth, Historia Regum, vi, 17–18, pp. 89–90. Cf. Gervase of Tilbury, Otia Imperialia, i, 17 (Leibnitz, I, 897; Liebrecht, p. 6). See Sir Thomas Browne, Pseudodoxia Epidemica, vii, 16, Works, ed. Wilkin, 1852, II, 260.

110. Caesarius Heisterbacensis, Dialogus, iii, 12, ed. Strange, I, 124.

111. William of Newburgh, Historia Rerum Anglicarum, Chronicles of the Reigns of Stephen, Henry II., and Richard I., ed. Howlett, I, 12: "Et hunc quidem Merlinum patre incubo daemone ex femina natum [Galfridus] fabulatur."

112. Scot, xii, 3, p. 219 (158), ed. Nicholson, p. 176. Cf. iii, 19, p. 72 (56), ed. Nicholson, p. 56; iv, 10, p. 85 (65), ed. Nicholson, p. 67. Belief in the existence of "agrestes feminae quas sylvaticas vocant" who have intrigues with mortal men is penalized in the Corrector, § 152, Schmitz, Bussbücher, II, 442.

113. Richard Coer de Lion, vv. 197–234, ed. Weber, Metrical Romances, 1810, II, 10–11; ed. Brunner, Wiener Beiträge, XLII (1913), 90–91; Giraldus Cambrensis, De Principis Instructione, iii, 27, ed. Warner, Opera, VIII, 301.

114. See Cross, Revue Celtique, XXXI (1910), 413–471 (see pp. 450–453 for the shape-shifting lover); Bruce, The Evolution of Arthurian Romance, 1923, II, 180–181. The parents of Eyvindr Kellda, according to his own account, being old and childless, hired Finnish wizards to procure them an heir. "Thus an evil spirit was sent into my mother's womb," said Eyvindr, "and that spirit I am" (Óláfssaga Tryggvasonar, cap. 41, Fornmanna Sögur, X [1835], 307).

115. See, for example, Ralph de Diceto, ed. Stubbs, II, 64, 67, 163; Flores Historiarum, ed. Luard, III, 57; Raynaldus, Annales Ecclesiastici,

ann. 1282, cap. 33, III (1748), 543–544; and in general Murray's Introduction to the romance of Thomas of Erceldoune.

116. Caesarius Heisterbacensis, Dialogus, iii, 6–11, ed. Strange, II, 116–124; v, 44, II, 328–329.

117. Herbert, Catalogue of Romances, III (1910), 496; cf. III, 636. See also III, 433, 566, 700.

118. Hector Boëthius, Scotorum Historia, viii, ed. 1574, fol. 149. Cf. Holinshed, V (1808), 146–147.

119. Walter Map, De Nugis Curialium, ii, 11–13, ed. Wright, pp. 77–82 (ed. James, pp. 72–78); Gervase of Tilbury, Otia Imperialia, i, 17 (Leibnitz, I, 897; Liebrecht, p. 6).

120. Leechdoms, ed. Cockayne, II, 344: "wiþ ælfcynne and nihtgengan and þam mannum þe deofol mid hæmð." Cf. I, xxxviii–xli.

121. Matthew Paris, Chronica Majora, ed. Luard, V, 82. He records the discovery of a strange dwarf in the Isle of Wight in that same year (1249).

122. Rigault, Le Procès de Guichard Évêque de Troyes, 1896, pp. 110–111, 116–119, 125–127, 283–284.

123. An Alphabet of Tales, No. 258, ed. Banks, I (1904), 180. Cf. Herbert, Catalogue of Romances, III, 423–426, 433.

124. Alphabet, No. 256, I, 179–180 (two stories), from Caesarius, iii, 8 (I, 121), and iii, 10 (I, 122–123).

125. Alphabet, No. 257, I, 180.

126. Walter de Hemingburgh, ed. Hamilton, II, 314–315; Walsingham, Historia Anglicana, ed. Riley, I, 199–200; Raynaldi, Annales Ecclesiastici, VI (1750), 46, ann. 1335, cap. 58 (from Walsingham).

127. Canterbury Tales, D 873–880.

128. The Pilgrim's Tale, vv. 85–100, ed. Furnivall, Thynne's Animadversions, Appendix I, pp. 79–80. Cf. Spurgeon, Five Hundred Years of Chaucer Criticism and Allusion, 1925, I, 82; Skeat's Chaucer, V, 313–314.

129. Scot, iv, 12, p. 88 (67–68), ed. Nicholson, pp. 69–70. On incubus see Scot, iii, 19–iv, 5, pp. 71–80 (56–62), ed. Nicholson, pp. 56–63; iv, 9–12, pp. 83–88 (64–68), ed. Nicholson, pp. 66–70.

130. Harsnet, A Declaration of Egregious Popish Impostures, 1603, pp. 137–138; cf. Kittredge, Publications of the Modern Language Association, XV, 422–428.

131. Grimm, Deutsche Mythologie, 4th ed., pp. 385–387, cf. p. 398.

132. Riddles Wisely Expounded, Child, The English and Scottish Popular Ballads, No. 1, V, 283.

133. Folk-Lore, XXII (1911), 330–331.

134. Bye-Gones for 1897–98, p. 437.

135. Giraldus Cambrensis, Itinerarium Kambriae, i, 5, Opera, ed. Dimock, VI, 57–58.

136. Scott, Minstrelsy, 5th ed., 1812, II, 427 (in the introduction to the ballad of "The Dæmon Lover," first printed in that edition).

137. A Treatise containing the Original of Unbelief, Mis-belief, or Misperswasions concerning the Verity, Unity, and Attributes of the Deity, Chapter 19, Works, I (1673), 915–916. The Dedication is dated March 2,

1624 (i.e. 1624-5). Compare the devil's rhyme in Freisauff, Salzburger Volkssagen, 1880, p. 529 ("Kudlkraut und Widrität Häb'n mi um mei' Madl brächt!").

138. Magna Vita S. Hugonis, v, 8, ed. Dimock, pp. 269-273.

139. Herbert, Catalogue of Romances, III (1910), 495, 527. Cf. Zingerle, Sitten, Bräuche und Meinungen der Tiroler, 2d ed., 1876, p. 106.

140. Holkot, Super Libros Sapientie, Lectio 190, Speyer, 1483, sig. pj v° (Reutlingen, 1489, sig. Miiij, lf. 5 r°). For St. John's wort (*Hypericum perforatum*) as *fuga daemonum* see The Book of Quinte Essence, ed. Furnivall, 1866, p. 19; Wier, De Praestigiis Daemonum, v, 18, ed. 1568, p. 508; Menghi, Flagellum Daemonum, Documentum 3, in Mallei Maleficarum, 1582, II, 106-107; Godelmann, Tractatus de Magis Veneficis et Lamiis, 1591, i, 8, 47, pp. 94-95; Harsnet, A Declaration of Egregious Popish Impostures, 1603, pp. 41, 45; Boguet, Discours des Sorciers, 1608, p. 287; Mylius, Antidotarium, 1620, p. 69; Baptista Codronchus, De Morbis Veneficis, iv, 8, 1618, p. 241; A Whip for the Devil, 1683, pp. 9, 82; Garmann, De Miraculis Mortuorum, 1709, ii, 8, 85, p. 673; Reling and Bohnhorst, Unsere Pflanzen, 4th ed., 1904, pp. 176-178; Sloet, De Planten in het Germaansche Volksgeloof en Volksgebruik, 1890, pp. 69-76; Rolland, Flore Populaire, III (1900), 169-181; Maury, La Magie, 1860, p. 164, note 2; Dyer, The Folk-Lore of Plants, New York, 1889, p. 62, cf. pp. 53, 84, 286; Frazer, The Golden Bough, 3d ed., XI, 54-57 (cf. IX, 160; XI, 74); Gessmann, Die Pflanze im Zauberglauben, [1899], pp. 49-51; De Gubernatis, La Mythologie des Plantes, II (1882), 173-174; Dodoens, translated by Lyte, 1578, i, 43, p. 64; Seligmann, Der Böse Blick, 1910, II, 68; Hewett, Nummits and Crummits, 1900, p. 75; J. G. Campbell, Witchcraft and Second Sight in the Highlands and Islands of Scotland, 1902, pp. 104-105; Carmichael, Carmina Gadelica, 1900, II, 96-97, 102-103; Zingerle, Sitten, Bräuche und Meinungen der Tiroler, 2d ed., 1871, p. 106; Lütolf, Sagen u.s.w. aus den Fünf Orten, 1865, p. 377; Kuhn, Sagen u.s.w. aus Westfalen, 1859, II, 29-30; Witzschel, Sagen, Sitten und Gebräuche aus Thüringen (Kleine Beiträge, II), 1878, p. 275; Zeitschrift für Oesterreichische Volkskunde, VI (1900), 124; Wuttke-Meyer, p. 104; Mélusine, VII (1894-95), p. 253; Blätter für Pommersche Volkskunde, I (1893), 18; V (1897), 106; VI (1898), 38-40, 95; VIII (1900), 139-140; IX (1901), 123-124; Zeitschrift des Vereins für Rheinische und Westfälische Volkskunde, VI (1909), 139; Frischbier, Hexenspruch und Zauberbann, 1870, p. 12; Am Ur-Quell, I (1890), 187; Germania, XXII (1877), 260. For the medicinal virtues of St. John's wort see, for example, Schöffler, Beiträge zur Mittelenglischen Medizinliteratur, 1919, pp. 207, 241. Cf. p. 214, above. According to a fifteenth-century note in Sloane MS. 2721, fol. 137 v°, you can handle snakes safely if your hands are rubbed with *herba Sancti Johannis*.

141. Spenser Society edition, p. 48 (56). For dill and vervain cf. Drage, Daimonomageia, 1665, p. 23.

142. Aubrey's Miscellanies, 2d ed., pp. 146-147; 4th edition, 1857, pp. 139-140; Remaines of Gentilisme and Judaisme, ed. Britten, 1881, pp. 82, 191, 231-232.

143. Halliwell, Popular Rhymes and Nursery Tales, 1849, pp. 225–226; Northall, English Folk-Rhymes, 1892, p. 180.

144. Peacock, A Glossary of Words used in the Wapentakes of Manley and Corringham, Lincolnshire (English Dialect Society), p. 85; Northall, p. 180. Similar rhymes are current in Germany: see, for example, Kuhn, Sagen u.s.w. aus Westfalen, 1859, II, 29; Kühnau, Schlesische Sagen, III (1913), 100; Samter, Geburt, Hochzeit und Tod, 1911, pp. 151–152.

145. Guy Mannering, chap. 3. For the medical and anti-magical virtues of vervain see Dioscorides, De Materia Medica, iv, 60, ed. Wellmann, II, 213–215; Leechdoms, ed. Cockayne, I, 90–95; II, 368; Middle English Medical Poem, vv. 775–826, ed. Stephens (Archæologia, XXX, 373–375), vv. 315–366, ed. Holthausen (Anglia, XVIII, 315–316); Alexander Neckam, De Laudibus Divinae Sapientiae, vv. 263–266, ed. Wright, p. 478; Boaistuau, Histoires Prodigieuses, ed. 1568, chap. 23, fol. 107 v° (ed. 1578, I, chap. 24, fol. 95); Dodoens, A Niewe Herball, translated by Henry Lyte, 1578, i, 86, pp. 127–128; Abt, Die Apologie des Apuleius, 1908, p. 72 (146); Wier, v, 19, ed. 1568, p. 510; Scot, xii, 18, p. 268 (193), ed. Nicholson, p. 218; Baxter, The Certainty of the Worlds of Spirits, 1691, p. 116; W. G. Black, Folk-Medicine, 1883, pp. 135, 153, 193–194; Dyer, The Folk-Lore of Plants, 1889, pp. 55–56, 282, 284–285; Seligmann, Der Böse Blick, 1910, II, 60–61; G. J. French, Bibliographical Notices of the Church Libraries at Turton and Gorton (Chetham Society, XXXVIII), p. 52; Brand's Popular Antiquities, ed. Hazlitt, III, 253, 255, 267; Henderson, 1879, p. 227; Leather, The Folk-Lore of Herefordshire, 1912, p. 21 (vervain and St. John's wort); Harland and Wilkinson, Lancashire Folk-Lore, 1867, pp. 76, 115; Folk-Lore Record, I (1878), 38; Folk-Lore, XVI (1905), 145, 150, n. 2; XXIII (1912), 491; XXV (1914), 250–251, 266; Clague, Manx Reminiscences, [1911], p. 163; Rolland, Flore Populaire, VIII, 38–43; A. DeCock, Volksgeneeskunde in Vlaanderen, 1891, pp. 156–158; Frazer, The Golden Bough, 3d ed., X, 162, 163, 165; XI, 62; De Gubernatis, La Mythologie des Plantes, II (1882), 367–369; Reling and Bohnhorst, Unsere Pflanzen, 4th ed., 1904, pp. 191–193; Wuttke-Meyer, p. 107; Mélusine, VII (1894–95), 283; Schöffler, Beiträge zur Mittelenglischen Medizinliteratur, 1919, p. 234; Germania, XXII (1877), 258; XXIV (1879), 75–76. Among other herbs of like potency may be mentioned fennel, because of the curious chapter in Gervase of Tilbury, Otia Imperialia, iii, 83 (Leibnitz, I, 987; Liebrecht, pp. 36–38, 142–143). See also Leechdoms, ed. Cockayne, I, 176 (mullein), 190 (wood chervil), 224 (wood thistle), 248 (mandrake), 312 (periwinkle); III, 30–39 (the Nine Worts charm: cf. Grendon, Journal of American Folk-Lore, XXII [1909], 190–195, 226–229). Cf. I, 318, 360, 364. "Si aliquis scire vult quid Jocularij faciunt tene verbenam in manu tua" (Sloane MS. 2628, fol. 9 r°).

146. Hewett, Nummits and Crummits, 1900, p. 80, cf. p. 68.

147. Vv. 801–804, ed. Stephens, Archæologia, XXX (1844), 374; vv. 341–344, ed. Holthausen, Anglia, XVIII (1896), 315; vv. 307–310, ed. Garrett, Anglia, XXXIV (1911), 172. Several other herbs are *fuga daemonum* if we may trust this poem: — betony, 471–472 (11–12 Holthausen, 45–46 Garrett); pimpernel, 693–696 (233–236, 215–218);

motherwort, 727–730, 757–760 (267–270, 297–300; 247–250, 275–278); henbane, 1061–1064 (601–604 Holthausen; not in Garrett); affodille, 1099–1104 (639–644, 506–511); aristologi, 1237–1238 (777–778, 579–580); baldmony, 1259–1262 (799–802, 595–598).

148. Vv. 805–814 (Stephens), 345–354 (Holthausen), 311–318 (Garrett).

149. Medical MS., ed. Stephens, Archaeologia, XXX (1844), 395–396.

150. Hale, pp. 107–108.

151. Boorde, The Breuyary of Helth, chap. 119, ed. 1552, fol. xlv, in Furnivall's ed. of Boorde's Introduction, etc., 1870, pp. 78–79. *Of* before *spirites* is misprinted *or*.

152. Harsnet, A Declaration of Egregious Popish Impostures, 1603, p. 45. Cf. Porphyry, De Abstinentia, ii, 42; Iamblichus, De Mysteriis, v, 10–15.

153. Proceedings against Dame Alice Kyteler, ed. Wright (Camden Society, XXIV), pp. 2–3, 32.

154. Wright, p. 15.

155. Wright, pp. 17 ("quidam aliegena de Anglia"), 14 ("ille vilis rusticus trutannus de Anglia").

CHAPTER V

MADNESS, CURSES, AND THE ELFSHOT

1. See p. 30.

2. See Tambornino, De Antiquorum Daemonismo (Religionsgeschichtliche Versuche und Vorarbeiten, VII, iii), 1909 (especially valuable for its collection of passages); A. Franz, Die Kirchlichen Benediktionen, 1909, II, 514–615.

3. See Thyraeus, Daemoniaci, 1603, cap. xvi, pp. 65–71; King James, Daemonologie, 1597, p. 47.

4. See Deacon and Walker, A Summarie Answere to Al the Material Points in any of Master Darel his Bookes, 1601, and Dialogicall Discourses of Spirits and Divels, 1601; cf. Thyraeus, Daemonicai, 1603, capp. ii, iiii.

5. For many instances from the Acta Sanctorum see Roskoff, Geschichte des Teufels, 1869, III, 169, 170, 173, 178–180, 185–189, 191–192. Demoniacs are often mentioned in the penitentials of the Anglo-Saxon time: see Schmitz, II, 237, 336, 356, 366, 539, 574, 627; Thorpe, pp. 308, 314, 333, 392 (cf. pp. 443, 458); Haddan and Stubbs, III, 197. For remedies for demoniacs see Leechdoms, ed. Cockayne, I, 102, 248, 312; II, 136, 352, 354 (cf. 334); ed. Leonhardi, pp. 41, 107, 108 (cf. 102). Cf. Jörimann, Frühmittelalterliche Rezeptarien (Beiträge zur Geschichte der Medizin, ed. Sigerist, I), 1925, pp. 22, 26.

6. On exorcists see the learned notes of Christopher Wordsworth, Yorkshire Archæological Journal, XVII (1903), 378–388. "Exorcista is on englisc se þe mid aðe halsað þa awyrgedan gastas þe wyllað menn dreccan" (Die Hirtenbriefe Ælfrics, i, 32, ed. Fehr, 1914, p. 9; cf. pp. 49, 108).

7. William Rishanger, Chronica, ed. Riley, p. 56.

8. Reginald, Libellus de Admirandis Beati Cuthberti Virtutibus, ed. Raine (Surtees Society, I), cap. 17, pp. 32–37. Cf. capp. 44, 98, 112, 114, pp. 90–91, 217–219, 248–254, 255–259. See also the metrical Vita Sancti Cuthberti, capp. 14, 40, in Miscellanea Biographica, ed. Raine (Surtees Society, VIII), pp. 96–97, 113–114. For cures by St. Egwin (died 717) see Chronicon Abbatiae de Evesham, ed. Macray, p. 50.

9. Reginald, cap. 122, pp. 268–269.

10. The Same, cap. 124, p. 270 ("eum colaphizando consuevit impetere"). Cf. II Corinthians, xii, 7: "Datus est mihi stimulus carnis meae angelus Sathanae qui me colaphizet."

11. Anonymous Legend of St. Hugh, cap. 7 (Dimock's ed. of Giraldus Cambrensis, VII, 179). See also Magna Vita S. Hugonis, v, 9, ed. Dimock, pp. 275–276.

12. Reginald, Libellus de Vita et Miraculis S. Godrici, ed. Stevenson (Surtees Society, XX), §§ 397, 456, 479, 520, 543, pp. 383, 400, 406–407, 422, 429–430; cf. § 524, p. 423.

13. Reginald, § 384, p. 381.

14. Vita Oswini, cap. 44, p. 58.

15. See pp. 221–222, above.

16. Liber Eliensis, ii, 128, ed. Stewart, 1848, I, 261–263. Compare the anecdote in Ælfric's Homily on St. Benedict, ed. Thorpe, II (1846), 160.

17. Annales de Wigornia, Annales Monastici, IV, 561; Knighton, ed. Lumby, II, 81–82. Cf. Anonimalle Chronicle, ed. Galbraith, 1927, p. 33.

18. R. R. Sharpe, Calendar of Letters from the Mayor and Corporation of the City of London circa A.D. 1350–1370, p. 136.

19. Gairdner, The Historical Collections of a Citizen of London, p. 239.

20. The Miracles of King Henry VI, ed. Knox and Leslie, 1923, pp. 125, 124.

21. More, Dyaloge . . . of the Veneracyon and Worshyp of Ymages, i, 16, ed. 1531, foll. xxvii (misprinted xxviii) v°–xxviii r°; Workes, 1557, p. 137.

22. A Confutation of Unwritten Verities, chap. xi, Remains of Cranmer, ed. Jenkyns, 1833, IV, 240.

23. Gregory, Dialogi, ed. Moricca, 1924, pp. 59–60.

24. Saxo Grammaticus, iii, p. 128 Müller and Velschow (p. 79 Holder).

25. Wier, iii, 39, ed. 1568, pp. 342–347; Scot, vi, 6–7, pp. 121–124 (90–92), ed. Nicholson, pp. 96–99. Cf. Alfonso el Sabio, Las Siete Partidas, vii, 23, 2 (ed. 1807, III, 668).

26. For some theories about fasting see Westermarck, Folk-Lore, XVIII (1907), 391–422. On long fasts see also the remark of Joubert, Seconde Partie des Erreurs Populaires et Propos Vulgaires touchant la Medecine, 1580, pp. 244–273.

27. Roger of Wendover, Flores Historiarum, ed. Coxe, I, 275. Cf. Vita Ludovici Pii, Recueil, VI, 106.

28. Roger of Wendover, ed. Coxe, IV, 113; ed. Hewlett, II, 294.

29. Capgrave, ed. Hingeston, p. 205.

30. Brut, ed. Brie, p. 503.

31. Rymer, Foedera, 2d ed., VI, 13; Somers Tracts, 3d Collection, I (1751), 54; Calendar of Patent Rolls 1354–1358, p. 529; Journal British Archæological Association, New Series, XV (1909), 164–165.

32. "Per fantasma daemonum incubarum" (Annales de Dunstaplia, Annals Monastici, ed. Luard, III, 353).

33. Kirk, Secret Commonwealth, 1690, § 15 (ed. 1815, p. 19). He is thinking of the hibernation of swallows, etc.: see Kircher, Mundus Subterraneus, viii, 1, 3d ed., 1678, II, 92–94; Burton, The Anatomy of Melancholy, Partition II, sect. 2, memb. 3 (New York, 1880, II, 127–129); Bewick, The History of British Birds, 1804, I, 258–260; Salgues, Des Erreurs et des Préjugés, 2d ed., I (1811), 222–228; Drayton, The Muses Elizium (Spenser Society), p. 24 (32); Fletcher, The Night-Walker, i, 1, 2–3.

34. See Rollins, Journal of American Folk-Lore, XXXIV (1921), 357–376; the Same, The Pack of Autolycus, 1927, pp. 36–37; Wier, De Commentitiis Ieiuniis, being cols. 107–134 appended to his De Lamiis, 1577; M. Casaubon, A Treatise Proving Spirits, Witches and Supernatural Operations, 1672, pp. 51–53; Kornmann, De Miraculis Vivorum, Opera Curiosa, 1694, pp. 107–113.

35. Cotton Mather, A Brand Pluck'd out of the Burning, § 11 (Burr, Narratives of the Witchcraft Cases, 1914, pp. 265–266). Cf. the case of Lady Jennings's daughter (1622), as recorded in Add. MS. 36674, fol. 134. See also the 1645 case in Add. MS. 27402, fol. 109 v°.

36. Dunton, The Post-Angel, 1701, II, 67–68.

37. Letters and Papers, Henry VIII, XIII, i, Nos. 487, 705, 1282, 1350, pp. 177–179, 267, 470, 502. Cf. the Transylvanian "black fast" (E. Gerard, The Land Beyond the Forest, New York, 1888, p. 214).

38. See Plummer, Vitae Sanctorum Hiberniae, 1910, I, cxx–cxxi, cxxxi; Clift, Journal British Archæological Association, New Series, XV (1909), 157–170.

39. The Injunctions, etc., of Richard Barnes, ed. Raine (Surtees Society, XXII), p. 17. For the use of the mass for cursing see p. 147, above.

40. On curses see J. G. Campbell, Superstitions of the Highlands and Islands, 1900, pp. 277–281; Gaskell, Old Wenlock and its Folklore, The Nineteenth Century, XXXV (1894), 264–265; Bye-Gones for 1899–1900, p. 43; York Powell in Elton's Saxo, 1894, p. lxxx; Hobley, Bantu Beliefs and Magic, 1922, pp. 145–153; Dundas, Kilimanjaro and its People, 1924, pp. 170–178; MacKenzie, The Spirit-Ridden Konde, 1925, pp. 268–269; G. Turner, Nineteen Years in Polynesia, 1861, p. 293; Hanson, The Kachins, 1913, pp. 145–147; Journal Royal Anthropological Institute, XLI (1911), 427–432; Westermarck, Ritual and Belief in Morocco, 1926, I, 479–492; Vallois, Bulletin de Correspondance Hellénique, XXXVIII (1914), 250–271. For Old Teutonic formulae of cursing see Weinhold, Die Altdeutschen Verwünschungsformeln, Berlin Academy, Sitzungsberichte, 1895, pp. 667–703.

41. Hale, pp. 36–37. Compare the Highland tinker-wife's curse: "I have made my wish before this, and I will make it now, and there was not yet a day I did not see my wish fulfilled" (J. G. Campbell, Superstitions

of the Highlands and Islands, 1900, p. 279). See also Strype, The Life of Sir Thomas Smith, 1698, pp. 131–132 (curses that cause the loss of an eye, 1570); Stearne, A Confirmation and Discovery of Witch-craft, 1648, pp. 34–35 (curses that kill).

42. Hale, p. 213. Cf. Philip Henry's Diary, December 9, 1663: "Mary Powel thought by some to bee bewitch't, her dame (cal'd Katharin of yᵉ Pinfold) is said to have kneel'd down and curst her; it seemes shee told some storyes of her about stealing — whether true or false doth not yet appear" (Diaries and Letters, ed. M. H. Lee, 1882, p. 152). For efficacious curses see the cases of 1645 (Add. MS. 27402, foll. 108 r°, 111 r°, 114 r°).

43. Robert Fox, The History of Godmanchester, 1831, pp. 124–125.

44. The Acts of the High Commission Court within the Diocese of Durham, ed. Longstaffe (Surtees Society, XXXIV), pp. 73–74.

45. Visitation in Beamont, Winwick, 2d ed., p. 42.

46. Child, The English and Scottish Popular Ballads, No. 120, III, 104–105.

47. Child, No. 79, II, 238–239.

48. Sharp, History of Hartlepool, 1851 (first ed. in 1816), p. 176.

49. Wickham, Records by Spade and Terrier, pp. 291–292.

50. Bye-Gones for 1886–87, pp. 232–233. Cf. Orde Browne, The Vanishing Tribes of Kenya, 1925, p. 183.

51. Transactions Devonshire Association, XXIV (1892), 54.

52. Sigebertus Gemblacensis, ed. Schard, Germanicarum Rerum Quatuor Chronographi, 1566, fol. 86 r°; Matthew Paris, Chronica Majora, ed. Luard, I, 262; Roger of Wendover, Flores Historiarum, ed. Coxe, I, 108; Flores Historiarum, ed. Luard, I, 292; Herbert, Catalogue of Romances, III (1910), 437; Folk-Lore, XII (1901), 164–165. Cf. Revue des Traditions Populaires, XXVII (1912), 325–326; J. W. Wolf, Niederländische Sagen, 1843, pp. 254–255, 436–437.

53. Archæologia Cambrensis, 6th Series, VII (1907), 271; 7th Series, I (1921), 306–307; Folk-Lore, XXII (1911), 50–51; XXXIII (1922), 392.

54. Archæologia Cambrensis, 3d Series, III (1857), 214; IV (1858), 205–206; Bye-Gones for 1888, pp. 47–48, 68; for 1899–1900, pp. 425–426, 431; for 1903–04, p. 197.

55. Hope, The Legendary Lore of the Holy Wells of England, 1893, pp. 71, 76, 83, 92–93, 107–108, 142, 143, 145, 185, 199.

56. See Grimm, Deutsche Mythologie, 4th ed., pp. 794–821.

57. Baildon, Proceedings Society of Antiquaries, 2d Series, XVIII (1899–1901), 140–147 (with figures). For the "magic squares" on such plates see The Reliquary, X (1869–70), 129–134, 139; XVII (1876–77), 141–146; Agrippa, Three Books of Occult Philosophy, transl. by J[ohn] F[rench], 1651, ii, 22, pp. 239–252; Bolte, Zeitschrift des Vereins für Volkskunde, XXVI (1916), 306–313.

58. Hartland, The Reliquary and Illustrated Archæologist, III (1897), 149–150 (with figure).

59. Whitaker, A History of Richmondshire, 1823, I, 195–196; County Folk-Lore, II (1901), 145–147.

60. Peacock, Proceedings Society of Antiquaries, 2d Series, VIII (1879–1881), 355.

61. Proceedings of the Privy Council, ed. Nicolas, VII, 12; Letters and Papers, Henry VIII, XV, No. 1006, p. 499. See further Nicolas, VII, 13–14, 24–25, 27, 30, 38; Letters and Papers, XV, Nos. 1008, 1011, pp. 499, 500; XVI, Nos. 8, 14, 55, pp. 3, 5, 16.

62. For elfshot see Sir John Rowll's Cursing, v. 68, Laing, Select Remains, ed. Small, p. 213; Logan, The Scottish Gaël, 1831, I, 339–342; Dalyell, The Darker Superstitions of Scotland, 1834, pp. 355–358; Burgess, The Scottish Review, XXV (1895), 99–102; Munro, Archæology and False Antiquities, 1905, p. 242; Walter Johnson, Folk-Memory, 1908, pp. 123–124; Henderson, Notes on the Folk Lore of the Northern Counties, 1879, pp. 185–187; Gomme, Ethnology in Folklore, 1892, pp. 54–56; Blakeborough, Wit, Character, etc., of the North Riding of Yorkshire, 2d ed., 1911, p. 137; E. M. Wright, Rustic Speech and Folk-Lore, 1913, pp. 210, 235; Gregor, The Folk-Lore of the North-East of Scotland, 1881, p. 184; J. G. Campbell, Superstitions of the Highlands and Islands, 1900, pp. 26–27, 88–89; Otway, Sketches in Erris and Tyrawley, 1841, pp. 379–382; The Reliquary, VIII (1867–68), 207–208 (with figures); Folk-Lore, XVII (1906), 200–210 (Ireland); County Folk-Lore, II (1901), 181–182; III (1903), 37–42, 45; Bishop Nicolson's Diary, 1712, Transactions Cumberland and Westmorland Antiquarian and Archæological Society, New Series, IV (1904), 58 (Bowness; elf-arrows valued "for the Cure of Cattle Elf-shot"); Carmichael, Carmina Gadelica, II, 58–59; Manninen, Die Dämonistischen Krankheiten im Finnischen Volksaberglauben (FF Communications, No. 45), XII (1922), 191–192; Fritzner, Historisk Tidsskrift, Christiania, IV (1877), 182–186; Det Arnamagnæanske Håndskrift Nr. 187 (Dansk Lægebog), ed. Såby, 1886, p. 47 ("Contra sagittas dyaboli"); Bang, Norske Hexeformularer, 1901, pp. 44–46, 60–61, 144–146, 163–164, 374–375, 407–408; Nyrop, "Elverskud," Dania, VIII (1901), 211–220; Ohrt, Trylleord (Danmarks Folkeminder, No. 25), 1922, pp. 100–101; Lid, Maal og Minne, 1921, pp. 37–66; Forsblom, Skrifter utgivna av Svenska Litteratursällskapet i Finland, CXXXV (1917), 96–112; F. S. Krauss, Volksglaube und Religiöser Brauch der Südslaven, 1890, pp. 93–95; Neues Archiv für Sächsische Geschichte und Alterthumskunde, IX (1888), 336; M. Höfler, Archiv für Religionswissenschaft, II (1899), 127–128; Bartels, Die Medicin der Naturvölker, 1893, pp. 25–27. Cf. Schönbach, Vienna Sitzungsberichte, Philosophisch-Historische Classe, CXLII (1900), No. 7, p. 133. For such arrows used as amulets see Bellucci, Il Feticismo Primitivo in Italia, 1907, pp. 45, 77–87. For "shotts" by means of sloe thorns, horseshoe nails, fish-hooks, the needle with which a corpse has been sewed "into its sheet," etc., see Sloane MS. 1983, fol. 72 v°.

63. The Private Correspondence of Pepys, ed. Tanner, 1926, I, 368–369; II, 26, 29–30.

64. The Æsir were Scandinavian and Germanic gods — Odin (Woden), Thor (Thunor), Tyrr (Tiw), etc.

65. Cockayne, Leechdoms, III, 52–55; Wülker, Bibliothek der Angelsächsischen Poesie, I, 317–319; Grendon, Journal of American Folk-Lore,

XXII (1909), 164–167, 214–215; Skemp, Modern Language Review, VI (1911), 289–293; W. Horn, Hoops Festschrift, 1925, pp. 88–104.

66. Leechdoms, ed. Cockayne, II, 156, 290; III, 46, 64; ed. Leonhardi, pp. 47, 88, 141, 148; Grendon, Journal of American Folk-Lore, XXII (1909), 208–209, 235. Cf. Cockayne, II, 110; Leonhardi, p. 34, line 5. See also Singer, Proceedings British Academy, 1919–1920, pp. 353–358. For elves as the cause of disease see also pp. 32, 147, above; cf. p. 218.

67. Pseudo-Paracelsus, De Summis Naturae Mysteriis, transl. Dorn, 1584, p. 85 (Paracelsus Of the Supreme Mysteries of Nature, transl. R. Turner, 1655, p. 88); Baxter, The Certainty of the Worlds of Spirits, 1691, pp. 65–69; Rowlands, Greenes Ghost Haunting Conie-Catchers, 1602, p. 12 (Works, Hunterian Club, I).

68. Greene, The Blacke Bookes Messenger, 1592, ed. Harrison (Bodley Head Quartos, X), 1924, p. 24.

69. Durbin, A Narrative of Some Extraordinary Things, 1800, pp. 18–20, 27, 28, 31–32, 43–51. Cf. Cotton Mather, Another Brand from the Burning, in Calef, More Wonders of the Invisible World, 1700, pp. 4, 5.

70. Wier, iv, 15, ed. 1568, pp. 394–395. See also iii, 14, pp. 253–254; iv, 1–2, pp. 352–358; iv, 5–9, pp. 364–374; iv, 13–14, pp. 385–393; iv, 16, pp. 395–401. Cf. Malleus Maleficarum, Pt. III, qu. 34, ed. 1620, pp. 448–449; Grillando, De Sortilegiis, ed. 1545, iii, 22, fol. xxiij (ed. 1592, iii, 27, pp. 38–39); Anania, De Natura Daemonum, 1581, pp. 193–194; Binsfeld, Commentarius in Titulum Codicis Lib. IX. De Maleficis et Mathematicis, 1591, pp. 510–521; Remy (Remigius), Daemonolatreia, 1595, pp. 220, 300–307; Boguet, Discours des Sorciers, 2d ed., 1608, pp. 214–221; Burr, Narratives of the Witchcraft Cases 1648–1706, 1914, pp. 28, 125, 134, 247, 312, 357; Webster, The Displaying of Supposed Witchcraft, 1677, pp. 35, 242–266; Baxter, The Certainty of the Worlds of Spirits, 1691, pp. 65–69, 93–94; Glanvil's Sadducismus Triumphatus, 4th ed., 1726, pp. 291–299, 315, 329, 332; New York Colonial Documents, IV (1854), 689; George Roberts, The Social History of the People of the Southern Counties, 1856, pp. 525–527; Proceedings Dorset Natural History and Antiquarian Field Club, XXXIV (1913), 22–23; Whitney and Bullock, Folk-Lore from Maryland, 1925, p. 79; W. J. V. Saville, In Unknown New Guinea, 1926, pp. 215–216; W. E. Armstrong, Rossel Island, 1928, pp. 174–175. See pp. 339–340, above.

71. Skeat and Blagden, Pagan Races of the Malay Peninsula, 1906, II, 233–234; Codrington, The Melanesians, 1891, p. 197; Ivens, Melanesians of the South-East Solomon Islands, 1927, pp. 200–204 (with figures); P. Amaury Talbot, The Peoples of Southern Nigeria, 1926, II, 175. Cf. Kroeber, Handbook of the Indians of California (Bureau of American Ethnology, Bulletin, LXXVIII), 1925, p. 68.

72. Horne and Aiston, Savage Life in Central Australia, 1924, pp. 149–152 (with figures).

73. Matthew Mayhew (d. 1710), A Brief Narrative, in Cotton Mather's Magnalia, 1702, Book vi, Chap. 6, section 1, p. 52. Cf. Reports Bureau of (American) Ethnology, VII (for 1885–86), 1891, pp. 336–337, 368, 385 (Cherokees); XI (for 1889–90), 1894, p. 418 (Siouan); XXIII (for 1901–02),

1904, p. 396 (Zuñi); XXX (for 1908–09), 1915, pp. 354–362 (Guiana); Kroeber, Handbook, as above, pp. 136, 197; Zeisberger, History of North American Indians (1779–80), Ohio Archæological and Historical Quarterly, XIX (1910), 126.

74. Cf. H. W. Bates, The Naturalist on the River Amazon, 1892, pp. 244–245; Bye-Gones for 1901–02, p. 68.

75. Codrington, The Melanesians, 1891, pp. 193, 199; cf. pp. 197 (elf-arrow), 200 (bit of stone or bone).

76. J. P. Mills, The Lhota Nagas, 1922, p. 166; Hutton, The Sema Nagas, 1921, pp. 213–214, 231–232.

77. Lercheimer (Witekind), Christlich Bedencken vnd Erinnerung von Zauberey, 1597, ed. Binz, 1888, pp. 54–55; M. Bartels, Die Medicin der Naturvölker, 1893, pp. 183–189; Maddox, The Medicine Man, 1923, pp. 79, 169, 190–195; Tschubinow, Beiträge zum Psychologischen Verständnis des Sibirischen Zauberers, 1914, pp. 67–68, 71–75; Charlevoix, Journal (1721), Histoire et Description Generale de la Nouvelle France, 1744, VI, 96; Alexander Henry, Travels and Adventures in Canada and the Indian Territories between the Years 1760 and 1776, 1809, pp. 118–121; Mooney, Bureau of Ethnology, 7th Report, 1891, pp. 334, 336, 369; Karl von den Steinen, Unter den Naturvölkern Zentral-Brasiliens, 1894, p. 492; Revue de l'Histoire des Religions, XXXII (1895), 148; The Native Tribes of South Australia, ed. Woods, 1879, pp. 46, 283–284; Mrs. James Smith, The Booandik Tribe of South Australian Aborigines, 1880, p. 29; Spencer and Gillen, The Northern Tribes of Central Australia, 1904, pp. 487–488; Howitt, The Native Tribes of South-East Australia, 1904, pp. 379–380, 383–386, 393; the Same, Journal Anthropological Institute, XVI (1887), 38–40; K. L. Parker, The Euahlayi Tribe, 1905, p. 27; Eylmann, Die Eingeborenen der Kolonie Südaustralien, 1908, pp. 224, 446–447; J. Mathew, Two Representative Tribes of Queensland, 1910, pp. 111–113; Spencer, The Native Tribes of the Northern Territory of Australia, 1914, pp. 319–320; Horne and Aiston, Savage Life in Central Australia, 1924, p. 122; Basedow, The Australian Aboriginal, 1925, pp. 181–182; Bonwick, Daily Life and Origin of the Tasmanians, 1870, p. 177; J. H. Holmes, In Primitive New Guinea, 1924, p. 212; Seligmann, The Melanesians of British New Guinea, 1910, pp. 167–170; E. B. Riley, Among Papuan Headhunters, 1925, p. 281; W. J. V. Saville, In Unknown New Guinea, 1926, p. 217; Jenness and Ballantyne, The Northern D'Entrecasteaux, 1920, pp. 139–140; Hose and McDougall, The Pagan Tribes of Borneo, 1912, II, 121–122; Skeat, Malay Magic, 1900, pp. 449–452; Gimlette, Malay Poisons and Charm Cures, 1922, pp. 50–51; Hewat, Bantu Folk Lore, pp. 36, 45–46; P. Amaury Talbot, The Peoples of Southern Nigeria, 1926, II, 167, 174; Mary H. Kingsley, Travels in West Africa, 1897, pp. 469–471; Am Ur-Quell, IV (1893), 38; Whitney and Bullock, Folk-Lore of Maryland, p. 82; Puckett, Folk Beliefs of the Southern Negro, 1926, pp. 302–304; Sir J. M. Campbell, The Indian Antiquary, XXIV (1895), 294; Archiv für Religionswissenschaft, XIV (1911), 204; Journal Anthropological Institute, VII (1878), 506; XIII (1884), 130–131; XVI (1887), 24–25, 38–40, 48, 254–255; XXI (1892),

116, 311; XXXI (1901), 290; Sudan Notes and Records, VI (1923), 90; Hodson, The Nāga Tribes of Manipur, 1911, pp. 135–136; J. H. Hutton, The Sema Nagas, 1921, pp. 213–214, 231–232; Sapir, Journal of American Folk-Lore, XX (1907), 42–44; Reports, Bureau of (American) Ethnology, VII (for 1885–86), 1891, pp. 336–338; XIV (for 1892–93), Part I, 1896, pp. 149–150; XXIII (for 1901–02), 1904, pp. 393–394, 396, 399–400, 402; XXV (for 1903–04), 1907, pp. 61–62; XXVI (for 1904–05), 1908, pp. 261, 262, 267; XXVII (for 1905–06), 1911, p. 583; XXX (for 1908–09), 1915, pp. 351, 352; Kroeber, Handbook of the Indians of California (Bureau of American Ethnology, Bulletin, LXXVIII), 1925, pp. 137, 150, 197, 423, 424, 472, 515–516, 627, 681, 855; Im Thurn, Among the Indians of Guiana, 1883, p. 349.

78. S. R. Maitland, Notes on the Contributions of the Rev. George Townsend, Part II, 1842, p. 132 (1574); Harsnet, Declaration of Egregious Popish Impostures, 1603, p. 253 (cf. pp. 214–216); James Mason, The Anatomie of Sorcerie, 1612, p. 42; The Boy of Bilson, pp. 48–49, 55, 62, 67; Wonderfull News from the North, 1650, p. 16; Tryal of Witches, 1682, pp. 21, 25–28, 31 (1664[–5]); Drage, Daimonomageia, 1665, pp. 3–6; Hansen's letter, March 29, 1682, Journal des Sçavans, April 13, 1682, p. 80 (Weekly Memorials for the Ingenious, No. 18, July 10, 1682, pp. 134–135); A True Account, etc., 1686 (case of John Tonken of Penzance); Sadducismus Debellatus, 1698, pp. 4, 33, 40, 41; A History of the Witches of Renfrewshire, ed. 1877, pp. xxvii, 75–76, 83, 109, 112, 116, 118, 121, 129 (Christian Shaw, 1696); Dunton, The Post-Angel, 1701, II, 67. Cf. Grillando, De Sortilegiis, ed. 1592, iii, 27–28, pp. 38–40; Bartholinus, Historiae Anatomicae Rariores, 1654, i, 52, pp. 81–82; Gaspar Schott, Magia Universalis, 1677, IV, 506, 524–538; T. Willis, An Essay of the Pathology of the Brain, transl. S. P., 1684, p. 44; Bovet, Pandaemonium, 1684, pp. 168, 170–171, 193; Baxter, The Certainty of the Worlds of Spirits, 1691, pp. 43–46, 60, 75–81, 93, 95–97, 100, 109–115; A. Glorez, Neuangeordnete Vollständige Haus- und Land-Bibliothec, Anderes Cabinet, 1719, pp. 185–196 (also in Glorez, Eröffnetes Wunderbuch, "1700," reprint, pp. 347–393: frogs, toads, lizards, puppies, needles, nails, etc., etc.).

79. Reading Records, Diary of the Corporation, ed. Guilding, III (1896), 230–233, 243; Historical MSS. Commission, 11th Report, Appendix, Part VII, p. 185. Cf. Drage, Daimonomageia, 1665, p. 20 (mouse jumps out of possessed person's mouth); Jörimann, Frühmittelalterliche Rezeptarien (Beiträge zur Geschichte der Medizin, ed. Sigerist, I), 1925, pp. 28, 29, 30, cf. pp. 25, 53 (snakes, frogs, lizards, etc., in one's body by witchcraft); A True and Exact Relation, 1645, p. 4 (toads). In 1651 Christiana Weekes was brought before the Wilts quarter sessions for charming an evil spirit out of a man's leg (Historical MSS. Commission, Various Collections, I, 120). In the Life of St. Waltheof, Abbot of Melrose in the twelfth century, we read of a horrible spider that emerged from a swelling on a man's finger (Acta Sanctorum, August 3, I, 255). A crippled Louisiana negro, who had a lump in his leg, declared "that it was a frog put there by a hoodoo" (Journal of American Folk-Lore, XL [1927], 205).

80. A True and Exact Relation, 1645, p. 4.

81. Drage, Daimonomageia, 1665, p. 20.

82. Remains of Denis Granville, ed. Ornsby (Surtees Society, XLVII), p. 31. A similar trick is recorded by Naudé (Naudaeus), Πέντας Quaestionum Iatro-Philologicarum, 1647, pp. 137–138.

CHAPTER VI

VENEFICA

1. Thucydides, ii, 48.

2. Boston Transcript, January 17, 1918.

3. The Times, November 19, 1920, p. 14.

4. Boston Evening Journal, October 3, 1884.

5. Atlanta Journal, February 11, 1911; the Constitution, Atlanta, February 12, 1911; Woman's World (magazine), Chicago, March, 1911, p. 18.

6. Boston Herald, December 29, 1927.

7. See, for example, Livy, viii, 18; xxxix, 41; xl, 37.

8. Dio Cassius, lxvii, 11; lxxii, 14.

9. Cardano, De Rerum Varietate, xv, 80, Opera, III (1663), 293. Cf. Webster, The Displaying of Supposed Witchcraft, 1677, pp. 244–245.

10. Processo Originale degli Untori nella Peste del M.DC.XXX, Milan, 1839; Manzoni, I Promessi Sposi.

11. Matthew Paris, Chronica Majora, ed. Luard, V, 705.

12. Anonymous Chronicle, Harleian MS. 3775, in Riley's ed. of Johannes Amundesham, Annales Monastici, I, 18–19; Gregory's Chronicle, Gairdner, The Historical Collections of a Citizen of London, p. 161.

13. Plato, Laws, xi, p. 933, brings magic into connection with poisoning. See the curious balade against poisoners by Chaucer's contemporary, Eustache Deschamps (No. 465, Œuvres, III, 283). Cf. the case of Eleanor Dulyne (p. 62, above).

14. Grillando, De Sortilegiis, ii, 3, ed. 1592, p. 7; iii, 25–26, pp. 36–38; v, 6–8, pp. 51–54.

15. Garmann, De Miraculis Mortuorum, 1709, i, 3, 65–67, pp. 140–141.

16. Garmann, i, 3, 65, p. 140; Cabanès and Nass, Poisons et Sortilèges, 1903, I, 153–170; Enthoven, The Folklore of Bombay, 1924, pp. 258–259.

17. Danaeus (Daneau), De Veneficis, cap. 3, ed. 1575, pp. 50–51.

18. See notes 9 and 10. Cf. Garmann, i, 3, 65, p. 140.

19. For Jews and lepers see Lehugeur, Histoire de Philippe le Long, I (1897), 422–429; Chroniques de Saint-Denis (Recueil, XX, 704–705); Continuatio Chronici Guillelmi de Nangiaco (XX, 628–629); Adam Murimuth, ed. Thompson, p. 32; Capgrave, ed. Hingeston, p. 186; Flores Historiarum, ed. Luard, III, 195–196; J. F. C. Hecker, Die Grossen Volkskrankheiten des Mittelalters, ed. Hirsch, 1865, pp. 65–72, 96–100; Garmann, i, 3, 65, p. 140.

20. Crawfurd, Plague and Pestilence in Literature and Art, 1914, pp. 54–55, 67, 112, 120–125, 156–158, 175–180, 183; Nohl, The Black Death, transl. C. H. Clarke, 1926, pp. 172–202.

21. Scot, vi, 3–7, pp. 116–124 (87–92), ed. Nicholson, pp. 93–99. See Wier, iii, 36–40, ed. 1568, pp. 332–348, whom Scot follows rather closely. Cf. Wier, vi, Epilogue, pp. 678–679. See also Cardano, De Rerum Varietate, xv, 80, Opera, III (1663), 293; Alfonso el Sabio, Las Siete Partidas, vii, 23, 2 (ed. 1807, III, 668).

22. Scot, iii, 7, p. 50 (41–42), ed. Nicholson, pp. 38–39.

23. On the whole imbroglio see Scofield, The Life and Reign of Edward the Fourth, 1923, II, 186–190, 206–209; Pike, History of Crime, 1876, I, 360–362, 494.

24. Indictments in Deputy Keeper's Third Report, Appendix II, p. 214; Rotuli Parliamentorum, VI, 173–175; Calendar of Patent Rolls 1476–1485, pp. 72–73; Coram Rege Roll, Vernon Harcourt, English Historical Review, XXIII (1908), 521–522, 524.

25. Third Report, as above, pp. 213–214; Coram Rege Roll, English Historical Review, XXIII, 521, 524; Stow, Annales, ed. 1631, p. 430; Hall's Chronicle, ed. 1809, pp. 326, 369; Calendar of Patent Rolls 1476–1485, pp. 40, 43, 50, 102.

26. See pp. 227–228, above.

27. Continuation of the Croyland Chronicle, Rerum Anglicarum Scriptores Veteres, 1684, I, 561–562.

28. Rotuli Parliamentorum, VI, 193–195; Croyland Continuation, I, 562.

29. Philippe de Comynes, i, 7, ed. de Mandrot, I (1901), 59; ed. Calmette, I (1924), 53; Autres Nouvelles Chroniques, appended to Monstrelet, Vol. III (1595), fol. 65 v°; Polydore Vergil, xxiv, ed. Basel, 1534, p. 530 ("in dolio uini Cretici"); Grafton, ed. 1569, pp. 741–742 (ed. 1809, II, 68).

CHAPTER VII

Charms Ghoulish and Profane

1. Pliny, xxviii, 4, 11–12, 45–49.

2. Tacitus, Annales, ii, 69. For other references see Abt, Die Apologie des Apuleius von Medaura und die Antike Zauberei (Religionsgeschichtliche Versuche und Vorarbeiten, IV, ii), 1908, pp. 141–144 (215–218).

3. Paulus Grillandus, De Sortilegiis, ed. 1545, v, 11, foll. xxvj v°–xxvij r° (ed. 1592, v, 8, p. 53). Cf. Remigius, Daemonolatreia, 1595, ii, 3, pp. 209–217; Guaccius (Guazzo), Compendium Maleficarum, 1608, ii, 2, pp. 105–107; Garmann, De Miraculis Mortuorum, 1709, Dissertatio Prooemialis, i, 172–196, pp. 112–123; Wm. Maxwell, De Medicina Magnetica, 1679, i, 6, p. 27 ("Notum est sagas veneficas mala inferre, absque cadaverum partibus, et illius, quem laedere desiderant, excrementis non posse"). For the use of such things in getting rid of demons see Arnaldus de Villa Nova, Libellus de Improbatione Maleficiorum, ed. Diepgen, Archiv für

Kulturgeschichte, IX (1911), 400. For their use in farm magic see Rantasalo, Der Ackerbau, IV (1924), 25–26, 57, 64–69, 141–153, 156–157, 159
(FF Communications, XVII, No. 55).

4. Bacon, Natural History, i, 26, Works, ed. Spedding, II, 348. Cf.
De Groot, The Religious System of China, IV (1901), 382–384.

5. Oldham, Satyrs upon the Jesuits, 5th ed., 1697, p. 81.

6. Seligmann, The Melanesians of British New Guinea, 1910, p. 551;
Driberg, The Lango, 1923, p. 242 (Uganda).

7. Folk-Lore, XXVI, 287–293. Compare the vain sacrifices of Gilles
de Rais.

8. W. G. Black, Folk-Medicine, 1883, pp. 95–107; Cabanès, Remèdes
d'Autrefois, 1905, pp. 46–65; Folk-Lore, XXVI (1915), 272; Löwenstimm,
Aberglaube und Strafrecht, 1897, pp. 95, 107–126; Hellwig, Verbrechen
und Aberglaube, 1908, pp. 63–78; the Same, Archiv für Kriminal-Anthropologie, XXXVII (1910), 384–389; Feilberg, Totenfetische im Glauben
Nordgermanischer Völker, Am Ur-Quell, III (1892), 1–7, 54–61, 87–91,
116–119; Schiffer and others, the same, III, 49–54, 81–86, 113–116, 126–
128, 147–151, 199–202, 209–212, 238–240; IV (1893), 16–20, 49–53, 68–
70, 98–100; Wuttke-Meyer, pp. 133–139; Fossel, Volksmedicin und Medicinischer Aberglaube in Steiermark, 1886, pp. 90–91; Seyfarth, Aberglaube
und Zauberei in der Volksmedizin Sachsens, 1913, pp. 286–292; Blätter
für Pommersche Volkskunde, I (1893), 62–64; De Cock, Volksgeneeskunde in Vlaanderen, 1891, pp. 72–74, 96; F. S. Krauss, Volksglaube und
Religiöser Brauch der Südslaven, 1890, pp. 134–147; Mansikka, Ueber
Russische Zauberformeln, 1909, pp. 90–93; Revue des Traditions Populaires, XX (1905), 251–253; De Groot, The Religious System of China,
IV (1901), 372–384; Sébillot, L'Homme, III (1886), 33–40; Doutté, Magie
et Religion dans l'Afrique du Nord, 1909, pp. 301–303; Roscoe, The
Bagesu, 1924, p. 108; Seligmann, The Melanesians of British New Guinea,
1910, pp. 289, 302, and Plate XL.

9. Pliny, xxviii, 4, 11, 45 ("inmatura morte raptorum manu strumas,
parotidas, guttura tactu sanari adfirmant, quidam vero cuiuscumque de-
functi, dumtaxat sui sexus, laeva manu aversa"); Fernel, De Abditis
Rerum Causis, ii, 16 (De Morbis, 1656, p. 520); Scot, xii, 14, p. 244 (176),
ed. Nicholson, p. 197 (cf. Garmann, Dissertatio Prooemialis, Sect. i,
§§ 174–179, pp. 112–115); Boyle, Some Considerations touching the Vse-
fulness of Experimental Philosophy, 2d ed., 1664, p. 230; Wheatcroft's
Autobiography, under 1686[–7], Journal of the Derbyshire Archæological
and Natural History Society, XXI (1899), 48–49; Letter from Dr. John
Beale to Robert Boyle, November 2, 1663, in Boyle, Works, ed. Birch,
1744, V, 441 (the remedy was used by the advice of "Dr. F. Cl." and was
completely successful; the gentlewoman who used it was a friend of
Beale's); Glyde, The Norfolk Garland, p. 36; the Same, A New Suffolk
Garland, 1866, p. 175; Henderson, ed. 1879, p. 154; Notes and Queries,
1st Series, II (1850), 36; Burne and Jackson, Shropshire Folk-Lore,
p. 202; Elworthy, Horns of Honour, 1900, pp. 192–193; Poole, The Customs, etc., of Somerset, 1877, p. 52; Hammond, A Cornish Parish, 1897,
p. 352; Leather, The Folk-Lore of Herefordshire, 1912, p. 84; Clague, Manx

Reminiscences, [1911,] p. 153 (birthmark); Thomas, Kentucky Superstitions, 1920, pp. 94 (birthmarks), 102 (eczema), 105 (goitre), 131 (wen cured by rubbing it against a dead man's neck); Folk-Lore Record, I (1878), 48, 227–228; V (1882), 174; Folk-Lore Journal, V (1887), 204–205; VII (1889), 55; Cambridge Antiquarian Society, Proceedings and Communications, XI (1907), 272, 274; Sussex Archæological Collections, XLV (1902), 215; Baltische Studien, XXXVI (1886), 332; De Cock, Volksgeneeskunde in Vlaanderen, 1891, p. 72 (birthmark); Am Ur-Quell, III (1892), 49; Zeitschrift der Gesellschaft für Schleswig-Holstein-Lauenburgische Geschichte, XVI (1886), 381 (pimples, tetter, warts).

10. Folk-Lore, XX (1909), 216; Browne, Pseudodoxia Epidemica, v, 24, 9, Works, ed. Wilkin, 1852, II, 101.

11. Bray, Traditions, Legends, etc., of Devonshire, 1838, II, 292; Glyde, The Norfolk Garland, p. 38; Henderson, ed. 1879, p. 145; Hewett, Nummits and Crummits, 1900, p. 67 (Devonshire); Transactions Devonshire Association, II (1867–68), 39; Folk-Lore, XXIII (1912), 476–477; Notes and Queries, 1st Series, II (1850), 37. Cf. Thomas, Kentucky Superstitions, 1920, p. 119; E. M. Wright, Rustic Speech and Folk-Lore, 1913, p. 249; Burne and Jackson, Shropshire Folk-Lore, p. 193; R. Kaufmann, Pratiques et Superstitions Médicales en Poitou, 1906, p. 55; Hovorka and Kronfeld, Vergleichende Volksmedicin, II (1909), 846–847; De Cock, Volksgeneeskunde in Vlaanderen, 1891, p. 163; Revue des Traditions Populaires, XVI (1901), 592; XX (1905), 252, 446.

12. Folk-Lore, XXXIII (1922), 396 (Connacht).

13. Scot, xii, 14, p. 244 (176), ed. Nicholson, p. 197, from Pliny, xxviii, 1, 2, 7. Cf. Fernel, De Abditis Rerum Causis, ii, 16 (De Morbis, 1656, p. 520); Thiers, Traité des Superstitions, 1741, I, 375; R. Kaufmann, Pratiques et Superstitions Médicales en Poitou, 1906, p. 55.

14. Bye-Gones for 1878–79, p. 114; for 1899–1900, pp. 293–294. For this remedy see also Corrector, § 177, Schmitz, Bussbücher, II (1898), 448; Leechdoms, ed. Cockayne, II, 126 (Leonhardi, p. 38).

15. Boston, Lincoln, Louth, and Spalding Herald, February 7, 1837, quoted in Folk-Lore Journal, VII (1889), 54. Earth from a skull is a depilatory; grass from a skull, if chewed, makes teeth fall out: Pliny, xxviii, 4, 11, 46.

16. Folk-Lore, XIV (1903), 370 (Ross-shire); XI (1900), 446 (Hebrides).

17. Folk-Lore, XXII (1911), 56 (Ireland).

18. Thomas, Kentucky Superstitions, 1920, p. 101.

19. Hammond, A Cornish Parish, 1897, p. 352.

20. Scot, xii, 14, p. 245 (177), ed. Nicholson, p. 197; Boston, Lincoln, Louth, and Spalding Herald, February 7, 1837, quoted in Folk-Lore Journal, VII (1889), 54. A wen on the neck may be cured by placing a string round the neck of a dead friend and then wearing it round your own neck (Thomas, p. 131). Cf. Grillando, De Sortilegiis, ed. 1545, v, 11, fol. xxvij r° (ed. 1592, v, 8, p. 53); Whitney and Bullock, Folk-Lore from Maryland, 1925, p. 92; Panjab Notes and Queries, III (1885–86), 26. For the use of the blood, etc., of executed criminals as medicine see De Groot, The

Religious System of China, IV (1901), 377–378; for coffin wood and grave plants see the same, IV, 405–406.

21. Pliny, xxviii, 4, 12, 49. Cf. Fernel, De Abditis Rerum Causis, ii, 16 (De Morbis, 1656, p. 520).

22. Folk-Lore, XI (1900), 217; XXVII (1916), 415. Cf. Hansen, Quellen, p. 451; Seyfarth, Aberglaube und Zauberei in der Volksmedizin Sachsens, 1913, pp. 287–288. In 1908 a piece of hangman's rope was begged in Delaware as a cure for fits (Chicago Inter-Ocean, December 27, 1908). Cf. de Rojas, Celestina, ed. Cejador y Frauca, 1913, I, 81.

23. Hewett, Nummits and Crummits, 1900, p. 65 (Devonshire); Thiers, Traité des Superstitions, 1741, I, 365. Shadwell, in a note to his comedy of The Lancashire Witches (1682), remarks: "The French gamesters . . . think that the noose of the rope that went about the neck of one that was hang'd will make them win. And here old women will prescribe a piece of the gallows for a cure for an ague" (ed. Halliwell, 1853, p. 58).

24. Transactions Devonshire Association, II (1867–68), 39.

25. Boston, Lincoln, Louth, and Spalding Herald, February 7, 1837, quoted in Folk-Lore Journal, VII (1889), 55. Cf. Sir Thomas Browne, Pseudodoxia Epidemica, v, 24, 9, Works, ed. Wilkin, 1852, II, 100.

26. Sussex Archæological Collections, XVIII (1866), 160–161; Transactions Cumberland and Westmorland Antiquarian and Archæological Society, XIV (1897), 373; Henderson, 1879, p. 145.

27. Thomas, Kentucky Superstitions, 1920, p. 125.

28. Transactions Devonshire Association, X (1878), 101. Cf. Glyde, The Norfolk Garland, p. 31; Kristensen, Danske Sagn, IV (1896), 581–584; Dieterich, Mutter Erde, 3d ed., 1925, pp. 28–29.

29. Bye-Gones for 1901–02, p. 116, cf. p. 99; Bergen, Animal and Plant Lore, 1898, p. 102. Cf. Thiers, Traité des Superstitions, 1741, I, 370.

30. Bray, as above, II, 291, note.

31. County Folk-Lore, III (1903), 151 (Shetland).

32. The same, I, No. 3 (1895), p. 54. Cf. Pitcairn, Criminal Trials in Scotland, 1833, I, 201–204.

33. Boston, Lincoln, Louth, and Spalding Herald, February 7, 1837, quoted in Folk-Lore Journal, VII (1889), 54; The East Anglian, II (1866), 216; Glyde, A New Suffolk Garland, 1866, p. 175; the Same, The Norfolk Garland, p. 36; Henderson, 1879, pp. 155–156.

34. See Seyfarth, Aberglaube und Zauberei in der Volksmedizin Sachsens, 1913, pp. 209–216; Am Ur-Quell, VI (1896), 36–37.

35. Wells Diocesan Records, Holworthy, Discoveries in the Diocesan Register, Wells, p. 7.

36. Leechdoms, ed. Cockayne, III, 68; Wülker, Bibliothek der Angelsächsischen Poesie, I, 327; Grendon, Journal of American Folk-Lore, XXII (1909), 208, 234.

37. Theodore as represented by Discipulus Umbrensium, i, 15, § 3 (Haddan and Stubbs, Councils, III, 190; Schmitz, Bussbücher, II, 556), by Canones Gregorii, § 117 (Schmitz, II, 535), and by Capitula Judiciorum, xvi, 4 (Schmitz, II, 237); Pseudo-Theodore, xxvii, 15 (Thorpe, Ancient

Laws, pp. 292–293); Pseudo-Ecgbert, Anglo-Saxon Confessionale, § 32 (Thorpe, p. 356: "þær man dead wære"; *var.*, "þær deade men beoð bebyrigde"); Pseudo-Bede-Ecgbert, i, 35 (Schmitz, II, 683); Pseudo-Cummean, vii (ix), 15 (Schmitz, II, 627); Corrector, § 95 (Schmitz, II, 430); Schmitz, I, 684, 749. Compare other rites mentioned in Corrector, §§ 95–97 (Schmitz, II, 430–431).

38. Raine, The Fabric Rolls of York Minster (Surtees Society, XXXV), p. 266.

39. Liebermann, Die Gesetze der Angelsachsen, I, 255.

40. Canons of Edgar, § 16, Thorpe, p. 396 (*lic-wiglunga*).

41. John of Salisbury, Policraticus, i, 12, ed. Webb, I, 51. Cf. Isidore, Origines, viii, 9.

42. Havamál, sts. 146–163, Bugge, Norrœn Fornkvæði, 1867, pp. 62–64.

43. An Apology for Lollard Doctrines, ed. Todd (Camden Society, XX), p. 95: "Nigromauncers are thei that bi figeris or markyngis vp-on the dead body of best or of man, thus enforcith to geit wityng, or to wirk, or thus to bow God." John of Salisbury calls those *aruspices* who "uaticinantur in ossibus animalium siue sanguine" (Policraticus, i, 12, ed. Webb, I, 51).

44. Chaucer, Parson's Tale, § 37 (Skeat, IV, 607); cf. Pardoner's Prologue, vv. 22–43, and Skeat's note, V, 271. See also Kirk, Secret Commonwealth, ed. 1815, p. 17 (ed. Lang, p. 31); J. G. Campbell, Superstitions of the Highlands and Islands, 1900, pp. 263–266; Curtin, Tales of the Fairies and of the Ghost World collected in South-West Munster, 1895, pp. 84–85; Thoms, Folk-Lore Record, I (1878), 176–179; J. C. Davies, Folk-Lore of West and Mid-Wales, 1911, pp. 275–276; Folk-Lore Journal, II (1884), 367–369; Folk-Lore, VI (1895), 157, 167; XIII (1902), 50–51; Beaumont, An Historical, Physiological and Theological Treatise of Spirits, 1705, pp. 295–296; Dalyell, Darker Superstitions, 1834, pp. 515–519; Bye-Gones for 1889–90, p. 19; H. C. Agrippa, De Occulta Philosophia, i, 33, ed. 1533, p. xxxix; Tylor, Primitive Culture, 1871, I, 112–113; Lubbock, The Origin of Civilization, 1870, pp. 142–143 (2d ed., 1870, pp. 163–164); Andree, Boas Anniversary Volume, 1906, pp. 143–165; Purchas his Pilgrimes, XII (1906), 18; Beiträge zur Geschichte des Niederrheins, XIII (1898), 234; F. S. Krauss, Volksglaube und Religiöser Brauch der Südslaven, 1890, pp. 169–170; L. de Milloué, Conférences au Musée Guimet (Annales, XIV), 1903, pp. 200–201; Curtin, A Journey in Southern Siberia, 1909, p. 99; Vreto (Bretos), Contes et Poèmes de la Grèce Moderne, 1858, p. 22 and note; G. F. Abbott, Macedonian Folklore, 1903, pp. 96–98; Elliot and Dowson, The History of India as told by its own Historians, I (1867), 331; Dornan, Pygmies and Bushmen of the Kalahari, 1925, p. 158. Cf. The Remains of Denis Granville (Surtees Society, XLVII), ed. Ornsby, pp. 31–32 (breastbone of woodcock or wild duck).

45. See Pseudo-Theodore, xxiii, 14, Thorpe, p. 290; Pseudo-Ecgbert, Excerptiones, § 75, Thorpe, p. 332; Schmitz, II, 181, 232, 321, 324, 328, 335, 342, 347, 352, 360, 378, 422, 619, 681, 696.

46. Year Book 45 Edward III, 1679, p. 17, § 7; Coke's Institutes, Third Part, cap. 6.

47. Contemporary Narrative, ed. Wright (Camden Society, XXIV), pp. 2, 32.

48. Du Bartas, La Seconde Sepmaine, 4th Day, Part 1 (Œuvres, 1611, p. 352); Sylvester, ed. 1633, p. 198.

49. Kathā-sarit-sāgara, xxxiv, Tawney's translation, I, 306; new ed. by Penzer, III (1925), 133.

50. Cardano, De Rerum Varietate, xvi, 90, Opera, III (1663), 310. Cf. Archiv für Kriminal-Anthropologie, XXXIX (1910), 301; Elworthy, Horns of Honour, 1900, pp. 190–191.

51. John Deacon and John Walker, Dialogicall Discourses, of Spirits and Divels, 1601, p. 143. Guilielmus Alvernus (Bishop of Paris 1228–1249) declares that a candle composed "ex cera et corio serpentis sulfurato," if it burns in a place where there is no other light, will make the straws and rushes on the floor seem to be "serpentes per domum dissilientes" (De Universo, ii, 3, 22, Opera, 1674, I, 1059). Cf. St. Bonaventura, Commentaria in Sententias, Lib. ii, dist. 8, part. 2, art. 1, qu. 3 (Opera, II [1885], 229; cf. II, 200–203, 436); Ulrich Molitoris, De Lamiis et Phitonicis Mulieribus, cap. 8 (error for 10), ed. 1489, sig. [D1] v°; Le Loyer, Discours et Histoires des Spectres, 1605, ii, 7, p. 145; Del Rio, Disquisitiones Magicae, Lib. ii, qu. 8, ed. 1616, p. 107; Thorndike, A History of Magic and Experimental Science, 1923, II, 345.

52. John Hawarde, Les Reportes del Cases in Camera Stellata, ed. Baildon, 1894, pp. 250–251. For a recipe "vt stramen appareat serpens" see Sloane MS. 2628, fol. 50 r° (cf. fol. 10 r°).

53. Thurston, Omens and Superstitions of Southern India, 1912, pp. 96–97.

54. Hildburgh, Journal Royal Anthropological Institute, XXXVIII (1908), 165. Cf. Basin, De Artibus Magicis ac Magorum Maleficiis, in Mallei Maleficarum, 1582, II, 20: "Est herba quaedam accensa fumigans quae facit trabes apparere serpentes." See also Journal of American Folk-Lore, XXXVIII (1925), 621.

55. Grimm, Deutsche Mythologie, 4th ed., pp. 897–898; Remi (Remigius), Daemonolatreia, 1595, ii, 3, pp. 212–215; Gaule, Πῦς-μαντία the Mag-astro-mancer, 1652, p. 355; Garmann, De Miraculis Mortuorum, 1709, Dissertatio Prooemialis, i, 194, pp. 122–123; Scheible, Das Kloster, VI (1847), 216–219; Lowes, The Road to Xanadu, 1927, pp. 556–557; Elworthy, Horns of Honour, 1900, pp. 178–191; Skeat, Philological Society Transactions, 1888–90, p. 295; Taylor, Journal of American Folk-Lore, XXXIV (1921), 327; Blakeborough, The Hand of Glory, 1924, pp. 16–23; J. S. Fletcher, A Book about Yorkshire, 1908, pp. 274–278; Folk-Lore, VII (1896), 269; XX (1909), 219–220; XXVI (1915), 293–294; Archiv für Kriminal-Anthropologie, XXIV (1906), 161; XXVI (1906), 222 (from Carpzov); LVI (1914), 269; Baring-Gould, Strange Survivals, 1892, p. 244; The Ocean of Story (Kathā-sarit-sāgara), transl. Tawney, ed. Penzer, note, III (1925), 150–154; Bergen, Animal and Plant Lore, 1899, p. 78; Frischbier, Hexenspruch und Zauberbann, 1870, p. 111; J. W. Wolf, Nederländische Sagen, 1843, pp. 363–365; Wuttke-Meyer, p. 134; E. Meier, Deutsche Sagen, Sitten und Gebräuche aus Schwaben, 1852,

pp. 175–176; Birlinger, Volksthümliches aus Schwaben, I (1861), 339; Witzschel, Kleine Beiträge, II (1878), 283; Bartsch, Sagen, Märchen und Gebräuche aus Meklenburg, II (1880), 332–333, 335; Strackerjan, Aberglaube und Sagen aus dem Herzogtum Oldenburg, 2d ed., 1909, I, 118; Vernaleken, Alpensagen, 1858, p. 422; U. Jahn, Volkssagen aus Pommern und Rügen, 1886, pp. 331–332; Zeitschrift des Vereins für Volkskunde, XXIII (1913), 126, 333; Am Ur-Quell, III (1892), 60–61, 92, 148, 210–211; V (1894), 163; Zeitschrift für Socialwissenschaft, VI (1903), 276; Archiv für Kriminal-Anthropologie, XXV (1906), 85–87; v. Hovorka and Kronfeld, Vergleichende Volksmedizin, II (1909), 537; Seyfarth, Aberglaube und Zauberei in der Volksmedizin Sachsens, 1913, pp. 288–289; Zeitschrift des Vereins für Rheinische und Westfälische Volkskunde, VI (1909), 64–65; XII (1915), 261–262; Kristensen, Danske Sagn, VI, i (1900), 393–395; Baltische Studien, XXXVI (1886), 330, cf. 338; F. S. Krauss, Volksglaube und Religiöser Brauch der Südslaven, 1890, pp. 144–146; Cosquin, Contes Populaires de Lorraine, [1886,] I, 178, 184; Sébillot, L'Homme, January 25, 1886, pp. 33–40; Cabanès, Remèdes d'Autrefois, 1905, p. 49; Grohmann, Aberglaube und Gebräuche aus Böhmen und Mähren, 1864, pp. 106, 205; Deutsche Volkskunde aus dem Oestlichen Böhmen, V (1905), 48; IX (1909), 57; Szulczewski, Allerhand Fahrendes Volk in Kujawien, 1906, pp. 27, 32; Mansikka, Ueber Russische Zauberformeln, 1909, p. 91; Wilken, De Indische Gids, VII, i (1885), 56; Mannhardt, Die Praktischen Folgen des Aberglaubens, 1878 (Deutsche Zeit- und Streit-Fragen, VII), pp. 21–24; Löwenstimm, Aberglaube und Strafrecht, 1897, pp. 113–126; Hellwig, Verbrechen und Aberglaube, 1908, pp. 72–73, 76–78; Henderson, Notes on the Folk Lore of the Northern Counties, 1866, pp. 200–206 (ed. 1879, pp. 239–244); Thomas and Katharine Macquoid, About Yorkshire, 1883, pp. 65–70. Cf. Roscoe, The Baganda, 1911, p. 329; Weeks, Among Congo Cannibals, 1913, p. 287; G. W. Briggs, The Chamārs, 1920, p. 169; Hobley, Bantu Beliefs and Magic, 1922, pp. 192–193; Milne, The Home of an Eastern Clan, 1924, p. 266; MacKenzie, The Spirit-Ridden Konde, 1925, p. 289; North Indian Notes and Queries, I (1891–92), 103; Journal of the Royal Anthropological Institute, XXXVIII (1908), 164; XL (1910), 302–303; XLI (1911), 301–302. It was a belief of Chinese bandits centuries ago that to eat of human flesh renders a burglar invisible by night (De Groot, The Religious System of China, IV [1901], 364). See also Journal of American Folk-Lore, XL (1927), 305.

56. For such abuses in great variety see A. Franz, Die Messe im Deutschen Mittelalter, 1902, pp. 87–114. Cf. Kotelmann, Gesundheitspflege im Mittelalter, 1890, pp. 240–242. It is reported that "in an interior city of Cuba not long since, a wooden image of Santa Barbara, known to the witches as Chango, was taken from the witch house in solemn procession to the . . . church accompanied by city officials and blessed by the priests. A banquet was given and the image returned to the temple of the witches" (E. P. Herrick, The Southern Workman, XXXVI [1907], 402).

57. See Wuttke-Meyer, pp. 139–144; Seyfarth, Aberglaube und Zauberei in der Volksmedizin Sachsens, 1913, pp. 273–275; Manz, Volks-

brauch und Volksglaube des Sarganserlandes, Schriften der Schweizerischen Gesellschaft für Volkskunde, XII (1916), 47–52; Revue des Traditions Populaires, XIV (1899), 560; XV (1900), 475–477.

58. Folk-Lore Record, I (1878), 46.

59. Canon 39, Mansi, Concilia, VII (1762), 883.

60. Forby, The Vocabulary of East Anglia, 1830, II, 406–407. Cf. Old Yorkshire, ed. Wm. Smith, II (1881), 170–171.

61. Pseudo-Ecgbert, Anglo-Saxon Confessionale, § 17 (Thorpe, Ancient Laws, 1840, p. 350), and Poenitentiale, Additamenta, § 27 (Thorpe, p. 392); cf. Pseudo-Theodore, xxxviii, 1–3 (Thorpe, p. 298). See Schmitz, Bussbücher, II (1898), 247, 524, 525, 635; cf. Grillando, De Sortilegiis, x, 18, ed. 1592, p. 164; Die Hirtenbriefe Ælfrics, ed. Fehr, 1914, p. 65.

62. Parochialia, Part III, Supplement to Archæologia Cambrensis, 6th Series, XI (1911), 84.

63. See also the cases of Joan Tyrrye in 1555 (p. 254) and Judith Phillips in 1595 (p. 206); cf. p. 215.

64. Notes and Queries for Somerset and Dorset, XII (1911), 33–34 (from Bishop Stafford's Register, Harleian MS. 6966). Cf. Holkot, Super Libros Sapientie, Lectio 190 (Speyer, 1488, sig. p ij r°; Reutlingen, 1489, sig. Miiij, lf. 5v°): "Inuocationes etiam quas vetule per nomina barbarica et extranea vel obseruationes infinitas pro morbis curandis sortilegia sunt quamuis admisceantur quedam de deo uel de euangelio."

65. See A. Franz, Die Kirchlichen Benediktionen, 1909, II, 436.

66. The Antiquary, XXXII (1896), 17–22.

67. Cf. Baxter, The Certainty of the Worlds of Spirits, 1691, p. 155; Hunt, Popular Romances of the West of England, 1865, II, 223–224 (Psalm lxviii, 1–2); Bang, Norske Hexeformularer, 1901, pp. 164–165, 168–169, 174–175, 527; Vassiliev, Anecdota Graeco-Byzantina, I (1893), 335. See Chapter II, note 83.

68. The Rev. Oliver Heywood, his Autobiography, etc., ed. Turner, I (1882), 344–345.

69. Burne and Jackson, Shropshire Folk-Lore, p. 150.

70. E. Owen, Welsh Folk-Lore, p. 245; Bye-Gones for 1886–87, p. 122.

71. Transactions Devonshire Association, X (1878), 103–104. Cf. Abbott, Macedonian Folklore, 1903, p. 227.

72. Blakeborough, Wit, Character, Folklore and Customs of the North Riding of Yorkshire, 2d ed., 1911, p. 183.

73. Giraldus Cambrensis, Itinerarium Kambriae, i, 5, Opera, ed. Dimock, VI, 58–59.

74. Articles to be Inquired Of, No. 64 (London, Richard Grafton, 1548), sig. Biiii, lf. 1 r°.

75. Cockayne, III, 10, 12; Leonhardi, p. 126.

76. Cockayne, II, 136; Leonhardi, p. 41. For the eating or drinking of magic words see Pradel, Griechische und Süditalienische Gebete (Religionsgeschichtliche Versuche und Vorarbeiten, III, iii), 1907, pp. 380–381; Dieterich, Abraxas, 1891, p. 159.

77. William of Malmesbury, Gesta Pontificum Anglorum, ed. Hamilton, i, 72, p. 137; iv, 156, p. 295. Cf. Crooke, Religion and Folklore of North-

ern India, 1926, pp. 434–435; La Tradition, VI (1892), 216–220. See p. 103, above.

78. See Cockayne, Leechdoms, I, xlvi–xlvii; Hälsig, Der Zauberspruch bei den Germanen, 1910, pp. 24–27. For devils or fiends see Cockayne, I, 102, 248, 312, 360, 386, 394; II, 136, 294, 306, 316, 322, 334, 342, 350, 352, 354; III, 10, 36, 70, 80; Kleinere Angelsächsische Denkmäler, ed. Leonhardi, I (1905), 41, 89, 94, 97, 98, 102, 104, 107, 108, 126, 151, 155. Cf. Rituale Ecclesiae Dunelmensis, ed. Stevenson (Surtees Society, X), pp. 115–116, 121, 129. For nightmare or nocturnal goblins see Cockayne, II, 140, 306, 342, 344; Leonhardi, pp. 42, 94, 104, 105. Cf. Heinrich, Ein Mittelenglisches Medizinbuch, 1896, p. 166. For elves see Cockayne, II, 138, 156, 290, 296, 334, 344, 348, 350; III, 10, 46, 54, 64 (cf. II, 348 [Castalides]; III, 32); Leonhardi, pp. 42, 47, 88, 90, 102, 105–107, 126, 141, 148. Cf. Yorkshire Archæological Journal, XVII (1903), 402–404; The Book of Cerne, ed. Kuypers, 1902, Appendix, p. 221; Klemming, Läke- och Örte-Böcker, 1883–86, pp. 394–395. For dwarfs see Cockayne, I, 364; III, 38, 40, 42, 118; Leonhardi, p. 138; Wülker, I, 326, 404; Grendon, pp. 166–167, 215–216; Skemp, pp. 293–295; Napier, Herrig's Archiv, LXXXIV (1890), 323. For witches or wizards see Cockayne, I, 190; II, 138, 298, 306, 342; III, 36, 52, 54 (cf. I, 402); Leonhardi, pp. 42, 90, 94. On "Krankheits-Dämonen" see M. Höfler, Archiv für Religionswissenschaft, II (1899), 86–164; Klemming, pp. 229–230; Manninen, Die Dämonistischen Krankheiten im Finnischen Volksglauben (FF Communications, XII, No. 45), 1922. On elves and dwarfs see Jente, pp. 167–180.

79. Cockayne, I, 388; II, 110, 136, 138, 140, 142, 334, 346, 348, 350, 352, 354; III, 54, 56; Leonhardi, pp. 33, 41–43, 102, 105–108, 144.

80. Cockayne, III, 46 (cf. II, 156); Leonhardi, p. 141 (cf. p. 47).

81. Cockayne, II, 344, 346, 350; III, 14, 24; Leonhardi, pp. 105, 107, 127, 132.

82. Cockayne, II, 296, 344, 346; Leonhardi, pp. 90, 105, 106.

83. Cockayne, II, 296, 350; Leonhardi, pp. 90, 107.

84. Cockayne, II, 334; Leonhardi, p. 102.

85. Cockayne, III, 14; cf. II, 334; Leonhardi, p. 127, cf. p. 102.

86. Cockayne, II, 138, 344, 346; Leonhardi, pp. 42, 105, 106.

87. Cockayne, II, 138, 140, 142, 156, 294, 334, 344, 346, 352, 354, 356; III, 6, 12, 28, 46, 56; Leonhardi, pp. 42, 43, 47, 89, 102, 105–108, 124, 126, 136, 141, 145. Cf. A. Franz, Die Messe, p. 87.

88. Giraldus Cambrensis, Gemma Ecclesiastica, i, 49, Opera, ed. Brewer, II, 137 (from Peter Cantor, Verbum Abbreviatum, cap. 29, Migne, CCV, 106). On priests who sing masses for the dead for a living man in order to kill him, see Grillando, De Sortilegiis, ed. 1592, x, 12, p. 159; xi, 17, p. 178. On those who, in celebrating mass, repeat evil prayers, naming the person to be witched, or who put *sortilegia* on the altar and offer them to God, see Grillando, iii, 22, p. 33; xvii, 1, pp. 221–222. See also A. Franz, Die Messe, pp. 87, 98–100. Compare the Black Fast to detect a thief or kill an enemy (p. 129, above). Bale, in a scurrilous passage, attacks the mass: "It serueth all wytches in their wytcherye, all sorcerers, charmers, inchaunters, dreamers, sothsayers, necromansers, coniures, crosse dyggers,

deuyll raysers, myracle doers, doggeleches, and bawdes. For without a masse, they can not wele worke their feates" (The Lattre Examinacyon of Anne Askewe, ed. Marpurg, January 16, 1547, fol. 60 r°).

89. See pp. 93–95. For "christening of a catt" (1632) see Reports of Cases in the Courts of Star Chamber and High Commission, ed. S. R. Gardiner (Camden Society, New Series, XXXIX), p. 275.

90. Criminal Chronology of York Castle, 1867, p. 29. Cf. Yorkshire Archæological Journal, XIV (1898), 115, note; Whitelock, Memorials of English Affairs, ed. 1853, II, 291.

91. Bray, Traditions, Legends, Superstitions, and Sketches of Devonshire, 1838, II, 291. Or you may walk thrice round the communion table at midnight: Notes and Queries, 1st Series, III (1851), 259.

92. For the cleft ash see, for example, Pengelly, Annual Reports and Transactions of the Plymouth Institution, VII (1881), 127–160; Glyde, The New Suffolk Garland, 1866, p. 171; Gilbert White, The Natural History of Selborne, Part II, Letter 28 (1776), Works, ed. 1802, I, 343–344; Gentleman's Magazine, LXXIV, ii (1804), 909 (with figure); Transactions Penzance Natural History and Antiquarian Society, 1st Series, II (1851–55), 240; The East Anglian, II (1866), 215–216, 250; Transactions Devonshire Association, VIII (1876), 54; IX (1877), 94–96 (arched bramble or cleft ash); Mead, Somersetshire Archæological and Natural History Association, XXXVIII (1892), 362–369; The Western Antiquary, III (1884), 38; Notes and Gleanings, Devon and Cornwall, II (1889), 79; By-Gones for 1891–92, p. 259; Folk-Lore, Record, I (1878), 40–41; Folk-Lore, VI (1895), 123–124; VII (1896), 303–306 (with figures); IX (1898), 333–334; Glyde, The Norfolk Garland, p. 41; F. Hancock, The Parish of Selworthy, Somerset, 1897, p. 238; Cecil Torr, Small Talk in Wreyland, 1st Series, 1918, pp. 7–8; Hartland, The Legend of Perseus, II (1895), 146–147; A. L. Humphreys, The Materials for the History of the Town of Wellington, 1889, pp. 244–245; J. Ll. W. Page, An Exploration of Exmoor, 4th ed., 1895, p. 32; Leather, The Folk-Lore of Herefordshire, 1912, pp. 80–81; E. M. Wright, Rustic Speech and Folk-Lore, 1913, p. 236. For the practice of creeping through trees, holed stones, etc., see Marcellus Empiricus, De Medicamentis, cap. 33, § 26, ed. Helmreich, 1889, p. 343; Gaidoz, Un Vieux Rite Médical, 1892 (with addenda in Mélusine, VIII [1896–97], 174–179, 201–208, 244–253, 282–285; IX [1898–99], 6–8, 33–34, 121–126, 226; X [1900–01], 254–255); Pseudo-Augustine, De Rectitudine Catholicae Conversationis, cap. 5, Migne, XL, 1172; Thiers, Traité des Superstitions, 1741, I, 383–384, 387; Liebrecht, Gervasius, pp. 170–171; Frazer, The Golden Bough, 3d ed., XI (1913), Balder the Beautiful, II, 168–195; Black, Folk-Medicine, 1883, pp. 65–70; Seligmann, Der Böse Blick, 1910, I, 327–328; Kristensen, Danske Sagn, IV (1896), 576–581; Zeitschrift des Vereins für Volkskunde, II (1892), 81–82; VII (1897), 42–53; XII (1902), 110–113; XX (1910), 167–181; XXIII (1913), 288–293; XXIV (1914), 201–206; Oertel, Studien zur Vergleichenden Literaturgeschichte, VIII (1908), 115–116; K. Kohler, Archiv für Religionswissenschaft, XIII (1910), 80; Burne and Jackson, Shropshire Folk-Lore, pp. 195–198; C. H. Poole, The Customs, Superstitions, and Legends of the

County of Stafford, pp. 81–82; Pitcairn, Criminal Trials in Scotland, 1833, II, 28; Hunt, Popular Romances of the West of England, 1865, II, 212, 215–216; Bye-Gones for 1871–73, p. 69; for 1899–1900, p. 268; for 1901–02, p. 440; Notes and Queries, 1st Series, I (1850), 397; Folk-Lore, XXXII (1921), 125; Wood-Martin, Traces of the Elder Faiths of Ireland, 1902, II, 226–243; Cross, Studies in Philology (University of North Carolina), XVI (1919), 260–261; Whitney and Bullock, Folk-Lore from Maryland, 1925, pp. 93–94; Am Ur-Quell, III (1892), 9–10, 66; Wuttke-Meyer, pp. 337, 338, 360; Seyfarth, Aberglaube und Zauberei in der Volksmedizin Sachsens, 1913, pp. 205–209; Schweizer Volkskunde, II (1912), 79; Knuchel, Die Umwandlung, 1919, pp. 55–56 (Schriften der Schweizerischen Gesellschaft für Volkskunde, XV); De Cock, Volksgeneeskunde in Vlaanderen, 1891, pp. 82–83; Skattegraveren, II (1884), 29; V (1886), 201–202; VII (1887), 31–32; VIII (1887), 116; R. Kaufmann, Pratiques et Superstitions Médicales en Poitou, 1906, p. 57; Zanetti, La Medicina delle nostre Donne, 1892, p. 211; The Indian Antiquary, XXVII (1898), 109. For the sacred character of the ash or the mountain ash see, for example, The Antiquary, XLII (1906), 367–372, 421–426; Devon and Cornwall Notes and Queries, XI (1921), 3–4, 97–100; XII (1923), 13–14; Notes and Gleanings, Devon and Cornwall, I (1888), 28–29; Bye-Gones for 1886–87, p. 38; Dawson, History of Skipton, 1882, pp. 388–389; J. C. Davies, Folk-Lore of West and Mid-Wales, 1911, pp. 240–242.

93. Folk-Lore, XIII (1902), 57.

94. Henderson, Notes on the Folk-Lore of the Northern Counties, 1879, pp. 142–143; Nicholson, Folk Lore of East Yorkshire, 1890, p. 141; Burne and Jackson, Shropshire Folk-Lore, pp. 203–204; Bergen, Animal and Plant Lore, 1899, p. 20 (Newfoundland). Cf. Hunt, Popular Romances of the West of England, 1865, II, 218–219; Hewett, Nummits and Crummits, 1900, p. 79; Leather, The Folk-Lore of Herefordshire, 1912, p. 82; Blakeborough, Wit, Character, etc., of the North Riding of Yorkshire, 2d ed., 1911, p. 133; Notes and Queries, 1st Series, I (1850), 397; County Folk-Lore, I, No. 2 (1893), pp. 18–20; Transactions Penzance Natural History and Antiquarian Society, 1st Series, II (1851–55), 240; Whitney and Bullock, Folk-Lore from Maryland, p. 83.

95. For the ass as a symbol of Holy Church see Old English Homilies, ed. Morris, I (1868), 9.

96. Burne and Jackson, Shropshire Folk-Lore, pp. 203–204, 209; Bye-Gones for 1897–98, p. 389; Baring-Gould, Devonshire Characters, 1908, pp. 76–77. Cf. Charles Kent, The Land of the "Babes in the Wood," [1910,] p. 86; Lovett, Magic in Modern London, 1925, pp. 31–33. For the Asinaria Festa see Chambers, The Mediæval Stage, 1903, I, 330–334.

97. Notes and Queries, 1st Series, III (1851), 179; Folk-Lore Record, I (1878), 46; Henderson, 1879, p. 146; Ditchfield, The Parson's Pleasance, pp. 185–186; Bang, Norske Hexeformularer, 1901, p. 180. Cf. A. Franz, Die Messe, p. 87. Gregory of Tours tells of a "Britannorum comes" who, to cure pains in his feet, washed them in the sacred paten: he lost the use of his legs. A similar punishment for a like offence came upon a Lombard duke (De Gloria Martyrum, cap. 85, Migne, LXXI, 781).

98. Scot, xii, 17, p. 260 (187), ed. Nicholson, p. 211.

99. Burne and Jackson, Shropshire Folk-Lore, p. 192; Notes and Queries, 1st Series, III (1851), 220.

100. Letters and Papers, Henry VIII, XIII, i, No. 1150, p. 430. Cf. Bale, Select Works, ed. Christmas (Parker Society), p. 527: "their sipping cups for the hiccough."

101. Leechdoms, ed. Cockayne, III, 10–13. Cf. A. Franz, Die Kirchlichen Benediktionen, 1909, I, 259–263, 280, 284–286.

102. Potts, The Wonderfull Discoverie of Witches, 1613, sig. H 3 r°.

103. Henderson, 1879, p. 146. For various misuses of the host see A. Franz, Die Messe, pp. 93–98.

104. Folk-Lore, XII (1901), 168; County Folk-Lore, V (1908), 131, cf. 64; Folk-Lore, XIII (1902), 427. Cf. Addy, Household Tales, 1895, p. 70; Clague, Manx Reminiscences, [1911], p. 173; Agnew, The Hereditary Sheriffs of Galloway, 1893, II, 82. See Malleus Maleficarum, Part II, qu. 1, cap. 5 (ed. 1620, p. 191); Hansen, Quellen, p. 166. See p. 181, above.

105. Lincolnshire Notes and Queries, II (1891), 43. Cf. Saga-Book of the Viking Club, III (1902–04), 51.

106. The Reliquary and Illustrated Archæologist, II (1890), 158. Cf. Salopian Shreds and Patches, V (1883), 207; Shropshire Notes and Queries, I (1886), 24–25, 71.

107. Grillando, De Sortilegiis, ed. 1545, iii, 15, fol. xxj r° (ed. 1592, iii, 19, p. 30).

108. Caesarius of Heisterbach, Dialogus de Miraculis, ix, 6, ed. Strange, 1851, II, 171; Herbert, Catalogue of Romances, III (1910), 362, § 139; cf. III, 514, § 39. Cf. Thiers, Traité des Superstitions, 1741, II, 336. For the host as a medicine see Thiers, II, 248–252; Bang, Norske Hexeformularer, 1901, p. 180.

109. Caesarius, ix, 9, ed. Strange, II, 173–174. Cf. Thiers, II, 336.

110. Herbertus Turrium, De Miraculis, iii, 28, ed. Chifflet, S. Bernardi Genus Illustre Assertum, 1660, pp. 376–377.

111. The same, iii, 29, pp. 377–378. Cf. Herbert, Catalogue of Romances, III (1910), 448, § 36.

112. Herbertus Turrium, De Miraculis, iii, 30, ed. Chifflet, pp. 378–379 (cf. Petrus Venerabilis, De Miraculis, i, 1, Migne, CLXXXIX, 851–853); Caesarius, ix, 8, ed. Strange, II, 172–173; Étienne de Bourbon, Septem Dona, ed. Lecoy de la Marche, Anecdotes Historiques, 1877, pp. 266–267, 328; Giraldus Cambrensis, Gemma Ecclesiastica, i, 11, Opera, ed. Brewer, II, 42–43; Herbert, Catalogue of Romances, III (1910), 23, 388, 448, 517, 647; An Alphabet of Tales, No. 695, ed. Banks, II (1905), 465 (from Caesarius). Cf. Deecke, Lübische Geschichten und Sagen, 5th ed., p. 280; Blätter für Pommersche Volkskunde, IX (1901), 3. Host buried in a garden to improve the crop (1482): Zeitschrift der Gesellschaft für Schleswig-Holsteinische Geschichte, XLV (1915), 199.

113. Ayenbite of Inwyt, ed. Morris, 1866, p. 40 (a translation of the Somme des Vices et des Vertus of Frère Lorens, 1279). Abuse of chalices, chrism, etc., is also mentioned (pp. 40–41).

114. Herbert, III, 643, § 22; cf. III, 547, § 91. See also Étienne de Bourbon, pp. 328–329; Hansen, Zauberwahn, p. 388.

115. Chronicle of the Grey Friars, ed. Nicholas (Camden Society, LIII), pp. 35–36; Grey Friars Chronicle, Monumenta Franciscana, ed. Howlett, II, 195. Cf. Schweizerisches Archiv für Volkskunde, XII (1908), 143–148; P. de l'Ancre, L'Incredulité et Mescreance du Sortilege, 1622, pp. 668–672; Summers, The Geography of Witchcraft, 1927, pp. 184, 444–445.

116. Act Books of the Archdeaconry Court of Lewes, Sussex Archæological Collections, XLIX (1906), 50. Cf. Cranmer, Miscellaneous Writings and Letters, ed. Cox (Parker Society), 1846, p. 66.

117. Archæologia Cambrensis, 6th Series, IX (1909), 106; Gloucestershire Notes and Queries, III (1887), 228; Folk-Lore, XI (1900), 444–445 Hunt, Popular Romances of the West of England, 1865, II, 213. Cf. Seyfarth, Aberglaube und Zauberei in der Volksmedizin Sachsens, 1913, pp. 273–274. Martin Plantsch (Opusculum de Sagis Maleficis, 1507, sig. b v, lf. 2 v⁰) speaks of the magical employment of masses, the eucharist, baptismal water, and holy wax.

118. Leechdoms, III, 14, 24; II, 344–346, 350.

119. Wilkins, Concilia, I, 576. Cf. Canon 20 of the Fourth Lateran Council (A.D. 1215), Mansi, Concilia, XXII (1778), 1007. See also A. Franz, Die Kirchlichen Benediktionen, 1909, I, 53; the Same, Die Messe, 1902, pp. 92–93.

120. Wilkins, II, 139.

121. F. Bond, Fonts and Font Covers, 1908, pp. 281–313; English Historical Review, XXVI (1911), 110–116 (1342); Peacock, English Church Furniture, 1866, pp. 178–179; Acts of Chapter of the Collegiate Church of SS. Peter and Wilfrid, Ripon, ed. Fowler (Surtees Society, LXIV), p. 222; J. C. Cox, Churchwardens' Accounts, [1913,] pp. 151–152; records of visitations in Raine, The Fabric Rolls of York Minster (Surtees Society, XXXV), pp. 247, 254, 258, 260, 272, cf. 243; Archæologia, X (1791), 206–207, 222; XLI (1867), 339, note; Archæologia Æliana, 3d Series, XVIII (1921), 49; Archæologia Cantiana, XXXII (1917), 148, 149, 162; XXXIII (1918), 73, 82, 88, 89; Kent Records, [I,] 1912, 23; The Reliquary and Illustrated Archæologist, XIV (1908), 208–212, 272–273; The Western Antiquary, II (1883), 155; County Folk-Lore, V (1908), 127–128; Frere and Kennedy, Visitation Articles and Injunctions (Alcuin Club, XV), 1910, II, 387.

122. Lyndewoode, Constitutiones Provinciales, iii, 1st ed., ca. 1480, sig. Giiij, lf. 3 r⁰ (ed. 1679, iii, 25, p. 247).

123. Grillando, De Sortilegiis, v, 3, ed. 1545, fol. xxv v⁰ (ed. 1592, pp. 47–48); x, 16, ed. 1545, fol. lij r⁰ (ed. 1592, x, 15, pp. 161–162).

124. See pp. 76, 82, 147–148, above.

125. Grillando, ed. 1545, iii, 15, fol. xxj v⁰ (ed. 1592, iii, 20, p. 31); ed. 1545, x, 18, fol. lij v⁰ (ed. 1592, x, 16, p. 163).

126. Notes and Queries, 1st Series, VIII (1854), 617 (cf. VI [1852], 50); 2d Series, I (1856), 331; Archæologia Cambrensis, 6th Series, IX (1909), 106; 3d Series, II (1856), 185; Black, Folk-Medicine, 1883, pp. 174–175;

Hunt, Popular Romances of the West of England, 1865, II, 212; Henderson, pp. 113–114; Burne and Jackson, Shropshire Folk-Lore, pp. 192–193; Bye-Gones for 1897–1898, p. 389; E. M. Wright, Rustic Speech and Folk-Lore, 1913, p. 244, cf. p. 245; Blakeborough, Wit, Character, etc., of the North Riding of Yorkshire, 2d ed., 1911, p. 134; Hewett, Nummits and Crummits, 1900, p. 72; County Folk-Lore, I, No. 2 (1893), p. 18. Cf. W. H. B. Saunders, Legends and Traditions of Huntingdonshire, 1888, pp. 274–275; Chr. Wordsworth, Yorkshire Archæological Journal, XVII (1903), 386. Cf. A. Franz, Die Messe, p. 87.

127. Brockett, A Glossary of English North Country Words, 1825, p. 219; Bye-Gones for 1903–04, p. 46; The Essex Review, V (1896), 160; Black, Folk-Medicine, 1883, p. 173; A. L. Humphreys, The Materials for the History of the Town of Wellington, 1889, p. 247; County Folk-Lore, I, No. 2 (1893), p. 23; Leather, The Folk-Lore of Herefordshire, 1912, p. 81; E. M. Wright, Rustic Speech and Folk-Lore, 1913, p. 247; Polson, Our Highland Folklore Heritage, 1926, p. 34; Thomas, Kentucky Superstitions, 1920, pp. 115–116; Clague, Manx Reminiscences, [1911,] p. 153; Bergen, Current Superstitions, 1896, pp. 99–100; Nicholson, Folk Lore of East Yorkshire, 1890, p. 88. Cf. Homilia de Sacrilegiis, ed. Caspari, 1886, p. 11; Siebourg, Bonner Jahrbücher, CIII (1898), 130, and (for eye amulets) CXVIII (1909), 158–175.

128. Letters of Eminent Men addressed to Ralph Thoresby, 1832, II, 196. Cf. Notes and Queries, 9th Series, V (1900), 104.

129. Cowper, Hawkshead, 1899, pp. 316–317.

130. Transactions Devonshire Association, X (1878), 102. Cf. Bang, Norske Hexeformularer, 1901, p. 179.

131. F. K. Robinson, A Glossary of Words used in the Neighbourhood of Whitby, 1876, p. 35.

132. Bye-Gones for 1874–75, pp. 222, 286; Burne and Jackson, Shropshire Folk-Lore, p. 191.

133. Leechdoms, ed. Cockayne, II, 136, 138; Leonhardi, p. 42. Cf. Bang, Norske Hexeformularer, 1901, p. 181 (filings from a church bell).

134. For the Office for Consecrating Cramp Rings see Burnet, The History of the Reformation, II (1681), Collection, pp. 295–297, cf. p. 294, and see p. 321 of the text; Pegge, Curialia Miscellanea, 1818, pp. 164–172; The Antiquarian Magazine, IV (1883), 293–297. Cf. Archæological Journal, XXI (1864), 103–113, 188; Archæologia, XXI (1827), 121–124; Letters and Papers, Henry VIII, XII, ii, No. 272, p. 114; XX, i, No. 542, p. 256; Tymms, Wills and Inventories (Camden Society, XLIX), pp. 41, 248; Collier's Dodsley's Old Plays, X, 212, and note; W. Jones, Finger-Ring Lore, 1877, 1898, pp. 162–165, 522–526; Boorde, Introduction to Knowledge, ed. Furnivall, 1870, p. 121.

CHAPTER VIII

WIND AND WEATHER

1. Ovid, Metamorphoses, vii, 202. With what Medea says of the moon (vii, 207–208) compare the prohibition of attempts by shouts and sorceries to relieve the moon in eclipse: Excarpsus Ecgberti, viii, 3 (Haddan and Stubbs, III, 424; Schmitz, II, 667); Pseudo-Theodore, xvii, 25 (Thorpe, p. 293). Cf. Schmitz, II, 423, 496; Homilia de Sacrilegiis, ed. Caspari, 1886, pp. 10, 30–32.

2. Agobard, Opera, ed. Baluze, I (1666), 162–163.

3. Schmitz, Die Bussbücher, I, 308–309; II, 425, 495. Cf. Council of Paris (A.D. 829), iii, 2, Mansi, Concilia, XIV, 595.

4. For wizardry in rain, hail, storm, and mist, see A. Franz, Die Kirchlichen Benediktionen, 1909, II, 12–123; W. J. Humphreys, Rain Making and other Weather Vagaries, 1926; Burdick, Magic and Husbandry, 1905, pp. 91–120; Fehrle, Antike Hagelzauber (from the Geoponica), Alemannia, XL (1912), 13–27; Seneca, Naturales Quaestiones, iv, 6–7; Grimm, Deutsche Mythologie, 4th ed., I (1875), 524–533; III (1878), 178–183; Uhland, Schriften zur Geschichte der Dichtung und Sage, VI (1868), 378, 382–383, 385–386, 388, 394–395, 397, 403–404, 409, 411–413; Frazer, The Golden Bough, 3d ed., I (1911), 247–311, 319–321; Hansen, Quellen, index, s. v. Wetterzauber; Weinhold, Zur Geschichte des Heidnischen Ritus (Berlin Academy, Abhandlungen, 1896), pp. 20–26; Soldan and Heppe, Geschichte der Hexenprocesse, ed. Bauer, index, s. v. Wettermachen; Mannhardt, Wald- und Feldkulte, 2d ed., I (1904), 214–216, 327–333, 553–554; U. Jahn, Die Deutschen Opfergebräuche bei Ackerbau und Viezucht, 1884, pp. 54–62 (especially on spells against bad weather); Wuttke-Meyer, pp. 159–160, 302–203; Corrector, § 194 (Schmitz, II, 452); Malleus Maleficarum, Pt. II, qu. 1, cap. 11 (ed. 1620, pp. 222–223), cap. 13 (pp. 237–238), and cap. 15 (pp. 243–247); Grillando, De Sortilegiis, ed. 1592, vi, 17, pp. 75–76; Boaistuau, Histoires Prodigieuses, 1568, chap. 8, fol. 29 v°; Ulrich Molitoris, De Pythonicis Mulieribus, cap. 7 (in 1620 ed. of Malleus, II, 53–59); B. Pererius, De Magia, i, 6, 1598, p. 32; Guaccius, Compendium Maleficarum, 1608, i, 7, pp. 22–24; G. Freygang, Disputatio Physica de Magis Tempestates Cientibus, 1676; Erasmus Francisci, Der Höllische Proteus, 2d ed., 1695, pp. 916–917; Roger Williams, A Key into the Language of America, 1643, chap. 28, p. 170 (ed. Trumbull, p. 195, and note); Dalyell, The Darker Superstitions of Scotland, 1834, pp. 242–257, 574–575; Mackinlay, Folklore of Scottish Lochs and Springs, 1923, pp. 213–229 (weather and wells); Temme, Die Volkssagen der Altmark, 1839, p. 92; Josef Müller, Sagen aus Uri (Schriften der Schweizerischen Gesellschaft für Volkskunde, XVIII), I (1926), 110–125, 135–136, 143–145, 242–243; Rosen, Bulgarische Volksdichtungen, 1879, p. 53; Archivio per lo Studio delle Tradizioni Popolari, XVIII (1899), 57–63; Rivista delle Tradizioni Popolari Italiane, I (1893), 75–77, 389–391; Biblioteca de las Tradiciones Populares Españolas, I (1883), 233; Gentleman's Magazine, January, 1763, XXXIII, 12–15; Mélusine, II (1884–85), 184–189, 205–

206, 237–238, etc.; Samter, Archiv für Religionswissenschaft, XXI (1922), 317–339 (cf. IX [1906], 518–520); Codrington, The Melanesians, 1891, pp. 200–202; Ivens, Melanesians of the South-East Solomon Islands, 1927, pp. 325–328; Seligmann, The Melanesians of British New Guinea, 1910, pp. 119, 174, 180–181, 291, 295, 643, 697, 735 (cf. p. 645); Horne and Aiston, Savage Life in Central Australia, 1924, pp. 110–120 (with figures), 147–148; Skeat, Malay Magic, 1900, pp. 107–109; Ribbe, Zwei Jahre unter den Kannibalen der Salomo-Inseln, 1903, pp. 173–174; Statham, Through Angola, 1922, p. 200 (with figure); Le Barbier, Bulletin de l'Académie Malgache, New Series, III (1922), 85; Pechuël-Loesche, Volkskunde von Loango, 1907, pp. 447–449; T. N. Goddard, The Handbook of Sierra Leone, 1925, p. 56; Capello and Ivens, From Benguella to the Territory of Yacca, 1882, I, 251–252; Talbot, In the Shadow of the Bush, 1912, pp. 71–73; J. H. Weeks, Among Congo Cannibals, 1913, pp. 280–281; Roscoe, The Northern Bantu, 1915, pp. 181–184; the Same, The Bakitara, 1923, pp. 28–34; the Same, The Banyankole, 1923, pp. 31–32; the Same, The Bagesu, 1924, p. 60; Hobley, Bantu Beliefs and Magic, 1922, p. 192; Boyes, A White King in East Africa, 1912, pp. 142–144, 155–156; Tauxier, Le Noir de Bandoukou, 1921, pp. 179, 184; Tremearne, The Ban of the Bori, pp. 185–193; Dornan, Pygmies and Bushmen of the Kalahari, 1925, pp. 291–292, 300; A. C. Hollis, The Nandi, 1909, p. 52; Hans Meyer, Die Barundi, 1916, p. 133; Driberg, The Lango, 1923, pp. 243–263; Dundas, Kilimanjaro and its People, 1924, pp. 167–169; Meek, The Northern Tribes of Nigeria, 1925, II, 63–68; D. R. MacKenzie, The Spirit-Ridden Konde, 1925, pp. 206–214; Atlantis, VII (1924), 42–43, 131–133 (Sudan); Journal Royal Anthropological Institute, XLIX (1919), 52–73; Marco Polo, ed. Pauthier, 1865, chap. 48, I, 125–126 (Yule, i, 31, ed. 1903, I, 166); chap. 74, I, 227–228, 231–232 (Yule, i, 61, I, 301–303); chap. 184, II, 675–676 (Yule, iii, 32, II, 407; see also note in Yule, I, 309–311); Andrew Battell, Purchas his Pilgrimes, Glasgow ed., VI (1905), 394 (ed. Ravenstein, Hakluyt Society, 2d Ser., VI, 46–47); Maddox, The Medicine Man, 1923, pp. 139–145; Crooke, Religion and Folklore of Northern India, 1926, pp. 69–80, 258, 406–407; The Imperial and Asiatic Quarterly Review, 3d Series, XIII (1902), 353, 360; XVII (1904), 140; Bureau of Ethnology, Report XI (for 1889–90), 1894, pp. 76–86, 91–97, 101–111, 113–116, 123–130; Report XXXV (for 1913–14), 1921, pp. 620–637; von Andrian-Werburg, Prähistorisches and Ethnologisches, 1915, pp. 160–224.

5. Ecgbert, iv, 14 (Haddan and Stubbs, Councils, III, 420; Schmitz, II, 664); Pseudo-Cummean, vii (ix), 8 (Schmitz, II, 627); Pseudo-Theodore, xxvii, 21 (Thorpe, p. 293).

6. Schmitz, I, 308, 460; II, 181, 238, 296, 321, 324, 328, 335, 342, 368, 377. Cf. Lea, A History of the Inquisition, 1888, III, 414–415.

7. Lex Visigothorum, vi, 2, 3 (4), Monumenta, Leges, Sect. I, I (1902), 259; Capitulary of 789, cap. 64 (Pertz, Leges, I, 64).

8. Bede, Historia Ecclesiastica, i, 17.

9. Leechdoms, ed. Cockayne, I, 388–391; Wülker, Bibliothek, I, 328–330; II, 202–203; Schlutter, Anglia, XXXI (1908), 58–62; Grendon, Journal of American Folk-Lore, XXII (1909), 176–179 (cf. 220–221);

Skemp, Modern Language Review, VI (1911), 296–298. Cf. A. Franz, Die Kirchlichen Benediktionen, 1909, II, 268–271; Leechdoms, I, 302, 308, 326.

10. Herbarium, 176, Leechdoms, I, 308; cf. I, 302 (peony), 326 (badger's teeth as amulet).

11. Reginald, Libellus de Vita et Miraculis S. Godrici, ed. Stevenson (Surtees Society, XX), cap. 128, p. 253. Compare the fighting storm-demons in 1256: Thomas Cantipratensis, Liber Apum aut de Apibus, ii, 57, 3, ed. Paris, ca. 1510, fol. lxxxij r°.

12. P. B. Watson, Marcus Aurelius Antoninus, 1884, pp. 195–198 (with discussion and full references).

13. Kromer, De Origine et Rebus Gestis Polonorum, viii, ed. Basel, 1568, p. 143 (Polonicae Historiae Corpus, 1582, II, 540). Cf. Guagnino, Compendium Chronicorum Poloniae, Corpus, 1582, II, 353; Ricardus Argentinus (Argentine), De Praestigiis et Incantationibus Daemonum et Necromanticorum, 1568, pp. 108–109.

14. Fabyan, ed. 1559, II, 504 (ed. Ellis, p. 661): "Of the mistes and other impedimentes, whiche fell vppon the lordes partie, by reason of the incantations, wroughte by Frere Bungey, as the fame then wente, me list not to write."

15. Saxo Grammaticus, vii, p. 324 Müller and Velschow (p. 219 Holder).

16. Symeon of Durham, Historia Regum, ed. Hinde (Surtees Society, LI), I, 17.

17. Radulfus Niger, Chronicon II, ed. Anstruther (Caxton Society), p. 173.

18. Letter of Bishop Gunther of Cologne, Annales Fuldenses (Recueil, VII, 166); Annales Bertiniani (VII, 72).

19. Chronicle of the Grey Friars, ed. Nichols, p. 3; Grey Friars Chronicle, Monumenta Franciscana, ed. Howlett, II, 146; Kingsford, Chronicles of London, p. 3; Chronicle of London, 1827, p. 10.

20. Flores Historiarum, ed. Luard, III, 216–217.

21. Chronicle of London, 1827, p. 65; Gregory's Chronicle, Gairdner, The Historical Collections of a Citizen of London, p. 86. For this portent of the devil's showing himself to wayfarers cf. Radulfus Niger, ed. Anstruther, p. 163; Eulogium Historiarum, ed. Haydon, III, 51; Brut, ed. Brie, p. 313.

22. John of Reading, ed. Tait, 1914, p. 167.

23. Brut, ed. Brie, pp. 477–478. The chronicler goes on to tell of the prosecution of Dame Eleanor Cobham (cf. p. 482). See pp. 81 ff., above.

24. Rushworth, Historical Collections, I (1659), 391.

25. Diary of William Whiteway, Proceedings Dorset Natural History and Antiquarian Field Club, XIII (1892), 69.

26. Brut, ed. Brie, p. 487.

27. Hale, p. 37: "Ipsa dixit, quod si mandaverit pluviam pluere, ad mandatum ejus pluit."

28. The Official Papers of Sir Nathaniel Bacon, ed. H. W. Saunders (Camden 3d Series, XXVI), pp. 31–32. Cf. (for fire) Baxter, The Cer-

tainty of the Worlds of Spirits, 1691, p. 55; Relation of the Most Remarkable Proceedings at the Late Assizes at Northampton, 1674, pp. 5-6.

29. Fuller, Church-History, Bk. ix (1655), 16th Century, i, 46, p. 71. See also W. Sparrow Simpson, Documents Illustrating the History of St. Paul's Cathedral (Camden Society, New Series, XXVI), pp. xxxvii–xxxix; Strype, Annals of the Reformation, I (1725), 260–262, 268.

30. An Addicion with an Appologie to the Causes of Brinnynge of Paules Church (in The Burnynge of Paules Church . . . in . . . 1561, London, 1563[-4], sig. Aiii r°: A Confutacion follows, commonly ascribed to Pilkington).

31. See Cotton Mather, The Wonders of the Invisible World, Boston, 1693, p. 19.

32. Sir Richard Baker (1588–1645), Chronicle, ed. 1653, p. 237, from Walsingham, Historia Anglicana, ed. Riley, II, 249–250.

33. Annales in Riley's ed. of Johannes de Trokelowe, p. 340.

34. Cf. Sir Thomas Browne, account of a thunderstorm at Norwich in 1665 (Works, ed. Wilkin, 1852, III, 341).

35. Chronicon Guillelmi de Nangiaco, Recueil, XX, 726.

36. Walsingham, II, 250; Annales in Riley's Trokelowe, p. 341.

37. Walsingham, II, 250–251; Annales, as above, pp. 343–344; Capgrave, Chronicle of England, ed. Hingeston, p. 279.

38. The Chronicle of Ihon Hardyng in Metre, ed. 1543, chap. 202, fol. cc v°; ed. Ellis, 1812, pp. 359–360.

39. Shrewsbury Chronicle, Transactions Shropshire Archæological and Natural History Society, 1st Series, III (1880), 255; Owen and Blakeway, A History of Shrewsbury, 1825, II, 269.

40. Cf. Remigius (Remi), Daemonolatreia, i, 27, ed. 1595, pp. 166–168 (ed. 1596, pp. 158–159).

41. A Straunge and Terrible Wunder, [1577,] reprint of 1820, pp. 11–14. See J. Harvey Bloom, English Tracts, I, 80, who gives a facsimile of the title-page (with a picture of the dog). See Holinshed's Chronicle, IV (1808), 344, which ascribes the damage to lightning and ignores the apparition. Cf. Stow, ed. 1592, pp. 1165–1166. The parish register, 1577, records the burial of "John Fuller and Adam Walker slayne in the tempest, in the belfry, in the tyme of prayer, upon the Lord's day, yᵉ iiijᵗʰ of August" (Suckling, The History and Antiquities of Suffolk, I, 126).

42. That is, "black, swarthy," like the charcoal-burners of Croydon. Cf. Richard Edwards, Damon and Pithias (Collier's Dodsley, I, 240):

> Byr ladie, you are of good complexion,
> A right Croyden sanguine.

43. J. G. Nichols, Narratives of the Days of the Reformation, p. 51.

44. Annales Bertiniani, Recueil, VII, 72.

45. A Second Relation, etc., 1638, reprinted in Harleian Miscellany, ed. Park, III (1809), 220–228; John Prince, Danmonii Orientalis Illustres or The Worthies of Devon, 1701 (ed. 1810, pp. 569–572); Increase Mather, Illustrious Providences, Boston, 1684, pp. 123–124.

46. Bray, Traditions, etc., of Devonshire, 1838, I, 310–314. Cf. Torr, Small Talk at Wreyland, 1918, pp. 12–13.

47. Prince, p. 570.

48. Wriothesley's Chronicle, ed. Hamilton (Camden Society, New Series, XI), I, 61.

49. Wier, ii, 19, ed. 1568, p. 203; iii, 16, pp. 262–273; iii, 34, p. 329; cf. v, 36, pp. 561–562.

50. Scot, i, 1, pp. 1–3 (1–2), ed. Nicholson, pp. 1–3. Cf. iii, 9, p. 55 (45), 43; iii, 13, pp. 60–63 (48–50), 47–49. Andrew Borde is more conservative: "With out any doute, in thunderynge and in lyghtenynge and tempestious wethers many euyl thynges hath ben sene and done," he tells us, and he adds, "Of all those aforesayde thynges, a whorlewynde I do not loue": Breuyary of Helth, chap. 183, ed. 1552, fol. lxv v°, in Furnivall's ed. of Borde's Introduction to Knowledge, etc., 1870, p. 75. Frederick, Duke of Württemberg, who visited England in 1592, remarks in his Badenfahrt, 1602, "Vil Hexen werden darinnen gefunden, und beschicht offtermahln durch Hagel unnd ander Ungewitter grosser Schaden" (W. B. Rye, England as Seen by Foreigners, 1865, p. 50).

51. J. Charles Cox, Churchwardens' Accounts, 1913, pp. 212–213. On bells as a protection against demons, witches, lightning, etc., see Durandus, Rationale Divinorum Officiorum, i, 4, Venice, 1589, fol. 13 v° (he was Bishop of Metz, 1237–1296); A. Franz, Die Kirchlichen Benediktionen, 1909, II, 40–43; Calfhill, An Aunswere to the Treatise of the Crosse, 1565, ed. Gibbings, Parker Society, pp. 15, 17; The Reliquary, XXII (1881–82), 10; MS. Cotton, Nero Diii, fol. 246 (quoted by Macray in his edition of Chronicon Abbatiae de Evesham, p. 297, note 1); Hooper, Early Writings, ed. Carr (Parker Society), 1843, p. 197 (cf. p. 533); Pilkington, Works, ed. Scholefield, Parker Society, 1842, pp. 177, 536; Wier, De Praestigiis Daemonum, ed. 1568, i, 8, pp. 53–54; v, 3, p. 453; v, 19, p. 513; Binsfeld, De Confessionibus Maleficorum et Sagarum, 1591, pp. 339–346; Guazzo (Guaccius), Compendium Maleficarum, 1608, pp. 244–245; Remy (Remigius), Daemonolatreia, 1596, i, 26, pp. 151–156; Aubrey, Miscellanies, 4th ed., 1857, p. 141; Fuller, Church-History, vi, 6, ed. 1656, pp. 300–301 (ed. 1837, II, 194–195); Sir J. M. Campbell, The Indian Antiquary, XXIV (1895), 121–124; Cambridge Antiquarian Society, Octavo Publications, XVIII, 2d ed. (1881), 121; William Robinson, The History and Antiquities of the Parish of Tottenham, 2d ed., 1840, II, 28; Dawson, History of Skipton, 1882, p. 384; Freisauff, Salzburger Volkssagen, 1880, pp. 498–500; Birlinger, Volksthümliches aus Schwaben, I (1861), 146–151, 322; Lütolf, Sagen, Bräuche und Legenden aus den Fünf Orten, Lucern u.s.w., 1865, p. 41; Rochholz, Schweizersagen aus dem Aargau, 1856, II, 378; Baumgarten, Aus der Volksmässigen Ueberlieferung der Heimat, Linz, 1864, I, 67; Chapiseau, Le Folk-Lore de la Beauce et du Perche, 1902, I, 208–209. Cf. E. von Lasaulx, Das Pelasgische Orakel des Zeus zu Dodc 1a, 1840, pp. 12–13; O. Jahn, Ueber den Aberglauben des Bösen Blicks bei den Alten, p. 79; Kitching, On the Backwaters of the Nile, 1912, p. 264.

52. The Pontifical of Egbert, Archbishop of York, A.D. 732–766, ed. Greenwell (Surtees Society, XXVII), p. 118.

53. Shrewsbury Chronicle, Transactions Shropshire Archæological and Natural History Society, 1st Series, III (1880), 255.

54. See pp. 207–209, above.

55. Wycherley's confession, Nichols, Narratives of the Days of the Reformation (Camden Society, LXXVII), pp. 332–333. Barron was one of the fiends conjured by Gilles de Rais in the fifteenth century (Bossard and de Maulde, Gilles de Rais, 2d ed., 1886, pp. xxii, xxvi, xlvi, li–liii, lxix–lxxii).

56. Aubrey, Brief Lives, ed. Clark, 1898, I, 212.

57. Transactions Lancashire and Cheshire Antiquarian Society, XXXIV (1917), 82–84. Compare the raising of the devil at Burnley Grammar School (Harland and Wilkinson, Lancashire Folk-Lore, 1867, p. 83), as well as the experiences of the schoolboys at Mousey Lea (Middleton, Annals of Hyde and District, 1899, p. 173) and of Dr. Lickbarrow's servant (J. Sullivan, Cumberland and Westmorland, 1857, pp. 150–151). These anecdotes look like faint reflections of the folk-tale known as "The Magician's Apprentice" (Lucian, Philopseudes, 34–36, ed. Reitz, III, 61–63); cf. Revue des Traditions Populaires, XXVI (1911), 6–8.

58. Folk-Lore, XII (1901), 74. See also Bovet, Pandaemonium, 1684, pp. 89–90.

59. John Heydon, Psonthonphanchia, 1664, p. 86; Mr. William Lilly's History of his Life and Times, 2d ed., 1715, p. 16 (storm of wind after Simon Forman's death); Henry More, An Antidote against Atheism, iii, 9, Philosophical Writings, 4th ed., 1712, p. 115; Gregor, The Folk-Lore of the North-East of Scotland, 1881, p. 136; Wilkinson and Tattersall, Memories of Hurstwood, 1889, p. 51; Halifax Antiquarian Society Papers, 1904–5, p. 4.

60. Mélusine, IV (1888–89), 13; Zeitschrift des Vereins für Volkskunde, IV (1894), 81; Zeitschrift für Oesterreichische Volkskunde, IV (1898), 151. See Herzog, Hessische Blätter für Volkskunde, XXV (1927), 223.

61. Radulphus de Coggeshall, ed. Stevenson, p. 184.

62. Matthew Paris, Historia Anglorum, ed. Madden, I, 249–250.

63. Rishanger, ed. Riley, p. 35.

64. Hancock, The Parish of Selworthy, 1897, pp. 234, 236; Wilkinson and Tattersall, Memories of Hurstwood, 1889, p. 51; Gregor, Folk-Lore of the North-East of Scotland, 1881, p. 136; F. K. Robinson, A Glossary of Words used in the Neighbourhood of Whitby, 1876, p. xxii; Krauss, Slavische Volkforschungen, 1908, p. 70; Fossel, Volksmedicin und Medicinischer Aberglaube in Steiermark, 1886, p. 171.

65. Higden, Polychronicon, i, 44 (with Trevisa's translation), ed. Babington, II, 43; Harrison, The Description of Britaine, in Holinshed, I (1807), 66. Cf. Skattegraveren, I (1884), 24–25.

66. Scheffer, Lapponia, 1674, pp. 144–145; Fritzner, Historisk Tidsskrift, Christiania, 1st Series, IV (1877), 200–202; Krohn, Finnisch-Ugrische Forschungen, VI (1906), 173–175; Kalevala, translated by Schiefner, 1852, x, 159–184, pp. 48–49; Bugge, The Home of the Eddic Poems, translated by Schofield, 1899, pp. 355–357; Blefken, Islandia, 1607, pp. 31, 70–71 (Purchas his Pilgrimes, Glasgow ed., XIII [1906], 498, 518–519); Gomme, Ethnology in Folklore, 1892, pp. 48–49; Uhland, Schriften, VI (1868), 403–404; Hibbert, A Description of the Shetland Islands, 1822,

p. 579; Mackinlay, Folklore of Scottish Lochs and Springs, 1893, pp. 219–220; J. H. Dixon, Gairloch, 1886, pp. 168–169; Celtic Magazine, XIII (1888), 93–94; Old-Lore Miscellany of Orkney, etc., VIII (1920), 2–4; Polson, Our Highland Folklore Heritage, 1926, pp. 73, 121–122; Mélusine, II (1884–85), 184; Giles Fletcher, Of the Russe Common Wealth, chap. 20, 1591, fol. 77. Cf. W. P. Bennett, The Sky-Sifter, pp. 152–153; Lovett, Magic in Modern London, 1925, p. 40.

67. Havamál, sts. 152–154 (Bugge, Norrœn Fornkvæði, 1867, pp. 62–63). Cf. Grógaldr, sts. 11–12 (Bugge, p. 341).

68. Saxo Grammaticus, bk. v, p. 192 Müller and Velshow (p. 128 Holder); cf. bk. i, p. 53 M. and V. (p. 32 Holder). There is a handy compendium of Saxo's folk-lore by York Powell in Elton's translation, 1894, pp. xxii–xcvii. Cf. Cockayne, Leechdoms, I, xlvii–liii; Gering, Ueber Weissagung und Zauber im Nordischen Altertum, 1902, pp. 19–20.

69. Alexander Roberts, A Treatise of Witchcraft, 1616, p. 21.

70. Ady, A Candle in the Dark, 1656, p. 116. Cf. [N. Orchard,] The Doctrine of Devils, 1676, p. 92.

71. See, for example, The Pedlers Prophecie, 1595, sig. D3, lf. 2 r°; Middleton and Rowley, The Spanish Gypsy, iv, 3, ed. Bullen, VI, 204; Middleton, The Changeling, i, 1, ed. Bullen, VI, 6; Dodsley's Old Plays, ed. Collier, IX, 342; Dodsley's Old Plays, ed. Hazlitt, VII, 468; Thomas Heywood, Pearson ed., 1874, IV, 245, 252; Fletcher, The Chances, v, 3, 34–36, ed. Dyce, VII, 294; the Same, The Fair Maid of the Inn, iv, 2, X, 79; Congreve, Love for Love, iii, 7, Works, ed. 1778, I, 222; Taylor the Water Poet, The Water-Cormorant his Complaint, 1622, sig. F2 r° (Workes, 1630, p. 13); John Heydon, Psonthonphanchia, 1664, p. 86; D'Avenant and Dryden, The Tempest, iv, 3, ed. Scott, III (1808), 178; Dryden, An Evening's Love, ii, 1, ed. Scott, III, 265; Oldham, Satyrs upon the Jesuits, iv, 5th ed., 1697, p. 79; Increase Mather, An Essay for the Recording of Illustrious Providences, Boston, 1684, pp. 127–128. See also the commentators on Macbeth, i, 3. For winds sold in Wales see Trevelyan, Folk-Lore and Folk-Stories of Wales, 1909, pp. 117–118.

72. Scott's Diary in Lockhart's Life, III (1827), 203–204.

73. Cf. Malleus Maleficarum, Pt. II, qu. 1, cap. 11, ed. 1620, pp. 222–223; Wier, iii, 34, ed. 1568, p. 329; Thiers, Traité des Superstitions, 1741, I, 153.

74. More, An Antidote against Atheisme, 1653, pp. 111–115.

75. Pitcairn, Criminal Trials in Scotland, 1833, III, 606–607. Careful directions for raising whatever wind one may wish at sea by means of the angels are found in a fifteenth-century Latin spell in Sloane MS. 75, fol. 186 r°.

76. Linderholm, De Stora Häxprocesserna i Sverige, I (1918), 114, 202–204, 225.

77. J. B. Baker, The History of Scarborough, 1882, pp. 474–475.

78. Bollettino Storico della Svizzera Italiana, VII (1885), 170. Cf. Archiv für Religionswissenschaft, XVIII (1915), 589–593. For whistling or sticking a knife in the mast to raise the wind see Gentleman's Magazine, January, 1763, XXXIII, 14–15 (sailors will not whistle); Polson, Our

Highland Folklore Heritage, 1926, p. 121; cf. M. H. Bradley, Caravans and Cannibals, 1927, pp. 73-74 (whistling for rain).

79. Norfolk Archæology, V (1859), 87. Cf. Folk-Lore, XIII (1902), 431; Hillen, History of the Borough of King's Lynn, II, 850.

80. Cf. Thorndike, A History of Magic and Experimental Science, 1923, II, 350; Whittier, Supernaturalism of New England, 1847, p. 64 (boats capsized, etc.). In 1610 when Prince Henry visited Woolwich to attend a launching, Mr. Phineas Pette, one of King James's master shipwrights, records a shrewd suspicion: "The beginning of the night was very fair, and bright moonshine, the moon being a little past full; but after midnight the weather was sore overcast, and a very sore gust of rain, thunder, and lightning, which made me doubt that there were some indirect working among our enemies to dash our launching" (Pette, Autobiography, Archæologia, XII, 2d ed. [1809], 263). For a curious instance of a bewitched ship see John Dunton's Athenian Mercury, Vol. IV, No. 20 (1691).

81. The Examination, Confession, Triall, and Execution, of Joane Williford, Joan Cariden, and Jane Hott, 1645, pp. 5, 2. For the sinking of the hoy by witchcraft see A True and Exact Relation of the Severall Informations, etc., of the Late Witches, 1645, p. 5.

82. Stearne, A Confirmation and Discovery of Witch-craft, 1648, p. 24; Pitcairn, Criminal Trials in Scotland, 1833, I, 235, 237, 254; Folk-Lore, XXXIII (1922), 211 (Isle of Skye); Hibbert, A Description of the Shetland Islands, 1822, p. 576.

83. Linderholm, De Stora Häxprocesserna i Sverige, I (1918), 114, 116, 142-144, 149-154, 158-159.

84. Picked up by me on Cape Cod. Cf. Polson, Our Highland Folklore Heritage, 1926, p. 122.

85. Folk-Lore Record, IV (1881), 93.

86. Cæsar Otway, Sketches in Erris and Tyrawly, 1841, pp. 387-388 (cats confined under metal pots to check a storm or prevent fair wind; vessel thus held in port). For other instances of ships detained by witchcraft see Chapter XI, note 105.

87. Fielding, A Voyage to Lisbon (under July 11), Works, 1784, X, 225-226.

88. Hussey, p. 60. Cf. Ady, A Candle in the Dark, 1656, p. 113: "God claimeth it as his own Prerogative to send Lightnings and Thunders, *Job* 38. 25, 35. but they say, when it Thundereth or Lighteneth, that Witches do sometimes cause it, especially if it be at an Assize time, when many Witches are condemned; and what hath been a more common report than this, when God hath sent thundring voyces from Heaven at an Assize time among the people, to warn them, instead of discerning that God was angry, they say, the Witches and the Devil was angry, and have caused that thunder?"

CHAPTER IX

The Witch in the Dairy

1. For witchcraft and magic in the dairy see, for example, Hansen, Quellen, 1901, pp. 210, 303, 536, 570–572, 589, 597, 605, 607, 612; Burdick, Magic and Husbandry, 1905, pp. 86–88, 139–141, 147; Grillando, De Sortilegiis, ed. 1545, vi, 10, foll. xxx v°–xxxj r° (ed. 1592, vi, 13, p. 71); A True and Iust Recorde of the Information [etc.] of all the Witches, taken at S. Oses (London, 1582), sigg. C4, lf. 4 v°; E3 v°; Lercheimer (Witekind), Christlich Bedencken vnd Erinnerung von Zauberei, 1597, ed. Binz, 1888, pp. 51–52; Boguet, Discours des Sorciers, 1608, Chap. 38, pp. 238–241; Bodin, De la Demonomanie des Sorciers, 1587, ii, 1, fol. 59 v°; iii, 1, fol. 140 r°; Carrichter, in Glorez, Neuangeordnete Vollständige Haus- und Land-Bibliothec, Anderes Cabinet, 1719, p. 226; Thiers, Traité des Superstitions, 1741, I, 153; Grimm, Mythologie, 4th ed., p. 897; Blagrave, Astrological Practice of Physick, 1671, p. 152; E. Mackenzie, An Historical [etc.] view of the County of Northumberland, 1825, II, 35–36; Brand, Popular Antiquities, ed. Hazlitt, 1870, III, 74; F. K. Robinson, A Glossary of Words used in the Neighbourhood of Whitby, 1876, p. xxii; Lincolnshire Notes and Queries, I (1889), 170; Blakeborough, Wit, Character, Folklore and Customs of the North Riding of Yorkshire, 2d ed., 1911, pp. 169–170; Folk-Lore, VI (1895), 158–159; County Folk-Lore, VII (1914), 53; Halifax Antiquarian Society Papers, 1904–5, p. 7; Bergen, Animal and Plant Lore, 1899, pp. 15, 34, 38; Thomas, Kentucky Superstitions, 1920, pp. 139, 248, 260, 272, 274; Whitney and Bullock, Folk-Lore from Maryland, 1925, pp. 80–81; Edmondston, A View of the Ancient and Present State of the Zetland Isles, 1809, II, 74; Dalyell, The Darker Superstitions of Scotland, 1834, pp. 261–265; The New Statistical Account of Scotland, XV (1845), Shetland, p. 142; Gregor, The Folk-Lore of the North-East of Scotland, 1881, pp. 189–195; Beveridge, Cullross and Tulliallan, 1885, II, 113; John Cameron, The Parish of Campsie, 1892, pp. 82–83; Wm. Mackay, Urquhart and Glenmoriston, 1893, pp. 431–432; Nicholson, Golspie, 1897, pp. 80–81; Warrick, The History of Old Cumnock, 1899, pp. 338–339; Spence, Shetland Folk-Lore, 1899, pp. 139–140; Maclagan, Evil Eye in the Western Highlands, 1902, passim; J. G. Campbell, Witchcraft and Second Sight in the Highlands and Islands of Scotland, 1902, pp. 7–15; Cowan, The Ancient Capital of Scotland, 1904, II, 131–132; Polson, Our Highland Folklore Heritage, 1926, pp. 64–67; Bottrell, Traditions and Hearthside Stories of West Cornwall, 1870, p. 85; Couch, The History of Polperro, 1871, p. 146; Collections Historical and Archaeological relating to Montgomeryshire, XV (1882), 134–135; A. W. Moore, The Folk-Lore of the Isle of Man, 1891, pp. 84, 100; Schönbach, Vienna Sitzungsberichte, Philosophisch-Historische Classe, CXLII (1900), No. 7, p. 132; J. W. Wolf, Niederländische Volkssagen, 1843, pp. 370–371; E. Meier, Deutsche Sagen, Sitten und Gebräuche aus Schwaben, 1852, pp. 177–180; Schambach and Müller, Niedersächsische Sagen und Märchen, 1855, pp. 166–167, 175–176;

Schönwerth, Aus der Oberpfalz, I (1857), 333–338; Frischbier, Hexen-spruch und Zauberbann, 1870, pp. 7, 8, 14–15, 18–19, 124–125; Germania, XXII (1877), 260–261; Witzschel, Sagen, Sitten und Gebräuche aus Thüringen (Kleine Beiträge, II), 1878, pp. 265, 271; Liebrecht, Zur Volks-kunde, 1879, p. 353; von Schulenburg, Wendische Volkssagen und Ge-bräuche, 1880, pp. 157–158, 170; Pauls, Beiträge zur Geschichte des Niederrheins, XIII (1898), 211; Alemannia, XI (1883), 92–93; Am Urdhs-Brunnen, III (1885–86), 24; Am Ur-Quell, V (1894), 281–282; VI (1896), 100–101, 131–132, 193–194; N. F., I (1897), 19–20; Knoop, Volkssagen aus dem Oestlichen Hinterpommern, 1885, pp. 16–17, 171; Blätter für Pommersche Volkskunde, III (1895), 150; IV (1896), 17–19; VII (1899), 23–27; Baltische Studien, XXXVI (1886), 179, 183, 184, 289–290, 319–320, 340–341; Neues Archiv für Sächsische Geschichte und Alterthums-kunde, IX (1888), 336–337; Vonbun, Die Sagen Vorarlbergs, 2d ed., 1889, pp. 150–153; Zeitschrift für Volkskunde, I (1889), 311; Zingerle, Sagen aus Tirol, 2d ed., 1891, pp. 234–235, 452–453, 467; Wuttke, Der Deutsche Volksaberglaube der Gegenwart, ed. Meyer, 1900, pp. 158–159, 265–267, 444–450; Korrespondenzblatt des Vereins für Siebenbürgische Landes-kunde, XXII (1899), 63–64; XXIII (1900), 92, 147–148; Deutsche Volkskunde aus dem Oestlichen Böhmen, IV (1904), 270–272; V (1905), 28–32, 34–35, 39–42, 149; IX (1909), 54–56, 61–62; XI (1911), 41–43; XII (1912), 35; John, Sitte, Brauch und Volksglaube im Deutschen West-böhmen, Beiträge zur Deutsch-Böhmischen Volkskunde, VI (1905), 321; Zeitschrift des Vereins für Rheinische und Westfälische Volkskunde, II (1905), 84; Drechsler, Sitte, Brauch und Volksglaube in Schlesien, II (1906), 104–105, 111–112; Archiv für Strafrecht, LIV (1907), 134; Lach-mann, Ueberlinger Sagen, Bräuche und Sitten, 1909, p. 393; Hessische Blätter für Volkskunde, VIII (1909), 48–51; Schweizerisches Archiv für Volkskunde, XIV (1910), 265–266; Festschrift Louis Gauchat, 1926, pp. 425–427; Kühnau, Schlesische Sagen, III (1913), 54, 57–59, 93–94; Jeger-lehner, Sagen und Märchen aus dem Oberwallis, Schriften der Schweizer-ischen Gesellschaft für Volkskunde, IX (1913), 176, 203–204; Manz, Volksbrauch und Volksglaube des Sarganserlandes, the same, XII (1916), 107, 117; Josef Müller, Sagen aus Uri, I (1926), 102–106, 241–243, the same, XVIII; Heberling, Zeitschrift der Gesellschaft für Schleswig-Holsteinische Geschichte, XLV (1915), 121–122; Skattegraveren, IV (1885), 56; IX (1888), 238; X₂ (1888), 14; Bang, Norske Hexeformularer, 1901, pp. 80–81, 85, 90, 105, 132–133, 207, 281, 283–284, 319, 322–323, 345–346, 577; Nyland, IV (1889), 72–73; Dania, II (1892–94), 225–226; Craigie, Scandinavian Folk-Lore, 1896, pp. 377–380, 387–388; Kristensen, Danske Sagn, VI, i (1900), 94, 285, 292–293, 298, 306–307, 319, 341; VI, ii (1901), 7, 133–134; Maal og Minne, 1913, p. 46; Ohrt, Trylleord (Dan-marks Folkeminder, No. 25), 1922, pp. 123–124, 127–128; Linderholm, De Stora Häxprocesserna i Sverige, I (1918), 127, 229, 244–245, 256; Hästesko, Motivverzeichnis Westfinnischer Zaubersprüche (FF Communi-cations, II, No. 19), 1914, pp. 48, 51; Mélusine, I (1877), 73; Chapiseau, Le Folk-Lore de la Beauce et du Perche, 1902, I, 205; Sudan Notes and Records, II (1919), 133; Westermarck, Ritual and Belief in Morocco, 1926,

I, 249–250; II, 170; D. R. MacKenzie, The Spirit-Ridden Konde, 1925, pp. 253–254, 258; Bourke, Scatalogic Rites of All Nations, 1891, pp. 395–396; Leland, Gypsy Sorcery, 1891, pp. 144–145.

2. Boston Herald, May 8, 1909.

3. Pliny, xxviii, 2, 4, 17. Cf. Corrector, § 103 (Schmitz, Bussbücher, II, 432); P. Massé, De l'Imposture et Tromperie des Diables, 1579, i, 11, fol. 47; Journal and Proceedings Asiatic Society of Bengal, New Series, X (1918), 352; E. W. Smith and A. M. Dale, The Ila-Speaking Peoples of Northern Rhodesia, 1920, I, 95; II, 91, 97.

4. Corrector, § 168 (Schmitz, II, 446; Hansen, Quellen, 1901, p. 42). Cf. Council of Paris (A.D. 829), iii, 2, Mansi, Concilia, XIV (1769), 595.

5. Freiburger Diöcesan-Archiv, XV (1882), 96–97; Hansen, Quellen, pp. 584–585.

6. Plantsch, Opusculum de Sagis Maleficis, 1507, sigg. bv lf. 1 r°–cii r°. Cf. the Hessian case in 1562 (Crecelius, Zeitschrift für Deutsche Mythologie, II [1855], 72). See also Lercheimer (Witekind), Christlich Bedencken vnd Erinnerung von Zauberey, 1587, ed. Binz, 1888, p. 51.

7. Geiler von Kaiserberg, Die Emeis, Strassburg, 1517, fol. liiii.

8. For a similar cut see Ulrich Tengler's Layenspiegel (1511), Hansen, Quellen, p. 298. Cf. Hans Sachs, Von Fünff Unhulden, ed. Keller, V, 286; Malleus Maleficarum, Part II, qu. 1, cap. 14, ed. 1620, p. 239; Guaccius (Guazzo), Compendium Maleficarum, 1608, i, 8, p. 27; Del Rio, Disquisitiones Magicae, ii, 12, ed. 1616, p. 129.

9. Kirk, Secret Commonwealth, § 3, ed. 1815, p. 5 (ed. Lang, p. 11). Cf. Bidrag till Södermanlands Äldre Kulturhistoria, I, i (1877), 103. For the belief that witches divert the fruit or substance or profit of their neighbors' milk see, for example, J. H. Dixon, Gairloch, 1886, pp. 164–166; James Campbell, Balmerino and its Abbey, 1899, pp. 404–405; Hossack, Kirkwall in the Orkneys, 1900, pp. 257–259; Old-Lore Miscellany of Orkney, V (1912), 132–133 (case of 1657). They may also take away the goodness of meal: Transactions Buchan Field Club, III (1892–95), 140. For eggs taken by magic see Skattegraveren, IX (1888), 15; XI (1889), 205–206. So a witch or wizard in East Sussex not long ago stopped a woman's hens from laying (Sussex Archæological Collections, LX [1909], 147).

10. For milking some object (a broomstick, a chair leg, an axe-handle, a fork, a knife-handle, a spigot, a rope, etc.) and similar magic see Kuhn and Schwartz, Norddeutsche Sagen, 1848, pp. 24–25; Rochholz, Schweizersagen aus dem Aargau, 1856, II, 167–168; Peter, Volksthümliches aus Oesterreichisch-Schlesien, II (1867), 252; Frischbier, Hexenspruch und Zauberbann, 1870, p. 14; von Schulenburg, Wendische Volkssagen und Gebräuche, 1880, pp. 160, 167; Gredt, Sagenschatz des Luxemburger Landes, 1883, p. 556; Knoop, Volkssagen aus dem Oestlichen Hinterpommern, 1885, p. 17; U. Jahn, Volkssagen aus Pommern und Rügen, 1886, p. 335; Blätter für Pommersche Volkskunde, IV (1896), 18; Vonbun, Die Sagen Vorarlbergs, 2d ed., 1889, pp. 150, 151; Wucke, Sagen der Mittleren Werra, 2d ed., 1891, p. 404; Zeitschrift des Vereins für Volkskunde, V (1895), 408; Am Ur-Quell, N. F., I (1897), 19; Wuttke-Meyer, 1900, pp. 158–159; E. H. Meyer, Badisches Volksleben, 1900, p. 557; Zeitschrift

für Oesterreichische Volkskunde, XIII (1907), 25, 132; XIV (1908), 136; Deutsche Volkskunde aus dem Oestlichen Böhmen, IV (1904), 268; V (1905), 31, 39, cf. 34–35; VI (1906), 201–202; XI (1911), 41; XII (1912), 35; Lachmann, Ueberlinger Sagen, Bräuche und Sitten, 1909, p. 393; Kühnau, Schlesische Sagen, III (1913), 84, 98–99, 104–105; Josef Müller, Sagen aus Uri, I (1926), 104–106 (Schriften der Schweizerischen Gesellschaft für Volkskunde, XVIII); De Cock and Teirlinck, Brabantsch Sagenboek, I (1909), 40–44; Kristensen, Jyske Folkeminder, VIII (1886), 260–261, 270; the Same, Danske Sagn, VI, i (1900), 276; VI, ii (1901), 61, 134; Skattegraveren, X (1888), 14, 26–28; Bidrag till Södermanlands Äldre Kulturhistoria, II, v (1884), 94; Sauvé, Le Folk-Lore des Hautes Vosges, 1889, pp. 183–184, 203–205; Revue des Traditions Populaires, XXVII (1912), 77; Korrespondenzblatt des Vereins für Siebenbürgische Landeskunde, XXVI (1903), 32–33; XXXVI (1913), 6; Krauss, Slavische Volkforschungen, 1908, pp. 40, 76; Journal of the Anthropological Institute, XXII (1893), 107–109; Enthoven, The Folklore of Bombay, 1924, p. 237.

11. Blakeborough, Wit, Character, Folklore and Customs of the North Riding of Yorkshire, 2d ed., 1911, pp. 174–175; Montgomerie, Poems, ed. Cranstoun, Scottish Text Society, 1887, p. 75; Minutes of Cupar Presbytery (1649), James Campbell, Balmerino and its Abbey, 1899, pp. 385–386; Pitcairn, Criminal Trials in Scotland, 1833, III, 605; J. G. Campbell, Witchcraft and Second Sight in the Highlands and Islands of Scotland, 1902, p. 9; James Napier, Notes and Reminiscences relating to Partick, 1875, pp. 187–188; Denham Tracts, II (1895), 83; Folk-Lore, V (1894), 186; XXXIII (1922), 210–212; Thomas, Kentucky Superstitions, 1890, p. 279. Cf. Gregor, The Folk-Lore of the North-East of Scotland, 1881, p. 189; Saga-Book of the Viking Club, III (1902), 51; Doddridge, Notes on the Settlement and Indian Wars of the Western Parts of Virginia and Pennsylvania, 1824, p. 163.

12. Bale, A Comedy concernynge Thre Lawes, 1538, sig. Biiij r° (ed. Schröer, Anglia, V [1882], vv. 463–466, p. 174); cf. sig. Biij r° (v. 414, p. 172).

13. Bale, sig. Biij r° (v. 419, p. 172).

14. Robert of Brunne, Handlyng Synne, vv. 74–82, ed. Furnivall (Roxburghe Club), 1862, pp. 3–4. See Paris, Histoire Littéraire, XXVIII, 179–207; Herbert, Catalogue of Romances, III (1890), 272–320; Wells, A Manual of the Writings in Middle English, 1916, pp. 342–344, 816.

15. Handlyng Synne, vv. 339–498 (Le Manuel des Pechiez, vv. 1078–1273), pp. 12–17.

16. Handlyng Synne, vv. 499–562, pp. 17–19. James Calfhill refers concisely to a similar story in the Preface to An Aunswere to the Treatise of the Crosse, 1565 (ed. Gibbings, Parker Society, p. 17): "when the witch, by her *Pater Noster*, made her pail go a milking." Cf. Boguet, Discours des Sorciers, 1608, p. 240.

17. Bartholomaeus de Spina, Quaestio de Strigibus, 1523, cap. 2 (ed. with Malleus, 1620, II, 150), following the report of an eye-witness.

18. Fournier, Revue d'Histoire et de Littérature Religieuses, IX, (1904), 97.

19. Arundel Penitential (Arundel MS. 201), § 79 (Schmitz, Bussbücher, I, 459: "aliqua incantatione aut maleficio"); Cotton MS. Faustina Aviii, Reliquiae Antiquae, 1845, I, 285; cf. Corrector, § 168 (Schmitz, II, 446).

20. See p. 179, above.

21. Atkinson, Forty Years in a Moorland Parish, 1891, pp. 87–90; Ditchfield, The Parson's Pleasance, pp. 191–192; Gregor, The Folk-Lore of the North-East of Scotland, 1881, p. 128, cf. p. 189; Nicholson, Golspie, 1897, p. 80; James Campbell, Balmerino and its Abbey, 1899, p. 387; J. G. Campbell, Witchcraft and Second Sight in the Highlands and Islands, 1902, pp. 7–8; Folk-Lore, XXVII (1916), 252; XXVIII (1917), 214; The Celtic Magazine, X (1885), 433; Seymour, Irish Witchcraft and Demonology, 1913, p. 241; Bardan, The Dead-Watchers and Other Folk-Lore Tales of Westmeath, 1891, p. 83; MacCulloch, Guernsey Folk Lore, 1903, pp. 361–365; Eisel, Sagenbuch des Voigtlandes, 1871, p. 140; Wuttke-Meyer, p. 160; Dykstra, Uit Friesland's Volksleven, II, 155. Cf. Garmann, De Miraculis Mortuorum, 1709, i, 3, 23–26 and 41, pp. 119–121, 127–128; F. W. Mathews, Tales of the Blackdown Borderland (Somerset Folk Series, No. 13), p. 108; Trotter, Galloway Gossip, 1901, p. 247; J. C. Davies, Folk-Lore of West and Mid-Wales, 1911, p. 243; Folk-Lore Journal, VII (1889), 60–61 (a Lancashire witch carries a goose, which is really a pitcher of stolen milk).

22. Giraldus Cambrensis, Topographia Hibernica, ii, 19, Opera, ed. Dimock, V, 106.

23. Hobthursts: The Reliquary, V (1864–65), 11–12. — Fairies: J. G. Campbell, Superstitions of the Highlands and Islands of Scotland, 1900, pp. 134–135; Folk-Lore, XXXIII (1922), 396; County Folk-Lore, III (1903), Orkney and Shetland Islands, pp. 31, 34, 42; Spence, Shetland Folk-Lore, 1899, pp. 166–167; Burgess, The Scottish Review, XXV (1895), 96–97 (Shetland trows); William Mackay, Urquhart and Glenmoriston, 1893, pp. 428–429. — Hedgehogs: Folk-Lore Record, I (1878), 183; Folk-Lore, XXVIII (1917), 102–103, 325–326 (Hampshire and Lincolnshire); Transactions Devonshire Association, XV (1883), 99; County Folk-Lore, I, No. 2 (1893), p. 7 (Suffolk); Notes and Queries, 6th Series, VII (1883), 309; VIII (1883), 32–33, 117–118, 317; E. M. Wright, Rustic Speech and Folk-Lore, 1913, p. 228. — Snakes: Notes and Queries, 10th Series, X (1908), 265, 316–317; Bergen, Animal and Plant Lore, 1899, pp. 86–87; Thomas, Kentucky Superstitions, 1920, p. 274 (black snakes: so also in New England); Revue des Traditions Populaires, XVIII (1903), 463; Mitteilungen der Schlesischen Gesellschaft für Volkskunde, VI, i (1904), 67–72; Revue de l'Histoire des Religions, XXXII (1895), 149 (snakes and nurses). In Poland toads play this trick: to thwart them, burn a live toad in a closed pot (Am Ur-Quell, III [1892], 272). Cf. Krauss, Slavische Volkforschungen, 1908, pp. 76–77; Knoop, Sagen und Erzählungen aus der Provinz Posen, 1893, p. 90 (witch as toad); Mitteilungen des Vereins für Anhaltische Geschichte und Altertumskunde, X (1907),

749; E. Gerard, The Land Beyond the Forest, New York, 1888, p. 196 (toad steals milk for witch).

24. Pliny, x, 40, 56, 115.

25. Blakeborough, Wit, Character, Folklore and Customs of the North Riding of Yorkshire, 2d ed., 1911, pp. 190–191; Árnason, Íslenzkar Þjóð-sögur, I (1862), 430–435; Maurer, Isländische Volkssagen, 1860, pp. 93–94; Hyltén-Cavallius, Wärend och Wirdarne, I (1863), 115, 225; Linder-holm, De Stora Häxprocesserna i Sverige, I (1918), 224; Jonsson, Folktro, Seder ock Bruk i Möre, 1881, pp. 9–10 (Nyare Bidrag till Kännedom om de Svenska Landsmålen, II, No. 5). Cf. Craigie, Scandinavian Folk-Lore, 1896, pp. 377, 379–380; Eisel, Sagenbuch des Voigtlandes, 1871, p. 158; Bang, Norske Hexeformularer, 1901, p. 322.

26. A Collection of Modern Relations, 1693, pp. 51–52.

27. More, An Antidote against Atheism, iii, 9, Philosophical Writings, 4th ed., 1712, p. 117. Compare the vampire-ghosts in Pechuël-Loesche, Volkskunde von Loango, 1907, pp. 317–318.

28. Skattegraveren, IV (1885), 56.

29. See pp. 224–225, above. Cf. Danaeus (Daneau), De Veneficis, cap. 3, ed. 1575, p. 46; Peter, Volksthümliches aus Oesterreichisch-Schlesien, II (1867), 24.

30. Good typical cases are those of Goody Malter in 1570 (Strype, The Life of Sir Thomas Smith, 1698, pp. 129–130) and Margaret Morton in 1651 (York Depositions, ed. Raine, p. 38). "Thou . . . art such a Witch for a cherne, or a cheese-presse," says Gabriel Harvey, "as is not to be found in the Mallet of Witches, or in Monsieur Bodines Daemono-mania" (An Aduertisement for Papphatchett, 1589, in his Pierces Super-erogation, 1593, Works, ed. Grosart, II, 231). For a blessing on milk and honey see Rituale Ecclesiae Dunelmensis, ed. Lindelöf (Surtees Society, CXL), pp. 129–130; cf. Leechdoms, ed. Cockayne, II, 142 (ed. Leonhardi, p. 43); II, 340 (Leonhardi, p. 104).

31. A True and Iust Recorde, of the Information [etc.] of all the Witches, taken at S. Oses (London, 1582), sig. E5, lf. 4 v°; Giffard, A Dialogue concerning Witches and Witchcraftes, 1593, sig. G v°; Bang, Norske Hexeformularer, 1901, p. 346. A bewitched spindle worked well when heated redhot and then cooled (A True and Iust Recorde, 1582).

32. Cf. Bombay Gazetteer, IX (1901), 430.

33. Giffard, sigg. T3–T4 (cf. B2 v°, C3 r°, G r°). See The Celtic Magazine, V (1880), 472 (witch's arm in the churn); Drage, Daimonomageia, 1665, p. 21 (redhot iron in churn burns witch); Whittier, The Supernaturalism of New England, 1847, p. 63 (redhot tongs in churn; witch burnt); Skattegraveren, XI (1889), 206–207.

34. Folk-Lore Record, III, i (1880), 134 (iron, wizard died of the burn; Suffolk, 1732); Harper's New Monthly Magazine, LXXXVII (1893), 797 (hot iron, witch burnt, Norfolk); W. H. Dawson, History of Skipton, 1882, p. 389 (poker, Yorkshire); Bye-Gones for 1895–96, p. 124 (poker, Welsh border); Henderson, Notes on the Folk-Lore of the Northern Counties, 1879, pp. 183–184 (hot iron, crooked sixpence, salt, etc.); Wil-

kinson and Tattersall, Memories of Hurstwood, 1889, p. 49 (iron); Gregor,
The Folk-Lore of the North-East of Scotland, 1881, p. 194 (horseshoe,
crooked sixpence, rowan — under the churn); E. Owen, Welsh Folk-Lore,
pp. 238–239 (crowbar); J. C. Davies, Folk-Lore of West and Mid-Wales,
1911, p. 238 (smoothing iron); Bergen, Animal and Plant Lore, 1899, pp.
21 (redhot horseshoe), 22 (horseshoe under the churn); Harper's New
Monthly Magazine, LXXXVII (1893), 797 (Norfolk: whip and bind the
churn); Thomas, Kentucky Superstitions, 1920, p. 248 (whip the churn);
Folk-Lore, XII (1901), 173–174 (salt, Lincolnshire; so Thiers, Traité des
Superstitions, 1741, I, 170: cf. County Folk-Lore, V, 76, 95, 97); Addy,
Household Tales, 1895, pp. 80–81 (shilling; house corners); County Folk-
Lore, II (1901), 155, and IV (1904), 53 (crooked sixpence) (cf. Bartsch,
Sagen, Märchen und Gebräuche aus Meklenburg, II [1880], 137: gold
coin in churn). Cf. Dalyell, The Darker Superstitions of Scotland, 1834,
pp. 263–265; Folk-Lore, XV (1904), 457–460 (Ireland); Vonbun, Die
Sagen Vorarlbergs, 2d ed., 1889, pp. 151–152 (hot iron; or shoot through
the churn and thus kill the witch); Heyl, Volkssagen, Bräuche und Mein-
ungen aus Tirol, 1897, p. 40 (kill the witch by firing a gun into the churn);
Kühnau, Schlesische Sagen, III (1913), 71–72 (iron); Schambach and
Müller, Niedersächsische Sagen und Märchen, 1855, pp. 175–176 (cream
put on the fire; witch came); Grohmann, Aberglaube und Gebräuche aus
Böhmen und Mähren, 1867, p. 139 (hot fork); Dania, II (1892–94), 223
(hot stone); Hyltén-Cavallius, Wärend och Wirdarne, I (1863), 192;
Bonnet, Revue des Traditions Populaires, XXVII (1912), 76 and note 2;
Wm. Hunter, Biggar and the House of Fleming, 1867, p. 390. For rowan
see Henderson, Notes on the Folk-Lore of the Northern Counties, 1879,
pp. 183–184; Peacock, A Glossary of Words used in the Wapentakes of
Manley and Corringham (English Dialect Society), 1877, p. 275; H. S.
Cowper, Hawkshead, 1899, pp. 309–310; Addy, Household Tales, 1895,
p. 79; Transactions Cumberland and Westmorland Antiquarian and
Archæological Society, XIV (1897), 375. For a queer variety of butter
sorcery see By-Gones for 1897–98, p. 209; cf. Malleus Maleficarum,
Part ii, cap. 14, ed. 1620, p. 240. Soap may be bewitched in the manufac-
ture; a hot poker acts as a counter-charm and burns the witch: Bergen,
Animal and Plant Lore, 1899, p. 21. For the virtues of salt see Samter,
Geburt, Hochzeit und Tod, 1911, pp. 151–161.

35. Old-Lore Miscellany of Orkney, etc., II (1909), 107; Wm. Wilson,
Folk Lore and Genealogies of Uppermost Nithsdale, 1904, pp. 22–24.

36. Odd Ways in Olden Days Down West or Tales of the Reformation
in Devon and Cornwall, 1892, p. xii.

37. Strype, The Life of Sir Thomas Smith, 1698, pp. 129–130.

38. Folk-Lore, IX (1898), 285 (Fife); XV (1904), 457 (Ireland);
A. W. Moore, The Folk-Lore of the Isle of Man, 1891, p. 91; Gredt, Sagen-
schatz des Luxemburger Landes, 1883, p. 563; Sébillot, Traditions et
Superstitions de la Haute-Bretagne, 1882, I, 276.

39. Transactions Devonshire Association, X (1878), 100–101; Palmer,
Odd Yarns of English Lakeland, 1914, p. 73; The Reliquary, V (1864–65),
11–12; Wentz, The Fairy-Faith in Celtic Countries, 1911, p. 43.

40. Scot, xii, 21, p. 281 (197–198), ed. Nicholson, p. 229; i, 4, p. 11 (7), ed. Nicholson, p. 8.

41. Folk-Lore, V (1894), 184–185 (Ireland); IX (1898), 285 (Fife). For another version of the Scottish charm see Robert Chambers, Popular Rhymes of Scotland, 1826, p. 279 (new ed., [1870,] p. 329); Adam Philip, The Parish of Longforgan, pp. 188–189. Cf. Krauss, Slavische Volk-forschungen, 1908, p. 41. For dew cf. Henderson, Notes on the Folk-Lore of the Northern Counties, 1879, p. 199; Wuttke-Meyer, p. 266; Kühnau, Schlesische Sagen, III (1913), 73–74; Schramek, Der Böhmerwaldbauer, 1915 (Beiträge zur Deutsch-Böhmischen Volkskunde, XII), p. 151; Am Ur-Quell, N. F., III (1892), 324–325; Deutsche Volkskunde aus dem Oestlichen Böhmen, VI (1906), 199 (cf. 200); Zeitschrift des Vereins für Volkskunde, XXII (1912), 95. Note the use of a supposed dead finger in Shetland in 1616 (Dalyell, The Darker Superstitions of Scotland, 1834, pp. 264–265).

42. Rochholz, Schweizersagen aus dem Aargau, 1856, II, 169; Kühnau, Schlesische Sagen, III (1913), 48–49; Strackerjan, Aberglaube und Sagen aus dem Herzogtum Oldenburg, 2d ed., 1909, I, 383–384. Cf. Mélusine, III (1886–87), 194; Am Ur-Quell, V (1894), 281; Nyare Bidrag till Kän-nedom om de Svenska Landsmål, IX, i (1900), 369; Linderholm, De Stora Häxprocesserna i Sverige, I (1918), 206; Kristensen, Efterslæt til Skat-tegraveren, 1890, pp. 195–196; Zeitschrift des Vereins für Rheinische und Westfälische Volkskunde, X (1913), 267–272; Josef Müller, Sagen aus Uri, I (1926), 102–103 (Schriften der Schweizerischen Gesellschaft für Volks-kunde, XVIII); Rantasalo, Der Ackerbau, IV (1924), 23–24 (FF Com-munications, XVII, No. 55).

43. Holinshed's Chronicles, VI (1808), 252; Wright, Proceedings against Dame Alice Kyteler (Camden Society, XXIV), 1843, p. 46 (not in the contemporary record); Blakeborough, Wit, Character, Folklore and Customs of the North Riding of Yorkshire, 2d ed., 1911, p. 143. Cf. Bergen, Current Superstitions, 1896, p. 82; E. M. Wright, Rustic Speech and Folk-Lore, 1913, p. 221; Puckett, Folk Beliefs of the Southern Negro, 1926, pp. 395–396; Panjab Notes and Queries, III (1885–86), p. 42; Samter, Geburt, Hochzeit und Tod, 1911, pp. 29–38.

44. Daily Chronicle, London, February 15, 1879, in Gomme, Folklore as an Historical Science, 1908, pp. 202–203.

45. Bye-Gones for 1893–94, p. 481. For drawing blood see Chapter II, note 190; cf. p. 236.

46. Sinclair, Satans Invisible World Discovered, 1685 (reprint, 1871, p. 127); Northall, English Folk-Rhymes, pp. 150–151; Hook's Original Christmas Box, Vol. III; Folk-Lore, XII (1901), 330; Brand-Hazlitt, III, 268–269; The Reliquary, V (1864–65), 12 (cf. VII [1866–67], 101); Bye-Gones for 1901–02, pp. 231–232; Hewett, Nummits and Crummits, 1900, p. 67; County Folk-Lore, II (1901), 214; Wood-Martin, Traces of the Elder Faiths of Ireland, 1902, II, 8–9. Cf. Hästesko, Motivverzeichnis Westfinnischer Zaubersprüche (FF Communications, No. 19, Vol. II), 1914, p. 51. For an elaborate churn-charm see Carmichael, Carmina Gadelica, 1900, II, 142–151.

47. Ady, A Candle in the Dark, 1659, p. 59.

48. A True and Iust Recorde, 1582, sigg. D4, lf. 5 r°, and E5, lf. 1 v° (beer and bread). John Carter testified that, after he had lost two brewings, "the third tyme . . . his sonne beeing a tall and lustie man, of the age of xxxvi. yeeres, was wished to take his Bowe and an arrowe, and to shoote to make his shaft or arrowe to sticke in the Brewing Fatte, and that he shotte twise and coulde not make the same to sticke, but at the thirde time that hee shotte, hee made the same to sticke in the brewinge Fatte, and after hee sayth they coulde brewe as well as before" (sig. E3 r°).

49. Jonson, The Devil is an Ass, 1616, i, 1, 12–15. Cf. Giffard, A Dialogue concerning Witches and Witchcraftes, 1593, sigg. H r°, K3 v°; A True Relation, 1645, p. 3; Pitcairn, Criminal Trials in Scotland, 1833, II, 525; III, 605–606; Hibbert, A Description of the Shetland Isles, 1822, p. 575; Hossack, Kirkwall in the Orkneys, 1900, pp. 258–259; De Cock and Teirlinck, Brabantsch Sagenboek, I (1909), 27–28; Revue des Traditions Populaires, XXIII (1908), 377; Cotton Mather, The Wonders of the Invisible World, 1693, p. 130; S. G. Drake, Annals of Witchcraft in New England, 1869, p. 96. For the cord see Scot, as quoted above, p. 168.

50. The Examination and Confession of Certaine Wytches at Chensforde, 1566, Philobiblon Society reprint, p. 31.

51. So in the Leventina (Switzerland) in 1457: Bollettino Storico della Svizzera Italiana, VI (1884), 234. Cf. A True and Exact Relation, 1645, p. 22; Folk-Lore, XXV (1914), 367 (Kent).

52. Wier rejects the notion that witches spoil ale (vi, 9, ed. 1568, pp. 596–597). Cf. Brand-Hazlitt, III, 271–272. Mischievous house-cobolds sometimes turn the beer sour: Transactions Devonshire Association, X (1878), 100–101; cf. County Folk-Lore, III (1903), 20–21. For Anne Whittle's charm "to helpe drinke that was forspoken or bewitched" see p. 39, above.

53. Bale's Comedy, 1538, sig. Biiij r° (vv. 447–454, ed. Schröer, p. 173).

54. The same, sig. Biiij r° (vv. 463–470, ed. Schröer, p. 174).

55. Rituale Ecclesiae Dunelmensis, ed. Lindelöf (Surtees Society, CXL), p. 116. Cf. Leechdoms, ed. Cockayne, II, 142; ed. Leonhardi, p. 43.

56. Herrick, Charmes, Riverside ed., II, 177.

57. Bye-Gones for 1897–98, p. 389; Salopian Shreds and Patches, I (1875), 121; J. C. Davies, Folk-Lore of West and Mid-Wales, 1911, p. 135; Zeitschrift des Vereins für Volkskunde, IV (1894), 81; Blätter für Pommersche Volkskunde, IV (1896), 72; Frischbier, Hexenspruch und Zauberbann, 1870, p. 122; Deutsche Volkskunde aus dem Oestlichen Böhmen, V (1905), 47; Kristensen, Jyske Folkeminder, IX (1888), 72; Archivio delle Tradizioni Popolari, V (1886), 285; XIV (1895), 283–284. If your batch of bread goes wrong, burn a loaf, and that will force the witch to come (Maryland): Journal of American Folk-Lore, XIV (1901), 43.

58. Potts, The Wonderfull Discoverie of Witches, 1613, sig. K.

59. Bye-Gones for 1878–79, p. 185; Folk-Lore, XXVI (1915), 198–199; A. W. Moore, The Folk-Lore of the Isle of Man, 1891, p. 83; Roscoe, The Bagesu, 1924, p. 108; Orde Browne, The Vanishing Tribes of Kenya, 1925,

p. 184; Sudan Notes and Records, II (1919), 133. Cf. Scot, xvi, 2, p. 472 (341), ed. Nicholson, p. 398; Hansen, Quellen, index, s. vv. *Zauberei*, *Feldfrüchte*; Pitcairn, Criminal Trials in Scotland, 1833, III, 603; Linderholm, De Stora Häxprocesserna i Sverige, I (1918), 127. For garden magic see Journal Royal Anthropological Institute, XLVI (1916), 385–388, 390–395. Cf. also Rantasalo, Der Ackerbau, IV (1924), FF Communications, XVII, No. 55. One of the Suffolk witches of 1645 confessed that she "usually bewitched standing corne" (A True Relation, 1645, p. 4, cf. p. 5).

60. Cf. Dieterich, Mutter Erde, 3d ed., 1925, p. 16.

61. Leechdoms, ed. Cockayne, I, 398–405; Wülker, Bibliothek der Angelsächsischen Poesie, I (1883), 312–316; Grendon, Journal of American Folk-Lore, XXII (1909), 172–177, 219–220. Bread hallowed on Lammas Day is to be crumbled on the four corners of the barn in some rural emergency that remains mysterious (Cockayne, III, 290). For "St. Columbkill's [magic] Circle," to be scratched with a knife on a millstone which is then to be partially buried in the hedge surrounding one's field, see Cockayne, I, 395; Grendon, p. 205. For blessing of fields, house, and barn see Rituale Ecclesiae Dunelmensis, ed. Stevenson (Surtees Society, X), pp. 117–118. Cf. Bale, Select Works, ed. Christmas (Parker Society), p. 528 ("conjuring of their ploughs").

62. See Rituale Ecclesiae Dunelmensis, pp. 118, 145–147 (cf. pp. 117–118, 130).

63. Wizards have killed trees in Suffolk in recent times (Zincke, Wherstead, 2d ed., 1893, pp. 229–230). In Dorset in 1912 a bottle containing two vipers and a centipede in spirits of wine was dug up near an apple-tree: it had caused two or three of the farmer's appletrees to be blown over, and one had died; the farmer himself was sick (Proceedings Dorset Natural History and Antiquarian Field Club, XXXVII [1916], 59–60).

64. Bale, A Comedy concernynge Thre Lawes, 1538, vv. 444–463, ed. Schröer, Anglia, V (1882), 173, 174.

65. Bye-Gones for 1895–1896, p. 149.

66. Cf. St. Augustine, De Civitate Dei, viii, 19.

67. Naturalis Historia, xviii, 6 (8), 41–43 (from Piso). Cf. Scot, xii, 4–5, pp. 220–222 (158–159), ed. Nicholson, pp. 177–178.

68. Abt, Die Apologie des Apuleius (Religionsgeschichtliche Versuche und Vorarbeiten, ed. by Dieterich and Wünsch, Vol. IV, Heft 2), pp. 266–267 (192–193).

69. Nider, Formicarius, v, 4, ed. 1516 (1517), fol. lxxv v°; repeated in Malleus Maleficarum, Part II, qu. 1, cap. 15 (ed. 1620, p. 245), and thence by Scot, xii, 5, p. 222 (159), ed. Nicholson, p. 178. Cf. Pitcairn, Criminal Trials in Scotland, 1833, III, 613, 614; Zeitschrift für Oesterreichische Volkskunde, I (1895), 303; D. Campbell, In the Heart of Bantuland, 1922, p. 240.

70. Enthoven, The Folklore of Bombay, 1924, p. 239.

71. See Chapter VIII. Cf. Hans Meyer, Die Barundi, 1916, p. 133.

72. Remy, Daemonolatreia, i, 21, 1595, pp. 145–146.

73. Folk-Lore, XXVI (1915), 199–200.

74. Drage, Daimonomageia, 1665, p. 41.

75. Charles Mackie, Norfolk Annals, 1901, I, 428. Cf. A True and Exact Relation, 1645, p. 23; A Tryal of Witches, 1682, p. 52 (1664[-5]); Folk-Lore, XXVI (1915), 197; Wuttke-Meyer, pp. 267–268; Josef Müller, Sagen aus Uri (Schriften der Schweizerischen Gesellschaft für Volkskunde, XVIII), I (1926), 106–108; Hobley, Bantu Beliefs and Magic, 1922, pp. 184–185; Orde Browne, The Vanishing Tribes of Kenya, 1925, pp. 201–202; D. R. MacKenzie, The Spirit-Ridden Konde, 1925, pp. 257–258. For charms, etc., against rats and mice see Geoponica, xiii, 5 (with an amusing skeptical comment); Cockayne, Leechdoms, I, 397 ("ut surices garbas non noceant": cf. Martin of Bracara, De Correctione Rusticorum, ed. Caspari, 1883, pp. 14–17); Furnivall, Political, Religious and Love Poems, 1866, p. 23 (2d ed., 1903, p. 43); Noreen, Altschwedisches Lesebuch, 1892–94, pp. 97–99 (cf. Holthausen, Arkiv för Nordisk Filologi, XIV [1898], 93–94); The Proceedings of the Great Bardic Institution, ed. Connellan (Ossianic Society, V), 1860, pp. 74–79; J. G. Campbell, Superstitions of the Highlands and Islands, 1900, pp. 225–226; Trevelyan, Folk-Lore and Folk-Stories of Wales, 1909, p. 230; Notes and Queries, 9th Series, III (1899), 395; Boston Evening Journal, February 8, 1884; Ons Volksleven, X (1898), 5–14, 66–68, 167; Wallonia, X (1901), 102–108; As You Like It, iii, 2, 186–188, and the commentators, particularly Halliwell, VI (1856), 188–189; Newell, Journal of American Folk-Lore, V (1892), 23–32 (cf. XI [1898], 161); F. N. Robinson, Studies in the History of Religions presented to C. H. Toy, 1912, pp. 95–98. For the plague of lice see also the examinations of 1645 in Add. MS. 27402, foll. 107 rᵒ, 114 rᵒ, 115 rᵒ.

76. Notes and Queries for Somerset and Dorset, X (1907), 49–50; County Folk-Lore, III (1903), 166; VII (1914), 124–131; Train, An Historical and Statistical Account of the Isle of Man, 1845, II, 170–171; Polson, Our Highland Folklore Heritage, 1926, p. 125.

77. Norfolk Archæology, II (1849), 306.

78. Torr, Small Talk at Wreyland, 2d Series, 1921, p. 51; Polson, as above, pp. 122–125. Cf. Northall, English Folk-Rhymes, 1892, p. 149; Bang, Norske Hexeformularer, 1901, pp. 515–518, 530; Journal Royal Anthropological Institute, XXXVII (1907), 172–174; Ivens, Melanesians of the South-East Solomon Islands, 1927, pp. 329–331.

79. Pitcairn, Criminal Trials in Scotland, 1833, III, 609; Gregor, The Folk-Lore of the North-East of Scotland, 1881, pp. 199–200; Linderholm, De Stora Häxprocesserna i Sverige, I (1918), 93–94, 96, 230; Sébillot, Le Folk-Lore des Pêcheurs, 1901, pp. 211–219; Zeitschrift der Gesellschaft für die Geschichte der Herzogthümer Schleswig, Holstein und Lauenburg, III (1873), 51. Cf. Deane, Fijian Society, 1921, pp. 167–168. For mediæval blessings on fishing nets, some of which include the idea that evil incantations may interfere, see A. Franz, Die Kirchlichen Benediktionen, 1909, I, 624–626. Cf. Zeitschrift für Romanische Philologie, XXXII (1908), 575. For blessings on the nets of hunters see Rituale Ecclesiae Dunelmensis, ed Stevenson (Surtees Society, X), p. 117; cf. Zeitschrift, as above, XXXII, 584–585.

CHAPTER X

METAMORPHOSIS

1. George Giffard, A Dialogue concerning Witches and Witchcraftes, 1593, sig. A3 v° (2d ed. in 1603); cf. B r° (cat, weasel, mouse), B4 v° (cat, weasel, toad, mouse), C r° (cat named Lightfoot; toad, Lunch; weasel, Makeshift), C4 (weasel), E r° (cat), K3 v°. Cf. The Wonderfull Discouerie of the Witch-crafts of Margaret and Philip Flower, 1619, sig. B2 r° (rat, cat, toad, bird, cricket), C2 (crow, dog), C3 (mouse, rat, owl, "kitlin," "moldiwarp"); A True and Exact Relation, 1645, pp. 2 (dog; also pp. 4, 6, 10, 14), 2 (polecat), 3 (cat), 14 ("two Kidyns"), 19 ("gray Kite"), 21 (rat), 27 (snake), 30 (gray bird), 34 (mice), 35 (black rabbits); The Examination, Confession, Triall, and Execution, of Joane Williford, Joan Cariden, and Jane Hott, 1645 (dog, mouse, hedgehog); Cross, Studies in Philology (University of North Carolina), XVI (1919), 244–245 (deer); Josef Müller, Sagen aus Uri (Schriften der Schweizerischen Gesellschaft für Volkskunde, XVIII), I (1926), 156 (fox); De Cock and Teirlinck, Brabantsch Sagenboek, I (1909), 26–27 (raven); G. F. Pico della Mirandola, Strix, 1523, sig. Dii, lf. 3 v°; Remigius, Daemonolatreia, 1595, ii, 5, p. 228; Krauss, Slavische Volkforschungen, 1908, p. 60 (crow); The Celtic Magazine, X (1885), 433–434 (otter); Revue des Traditions Populaires, IX (1894), 457–458; Speck, Memoirs American Anthropological Association, VI (1919), 251, 260–262, 269–271; Pechuël-Loesche, Volkskunde von Loango, 1907, pp. 343–344; P. A. Talbot, The Peoples of Southern Nigeria, 1926, II, 213. Verse spells for transformation, as well as for returning to humanity, were recited by Isobel Gowdie in her Second Confession, 1662 (Pitcairn, Criminal Trials in Scotland, 1833, III, 607–608). For shape-shifting and for transformation of men into beasts see Gering, Ueber Weissagung und Zauber im Nordischen Altertum, 1902, pp. 12–16. Harsnet scouts this superstition: "What man iudging according to wit, vnderstanding, or sence, can imagine that a Witch can transforme her selfe into the likenes of a Cat, a Mouse, or an Hare: and that shee being hunted with Hounds, in the forme of an Hare, and pinched by the breech, or whipped with scourges, in the similitude of a Cat, the same pinch or marke, shal be found in the breech of the Witch, that was before made by the Hounds in the breech of an Hare" (A Declaration of Egregious Popish Impostures, 1603, p. 111).

2. Journal Anthropological Institute, XVI (1887), 30.

3. Theal, Ethnography and Condition of South Africa before A.D. 1505, 2d ed., 1919, pp. 245–246; Tremearne, The Ban of the Bori, p. 151; Seligmann, The Melanesians of British New Guinea, 1910, pp. 282–284; N. W. Thomas, Anthropological Report on the Ibo-Speaking Peoples of Nigeria, I (1913), 41; Weeks, Among the Primitive Bakongo, 1914, pp. 224–225. Cf. E. W. Smith and A. M. Dale, The Ila-Speaking Peoples of Northern Rhodesia, 1920, II, 92; D. Campbell, In the Heart of Bantuland, 1922, p. 240; Journal (Royal) Anthropological Institute, XVI (1887), 34; XLIX (1919), 296; Massam, The Cliff Dwellers of Kenya, 1927, pp. 182, 184

(snakes). For the use of bits of lizards etc. in black magic see pp. 48–49, above.

4. P. Amaury Talbot, In the Shadow of the Bush, 1912, pp. 194–195; cf. Revue de l'Histoire des Religions, XXIX (1894), 292–294. Sometimes the familiars are nondescript: thus an eighteenth-century witch's imps are noted as between rats and bats (Zincke, Wherstead, 2d ed., 1893, pp. 227–228). A rat was the familiar spirit of Joan Cason of Kent in 1586 (Waller, in Holinshed, IV [1808], 891–893).

5. See Corrector, § 151 (Schmitz, II, 442); Guilielmus Alvernus, De Universo, ii, 3, 13, Opera, 1674, I, 1043–1044; Vincent of Beauvais, Speculum Historiale, ii, 64–65, ed. 1494, fol. 22 v°; Bodin, Demonomanie, ii, 6, ed. 1580, foll. 94 v°–104 r°; Binsfeld, De Confessionibus Maleficorum et Sagarum, 1591, pp. 180–189; Remy, Daemonolatreia, 1595, ii, 5, pp. 227, 229–232; Claude Prieur, Dialogue de la Lycanthropie, 1596; Deacon and Walker, Dialogicall Discourses of Spirits and Divels, 1601, pp. 158–163; Le Loyer, Discours et Histoires des Spectres, 1605, pp. 139–145; de Nynauld, De la Lycanthropie, 1615; P. de l'Ancre, Tableau de l'Inconstance des Mauvais Anges et Demons, 2d ed., 1613, pp. 252–326 (for the Arrest of 1603, pp. 262–305, see also Bernou, La Chasse aux Sorcières dans le Labourd, 1897, pp. 363–414); the Same, L'Incredulité et Mescreance du Sortilege, 1622, pp. 785–790; Rowlands, The Knave of Harts, 1622, Hunterian Club reprint (Works, II), p. 47 (case of Peter Stumpe); Edward Fairfax, Daemonologia, ed. Grainge, 1882, p. 97 (Stub Peter, etc.); Burton, The Anatomy of Melancholy, i, 1, 1, 4, ed. 1628, p. 9; Birch, The History of the Royal Society, I (1756), 300 (letter from the Palatinate, read by Sir Kenelm Digby, meeting of September 2, 1663); Webster, The Displaying of Supposed Witchcraft, 1677, pp. 33, 68–69, 86, 91–97; Increase Mather, Illustrious Providences, Boston, 1684, pp. 172–174, 177–179; Erasmus Francisci, Der Höllische Proteus, 2d ed., 1695, pp. 334–364, 378–386; Sir William Temple, Of Poetry, Works, 1757, III, 418 (France and Ireland); Hauber, Bibliotheca, Acta et Scripta Magica, chap. 243, Stück 29 (1742), pp. 284–289; The London Magazine, May, 1765, XXXIV, 215 (with fine plate: the Beast of Gevaudun); Hecker, The Epidemics of the Middle Ages, transl. Babington, 1835, II, 55–59 (cf. 130–131); Bourquelot, Recherches sur la Lycanthropie, Mémoires, Société des Antiquaires de France, 2d Series, IX (1849), 193–262; Leubuscher, Ueber die Wehrwölfe und Thierverwandlungen im Mittelalter, 1850; W. Hertz, Der Werwolf, 1862; Baring Gould, A Book of Were-Wolves, 1865; Tylor, Primitive Culture, 1871, I, 279–284; Rolland, Faune Populaire de la France, I (1877), 153–159; Andree, Ethnographische Parallelen und Vergleiche, I (1878), 62–80; Sloet van de Beele, Le Loup-Garou (Extrait de la Revue Internationale, VII), 1885; the Same, De Dieren in het Germaansche Volksgeloof en Volksgebruik, 1887, pp. 42–72; U. Jahn, Volkssagen von Pommern und Rügen, 1886, pp. 379–387; E. Gerard, The Land Beyond the Forest, New York, 1888, pp. 186–187; Ons Volksleven, II (1890), 101–102; IV (1892), 150–152, 221–222; Riezler, Geschichte der Hexenprozesse in Bayern, 1896, pp. 293–294 (A.D. 1717 and 1720); Löwenstimm, Aberglaube und Strafrecht, 1897, pp. 21, 182; Richel, Zeitschrift

für Kulturgeschichte, Ergänzungsheft III (1898), p. 3 (A.D. 1593); Chapiseau, Le Folk-Lore de la Beauce et du Perche, 1902, I, 217–220, 239–240; II, 206–209; E. MacCulloch, Guernsey Folk Lore, 1903, pp. 230–232; Abt, Die Apologie des Apuleius, 1908, p. 126 (52); Annalen des Historischen Vereins für den Niederrhein, LXXXV (1908), 52–53, 68; C. T. Stewart, The Origin of the Werewolf Superstition (University of Missouri Studies, Social Science Series, II, iii), 1909; the Same, Zeitschrift des Vereins für Volkskunde, XIX (1909), 30–51; Trevelyan, Folk-Lore and Folk-Stories of Wales, 1909, pp. 295–297; Elliott O'Donnell, Werwolves, 1912. See also Lingua, i, 7 (Dodsley, Old Plays, ed. Collier, V, 117); Drayton, The Man in the Moone, vv. 5–14; Middleton, The Changeling, iii, 3, ed. Bullen, VI, 49; Ford, The Lover's Melancholy, iii, 2, ed. Dyce, I, 64; the Same, Perkin Warbeck, v, 3, II, 212. Cf. Malleus Maleficarum, Part I, qu. 10, ed. 1620, pp. 96–103; Part II, qu. 1, cap. 8, pp. 200–204; M. G. Lewis, Journal of a West India Proprietor, 1834, p. 295 (hyena); Granada, Reseña Histórico-descriptiva de Supersticiones del Río de la Plata, 1896, pp. 581–627; Ambrosetti, La Leyenda del Yaguareté-Abá, Buenos Aires, 1896 (also Globus, LXX [1896], 272–273); Mary H. Kingsley, Travels in West Africa, 1897, pp. 536–539; Basset, Les Apocryphes Éthiopiens, IV (1894), 24; Baissac, Le Folk-Lore de l'Île Maurice, 1888, pp. 146–179; Bezemer, Volksdichtung aus Indonesien, 1904, pp. 363–365, 422–423; Bompas, Folklore of the Santal Parganas, 1909, pp. 229, 256; Wilken, De Indische Gids, 1884, pp. 945–950; Skeat, Fables and Folk-Tales from an Eastern Forest, 1901, p. 26; K. J. Beatty, Human Leopards, 1915; Crooke, Religion and Folklore of Northern India, 1926, pp. 354–355; Willoughby-Meade, Ghost and Vampire Tales of China, 1925, pp. 8–11; Roscher, Das von der "Kynanthropie" handelnde Fragment des Marcellus von Side, Leipzig, Gesellschaft der Wissenschaften, Philologisch-historische Classe, Abhandlungen, XVII (1897), No. 3; the Same, Die Hundekrankheit der Pandareostochter und andere Mythische Krankheiten, Rheinisches Museum, LIII (1898), 169–204, 639–640; G. F. Abbott, Macedonian Folklore, 1903, pp. 215–218; F. Hamel, Human Animals, 1915. Werewolves, who in one interpretation are sorcerers, recover their human shape when wounded, and show the hurts as men that they have received as beasts (Hertz, Der Werwolf, 1862, pp. 69, 78–83; Bodin, Demonomanie, ii, 6, ed. 1587, fol. 107 v°).

6. Jente, Die Mythologischen Ausdrücke im Altenglischen Wortschatz, 1921, pp. 143–144; Asser, De Rebus Gestibus Ælfridi, cap. 77, ed. Stevenson, 1904, p. 62 (cf. pp. 304–305; Haupt's Zeitschrift, XII [1865], 252); Cnut, i, 26 (Liebermann, I, 306; Thorpe, p. 161: "se wodfreca werewulf"; cf. Napier's Wulfstan, p. 191); Gervase of Tilbury, Otia Imperialia, iii, 120 (Leibnitz, p. 1003; Liebrecht, pp. 51–52, cf. pp. 161–163); Giraldus Cambrensis, Topographia Hibernica, ii, 19, Opera, ed. Dimock, V, 101–105; the Same, Expugnatio Hiberniae, ii, 23, V, 356; the Wonders of Ireland, etc. Cf. Kittredge, [Harvard] Studies and Notes, VIII (1903), 257–260; Ériu, V (1911), 203.

7. See, for example, Arthur and Gorlagon, ed. Kittredge, as above, VIII, 149–275; the romance of William of Palerne, ed. Skeat, 1867 (cf.

Wells, A Manuel of the Writings in Middle English, 1916, p. 765); Marie's Lai de Bisclavret, written in England in the twelfth century. Cf. K. F. Smith, Historical Study of the Werwolf in Literature, Publications Modern Language Association, IX (1894), 1–42.

8. Matthew Paris, Chronica Majora, ed. Luard, II, 113; Eulogium Historiarum, ed. Haydon, III, 51.

9. Remigius (Remy), Daemonolatreia, i, 23, ed. 1595, pp. 154–157. Cf. P. de l'Ancre, Tableau de l'Inconstance des Mauvais Anges et Demons, 1613, pp. 67–69, 135; Roskoff, Geschichte des Teufels, 1869, I, 358–359. According to the Anjou Chronicle demons in wolf form, but with the voice of goats, appeared in various places A.D. 965 (Recueil, VIII, 252).

10. Vita Bartholomaei Farnensis, in Arnold's ed. of Symeon of Durham, I, 314.

11. Memorials of St. Dunstan, ed. Stubbs, pp. 84–85, 262–263; Matthew Paris, Chronica Majora, ed. Luard, I, 474; Flores Historiarum, ed. Luard, I, 520–521.

12. Memorials of St. Dunstan, pp. 26–27, 59, 100. Cf. the Life of St. Waltheof, twelfth-century Abbot of Melrose, Acta Sanctorum, August 3, I, 264 (mouse, cat, pig, dog, wolf, bull).

13. Acta Sanctorum, April 29, III, 659–660.

14. Reginald, Libellus de Admirandis Beati Cuthberti Virtutibus, cap. 17, ed. Raine (Surtees Society, I), pp. 32–37. Cf. Jacoby, Archiv für Religionswissenschaft, XXI (1922), 219–220.

15. Reginald, Libellus de Vita et Miraculis S. Godrici, ed. Stevenson (Surtees Society, XX), §§ 187, 188, 236, 320 (Appendix, cap. 2), pp. 196–198, 250–251, 337–338.

16. The Confession of Mr. Richard Allington before Mr. Doctor Caldewell and Sir John of the Rolls, The Warwickshire Antiquarian Magazine, I (1859), 191.

17. Joannis Rossi Historia Rerum Angliae, ed. Hearne, 1745, pp. 206–207. A witch or wizard (or a familiar spirit) may take the form of a bird: A True and Exact Relation, 1645, pp. 30, 34 (small gray bird; sparrow); A True and Impartial Relation of the Informations against Three Witches, 1682, pp. 11–12 (magpie); see also, Lincolnshire Notes and Queries, II (1891), 143; Folk-Lore, XII (1901), 172; Edmondston, A View of the Ancient and Present State of the Zetland Islands, 1809, II, 74, and Gregor, The Folk-Lore of the North-East of Scotland, 1881, pp. 135–136 (raven or crow); Addy, Household Tales, 1895, pp. 36–37 (blackbird: cf. Lincolnshire Notes and Queries, II [1891], 143); S. G. Drake, Annals of Witchcraft in New England, 1869, pp. 87–88, 113–114 (Andover, deposition of 1659; blackbird); yellowbird (Deodat Lawson, A Brief and True Narrative, 1692, Burr, Narratives of the Witchcraft Cases 1648–1706, 1914, pp. 154–156). For a fiend's assuming bird-form see Salomon and Saturn, i, 149–151, ed. Kemble, 1848, p. 143; ed. Wülker, Bibliothek, III, ii (1898), 66 (312). For the magpie as an ominous bird see Burne and Jackson, Shropshire Folk-Lore, pp. 223–224; Bye-Gones for 1897–98, p. 389; E. M. Wright, Rustic Speech and Folk-Lore, 1913, pp. 217–218.

18. English Chronicle, ed. Davies (Camden Society, LXIV), p. 74.

19. Wilkinson and Tattersall, Memories of Hurstwood, 1889, pp. 60–61; Halifax Antiquarian Society Papers, 1904–05, p. 4; A. L. Humphreys, The Materials for the History of the Town of Wellington, Co. Somerset, 1889, p. 243; Speight, Lower Wharfedale, 1902, p. 158; Couch, The History of Polperro, 1871, pp. 140–141; Suffling, History and Legends of the Broad District, [1890,] pp. 106–107; T. and K. Macquoid, About Yorkshire, 1883, p. 70; Rye, The Norfolk Antiquarian Miscellany, I (1877), 292–293; Norfolk Archæology, II (1849), 307; Notes and Queries, I (1850), 468; the same, 9th Series, II (1898), 336; County Folk-Lore, II (1901), 126–127; V (1908), 53–54; Lincolnshire Notes and Queries, IV (1896), 147; Bye-Gones for 1905–06, p. 99; Folk-Lore, XII (1901), 74; Waldron, A Description of the Isle of Man, 1726, ed. Harrison (Manx Society), 1865, pp. 12–13; Folk-Lore Journal, VII (1889), 287; E. M. Wright, Rustic Speech and Folk-Lore, 1913, pp. 193–195. Cf. Kristensen, Danske Sagn, VI, i (1900), 190–215. For a Latin charm to keep the hounds of hell away from one's cattle see Wünsch, Antikes Zaubergerät aus Pergamon, 1905, p. 43.

20. F. K. Robinson, A Glossary of Words used in the Neighbourhood of Whitby, 1876, p. 74; County Folk-Lore, II (1901), 71–73; IV (1904), 17; E. M. Wright, Rustic Speech and Folk-Lore, 1913, pp. 195–197; Wordsworth, ed. Knight, 1896, IV, 68–73.

21. English Dialect Dictionary, s. v. shuck; Jente, Die Mythologischen Ausdrücke im Altenglischen Wortschatz, 1921, pp. 150–153.

22. Notes and Queries, 9th Series, II (1898), 336; Folk-Lore, XII (1901), 172; Page, An Exploration of Exmoor, 4th ed., 1895, p. 308.

23. Stearne, A Confirmation and Discoverie of Witch-craft, 1648, p. 19.

24. The Examination and Confession of Certaine Wytches at Chensford, 1566; The Examination, Confession, Triall, and Execution, of Joane Williford, Joan Cariden and Jane Hott, 1645, p. 3.

25. Beamont, Winwick, 2d ed., p. 42.

26. See Thomason Catalogue, I, 229, 237, 242, 243. Cf. Mrs. Steuart Erskine, A Royal Cavalier, 1910, pp. 111–112, 230–231; Cleveland's poem To Prince Rupert. In 1645 James More confessed "that his sister Euerard required his imp Nan to send with 2 of her husbands to send to Pr. Ru. wᶜʰ accordingely he deliuered and haue not seene since" (Add. MS. 27402, fol. 121 rᵒ).

27. County Folk-Lore, II (1901), 147–149.

28. Canterbury MS. M295, Historical MSS. Commission, 5th Report, Appendix, p. 455.

29. The Miracles of King Henry VI, ed. Knox and Leslie, 1923, pp. 128–129. Cf. Fernel, De Abditis Rerum Causis, ii, 16 (De Morbis, 1656, pp. 517–518).

30. Contemporary Narrative, ed. Wright, pp. 3, 32.

31. Wier, ed. 1582, col. 112, l. 40; Cranmer, Miscellaneous Writings and Letters, ed. Cox (Parker Society), 1846, p. 66; Harland and Wilkinson, Lancashire Folk-Lore, 1867, p. 59; County Folk-Lore, V (1908), 53, 55–56; Folk-Lore Journal, VI (1889), 26; Folk-Lore, XII (1901), 172; Gregor, The Horse in Scottish Folk Lore, 1890, pp. 4–5; E. M. Wright,

Rustic Speech and Folk-Lore, 1913, p. 195; Nicholson, Golspie, 1897, pp. 15–16; James, English Historical Review, XXXVII (1922), 414; Étienne de Bourbon, Anecdotes, ed. Lecoy de la Marche, 1877, pp. 32, 37; Bosquet, La Normandie Romanesque, 1845, pp. 128–129; Monnier and Vingtrinier, Croyances et Traditions Populaires, 1874, pp. 696–698; Meyrac, Traditions des Ardennes, 1890, pp. 330–331; Kristensen, Danske Sagn, II (1893), 370–378; Storaker, Historisk Tidsskrift, Christiania, I (1871), 479–480; F. Wolf, Scheible's Kloster, XI (1844), 1094–1095; Bechstein, Mythen und Sagen Tirols, 1857, pp. 210–211; Birlinger, Aus Schwaben, 1874, I, 194–195; U. Jahn, Volkssagen aus Pommern und Rügen, 1886, p. 304, cf. 375. Cf. von Negelein, Zeitschrift des Vereins für Volkskunde, XI (1901), 406–420; XII (1902), 14–25, 377–390.

32. For witches wounded or killed in cat shape see, for example, Wilkinson and Tattersall, Memories of Hurstwood, 1889, pp. 57–58; Transactions Lancashire and Cheshire Antiquarian Society, XXXIV (1917), 104–105; Lincolnshire Notes and Queries, I (1889), 246, 247; County Folk-Lore, II (1901), 155; Halifax Antiquarian Society Papers, 1904–05, p. 6; Journal of American Folk-Lore, IV (1891), 324; E. Owen, Welsh Folk-Lore, pp. 224–226; J. G. Campbell, Witchcraft and Second Sight in the Highlands and Islands, 1902, pp. 49–50; Agnew, The Hereditary Sheriffs of Galloway, 1893, II, 82–83; W. Ross, Aberdour and Inchcolme, 1885, p. 327; Polson, Our Highland Folklore Heritage, 1926, p. 70; Kristensen, Danske Sagn, VI, ii (1901), 38–39; Dykstra, Uit Friesland's Volksleven, II, 153–155; Ons Volksleven, V (1893), 115–116; E. Meier, Deutsche Sagen, Sitten und Gebräuche aus Schwaben, 1852, pp. 184–186; Bartsch, Sagen, Märchen und Gebräuche aus Meklenburg, I (1879), 114; Gredt, Sagenschatz des Luxemburger Landes, 1883, p. 559; Schambach and Müller, Niedersächsische Sagen und Märchen, 1855, pp. 179–181; Zeitschrift des Vereins für Rheinische und Westfälische Volkskunde, IV (1907), 117; Rochholz, Schweizersagen aus dem Aargau, 1856, II, 55; Schweizerisches Archiv für Volkskunde, II (1898), 109; Hertz, Der Werwolf, 1862, pp. 71–74; Archivio per lo Studio delle Tradizioni Popolari, V (1886), 285; Journal Royal Anthropological Institute, XLIV (1914), 338; Puckett, Folk Beliefs of the Southern Negro, 1926, p. 149. Cf. Folk-Lore, XII (1901), 172.

33. Gervase of Tilbury, Otia Imperialia, iii, 93 (Leibnitz, Scriptores Rerum Brunsvicensium, I, 992; Liebrecht, Gervasius, p. 45). Cf. Malleus Maleficarum, Pt. II, qu. 1, cap. 9, ed. 1620, pp. 208–210; Bartholomaeus de Spina, Quaestio de Strigibus, cap. 19 (in 1620 ed. of Malleus, II, 213–214); Guaccius, Compendium Maleficarum, 1608, i, 13, pp. 61–62; Hansen, Zauberwahn, p. 350; George Henderson, Survivals in Belief among the Celts, 1911, pp. 107–109.

34. John Hale, A Modest Enquiry into the Nature of Witchcraft, 1702, pp. 64–65.

35. Bodin, De la Demonomanie des Sorciers, ii, 6, ed. 1587, foll. 107 v°–108 r°. See Chapter XVI, note 135. Cf. Mielke, Archiv der Brandenburgia, XII (1907), 135. For witch-cats holding a Sabbath see Sébillot, Traditions et Superstitions de la Haute-Bretagne, 1882, II, 44–45.

36. The Examination and Confession of Certaine Wytches at Chensford, 1566 (Philobiblon Society reprint).

37. Alanus de Insulis, Contra Haereticos, i, 63 (Migne, CCX, 366): "quia, ut dicitur, osculantur posteriora catti, in cuius specie, ut dicunt, apparet eis Lucifer." Cf. Reliquiae Antiquae, ed. Wright and Halliwell, 1845, I, 248.

38. See Chapter XIII, note 34.

39. A witch-cat caused intense excitement at Pottsville, Pennsylvania, in 1911. See The Public Ledger, Philadelphia, September 24, 27, 30, and October 1, 1911.

40. Glyde, The Norfolk Garland, p. 6. Cf. Gregor, Folk-Lore of the North-East of Scotland, 1881, p. 123 (with references); Middleton, Anything for a Quiet Life, v, 1, ed. Bullen, V, 324.

41. County Folk-Lore, I, No. 2 (1893), p. 11; Bergen, Animal and Plant Lore, 1899, p. 81. Cf. John Thomlinson's Diary, October 1, 1718 (Six North Country Diaries, ed. Hodgson, Surtees Society, CXVIII, 141); Schönwerth, Aus der Oberpfalz, I (1857), 247; Skeat, Malay Magic, 1900, pp. 191, 398. For miscellaneous cat magic see Rochholz, Schweizersagen aus dem Aargau, 1856, II, 54–56 (cat-ghost, cat-spooks, cat-witch, cat guarding treasure or sacrificed in a treasure hunt); Josef Müller, Sagen aus Uri (Schriften der Schweizerischen Gesellschaft für Volkskunde, XVIII), I (1926), 168–172, 176–177. For cats and storms, see p. 161, above.

42. Increase Mather, Illustrious Providences, Boston, 1684, p. 101.

43. John Bramhall, A Vindication of True Liberty, 1655, Works, 1844, IV, 161.

44. Mr. Henry W[atso]n's Answer to Bully Dawson (A Continuation or Second Part of The Letters from the Dead to the Living, by Tho. Brown and Others, 1703, pp. 148–149). Cf. John Trenchard (1662–1723), The Natural History of Superstition (Somers Tracts, III [1748], 211); Otway, The Soldier's Fortune, Works, 1728, II, 343 ("I dare swear he wou'd smell out a Rival if he were in the House, only by natural Instinct, as some that always sweat when a Cat's in the Room"); Cibber, The Double Gallant, ed. 1749, p. 58 (Works, 1754, III). "But it seemeth not strange, bicause it is common," says Reginald Scot, "that some man otherwise hardie and stout enough, should not dare to abide or endure the sight of a cat" (xiii, 8, p. 301 [212], ed. Nicholson, p. 245).

45. For the devil as a hare see, for example, Folk-Lore, XII (1901), 74; Bygone Lincolnshire, ed. W. Andrews, 1891, I, 84–85. Cf. County Folk-Lore, V (1908), 53–55 (rabbits or hares as boggarts). On various superstitions with regard to hares see W. G. Black, Folk-Lore Journal, I (1883), 84–90; The Cornish Magazine, II (1899), 267–268; Billson, Folk-Lore, III (1892), 441–466; The Essex Review, V (1896), 159; Hopf, Thierorakel und Orakelthiere, 1888, pp. 66–67; Mélusine, III (1886–87), 265–269; VIII (1896–97), 25–29; Puckett, Folk Beliefs of the Southern Negro, 1926, pp. 472–476.

46. Holkot (died 1349), Super Libros Sapientie, Lectio 190, Reutlingen,

1489, sig. Miiij, lf. 4 r° ("obuiare lepori est malum, et obuiare bufoni signi-
ficat bonum"); Ben Jonson, Tale of a Tub, iv, 3, 18; Beaumont and
Fletcher, Thierry and Theodoret, iv, 1 (Dyce, I, 162); Aubrey, Remaines
of Gentilisne and Judaisme, ed. Britten, 1881, p. 26; Sir Thomas Browne,
Pseudodoxia Epidemica, v, 23, 1 (Works, ed. Wilkin, 1852, II, 79); Burne
and Jackson, Shropshire Folk-Lore, p. 212; Nicholson, Golspie, 1897,
p. 55; County Folk-Lore, IV (1904), 9; Bergen, Animal and Plant Lore,
1899, p. 29; Birlinger, Volksthümliches aus Schwaben, I (1861), 476;
Zeitschrift des Vereins für Volkskunde, V (1895), 411–412. Cf. Transactions Devonshire Association, XXVIII (1896), 95 (rabbit).

47. See p. 166.

48. Ibid.

49. George Henderson, Survivals in Belief among the Celts, 1911, pp.
102–107; Nicholson, Golspie, 1897, pp. 76–78; Rhŷs, Hibbert Lectures
for 1886, pp. 199–200; the Same, Celtic Folklore, 1901, I, 294–296;
Bartsch, Sagen, Märchen und Gebräuche aus Maklenburg, I (1879), 114,
133; Burne and Jackson, Shropshire Folk-Lore, p. 156; H. S. Cowper,
Hawkshead, 1899, pp. 319–320; Proceedings Dorset Natural History and
Antiquarian Field Club, XXXVII (1916), 60; Notes and Queries for
Somerset and Dorset, IV (1895), 77; Folk-Lore, XII (1901), 172.

50. Harsnet, A Declaration of Egregious Popish Impostures, 1603,
p. 111; Bray, Traditions, etc., of Devonshire, 1838, II, 277–278; Walter,
Records, Historical and Antiquarian, of Parishes round Horncastle, 1904,
pp. 214–216; Monk, History of Witney, 1894, p. 53; J. Ll. W. Page, An
Exploration of Exmoor, 4th ed., 1895, p. 309; Blakeborough, Wit, Character, Folklore and Customs of the North Riding of Yorkshire, 2d ed.,
1911, pp. 170–171; Couch, The History of Polperro, 1871, p. 145; Folk-
Lore, IX (1898), 285 (Fife); M. H. Miller, Olde Leeke, 1891, p. 314;
Gregor, The Folk-Lore of the North-East of Scotland, 1881, pp. 128–129;
Henderson, Notes on the Folk-Lore of the Northern Counties, 1879, pp.
201–204; F. W. Mathews, Tales of the Blackdown Borderland, 1923
(Somerset Folk Series, No. 13), pp. 103, 108; Bye-Gones for 1897–98,
p. 209; County Folk-Lore, II (1901), 156; VII (1914), 57–58; The Reli-
quary, XIV (1873–74), pp. 253–254; Lincolnshire Notes and Queries, I
(1889), 248; II (1891), 233–234; Notes and Queries for Somerset and Dorset, III (1893), 3; Warrick, The History of Old Cumnock, 1899, p. 339;
Trotter, Galloway Gossip, 1901, pp. 247–248; W. Wilson, Folk Lore and
Genealogies of Uppermost Nithsdale, 1904, p. 20; Polson, Our Highland
Folklore Heritage, 1926, p. 70; E. Owen, Welsh Folk-Lore, pp. 227–230;
The Cambrian Journal, II (1855), 118; J. C. Davies, Folk-Lore of West
and Mid-Wales, 1911, pp. 242–245; Kristensen, Jyske Folkeminder, VIII
(1886), 261–262; the Same, Danske Sagn, VI, i (1900), 328; VI, ii (1901),
5, 7–8, 33–37, 76–88; Bartsch, Sagen aus Meklenburg, I (1879), 114, 133–
134; Am Urdhs-Brunnen, I (1881–82), 15; MacCulloch, Guernsey Folk
Lore, 1903, pp. 360–361; Sauvé, Le Folk-Lore des Hautes-Vosges, 1889,
pp. 176–177.

51. The Second Examination and Confession of Mother Agnes Waterhouse, 1566, Philobiblon Society reprint, p. 46. She had been a witch for

fifteen years (The End and Last Confession of Mother Waterhouse, 1566, reprint, p. 47). Cf. The Examination and Confession of Certaine Witches at Chensforde, 1566, reprint, p. 26.

52. See pp. 207–209.

53. Document published by Raine, Archæological Journal, XVI (1859), 80–81. Cf. Winstedt, Shaman, Saiva, and Sufi, a Study of the Evolution of Malay Magic, 1925, p. 21 (civet-cat fed with blood from the finger). The witch who was thought to have afflicted Rachel Pindar (1574) was believed to feed a demon with a drop of blood from the forefinger of her left hand (contemporary narrative, The Disclosing of a Late Counterfeyted Possession, sig. Aiiij, lf. 3 v°).

54. Winstedt, as above, pp. 21–22 (house cricket); Talbot, In the Shadow of the Bush, 1912, p. 195 (Nigeria; black butterfly); Karsten, The Civilization of the South American Indians, 1926, pp. 292–293 (venomous insects sent as demons by wizards); Dalyell, The Darker Superstitions of Scotland, 1834, pp. 562–565 (fly, wasp, bee, beetle); Drage, Daimonomageia, 1665, p. 10 (witch as fly enters the body of her victim). In some parts of Scotland moths are called "witches" (Gregor, Folk-Lore of the North-East of Scotland, 1881, p. 147). In 1692 Abraham de la Pryme, himself a student of the occult, enjoyed a conversation with a substantial farmer who had lost a great many cattle by witchcraft. About thirteen years before, the farmer said, he was "with several others set to keep a witch in a room," when "before them all sehe chang'd herself into a beetle or great clock [i.e. cockchafer], and flew out of the chimney, and so escaped" (Diary, ed. Jackson, Surtees Society, LIV, pp. 22–23).

55. For bees see A Tryal of Witches at Bury St. Edmonds, 1664[-5], London, 1682, pp. 26–28 (bee; flies); Drage, Daimonomageia, 1665, pp. 18–19 (witch as bumblebee); York Depositions, ed. Raine (Surtees Society, XL), p. 67 (witch in shape of bee, 1654); Samuel Clarke, A Mirrour or Looking-Glasse both for Saints and Sinners, 2d ed., 1654, p. 462 (1653); Folk-Lore, XI (1900), 438; Walter, Records of Parishes round Horncastle, 1904, p. 216. Cf. A History of the Witches of Renfrewshire, 1809, p. 101 (bumblebee); Henderson, Survivals in Belief among the Celts, 1911, pp. 82–88 (bee-soul; fly); A True and Exact Relation, 1645, p. 21 (hornet); A True Relation, 1645, p. 5 (hornets; wasps). For flies see Gregory of Tours, De Gloria Martyrum, i, 107. Opera, 1699, cols. 843–844 (demon fly); Nider, Formicarius, v, 2, ed. 1516 (1517), fol. lxxii v° (demon as big fly); Remy (Remigius), Daemonolatreia, i, 23, pp. 152–153 (demons as flies); Nashe, Have with You to Saffron-Walden, 1596, Works, ed. McKerrow, III (1905), 37 (fly in a box); Stearne, A Confirmation and Discovery of Witch-craft, 1648, pp. 54–55; Bartholinus, Historiae Anatomicae Rariores, 1654, p. 80 (big fly); Drage, Daimonomageia, 1665, p. 15; Baxter, The Certainty of the Worlds of Spirits, 1691, p. 153 (fly or flea); Glanvil's Sadducismus Triumphatus, 4th ed., 1726, pp. 299–301 (flies, miller); Matthew Mayhew, A Brief Narrative, in Cotton Mather's Magnalia, 1702, Book vi, chap. 6, sect. 1, p. 52 (part of the soul of a person kept imprisoned in the form of a fly by Martha's Vineyard powwaws); Archiv für Kultur-Geschichte, VII (1909), 44 (fly). A Melanesian wizard often

comes as a blowfly to inflict disease (Codrington, The Melanesians, 1891, p. 207).

56. Scot, Dedication, ed. Nicholson, p. ix. Odo of Cheriton (Kent) in a sermon tells about the Carthaginian wizard Cyprian, who kept demons in a box and used to send them "to carry out his business" whenever he liked (Hervieux, Les Fabulistes Latins, IV [1896], 281).

57. Nashe, The Unfortunate Traveller, 1594, Works, ed. McKerrow, II, 233.

58. Wood, Athenae Oxonienses, ed. Bliss, II (1815), 541–545. Cf. Bruce in his ed. of Sir Kenelm Digby, Journal of a Voyage into the Mediterranean (Camden Society), pp. xvii–xix, 95–96.

59. Leycester's Commonwealth, 1641, ed. Burgoyne, 1904, pp. 99–100.

60. Aubrey, Brief Lives, ed. Clark, 1898, I, 26–29.

61. Account of the Manner of the Death of Mr. J. Sharp, in Kirkton, The Secret and True History of the Church of Scotland, ed. Sharpe, 1817, p. 421. Cf. Pitcairn, Criminal Trials in Scotland, 1833, III, 601.

62. Dalyell, The Darker Superstitions of Scotland, 1834, pp. 563–564.

63. Scot, iii, 15, p. 65 (52), ed. Nicholson, p. 51.

64. Scheffer, Lapponia, 1674, pp. 146–148; Fritzner, Historisk Tidsskrift, Kristiania, IV (1877), 188–190; Lid, Maal og Minne, 1921, pp. 46–49.

65. Paulus Diaconus, Historia Lombardica, vi, 6.

66. Eulogium Historiarum, Continuatio, ed. Haydon, III, 417. Cf. Thyraeus, Daemoniaci, 1603, p. 15; the Same, De Apparitionibus (Tractatus Duo, 1600), cap. 9, p. 27 ("Frequentius habitum canis induunt, et serpentis, et hirci, et capri, et araneae").

67. See, for example, Lewin, Die Gifte in der Weltgeschichte, 1920, pp. 13–14, 102, 368, 485, 573; Kittredge, The Old Farmer and his Almanack, 1904, pp. 104–107, 114–120. For the *rubeta* see Aelian, De Natura Animalium, xvii, 12; Pliny, viii, 31, 48, 110; xxv, 10, 76, 123 (cf. xxxii, 5, 18: frogs); Ramesey, Lifes Security, 1665, pp. 226–229.

68. Kittredge, as above, pp. 117–119; H. de Rochas, La Physique Réformée, 1647, p. 475; Digby, The Nature of Bodies, chap. 18, § 8, ed. 1645, p. 203; the Same, Discovrs tovchant la Gverison des Playes par la Poudre de Sympathie, 1658, p. 104 ("l'on porte autour de soy de la poudre des crapeaux ou méme vn crapaut ou arraignée viue, . . . ou de l'arsenic"). Cf. Sussex Archæological Collections, XXXI (1881), 137; Proceedings Dorset Natural History and Antiquarian Field Club, XXXV (1914), 85; Devon Notes and Queries, IV, i (1907), 124; The Essex Review, V (1896), 160 (frog's leg as charm against toothache). For frog-amulets against the evil eye see Elworthy, The Evil Eye, 1895, pp. 308–311, 318–319, 327; Bellucci, Il Feticismo Primitivo in Italia, 1907, pp. 113 –116.

69. Hewett, Nummits and Crummits, 1900, pp. 76–77.

70. Wier, De Praestigiis Daemonum, iii, 36, ed. 1568, p. 335.

71. Brut, ed. Brie, pp. 169–170; Eulogium Historiarum, ed. Haydon, III, 109–111.

72. Cf. Bodin, Demonomanie, ii, 8, ed. 1580, fol. 114 r°. See p. 149, above.

73. For a familiar spirit as a frog see A True and Exact Relation, 1645, p. 34.

74. For a toad in the house taken for a ghost see Saga-Book of the Viking Club, III (1902), 59.

75. A pet guinea pig, which she said was her familiar spirit, was carried about by a professed witch, Kilnsey Nan, ca. 1820 (Cobley, On Foot through Wharfedale, [1882,] pp. 240–241). Cf. Ady, A Candle in the Dark, 1656, p. 135 (pet frog taken for a devil).

76. Strype, The Life of Sir Thomas Smith, 1698, p. 130 (case in 1570); The Norfolk Antiquarian Miscellany, I (1877), 298–299; George Roberts, The History and Antiquities of the Borough of Lyme Regis and Charmouth, 1834, p. 262; Roskoff, Geschichte des Teufels, 1869, I, 346. Cf. Thurnwald, Forschungen auf den Salomo-Inseln und dem Bismarck-Archipel, I (1912), 446.

77. The Examination and Confession of Certaine Wytches at Chensforde, 1566, Philobiblon Society, p. 32; The Second Examination, id., p. 40.

78. Report, in The Triall of Maist. Dorrell, 1599, pp. 92–93. Compare the case of John Chambers, 1645, in Add. MS. 27402, foll. 108 v°–109 r°, and see foll. 110 r°, 114 v°.

79. Folk-Lore Record, II (1879), 207–209.

80. The Antiquary, XLI (1905), 363.

81. P. de l'Ancre, Tableau de l'Inconstance des Mauvais Anges et Demons, 1613, sig. ō.

82. Contemporary narrative, as above (note 53), sig. Aiiij, lf. 4 r°.

83. Folk-Lore, XI (1900), 215.

84. Burne and Jackson, Shropshire Folk-Lore, p. 161.

85. Mathews, Tales of the Blackdown Borderland, p. 107, cf. 103.

86. Bodin, Demonomanie, 1580, iv, 4, fol. 194 v°.

87. A Detection of Damnable Driftes, 1579; Alexander Roberts, A Treatise of Witchcraft, 1616, p. 58; State Trials, II (1816), 1058. See also A Tryal of Witches at Bury St. Edmonds (London, 1682), pp. 5–8 (toad exploded); Marlowe, Legends of the Fenland People, 1926, p. 224 (toad exploded at the fire; witch scorched); Skattegraveren, IX (1888), 239; Ons Volksleven, IX (1897), 14; E. John, Aberglaube, Sitte und Brauch im Sächsischen Erzgebirge, 1909, p. 134; Wuttke-Meyer, p. 117; Folk-Lore, XII (1901), 172; De Cock and Teirlinck, Brabantsch Sagenboek, I (1909), 30. Cf. Guazzo (Guaccius), Compendium Maleficarum, 1608, i, 13, p. 63. For a very curious example of charm and counter-charm (a witch turns a man into a fox and is herself transformed into a toad) see the romance of Walewein, vv. 5694–5755, ed. Jonckbloet, I (1846), 189–191. For toad see also The Disclosing (as in note 53), sig. Av, lf. 2 r°.

88. Croniques de London, ed. Aungier (Camden Society, XXVIII), pp. 3–4.

89. Holkot (died 1349), Super Libros Sapientie, Lectio 190, Reutlingen, 1489, sig. Miiij, lf. 4 r°.

90. See p. 159, above. In Transylvania, if you kill a frog, rain ensues (E. Gerard, The Land Beyond the Forest, New York, 1888, p. 203).

91. See p. 219. Cf. C. K. Sharpe, Historical Account of the Belief in Witchcraft in Scotland, 1884, p. 199 (horse).

92. See p. 232, above. Compare the Jewish story in Blau, Das Altjüdische Zauberwesen, 1898, p. 158: Zeiri bought an ass at Alexandria, but when he wished to water him, the spell dissolved and the ass became a plank. See also Dr. Faustus, chap. 34, Thoms, Early English Prose Romances, 2d ed., 1858, III, 259–260; Prato, La Tradition, V (1891), 360–367; VI (1892), 69–72, 138–142; VII (1893), 295–300; Bladé, Contes Populaires de la Gascogne, 1886, II, 152–157.

93. William of Malmesbury, Gesta Regum, ii, 171, ed. Stubbs, I, 201–202; Matthew Paris, Chronica Majora, ed. Luard, I, 518–519; Flores Historiarum, ed. Luard, I, 567–568; Roger of Wendover, Flores Historiarum, ed. Coxe, I, 485–486; Bromton, Twysden, Scriptores X, col. 940; Radulfus Niger, ed. Anstruther, pp. 155–156; Vincent of Beauvais, Speculum Naturale, iii, 109; Bodin, ed. 1587, ii, 6, fol. 111; Ulrich Molitoris, De Pythonicis Mulieribus, cap. 3 (in 1620 ed. of Malleus, II, 43); A Pleasant Treatise of Witches, 1673, pp. 22–23 (from William). One manuscript of the Flores (Luard, I, 568) cites St. Augustine and the Life of St. Macarius (Acta Sanctorum, January 15, p. 1013). On the popularity of Apuleius in the middle ages see Traube, Munich Academy, Abhandlungen, Philosophisch-Philologische Classe, XIX, 308. He does not mention William's story. Neither does Weinhold, Ueber das Märchen vom Eselmenschen, Berlin Academy, Sitzungsberichte, 1893, pp. 475–488.

94. De Civitate Dei, xviii, 17 (Pliny, viii, 22, 34).

95. De Civitate Dei, xviii, 18. Here also is the story of Prestantius' father transformed into a horse by magic cheese (cf. Cotta, The Infallible True and Assured Witch, 1624, p. 37).

96. Scot, v, 3–5, pp. 94–101 (72–77), ed. Nicholson, pp. 75–80, from Malleus Maleficarum (Pt. II, qu. 2, cap. 4, ed. 1620, pp. 285–286) and Bodin (ed. 1587, ii, 6, fol. 110 v°); A Pleasant Treatise of Witches, 1673, pp. 23–24 (from Malleus).

97. Bolte and Polívka, Anmerkungen zu den Kinder- 1. Hausmärchen der Brüder Grimm, II (1915), 60–69. A witch in Bohemia had a magic halter by means of which she transformed a man into a horse and worked him on her farm; but the tables were turned on her (Deutsche Volkskunde aus dem Oestlichen Böhmen, IX [1909], 61).

98. Ovid, Metamorphoses, viii, 837–865; Crusius in Roscher's Lexikon der Mythologie, I, 1375–1377; Zielinski, Philologus, L (1891), 137–162 (especially pp. 139–140, 144–151).

99. Acta Sanctorum, January 15, I (1643), 1013; An Alphabet of Tales, No. 237, ed. Banks, I (1904), 166. The legend is often cited, as, for example, by Ulrich Molitoris, De Pyrhonicis Mulieribus, cap. 8 (in 1620 ed. of Malleus, II, 60–61), and in Malleus Maleficarum, Part I, qu. 10, ed. 1620, p. 99.

100. Cf. A True and Impartial Relation of the Informations against Three Witches, 1682, p. 19.

101. Giraldus Cambrensis, Topographia Hibernica, ii, 19, Opera, ed. Dimock, V, 106. In the same chapter he tells of Irish werewolves and cites

St. Augustine and his reference to Apuleius. Cf. Kittredge, [Harvard] Studies and Notes in Philology and Literature, VIII (1903), 257–260.

102. See Nyrop, Navnets Magt, 1887.

103. Reginald, Libellus de Admirandis Beati Cuthberti Virtutibus, cap. 15, ed. Raine (Surtees Society, I), pp. 26–28.

CHAPTER XI

MIRRORS AND THIEVES

1. For crystallomancy and mirror magic see, for example, Haberland, Die Spiegel im Glauben und Brauch der Völker, Zeitschrift für Völkerpsychologie, XIII (1882), 324–347; Wm. Jones, Finger-Ring Lore, 1877, 1898, p. 101 (figure); Tuchmann, Mélusine, IV (1888–89), 278–282; Archivio per lo Studio delle Tradizioni Popolari, XVI (1897), 422–431 (hydromancy); Alfonso el Sabio, Las Siete Partidas, vii, 23, 1 (ed. 1807, III, 667); Speculum Morale, Book iii, Part iii, dist. 17 (error for 27), 1493, fol. 190 vº; Étienne de Bourbon, Septem Dona Spiritus Sancti, ed. Lecoy de la Marche, 1877, pp. 317–318; Cardano, De Rerum Varietate, xvi, 93, Opera, III (1663), 325–326; Fortunatus de Grippis, De Superstitione et Vinculis Daemonum, pp. 13–15; Ricardus Argentinus, De Praestigiis et Incantationibus Daemonum et Necromanticorum, 1568, cap. 3, pp. 23–27; Rowlands, The Letting of Humours Blood in the Head-Vaine, 1600, Hunterian Club, p. 60; Giffard, A Dialogue concerning Witches and Witchcraftes, 1593, sigg. D4 vº, E4, F; Wm. Perkins, The Combat betweene Christ and the Devil Displayed, 2d ed., 1606, p. 37 (the visions in the mirror are sent by Satan); Bernard, A Guide to Grand-Iury Men, 2d ed., 1629, p. 134; Bower, Doctor Lamb Revived, 1653, pp. 2–3, 6; Wm. Turner, A Compleat History of the Most Remarkable Providences, 1697, Part I, chap. xi, pp. 59–60; Mr. William Lilly's History of his Life and Times, 2d ed., 1715, pp. 101–103; Archæologia, XL (1866), 396; Hans Sachs, Von Fünff Unhulden, ed. von Keller, V, 286; Wuttke-Meyer, pp. 245–246; Josef Müller, Sagen aus Uri (Schriften der Schweizerischen Gesellschaft für Volkskunde, XVIII), I (1926), 224–225; Notices et Extraits, XIX, i (1862), 221–222 (from Ibn Khaldun, born 1332, died 1406); Mittheilungen der Deutschen Gesellschaft für Natur- und Völkerkunde Ostasiens, VI (1893–97), 28–30 and fig. 43 (China); K. L. Parker, The Euahlayi Tribe, 1905, p. 36 (Australia); Rattray, Ashanti, 1923, p. 163. Much valuable material (with a welter of Freudian psychology) may be found in Géza Róheim, Spiegelzauber, 1919.

2. John Wesley's Journal, July 24, 1761, Standard Edition, IV, 472.

3. Dawson, The Reliquary, XXIII (1882–83), 197–202. See also his History of Skipton, 1882, pp. 390–394.

4. Gervase of Tilbury, Otia Imperialia, i, 17 (Leibnitz, Scriptores Rerum Brunsvicensium, I, 897; Liebrecht, p. 6); Guilielmus Alvernus, De Universo, ii, 2, 35, Opera, 1674, I, 878; Wier, De Praestigiis Daemonum, v, 5, ed. 1568, pp. 460–463; Del Rio, Disquisitiones Magicae, iii, 2, 4, 9, ed. 1616, p. 475; Cardano, De Subtilitate, xix, Opera, III (1663),

655–656; P. de l'Ancre, Le Incredulité et Mescreance du Sortilege, 1622, p. 777; Abt, Die Apologie des Apuleius, pp. 171–177 (245–251), 184–185 (258–259); Alemannia, XVII (1889), 240–241; McBryde, Modern Language Notes, XXI (1906), 182; Purchas his Pilgrimes, Glasgow ed., V (1905), 434; Hopfner, Griechisch-Ägyptischer Offenbarungszauber, I (Studien zur Paläographie und Papyruskunde, ed. Wessely, XXI), 1891, § 846, p. 236; B. M. Papyrus xlvi (fourth century), Kenyon, Greek Papyri in the British Museum, I (1893), 65–67.

5. John of Salisbury, Policraticus, ii, 28, ed. Webb, I, 161.

6. Chaucer, The Parson's Tale, § 37, ed. Skeat, IV, 607. For scapulimancy see Chapter VII, note 44.

7. Le Manuel des Pechiez, vv. 1090–1091; Handlyng Synne, vv. 351–354 (ed. Furnivall, Roxburghe Club, 1862, pp. 12–13). Cf. Bishop Peter Quivil, Modus Exigendi Confessiones (Synod of Exeter, 1287), Wilkins, Concilia, II, 162 (p. 48, above). For "turning the psalter" see pp. 196 ff.

8. John of Salisbury, Policraticus, ii, 28, ed. Webb, I, 164–165.

9. See p. 208.

10. Document printed by Raine, Archæological Journal, XVI (1859), 80.

11. Registrum Radulphi Baldock, ed. Fowler (Canterbury and York Series, VII), I, 144–145.

12. Wilkins, Concilia, III, 394: "Unus lapis de birillo, artificialiter in corio nigro suspensus."

13. Visitations of Religious Houses in the Diocese of Lincoln, ed. Thompson (Canterbury and York Series, XXIV), II, 208–213.

14. Document printed by Raine, Archæological Journal, XIII (1856), 372–374.

15. Hale, pp. 10–11.

16. Lee's petition, Archæologia, LX (1907), 377–378.

17. Hale, p. 84.

18. Cf. Letters and Papers, XIII, i, No. 1383, p. 512: 1538, information about a priest who "said he had for four years dwelt with my Lord Cardinal, and had made him a ring with a stone that he wrought many things with."

19. Ellis, Original Letters, 3d Series, III (1846), 41–42; Letters and Papers, IX, No. 551, p. 182.

20. Statutes of the Realm, III (1817), 837.

21. Wycherley's deposition in J. G. Nichols, Narratives of the Days of the Reformation (Camden Society, LXXVII), pp. 333–334.

22. Scot, xv, 8, 12, 16, pp. 401–407, 411–414, 422–423 (285–289, 293–295, 304–305), ed. Nicholson, pp. 335–340, 344–346, 354–355.

23. A True and Faithful Relation of What Passed for Many Years between Dr. John Dee and some Spirits, 1659.

24. Cuming, Journal of the British Archæological Association, V (1850), 52; Proceedings Society of Antiquaries, 2d Series, XXI (1906–07), 382–383; Horace Walpole's Letters, ed. Toynbee, VIII, 22–23; XII, 145.

25. See, for example, E. W. Lane, Manners and Customs of the Modern Egyptians, I (1837), 365–376; Lefébure, Le Miroir d'Encre dans la Magie Arabe, Revue Africaine, XLIX (1905), 205–227; Doutté, Magie et Religion de l'Afrique du Nord, 1909, pp. 387–394 (water, basin, mirror, sword, ink); Westermarck, Ritual and Belief in Morocco, 1926, I, 353–355 (ink); Lyall, Asiatic Studies, 1882, p. 93 (black paste); The Indian Antiquary, XXXIII (1904), 56; Bompas, Folklore of the Santal Parganas, 1919, p. 419 (oiled leaf); Melland, In Witch-Bound Africa, 1923, p. 225 (water turning black; Northern Rhodesia); E. W. Smith and Dale, The Ila-Speaking Peoples of Northern Rhodesia, 1920, I, 271 (blackened water); P. A. Talbot, The Peoples of Southern Nigeria, 1926, II, 190 (blackened water, etc.); Seligmann, The Melanesians of British New Guinea, 1910, pp. 654–655 (red juice); Gomes, Seventeen Years among the Sea Dyaks of Borneo, 1911, p. 166 (crystal); Am Ur-Quell, N. F., III (1892), 63 (blood on fingernail).

26. Scott's Journal, October 16, 1831, ed. 1890, III, 420–421.

27. Aubrey's Miscellanies, 2d ed., 1721, p. 135; 4th ed., 1857, p. 130. For crystal or beryl see 2d ed., pp. 165–168 (with figure opposite p. 1); 4th ed., pp. 154–157.

28. For thief magic of one sort or another see Middle English versified Herbal, vv. 621–626, ed. Stephens, Archæologia, XXX (1844), 369 (vv. 161–166, ed. Holthausen, Anglia, XVIII [1896], 311; vv. 181–186, ed. Garrett, Anglia, XXXIV [1911], 169); Richard Argentine (Argentinus), De Praestigiis et Incantationibus Daemonum et Necromanticorum, 1568, pp. 180–181; Bernard, A Guide to Grand-Iury Men, 2d ed., 1629, pp. 134–135; Couch, The History of Polperro, 1871, p. 126; Old Yorkshire, ed. by William Smith, IV (1883), 267–269; The Reliquary, VI (1865–66), 14; Transactions Devonshire Association, II (1867–68), 73–74; Bye-Gones for 1876–77, pp. 112, 161–162, 170; for 1878–79, p. 188; for 1905–06, pp. 299–300; Lincolnshire Notes and Queries, II (1891), 143 (figure of thief on wall); Folk-Lore, XV (1904), 80–81; J. Hunter, The Diocese and Priory of Dunkeld, II, 61–65, 67–68; Puckett, Folk Beliefs of the Southern Negro, 1926, pp. 278–282; The Occult Review, XL (1924), 20–21 (Wales); Skattegraveren, X (1888), 102–103; Det Arnamagnæanske Håndskrift Nr. 187, ed. Såby, 1886, p. 97; Kristensen, Danske Sagn, VI, i (1900), 70–71, 78–80, 86–87, 89–91, 271–272, 275, 285, 287–290, 301–303, 323–327; Ohrt, Trylleord (Danmarks Folkeminder, No. 25), 1922, pp. 22–27; Bidrag till Södermanlands Äldre Kulturhistoria, I, iv (1883), 74; Bang, Norske Hexeformularer og Magiske Opskrifter (Videnskabs-sellskabet i Christiania), 1901, pp. 337–338, 363–364, 407–408, 462–463, 468–469, 476, 484, 490, 493, 502–503, 510, 513–514, 532, 536–537, 571–572, 575–576, 580–582, 639–640, 647–686, 756–757; Renvall, Äländsk Folktro, 1890, pp. 35–37 (Nyare Bidrag till Kännedom om de Svenska Lands-målen, VII, No. 9); Svenska Landsmål, 1906, i, p. 22; Hästesko, Motivverzeichnis Westfinnischer Zaubersprüche (FF Communications, II, No. 19), 1914, pp. 55–56; Skrifter utgivna av Svenska Litteratursällskapet i Finland, XVIII (1891), 187; Schönbach, Vienna Sitzungsberichte, Philosophisch-Historische Classe, CXLII (1900), No. 7, p. 149; Ons Volksleven,

X (1898), 133–134; XI (1899), 43–44; Am Ur-Quell, II (1891), 126–127, 185–187; III (1892), 219–220, 232; V (1894), 289–290; Beiträge zur Volkskunde, 1896 (Germanistische Abhandlungen, XII), pp. 114–116, 118; Reiser, Sagen, Gebräuche und Sprichwörter des Allgäus, I (1895), 211–212; Blätter für Pommersche Volkskunde, IV (1896), 119–120, 139–141; V (1897), 56–58; X (1902), 165; Zeitschrift für Oesterreichische Volkskunde, II (1896), 151–153; VI (1900), 118–119; Niederlausitzer Mittheilungen, II (1892), 47–48; VII (1903), 375–376; Schweizerisches Archiv für Volkskunde, I (1897), 232–233; XV (1911), 188; Kleeberger, Volkskundiges aus Fischbach i. d. Pfalz, 1902, pp. 56–58; Zeitschrift des Vereins für Rheinische und Westfälische Volkskunde, II (1905), 298–299; Mitteilungen der Schlesischen Gesellschaft für Volkskunde, IX, ii (1907), 24; John, Sitte, Brauch und Volksglaube im Deutschen Westböhmen, Beiträge zur Deutsch-Böhmischen Volkskunde, VI (1905), 275–278, 299–302, 322–323; Deutsche Volkskunde aus dem Oestlichen Böhmen, IX (1909), 57; Schweizer Volkskunde, II (1912), 10–11; Manz, Volksbrauch und Volksglaube des Sarganserlandes, Schriften der Schweizerischen Gesellschaft für Volkskunde, XII (1916), 114–116; Knuchel, Die Umwandlung, the same, XV (1919), 85–86; B. M. Papyrus xlvi, ll. 172–201, 295–303, Kenyon, Greek Papyri in the British Museum, I (1893), 70–71, 74 (cf. Kuhnert, Rheinisches Museum, XLIX [1894], 38–39); A. Vassiliev, Anecdota Graeco-Byzantina, I (1893), 340–341; Jacoby, Hessische Blätter für Volkskunde, XXV (1927), 200–208; Pseudo-Augustine, Sermon 279, § 4 (Migne, XXXIX, 2272–2273); Bartholomaeus Sibylla, Speculum Peregrinarum Quaestionum, 1493, fol. cclxxi r°; Germania, I (1856), 105–107; XXII (1877), 258; XXVI (1881), 241; XXXI (1886), 346; Haupt's Zeitschrift, XXXV (1891), 248–249; Alemannia, II (1875), 128–129, 131–132, 134–135; XXXI (1903), 184; Wolf, Beiträge zur Deutschen Mythologie, I (1852), 257–258; Wuttke-Meyer, pp. 175–177, 254–255, 413–415; Frischbier, Hexenspruch und Zauberbann, 1870, pp. 111–122; Dieterich, Kleine Schriften, 1911, p. 197; Löwenstimm, Aberglaube und Strafrecht, 1897, pp. 84–92; the Same, Zeitschrift für Socialwissenschaft, VI (1903), 224–227; Archiv für Kriminal-Anthropologie, III (1900), 89–90, 92, 96–97; XIX (1905), 294–295; LVI (1914), 270–273; Seligmann, The Melanesians of British New Guinea, 1910, pp. 133, 182, 654–655; Folk-Lore, XV (1904), 246–248 (Basuto); Thurston, Omens and Superstitions of Southern India, 1912, pp. 270–271, 287–288; Crooke, Religion and Folklore of Northern India, 1926, p. 311; Orde Browne, The Vanishing Tribes of Kenya, 1925, pp. 185–188; Gimlette, Malay Poisons and Charm Cures, 1923, pp. 61–68; I. H. N. Evans, Studies in Religion, etc., in British North Borneo and the Malay Peninsula, 1923, p. 26; Bentley, Pioneering on the Congo, 1900, I, 279; João dos Santos, Ethiopia Oriental, v, 13, ed. 1608, fol. 129 (Purchas his Pilgrimes, Glasgow ed., IX [1905], 254); Westermarck, Ritual and Belief in Morocco, 1926, I, 353, 356; Journal of the Gypsy Lore Society, 2d Series, V (1911–12), 275–276; E. W. Smith and A. M. Dale, The Ila-Speaking Peoples of Northern Rhodesia, 1920, I, 265–267; Alldridge, The Sherbro and its Hinterland, 1901, pp. 162–163; Boyes, A White King in East Africa, 1912, pp. 245–247; Journal Royal

Anthropological Institute, XXIII (1894), 161; XXIV (1895), 44; XXIX (1899), 51–52; XXXVIII (1908), 164–165, 167–168; XLI (1911), 303–304; XLV (1915), 137; XLVII (1917), 157; LV (1925), 231, 262, 263, 462; Panjab Notes and Queries, II (1884–85), 4, 23, 78, 167–168; Purchas his Pilgrimes, XV (1906), 351; Mittheilungen der Deutschen Gesellschaft für Natur- und Völkerkunde Ostasiens, VI (1893–97), 28–29; Lefèvre-Pontalis, Annales du Musée Guimet, XXVI, iv (1900), 102, 104; Mooney, Bureau of Ethnology, 7th Report (for 1885–86), 1891, pp. 386–387; Leland, Gypsy Sorcery, 1891, pp. 85–87, 108–110.

29. See pp. 196–200.

30. Audollent, Defixionum Tabellae, 1904, Nos. 2–4B, pp. 8–12; No. 6, pp. 13–14; Nos. 11–12, pp. 18–19; No. 42, pp. 77–78; Nos. 74–75, pp. 102–104; No. 104, pp. 156–159 (Bath); No. 122, pp. 177–178; No. 212, pp. 283–286.

31. Wier, v, 5, ed. 1568, pp. 463–464; Godelmann, Tractatus de Magis, Veneficis et Lamiis, 1591, i, 5, 7–9, p. 42; A. Taylor, Hessische Blätter für Volkskunde, XXII (1924), 59–63; cf. XII (1913), 139–143. See also Mitteilungen der Schlesischen Gesellschaft für Volkskunde, IX, i (1907), 44–45; Kristensen, Danske Sagn, VI, i (1900), 70–71, 383–389; Bang, Norske Hexeformularer (Videnskabssellskabet i Christiania), 1901, No. 1376, pp. 647–655; Wigström, Folktro ock Sägner, p. 302 (Nyare Bidrag till Kännedom om de Svenska Landsmålen, VIII, No. 3, 1902); Ohrt, Trylleord (Danmarks Folkeminder, No. 25), 1922, pp. 22–24. Cf. Skeat, Malay Magic, 1900, pp. 155, 310; Papyrus xlvi (4th century), Kenyon, Greek Papyri in the British Muesum, I (1893), 67–68; A. Vassiliev, Anecdota Graeco-Byzantina, I (1893), 341; M. Bartels, Die Medicin der Naturvölker, 1923, p. 97, cf. 98–101; Archiv für Religionswissenschaft, XVI (1913), 122–126; XVIII (1915), 585–587; XXI (1922), 485–491. For a witch's curse that makes one lose an eye see Strype, The Life of Sir Thomas Smith, 1698, pp. 131–132; cf. A True and Impartial Relation of the Informations against Three Witches, 1682, p. 25. For a sacrilegious thief struck blind by miracle see Gregory of Tours, De Gloria Martyrum, cap. 66 (Migne, LXXI, 765). In a very interesting charm against a thief (fifteenth century), with directions in English and prayer in Latin, a delineated eye is to be struck out with a copper nail and a copper hammer (Sloane MS. 2721, fol. 137).

32. Archæologia Cambrensis, 3d Series, II (1856), 185; Germania, XXXI (1886), 346. Cf. Wuttke-Meyer, pp. 186–187, 413; Schambach and Müller, Niedersächsische Sagen und Märchen, 1855, pp. 172–173; Bartsch, Sagen, Märchen und Gebräuche aus Meklenburg, II (1880), 334; Strackerjan, Aberglaube und Sagen aus dem Herzogtum Oldenburg, 2d ed., 1909, I, 122–123; Knoop, Volkssagen aus dem Oestlichen Hinterpommern, 1885, p. 169; Am Ur-Quell, II (1891), 125–126; III (1892), 200; Zeitschrift der Gesellschaft für die Geschichte der Herzogthümer Schleswig, Holstein und Lauenburg, III (1873), 135–140; Merker, Die Masai, 1904, p. 254; Hobley, Bantu Beliefs and Magic, 1922, p. 171. Cf. Panjab Notes and Queries, II (1884–85), 4, 23; Ivens, Melanesians of the South-East Solomon Islands, 1927, p. 268; W. J. V. Saville, In Unknown New

Guinea, 1926, pp. 269–270; M. H. Bradley, Caravans and Cannibals, 1927, pp. 71–72.

33. See p. 129.

34. Dawson, History of Skipton, 1882, pp. 392–393; The Reliquary, XXIII (1883), 198.

35. Scot, xii, 17, pp. 260–266 (188–192), ed. Nicholson, pp. 211–216. He is largely indebted to Wier, v, 5–6 (ed. 1568, pp. 460–467).

36. Reliquiae Antiquae, 1845, I, 260; Henslowe's Diary, ed. Greg, p. 33; Coulton, Social Life in Britain, 1918, p. 527. Cf. Bang, Norske Hexeformularer, 1901, Nos. 1091, 1109, 1172, 1173, pp. 484, 490, 513–514. See also Sloane MS. 2628, foll. 10 v°, 51 r° (the latter is like Henslowe).

37. See Wülker, Bibliothek der Angelsächsischen Poesie, I, 323–325; McBryde, Modern Language Notes, XXI (1906), 180–183; Grendon, Journal of American Folk-Lore, XXII (1909), 168–169, 178–187, 206–207, 218, 221–223, 224, 234; Skemp, Modern Language Review, VI (1911), 298–299.

38. (1) Leechdoms, ed. Cockayne, I, 390–393 (practically identical with III, 60). (2) I, 392. (3) III, 286–289; McBryde, p. 181. (4) McBryde, p. 181 (cf. a seventeenth-century charm, p. 182). For a twelfth-century English charm against thieves see Priebsch, Modern Language Review, XVII (1922), 81.

39. Rituale Ecclesiae Dunelmensis, ed. Stevenson (Surtees Society, X), p. 119.

40. Leechdoms, I, 384.

41. Leechdoms, III, 58; Leonhardi, Kleinere Angelsächsische Denkmäler, I (1905), 145.

42. Leechdoms, I, 396, 397.

43. An English protective charm against thieves (ca. 1450) is eminently religious (Ein Mittelenglisches Medizinbuch, ed. Heinrich, 1896, p. 170). Modernized: "Carmen contra latrones. In Bethlehem God was born. Between two beasts to rest he was laid. In that place was neither thief nor man, but the Holy Trinity. That same God that there was born defend our bodies and our chattels from thieves and all manner of mischiefs and harms wherever we wend, by land, by water, by night or by day, by tide or by time! Amen." This is a fuller version of a vernacular formula in Leechdoms, I, 390, and III, 60. See a seventeenth-century English version in Sloane MS. 2628, fol. 6 r° (cf. fol. 46).

44. Compare a similar case in Gregory of Tours, vii, 44. See also Giraldus Cambrensis, Itinerarium Kambriae, i, 2, Opera, ed. Dimock, VI, 94–95.

45. Magna Vita S. Hugonis, v, 8, ed. Dimock, pp. 267–269.

46. John of Salisbury, Policraticus, ii, 28, ed. Webb. I, 161.

47. Robert of Brunne, Handlyng Synne, vv. 339–354, ed. Furnivall (Roxburghe Club), 1862, pp. 12–13. The French does not mention lost goods, but it does specify divination by "turning the psalter," which was often used for the detection of a thief.

48. Registrum Radulphi Baldock, ed. Fowler (Canterbury and York Series, VII), I, 144–145.

49. Royal MS. 15. Axx (ca. 1400), ed. M. R. James, English Historical Review, XXXVII (1922), 420–421.

50. See pp. 187–189, above.

51. Letter-Book H, fol. cxliii (Riley, Memorials of London, pp. 462–463; R. R. Sharpe, Calendar of Letter-Books, H, p. 181).

52. Foxe, Acts and Monuments, ed. 1583, II, 43 ("Ex Regist. Longland, fol. 50").

53. Modus Exigendi Confessiones, Synod of Exeter, Wilkins, Concilia, II, 162. Cf. Glyde, The Norfolk Garland, p. 13 (love divination); P. Massé, De l'Imposture et Tromperie des Diables, 1579, i, 8, fol. 32 (names written on slips of paper and put into holy water: see also Wallonia, I [1893], 150); Hessische Blätter für Volkskunde, XXV (1927), 203–208; Sloane MS. 121, fol. 36 v°, and 2721, fol. 137 r° (both of fifteenth century).

54. The Connoisseur, No. 56, I (1755), 331–336. See Burne and Jackson, Shropshire Folk-Lore, p. 179. Cf. Roscoe, The Banyankole, 1923, p. 29; M. H. Bradley, Caravans and Cannibals, 1927, p. 67.

55. Letter-Book H, fol. clv (Riley, pp. 472–473; Sharpe, p. 198).

56. Registrum Radulphi Baldock, ed. Fowler (Canterbury and York Series, VII), I, 144–145.

57. Letter-Book H, fol. clx (Riley, pp. 475–476; Sharpe, p. 207).

58. The same, fol. cxlv (Riley, pp. 464–466; Sharpe, p. 184). For the whetstone see Riley, pp. 316, 353, 423, 432, 477, 493, 497, 584; Hall's Satires, iv, 6, ed. Singer, 1824, p. 115 and note; Harington, Nugae Antiquae, ed. Park, 1804, II, 240; Summer's Last Will and Testament, Collier's Dodsley, IX, 24; Hazlitt, English Proverbs, 1869, pp. 156, 489 (1907, pp. 181, 497, 560).

59. Walsingham, Historia Anglicana, ed. Riley, II, 63; Holinshed, II (1807), 754.

60. Letter-Book H, fol. ccxlviii (Riley, pp. 518–519; Sharpe, p. 351).

61. Town Clerk's proclamation, Sharpe, Calendar of Letter-Books, I, 196–197.

62. Paule's petition, Martin, Archæologia, LX (1907), 371–372. Fereby's answer (pp. 372–373) naturally tells a different story; it ignores the necromancers.

63. Petition, Archæologia, LX, 377.

64. Hale, p. 63.

65. For the similar iudicium in psalterio see A. Franz, Die Kirchlichen Benediktionen, 1909, II, 362–364, 391–392; Zeumer, Formulae Aevi Merowingici et Karolini, 1886 (Monumenta, Leges, Section V), pp. 636–637; Patetta, Le Ordalie, 1890, pp. 216–217. Compare the ordeal of the suspended bread (Zeumer, pp. 630–632; Sloane MS. 3846, fol. 27 v°).

66. Le Manuel des Pechiez, v. 1090, ed. Furnivall (Roxburghe Club), 1862, p. 12.

67. Hale, p. 61.

68. Scot, xvi, 5, pp. 477–478 (344), ed. Nicholson, pp. 401–402. Cf. Del Rio, Disquisitiones Magicae, lib. iv, cap. 2, qu. 6, sect. 4, § 12, ed. 1616, p. 545; Brand's Popular Antiquities, ed. Hazlitt, 1870, III, 302–303. See note 79.

69. Hale, p. 61.

70. Document printed by Raine, Archæological Journal, XVI (1859), 81.

71. Lincoln Episcopal Visitations, Peacock, Archæologia, XLVIII (1885), 262.

72. Cf. p. 167, above.

73. J. G. Nichols, Narratives of the Days of the Reformation (Camden Society, LXXVII), p. 332.

74. See Patriche's Complaint and Information, with Lamkyn's answer, summarized by W. J. Hardy, The Antiquary, XXI (1890), 4–6; other answers in G. W. Macdonald's Historical Notes of the Parish of Holbeach, 1890, pp. 104–106, cf. pp. 163–164.

75. Historical MSS. Commission, Various Collections, VII, 53.

76. J. C. Cox, Churchwardens' Accounts, 1913, p. 320.

77. Giffard, A Dialogue concerning Witches and Witchcraftes, 1593, sig. E3 v°.

78. For the seventeenth century see, for example, Dalyell, The Darker Superstitions of Scotland, 1834, p. 522 (1617); Records of the Borough of Leicester, ed. Stocks, IV (1923), 210 (1624); County Folk-Lore, VII (1914), 116–117 (1646); William Ross, Aberdour and Inchcolme, 1885, pp. 335–336 (1669, 1678); Dunton, The Athenian Mercury, October 16, 1694, Vol. XV, No. 13; Gaspar Schott, Magia Universalis, 1677, IV, 557–558.

79. Mackie, Norfolk Annals, II (1901), 156; The East Anglian, III (1869), 21–22; Henderson, 1879, pp. 235–236; Burne and Jackson, Shropshire Folk-Lore, pp. 173–174; Folk-Lore Journal, I (1883), 333; Bye-Gones for 1882–83, p. 194; Journal of the British Archæological Association, XLVIII (1892), 48–49. Cf. Notes and Queries, 1st Series, I (1850), 412. For further modern evidence see Bray, Traditions, etc., of Devonshire, 1838, II, 294; Mortimer M. Thompson, The Witches of New York, 1859, pp. 300–303; Saga-Book of the Viking Club, III (1902–04), 54; James Napier, Notes and Reminiscences relating to Partick, 1875, pp. 199–201; Trotter, Galloway Gossip, 1901, pp. 129–130; Hewett, Nummits and Crummits, 1900, p. 24; Bergen, Current Superstitions, 1896, p. 144 (Labrador); Transactions Glasgow Archæological Society, I (1868), 392–393 (theft or love); Folk-Lore Journal, II (1884), 380–381; Bye-Gones for 1888, p. 78; Folk-Lore, VI (1895), 118 (to detect a witch); VII (1896), 145 (Lesbos); Transactions Cumberland and Westmorland Archæological Society, XIV (1897), 374 (malice or mischief); Cowper, Hawkshead, 1899, pp. 317–318; Wuttke-Meyer, pp. 254–255; A. Baumgarten, Aus der Volksmässigen Ueberlieferung der Heimat, Linz, 1864, II, 10; Grohmann, Aberglaube und Gebräuche aus Böhmen und Mähren, 1864, p. 204; Mannhardt, Die Praktischen Folgen des Aberglaubens, 1878, pp. 25–26; Frischbier, Hexenspruch und Zauberbann, 1870, pp. 118–119; Bartsch, Sagen, Märchen und Gebräuche aus Meklenburg, II (1880), 333–334; Baltische Studien, XXXVI (1886), 336–337; Am Ur-Quell, I (1890), 47; II (1891), 126, 203; Niederlausitzer Mittheilungen, II (1892), 153; Blätter für Pommersche Volkskunde, IV (1896), 120; Zeitschrift für

Oesterreichische Volkskunde, VI (1900), 118; Alemannia, XXXVII (1909), 16; E. H. Meyer, Badisches Volksleben, 1900, p. 567; Huss, Von Aberglauben, Beiträge zur Deutsch-Böhmischen Volkskunde, IX, ii (1910), 24 (with figure); Archiv für Strafrecht, LXII (1916), 456 (to detect witch); Dykstra, Uit Friesland's Volksleven, II, 170–171; Kristensen, Danske Sagn, VI, i (1900), 389–391; Bang, Norske Hexeformularer, 1901, pp. 581, 582; H. J. Bell, Obeah, 2d ed., 1893, pp. 66–67 (West Indies).

80. Dunton, The Athenian Mercury, Vol. IV, No. 22 (1691); Forby, The Vocabulary of East Anglia, 1830, II, 398–399 (love or theft); Glyde, The New Suffolk Garland, 1866, p. 176 (Canticles, viii, 6–7); Henderson, Notes on the Folk-Lore of the Northern Counties, 2d ed., 1879, pp. 236–237; Northall, English Folk-Rhymes, 1892, p. 124; Addy, Household Tales, 1895, p. 74 (Ruth, i, 16, or Canticles, viii, 7); Peacock, A Vocabulary of Words used in the Wapentakes of Manley and Corringham, 1877, p. 23 (love, theft, strayed cattle); County Folk-Lore, I, No. 3 (1895), p. 58 (Canticles, viii, 7); V (1908), 140; Saga-Book of the Viking Club, III (1902), 54 (love or theft); Proceedings Dorset Natural History and Antiquarian Field Club, XIII (1892), 55; Folk-Lore, XXIV (1913), 80; XXXV (1924), 352; Bergen, Current Superstitions, 1896, p. 41 (Canticles, vi, 3); J. C. Davies, Folk-Lore of West and Mid-Wales, 1911, pp. 13–14; Trotter, Galloway Gossip, 1901, p. 130.

81. Henderson, 1879, p. 235; Bye-Gones for 1882–83, p. 194; Burne and Jackson, Shropshire Folk-Lore, pp. 173–174; Folk-Lore Journal, I (1883), 333.

82. Folk-Lore, XVI (1905), 169–170.

83. Wier, ii, 12, ed. 1568, pp. 176–177. See also P. Massé, De l'Imposture et Tromperie des Diables, 1579, i, 6 and 9, foll. 25 v°–26 r°, 35 r°; Bodin, Demonomanie, ii, 1, ed. 1587, fol. 59; Godelmann, Tractatus de Magis, Veneficis et Lamiis, 1591, i, 5, 19, pp. 45–46; Peucer, Commentarius, De Praecipuis Divinationum Generibus, 1593, p. 321; Lercheimer (Witekind), Christlich Bedencken vnd Erinnerung von Zauberey, 1597, ed. Binz, 1888, p. 17; Gaule, Select Cases of Conscience touching Witchcrafts, 1646, p. 76; Del Rio, Disquisitiones Magicae, lib. iv, cap. 2, qu. 6, sect. 4, § 9, ed. 1616, p. 544; Prætorius, De Coscinomantia, 1677 (with a discussion of all manner of divining); Gaspar Schott, Magia Universalis, 1677, IV, 556–557; Henry More, Antidote against Atheism, 1653, p. 109 ("that ordinary way of Divination which they call *Coskinomancy*"); Increase Mather, An Essay for the Recording of Illustrious Providences, 1684, p. 287; Dunton, The Athenian Mercury, October 16, 1694, Vol. XV, No. 13; Brockett, A Glossary of English North Country Words, 1825, p. 174; G. Roberts, The Social History of the People of the Southern Counties, 1856, p. 532; John Hunter, The Diocese and Priory of Dunkeld, I, 101; Brand's Popular Antiquities, ed. Hazlitt, 1870, III, 301–303; Scheible's Kloster, III (1846), 621–622 (with figure); Wuttke-Meyer, p. 255; Am Ur-Quell, II (1891), 126; Zeitschrift für Oesterreichische Volkskunde, II (1896), 319; VI (1900), 118; Huss, Von Aberglauben, Beiträge zur Deutsch-Böhmischen Volkskunde, IX, ii (1910), 24–25 (with figure); Deutsche Volkskunde aus dem Oestlichen Böhmen,

V (1905), 39; Grohmann, Aberglaube und Gebräuche aus Böhmen und Mähren, 1864, p. 204; Baltische Studien, XXXVI (1886), 336; Fritzner, Historisk Tidsskrift, Kristiania, IV (1877), 192–194; Kristensen, Danske Sagn, VI, i (1900), 389–391; Skattegraveren, V (1886), 204; X (1888), 33; Bang, Norske Hexeformularer, 1901, pp. 580–582; Wallonia, I (1893), 149; Fehrle, Archiv für Religionswissenschaft, XIX (1919), 547–551 (cf. Marmorstein, the same, XXI [1922], 235–238).

84. Hale, p. 139.

85. J. G. Nichols, Narratives of the Days of the Reformation (Camden Society, LXXVII), p. 334. Cf. Baumgarten, Aus der Volksmässigen Ueberlieferung der Heimat, Linz, 1864, II, 10; Giambattista Basile (journal), II (1884), 41.

86. Raine, Depositions from the Castle of York (Surtees Society, XL), p. 82, note. Cf. Notes and Queries, 8th Series, II (1892), 305; Henderson, Notes on the Folk-Lore of the Northern Counties, 1879, p. 236; Journal of American Folk-Lore, XXXI (1918), 140; Puckett, Folk Beliefs of the Southern Negro, 1926, pp. 280–282.

87. Scot, xii, 17, p. 262 (189), ed. Nicholson, p. 213; cf. xvi, 5, pp. 477–478 (344), ed. Nicholson, pp. 401–402; Aubrey, Remaines of Gentilisme and Judaisme, ed. Britten, 1881, p. 25. Cf. Henderson, 1879, p. 236; H. J. Bell, Obeah, 2d ed., 1893, p. 64.

88. Worcester County Records, Calendar of Quarter Sessions Papers (Worcestershire Record Society), I, 492; Historical MSS. Commission, Various Collections, I, 307.

89. William Ross, Aberdour and Inchcolme, 1885, pp. 335–336 (1678); Northall, English Folk-Rhymes, 1892, p. 124.

90. Durham Depositions, ed. Raine, pp. 251–252. See the same for 1567 (p. 84), ca. 1570 (p. 117); for 1598 see York Depositions, ed. Raine, p. 82, note; for 1602 see Goudie, The Diary of the Rev. John Mill (Scottish History Society, V), 1889, pp. 185–187; for 1603, 1604, 1619, and 1641 see Dalyell, p. 521; for 1669 see William Ross, Aberdour and Inchcolme, 1885, p. 334. Cf. George Giffard, A Discourse of the Subtill Practises of Deuilles by Witches and Sorcerers, 1587, sig. G v°: "The charmer often times knoeth no deuil; but with his charme of words he can catch rattes, and burst snakes, take away the paine of the tooth ache, with a paire of sheares and a siue, find out a theife." Cf. the Same, A Dialogue concerning Witches and Witchcraftes, 1593, sig. F4 v°. See also Bodin, De la Demonomanie des Sorciers, ii, 1, fol. 59; iii, 5 (ed. 1587, foll. 163 [misprinted 273] v°–164 [misprinted 264] r°); Thomas Brattle, Letter, 1692 (Burr, Narratives of the Witchcraft Cases 1648–1706, 1914, p. 181); Bernard, A Guide to Grand-Iury Men, 2d ed., 1629, pp. 208–209 (to discover a witch); Gaule, Select Cases of Conscience touching Witches and Witchcrafts, 1646, p. 76; Increase Mather, An Essay for the Recording of Illustrious Providences, 1684, p. 287; Brand-Hazlitt, III, 301–302.

91. Holyday, Τεχνογαμια or The Marriage of the Seven Arts, ii, 3, 1st ed., 1618, sigg. G2–G3. Cf. Folk-Lore, XXXV (1925), 254.

92. Cotton Mather, The Wonders of the Invisible World, Boston, 1693, pp. 66–67; the Same, Late Memorable Providences, 2d Impression, London, 1691, p. 117. For a New England seer in the lost-and-stolen line see President Stiles's account of Mr. Stafford of Tiverton, who died in 1773 (Literary Diary, ed. Dexter, 1901, I, 386). See also Daniel Webster, Defence of the Kennistons (1817), Works, 1851, V, 455, cf. 443.

93. Gurdon, The Khasis, 2d ed., 1914, p. 119; Melland, In Witch-Bound Africa, 1923, pp. 227–230; Codrington, The Melanesians, 1891, pp. 211–212, 223; Skeat, Malay Magic, 1900, pp. 536–542. Cf. Hilton-Simpson, Land and Peoples of the Kasai, 1911, pp. 210–211, 329–330; Stack, The Mikirs, 1908, p. 35; The Indian Antiquary, XIV (1885), 131; XV (1886), 327; XXXIII (1904), 58 (Ceylon); Panjab Notes and Queries, II (1884–85), 114; Gouldsburg and Sheane, The Great Plateau of Northern Rhodesia, 1911, p. 92; E. W. Smith and A. M. Dale, The Ila-speaking Peoples of Northern Rhodesia, 1920, I, 268–269; Ivens, Melanesians of the South-East Solomon Islands, 1927, pp. 346–347; Journal (Royal) Anthropological Institute, XXXII (1902), 326; LIII (1923), 73–74; Mooney, 7th Report, Bureau of Ethnology, 1921, pp. 386–387 (Cherokees).

94. Theocritus, iii, 31; Aelian, De Natura Animalium, viii, 5; Artemidorus, Oneirocritica, ii, 69; Lucian, Alexander, 9; Philippides in Pollux, Onomasticon, vii, 188 (Meineke, Fragmenta, IV [1841], 478).

95. Halliwell, Popular Rhymes and Nursery Tales, 1849, p. 207. For further examples of spells and rites to "bind" thieves, see Hollingsworth, The History of Stowmarket, 1894, p. 247 (thief wanders round and round); F. Hancock, Parish of Selworthy, 1897, p. 243 (magic bag in chimney; thief cannot pass house); Cowper, Hawkshead, 1899, pp. 313–314 (thief is to find himself on rooftree of church during morning service); The Eastern Counties Collectanea, ed. L'Estrange, 1872–73, p. 29; Folk-Lore, XXI (1910), 377–378; Baumgarten, Aus der Volksmässigen Ueberlieferung der Heimat, Linz, 1864, II, 5–9; Kristensen, Danske Sagn, VI, i (1900), 265, 287, 290–291, 293, 305, 329, 331; cf. pp. 263–266; Bang, Norske Hexeformularer, 1901, pp. 337, 363–364, 462–463, 510, 532, 756–757; Zeitschrift für Oesterreichische Volkskunde, II (1896), 151–152; IV (1898), 265–266; Wuttke-Meyer, p. 413; Am Ur-Quell, II (1891), 125–126, 185–187; V (1894), 289; Zeitschrift für Volkskunde, I (1889), 346; IV (1892), 259; Kleeberger, Volkskundiges aus Fischbach i.d. Pfalz, 1902, pp. 56–57; Bartsch, Sagen, Märchen und Gebräuche aus Meklenburg, II (1880), 335–341; Blätter für Pommersche Volkskunde, IV (1896), 158–160, 169–170; V (1897), 57; Strackerjan, Aberglaube und Sagen aus dem Herzogtum Oldenburg, 2d ed., 1909, I, 119–122; Mélusine, III (1886–87), 110; Reiser, Sagen, Gebräuche und Sprichwörter des Allgäus, I (1895), 209; Manz, Volksbrauch und Volksglaube des Sarganserlandes, Schriften der Schweizerischen Gesellschaft für Volkskunde, XII (1916), 114–115; Jegerlehner, Sagen aus dem Unterwallis, the same, VI (1909), 15, 132–133 (thief died), 178; the Same, Sagen und Märchen aus dem Oberwallis, the same, IX (1913), 98; Josef Müller, Sagen aus Uri, I (1926), 233–236, the same, XVIII; Schweizerisches Archiv für Volks-

kunde, XIV (1910), 253–254; XVI (1911), 116; Festschrift Louis Gauchat, 1926, p. 426; Zeitschrift des Vereins für Rheinische und Westfälische
Volkskunde, I (1904), 151, 300–301; VIII (1911), 147–148; IX (1912),
155; Archiv für Kriminal-Anthropologie, III (1900), 92, 97; XIX (1905),
294–295; Grohmann, Aberglaube und Gebräuche aus Böhmen und
Mähren, 1864, pp. 202–204; Dunger, Rundâs und Reimsprüche aus dem
Vogtlande, 1876, pp. 283–284; Baltische Studien, XXXVI (1886), 219–
227; Knoop, Volkssagen aus dem Oestlichen Hinterpommern, 1885,
p. 170; Szulczewski, Allerhand Fahrendes Volk in Kujawien, 1906, pp. 27–
28; Alemannia, II (1875), 128; XVI (1888), 55–56; Germania, I (1856),
106–107; XXXVI (1891), 404; Gredt, Sagenschatz des Luxemburger
Landes, 1883, p. 569; E. H. Meyer, Badisches Volksleben, 1900, p. 566;
P. A. Talbot, The Peoples of Southern Nigeria, 1926, II, 181; Ivens,
Melanesians of the South-East Solomon Islands, 1927, pp. 358–359;
Rantasalo, Der Ackerbau, IV (1924), 140–158 (FF Communications,
XVII, No. 55); Rivista delle Tradizioni Popolari Italiane, I (1893–94),
935 (binding a witch). See also Sloane MS. 3846, foll. 26 r°–27 r°.

96. Gregory, Dialogi, iii, 22, ed. Moricca, 1924, pp. 190–191. Cf. Ons
Volksleven, III (1891), 76, 112.

97. Reginald, Libellus de Admirandis Beati Cuthberti Virtutibus,
capp. 71, 80, ed. Raine (Surtees Society, I), pp. 145–146, 165–168; cf.
cap. 81, pp. 168–172.

98. Chronicon Abbatiae de Evesham, ed. Macray, pp. 55–56.

99. Acta Sanctorum, July, VII, 214.

100. Giraldus Cambrensis, Gemma Ecclesiastica, i, 32, Opera, ed.
Brewer, II, 104–105. Cf. Caesarius of Heisterbach, ix, 6 (ed. Strange,
1851, II, 171), of a wicked priest who could not get out of his church.

101. Giraldus Cambrensis, Itinerarium Kambriae, i, 2, Opera, VI,
23–24. For similar marvels see VI, 24–25. Compare the tale of the
sacrilegious husband and wife in Le Manuel des Pechiez, 6836–6869
(Handlyng Synne, 8939–8978), ed. Furnivall (Roxburghe Club), 1862,
pp. 277–278. See also Ælfric, Homilies, ed. Thorpe, II (1846), 508, and
Lives of Saints, ed. Skeat, II (1900), 280–283 (miracles of St. Martin).

102. The Tale of the Basyn, ed. Wright, 1836; Jamieson, Popular
Ballads, 1806, I, 272–282; Hartshorne, Ancient Metrical Tales, 1829,
pp. 198–208; Hazlitt, Early Popular Poetry, 1866, III, 42–53; Neumeister,
Der Verzauberte Topf, 1906. Cf. Dorsey, Traditions of the Osage (Field
Columbian Museum, Anthropological Series, VII), 1904, pp. 24–25.

103. Κρυπτάδια, II (1884), 62–67; Bladé, Contes Populaires de la
Gascogne, 1886, III, 65–70; W. P. Greenough, Canadian Folk-Life and
Folk-Lore, 1897, pp. 52–56. Cf. Grimm, No. 64 (Die Goldne Gans), with
Bolte and Polívka's Anmerkungen, II (1915), 39–44, 495.

104. Kristensen, Danske Sagn, VI, i (1900), 378–382; cf. 282, 283, 294.

105. Cf. Agrippa, De Occulta Philosophia, i, 40, ed. 1533, p. xxxvi
(misprint for xlvi); Guazzo (Guaccius), Compendium Maleficarum, 1608,
i, 8, p. 28; i, 13, p. 63; Blefken, Islandia, 1607, p. 32; Lercheimer (Witekind), Christlich Bedencken vnd Erinnerung von Zauberey, 1597, ed.
Binz, 1888, p. 47; João dos Santos, Ethiopia Oriental, v, 13, ed. 1608, fol.

128; Purchas his Pilgrimes, Glasgow ed., IX (1905), 254; Chau Ju-kua, transl. Hirth and Rockhill, 1911, p. 131; Cordier, Ser Marco Polo, 1920, pp. 121–122; Davies, Folk-Lore of West and Mid-Wales, 1911, pp. 236–237; Kristensen, Danske Sagn, VI, i (1900), 330. Cf. p. 161, above.

106. Helgakviða Hundingsbana II, sts. 32–33, Bugge, Norrœn Forn-kvæði, 1867, p. 197.

107. Von Wilamowitz-Moellendorff, in the Göttingen Nachrichten, 1895, pp. 217–223; J. F. Campbell, Popular Tales of the West Highlands, II (1860), 170; J. G. Campbell, The Fians, 1891, p. 74; P. Kennedy, Legendary Fictions of the Irish Celts, 1866, p. 208; Curtin, Myths and Folk-Lore of Ireland, 1890, pp. 223, 290, 300–301; Göngu-Hrólfs Saga, cap. 6, Ásmundarson, Fornaldarsögur Norðrlanda, III (1889), 157; Fornaldar Sögur, ed. Rafn, III (1830), 253. See Bolte and Polívka, Anmerkungen zu den Kinder- u. Hausmärchen, II (1915), 163–189.

108. Tallqvist, Die Assyrische Beschwörungsserie Maqlû, pp. 54–55; Pliny, xxviii, 2, 3, 13; Anania, De Natura Daemonum, 1581, pp. 206–207; Ælfric, Homilies, ed. Thorpe, II (1846), 486; A True and Iust Recorde, of the Information [etc.] of all the Witches, taken at S. Oses (London, 1582), sigg. C4, lf. 3 v°; D4, lf. 4 r°; A Tryal of Witches at Bury St. Edmonds, 1664 (London, 1682), pp. 48–51 (cart). Cf. Samuel Clarke, A Mirrour or Looking-Glasse both for Saints and Sinners, 2d ed., 1654, p. 213; J. M. Taylor, The Witch Delusion in Colonial Connecticut, pp. 64–65; Add. MS. 27402, fol. 109 v° (1645).

109. Harper's New Monthly Magazine, October, 1903, LXXXVII, 796 (Norfolk); Ditchfield, The Parson's Pleasance, p. 190; Saga-Book of the Viking Club, III (1902–04), 47–48; County Folk-Lore, II (1901), 60; Edmondston and Saxby, The Home of a Naturalist, 2d ed., 1889, p. 124; Lincolnshire Notes and Queries, I (1889), 249; Salopian Shreds and Patches, V (1883), 207; Burne and Jackson, Shropshire Folk-Lore, pp. 152–154; Christopher Marlowe, Legends of the Fenland People, 1926, pp. 223, 225; Durbin, A Narrative of some Extraordinary Things, 1800, pp. 21, 38–39, 41–42; Nicholson, Folk Lore of East Yorkshire, 1890, pp. 94–95; Blakeborough, Wit, Character, etc., of the North Riding of Yorkshire, 2d ed., 1911, pp. 177–178; Addy, Household Tales, 1895, pp. 45–46; Sussex Archæological Collections, XIII (1861), 219; Gregor, The Horse in Scottish Folk Lore, 1890, p. 5; Dick, Highways and Byways in Galloway and Carrick, 1916, p. 371; MacCulloch, Guernsey Folk Lore, 1903, p. 353; Whittier, The Supernaturalism of New England, 1847, p. 51; Kristensen, Danske Sagn, VI, i (1900), 69, 133–136; VI, ii (1901), 7; Bang, Norske Hexeformularer, 1901, pp. 166, 168–169, 363–364, 462–463, 510, 532, 756–757; Wuttke-Meyer, pp. 159, 267; Witzschel, Sagen, Sitten und Gebräuche aus Thüringen (Kleine Beiträge, II), 1878, pp. 290–291; A. Baumgarten, Aus der Volksmässigen Ueberlieferung der Heimat, Linz, 1864, II, 3–5; E. Meier, Deutsche Sagen, Sitten und Gebräuche aus Schwaben, 1852, pp. 199–200; Josef Müller, Sagen aus Uri (Schriften der Schweizerischen Gesellschaft für Volkskunde, XVIII), I (1926), 230–233; Rheinische Geschichtsblätter, II (1896), 156–157; John, Sitte, Brauch und Volksglaube im Deutschen Westböhmen, Beiträge zur Deutsch-

Böhmischen Volkskunde, VI (1905), 310–311; Korrespondenzblatt des Vereins für Siebenbürgische Landeskunde, XXII (1899), 35; E. H. Meyer, Badisches Volksleben, 1900, pp. 557–558; Ons Volksleven, IV (1892), 50–51, 103–104; Wallonia, X (1902), 182. Cf. Thiers, Traité des Superstitions, 1741, I, 431; Sauvé, Le Folk-Lore des Hautes-Vosges, 1889, p. 202; Volkskunde, XXIV (1913), 142–149, 207–209; Storaker, Historisk Tidsskrift, Christiania, I (1871), 464–465; Baltische Studien, XXXVI (1886), 179; Zeitschrift für Deutsche Philologie, XXXVIII (1906), 366; Alemannia, XIX (1892), 137–138; XXVII (1900), 106; Gredt, Sagenschatz des Luxemburger Landes, 1883, p. 557.

110. See, for example, Hálfdanar Saga Brönufóstra, chap. 12, Asmundarson, Fornaldarsögur, III (1889), 453; Campbell, Popular Tales of the West Highlands, II (1860), 265 (cf. I, 215); P. W. Joyce, Old Celtic Romances, 1879, p. 237 (cf. pp. 193, 376); Celtic Magazine, XII (1887), 512; Nicholson, Golspie, 1897, pp. 21–23; Kroeber, Cheyenne Tales, Journal of American Folk-Lore, XIII (1900), 184; Rua, Novelle del Mambriano, 1888, p. 99; Prato, Zeitschrift für Volkskunde, I (1889), 113; Revue Celtique, V (1881–83), 232, note 1; Mabinogion transl. by Loth, 1889, I, 106–107 (2d ed., 1913, I, 160–161); MacDougall, Folk and Hero Tales, 1891, pp. 164–165; MacManus, In Chimney Corners, 1899, pp. 95–98, 108–109; H. Parker, Village Folk-Tales of Ceylon, III (1914), 65–67, 69–70; Callaway, Nursery Tales of the Zulus, 1868, p. 189; Boas, Bulletin Bureau of American Ethnology, XXVII (1902), 95; The Tempest, i, 2, 466.

111. Bede, Historia Ecclesiastica, iv, 22 (20); Ælfric's Homilies, ed. Thorpe, II (1846), 358 (*drycræft, runstafas*); Robert of Brunne, Handlyng Synne, vv. 10510–10705, ed. Furnivall (Roxburghe Club), 1862, pp. 324–330; Gregory, Dialogi, iv, 59, ed. Moricca, 1924, p. 320 (repeated in Le Manuel des Pechiez, vv. 7535–7552, ed. Furnivall, pp. 326–327). Bede mentions "litteras solutorias, de qualibus fabulae ferunt." For bonds loosed by miracle see Ælfric, ed. Thorpe, II, 414 (cf. Acts, v, 17–23). For loosing spells see Sloane MS. 2628, foll. 7 v°, 13 v°–14 r°, 35 v°, 36 r°.

112. Judges, viii, 33; ix, 46; Wier, i, 10, ed. 1568, p. 61; Scot, xv, 2, p. 384 (271), ed. Nicholson, p. 319.

113. Continuation of Chronicon Girardi de Fracheto (Recueil, XXI, 60–61); Chroniques de Saint-Denis (Recueil, XX, 711–712; cf. XXI, 680, note 3); Lea, A History of the Inquisition, 1888, III, 454–455.

CHAPTER XII

Treasure Trove

1. William of Malmesbury, Gesta Regum Anglorum, ii, 170, ed. Stubbs, I, 198–201; Matthew Paris, Chronica Majora, ed. Luard, I, 478–479; Eulogium Historiarum, ed. Haydon, I, 396–400; Flores Historiarum, ed. Luard, I, 526; Radulfus Niger, ed. Anstruther (Caxton Society), p. 155.
2. Leland, Itinerary, ed. L. Toulmin Smith, V, 85; Wm. Phelps, The

History and Antiquities of Somersetshire, Historical Introduction (appended to Vol. II), pp. 99-100.

3. J. W. Collins, Journal British Archæological Association, XIII (1857), 296-297.

4. La Estoire de Seint Aedward le Rei, vv. 934-961, ed. Luard, Lives of Edward the Confessor, pp. 51-52.

5. Odo of Cheriton, Herbert, Catalogue of Romances, III (1910), 70.

6. Legend of Fulk Fitz-Warin, in Stephenson's ed. of Radulphus de Coggeshall, pp. 280-286. Cf. Gull-Þoris Saga, end.

7. Walsingham, Historia Anglicana, ed. Riley, I, 264; Monk of St. Albans, ed. Thompson, p. 18.

8. Saxo Grammaticus, ii, pp. 61-63 Müller and Velschow (pp. 38-39 Holder). Cf. Jente, Die Mythologischen Ausdrücke im Altenglischen Wortschatz (Anglistische Forschungen, ed. Hoops, LVI), 1921, pp. 132-136. For a variety of uncanny creatures guarding treasure (ghosts, demons, serpents, dragons, toads, etc.) see Notes and Queries, 1st Series, XII (1855), 487; County Folk-Lore, V (1908), 339; Folk-Lore, XVII (1906), 412-414; Bye-Gones for 1899-1900, p. 489; Sussex Archæological Collections, LXVI (1925), 235; Trevelyan, Folk-Lore and Folk-Stories of Wales, 1909, pp. 141-149; Kristensen, Danske Sagn, I (1892), 369-391; III (1895), 447, 454-460; von Sydow, Troldesagn og Dunkel Tale (Danmarks Folkeminder, No. 17), 1917, pp. 103-115; Rosén, Folkminnen och Folktankar, V (1918), 107-108; Mannhardt, Germanische Mythen, 1858, pp. 149-153; Rochholz, Schweizersagen aus dem Aargau, 1856, II, 49-50; Birlinger, Volksthümliches aus Schwaben, I (1861), 86; Lütolf, Sagen, Bräuche und Legenden aus den Fünf Orten, 1865, pp. 315, 350; Calmet, Traité sur les Apparitions, 1751, I, 269-284; Herbert of Torre, De Miraculis, iii, 33, Migne, CLXXXV, 1378-1379 (ed. Chifflet, pp. 385-386); The Indian Antiquary, XLV (1916), Supplement (Barnett), p. 2; Crooke, Religion and Folklore of Northern India, 1926, pp. 217-218; Panjab Notes and Queries, I (1883-84), 135-136; II (1884-85), 41-43.

9. Rituale Ecclesiae Dunelmensis, ed. Lindelöf (Surtees Society, CXL), pp. 97-98: "sint libera ab omni inpugnatione fantasmatica." The last word is glossed by the Anglo-Saxon scinlacvm. See also A. Franz, Die Kirchlichen Benediktionen, 1909, I, 621-623.

10. Azo of Bologna, the celebrated civilian of the fourteenth century, lays down the principle that, if a man finds treasure in his own ground, it belongs to him unless he has used art magic in the discovery; in that case it belongs to the fiscus (Select Passages from the Works of Bracton and Azo, ed. Maitland, Selden Society, VIII [1894], 128; cf. Bodin, Demonomanie, ed. 1587, fol. 151 r°). This is a variation on the law in Justinian's Institutes (ii, 1, 39), which makes no mention of magic.

11. Boyle, The General History of the Air, Works, ed. Birch, 1744, V, 197. See also, for example, Wier, De Praestigiis Daemonum, i, 20, ed. 1568, pp. 110-111; Anania, De Natura Daemonum, 1581, pp. 190-193; Nashe, Pierce Penilesse, 1592, Works, ed. McKerrow, I, 231-232; Kircher, Mundus Subterraneus, viii, 4, 3d ed., 1678, II, 122-124; Garmann, De Miraculis Mortuorum, 1709, i, 3, 27, p. 122; ii, 10, 140, p. 795; Georgius

Agricola, De Re Metallica, vi, 1556, pp. 173–174; the Same, De Animantibus Subterraneis, cap. 37, 1614, pp. 77–79; Hallywell, Melampronoea, 1681, p. 61; Lewis Morris, Gentleman's Magazine, July, 1795, LXV, ii, 559–560; Keys[s]ler's Travels, III (1757), 377; Hunt, Popular Romances of the West of England, 1865, II, 118–122; Bottrell, Traditions and Hearthside Stories of West Cornwall, I (1870), 74–76; II (1873), 185–190; Hammond, A Cornish Parish, 1897, pp. 359–360; Courtney, Cornish Feasts and Folk-Lore, 1890, pp. 128–129; The Cornish Magazine, II (1899), 267–273; Bye-Gones for 1876–77, p. 161; for 1907–08, p. 294; E. M. Wright, Rustic Speech and Folk-Lore, 1913, pp. 199–200; Folk-Lore, VII (1896), 371; J. C. Davies, Folk-Lore of West and Mid-Wales, 1911, pp. 136–138; Revue des Traditions Populaires, II (1887), 57–58, 410–417, 472–474; III (1888), 498bis–502; V (1890), 531–533; VI (1891), 487; Wuttke-Meyer, p. 47; Mélusine, III (1886–87), 469–470; Crooke, Religion and Folklore of Northern India, 1926, p. 218.

12. Cf. Peacock, Archæologia, XLVIII (1885), 254.

13. 33 Henry VIII, chap. 8, Statutes of the Realm, III (1817), 837. For hill-digging see Jessopp, Random Roaming, 1894, pp. 84–121; Transactions Shropshire Archæological and Natural History Society, 3d Series, III (1903), 349–350 (1574); Harsnet, A Declaration of Egregious Popish Impostures, 1603, pp. 13–14 (1584); Diary of William Whiteway, October 2, 1621, Proceedings Dorset Natural History and Antiquarian Field Club, XIII (1892), 61; Bye-Gones for 1891–92, p. 339 (ca. 1630); Notes and Queries for Somerset and Dorset, XV (1917), 257–258 (1662); Transactions Shropshire Archæological and Natural History Society, 3d Series, III (1903), 348–350 (1669); Journal of the British Archæological Association, New Series, IX (1903), 8–32. Cf. Kristensen, Danske Sagn, I (1892), 355–391; III (1895), 419–491; Josef Müller, Sagen aus Uri (Schriften der Schweizerischen Gesellschaft für Volkskunde, XVIII), I (1926), 261–302.

14. See p. 282, above.

15. The Antiquary, XLII (1906), 46–51. See also Archivio per lo Studio delle Tradizioni Popolari, XVII (1898), 113; Hellwig, Verbrechen und Aberglaube, 1908, pp. 108–110; E. Thurston, Omens and Superstitions of Southern India, 1912, pp. 215–220. For candles made of human tallow see p. 144, above.

16. Löwenstimm, Zeitschrift für Socialwissenschaft, VI (1903), 215–216.

17. Jessopp, Random Roaming, 1894, pp. 109–112. For the sacrifice of a cock in treasure-digging see The Indian Antiquary, XXXIX (1910), 224. Cf. pp. 93–94, above.

18. Historical MSS. Commission, MSS. at Hatfield House, V, 81–83. See the cases of Agnes Hancok in 1438 and Joan Tyrrye in 1555 (pp. 145–146, 254, above); cf. p. 215.

19. Bye-Gones for 1907–08, pp. 5, 22; W. T. Palmer, Odd Yarns of English Lakeland, 1914, pp. 71–72; County Folk-Lore, II (1901), 19. Cf. Wilkinson and Tattersall, Memories of Hurstwood, 1899, pp. 56–57; Trevelyan, Folk-Lore and Folk-Stories of Wales, 1909, p. 153; J. C. Davies, Folk-Lore of West and Mid-Wales, 1911, p. 179; Baumgarten,

Aus der Volksmässigen Ueberlieferung der Heimat, Linz, 1864, II, 43; Zeitschrift für Volkskunde, III (1891), 186; Jegerlehner, Sagen und Märchen aus dem Oberwallis, Schriften der Schweizerischen Gesellschaft für Volkskunde, IX (1913), 80; Revue des Traditions Populaires, VI (1891), 280–282, 284–287, 403; VIII (1893), 422.

20. Bye-Gones for 1907–08, p. 42 (Wales). Cf. Baumgarten, II, 42–43; Köhler, Kleinere Schriften, III (1900), 581–582; von Schulenburg, Wendische Volkssagen und Gebräuche, 1880, p. 184; Schambach and Müller, Niedersächsische Sagen und Märchen, 1855, pp. 152–154; Kristensen, Danske Sagn, VI, i (1900), 255–256; Revue des Traditions Populaires, VI (1891), 279, 282–283, 285.

21. S. G. Drake, Annals of Witchcraft in New England, 1869, pp. 156–157; A. F. Moulton, Some Descendants of John Moulton and William Moulton, [1893,] p. 18; Whittier, The Supernaturalism of New England, 1847, p. 31. See also Mixer, Old Houses of New England, 1927, p. 200. For stories of this kind see Bolte and Polívka, Anmerkungen zu den Kinder- u. Hausmärchen der Brüder Grimm, III (1918), 421–423; Seymour, Irish Witchcraft and Demonology, 1913, pp. 132–134 (cf. p. 83).

22. See in general A. Wünsche, Der Sagenkreis vom Geprellten Teufel, 1905. Cf. Henderson, The Folk-Lore of the Northern Counties, 1879, p. 279; Archæologia Cambrensis, 6th Series, XIX (1919), 538–540; Bolte and Polívka, III, 355–364; Bolte, Zeitschrift des Vereins für Volkskunde, VIII (1898), 21–25; Hackman, Skrifter utgivna av Svenska Litteratursällskapet i Finland, CLXV (1922), 140–170; Aarne, Finnische Märchenvarianten (FF Communications, I, No. 5), 1911, Nos. 1000–1199, pp. 79–114; the same (V, No. 33), 1920, Nos. 1000–1191, pp. 22–26; the Same, Estnische Märchen- und Sagenvarianten (III, No. 25), 1918, Nos. 1000–1192, pp. 64–79; Hackman, Katalog der Märchen der Finnländischen Schweden (I, No. 6), 1911, Nos. 1000–1182, pp. 18–22; De Meyer, Les Contes Populaires de la Flandre (VII, No. 37), 1921, Nos. 1002–1184, pp. 60–62; Christiansen, The Norwegian Fairytales (XII, No. 46), 1922, Nos. 1000–1185, pp. 32–34.

23. Parsons, Proceedings Cambridge Antiquarian Society, XIX (1915), 37–38 (from Bishop Gray's Register).

24. Cf. Mr. William Lilly's History of his Life and Times, 2d ed., 1715, pp. 32–33. See p. 158, above.

25. Original record from the Archiepiscopal Register of York, Raine, Archæological Journal, XVI (1859), 71–81.

26. Documents, Norwich Archæology, I (1847), 50–57. Cf. Jessopp, Random Roaming, 1894, pp. 103–109.

27. Peacock, Archæologia, XLVIII (1885), 255–256.

28. The letter is not dated, but the narrative begins in the 19th year of Henry VIII (1527–28), and Wolsey died on November 29, 1530.

29. Stapleton's letter to Wolsey, Norfolk Archæology, I (1847), 57–64, cf. 220, note.

30. Cf. Wier, i, 4, ed. 1568, p. 41; Scot, p. 519 (372), ed. Nicholson, p. 435.

31. Durbin, A Narrative of some Extraordinary Things, 1800, pp. 54–55.

32. The same, p. 29. *"Malchi* (that is, *my King*)" was a familiar spirit of Thomas Perkes of Mangotsfield. Perkes's devils wore him out at last: "They appeared faster than he desired, and in most dismal shapes, like serpents, lions, bears, &c. hissing and roaring, and attempting to throw spears and balls of fire at him." So he told the Rev. Arthur Bedford, whose letter of August 2, 1703, is appended to Durbin's Narrative (p. 59).

33. See p. 64, above.

34. Letters and Papers, Henry VIII, XIII, i, No. 41, p. 13.

35. See p. 189, above.

36. Deposition (MS. Lansdowne 2, art. 26), J. G. Nichols, Narratives of the Days of the Reformation (Camden Society, LXXVI), pp. 334–335.

37. "Wyth a screpture on hys brest for coungerynge": Chronicle of the Grey Friars, ed. Nichols (Camden Society, LIII), p. 63. I am confident of the identification. Wycherley lived in Charterhouse Lane, and his examination took place in August, 1549. For examples of later treasure-quests see: — 1570: Hart, Archæologia, XL (1866), 391–394. — 1572: T. Wright, Queen Elizabeth and her Times, 1838, I, 441–442. — 1573: Wright, I, 457–459 (Earl of Shrewsbury to Lord Burghley, January 20, 1572 [–3]); Lodge, Illustrations of British History, 2d ed., 1838, II, 3–5 (Shrewsbury to the Privy Council, Feb. 1, 1572 [–3]); the same, II, 4–5 (Sir Thomas Smith to Shrewsbury, February 17, 1572 [–3]); Strype, Life of Sir Thomas Smith, 1698, pp. 170–173; the Same, Annals of the Reformation, II (1725), 181–182. — 1574: pardon to Thomas Heather for invocation and conjuration (in 1573) to gain great sums of money (Rymer, Foedera, 2d ed., XV, 730). — 1580: Holinshed, IV (1808), 433; Stow, ed. 1631, p. 688. — 1589: Wright, II, 397–398. — 1591: The Essex Review, XVI (1907), 68–71. — 1595: Historical MSS. Commission, MSS. at Hatfield House, V, 81–83. — Ca. 1600: Calendar of State Papers, Domestic, 1598–1601, p. 523. — 1611: Calendar, as above, 1611–1618, p. 29. — 1692: Historical MSS. Commission, Various Collections, I, 160.

38. Add. MS. 27402, foll. 120 v°, 121 v°, 111 v°.

39. Pseudo-Paracelsus, De Summis Naturae Mysteriis, transl. Dorn, 1584, pp. 60–66 (Of the Supreme Mysteries of Nature, transl. R. Turner, 1655, pp. 64–70). Cf. Archivio per lo Studio delle Tradizioni Popolari, XX (1901), 323–329, 540–550. Whoever wishes to acquire money by means of the spirits Sathan, Barentur, and Barbason, may find the formula in Sloane MS. 3846, foll. 27 v°–29 r°.

40. Blau, Das Altjüdische Zauberwesen, 1898, p. 59, note.

41. Grillando, De Sortilegiis, iii, 12, ed. 1592, p. 24.

42. See Iamblichus, De Mysteriis, ii, 10, and iii, 31 (ed. Parthey, 1857, pp. 91, 177); Arnobius, iv, 12; Lobeck, Aglaophamus, p. 58.

43. See F. B. Bond, The Gate of Remembrance, the Story of the Psychological Experiment which Resulted in the Discovery of the Edgar Chapel at Glastonbury (Oxford, 1918).

CHAPTER XIII

HAUNTED HOUSES AND HAUNTED MEN

1. Plot, The Natural History of Oxford-shire, 1677, viii, 37–45, pp. 206–210; E. Marshall, The Early History of Woodstock Manor, 1873, pp. 204–205.

2. The Kingdoms Intelligencer, April 20–27, 1663, pp. 257–261; Glanvil, Palpable Evidence of Spirits and Witchcraft, 1668; the Same, Sadducismus Triumphatus, 4th ed., 1726, pp. 270–285; A Wonder of Wonders (ballad), Rollins, The Pack of Autolycus, 1927, pp. 114–121. Cf. John Wesley's Journal, May 25, 1768, Standard Edition, V, 266; Webster, The Displaying of Supposed Witchcraft, 1677, p. 11; Hudibras, ii, 1, 131–132; Oldham, Satyrs upon the Jesuits, iv, 5th ed., 1697, p. 78; Bovet, Pandaemonium, 1684, p. 61; H. Addington Bruce, Historic Ghosts and Ghost Hunters, 1905, pp. 15–35.

3. Diary of Abraham de la Pryme, ed. Jackson (Surtees Society, LIV), 1870, pp. 39–42, 45.

4. Richard Chamberlaine, Lithobolia, 1698; reprinted in The Historical Magazine, V (1861), 321–327, and by Burr, Narratives of the Witchcraft Cases 1648–1706, pp. 58–77.

5. Southey, Life of John Wesley, New York, 1847, I, 64–68, 412–435; H. Addington Bruce, Historic Ghosts and Ghost Hunters, pp. 36–55. For a variety of examples see Nider, Formicarius, v, 2, ed. 1516 (1517), foll. lxxi v°–lxxiii v°; Binsfeld, De Confessionibus Maleficorum et Sagarum, 1591, pp. 83–99; York Depositions, ed. Raine, p. 74 (1656); Strange and Wonderful News from Yowel in Surry, 1681; Increase Mather, An Essay for the Recording of Illustrious Providences, 1684, pp. 142–167; Glanvil's Sadducismus Triumphatus, 4th ed., 1726, pp. 361–380, 412–420, 429–439; Baxter, The Certainty of the Worlds of Spirits, 1691, passim; Beaumont, An Historical, Physiological and Theological Treatise of Spirits, 1705, pp. 306–312; An Exact Narrative of Many Surprizing Matters of Fact, 1709; New England Historical and Genealogical Register, XXXII (1878), 134 (1724); Malcolm, Anecdotes of the Manners and Customs of London during the Eighteenth Century, 2d ed., 1810, I, 376–382 (1772), 402 (1716); County Folk-Lore, VI (1912), 51; W. V. Ingram, An Authenticated History of the Famous Bell Witch, 1924, pp. 236–241; P. de l'Ancre, L'Incredulité et Mescreance du Sortilege, 1622, pp. 817–818; Andrew Lang, Cock Lane and Common Sense, 1894, pp. 127–179; Flammarion, Haunted Houses, 1924; Summers, The Geography of Witchcraft, 1927, pp. 263–286. For a recent American case see the New York Herald, August 27, 1908.

6. William Hayley's narrative, Sussex Archæological Collections, XVIII (1866), 111–113.

7. Cf. J. C. Davies, Folk-Lore of West and Mid-Wales, 1911, pp. 150–152; H. J. Bell, Obeah, 2d ed., 1893, pp. 93–97; Journal of the Burma Research Society, II (1912), 45–47.

8. Annales Fuldenses, Recueil, VII, 168. This case was known to Cotton Mather (The Wonders of the Invisible World, Boston, 1693, p. 61).

9. Giraldus Cambrensis, Itinerarium Kambriae, i, 12, Opera, ed. Dimock, VI, 93.

10. Wright and Halliwell, Reliquiae Antiquae, 1845, I, 53. For vervain and St. John's wort as *fuga daemonum*, see pp. 119–122, above.

11. Leechdoms, ed. Cockayne, II, 342; ed. Leonhardi, I 104: "If thou hast it on thee and under thy pillow and over the doors of thy house, no devil can harm thee, within or without." Cf. Cockayne, I, 174–177, 248, 328–331; Klemming, Läke- och Örte-Böcker, 1883–86, p. 438.

12. Cf. Cockayne, I, 70, 176, 248, 350 (*scinlac*), 360, 364; Det Arnamagnæanske Håndskrift Nr. 187 (Dansk Lægebog), ed. Såby, 1886, p. 48.

13. The midday demon (δαιμόνιον μεσημβρινόν) appears in the Septuagint version of Psalm xci, 6, for "the destruction that wasteth at noonday." So also in the Vulgate (*daemonium meridianum*). Cf. Henry Howard, Earl of Northumberland, A Defensative against the Poyson of Supposed Prophecies, 1583, sig. Yij v°; Pitrè, Usi e Costumi, Credenze e Pregiudizi del Popolo Siciliano (Biblioteca, XVII), 1889, IV, 33, 98–100. Cf. J. W. Wolf, Deutsche Märchen und Sagen, 1845, pp. 239, 318–321; the Same, Hessische Sagen, 1853, pp. 32–34; Panzer, Beiträge zur Deutschen Mythologie, II (1855), 107; Grässe, Der Sagenschatz des Königreichs Sachsen, 1874, II, 187–188; U. Jahn, Volkssagen aus Pommern und Rügen, 1886, pp. 142–143.

14. Rituale Ecclesiae Dunelmensis, ed. Stevenson (Surtees Society, X), p. 129 (cf. pp. 117–118); see also Revue des Langues Romanes, V (1874), 105. For an interesting essay by G. Hübener on "Beowulf und Nordische Dämonenaustreibung" see Englische Studien, LXII (1928), 293–327.

15. See Jente, Die Mythologischen Ausdrücke im Altenglischen Wortschatz, 1921, pp. 177–179.

16. Grimm, Deutsche Mythologie, 4th ed., I, 391–392; III, 137–138; E. H. Meyer, Germanische Mythologie, 1891, pp. 118–119, 121, 132, 138–139, 232, 249; Golther, Handbuch der Germanischen Mythologie, 1895, pp. 157–158; Child, The English and Scottish Popular Ballads, I, 67, 73, 86, 466–467; II, 458, 464, 470, 472; IV, 494; V, 239, 285. The adjective *bilewit* occurs in Anglo-Saxon, but without mythological significance: see Jente, as above, p. 166.

17. For such exchange see Kittredge, The Friar's Lantern and Friar Rush, Publications Modern Language Association, XV (1900), 430–432. For house-cobolds, serviceable or mischievous or both, see Roscher, Ephialtes, pp. 74–75; Guilielmus Alvernus, De Universo, ii, 3, 8, Opera, Paris, 1674, I, 1030; Georgius Agricola, De Animantibus Subterraneis, cap. 37, 1614, p. 79; Guazzo, Compendium Maleficarum, 1608, i, 18, pp. 89–90; Prätorius, Anthropodemus Plutonicus, Part I, 1666, pp. 359–378; Erasmus Francisci, Der Höllische Proteus, 2d ed., 1695, chap. 75, pp. 790–800; Calmet, Traité sur les Apparitions des Esprits, 1751, I, 243–269, cf. I, 305–321; Henderson, Notes on the Folk-Lore of the Northern Counties, 1879, pp. 246–280; Burne and Jackson, Shropshire Folk-Lore,

pp. 45-51; Addy, Household Tales, 1895, pp. 39-40; Archæologia, XVII (1814), 144; Gomme, Folk-Lore Relics of Early Village Life, 1883, pp. 72-123; Transactions of the Devonshire Association, X (1878), pp. 100-101; Lincolnshire Notes and Queries, II (1891), 146; Folk-Lore, VIII (1897), 68-69; XII (1901), 73; County Folk-Lore, II (1901), 132, 133; Wilkinson and Tattersall, Memories of Hurstwood, 1889, pp. 62-63; E. M. Wright, Rustic Speech and Folk-Lore, 1913, pp. 201-202; H. S. Cowper, Hawkshead, 1899, pp. 307, 309; Bye-Gones for 1876-77, p. 43; Transactions Lancashire and Cheshire Antiquarian Society, XXV (1907), 69-70; J. G. Campbell, Superstitions of the Highlands and Islands of Scotland, 1900, pp. 155-194; the Same, Witchcraft and Second Sight, 1902, pp. 217-220; Papers of the Manchester Literary Club, VI (1880), 278-283; Harland and Wilkinson, Lancashire Folk-Lore, 1867, pp. 56-59; Henderson, The Norse Influence on Celtic Scotland, 1910, pp. 79-84; Proceedings Society of Antiquaries of Scotland, XXXIV (1900), 328-330; Bosquet, La Normandie Romanesque, 1845, pp. 126-134; Sébillot, Traditions et Superstitions de la Haute-Bretagne, 1882, I, 129-137; Chapiseau, Le Folk-Lore de la Beauce et du Perche, 1902, I, 248-250; Wuttke-Meyer, 1900, pp. 43-46; Haag, Baltische Studien, XXXII (1882), 187-192; Journal Anthropological Institute, V (1876), 420-422; Zeitschrift für Volkskunde, I (1889), 74-78; Holmberg, Finno-Ugric, Mythology of All Races, ed. J. A. MacCulloch, IV (1927), 163, 166.

18. See pp. 145-146, 206, 254.

19. Transactions Devonshire Association, XXXVII (1905), 112; Hammond, A Cornish Parish, 1897, pp. 360-361. Cf. Bray, Traditions, etc., of Devonshire, 1836, I, 168-169, 175, 182-183; Leechdoms, ed. Cockayne, II, 290 (ed. Leonhardi, I, 88).

20. J. Ll. W. Page, An Exploration of Exmoor, 4th ed., 1895, p. 308; The Antiquary, VI (1882), 210; Folk-Lore, XXVI (1915), 195-196 (Guernsey). Cf. Lucian, Philopseudes, 20. See p. 21, above.

21. Bray, I, 183; Bye-Gones for 1878-79, p. 299, cf. 348; F. Hancock, The Parish of Selworthy, Somerset, 1897, p. 248; The East Anglian, III (1869), 22; E. M. Wright, Rustic Speech and Folk-Lore, 1913, p. 201; Whittier, Supernaturalism of New England, 1847, p. 52; Cross, Studies in Philology (University of North Carolina), XVI (1919), 276; Abbott, Macedonian Folklore, 1903, p. 144. Cf. J. C. Davies, Folk-Lore of West and Mid-Wales, 1911, p. 189; John Hunter, The Diocese and Priory of Dunkeld, II, 59-60; Maclagan. Evil Eye in the Western Highlands, 1902, pp. 43-44, 131; Wentz, The Fairy-Faith in Celtic Countries, 1911, p. 183; Hessische Blätter für Volkskunde, XX (1921), 22-23; Kristensen, Danske Sagn, II (1893), 487-488, 490; Dania, II (1892-94), 227; Krauss, Slavische Volkforschungen, 1908, p. 71; Holmberg, Finno-Ugric, The Mythology of All Races, ed. J. A. MacCulloch, IV (1927), 186.

22. Diary of Abraham de la Pryme, June 27, 1695, ed. Jackson (Surtees Society, LIV), pp. 63-64. For witches and wizards as Will-o'-the-Wisps see Tauxier, Le Noir de Bondoukou, 1921, p. 195. Cf. Puckett, Folk Beliefs of the Southern Negro, 1926, pp. 133-136.

23. Radulphus de Coggeshall, Chronicon Anglicanum, ed. Stevenson,

pp. 120–121. Cf. pp. 134–135 for mysterious visitors to the Abbey of Coggeshall: they had caps of invisibility.

24. Cf. Champier, Dyalogus in Magicarum Artium Destructionem, ca. 1500, iii, 1, sig. bij, lf. 4 v°.

25. Giraldus Cambrensis, Itinerarium Kambriae, Opera, ed. Dimock, VI, 96–99.

26. John of Worcester, ed. Weaver, Anecdota Oxoniensia, XIII (1908), 46–48 (Thorpe's ed. of Florence of Worcester, II, 102–105); Gervase of Canterbury, ed. Stubbs, I, 102–103.

27. Stationers' Registers, ed. Arber, I, 389.

28. Laneham's Letter, 1575, ed. Furnivall, Captain Cox (Ballad Society), 1871, p. 30.

29. Scot, A Discourse upon Divels and Spirits, chap. 21, Discoverie, 1584, p. 522 (374), ed. Nicholson, p. 438.

30. Trithemius, Chronicon Monasterii Hirsaugiensis, ed. 1559, pp. 160–162. Cf. Kittredge, Publications Modern Language Association, XV (1900), 415, note; Anz, Jahrbuch des Vereins für Niederdeutsche Sprachforschung, XXIV (1899), 76–112; Priebsch, Prager Deutsche Studien, VIII (1908), 423–434; Danske Studier, 1912, pp. 15–17.

31. Gammer Gurton's Needle, iii, 2, ed. Manly, Specimens of the Pre-Shaksperean Drama, II (1900), 123; ed. Bradley, Gayley's Representative Comedies, I (1903), 231.

32. Poetria Magistri Johannis Anglici de Arte Prosayca, Metrica, et Rithmica, ed. Mari, Romanische Forschungen, XIII (1902), 916–917. Cf. Hauréau, Notices et Extraits, XXVII, ii, 83–84; Paetow, Morale Scolarium (Memoirs University of California, IV), 1927, pp. 126–127.

33. Le Roux de Lincey, Le Livre des Légendes, 1836, pp. 251–257.

34. Freymond, Artus' Kampf mit dem Katzenungetüm (Beiträge zur Romanischen Philologie, Festgabe für Gustav Gröber, 1899, pp. 311–396); Lot, Romania, XXX (1901), 7; Skene, The Four Ancient Books of Wales, 1868, II, 460–461; Loth, Les Mabinogion, 1889, II, 249 (2d ed., 1913, II, 272); Kittredge, A Study of Gawain and the Green Knight, 1916, p. 171; the Same, [Harvard] Studies and Notes, VIII (1903), 259; J. D. Bruce, The Evolution of Arthurian Romance (Hesperia, ed. Bright), 1923, I, 41, note 9, 147.

35. Froissart, ed. Kervyn de Lettenhove, XI, 192–201; Henry Howard, Earl of Northampton, A Defensative against the Poyson of Supposed Prophecies, 1583, sig. Yiii, lf. 2 v°; A Pleasant Treatise of Witches, 1673, pp. 49–52.

36. Froissart, XI, 200–201.

37. Guilielmus Alvernus, De Universo, ii, 3, 8, Opera, 1674, I, 1030. For further references see Kittredge, Publications Modern Language Association, XV (1900), 436, note 3. Add Nider, Formicarius, v, 2, ed. 1517 (1516), fol. lxxiii r°; Doctor Lamb's Darling, 1653, p. 6; Bower, Doctor Lamb Revived, 1653, p. 17; Glanvil, Sadducismus Triumphatus, 4th ed., 1726, p. 318; Henry More, An Antidote against Atheism, iii, 9, Philosophical Writings, 4th ed., 1712, p. 116; Ancient Town Records (New Haven), ed. Dexter, I (1917), 251; Increase Mather, Illustrious Provi-

dences, 1684, pp. 149–151; Bovet, Pandaemonium, 1684, pp. 222–225; Baxter, The Certainty of the Worlds of Spirits, 1691, pp. 69–70; Cotton Mather, Memorable Providences, 1691, p. 16; Durbin, A Narrative of some Extraordinary Things, 1800, pp. 10, 35–40, 42; Harland and Wilkinson, Lancashire Folk-Lore, 1867, p. 61; Pitcairn, Criminal Trials in Scotland, 1833, II, 525; E. M. Wright, Rustic Speech and Folk-Lore, 1913, pp. 192–193; Flammarion, Haunted Houses, 1924, pp. 115, 119, 292; Ingram, An Authenticated History of the Famous Bell Witch, 1924, p. 238; County Folk-Lore, II (1901), 109; Folk-Lore, XII (1901), 73; Basile, Pentamerone, i, 2, ed. 1674, p. 34; iii, 7, p. 351; Kristensen, Danske Sagn, V (1897), 528; VI, i (1900), 148, 209; Archivio per lo Studio delle Tradizioni Popolari, XVIII (1899), 459–460; Skrifter utgivna av Svenska Litteratursällskapet i Finland, XVIII (1891), 209.

38. Roxburghe Ballads, ed. Chappell, II (1874), 84. Cf. Harman, A Caveat for Common Cursetors, Early English Text Society, p. 36.

39. Suetonius, Otho, 7.

40. James, English Historical Review, XXXVIII (1923), 86.

41. Kittredge, as above (note 37).

42. Addy, Household Tales, 1895, p. 42; J. G. Campbell, Superstitions of the Highlands and Islands, pp. 159, 164, 167.

43. Report, in The Triall of Maist. Dorrell, 1599, pp. 97–98.

44. Folk-Lore, XXVII (1916), 299–300.

45. Gervase of Tilbury, Otia Imperialia, i, 18(Leibnitz, I, 897; Liebrecht, p. 6; and note, pp. 74–76).

46. There are good examples in Roskoff, Geschichte des Teufels, 1869, II, 190–191.

47. Reginald, Libellus de Vita et Miraculis S. Godrici, ed. Stevenson (Surtees Society, XX), cap. 38, §§ 82–84, pp. 93–95.

48. Cap. 135, § 248, pp. 261–262.

49. Cap. 119, § 229, p. 242.

50. Cap. 112, § 218, pp. 231–232; cap. 165, §§ 294–296, pp. 313–315 (repeated by Matthew Paris, Chronica Majora, ed. Luard, II, 273).

51. Cap. 90, §§ 187–188, pp. 196–198. Cf. cap. 126, § 236, pp. 250–251; Appendix, cap. 2, § 320, pp. 337–338.

52. Cap. 125, § 225, pp. 249–250. For the normal shape of demons note the account of the monk who used to see them often, as reported by Herbertus Turrium, Archbishop of Sardinia, De Miraculis, i, 19 (Migne, CLXXXV, 1294–1295).

53. Vita Bartholomaei Farnensis (born ca. 1120), in Arnold's ed. of Symeon of Durham, I, 321.

54. See Jeremiae Lossii Curiose Gedancken vom Alpe übersetzet von M. M., 1704; E. H. Meyer, Germanische Mythologie, 1891, pp. 76–79; M. Höfler, Janus, V (1900), 512–518; the Same, Archiv für Religionswissenschaft, II (1899), 86–94; the Same, Deutsches Krankheitsnamen-Buch, 1899, pp. 10–13, s. v. Alb; Manninen, Die Dämonistischen Krankheiten im Finnischen Volksaberglauben (FF Communications, No. 45, XII), 1922, pp. 174–183; Hästesko, Motivverzeichnis Westfinnischer Zaubersprüche (the same, No. 19, II), 1914, pp. 28–31; Forsblom, Skrifter

utgivna av Svenska Litteratursällskapet i Finland, CXXXV (1917), 113–130; Kristensen, Danske Sagn, II (1893), 241–251; De Cock, Volksgeneeskunde in Vlaanderen, 1891, pp. 177–183; Wuttke-Meyer, pp. 272–276, 285–286; Schönwerth, Aus der Oberpfalz, I (1867), 208–232; Bieber, Kaffa, II (1923), 347; Ernest Jones, Der Alptraum, transl. Sachs (Schriften zur Angewandten Seelenkunde, ed. Freud, XIV), 1912.

55. See references in Roscher, Ephialtes, p. 22. Cf. Robert Fludd, Microcosmi Historia, Tom. II, Tract. i, Sect. 1, Lib. x, cap. 3, p. 209. King James pronounces "the Mare" "but a naturall sicknes," not a spirit (Daemonologie, 1597, iii, 3, p. 69).

56. Laistner, Das Rätsel der Sphinx, Grundzüge einer Mythengeschichte, 1889.

57. Cockayne, Leechdoms, I, 70; II, 342, 344 (where the incubus is also mentioned); Leonhardi, pp. 104, 105.

58. Cockayne, II, 140; Leonhardi, p. 42.

59. Cockayne, II, 306; Leonhardi, p. 94.

60. Cockayne, III, 42; Wülker, I, 326, 404; Napier, Herrig's Archiv, LXXXIV (1890), 323; Schlutter, Anglia, XXX (1907), 257–258; Grendon, Journal of American Folk-Lore, XXII (1909), 166–167, 215–216; Skemp, Modern Language Review, VI (1911), 293–295; Holthausen, Anglia, Beiblatt, XXXI (1920), 30, 118–119; Grattan, Modern Language Review, XXII (1927), 4–6.

61. See Chapter VII, note 78.

62. Heimskringla, Ynglinga Saga, 16 (13), Konunga Sögur, I (1816), 19; ed. Jónsson, I, i (1893), 28.

63. The Oldest English Texts, ed. Sweet, 1885, pp. 71, 72. Cf. Wright's Vocabularies, ed. Wülcker, 1884, I, 27, line 34; I, 597, lines 35–37. On the whole matter see Jente, Die Mythologischen Ausdrücke im Altenglischen Wortschatz, 1921, pp. 124–127, 173.

64. Canterbury Tales, A 3474–3486, ed. Skeat, IV, 100. See Skeat's note, V, 105–106; Folk-Lore Record, I (1878), 145–154; II (1879), 127–134; Denham Tracts, II (1895), 11–13; Northall, English Folk-Rhymes, 1892, pp. 144–149; Vansittart, The Antiquary, XL (1904), 76–81; Thiers, Traité des Superstitions, 1741, I, 97–98; R. Köhler, Germania, V (1860), 448–456, and XI (1866), 435–445 (Kleinere Schriften, III [1900], 320–341); the Same, Jahrbuch für Romanische und Englische Literatur, VIII (1867), 409–417 (Kleinere Schriften, III, 341–351); Mélusine, I (1878), 308–309; Carnoy, Littérature Orale de la Picardie, 1883, p. 375. For the mysterious Paternoster Verde see Rivista delle Tradizioni Popolari Italiane, I (1893), 75–77, 389–391.

65. Roscher, Ephialtes, pp. 61–62, 72–76 (Sächsische Gesellschaft der Wissenschaften, Philologisch-Historische Classe, Abhandlungen, XX); Guilielmus Alvernus, De Universo, ii, 3, cap. 8, 24, Opera, Paris, 1674, I, 1030, 1066; Garmann, De Miraculis Mortuorum, 1709, i, 3, 27, pp. 121–122 (cf. i, 1, 116–119, pp. 75–78); Douce, Illustrations of Shakspeare, 1839, pp. 425–426 (on A Midsummer Night's Dream, i, 4; cf. New Shakspere Society Transactions, 1875–6, pp. 191–193); Couch, The History of

Polperro, 1871, p. 133; Burne and Jackson, Shropshire Folk-Lore, pp. 149, 157; Bye-Gones for 1893-94, p. 205; for 1895-96, pp. 72, 80, 492; Palmer, Odd Yarns of English Lakeland, 1914, p. 73; E. M. Wright, Rustic Speech and Folk-Lore, 1913, p. 210; Train, An Historical and Statistical Account of the Isle of Man, 1845, II, 153; J. W. Wolf, Nieder-ländische Sagen, 1843, pp. 347-348; Sébillot, Traditions et Superstitions de la Haute-Bretagne, 1882, I, 141-144; Bladé, Contes Populaires de la Gascogne, 1886, II, 262-263; Orain, Folk-Lore de l'Ille-et-Vilaine, II (1898), 179, 188-191; La Tradition, III (1889), 53-54; Carnoy and Nico-laides, Traditions Populaires de l'Asie Mineure, 1889, p. 364; Schönwerth, Aus der Oberpfalz, I (1857), 327-331; Storaker, Historisk Tidsskrift, Christiania, I (1871), 460-464; Nyland, II (1887), 79; IV (1889), 67-68; Craigie, Scandinavian Folk-Lore, 1896, pp. 274-275; Wuttke-Meyer, p. 274; Manz, Volksbrauch und Volksglaube des Sarganserlandes, Schrif-ten der Schweizerischen Gesellschaft für Volkskunde, XII (1916), 106; Grohmann, Aberglaube und Gebräuche aus Böhmen und Mähren, 1864, p. 16; Holmberg, Finno-Ugric, The Mythology of All Nations, ed. J. A. MacCulloch, IV (1927), 162, 166-167. Note also the actions of the Buck-inghamshire vampire in the twelfth century (William of Newburgh, v, 22, ed. 1610, p. 638; cf. Havekost, Die Vampirsage in England, 1914).

66. Potts, The Wonderfull Discoverie of Witches, 1613, sig. S3, lf. 2 v°; Elworthy, West Somerset Word-Book, 1886, p. 311, cf. p. 578; E. M. Wright, as above, p. 211; Whitney and Bullock, Folk-Lore from Mary-land, 1925, p. 79. Cf. E. H. Meyer, Badisches Volksleben, 1900, pp. 371, 554, 555; Theodor Lachmann, Ueberlinger Sagen, Bräuche und Sitten, 1909, pp. 392-393; Zeitschrift des Vereins für Rheinische und Westfälische Volkskunde, IV (1907), 117; Skrifter utgiva av Svenska Litteratursäll-skapet i Finland, XVIII (1891), 206; Bergen, Animal and Plant Lore, 1899, p. 82; Puckett, Folk Beliefs of the Southern Negro, 1926, pp. 152-153; Bang, Norske Hexeformularer, 1901, p. 336 (cf. Samter, Geburt, Hochzeit und Tod, 1911, pp. 29-30, 48-52).

67. Ælfric, Lives of Saints, xxxi, 34, ed. Skeat, II, 284-285. See Surius, 1618, De Probatis Sanctorum Vitis, November 11, pp. 254-255 (St. Martin of Tours); cf. Ælfric's Homilies, ed. Thorpe, II (1846), 514. For the be-lief that devils may possess cattle (cf. Mark, v, 1-20; Luke, viii, 26-39) see Salomon and Saturn, ed. Kemble, 1848, p. 148.

68. Rituale Ecclesiae Dunelmensis, ed. Stevenson (Surtees Society, X), p. 119. Cf. Bang, Norske Hexeformularer, 1901, pp. 238, 258.

69. Folk-Lore, II (1891), 248.

70. Henderson, Notes on the Folk-Lore of the Northern Counties, 1879, pp. 190-192; Folk-Lore, XIII (1902), 424-425 (Berkshire); XXXII (1922), 307 (Isle of Skye); J. G. Campbell, Witchcraft and Second Sight, 1902, pp. 48-49 (Perthshire). Cf. Puckett, Folk Beliefs of the Southern Negro, 1926, pp. 151-152; Niderberger, Sagen, Märchen und Gebräuche aus Unterwalden, II (1910), 163-164; Gredt, Sagenschatz des Luxem-burger Landes, 1883, pp. 559-560; De Cock and Teirlinck, Brabantsch Sagenboek, I (1909), 46-48; Josef Müller, Sagen aus Uri (Schriften der Schweizerischen Gesellschaft für Volkskunde, XVIII), I (1926), 91;

Bombay Gazetteer, IX, i (1901), 430; von Sydow, Festskrift til H. F. Feilberg, 1911, pp. 594–605.

71. Boston Herald, February 6, 1919 (as reported by the grandson of one of the man's shipmates). I heard a version of this story forty-odd years ago from an old Provincetown man, a native of Truro.

72. For the nightmare witch see also Transactions Lancashire and Cheshire Antiquarian Society, XXXIV (1910), 105–106. Cf. Promptorium Parvulorum, ed. Way, II (1851), 326; ed. Mayhew, 1908, col. 282: "Mare or wych."

73. Blundevill, Fower Chiefest Offices belonging to Horsemanship, 1571, as quoted in Notes and Queries, 6th Series, I (1880), 54.

74. Scot, iv, 11, p. 87 (67), ed. Nicholson, p. 68; Fletcher, Monsieur Thomas, iv, 6; Edmondston and Saxby, The Home of a Naturalist, 2d ed., 1889, pp. 186–187.

75. Scot, ibid.; Aubrey, Remaines of Gentilisme and Judaisme, ed. Britten, 1881, p. 28; Browne, Pseudodoxia Epidemica, v, 24, 9, Works, ed. Wilkin, 1852, II, 100; The Table Book, ed. Hone, II (1828), 583; Boston, Lincoln, Louth, and Spalding Herald, February 7, 1837, in Folk-Lore Journal, VII (1889), 55; J. Sullivan, Cumberland and Westmorland, 1857, p. 153; Glyde, The New Suffolk Garland, 1866, pp. 175, 179; Wilkinson and Tattersall, Memories of Hurstwood, 1889, p. 49; E. M. Wright, Rustic Speech and Folk-Lore, 1913, pp. 226, 233–234; F. K. Robinson, A Glossary of Words used in the Neighbourhood of Whitby (English Dialect Society), 1876, pp. 85–86; County Folk-Lore, I, No. 2 (1893), pp. 22, 39; IV (1904), pp. 51–52; VI (1912), 62; Palmer, Odd Yarns of English Lakeland, 1914, p. 81. Cf. Cuming, Journal British Archæological Association, XXI (1865), 323–329; Transactions Lancashire and Cheshire Antiquarian Society, XXVII (1910), 108–110; Proceedings Society of Antiquaries of Newcastle-upon-Tyne, 3d Series, II (1907), 240–243 (with figures); Halifax Antiquarian Society Papers, 1904–5, p. 7; Folk-Lore, XII (1901), 175; XVI (1905), 335–336; County Folk-Lore, V (1908), 99–100; Saga-Book of the Viking Club, III (1902), 51–52; Lovett, Magic in Modern London, 1925, p. 90; Maclagan, Evil Eye in the Western Highlands, 1902, p. 169; Warden, Angus, IV (1884), 167; Clague, Manx Reminiscences, [1911,] p. 153; Thiers, Traité des Superstitions, 1741, I, 384; Seligmann, Der Böse Blick, 1910, II, 27; Hyltén-Cavallius, Wärend och Wirdarne, I (1863), 256–258; Wallonia, I (1893), 106; XIII (1905), 49; The Indian Antiquary, XXVII (1898), 108–109.

76. See Chapter VII, note 92.

77. Herrick, Another Charme for Stables, Riverside ed., II, 116. For a witch that rode a cow (1650) see York Depositions, ed. Raine, pp. 28–30.

78. Wuttke-Meyer, pp. 477–478, 483; Sussex Archæological Collections, XIII (1861), 222–223; Archæologia, XVII (1814), 144; Brockett, A Glossary of English North Country Words, 1825, p. 57; E. M. Wright, Rustic Speech and Folk-Lore, 1913, pp. 193–194. Cf. S. G. Drake, Annals of Witchcraft in New England, 1869, p. 279; J. Ll. W. Page, An Exploration of Exmoor, 4th ed., 1895, p. 310; Wm. Mackay, Urquhart and

Glenmoriston, 1893, pp. 419–420; Revue des Traditions Populaires, XXIII (1908), 11, 379; Knoop, Volkssagen aus dem Oestlichen Hinterpommern, 1885, pp. 138–139; Deutsche Volkskunde aus dem Oestlichen Böhmen, VI (1906), 181–182; Pechuël-Loesche, Volkskunde von Loango, 1907, p. 319; Journal Ceylon Branch Royal Asiatic Society, IV (1865–66), 37.

79. Vita Oswini Regis Deirorum, cap. 15, Raine, Miscellanea Biographica (Surtees Society, VIII), p. 29.

80. For spectral evidence see pp. 363–364.

81. Bovet, Pandaemonium, 1684, p. 194; A Collection of Modern Relations, 1693, pp. 50–51 (1649); Glanvil's Sadducismus Triumphatus, 4th ed., 1726, pp. 328–329 (1663).

82. See pp. 174, 177, 179.

83. Weinreich, Antike Heilungswunder, 1909 (Religionsgeschichtliche Versuche und Vorarbeiten, ed. Wünsch and Deubner, VIII, i), p. 30; cf. pp. 80–109 ("Heilung durch Handlung im Traum"), 110–136 ("Heilung durch Weisung im Traum"). Cf. Maury, La Magie, 1860, pp. 236–249; B. Schmidt, Das Volksleben der Neugriechen, I (1871), 77–82; A. Franz, Die Kirchlichen Benediktionen, 1909, II, 405–406; Glanvil's Sadducismus Triumphatus, 4th ed., 1726, pp. 359–361.

84. See Deubner, De Incubatione, 1900, pp. 56–109, especially pp. 59–64, 72, 82, 99; the Same, Kosmas und Damian, 1907; A. Franz, II, 441–449; H. Magnus, Der Aberglauben in der Medicin, 1903, pp. 28–35. Cf. Vita S. Germani, cap. 3, § 21, Acta Sanctorum, May 28, VI (1688), 782; Magnúss Saga hin Lengri, Vigfusson, Icelandic Sagas (Rolls Series), I, 273–274 (ed. Jónsson, 1780, pp. 514–518); Gregory, Dialogi, iv, 49, ed. Moricca, 1924, p. 308. At Clirok in Wales incubation was practised in 1756. People came to bathe in St. Beuon's Well, and rickety children were left to sleep on the saint's tomb after bathing (The Travels through England of Dr. Richard Pococke, II, 175, Camden Society, N. S., XLIV). Incubation for lunacy was practised in Scotland as late as 1850 (Archæologia Cambrensis, 6th Series, XII [1912], 234). Cf. Folk-Lore, VII (1896), 148 (Lesbos); XIX (1908), 313–315 (the Abruzzi).

85. Chronicon Frodoardi, Recueil, VIII, 198.

86. Caesarius Heisterbacensis, Dialogus, vii, 48, ed. Strange, 1851, II, 68.

87. Martyrdom of Indracht (Digby MS. 112), Notes and Queries for Somerset and Dorset, XVII (1923), 21.

88. Miracula Simonis de Montfort, in Halliwell's ed. of Rishanger (Camden Society), 1840, p. 72.

89. Fornmanna Sögur, III (1827), 102–103; Memorials of St. Dunstan, ed. Stubbs, pp. 40–42, cf. 48–49; Caesarius Heisterbacensis, x, 3, ed. Strange, II, 219–220. See also Weinreich, Antike Heilungswunder, 1909, pp. 5–6, 91. Compare the Sleeping Preacher (p. 320, above). A story which shows striking resemblances to the Cædmon legend occurs in the Life of St. Waltheof (Acta Sanctorum, August 3, I, 270–271; noted by Wüst, Anzeiger für Deutsches Altertum, XXXV [1912], 164–167).

90. Bede, Historia Ecclesiastica, ii, 6. There is a similar miracle in St. Peter Damiani's 19th Opusculum, cap. 8 (Migne, CXLV, 437-438). As St. Paul had a messenger of Satan to buffet him, so, by a literal interpretation, St. Godric of Finchale was diabolically buffeted; for once, while he was sitting by the fire, an invisible demon dealt him a blow that almost dashed him headlong to the ground: Reginald, Libellus de Vita et Miraculis S. Godrici, ed. Stevenson (Surtees Society, XX), cap. 35, p. 88.

91. Lucian, Philopseudes, 20.

92. Capgrave, ed. Hingeston, p. 156.

93. Gregory, Dialogi, i, 4, ed. Moricca, 1924, p. 28; Wærferth's Anglo-Saxon version, ed. Hecht, 1900, p. 26. Cf. Nider, Formicarius, v, 6, ed. 1516 (1517), fol. lxxix vº.

94. Perceval li Gallois, ed. Potvin, I, 7-8; Sebastian Evans, The High History of the Holy Grail, I, 13-15.

95. Serglige Conculaind, 8-9, Windisch, Irische Texte, I (1880), 207-208.

96. Reginald, Libellus de Admirandis Beati Cuthberti Virtutibus, ed. Raine (Surtees Society, I), cap. 112, pp. 248-254.

97. Im Thurn, Journal Anthropological Institute, XI (1882), 384; the Same, Among the Indians of Guiana, 1883, p. 345. Cf. Krauss, Slavische Volkforschungen, 1908, p. 36; Speck, Memoirs American Anthropological Association, VI (1919), 269-271.

98. Cf. Malleus Maleficarum, Pt. II, qu. 1, cap. 11, ed. 1620, pp. 223-224.

99. Walter Map, De Nugis Curialium, ii, 14, ed. Wright, pp. 82-83 (ed. James, pp. 78-79). The work was written at intervals ca. 1181-1193: see Hinton, Publications Modern Language Association, XXXII (1917), 81-132. The same story is told by Étienne de Bourbon Septem Dona Spiritus Sancti (thirteenth century), ed. Lecoy de la Marche, Anecdotes Historiques, 1877, pp. 320-322. For a startling case of a boy killed by a spectral woman (1661) see Diary and Correspondence of Dr. John Worthington, ed. Crossley (Chetham Society, XXXVI), II, 66 and note, 69; Drage, Daimonomageia, 1665, p. 12. For spectral evidence see Drage, p. 6; James I, Daemonologie, 1597 (1603), pp. 79-80.

100. Cf. Corrector, § 153 (Schmitz, Bussbücher, II, 443). For the dominae nocturnae or bonae res see Hansen, Zauberwahn, pp. 134-140.

101. Champier, Dyalogus in Magicarum Artium Destructionem, tract iii (ii), chap. 3, Lyons, ca. 1500, sig. bij, lf. 2 vº-3 rº. For the same legend see Själens Tröst, ed. Klemming, pp. 31-32; Nider, Formicarius, ii, 4, ed. 1517 (1516), fol. xxvi rº; An Alphabet of Tales, ed. Banks, I, (1904), No. 247, p. 173; Bartholomaeus de Spina, Quaestio de Strigibus, cap. 28 (in 1620 ed. of Malleus Maleficarum, II, 243-244); Scot, iii, 16, p. 66 (52-53), ed. Nicholson, p. 52. The anecdote does not appear in the best accounts of St. Germanus, but may be found in Legenda Aurea, Koburger, 1478, fol. cxxxiij rº (ed. Grässe, 1850, cap. 107 [102], p. 449), and elsewhere (see Acta Sanctorum, July, VII, 287-288). Cf. Schmeller, Bayerisches Wörterbuch, I (1872), 270-271; Hansen, Zauberwahn, p. 136; the Same, Quellen, p. 235.

102. York Depositions, ed. Raine, p. 58.

103. For *striges* and the like see, for example, Gaster, Two Thousand Years of a Charm against the Child-Stealing Witch, Folk-Lore, XI (1900), 129–162; Ovid, Fasti, vi, 131–168; Pliny, xi, 39, 95, 232; Festus, De Verborum Significatione, p. 314 Müller; Petronius, Saturae, 63; Q. Serenus Sammonicus, De Medicina, lix, 1044–1047, ed. Keuchen, 1662, p. 34; Bücheler and Riese, Anthologia Latina, II, ii (1887), No. 987, p. 456 (cf. Philologus, LXX [1911], 507–508); Torrentius on Horace, Epodes, v, 20 (1608, pp. 352–353); Isidore, Etymologiae, viii, 11, 102; Guilielmus Alvernus, De Universo, ii, 3, 12, Opera, 1674, I, 1036; ii, 3, 24, I, 1066; Archivio Storico Lombardo, XVII (1890), 881 (A.D. 1520); Nider, Formicarius, v, 3, ed. 1517 (1516), fol. lxiiii rº; G. F. Pico della Mirandola, Strix, 1523, sigg. B vº–Bii rº; Bartholomaeus de Spina, Quaestio de Strigibus, capp. 2 (ed. 1620, with Malleus, II, 152–153), 8 (p. 179), 18 (p. 210), 19 (pp. 212–214); Wier, iii, 4, ed. 1568, pp. 219–220; Ponzinibius, De Lamiis, cap. 63, ed. 1592 (in Tractatus Duo), p. 279; Cardano, De Rerum Varietate, xvi, 93, Opera, 1663, III, 323; Kornmann, De Miraculis Mortuorum, 1610, v, 1 (Opera Curiosa, 1694, pp. 193–195); Leo Allatius, De Graecorum Hodie quorundam Opinationibus, capp. 2–3 (De Templis Graecorum, etc., 1645, pp. 115–118); Bochart, Hierozoicon, vi, 9, ed. 1675, II, 831–833; Bartholinus, Historiae Anatomicae Rariores, 1654, pp. 20–22; Webster, The Displaying of Supposed Witchcraft, 1677, pp. 22–23; Garmann, De Miraculis Mortuorum, 1709, i, 3, 23–26, 30, pp. 119–121, 123; Samter, Geburt, Hochzeit und Tod, 1911, pp. 21–25; Roskoff, Geschichte des Teufels, 1869, I, 146–147, 297; B. Schmidt, Das Volksleben der Neugriechen, I (1871), 136–138; Lea, A History of the Inquisition, 1888, III, 502; Potts, The Wonderfull Discoverie of Witches, 1613, sig. L2 rº; Kuhn und Schwartz, Norddeutsche Sagen, 1848, pp. 25–26; Panzer, Beiträge zur Deutschen Mythologie, II (1855), 111; Peter, Volksthümliches aus Oesterreichisch-Schlesien, II (1867), 24; Zeitschrift für Oesterreichische Volkskunde, II (1896), 151; Schweizerisches Archiv für Volkskunde, XII (1908), 7–9; Deutsche Volkskunde aus dem Oestlichen Böhmen, IX (1909), 53; Sébillot, Traditions et Superstitions de la Haute-Bretagne, 1882, I, 180; Revue des Traditions Populaires, IX (1894), 457–458; Archivio per lo Studio delle Tradizioni Popolari, XX (1901), 103; XXII (1903), 7–9; Zanetti, La Medicina delle Nostre Donne, 1892, p. 11; Philologus, LXVI (1907), 342–345; Krauss, Slavische Volkforschungen, 1908, pp. 60–66; Panjab Notes and Queries, II (1884–85), 6; Journal (Royal) Anthropological Institute, XXVI (1897), 149–150; XL (1910), 463; J. H. Knowles, Folk-Tales of Kashmir, 1888, p. 59; E. Thurston, Omens and Superstitions of Southern India, 1912, pp. 261–262; Crooke, Religion and Folklore of Northern India, 1926, pp. 207–208; Skeat, Malay Magic, 1900, pp. 325–328; Zeitschrift der Deutschen Morgenländischen Gesellschaft, XXXVI (1882), 85; R. Austin Freeman, Travels and Life in Ashanti and Jaman, 1898, pp. 291–293; T. N. Goddard, The Handbook of Sierra Leone, 1925, p. 56; Rattray, Ashanti, 1923, p. 265; P. Amaury Talbot, The Peoples of Southern Nigeria, 1926, II, 214, 222; Oviedo, Historia General y Natural de Indias, xxix, 31, ed. Amador de los Rios, III (1853), 159–160.

104. Weicker, Der Seelenvogel, 1902, pp. 32–33, 308.

105. Duris Samius, frag. 37, ed. Hulleman, 1841, pp. 123–124 (from scholium on Aristophanes, Wasps, 1030 [1035], where further references are given). Cf. Wagstaffe, The Question of Witchcraft Debated, 1669, p. 20; B. Schmidt, Das Volksleben der Neugriechen, I (1871), 131–135; M. Mayer, Archäologische Zeitung, XLIII (1886), 119–130; Basset, Les Apocryphes Ethiopiens, IV (1894), 18–22; Abbott, Macedonian Folklore, 1903, pp. 265–266.

106. Zenobius, Epitome, iii, 3 (Paroemiographi Graeci, ed. Gaisford, 1836, p. 280; ed. von Leutsch and Schneidewin, 1839, I, 58); Suidas, ed. Bernhardy, I, i, 1079; Hesychius, s. vv. Γελλώ, Γελλῶς; Roscher, Ephialtes, p. 59; Leo Allatius (Allacci), De Psellis, p. 41 (Fabricius, Bibliotheca Graeca, Vol. V, 1712); the Same, De Graecorum Hodie Quorundam Opinationibus, cap. 3 (De Templis Graecorum, etc., 1645, pp. 146–147); Mansikka, Ueber Russische Zauberformeln, pp. 48–49, 58–59; Gaster, Folk-Lore, XI (1900), 142–148; Wesselofsky, Giornale Storico della Letteratura Italiana, XI (1888), 342–343.

107. Rouse, Folk-Lore, X (1899), 151–152; B. Schmidt, I (1871), 139–140; Du Cange, s. v. Γελλώ.

108. B. Schmidt, I, 133.

109. Nicephorus Callistus, xviii, 9 (Migne, CXLVII,. 348). Cf. Evagrius, v, 21. See Delrio, Disquisitiones Magicae, lib. ii, qu. 6, ed. 1616, p. 99; qu. 27, sect. 2, p. 275.

110. Hansen, Zauberwahn, 1900, pp. 58–60; cf. pp. 81, 84, 132–140, 149.

111. Gervase of Tilbury, Otia Imperialia, iii, 85–86 (Leibnitz, I, 987–988; Liebrecht, pp. 38–40, cf. pp. 143–146); John of Salisbury, Policraticus, ii, 17, ed. Webb, I, 101.

112. Garmann, De Miraculis Mortuorum, 1709, i, 3, 41, p. 128. Cf. Grillando, De Sortilegiis, ed. 1545, vi, 10, fol. xxx v° (ed. 1592, vi, 13, p. 71).

113. Kathā Sarit Sāgara, ch. 32, Tawney, I (1880), 288–289 (ed. Penzer, III [1925], 102–103); Plautus, Pseudolus, iii, 2, 30–32. Cf. Grimm, Deutsche Mythologie, 4th ed., I (1875), 226–232; IV (1878), 88–90; Revue Celtique, XII (1891), 84–85; Krauss, Slavische Volkforschungen, 1908, pp. 61–64; Höfler, Die Volksmedizinische Organotherapie, pp. 233–234; Bompas, Folklore of the Santal Parganas, 1909, p. 419; Enthoven, The Folklore of Bombay, 1924, p. 239; Talbot, In the Shadow of the Bush, 1912, pp. 192–193; Wilken, Het Animisme, De Indische Gids, VI, i (1884), 950–955; Bombay Gazetteer, IX, i (1901), 429; Tod, Annals and Antiquities of Rajast'han, II (1832), 587; Sir John Malcolm, A Memoir of Central India, 2d ed., 1824, II, 212; Silas, A Primitive Arcadia, 1926, p. 48 (Papua); W. J. V. Saville, In Unknown New Guinea, 1926, pp. 216, 272; Sir George Grey, Journals of Two Expeditions of Discovery in North-West and Western Australia, 1841, II, 314–316, 323. See also Apuleius Metamorphoses, i, 12–19; Petronius, Saturae, 134.

114. Philostratus, Apollonius of Tyana, iv, 25. Cf. Jātaka, i, 96, Cowell, I (1895), 232–237; ii, 196, II (1895), 89–91; J. H. Knowles, Folk-Tales of Kashmir, 1888, pp. 233–239; B. Schmidt, Das Volksleben der Neu-

griechen, I (1871), 111–112; Krauss, Slavische Volkforschungen, 1908, pp. 61–62.

115. The cannibalism and preparation of ointment in Potts (The Wonderfull Discoverie of Witches, 1613, sig. L2 r°) are late and exceptional in English cases.

116. See, for example, Hansen, Quellen, p. 141 (cf. 552); Bossard and Maulde, Gilles de Rais, 2d ed., 1886, pp. xx, xxiv, li–lii; Guazzo (Guaccius), Compendium Maleficarum, 1608, i, 6, p. 16; Boguet, Discours des Sorciers, ch. 38, 2d ed., 1608, pp. 205–206. Cf. pp. 141, 206, 243, above.

117. Hansen, Quellen, pp. 211, 237, 308, 570 (cf. 497); Nider, Formicarius, v, 3, ed. 1516 (1517), fol. lxxiiii; Wier, iii, 2, ed. 1568, p. 215 (cf. iii, 4, pp. 218–223); Bodin, Demonomanie, iv, 5, ed. 1580, foll. 198 v°–199 r°; Jonson, Masque of Queens, 1609. Cf. de l'Ancre, L'Incredulité et Mescreance du Sortilege, 1622, p. 790. See pp. 141, 245, above.

118. Hansen, Quellen, pp. 93, 120, 233; Nider, v, 3, ed. 1516 (1517), fol. lxxiiii; G. F. Pico della Mirandola, Strix, 1523, sigg. E v°, Eii, lf. 3 v°; Wier, iii, 2, ed. 1568, pp. 214–215 (cf. iii, 4, pp. 218–223); Scot, iii, 3, p. 44 (37), ed. Nicholson, p. 34; iii, 12, pp. 59–60 (48), ed. Nicholson, p. 46; Jonson, The Masque of Queens, 1609 (with learned notes); Boguet, pp. 165–168 (cf. pp. 204–207). Cf. Cardano, De Subtilitate, xviii, Opera, 1663, III, 639; Hansen, p. 497. See also pp. 243, 268, above.

CHAPTER XIV

The Seer

1. On the whole subject see Rupert Taylor, The Political Prophecy in England, 1911. Cf. Dodds, Modern Language Review, XI (1916), 276–284.

2. Norfolk Archæology, I (1847), 209–216. There is an excellent "line" of prophecies in William of Malmesbury's Gesta Pontificum (see Hamilton's edition, p. 570). Cf. A Discovrsive Probleme concerning Prophesies by I[ohn]. H[arvey]. Physition, 1588 (twelve British prophets are mentioned and derided, pp. 56–58).

3. We have already noted evidence from the Anglo-Saxon age and from the eleventh, twelfth, and thirteenth centuries (pp. 27–30, 41–48).

4. Matthew Paris, Chronica Majora, ed. Luard, II, 535, 541, 546–547; the Same, Historia Anglorum, ed. Madden, II, 129, 136 (cf. III, 227); Annales Monastici, ed. Luard, I, 60; II, 278; III, 34; IV, 56–58, 401; Walter of Coventry, ed. Stubbs, II, 208, 212; Gaufridus de Coldingham, Raine, Historiae Dunelmensis Scriptores Tres (Surtees Society, IX), pp. 27–28; Boothroyd, History of Pontefract, 1807, pp. 73–75.

5. Knighton, ed. Lumby, I, 276–277.

6. Chaucer, Troilus, iv, 1406–1407. Cf. Holkot, Super Libros Sapientie, Lectio 190, Speyer, 1483, sigg. oiiij, lf. 5 v°–pj r° (Reutlingen, 1489, sig. Miiij, lf. 4 v°).

7. Guillelmus Armoricus, Gesta Philippi Augusti, cap. 202, Œuvres de Rigord et de Guillaume le Breton, ed. Delaborde, I (1882), 295–296.

8. Giovanni Villani, Storia, vii, 31, ed. 1587, p. 212.

9. Registrum Radulphi Baldock (Canterbury and York Series, VII), I, 144–145. Cf. Council of Paris, A.D. 829, iii, 2, Mansi, Concilia, XIV, 595.

10. Cardwell, Documentary Annals, 1844, I, 30; Frere and Kennedy, Visitation Articles and Injunctions (Alcuin Society), 1910, II, 111.

11. Cranmer, Miscellaneous Writings and Letters, ed. Cox (Parker Society), 1846, p. 158; Cardwell, I, 58; Frere and Kennedy, II, 188. Cf. Strype, Memorials of Cranmer, I (1694), 183.

12. Cardwell, I, 161; Frere and Kennedy, II, 353.

13. Strype, Historical Memorials, III (1721), Appendix, p. 183; Frere and Kennedy, II, 398.

14. Cardwell, I, 226, 246; Frere and Kennedy, III, 5, 20.

15. Strype, Annals of the Reformation, I (1725), Appendix, p. 59; Frere and Kennedy, III, 92.

16. Frere and Kennedy, III, 106.

17. The Same, III, 204.

18. The Same, III, 227–228.

19. Cardwell, II, 34.

20. See pp. 194–195, above.

21. Palgrave, An Essay upon the Original Authority of the King's Council, 1834, pp. 87–88; Select Cases before the King's Council, ed. Leadam and Baldwin (Selden Society, XXXV), 1918, p. xxxiv.

22. English Chronicle, ed. Davies (Camden Society, LXIV), p. 69. Cf. The First Part of the Contention of the Two Famous Houses, of Yorke and Lancaster, [i, 4, and iv, 1,] Shakespeare's Works, ed. Wright, IX (1895), 522, 548–550; 2 Henry VI, i, 4, and iv, 1; Boswell-Stone, Shakspere's Holinshed, 1896, pp. 252–253, 270–271. See also Chronicle of London, 1827, pp. 135–136; Gregory's Chronicle, ed. Gairdner, p. 190; Kingsford, Chronicles of London, 1905, pp. 159, 276.

23. See Sir William Lomner to John Paston, May 5, 1450, Paston Letters, ed. Fenn and Ramsay, 1840, I, 18–19.

24. See pp. 138–139, above.

25. Gairdner, Three Fifteenth-Century Chronicles, p. 163.

26. Cambridge Antiquarian Communications, No. 67, XIX (1915), 37–38.

27. Warkworth's Chronicle, ed. Halliwell (Camden Society), 1839, p. 24.

28. Hale, pp. 36–37.

29. Lincoln Episcopal Visitations, Peacock, Archæologia, XLVIII (1885), 251–253.

30. Third Report of the Deputy Keeper, Appendix II, pp. 230–232. Cf. Pike, History of Crime, II (1876), 20–21, 605.

31. See p. 127, above.

32. Letters and Papers, IX, No. 846, p. 284. Other friars were in trouble for seditious words and necromancy in 1535. See Cromwell to Rutland, August 9 (Historical Manuscripts Commission, 12th Report, Appendix, IV, Duke of Rutland's MSS., I, 25); Gervase Tyndall to Crom-

well, Letters and Papers, IX, No. 740, p. 252 (cf. No. 551, p. 182); Ellis, Original Letters, 3d Series, III, 41–42.

33. Letters and Papers, XII, ii, No. 1212, pp. 426–428; No. 1231, pp. 432–433; XIII, i, No. 107, p. 37; No. 705, p. 267. 1535 and 1537 were bad years for prophets: see VIII, Nos. 1, 327, 565, 567, 736, 771, pp. 2, 131, 214–215, 275, 290; XII, i, Nos. 318, 534, 841, pp. 145, 248, 371–372; XII, ii, Nos. 74, 80, pp. 25, 28. Cf. XIV, No. 806, p. 382 (1539; Leynham, a "mad prophet").

34. Letters and Papers, XIII, i, Nos. 487, 705, 1282, 1350, pp. 177–179, 267, 470, 503.

35. See Underhill's Autobiography, J. G. Nichols, Narratives of the Days of the Reformation, pp. 159, 172–175, cf. 326–330.

36. Acts of the Privy Council, New Series, III, 279; Nichols, as above, p. 335.

37. Acts of the Privy Council, New Series, IV, 12–13, 20, 94, 131.

38. Strype, Historical Memorials, III (1721), Appendix, p. 35.

39. Acts of the Privy Council, New Series, V, 362.

40. Strype, Historical Memorials, III (1721), Catalogue, p. 164.

41. Commons' Journals, I, 57, 59, 65, 69; Lords' Journals, I, 591, 601, 602, 606; Statutes of the Realm, IV, i (1819), 445–446 (5 Elizabeth, chap. 15).

42. "I will here also omitte to talke of Grigge the poulter, with divers other, whose endes have made their doinges knowne," writes John Halle, Chyrurgyen, in An Historiall Expostulation: against the Beastlye Abusers, both of Chyrurgerie, and Physycke, in Oure Tyme, 1565, ed. T. J. Pettigrew (Percy Society, XI), 1844, p. 26.

43. Wriothesley's Chronicle, ed. Hamilton (Camden Society), II, 42; Stow, Annales, ed. 1631, p. 604. For later prophets, among a countless multitude, see Depositions Taken before the Mayor and Aldermen of Norwich, ed. Rye, 1905, pp. 61–62 (1559); Diary of Walter Yonge, ed. Roberts (Camden Society, XLI), p. 38 (1621); Diary of John Rous, ed. Green (Camden Society, LXVI), p. 36 (1629); Devon and Cornwall Notes and Queries, XIII (1925), 312–314 (Anne Jefferies, 1647, instructed by the fairies); Ashmole's Diary, April 20, 1653, ed. Burman, 1774, pp. 318–319 (ed. Gunther, 1927, p. 51: Arise Evans, the Welsh seer; cf. Aubrey, Miscellanies, 2d ed., 1721, pp. 124–128, and Archæologia Cambrensis, 4th Series, X [1879], 233–234); William Robinson, The History and Antiquities of the Parish of Hackney, 1842, I, 219–220 (1654); Diary and Correspondence of Dr. John Worthington, ed. Crossley (Chetham Society, XIII), I, 357 (1661). Cf. Notes and Queries for Somerset and Dorset, VIII (1903), 106–108. Henry Howard, Earl of Northampton, published his laborious work, A Defensative against the Poyson of Supposed Prophecies, in 1583; it was reissued in 1620.

CHAPTER XV

COLD WATER

1. On the *judicium aquae frigidae* see Patetta, Le Ordalie, 1890, pp. 33, 34, 41, 52, 60–61, 98, 101, 113, 116–117, 135–137, 158–161, 191–194, 213–214, 341, 344–345, 372, 376–378, 431; A. Franz, Die Kirchlichen Benediktionen, 1909, II, 313–328, 355–357, 377–384; Lea, Superstition and Force, 4th ed., 1892, pp. 318–334; Thiers, Superstitions Anciennes et Modernes, 1733, vi, 1–2, I, 216–227; P. le Brun, Histoire Critique des Pratiques Superstitieuses, 1750, II, 240–317; Tuchmann, Mélusine, IV (1888–89), 184–188; Soldan und Heppe, Geschichte der Hexenprocesse, I, 394–397 (ed. Bauer, I, 380–384); Liebermann, Die Gesetze der Angelsachsen, II, 530; W. R. Halliday, Greek Divination, 1913, pp. 109–115; Aubrey, Remaines of Gentilisme and Judaisme, ed. Britten, 1881, p. 126; Shirley, The Sisters (licensed 1642), ii, 1 (Works, ed. Gifford and Dyce, V, 369); Stearne, A Confirmation and Discovery of Witch-craft, 1648, pp. 15, 18–19; Dugdale, Origines Juridiciales, 1671, pp. 86–88; Drage, Daimonomageia, 1665, pp. 40–41; Filmer, An Advertisement to the Jury-Men of England touching Witches, 1679, p. 327; Train, An Historical and Statistical Account of the Isle of Man, 1845, II, 167–168; Hyltén-Cavallius, Wärend och Wirdarne, I (1863), 447–449; Linderholm, De Stora Häxprocesserna i Sverige, I (1918), 51–53, 79–83, 204, etc.; Rick, Defensio Compendiosa Probae Aquae Frigidae, 1597; Godelmann, Tractatus de Magis, Veneficis et Lamiis, 1591, iii, 5, pp. 30–45; Hauber, Bibliotheca Magica, 3. Stück, 1738, pp. 147–148; 8. Stück, 1739, pp. 502–506; 9. Stück, 1739, pp. 567–591; Zeitschrift der Gesellschaft für Schleswig-Holsteinische Geschichte, XLV (1915), 183–184, 192–193, 203, 206, 216, 221–222, 229, 232, 235, 237; Blätter für Pommersche Volkskunde, XI (1902), 83–84 (ca. 1835); Krauss, Slavische Volkforschungen, 1908, pp. 67–68.

2. Grimm, Deutsche Rechtsalterthümer, 4th ed. (Heusler and Hübner), 1899, II, 582–586 (923–926).

3. See pp. 290–291, above.

4. Child, The English and Scottish Popular Ballads, I, 338; II, 505; III, 505; Laistner, Das Rätsel der Sphinx, 1889, I, 196–197, 252–253, 257–258; Blau, Das Altjüdische Zauberwesen, 1898, pp. 158–159; Goldziher, Archiv für Religionswissenschaft, XIII (1910), 20–46; Durham Depositions, ed. Raine (Surtees Society, XXI), p. 100; Dryden, An Evening's Love, iii, 1, ed. 1671, p. 35 (ed. Scott, 1808, III, 275); Middleton, Annals of Hyde and District, 1899, p. 174; J. G. Campbell, Witchcraft and Second Sight, 1902, p. 184; Torr, Small Talk at Wreyland, 1918, p. 13; Folk-Lore, XIII (1902), 428; Dorsey, Traditions of the Arikara, 1904, p. 132; the Same, The Mythology of the Wichita, 1904, pp. 107–108, 216; Samter, Geburt, Hochzeit und Tod, 1911, pp. 85–89.

5. William of Malmesbury, Gesta Regum, ii, 170, ed. Stubbs, I, 201.

6. Pliny, vii, 2, 17. Cf. Wier, iii, 35, ed. 1568, pp. 330–331.

7. Map, De Nugis Curialium, iii, 3, ed. Wright, p. 125 (ed. James, p. 124). Map cites Solinus (i, 101, ed. Mommsen², 1895, p. 26), who cites

Apollonides. Cf. Tuchmann, Mélusine, IV (1888–89), 33. J. G. Campbell mentions a witch with eyes of different colors, one black or brown and one blue (Witchcraft and Second Sight in the Highlands and Islands, 1902, pp. 50–51). Alexander the Great had one blue and one black eye according to Michael Glycas, Annales, Byzantine Corpus, ed. Bekker, [XXVI,] 268.

8. Anthologia Palatina, ix, 125 (ed. Jacobs, II, 42–43, cf. his Animadversiones, III, i, 285; ed. Dübner, II, 24–25; ed. Stadtmüller, III, i, 97–99); Julian, Oratio ii, p. 81D Spanheim (ed. Hertlein, I, 104), and Epistola xvi, p. 383D (II, 495 Hertlein: rejected as spurious by Bidez, Œuvres Complètes, I, ii, 247 [1924]; cf. ed. Bidez and Cumont, 1922, p. 260); Claudian, In Rufinum, ii, 112; Nonnus, Dionysiaca, xxiii, 94–97; Eustathius, Hysmine and Hysminias, viii, 7, Hercher, Erotici Scriptores Graeci, II, 241–242 (cf. xi, 17, Hercher, II, 282–283); Gregory Nazianzen, Carmina, ii, 2, 4, 142–143 (Migne, Patrologia Graeca, XXXVII, 1516; xlix, Opera, II [1611], 114 C); Tzetzes, Chiliades, iv, 339–341, ed. Kiesseling, p. 133; Georgius Pisida, De Expeditione Heraclii Imperatoris contra Persas, i, 41 (Byzantine Corpus, XXXI, ii, 5).

9. Pseudo-Aristotle, De Mirabilibus Auscultationibus, cap. 57, p. 834 (Didot ed., IV, 83); Stephanus Byzantinus, Ethnica, s. v. Παλική, ed. Meineke, p. 497. Cf. Achilles Tatius, Clitophon, viii, 12 and 14 (Hercher, Erotici Scriptores Graeci, I, 205, 207); Diodorus Siculus, xi, 89; Macrobius, v, 19; Silius Italicus, Punica, xiv, 219–220; Solinus, 4, §§ 5–7, ed. Mommsen, p. 47; Priscian, Periegesis, 466–469, ed. Krehl, p. 495; Isidore, Origines, xiv, 6. See Glotz, L'Ordalie dans la Grèce Primitive, 1904, pp. 80–85; Patetta, Le Ordalie, 1890, p. 135. Cf. Dalyell, The Darker Superstitions of Scotland, 1834, pp. 513–514; Frazer's Pausanias, 1898, III, 388–389. On this ordeal and others in classic lands see Halliday, Greek Divination, 1913, pp. 99–115.

10. Zosimus, Historia Nova, i, 58, 1–3.

11. Gesta Hammaburgensis Ecclesiae Pontificum, iv, 26, schol. 134 (Pertz, Monumenta Germaniae Historica, Scriptores, VII, 379). Compare the buffalo sacrifice (Crooke, Religion and Folklore of Northern India, 1926, pp. 61–62).

12. Pausanias, iii, 23, 5. Compare the crocodile ordeal: Codrington, The Melanesians, 1891, p. 213; Meek, The Northern Tribes of Nigeria, 1925, I, 268; Sibree, The Great African Island, 1880, p. 284; Osborn, Madagascar, 1924, p. 226; The Antananarivo Annual, No. 2 (1876, reprinted 1885), I, 222; No. 12 (1888), III, 421–426.

13. Mansikka, Die Religion der Ostslaven, I (1922), 218 (FF Communications, Vol. X, No. 43). Cf. Löwenstimm, Aberglaube und Strafrecht, 1897, pp. 81–82; the Same, Zeitschrift für Socialwissenschaft, VI (1903), 224.

14. Capitularia Regum Francorum, II (1897), 16; cf. II, 7. For Frankish rites see Zeumer, Formulae Aevi Merowingici et Karolini, 1886 (Monumenta, Leges, Section V), pp. 617–629.

15. See, for instance, Keutgen, Urkunden zur Städtischen Verfassungsgeschichte, 1901, pp. 92, 196, 205, 453.

16. Letter of Scribonius (Wilhelm Adolf Schreiber), October 4, 1580. See Tractatus Duo Singulares de Examine Sagarum super Aquam Frigidam Projectarum, 1686; Hauber, Bibliotheca, Acta et Scripta Magica, 9tes Stück, 1739, pp. 567–591; Erasmus Francisci, Der Höllische Proteus, 2d ed., 1695, pp. 108–114.

17. Æthelstan, ii, 23 (Liebermann, Die Gesetze der Angelsachsen, I, 162; i, 23, Thorpe, Ancient Laws, folio, 1840, p. 90; cf. Fuller, Church-History, 1656, Book ii, Century X, chap. 9, p. 127); Be Blaserum ond be Morðslihtum, of uncertain date, ca. 930–975, § 2 (Liebermann, I, 388; Thorpe, as Æthelstan, iv, 6, p. 95); Æthelred, iii, 6 (Liebermann, I, 230; Thorpe, p. 126); Leis Willelme, xv, 3 (Liebermann, I, 502–503; Thorpe, p. 204; Matzke, Lois de Guillaume le Conquérant, p. 13); Assize of Clarendon, §§ 1–2 (Benedict of Peterborough, Gesta Regis Henrici Secundi, ed. Stubbs, Appendix, II, cxlix–cl); Assize of Northampton (the same, I, 108). Cf. Glanville, Tractatus de Legibus, ed. 1604, fol. 114 r°. In some of these cases the hot-water ordeal may possibly be meant rather than the *judicium aquae frigidae:* see Liebermann, II, 530, 534.

18. Historical MSS. Commission, 8th Report, Appendix, Part I, p. 270; Boothroyd, History of Pontefract, 1807, Appendix, p. ii; Wardell, Municipal History of Leeds, 1846, Appendix, p. vi; Gross, Harvard Law Review, XV (1902), 692–693.

19. Liebermann, I, 401–405, 413–415, 417–418, 422–424, 427. Cf. Textus Roffensis, ed. Hearne, 1720, pp. 19–28.

20. Liebermann, I, 415 (Late West Saxon, scincræft), 418 (Latin, "per aliquod maleficium uel per herbas seu per causas diabolicas"), 423 (*maleficium, praestigium*), 424 (*maleficium*). Cf. Schmitz, Die Bussbücher, I (1883), 457–459; II (1898), 496. See p. 28, above.

21. For witchcraft (*maleficium*) see Ritual XIII, § 7 (Liebermann, I, 423), in manuscripts of about 1130–1150. See also Ritual I, § 20 (Liebermann, I, 404, note 38), in a manuscript of about 1060 (*ueneficium*).

22. Ritual I, Liebermann, I, 405.

23. Ritual X, Liebermann, I, 417–418. Cf. Hincmar, De Divortio Lotharii, Responsio to Sixth Question, Opera, Paris, 1645, I, 604–613; Peter Cantor, Verbum Abbreviatum, cap. 78, Magne, CCV, 233.

24. Pipe Roll, 12 Henry II (Pipe Roll Society IX [1888]), pp. 5, 13, 14, 33, etc. (see index, *judicium aque*); 22 Henry II (XXV [1904]), pp. 15, 26, 34, etc. ("per assisam de Norhant'" is regularly added), 198. See also 18 Henry II (XVIII [1894]), p. 10; 23 Henry II (XXVI [1905]), p. 79; 25 Henry II (XXVIII [1907]), p. 106 ("pro justicia facienda de Waltero qui periit judicio aque"); 26 Henry II (XXIX [1908]), p. 52, and 28 Henry II (XXXI [1910]), p. 53 ("de misericordia pro judicio aque"). Cf. 13 Henry II (XI [1889]), p. 1; 16 Henry II (XV [1892]), p. 16. See Gross, Harvard Law Review, XV (1902), 692–693.

25. Pipe Roll, 12 Henry II (IX [1888]), p. 18: "pro benedictione fossarum apud Sanctum Ædmundum."

26. Pipe Roll, 14 Henry II (XII [1890]), pp. 198, 48.

27. Pipe Roll, 15 Henry II (XIII [1890]), p. 24.

28. T. D. Whitaker, An History of Richmondshire, 1823, II, 422, 424; Dobson and Harland, A History of the Preston Guild, 3d ed. [1862], p. 75; Bateson, The English Historical Review, XV (1900), 497.

29. Pipe Roll, 31 Henry II (XXXIV [1913]), p. 4; Receipt Roll of the Exchequer, ed. Hall, 1899, p. 23.

30. Pipe Roll, 31 Henry II, p. 15.

31. The same, p. 17.

32. The same, p. 17. Cf. 32 and 33 Henry II, XXXVI (1914), 19; XXXVII (1915), 2. Cf. the Alverton case in 1167, but this may have been an execution (Pipe Roll, 13 Henry II, XI [1889], 91).

33. Pipe Roll, 31 Henry II, p. 70.

34. Benedict of Peterborough, ed. Stubbs, I, 156; Roger of Hoveden, ed. Stubbs, II, 131. A twelfth-century tract remarks that the citizens of London "non lege duelli, non examine aquae vel ferri candentis se purgabunt, nisi sponte elegerint, sed ibi finis est omnis controversiae sacramentum" (Materials for the History of Thomas Becket, ed. Robertson, IV, 148).

35. Maitland, Three Rolls of the King's Court (Pipe Roll Society, XIV), 1891, pp. 80, 86, 89, 98, 101, 105, 143; the Same, Select Pleas of the Crown (Selden Society, I), I (1888), pp. 1, 3–5, 8, 29, 55, 75, 79, 80; Placitorum Abbreviatio, 1811, p. 43a, b, 68b, 90b; Palgrave, Rotuli Curiae Regis, 1835, I, 204.

36. Rymer, Foedera, 2d ed., I, 228; Patent Rolls of the Reign of Henry III, 1216–1225, p. 186 (January 26, 1219); Dugdale, Origines Juridiciales, 1671, pp. 87–88. For William Rufus's angry outburst against the ordeal by fire (hot iron) see Eadmer, Historia Novorum in Anglia, ed. Rule, p. 102.

37. Canon 18, Mansi, Concilia, XXII (1778), 1007.

38. Roger Bacon, De Nullitate Magiae, cap. 2, Opera Inedita, ed. Brewer, 1859, p. 526.

39. Nathaniel Bacon, The Annalls of Ipsw^che, ed. Richardson, 1884, p. 44 (29 Edw. I).

40. James I, Daemonologie, 1597 (1603), iii, 6, pp. 80–81.

41. Wm. Perkins, A Discourse of the Damned Art of Witchcraft, 1608, p. 208; Cotta, The Triall of Witch-craft, 1616, pp. 104–114; the Same, The Infallible True and Assured Witch, 1624, pp. 127–137 (cf. his tract, A Short Discoverie of the Vnobserved Dangers of Seuerall Sorts of Ignorant and Vnconsiderate Practisers of Physicke in England, 1612, p. 54); Bernard, A Guide to Grand-Iury Men, 2d ed., 1629, pp. 209–211; Hopkins, The Discovery of Witches, 1647, pp. 5–6 (see also The Examination, Confession, Triall, and Execution of Joane Williford, Joan Cariden, and Jane Hott, 1645, pp. 2, 4); Stearne, A Confirmation and Discovery of Witchcraft, 1648, pp. 18–19. Cf. Drage, Daimonomageia, 1665, pp. 40–41.

42. Stearne, p. 18. He remarks that "it is held unlawfull" and rejects the test, but mildly and (as it were) wistfully.

43. Historical MSS. Commission, Various Collections, I, 160–161.

44. John Bufton's Diary, Proceedings Essex Archæological Society, I (1855), 126 (cf. New Series, XI [1911], 211–218); Boys, The Case of Witchcraft at Coggeshall, Essex, in the Year 1699 (London, 1901), p. 21.

45. J. M. Taylor, The Witchcraft Delusion in Colonial Connecticut, pp. 41, 65–66, 71, 73, 75; Increase Mather, An Essay for the Recording of Illustrious Providences, 1684, pp. 139, 280–287. The swimming ordeal is also rejected by Wier, vi, 7, ed. 1568, pp. 588–589; by Binsfeld, Tractatus de Confessionibus Maleficorum et Sagarum, 1579, pp. 41, 148–157; by Bodin, Demonomanie, 1580, iv, 4, fol. 194 r° (cf. iv, 5, fol. 201); by Godelmann, Tractatus de Magis, Veneficis et Lamiis, 1591, iii, 5, 26–35, pp. 41–45; by Binsfeld, De Confessionibus Maleficorum et Sagarum, 1591, pp. 146, 314–322; by Lercheimer (Witekind), Christlich Bedencken vnd Erinnerung von Zauberey, 1597, ed. Binz, 1888, pp. 105–107; by Purchas, Pilgrimes, Part I, Bk. vii, chap. 3, § 6, note, Glasgow ed., VI (1905), 402 ("deceivable superstition," still practised in "the East parts"); by P. de l'Ancre, Tableau de l'Inconstance des Mauvais Anges et Demons, 1613, p. 11; by Bernard, A Guide to Grand-Iury Men, 2d ed., 1629, pp. 209–211; by Filmer, An Advertisement to the Jury-Men, 1653, p. 11; by Fuller, Church-History, 1656, Book ii, Century XI, chap. 14, p. 141 (cf. Book ii, Century X, chap. 9, p. 127); by Ady, A Candle in the Dark, 1656, pp. 7, 100–102; by Ramesey, Ελμινθολογια, 1668, p. 74; by Orchard, The Doctrine of Devils, 1676, p. 89; by Bekker, Le Monde Enchanté, 1694, i, 21, 5 and 8, I, 316–318; by Erasmus Francisci, Der Höllische Proteus, 2d ed., 1695, p. 108; by Meinders, Unvorgreifliche Bedancken und Monita, 1716, pp. 121–126. Cf. Gaule, Select Cases of Conscience touching Witches and Witchcrafts, 1646, p. 76; Zeitschrift für Schleswig-Holsteinische Geschichte, XLV (1915), 165–167. Swimming is approved by the author of The Wonderfull Discouerie of the Witch-crafts of Margaret and Philip Flower, 1619, sig. D3.

46. Scot, xiii, 9, p. 303 (213), ed. Nicholson, p. 247. He cites Wier (see De Praestigiis Daemonum, vi, 7, ed. 1568, pp. 588–589).

47. Court Rolls of the Manor of Hales, ed. Amphlett (Worcestershire Historical Society), Part II (1912), p. 449. Note that William Byg, a fifteenth-century wizard, had the alias of Lech, doubtless because he professed the healing art (see p. 187, above).

48. Most of these cases are collected by W. C. Sydney, England and the English in the Eighteenth Century, 1891, I, 281–288; some appear in Inderwick, Side-Lights on the Stuarts, 2d ed., 1891, pp. 185–187. Their references have required correction and supplementing. Some cases are discussed in one of a good series of articles "On the Progress and Decline of Witchcraft," Gentleman's Magazine, January, 1830, C, i, 27–29. Strutt in his Horda Angel-cynnan, I (1774), 20, reports that the swimming ordeal was "lately put in practice on two poor old people in the Hundreds of Essex, by several stupid, illiterate blockheads, who affirmed that they had bewitched their cattle."

49. The Tryal of Richard Hathaway (London, 1702); Howell, State Trials, XIV (1816), 639–695; Luttrell, A Brief Historical Relation (under November 15, 1701, and May 9, 1702), V, 110, 172; Pike, History of Crime, II, 289–290; Inderwick, Side-Lights on the Stuarts, 2d ed., 1891, pp. 180–185.

50. Wickwar, Witchcraft and the Black Art, 1926, pp. 271–272 (from a "leaflet" of 1702). I have not found this case elsewhere.

51. Rev. Humphrey Michel's MS. Diary, June 11 and 17, 1709, in Sydney, I, 281.

52. Add. MS. 35838, fol. 404.

53. Gentleman's Magazine, January, 1731, I, 29–30, citing the Daily Journal, January 15, 1731 (the woman died).

54. Wickwar, pp. 292–293, from the Northampton Mercury, June 30, 1735.

55. Rev. Joseph Juxon, A Sermon upon Witchcraft. Occasion'd by the Late Illegal Attempt to Discover Witches by Swimming. Preach'd at Twyford, in the County of Leicester, July 11, 1736.

56. The Whitehall Morning Post, July 19–21, 1737; London Magazine for July, 1737, VI, 395–396; Caledonian Mercury, July 26, 1737. The witch floated three times, but was subsequently weighed against the church bible and outweighed it. See also (for weighing) Gentleman's Magazine, February, 1759, XXIX, 93; Strutt, Horda Angel-cynnan, I (1774), 20; Forby, The Vocabulary of East Anglia, 1830, II, 397; Tuchmann, Mélusine, IV (1888–1889), 197–198; Bekker, Le Monde Enchanté, 1694, i, 21, 9–11, I, 318–321. Cf. Viṣṇu-Sūtra, x (transl. Jolly, 1880, pp. 55–57); Asiatick Researches, I (1788), 389–390, 402–403; Traill, the same, XVI (1828), 173; J. A. Dubois, Mœurs, Institutions et Cérémonies des Peuples de l'Inde, 1825, II, 550; Stenzler, Zeitschrift der Deutschen Morgenländischen Gesellschaft, IX (1855), 665–669; Schlagintweit, Die Gottesurtheile der Indier, 1866, pp. 31–32; Heuen-Tsang, transl. S. Beale, Buddhist Records of the Western World, 1884, I, 84; Patetta, Le Ordalie, 1890, pp. 33, 97, 214–215. On various magical means to know a witch see Tuchmann, Mélusine, IV (1888–89), 251–258, 278–286, 289–295, 317–323.

57. Parish Register, Monk's Sleigh, December 19, 1748, in The East Anglian, I (1864), 48.

58. The Tryal of Thomas Colley, at the Assizes at Hertford, on Tuesday the 30th of July, 1751, . . . for the Cruel and Inhuman Murder of Ruth Osborne, Wife of John Osborne, of Tring, in Hertfordshire, by Ducking her in Marlston-Mere, . . . under Supposition of her being a Witch. London, [1751]. The murder occurred on April 22, 1751; Colley was hanged on August 24. Cf. Gentleman's Magazine, 1751, XXI, 186, 198, 375, 378; The Midwife, or The Old Woman's Magazine, 1751, Vol. II, No. 2, pp. 61–63; The Eastern Counties Collectanea, ed. by L'Estrange, 1872–73, pp. 207–208 (from Norwich Gazette, April 24, 1751).

59. Norwich Gazette, September, 1752, in The Eastern Counties Collectanea, 1872–73, p. 208.

60. Annual Register for 1760, 3d ed., 1764, pp. 112–113; Gentleman's Magazine, July, 1760, XXX, 346; Leicestershire and Rutland Notes and Queries, III (1895), 265–266.

61. Public Advertiser, January 1, 1761, in Sydney, I, 286.

62. Gentleman's Magazine, December, 1762, XXXII, 596.

63. The same, August, 1769, XXXIX, 411.

64. The same, July, 1776, XLVI, 332; Leicester and Nottingham Journal, July 6, 1776, as quoted in County Folk-Lore, I, No. 3 (1895), pp. 50–51; Nichols, Leicestershire, IV, ii (1811), 778.

65. Gentleman's Magazine, August, 1785, LV, ii, 658; Drake, Annals of Witchcraft in New England, 1869, p. 125.

66. Proceedings Suffolk Institute of Archæology, III (1863), 309; The East Anglian, I (1864), 406. This may or may not be the same case that is reported from 1792 in County Folk-Lore, I, No. 2 (1893), p. 185.

67. Gentleman's Magazine, August, 1751, XXI, 378.

68. Burr, Narratives of the Witchcraft Cases 1648–1706, 1914, pp. 441–442.

69. Pennsylvania Gazette, October 15–22, 1730, in New Jersey Archives, 1st Series, XI (1894), 220–223; Gentleman's Magazine, January, 1731, I, 29.

70. A Brief Account, prefixed to the Rev. Isaac Nicholson's Sermon against Witchcraft, London, 1808; the Same, An Abstract of the Proceedings had against Joseph Harper [and others] for assaulting Ann Izzard, London, 1810.

71. The Times (London), July 19, 1825, from the Suffolk Chronicle (newspaper). See also Forby, The Vocabulary of East Anglia, 1830, II, 391–392.

72. At some time in the first quarter of the seventeenth century Joan Harvye of Hockam, Norfolk, was in trouble "for scratching of an old witch there, nowe dead" (Add. MS. 28223, fol. 15; Notestein, p. 400). Cf. Chapter II, note 190.

73. Gentleman's Magazine, 1830, C, i, 107; Bye-Gones for 1882–83, p. 118.

74. Essex Review, XVIII (1909), 121–129.

75. Essex Review, V (1896), 159; Folk-Lore Record, III, ii (1881), 292 (from the Daily Telegraph, June 23, 1880). For Norfolk see Charles Kent, The Land of the "Babes in the Wood," 1910, p. 84.

76. Boston Herald, March 22, 1923.

77. Neuwald, Exegesis Purgationis, etc., Tractatus Duo, 1686, p. 154.

78. Laws of Manu, viii, 114–115 (transl. Burnell and Hopkins, 1884, pp. 196–197; transl. Gangā-Nātha-Jhā, IV, i [1924], 143–144); The Indian Antiquary, XIV (1885), 132; Tod, Annals and Antiquities of Rajast'han, II (1832), 587; R. V. Russell, The Tribes and Castes of the Central Provinces of India, 1916, II, 290 (cf. III, 111); Bombay Gazetteer, IX, i (1901), 302, 426; Sangermano, A Description of the Burmese Empire, transl. Tandy, 1833, p. 117. Cf. Sir John Malcolm, A Memoir of Central India, 2d ed., 1824, II, 216–217; C. Grant, The Gazetteer of the Central Provinces of India, 2d ed., 1870, pp. cxxxi, 39; The Asiatic Journal, XII (1821), 404–405; New Series, XXIV, i (1837), 64; Panjab Notes and Queries, II (1884–85), 6–7, 94; Indian Notes and Queries, IV (1886–87), 47; Stenzler, Zeitschrift der Deutschen Morgenländischen Gesellschaft, IX (1855), 662–663; Schlagintweit, Die Gottesurtheile der Indier, 1866, p. 25.

79. Voyages d'Ibn Batoutah, ed. and transl. by Dufrémery and Sanguinetti, IV, 36–38. Cf. H. Winckler, Altorientalische Forschungen, I, iv (1896), 339, note.

80. O. Hanson, The Kachins, 1913, p. 143.

81. Mrs. L. Milne, The Shans at Home, 1910, pp. 192–193. Cf. North Indian Notes and Queries, II (1892–93), 113; Journal of the Anthropological Institute, XXIII (1894), 163–164 (Borneo); Tijdschrift voor Indische Taal- Land- en Volkenkunde, XIV (1864), 506–510.

82. Sir H. M. Elliot, The History of India as Told by its own Historians, I (1867), 330; Sir A. C. Lyall, Asiatic Studies, 1882, p. 83; Skeat, Malay Magic, 1900, pp. 542–544. Cf. Viṣṇu-Sūtra, xii (transl. Jolly, The Institutes of Vishnu, 1880, pp. 59–60); Asiatick Researches, I (1788), 390–391, 404; Stenzler, as above, pp. 671–674; Schlangintweit, p. 27; Folk-Lore Journal, II (1884), 89 (Burma); Journal of the Anthropological Institute, II (1873), 241 (Burma); Gurdon, The Khasis, 2d ed., 1914, pp. 94–95; E. H. Gomes, Seventeen Years among the Sea Dyaks of Borneo, 1911, pp. 316–320; J. A. Dubois, Mœurs, Institutions et Cérémonies des Peuples de l'Inde, 1825, II, 553; Traill, Asiatic Researches, XVI (1828), 173.

83. Hammurabi, §§ 2, 132. The law (§ 2) is not quite clear as to witchcraft. It reads, "If a man has cast a spell upon a man and has not established it, he upon whom the spell was cast shall go to the divine river," etc. This may well mean "If a man has accused another of sorcery." Professor Lyon has kindly helped me here.

84. Van Nyendael, Beschryving van Rio Formosa, 1701 (Bosman, Nauwkeurige Beschryving van de Guinese Goud- Tand- en Slavekust, ed. 1737, Part II, pp. 241–242). See also Bosman, II, 131.

85. The Wonderfull Discoverie of the Witch-crafts of Margaret and Philip Flower, 1619, Sig. C v°; Damnable Practises (ballad), 1619, Rollins, A Pepysian Garland, 1922, pp. 102–103.

86. Diary of Walter Yonge, ed. Roberts (Camden Society, XLI), pp. 82–83.

87. Cf. Ezekiel, iii, 26; Lamentations, iv, 4.

88. On the bread (or bread-and-cheese) ordeal see Jacoby, Der Ursprung des Judicium Offae, Archiv für Religionswissenschaft, XIII (1910), 525–566; Zeumer, Formulae Aevi Merowingici et Karolini (Monumenta, Leges, Sect. V), 1886, pp. 629–636 (hanging bread, pp. 630–632); A. Franz, Die Kirchlichen Benediktionen, 1909, II, 335–336, 341–342, 358–360, 384–390; Recueil des Historiens, IV, 604–605, 607–608; Vassiliev, Anecdota Graeco-Byzantina, I (1893), 340 (cf. pp. 330, lxiii–lxvii); Lercheimer (Witekind), Christlich Bedencken vnd Erinnerung von Zauberey, 1597, ed. Binz, 1888, p. 18; Ohrt, Trylleord (Danmarks Folkeminder, No. 25), 1922, pp. 24–27; Mittheilungen der Schlesischen Gesellschaft für Volkskunde, IX, i, Heft 17 (1907), p. 45. Cf. B. M. Papyrus XLVI, ll. 172–201, 295–303, Kenyon, Greek Papyri in the British Museum, I (1893), 70–71, 74. For the oracle of the hanging bread to detect a thief see Sloane MS. 3846, fol. 27 v°.

89. Rituals III (ninth or tenth century) and XIV (eleventh or early twelfth century), Liebermann, I, 408–409, 425–427; Æthelred, viii, 22–24, Liebermann, I, 266 (Thorpe, ix, 22–24, p. 147); Cnut, i, 5, 2a–c, Liebermann, I, 286 (Thorpe, p. 155). The morsel was styled corsnæd, which is explained in the Quadripartitus by "panis coniuratus," in the Instituta Cnuti by "panis benedictus," and in the Consiliatio Cnuti by "offa iudicialis": Liebermann, I, 286, 287: see also II, 472–473. Cf. Textus Roffensis,

ed. Hearne, 1720, pp. 33–37; Patetta, Le Ordalie, 1890, pp. 34, 202–203, 209–211, 431.

90. Aelred, Vita Sancti Edwardi, Twysden, Scriptores X, 1652, col. 395; Lives of Edward the Confessor, ed. Luard, pp. 117–119, 372; Henry of Huntingdon, vi, 23, ed. Arnold, pp. 194–195; William of Malmesbury, Gesta Regum, ii, 197, ed. Stubbs, I, 240; Chronica Monasterii de Hida, in Edwards's ed. of Liber Monasterii de Hyda, p. 289; illustration in Cotton MS. Vitellius Axiii, reproduced by Strutt, The Regal and Ecclesiastical Antiquities of England, ed. Planché, 1842, p. 3, plate ii; Freeman, Norman Conquest, 3d ed., II (1877), 656–661.

91. Tremearne, The Tailed Head-Hunters of Nigeria, 1912, p. 200; Ivens, Melanesians of the South-East Solomon Islands, 1927, pp. 343, 344; Lewin, The Hill Tracts of Chittagong, 1869, p. 75; Krapf, Travels . . . in East Africa, Boston, 1860, p. 142. Cf. Asiatick Researches, I (1788), 391–392; Stenzler, Zeitschrift der Deutschen Morgenländischen Gesellschaft, IX (1855), 676; Schlagintweit, Die Gottesurtheile der Indier, 1866, pp. 33–36; Patetta, Le Ordalie, 1890, pp. 50–51. See also the curious note of Pseudo-Acron on Horace, Epistola i, 10, 10 (ed. Hauthal, II, 422; ed. Kellner, II, 242), quoted by Patetta, p. 140.

CHAPTER XVI

The Compact and the Witches' Sabbath

1. St. Augustine, De Doctrina Christiana, ii, 20–24; De Diversis Quaestionibus LXXXIII, 79, 1 and 4.

2. Rosweyde, Vitae Patrum, 2d ed., 1628, pp. 156–158; Acta Sanctorum, June 14, II (1698), 949–951; W. Meyer, Munich Academy, Sitzungsberichte, III (1873), 50–53; An Alphabet of Tales, No. 64, ed. Banks, I (1904), 45–47; Själens Tröst, ed. Klemming, pp. 26–30. Cf. Herbert, Catalogue of Romances, III (1910), 257, 440; Hansen, Zauberwahn, pp. 167–168.

3. See the Latin text in Petsch, Theophilus, 1908, pp. 1–10.

4. E. Sommer, De Theophili cum Diabolo Foedere, 1844; Dasent, Theophilus, 1845; Hansen, Zauberwahn, 1900, pp. 167–168 (St. Basil; Theophilus); Lundgren, Studier öfver Theophilus-Legendens Romanska Varianter, 1913; Waxman, Chapters on Magic in Spanish Literature (from La Revue Hispanique, XXXVIII), 1916, pp. 43–62; Plenzat, Die Theophiluslegende in den Dichtungen des Mittelalters, 1926 (Germanische Studien, XLIII); Beaumanoir, La Manekine, vv. 5739–5756, Œuvres, ed. Suchier, I (1884), 177; Grace Frank, ed. of Rutebuef's Théophile, 1925, Introduction.

5. Homilies of Ælfric, ed. Thorpe, I (1844), 448.

6. For the South English version see The Early South-English Legendary, ed. Horstmann, 1887, I, 288–293. For that in the North English collection see Kölbing, Englische Studien, I (1877), 16–57, 186, 540. For a third version see Heuser, Englische Studien, XXXII (1903), 1–23. Cf. also Kölbing, Beiträge zur Vergleichenden Geschichte der Romantischen

Poesie und Prosa des Mittelalters, 1876, pp. 1-41; Gerould, The North-English Homily Collection, 1902, pp. 75-79, and Modern Language Notes, XVIII (1903), 145-146; the Same, Saints' Legends, 1916, pp. 252-253, 317-318; The Minor Poems of the Vernon MS., xxv, 376-378, ed. Horstmann, I (1892), 130.

7. Speculum Historiale, xxi, 69-70, ed. 1494, fol. 277; Ward, Catalogue of Romances, II (1893), 595, 599-600, 602, 675-677, 710, 713, 730, 735-740; Herbert, the same, III (1910), 454, 523, 534-535, 543, 608, 717; An Alphabet of Tales, No. 467, ed. Banks, II (1905), 318-319.

8. Edited by Ludorff, Anglia, VII (1884), 60-115; cf. Logeman, Anglia, X (1888), 533-541.

9. Heywood, The Hierarchie of the Blessed Angells, 1635, pp. 471-472.

10. Bilson, The Yorkshire Archæological Journal, XXIV (1917), 221-225; M. R. James, The Sculptures in the Lady Chapel at Ely, 1895, p. 17. For the iconography of the subject see also Faligan, Revue des Traditions Populaires, V (1890), 1-14.

11. Celestyn, ed. Horstmann, Anglia, I (1878), 55-85. Cf. Gerould, Saints' Lives, 1916, pp. 228-229.

12. William of Malmesbury, Gesta Regum, ii, 167-169, 172, ed. Stubbs, I, 193-198, 202-203; Roger of Wendover, Flores Historiarum, ed. Coxe, I, 431-434; Radulfus Niger, ed. Anstruther, pp. 154-155; Chronicon Anglicum Petriburgense, ed. Giles, pp. 36-37; Chronicle in Liber de Legibus Antiquis, ed. Stapleton (Camden Society, XXXIV), p. 180; Vincent of Beauvais, Speculum Historiale, xxiv, 98, Venice, 1494, fol. 320 v°; Holkot, Super Libros Sapientiae, Lectio 190, Reutlingen, 1489, sig. Miiij, lf. 4 v°; An Alphabet of Tales, ed. Banks, No. 50, I (1904), 34-35; Giraldus Cambrensis, Gemma Ecclesiastica, i, 9, Opera, ed. Brewer, II, 34; Hansen, Zauberwahn, p. 169; R. Allen, English Historical Review, VII (1892), 625-668, especially pp. 663-668; A. Graf, Miti, Leggende e Superstizioni del Medio Evo, II (1893), 1-75; Hock, Gerbert, 1837, pp. 159-165, 229-238; Picavet, Gerbert, 1897, pp. 197-217; de la Salle, Gerbert, 1914, pp. 51-68. Cf. Bale's Select Works, ed. Christmas (Parker Society), 1849, pp. 560, 561, 592-593; Bale, The Pageant of Popes, transl. John Studley, 1574, foll. 72-73; Calfhill, An Aunswere to the Treatise of the Crosse, 1565, ed. Gibbings (Parker Society), 1846, pp. 91-92.

13. Pilkington, Works, ed. Scholefield (Parker Society), 1842, pp. 602-603. As to Benedict IX see Bale, Select Works, pp. 592-593; the Same, The Pageant of Popes, 1574, foll. 75-76. Cf. Bovet, Pandaemonium, 1684, p. 121: "*Benedict* the ninth, a *Conjurer*, wont with *Laurence* and *Gratian* (two *Conjurers*) whom he made Cardinals, to wander in the Woods, to *invocate Devils*, and bewitch Women to follow them." His source is Cardinal Ben(n)o's Vita et Gesta Hildebrandi (Flacius Illyricus, Catalogus Testium Veritatis, ed. 1556, pp. 330-333). Platina says of Benedict: "Constat ... simulacrum eius admodum monstruosum post mortem cuidam apparuisse" (De Vita et Moribus Summorum Pontificum, 1529, cliii, p. 129). Cf. Del Rio, Disquisitiones Magicae, ii, 12, § 9, ed. 1616, p. 134.

14. Kittredge, A Study of Gawain and the Green Knight, 1916, pp. 184-185; Nashe, Have with You to Saffron-Walden, 1596, Works, ed.

Grosart, III, 42 (ed. McKerrow, III, 30). Cf. Comparetti, Virgilio nel Medio Evo, 2d ed., 1896, II, 196–197, 259.

15. Walter Map, De Nugis Curialium, iv, 11, ed. Wright, pp. 170–176; ed. James, pp. 176–183. For the *daemonium meridianum* see Chapter XIII, note 13, above.

16. Matthew Paris, Chronica Majora, ed. Luard, II, 207–209 (from the Vita Sancti Wlfrici by John, Abbot of Forda).

17. Cf. Chaucer, Troilus, iv, 1544–1545; Ovid, Metamorphoses, i, 192–193.

18. Walter Map, De Nugis Curialium, iv, 6, ed. Wright, pp. 154–166 (ed. James, pp. 159–171).

19. For the suits against him see State Trials of the Reign of Edward I, ed. Tout and Johnstone, 1906, pp. 49–51, 53–67, cf. p. 98 (cf. also Thoroton, The Antiquities of Nottinghamshire, 1677, pp. 32–33). See also Calendar of Fine Rolls, I, 269 (arrest: roll of January 21, 1290); Palgrave, Parliamentary Writs, I (1827), 14, note 1 (fine); Calendar of Patent Rolls 1281–1292, p. 421 (pardon, February 12, 1291); Calendar of Fine Rolls, I, 347 (cf. p. 352), and Calendar of Inquisitions post Mortem, III, 131–134, No. 207 (writ to escheator, November 5, 1294); Calendar of Inquisitions, III, 134, Nos. 207, 208 (Joan's dower, 1395; cf. Calendar of Close Rolls 1288–1296, pp. 412, 413, 415, 435, 441, 459). On the connection of the bishop with the Briançon property see Calendar of Patent Rolls 1281–1292, pp. 362, 439; the same, 1301–1307, p. 56; cf. Morant, The History and Antiquities of the County of Essex, 1816 reprint, I, Appendix, p. 91; Calendar of Inquisitions, V, 149, No. 273.

20. Bartholomew de Briançon died on November 25, 1286 (Calendar of Inquisitions post Mortem, II, 378, No. 624; cf. Calendar of Fine Rolls, I, 233). On him and his family and property see further Calendar of Fine Rolls, I, 154; II, 87, 277, 332, 348; Calendar of Charter Rolls, III, 462; Calendar of Inquisitions, II, 78, 465, Nos. 116, 766; III, 342, No. 450; V, 149–150, 379–381, Nos. 273, 599 (cf. Calendar of Fine Rolls, II, 75, 78); Calendar of Inquisitions Miscellaneous (Chancery), I, 382, No. 1318; Morant, as above, I, Appendix, pp. 77, 306.

21. Calendar of Inquisitions post Mortem, III, 131–134.

22. Cf. Roskoff, Geschichte des Teufels, 1869, I, 330, 346, 358, 359; Sebastien Champier, Dyalogus in Magicarum Artium Destructionem, Lyons, ca. 1500, iii, 3, sig. bij, lf. 2 r°; Hansen, Quellen, p. 496; Bodin, ed. 1587, ii, 4, foll. 91 r°, 93 r°, 95 r°, 96 r°; ii, 5, fol. 102 r°; Scot, iii, 2, p. 42 (36), ed. Nicholson, p. 32; Pitcairn, Criminal Trials in Scotland, 1833, III, 613.

23. Boniface VIII to the Archbishop of Canterbury, February 6, 1301 (Register of John de Halton, Bishop of Carlisle, I, 174–175, Canterbury and York Series, XII; Chronicon de Lanercost, ed. Stevenson, Maitland Club, pp. 200–201; same, translated by Maxwell, pp. 172–173); the same to the same, March 1, 1302 (Papal Letters, I, 607); Boniface VIII to Edward I, April 6, 1302 (Rymer, Foedera, 2d ed., II, 900); the Pope to the Archbishop, April 6, 1302 (Papal Letters, I, 600); Edward I to the Pope, August 24, 1302 (Prynne, Records, III, 926; Calendar of Close Rolls 1296–1302, p. 604); the same to the same, August 24, 1302 (Prynne, III, 925;

Rymer, II, 907; Calendar, pp. 603–604); Edward I to three Cardinals, August 24, 1302 (Prynne, III, 927; Rymer, II, 907–908; Calendar, p. 604); Edward I to the Pope, September 13, 1302 (Prynne, III, 926; Calendar, p. 602); the Pope's mandate to the Archbishop of Canterbury, December 6, 1302 (Papal Letters, I, 605); Edward I to the Pope, 1303 (Rymer, II, 931–932; Calendar of Close Rolls 1302–1307, pp. 81–82); Relaxation of Suspension, etc., June 8, 1303 (Papal Letters, I, 610), with concurrent letters to Edward I (Rymer, II, 932–934) and the Chapters of Coventry and Lichfield; the Pope's license to the Bishop to borrow 7000 florins, June 15, 1303 (Papal Letters, I, 610).

24. Chronicle of London, 1827, pp. 44–45; cf. Gregory's Chronicle, in Gairdner, The Historical Collections of a Citizen of London (Camden Society, XVII), pp. 74–75.

25. Johannes de Reading, Chronicon, ed. Tait, p. 176.

26. Bray, Traditions, Legends, Superstitions, and Sketches of Devonshire, 1838, II, 283–284, cf. p. 285. The folk-tale of The Wasted Wishes has been found in the North of England within a generation or so. As there told, it involves a compact signed with blood, and the third wish is used to cheat the devil (Transactions Lancashire and Cheshire Antiquarian Society, XXXIV [1917], 88–89).

27. Thoms, Altdeutsche Blätter, II (1840), 78; Herbert, Catalogue of Romances, III (1910), 169, 385, 445.

28. Thoms, II, 76–77; Herbert, III, 381.

29. Thoms, II, 76; Herbert, III, 119, 138, 145, 148, 380. For the devil's mark as *signum pacti* see Hansen, Zauberwahn, pp. 442, 443, 449; the Same, Quellen, pp. 137, 155, 178, 493, 558, 582 (note 1), 600; Danaeus (Daneau), De Veneficis, 1575, cap. 4, pp. 58–59; Bodin, Demonomanie, 1587, ii, 4, foll. 87 r°–88 r°; Guaccius (Guazzo), Compendium Maleficarum, 1608, i, 6, p. 17.

30. Herbert, III, 448.

31. See Malleus Maleficarum, Part II, qu. 1, cap. 2, ed. 1620, p. 164; Perkins, A Discourse of the Damned Art of Witchcraft, 1608, pp. 51–55; Glanvil, A Blow at Modern Sadducism, 1668, p. 79 (Saducismus Triumphatus, 1682, Part I, p. 60).

32. Event Book, in The Rev. Oliver Heywood his Autobiography, ed. Turner, I (1882), 344–345 (see p. 146, above); Middlesex County Records, ed. Jeaffreson, III, 88. Cf. Rollins, Cavalier and Puritan, 1923, pp. 372–378.

33. On the Witches' Sabbath and transportation see, for example, Malleus Maleficarum, Part II, qu. 1, capp. 2–3 (ed. 1620, pp. 160–169, compact, meetings, homage, etc.; pp. 169–177, transportation); Grillando, De Sortilegiis, 1545, ii, 3, §§ 2–5, foll. xvij v°–xviij r°; ii, 7, §§ 1–27, foll. xxxiiij r°–xliij v°; Daneau (Danaeus), De Veneficis, 1575, chap. 4; cf. chap. 2, p. 41 (wax candles offered; kiss); English translation, A Dialogue of Witches, 1575, sigg. Fiij, lf. 2 r°–Hiiij, lf. 4 v°; cf. Dv, lf. 2 r°, Ei v°; Bodin, De la Demonomanie des Sorciers, 1580 (dedication dated December 20, 1579), ii, 4 and 5, foll. 79 r°–93 r° (uses Grillando and Daneau); Anania, De Natura Daemonum, 1581, pp. 147–152; Binsfeld, De Confessionibus Male-

ficorum et Sagarum, new ed., 1591 (dedication dated 1591), pp. 34, 54–59, 221–226, 236–237, 346–364; the Same, Commentarius in Titulum Codicis Lib. IX. De Maleficis et Mathematicis (in same volume), pp. 537–553; Remy (Remigius), Daemonolatreia, 1595, i, 11–20, pp. 98–145; i, 22, pp. 148–149; i, 24, pp. 157–158; i, 29, pp. 177–183 (cites many witch-trials of 1581–1591, and one [p. 121] of 1574); James I, Daemonologie, 1597 (1603), i, 3–4, pp. 35–41; Guazzo (Guaccius), Compendium Maleficarum, 1608 (dedication dated May, 1608), i, 6, pp. 13–18; i, 7, p. 22; i, 8, p. 25; i, 12, pp. 38–59 — with woodcuts illustrating everything described in the text; Boguet, Discours des Sorciers, 1608, pp. 94–143; P. de l'Ancre, Tableau de l'Inconstance des Mauvais Anges et Demons, 1613, pp. 61–227; Margaret Murray, The Witch-Cult in Western Europe, 1921; Summers, The History of Witchcraft and Demonology, 1926, pp. 110–172; Gomme, Ethnology in Folklore, 1892, pp. 57–58. For the history of the Sabbath, etc., see Hansen, Zauberwahn, Chaps. iv.–vi, with the documents in his Quellen. Cf. Lea, History of the Inquisition, 1888, III, 493–501; Reitzenstein, Hellenistische Wundererzählungen, 1906, p. 143, and note 2. For an emphatic assertion of a witch-epidemic affecting thousands of hysterical women see J. Kohler, Archiv für Strafrecht, LIX (1912), 387. The whole business of the Witches' Sabbath, or almost all of it (involving the amalgamation of the Diana-Herodias idea with the belief in child-devouring *striges*) was known to John of Salisbury. He rejected it as an evil dream: "Qui uel cecus hoc ludificantium demonum non uideat esse nequitiam?" (Policraticus, ii, 17, ed. Webb, I, 100–101.) For a famous mediæval anecdote about a deluded old woman who thought she shared in these night-rides but was undeceived by her priest see Thomas Wright, Latin Stories (Percy Society, 1842), No. 19, p. 21; Crane, The Exempla of Jacques de Vitry, 1890, No. 269, pp. 112–113, 251; Herbert, Catalogue of Romances, III (1910), 555. The tale is very similar to Porta's account of an experiment which he tried with a witch (see also note 125, below). Bishop Baldock in 1311 speaks of sorcerers and enchanters in the diocese of London as holding "conventiculas" (Registrum, ed. Fowler, I, 145, Canterbury and York Series). Some connection might conceivably be traced between the witches' sabbath and the mummings, animal disguises, New Year's rites, revelries at wakes, etc., so often denounced by early councils and preachers and condemned in the penitentials of Anglo-Saxon times. See, for example, Schmitz, Bussbücher, I, 303, 311, 379, 413, 462, 479, 480, 581, 633, 666, 749, 786, 810; II, 181, 237–238, 296, 322, 325, 329, 336, 337, 343, 347, 353, 361, 377, 423, 429, 431, 496, 627, 682; Thorpe, pp. 293, 298 (Pseudo-Theodore, xxvii, 19; xxxviii, 9); so-called Canons of Ælfric (Thorpe, p. 448); Wasserschleben, p. 368; Concilia Aevi Merovingici, ed. Maassen, 1893, p. 179; Pseudo-Augustine, De Rectitudine Catholicae Conversationis, cap.5 (Migne, XL, 1172), and Sermons 129, 130, 265 (Migne, XXXIX, 2001–2004, 2239); Homilia de Sacrilegiis, ed. Caspari, 1886, pp. 10–11, 14, 34–35; Grimm, Deutsche Mythologie, 4th ed., III (1878), 401; Kögel, Geschichte der Deutschen Litteratur, I, i (1894), 51–55; Crusius, Philologus, LXVIII (1909), 579; F. Schneider, Archiv für Religionswissenschaft, XX (1920–21), 91–114, 121–122, 408; E. K. Chambers, The Mediaeval Stage,

1903, I, 237–238, 244–246, 258–259, 330–332; II, 290–306; Enid Walford, The Court Masque, 1927, pp. 3–21; Summers, The Geography of Witchcraft, 1927, pp. 89, 65, 68–71 (he takes the ninth-century Frankish compilation for the genuine work of St. Theodore, the seventh-century Archbishop of Canterbury).

34. Regino of Prüm, Libri Duo de Synodalibus Causis et Disciplinis Ecclesiasticis, ii, 371, ed. Wasserschleben, 1840, pp. 354–356; cf. ii, 5, 45, p. 212. See Hansen, Zauberwahn, pp. 78–88, 190–209, 235. Cf. Kauffmann, Paul and Braune's Beiträge, XVIII (1894), 148–157; J. A. Schmeller, Bayerisches Wörterbuch, I (1872), 270–271.

35. Ivo Carnotensis, Decretum, xi, 30 (Panormia, viii, 75, ed. 1499, Furter, fol. clxvi). Cf. Corrector, §§ 70, 90, 170–171 (Schmitz, II, 425, 429, 446–447).

36. Regino, ii, 5, 45, p. 212.

37. See Malleus Maleficarum, ii, 1, 3, ed. 1620, p. 177; P. de l'Ancre, L'Incredulité et Mescreance du Sortilege, 1622, pp. 523–597.

38. Thomas Wright long ago noted the fact that English witchcraft in Queen Elizabeth's time "seems to have been entirely free from the romantic incidents which form so striking a characteristic of the popular creed in other countries. We have no voyages out to sea in sieves; no witches' sabbaths" (Narratives of Sorcery and Magic, 1851, I, 280–281). On the Continental Sabbath see Wright, I, 297–333. For the Sabbath in Guernsey in 1617 see J. L. Pitts, Witchcraft and Devil Lore in the Channel Islands, 1886, pp. 12–20.

39. It is barely possible that the evidence in two cases mentioned by Henry Holland in A Treatise against Witchcraft (1590) included something about the Witches' Sabbath. Holland has been discussing the aërial flight "to meete with Herodias, Diana, and Minerva," and has admitted that "whatsoeuer is saide of transportations, contrarie to the nature of our bodies, as to ride on the moone to meete Herodias &c. all such thinges are indeede but meere delusions." Yet he holds that the transportation of witches by Satan is possible in nature (sigg. E3 v°–E4 r°). So far he is merely repeating Continental arguments with reference to the magic flight pronounced delusion by the Canon Episcopi, and is following Continental authorities. He refers, for example, to Bodin and Danaeus, and he adds nothing to the reasoning of the Malleus Maleficarum (Part II, qu. 1, cap. 3), which distinguishes between the imaginary experiences contemplated in the Canon and the actual experiences of more recent times. Next he takes up the formal compact, which he avers is made at the witches' "common meetings, which they cal their sabboth" (sig. F1 r°). These he describes, still using Continental authors. "In these horrible meetings," he avers, "Sathan himselfe appeares sometime in one forme, sometime in another: . . . for somtimes his ministers behould him in the likenes of a man, but most commonly of a foule stinking goate," etc. This is almost word for word from Danaeus (A Dialogue, 1575, sig. Fiij, lf. 5 v°). Then comes a remark which seems, at the first blush, to accept all these gruesome details as applicable to English conditions: "See I pray thee, the ex-

aminations, confessions, and practise of M. A. of Barking, and M. B. of
Rochester, confirmed by sufficient credible witnesses. Ann. 1584." It is
not clear whether he means to cite these two cases in confirmation of what
he has said about the "sabboth" or merely in support of the proposition
that witches make a contract with Satan and receive assistance from him.
In the absence of confirmatory testimony, I am forced to infer that he did
not intend to declare that these cases involved evidence about the "sabboth." Indeed Holland himself seems to exonerate the general run of contemporary witches, so far as this article of faith is concerned, when he
states expressly that "the common sort of our witches" have no formal
covenant with Satan, no such covenant, that is to say, as Danaeus describes as ratified in witch-meetings, with renunciation of one's faith in God
and definite acceptance of Satan as God (F v°–F2 r°). I am inclined to interpret "M. A. of Barking" as the Mother Arnold who seems to have been
executed at that place in 1575. Lowndes (Bohn's ed., X, 2959), at all
events, registers "The Examination and Confession of a notorious Witch
named Mother Arnold, alias Whitecote, alias Glastonbury, at the Assise of
Burntwood in July, 1574; who was hanged for Witchcraft at Barking.
1575." Notestein (p. 350) was unable to find this tract, and I have had no
better fortune. 1584 for 1574 would not be a remarkable erratum or slip of
Holland's pen. As to "M. B. of Rochester," I have little doubt that she
was the famous Mother Bungie of whom Scot has such interesting things
to tell. She was, he says, "a principall witch, so reputed, and condemned
of all men, and continuing in that exercise and estimation manie yeares
(having cousened & abused the whole realme, in so much as there came to
hir, witchmongers from all the furthest parts of the land, she being in diverse bookes set out with authoritie, registred and chronicled by name of
the great witch of *Rochester*, and reputed among all men for the cheefe
ringleader of all other witches)." She was found, he says, "to be a meere
cousener; confessing in hir death bed freelie, without compulsion or in-
forcement, that hir cunning consisted onlie in deluding and deceiving the
people: saving that she had . . . some sight in physicke and surgerie, and
the assistance of a freend of hirs, called *Heron*, a professor thereof. And
this I know, partlie of mine owne knowledge, and partlie by the testimonie
of hir husband, and others of credit, to whome (I saie) in hir death bed,
and at sundrie other times she protested these things; and also that she
never had anie materiall spirit or divell (as the voice went) nor yet knew
how to worke anie supernaturall matter, as she in hir life time made men
beleeve she had and could doo" (Discoverie, xvi, 3, pp. 473–474 [341–342],
ed. Nicholson, pp. 398–399). When she died we do not know, but she was
dead when Scot wrote the latter part of his Discoverie in or shortly before
1584. Nor do we know whether she was ever brought to trial. Manifestly,
however, she was not hanged. That she ever made any revelations about
Witches' Sabbaths is to the last degree improbable. If she had pretended
to know something about such meetings, Scot would assuredly have said
so, for her recantation would have been a strong argument in favor of his
thesis that these are either imaginary or fictitious.

40. Strype, The Life of Sir Thomas Smith, 1698, pp. 128–132.

41. A True and Iust Recorde, of the Information, Examination and Confession of all the Witches, taken at S. Osees (London, 1582), sig. B2, lf. 2; Mrs. E. Lynn Linton, Witch Stories, 1861, pp. 209, 220.

42. The English physician Richard Argentine, in his De Praestigiis et Incantationibus Daemonum et Necromanticoram (Basel, 1568), has a chapter "De Pactis et Conuentionibus inter incanta·orem et Daemonem" (cap. 5, pp. 31–35), but says nothing of the Sabbath. He dates his dedication at Exeter "pridie Calendas Februarii Anno 1563" and says he wrote in the preceding year.

43. Giffard, A Dialogue concerning Witches and Witchcraftes, 1593, sig. K r°.

44. Scot, iii, 1–3 and 6, pp. 40–44, 47–48 (35–38, 40), ed. Nicholson, pp. 31–34, 37. Cf. iii, 12 and 16, pp. 59–60, 65–67 (48, 52–53), ed. Nicholson, pp. 46–47, 51–52; x, 8 and 9, pp. 184–187 (135–137), ed. Nicholson, pp. 148–150. Scot's account of the witch's "bargaine or profession" (which he scouts) is quoted almost word for word from the Malleus, Part II, qu. 1, cap. 2.

45. Strype, Life of Smith, 1598, Appendix, p. 139; Dee's Diary, ed. Halliwell (Camden Society), 1842, p. 59; Gabriel Harvey, Pierces Supererogation, 1593, Works, ed. Grosart, II, 291.

46. Danaeus's De Veneficis was issued in 1575 (the address to the Reader is dated July 1, 1574). The English translation (1575) is entitled A Dialogue of Witches. The Sabbath is treated in Chapter IV.

47. Newes from Scotland, [1591] (reprinted in Bodley Head Quartos, ed. G. B. Harrison, No. IX, 1924).

48. William Perkins, A Discourse of the Damned Art of Witchcraft, 1608, pp. 194–196. Cf. pp. 47, 48, 193, 202–203, 250–251. He believes in Satanic transportation (pp. 21, 49).

49. Notestein, pp. 17–18. Cf. Summers, The Geography of Witchcraft, 1927, pp. 115–116: "There is, in truth, no controversialist of the day who exceeds Jewel in the reckless violence of his abuse. His impudence, profanity, unblushing mendacity, and downright forgery are beyond belief . . . . It is important that we should appreciate a just character of the man to whom the witch-trials in England are largely due, not that he acted from any hatred to Witchcraft and Satanists, but solely from political motives." — "By my troth, Captain, these are very bitter words!"

50. Jewel to Peter Martyr, August 1, 1559 (Zurich Letters, No. 16, I, 22 [39]; Jewel's Works, ed. Ayre, Parker Society, IV, 1213–1215); November 2, 1559 (Zurich Letters, No. 19, I, 25 [44–45]; Works, IV, 1216: "Magarum et veneficarum numerus ubique in immensum excreverat").

51. This sermon (Jewel's Works, II, 1025–1034) is undated. Clearly, however, it was preached after Jewel's return from his visitation, — that is, after November 1, 1559 (see Works, IV, 1216, 1221), — and probably soon after, while his experiences were still fresh in mind (cf. Burr in Notestein, p. 16, note). Doubtless it was delivered before May 24, 1560, when Jewel left London for Salisbury (Works, IV, 1233, 1235). There are strong arguments for identifying it with his court sermon of March 17, 1560 (see I, 26): cf. I, 27–28, with II, 1030, 1031 ¶ 2; and note what Jewel says in a let-

ter of February 8, 1566 (IV, 1266), about the argument of his sermon at court "ante sex annos." Strype (Annals of the Reformation, I [1725], 201) asserts that the sermon at Paul's Cross on March 31, 1560, was a repetition of the court sermon of March 17, but I think he is mistaken. He cites no evidence. Perhaps he was inferring such identity from the title-page of the contemporary edition of the sermon of March 31 (Jewel's Works, I, 2).

52. Jewel's Works, ed. Ayre, II, 1025–1034 (witchcraft passage, p. 1028).

53. If Jewel had imbibed Continental notions about the Witches' Sabbath, he had every occasion to mention them (as he does not) in this very sermon, apropos of the pagan idea of the early Christians, which he does mention in plain terms: "Whereas the Christian men, soon after the apostles' time, used to resort together in the night-time, or in the morning before day, into some private house, there to call upon the name of God, and to receive the sacrament together, for fear of the cruelty of tyrants; the enemies reported that, being thus together, they killed a child amongst them, and so devoured up his flesh, and drank his blood, and after put out the lights, and so committed incest and adultéry one with another" (Works, II, 1026).

54. Jewel's Articles of Enquiry for Salisbury Cathedral, 1568, include the following question: "An aliquis ax predictis prebendariis sit aut fuerit invocator diaboli sive malus divinator aut in huiusmodi diabolice invocacionis sive male divinacionis facinore respersus sive notatus" (Frere and Kennedy, Visitation Articles, III, 204). But this is a different matter, to say nothing of the fact that the date is about ten years after his return from the Continent. Anyhow, clerics did often dabble in the arts here mentioned. Note, for example, the case of Leonard Bilson, prebendary of Winchester, in 1561 (p. 258, above). Such references to sorcery as the following also have no bearing on my argument: (1) In refuting the allegation that St. Peter said mass at Rome, Jewel says, "This have men told you, and with such things as they have found out themselves they have infeoffed and fathered the apostles of Christ. So commonly conjurers and sorcerers make their vaunts, that they have all their books and their cunning from Athanasius, from Moses, from Abel, from Raphael the archangel" (Jewel's Works, I, 23); (2) "The conjurers and sorcerers say that their books of conjuration and sorcery came from Moses, from Enoch, and from Abel" (the same, II, 991). As to the cessation of the exorcist's office in the Church, see III, 273.

55. On the Royal Visitations of 1559 see Gee, The Elizabethan Clergy and the Settlement of Religion 1558–1564, 1898, pp. 41–129; Birt, The Elizabethan Religious Settlement, 1907, pp. 140–182.

56. Zurich Letters, Nos. 16, 19, 23, I, 22–23 (38–41), 25–26 (44–45), 30 (52); Jewel's Works, IV, 1213–1218, 1221.

57. Gee, pp. 74–76.

58. Articles to be enquyred in the visitation, in the fyrste yeare of the raygne of our moost drad soueraygne Lady, Elizabeth (London, Richard Iugge and Iohn Cawood, 1559), § 37, sig. Bj r°; Cardwell, Documentary Annals, 1844, I, 246; Frere and Kennedy, Visitation Articles and Injunc-

tions (Alcuin Club), 1910, III, 5; Gee, p. 68. On June 13, 1559, Cecil wrote, "The Queen, on the advice of the Council, is determined to have a great visitation; whereupon the Injunctions and Articles of Inquisition are already formed" (Gee, p. 43).

59. Articles to be enquired of, in the Kynges Maiesties Visitacion (London, Richard Grafton, no date), sig. Bj v°: "Whether you knowe any that vse Charmes, Sorcery, Enchauntmentes, Witchecrafts, sothe saiyng, or any other like crafte inuented by the deuill." Cf. Frere and Kennedy, II, 111.

60. Frere and Kennedy, II, 353; cf. II, 356, 372 (1555).

61. The same, II, 398, 388, 425.

62. See Shaxton's articles for Salisbury in 1538 (Frere and Kennedy, II, 58); Cranmer's for Canterbury in 1548 (II, 188); Hooper's for Gloucester and Worcester in 1551–52 (II, 300–301); Parker's for Canterbury in 1560 and for Winchester in 1575 (III, 85, 381); Parkhurst's for Norwich in 1561 and 1569 (III, 106, 214); Sandys's for Worcester in 1569 and for London in 1571 (III, 227–228, 313); Grindal's for York in 1571 and for Canterbury in 1576 (III, 270; Cardwell, I, 413–414); Freke's for Rochester in 1572 (Frere and Kennedy, III, 343); Whitgift's for Salisbury in 1588 (Cardwell, II, 34). Sandys's Articles of 1569 are interesting for their details: "Whether any manner of person use any kind of sortilege, that is to say, witchcraft, enchanting, charms to cure men or beast, invocations of wicked spirits, telling where things lost or stolen are become, by key, book, tables, shears, sieves, looking in crystals, or any other means casting of figures." Freke's Rochester Articles of 1572 mention *maleficium* specifically: "Whether that there be any suspected of coining, enchantments, sorcery, or witchcraft; and who they are, what are their doings, and what hurt or displeasure hath ensued unto any of your neighbours by them or by any of their doings." Archbishop Abbot's Articles for Canterbury in 1616 make a distinction: "Any which have used any enchantments, sorceries, incantations, or witchcrafts, which are not made felony by the statutes of this realm" (Cardwell, II, 181). Nowhere in the long list just cited is there a hint of Continental specialties. In Freke, *coining* is somebody's misprint for *coniuring*.

63. Acts of the Privy Council, New Series, V, 137 (May 28, 1555), 139 (June 1), 143–144 (June 7), 176 (August 29). John Fielde, one of the alleged conspirators, had been entrusted to the custody of Bonner. Dee, too, was in Bonner's custody when discharged. For Benger see also VI, 81, 82, 101, 108–109, 191, in connection with another affair — not conjuring, apparently.

64. See the cases of Agnes Hancok in 1438 (p. 145) and Judith Phillips in 1595 (p. 206). For a fairy "haunting" a woman see Giffard, A Dialogue concerning Witches and Witchcraftes, 1593, sig. B v°. Cf. A Pleasant Treatise of Witches, 1673, pp. 53–69; J. A. MacCulloch, The Mingling of Fairy and Witch Beliefs in Sixteenth and Seventeenth Century Scotland, Folk-Lore, XXXII (1921), 227–244. Cf. p. 215, above. Miss Murray has brought together a good deal of material on fairies (The Witch-Cult, pp. 238–246).

65. Holworthy, Discoveries in the Diocesan Registry, Wells, p. 6.

66. Child, The English and Scottish Popular Ballads, I, 339. See also II, 505; III, 505; V, 290.

67. Acts, as above, VII, 6, 7.

68. Acts, VII, 5, 7; cf. VII, 123, 401, for John Ke(e)le.

69. Acts, VII, 22. It was also in 1558 that Thomas Lufkyn, by trade a fuller, began to practise at Maidstone. "He had by roving abroade," writes John Halle, "become a phisician, a chirurgien, an astronomier, a palmister, a phisiognomier, a sothsayer, a fortune devyner, and I can not tell what. . . . Unto this divell incarnate, resorted all sortes of vayne and undiscrete persons, as it were to a God, to knowe all secretes, paste and to come, specially women, to know how manie husbandes and children they shoulde have, and whether they shoulde burie their husbandes then lyving. . . . All this he boasted that he could do by astronomie; but when he was talked with of one that had but a yonge and smalle skyll in that arte, he coulde make no directe answere no more then puppe my dogge" (An Historiall Expostulation: against the Beastlye Abusers, bothe of Chyrurgerie, and Physyke, in Oure Tyme, 1565, ed. Pettigrew, Percy Society, 1844, pp. 8–9). Cf. note 90, below.

70. In a letter of March 20, 1559, to Peter Martyr, Jewel writes, "Tandem tamen aliquando, quinquagesimo videlicet septimo post die quam solvissemus Tiguro, pervenimus in Angliam" (Works, ed. Ayre, IV, 1198; Zurich Letters, I, 5 [9]).

71. Commons' Journals, I, 57, 59, 60; Lords' Journals, English Historical Review, XXVIII (1913), 538, 539.

72. Jewel's Works, ed. Ayre, IV, 1199; Zurich Letters, No. 4, I, 5: "Magno nobis impedimento sunt episcopi" or (to adopt a variant, involving a pun) "aposcopi," etc.

73. Jewel's Works, IV, 1201–1209; Zurich Letters, Nos. 5–7, I, 7–12 (13–22).

74. Cecil's memoranda for the parliament of 1559 do not mention witchcraft (Marquis of Salisbury's MSS., I, 162–165).

75. To avoid the possibility of misunderstanding, I must add that the act of 1542 contained a provision about digging down crosses (there mentioned in connection with treasure-digging sorcery) which was probably omitted from the bill of 1559 as it was from the act of 1563.

76. Calendar of State Papers, Domestic, 1547–1580, p. 137 (August 20, 1559); cf. Add. MS. 32091, fol. 176.

77. The same, p. 142.

78. Archæologia Cantiana, XXVI (1904), 31.

79. Notes and Queries for Somerset and Dorset, II (1891), 62.

80. Transactions Devonshire Association, XLIV (1912), 221–222.

81. See p. 155, above.

82. Diary of Henry Machyn, ed. J. G. Nichols (Camden Society, XLII), pp. 251, 261.

83. "The unfained retractation of Fraunces Cox, which he uttered at The Pillery in Chepesyde and elswhere, accordyng to the Counsels commaundment. Anno 1561. The 25 of June" (Lemon, Catalogue of a Collection of Broadsides in the Possession of the Society of Antiquaries, 1866,

No. 55, p. 19). There is an extract in Brand-Hazlitt, Popular Antiquities, III, 114. Cf. Rollins, Analytical Index, 1924, No. 623, p. 59; Notestein, p. 31, note.

84. Francis Coxe, A Short Treatise Declaringe the Detestable Wickednesse of Magicall Sciences, as Necromancie, Coniurations of Spirites, Curiose Astrologie and Such lyke. See S. R. Maitland, Notes on the Contributions of the Rev. George Townsend to the New Edition of Fox's Martyrology, Part II, 1842, pp. 104–106. Cf. Notestein, p. 351.

85. See Joseph Hunter, Memoirs of Sir William Saint Loe, Retrospective Review, 2d Series, II (1828), 314–325; Robert Simpson, A Collection of Fragments Illustrative of the History of Derby, 1826, I, 340; S. Rudder, A New History of Gloucestershire, 1779, p. 774; Historical MSS. Commission, Marquis of Salisbury's MSS., I, 325, 499; III, 164–165; Doyle, Official Baronage, III, 320; Dictionary of National Biography, XIX, 309–311.

86. Some of these details about Hugh Draper and Francis Cox come from two lists of prisoners drawn up for the Council by the Lieutenant of the Tower in 1561 (May 26 and July 3). Draper had been committed on March 21 and Cox on March 25. According to this document, Draper made a confession (before that which he made in open court), and therein "it aperithe that before time he hathe ben busie and doinge with suche matters; but he deniethe any matter of weight touchinge Sr William Sentlo or my ladie, and also affirmethe y^t longe since he so misliked his science that he burned all his bookes." In a bill for the diet of prisoners rendered by the Lieutenant in 1562 (including Cox's board from March 25 to December 19, 1561), he remarks "This Francis Coxe was one of those that were committed for s^r Wm Seintlewes matter, and was after found faultie for conjuringe." Ralph Davis is mentioned in the 1561 returns as committed on April 1 and as accused by "Mr Sentlo his daughter" [i. e., apparently, by the daughter of Edward St. Loe, Sir William's brother] of being concerned with her in a plot "for ye poisoninge of my ladie Sentlo. The which he also deniethe." From the 1562 bill we hear that he remained in the Tower until February 11, 1562, when "he was delivered from the Tower to the Kings Bench, and since that time was set at liberty upon sureties." Davis was not one of the nine pilloried sorcerers. See the documents in John Bayley, The History and Antiquities of the Tower of London, 1821, Part II, Appendix, pp. l–lii; Miscellanea (Catholic Record Society), I (1905), 55, 56. Hunter (Retrospective Review, 2d Series, II [1828], 322–323) prints a letter from Sir William's mother to his wife in which she says: "I told hur [an unnamed lady] I was suer yow wher powsonyd when I was at London, and yff yow had not had a present remedy ye had dyed." For interesting St. Loe letters see Hunter, Hallamshire, ed. Gatty, pp. 107–108. One of them was written by Sir William from the house of "Maester Man" in Redcross Street, London. Draper, while confined in the Salt Tower, whiled away his time by engraving astrological figures (reproduced by Bayley, Part I, opp. p. 210) on the wall with the inscription "Hew Draper of Brystow made thys spheer the 30 daye of Maye Anno 1561."

The case of the nine sorcerers, with their oath, is fully reported by

Coke, A Booke of Entries, 1614, fol. 1 rº, to whom Francis Hutchinson refers in An Historical Essay concerning Witchcraft, 2d ed., 1720, pp. 33–34 (not in 1st ed., 1718). Machyn (Diary, p. 261) registers on June 20 the arraignment of "seven men" at Westminster "for kungeryng and odur maters." *Seven* should be *nine* and the date should be the 23d, as the record in Coke shows. Cf. Strype, Annals of the Reformation, I (1725), 269; Notestein, p. 385. Leonard Bilson was installed as a prebendary of Winchester on July 7, 1551 (Le Neve, Fasti, ed. Hardy, 1854, III, 32). He suffered a long imprisonment. We hear of him in the Tower in 1562 (Miscellanea, Catholic Record Society, I, 56), 1564 (Acts of the Privy Council, VII, 163), in 1570 (Miscellanea, I, 57), and on March 29, 1571 (Acts, VIII, 21). On October 14, 1571, he was transferred to the Marshalsea, whence he was discharged in 1582 (the same, I, 70; II, 231; cf. I, 60). His confinement was rather for recusancy than for sorcery. The account in Sloane MS. 3943, fol. 19, is merely translated from Coke's Entries.

87. Grindal's letter to Cecil (April 17, 1561) enclosing the confession of John Coxe *alias* Devon, priest, "for mass matters, taken this day after receipt of your letters," is printed by Pike, History of Crime, II, 22–23. It also enclosed an examination of Coxe taken by a justice of the peace on April 14 (Calendar of State Papers, Domestic, 1547–1580, pp. 173–174). Grindal's comments are interesting: "Surely for this magic and conjuration your honours the Council must appoint some extraordinary punishment for example. My Lord Chief Justice sayeth the temporal law will not meddle with them. Our ecclesiastical punishment is too slender for so grievous offences." Neither of the documents enclosed mentions sorcery, and it is possible that by "magic and conjuration" Grindal meant merely the mass and other Catholic rites (which the Reformers often styled conjuration or the like: cf. the habitual language of Bale, as, for example, in his Select Works, ed. Christmas, pp. 16, 259, 326, 329, 367, 381, 384, 393, 395, 423, 424, 439, 494, 501, 536, 537, 539, 592, 630). Yet the oath of abjuration which this John Coxe (Cocks) took on June 23, 1561, after confession in open court, specifies several varieties of witchcraft and sorcery. Besides, the Chief Justice to whom Grindal refers was apparently Sir Robert Catlyn of the Common Pleas, whom Cecil was consulting about this time as to the state of the law on witchcraft. A letter from Catlyn to Cecil on this subject (April 20, 1561) is preserved (Calendar, 1547–1580, p. 174). Finally, the Midsummer Returns, 1561, of prisoners in the King's Bench mention "John Devon *als* Cox, clerke, sent in the xv daie of Aprill 1561, vpon my Lord of Londons commaundyment and others the Quenes comissimers, viz: for saying of Masse and coniorynge" (Miscellanea, Catholic Record Society, I, 52–53). On Coxe-Devon see also Birt (The Elizabethan Religious Settlement, 1907, pp. 331, 440–441, 528–529), who does not discuss the question of conjuring.

88. Thomas Gale, Certaine Workes of Galens, 1586, fol. 33, quoted in New Shakspere Society Transactions, 1877–79, p. 459, and by John Timbs, Doctors and Patients, 1873, I, 243–244. Cf. John Cotta, the Northampton physician (ca. 1575–1650): "A sort of practitioners, whom our custome and country doth call wisemen and wisewomen, reputed a kind of good and

honest harmles witches or wisards, who by good words, by hallowed herbes and salues, and other superstitious ceremonies promise to allay and calme diuels, practises of other witches, and the forces of many diseases" (A Short Discoverie of the Vnobserued Dangers of Seuerall Sorts of Ignorant and Vnconsiderate Practisers of Physicke in England, 1612, p. 71).

89. Bulleins Bulwarke of Defence againste all Sicknes (finished in March, 1562-3; 1st ed. in that year; 2d ed., 1579). This contains both The Booke of Simples and the Dialogue betwene Sorenes and Chyrurgi. The passage here quoted is given by Strype, Annals, II (1725), 611. Cf. A. H. Bullen's life of Bullein in the Dictionary of National Biography. For further items relative to witchcraft see Bullein, A Dialogue wherein is a Goodly Regimente against the Feuer Pestilence (first published in 1565), ed. Bullen, Early English Text Society, 1888, pp. 104, 114.

90. John Halle, An Historiall Expostulation, 1565, ed. Pettigrew (Percy Society, 1844), pp. 11-15. See also his account of Robert Haris (1556) and of Kiterell, "a physitien, or rather a detestable decavyng sorcerer" (pp. 6-7, 28-29). Halle believes that some diseases come "by enchauntement" (p. 29). See also note 69, above. Cf. Caius (1552), pp. 68-69, above.

91. 4th Report of the Deputy Keeper, 1843, Appendix II, pp. 263-264 (indictment and proceedings). Cf. Thomas Wright, Queen Elizabeth and her Times, 1838, I, 121, 127, 129; Calendar of State Papers, Spanish, 1558-1567, pp. 259-260, 262, 275, 278-279, 288, 292-293, 331; Calendar of State Papers, Foreign, 1562, pp. 423-424, 460, 480, 484, 492, 519, 551, 564, 566-567; the same, 1563, pp. 27, 191, 338. See also the articles on Arthur Pole and Sir Anthony Fortescue in the Dictionary of National Biography.

92. Sir John Mason to Sir Thomas Challoner, February 27, 1563 (Wright, as above, I, 129). Cf. Cecil's letter to Sir Thomas Smith (Wright, I, 127), which says that the conspirators "were persuaded by one Prestall" that the queen was to die soon. Prestall and Comyn embarked on October 10, 1562; the others tried to follow on the 14th, but were arrested. See 4th Report, as above.

93. Prestall "vaunts himself to be of high blood, and next heir to the Poles" (Margery Kinnersley's declaration, March 16, 1591, Calendar of State Papers, Domestic, 1591-1594, p. 19).

94. I cannot be quite sure of this item about Prestall's release, for there is a possibility of confusion with Cornelius de Alneto (Lannoy), the notorious alchemist, as to whom see Calendar of State Papers, Foreign, 1564-1565, p. 267; Domestic, 1547-1580, pp. 249, 256, 275-277, 289, 292, cf. 273; Marquis of Salisbury's MSS., I, 318, 325-333, 336, 337. However, Anthony Spencer and Richard Bingham, two of the Pole conspirators, were discharged from the Tower on May 3, 1567 (Acts of the Privy Council, VII, 351). For another alchemist, Alexander Bonus, see Marquis of Salisbury's MSS., III, 414; Acts, XVII, 31-32. On August 7, 1565, Armagill Waade wrote to Cecil recommending the suit of Mr. Prestoll (Calendar, Domestic, 1547-1580, p. 256).

95. Lord Scrope to Cecil, August 29, 1569, Calendar, Foreign, 1569-1571, p. 118.

96. Acts of the Privy Council, X, 382.

97. See the interesting examination of William Kinnersley, March 8, 1591 (Calendar, Domestic, 1591–1594, pp. 17–18, cf. p. 19).

98. On November 30, 1563, Prestall wrote to Cecil for letters of protection "that he may safely come to make answer to certain charges preferred against him" (Calendar, Domestic, 1547–1580, p. 231). Whether he got such letters I do not know. On August 7, 1565, he was in the Tower, it seems (the same, p. 256), where he remained until 1567, when he was released on his promise to turn silver into gold (note 94, above). Soon after he must have absconded. From some time before August 29, 1569, to March 23, 1572(or later), he was actively engaged in plots in Scotland and Flanders; and towards the end of that period he was negotiating with John Lee, one of Cecil's agents at Antwerp, with a view (so Lee thought) of becoming reconciled to the English government and giving information against some of his fellow-conspirators (Calendar, Foreign, 1569–1571, pp. 118, 217, 220, 330, 400; 1572–1574, p. 223; Calendar, Domestic, Addenda, 1566–1579, pp. 338, 341, 348, 354, 356, 358, 372, 379, 384; Historical MSS. Commission, Marquis of Salisbury's MSS., I, 466, 476). Apparently he was induced to return to England by a letter from Cecil in 1571 (see Prestall's own statements as reported by William and Margery Kinnersley: Calendar, Domestic, 1591–1594, pp. 17–19; cf. Marquis of Salisbury's MSS., II, 552). But he was confined in the King's Bench for two years, from 1572 to July 5, 1574, when he was released under bonds (for his release see Acts of the Privy Council, VIII, 264–265; for the length of his confinement see his letter of 1585 in Strype, Annals, III [1728], 312). In this interval Dr. John Story, Prestall's fellow-plotter, was kidnapped, taken to England, tried, and (in June, 1571) executed. There was some idea of kidnapping Prestall in September, 1570 (Thomas Wright, Queen Elizabeth and her Times, 1838, I, 378; Calendar, Foreign, 1569–1571, p. 330). He was at liberty in England, under bonds, on June 11, 1576 (Acts, IX, 138–139; Calendar, Domestic, 1547–1580, p. 520), but on December 26, 1576, and January 29, 1577, we find his name in lists of fugitives beyond the sea (see Historical MSS. Commission, Report on MSS. of Lord Montagu of Beaulieu, p. 83; Calendar, Domestic, 1547–1580, p. 532; Strype, Annals, II [1725], Appendix, p. 102; Peck, Desiderata Curiosa, 1779, I, 78). On October 12, 1578, however, he was in the Tower (Acts, X, 344; Calendar, Domestic, 1547–1580, p. 601), to which (according to a record of November 10, 1578) he had been "latelie committed" (Acts, X, 382). He remained a prisoner there until July 22, 1588. On this date his name occurs in the bills of the Lieutenant of the Tower, but it is absent from the next bill on Lady Day, 1589 (Miscellanea, Catholic Record Society, III [1906], 8–28). Presumably he was released in July, 1588. The cause of his long confinement appears to be his conviction for high treason, for which he was indicted in 1578 (in 13 Elizabeth according to Acts, X, 344; "He standeth attainted of highe treason for more then seven yeeres past" according to documents of November 30, 1586, Miscellanea, II, 264, cf. 238). He was condemned to death, but spared by the queen (Calendar, Domestic, 1591–1594, pp. 17–19). From various sources we learn of his presence in the Tower in

1579 (Acts, XI, 102), 1585 (Strype, Annals, III [1728], 312–313; Miscellanea, II, 238, cf. 132), 1586 (Miscellanea, II, 261, 264), and 1587 (letter of the Earl of Arundel: see Calendar of State Papers, Domestic, 1581–1590, p. 419, and Pollen and MacMahon, English Martyrs, II [1919], 161, Catholic Record Society). For his continuous imprisonment from June 24, 1579, to July 22, 1588, we have the authority of the Tower Bills (Miscellanea, II, 8–27). After his release from the Tower we hear of him in 1590 and 1591 only (note 97, above); then he vanishes.

99. Commons' Journals, I, 63, 65, 69, 70; Lords' Journals, I, 591, 600, 601, 602, 603, 606. In support of the theory that the Marian exiles learned Continental views of witchcraft during their enforced residence in Germany and Switzerland, certain phrases of the law of 1604 are quoted by Professor Burr as embodying these novel ideas (Proceedings American Antiquarian Society, New Series, XXI [1911], 196). "To 'use, practise, or exercise any invocations or conjurations of evil and wicked spirits to or for any intent or purpose,'" he remarks, "is specified first of all as enough by itself to warrant [the witches'] death as felons; and to their witchcrafts against their neighbors are now assimilated 'other lewd intents and purposes contrary to the laws of God and to the peril of their own souls.'" Thus, he argues, the Elizabethan law shows "a new diction and a new spirit": it punishes *sin* as well as *crime*. This argument comes to naught as soon as one compares the law of 1603 with the law of 1542. Henry's statute punished with death all who should "use, devise, practise, or exercise, or cause to be used, devysed, practised, or exercised, any Invocacions or conjuracions of Sprites" for any "unlawfull intent or purpose." And Henry's statute declared that such invocations "cannot be used and exercised but to the great Offence of Godes lawe, hurt and damage of the Kinges Subjectes, and losse of the sowles of suche Offenders."

100. Zurich Letters, Nos. 54–56, I, 73–76 (123–128); Jewel's Works, IV, 1257–1262.

101. John Parkhurst, Bishop of Norwich, to Josiah Simler and Ludwig Lavater, April 29, 1562 (Zurich Letters, No. 47, I, 63 [109]): "Ovis in Essexia non ita pridem prodidit homicidam, quemadmodum corvi in Helvetia."

102. Jewel to Bullinger, August 14, 1562 (Zurich Letters, No. 50, I, 68–69 [116–117]). Cf. Parkhurst to Simler, June 30, 1574 (No. 119, I, 179 [305]): "Mirum est quod vacca cervum peperit," etc.

103. Parkhurst to Bullinger, August 21, 1566 (No. 72, I, 98 [164–165]): "Vocatur senior David, necromanticae artis peritus."

104. Robert Horn, Bishop of Winchester, to Bullinger, August 3, 1571 (No. 98, I, 148 [282]): "et veneno et violentia et fascinatione et proditione."

105. Parkhurst to Bullinger, June 29, 1574 (No. 118, I, 178 [303]).

106. Parkhurst to Bullinger, April 26 and August 13, 1563 (Nos. 57, 59, I, 76–77 [128–129], 78–79 [131–132]). Cf. I, 119 [201]; II, 360.

107. The Acts of the Parliament of Scotland, II (1814), 539 (June 4, 1563); cf. III (1814), 38, 44.

108. Strype, Annals of the Reformation, I (1725), 349, from Bishop Alley's own copy. To balance this, I may quote Cecil's letter to Sir Thomas Smith (January 14, 1563), in which he mentions as one of the "matters of moment lyke to pass" in the parliament, "reviving of some old lawes for penalties of some fellonyes" (Wright, Queen Elizabeth, 1838, I, 121).

109. See Notestein, pp. 17–18; Summers, The Geography of Witchcraft, 1927, p. 114. Lecky (History of the Rise and Influence of the Spirit of Rationalism in Europe, New York, 1866, I, 121, note 2) misunderstands Strype (Annals, I [1725], 8), and so do Notestein (p. 17) and Summers (p. 116), though Notestein gives the right interpretation in a note.

110. Notestein, p. 18; echoed by Summers, Geography, p. 193.

111. A True and Iust Recorde, of the Information, Examination and Confession of all the Witches, taken at S. Oses (London, 1582), sig. B5, lf. 2.

112. Compare Darcey's method in dealing with Ursley Kempe and its success. "The saide Brian Darcey then promising to the saide Vrsley, that if shee would deale plainely and confesse the trueth, that she should haue fauour: and so by giuing her faire speeches shee confessed as followeth. The saide Ursley bursting out with weeping, fel vpon her knees, and confessed," etc. (sig. A4, lf. 4 vᵒ). His *fraus pia* no doubt was regarded by his contemporaries as justifiable. It had long been maintained by some casuists that an inquisitor in such cases might delude an accused person thus. See the discussion in the Malleus Maleficarum. "An hic iudex super delatum infamatum, et per testes, et indicia facti legitime conuictum, cum nihil desit nisi in ore proprio crimen fateatur, possit licite conseruationem vitae compromittere, cum tamen, si crimen fatetur, vltimo supplicio punitur" (Part III, qu. 14, ed. 1620, pp. 371–372).

113. Newes from Scotland (Roxburghe Club reprint, 1816; Bodley Head Quartos).

114. Note that by "our witches" Jonson means "modern witches," not "those of our own country." Shadwell, in his comedy of The Lancashire Witches (1682) imitates Jonson in supplying a commentary with a plethora of references to classical and modern Continental authorities — Ovid, Horace, Lucan, Del Rio, Remigius, Bodin, Guaccius, the Malleus, etc. Much of his erudition is borrowed from Jonson.

115. Thomas Potts, The Wonderfvll Discoverie of Witches in the Covnty of Lancaster. With the Arraignement and Triall of Nineteene Notorious Witches, at the Assizes and Generall Gaole Deliuerie, holden at the Castle of Lancaster, vpon Munday, the Seuenteenth of August last, 1612 (London, 1613), sig. B3, lf. 2 (The Confession and Examination of Anne Whittle *alias* Chattox, being Prisoner at *Lancaster;* taken the 19. day of May, *Annoq; Regni Regis Iacobi Angliae, Decimo*).

116. "Malkin" is often used for "hare" and Crossley is probably right in interpreting the name of Mother Demdike's house as "the Witches' Tower" (reprint of Potts for the Chetham Society, 1845, Notes, p. 16). Potts tells us how the Lancashire prosecution originated: "The Iustices of those partes, vnderstanding by a generall charme and muttering, the great

and vniuersall resort to *Maulking Tower*, the common opinion, with the report of these suspected people, the complaint of the Kinges subiectes for the losse of their Children," etc., "sent for some of the Countrey, and took great paynes to enquire after their proceedinges" (sig. B2).

117. Potts, sigg. G3, I3, P, P2, Q, R, Z.

118. Sigg. G3, I2, I3, P, Q3, Y3.

119. Sig. I2 v°.

120. Sig. H3.

121. Sigg. G3, I3, P, Q3, Y3 (Jennet Preston "had a Spirit with her like vnto a white Foale, with a blacke-spot in the forehead").

122. Sig. R r°.

123. Sigg. F2, F3, G3.

124. Potts, sigg. L2–N3. Cf. Webster, pp. 275–276; Notestein, pp. 128–129. That James Mason in The Anatomie of Sorcerie, 1612, has nothing to say of the Sabbath is not necessarily significant, for his treatise concerns rather divination than malefic magic.

125. Cotta, The Triall of Witch-craft, 1616, p. 35. Cotta is not quite accurate. Porta does not say that this particular hag (a *strix* who was "in his hands") imagined that she had visited a Witches' Sabbath on this occasion (as Cotta implies); but he does bring her experience into connection with such imaginings, and it is clear that he regards her as one of those who now and then, after anointing themselves, fancy that they are rapt to such assemblies and there enjoy "conuiuia, sonos, tripudia, et formosorum iuuenum concubitus" (Magia Naturalis, ii, 26, ed. 1558, p. 102: see also note 33, above). H. F. borrows the Porta story from Cotta, retailing it almost word for word (Preface to A True and Exact Relation of the Severall Informations, Examinations, and Confessions of the late Witches, Arraigned and Executed in the County of Essex, 1645). William Foster, in 1631, remarks that "Witches by annointing themselves with their venificall ointments are carried up in the airy Heaven" (Hoplocrisma-spongus, p. 21). Cf. Thomas Wright, Proceedings against Dame Alice Kyteler, 1843, p. 46.

126. Cotta, pp. 38–40.

127. "Some late Writers haue obserued, that diuers Witches by such pictures, haue caused the persons thereby represented secretly to languish and consume, as was lately proued against some late famous Witches of *York-shire* and *Lancaster*" (Cotta, p. 90). Webster in 1677 laughs the Lancashire cases to scorn. He derides the notion "that the Devil should carry an old Witch in the Air into foraign Regions, that can hardly crawl with a staff, to dancing and banqueting, and yet to return with an empty belly, and the next day to be forced, like old *Dembdike* or *Elizabeth Sothernes*, and *Alizon Denice*, to go a begging with the sowr-milk Can." Witches who confess such things are merely deluded by Satan, who "doth nothing but dart and cast in these filthy and fond cogitations into their minds agreeable to their wicked wills and corrupted desires" (The Displaying of Supposed Witchcraft, pp. 68, 74–75). Webster has no respect for "that old Platonical Whimsie," revived of late by Glanvil and others, "of the Souls

real egression forth of the body into far distant places, and its return again, with the certain knowledge of things there done or said." See Glanvil, A Blow at Modern Sadducism, 1668, pp. 15–17 (Saducismus Triumphatus, 1681, pp. 13–15). Glanvil, in Webster's opinion, gives "too much credit to the things related by the Witches in their confessions, to be stories of things really performed at a great distance." "These Relations of the Witches are meer lyes and forgeries, and are but taught them by the spiritual craft of the Devil." Of course he repeats Porta's story, of which he gives a racy translation. "It appeareth," therefore, "that the Witches are under a melancholy and passive delusion, promoted by the help of soporiferous Oyntments, whereby they fancy and think they are carried into far remote places, where they hear and see strange things, and do and suffer that which is not at all performed, but only as in a dream, their bodies in the mean time lying immoveable, and so do but relate falsities and lyes" (pp. 69–70). Webster probably had no knowledge of the Somerset cases of 1665, which are not mentioned in A Blow at Modern Sadducism (1668) but make their first appearance (from Robert Hunt's manuscript) in the enlarged edition, Part II, pp. 127–165 (entitled Saducismus Triumphatus), which appeared in 1681 (reprinted in 1682, 1689, 1700, and 1726). The case of Julian Cox (1663) is also first reported in the volume of 1681, Part II, pp. 191–209. On Sad(d)ucismus Triumphatus see Greenslet, Joseph Glanvil, 1900, pp. 70, 144–176. Orchard (The Doctrine of Devils, 1676, p. 55) explodes the belief that "the Devil out of a glewish dew, can and often doth, mould up so many various dishes of choice Viands, and Butts of lascivious Wines, that many Thousands may fill, and feed, and feast themselves most deliciously."

128. Thomas Cooper, The Mystery of Witch-craft, 1617, pp. 89–94, cf. pp. 114–115. In pp. 88–91 he borrows more or less from King James, whom he cites (see the Dæmonologie, 1597, 1603, pp. 33, 36–37, 43, 44). Note also his mention of King James on pp. 6–7.

129. Cooper, p. 16. Just before (p. 15), he has mentioned "the late Assise at *Lancaster*" in 1612.

130. Edward Fairfax, Daemonologia, ed. Grainge, 1882, pp. 86, 110, 114–115, 107–108.

131. The same, pp. 94, 126–127; cf. p. 98, note.

132. Edmund Robinson's examination, February 10, 1633–4, in Webster, The Displaying of Supposed Witchcraft, 1677, pp. 347–349; cf. another text (from Harleian MS. 6854) in Baines, History of the County Palatine and Duchy of Lancaster, 1836, I, 604–606. Webster, who knew the boy, gives interesting details (pp. 276–278).

133. Margaret Johnson's examination, March, 1633–4 (Baines, I, 607–608). Susanna Edwards "confesseth, that she can go unto any place invisible, and yet her Body shall be lying in her Bed": A True and Impartial Relation of the Informations against Three Witches . . . Who were Indicted, Arraigned, and Convicted at the Assizes holden for the County of Devon at the Castle of Exon, Aug. 14. 1682 (London, 1682), p. 37.

134. Robinson's examination, July 16, 1634, Calendar of State Papers, Domestic, 1634–1635, p. 152; cf. pp. 141, 153. On the whole case see Web-

ster, pp. 276–278; Thomas Wright, Narratives of Sorcery and Magic, 1851, II, 108–117; Notestein, pp. 146–157.

135. The plot of The Late Lancashire Witches includes most of Robinson's details. Interwoven, as an episode, is the celebrated tale of the brave soldier who ventures to spend three nights in a haunted mill and on the third is well "nipt and pull'd and pinch'd" by the cat-witches, but cuts off the paw of one of them (Halliwell's reprint in The Poetry of Witchcraft, 1853, pp. 171–174, 221–222, 225–227). This is to all intents and purposes Bodin's narrative of the witches of Vernon Castle in 1561 (see p. 177, above). It is related somehow to an incident in No. 4 of the Grimms' Kinder- und Hausmärchen (cf. Bolte and Polívka, Anmerkungen, II, 165). Cleveland recalls the play rather than the case itself in his satirical verses in "Upon a Miser":

> Have you not heard th' abominable sport
> A Lancaster grand-Jurie will report?
> The Souldier with his Morglay watch't the Mill,
> The Cats they came to feast, when lustie Will
> Whips off great Pusses leg, which by some charme
> Proves the next day such an old womans arme.

136. Matthew Hopkins, The Discovery of Witches, 1647, p. 2. Gaule, the opponent of Hopkins, seems to believe that witches hold meetings by night (Select Cases of Conscience touching Witchcrafts, 1646, p. 82). He repeats the well-known details with an eye to Danaeus and especially to the Malleus (Part II, qu. 1, cap. 2, foll. xxvi[i] v°–xxxviii r°, Koelhoff ed., 1494). Yet he derides the elaborate accounts of the Sabbath (pp. 56–65). After mentioning with scorn the notion that witches use ointment of stolen infants or of dead men's flesh, and particularizing as an absurdity the idea that the devil "oft times marries them ere they part, either to himselfe, or their Familiar, or to one another, and that by the Book of Common prayer (as a pretender to witchfinding lately told me in the Audience of many)," he concludes: "Thus you see what we are likely to attain to, by searching too precisely into Diabolicall solemnities; among some probabilities to manifold Impossibilities, and absurdities, among some truths, to manifold superstitions."

137. John Stearne, A Confirmation and Discovery of Witch-craft, 1648, p. 11. Meetings are mentioned in The Witches of Huntingdon (Preface signed John Davenport), 1646, pp. 14, 15.

138. Stearne, p. 52, cf. p. 53.

139. A True and Exact Relation of the Severall Informations, Examinations, and Confessions of the Late Witches, Arraigned and Executed in the County of Essex, 1645, pp. 12–15. Cf. Anne Leech's confession (p. 9) that she and Elizabeth Gooding and Anne West "met together at the house of the said Elizabeth Clark, where there was a book read, wherein shee thinks there was no goodnesse." All three, as well as Elizabeth Clark, were executed in 1645. Stearne adverts to these Manningtree meetings more than once (A Confirmation and Discovery of Witch-craft, 1648, pp. 38, 52, 53).

140. The Examination, Confession, Triall, and Execution, of Joane Williford, Joan Cariden, and Jane Hott, 1645, p. 3, cf. p. 6.

141. Wonderfull News from the North, 1650, p. 24.

142. Bernard, A Guide to Grand-Iury Men, 2d ed., 1629, pp. 260–266, cf. pp. 110, 219. He adverts to the Lancashire cases again and again (pp. 88, 90, 100, 152–155, 161–162, 207, 219–220). He also mentions the romancing of Grace Sowerbutts (pp. 194–195). On Bernard and his book see Notestein, pp. 234–236, 241, 361, 401. I cannot agree with Notestein, that Bernard's main interest was "to warn those who had to try cases to be exceedingly careful" (p. 241). Bernard regards it as our duty to "hate Witches" (p. 247), and he agrees with Perkins (see p. 292, above) in holding that the white witches deserve death as well as the black (pp. 249–254).

143. Bernard, pp. 216–217.

144. "Bodin, his Daemono. Delrio, lib. 2. q. 16. de disq. magice." See Del Rio, Disquisitiones Magicae, ii, 16, ed. 1616, pp. 154–171: "De nocturnis sagarum conuentibus, et an vera sit earum translatio de loco ad locum?"

145. Bernard, pp. 231–232.

146. Compare Stearne, pp. 3–4, with Bernard (2d ed., 1629), pp. 83–86; pp. 8–9 with pp. 240–244, 249–250; pp. 10–12, 20, 23, with pp. 87–91; pp. 25–26 with pp. 91–95; pp. 33–34, 36, with pp. 98–99, 193–197, 200–201; p. 37 with p. 202; pp. 39, 40, with pp. 205, 212–214; pp. 42–43 with pp. 214–215; pp. 50–52 with pp. 120–125, 260–261, 264–265; pp. 53–57 with pp. 216–220, 246–249, 257. Notestein (p. 361) remarks that Bernard's book "had been used by Stearne and doubtless by Hopkins," but he seems not to have observed Stearne's enormous plagiarism.

147. Stearne, p. 53. Burton-Old is misprinted "Burton, Old."

148. Glanvil, Saducismus Triumphatus, 1681, Part II, pp. 127–167.

149. Glanvil, p. 127.

150. Ady, in 1656, makes it clear that he derives "from Bodinus and other Popish Writers" his knowledge of witch-rides by means of "the broth of a sodden Infant," which he regards as a mere superstition, and that he thinks of the belief as especially entertained in Germany (A Candle in the Dark, p. 111; cf. pp. 122–123). See also his quotation of the Canon Episcopi from Scot (whom he mentions) about the false belief of riding with Diana or Herodias "with an innumerable multitude" (pp. 108–109). On this matter see also Wagstaffe, The Question of Witchcraft Debated, 1669, pp. 52–55; R. T., The Opinion of Witchcraft Vindicated, 1670, pp. 53–54. William Drage is an enlightening witness. In his "Daimonomageia. A Small Treatise of Sicknesses and Diseases from Witchcraft" (1665) he refers constantly to learned Continental authorities and also cites a good many instances of witch-sent ailments or symptoms that have come to his attention in England. His only example of the Sabbath is an elaborate account of the confession of three men and a woman burned at Poitou in 1564. This includes the journey through the air, "huge meetings," homage to the goat-shaped devil, feasting, and lascivious revels (pp. 17–18). "Many Histories," says Drage, "confirm these things; we make but a brief abstract of them, the foresaid Authors may satisfie the Reader fully

therein." The foresaid authors are all Continental (Remigius, Bodin, Grillando, and so on). No English evidence is adduced. When Henry Hallywell (Melampronoea, 1681, pp. 66–75) treats of witches' "Nocturnal Conventicles and Diabolical meetings," he says not a word of such affairs as held in England. He is discussing the general objection to the credibility of witchcraft involved in the proposition (which he refutes) "That these Witches are supposed to be present at their Nocturnal Conventicles and Diabolical meetings, when their Bodies are at home; which is impossible." He admits (p. 70) that "the Soul may be rapt from this Terrestrial Body, and carried to remote and distant places, from whence she may make a Postliminiar return." He remarks "I would not so be understood as if I thought that Witches did never bodily assist at the performance of their Hellish Rites, but only that sometimes they may be present at them, when their Bodies are at home" (pp. 74–75). Bovet (Pandaemonium, 1684, p. 31) remarks that "Sometimes personally, and sometimes in a Dream, or Trance they revel with the evil Spirit in nightly Cabals and Consults." Baxter, in his Preface (dated 1690) to Cotton Mather's Late Memorable Providences (2d impression, London, 1691), accepts Bodin and Remigius on witches' meetings. The Goodwin girl of whom Mather tells went on "Fantastick Journeys" to the witches' "Randezvouse," when in fact she was simply riding a chair (pp. 25–31). This is, of course, the same sort of imaginary journey instanced from Porta by H. F. in his Preface to A True and Exact Relation of the Severall Informations, Examinations, and Confessions of the late Witches . . . in the County of Essex, 1645.

151. For alleged witch-meetings in New England see, for example, Cotton Mather, The Wonders of the Invisible World, Boston, 1693, pp. 49, 94–96, 99, 106–107, 125, 133, 137–138. Our scholars were well acquainted with the literature of the subject. For the influence of Bernard see The Wonders, sig. bb, lf. 4 1°; for Anthony Horneck's Swedish cases (Glanvil's Saducismus Triumphatus, 1681, Part II, pp. 311–328) see pp. 54, 148–149. "In these Hellish Meetings," writes Mather, "these Monsters have associated themselves to do no less a Thing than, *To destroy the Kingdom of our Lord Jesus Christ, in these parts of the World*" (p. 49). "The Witches say, that they form themselves much after the manner of *Congregational Churches*" (p. 140). Miss Murray takes all this sort of thing seriously (The Witch-Cult, 1921, pp. 151 etc.). Mr. Summers, too, believes in the existence of "a coven of witches" (The Geography of Witchcraft, 1927, p. 346). "There can be no doubt that at Salem the traditional rites of the hideous black worship were precisely observed, allowing, of course, that it was a Protestant Communion and not the Holy Mass which was the model of their hellish liturgy. These practices must have been carefully handed down and taught to the New England representatives of the witch society" (p. 348).

CHAPTER XVII

KING JAMES THE FIRST

1. For other pronouncements of a more or less similar nature, see Sir Walter Scott, Introduction to Potts's Discoverie, Somers Tracts, 2d ed., 1810, III, 95; Mrs. Lucy Aitkin, Memoirs of the Court of King James the First, 1822, II, 166–167; Retrospective Review, V (1822), 90; Scott, Letters on Demonology and Witchcraft, 1830, pp. 227, 246–247; Crossley, Introduction to Potts, Chetham Society, 1845, pp. xviii, xlv; Thomas Wright, Narratives of Sorcery and Magic, 1851, I, 284; II, 143–144; Charles Hardwick, History of Preston, 1857, p. 146; P. Q. Karkeek, Transactions of the Devonshire Association, VI (1874), 736; F. A. Inderwick, Side-Lights on the Stuarts, 2d ed., 1891, pp. 154–155; Engelbert Horley, Sefton, 1893, p. 115, note 1; H. M. Doughty, Blackwood's Magazine, March, 1898, CLXIII, 388; W. O. Roper, Materials for the History of Lancaster, Part I, Chetham Society, 1907, pp. 26–27.

2. Mrs. Linton, Witch Stories, 1861, p. 20.

3. Pages 259–260.

4. Page 259.

5. Page 261.

6. Page 195.

7. Page 195.

8. R. Steele, in Social England, ed. H. D. Traill, IV, 85–86.

9. Trevelyan, England under the Stuarts, [1904,] p. 32.

10. The same, p. 33.

11. A brief but powerful vindication of King James was inserted by William Gifford in his edition of Ford (I, clxxi, Dyce's revision, 1869, III, 276; cf. Quarterly Review, XLI [1829], 80–82), but it has attracted little attention. See also Disraeli's Character of James the First (Miscellanies of Literature, New York, 1841, III, 355–360).

12. See particularly Mr. F. Legge's paper on Witchcraft in Scotland, in The Scottish Review for October, 1891, XVIII, 257–288.

13. Newes from Scotland, 1591, sig. B2 (Roxburghe Club reprint).

14. King James, Basilikon Doron, 1599, Roxburghe Club reprint, p. 97.

15. Spottiswood, History of the Church of Scotland, Bannatyne Club, II, 412; Pitcairn, Criminal Trials, I, 230, 240, note; Legge, Scottish Review, XVIII, 262.

16. A. Lang, History of Scotland, II, 353.

17. Pitcairn, Criminal Trials, I, 357.

18. See p. 371, above.

19. Privy Council Register, V, 409–410; Spottiswood, III, 66–67; Legge, p. 264; Lang, History of Scotland, II, 433.

20. Gardiner, History of England, 1603–1642, VII (1899), 322–323.

21. John Hawarde (born about 1571) makes a curious note in his manuscript, Les Reportes del Cases in Camera Stellata (ed. Baildon, pp. 179–180): "Nothinge now was talked of but the relligion, vertue, wisedome, learninge, Justice, & manye other most noble & woorthye prayses of

K. James, . . . his bookes new printed, (Βαζιλιχον δορων, Free monarchies, Monologie, Expositions upon the Reuelacions & the Kings, the Lepanto)."

22. There are two 1603 London editions of King James's Dæmonologie. See the details in Ferguson, Publications of the Edinburgh Bibliographical Society, III, 51.

23. See the Roxburghe Club reprint of the 1599 edition of the Basilikon Doron. On the attention which the book attracted, see Calendar of State Papers, Venetian, 1603–1607, pp. 10, 65.

24. Wright, Narratives of Sorcery and Magic, 1851, I, 279. See also the authors cited above (note 1).

25. Wright, Narratives, I, 279.

26. John Darrel, A True Narration, etc., 1600, p. 1.

27. Darrel, p. 7.

28. Another case occurred in 1580. William Randoll was hanged for conjuring to discover hidden treasure and stolen goods. Four others were tried for aiding and abetting, and three of them were sentenced to death, but reprieved. The trial was held at the King's Bench (Holinshed, IV, 433). An excessively curious case is that of a woman tried by the mayor of Faversham, Kent, in 1586. The court and jury were convinced that she was not guilty of witchcraft. In order to clear her of the capital charge, a verdict of guilty of invocation and conjuration was brought in. The mayor was about to congratulate the defendant on escaping with her life, when the legal adviser of the corporation informed him that invocation and conjuration amounted to felony, and she was hanged accordingly. Full details are given by John Waller in Holinshed, IV, 891–893.

29. Wright, I, 284.

30. As to this latter dictum, it is instructive to observe that in 1578 one Dr. Browne was in trouble because he "spread misliking of the laws, by saying there are no witches" (Calendar of State Papers, Domestic, Addenda, 1566–1579, p. 551).

31. There is some difference between the two statutes in defining the minor varieties, but it is slight and not in the direction of severity.

32. See the extraordinary passage in Webster's Displaying of Supposed Witchcraft, 1677, pp. 245–246.

33. Walsingham to Leicester, Leycester Correspondence (Camden Society, XXVII), p. 224; Hooker (alias Vowell), in Holinshed, IV (1808), 868; Thomas Cogan, The Haven of Health, 1589, pp. 272 ff. See also an important paper on the Black Assizes in the West, by F. Willcocks, M.D., in Transactions of the Devonshire Association, XVI, 595 ff. For Vowell, see Charles Worthy, in the same Transactions, XIV, 631 ff. (cf. XI, 442 ff.).

34. 13th Report of the Commission on Historical MSS., Appendix, Part IV, pp. 139–140.

35. A possible exception is Susan Swapper, of Rye. She was condemned in 1607, but I cannot find that she was ever executed. The case is exceedingly curious (see Commission on Historical MSS., 13th Report, Appendix, Part IV, pp. 136–137, 139–140, 144, 147–148). For what happened after 1643, when James had been in his grave a score of years, it is absurdly cruel to hold him accountable.

36. Cf. the observations of Mr. J. W. Brodie-Innes in his interesting brochure on Scottish Witchcraft Trials, pp. 21–24 (Privately Printed Opuscula issued to Members of the Sette of Odd Volumes, No. 25, 1891).

37. A True and Iust Recorde, of the Information [etc.] of all the Witches, taken at S. Oses (London, 1582). Mrs. Linton gives a good summary in her Witch Stories, 1861, pp. 205–221.

38. Potts, The Wonderfull Discoverie of Witches in the Countie of Lancaster. . . . Together with the Arraignement and Triall of Iennet Preston, at . . . Yorke, London, 1613. Cf. Farington Papers (Chetham Society, XXXIX), 1856, p. 27. One other died before trial.

39. The Witches of Northamptonshire, 1612 (reprint, 1867).

40. See, for example, Horley, Sefton, 1893, p. 115, note 1; Roper, Materials for the History of Lancaster, Part I, Chetham Society, 1907, pp. 26–27.

41. Ainsworth, The Lancashire Witches, 1849, I, 199–200.

42. The same, I, 207 (cf. I, 244, 247).

43. Potts, Wonderfull Discoverie, sig. T2.

44. Ainsworth, III, 241 ff.

45. Journal of Nicholas Assheton, ed. Raines, Chetham Society, 1848, pp. 32 ff.

46. Crossley, Introduction to his reprint of Potts (Chetham Society, VI), p. xviii.

47. The same, p. xlv.

48. Exact figures are unattainable, but the records are quite as trustworthy for 1603–1625 as for 1581–1603. It is altogether unlikely that a complete scrutiny would bring to light more new cases of execution for the later period than for the earlier.

49. That is, not more severe during James's reign. For what occurred long after the king's death, he cannot be blamed.

50. It is to be hoped that what Thomas Cooper says in The Mysterie of Witch-craft, 1617, p. 7, will not be taken as evidence in favor of the current view. Heretofore it has not been so utilized.

51. Hutchinson, Historical Essay concerning Witchcraft, 1718, p. 179 (ed. 1720, p. 224).

52. The same, p. 180. Here Hutchinson is referring to a particular part of the statute (about the violation of graves).

53. Page 178.

54. The same, p. 180.

55. William Harris, An Historical and Critical Account of the Life and Writings of James the First, 1753, pp. 40–41.

56. Somers Tracts, 2d ed., III, 95.

57. In a series of articles on the Rise and Progress of Witchcraft, containing much valuable material. Gentleman's Magazine Library, Popular Superstitions, p. 233.

58. See Chapter I.

59. Perkins, A Discourse of the Damned Art of Witchcraft, 1608, pp. 200 ff.

60. The same, pp. 206 ff.

61. James I, Dæmonologie, London, Printed for William Apsley and W. Cotton, 1603, p. 80 (misprinted, "64").

62. Perkins, p. 208.

63. Page 55.

64. Page 128.

65. Pages 191–196.

66. Page 247.

67. Pages 256–257. For other expressions of opinion on witchcraft, see Perkins's Golden Chaine, ed. 1605, pp. 34–36, and his Combate betweene Christ and the Diuell, ed. 1606, pp. 16, 25, 37.

68. Samuel Clarke, Life of Perkins (The Marrow of Ecclesiastical History, Part I, 3d ed., 1675, p. 416); cf. John Manningham's Diary, ed. Bruce, Camden Society, p. 104; Fuller, Holy State, ed. 1840, p. 71.

69. Bishop Hall, Works, Oxford, 1837, VI, 340.

70. See note 68, above.

71. Cotta, The Triall of Witch-craft, 1616, pp. 53, 57, 89, 91, 95.

72. Cotta, pp. 77, 90.

73. Page 80.

74. Ormerod, County of Chester, ed. Helsby, I, 611; Joseph Welch, List of the Queen's Scholars of St. Peter's College, Westminster, ed. Phillimore, p. 59; Foster, Alumni Oxonienses, I, 325; Dictionary of National Biography; Cooper, The Mystery of Witch-craft, 1617, sig. A2.

75. Cooper, Mystery, pp. 12–13.

76. The same, sigg. A3, A4, p. 13.

77. Deacon and Walker refer to the case in their Summarie Answere to Darrel, 1601, p. 237 Darrel, in A Survey of Certaine Dialogical Discourses, 1602, p. 54, gives the boy's name ("*Tho. Harison of North Wych in Ches shire*"), and says that he is "at this present very greuously vexed by Sathan."

78. Compare, for instance, Cooper, pp. 52–55, with Perkins, pp. 19–22, 26, 27, 28, 30, 31, 33, 34; Cooper, pp. 64–65, with Perkins, pp. 41–43; Cooper, p. 68, with Perkins, pp. 47–48; Cooper, pp. 128–133, 136, with Perkins, pp. 55–67, 73, 92, 104.

79. Cooper, p. 314.

80. Page 232.

81. The Dictionary of National Biography and Dr. Usher date Giffard's death 1620. But he was doubtless the George Giffard of Maldon whose will was proved in 1600 (Transactions of the Essex Archæological Society, New Series, VII, 46). For Giffard's connection with the Classical Movement of 1573–1592, see R. G. Usher, Presbyterian Movement, 1905, pp. xli, 9, 16, 19, 42, 94. For Giffard's reputation see D'Ewes, Autobiography, ed. Halliwell, I, 114.

82. Dedicatory Epistle.

83. Giffard, ed. 1603, sig. A3.

84. A True and Exact Relation of the severall Informations [etc.] of the late Witches, 1645, pp. 8, 15, 32, 34.

85. The general anxiety of Englishmen as Elizabeth's death drew nigh is graphically described by Dekker, The Wonderfull Yeare, 1603 (Works, ed.

Grosart, I, 94–96). Such crises are always favorable to outbreaks of witch-prosecution.

86. Harsnet, Discovery, 1599, pp. 8–9.

87. Deacon and Walker, Summarie Answere, and Dialogicall Discourses.

88. "Phantastical giddy-headed Puritans" Archbishop Matthew Hutton of York calls them in a letter to Whitgift, October 1, 1603 (Strype's Life of Whitgift, 1718, p. 570).

89. The exorcisms of the Jesuit Edmunds (alias Weston) and his associates in 1585 and 1586 were similarly attacked by Bancroft and Harsnet. See Harsnet's famous diatribe, A Declaration of Egregious Popish Impostures, 1603 (2d ed., 1605). The Roman Catholics were no more convinced in this case than the Puritans were in that of Darrel (see the references to Yepez and others in Mr. T. G. Law's article on Devil-Hunting in Elizabethan England, in the Nineteenth Century for March, 1894, XXXV, 397 ff.). On Sir George Peckham, who was involved in this affair, see Merriman, American Historical Review, XVII, 492 ff. Compare Sir George Courthop on the Nuns of Loudun (Memoirs, Camden Miscellany, XI, 106–109); see also Evelyn's Diary, August 5, 1670. Darrel's opponents did their best to stigmatize his principles and practices with regard to demoniacal possession as identical with those of the Roman Catholic Church. Thus Deacon and Walker, speaking of Darrel, inform their readers that "he hath for a season (though feare and shame enforceth him now to pluck in his head) very prowdlie *ietted* from countrie to countrie like a pettie new *Pope* among his owne *Cardinals*; yea and that also in his *pontificalities*, portrayed and contriued after the *new-found popelike cut*" (Summarie Answere, 1601, Address to the Reader).

90. Lewis Hughes, Certaine Grievances, 1641, p. 20. See George Sinclair, Satan's Invisible World Discovered, 1685, Relation XII (reprint, 1871, pp. 95–100; cf. Ferguson, Publications of the Edinburgh Bibliographical Society, III, 56–57); Commission on Historical MSS., 8th Report, Appendix, Part I, p. 228. An account of the affair, by George Swan, was published in 1603, under the title, A True and Brief Report, etc. On Lewis Hughes see Kittredge, George Stirk, Minister (reprinted from the Publications of the Colonial Society of Massachusetts), 1910, pp. 18–21; G. W. Cole, Proceedings American Antiquarian Society, New Series, XXXVII (1927), 247–311 (pp. 249–257 for the case).

91. Darrel, Replie, 1602, p. 21.

92. Darrel, pp. 21–22.

93. John Bruen's memoranda, in William Hinde's Life of John Bruen (born 1560, died 1625), in Samuel Clarke, The Marrow of Ecclesiastical History, Part II, Book ii, 1675, p. 95. Bruen (who was a Cheshire man) was an eyewitness of the boy's fits, and his notes, as excerpted by Hinde, give a good idea of his ravings (pp. 94–96). The boy cried out against "the witch," but I do not find that anybody was brought to trial.

94. Hall, Autobiography, Works, ed. Hall (1837), I, xxi. Hall may have had in mind the case reported by Bishop Parkhurst in a letter to Bullinger,

June 29, 1574 (Zurich Letters, I [1842], No. 118, translation, p. 303, original, p. 178).

95. Hall, Works, VI, 136–137; VII, 245–246; Contemplations, Works, ed. 1628, pp. 1134–1135.

96. Aubrey, Brief Lives, ed. Clark, I, 138. See also Proceedings Cambridge Antiquarian Society, XV, 248 ff.; James Primerose, Popular Errours, transl. Robert Wittie, 1651, Preface by translator; Nashe's Works, ed. McKerrow, I, 300.

97. The Witches of Warboys, 1593, sig. B2 r°.

98. See the Throckmorton pedigree (drawn up by Robert Throckmorton himself in 1613) in Charles's Visitation of the County of Huntingdon, ed. Ellis, Camden Society, 1849, pp. 123–124, and the Pulter pedigree, in the same, p. 101. Cf. the Pickering pedigree in Bridges, Northamptonshire, II, 383–385.

99. Dorington was A.B. 1555, Fellow of St. Catherine's College 1558, A.M. 1559, S.T.B. Queen's College 1565, S.T.P. 1575. Nutt matriculated at Peterhouse 1568; he was A.B. 1573, A.M. 1577. For this information, as well as the university record of Henry and Thomas Pickering (the editor of Perkins's Discourse), I am indebted to the kindness of the Registrary, Dr. J. N. Keynes, and the good offices of Professor Skeat.

100. Henry Pickering was a younger son of Sir Gilbert Pickering, Knight, of Tichmarsh, Northamptonshire. He matriculated at Christ's College, as a Pensioner, March 16, 1582–3, was A.B. 1586, A.M. 1590, and incorporated at Oxford 1593 (see note 99, above).

101. Witches of Warboys, sig. E3.

102. The year when Pickering became rector of Aldwincle All Saints, and the date of his death (1637, aged 75), were first correctly given (from his tombstone) by Mr. W. D. Christie in the Globe Edition of Dryden's Poetical Works, 1870, p. xvi, note †.

103. Thomas Pickering was admitted at Emmanuel College as a Pensioner in 1589. He was A.B. 1592, A.M. and Fellow 1596, B.D. 1603. He became Vicar of Finchingfield, Essex, March 9, 1605–6, and died there in 1625. For these facts I am indebted to the Registrary of the University, Dr. J. N. Keynes, and to Mr. J. B. Peace, Bursar of Emmanuel. His marriage license was issued May 4, 1611; his will was proved 1627, and administration was granted March 13, 1625–6 (Transactions of the Essex Archæological Society, New Series, VI, 299).

104. Cotta, The Triall of Witch-craft, 1616, p. 77.

105. Samuel Harsnet, when in full c. y after Darrel, did not venture to attack the Warboys case directly. True, he refers slightingly to the printed narrative as a "silly book," but in the same breath he suggests that one of Darrel's patients had taken a leaf out of it. And Darrel, in replying, taunts Harsnet with not daring to assail the case openly. That Mr. Throckmorton's children, says Darrel, "were tormented by the diuell, even 5. of his daughters, it is notoriously knowne, and so generally receaued for truth, as the Dis[coverer]. himselfe [i. e. Harsnet] dareth not deny it, though fayne he would, as appeareth by his nibling at them" (Detection of Harshnet, 1600, p. 39; cf. pp. 20–22, 36, 40). And again, he does not hesitate to declare that

Harsnet refrained from accusing the Throckmorton girls of counterfeiting because he did not dare: "He thought it best and meet for his safety becaus they were the children of an Esquier, not to say so in plaine tearmes" (p. 21).

106. J. H. Gray, Queen's College, 1899, pp. 128–129.

107. That offence, under the Elizabethan statute, was punishable only by imprisonment and the pillory, for none of the girls had died.

108. The Witches of Warboys, sig. I r°; cf. sig. P 2 v°.

109. Sig. N3.

110. Sig. E3 r°.

111. Lords' Journals, II, 267, 269, 271, 272, 275, 276, 293, 294, 316; Commons' Journals, I, 204, 207, 227, 232, 234, 236. There is no reason to suppose that the "attending" on the king by a part of the Lords' committee on April 12 had to do with the bill (Lords' Journals, II, 276).

112. The object of the law was not to multiply culprits, but to deter men from committing the crime. The idea that very great severity defeats its object did not then obtain among penologists. Take an example of the temper of intelligent men in this regard. In May, 1604, William Clopton writes to Timothy Hutton: "There is an act passed to take away the clergie from stealers of sheep and oxen, which will do much good" (Hutton Correspondence, Surtees Society, 1843, p. 195).

113. Stow, ed. Howes, 1631, pp. 767–768.

114. Howard, Defensative, ed. 1620, p. 81.

115. The same, p. 85. Bishop Bancroft and the Earl of Shrewsbury were on the Lords' Committee. The bishop had been the leading spirit in the prosecution of Darrel, and the earl had been present at the trial. But this is no reason why they should have opposed the statute. As we have seen, Bancroft was a prosecutor of exorcists, not a protector of alleged witches. In the Synod called by James (which sat concurrently with Parliament, and broke up on July 9, 1604, two days after Parliament rose) a canon (written by Bancroft) was adopted, forbidding clergymen, without proper license, "to attempt upon any pretence whatsoever, eyther of Possession or Obsession, by fasting, and prayers to cast out any Devill or Devills" (Canon 72, Constitutions and Canons of the Synod of 1603, ed. 1633; cf. J. W. Joyce, England's Sacred Synods, 1855, pp. 620 ff.; Cardwell, Synodalia, II, 583 ff.). This canon was in no wise inconsistent with the statute, nor can it have been so regarded by the twelve bishops who sat on the Lords' Committee. At all events, James I showed himself quite as skeptical as Bancroft in cases of alleged possession (see pp. 318 ff., above).

116. Notestein, pp. 39–40, 347.

117. The Same, pp. 40, 347–348; Rollins, Analytical Index, p. 131.

118. On the Wroth family see a series of papers by Mr. W. C. Waller in the Transactions of the Essex Archæological Society, New Series, VIII, 145 ff., 345 ff.; IX, 1 ff. On Sir Robert Wroth (1540–1606) see especially VIII, 150 ff. His son Robert (1576–1614, knighted in 1603) was one of Ben Jonson's patrons (see VIII, 156 ff.).

119. See p. 324, above.

120. See pp. 322–323, above.

121. Montagu became Recorder in 1603 (Calendar of State Papers, Domestic, 1603–1610, pp. 10, 14; cf. Foss, Judges of England, VI, 167 ff.; Peile, Biographical Register of Christ's College, 1910, I, 173).

122. Life of Cooper in Dictionary of National Biography.

123. See p. 293, above. Cf. Peile, as above, I, 181.

124. See pp. 7–22, above.

125. See pp. 315, 319, 326–327, above.

126. Cotta, The Triall of Witch-craft, p. 90.

127. Potts, The Wonderfull Discoverie, 1613, sigg. K3–N2.

128. See p. 300, above.

129. Hutchinson, p. 179.

130. See Pitcairn, Criminal Trials, I, 218, 233, 237, and especially 239 (cf. II, 478); Newes from Scotland, Sig. B3.

131. James I, Dæmonologie, 1603, pp. 43, 58.

132. Lucan, Pharsalia, vi, 507 ff.

133. Marston, Sophonisba, act iv, scene 1, vv. 99–125 (Works, ed. Bullen, II, 290–291).

134. John Weever, Ancient Funerall Monuments, 1631, pp. 45–46. Cf. Reginald Scot, xv, 8, 17; Baines, History of Lancashire, ed. Harland, I, 199.

135. Sir John Knyvet was appointed Chief Justice of the King's Bench in 1357 and Lord Chancellor in 1372 (Campbell, Lord Chancellors, 1846, I, 267–268).

136. Coke's Institutes, Third Part, cap. 6. See Gentleman's Magazine, 1829, Part II, XCIX, 515.

137. Truth Brought to Light by Time, 1651, p. 140; Egerton Papers, Camden Society, pp. 472–473.

138. Truth Brought to Light, p. 138.

139. As to Forman, see pp. 316–317, above.

140. No doubt James approved of the statute. He certainly believed in witchcraft and thought that proved witches ought to be put to death. In the Basilikon Doron, addressed to Prince Henry, he mentions witchcraft among the "horrible crymes that yee are bounde in Conscience neuer to forgiue" (1599, Roxburghe Club reprint, p. 37; London edition of 1603, p. 31). But the question is not whether he was a believer in the actuality of such offences, but whether he was a blind and maniacal persecutor who misled the English nation, to its everlasting disgrace.

141. Cf. Inderwick, Side-Lights on the Stuarts, 2d ed., p. 150.

142. Calendar of State Papers, Domestic, 1603–1610, p. 96.

143. Calendar, p. 406.

144. Jonson, The Alchemist, i, 1.

145. Reade stood suit with the College of Physicians in 1602 for practising without a license and was cast, as Whalley remarks in his note on the passage in The Alchemist. In the pardon he is styled "in medicinis professor." Cf. Historical MSS. Commission, 8th Report, Appendix, Part I, p. 228.

146. The pardon, giving these details, is printed in Rymer's Foedera, 2d ed., XVI, 666–667.

147. Calendar, 1603–1610, p. 598.

148. Calendar, 1611–1618, p. 29.

149. Francis Osborne, Essay 1, A Miscellany of Sundry Essayes, etc., 1659, pp. 4–5.

150. See Manly, Macbeth, 1900, pp. xvi–xviii.

151. Calendar of State Papers, Venetian, 1603–1607, pp. 44 (June 4, 1603).

152. In 1604, 1608, 1610, and 1617, for instance (Calendar, as above, 1603–1607, p. 193; 1607–1610, pp. 116, 465; F. Drake, Eboracum, 1736, p. 134).

153. Arthur Wilson, History of Great Britain, 1653, p. 289.

154. See Lee's life of Forman in the Dictionary of National Biography, XIX, 438 ff. Cf. the Ashmole MS. quoted by Wood, Athenae Oxonienses, ed. Bliss, II (1815), 100. The Venns date the license 1604 and ignore the alleged degree: Alumni Cantabrigienses, Part I, Vol. II (1922), 158.

155. William Lilly, History of his Life and Times, 2d ed., 1715, p. 16.

156. Forman was twice imprisoned, at the instance of the Royal College of Physicians, as an unauthorized and ignorant practitioner (in 1595 and 1596). In 1601 he was again complained of. In 1606 and 1607, after obtaining his Cambridge degree, he was cited to appear before the College, but refused to obey. See the records in the 8th Report of the Commission on Historical MSS., Appendix, Part I, p. 228.

157. Truth Brought to Light by Time, 1651, pp. 135–138; Letter from Thomas Bone to Sir John Egerton, November 9, 1615, Egerton Papers, Camden Society, pp. 470–473.

158. See Lilly, pp. 12–16.

159. The indictments are printed (in translation) in A Briefe Description of the Notorious Life of Iohn Lambe, Amsterdam, 1628, pp. 3–6. They are not dated. The bewitching of Lord Windsor is stated in the first indictment to have occurred on December 16, 5 Jac. I (i. e. 1607), and at divers times afterward; the second indictment dates the invocation of evil spirits, May 13, 6 Jac. I (i. e. 1608), and before and after. Lee (Dictionary of National Biography, XXXII, 1) shifts the second of these dates, inadvertently, from the *offence* to the *trial*. We do not, in fact, know when Lambe was tried, but it was before 1617.

160. Briefe Description, p. 14.

161. The same, pp. 14 ff.

162. The indictment dates the offence June 10, 21 Jac. I, i. e. 1623 (Briefe Description, p. 15). The conviction was in 1624 (Calendar of State Papers, Domestic, 1623–1625, p. 485).

163. Calendar, 1623–1625, pp. 241, 243, 261, 266, 280.

164. Briefe Description, 1628, p. 20.

165. The same, pp. 20–21; Rushworth, Historical Collections, I, 618 (cf. I, 391); Reign of Charles I, continuation of Baker's Chronicle, ed. 1660, p. 493; Diary of William Whiteway, June 13, 1628 (Proceedings Dorset Natural History and Antiquarian Field Club, XIII, 69); Historical MSS. Commission, 8th Report, Appendix, Part I, p. 229; Richard Smith, Obituary, in Peck, Desiderata Curiosa, Vol. II, Book xiv, p. 11; Jupp, Historical Account of the Company of Carpenters, 1887, pp. 84–85.

166. Continuation of Baker's Chronicle, as above, p. 493. Cf. Fairholt, Poems and Songs relating to George Villiers, Duke of Buckingham, Percy Society, 1850, pp. xiv–xv, 58–63, 65.

167. Calendar of State Papers, Domestic, 1623–1625, p. 476. Lady Purbeck had visited Lambe in prison to procure charms from him (p. 474; cf. p. 497).

168. Another infamous person who drove a thriving trade with the court ladies was Mrs. Mary Woods, who practised her arts at Norwich, and removed to London in 1612. She was involved in the alleged plot of the Countess of Essex to poison the Earl. She was arrested and examined, but it does not appear that she was proceeded against under the statute of 1604, although one witness declared that she professed to have a familiar spirit. Obviously she was regarded as a mere charlatan, yet it would have been easy enough to hang her for a witch if the king had favored such a prosecution (Calendar of State Papers, Domestic, 1611–1618, pp. 134, 161, 173, 183, 187; Inquiry into the Genuineness of a Letter, etc., pp. 17–19, Camden Miscellany, V; Gardiner, History of England, 1603–1642, 4th ed., II [1895], 169, note 1).

169. See Dee's own account of the affair in his Compendious Rehearsall, 1592, printed by Crossley, in Autobiographical Tracts of Dr. John Dee, pp. 20–21 (Chetham Miscellany, I), and cf. the Necessary Advertisement prefixed to his General and Rare Memorials pertayning to the Perfect Arte of Navigation, 1577 (Crossley, p. 57). See also Calendar of State Papers, Domestic, 1547–1550, p. 67; Charlotte Fell Smith, John Dee, 1909, pp. 14–15.

170. Dee's Preface to Henry Billingsley's translation of Euclid's Elements, 1571 (Smith, pp. 24–28).

171. Necessary Advertisement, 1577 (Crossley, p. 53).

172. Compendious Rehearsall, 1592 (Crossley, pp. 27 ff.).

173. Aubrey, Brief Lives, ed. Andrew Clark, I, 212–214.

174. Smith, John Dee, p. 293. The petition is printed by Ellis, Original Letters of Eminent Literary Men, Camden Society, pp. 47–48.

175. MS. College of Arms c. 37, 168, quoted by F. R. Raines, Rectors of Manchester and Wardens of the Collegiate Church, Part II, 1885, p. 110 (Chetham Society).

176. James has been derided for maintaining the doctrine of witchcraft in the Essex divorce case (see his answer to Archbishop Abbot in Truth Brought to Light by Time, 1651, pp. 103 ff.). This discredit, however, such as it is, is cancelled by his conduct in the case of Sir Thomas Lake (involving a precisely similar allegation of witchcraft), in which he showed much acumen in unravelling a tangled skein of malice and perjury. See Gardiner, History, III (1895), 189–194. Gardiner remarks that James "prided himself upon his skill in the detection of imposture" (III, 192).

177. Harleian MS. 6986, art. 40 (autograph), as printed by Sir Henry Ellis, Original Letters, 1st Series, 1824, III, 80–81. The letter may also be found in Birch, Life of Henry Prince of Wales, 1760, p. 37; Letters to King James the Sixth, Maitland Club, 1835, p. xxxv (where it is said, erroneously, to be in reply to an extant letter of January 1, 1603–4, from Prince

Henry); Nichols, Progresses of James I, I, 304; Halliwell, Letters of the Kings, 1848, II, 102. Cf. Gifford's edition of Ford, I, clxxi (ed. Dyce, 1869, III, 276); Quarterly Review, XLI (1829), 80–82.

178. James I, Counterblast, ed. Arber, p. 108.

179. James I, letter dated March 5th (no year), Halliwell (from Rawlinson MS.), Letters of the Kings, II, 124–125. It does not appear to whom the letter was addressed. Such cases of real or pretended fasting are common. See, for example, John Reynolds, A Discourse upon Prodigious Abstinence: occasioned by the Twelve Moneths Fasting of Martha Taylor, the famed Derbyshire Damosell, 1669. See pp. 128–130, above.

180. Journal of Sir Roger Wilbraham, 1593–1616, ed. by H. S. Scott, p. 70 (Camden Miscellany, X). This is clearly the case mentioned by Walter Yonge in his Diary (ed. Roberts, Camden Society, 1848, p. 12). If so, the bewitched person was "near kinswoman to Doctor Holland's wife, Rector of Exon College in Oxford." This was Thomas Holland, on whom see Wood, Athenae Oxonienses, ed. Bliss, II, 111–112; Foster, Alumni Oxonienses, II, 731.

181. King James his Apophthegmes, 1643, pp. 8–9; Calendar of State Papers, Domestic, 1603–1610, pp. 212, 213; Venetian, 1603–1607, pp. 238, 240–241; letters in Lodge, Illustrations of British History, 2d ed., 1838, III, 143–144, 153–155, 157–160; Arthur Wilson, History of Great Britain, 1653, p. 111; Baker's Chronicle, ed. 1660, p. 431; Fuller, Church-History, Book x, Century xvii, sect. 4, § 56, 1656, p. 73; Aubrey, MS. History of Wiltshire, pp. 362–363, as quoted by Halliwell, Letters of the Kings, II, 124, note; Foster, Alumni Oxonienses, II, 679; Dictionary of National Biography.

182. State Papers, James I, Vol. XIII, No. 80. It is an obscure and rambling document.

183. King James his Speech to both Houses of Parliament on Occasion of the Gunpowder-Treason, ed. 1679, p. 7; cf. Journal of Sir Roger Wilbraham, pp. 70–71.

184. Calendar of State Papers, Venetian, 1603–1607, p. 327 (cf. pp. 316–317).

185. Discourse, appended to King James his Speech (see note 183, above), pp. 28–29 (cf. pp. 30–31).

186. Cotta, The Triall of Witch-craft, p. 76.

187. Wright, Narratives of Sorcery and Magic, II, 144.

188. Aubrey, MS. History of Wiltshire, pp. 362–363 (Halliwell, Letters of the Kings, II, 124, note).

189. See p. 300, above.

190. Calendar of State Papers, Domestic, 1603–1610, p. 218.

191. Calendar, 1611–1618, p. 53.

192. Calendar, 1634–1635, pp. 26, 77–79, 98, 129–130, 141, 152–153.

193. Thomas Guidott, Preface to his edition of Jorden's treatise, A Discourse of Natural Bathes and Mineral Waters, 1673, as quoted by Bliss in his edition of Wood's Athenae Oxonienses, II (1817), 550. See G. W. Cole, Lewis Hughes, in the Proceedings of the American Antiquarian Society for October, 1927, New Series, XXXVII, 249–257. Fuller

mentions the case, but without details: "*Anne Gunter*, a Maid of *Windsor*, gave it out she was *possessed of a Deuil*, & was transported with strange *Extaticall Phrensies*."

194. On Smythe's identity see Kittredge, Modern Philology, IX (1911), 195–200.

195. Letter from Alderman Robert Heyrick of Leicester to his brother Sir William in London, dated July 18, 1616 — the very day of the execution (printed by Nichols, Leicestershire, Vol. II, Part II, p. 471*).

196. See p. 302, above.

197. The Witches of Warboys, 1593, sig. P2 r°.

198. Heyrick's letter.

199. Nichols, Progresses of James I, III, 192; Calendar of State Papers, Domestic, 1611–1618, p. 398.

200. Sir Humphrey Winch was M.P. for the Borough of Bedford (Members of Parliament, I, 442a).

201. The king went from Nottingham to Leicester on August 15th, spent the night there, and proceeded to Dingley, on the 16th (Nichols, Progresses, III, 180–181, cf. III, 175). Cf. Wm. Kelly, Royal Progresses and Visits to Leicester, 1884, pp. 365–369.

202. Archbishop of Canterbury.

203. Osborne, Essayes, 1659, p. 8.

204. Robert Heyrick's letter, October 15, 1616 (printed by Nichols, Leicestershire, Vol. II, Part II, p. 471*).

205. Nichols, Progresses, III, 192–193; Calendar of State Papers, Domestic, 1611–1618, p. 398. We can make out a satisfactory account of the case by comparing Osborne with Heyrick's two letters (one of July 18, the other of October 15, 1616, both printed by Nichols, Leicestershire, Vol. II, Part II, p. 471*). I have followed Heyrick (as being absolutely contemporary and on the spot) wherever he differs from Osborne. Heyrick does not mention the king, but Osborne's testimony as to James's intervention is corroborated in all essentials by Chamberlain's letter of October 12, 1616 (Nichols, Progresses, III, 192–193; Calendar, 1611–1618, p. 398). Osborne, by the way, speaks of his narrative as follows: "I will here relate a Story of my own Knowledge" (p. 5).

206. Mr. William Wheater's statement that six persons suffered death for witchcraft at York in 1622 (Old Yorkshire, ed. by William Smith, IV, 266) is a mistake. This was the Fairfax case. Six persons were indicted, but all of them were discharged without a complete trial.

207. John Latimer, The Annals of Bristol in the Seventeenth Century, 1900, p. 91.

208. There was no torture. She confessed to the minister, Henry Goodcole, for her soul's sake. See Goodcole's narrative, The Wonderfull Discoverie of Elizabeth Sawyer, 1621, reprinted in The Works of John Ford, ed. 1895 (Bullen), I, lxxxi ff. Goodcole was the ordinary of Newgate. His wife, who practised medicine, became involved, in 1622, in the case of Lady Jennings's daughter, supposed to be bewitched (Add. MS. 36674, foll. 134 r°–137 r°).

209. The Wonderfull Discoverie of the Witchcrafts of Margaret and Philip Flower, 1619. Cf. pp. 237–238, above.

210. We may laugh at witchcraft, but it by no means follows that all the afflicted persons were impostors or that the defendants were always guiltless. The children who cried out on the Salem goodwives and the numerous other "young liars" (as one unsympathetic writer has called them) were *really* afflicted, though the cause was mistaken. Much of their play-acting was a part of their disease. As for the witches themselves (I do not here refer to Salem in particular), it is clear that many of them were malignant creatures who did what they could to get into communion with the fiend and thought they had succeeded. As Mr. Andrew Lang well remarks, "There can be little doubt that many witches were in intention malevolent enough. They believed in their own powers, and probably dealt in poison on occasion" (History of Scotland, II, 352). Others were precocious experimenters in supernormal mental states. I need but refer to Professor Wendell's suggestive essay on the Salem witches (Stelligeri, 1893; cf. his Cotton Mather, pp. 93 ff.) and to Mr. Brodie-Innes's paper on Scottish Witchcraft Trials, in which this fruitful subject of investigation is broached, with illuminating remarks. Neither professes to do more than raise the question. The undiscovered country of witch pathology awaits its trained explorer. Dr. E. W. Taylor's recent paper on Some Medical Aspects of Witchcraft leads one to hope that he will pursue the subject. Meantime we may speak respectfully of some of our elders — Wierus, Scot, Webster, Bekker, and Meric Casaubon (not all of them on the same side) — who have made wise observations needing only to be translated from the obsolete technical language of their day in order to appeal to the modern alienist. For cases of genuine and indubitable attempts at sorcery, see, for example, Proceedings of the Society of Antiquaries, 2d Series, XVIII, 140 ff.; W. H. Hart, Archæologia, XL, 397. Examples are countless.

211. Hutchinson, Historical Essay, 1718, pp. 217 ff. (from the narrative). Cf. The Boy of Bilson, 1622, pp. 55–73; The Second Part of the Boy of Bilson, 1698, pp. 1–9; Gee, The Foot out of the Snare, 1624, pp. 53–54.

212. A. Wilson, History of Great Britain, 1653, pp. 111–112. For Wilson's own skepticism on the subject of witchcraft, see his Autobiography, in Peck, Desiderata Curiosa, Vol. II, Book xii, pp. 26–27.

213. John Gee, Hold Fast, a Sermon Preached at Pauls Crosse vpon Sunday being the XXXI. of October, Anno Domini 1624 (London, 1624), pp. 45–46 (Kittredge, American Historical Review, XX [1915], 570).

214. Osborne, Essay i (A Miscellany, 1659, p. 4). Cf. p. 315, above.

215. Goodman, Court of King James the First, ed. Brewer, 1839, I, 3.

216. Bernard, A Guide to Grand-Iury Men, 2d ed., 1629, p. 34.

217. Fuller, Church-History, Book x, Cent. cxvii, sect. 4, §§ 54–57, 1656, pp. 73–74. Cf. Gifford's Jonson, VII, 140, note 4.

218. Fuller, § 56. The only case that we can date is Haydock's (see p. 320, above).

219. Fuller, § 57.

220. Osborne, Essay i.

221. The Dæmonologie (unmodified) was included in the authorized edition of the king's Works in 1616.

222. Spectator for July 14, 1711 (No. 117); cf. Blackstone, Commentaries, Book iv, chap. 4, sect. 6 (4th ed., 1770, IV, 60–61).

223. Full details of this case are given in Fairfax's own narrative, entitled Dæmonologia (edited by William Grainge, Harrogate, 1882).

224. Fairfax says this message was delivered to the grand jury in his hearing (p. 126).

225. Fairfax, p. 126.

226. Pages 123–127.

227. Page 127.

228. Page 124.

229. Page 81.

230. Crossley in his edition of Potts's Discoverie, p. lxxviii.

231. Wright, Narratives of Sorcery and Magic, II, 117.

232. I do not include the Bakewell cases, as to which the evidence is too uncertain to trust. See Notestein, pp. 137, 384, 396.

233. Jeaffreson, Middlesex County Records, II, xvii–xviii, liii.

CHAPTER XVIII

WITCHCRAFT AND THE PURITANS

1. The Rambler, No. 2.

2. That the New Englanders brought their views on demonology and witchcraft with them from the Mother Country is a self-evident proposition, but it may be worth while to refer to a striking instance of the kind. The Rev. John Higginson, writing from Salem to Increase Mather in 1683, sends him two cases for his Illustrious Providences, — both of which he "believes to be certain." The first is an account of how a mysterious stranger, thought to be the devil, once lent a conjuring book to "godly Mr. [Samuel] Sharp, who was Ruling Elder of the Church of Salem allmost 30 years." The incident took place when Sharp was a young man in London. The second narrative Mr. Higginson "heard at Gilford from a godly old man yet living. He came from Essex, and hath been in N. E. about 50 years." It is a powerfully interesting legend of the Faust type, localized in Essex. In a postscript Mr. Higginson adds, "I had credible information of one in Leicestershire, in the time of the Long Parliament, that gave his soul to the Divel, upon condition to be a Famous Preacher, which he was for a time, &c., but I am imperfect in the story" (Mather Papers, Massachusetts Historical Society Collections, 4th Series, VIII, 285–287). See also the cases of witchcraft before 1692 collected in S. G. Drake's Annals of Witchcraft in New England. Dr. Poole is far nearer the truth in saying that "the New-England colonists had no views concerning witchcraft and diabolical agency which they did not bring with them from the Old World" (Witchcraft in Boston, in Winsor, Memorial History of Boston, II, 131) than President White is when he remarks that "the life of the early colonists in New England was such as to give rapid growth to the germs of the doctrine

of possession brought from the mother country" (Warfare of Science with Theology, II, 145).

3. A masterly short account of the various elements which made up the fully developed doctrine of witchcraft as it was held during the three centuries of especial prosecution (1400–1700), and of the sources from which these elements were derived, may be found in the first chapter of Joseph Hansen's Zauberwahn, Inquisition und Hexenprozess im Mittelalter (Munich and Leipzig, 1900). A learned and able essay by Professor George L. Burr, The Literature of Witchcraft, reprinted from the Papers of the American Historical Association, New York, 1890, should also be consulted.

4. See Bacon's Works, ed. Spedding, I, 193, 498, 608–609; II, 634, 641–642, 657–658, 664; III, 490; VI, 392–393, 395–396; VII, 738; Life and Letters, VII, 30–31.

5. King James did not force this act through parliament, but he must have approved it. See Chapter XVII.

6. See F. Legge, Witchcraft in Scotland (Scottish Review, XVIII, 267); Thomas Wright, Narratives of Sorcery and Magic, chap. xxv. Whitelocke, under date of October 4, 1652, notes "Letters that sixty Persons Men and Women were accused before the Commissioners for Administration of Justice in *Scotland* at the last Circuit for Witches; but they found so much Malice and so little Proof against them that none were condemned" (Memorials, 1732, p. 545). Cf. also his very important entry on the same subject under October 29, 1652 (pp. 547–548).

7. Epistolæ Ho-Elianæ, Familiar Letters, edited by Joseph Jacobs, 1890, Book ii, letter 76, p. 506: "To my Honourable Friend, Mr. E. P., at Paris" (cf. Jacobs's notes, pp. 783–784). The letter is dated "Fleet, 3 Feb. 1646." This is certainly Old Style. Howell is a queer dater, but a reference in this letter to the departure of the Scottish army (p. 505) proves that the letter was written after December 21, 1646. There is a similar passage about witches in Book iii, letter 2, p. 515 (also to Porter), dated "Fleet, 20 Feb. 1646."

8. Letters, as above, Book iii, No. 23, pp. 547 ff., dated "Fleet, 20 Feb. 1647," i. e. doubtless 1648.

9. See Jacobs's Introduction, pp. xlii–xliii. The question whether Howell's letters were actually sent to the persons to whom they are addressed or whether they are to be regarded merely as literary exercises composed during his imprisonment (see Jacobs, pp. lxxi ff.) does not affect, for our purposes, the value of the quotations here made, since the letters to which we now refer actually purport to have been written in the Fleet, and since they were first published in the second edition (1650) in the additional third volume and from the nature of things could not have appeared in the first edition (1645). They must, at all events, have been composed before 1650, and are doubtless dated correctly enough.

10. See p. 371, above.

11. Taylor, Sermon xvii (Whole Works, ed. Heeber and Eden, 1861, IV, 546).

12. Taylor, Whole Works, III, 57; cf. Sermon vii (Works, IV, 412).

13. I. e. the statute of 1604.

14. A Tryal of Witches at the Assizes held at Bury St. Edmonds . . ., 1664 (London, 1682), pp. 55–56. This report is reprinted in Howell's State Trials, VI, 647 ff., and (in part) in H. L. Stephen's State Trials Political and Social (1899), I, 209 ff. See also Hutchinson, An Historical Essay concerning Witchcraft, chap. viii (1718, pp. 109 ff.; 2d ed., 1720, pp. 139 ff.); Thomas Wright, Narratives of Sorcery and Magic, II, 261 ff. Hale's opinion was regarded as settling the law beyond peradventure. It is quoted in A True and Impartial Relation of the Informations against Three Witches . . . Assizes holden for the County of Devon at the Castle of Exon, August 14. 1682 (London, 1682), Address to the Reader. For Roger North's comments on the Exeter case, see pp. 3–4, above. A Collection of Modern Relations of Matters of Fact, concerning Witches & Witchcraft, Part I (London, 1693), contains "A Discourse concerning the great Mercy of God, in preserving us from the Power and Malice of *Evil Angels. Written by Sir* Matt. Hale *at Cambridge* 26 Mar. 1661. *Upon occasion of a Tryal of certain Witches before him the Week before at St.* Edmund's-Bury." The date is wrong (1661 should be 1664) but the trial is identified with that which we are considering by the anonymous compiler of the Collection in the following words: "There is a Relation of it in print, written by his Marshal, which I suppose is very true, though to the best of my Memory, not so compleat, as to some observable Circumstances, as what he related to me at his return from that Circuit." The date of the trial is given as "the Tenth day of March, 1664" on the title-page of the report (A Tryal of Witches) and on page 1 as "the Tenth day of March, in the Sixteenth Year of the Reign of . . . Charles II." On p. 57 the year is misprinted "1662." Howell's State Trials, VI, 647, 687, makes it 1665, but 16 Charles II corresponds to January 30, 1664–January 29, 1665: hence 1664 is right. The (unfinished) Discourse just mentioned must not be confused with Hale's Motives to Watchfulness, in reference to the Good and Evil Angels, which may be found in his Contemplations Moral and Divine, London, 1682 (licensed 1675–6), Part II, pp. 67 ff.

15. Roger North, Life of the Lord Keeper Guilford, ed. 1826, I, 121.

16. Cotton Mather, Wonders of the Invisible World (London, 1693), p. 55. Mather also reproduces the substance of the report above referred to (note 14) in the same work. Bragge, too, reproduces it, in the main, in his tract, Witchcraft Farther Display'd, 1712, in support of the accusation against Jane Wenham.

17. Campbell, Lives of the Chief Justices, 1849, I, 561 ff., chap. xvii. See also the criticism of Hale in a memoir of George Onslow's, 1770, 14th Report of the Historical MSS. Commission, Appendix, Part IX, p. 480.

18. Burnet's Life of Hale was published in 1682.

19. Roger North, Life of the Lord Keeper Guilford, ed. 1826, I, 117 ff.

20. State Papers (Domestic), 1682, August 19, bundle 427, No. 67, as quoted by Pike, History of Crime in England, II, 238.

21. A Tryal of Witches, as above, p. 41.

22. A Tryal, as above, p. 42. Cf. the Supplementary Memoir, in Simon Wilkin's edition of Browne's Works, 1852, I, liv–lvi.

23. See pp. 124 ff., above.

24. Burton, Anatomy of Melancholy, 1621, Part I, section 2, member 1, subsection 3. I quote from the edition of 1624.

25. The following short character of Glanvil by Bishop Kennet, may be quoted, not because it is just, but because it might conceivably be brought forward by somebody in rebuttal of this proposition: — "Mr. *Joseph Glanvill* of *Lincoln* College, *Oxon.* taking the Degree of M.A. in the beginning of 1658. was about that Time made Chaplain to old *Francis Rous* one of *Oliver*'s Lords, and Provost of *Eaton* College. — He became a great Admirer of Mr. *Richard Baxter*, and a zealous Person for a Commonwealth. After his Majesty's Restauration he turn'd about, became a Latitudinarian, — Rector of *Bath*, Prebendary of *Worcester*, and Chaplain to the King" (White Kennet, Register, 1728, p. 931).

26. See Dr. Ferris Greenslet's Joseph Glanvill, A Study in English Thought and Letters of the Seventeenth Century, New York, 1900, especially chap. vi. For a bibliography of Glanvil, see Emanuel Green, Bibliotheca Somersetensis, Taunton (Eng.), 1902, I, 206 ff.

27. More's theories on the subject of apparitions, demons, and witches may also be read, at considerable length, in his Antidote against Atheism, Book iii, chaps. 2–13 (Philosophical Writings, 2d ed., 1662, pp. 89 ff.); cf. the Appendix to the Antidote, chaps. 12–13 (pp. 181 ff.), and The Immortality of the Soul, chap. 16 (pp. 129 ff.).

28. John Hale, A Modest Enquiry into the Nature of Witchcraft, Boston, 1702.

29. Mr. Higginson's Epistle is dated 1697–8.

30. John Hale, A Modest Enquiry, 1702, p. 12.

31. Meric Casaubon was born in 1599 and died in 1671. His learned, lively, and vastly entertaining work, A Treatise concerning Enthusiasme, as it is an Effect of Nature: but is mistaken by many for either Divine Inspiration, or Diabolicall Possession, appeared in 1655, and in a "Second edition: revised, and enlarged" in 1656. It shows an open mind and a temper rather skeptical than credulous. Passages of interest in our present discussion may be found on pp. 37–41, 44, 49, 94–95, 100, 118, 174 (Quakers), 286, of the second edition. Of particular significances is the Doctor's account of his visit to a man who was thought to be possessed but whom he believed to be suffering from some bodily distemper (pp. 97 ff.). Casaubon's treatise (in two parts) Of Credulity and Incredulity, in Things Natural, Civil, and Divine, came out in 1668, and was reissued, with a new title-page (as above), in 1672. A third part, Of Credulity and Incredulity in Things Divine and Spiritual, appeared in 1670. Webster's assault upon Casaubon in his Displaying of Supposed Witchcraft was made in apparent ignorance of the fact that the venerable scholar had been dead for some years (see p. 343, above).

32. Compare Reginald Scot's chapter "Of Theurgie, with a confutation thereof" (Discoverie of Witchcraft, Book xv, chap. 42, pp. 466–467 [336–337], ed. Nicholson, pp. 392–393). See also Henry Hallywell, Melampronoea: or A Discourse of the Polity and Kingdom of Darkness. Together with a Solution of the Chiefest Objections brought against the Being of Witches, 1681, pp. 50–51.

33. Cudworth, Intellectual System, Book i, Chap. 4, § 15, ed. 1678, pp. 265–269.

34. Sadducismus Triumphatus, ed. 1726, p. 336; see James Crossley's Introduction to Potts, Discoverie (Chetham Society, 1845), p. vi, note 2. This experiment was twice tried as late as 1712, in the case of Jane Wenham, by the Rev. Mr. Strutt, once in the presence of Sir Henry Chauncy, and again in the presence of the Rev. Mr. Gardiner. Its ill success is recorded by a third Anglican clergyman, — Mr. Francis Bragge (A Full and Impartial Account of the Discovery of Sorcery and Witchcraft, Practis'd by Jane Wenham, London, 1712, pp. 11, 15).

35. Boyle, Letter to Glanvil, September 18, 1677, Works, ed. Birch, V, 244. Compare Dr. Samuel Collins's letter to Boyle, September 1, 1663 (Boyle's Works, V, 633–634).

36. Boyle, letter to Glanvil (Works, V, 245).

37. See Demonologie ou Traitte des Demons et Sorciers . . . Par Fr. Perreaud. Ensemble l'Antidemon de Mascon, ou Histoire Veritable de ce qu'un Demon a fait & dit, il y a quelques années, en la maison dudit S^r. Perreaud à Mascon. Geneva, 1653.

38. Barrow, Theological Works, ed. 1830, IV, 480–482.

39. Hickes, Ravillac Redivivus, reprinted in the Somers Tracts, 2d ed., VIII, 510 ff. (see especially pp. 546 ff.). Weir, who was unquestionably insane, was executed in 1670.

40. Diary and Correspondence of Samuel Pepys, London, 1885, IV, 275. On elf-arrows, see pp. 133–134, above.

41. Evelyn may have derived his information from Sir William Phips's letter to the home government (October 14, 1692), as Dr. G. H. Moore suggests (Final Notes on Witchcraft in Massachusetts, N. Y., 1885, p. 66). For the letter see Goodell, Essex Institute Collections, 2d Series, I, ii, 86 ff. Phips's second letter (Feb. 21, 1692–93, to the Earl of Nottingham) is printed by Moore, pp. 90 ff.

42. The remark, sometimes heard, that Calvinism was especially responsible for witch-trials is a loose assertion which has to reckon with the fact that the last burning for witchcraft at Geneva took place in 1652 (see Paul Ladame, Procès Criminel de la Dernière Sorcière Brulée à Genève, Paris, 1888).

43. Burton, Anatomy of Melancholy, Part I, section 2, member 1, subsection 3: — "Many deny Witches at all, or if there be any, they can doe no harme: of this opinion is Wierus, lib. 3. cap. 53, de præstig. dæm. Austin Lerchemer, a Dutch writer, Biarmanus, Ewichius, Euwaldus, our countryman Scot: but on the contrary are most Lawyers, Diuines, Physitians, Philosophers."

44. Wier's great work, De Praestigiis Dæmonum, was published in 1563, and was afterwards much enlarged. It went through several editions.

45. See the extraordinary list in William Drage, Daimonomageia. A Small Treatise of Sicknesses and Diseases from Witchcraft, and Supernatural Causes, 1665. Webster considers this subject at length in chap. xii of his Displaying of Supposed Witchcraft, 1677, with a full discussion of

van Helmont's views. Cf. Henry More, Antidote against Atheism, chaps. 4–5 (Philosophical Writings, 2d ed., 1662, pp. 97 ff.). See p. 134, above.

46. "Ea dæmonis subtilitate uelocitateque imperceptibili, ori ingesta, nostris ad hæc oculis uel celeritate eius uictis, uel fascino delusis, uel interiecto corpore aereo aut aliter motis eo intus uel foris uel utrinque humoribus aut spiritu caligantibus." De Præstigiis Dæmonum (Basileae, 1568), iv, 2, pp. 352–353.

47. Even Bekker (see p. 351, above), who approaches the subject from the philosophical direction, and whose logical process is different from Wier's, is greatly indebted to him.

48. Compare the fate of Bekker in 1692 (p. 39).

49. Meric Casaubon, A Treatise Proving Spirits, Witches and Supernatural Operations, 1672, p. 35.

50. The same, p. 46.

51. James I, Dæmonologie, Workes, 1616, p. 92. On Wier in general, see Carl Binz, Doctor Johann Weyer, ein Rheinischer Arzt, der erste Bekämpfer des Hexenwahns, Berlin, 1896.

52. Scot expressly asserts his belief in the existence of evil spirits (A Discourse upon Divels and Spirits, chap. 32, p. 540; cf. chap. 16, p. 514).

53. Discoverie of Witchcraft, xiii, 22–34, pp. 321 ff. (226 ff.), ed. Nicholson, pp. 262 ff. (with cuts). Most of the tricks which Scot describes are identical with feats of legerdemain that are the stock in trade of every modern juggler: — "To throwe a peece of monie awaie, and to find it againe where you list" (p. 326); "To make a groat or a testor to sinke through a table, and to vanish out of a handkercher verie strangelie" (p. 327); "How to deliver out foure aces, and to convert them into foure knaves" (p. 333); "To tell one without confederacie what card he thinketh" (p. 334); "To burne a thred, and to make it whole againe with the ashes thereof" (p. 341); "To cut off ones head, and to laie it in a platter, &c.: which the jugglers call the decollation of John Baptist" (p. 349). The picture of the apparatus required for the last-mentioned trick is very curious indeed.

54. King James remarks, in the Preface to his Dæmonologie, that Scot "is not ashamed in publike Print to deny, that there can be such a thing as Witch-craft: and so maintaines the old errour of the Sadduces in denying of spirits" (Workes, 1616, pp. 91–92).

55. In what an orderly way one may proceed from an admission of the doctrine of fallen angels to the final results of the witch-dogma may be seen, for instance, in Henry Hallywell's Melampronoea: or A Discourse of the Polity and Kingdom of Darkness, 1681. Hallywell had been a Fellow of Christ's College, Cambridge.

56. See p. 332, above.

57. 1665 ed. of Scot, p. 39 (see Nicholson's reprint of the 1584 edition, p. xlii).

58. The same, p. 46.

59. Crossley, Introduction to the Chetham Society reprint of Potts's Discoverie of Witches, pp. xxxviii–xxxix.

60. Webster, The Displaying of Supposed Witchcraft, 1677, p. 202.

61. Page 228. Perhaps Webster is merely "putting a case" here; but he certainly seems to be making an admission, at least in theory.

62. Page 230.

63. Pages 294 ff.

64. Page 294.

65. Pages 297–298.

66. Pages 302–310.

67. Page 308.   On the astral spirit, see also pp. 312 ff.

68. Page 310.

69. Pages 10–11.

70. See also pp. 267 ff.

71. Page 73.

72. Page 231.

73. Pages 242–243.

74. Page 244.

75. Pages 245–246.

76. Page 247.

77. Page 260.

78. Page 267.

79. Note, however, that the upholders of the current beliefs on witchcraft are also many times emphatic enough in similar cautionary remarks. A first-rate example is the following characteristic passage from Dr. Casaubon, whom Webster calls a "witchmonger": "And indeed, that the denying of *Witches*, to them that content themselves in the search of truth with a superficial view, is a very plausible cause; it cannot be denied. For if any thing in the world, (as we know all things in the world are) be liable to fraud, and imposture, and innocent mistake, through weakness and simplicity; this subject of Witches and Spirits is. . . . How ordinary is it to mistake natural melancholy (not to speak of other diseases) for a Devil? And how much, too frequently, is both the disease increased, or made incurable; and the mistake confirmed, by many ignorant Ministers, who take every wild motion, or phansie, for a suggestion of the Devil? Whereas, in such a case, it should be the care of wise friends, to apply themselves to the Physician of the body, and not to entertain the other, (I speak it of *natural* melancholy) who probably may do more hurt, than good; but as the learned Naturalist doth allow, and advise? Excellent is the advice and counsel in this kind, of the Author of the book *de morbo Sacro* attributed to *Hippocrates*, which I could wish all men were bound to read, before they take upon them to visit sick folks, that are troubled with melancholy diseases" (A Treatise proving Spirits, etc., 1672, pp. 29–30; cf. note 31, above).

80. Webster, pp. 219, 220, 224.

81. Glanvil, Saducismus Triumphatus, Part II, ed. 1681, p. 4 (ed. 1726, pp. 225–226). Glanvil is here replying to Webster, whose book, it will be remembered, appeared in 1677.

82. Increase Mather's copy of Webster is in the Harvard College Library.

83. Lowell, New England Two Centuries Ago, Writings, Riverside edition, II, 73.

84. Hobbes, Leviathan, i, 2 (English Works, ed. Molesworth, III, 9). Compare Hobbes's Dialogue between a Philosopher and a Student of the Common Laws of England (English Works, VI, 96): "L. I know not. Besides these crimes, there is conjuration, witchcraft, sorcery and enchantment; which are capital by the statute 1 James, c. 12. — P. But I desire not to discourse of that subject. For though without doubt there is some great wickedness signified by those crimes; yet I have ever found myself too dull to conceive the nature of them, or how the devil hath power to do so many things which witches have been accused of." Wier is far more humane, as well as more reasonable. If one holds, he writes, that witches are to be severely punished for their evil intent, let it be remembered that there is a great difference between sane and insane will. "Quod si quis contentiose uoluntatem seuerius puniendam defendat, is primum distinguat inter uoluntatem hominis sani perfectam, quae in actum uere dirigi coeperit: et inter uitiatae mentis sensum, uel (si uoles) corruptam amentis uoluntatem: cui suo opere, quasi alterius esset, colludit diabolus, nec alius insulse uolentem subsequitur effectus." De Præstigiis Dæmonum, vi, 21, ed. 1568, pp. 641–642.

85. Selden, Table-Talk, 1689, p. 59 (the first edition). Selden died in 1654.

86. Soldan, Geschichte der Hexenprozesse, ed. Heppe, II, 243.

87. Ady, A Candle in the Dark: or, A Treatise concerning the Nature of Witches & Witchcraft, 1656, p. 41.

88. Sir Robert Filmer's brief tract, An Advertisement to the Jury-men of England, touching Witches, was occasioned, according to the Preface, by "the late Execution of Witches at the Summer Assises in Kent." It was first published in 1653, and may be found annexed to the Free-holders Grand Inquest, 1679. The case which elicited Sir Robert's little book is reported in A Prodigious & Tragicall History of the Arraignment, Tryall, Confession, and Condemnation of six Witches at Maidstone, in Kent, at the Assizes there held in July, Fryday 30, this present year, 1652 (London, 1652, reprinted 1837).

89. A. D. White, A History of the Warfare of Science with Theology, 1896, I, 362.

90. Wood, Athenae Oxonienses, ed. Bliss, III, 1114.

91. Dr. Hutchinson's admirable work, An Historical Essay concerning Witchcraft, which still remains one of the most valuable treatises on this subject that we have, was published in 1718. It appeared in a second edition in 1720, in which year he was appointed Bishop of Down and Connor.

92. I have used a copy of the French translation, — Le Monde Enchanté, Amsterdam, 1694. This was made by Bekker's direction and revised by him. Each of the four volumes has a separate dedication, and each dedication (in the Harvard College copy) is authenticated by Bekker's autograph signature.

93. This concludes Bekker's First Book.

94. What precedes is, in substance, Bekker's Book II.

95. This is the substance of Bekker's Third Book.

96. "De Christelijke Synodus . . . heeft, . . . met eenparigheyd van stemmen, den selven Dr. Bekker verklaart intolerabel als Leeraar in de Gereformeerde Kerke; en vervolgens hem van sijn Predik-dienst geremoveert" (decree in W. P. C. Knuttel, Balthasar Bekker de Bestrijder van het Bijgeloof, the Hague, 1906, p. 315).

97. Knuttel, p. 319.

98. Knuttel, p. 357. Strictly speaking, it was not for his denial of modern witchcraft that Bekker was punished, for it is in the last two books of his treatise that he deals particularly with this subject, and these did not appear until after he had been unfrocked. Still, his Second Book, which got him into trouble, contains all the essentials. It denies the power of the devil and wicked spirits to afflict men, and holds that the demoniacs of the New Testament were neither possessed nor obsessed, but merely sufferers from disease. For a full analysis of Bekker's work and an account of the opposition which it roused, see Knuttel, chap. v, pp. 188 ff.; for the ecclesiastical proceedings against Bekker, see chap. vi, pp. 270 ff. The various editions and translations of De Betoverde Weereld are enumerated by van der Linde in his Balthasar Bekker, Bibliografie (the Hague, 1869), where may also be found a long list of the books and pamphlets which the work called forth. There is a good account of Bekker's argument in Soldan's Geschichte der Hexenprozesse, neu bearbeitet von Dr. Heinrich Heppe (Stuttgart, 1880), II, 233 ff. See also Roskoff, Geschichte des Teufels, Leipzig, 1869, II, 445 ff.

99. Theologians took infinite pains to distinguish between miracles (miracula), which could be wrought by divine power only, and the kind of wonders (mira) which Satan worked. See, for example, William Perkins, A Discourse of the Damned Art of Witchcraft, 1608, pp. 12 ff., 18 ff.; Del Rio, Disquisitiones Magicæ, lib. ii, quæstio 7, ed. 1616, pp. 103 ff. Sir Robert Filmer, in An Advertisement to the Jury-men of England, Touching Witches (appended to The Free-holders Grand Inquest, 1679; see note 88, above), makes merry with such fine-spun distinctions. "Both [Perkins and Del Rio]," he says, "seem to agree in this, that he had need be an admirable or profound Philosopher, that can distinguish between a Wonder and a Miracle; it would pose Aristotle himself, to tell us every thing that can be done by the power of Nature, and what things cannot; for there be daily many things found out, and daily more may be, which our Forefathers never knew to be possible in Nature" (pp. 322-323). Cf. Calef, More Wonders of the Invisible World, 1700, p. 35.

100. Cf. Soldan, Geschichte der Hexenprozesse, ed. Heppe, II, 243: — "Zu derjenigen freieren Kritik der biblischen Schriften selbst sich zu erheben, welche das Vorhandensein gewisser, aus den Begriffen der Zeit geschöpfter dämonologischen Vorstellungen in der Bibel anerkennt, ohne daraus eine bindende Norm für den Glauben herzuleiten, — diess war frelich erst einem späteren Zeitalter vorbehalten. Bekker kannte, um seine sich ihm aufdringende philosophische Ueberzeugung mit der Bibel zu versöhnen, keinen andern Weg, als den der üblichen Exegese, und daher kommt es, dass diese nicht überall eine ungezwungene ist." It is instruc-

tive to note the pains which Sir Walter Scott takes, in his Second Letter on Demonology and Witchcraft, to harmonize the Bible with his views on these subjects.

101. To avoid all possibility of misapprehension I shall venture to express my own feelings. The two men who appeal to me most in the whole affair of witchcraft are Friedrich Spee, the Jesuit, and Balthasar Bekker, the "intolerable" pastor of Amsterdam. But what I *feel*, and what all of us feel, is not to the purpose. There has been too much feeling in modern discussions of witchcraft already.

102. Sigmund Riezler, Geschichte der Hexenprozesse in Bayern, Stuttgart, 1896, p. 143.

103. Ibid.

104. Soldan, Geschichte der Hexenprozesse, revised by Heppe, II, 37; cf. G. L. Burr, The Fate of Dietrich Flade, 1891 (reprinted from the Papers of the American Historical Association, V).

105. Jean d'Espaignet and Pierre de l'Ancre, the special commissioners, are said to have condemned more than 600 in four months (Soldan, ed. Heppe, II, 162; cf. Baissac, Les Grands Jours de la Sorcellerie, 1890, p. 401). I do not find that de l'Ancre makes a distinct statement of the number convicted. He makes various remarks, however, which seem to show that 600 is no exaggeration. Thus he says that the Parliament of Bordeaux, under whose authority he acted, condemned "an infinity" of sorcerers to death in 1609 (Tableau de l'Inconstance des Mauvais Anges et Demons, Paris, 1613, p. 100). "On fait estat qu'il y a trente mille ames en ce pays de Labourt, contant ceux qui sont en voyage sur mer, & que parmy tout ce peuple, il y a bien peu de familles qui ne touchent au Sortilege par quelque bout" (p. 38). The commission lasted from July to November (pp. 66, 456, 470); besides those that the two commissioners tried during this period, they left behind them so many witches and wizards that the prisons of Bordeaux were crowded and it became necessary to lodge the defendants in the ruined château du Hâ (pp. 144, 560). Cf. pp. 35 ff., 64, 92, 114, 546. The panic fear that witchcraft excites is described by de l'Ancre in a striking passage: — "Qu'il n'y ayt qu'vne seule sorciere dans vn grand village, dans peu de temps vous voyez tant d'enfans perdus, tant de femmes enceintes perdâs leur fruit, tant de haut mal donné à des pauures creatures, tant d'animaux perdus, tant de fruicts gastez, que le foudre ni autre fleau du ciel ne sont rien en comparaison" (pp. 543–544).

106. An Account of what Happened in the Kingdom of Sweden, in the Years 1669, 1670 and Upwards, translated from the German by Anthony Horneck, and included in Glanvil's Saducismus Triumphatus, ed. 1682 (ed. 1726, pp. 474 ff.). Horneck's version is from a tract entitled, Translation . . . Der Königl. Herren Commissarien gehaltenes Protocol über die entdeckte Zauberey in dem Dorff Mohra und umbliegenden Orten, the Hague, 1670. Cf. Thomas Wright, Narratives of Sorcery and Magic, II, 244 ff.; Soldan, ed. Heppe, II, 175 ff.; Vilhelm Bang, Hexevæsen og Hexeforfølgelser især i Danmark, Copenhagen, 1896, pp. 48 ff. This is what Mr. Upham calls Cotton Mather's "favorite Swedish case" (Salem Witchcraft and Cotton Mather, Morrisania, 1869, p. 20). It was, in a manner, "Leo-

nato's Hero, your Hero, every man's Hero" toward the end of the seventeenth century, since it was one of the most recent instances of witchcraft on a large scale. The good angel in white who is one of the features of the Mohra case appears much earlier in England: see Potts, Wonderfull Discoverie of Witches, 1613, sig. L (a reference which may serve as a note to Mr. Upham's essay, just cited, p. 34).

107. Franz Volk, Hexen in der Landvogtei Ortenau und Reichsstadt Offenburg, Lahr, 1882, pp. 24–25, 58 ff.

108. Scot, p. 543; Hutchinson, Historical Essay, 2d ed., p. 38; A True and Iust Recorde, of the Information [etc.] of all the Witches, taken at S. Oses (London, 1582).

109. F. Legge, The Scottish Review, XVIII, 261 ff.

110. Thomas Potts, The Wonderfull Discoverie of Witches in the Countie of Lancaster (London, 1613); Thomas Wright, Narratives of Sorcery and Magic, Chap. xxiii.

111. Whitaker, Whalley, I (1800), 184 ff; Baines, History of the County Palatine of Lancaster, I (1836), 605–606; Crossley, Chetham Society reprint of Potts, pp. lix ff.; Wright, chap. xxiii; Heywood and Brome's play, The Late Lancashire Witches, 1634; Calendar of State Papers, Domestic Series, 1634–1635, pp. 77–79, 98, 129–130, 141, 152; Historical Manuscripts Commission, 10th Report, Appendix, Part IV, p. 433; 12th Report, Appendix, Part II, p. 53, cf. p. 77; Notes and Queries, 3d Series, V, 259, 385.

112. Nichols, History and Antiquities of the County of Leicester, II, 471*.

113. See p. 331, above, and note 176, below.

114. Whitelocke's Memorials, December 13, 1649, ed. 1732, p. 434; Brand, Popular Antiquities, ed. Hazlitt, III, 80; Ralph Gardner, England's Grievance Discovered, in Relation to the Coal-Trade, 1655 (reprinted, 1796, chap. 53, pp. 114 ff.).

115. A Prodigious & Tragicall History of the Arraignment [etc.] of Six Witches at Maidstone . . . Digested by H. F. Gent, 1652 (reprinted in an Account, etc., London, 1837).

116. A True and Impartial Relation of the Informations against Three Witches, 1682.

117. Sir J. H. Lefroy, Memorials of the Discovery and Early Settlement of the Bermudas or Somers Islands, II, 601 ff.

118. A Full and True Relation of the Tryal [etc.] of Ann Foster, London, 1674 (Northampton, reprinted by Taylor & Son, 1878); Relation of the Most Remarkable Proceedings at the late Assizes at Northampton, 1674. Cf. W. Ruland, Steirische Hexenprozesse, in Steinhausen's Zeitschrift für Kulturgeschichte, 2. Ergänzungsheft, Weimar, 1898, pp. 45 ff.

119. New England Historical and Genealogical Register, XXIV, 382.

120. Thomas Brattle, Letter of October 8, 1692, Massachusetts Historical Society Collections, V, 65. Compare, on the whole question, the remarks of Professor Wendell in his interesting paper, Were the Salem Witches Guiltless? (Historical Collections of the Essex Institute, XXIX

republished in his Stelligeri and Other Essays concerning America, New York, 1893) and in his Cotton Mather, pp. 93 ff.

121. A long and curious list of cases of defamation may be seen in a volume of Depositions and other Ecclesiastical Proceedings from the Courts of Durham, extending from 1311 to the Reign of Elizabeth, edited by James Raine for the Surtees Society in 1845 (Publications, XXI). Thus, in 1556–57, Margaret Lambert accuses John Lawson of saying "that she was a chermer" (p. 84); in 1569–70 Margaret Reed is charged with calling Margaret Howhett "a horse goodmother water wych" (p. 91); in 1572. Thomas Fewler deposed that he "hard Elizabeth Anderson caull . . . Anne Burden 'crowket handyd wytch.' He saith the words was spoken audiently there; ther might many have herd them, beinge spoken so neigh the crose and in the towne gait as they were" (p. 247). So in 1691 Alice Bovill complained of a man who had said to her, "Thou bewitched my stot" (North Riding Record Society, Publications, IX, 6). See also Historical Manuscripts Commission, Report on Manuscripts in Various Collections, I, 283; Lefroy, Bermudas or Somers Islands, II, 629 (No. 15).

122. See, for example, Mr. Noble's edition of the Records of the Court of Assistants, II, 43, 72, 85, 94, 95, 104, 131, 136, — all between 1633 and 1644.

123. See Drake's Annals of Witchcraft in New England; Noble's Records, as above, I, 11, 31, 33, 159, 188, 228, 229, 233.

124. "Quia vulgo creditum, multorum annorum continuatam sterilitatem à strigibus et maleficis diabolicâ invidiâ causari; tota patria in extinctionem maleficarum insurrexit" (as quoted from the autograph MS. in the Trier Stadt-Bibliothek by G. L. Burr, The Fate of Dietrich Flade, p. 51, Papers of the American Historical Association, V).

125. "Incredibile vulgi apud Germanos, & maxime (quod pudet dicere) Catholicos superstitio, invidia, calumniæ, detractationes, susurrationes & similia, quæ nec Magistratus punit, nec concionatores arguunt, suspicionem magiæ primum excitant. Omnes divinæ punitiones, quas in sacris literis Deus minatus est, à Sagis sunt. Nihil jam amplius Deus facit aut natura, sed Sagæ omnia. 2. Unde impetu omnes clamant ut igitur inquirat Magistratus in Sagas, quas non nisi ipsi suis linguis tot fecerunt" (Spee, Cautio Criminalis, seu de Processibus contra Sagax Liber, 2d ed., 1695, pp. 387–388; cf. Dubium xv, pp. 67–68, Dubium xxxiv, pp. 231–232). Spee's book came out anonymously in 1631, and, unlike most works on this side of the question, had immediate results. Spee had no doubt of the existence of witchcraft (Dubium i, pp. 1 ff., Dubium, iii, pp. 7–8); his experience, however, had taught him that most of those condemned were innocent.

126. The case is reported in A True and Impartial Relation of the Informations against Three Witches [etc.], 1682, which is reprinted in Howell's State Trials, VIII, 1017 ff.

127. Roger North, Autobiography, chap. x, ed. Jessopp, 1887, pp. 131–132. North gives a similar account of the same trial, with some general observations of great interest, in his Life of the Lord Keeper Guilford, I, 267–269 (ed. 1826). It is not clear whether North was present at the trial or not.

It is important to notice that North wrote his biographies late in life and that his death did not take place until 1734, only two years before the statute against witchcraft was repealed.

128. North remarks that Guilford (then Francis North, Chief Justice of the Common Pleas) "had really a concern upon him at what happened; which was, that his brother Raymond's passive behavior should let those poor women die" (Life of the Lord Keeper Guilford, I, 267). Raymond was, to be sure, the judge who presided at the trial, but Francis North cannot be allowed to have all the credit which his brother Roger would give him, for he refused to reprieve the convicted witches (see his letter, quoted at p. 334, above).

129. There was a fierce war of pamphlets over Jane Wenham's case. See the bibliography in Notestein, pp. 373–375. Cf. Memoirs of Literature, 1722, IV, 357; Wright, Narratives of Sorcery and Magic, 1851, II, 319–326. Jane Wenham lived nearly twenty years after her trial; she died in 1730 (Clutterbuck, History and Antiquities of the County of Hertford, II, 461; W. B. Gerish, A Hertfordshire Witch, p. 10).

130. I refer to such remarks as the following: "As the devil lost his empire among us in the last age, he exercised it with greater violence among the Indian Pawwaws, and our New England colonists" (Richard Gough, British Topography, 1780, II, 254, note P); "The colonists of [Massachusetts] appear to have carried with them, in an exaggerated form, the superstitious feelings with regard to witchcraft which then [at the time of the settlement] prevailed in the mother country" (Introduction to the reprint of Cotton Mather's Wonders of the Invisible World, in the Library of Old Authors, 1862); "In the dark and dangerous forests of America the animistic instinct, the original source of the superstition, operated so powerfully in Puritan minds that Cotton Mather's *Wonders of the Invisible World* and the Salem persecution surpassed in credulity and malignity anything the mother country could show" (Ferris Greenslet, Joseph Glanvill, New York, 1900, pp. 150–151); "The new world, from the time of its settlement, has been a kind of health resort for the worn-out delusions of the old. . . . For years prior to the Salem excitement, European witchcraft had been prostrate on its dying bed, under the watchful and apprehensive eyes of religion and of law; carried over the ocean it arose to its feet, and threatened to depopulate New England" (George M. Beard, The Psychology of the Salem Witchcraft Excitement, New York, 1882, p. 1).

131. Wright, Narrative of Sorcery and Magic, II, 284.

132. Proceedings American Antiquarian Society, New Series, V, 267.

133. F. Legge, Witchcraft in Scotland, in The Scottish Review, October, 1891, XVIII, 263.

134. On modern savages as devil-worshippers, see, for example, Henry More, Divine Dialogues, 1668, I, 404 ff. (Dialogue, iii, sections 15–16).

135. Mather, Magnalia, Book i, chap. i, § 2, ed. 1853, I, 42; Book, vi, chap. vi, §3, III, 436; Jesuit Relations, ed. Thwaites, I, 286; II, 76; VIII, 124, 126. See also Thomas Morton, New English Canaan, 1637, chap. ix, ed. Adams (Prince Society), p. 150, with the references in Mr. Adams's note. Cf. Hutchinson, History of Massachusetts, chap. vi, ed. 1795, I,

419 ff.; Diary of Ezra Stiles, June 13, 1773, ed. Dexter, I, 385–386. Captain John Smith says of the Virginia Indians: "Their chiefe god they worship is the Diuell" (A Map of Virginia, 1612, p. 29).

136. Mayhew's letter of October 22, 1652, in Eliot and Mayhew's Tears of Repentance, 1653 (Massachusetts Historical Society Collections, 3d Series, IV, 203–206); Gookin, Historical Collections of the Indians in New England (Massachusetts Historical Society Collections, I, 154). See the references in Mr. Adams's note to Morton's New English Canaan, Prince Society edition, p. 152, and compare the following places in the Eliot Tracts (as reprinted in the Massachusetts Historical Society, Collections, 3d Series, IV), — pp. 17, 19–20, 39, 50–51, 55–57, 77, 82, 113–116, 133–134, 156, 186–187. See, for the impression that Indian ceremonies made on a devout man in 1745, David Brainerd's Journal, Mirabilia Dei inter Indicos, Philadelphia, [1746,] pp. 49–57: — "I sat," writes Brainerd, "at a small Distance, not more than Thirty Feet from them, (tho' undiscover'd) with my Bible in my Hand, resolving if possible to spoil their Sport, and prevent their receiving any Answers from the *infernal* World" (p. 50).

137. Gookin, Historical Collections (Massachusetts Historical Society, Collections, I, 154); Massachusetts Records, ed. Shurtleff, II, 177; III, 98.

138. The Most Strange and Admirable Discoverie of the Three Witches of Warboys, 1593, sigg. B2 r°, P v°.

139. Thomas Potts, The Wonderfull Discoverie of Witches, 1613, sig. S; The Arraignment and Triall of Iennet Preston, of Gisborne in Craven, in the Countie of York, London, 1612 (in the same, sig. Y2).

140. Mary Smith's case, Alexander Roberts, A Treatise of Witchcraft, 1616, pp. 52, 56, 57; the Husbands Bosworth case, Letter of Alderman Robert Heyrick, of Leicester, July 18, 1616, printed in Nichols, History and Antiquities of the County of Leicester, II, 471*.

141. Edward Fairfax, Dæmonologia, 1621 (ed. Grainge, 1882).

142. Chetham Society Publications, VI, lxiv.

143. A True and Exact Relation of the Severall Informations [etc.] of the late Witches, London, 1645, p. 20; T. B. Howell, State Trials, IV, 846.

144. Depositions from the Castle of York, [edited by James Raine,] Surtees Society, 1861 (Publications, XL), pp. 28–30.

145. The same, p. 58.

146. The same, pp. 64–65, 67.

147. Glanvil, Saducismus Triumphatus, ed. 1682, Relations, pp. 96, 98, 100 (ed. 1726, pp. 286, 288, 289).

148. York Depositions, p. 82.

149. The same, pp. 88–89, 92.

150. The same, pp. 112–114; Glanvil, ed. 1682, pp. 160–161 (ed. 1726, pp. 328–329).

151. A Tryal of Witches . . . at Bury St. Edmonds . . . 1664, London, 1682, pp. 18, 20, 23, 26, 29, 34, 38 (Sir Matthew Hale's case); York Depositions, pp. 124–125.

152. Glanvil, ed. 1682, pp. 103–104, 109 (ed. 1726, p. 291).

153. Calendar of State Papers, Domestic, 1667–1668, p. 4; York Depositions, p. 154.

154. York Depositions, p. 176.

155. Ann Tilling's case, Gentleman's Magazine for 1832, Part I, CII, 489 ff.; Inderwick, Side-Lights on the Stuarts, 2d ed., 1891, pp. 171–172, 191.

156. York Depositions, pp. 192, 202–203.

157. The same, p. 247.

158. An Account of the Tryal and Examination of Joan Butts, 1682.

159. Margaret Stothard's case, The Monthly Chronicle of North-Country Lore and Legend, [II,] 1888, p. 395.

160. Hutchinson, Historical Essay, 1718, pp. 44–45 (ed. 1720, pp. 61–62). There is a very interesting account of the second of these trials (that of Elizabeth Horner or Turner) in a letter to the Bishop of Exeter from Archdeacon (?) Blackburne, who attended at the bishop's request. This letter, dated September 14, 1696, has been printed by Mr. T. Quiller-Couch in Notes and Queries, 1st Series, XI, 498–499, and again in Brand's Popular Antiquities, ed. Hazlitt, III, 103–104. The spectral evidence comes out clearly. Of Holt, Blackburne remarks: "My Lord Chief Justice by his questions and manner of summing up the Evidence seem'd to me to believe nothing of witchery at all."

161. Dalton, Country Justice, chap. 160, § 5, p. 384. "The court justified themselves from books of law, and the authorities of Keble, Dalton and other lawyers, then of the first character, who lay down rules of conviction as absurd and dangerous, as any which were practised in New England" (Hutchinson, History of Massachusetts, ed. 1795, II, 27).

162. James Burvile testified "That hearing the Scratchings and Noises of Cats, he went out, and saw several of them; that one of them had a Face like *Jane Wenham;* that he was present several Times when *Anne Thorn* said she saw Cats about her Bed; and more he would have attested, but this was thought sufficient by the Court" ([F. Bragge,] A Full and Impartial Account of the Discovery of Sorcery and Witchcraft, practis'd by Jane Wenham, London, 1712, p. 29). After the conviction of the witch, Ann was still afflicted: "*Ann Thorn* continues to be frequently troubl'd with the Apparition either of *Jane Wenham* in her own Shape, or that of a Cat, which speaks to her, and tempts her to destroy her self with a Knife that it brings along with it" ([Bragge,] Witchcraft Farther Display'd, 1712, Introduction). In 1711 spectral evidence was admitted at the trial of eight witches at Carrickfergus, in Ireland (A Narrative of some Strange Events that took place in Island Magee, and Neighbourhood, in 1711, by an Eye Witness, Belfast, 1822, Appendix, pp. 49–50).

163. A Tryal of Witches, as above, p. 40.

164. "The Judge and all the Court were fully satisfied with the Verdict" (A Tryal, etc., p. 58).

165. For a learned discussion of spectral evidence, see J. B. Thayer, Atlantic Monthly, April, 1890, LXV, 471 ff.

166. Dr. Hutchinson, who acknowledges his indebtedness to Holt, mentions six witches as tried by the Chief Justice from 1691 to 1696, and adds, "Several others in other Places, about Eleven in all, have been tried for Witches before my Lord Chief Justice *Holt*, and have all been acquitted.

The last of them was *Sarah Morduck*, accused by *Richard Hathaway*, and tried at *Guilford* Assize, *Anno* 1701" (Historical Essay, 2d ed., pp. 58–63). It is not clear whether the "eleven in all" includes the seven previously mentioned. On the Morduck-Hathaway case, cf. Howell, State Trials, XIV, 639 ff.

167. Drake, Annals of Witchcraft in New England, pp. 136, 138; Noble, Colonial Society Publications, X (1907), 21–23.

168. Compare Goodell's remarks on the reversal of attainder, in his Reasons for Concluding that the Act of 1711 became a Law, 1884. I have not considered here the bearing of this reversal, or of the attempt to pay damages to the survivors or their heirs, because these things came somewhat later. It must be noted, however, that all such measures of reparation, whatever may be thought of their sufficiency, were unexampled in the history of witch-trials the world over, and that they came before the last condemnation for witchcraft in England (1712). See the references appended by Goodell to the Act of 1703 in The Acts and Resolves of the Province of the Massachusetts Bay, VI, 49–50.

169. See p. 338, above.

170. Legge, as above, p. 264; Register of the Privy Council of Scotland, V (1882), 409–410.

171. Hutchinson, p. 83; 2d ed., p. 108.

172. See W. F. Poole in Winsor's Memorial History of Boston, II, 133; cf. Noble, Colonial Society Publications, X (1907), 20–23.

173. See Poole, II, 133. Dr. Poole finds twelve executions in New England before 1692. This makes the total for all New England, from 1620 to the present day, 34 (including two who died in jail). Cf. C. W. Upham, Salem Witchcraft, Boston, 1867, II, 351; S. G. Drake, Annals of Witchcraft, 1869, pp. 191 ff. In this part of the chapter I have made a few quotations from a book of my own, The Old Farmer and his Almanack (Boston, 1904).

174. "They were the first of all people," writes Mr. Goodell, "to escape the thraldom" (Reasons for Concluding that the Act of 1711 became a Law, 1884, p. 21).

175. See Hutchinson, Historical Essay, 2d ed., 1720, pp. 45 ff.

176. John Stearne, Hopkins's associate, speaks of what he has himself "learned and observed since the 25. of March 1645 as being in part an agent in finding out or discovering some of those since that time, being about two hundred in number, in Essex, Suffolke, Northamptonshire, Huntingtonshire, Bedfordshire, Norfolke, Cambridgeshire, and the Isle of Ely in the County of Cambridge, besides other places, justly and deservedly executed upon their legall tryalls" (A Confirmation and Discovery of Witch-craft, London, 1648, To the Reader). Stearne wrote his book after the death of Hopkins, which took place in 1647. In the life of Hopkins in the Dictionary of National Biography, the Witch-Finder is said to have begun operations in 1644. This is a manifest error. Hopkins himself (Discovery of Witches, 1647, p. 2, see below) says that his experiences began at Manningtree "in *March* 1644," but Stearne's statement makes it clear that this is Old Style, for Stearne was also concerned in the Manningtree busi-

ness, and the year is completely established by the report of the proceedings, — A True and Exact Relation of the severall Informations [etc.] of the late Witches, London, 1645 (cf. T. B. Howell's State Trials, IV, 817 ff.). The traditional statement that Hopkins was hanged as a wizard (cf. Hudibras, Part II, canto 3, ll. 139 ff.) is disproved by the following passage in Stearne: "I am certain (notwithstanding whatsoever hath been said of him) he died peaceably at Manningtree, after a long sicknesse of a Consumption, as many of his generation had done before him, without any trouble of conscience for what he had done, as was falsly reported of him" (p. 61). For the record of his burial, August 12, 1647, see Notes and Queries, 1st Series, X, 285. The notion that Hopkins was "swum" and, since he floated, was subsequently hanged, most likely originated in a document criticising his performances which was brought before the Norfolk judges in 1646 or (more probably) in 1647. Hopkins printed a reply to this document shortly before his death, — The Discovery of Witches: in Answer to severall Queries, lately delivered to the Judges of Assize for the County of Norfolk. And now published by Matthew Hopkins, Witch-finder (London, 1647). The first "querie," as printed by Hopkins, was this: — "That he must needs be the greatest Witch, Sorcerer, and Wizzard himselfe, else hee could not doe it." Cf. Wright, Narratives of Sorcery and Magic, II, 145 ff.; Lives of Twelve Bad Men, edited by Thomas Seccombe, London, 1894, p. 64; Ady, A Candle in the Dark, 1656, pp. 101–102; James Howell, as above (note 7); Gough, British Topography, 1780, II, 254.

177. Legge, Scottish Review, XVIII, 273–274. Ady (A Candle in the Dark, 1656, p. 105) says: "A little before the Conquest of *Scotland* (as is reported upon good intelligence) the Presbytery of *Scotland* did, by their own pretended authority, take upon them to Summon, Convent, Censure, and Condemn people to cruel death for Witches and (as is credibly reported) they caused four thousand to be executed by Fire and Halter, and had as many in prison to be tried by them, when God sent his conquering Sword to suppress them." The "conquest" to which Ady refers is Cromwell's, in 1650. It is well known that from 1640 to Cromwell's invasion, witch prosecution ran riot in Scotland, but that during his supremacy there were very few executions in that country (see Legge, pp. 266–267).

178. Mannhardt, Die Praktischen Folgen des Aberglaubens, p. 34.

179. Soldan, Geschichte der Hexenprozesse, ed. Heppe, I, 492.

180. Remy, Daemonolatreia, Lugduni, 1595.

181. See note 105, above.

182. Soldan, Geschichte der Hexenprozesse, ed. Heppe, II, 38 ff.

183. See the extraordinary enumeration in Roskoff, Geschichte des Teufels, Leipzig, 1869, II, 293 ff.; cf. S. Riezler, Geschichte der Hexenprozesse in Bayern, pp. 141 ff., 283 ff.

184. Potts, The Wonderfull Discoverie of Witches, 1613.

185. Matthew Hopkins, Discovery of Witches, 1647, p. 3.

186. John Stearne, A Confirmation and Discovery of Witch-craft, 1648, p. 14.

187. Wright, Narratives of Sorcery and Magic, chap. xxv.

188. Memorials, 1732, pp. 163, 450.

189. Hugh Hare, Justice of the Peace, in his charge at the General Quarter Sessions for Surrey, at Dorking, on April 5, 1692, spoke as follows: "Besides these Crimes which are so frequently and so imprudently perpetrated, there are some others also which may not improperly be ranked among the offences against Moral Justice. But, Gentlemen, the proof of some of them is so difficult, and they are so seldom practised, that I shall but just put you in mind of them, and that you are to enquire and present all Persons that have invocated, entertained or employed any wicked Spirit, or have used any Witchcraft, Charm, or Sorcery; this is a sin of a very deep die, being directly against the first Commandment, and is punished with Death both by the Law of God, and by a Statute made in the first Year of King *James* the First; but it is so hard a matter to have full proof brought of it, that no Jury can be too cautious and tender in a prosecution of this Nature. However, where the evidence is clear and undeniable, you must proceed according to your Oaths." (Surrey Archæological Collections, XII [1895], 128–129.) Coincidence in date justifies the quotation.

190. A Relation of the Diabolical Practices of above Twenty Wizards and Witches, 1697; Sadducismus Debellatus, 1698; A History of the Witches of Renfrewshire, 1877. A seventh committed suicide in prison.

191. See Inderwick, Side-Lights on the Stuarts, 2d ed., 1891, pp. 193–194; Notestein, pp. 313–333, 418–419.

192. That is, Francis Bragge, who was also a clergyman, being Curate of Biggleswade according to W. B. Gerish (A Hertfordshire Witch, p. 8). For details, see pp. 361–362, above.

193. Blackstone, Commentaries, Book iv, chap. 4, sec. 6 (4th ed., 1770, IV, 60–61); cf. Dr. Samuel A. Green, Groton in the Witchcraft Times, 1883, p. 29. In 1715 and 1716 there appeared, in London, A Compleat History of Magick, Sorcery, and Witchcraft, in two volumes, which asserted the truth, and gave the particulars, of a long line of such phenomena, from the case of the Witches of Warboys (in 1592) to the Salem Witchcraft itself. The book was the occasion of Dr. Francis Hutchinson's Historical Essay, published in 1718, and in a second edition in 1720. Richard Boulton, the author of the Compleat History, returned to the charge in 1722, in The Possibility and Reality of Magick, Sorcery, and Witchcraft, Demonstrated. Or, a Vindication of a Compleat History of Magick, etc. The Compleat History came out anonymously, but Boulton, who describes himself as "sometime of Brazen-Nose College in Oxford," acknowledges the authorship in his reply to Hutchinson.

194. British Museum, Additional MS. 35838, fol. 404; Notestein, pp. 330–331, 419; Summers, The Geography of Witchcraft, 1927, pp. 160–161. I leave in suspense the statement that Jane Clarke of Great Wigston and her son and daughter were tried at Leicester in 1717 (Leicestershire and Rutland Notes and Queries, I [1891], 247). I suspect this is the same case. On the alleged executions at Northampton in 1705 and Huntingdon in 1716 see Notestein, pp. 375–383, who makes out a very strong case for the fictitious character of the pamphlets that profess to record them. In the Proceedings of the American Antiquarian Society, New Series, XVIII (1907),

206, I accepted the 1705 case and rejected (though not decidedly) that of 1716.

195. The Case of Witchcraft at Coggeshall, Essex, in the year, 1699, being the Narrative of the Rev. J. Boys, Minister of that Parish. Printed from his Manuscript in the possession of the Publisher. London, A. Russell Smith, 1901 (50 copies only).

196. In Calef, More Wonders of the Invisible World, 1700, pp. 3 ff.

197. An Answer of a Letter from a Gentleman in Fife, 1705; cf. also A Collection of Rare and Curious Tracts on Witchcraft and the Second Sight, Edinburgh, 1820, pp. 79 ff.

198. Daily Journal, January 15, 1731, as quoted in the Gentleman's Magazine for 1731, I, 29.

199. Daines Barrington points with pride to this early abolition of penalties: "It is greatly to the honour of this country, to have repealed all the statutes against this supposed crime so long ago as the year 1736, when laws of the same sort continue in full force against these miserable and aged objects of compassion, in every other part of Europe" (Observations on the More Ancient Statutes, 3d ed., 1769, p. 367, on 20 Henr. VI).

200. Gough, British Topography, 1780, I, 517.

201. Gentleman's Magazine for 1751, XXI, 186, 198; Wright, Narratives of Sorcery and Magic, II, 326 ff.; Gough, as above, I, 431.

202. Soldan, ed. Heppe, II, 314, 322, 327.

203. See, for example, A. Löwenstimm, Aberglaube und Strafrecht, Berlin, 1897; W. Mannhardt, Die Praktischen Folgen des Aberglaubens, 1878 (Deutsche Zeit- und Streit-Fragen, ed. by F. von Holztendorff, VII, Nos. 97, 98); Wuttke, Der Deutsche Volksaberglaube der Gegenwart, 2d ed., 1869; the chapter on Hexerei und Hexenverfolgung im Neunzehnten Jahrhundert, in Soldan, Geschichte der Hexenprozesse, ed. by Heppe, II, 330 ff.; cf. The Monthly Chronicle of North-Country Lore and Legend, [II,] 1888, p. 394; North Riding Record Society, Publications, IV, 20, note; History of Witchcraft, sketched from the Popular Tales of the Peasantry of Nithsdale and Galloway (R. H. Cromek, Remains of Nithsdale and Galloway Song, 1810, pp. 272 ff.); H. M. Doughty, Blackwood's Magazine, March, 1898, CLXIII, 394–395; Brand's Popular Antiquities, ed. Hazlitt, III, 71, 95, 96, 100 ff.; The Antiquary, XLI, 363; W. G. Black, Folk-Medicine, 1883; Miss Burne, Shropshire Folk-Lore, chap. xiii; W. Henderson, Notes on the Folk-Lore of the Northern Counties, 1879, chap. vi; J. G. Campbell, Witchcraft and Second Sight in the Highlands and Islands of Scotland, 1902; Notes and Queries, 1st Series, VII, 613, XI, 497–498; 3rd Series, II, 325; 4th Series, III, 238, VII, 53, VIII, 44; 5th Series, V, 126, 223, IX, 433, X, 205, XI, 66; 6th Series, II, 145, IV, 510; 7th Series, IX, 425, XI, 43; 8th Series, IV, 186, 192, V, 226, VI, 6, VII, 246; 9th Series, II, 466, XII, 187; the journal, Folk-Lore, *passim*.

204. Cf. Allen Putnam, Witchcraft of New England explained by Modern Spiritualism, Boston, 1880.

205. See pp. 251 ff., above. On the prevalence of occult phenomena in troublous times cf. Froude, History of England from the Fall of Wolsey to the Death of Elizabeth, II (1856), 182–183.

206. Legge, The Scottish Review, XVIII, 262. See also Newes from Scotland declaring the Damnable Life of Dr. Fian, 1591 (Roxburghe Club reprint).

207. Mather Papers, Massachusetts Historical Society Collections, 4th Series, VIII, 366–368. This was the same Joshua Moodey, it will be remembered, who afterwards assisted Philip English and his family to escape from jail in Boston, and thus saved them from being executed as guilty of witchcraft (Sibley, Harvard Graduates, I, 376–377).

208. Professor G. L. Burr, in an eloquent essay entitled "New England's place in Witchcraft" (Proceedings American Antiquarian Society, New Series, XXI [1911], 185–217), joins issue vigorously on these theses. But I let them stand as they were originally printed (in 1907), except with regard to a detail in the fifteenth thesis, for I have never seen any reason to modify them further.

INDEX

INDEX

Aarne, A., 519
Abbot, George, 323, 553, 575
Abbott, G. F.: see Macedonia
Abdias, 383
Abingdon, 419; Thomas of, 65, 189, 439
abortion, 32, 444, 588
Abt, Adam, 172, 448, 458, 493, 504
Acca, St., 153
Achelous, 407
Achilles Tatius, 537
Acron, 544
Acta Sanctorum, 383, 449, 456, 494, 502, 514, 529, 544
Adams, C. F., 591 f.
Addicion (1564), An, 475
Addison, Joseph, 214, 326, 369
Additional MSS., 391, 406, 435, 451, 490, 495, 501, 515, 520, 541 f., 554, 577, 596
Addy, S. O., 400, 423, 431 f., 469, 486, 494, 511, 515, 523, 525
Adelbert, St., 190
Adowne, John, 61
Adrammelech, 210
Adso, 380
Ady, Thomas, 159, 350 f., 377, 405, 479, 488, 501, 540, 564, 595
Ælfric, 30, 145, 202, 219, 239, 379 f., 385 ff., 393, 398, 449 f., 514 f., 548
Ælian, 500, 513
Ælred, 544
Ælsi, 75
Æquitius, 222
aëromancy, 57
Æsculapius, 221
Æsir, 133
Æsop, 106
Ætheldreda, St., 125
Æthelred, 28, 233, 238, 383, 385
Æthelstan, 29, 143, 415
affodille, 449
Africa, 26 f., 49, 55, 92 f., 134, 172, 174 f., 237 f.; Notes, passim
Agnew, Sir Andrew, 469, 496
Agobard, 152
Agricola, Georgius, 517 f., 522

agriculture: see Burdick; crops; Rantasalo
Agrip, 439
Agrippa, H. C., 74, 452, 462, 514
ague, 34, 142, 218, 461
Ailsworth, 75
Ainsworth, W. H., 286 ff.
Ainu, 413
air poisoned, 27
Aiston, G., 402, 454 f., 473
Aitkin, Lucy, 566
alchemy, 64 f., 114, 187, 261
Aldhelm, 382, 397
Aldo, 180 f.
ale, procured by witchcraft, 34, 171; bewitched: see brewing
Alexander the Great, 105 f., 116, 537
Alfonso el Sabio, 412, 450, 458, 503
Alfred, King, 27, 175
Allan, Ann, 164
Allatius (Allacci), Leo, 531 f.
Alldridge, T. J., 506
Allein: see Alley
Allen, Robert, 229; Thomas, 180
Alley (Allein), William, 263
alligator, 49
Allington, Richard, 176
Alne, 107
Alneto (Lannoy), Cornelius de, 557
Alnwick, William, 187
Alphabet of Tales, 44, 118, 224, 239 f., 440, 469, 502
Alphabetum Narrationum, 44, 118, 132, 440
Alsace, 368
Altafex, William, 53
Alvernus: see Guilielmus
Alverton, 539
Alwincle, 230
Ambrose Waterduke, 211 f.
Ambrosetti, J. B., 493
Amos, Andrew, 409
Amphlett, John, 540
amulets, 31, 52 ff., 146, 389, 396, 453, 471, 500
Amundesham, John, 416, 418, 457

Amylyon, ——, 209
Anabaptists, 180, 246
Anania, G. L. d', 402, 454, 515 f., 533, 547
Ancetyr, Alice, 188 f.
Ancre, Pierre de l', 292, 368, 441, 445, 470, 494, 501, 504, 521, 540, 548 f., 588
Ancyra, Synod of, 244, 384, 394
Andel, M. A. van, 391
Anderson, Sir Edmund, 298, 300, 307, 311 f.; Elizabeth, 590
Andover, Mass., 494
Andree, R., 412, 423, 434, 462, 492
Andrew Malchus, 110, 210
Andrian-Werburg, F. von, 473
Andros, Sir Edmund, 371
angels, 67, 86, 240 f., 344, 414
Anglo-Saxon period, 27 ff., 74 f., 95, 104, 113, 117, 133, 143, 145 ff., 151 ff., 170 ff., 175, 191, 205, 214 f., 218 f., 449, 530, 538. See Cockayne
animal disguises, 548
animal shape: see metamorphosis
animals, demons as, 134 f.
animals inside one, 134 f.
animals, spells against, 32
anise: see dill
Anjou Chronicle, 494
Anonimalle Chronicle, 450
Anthologia Palatina, 537
Antichrist, 28
Anz, H., 524
Aphaca, 233
Apollodorus, 441
Apollonia, St., 391
Apollonides, 537
Apollonius of Tyana, 336
apparitions, 58, 62, 154, 175, 228, 344 f. See ghosts
Apuleii Herbarium, 388 f., 474
Apuleius, 114, 183, 448, 458, 493, 532
archery, 180
Arderne, John, 389
Argentine, Richard, 399, 474, 503, 505, 551
Argo, 16
aristolagi, 449
Aristophanes, 532
Aristotle, 537
Arkillus, 221
Arles, Council of, 145; Cæsarius of, 398: see Augustine
Armoricus, Guillelmus, 534
Armstrong, W. E., 434

Árnason, J., 485
Arnobius, 410, 520
Arnold of Liége, 118
Arnold, Mother, 550
Arnuphis, 153
Arphaxat, 30
arrow turned, 79
arrowheads, 133 f.
arrows: see elfshot
Artemidorus, 513
Arthur, King, 116, 178, 222, 524
Arthur and Gorlagon, 493
Arundel, Earls of: Richard Fitz-Alan, 176; Philip Howard, 559
Arundel MSS., 395; Penitential, 54, 166, 384, 404, 437, 441
Asclepias, 221
ash, cleft, etc., 148
Ashmole, E., 535; MSS., 574
Ashtaroth, 30
Asia Minor, 527
Askewe, Anne, 467
Asmodeus, 172, 212
Aspinwal, Thomas, 131
ass, 148, 183
assault, 47 f. See scratching
Asser, 493
Asshewell, John, 83
Assmann, B., 385 f., 393
Assyrians, 27, 73, 432. See Tallqvist
Aston, Sir Roger, 309
astrology, 26, 45, 70, 73, 82, 226 ff., 258 f., 383, 414, 555
Atharva-Veda, 442
Athens, plague at, 136
Atkinson, J. C., 98, 429, 484; W., 230
attainder, 594
Auberi, 440
Aubrey, John, 55, 121, 158, 190, 199, 220, 302, 318, 321, 421, 435, 437, 476, 498, 535 f., 576
Audollent, A., 408, 414, 424, 440, 507
aufhock, 220 f.
augury, 30, 45, 51, 57, 165, 383 f. See divination
Augustine, St., 42, 116, 183 f., 239, 380, 385 ff., 389, 393, 398, 467, 489, 506, 548
Augustus, 116
Aun, King, 438
aurum potabile, 69, 86
Australia, 134, 175, 401 f., 405 f., 413, 433 f., 455, 473, 503, 532
automatic writing, 213

Auvergne, Guillaume d': see Alvernus
ave, 36 f.
Avesbury, Robert of, 403
Awder, William, 88
Axminster, 238
Azo, 517
Aztecs, 112

Babcock, J. W., 434 f.
Babraham, 207
Babylonia, 73, 237
Bacon, Francis, 50, 141, 331, 377, 406, 420; Nathaniel, 539; Sir Nathaniel, 474; Roger, 235, 240
Badby, Thomas, 181
Baddaford, John and Joan, 9 ff.
badger, 54
bag, magic (hoodoo, conjure), 48 ff. See milk-sucking
Baildon, W. P., 416, 452
Baines, Edward, 562, 573, 589
Baissac, Charles, 493; Jules, 588
Baker, J. B., 424, 478; Mother, 87; Sir Richard (chronicle), 420, 475, 574 ff.; William, 71
Bakewell, 579
baking, 35, 170 f.
Baldewyne, Dionisia, 51
baldmony, 449
Baldock, Ralph, 51, 187, 192 f., 227, 548
Baldwin, J. F., 534
Bale, John, 34 ff., 58, 84, 164, 170 ff., 391, 439, 443, 466 f., 469, 488 f., 545, 556; Robert, 417
Ballantyne, A., 455
balls of clay, 48, 192 f.
Baltisham, 230
Bamberg, 368
Banastre, William, 187
Bancroft, Richard, 298 ff., 572
Bang, A. C., 388, 390 ff., 406, 433, 435, 444, 453, 465, 468 f., 471, 481, 485, 490, 505, 507 f., 511 ff., 515, 527; V., 588
Banticke, Jonathan, 14
baptism, repeated, 145; of image, 76, 82, 148, 151; of cock, cat, or dog, 94, 148, 206, 208. See font water
Barbason, 424, 520
Bardan, P., 422, 484
Barentur, 424, 520
barguests, 176
Barham, R. H., 79

Baring-Gould, S., 390, 463, 468, 492
Barker, Robert, 207, 228
Barking, 550
Barley, Thomas, 188
Barnes, Richard, 115, 129 f.
Barnet, Battle of, 153
Barnett, L. D., 402, 517
Barnstable, 20 f.
Barnstaple, 20
Baro, 158, 211
barrel, spiked, 97
barrenness, 26 f., 32, 113
Barrington, Daines, 597; Sir Francis, 309
Barron (fiend), 477
Barrow, Dr., 302; Isaac, 336 f.
Bartels, M., 434, 444, 453, 455, 507
Bartholin, Thomas, 456, 499, 531
Bartholomew, St., 30
Bartholomew of Farne 175, 218
Barthram, Oliffe, 182, 217
Barton, Elizabeth, 64 f.
Bartsch, K., 391 f., 433, 464, 486, 496, 498, 507, 510, 513
Basedow, H., 455
Basil of Cæsarea, 239
Basile, Giambattista, 525
basin, 57, 165, 186. See mirror
Basin, The, fabliau, 201
Basin, Bernard, 463
Basques: see Labourd
Basset, R., 493, 532
bat, 135, 175, 492
Batchelor, J., 413
Bate (Batte), Richard, 89 f.; William, 89 f., 315
Bates, H. W., 455
Bateson, M., 539
bath, 79
Bath, 44, 75
Batte: see Bate
Battell, Andrew, 473
battle charms, 31 ff., 53 f.
battle maidens, 29 f.
Batutah, Ibn, 542
Baum, P. F., 440
Baxter, Richard, 133, 448, 454, 456, 465, 474 f., 499, 521, 525, 565, 582
Bayle, Pierre, 350
Bayley, John, 555
Bayly, Joan, 99; Robert, 189
Beale, John, 459; S., 541
Beamont, W., 452, 495
bear, 175 f.

Beard, G. M., 591
Beatty, K. J., 493
Beauchamp, Richard Lord, and Lady, 139
Beaumanoir, Philippe de Remi, Sire de, 544
Beaumont, and Fletcher, 498; John, 462, 521. See Fletcher
Beauvais, Vincent of, 43, 106, 239 f., 440, 492, 502
Beaver, W. N., 424, 434
Bechstein, L., 496
Becket, Thomas, 226
bed, throwing out of, 217
bedclothes twitched off, 217
Bede, 29, 31, 58, 152, 202, 222, 226, 380 f., 384 ff., 393, 462
Bedford, Arthur, 520
Bedford, 58, 173; John of Lancaster, Duke of, 83. See Jacquette
Bedfordshire, 236, 272 f., 594
bee-charms, 32, 163, 191
Beere, Alice, 8
bees and host, 150; imps as bees, 179 ff., 208
beetle, 499
Beggar's Curse, The, 132
Bekker, Balthasar, 340, 351 ff., 541, 578, 584
belemnites, 49
Belfour, A. O., 397
Belgium: see Low Countries
Bell Witch, The, 521, 525
Bell, J. H., 401, 419, 435, 511 f., 521; John, 199
Bellie Blind, 113, 215
bells against demons and storms, 158
Bellucci, G., 401, 453, 500
Belly Blind, 113, 215
Belphares, 208
Belton, Mariot de, 107
Benedict IX, 240; XII, 53
Benet, Johanna, 85; Thomas, 86
Bénévent, ——, 378
Benger, Sir Thomas, 69, 254
Bennet, Elizabeth, 248, 264 f.
Bennett, W. P., 478
Ben(n)o, 545
Bensart, Maturyn, 86
Bentham, Thomas, 250
Bentley, W. H., 401, 506
Beowulf, 205, 522
Berçuire (Bersuire), Pierre, 437 f.
Bere, John, 36

Berewold, Richard, 193, 403
Bergen, Fanny D., 390, 402, 423, 431, 436, 461, 463, 468, 471, 480, 484, 486 f., 497 f., 510 f., 527
Berith, 30, 202
Berkeley, the Witch of, 43 f.
Berkshire, 527
Berkyng, John, 195
Bermuda, 358
Bernard, Richard, 235, 273 f., 325, 377, 400, 421, 427 f., 435, 503, 505, 512, 536, 540, 565
Bernou, Jean, 492
Berthold of Regensburg, 42
Berthold, O., 405
Bertiani, Annales, 474 f.
beryl, 80, 187 f.
Best, Edetha, 108
betony, 448
Beuon, St., 529
Beveridge, D., 421, 480
Beverley, Johanna, 107
Beverley Minster, 239
Bewick, Thomas, 451
Bezemer, T. J., 493
Bianchi, V., 399
bible as charm, 146 f.; texts as spells, 52, 146, 196 ff., 436; bible (or psalter) and key, 71, 186, 190, 196 ff., 553
biblical exegesis, 355 ff.
Bidez, J., 537
Bieber, F. J., 398, 526
bier, ordeal of the, 345
bilewit, 522
Billie Blin, 215
Billington, Isabella, 148
Billson, C. J., 497
Bilson, John, 545; Leonard, 258, 552, 556
Bilson, the Boy of, 324 f., 456, 578
Bilwiz, 215
binding spells, 3, 31, 200 ff., 361
Bingen, 214
Bingham, Richard, 557
Binsfeld, Peter, 443, 454, 476, 492, 521, 540, 547 f.
Binz, Carl, 584
Birch, Thomas, 406, 492, 517, 575, 583; W. de G., 388, 415
birds, demons and witches as, 64, 161; 167 f., 176, 494. See augury, striges
Birlinger, A., 464, 476, 496, 498, 517
Birt, H. N., 552, 556
birthmarks, 142

Bisclavret, Lai de, 494
Bishopwilton, 34
Blachford, Mother, 20
Black Assize, 283, 347
Black Dog of Bungay, 156 f.
black fast, 129 f., 229, 466
Black, W. G., 390 f., 424 f., 427, 448, 459, 467, 470, 497, 597
Blackburne, ——, 593
Blackstone, Sir William, 326, 369
Bladé, J. F., 428, 502, 514, 527
bladebone, 100. See scapulimancy
Blagden, C. O., 442
Blagrave, Joseph, 421, 434 f., 480
Blair, E. H., 413
Blake, Thomas, 138 f., 228; Lady, her son, 90
Blakeborough, R., 422, 430 f., 453, 465, 468, 471, 480, 483, 485, 487, 498, 515. See Fairfax-Blakeborough
Blakeway, J. B., 475
Blanche d'Artois, 76
Blandy, Mary, 438
Blashill, Thomas, 400
blasting trees, etc., 35. See crops
Blatchford, Lizzie, 20 f.
Blau, L., 425, 440, 444, 502, 536
bleeding of corpse, 345
Blefken, Dithmar, 477, 514
blessings, 214 f.
Blickling Homilies, 28
blindness, 190
Blinkenberg, C., 401
Bliss, Philip, 576
Blois, Peter of, 44 f., 75
blood, as medicine, 31, 383, 460; staunching, 32; feeding imps with, 177, 179, 208 f.; sucking, 166 f., 224, 245, 268
blooding: see scratching
bloody milk, 163, 166
Bloom, J. H., 475
blue, 37
Blundevill, Thomas, 220
Boaistuau, Pierre, 448, 472
Boas, F., 516
boats: see seafaring
Bochart, Samuel, 397, 531
Bodin, Jean, 25, 88, 182, 249, 273, 425, 431, 441, 480, 485, 492 f., 496, 500, 502, 511 f., 517, 533, 540, 546 f., 549, 560, 563 ff.
Bodmin, 55, 103, 175
Boece, Hector, 86, 117

Böttiger, C. A., 443
Bogg, Edmund, 402, 436
boggarts, 176
Boguet, Henry, 412, 447, 454, 480, 483, 533, 548
Bohnhorst, J., 447 f.
Bois, Jules, 91
Bold, Henry, 435 f.
Boleyn, Anne, 107
Bolingbroke, Roger, 81 ff.
Bolte, Johannes, 452, 502, 514 f., 519, 563
Bompas, C. H., 493, 505, 532
Bonavant, Edward, 134
Bonaventura, St., 444, 463
Bond, F., 470; F. B., 520
Bone, Thomas, 574
Boniface VIII, 241 f.; IX, 403
Bonner, Edmund, 114 f., 227, 253 ff., 553
Bonnet, M., 486
Bonus, Alexander, 557
Bonwick, J., 414, 455
Book of Quinte Essence, 447
books of magic, 38, 58, 65, 70, 80, 83, 110, 189, 207 f., 210, 228, 552
boot, devil in, 110
bootfull of gold, 206
Boothroyd, B., 533, 538
Borde: see Boorde
Borneo, 399, 413, 455, 505 f., 543
Borrowby, Prior, 229
Bosman, W., 543
Bosquet, A., 496, 523
Boston, Mass., 129
Boswell-Stone, W. G., 534
Bothwell, Francis, 278, 371
Botreaux, William Lord, 80; Sir Ralph, 80
Bottle Imp, 105
bottles buried or heated, 49, 102 f.
Bottrell, William: see Cornwall
Boulton, Richard, 596
Bourbon, Étienne de, 417, 469 f., 496, 503, 530
Bourke, J. G., 443, 482
Bourn, Dr., 435
Bourquelot, F., 492
Bouvet, ——, 405
Bovet, Richard, 421, 456, 477, 521, 525, 529, 545, 565
Bovill, Alice, 590
Bower, Edmond, 503, 524
Bowmer, Agnes, 38

Boy, Prince Rupert's dog, 176 f.
Boyes, J., 473, 506
Boyle, Robert, 205, 336, 459
Boys, J., 369 f., 421, 539
Brabant: see Low Countries
Bracara, Martin of, 490
Bradewelle, Sir Osbern de, 215
Bradley, Henry, 524; M. H., 479, 508 f.
Bragge, Francis, 581, 583, 593, 596
Brainerd, David, 592
bramble, 386
Bramhall, John, 178
Brampton, 66
Brand, John, 434 f., 440, 448, 480, 487 f., 509, 511 f., 555, 589, 593, 597
Brandon, juggler, 86 f.
Brattle, Thomas, 358 f., 512
Bray, Mrs. E. A., 460 f., 467, 475, 498, 510, 523, 547
brazen head, 240; horse, 56
bread, 489; ordeal of, 237 f.; holy bread, 147; loaf burned, 488. See baking; host; loaf
Bremen, Adam of, 233
Brereton, Sir William, 401
brewing, 19, 27, 35, 39 f., 103, 170 f., 385
Brewster, A. B., 402, 433
Brian, Robert, 199
Brianzun (Briançon), Bartholomew de, 241; Joan de, 241
Bridgman, John, 321
Bridlington, the Hermit of, 226
Brie, Maria, 378, 387, 390, 392 f.
Brigge, Mabel, 129, 229
Briggs, G. W., 399, 411, 423, 432, 464
Brightling, 214
bristles, 88, 90, 134, 160
Bristol, 134
Brockett, J. T., 425, 432, 471, 511, 528
Brodie-Innes, J. W., 568, 578
Brome, Richard, 271, 589
Bromley, Sir Edward, 287, 311 f.
Brom(p)ton, John, 397, 440, 502
Bromyard, Johannes de, 437
Brotanek, R., 379, 385, 387, 393
Brown, William, 404
Browne, Sir Thomas, 142, 220, 334 f., 384, 398, 442 f., 445, 461, 475, 498; Thomas, 243; William, 36. See Orde Brown
brownies, 215
Browning, Robert, 437
Bruce, H. A., 521; J. D., 445, 524; John, 500

Bruen, John, 570
Brugges, John, 56
Brun, P. le, 536
Brunfeld, 205
Brunne, Robert of, 43, 51, 164 ff., 186, 192, 202, 398, 514
Brunswick, 410
Brut, 128, 416 ff., 450, 474, 500
Brutus, 47
Buckingham, Dukes of: Edward, 228 f.; George, 317; Henry, 61
Buckinghamshire, 100, 110, 439, 527
Budge, E. A. W., 411
Bücheler, F., 531
Bühler, G., 402, 411
Bürger, G. A., 431
buffalo, 537
Bufton, John, 539
Bugge, S., 438, 477 f. See Edda
Bulcock, John, 10; Joan, 10
Bulgaria, 472
bull, 494
Bullein, William, 259 f.
Bullen, A. H., 557
Bullinger, Henry, 262 f., 409, 559, 570 f.
Bullock, C. C.: see Maryland
bumblebees, 179, 208
Bungay, Friar, 153
Bungay, 156
Bungie, Mother, 66, 550
Burchard, 29, 47, 54, 104, 163, 382, 384 ff., 393, 404. See Corrector
Burden, Anne, 590
Burdett, Thomas, 138 ff.
Burdick, L. D., 425, 433, 472, 480
Burgess, J. J. H., 453, 484
Burgh, Hubert de, Earl of Kent, 108
Burghley, Lord, 88, 520
burglar's magic, 144 f., 464
Burgt, J. M. M. van der, 378, 401
burial, imitative, 142
Burma, 237
Burne, C. S.: see Shropshire
Burnet, Gilbert, 333, 409, 443, 471
burning by witchcraft, 11 f., 49, 155; burning grain, 143; burning bewitched animal, 95 ff.; burning heart, etc., 97 ff.; burning thatch, etc., 102
Burnley, 477
Burnynge of Paules Church, The, 475
Burr, G. L., 23 f., 376 f., 421 f., 430, 451, 454, 494, 512, 521, 542, 551, 559, 580, 588, 590, 598
Burroughs, George, 90

Burton, Robert, 335, 451, 492, 583
Burton Old, 272 f.
Burton-on-Trent, 89
Bury, Lady Charlotte, 90 f.
Bury St. Edmunds, 182, 217, 234, 332 ff., 342, 364, 368, 499, 501, 515, 592
burying alive, 95; burying bottles, etc., 102 f.
Bushe, Mother, 257
Butler, Alice, 8 f.; William, 302. See Hudibras
butter bewitched, 167 f. See dairy
butterfly, 499
Butts, Joan, 420, 435, 590
Byg, William, 187 f., 540
Byntham, Alice, 193 f.
Byx (alias Elwin), Margaret, 155

Cabanès, Auguste, 391, 393, 412, 425, 431, 442, 457, 459, 464
Cade, Jack, 177
Cædmon, 222
Cælestinus, 240
Caerleon, 119
Cæsar, Sir Julius, 318
Cahors, 77
Caius, John, 68 f., 557
cake, 91, 103, 432
Calais, 157 f.
Calamy, Edmund, 331
Caland, W., 411, 423 f., 434
calculating the king's death, 139
Calef, Robert, 351, 422, 454, 587
calf, 148
Calfhill, James, 476, 483, 545
Callaway, H., 405, 516
Callisthenes, 437
Calmet, A., 412, 517, 522
Calton, Edmund, 261
Calvert, J., 402, 433
Cambridge, Eng., 61, 207, 228; University, 68, 290 ff., 304 ff., 317
Cambridge, Mass., 162
Cambridgeshire, 100, 236, 422, 594
Camden, William, 420
Cameron, John, 480
Campbell, Lady Charlotte, 90 f.; Dugald, 489, 491; James, 482 ff.; J. F. (of Islay), 515 f.; J. G., 422, 435, 447, 451 ff., 462, 476, 480, 483 f., 490, 496, 515, 523, 527, 536 f., 597; John Lord, 333 f., 573; Sir J. M., 378, 455, 476
Canada, 413, 455, 514
Canary Islands, 55

candle, 85, 89, 100, 140, 144, 347, 518, 547. See Hand of Glory
Canne: see Tannere
cannibalism, 29, 141, 225
Cannon, H. L., 399
Canon Episcopi, 243 ff., 246, 549, 564
Cans, John, 206
Canterbury, 195; Gervase of, 524
Cantipratensis, Thomas, 474
cap of invisibility, 524
Cape Cod, 20 f., 146, 183, 219, 479
Capello, H., 405, 473
Capgrave, John, 42, 58, 222, 397, 450, 457, 475
capitularies, 384, 537
caprimulgus, 166
Cardano, Girolamo, 144, 433, 441, 457 f., 503 f., 531, 533
Cardinall, A. W., 442
Cardwell, Edward, 443 f., 534, 552 f., 572
Cariden, Joan, 272, 491, 495, 539
Carleton, Sir Dudley, 323
Carmichael, A., 405, 447, 453, 487
Carnavon, 321
Carnoy, H., 526 f.
Caroline of Brunswick, 90 f.
Carpzov, B., 463
Carr, William, 390
Carrichter, B., 480
Carrowe, Sir William, 62
Cartar, George, 228
Carter, John, 488
Carthage, 112, 172, 500
Cary, Christopher, 69
Casanova, P. G., 112
Casaubon, Meric, 189, 335, 340, 343, 350, 421, 451, 578, 585
Cason, Joan, 102, 492
Caspari, C. P.: see Homilia; Martin of Bracara
cassowary, 49
castor-oil plant, 153
cat, 52, 93, 95, 97, 160, 174, 177 ff., 202, 216, 403, 424, 496; and corpse, 178; sucks breath, 178
caterpillar, 94
cat-fear, 178 f.
Cathari, 245 f.
Catlyn, Sir Robert, 556
Catonis Disticha, 398
cattle, and sheep, 4, 26 f., 32, 41, 95 ff., 103, 143, 146 f., 163 ff., 172, 174, 191, 219, 389, 495, 499, 527 f. See dairy; murrain

Cauzons, T. de, 413
Cavazzi, G. A., 401
Cawnton, 38
Cecil, William, 257, 259, 553 f., 556 ff., 560
Celtic, 92, 201, 396. See Cornwall; Ireland; Scotland; Wales; Man; Wentz
centipede, 49, 402, 436, 489
Cerne, Book of, 387, 466
Ceylon, 145
Chaderton, William, 308 f.
chair, magic, 201
Challoner, Richard, 420; Sir Thomas, 557
Chamberlain, John, 323
Chamberlaine, Richard, 521
Chambers, Sir E. K., 468, 548 f.; John, 501; R., 487
chameleon, 404
Champier, Symphorien, 224, 407, 524, 546
champion, 53
chancery, 55 f., 62, 85 f., 188, 195 f.
Chandos, Lady, 257
Chapalu, 178, 216
Chapiseau, F., 413, 476, 481, 493, 523
Chappell, W., 525
Chapuys, Eustace, 107
Charlemagne, 109, 152, 225
Charles I, 321, 328; II, 334
Charles, Nicholas, 571
Charlevoix, P. F. X. de, 413, 455
charms, 141 ff., 219 f. See spells
Charrette, Roman de la, 440
Chastiel Bran, 204
Chatton, 272
Chattox: see Whittle
Chaucer, 9 f., 46, 56 f., 73, 106, 118 f., 144, 185 ff., 219, 227, 398, 457, 546
Chau-Ju-Kua, 515
Chauncy, Sir Henry, 361, 583
cheating the devil, 206
cheese, magic, 184
Chelmsford, 170, 177 ff., 182, 236 f., 248, 310, 495, 501
Cheney, A. D., 409
Cheriton, Odo of, 500, 517
Chesham, 193
Cheshire, 301
child as scryer, 51. See mirror
Child, F. J., 119, 254 f., 394, 400, 429, 431, 439 f., 442 ff., 446, 452, 522, 536, 554
childbirth, 26, 34, 81 f., 113 ff., 143, 253
Chilperic, 108

China, 413, 459, 464, 493, 503. See De Groot
cholera, 136, 426
chrism, 42, 51, 202
Christiansen, R. T., 396, 519
Christie, W. D., 571
Chronique Rimée, 415
church bell, 151; rung in storms, 158; blessed, 158; church leads, 151
churches struck by lightning, 154 ff.
churching, 145
churn magic, 167 ff.
Cibber, Colley, 497
Cicero, 55, 398
Circe, 57, 184
circle, 52, 105, 202, 208, 210 f., 282; St. Columbkill's, 489
Cirencester, 63, 197
cistern, demon in, 216
Clague, J.: see Man
Clarence, George of, 138 f.
Clarendon, Assize of, 233 f.
Claridge, G. C., 378
Clark, Andrew, 395, 420; Elizabeth, 272
Clarke, Jane, and son and daughter, 596; Samuel, 499, 515, 569 f.
Clarkson, John, 377
Claudian, 537
clay balls, 48, 192 f.
cleft ash, etc., 148
Clene, Dr., 110
Clerk, Joan, 71; Roger, 194
Clerke, ——, 229
Cleveland, John, 495, 563
Cleveland, 98
Cleveton, 315
Clifford, Rosamond, 182 f.
Clift, J. G. N., 451
Clitheroe, 158
Clopton, William, 572
clothing burned, 428
Clovesho, Council of, 27, 383, 386
Clutterbuck, Robert, 591
Cnidos, 60, 112
Cnut, 28 f., 175, 238, 383, 385, 387, 493
Cobham, Eleanor, 81 ff., 115, 474
Cobley, F., 501
cobolds, house and stable, 215
cock, 52, 93 ff., 97 f., 148, 176, 206, 208, 529
Cockayne, T. O., 382, 386 ff., 394 f., 404, 425, 441, 444, 446, 448 f., 453 f., 460 f., 465 f., 469 ff., 473 f., 478, 485, 488 ff., 508, 522 f., 526

cockchafer, 499
cockfighting, 149
cocklebread, 104
Cocks: see Cox(e)
cocoanut, 101
Codrington, R. H., 454 f., 473, 500, 513, 537
Codronchus, Baptista, 447
coffin, 142
Cogan, Thomas, 420, 567
Coggeshall, 369, 421, 539; Radulphus de, 399, 477, 523 f.
Coke, Sir Edward, 290, 293, 307, 311 ff., 417, 462, 556
cold water ordeal, 232 ff.
Coldingham, Gaufridus de, 533
Cole, G. W., 570, 576
Coleridge, S. T., 222
Colin T., 56
Colle Tregetour, 56
Collection of Matters of Fact (1693), A, 421
Collection of Modern Relations (1693), A, 421, 485, 529, 581
Colley, Thomas, 236
Collins, J. W., 517; Samuel, 583
Cologne, 154
Colsell, John, 65
Columban, 29, 382
Columbkill, St., 489
Coman, Widow, 235, 369 f.
Commons' Journals, 535, 554, 559, 572
communion, 145; table, 148. See eucharist
compact, 42, 146, 239 ff., 346
Comparetti, D., 546
Comus, 201
Comynes, Philippe de, 458
Condé, Jean de, 111
confessionals, 29, 48
confirmation, 145
Congreve, William, 478
conjure bags, 49
Connecticut, 97, 237, 515, 524, 540
Connellan, O., 490
Connoisseur, The, 193
Connyngton, Johanna, 39
contract: see compact
Convertimini, 106
Cook, Jonet, 195
Cooke, John, 157
Cooper, Thomas, 269, 294 f., 310, 420 f., 568
Corbet, Miles, 21

Cordier, H., 515
corns, 142
Cornwall, 51, 55 f., 80, 219 f., 390 f., 422, 435, 459 f., 467 f., 480, 495, 497 f., 505, 518, 523, 526 f.
Cornwalyse, Joan La, 51
corp criadhach, 91 f.
corpse, bits of, etc., 52, 141 ff., 225, 243, 268, 283 f., 312 ff., 431
Corrector, 29, 47, 163, 386, 398, 433, 437, 441, 445, 460, 462, 472, 482, 484, 492, 530, 549
corsnæd, 543
Corson (Curson), Lord, 209
coscinomancy: see sieve
Cosmas, St., 221
Cosquin, E., 464
Cosyn, Edward, 260 f.
Cotta, John, 235, 269, 293 f., 305 f., 311, 320 f., 400, 410, 418, 420, 426 f., 502, 556 f.
Cotton, Bartholomew de, 401
Cotton MSS., 402, 404, 417 f., 476, 544
Couch, T. Q., 390, 480, 495, 498, 505, 526 f.
Coulton, G. G., 398, 508
councils and synods, 41, 46, 48, 104, 145, 150, 234 f., 244, 384 f., 394, 472, 482, 509, 534, 548, 572. See Haddan; Wilkins
Courthop, Sir George, 570
Courtney, M. A., 391. See Cornwall
Coventry, 77 f., 188, 241, 269, 295; Walter of, 533
Cowan, Samuel, 427, 480
Cowper, H. S., 389, 471, 486, 498, 510, 513, 523
Cox, J. C., 470, 476, 510; Julian, 562; Richard, 250; Captain, 216
Cox (alias Devon), John, 259
Cox(e), Francis, 258 f.
Cozen, William, 17 f.; Joan, 18
Crabbe, Stephen, 46
Craigie, W. A., 426, 481, 485, 527
cramp, 142; cramp rings, 151
Crane, T. F., 548
Cranmer, Thomas, 127, 227, 229, 408, 470, 495, 553
Crawfurd, Raymond, 458
cream, 167 ff.
Crecelius, W., 482
creed, 31, 36 f.
creeping through, 31, 148, 220
Cresimus, C. Furius, 172

Creton, Jean, 407
Crew, Sir Randolph, 322 f.
cricket, 491, 499
Crickstone, 220
crocodile, 174; ordeal, 537
Croft, Elizabeth, 69
Croke, Sir John, 300, 307, 311 f., 321
Cromek, R. H., 597
Cromwell, Sir Henry and family, 303 ff., 322; Oliver (Protector), 331, 595; Thomas, 63 ff., 110, 189, 408 f., 534 f.
Crooke, W., 378, 399, 402, 411, 423, 432, 434, 465 f., 473, 493, 506, 517 f., 531, 537
crooked sixpence, 167
crops, 27, 32, 34, 95, 149, 163, 171 f., 388, 459, 469
cross dug up, 205 f., 210, 554; over treasure, 209
Cross, T. P., 401, 427, 435, 445, 468, 491, 523
crossed by hare, 179
Crossley, James, 288, 328, 343 f., 410, 560, 566, 575, 583
crossroads, 31, 94, 202
crow, 176, 491
Crowther, Timothy, 97, 185, 190
Croxton, ———, 199
Croydon complexion, 157
Croyland Chronicle, 458
crucifying, 148
Crushe, John, 96
Crusius, Otto, 502, 548
crystallomancy: see mirror
Cuba, 425, 464
Cuchulinn, 223, 530
Cudworth, Ralph, 335 f.
Cuirrech, 92
Cuming, H. S., 412, 504, 528
Cummean, 381 ff., 393 f., 444, 462, 473
Cumont, Franz, 414, 537
Cupid and Psyche, 117
cures: see white witchcraft
Curio, 55
curses, 28, 101, 130 ff., 141, 147, 507. See defixiones; tablets
cursing stones and wells, 34, 132
Curson, John, 209; Lord, 209
Cursor Mundi, 380
Curteys, Thomas, 38
Curtin, Jeremiah, 462, 515
Curtis, ———, 100 f.
Cuthbert, St., 31, 124 f., 176, 184, 201, 223, 393

cynanthropy, 493
Cyprian, wizard, 500
Cyrus, St., 74, 221
Czecho-Slovak, 433

Dacre, Lord, 62
Dæmon Lover, The, 119
dairy, witchcraft in the, 34 f., 42, 51, 92, 103, 163 ff., 214 f.
Dale, A. M.: see Smith, E. W.
Dalok, Elena, 130, 155, 228
Dalton, Michael, 364
Dalyell, J. G., 395, 419, 425 ff., 453, 462, 472, 480, 486 f., 499 f., 510, 512, 537
Dame Sirith, 104 f.
Damian, St., 221
Damiani, St. Peter, 530
damnum minatum, 9
damp (vapor), 89, 347
Danbury, 155 f.
Daneau (Danæus), Lambert, 25, 249, 441, 457, 485, 547, 549, 563
Darcey, Brian, 264 f., 285, 309
Darel, Godfrey, 48
Darrel, John, 297 ff., 311, 428, 449, 501, 525, 567, 569, 571 f.
Dartmouth, 7, 12
Dasent, Sir G. W., 544
D'Avenant, Sir William, 478
Davenport, John, 563
Davies, J. C.: see Wales
Davis, J. E., 418; Ralph, 5
Davison, Alice, 38
Davye, George and Joan, 17
Davys, John, 230
Dawson, Bully, 179; W. H., 389, 428 f., 468, 476, 485, 503, 508
Deacon, John, 144, 298 ff., 449, 492, 569 f.
dead hand, 168 f.
dead men: see bier; corpse; necromancy
Deane, Jennet, 10; Wallace, 402, 433, 490
death, storms at, 183; death stones, 49
Decle, L., 405, 413
De Cock, A., 391, 424, 448, 459 f., 468, 483, 488, 491, 501, 526 f.
Dedo, R., 412
Dee, John, 69, 158, 180, 185, 189, 249, 254, 313, 318
Deecke, E., 469
deer, 491
defamation, 36, 51, 59 f., 62, 188 f., 192 f., 196, 360, 590

defixiones, 74, 93, 190. See curses; tablets

De Groot, J. J. M., 383, 413, 459, 464. See China

De Gubernatis, A., 447 f.

Dekker, Thomas, 434, 569 f.

Delatte, A., 443 f.

Delcourt, Joseph, 404

Del Rio, Martin, 24 f., 273, 441, 463, 482, 503, 509, 511, 532, 545, 560, 587

Demdike (Southerns), Elizabeth, 18, 265 ff., 561

De Meyer, M., 519

demoniacs: see possession

demons of disease, 147, 466

Denbighshire, 132

Denmark, 16, 28, 159, 216, 461, 495 ff., 501. See Kristensen; Saxo; Scandinavian; Thiele

Dennys, N. B., 413

Derby, Ferdinando, Earl of, 90, 308 f.; William, Earl of, 309

Derbyshire, 576

Deschamps, Eustache, 457

Despensers, 77 f.

Detection of Damnable Driftes (1579), A, 501

Deubner, Ludwig, 529

Devell, Henry, 107

Device family, 18, 149, 171, 266 f.

devil: see compact; possession; apparitions; incubus; weather; cheating

devils as animals, 175 ff.

devil's barn, 206

devil's bridge, 206

devil's mark, 242, 547

devil's thumb, 242

Devon, F., 416, 418; John (alias Cox), 259, 556

Devonshire, 6 ff., 91, 93, 95, 98 f., 103, 121, 132, 146, 148, 157, 181 f., 290, 334, 381, 390, 396, 400, 424, 429, 432 f., 447 f., 460 f., 467 f., 471, 475, 484, 486 ff., 498, 500, 505, 510, 523, 562. See Bray

dew, 168

D'Ewes, Sir S., 569

Dewse, Mrs., 89

Diana, riding with, 244 ff., 250, 549, 564

Dibb, Mrs., 269

Diceto, Ralph de, 445

Dick, C. H., 515

Dickman, A. J., 439 f.

Dieterich, A., 385, 461, 465, 489, 506

Digby, Sir Kenelm, 433, 492, 500

Digby MSS., 390, 529

dill, 37, 121 f.

Dindśenchas, 423

Dio Cassius, 457

Diodorus Siculus, 537

Dioscorides, 448

Disant, John, 50

disease, 174 ff., 466. See white witchcraft; murrain

Disraeli, I., 566

Distracted Emperor, The, 439

Ditchfield, P. H., 428, 468, 484, 515

divination, 30, 41, 48, 57, 70, 143 f., 185 ff. See bible and key; sieve and shears; clay balls; loaf and knives

Dixon, J. H., 478, 482

dobbies, 215, 220 f.

Dobeneck, F. L. F. von, 412, 442

Dobson, John, 229; William, 539

Doddridge, J., 423, 427 f., 483

Dodds, M. H., 533

Dodoens, R., 447 f.

Dodsley's Old Plays, 405, 471, 475, 478, 493

dog, 32, 52, 95, 123 f., 142, 157, 175 ff., 182, 271, 389, 491. See Black Dog

Doland, Elizabeth, 196

Dolebury Camp, 204

Dolloff, Stephen, 160

Done, Sir G., 64

Dorchester, Dorset, 407

Dorington, Francis, 303 f.; John, 304

Dornan, S. S., 402, 462, 473

Dorset, 80, 98 f., 108, 257, 390, 402, 436, 454, 489, 498, 500, 511, 518

Dorsey, J. O., 536

Dottin, G., 400

Douai Diaries, 420

Douce, F., 526

dough, 422

Doughty, H. M., 566, 597

Doutté, E., 413, 442, 459, 505

Dowsing, George, 209

Dowson, J., 462

Doyle, J. L., 410, 555

Drage, William, 103, 135, 400, 421, 424, 427 f., 447, 456, 485, 489, 499, 530, 536, 539, 564 f., 583

dragon, 153 f., 205; dragon's blood, 100

Drake, F., 574; S. G., 488, 494, 519, 528, 542, 579, 590, 594

Draper, Hugh, 258 f.; Robert, 196

Drayton, Michael, 121, 416, 451, 493

dream, 45, 47, 100, 165, 244; cure or in-
    jury in, 221 ff.; composition in, 222
Drechsler, P., 392, 430, 481
Driberg, J. H., 459, 473
dropsy, 181
drowned, 48
drowning, as punishment, 75; charm
    against, 443; cat drowned, storm, 161
Druids, 153
Drummer, The, 214
Dryden, Sir Erasmus, 305; Erasmus,
    305; John, 305, 478, 536
Du Bartas, 144
Dubois, J. A., 541, 543
Du Cange, 412, 532
duck, 462
Duff, King, 86
Dugas, C., 414
Dugdale, Sir William, 404, 536, 539
Dulyne, Eleanor, 62, 457
dumb cake, 432
Du Méril É., 439
Dundas, Sir Charles, 473
Dunger, H., 391, 393, 514
Dunmow, 237
Dunn, Mark, 344 f.; Mary, 20
Dunstan, St., 175, 222
Dunstaplia, Annales de, 401, 451
Dunton, John, 451, 456, 479, 510 f.
Durandus, G., 476
Durbin, Henry, 134, 435, 515, 520, 525
Durham, 37 f., 46 f., 59 f., 93, 98 f., 107,
    113, 125, 129 f., 135, 150, 153, 184,
    201, 432, 443, 452, 512; Ritual, 170 ff.,
    205, 214 f., 219, 466, 485, 489 f., 508,
    536, 590
Durham, Symeon of, 397, 474
Duris Samius, 532
dwarfs, 41, 52, 176, 205, 218, 221, 437,
    446, 466
Dyer, T. F. T., 447 f.
Dykstra, W., 484, 496, 511
Dymock, 133
Dyrim, Frances, 257

E., T., 69 f.
Eadmer, 539
eagle, 176
Earth, Mother, 171
East Dereham, 66
Ebel, K., 413, 436
Ebermann, O., 388, 390, 396
Ecgbert, 29 f., 74 f., 152, 381 ff., 393,
    462, 465, 472, 476

Ecgwin, St., 201, 450
eclipse, 418, 472
Edda, Elder, 55, 143, 159, 201, 406, 462,
    478
Edgar, King, 28 f., 75, 143, 383, 386 f.,
    393, 462
Edmondston, Arthur, 480, 494; Biot,
    515, 528
Edmonton, 323, 434
Edmund, King, 28; Earl of Kent, 53
Edmunds: see Weston
Edward and Guthrum, 27, 383; the
    Confessor, 124, 204, 544; I, 76, 241 f.,
    403; II, 53, 76, 108; III, 78, 105 f.,
    403; IV, 85, 106 f., 139, 228; VI, 86,
    229, 253
Edwards, Richard, 475; Susanna, 562
Egeria, 47
Egerton, Sir J., 574; MSS., 428; Papers,
    420
eggs, 102, 160, 190, 427, 480
Egliston, Thomas, 37
Egypt, 40, 57, 73, 105, 112, 153, 424,
    505
Eisel, R., 485
Eitrem, S., 387, 424
Eleanor, Queen, 183
elf-disease, 32, 147
elfshot, 133 ff., 147, 337 f., 395, 428
Eliot, John, 592; Tracts, 592
Elizabeth, Queen of Edward IV, 85,
    106 f.
Elizabeth, Royal Acts of, 1559, 115,
    227, 253
Elizabethan witchcraft, 25 f., 246 ff.
Elkes, ——, 90
Elliot, Sir H. M., 462, 543
Ellis, Sir Henry, 319, 408, 439, 504, 535,
    575; W., 401
Elton, O., 380, 451, 478
elves, 32, 117 ff., 147. See elfshot
Elwin: see Byx
Elworthy, F. T., 381, 429 f., 432 f., 459,
    463, 500, 527
Ely, 125, 207, 228; Lady Chapel at,
    239 f.; siege of, 33; Thomas of, 217
Emet, Mother, 37, 122
Endor, Witch of, 57, 144, 407
English, Philip, 598
Enthoven, R. E., 402, 411, 425, 433, 436,
    442, 457, 483, 489
envoûtement: see image
Epanamon, 105
Ephesian letters, 54

epic charms, 40
Epidaurus Limera, 233
epilepsy, 95 f., 102, 142
Epistle of the Persecution (1582), 419
Epworth, 214
Erceldoune: see Thomas
Erskine, Mrs. Steuart, 495
Espaignet, Jean d', 588
Essex, 96, 130, 134 f., 155 f., 217, 262, 271 f., 284 f., 295 f., 309 f., 331 f., 358, 368, 421, 425, 471, 497, 500, 520, 539 f., 542, 565, 579, 594. See Giffard
Essex, Robert, Earl of, 575; Frances, Countess of, 575
Esthonia, 519
eucharist, 51, 148 f.
Eudo, 240 f.
Eulogium Historiarum, 397, 440, 474, 494, 500, 516
Eustace the Monk, 45 f.
Eustathius, 404, 441; romancer, 537
Evagrius, 532
Evans, Arise, 535; I. H. N., 399, 506; Joan, 438 f.; R. H., 417; Sebastian, 530; Thomas, 417
Evelyn, John, 338, 570
Evesham, 450, 514
evil eye, 95, 232, 388, 500
Evrard of Trèves, 75 f.
Exact Narrative (1709), An, 521
Examination and Confession of a Notorious Witch (1574), The, 550
excommunication, mock, 52
exempla, 44, 78 f., 106, 117 f., 239
Exeter, 3 f., 48, 50 f., 104, 150, 166, 192 f., 263, 358, 361
exorcists, 449, 552, 572
explosion, 501
eye, amulets for the, 471; peculiar eyes, 232; loss of eye, 190. See evil eye; blindness
Eye-next-Westminster, 83
Eylmann, E., 413, 455
Eyvindr Kellda, 445

Fabate, ——, 235
Fabricius, J. A., 383, 532
Fabyan, Robert, 82, 416 ff., 474
Fahz, L., 412, 436
Fairfax, Edward, and his children, 269, 326 f., 400, 421, 427, 492, 577, 592
Fairfax-Blakeborough, J., 463
Fairholt, F. W., 575

fairies, 26, 128, 146, 166, 199, 215, 217, 254 f., 389, 535
Faligan, E., 398, 545
familiars, 52; as animals, 174 ff.; as insects, 179 ff.; as toads, 181 ff.
Fantom, Carlo, 55
Farington Papers, 568
Farne, 175, 218
Farrow, S. S., 413
fasting, 31, 128 ff., 229; for distraint, 129. See black fast
Fasting Nun of Leicester, the, 128
Fastrada's ring, 439
fat, human, 142, 144, 518
Faternon, 315
Faunus, 46 f.
Faustus, 146, 239, 502, 579
Favelle, Elias, 48
Favent, Thomas, 405
Faversham, 161, 272, 567
favor, 77. See love
Feast of Asses, 148
Fehrle, E., 472, 512
Feilberg, H. F., 412, 459
Female Tatler, 159
fennel, 448
Fenner, Edward, 303, 305, 322
Fenwick, George, 131; Ralph, 131
Ferguson, J., 567, 570
Fernel, Jean, 142, 441, 459 ff., 495
Ferrys, George, 69, 254
Festus, 531
fever, 392 f.
Fewler, Thomas, 590
Fian, John, 265, 278, 598
field magic: see crops
Field(e), John, 69, 553
Fielding, Henry, 161
fight: see battle
figure-flinger, 408
Filmer, Sir Robert, 351, 536, 540, 587
Finchale, 153, 176, 217. See Godric
Find, 92
Finland, 40, 159, 180, 396, 414, 423, 445, 453, 466, 481, 487, 505, 519, 523, 525 ff.
Finnian, 29, 382
fire by witchcraft, 12, 155, 377; quenching fire, 159
fish-bones, 134
fishing, 98, 173, 384
fits, 142
Fitz-Simon, Silvester, 234
Five Wounds, 46, 443.
Flacius Illyricus, 545

Flamank, Richard, 55
Flammarion, C., 521, 525
Flanders: see Low Countries
Flateyjarbók, 439
flea, 499
Fleming, Abraham, 156 f.
Flenley, R.: see London Chronicles
Fletcher, ——, 344 f.; Giles, 478; John, 220, 405, 451, 478, 498; J. S., 463; R. H., 445
flies, 180 f.
flints, 160
Flodder: see Pendleton
Floire et Blanceflor, 440
Flores Historiarum, 397, 399, 403, 440, 445, 452, 457, 474, 494, 502, 516. See Wendover
Flower family, 237 f., 310, 323 f., 421, 428, 491, 540; J. W., 416
Fludd, Robert, 526
Flügel, E., 416 f.
flying witches, 29. See transportation
Förster, Max, 389
Foix: see Gaston
Foliot, Gilbert, 43
folleti, 217
font, locked, 150 f.; water of, 147, 150 f.
footprint, 101 f.
Forby, Robert, 427, 432, 435, 465, 511, 541 f.
Ford, John, 434, 493
Forda, John of, 546
Forde, ——, 66; Thomas, 195
Forgues, E. D., 413
Forman, Simon, 314, 316 f., 477
Forrest, William, 239
Forsblom, V. W., 453, 525 f.
Fortescue, Sir Anthony, 255, 260 f.
Fortunatus, Bishop, 128
Foss, Edward, 573
Fossel, V., 391 f., 459, 477
Fossey, Charles, 411, 432
Fossez, 153 f.
Foster, Ann, 358; Joseph, 569, 576; William, 561
Fotman, Elizabeth, 37
Fournier, P., 394, 404, 437, 484
fox, 175, 184
Fox, Robert, 452
Foxe, John, 84, 193
Fracheto, Girardus de, 415, 516
France, 75 ff., 86, 108 f., 135, 163, 177, 182, 202 f., 358, 368; Notes, passim
Francis, St., 46

Francisci, Erasmus, 427, 445, 472, 492, 522, 538, 540
Frank, Grace, 544; Ortillus, 126
Franz, A., 386 ff., 395, 404, 443 f., 449, 464 ff., 468 ff., 474, 476, 490, 509, 517, 529, 536, 543
Frauncis, Elizabeth, 178
Frazer, Sir J. G., 82, 402, 412, 425, 433, 441 f., 444, 447 f., 467, 472, 537
Freeland, L. S., 413
Freeman, E. A., 544; R. A., 531
Freeston, Mary, 315
Freisauff, R., 476
Freke, Edmund, 553
French, G. J., 448
Frere, W. H., 443 f., 470, 534, 552 f.
Freygang, G., 472
Freymond, E., 524
friar, devil as, 155
Friar Rush, 216.
Friday, 100
Frischbier, H., 402, 424, 430, 447, 463, 481 f., 488, 506, 510
Frisians, 484, 496, 511
Frisius, Paulus, 412
Fritzner, J., 413, 444, 453, 477, 500, 512
Frodoard, 529
frog, 94 f., 100, 103, 175, 181, 501
Froissart, Jean, 216
Froude, J. A., 408, 597
fuga daemonum, 37, 119 ff., 388
Fuldenses, Annales, 474, 522
Fulk Fitz-Warin, 517
Fuller, John, 475; Thomas, 325 f., 420, 475 f., 540, 569, 576 f.
fumigation, 69, 135, 172, 319
furies, 30
Furnivall, F. J., 409, 446 f., 449, 471, 476, 490, 509, 516, 524. See Brunne
Furseman, William, 12

Gabley, Mother, 160
Gabriel's Hounds, 176
Gaidoz, H., 467
Gairdner, James, 84, 402, 408 f., 416, 418, 450
Galanthis, 114
Galba, 217
Gale, Thomas, 259
gallows, 141 ff.
Galsworthie, John, 21 f.
gambling magic, 67, 142, 229, 439
games, charms, 54; racing, 93; swimming, 54

Gammer Gurton's Needle, 216
garden: see crops
Gardiner, S. R., 280, 467, 575
Gardner, ——, the witch of Thorpe, 96; Ralph, 589
Garlandia, Johannes de, 216
garlic, 147, 151
Garmann, C. F., 439, 441, 447, 457 ff., 463, 484, 517, 526, 531 f.
Garrett, R. M., 393 f., 439, 448 f., 505
Gasquet, F. A., 395, 407, 409
Gaster, M., 390, 442, 531 f.
Gaston Phébus, 216 f.
Gatherley Moor, 133
Gaule, John, 25, 398, 400, 403, 405, 421, 427, 434, 463, 511 f., 540, 563
Gauls, Rhine ordeal, 232
Gaupp, R., 442
Gaveston, Piers, 108
Gawe, Mother, 95
Gee, Henry, 552 f.; John, 325, 578
Geffrey, Margaret, 61
Geiger, W., 411 f.
Geiler von Kaiserberg, 163 f.
Gello, 224 f.
Gembloux, Sigebert of, 132
gems, 108, 393 f., 438. See rings
Geneva, 358, 583
geomancy, 57
Geoponica, 472, 490
George, St., 220
Georgeakis, G., 442 f.
Georgia, 422
Georgius Pisida, 537
Gerard, E., 485, 492, 501; or Gerold, Hugo, 41
Géraud, Hugues, 77
Gerbert: see Silvester II
Gering, H., 383, 398, 405, 478, 491
Gerish, W. B., 591, 596
Germanicus, 141
Germanus, St., 152, 201, 224, 529
Germany, 40, 42, 44, 102, 119, 159, 163, 169, 221, 250, 358, 360, 368, 370; Notes, *passim*
Gerould, G. H., 545
Gessmann, G. W., 447
Gesta Romanorum, 78 f., 106
Gevaudun, 492
ghosts, 26, 84, 134, 177, 217, 344 f., 377, 501, 517
Gibbons, ——, 135
Giffard, George, 96, 103, 167, 174, 198,

248, 295 ff., 310 f., 398 f., 428, 488, 503, 512, 553
Gifford, William, 278, 566, 576
gift of witch, 11
Giles, Dobby and Molly, 134, 210 f.
Gillams, Mother, 428
Gillen, F. J., 405 f., 455
Gilo, 224
Gimlette, J. D., 402, 413, 455, 506
Ginnechochet, 216
Giraldus Cambrensis, 75, 117, 147 f., 150, 166, 179, 184, 201, 214 ff., 446, 469, 493, 508, 545
girdles, 114, 143, 405 f., 438
Giustinian, G., 320
glamour, 28
glanders, 136
Glanvil, Joseph, 6, 274, 335, 343, 349 f., 354, 421, 424 f., 427, 434 f., 454, 499, 521, 524, 529, 547, 561 f., 565, 583, 592
Glanvill(e), Ranulf de, 538
Glastonbury, 213, 221 f.; Mother, 550
Glendower, Owen, 156, 176, 226
Glorez, A., 456
Glotz, G., 537
Gloucester, 197; Humphrey, Duke of, 81 ff., 106; Eleanor, Duchess of, 81 ff., 106
Gloucestershire, 70 f., 212, 470
Glover, Goody, 90; James the, 11; Mary, 300, 321
Glycas, Michael, 537
Glyde, John: see Norfolk; Suffolk
Gmelin, Julius, 403
gnomes, 205
goat, 175, 243, 398, 494, 500, 549
goatsucker, 166
goblins, 32, 176 f., 215
Goddard, T. N., 473, 531; William, 139
Godelmann, J. G., 447, 507, 511, 536, 540
Godely, William, 209 f.
Godmanchester, 130
Godric, St., 125, 153, 176, 217, 530
Godwine, Earl, 238
Göngu-Hrólfs Saga, 515
Gogmagog, 204
gold for eyes, 151
Goldne Gans, Die, 514
Goldziher, I., 536
Gollancz, H., 396
Golther, W., 382, 396, 522
Gomes, E. H., 505, 543

Gomme, Sir G. L., 399, 412, 423, 453, 477, 487, 523, 548
Gonzenbach, L., 442
Goodcole, Henry, 577; Mrs., 577
Goodell, A. C., 421, 583, 594
Gooding, Elizabeth, 563
Goodman, Godfrey, 325
Goodwin, John, his children, 371, 565
Gookin, Daniel, 592
goose, 484
Gorman, H., 421
Goslyng, Thomas, 158
Gough, Richard, 591, 595, 597
Gouldsbury, C., 434, 513
Gowdie, Isobel, 160, 491
Gower, John, 57 f., 104 f.
Gowghter, 117
Grässe, J. G. T., 522
Graf, A., 545
Grafton, Richard, 408, 458
grain, 172; burning grain, 31; grain ordeal, 238
Granada, D., 493
Granso, 180 f.
Grant, C., 542
Granville, Denis, 135, 462
Gratian, 244
Grattan, J. H. G., 526
grave mould, 49, 142 f.
Gray, J. H., 572; William, 519
Great Paxton, 236
Gredt, N., 482, 486, 496, 514, 516, 527
Greece, 54, 60, 93, 111 f., 172, 183 f., 190, 201, 218, 224, 378, 384, 396, 414, 442 ff., 451, 462, 465, 506 f., 510, 529, 531 ff., 536 f., 543. See Macedonia
Green, Emanuel, 582; S. A., 596
Greene, Robert, 133 f., 439
Greenough, W. P., 514
Greenslet, F., 562, 582, 591
Greenwood, Sir Hamar, 136; Richard, 207 f.
Gregor, W., 390, 426 ff., 430, 453, 477, 480, 483 f., 486, 490, 494 f., 497 ff., 515
Gregory Nazianzen, 537
Gregory the Great, 43, 127 f., 200 f., 202, 222, 529
Gregory, William, 126, 407, 416 f., 457, 474, 534, 547
Grendon, Felix, 387 ff., 441, 444, 448, 453 f., 461, 466, 473, 489, 508, 526
Grey Friars Chronicle, 408 ff., 416, 470, 474, 520
Grey, Sir George, 532

Grienberger, T., 396
Griffith, F. Ll., 396
Grig, ——, 230 f.
Grillando, Paolo, 141, 149, 151, 212 f., 384, 387, 402, 412, 436, 441, 454, 456 ff., 460, 465 f., 472, 480, 520, 532, 547, 565
Grimm, Jakob, 425, 427, 446, 452, 463, 472, 480, 514, 522, 532, 536, 548, 563; Wilhelm, 514, 563
Grindal, Edmund, 115, 250, 259, 553
Grippis, Fortunatus de, 503
Grógaldr, 438, 478
Grohmann, J. V., 392, 464, 486, 510, 512, 514, 527
Gross, Charles, 538
Grosseteste, Robert, 222, 240
Grundtvig, S., 376, 437
Guagnino, A., 474
Guazzo (Guaccius), F. M., 440 f., 445, 458, 472, 476, 482, 496, 501, 514, 522, 533, 547 f., 560
Guernsey, 430, 484, 515, 549
Guichard, 83, 108 f., 117 f.
Guidott, T., 576
Guigemar, 16
Guignehochet, 216
Guilford, Francis Lord, 333 f., 590 f.
Guilielmus Alvernus, 217, 406 f., 444, 463, 492, 503, 522, 526, 531
Guillaume de Palerne, 440; le Breton, 534
guinea pig, 501
Gull-þoris Saga, 517
Gunpowder Plot, 320
Gunter, Anne, 321 f., 577
Gunther, Bishop, 474
Gurdon, P. R. T., 513, 543
Guthrum, 27, 383
Gybbys, John, 130
Gyges, 111
Gylou, 224
Gypsies, 390, 414, 434, 482, 506 f.

Haag, G., 523
Haberland, Karl, 503
Habington, William, 405
Hache, Roger atte, 194
Hackett, Margaret, 85
Hackman, J., 519
Haddan, A. W., 378, 381 ff., 393, 449, 461, 472 f.
Haddon, A. C., 412, 432; John, 188
Hadrumetum, 111 f.

Hälsig, F., 387, 390, 396, 436, 444, 466
Hästesko, F. A.: see Finland
hail: see weather
hair, 48 f., 90, 97, 102 f., 134, 142, 436
Hairy Jack, 176
Hale, John, 177, 335, 428, 435; Sir Matthew, 332 ff., 364, 592; W. H. H., 36 f., 407 f., 419, 438, 449, 451 f., 474, 504, 509 f., 512
Hálfdanar Saga, 516
Halifax, 207 f., 436, 477, 480, 495 f., 528
Halitgar, 384, 386
Hall, Alice, 196; Edward, 82, 408, 416 f.; Hubert, 401; Joan, 107; Joseph, 293, 301 f., 509; Richard, 107; Thomas, 38
Hallbjörn, 222
Halle, John, 260, 535, 554
Halliday, W. R., 536 f.
Halliwell, J. O., 389 f., 421, 437, 448, 461, 497, 513, 522, 534, 551, 563, 576
Hallywell, Henry, 518, 565, 582, 584
halter, 142
Halton, John de, 403, 546
Ham, 42
Hamel, F., 493
Hammond, J., 459 f., 518, 522
Hammurabi, 237
Hamper, ——, 148 f.
Hampshire, 484
Hampton, N. H., 206
Hancock, F., 400, 430, 467, 477, 513, 523
Hancok, Agnes, 38, 145 f., 443, 518, 553
hand of corpse, 142; of glory, 145, 463 f.
hanged man, 141 f.
hangman's rope, 142
hansel, 165
Hansen, Joseph, 24, 376 f., 382, 403 f., 412, 415, 417, 441, 445, 461, 469 f., 472, 480, 482, 489, 496, 530, 532 f., 544 ff., 580
Hanson, O., 451, 542
Harcourt, Vernon, 458
hardman, 55
Hardness, 7 ff.
Hardwick, C., 417, 566
Hardy, W. J., 407 f., 510
Hardyng, John, 156
hare, 45, 149, 166, 174, 179, 427
Hare, Hugh, 596
Harington, Sir John, 509
Haris, Robert, 557
Harland, John, 389 f., 422, 424, 448, 477, 523, 525; John (and Dobson, W.), 539

Harleian MSS., 399, 416, 418, 457, 562, 575
Harley, ——, 95 f.
Harman, Thomas, 525
Harold Fairhair, 439
Harper, Joseph, 542
Harpsfield, N., 408 f.
Harris, Elizabeth, 161; William, 289
Harrison, Thomas, 301, 569; William, 477
Harry, John, 55 f.
Harsnet, Samuel, 122, 298, 402, 412, 427 f., 447, 456, 491, 498, 518, 571 f.
Hart, Thomas, 99; W. H., 424, 520, 578
Hartland, E. S., 433 f., 452, 467
Hartlay, Edmund, 282
Hartlepoole, Richard, and wife, 229 f.
Hartshorne, C. H., 514
Harvey, Gabriel, 249, 485; John, 533; ——, 301
Harvie, Isobel, 39
Harvye, Joan, 542
Hasylwoode, William, 198 f.
hate, 51, 121. See love
Hathaway, Richard, 540, 594
Hauber, E. D., 492, 536, 538
Hauksbók, 386
haunted houses, 214 ff.
Hauréau, B., 524
Havekost, E., 397, 527
Hawarde, John, 424, 463, 566
Hawkwell, 96
hay burned, 428
Haydock, Richard, 320, 325, 529, 578
Hayley, William, 521
hazelwood, 10
Hazlitt, W. C., 509. See Brand
head down, 74; head that speaks, 240; head as idol, 403
headache, 142
head-band, 443
headless man, 220, 228
healers: see white witchcraft
Heanley, R. M., 431
heart pierced and roasted, 97 ff.; extracted, 42
Heather, Thomas, 520
Heawelon, 315
Heberling, R., 481
Hecker, J. F. C., 413, 457, 492
Heddon, 131
hedgehogs, 49, 166, 491
Hefele, C. J. von, 384
Heim, R., 396, 425, 444

Heimskringla, 438, 526

Heinrich, Fritz, 389 ff., 408, 444, 466, 508

Heisterbach, Cæsarius of, 116 ff., 149, 221 f., 514, 529

Heiward, Robert le, 234

Heldenbuch, 440

helenium, 32

Helgakviða, 515

Heliand, 222

Hellwig, A., 399 f., 406, 459, 464, 518

Helmont, J. B. van, 348, 412, 430, 584

Heming(s)burgh (-ford), Walter of, 403, 446

henbane, 449

Henderson, George, 496, 498 f., 523; William, 390, 424 f., 426 ff., 430, 432, 453, 459 ff., 464, 468 f., 485 ff., 498, 510 ff., 519, 522, 527, 597

Henrici, Leges, 29, 75, 383

Henry I, 159; II, 183; III, 235; IV, 156; V, 79, 411; VI, 61, 83, 115, 126 f., 177; VII, 50; VIII, 38, 66, 86, 107 ff., 189; son of James I, 265, 319, 479, 573

Henry, Alexander, 413, 455; Philip, 452

Henslow, George, 389, 444

Henslowe, Philip, 92 f., 190 f.

Heppe, H.: see Soldan

Herbert, J. A., 398, 438, 445 ff., 452, 469 f., 483, 517, 544 f., 547 f.

herbs, spells for, 31 f.

Hercules, 114, 116

Hereford, 34, 59; Duke of (Henry IV), 404

Herefordshire, 117, 390, 408, 425, 448, 459, 467 f., 471

heresy, 38, 80 f., 187, 245 ff.

Hereward, 33

Herle, Charles, 176

Hermogenes, 30

Herodias, 250, 549, 564

Heron, John, 66, 133, 550

Herrick, E. P., 405, 425, 464; Robert, 171, 220, 436

Hertford, 38

Hertfordshire, 211 f., 236, 591

Hertz, W., 407, 492, 496

Hervieux, L., 500

Hesychius, 404, 532

Heuen-Tsang, 541

Heuser, W., 544

Hewat, M. L., 405, 455

Hewett, S., 390, 400, 436, 447 f., 460 f., 468, 471, 487, 500, 510

Heydon, John, 54 f., 406, 477 f.

Heyl, J. A., 486

Heyrick, Robert, 577, 592; Sir William, 577

Heyward, Sir Rowland, 89

Heywood, John, 110 f.; Oliver, 400, 435, 465; Thomas, 14 f., 239, 271, 402, 441, 478, 589

Hibbert, S., 477 f., 479, 488

hibernation, 129, 451

Hickes, George, 133, 337 f., 421

Hicks, Elizabeth, 71

hide, sleeping on or in a, 46 f.

Higden, Ranulf, 159, 397

Higginson, John, 335, 579

Hikkes, Robert, 206

Hildburgh, W. L., 411, 463

Hill, Richard, 408, 416 f.

hill-digging, 204 ff.

Hillebrandt, A., 402, 411

Hillen, H. J., 479

Hilles, Richard, 409

hillmen, 119

Hilton-Simpson, M. W., 431, 513

Hincmar, 380, 538

Hind Etin, 119

Hinde, William, 570

Hinton, J., 530

Hippocrates, 218, 585

Hoare, Christobel M., 401

Hobart, Sir Henry, 308, 310

Hobbes, Thomas, 178, 335, 350

Hobley, C. W., 432, 442, 451, 464, 473, 490, 507

hobthursts, 166, 215

Hock, K. F. von, 545

Hodson, T. C., 411, 456

Höfler, M., 395, 424, 453, 466, 532

Hoffmann-Krayer, E., 396

Hoghton, Sir Richard, 287 f.

Hoigges, Henry, 55 f.

Holbeach, 197

holed stones, 148, 220

Holinshed, Raphael, 169, 399, 410, 419, 434, 446, 475, 477, 492, 509, 520, 534, 567

Holkot, Robert, 79, 106, 121, 240, 465, 497 f., 501, 533

Holland, Henry, 549; Thomas, 576

Holland: see Low Countries

Hollingsworth, A. G. H., 433, 513

Hollis, A. C., 434, 444, 473

Holmberg, Uno, 414, 423, 523, 527

Holmes, J. H., 401, 455

Holond, John, 196
Holonde, Richard, 65
Holt, Sir John, 364 f.
Holthausen, F., 389, 394, 448 f., 490, 505, 526
Holworthy, R., 461, 553
Holy Maid of Kent, 64 f.
holy oil, 147, 151, 202; water, 41, 48, 122, 147, 151, 202, 211; wax, 470
Holyday, Barten, 200
homage, 42, 240 ff.
Homer, 113 f., 384, 441 f.
Homilia de Sacrilegiis, 384, 386 f., 398, 444, 471 f., 548
Hone, William, 528
honey, 163, 214 f.
Honeywell, Christopher, 15 f.
Honorius IV, 399
hoodoo bag, 48 f.
Hooker (alias Vowell), John, 567
Hooper, John, 40, 70 f., 476, 553
Hoops, Johannes, 386
Hope, John, 207; R. C., 394, 439, 452
Hopf, L., 398, 497
Hopfner, T., 504
Hopkins, Matthew, 6, 134, 176, 236, 271 ff., 296, 331 f., 358, 367 f., 371, 564, 594 f.; Nicholas, 229
Horace, 531, 544, 560
Horley, E., 566, 568
Horn, 440
Horn, Robert, 559; W., 454
Horne, G., 402, 454 f., 473
Horneck, Anthony, 565, 588
Hornegild, ——, 14
Horner, Elizabeth, 593
hornet, 499
horse, 36 f., 95 ff., 133, 147, 395, 431; transformation to, 184; ridden by nightmare, 219 f.; demon horse, 177, 266 f.; brazen horse, 56
horseshoe, 167, 200
Horsey, William, 50
Horstmann, C., 544 f.
Horton (Orthon), 216
Horwood, A. J., 404
Hose, C., 399, 413, 455
Hossack, B. H., 482, 488
host, 42, 149 f., 181
Hott, Jane, 272, 491, 495, 539
Houell, Robert, 403 f.
house cobolds, 41, 215 ff., 221, 488
Hoveden, Roger of, 539
Hovorka, O. v., 460, 464

Howard, Henry: see Northampton; Surrey
Howell, James, 331 f., 595
Howhett, Margaret, 590
Howitt, A. W., 413, 433, 455
huckauf, 220 f.
Hudgin, 216
Hudibras, 521, 595
Hudson, Mrs., 107
Hübener, G., 522
Hugh, St., 120, 125, 175
Hughes, Lewis, 300
Hull, William, 38
human sacrifice, 206, 233, 243
humblebees, 179, 208
Humm, John, 417
Humphreys, A. L., 430, 433, 467, 471, 495; W. J., 472
hunger borns, 34
Hungerford, Walter Lord, 65 f.
Huns, 116
Hunt, Alice, 248; Margaret, 37, 122; Justice Robert, 274, 562; Robert, 391, 427 f., 435 f., 465, 468, 470 f., 518
Hunter, John, 505, 511, 523; Joseph, 555; William, 426, 486
hunting, 384, 490
Huntingdon, 95, 135, 271, 306, 563, 596
Huntingdonshire, 96, 228, 236, 435, 471, 594. See Warboys
Huntley, Alice, wife of John, 85; Mother, 66
Huss, K., 511
Hussey, Joseph, 162
Hutchinson, Francis, 288 f., 312, 351, 366, 556, 581, 589, 593 f., 596; Roger, 68; Thomas, 591 ff.
Hutgin, 216
Hutton, J. H., 411, 423 f., 455 f.; Matthew, 570; Timothy, 572
Hyde, Douglas, 388, 390, 396
Hyde, 544
hydromancy, 57, 186, 503
hyena, 237, 493
Hyltén-Cavallius, G. O., 391, 485 f., 528, 536
hypericon, 119 ff.
hysteria, 267, 322, 334 f., 354

Iamblichus, 410, 449, 520
Ilithyia, 114
im Thurn, Sir E. F., 223, 456

image magic, 27, 29, 42, 56, 73 ff., 80, 105, 113, 115, 147 f., 270, 308, 398; milking an, 163
Image of Ypocresye, 64
Imbert-Gourbeyre, A., 46
Imma, 202
imposture, 61 ff., 87, 192 ff., 319 ff., 341, 354, 429
impotence, 26 f., 113
imps: see familiars
Inchubus, 110, 210
incubation, 46 f., 94, 125, 221 f.
incubus, 42, 52, 64, 115 ff., 219, 225, 332
Inderwick, F. A., 540, 566, 573, 593, 596
India, 73 f., 101 f., 134, 144, 172, 237; Notes, passim
Indians, 20, 103, 134, 362 f., 371, 413, 423, 434, 454 ff., 472 f., 499, 507, 513 f., 516, 530, 536, 591
Indracht, St., 222
infanticide, 224 f., 243, 245, 268
Ingram, W. V., 521, 525
ink, 189 f.
Ino, 233
Inquisition, 25, 246
insects, 172 ff., 179 ff., 491
Institoris, Heinrich, 25
Insulis, Alanus de, 178
inversion, 21, 40 f., 74, 103, 215
invincibility, 108
invisibility, 176, 464, 524
invulnerability, 55
invultuacio: see image
Iphiclus, 113
Ipswich, 14, 96, 236
Ireland, 52 f., 92, 122 ff., 132, 136, 161, 166, 168, 175, 223; Notes, passim. See Kyteler
Iscanus, Bartholomew, 166
Isidore, 403, 444, 462, 531, 537
Isidorus Mercator, 384
Isis, 40
Islington, 88
Italy, 136 f., 172, 183 f., 206, 346 f.; Notes, passim
Ivanow, W., 411
Ivens, R., 388, 405, 436, 454, 473, 490, 507, 513 f., 544
Ivo of Chartres, 244
Izzard, Ann, 236

Jackson, ——, 210; Elizabeth, 300; G. F. (see Shropshire); Thomas, 120, 429
Jacobs, F., 537; J., 580

Jacoby, A., 443, 494, 506, 543
Jacquette de Luxembourg, 84, 106 f.
Jacson, Mariot, 38
Jahn, O., 476; U., 377 f., 425, 464, 472, 482, 492, 496, 522
jail fever: see typhus
James, St., 30, 391 f.
James I, 6, 14, 22, 235, 276 ff., 331, 340 f., 366, 406, 420, 449, 526, 530, 548, 562, 584
James, M. R., 389, 496, 509, 525, 545. See Map
Jameson, Thomas, 208
Jamieson, Robert, 514
Jamnes, 385
Jane, Queen, 410
Jaquett: see Jacquette
Jarbrey, Nazareth, 188
Jastrow, M., 411
Jātaka, 532
Jeaffreson, J. C., 547, 579
Jeanne de Navarre, 76, 83, 109
Jefferies, Anne, 535
Jeffray, John and Maud, 327
Jegerlehner, J., 481, 513, 519
Jenks, Roland, 89, 347
Jenness, D., 455
Jennings, Lady, and daughter, 451, 577
Jente, R., 379, 383, 385, 393, 415, 441, 466, 493, 495, 517, 522, 526
Jerome, St., 239
Jessopp, A., 408, 518 f., 590
Jesuit Relations, 363, 591
Jewel, John, 23, 227, 250 ff., 371
Jews, 46, 68, 75 f., 111 f., 137, 195, 399, 425, 440, 442, 444, 502, 520
Joan of Arc, 83, 399; of Navarre, 79 f.
Job, 40, 391 f.
Jörimann, J., 387 f., 441, 449, 456
John, St., 74, 221
John XXII, 77 f.
John, King, 159, 181, 226
John, A., 425, 481, 506, 515 f.; E., 392, 501
Johnson, Margaret, 270 f.; Samuel, 329; Walter, 453
Johnstone, H., 546
Jones, Edward, his wife, 150; Ernest, 526; Maurice, his wife, 130; Nicholas, 88; Richard, 63 f., 110, 211; William, 439, 471, 503
Jonson, Ben, 88, 170, 265, 315, 498, 533, 572
Jonsson, M., 485

Jooly, Katherine, 212
Jorden, Edward, 322; Joan, 182
Josaphat, 392
Josephus, 438
Josiah, 380
Jost, St., 392
Joubert, Laurent, 450
Jourdemayne, Margery, 81 ff., 106, 115
Journeman, Mrs., 238
Joyce, J. W., 572; P. W., 516
Jude, St., 30
Judy, ——, 209
Jülich, Johann Wilhelm, Graf von, 442
jugglers, 56, 86 f., 350 f., 448
jugs: see bottles
Julian, 41, 537
Jupp, E. B., 574
Justinian, 517
Juxon, Joseph, 370, 541

Kaiserberg: see Geiler
Kalevala, 477
kangaroo, 174
Karkeek, P. Q., 566
Karsten, R., 499
Kathā-sarit-sāgara, 463, 532
Kauçika Sūtra, 424
Kauffmann, F., 549
Kaufmann, R., 460, 468
Keats, John, 225
Ke(e)le, John, 255, 554
Keeling, Serjeant, 364
Kelley, Sir Edward, 312 f.
Kelly, William, 577
Kemble, J. M., 387, 389, 415, 494, 527
Kemp, D., 401, 405
Kempe, Ursley, 248, 264, 284 f., 560
Kendal, John, 50
Kene, Reginald, 51
Kennedy, P., 515; W. M.: see Frere
Kennet, White, 582
Kenniston trial, 513
Kent, Charles, 425, 427, 468, 542
Kent, 51, 64, 66, 87, 108, 150, 180, 236,
    257, 260, 272, 358, 393, 439, 470, 488,
    492, 554, 567, 586; Holy Maid of,
    64 f. See Edmund
Kentucky, 49, 164, 401, 460 f., 471, 480,
    484, 486
Kenyon, Sir F. G.: see papyri
Kerke, Anne, 428
Kerneslawe, John de, 47 f.
Kettering, 209
Kettleby, 133

Keutgen, F., 537
key, 444. See bible
Keynes, J. N., 571
Keyssler, J. G., 518
Khaldun, Ibn, 503
Kilkenny: see Kyteler
king devils, 63
Kingdoms Intelligencer (1663), The,
    521
king's evil, 142, 151, 316
Kingsford, C. L.: see London Chronicles
Kingsley, M. H., 405, 493; Joan of, 118
Kircher, A., 451, 517
Kirchmann, J., 440
Kirk, Robert, 128 f., 164, 462
Kirkton, J., 500
kiss, 241, 272, 403, 497
kistvaen, 103
Kitching, A. L., 434, 476
Kiterell, ——, 557
Kittredge, G. L., 446, 493, 500, 503,
    522, 524 f., 545, 570, 577 f., 594
Klapper, J., 387
Kleeberger, C., 392, 405, 506, 513
Klemming, G. E., 391 f., 396, 444, 466,
    522
Knaresborough: see Steward
knife in mast, 478
Knighton, Henry, 125 f., 397, 401, 403,
    533
Knivet (Knevett), Sir John, 144, 313
knockers, 205
Knoop, O., 393, 430 f., 481 f., 484, 507,
    514, 529
Knortz, K., 390
knots, 444
Knowles, J. H., 531 f.
Knuchel, E. F., 468, 506
Knuttel, W. P. C., 587
Knyght, John, 85
Kögel, R., 387, 548
Köhler, R., 390 f., 398, 519, 526
Kölbing, E., 544 f.
Kohl, J. G., 413
Kohler, J., 548; K., 467
Kormaks Saga, 404
Kornmann, H., 438 f., 445, 451, 531
Kotelmann, L., 397, 464
Krapf, L., 544
Krauss, F. S.: see Slavic
Kristensen, E. T., 401, 405, 410, 425 f.,
    428, 461, 464, 467, 483, 487 f., 495 f.,
    498, 505, 507, 511 ff., 515, 517 ff., 523,
    525 f.

Kroeber, A. L., 454 ff., 516
Krohn, K., 396, 477
Kromer, M., 474
Kronfeld, A., 460
Kühnau, R., 448, 481, 483, 486 f.
Kuhn, A., 447 f., 482, 531
Kuhnert, E., 404, 412, 436, 506
Kuninkpert, 180 f.
Kyme, John, 58, 227
Kymer, Gilbert, 417
Kyteler, Alice, 52 f., 94, 122 f., 144, 177, 415

Labourd, 182, 358, 368
Labrador, 510
Lachmann, T., 481, 483, 527
Laconia, 233
Ladame, Paul, 583
Lady fast, the, 130
Lady Isabel and the Elf-Knight, 119
Laing, D., 453
Laishe, Joan, 19
Laistner, Ludwig, 218, 536
Lake, Sir T., 406, 575
Lambe, Elizabeth, 224; John, 154, 317 f., 503, 524
Lambert, Cecilia, 257; Margaret, 60, 590
lameness, 18, 60 f., 92, 101 f.
Lamia, 224, 382
Lamkyn, John, 197
Lammert, G., 391, 395
Lancashire, 7, 10 f., 17 f., 39, 90, 149, 171, 265 ff., 269 ff., 273 f., 282, 285 ff., 294, 309, 321, 328, 358, 368, 389 f., 421, 448, 484, 495, 523, 525, 561. See Potts
Lancre: see Ancre
Laneham, Robert, 524
Lanercost, 546
Lang, A., 279, 521, 578
Langkelly, William, 80
Langley, Thomas, 37
Langlois, C. V., 415
Langton, Stephen, 46; Walter de, 241 f.
Lanman, C. R., 442
Lannoy, C. de, 557
Lansdowne MSS., 520
Lanval, 240
Lapland, 159, 180
La Salle, G. L. de, 430; L. F. de, 545
Lasaulx, E. von, 476
Lateran Council (1215), 470
Latimer, Hugh, 71; John, 577

Latinus, 47
Latona, 114
Laudun, William, 43
Laukiston, Richard, 61, 107
Laurentius, 222
Lavater, L., 559
Law, A., 18; T. G., 570
Lawes against Witches (1645), The, 421
Lawes, Henry, 121
laws, 4, 6, 27 ff., 38, 66, 86, 104, 143, 152, 189, 205 f., 212, 225 f., 230, 236, 255 ff., 261 ff., 278, 281 ff., 363, 559, 586, 596
Lawson, Deodat, 103, 494; Elizabeth and John, 60, 590
lawsuits, 55
Lea, H. C., 403, 412, 473, 516, 531, 536, 548
Leach, A. F., 395
Leadam, I. S., 534
Leather, E. M.: see Herefordshire
Le Barbier, C., 473
Le Braz, A., 400
Lech: see Byg
Leche, Margery la, 236
Lecky, W. E. H., 560
Le Clercq, C., 413
Lecoy de la Marche, A.: see Bourbon
Ledrede, Richard, 53, 123
Lee, John, 558; Sir Sidney, 574; William, 188
Leech, Anne, 563
Lefébure, E., 505
Lefèvre-Pontalis, P., 507
Lefroy, Sir J. H., 589 f.
Legenda Aurea, 224, 391, 530
Leges Henrici, 29, 75, 383
Legge, F., 566, 580, 589, 591, 594 f., 597
Legibus, De Antiquis, 397, 545
legitimacy, 232
Lehugeur, P., 412, 415, 417, 457
Leicester, 77, 188, 228, 322 ff., 510, 592; Robert, Earl of, 69 f., 180; the Fasting Nun of, 128
Leicestershire, 63, 66, 236, 358, 435, 596 f.
Leigh, Sir T., 377
Leland, C. G., 434, 482, 507; John, 204
Le Loyer, P., 463, 492
Lemgo, 233
lemon, 101
Lemon, R., 554
Leonard, Lord, 210
Leonhardi, G.: see Cockayne

lepers, 45, 137
Lercheimer, A.: see Witekind
L'Estrange, J., 408, 513
letters (Schutzbriefe), 406
Leubuscher, R., 492
Leventhorp, ——, 207
levitation, 146
Lewes, 150
Lewin, L., 412, 500; T. H., 544
Lewis, M. G., 48, 493
Leyden, John of, 246
Leynham, ——, 535
Lhwyd, E., 145
lice, 173
lichen, 147, 151
Lichfield, 241
Lickbarrow, Dr., 477
Lid, Nils, 453, 500
Liebermann, F., 379 ff., 387, 393, 397,
    404, 414 f., 462, 493, 536, 538, 543
Liebrecht, F., 467, 481, 493. See Til-
    bury
Liége, 156; Arnold of, 118
Liegnitz, Battle of, 153
lightning, 154 ff., 257
Lilly, William, 316, 424, 477, 503, 519
lime, 102
Lincey, A. J. V. Le Roux de, 524
Lincoln, 38 f., 58 f., 120, 125, 191, 193,
    197, 228, 238, 323
Lincolnshire, 100, 102, 132, 149, 381,
    422, 431, 480, 484, 486, 494 ff., 504 f.,
    515, 523
Linde, A. van der, 587
Linden, Johann, 360
Linderholm, E., 441 f., 478 f., 481, 485,
    487, 489 f., 536
Lingua, 493
Linton, Mrs. E. Lynn, 276, 551, 568
Livy, 457
lizard, 49, 424
Llanfaes, 201
Llewellyn, 108, 226 f.
Lloyd, Meredith, 158
loaf floated, 48; and knives, 52, 193
Lobeck, C. A., 404, 410, 520
Loch, S.: see Longman
Lockhart, J. G., 478
locks, for fonts, etc., 150 f.; unlocking
    charm, 115
Lodge, Edmund, 420, 520, 576; Thomas,
    90
Löwenstimm, A., 399, 406, 426, 442,
    459, 464, 492, 506, 518, 537, 597

Logan, James, 429, 453
Logeman, W. S., 545
Lollard Apology, 52, 143; Lollards, 403
Lombards, 180 f.
Lomner, Sir W., 534
London, 36, 41, 51 f., 56, 59, 61 f., 69,
    83, 85 ff., 99, 107 f., 122, 126, 132,
    150, 154 f., 187 ff., 192 ff., 198 f.,
    211 f., 227, 229 f., 234, 236, 255,
    257 ff., 261, 304, 313, 315, 317, 321 f.;
    Notes, passim
London Chronicles, 401, 409 f., 416 ff.,
    501, 534, 547, 574
Long, Sir Richard, 133
Longland, John, 193
Longman, E. D., 412, 422, 429 f., 436
loosing spells, 113, 115, 202
Lor, Jacobus de, 77
Lords' Journals, 535, 554, 559, 572
Lorens, Frère, 403, 469
Loring, Mrs. D., 20 f.
Lorraine, 66
Losinga, Herbert de, 42
Loss, Jeremiah, 525
lost articles, 165. See thieves
Lot, F., 524
Loth, J., 516, 524
Lothaire I, 113
lots, 385
Loudun, the nuns of, 570
Louis I, 233, 450; X, 76, 83
Louisiana, 401, 434, 456
Louthe, John, 157
love and hate, 26 f., 30, 41 f., 48, 51 f.,
    61, 77, 84 f., 87, 90 f., 99 f., 102,
    104 ff., 128, 149, 151, 229, 433
Lovetot, Sir John, 241 f.; Joan, 241
Lovett, E., 401, 406, 430, 432, 468, 478,
    528
Low Countries, 14, 93, 128, 391, 400,
    413, 424, 430 ff., 448, 452, 459 f., 463,
    468, 480, 483 f., 488, 490 ff., 496, 501,
    505 f., 509, 511 f., 514, 516, 519,
    526 ff. See Bekker
Lowell, J. R., 349
Lowes, J. L., 463
Lowth, ——, 189
Lubbock, Sir John, 462
Lucan, 312, 378, 560
Lucian, 222, 433, 477, 513, 523
Lucifel, 160
Lucifer, 178, 241
Luciferians, 437
Lucina, 114

Ludorff, F., 545
Lütolf, A., 447, 476, 517
Lufkyn, Thomas, 554
lunar venom, 26, 378
Lundgren, H., 544
Lupton, T., 441
Lupus, Bishop, 152
lutins, 215
Luttrell, N., 540
Lyall, Sir A. C., 411, 505, 543
lycanthropy: see werewolves
Lycosthenes, Conrad, 43
Lydwith, 128
Lyme, Conn., 237
Lyndewoode, William, 150 f., 387
Lyndyssay, Margaret, 113
Lyon, D. G., 543

Maassen, F., 384 f.
Mabinogion, 516, 524
Macarius, St., 184
Macbean, L., 395
Macbeth, 13 f., 86
McBryde, J. M., 389, 504, 508
MacCulloch, Sir E. (see Guernsey);
    J. A., 553: see Holmberg
Macdonald, A., 390; G. W., 510
MacDougall, James, 516
McDougall, W., 399, 413, 455
Macedonia, 423, 436, 442, 462, 465,
    493, 523, 532
Machyn, Henry, 257 f., 410, 556
Mackay, W., 422, 426, 480, 484, 528 f.
Mackel, E., 396
McKenzie, D., 412
MacKenzie, D. R., 402, 413, 432, 442,
    451, 464, 473, 482, 490; E., 480
Mackie, C., 400, 432, 490, 510
Mackinlay, J. M., 472, 478
McKinley, William, 422
McKnight, G. H., 437
Maclagan, R. C., 422, 426 f., 434, 480,
    523, 528
MacMahon, W., 559
MacManus, S., 516
Macquoid, T. and K.: see Yorkshire
Macrobius, 537
Madden, Sir F., 402, 438
madder, 191
Maddox, J. C., 455, 473
madness, 10, 27, 30, 98, 112, 124 ff.,
    529. See possession
Magician's Apprentice, The, tale, 477
Magnus, H., 529

Magnúss Saga, 529
magpie, 494
Maidstone, 358
Maitland, F. W., 517, 539; Sir John
    (Chancellor), 278; S. R., 439, 456,
    555
Malays, 101 f., 134, 237, 399, 402, 405,
    413, 434, 442, 455, 473, 497, 499, 506,
    513
Malborne, John, 70
Malchi, 210 f.
Malchus, 110, 210
Malcolm, King, 153
Malcolm, Sir John, 532, 542; J. P., 521
Maldon, 182, 295
maleficium, 4 ff., 22, 24 ff., 253, 553
Malekin, 215
Malfrey, Thomas, 189
Malkin Tower, 271, 273
Malleus Maleficarum, 24, 168, 249,
    412, 430, 441, 454, 469, 472, 478, 482,
    485 f., 489, 493, 496, 502, 530, 547,
    549, 551, 560, 563
Malling, 180
Malmesbury, William of, 43, 111, 147,
    183, 204, 232, 240, 397, 533, 544
Malter, Goodwife, 167 f., 485
malum secutum, 9
Malvenda, T., 380, 445
Mambres, 385
Man, Isle of, 84, 159, 390, 405, 422,
    428 f., 433, 448, 459 f., 469, 471, 480,
    486, 488, 490, 495, 527 f., 536
Mandeville, Sir John, 45
mandrake, 448
Manichæans, 245
Maniere de Langage, La, 406
Manly, J. M., 439, 524, 574
Mannhardt, W., 368, 441, 464, 472, 510,
    517, 595, 597
Manninen, I.: see Finland
Manningham, John, 569
Manningtree, 271, 273
Mansikka, V. J.: see Russia
Manu, 542
Manucci, N., 411
Manz, W., 392, 414, 442, 464 f., 481,
    506, 513, 527
Manzoni, A., 137
Map, Walter, 117, 223 f., 232, 240 f.,
    397
Marcellus Empiricus (Burdigalensis),
    386, 425, 467; Sidetes, 493
Marco Polo, 473, 515

Marcus Aurelius, 153
Mareschal, Robert le, 77 f.
Margaret, Queen of Edward IV, 60 f.
Marguerite of Navarre, 412
Marian exiles, 250 ff.
Mariani, L., 414
Marie de France, 16, 240, 494
Marigny, Enguerrand de, 76 f., 83, 109
marigold, 37, 122
Marillac, Charles de, 409
Marin, F. R., 391
Marisco, Richard de, 46, 150
Marlowe, C., 501, 515
Marmorstein, A., 512
marriage, 105 ff., 111, 113, 190, 385.
    See love
Marshall, Agnes, 38; E., 521
Marston, John, 312
Martha's Vineyard, 134, 499
Martin, St., 514, 527; of Bracara, 387
Martin, C. Trice, 408, 410, 509
Martyn, Alse, 167
Martyr, Peter, 251, 253, 256, 554
Mary, the Virgin, 390 ff.
Mary I, 69, 180; Queen of Scots, 260
Maryland, 423, 428, 433, 435, 454 f.,
    460, 468, 480, 488, 527
Mascall, Robert, 34, 59
Mascon, 336
Mason, James, 456, 561; Sir John, 557
mass, 75, 82, 147, 451, 470
Massam, J. A., 398, 491 f.
Massé, P., 482, 509, 511
Mather, Cotton, 102, 200, 333, 349, 363,
    370, 421 f., 428, 451, 454, 475, 488,
    499, 522, 525, 565, 578, 585, 591; In-
    crease, 102, 178, 235, 349, 371, 435,
    445, 475, 478, 492, 511 f., 521, 524 f.,
    579
Mathew, J., 455; Toby, 315
Mathews, F. W., 429 f., 432, 484, 498,
    501
Matthew, St., 30
Matthews, Albert, 399
Matthys, Jan, 246
Mattsson, Per, 160
Matzke, J. E., 538
Mauchamp, É., 378, 413, 442
Maurer, K., 485
Mauricius, 224 f.
Maury, L. F. A., 447, 529
Mawdelyn, Dr., 65
Maxwell, W., 458
May, 121 f.

Maydland, Dr., 229
Mayer, M., 532
Mayhew, Matthew, 134, 499; Thomas,
    592
Mead, F. H., 467
measures, 114
Medea, 58, 75, 152
Medical Act, 38; treatises, 389, 404, 444.
    See Cockayne; Heinrich; Henslow
Medicina de Quadrupedibus, 404
medicine: see quacks; white witchcraft
Meek, C. K., 473, 537
Meere, John, 108
meeting, 44 f., 51, 183
Meier, E., 392, 430, 463 f., 480, 496, 515
Meilerius, 119
Meinders, H. A., 540
Melanesians, 134, 388, 401, 436, 442,
    444, 454, 459, 473, 490 f., 499 f.,
    505 ff., 513 f., 537, 544
Melland, F. H., 402, 505, 513
Melsa Chronicle, 401
Melville (Menville), Ninian, 67 f.
Men-an-Tol, 220
Mendoza, Bernardino, 88
Menghi, Girolamo, 423, 447
menses, 383
Mercurio, Scipione, 432
Meridiana, 240
Merker, M., 507
Merlin, 58, 116 f., 226, 229
Merriman, R. B., 409, 570
Merseburg Spell, 40
Mesopotamia, 172
metamorphosis, 13, 28, 41, 57, 161, 166,
    174 ff., 248, 250, 348
Metles, Jewet, 128
Mexico, 413
Meyer, Carl, 412, 436; E. H., 392, 482,
    511, 514, 516, 522, 525, 527 (see
    Wuttke); Hans, 378, 402, 442, 473,
    489; R. M., 396; W., 380, 544
Meyrac, A., 391, 431, 496
Michel, Dan, 51, 150, 437; Humphrey,
    541
midday, 58, 215, 240
Middlesex, 243, 328
Middleton, Christopher, 416; Thomas,
    478, 493, 497; Thomas (of Hyde),
    477, 536
Midia, Petronilla de, 52 f.
Midsummer Eve, 148
midwives, 34, 114 f.
Mielke, R., 496

milk: see dairy
milk-hares, 166
milking an axe-handle, etc., 163 f.
milk-sucking bag, 51, 165 f.
Mill, John, 512
Miller, Anna, 62; M. H., 498
Millie, Bessie, 159
Milloué, L. de, 462
Mills, J. P., 411, 455
Milne, Mrs. L., 411, 434, 464, 543
Milton, 201, 224
mine-spirits, 205
miracles, 587
Mirandola: see Pico
Mirk, John, 59, 407
mirror, breaking a, 93
mirror magic and crystallomancy, 41,
    48, 51 f., 68, 79 f., 165, 185 ff., 206,
    209 f., 260, 313, 318, 553
Mirror for Magistrates, 416
Misselden, John and Robert, 65
mist: see weather
Mitton, Arthur, 188
Mixer, K., 519
Mixindale Head, 207 f.
Mody, John, 51
Mogk, E., 396
Mohra, 358, 565, 588
mole, 491
molin, red, 214
Molitoris, Ulrich, 378, 463, 472, 502
Molyneux, Sir R., 309
Mompesson, John, 214
Monaciello, 217
Money Field, the, 204
monk, devil as, 216
Monk, W. J., 498
Monmouth, 236; Geoffrey of, 43 f., 47,
    116, 204, 232
Monmouthshire, 433
Monnier, D., 496
Monseur, E., 431 f.
Montagu, Sir Edward, 310; Henry, 310;
    James, 293, 310
Montfort, Simon de, 159
Montgomerie, A., 483
Moodey, Joshua, 371
moon, 26, 31, 472
Mooney, J., 455, 507, 513
Moonstone, The, 189
Moore, A. W. (see Man); G. H., 362,
    583
Morant, Philip, 546
morð, 29

Morduck, Sarah, 236, 594
More, George, 298; Henry, 159 f., 166,
    335 f., 477, 511, 524, 584, 591; James,
    495; Sir Thomas, 60 f., 64, 127, 210,
    229
Moréas, Jean, 397
Moret, A., 411
Morgan, Christopher, 199; Nanny, 182
Morpeth, 199
Morris, John, 66; Lewis, 518; William,
    111
Mortimer, Roger, 53
Morton, Cardinal John, 110; Margaret,
    485; Bishop Thomas, 325; Thomas,
    591 f.
Moses, 105 f.; Law of, 27, 363, 439
moss from skull, 142
moth, 499
Moth, F., 439
motherwort, 449
Moule, H. J., 408
Moulton, A. F., 519; Jonathan, 206
mountain ash, 167
mouse, 135, 389, 490 f.; soul as mouse,
    178
Mousey Lea, 477
Müllenhoff, K., 390, 394 f.
Müller, Josef, 472, 481, 483, 487, 490 f.,
    497, 503, 513, 515, 518, 527; W.: see
    Schambach
mugwort, 214
mullein, 448
mumming, 548
Mummolus, 108
Munday, Anthony, 391
Mundy, P., 409
Munro, Robert, 453
murdrum, 29
Mure, Isabel, 34
Murimuth, Adam, 403, 415, 457
murrain, 4, 38 f., 41, 95 ff., 174. See
    cattle
Murray, Sir J. A. H., 446; Margaret A.,
    421, 548, 553, 565
Myddvai, the Physicians of, 391
Mylius, J. D., 447
Myrc: see Mirk

nail of thumb or finger in image magic,
    51 f., 165, 186, 192
nails, 200; in roll, image, heart, or skull,
    73 ff., 97 ff., 142; in footprint, 102; in
    charm bottle, 102; boiled, 103
nails, parings of, 48 f., 96, 99, 101, 103

name, 74, 99, 422
Nan, Kilnsey, 501
Nandick, Thomas, 61
Nangiaco, Guillelmus de, 415, 457, 475
Napier, A. S., 382, 389, 466, 526 (see Wulfstan); James, 400, 422, 483, 510
Naples, 101
Nasche: see Nashe
Nashe, Edmund, 63, 197; Thomas, 69, 180, 399, 420, 499, 509, 517, 545 f., 571
Nassau, R. H., 401
Naudé, G., 457
Neckam, Alexander, 448
necromancy, 46, 70, 143 f., 312 f., 380
Nectanebus, 57, 105 f.
needles, 87, 90, 97 ff., 133 f., 167
Negelein, J. von, 412, 496
negroes, 48 f., 91, 406, 413, 422 f., 431 f., 434, 455 f., 487, 496 f., 505, 512, 523, 527. See Africa
Neilson, George, 404
neton, 118
nets, 173
Neumeister, R., 514
Neuwald, Hermann, 237
Nevell, Lord Harry, 67 f., 439
Neville, Sir William, 62 ff., 110, 211
New England, 90, 93, 129, 160 f., 178, 183, 200, 206, 214, 235, 237, 279, 331 ff., 428, 484, 494, 521. See Whittier
New Guinea, 49, 115, 424, 434, 454 f., 507 f., 532. See Melanesians
New Hampshire, 93, 160 f., 206, 214
New Jersey, 236
New Romney, 87
New Year's Day, 47, 548
New York, 454, 510
Newbald, 143
Newburgh, William of, 43, 116, 397, 527
Newcastle, 200, 358
Newell, W. W., 490
Newfoundland, 468
Newport, William, 71, 197
Newton, Sir Isaac, 336
Nicander, 114
Nicephorus Callistus, 532
Nichols, John, 541, 576 f., 589, 592; J.G., 389, and Notes, passim
Nicholson, E. W. B., 422, 480, 484, 496, 498, 516; Isaac, 435, 542; John, 424, 429, 468, 471, 515

Nicolaides, J., 527
Nicolas, Mary, 236
Nicolson, William, 453
Nider, J., 378, 402, 412, 499, 521, 524, 530 f., 533
Niderberger, F., 527
Niger, Antonius, 410; Radulphus, 153, 397, 474, 502, 516, 545
nightmare, 147, 149, 183, 218 ff., 389, 466
nihtgenga, 218
nine, 98
Nine Worts, 32
Ninian: see Saint Trinian
Noble, John, 590, 594
Nogara, B., 414
Nohl, J., 458
Nonmete Hill, 206
Nonnus, 537
Noreen, A., 490
Norfolk, 66, 97, 155, 173, 182, 198, 206, 211, 236, 315, and Notes, passim; Thomas Howard, Duke of, 210; Thomas Mowbray, Duke of, 404
Norhamptone, William, 193 ff.
north, 154
North, Roger, 3 f., 333, 361, 581. See Guilford
North Carolina, 92, 442
North English Homilies, 239
North Marston, 110
Northall, G. F., 390, 432, 437, 440, 448, 487, 490, 511 f., 526
Northampton, 197, 293, 358, 428, 475, 596 f.; Assize of, 233 f.; Henry Howard, Earl of, 309, 424, 522, 535
Northamptonshire, 38, 84, 236, 286, 427, 594
Northfelde, Thomas, 83 f.
Northumberland, 272, 480; Henry Percy, Earl of, 307, 309
Northumbrian Priests, 28, 383
Northwich, 295; the Boy of, 301
Norwich, 60, 62, 100, 107, 173, 209, 262, 408, 535, 575
Notestein, Wallace, 251, 419, 542, 550 f., 555 f., 560 f., 563 f., 572, 579, 591, 596
Notingham, John de, 77 f.
Nottingham, 146, 243
Nourry, É., 398, 425
Nova Scotia, 92
Numa, 46
nut, 101
Nutt, Thomas, 304

Nyendael, D. van, 543
Nynauld, J. de, 492
Nyrop, K., 412, 453, 503

oak pin, 347
oaths, 232
obeah, 48 f., 141. See Bell, H. J.
Oberion, 110, 208, 210
Oberycom, 59
Octavian's treasure, 204
Oddo, 159
Odin, 55, 143, 159
O'Donnell, E., 493
Oertel, H., 467
offertory, 151
Ohrt, F., 396, 453, 481, 505, 507, 543
ointment, 50, 144, 166, 225, 243, 268
Oláfssaga, 445
Olaus Magnus, 43
Olbrich, K., 405
Old English Homilies, 468
Old Norse, 54 f., 438 f. See Edda; Odin; sagas; Gering
Old Shuck, 176
Oldham, John, 141, 478, 521
Oldreeve, Henry, 17
Oman, J. C., 411, 432
omens, 44 f., 51
onion, 101
Onley, Roger, 84
Onslow, George, 581
Opinion of Witchcraft Vindicated(1670), The, 564
oracles, 47, 227
Orain, A., 527
orange, 101
Orchard, N., 378, 405, 478, 540, 562
Orde Browne, G. St. J., 452, 488 ff., 506
ordeal, 54. See bread; grain; rice; stones; swimming; wager
Ordrych, Roger, 236
Orleans, 46, 56 f., 186 f.
Ormerod, George, 569
Orpheus, 67
Ortenau, 358
Orthon, 216
Osborn, C. S., 537
Osborne, Francis, 315 f., 323, 325 f.; John, 541; Ruth, 370, 541
Ossory, 53
Oswin, St., 125, 221
Otho, 217
Otway, Cæsar, 453, 479; Thomas, 497
Outlawe, William, 122, 169

oven, 31
Overbury, Sir T., 90, 314, 317
Ovid, 46, 75, 113 f., 152, 472, 502, 531, 546, 560
Oviedo, G. F. de, 531
Owen, E. (see Wales); H., 475
owl, 491
Owst, G. R., 398
Oxenedes, Johannes de, 401
Oxford, 46, 63, 70; Black Assize at, 89; University, 294 f.
Oxfordshire, 432
Oxley, Isabel, 131

Paetow, L. J., 524
Page, J. Ll. W., 400, 433, 467, 495, 498, 523, 528; Roger, 196
Paget, Sir W., 66 f.
Palgrave, Sir F., 226, 401, 407 f., 415, 418, 534, 539, 546
Palici, 232
Palmer, C. T., 428; John, 371; W. T., 486, 518, 527 f.
palmistry, 70
Palumbus, 111
Pandareus, 493
Panter, Goody, 272
Panzer, F., 522, 531
papyri, 384, 387, 411, 414, 424, 440, 504, 506 f., 543
Paracelsus, 212, 348, 412, 454
Parcae, 382
Paris, Gaston, 439, 483; Matthew, 397, 399, 438, 440, 446, 452, 457, 477, 494, 502, 516, 525, 533, 546
Paris, Council of (829), 472, 482, 534
Parisot, R., 441
Parker, Ann, 212; H., 516; K. L., 401, 455, 503; Mary, 60; Matthew, 115
Parkhurst, John, 227, 250, 262 f., 553, 559, 570 f.
Parkyn, John, 38
Parlaben, Richard, 255
Parris, Samuel, 102 f., 367
Parsons, C. E., 519; E. C., 434
Paston, John, 534
pater noster, 31, 36, 483
Patetta, F., 509, 536 f., 541, 543 f.
Patriche, John, 197
Patrick, St., 390
Paul, St., 30, 393, 530
Paule, William, 195 f.
Paulicians, 245
Paulini, Annales, 403 f.

Pauls, A., 439; E., 442, 481
Paulus Diaconus, 500
Pausanias, 114, 537
Payne, J. F., 387, 390
Peace, J. B., 571
Peacock, E., 395, 429 f., 435, 448, 453,
    470, 486, 510 f., 518 f., 534; ———, 406
peas, 200
Pechuël-Loesche, E., 413, 434, 473, 485,
    491, 529
Peck, Francis, 558, 574, 578
Peckham, Sir George, 570
Pedlers Prophecie, The, 478
Pegge, Samuel, 471
Peile, John, 573
Pembroke, 216
Pendle: see Lancashire
Pendleton, Ellen, 155
Pengelly, W., 467
penitentials, 29 f., 54, 74 f., 143, 152,
    166, 383 f., 444, 449, 548. See Bede;
    Corrector; Columban; Cummean;
    Finnian; Ecgbert; Schmitz; Theodore;
    Wasserschleben
Pennsylvania, 430, 497. See Doddridge
Penzance, 456
peony, 474
Pepys, Samuel, 133, 337, 421
Perceval, romance, 222
Percy, H. B., 60
Pererius, B., 395, 472
periwinkle, 448
Perkes, Thomas, 520
Perkins, Clarence, 403; William, 27,
    232, 235, 249 f., 290 ff., 295 ff., 305,
    310 f., 378, 399, 420, 426, 434, 503,
    547, 564, 587
Perreaud (Perrault), F., 583
Perrers, Alice, 78, 105 f.
Perry, William, 324 f.
Persant, Jean de, 203
Peryam, Sir W., 307
Peter, St., 30, 33, 40, 222, 392 f.
Peter Cantor, 466, 538; Comestor, 106;
    of Wakefield, 226
Peter, A., 391 f., 485, 531
Peterborough, Benedict of, 539
Peterson, William, 65
Petit, J., 415
Petrarch, 109
Petriburgense, Chronion, 545
Petronius, 531 f.
Petrus Venerabilis, 469
Petsch, R., 544

Pette, Phineas, 479
Pettigrew, T. J., 396, 535, 554, 557
Peucer, Kasper, 511
Phæacians, 16
Phelps, William, 516
Pherecydes, 113
Philip IV, 76, 109
Philip, Adam, 487
Philippides, 513
Philippines, 413
Phillips, Judith, 206, 465, 553
Philosophical Transactions, 420
Philostratus, 225
philtres: see love
Phips, Sir William, 583
Phœnicia, 233
Phylarchus, 232
physiognomy, 70
Pickering, Sir Gilbert, 304, 571; Henry,
    304 f.; John, 302; Mary, 305; Thomas,
    290, 305
Pico della Mirandola, G. F., 250, 491,
    531, 533
picture, 92 f. See image
pigs, 96 f., 184, 494
Pike, L. O., 378, 403, 458, 534, 540, 556,
    581
Pilgrim's Tale, The, 119
Pilkington, James, 240, 475 f.
pillory, 59, 212, 257 f., 282, 286
pimpernel, 448
Pindar, Rachel, 182, 499
Pineau, L., 442 f.
pins and needles: see image
Piozzi: see Thrale
pipe, 160
Pipe Roll, 234 f., 538 f.
Piso, 489
Pitcairn, Robert, 279, 401, 421 f., 424,
    426, 441, 461, 468, 478 f., 483, 488 ff.,
    500, 525, 546, 566, 573
Pitrè, G., 433, 442, 522. See Italy
pits, ordeal, 234 f.
Pittenweem, 421
Pitts, J. L., 549
pixies, 219; pixey-led, 20 f., 215, 513
plague, 31, 136 ff., 181, 346 f.
Plantagenets, 116 f.
plantain, 101
Plantsch, Martin, 163, 405, 412, 470
Platina, B., 545
Plato, 105 f., 111, 116, 412, 457, 561
Plautus, 532
Plaxton, George, 151

Pleasant Treatise of Witches (1673), A, 502, 524, 553

Plenzat, Karl, 544

Pliny, 114, 141 f., 166, 172, 232, 398, 404, 414, 424, 444, 460, 482, 500, 502, 531

Ploss, H. H., 444

Plot, R., 420, 521

plough, 171

ploughstave, 143

Plummer, Charles, 451

Pocock(e), Richard, 34, 529

Poer, John le, 122 f.

pointing bones, 134

poison, 32, 62, 90, 136, 181, 346 f.

Poland, 153, 159, 370, 484

Pole, ——, 211; Arthur and Edmund, 260; Reginald, Cardinal, 227, 230, 254, 260; William de la, Duke of Suffolk, 227 f.

polecat, 491

Pollard, A. F., 402; F., 420

Pollen, J. H., 420, 559

Pollux, Julius, 403, 513

Polson, A., 390, 400, 422, 425 f., 471, 478 ff., 490, 496, 498

poltergeister, 35, 41, 214 ff.

Polynesia, 451

Pontus, 232

Ponzinibius, J. F., 531

pool, 233

Poole, ——, 86; C. H., 467 f. (see Somerset); W. F., 358, 579, 594

Porphyry, 449

Porta, G. B. della, 269, 548, 561 f., 565

Porter, Endymion, 331; Thomas, 377

Portland, 176

portraits, 92 f.

possession, demoniacal, 27, 124 ff., 134 f., 145, 175 f., 229, 262, 297 ff., 339, 352, 582

Post-Angel, 129

Pot, Henry, 192 f.

potato, 101

Potts, Thomas, 7, 10 f., 269, 274, 285 ff., 376, 395, 420, 469, 488, 527, 531, 533, 560 f., 573, 589, 592, 595

Poughkeepsie, 47

poultry, 35, 96, 482

Powel, Mary, 452

Powell, F. Y., 380, 404, 406, 451, 478; Sir John, 4, 361 f., 364

Power, D'Arcey, 389

powwaws, 134, 363, 499, 591

Pozzuoli, 74

Pradel, Fritz, 423, 443, 465

Praepositi, Johannes, 203

Prätorius, Johannes, 511, 522

Prato, S., 502, 516

prayers, 145 ff., 387

pressing to death, 328

Prestall, John, 108, 255, 260 f.

Prestantius, 502

Preston, 234

Preston, Jennet, 267, 286, 592

Preusler, W., 396

Preuss, Hans, 380

Prick of Conscience, The, 380

Priebsch, R., 389, 524

Priest's Wife, The, tale, 43 f.

Prieur, Claude, 492

Prim(e)rose, James, 74, 421, 571

Prince, John, 157

Priscian, 537

Prodigious and Tragicall History (1652), A, 586, 589

profanation of host, etc., 41, 51, 75, 82, 145 ff.

Promptorium Parvulorum, 528

prophecy, 58, 63, 116 f., 226 ff., 309

Proteus, 57

Prüm, 216, 244

Pryme, A. de la, 499, 521, 523

Prynne, William, 546 f.

psalter: see bible

Puck, 21, 42, 215, 217, 377

Puckering, Sir T., 377

Puckett, N. N.: see negroes

Purbeck, Lady, 317

Purchas, Samuel, 462, 473, 477, 504, 506, 515, 540

Puritans, 329 ff.

purses, 114

Pursever Wood, 9

Putnam, Allen, 597

Pye, Sir Robert, 55

pygmies: see dwarfs

pyromancy, 57, 186

Pyrrhus, 227

quacks, 38, 68 f., 259 f.

Quadi, 153

Quadripartitus, 41, 379

Quakers, 582

Quicherat, J., 418

Quiller-Couch, T., 593

Quivil, Peter, 48, 104, 150, 193, 504

Rabbet, Thomas, 285
rabbit, 491, 497; foot, 49, 404. See hare
rabies, 389
racing, 93
Radin, Paul, 433
Radnorshire, 106
rain: see weather
Raine, James, 499, 504, 510, 590. See Durham; Reginald; York
Raines, F. R., 575
Rais, Gilles de, 459, 477, 533
Ramesey, W., 400, 500, 540
Ramsay, Sir J. H., 403
Randolf, John, 79 f.
Randoll, William, 567
Rank, J., 392
Rantasalo, A. V., 434, 459, 487, 489, 514
rat, 13, 389, 490 f., 492, 512
Rattray, R. S., 503, 531
raven, 95, 176, 437
Ravisius Textor, 394
Raymond, Thomas, 591
Raynaldus: see Rinaldi
Raynard, Ralph, 344 f.
Reade, Simon, 315
Reading, 134, 154; John of, 474, 547
Rebus in Oriente Mirabilibus, De, 382
red, 49, 94, 99 f., 184, 271, 437; red plague, 130 f.
Redferne, Anne, 266 f.
Redman, Richard, 38, 58
Reed, Margaret, 590
Reede, 131
Reformers, 250 ff.
Regensburg: see Berthold
Reginald of Durham, 125, 184, 223, 393, 474, 494, 514, 525, 530
Regino of Prüm, 244 f., 254
Reinfried von Braunschweig, 440
Reiser, K. A., 506, 513
Reitzenstein, R., 378, 396, 445, 522, 548
Relation of the Diabolical Practices (1697), A, 596
Relation of the Most Remarkable Proceedings (1674), 428, 589
Reling, H., 447 f.
Reliquiae Antiquae, 389, 484, 497, 508
Remy (Remi, Remigius), Nicholas, 175, 250, 368, 454, 458, 463, 475 f., 489, 491 f., 499, 548, 560, 565
Renfrewshire, 456, 499, 596
Renvall, L. T., 505
Reynolds, John, 576
Rhine ordeal, 232

Rhode Island, 513
Rhymer: see Rymer
Rhŷs, Sir John, 426, 433, 498
Ribadeneira, P. de, 419
Ribbe, C., 414, 473
rice ordeal, 238
Richard III, 60 f., 84 f., 106 f., 116 f.
Richardson, James, 207 f.; William, 65
Richel, A., 492 f.
Rick, J., 536
Ridder Stig, 436 f.
Riddles Wisely Expounded, 446
Ridgeway, Sir Thomas, 7 ff., 290, 308, 310 f.
riding: see nightmare; Diana
Riegel, J., 440
Riese, A., 531
Rievaulx, 48
Riezler, S. von, 492, 588, 595
Rigault, A., 415, 417, 438, 446
Riley, E. B., 455; H. T., 509
Rinaldi, O., 118, 445 f.
rings, 52, 55, 63, 67, 105 f., 109, 142, 151, 189, 211; of Moses, 105 f.
Ripon, 470
Rishanger, William, 401, 449, 477
Rishton, E., 419
ritual for ordeal, 233 f.
Rizzio, David, 262
Robert (Robin) filius Artis, 123; le Diable, 117
Roberts, Alexander, 159, 399 f., 435, 501; George, 429, 454, 501, 511
Robertson, J. A., 413
Robey, Isabel, 11
Robgente, ——, 130
Robin Goodfellow (see Puck); Hood, 131, 394
Robinson, Edmund, 164, 270 f.; F. K., 430, 471, 477, 480, 495, 528; F. N., 490; William, 476, 535
Robson, Agnes, 39
Rochas, H. de, 91, 500
Roche, Mother, 65 f.
Rochester, 242, 550
Rochholz, E. L., 436, 476, 482, 487, 496 f., 517
Rockley, 34
rod, 37
Róheim, G., 423, 503
Rojas, F. de, 404, 431, 461
Rolland, E., 447 f., 492
Rollins, H. E., 451, 521, 543, 547, 572, 555

Rome, 50, 181; plague, 136
Romeyn, John le, 400
roof, 31
Roper, W. O., 566, 568
ropes pulled, 270. See tether
Rosamond, Fair, 182 f.
Roscher, W. H., 399, 443, 445, 493, 502, 522, 526, 532
Roscoe, John, 402, 423, 426, 428, 459, 464, 473, 488, 509
Rose, Goody, 173
Rosen, G., 472
Rosén, H., 517
Roskoff, G., 449, 494, 501, 525, 531, 546, 587, 595
Ross, Alexander, 421; John, 494; William, 496, 510, 512
Rosweyde, H., 544
Rous, John, 535
Rouse, W. H. D., 532
Routledge, W. S., 402
rowan, 167
Rowlands, Samuel, 133, 431, 437, 492, 503
Rowley, Samuel, 434; William, 478
Rowll, Sir John, 453
Roxburghe Ballads, 525
Royal MSS., 509
Royster, J. F., 56
Rua, G., 516
Rube, 392
rubeta, 500
Ruborough, 204
Rudder, S., 555
rue, 122
Ruland, W., 589
Rule, Margaret, 370
runes, 31, 437
Rupert, Prince, 495; his dog Boy, 176 f.
Rush, Friar, 216
Rushworth, John, 474, 574
Russell, R. V., 411, 425, 444, 542
Russia, 206, 233, 396, 413 f., 426, 433, 459, 464, 532
Rutebuef, 544
Rutland, Francis Manners, Earl of, 310, 323 f., 421; Countess of, 323 f.; Thomas Manners, 534
Rutton, W. L., 418
Ryan, John, 196
Rye, W., 389, 408, 495, 535; W. B., 476
Rye, 99, 148 f., 283, 567
Rygeway, Cecilia de, 128
Rymer, Thomas the, 226, 229, 446

Rymer's Foedera, 403, 407, 416, 418, 438, 451, 520, 539, 546 f., 573

Såby, U., 453, 505, 522
Sachs, Hans, 482, 503
sacrifice, 93 ff., 148; human, 93, 148, 233
Sadducismus Debellatus, 421, 456, 596
Sadyngstone, William, 187
sagas, 380, 516 f., 529
sailing in a kettle, 15
Saint Albans, Monk of, 437, 517
Saint Denis, Chroniques de, 415, 417, 457, 516
Saint John's gospel, 147, 443; wort, 119 ff.
St. Johnston, T. R., 402, 437
Saint Loe, Sir William and Lady Elizabeth, 258 f.
Saint Margaret's fast, 130
Saint Ninian's fast, 129 f.
Saint Osyth, 153, 248, 264 f., 284 f., 309, 358, 485, 515
Saint Paul's steeple, 154 f., 257
Saint Trinian's fast, 129 f.
Saintyves, P.: see Nourry
Sakevyle, Sir Richard, 257
sale of curses, 132; of winds, 159; of ailment, 143
Salem, 90, 102 f., 129, 279, 329 ff., 338, 578
Salgues, J. B., 442, 451.
Salisbury, 86, 262; John of, 32, 75, 143, 185 f., 225, 403, 462, 508, 548; William de Montagu, Earl of, 53 f.; Thomas de Montagu, Earl of, 83; Robert Cecil, Earl of, 321. See Wyville
saliva, 90, 402
Sall, Thomas, 62
Salmesbury, 267 f., 311 f.
Salomon and Saturn, 31, 389, 494, 527
salt, 49, 101, 147, 167, 171
Saltrey, 228
Salvani, Provenzano, 227
salve, fairies', 254 f.
Sammonicus, Q. Serenus, 531
Sampson, Agnes, 278, 312
Samter, E., 385, 442, 444, 448, 473, 486 f., 527, 531, 536
Samuel, Agnes, 303; Alice, 302 ff.; John, 303, 322
Sancto Victore, Johannes de, 415
Sanders, Nicholas, 419
Sandon, Christopher, 188 f.
Sandys, Edwin, 227, 553

Sangermano, V., 542
Santos, João dos, 506, 514 f.
Sapir, E., 456
Saracens, 204
Sargeant, Joan, 143
Sathan, 424, 520
satyrs, 219
Saunders, W. H. B., 435, 471
Sauvé, L. F., 391, 430, 483, 498
Saville, W. J. V., 434, 455, 507 f., 532
Sawndie, William, 126 f.
Sawyer, Elizabeth, 323
Saxby, J. M., 515, 528
Saxo Grammaticus, 28, 205, 433, 450, 474, 478
Scandinavia, 28, 40, 49, 119, 153, 159, 180, 201, 210, and Notes, *passim*. See Bang; Denmark; Edda; Old Norse; sagas; Saxo; Sweden
scapulimancy, 57, 100, 144
Scaramelli, G., 316
Scarborough, 229, 424
Scariot, 189, 211 f.
sceptre, 81, 211
Schambach, G., 480, 486, 496, 507, 519
Schedel, Hartmann, 43
Scheffer, J., 500
Scheftelowitz, I., 424
Scheible, J., 405, 442, 463, 496, 511
Scherer, W., 390, 394 f.
Schiefner, A., 477
Schiffer, B. W., 459
Schlagintweit, E., 541, 542 ff.
Schlutter, O. B., 473, 526
Schmeller, J. A., 530, 549
Schmidt, B., 529, 531 ff.
Schmitz, H. J., 381 ff., 393 f., 404, 433, 437, 441, 444 f., 449, 460 ff., 465, 472 f., 482, 484, 492, 530, 538, 548 f.
Schneider, F., 548
Schöffler, H., 447 f.
Schönbach, A. E., 383, 388, 453, 480, 505
Schönwerth, F., 432, 481, 526 f.
Schofield, W. H., 477
Schorn: see Shorn
Schott, Gaspar, 397, 456, 510 f.
Schottmüller, K., 403
Schramek, J., 487
Schreiber, W. A., 233, 237
Schröer, A., 394, 483, 488 f.
Schulenburg, W. von, 481 f., 519
Schwartz, W., 482, 531
Scofield, C. L., 458
scorpion, 49, 174

Scot, Reginald, 25, 65 f., 69 f., 86 ff., 112, 119, 122, 137 f., 148, 158, 168, 180, 184, 189 f., 196, 199, 216, 220, 235, 248 f., 265, 285, 291, 297, 340 ff.; Notes, *passim*
Scotland, 39 f., 91 f., 95, 98 f., 102, 113, 117, 119, 128 f., 148, 159 f., 164, 166 f., 169, 172, 180, 217, 220, 249, 262 f., 277 ff.; 312, 319, 331 f., 358, 362, 366, 368 f., 370; Notes, *passim*. See Dalyell; James I
Scott, Sir Walter, 99, 119 ff., 289, 478, 536, 566, 588
scratching, 47, 169, 236, 290, 428
Scribonius: see Schreiber
scrofula, 142, 151, 316
Scrope, Lord, 557; Ralph, 132
scryer, 51, 186 f., 208, 210, 313. See mirror
scucca, 176
Scythians, 232
seafaring, boats, and ships, 12 ff., 18, 40, 152 f., 159 ff., 173, 190, 201
seals, 37
Sébillot, P., 398, 423, 425, 429, 431, 459, 464, 490, 496, 523, 531
Seccombe, Thomas, 595
seers, 226 ff. See divination; prophecy; soothsaying
Selden, John, 350
Selen Troist, 398
Seleucus, 116
Seligmann, C. G., 401, 436, 442, 444, 455, 459, 473, 491, 505 f.; Siegfried, 447 f., 467, 528
Sell the Horse but Keep the Bridle, 184
semen, 382 f.
semipedales, 218
Seneca, 401, 472
Senex, Johannes, 234
Serapion, 233
Serbia, 206
Serglige Conculaind, 530
Sewall, Samuel, 366
Seyfarth, C., 392, 395, 402, 413, 423, 425, 433, 442, 461, 464, 468, 470
Seymour, St. J. D., 433, 484, 519
shadow, 92
Shadwell, Thomas, 421, 437, 461, 560
Shagfoal, 177
Shakespear, John, 411, 433
Shakilton, Thomas, 199
Shakspere, 13 f., 34, 86, 108, 131, 181, 219, 378, 399, 417, 478, 490, 516, 526, 534

Sharp, Sir Cuthbert, 132, 452; James (Archbishop), 180; Samuel, 579

Sharpe, C. K., 502; R. R., 450, 509

Shaw, Christian, 456

Shaxton, Nicholas, 114, 553

Sheane, H., 434, 513

Shedewater, William, 195

Sherborne, 86

Sherwood, Grace, 236, 422

shift of ailment, 32, 94 f., 142 f., 529

ships: see seafaring

Shirley, James, 536; Serjeant, 308

shoe, 443

shooting a figure, 92; the witch in the churn or vat, 486, 488

Shore, Jane, 60 f.

Shorn, John, 110 f.

Short, Mercy, 129

shot-free, 55

shoulder-bone: see scapulimancy

shrewmouse, 94

Shrewsbury, 95, 156, 158; George, Earl of, 258, 520; Elizabeth, Countess of, 258 f.

Shrewsbury Chronicle, 475 f.

Shropshire, 47, 115, 146, 182, 390, 425, 459, 467 f., 469, 471, 488, 494, 498, 509 ff., 515, 518, 522, 527

Shuck, Old, 176

Siberia, 455, 462

Sibley, J. L., 598

Sibree, J., 401, 434, 537

Sibylla, Bartholomaeus, 506

Sicily, 101, 232

Siebourg, Max, 471

sieve and shears, 60, 190, 198 ff., 211, 553

signet, 37

Silas, E., 532

Silius Italicus, 537

silver bullet, 92

Silvester II, 240

simia Dei, 128

Simler, Josiah, 559

Simon, St., 30

Simon Magus, 30, 350

Simpson, R., 555; W. S., 443, 475

Sinclair, George, 421, 487, 570

Singer, Charles, 387 f., 454

Sion Monastery, 395

Sirens, 224

Själens Tröst, 398, 530, 544

Skarme: see Shorn

Skeat, Professor W. W., 446, 462 f., 493, 526, 571 (see Ælfric); W. W.: see Malays

Skelton, John, 39 f., 109

Skemp, A. R., 388, 454, 466, 474, 508, 526

Skene, W. F., 524

skull, 52, 142, 144

slander: see defamation

Slavic, 399, 431, 434, 453, 459, 462, 464, 477, 483 f., 487, 491, 523, 530 ff., 536 f.

sleep, magic, 145; sleep charms, 145. See Hand of Glory

sleeping on hide, 46 f. See incubation

Sleeping Preacher, the, 320, 325, 529, 578

Sloane MSS., 389 f., 406, 414, 423 f., 428, 435 f., 441 f., 444, 447 f., 453, 463, 478, 507 ff., 514, 516, 520, 543, 556

Sloet van de Beele, L. A. J. W., 447, 492

Smith, Ann, 406; C. F., 575; E. W. (and A. M. Dale), 406, 423, 434, 482, 491, 505 f., 513; Mrs. James, 455; Captain John, 592; John, 322; K. F., 494; L. Toulmin, 516; Mary, 182, 592; Richard, 574; Sir Thomas, 167 f., 197, 211 f., 248 f., 452, 485, 501, 507, 520, 557, 560; William, 209; William (editor), 433 f., 437, 465

Smythe (Smith), John, 322

Smythson, Johanna, 60

snail, 94

snakes, 32, 174, 447, 491 f., 517; snake spells, 146, 512; snake oil, 91, 144 f.; candle makes snake appear, 144 f.; suck cows, 166

sneezing, 44, 385

soap, 486

Soldan, W. G., 472, 536, 586 ff., 595, 597

Solinus, 536 f.

Solomon, 63, 106, 110; Solomon's circle, 211. See Salomon

Solomon Islands, 238, 414, 434, 501. See Ivens

Somer, Thomas, 199 f.

Somerset, 65, 80, 97 ff., 101, 132, 204, 236, 274, 370, 386, 407, 422, 425, 429 f., 433, 459, 467, 484, 495, 498, 523, 527, 562; the Protector, 189

Sommer, E., 544

soothsaying, 30 f., 41, 226 ff., 383 f. See divination; prophecy

Sophronius, 74
Sorel, Charles, 412
sortes, 30, 41, 384 f.
Soubiete, Saubadine de, 182
soul as bee, 499; as mouse, 178
South America, 223, 455 f., 493, 499
South Carolina, 434
South English Legendary, 239
Southerne, Elizabeth, 212
Southerns: see Demdike
Southey, Robert, 43, 109, 521
Southwell, Thomas, 81 ff.
Southwell Minster, 395
Sowe, Richard de, 77 f.
Sowerbutts, Grace, 267 f., 564
Spain, 370, 391, 423, 472
Sparam, Margery, 406
Sparke, John, 193
sparrow, 494
Speck, F. G., 413, 423, 491, 530
spectral evidence, 42, 221, 223 f., 307, 363 f.
Speculum Laicorum, 44; Morale, 503
Spee, Friedrich, 360, 588
Speed, John, 406
Speight, H., 495
spells and charms, 31 ff., 93, 98, 100 f., 114 f., 145 ff., 160, 169 ff., 491. See Bang
Spence, John, 480, 484
Spencer, Anthony, 557; Baldwin, 434, 455
spiders, 32, 52, 94, 218
Spina, B. de, 483, 496, 530 f.
Spottiswood(e), John, 566
springs, 232, 472. See wells
Spurgeon, C. F. E., 446
squares, magic, 452
stable goblins and charms, 215, 219 f.
Stack, E., 402, 513
Stacy, John, 138 f., 228
Stafford, Bishop Edmund, 465; Mr., a wizard, 67, 513
Staffordshire, 100, 325, 467 f.
stairs, 17
Staplehurst, 260
Stapleton, William, 110, 210
State Trials, 401, 405, 501, 581, 590, 592, 594 f.
Statham, J. C. B., 402, 473
Stearne, John, 6, 134 f., 176, 235, 272 ff., 400, 421, 434, 452, 479, 499, 536, 594 f.
Steele, Robert, 276 f.

Steinen, Karl von den, 455
Steinmeyer, E. von, 388, 396
Stenzler, A. F., 541 f., 544
Stephanus Byzantinus, 537
Stephens, G., 448 f., 505; H. L., 581
stercus, 383
Steward (Styward), John, 179, 196 f., 207 ff.
Stewart, C. T., 493; William, 419
stigmata, 46
Stile, Elizabeth, 419
Stiles, Ezra, 513, 592
Stokes, Whitley, 423
Stokys, John, 36
stone, magic, 176
stones, ordeal of, 238; food turned to, 132
stone-throwing, 214, 217
stone-worship, 33
Storaker, J. T., 496, 516, 527
Storax, 208
storms: see weather
Story, John, 261
Stothard, Margaret, 593
Stow, John, 408, 410, 416 ff., 420, 458, 475, 520, 535, 572
Strackerjan, L., 425, 464, 487, 507, 513
Strange and Wonderful News (1681), 521
strangury, 102
Stratton, Adam de, 48 ff.
striges, 167, 224, 245, 382, 548
stroking, 90, 142
Strutt, J., 540 f., 544
Strype, John, 410, 452, 475, 485 f., 501, 507, 520, 534 f., 550 ff., 556 ff., 570
Stub Peter, 492. See Stumpe
Stubbs, William: see Haddan
stumbling, 147
Stumpe, Peter, 492. See Stub
styes, 151
Style, Elizabeth, 274
Styward: see Steward
succuba: see incubus
sucking breath, 178
Suckling, A., 475
Suetonius, 525
Suffling, E. R., 495
Suffolk, 96, 215, 236, 331 f., 368, 381, 425, 459, 461, 467, 484 f., 489, 511, 528, 594. See Bury
Suffolk, William de la Pole, Duke of, 139, 227 f.
suicide, 142, 159

Suidas, 404, 532
Sulby, 38, 48, 58
Sullivan, J., 430, 477, 528
Summers, M., 421, 470, 521, 548 f., 551, 560, 565, 596
Surius, Laurentius, 527
Surrey, 230 f., 521, 596; Henry Howard, Earl of, 62
Sussex, 91, 102, 214, 424, 460 f., 482, 500, 515, 517, 528
Svend Ranild, 16
swallows, 54, 451
Swan, George, 570
Swane, Goodwife, 108
Swapper, Susan, 567
Sweden, 44, 160 f., 358, 391, 441 f., 489 f., 565. See Linderholm
Sweet, Henry, 526
Swift, Abraham, 435
swimming ordeal, 28, 232 ff., 290 f., 370; match, 54
Swinefeld, Richard de, Bishop of Hereford, 399
Swinow, Dorothy, 272
Switzerland, 160, 169, 250, 370; Notes, *passim*
sword, 57, 81, 165, 186, 210 f. See mirror
Sybel, L. von, 443
Sydney, W. C., 540
Sydow, C. W. von, 517, 528
Sylvester, Joshua, 463
sympathetic magic, 17, 74, 160. See footprint; image; thatch; urine
Syriac, 396
Szulczewski, A., 464. 514

tablets, 53, 60, 66, 74, 93, 132 f., 141, 208, 210. See defixiones
Tacitus, 141
Talbot, D. Amaury, 442 f.; P. Amaury, 401, 413, 423, 434, 442 f., 454 f., 473, 491 f., 499, 505, 514, 531
Tallqvist, K. L., 378, 411, 515
Talmud, 399
Tambornino, J., 449
Tanglost, ——, 85 f.
Tanner, John, 413
Tannere, John, 242
Tarbis, 106
Tartars, 153
Tasmania, 414, 455
Tassell, John, 230; William, 229
Tatlock, J. S. P., 407
Tatterfoal, 177

Tattersall, J. F.: see Wilkinson, T.
Taunton, 93, 254
Tausserat, A., 398
Tauxier, L., 401 f., 405, 473, 523
Tavenner, E., 396
Taxone, Liber de, 441
Taylor, Archer, 463, 507; E. W., 578; J. M., 427, 515, 540; John, the Water Poet, 408, 478; Jeremy, 332; Martha, 576; Rupert, 533; Silas, 14
Tecla, St., 94
Tedworth, the Drummer of, 214
teeth, 117
Teignmouth, 51
Teirlinck, I., 483, 488, 491, 501, 527
Temme, J. D. H., 434, 472
tempestarii, 152 ff.
Templars, 51
Temple, Sir W., 396, 492
Tengler, Ulrich, 482
tether, 164, 169. See ropes
Tettau, W. J. A. von, 434
Textor: see Ravisius
Textus Roffensis, 538, 543 f.
Thales, 106
thatch fired, 102, 290
Thayer, J. B., 593
Theal, G. McC., 491
theft, charms, etc., 32, 36, 41, 51 f., 60, 71, 165, 185 ff., 208, 214, 229, 393, 424, 435, 505 ff., 553, 567
Theocritus, 412, 441, 513
Theodore, St., 29 f., 381 ff., 393 f., 444, 461 f., 465, 472, 548 f.
Theophilus, 239; of Alexandria, 74
Thersytes, 35 f.
Thetford, 88
theurgy, 336
Thiele, J. M., 439
Thiers, J. B., 412, 426, 430, 442, 460 f., 467, 469, 478, 480, 486, 516, 526, 528, 536
Thirkle, John, 255
Thomas of Erceldoune, romance, 446
Thomas the R(h)ymer: see Rymer
Thomas, D. L. and L. B. (see Kentucky); N. W., 491
Thomlinson, John, 497
Thompson, M. M., 510; R. C., 411
Thoms, W. J., 405, 412, 437, 462, 502, 547
Thomson, Agnes, 60
Thonge, Sir John, 50
Thoresby, Ralph, 151

Thorleifr Jarlaskjáld, 222

Thorn, Anne, 593

Thorndike, Lynn, 442, 463, 479

thorns, 99, 103, 134

Thoroton, Robert, 546

Thorpe, Benjamin, 379 ff., 393 f., 414 f., 444, 449, 461 f., 465, 473, 493, 516, 524, 527, 538, 543 f., 548

Thorpe, 96

Thrale, H. L., 242

Three Biters, 39 f.

Three Warnings, The, 242

threshold, 49, 102

Throckmorton family, 302 ff., 310

Throgmorton, George, 257; Lady Frances, 257

Thucydides, 457

thunder stones, 49

Thundering Legion, 153

Thuresby, John, 138

Thurlow, Grace, 285

Thurnwald, R., 434, 501

Thursday, 32

Thurston, E., 399, 411, 426, 463, 506, 518, 531

Thyraeus, Petrus, 449, 500

Thweng: see Thonge

Tighe, R. R., 418

Tilbrook Bushes, 271 ff.

Tilbury, Gervase of, 106, 117, 175, 177, 217, 225, 445, 448, 493, 503

tile, 102, 434

Tilling, Ann, 593

Tilluth, Francis, 155

Timble Gill, 269

Timbs, John, 556

Tindall, Sir John, 307

Titinia, 55

toad in witchcraft, 47, 95, 99, 135, 149, 168, 178, 181 ff., 204, 484 f., 491; in medicine, 181; guards treasure, 517

tobacco, 319

Tobit, 172, 319

Tocotes, Sir Roger, 138

Tod, James, 532, 542

Todd, 184

Toland, John, 25 f.

Toldo, P., 440

Toledo, 45, 105

Tompson, William and Elizabeth, 12 f.

Toncroy, Nicholas, 47

Tongans, 106

Tonken, John, 456

Tooker (Turke), Susan, 18 f.; Walter, 18

toothache, 30, 32 ff., 37, 40, 142, 500, 512; St. Peter charm for, 32 f.

Torr, C., 467, 475, 490, 536

Torre: see Turrium

Torrentius, Laevinus, 531

Tours, Gregory of, 48 f., 399, 438, 468, 499, 507 f.

Tout, T. F., 546

Tozar, Isabel, 17

Traill, G. W., 543

Train, J., 422, 490

transference of milk, etc., 163 ff., 172. See shift

transformation: see metamorphosis

transportation, magic, 29, 125, 243, 270 f., 273. See Diana

Transylvania, 451, 485, 492, 501

Traube, L., 502

travel charms, 32, 152 f.; omens, 44 f., 51, 183, 385

Trawlove, John, 209

treasure, 68, 90, 94, 132, 144, 158, 195, 204 ff., 315, 497, 554, 567

trees dried up, 172

tree-worship, 33, 42

trefoil, 121

tregetours: see jugglers

Tremearne, A. J. N., 423, 433 ff., 442, 473, 491, 544

Trenchard, John, 497

Tresilian, Sir Robert, 54

Trevelyan, G. M., 276 f.; Marie: see Wales

Trèves, 75 f., 157, 358, 360, 415

Trevisa, John, 397, 477

Trevisard, Michael, Alice, and Peter, 7 ff., 290, 311

triangle, 95

tricksy spirits, 215

Trier: see Trèves

Trig, Alice, 193 f.

Tring, 236

Trithemius, J., 524

Trium Fontium, Albericus, 437

Trokelowe, Johannes de, 438, 475

trolls, 119

Trotter, R. De Bruce, 422, 425, 429, 484, 498, 510 f.

True Account (1686), A, 456

True and Exact Relation (1645), A, 400, 456 f., 479, 488, 490 f., 494, 499, 501, 561, 563, 565, 569, 592, 595

True and Full Relation (1704), A, 426

True and Impartial Relation (1682), A, 421, 494, 502, 507, 562, 581, 589 f.
True and Iust Recorde (1582), A, 428, 480, 485, 488, 515, 551, 560, 568, 589
True Relation (1645), A, 488 f., 499
Truth Brought to Light (1651), 420, 573 ff.
Tryal of Witches (1682), A, 456, 490, 581
Tschubinow, G., 455
Tuchmann, J., 441, 503, 536 f., 541
Tübingen, 163. See Plantsch
Türlîn, Heinrich von dem, 405
Tunna, 202
turf, 102, 167
Turke: see Tooker
Turnaston(e), 34, 59
Turner, Ann, 90, 314, 317; Elizabeth, 593; G., 451; William, 503
turning one's coat, etc., 21, 215. See inversion
Turrium, Herbertus, 469, 517, 525
Twinnowe (Twynmowe, Twynyho), Ankerett, 138 f.
Two Witches of Rome, 183 f.
Tyffyn, 248
Tylor, Sir E. B., 462, 492
Tymms, S., 471
Tyndale, William, 109 f., 419; Sir William and Lady, 62
Tyndall, Gervase, 534 f.
typhoid, 136
typhus, 89, 283, 347
Tyrrel, Wat, 175
Tyrrye, Joan, 254, 465, 518
Tzetzes, 537

Uhland, L., 439, 472, 477
unbaptized infant, 52
unctores, 346 f., 457
Underhill, Edward, 535
unguent: see ointment
unlocking charm, 115
Upham, C. W., 588 f., 594
Uppsala, 233
urine, 102 f., 160, 383
Usher, R. G., 569
Usk, Adam of, 404

Valentyne, ——, 260
valkyries, 29 f.
Vallois, R., 451
Valois, Charles de, 76 f.
vampires, 43, 166, 245, 527

Vanlandi, 219
Vansittart, E. C., 526
Vassiliev, A., 444, 465, 506 f., 543
Vaughan, Richard, 301
vehicles stopped, 3
veneficae, 136 ff.
Venn, J. and J. A., 574
ventriloqui, 65
Venus, 111, 382
verbena: see vervain
Vergil, Polydore, 458
vermin, 172 f.
Vernaleken, T., 464
Vernon, cats of, 177, 563
Vernon MS., 545
vervain, 37, 119 ff.
Vickers, K. H., 416
victory, 32
Vigfusson, G., 404, 406, 529
Vignay, Jean de, 397
Vignolles, Bernard de, 50
Villa Nova, Arnaldus de, 458 f.
Villani, Giovanni, 534
Vincenti, A. von, 387
Vingtrinier, A., 496
Vinnianus: see Finnian
vipers, 181, 402, 436, 489
Virgil, 47, 75, 384, 398
virgin parchment, 208; scryer: see scryer
Virginia, 236, 422, 592. See Doddridge
Virley, John, 83
Visigoths, 152
visitations, 34, 38, 114 f., 150, 227, 251, 253 f., 443 f., 465, 470, 504, 552 f.
Viṣṇu-Sūtra, 541, 543
Vitry, Jacques de, 548
Vogt, W. H., 406
voice in the air, 228
Volk, Franz, 589
vomiting pins, etc., 320 f., 339 f.
Vonbun, F. J., 427, 481 f., 486
Vordemfelde, H., 382, 394
Vowell: see Hooker
Vreto (Bretos), M., 462
vulture, 174, 437

Waade, Armagill, 557
Waddam, Margaret, 235
Waddington, William of, 43, 51, 164 f., 186, 398, 514, 516. See Brunne
Wærferth, 530
wager of battle, 53 f.
Wagstaffe, John, 351, 532, 564

Wake, Thomas, 84
Wakefield, 186. See Peter
wakes, 548
walcyries, 29 f.
Waldemar, 439
Waldenses, 245 f.
Waldron, G. (see Man); Katharine, 321
Wales, 37, 43, 94, 122, 132, 145 f., 156, 166, 169, 175, 201, 230; Notes, *passim*
Walewein, 501
Walford, Enid, 549
Walker, Adam, 475; John, 144, 298 ff., 449, 492, 569 f.; Richard, 80, 187
walking toad, 182
Wall Spirit, 69
Waller, John, 434, 492, 567; Richard, 160; Thomas, 230; W. C., 572
Walles, William, 134
Walloons: see Low Countries
Walpole, Horace, 504; Thomas, 66
Walpoole, Dorothy, 130 f.
Walsingham, Thomas, 397, 403, 416, 446, 475, 509, 517
Walsingham, 128
Walter, J. C., 498 f.
Waltheof, St., 226, 456, 494, 529
war: see battle
Warboys, 248, 294, 302 ff., 322, 428, 592
Ward, H. L. D., 545
Wardell, J., 538
Warden, A. J., 528
Ward-house, 159
Warenne, Earl of, 204 f.
Waring, P., 313
Warkworth, John, 34, 534
Warren, son of Baldwin, 234
Warrick, J., 480, 498
warts, 94, 142
Warwickshire, 138, 234
wasp, 499
Wasserschleben, H., 383 ff., 548 f.
waste lands, 132
Wasted Wishes, The, 547
watch, 180
water dissolves spell, 79, 127, 183 f., 232. See font; holy
water ordeal: see swimming
Waterhouse, Agnes, 170, 178 f., 182
Watson, Henry, 179; P. B., 474
Waxman, S. M., 544
Wayd, ——, 63 f.
weapon salve, 74
weapons, 28, 31, 53 ff.
weasel, 174

weather (wind, storm, etc.) 13 ff., 27 f., 32, 152 ff., 159, 183, 208
Webbar, Christian, 15 ff.
Webster, Daniel, 513; John, 113, 343 ff., 420, 441, 454, 457, 492, 521, 531, 561 ff., 567, 578, 582 ff.
Wed, John, 228
Weech, Christian, wife of Thomas, 315
weeds, 95
Weekes, Christiana, 456
Weeks, J. H., 413, 436, 464, 473, 491
Weever, John, 313
Weicker, G., 532
weighing, 541
Weinhold, K., 393, 451, 472, 502
Weinreich, O., 437, 445, 529
Weir, Major Thomas, 337
Weisse Frauen, 132
Welch, Joseph, 569
Welcker, F. G., 443
Welford, John, 197
wells dried up, 172; worship of, magic at, 33 ff., 42, 94, 132; poisoning of, 136. See springs
Wells, J. E., 483, 494
Wells, Norfolk, 160; Somerset, 461
Wendell, Barrett, 578, 585 f.
Wendover, Roger of, 397, 438, 440, 450, 452, 502, 545
Wenham, Jane, 4, 315, 361 f., 364, 369, 581, 583
Wenlock, 47
wens, 142
Wentworth, Anne, 127, 229; Sir Roger, 127, 229
Wentz, W. Y. E., 486, 523
were-leopards, 493
werewolves, 111, 175, 184, 248, 503
Wermhille, John and Agnes de, 51
Wesley family, 214; John, 185, 521
Wesselofsky, A., 532
West, Andrew, 427 f.; Anne, 563; Rebecca, 272
West Indies, 48, 141, 493, 511 f. See Bell, H. J.; Cuba; obeah
Westermann, D., 402
Westermarck, E., 434, 442, 450 f., 481 f., 505 f.
Westminster, 99
Westmoreland, Ralph, Earl of, 67 f.
Weston, William, 570
Weyer: see Wier
Weymouth, 408
Whalley, Peter, 573

Whalley, Thomas of, 48
Wharfedale, 103
Wheatcroft, Leonard, 459
Wheater, William, 577
Wherstead, 96
whetstone, 194 f.
Whip for the Devil, A, 447
whipping the churn, 167
whirlwind, 476
whistling, 160
Whitaker, T. D., 452, 539, 589
white pater noster, 219
white witchcraft, 19 f., 23, 27, 30 ff., 89,
    97, 132, 142 ff., 185 ff., 230 f., 236,
    292, 295 f., 351, 550
White, A. D., 351, 377, 579 f.; Gilbert,
    467; John, 196; Bishop John, 227,
    254; Margaret, 272
Whitecote, Mother, 550
Whitehead, ——, 144
Whitelocke, Sir B., 467, 589
Whiteway, William, 474, 518, 574
Whitgift, John, 227, 298, 553, 570
Whitney, A. W. (see Maryland); W. D.,
    442
Whittier, J. G., 479, 485, 515, 519, 523
Whittle, Anne, 39, 265 ff., 488
whooping cough, 94 f., 148 f.
Wickham, J. D. C., 422, 429, 452
Wickwane, William, 400
Wickwar, J. W., 400, 540 f.
Widdicombe, 157
Wieger, L., 413
Wier, Johann, 112, 134, 158, 198, 291,
    293, 297, 339 ff., 354; Notes, passim
Wiesensteig, 358
Wife of Usher's Well, The, 131 f.
Wigornia, Annales de, 401, 450
Wigström, E., 405, 507
Wihtræd, King, 393
Wilamowitz-Moellendorff, U. von, 515
Wilbraham, Sir Roger, 95 f., 320, 576
Wilfred, St., 37
Wilken, G. A., 464, 493, 532
Wilkin, Simon, 581
Wilkins, David, 397, 399, 411, 416, 470,
    504, 509; Simon: see Browne, Sir T.
Wilkinson, John, 186 f., 207 f.; T., 477,
    485 f., 495 f., 518, 523, 528; T. T.,
    389 f., 422 ff., 448, 477, 523, 525
Willcocks, F., 567
William I, 33, 40 f., 233; II, 175, 398,
    539
William of Palerne, 440, 493

Williams, Sir David, 307; Roger, 472;
    Thomas, 402, 433
Williamson, Joseph, 14
Willie's Lady, 113 f.
Williford, Joan, 161, 491, 495, 539
Willis, T., 456
Will-o'-the-Wisp, 215
Willoughby-Meade, G., 493
Wilson, Arthur, 316, 325, 576; W., 486,
    498
Wiltshire, 159, 214, 235 f., 407, 421, 456
Wimondham, 155
Winch, Sir Humphrey, 310, 322 f.
Winchester, 118, 125, 187
Winckler, H., 542
wind: see weather
Windisch, E., 530
Windsor, 87, 234, 577; Thomas, Lord,
    317
Winsor, Justin, 579, 594
Winstedt, R. O., 433, 499
Winwick, 131, 176
Wisdom, ——, 67 f., 439
wishing wells, 34, 132
Witch of Berkeley, 43 f.
Witches' Sabbath, 25, 42, 90, 243 ff.; of
    cats, 496
witch-marks, 236
Witekind, H., 455, 480, 482, 511, 514,
    540, 543, 583
Withold, St., 219
Wittie, Robert, 571
Witzschel, A., 430, 447, 464, 481, 515
Wlislocki, H. von, 414
Wodham, William, 417
Wolf, F., 496; J. W., 391 f., 395, 406,
    452, 480, 506, 522, 527
Wolfdietrich, 440
Wolsey, Cardinal, 62 f., 86, 109 f., 210,
    519
wolves, charm for, 393. See werewolves
Wonderfull News from the North(1650),
    400, 456, 564
wood thistle, 448
Wood, Anthony à, 420, 500, 574, 576,
    586; Thomas, 408
woodcock, 462
Woodcott, John, 161
Woodes, Hugh, 65
Wood-Martin, W. G., 468, 487
Woods, J. D., 413, 455; Mary, 575
Woodstock, 214
wool, black, 143
Worcester, 83, 125; John of, 397, 524

Worcestershire, 71, 199, 212, 235 f., 407
Wordsworth, Christopher, 396, 449, 471;
    William, 176
worms, 36 f., 40
Worthington, John, 530, 535
Worthy, Charles, 567
Wotton, Nicholas, 66
wounds, 32; transferred, 176 ff. See
    Five Wounds
wrecks: see seafaring
Wrede, F., 396
Wright, E. M., 390, 453, 460, 467, 471,
    484, 487, 494 ff., 518, 523, 525, 527 f.;
    Thomas, 281 ff., 328, 362, and Notes,
    passim: see Kyteler; Map
Wriothesley, Charles, 157 f., 408 ff., 535
Wroth, Sir Robert, 309 f.
Wryght, Thomas, 38, 58
Wucke, C. L., 482
Wülker (Wülcker), R., 382, 387 ff., 453,
    461, 466, 473, 489, 494 f., 508
Wünsch, R., 74, 414, 495
Wünsche, A., 519
Württemberg, Frederick Duke of, 476
Würzburg, 368
Wüst, Paul, 529
Wulfric, St., of Haselbury, 240
Wulfstan, 30, 33, 379 f., 382, 385, 387,
    393 f., 493
Wuttke, A., ed. E. H. Meyer, 392, and
    Notes, passim
Wycherley, William, 71, 158, 189, 197,
    199, 211 f.
Wyghton, John, 56
Wynick, John, 271
Wyrcester, William, 82, 416 f.
Wyriott, Thomas, 85 f.
Wyville, Robert, Bishop of Salisbury, 53

Yardwell, 230
Yarmouth, 428
Yatton, 65
Year Books, 404, 462
yellowbird, 494
Yelverton, Sir Christopher, 307
Yepes, Diego de, 419 f.
Ynglinga Saga, 438, 526
Yonec, Lai de, 117
Yonge, Walter, 535, 543, 576
York, 34, 38, 41, 75, 114, 129, 143, 148,
    152, 158, 187, 229, 270, 400, 512, 519,
    521, 528, 530, 592
Yorkshire, 97 ff., 101, 106 f., 146 f., 164,
    166, 179, 185, 190, 220 f.; Notes,
    passim
Young, Robert, 427
Yowel, 521
Yule, Henry, 473
Yvain, 440

Zanetti, Z., 391, 468, 531
Zaroes, 30
Zeiri, 502
Zeisberger, D., 455
Zenobius, 532
Zettinger, J., 381
Zeumer, K., 404, 509, 537, 543
Zezschwitz, K. A. G. von, 380
Zielinski, T., 502
Zincke, F. B., 427, 489, 492
Zingerle, I. V. von, 447, 481
Zoroaster, 42, 57
Zosimus, 537
Zürich, 251, 256, 262 f.; Letters, 551 f.,
    554, 559, 570 f.
Zulus, 516
Zupitza, Julius, 389